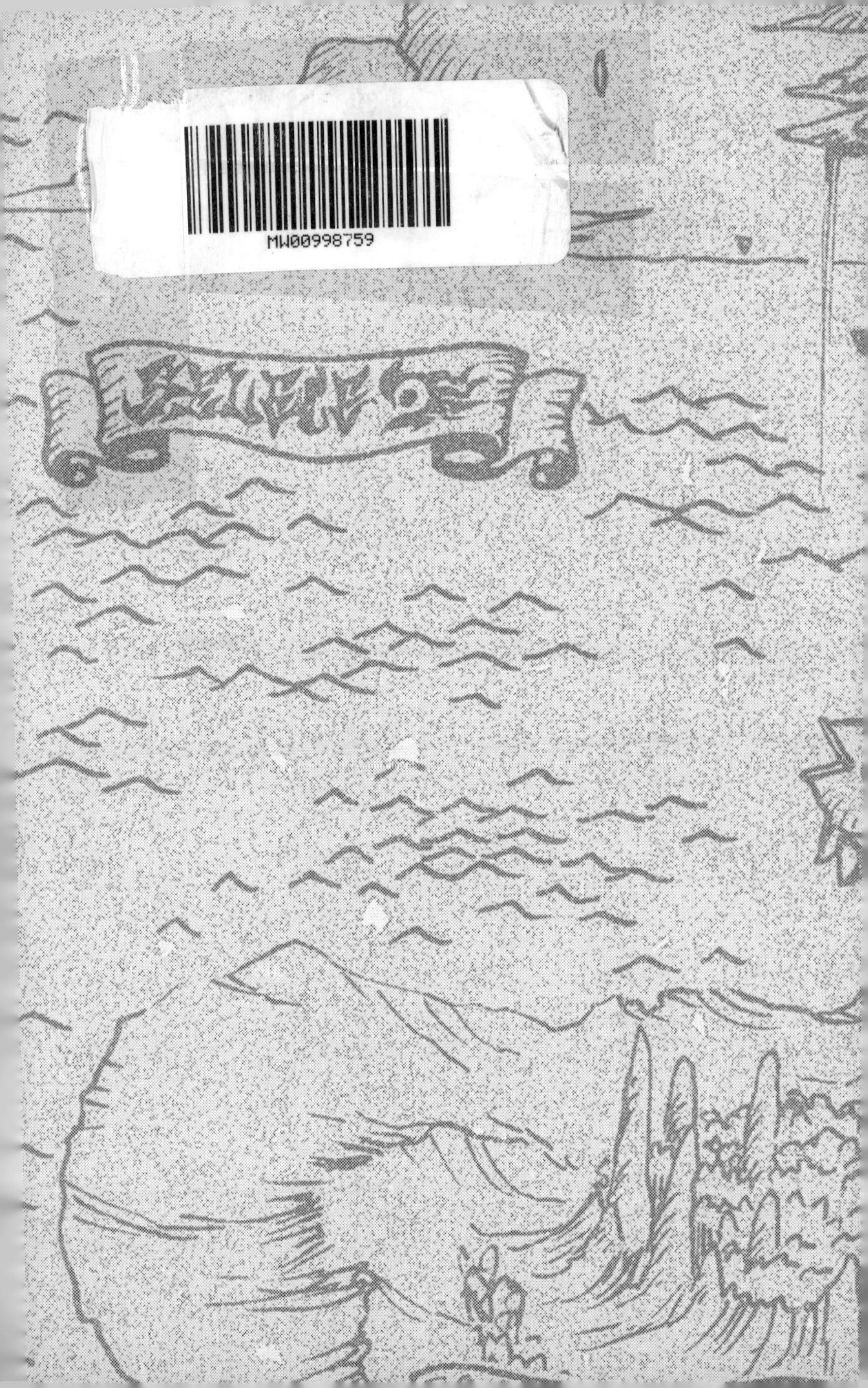

CLAMP's

MAGIC · KNIGHT
RAYEARTH II

Volume 1 (of 3)

TOKYOPOP

LOS ANGELES * TOKYO

Translator - Anita Sengupta
English Adaption - Jamie S. Rich
Copy Editors - Bryce Coleman, Carol Fox
Retouch - Paul Morrissey
Lettering - Monalisa de Asis
Cover Layout - Patrick Hook

Editor - Jake Forbes
Managing Editor - Jill Freshney
Production Coordinator - Antonio DePietro
Production Manager - Jennifer Miller
Art Director - Matthew Alford
Director of Editorial - Jeremy Ross
VP of Production & Manufacturing - Ron Klamert
President & C.O.O. - John Parker
Publisher & C.E.O. - Stuart Levy

Email: editor@TOKYOPOP.com
Come visit us online at www.TOKYOPOP.com

A ❧ TOKYOPOP® Manga

TOKYOPOP® is an imprint of Mixx Entertainment, Inc.
5900 Wilshire Blvd. Suite 2000, Los Angeles, CA 90036

Magic Knight Rayearth II Vol. 1 ©1995 CLAMP.
First published in 1995 by Kodansha Ltd., Tokyo.
English publication rights arranged through Kodansha Ltd.

English text © 2003 by Mixx Entertainment, Inc.
TOKYOPOP is a registered trademark of Mixx Entertainment, Inc.

ISBN: 1-59182-266-1

First TOKYOPOP® printing: April 2003

10 9 8 7 6 5 4 3 2 1
Printed in Canada

Introduction...

Welcome to Magic Knight Rayearth II! Here begins Hikaru, Umi and Fuu's second adventure in the magical realm of Cephiro. This new adventure stands on its own, but it does help if you know a bit about the first series before you begin. For those of you who are new to Rayearth, or if you just need a little refresher course, here's what happened in the first series...

Hikaru, Umi and Fuu were three Tokyo schoolgirls with nothing in common, that is until they were magically summoned to the land of Cephiro. An ancient wizard (with a childlike body) named Guru Clef told the girls that they were the Magic Knights, the legendary heroes from another world who were prophesized to save Cephiro from Zagato, a sinister man who held the land's ruler captive. After receiving some magical armor, called "guards," the girls began their quest.

Along the way they befriended Presea, the blacksmith, Ferio, a wandering swordsman, and Mokona, a bizarre white puffball who became their guide. In order to become true Magic Knights, the girls first had to unlock the Mashin (or Rune Gods, as they're called in the anime). These ancient spirits function like "mecha" in combat, as well as providing guidance to the girls from within their own souls.

Armed with new powerful weapons and even more powerful Mashin, the girls journeyed to Zagato's fortress to rescue Princess Emeraude. Much to their surprise, the Magic Knights discovered that Emeraude wanted the Magic Knights to slay her. Zagato was bent on destroying the knights only to protect Emeraude, the woman he loved. The tragic nature of Cephiro's existence is based on the leader, or "Pillar," devoting herself 100% to her country. When Emeraude fell in love with Zagato, she could not be with him because of her duty, and so she chose to die rather than live in sorrow. The Magic Knights defeated Emeraude, but it left the three girls scarred for life and sent them back to earth in tears.

Now we rejoin the girls one year later, more mature for their experiences, holding many regrets for what they were forced to do. Perhaps the future holds happier times for these young ladies from another world who are so pure of heart.

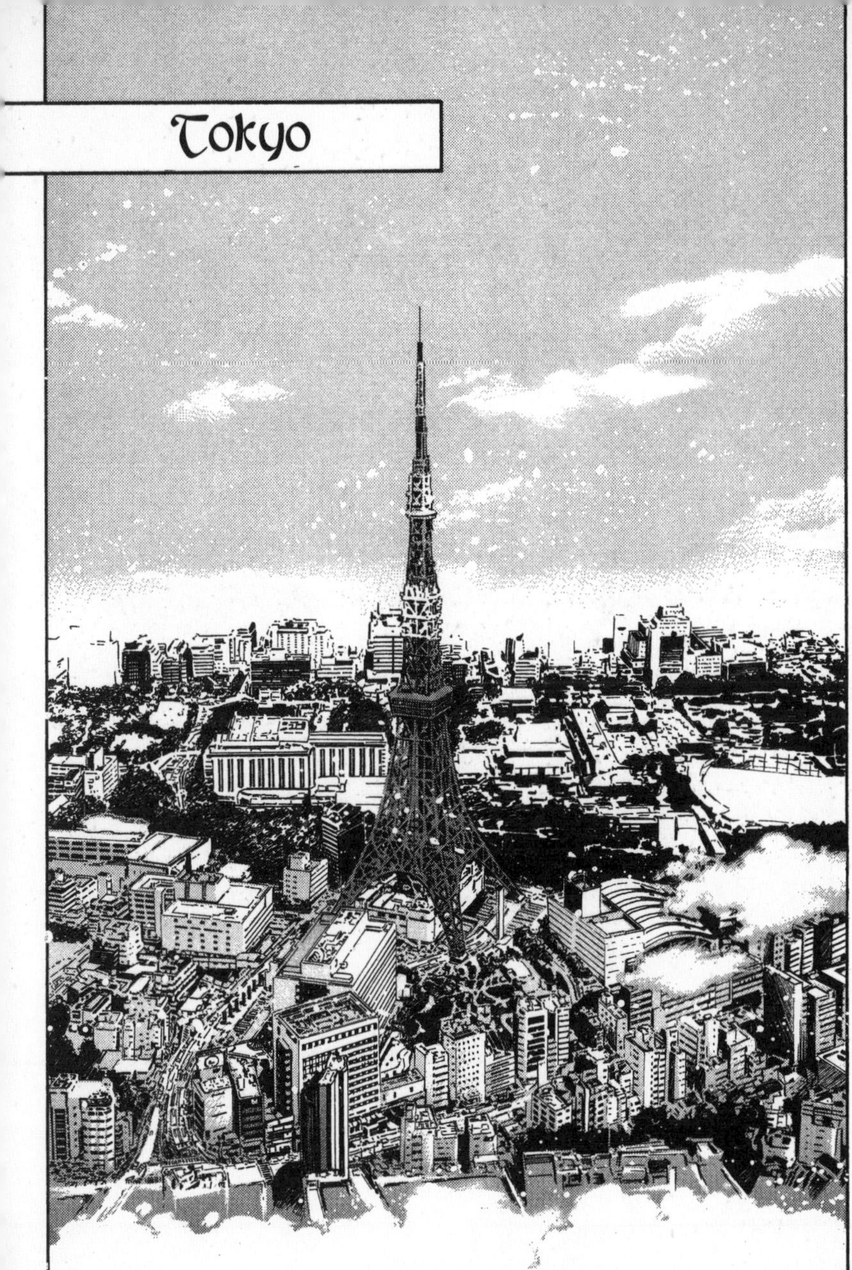
Tokyo

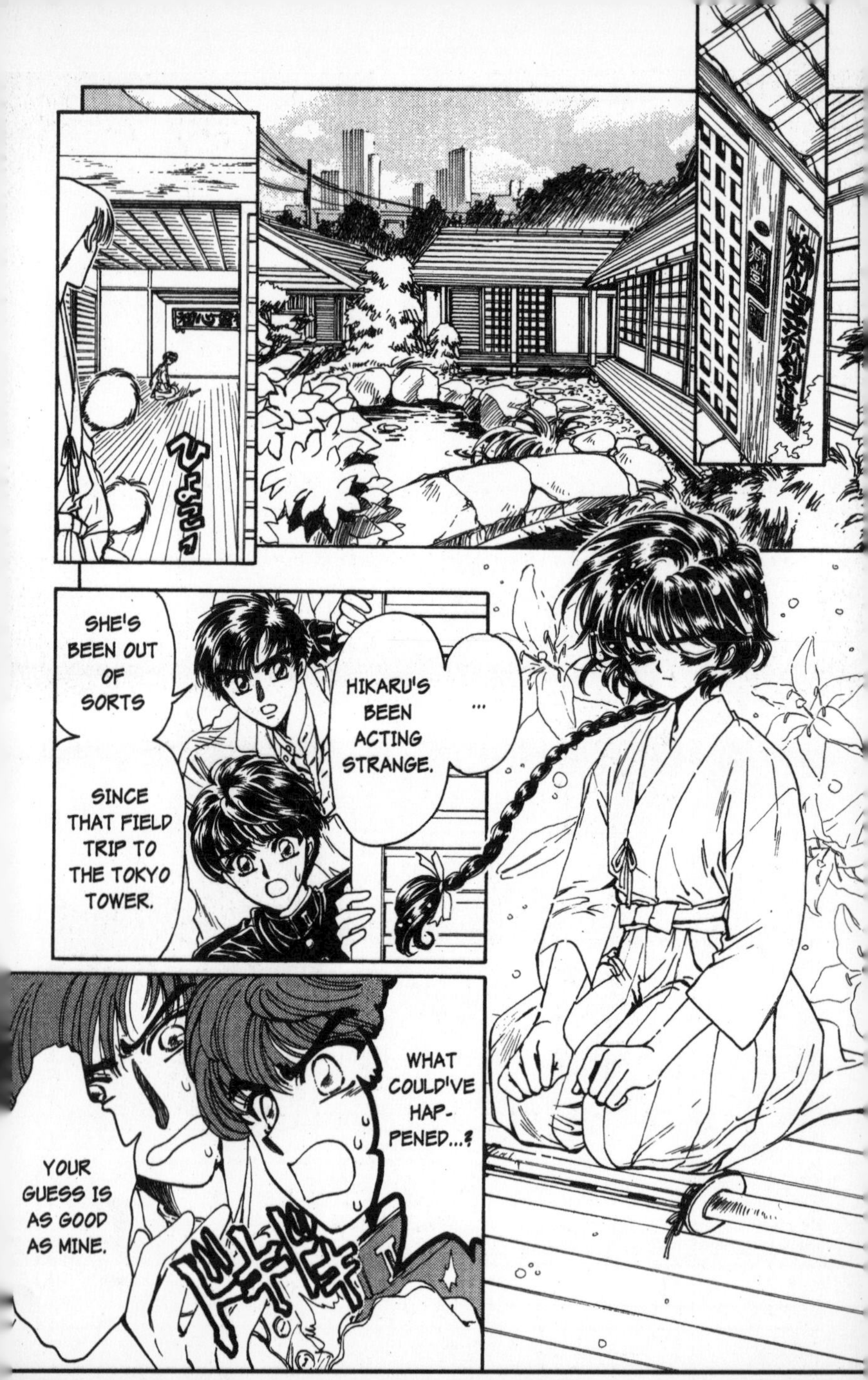
...
HIKARU'S BEEN ACTING STRANGE.
SHE'S BEEN OUT OF SORTS
SINCE THAT FIELD TRIP TO THE TOKYO TOWER.
WHAT COULD'VE HAP-PENED...?
YOUR GUESS IS AS GOOD AS MINE.

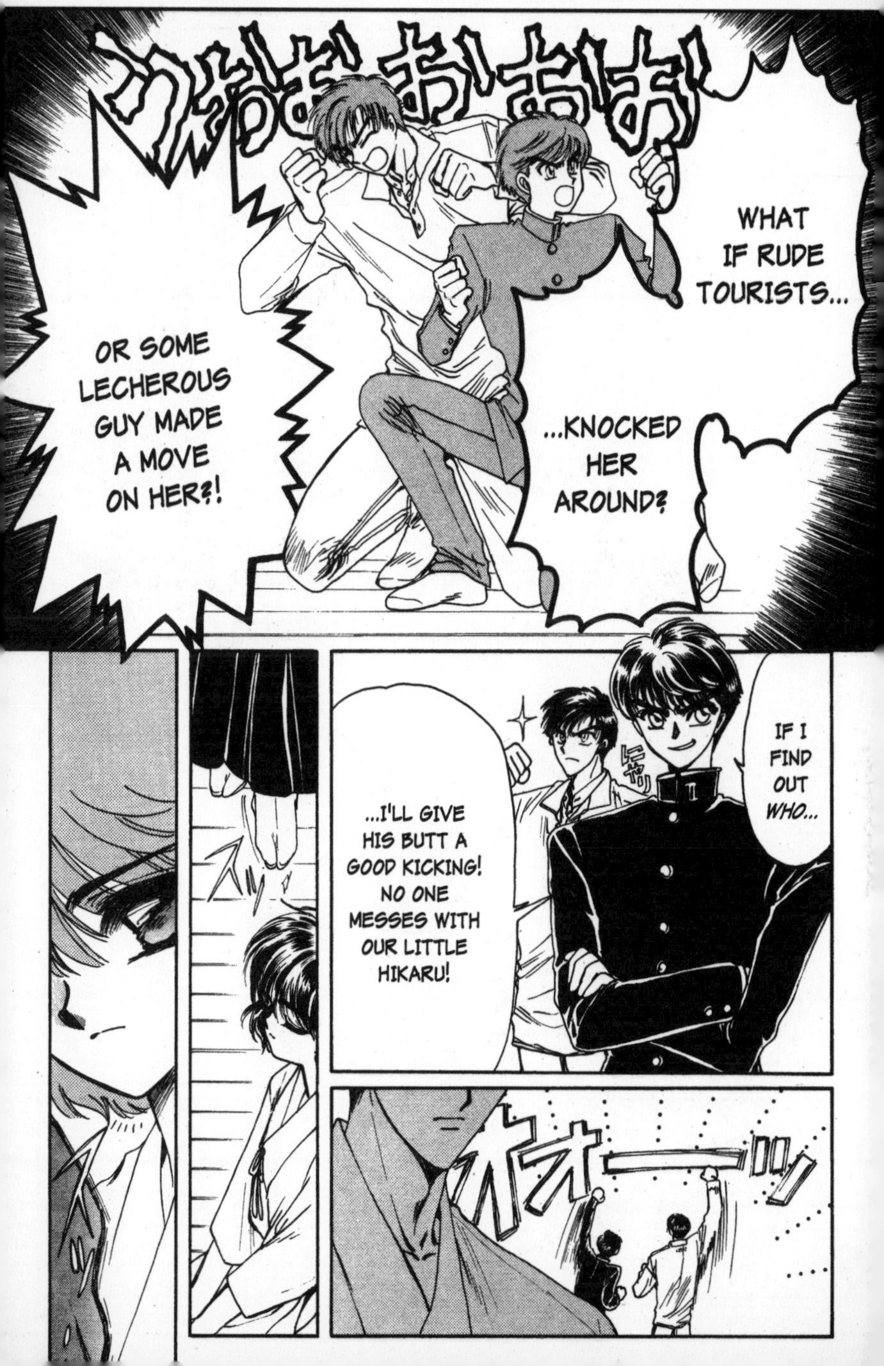
WHAT IF RUDE TOURISTS...
...KNOCKED HER AROUND?
OR SOME LECHEROUS GUY MADE A MOVE ON HER?!
IF I FIND OUT WHO...
...I'LL GIVE HIS BUTT A GOOD KICKING! NO ONE MESSES WITH OUR LITTLE HIKARU!

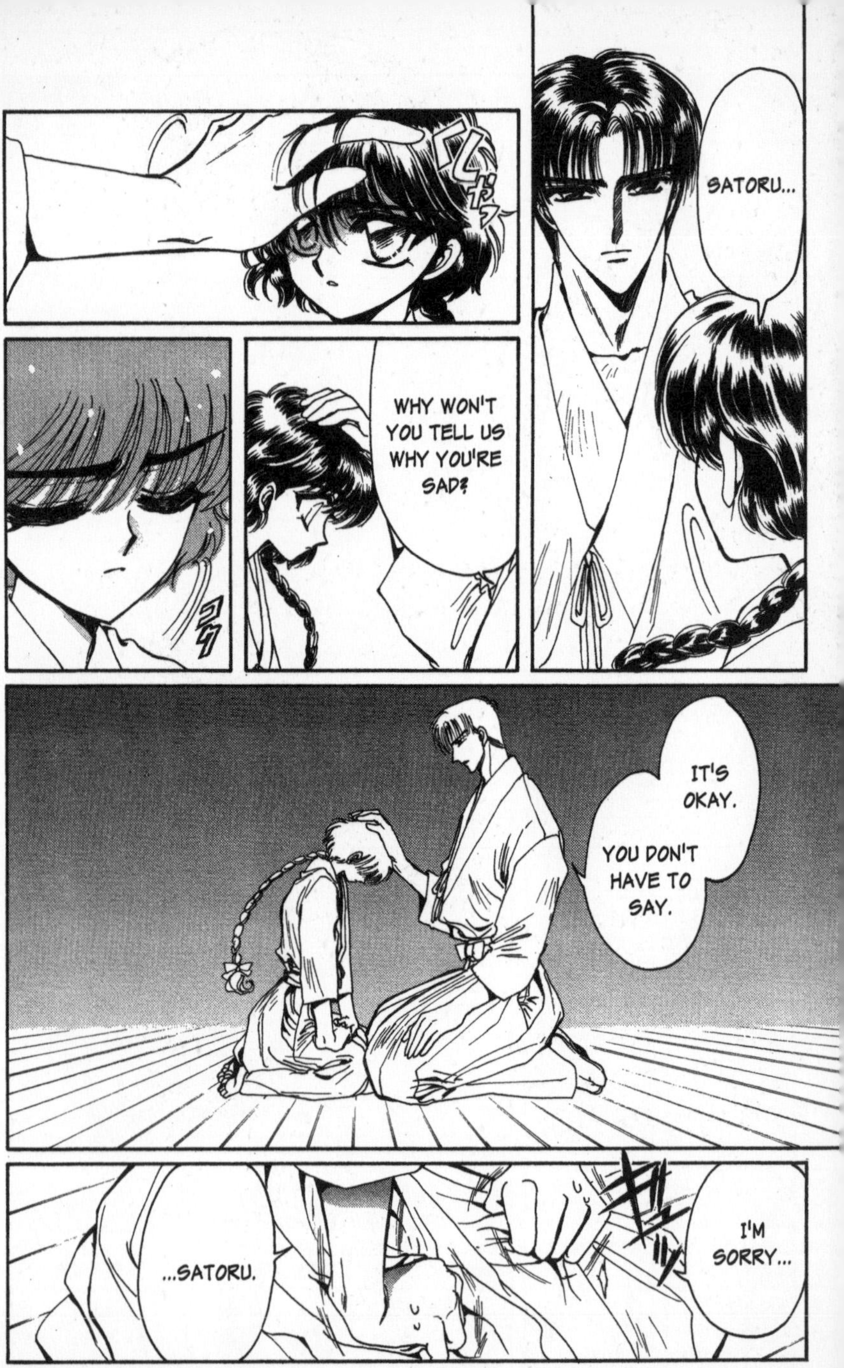
SATORU...
WHY WON'T YOU TELL US WHY YOU'RE SAD?
IT'S OKAY.
YOU DON'T HAVE TO SAY.
I'M SORRY...
...SATORU.

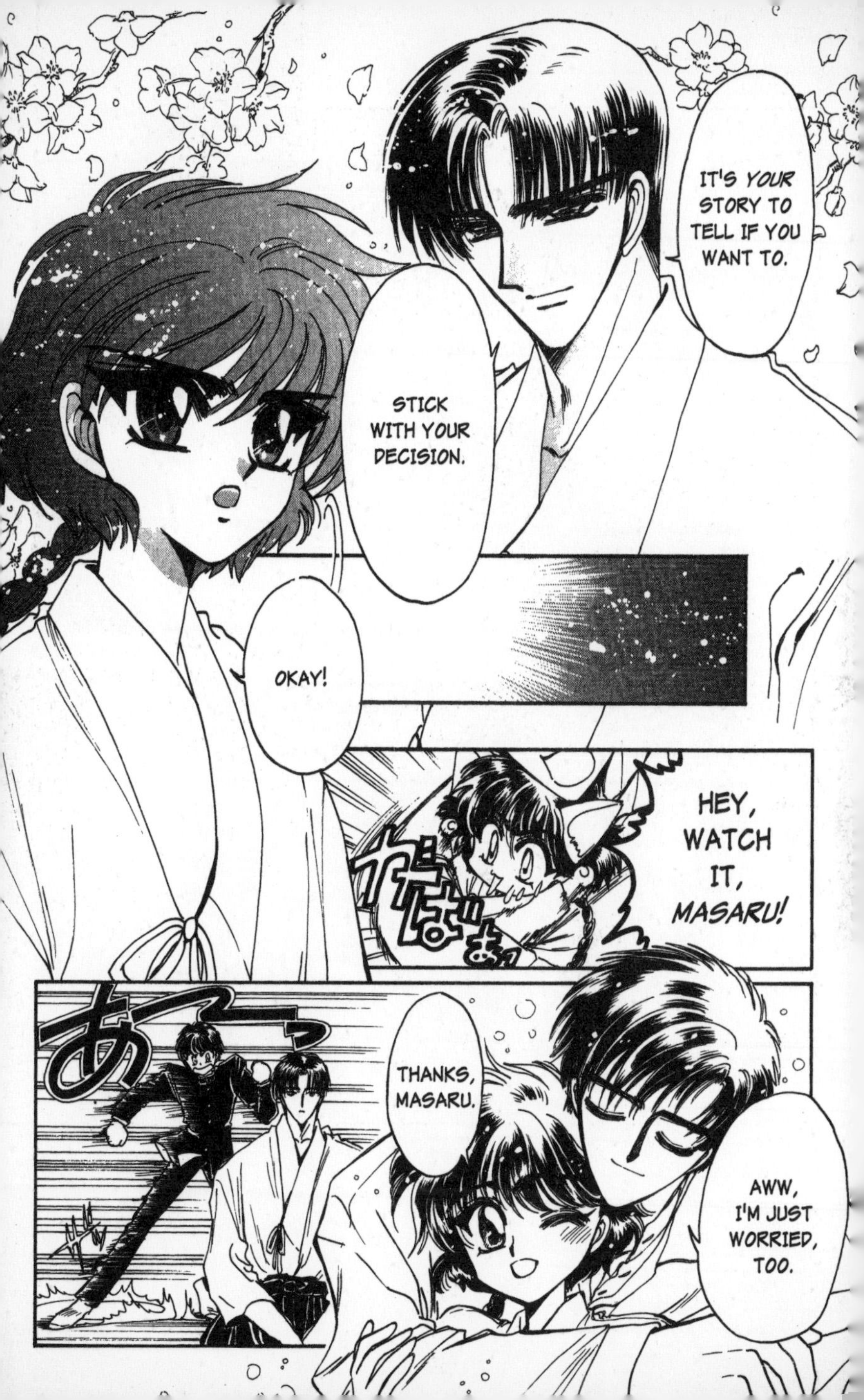
IT'S YOUR STORY TO TELL IF YOU WANT TO.
STICK WITH YOUR DECISION.
OKAY!
HEY, WATCH IT, MASARU!
THANKS, MASARU.
AWW, I'M JUST WORRIED, TOO.

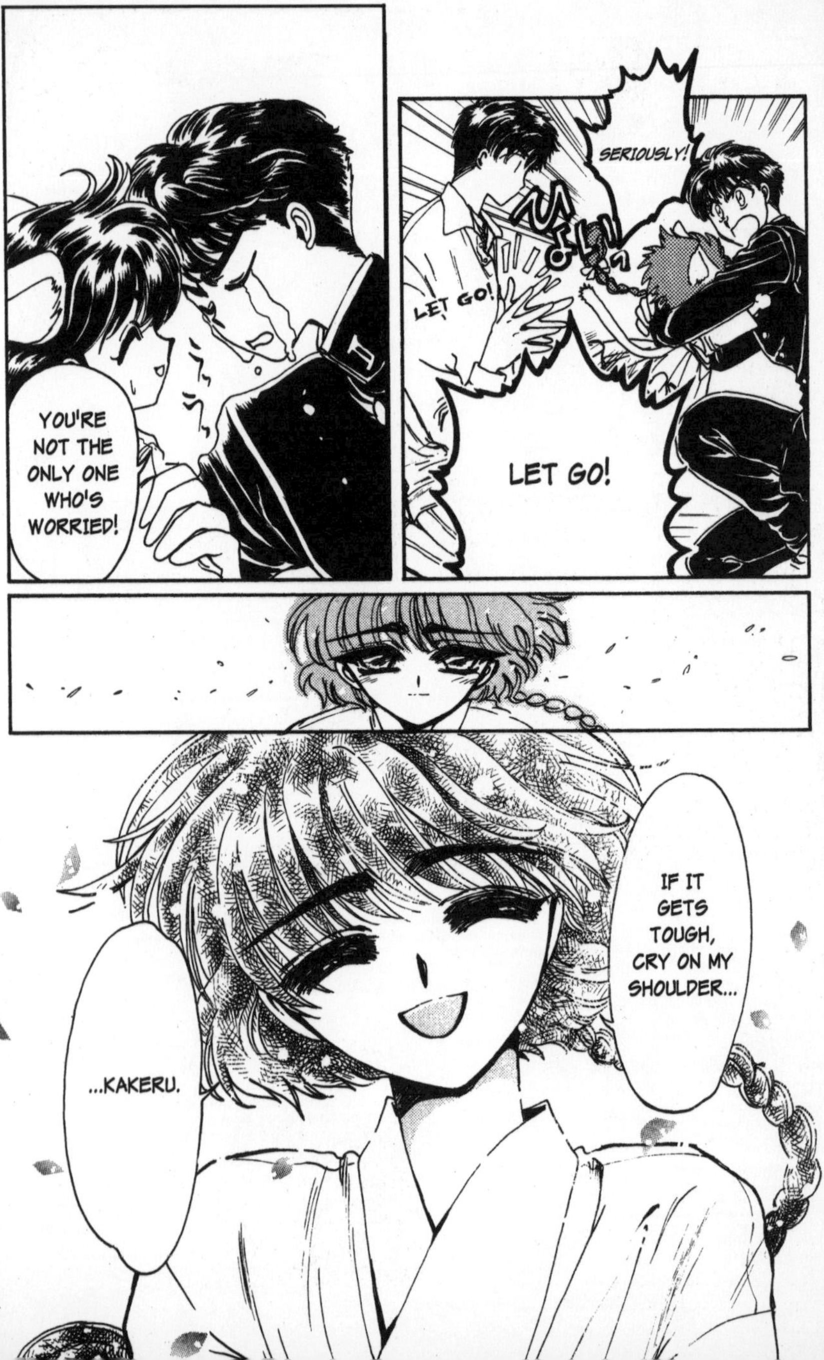
SERIOUSLY!
LET GO!
LET GO!
YOU'RE NOT THE ONLY ONE WHO'S WORRIED!
IF IT GETS TOUGH, CRY ON MY SHOULDER...
...KAKERU.

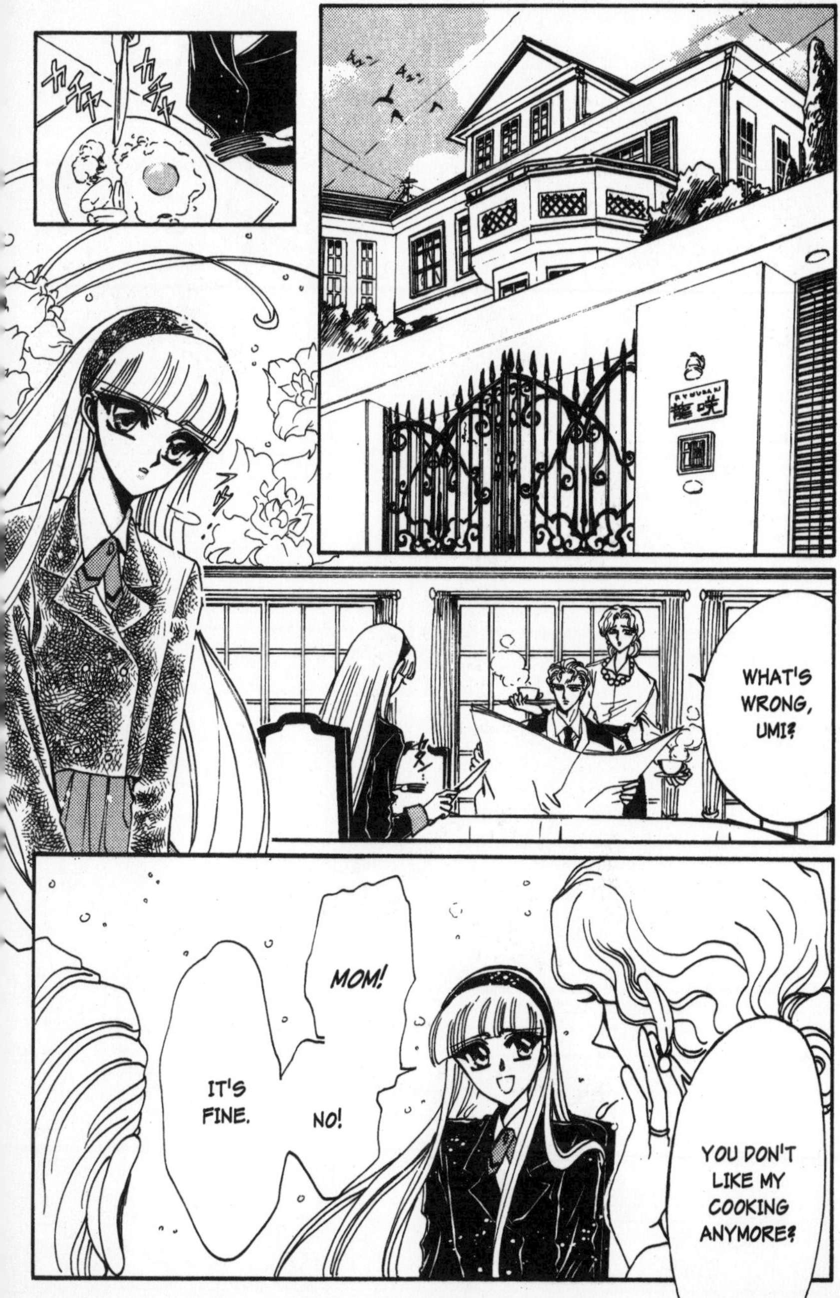
龍咲
カチャ
カチャ
WHAT'S WRONG, UMI?
YOU DON'T LIKE MY COOKING ANYMORE?
MOM!
NO!
IT'S FINE.

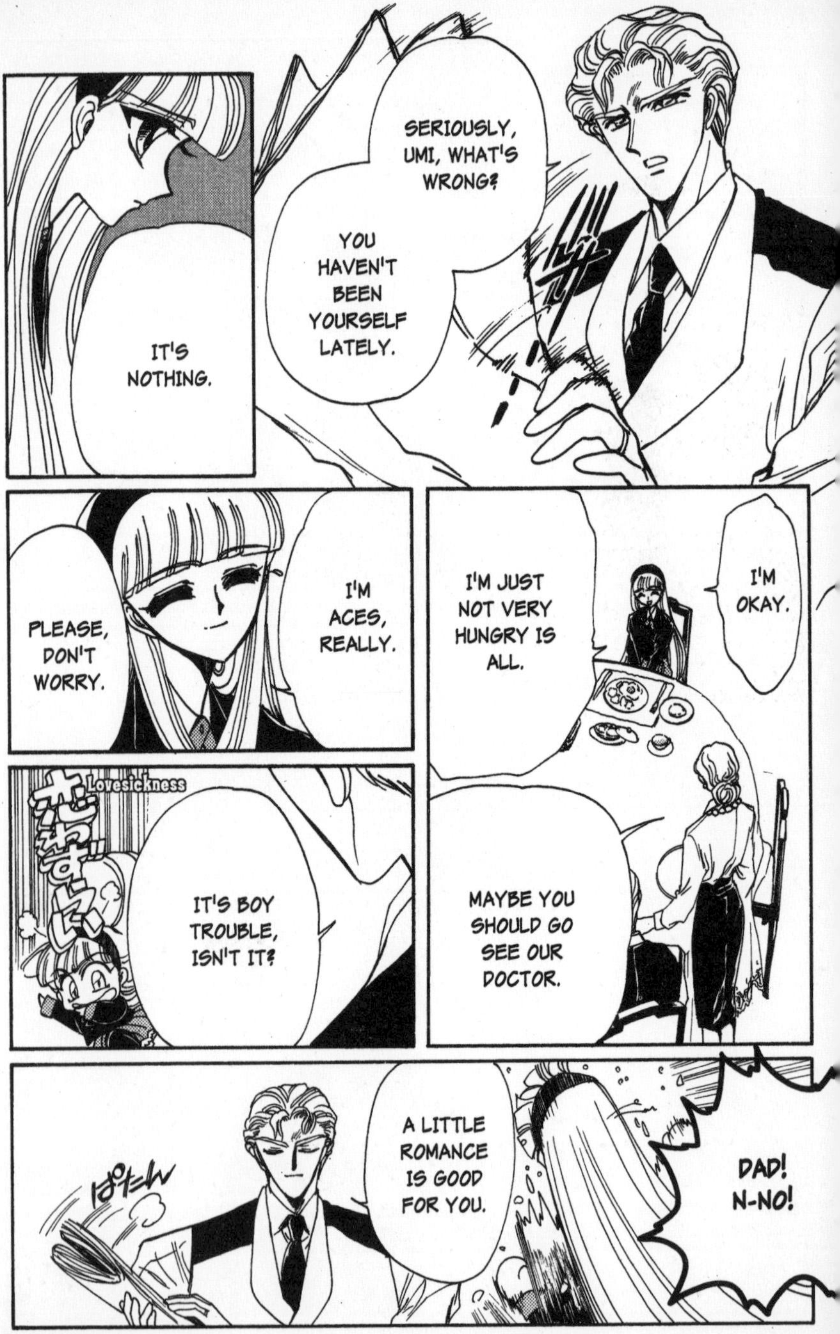
SERIOUSLY, UMI, WHAT'S WRONG?
YOU HAVEN'T BEEN YOURSELF LATELY.
IT'S NOTHING.
I'M OKAY.
I'M JUST NOT VERY HUNGRY IS ALL.
MAYBE YOU SHOULD GO SEE OUR DOCTOR.
I'M ACES, REALLY.
PLEASE, DON'T WORRY.
Lovesickness
IT'S BOY TROUBLE, ISN'T IT?
A LITTLE ROMANCE IS GOOD FOR YOU.
DAD! N-NO!

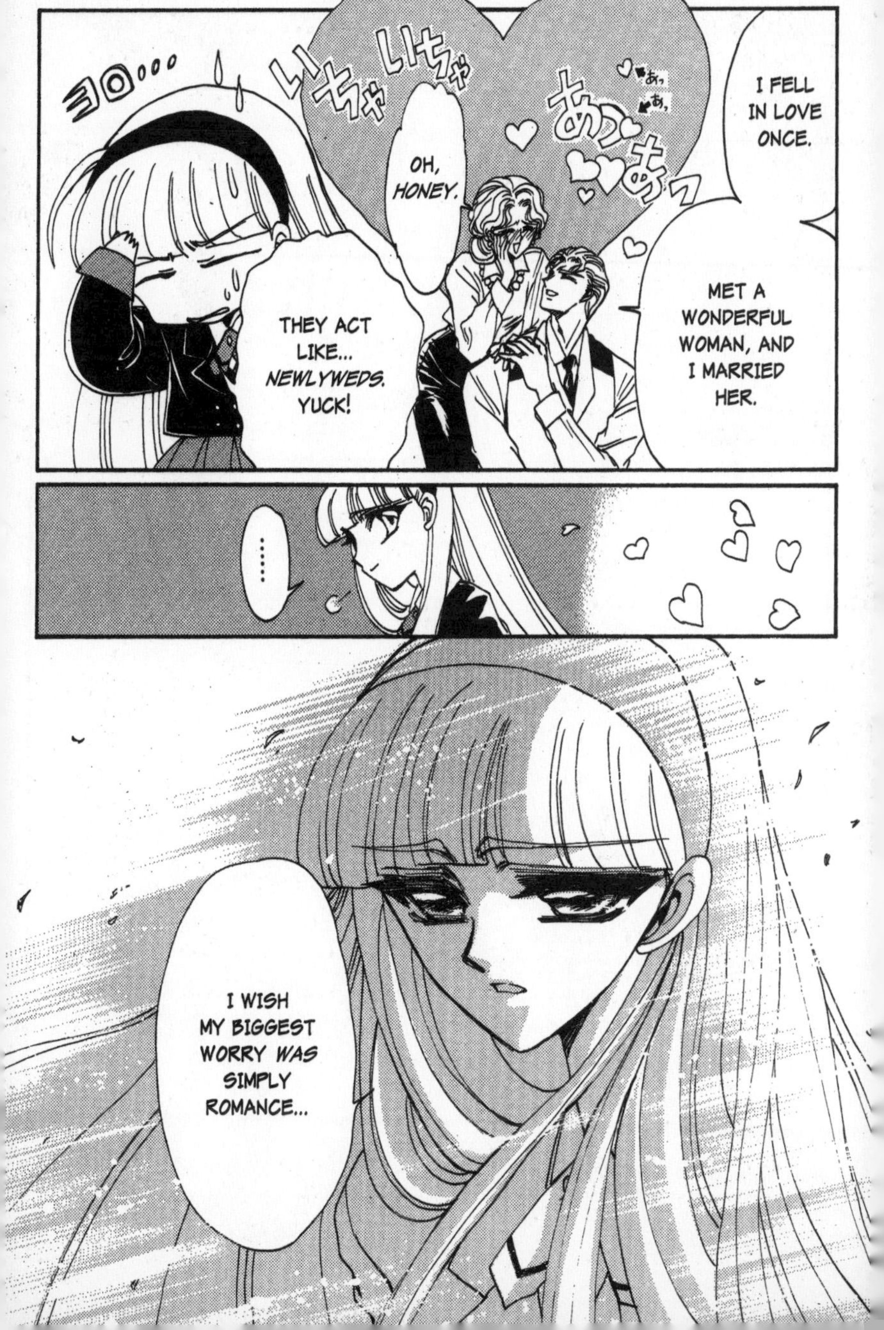
I FELL IN LOVE ONCE.
MET A WONDERFUL WOMAN, AND I MARRIED HER.
あっ
あっ
あっあっ
OH, HONEY.
いちゃいちゃ
THEY ACT LIKE... NEWLYWEDS. YUCK!
ヨロ
……
I WISH MY BIGGEST WORRY WAS SIMPLY ROMANCE...

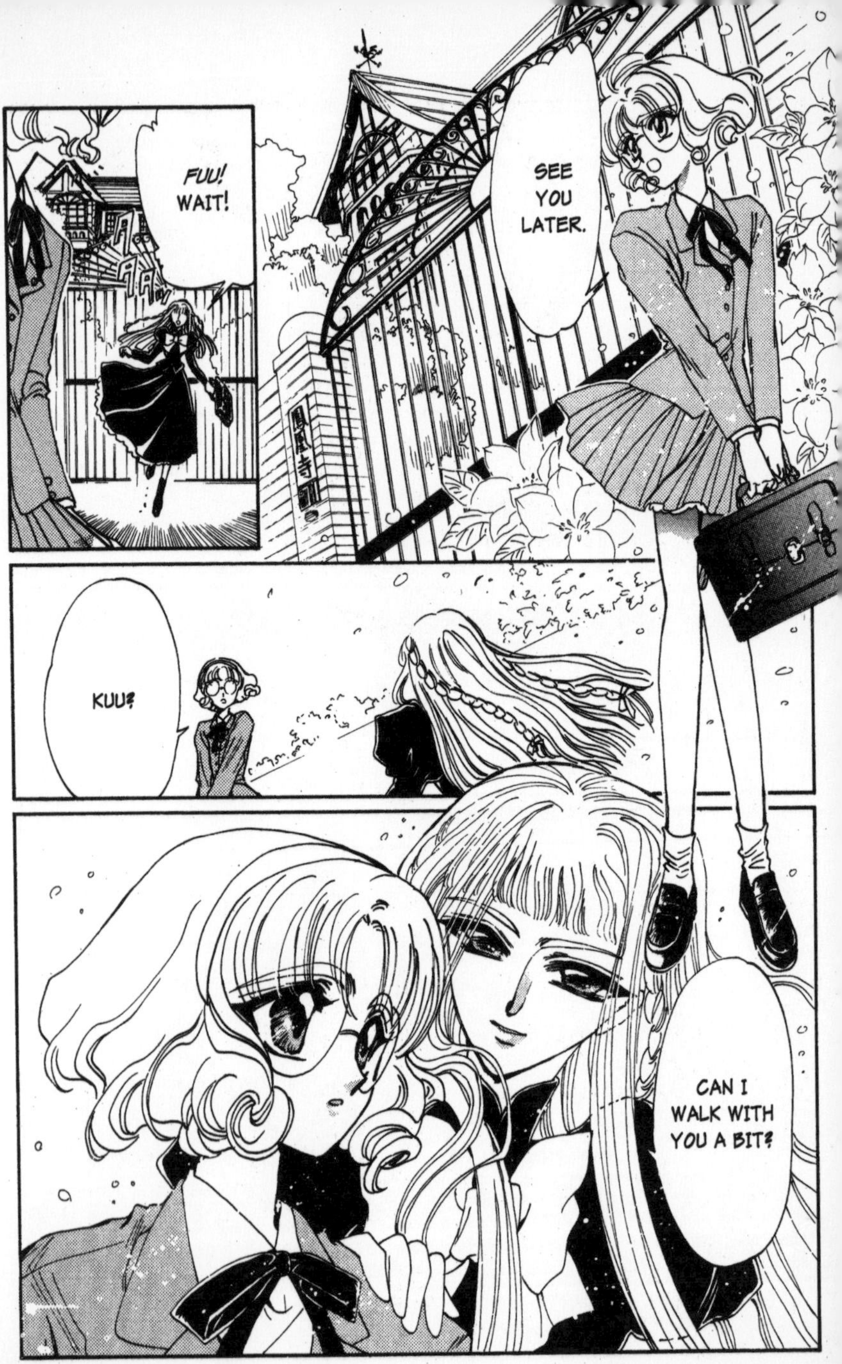
SEE YOU LATER.
FUU! WAIT!
KUU?
CAN I WALK WITH YOU A BIT?

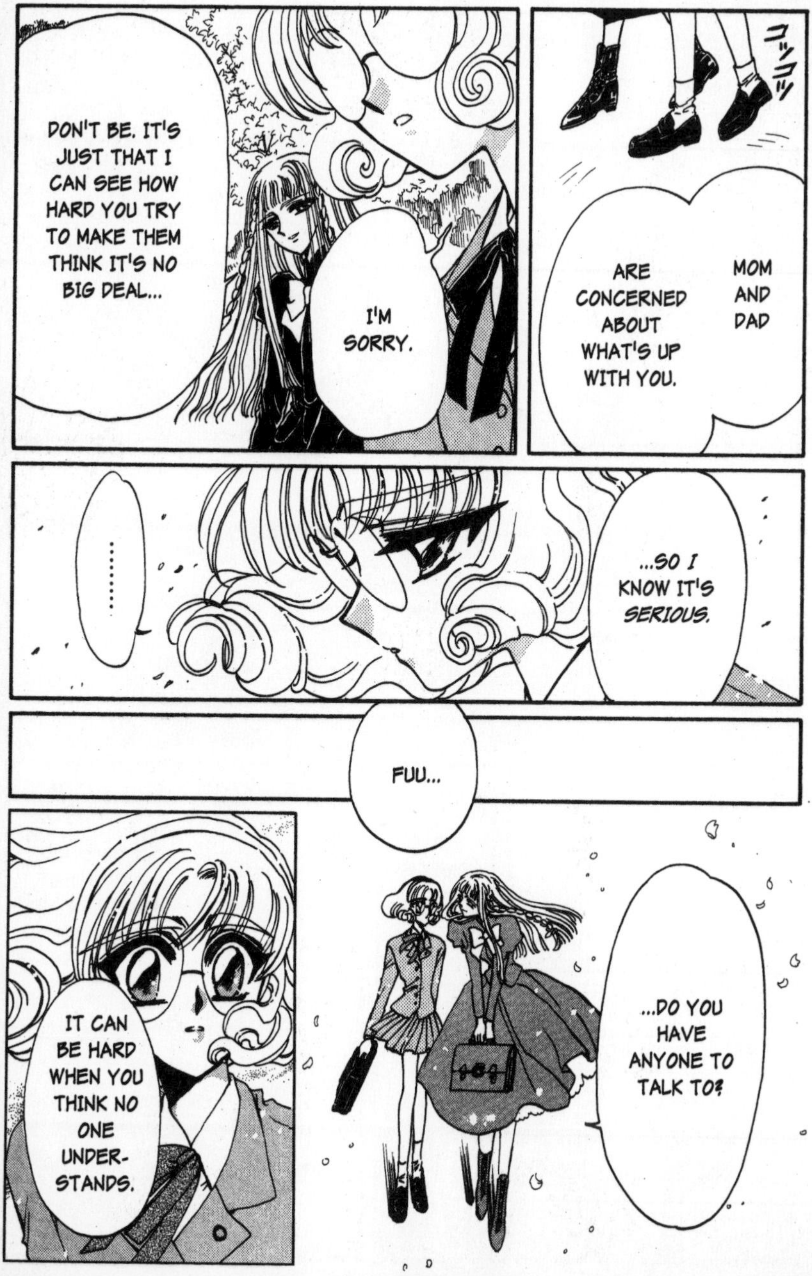
コツコツ
MOM AND DAD ARE CONCERNED ABOUT WHAT'S UP WITH YOU.
I'M SORRY.
DON'T BE. IT'S JUST THAT I CAN SEE HOW HARD YOU TRY TO MAKE THEM THINK IT'S NO BIG DEAL...
...SO I KNOW IT'S *SERIOUS.*
....
FUU...
...DO YOU HAVE ANYONE TO TALK TO?
IT CAN BE HARD WHEN YOU THINK NO ONE UNDER-STANDS.

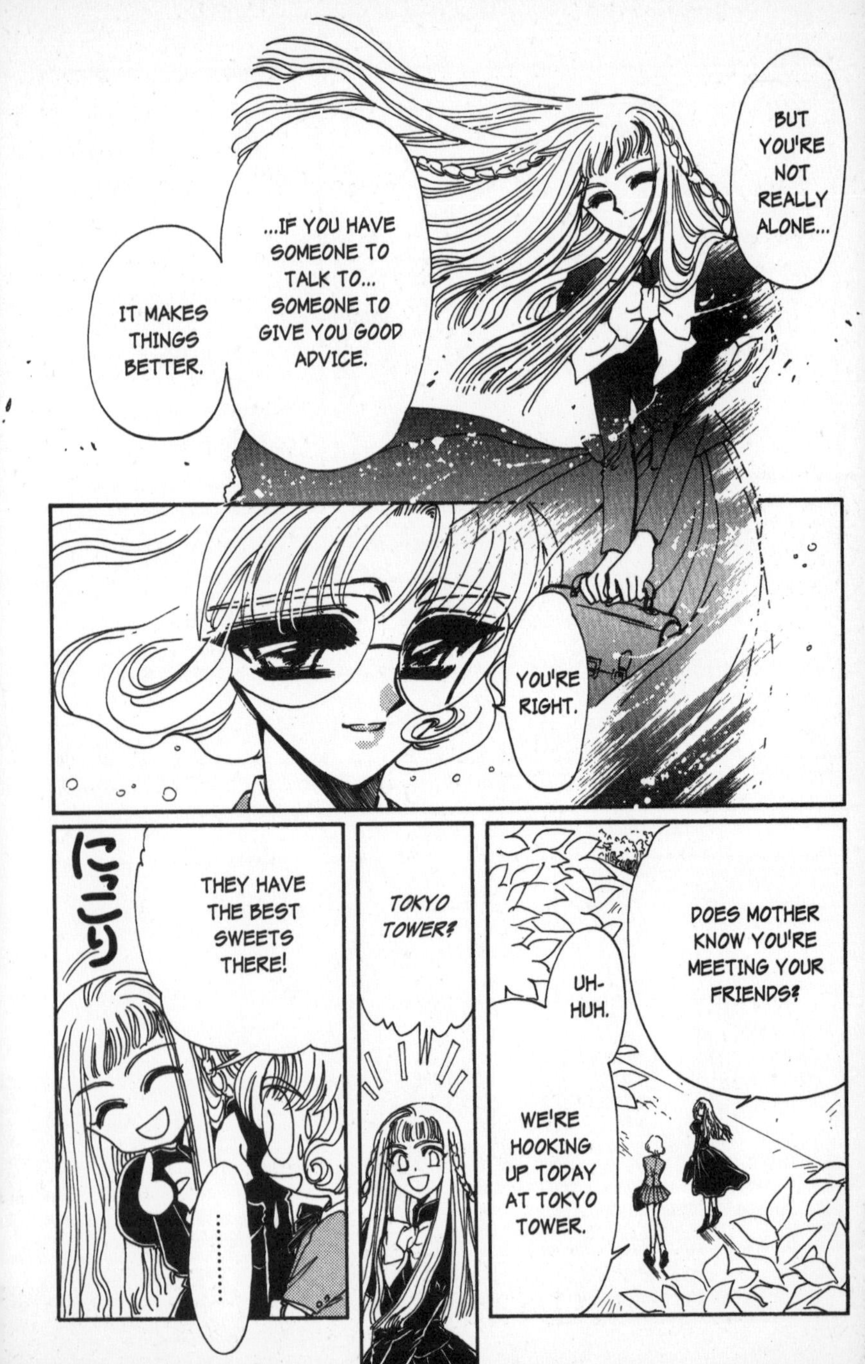
BUT YOU'RE NOT REALLY ALONE...
...IF YOU HAVE SOMEONE TO TALK TO... SOMEONE TO GIVE YOU GOOD ADVICE.
IT MAKES THINGS BETTER.
YOU'RE RIGHT.
DOES MOTHER KNOW YOU'RE MEETING YOUR FRIENDS?
UH-HUH.
WE'RE HOOKING UP TODAY AT TOKYO TOWER.
TOKYO TOWER?
THEY HAVE THE BEST SWEETS THERE!
にっこり
......

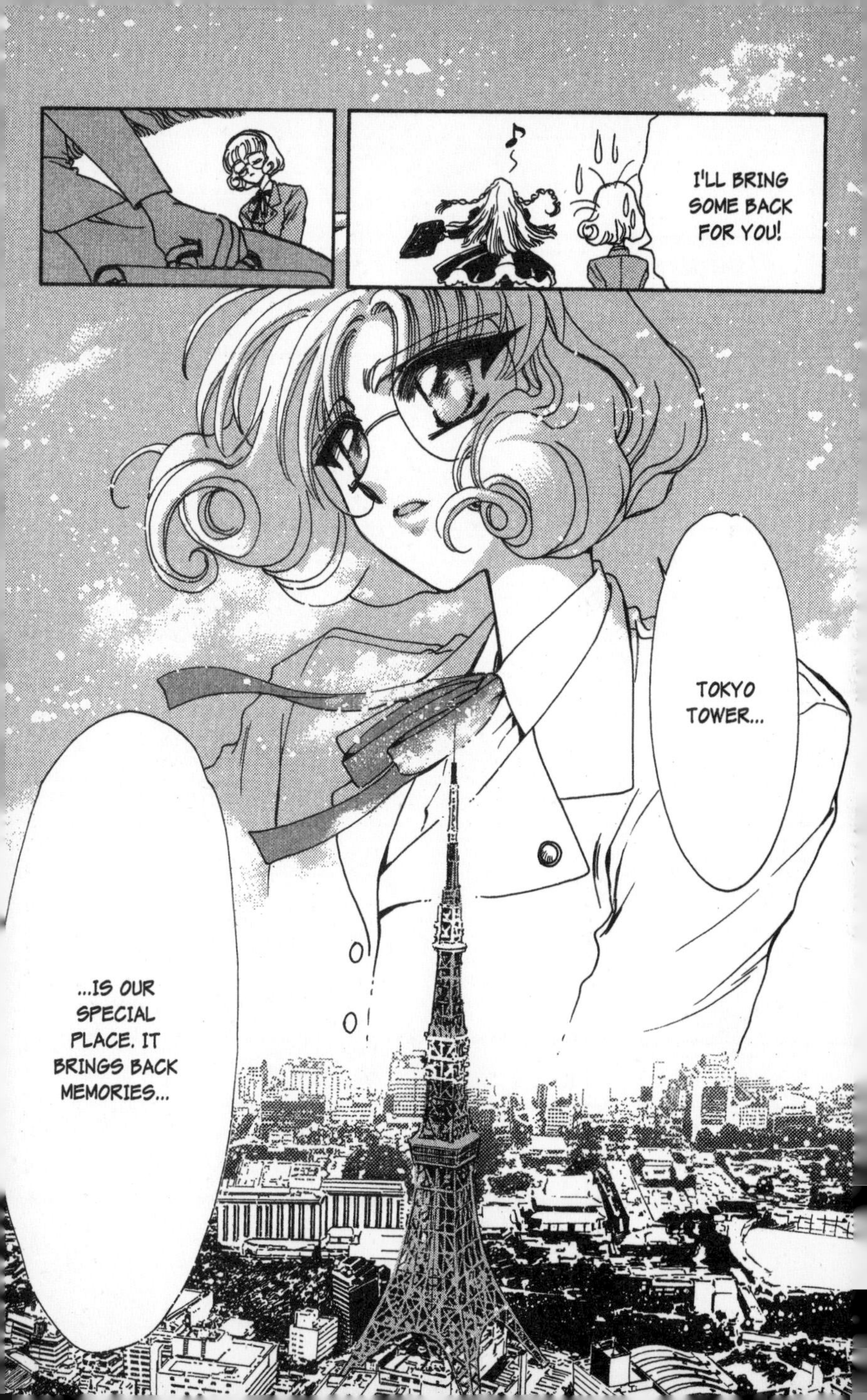
I'LL BRING SOME BACK FOR YOU!
TOKYO TOWER...
...IS OUR SPECIAL PLACE. IT BRINGS BACK MEMORIES...

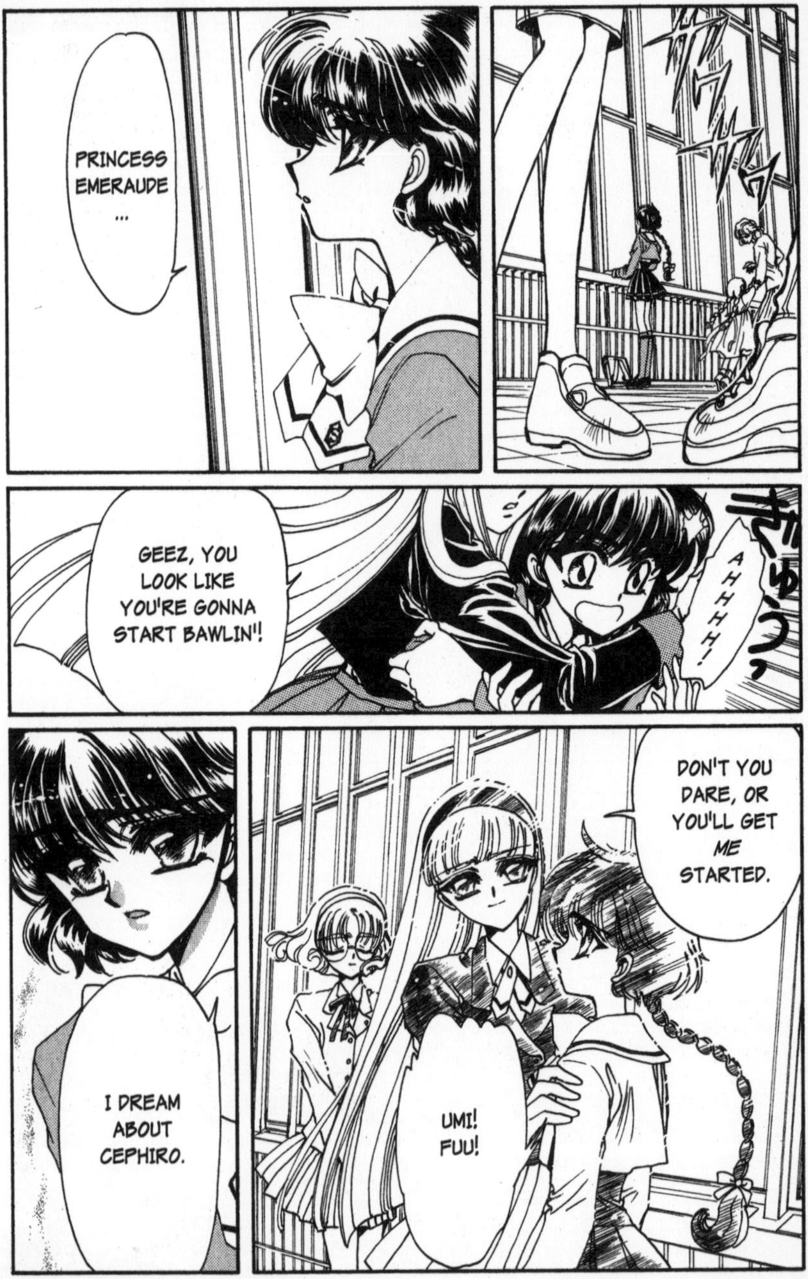
PRINCESS EMERAUDE ...
AHHHH!
GEEZ, YOU LOOK LIKE YOU'RE GONNA START BAWLIN'!
DON'T YOU DARE, OR YOU'LL GET *ME* STARTED.
UMI! FUU!
I DREAM ABOUT CEPHIRO.

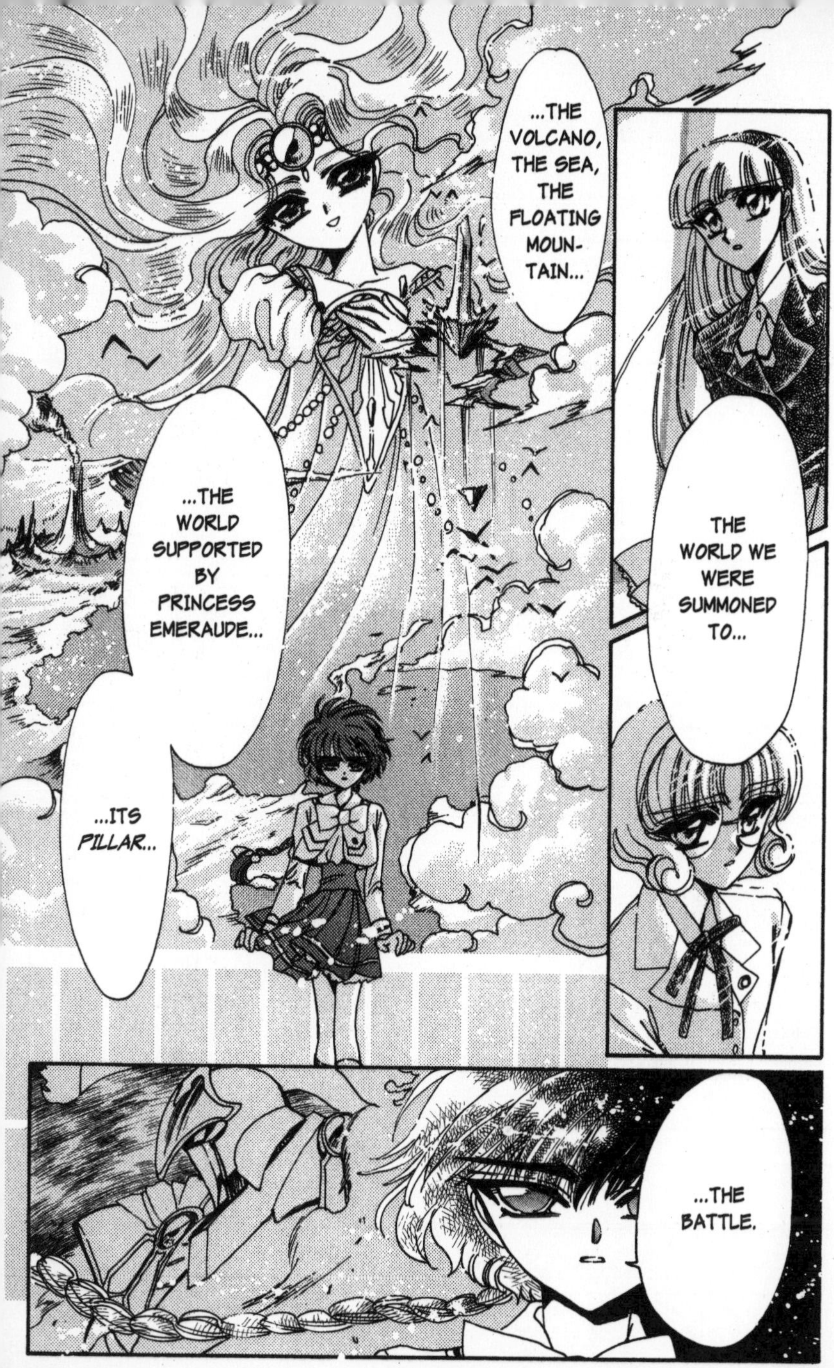
THE WORLD WE WERE SUMMONED TO...
...THE VOLCANO, THE SEA, THE FLOATING MOUN-TAIN...
...THE WORLD SUPPORTED BY PRINCESS EMERAUDE...
...ITS *PILLAR*...
...THE BATTLE.

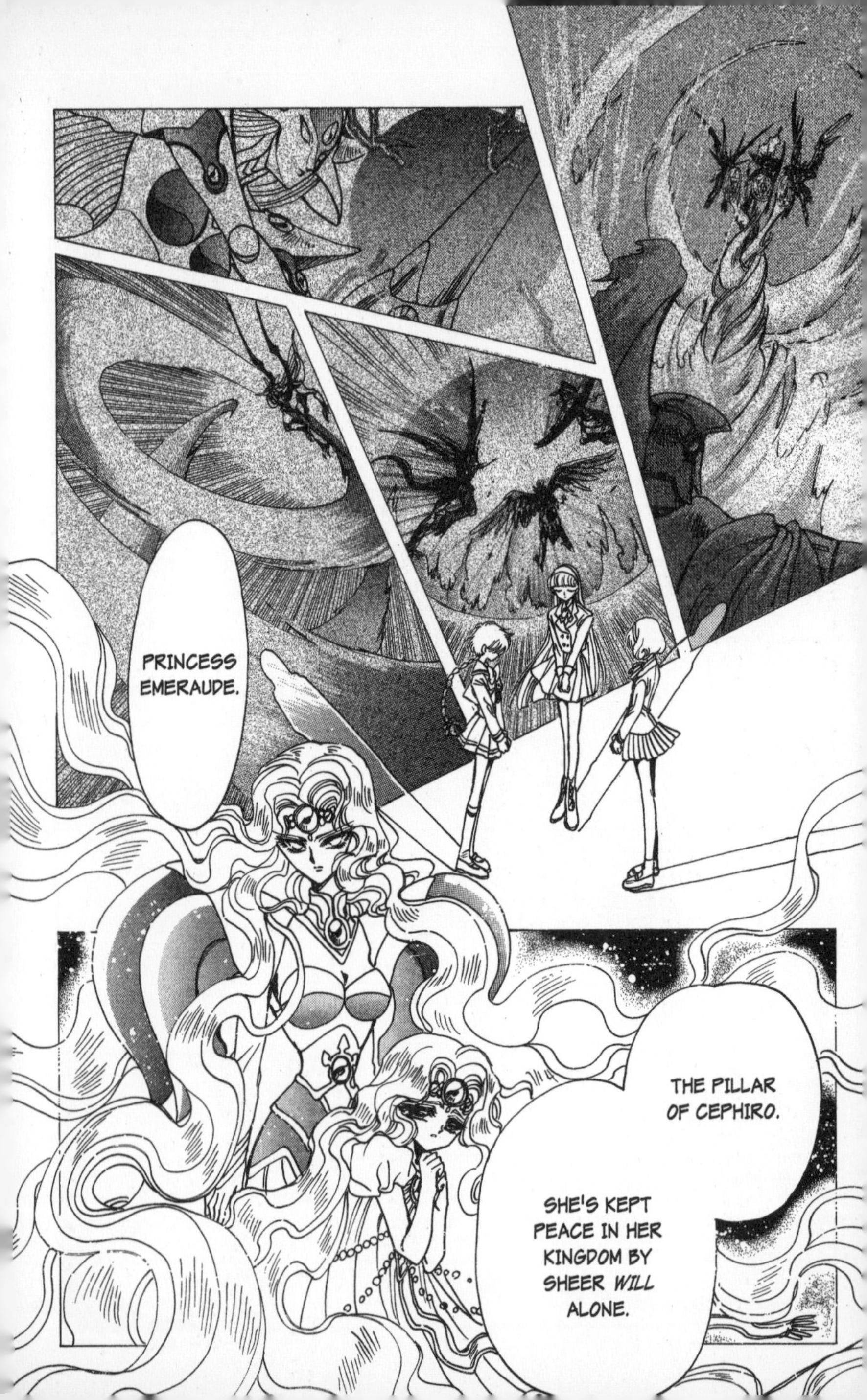
PRINCESS EMERAUDE.
THE PILLAR OF CEPHIRO.
SHE'S KEPT PEACE IN HER KINGDOM BY SHEER *WILL* ALONE.

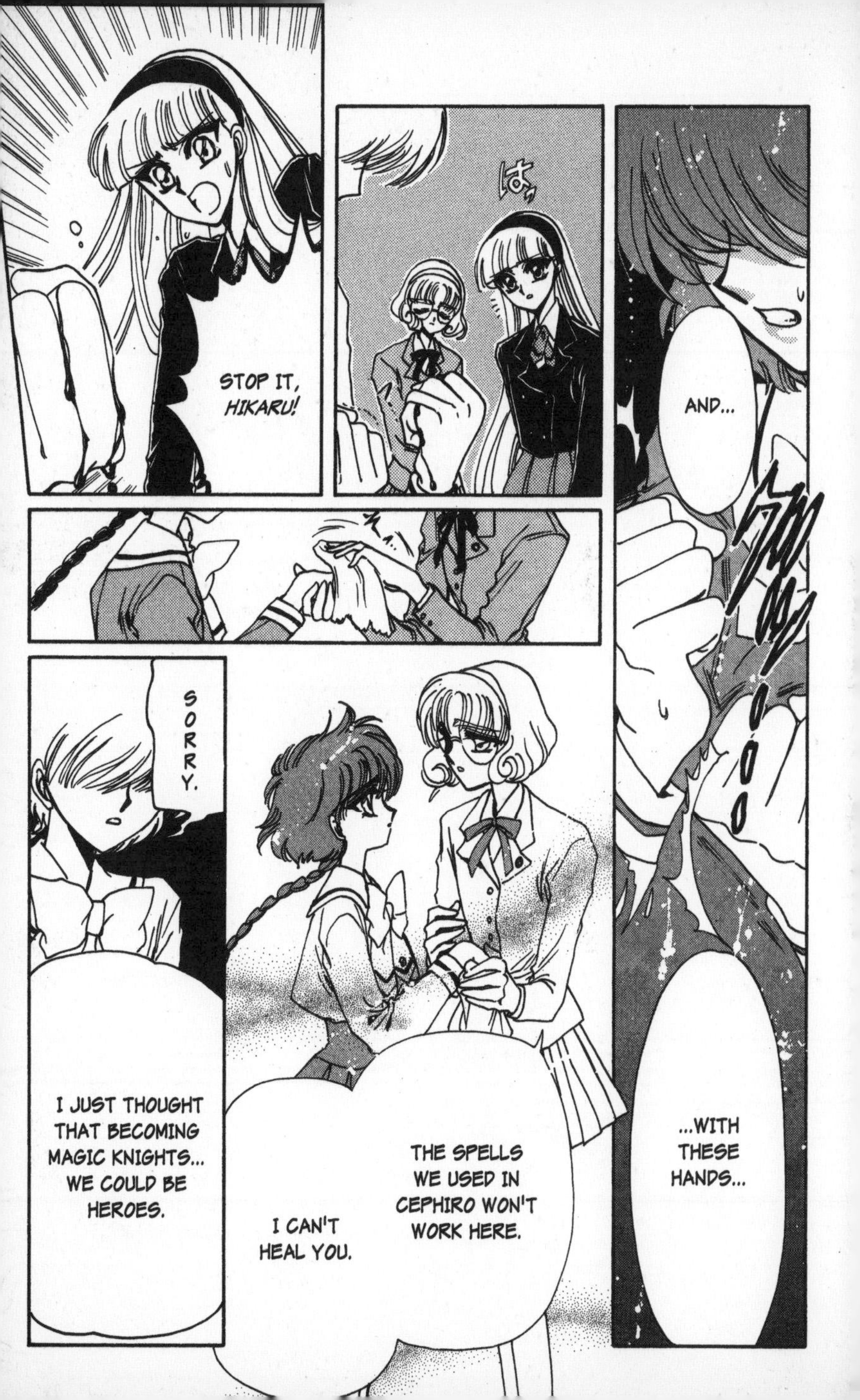
AND...
...WITH THESE HANDS...
はっ
STOP IT, HIKARU!
THE SPELLS WE USED IN CEPHIRO WON'T WORK HERE.
I CAN'T HEAL YOU.
SORRY.
I JUST THOUGHT THAT BECOMING MAGIC KNIGHTS... WE COULD BE HEROES.

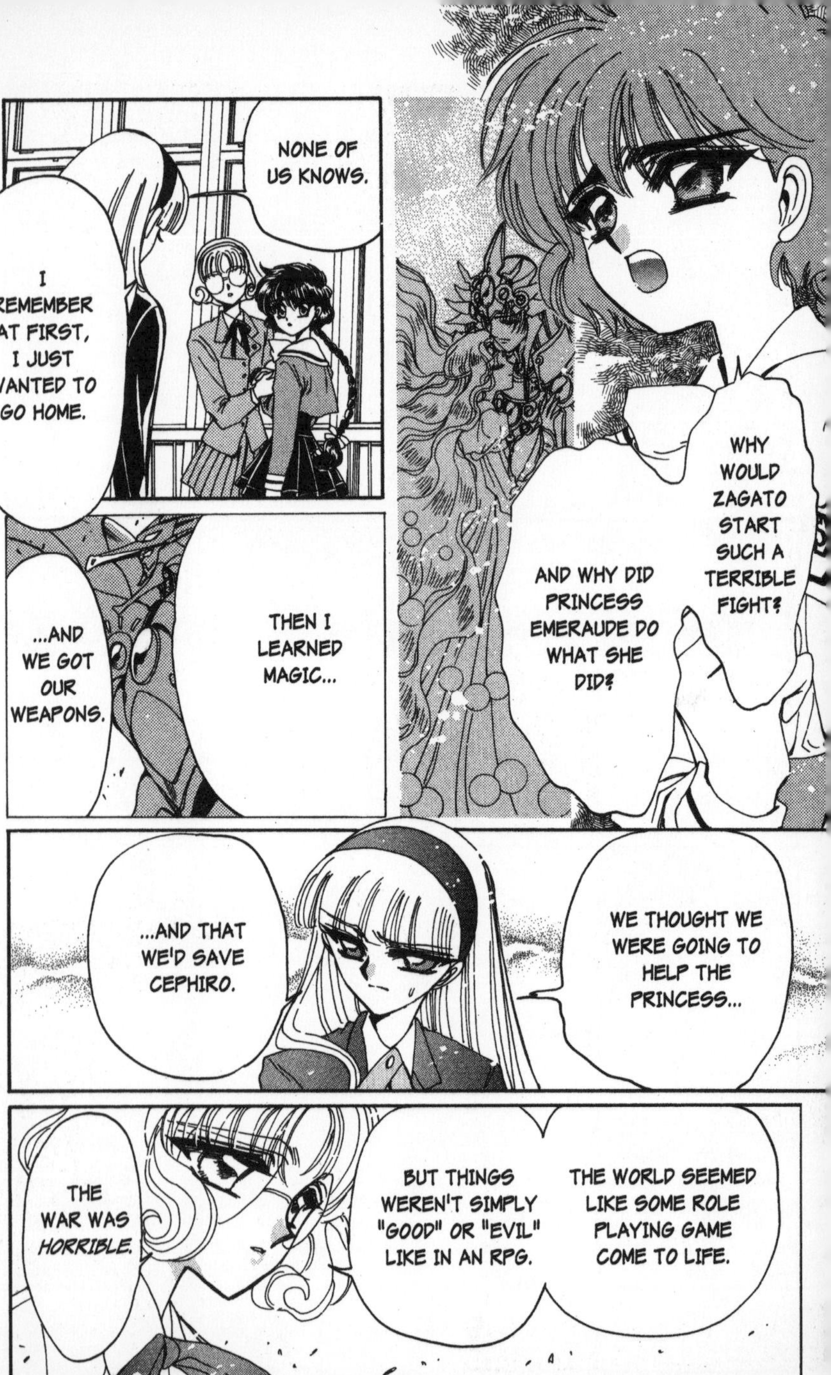
WHY WOULD ZAGATO START SUCH A TERRIBLE FIGHT?
AND WHY DID PRINCESS EMERAUDE DO WHAT SHE DID?
NONE OF US KNOWS.
I REMEMBER AT FIRST, I JUST WANTED TO GO HOME.
THEN I LEARNED MAGIC...
...AND WE GOT OUR WEAPONS.
WE THOUGHT WE WERE GOING TO HELP THE PRINCESS...
...AND THAT WE'D SAVE CEPHIRO.
THE WORLD SEEMED LIKE SOME ROLE PLAYING GAME COME TO LIFE.
BUT THINGS WEREN'T SIMPLY "GOOD" OR "EVIL" LIKE IN AN RPG.
THE WAR WAS *HORRIBLE.*

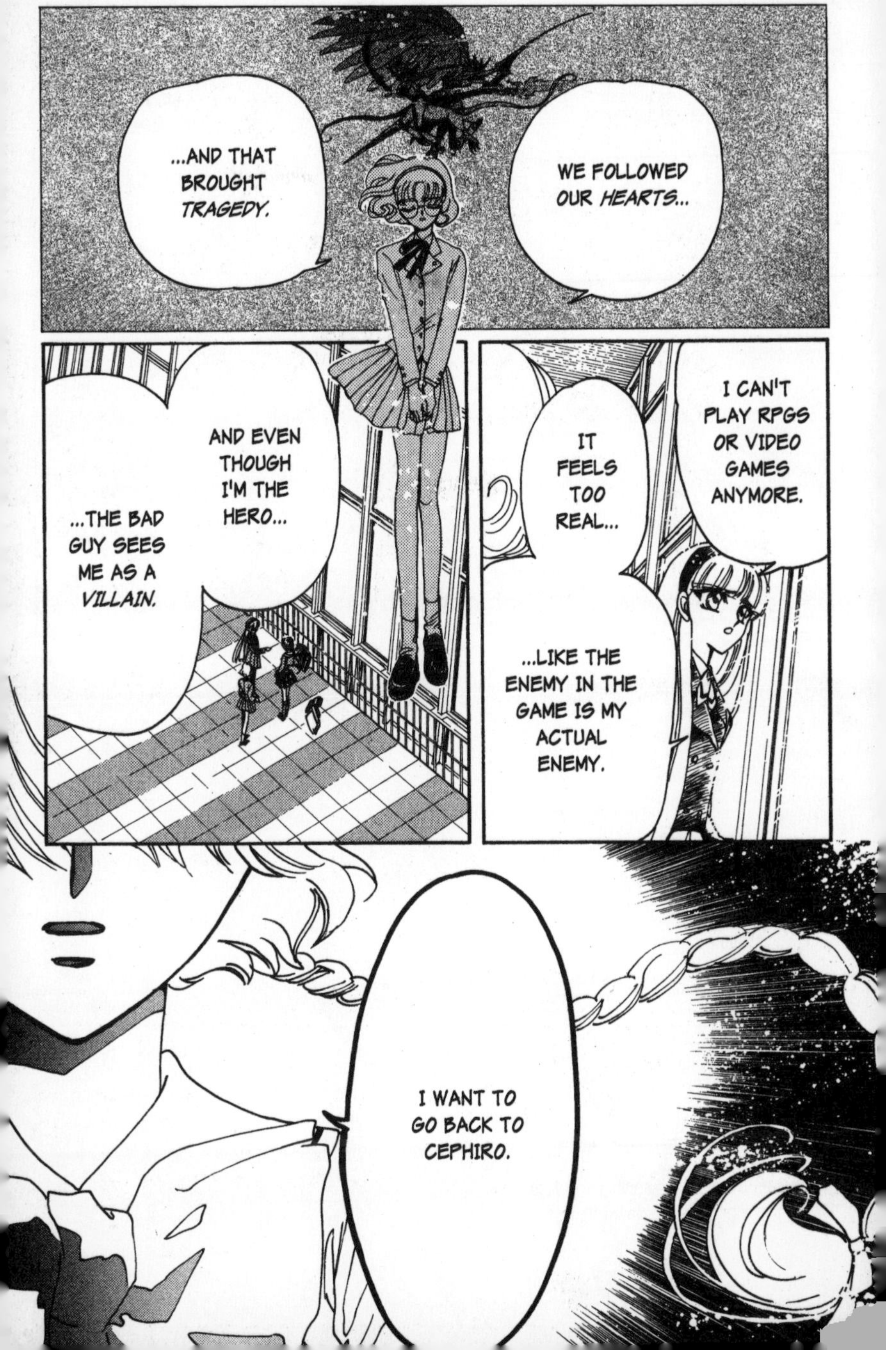
WE FOLLOWED OUR HEARTS...
...AND THAT BROUGHT TRAGEDY.
I CAN'T PLAY RPGS OR VIDEO GAMES ANYMORE.
IT FEELS TOO REAL...
...LIKE THE ENEMY IN THE GAME IS MY ACTUAL ENEMY.
AND EVEN THOUGH I'M THE HERO...
...THE BAD GUY SEES ME AS A VILLAIN.
I WANT TO GO BACK TO CEPHIRO.

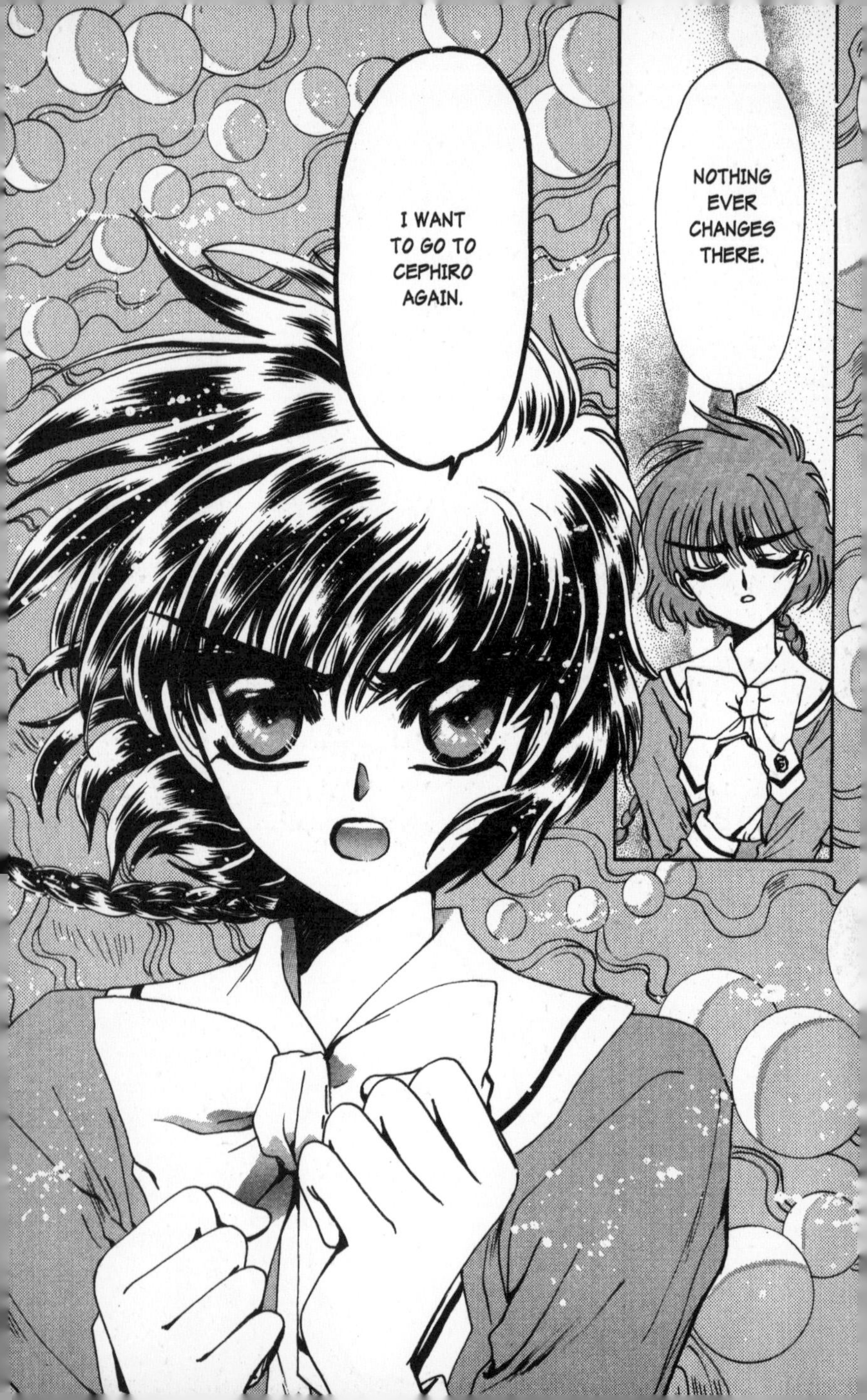
NOTHING EVER CHANGES THERE.
I WANT TO GO TO CEPHIRO AGAIN.

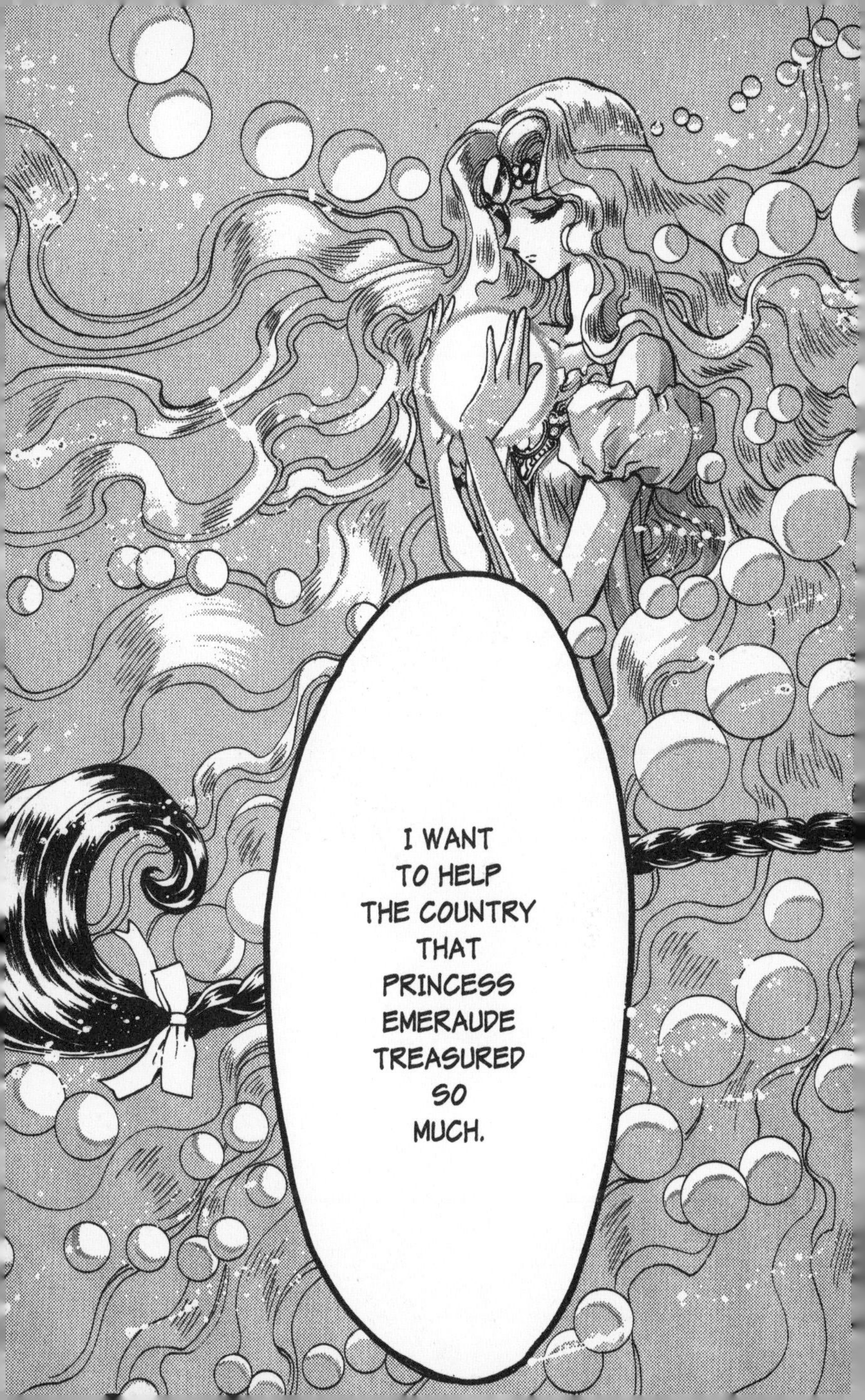
I WANT TO HELP THE COUNTRY THAT PRINCESS EMERAUDE TREASURED SO MUCH.

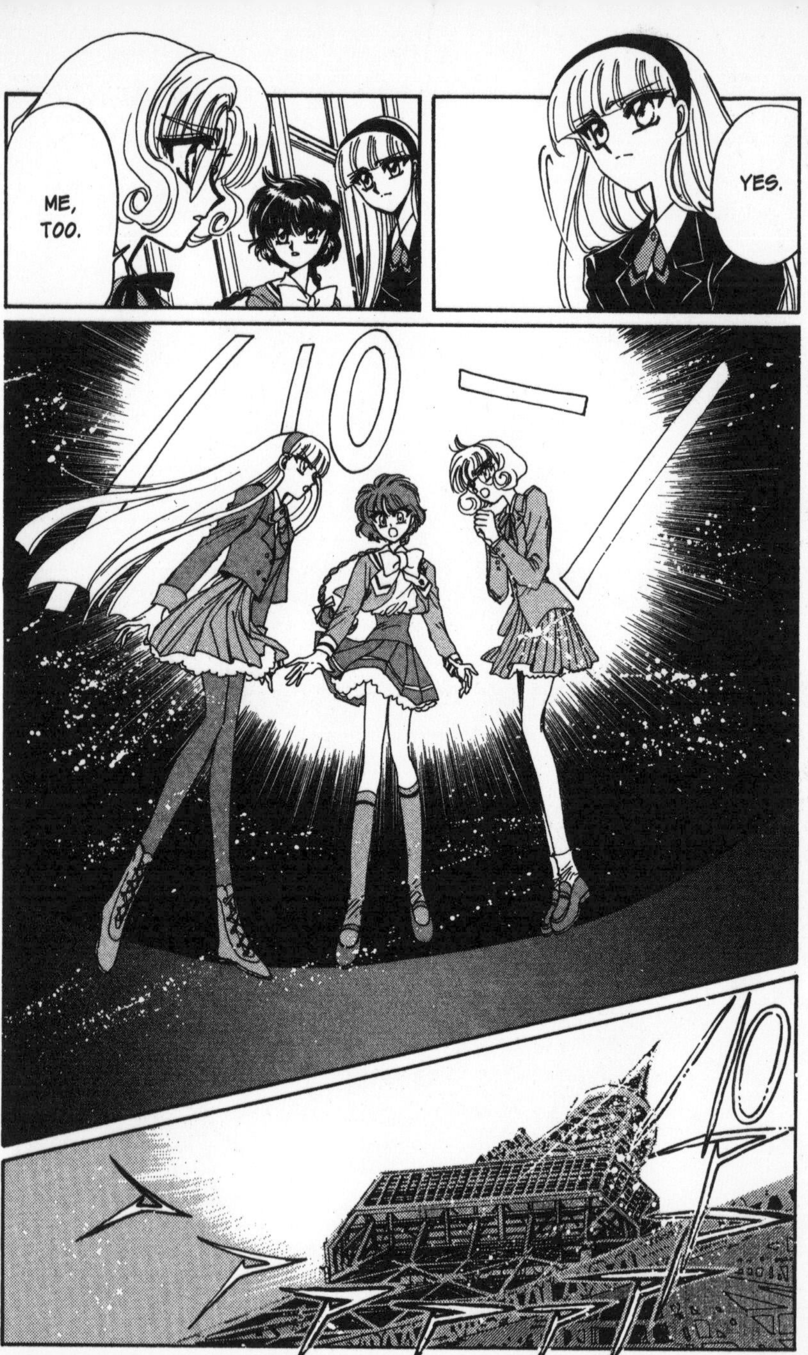
YES.
ME, TOO.

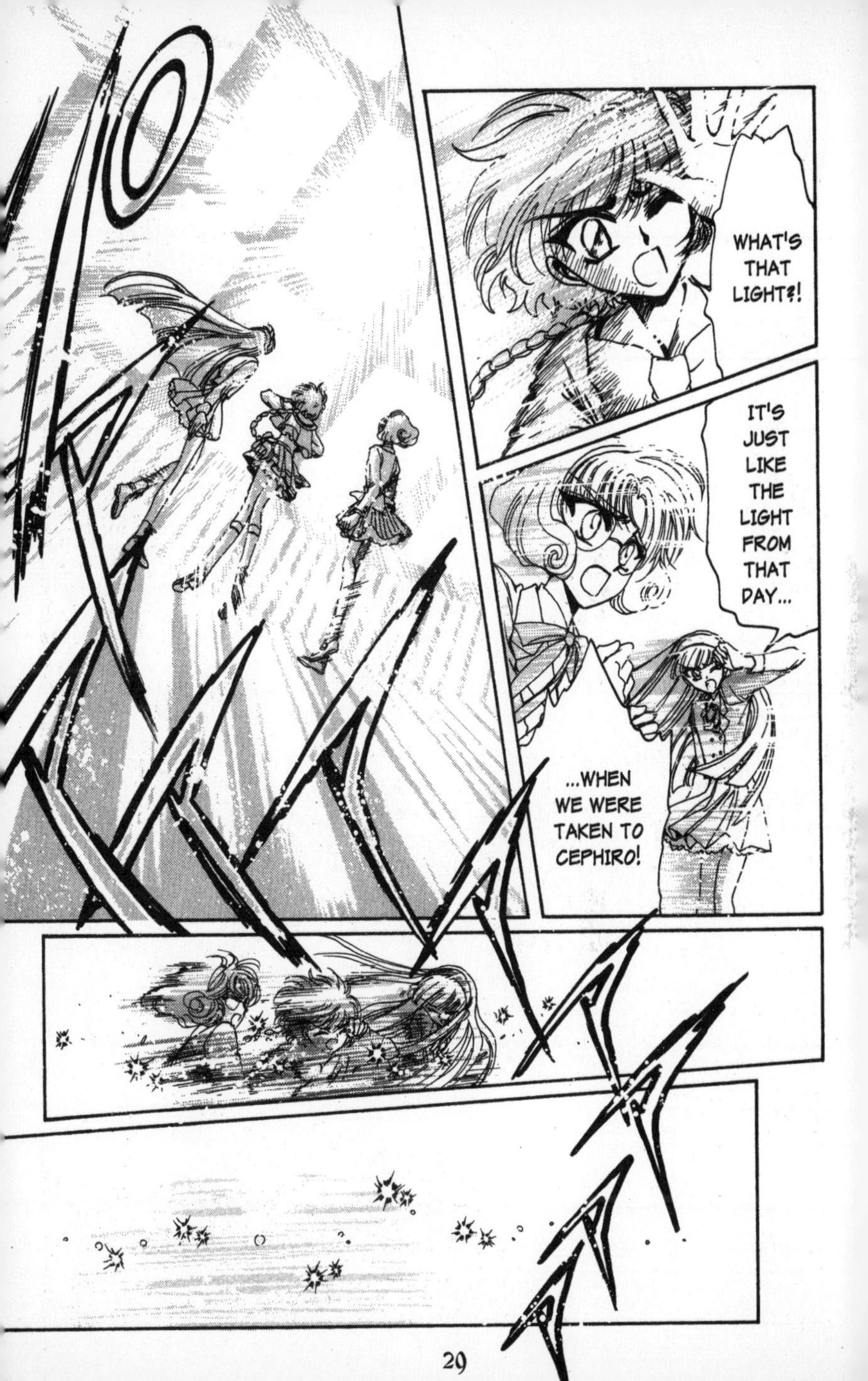
WHAT'S THAT LIGHT?!
IT'S JUST LIKE THE LIGHT FROM THAT DAY...
...WHEN WE WERE TAKEN TO CEPHIRO!

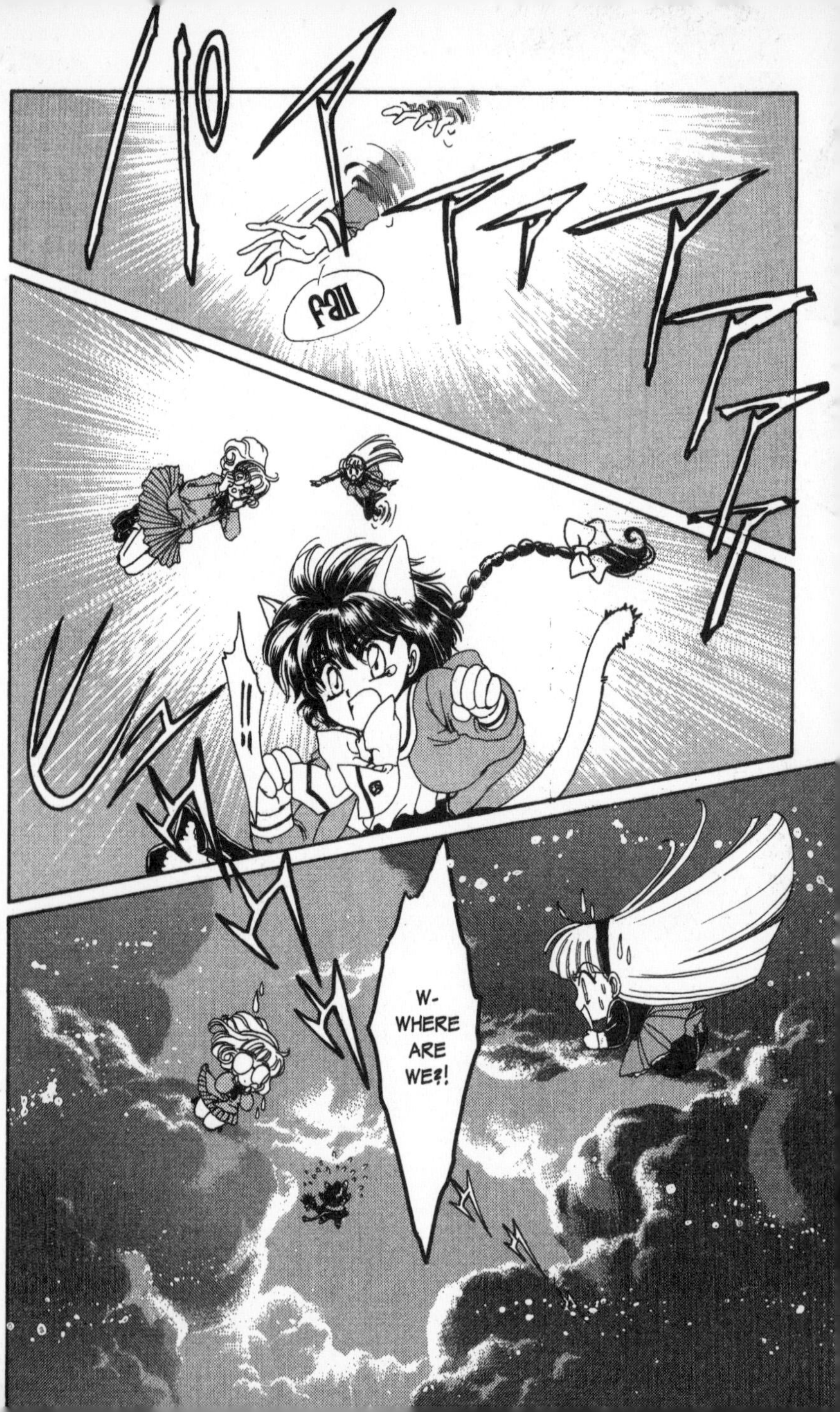

fall
W-
WHERE
ARE
WE?!

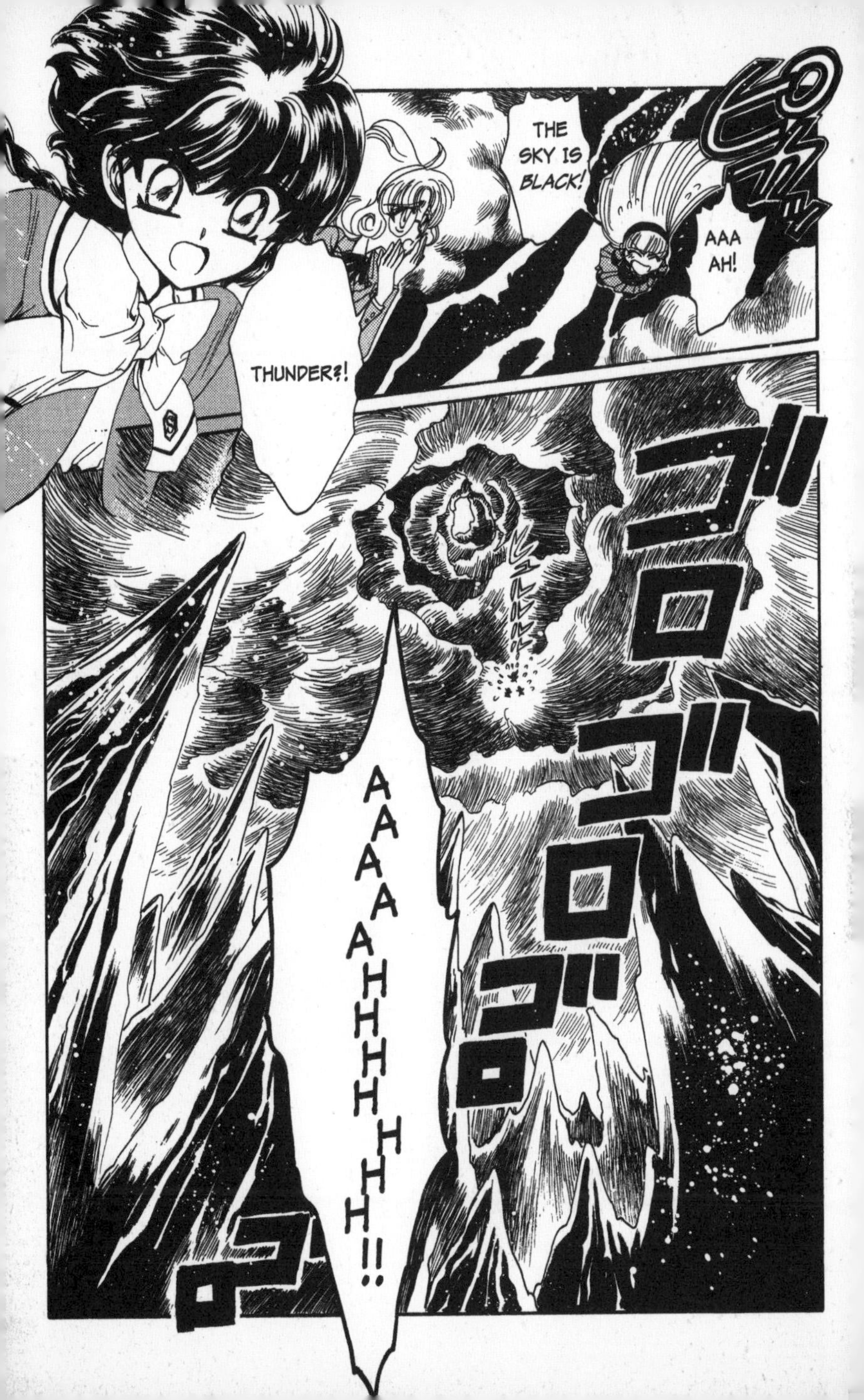
AAA AH!
THE SKY IS BLACK!
THUNDER?!
ゴロゴロゴロ
AAAAAHHHHHHH!!

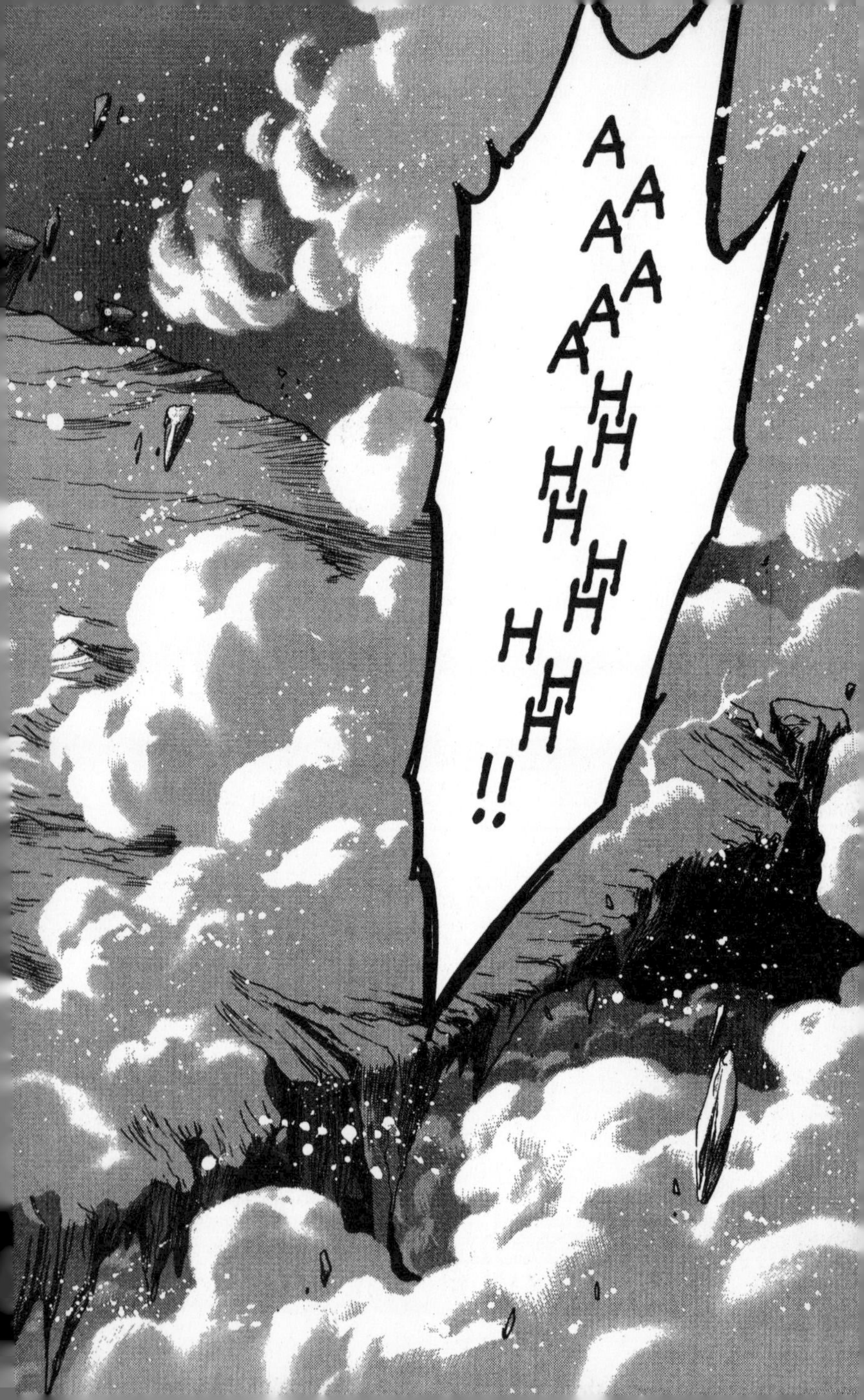
AAAAAAHHHHHHHHH!!

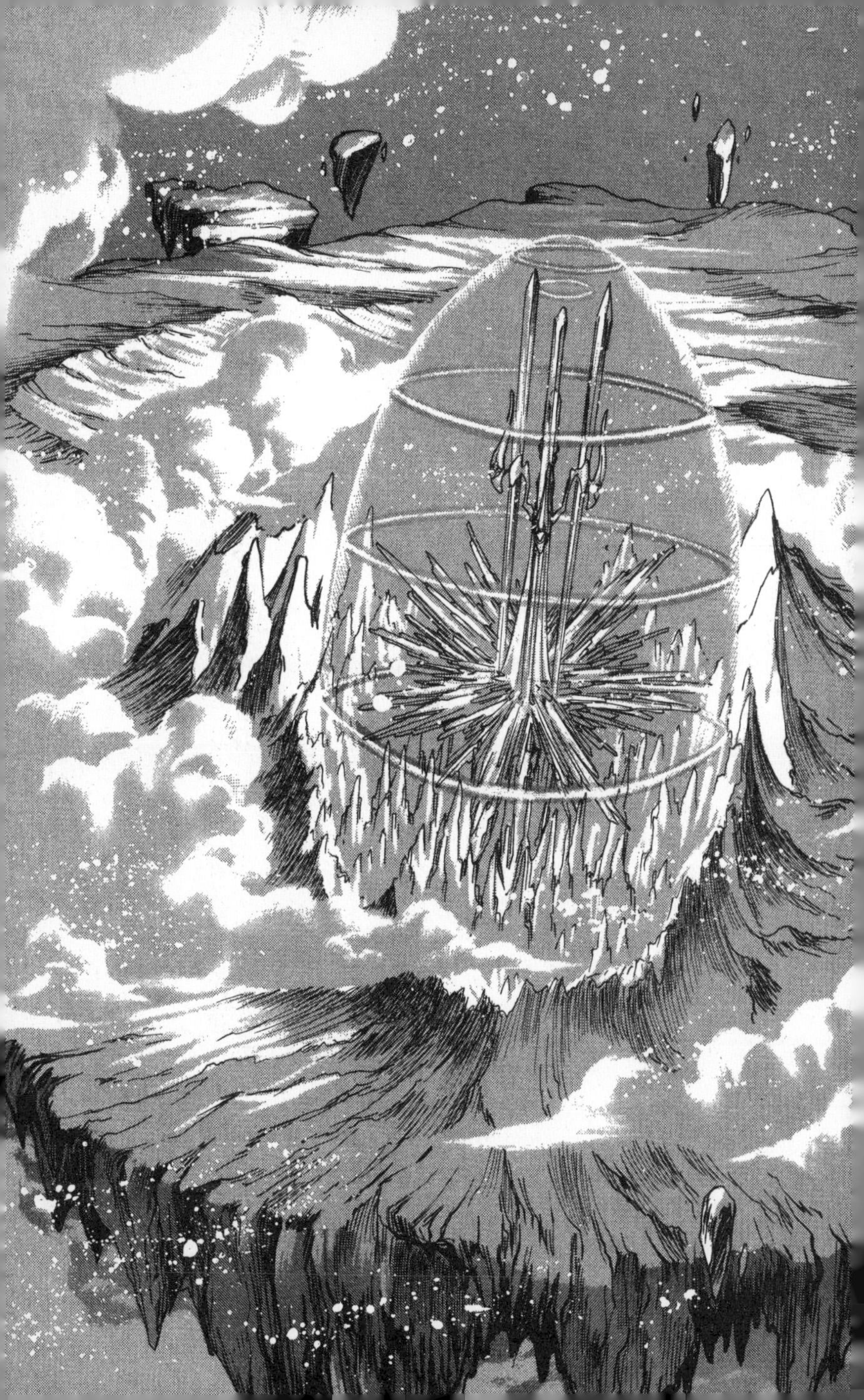

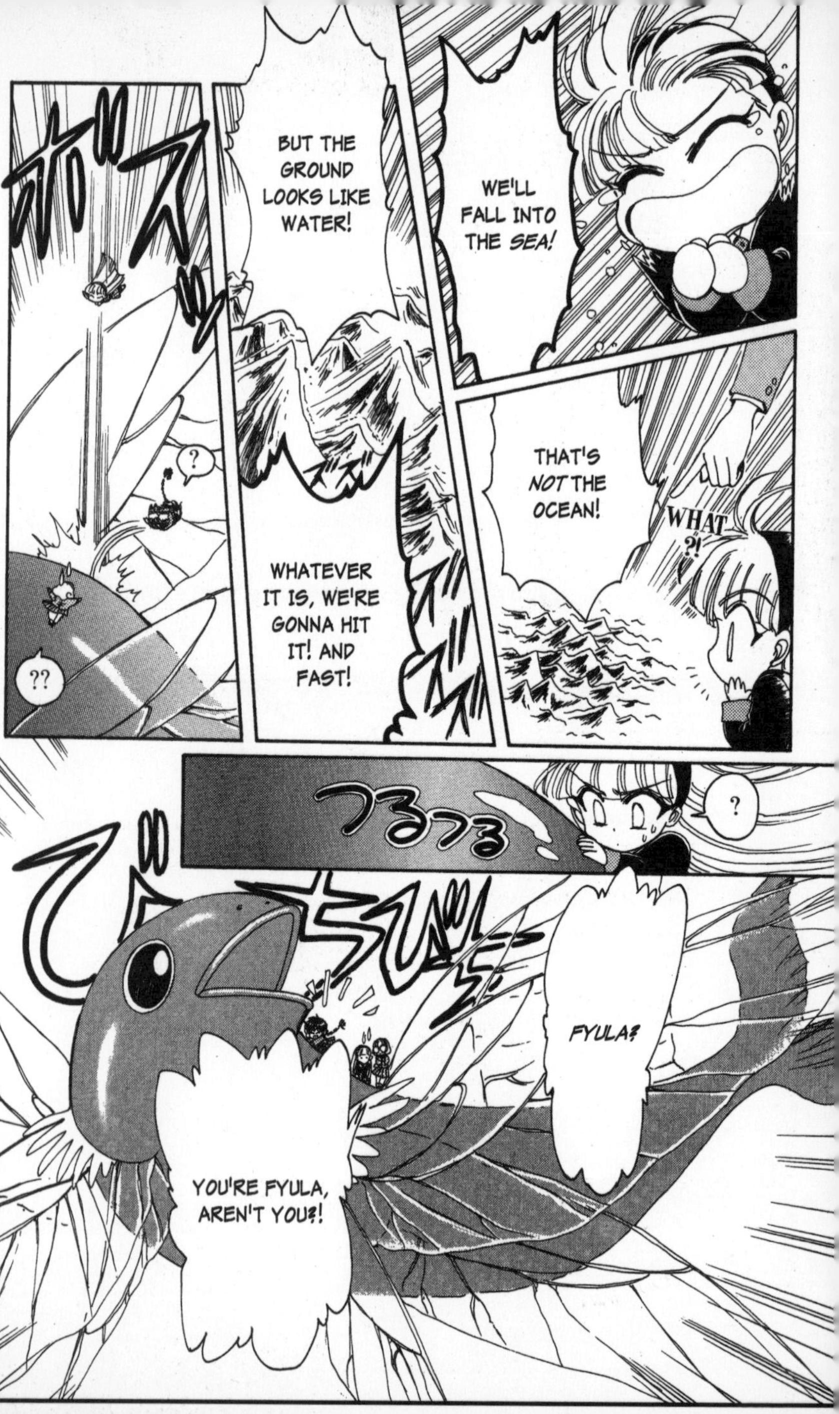
WE'LL FALL INTO THE *SEA!*
THAT'S *NOT* THE OCEAN!
WHAT?!
BUT THE GROUND LOOKS LIKE WATER!
WHATEVER IT IS, WE'RE GONNA HIT IT! AND FAST!
?
??
?
つるつる
FYULA?
YOU'RE FYULA, AREN'T YOU?!

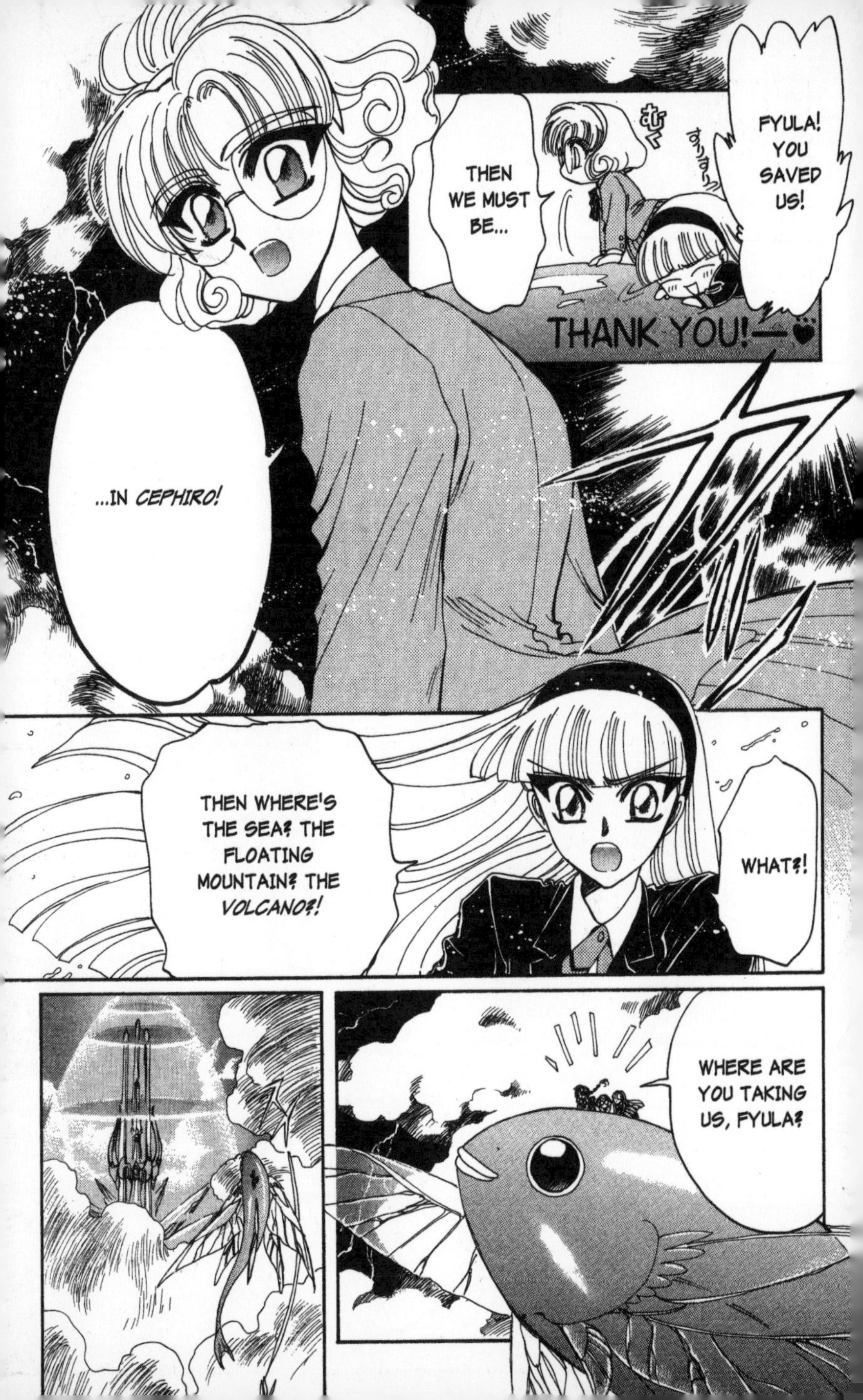
FYULA! YOU SAVED US!
THEN WE MUST BE...
THANK YOU!—♥
...IN CEPHIRO!
WHAT?!
THEN WHERE'S THE SEA? THE FLOATING MOUNTAIN? THE VOLCANO?!
WHERE ARE YOU TAKING US, FYULA?

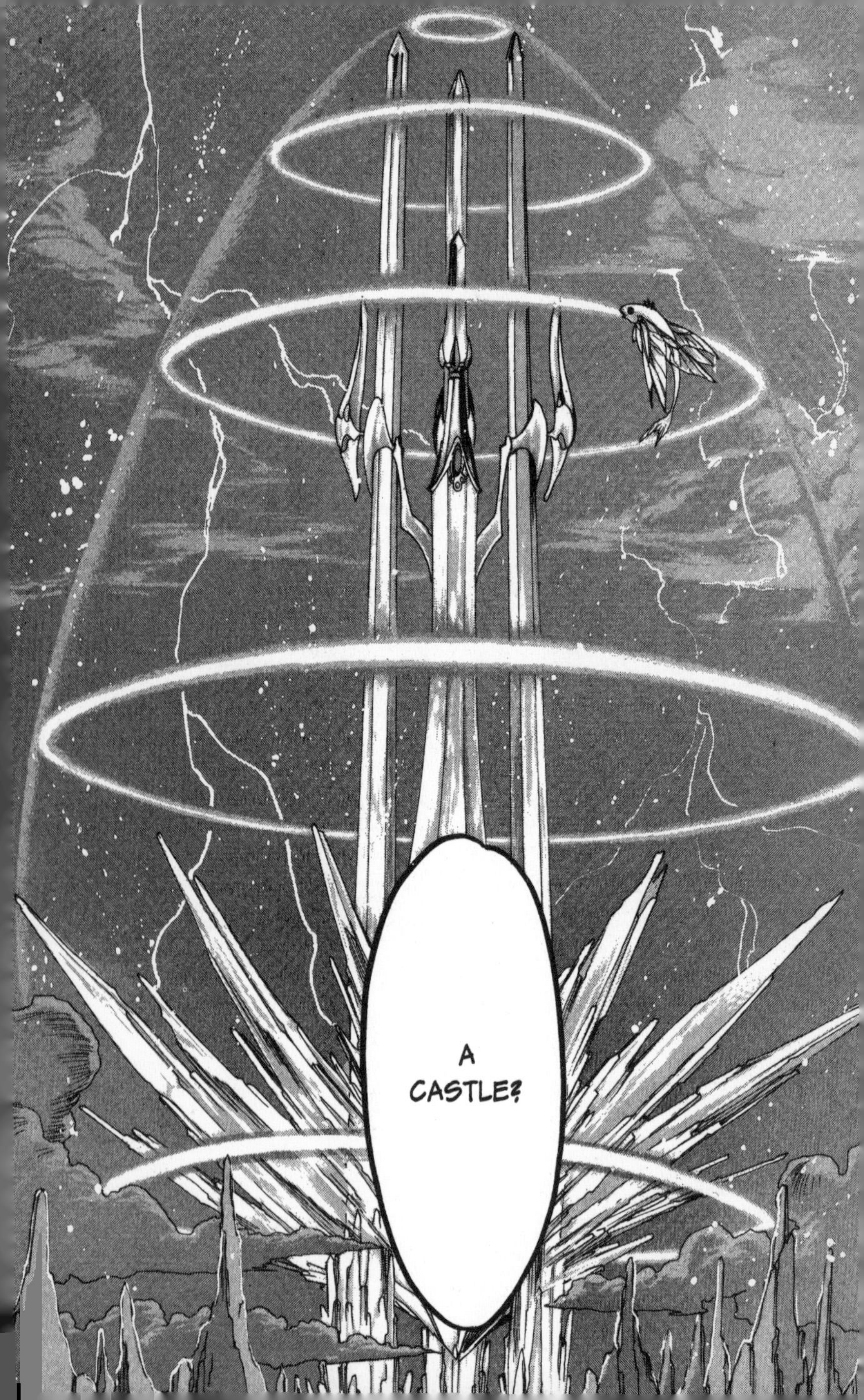
A CASTLE?

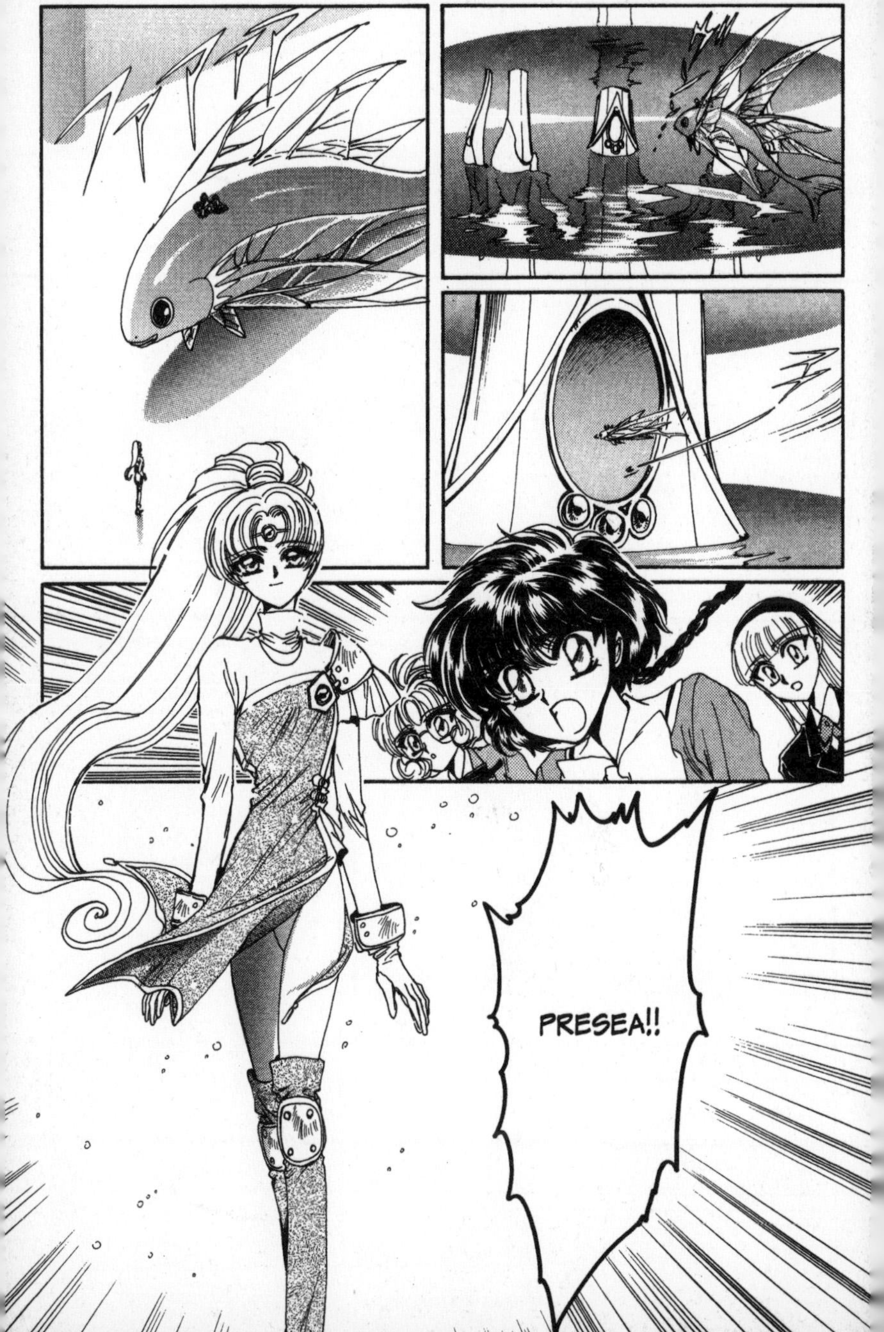
PRESEA!!

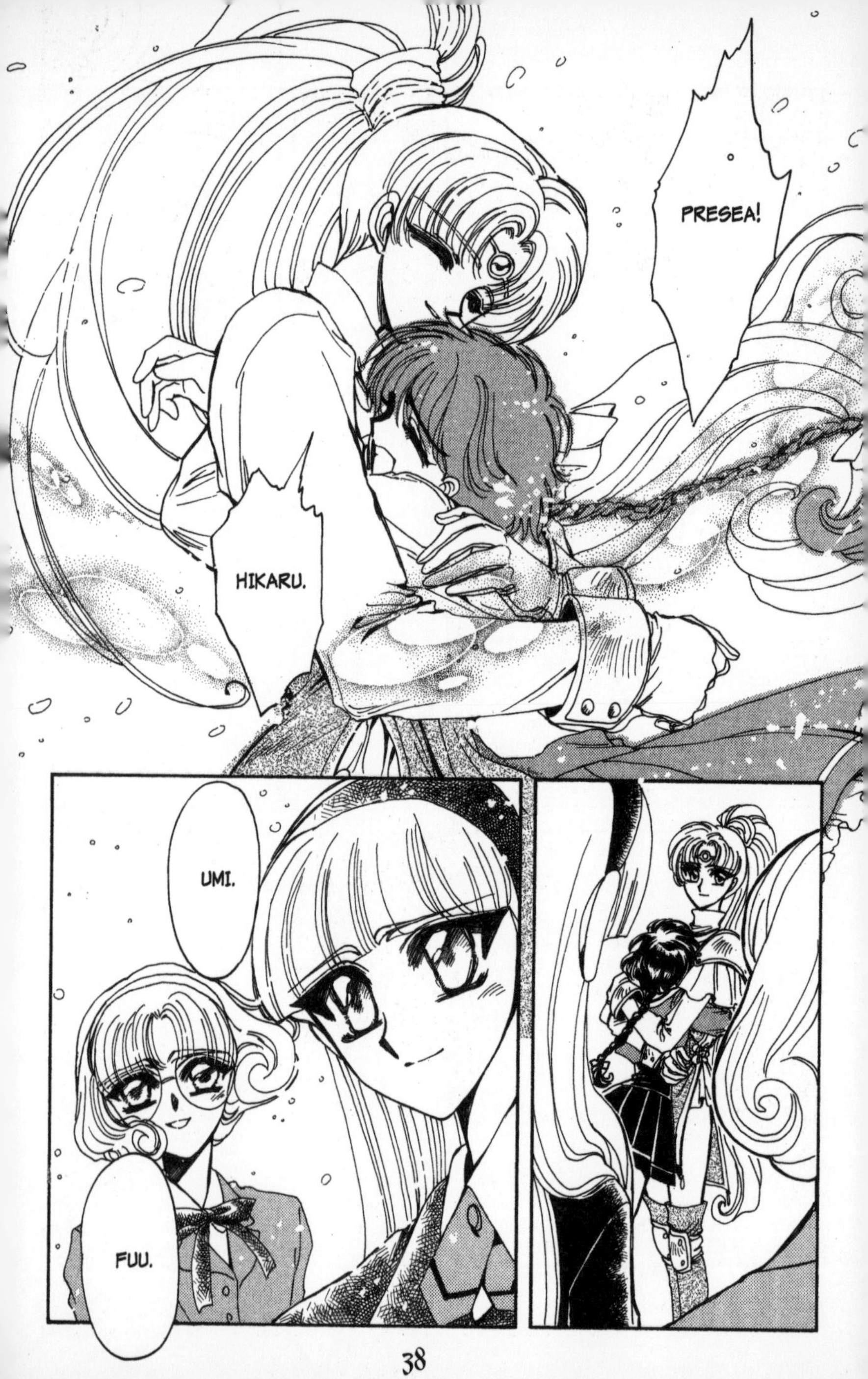
PRESEA!
HIKARU.
UMI.
FUU.

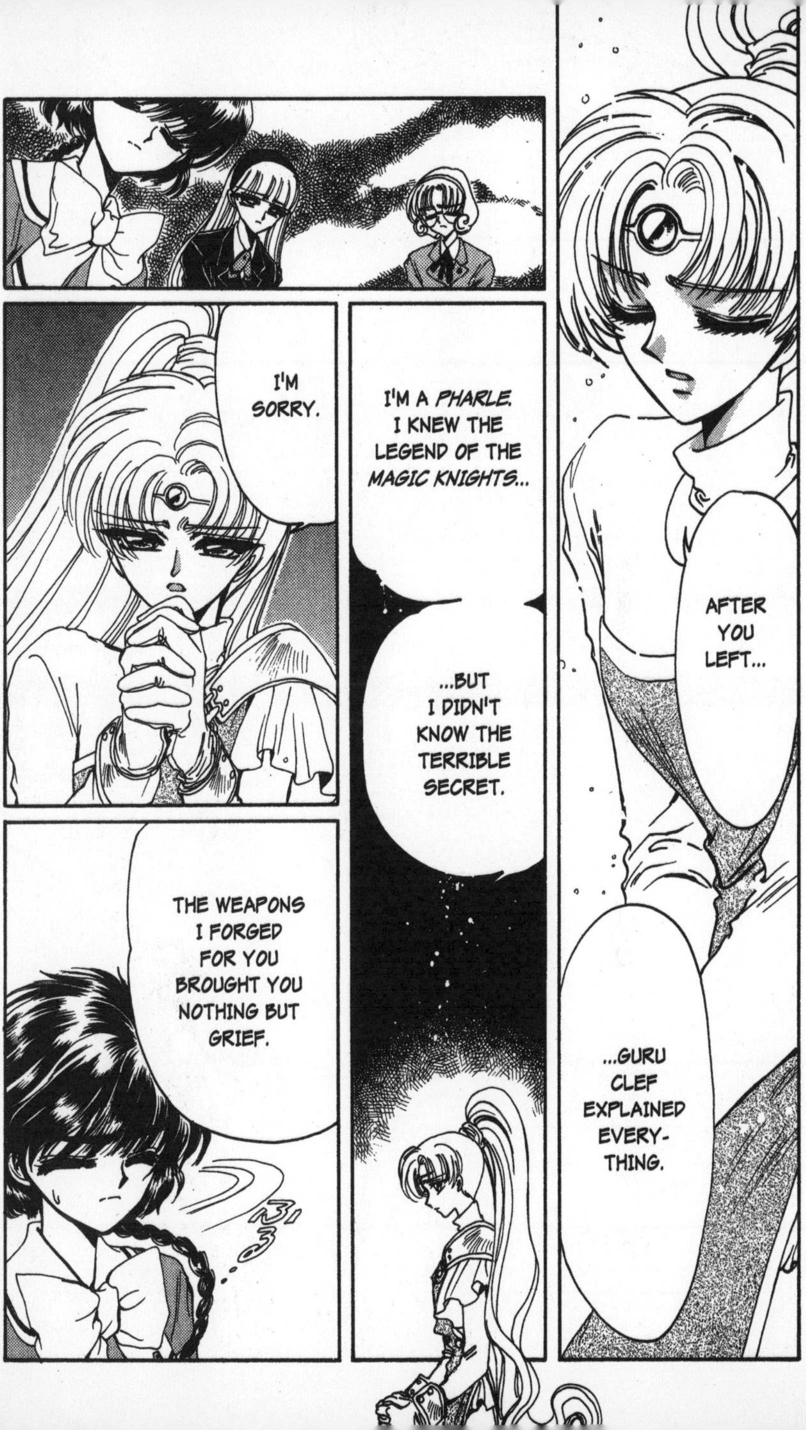
AFTER YOU LEFT...
...GURU CLEF EXPLAINED EVERY-THING.
I'M A PHARLE. I KNEW THE LEGEND OF THE MAGIC KNIGHTS...
...BUT I DIDN'T KNOW THE TERRIBLE SECRET.
I'M SORRY.
THE WEAPONS I FORGED FOR YOU BROUGHT YOU NOTHING BUT GRIEF.

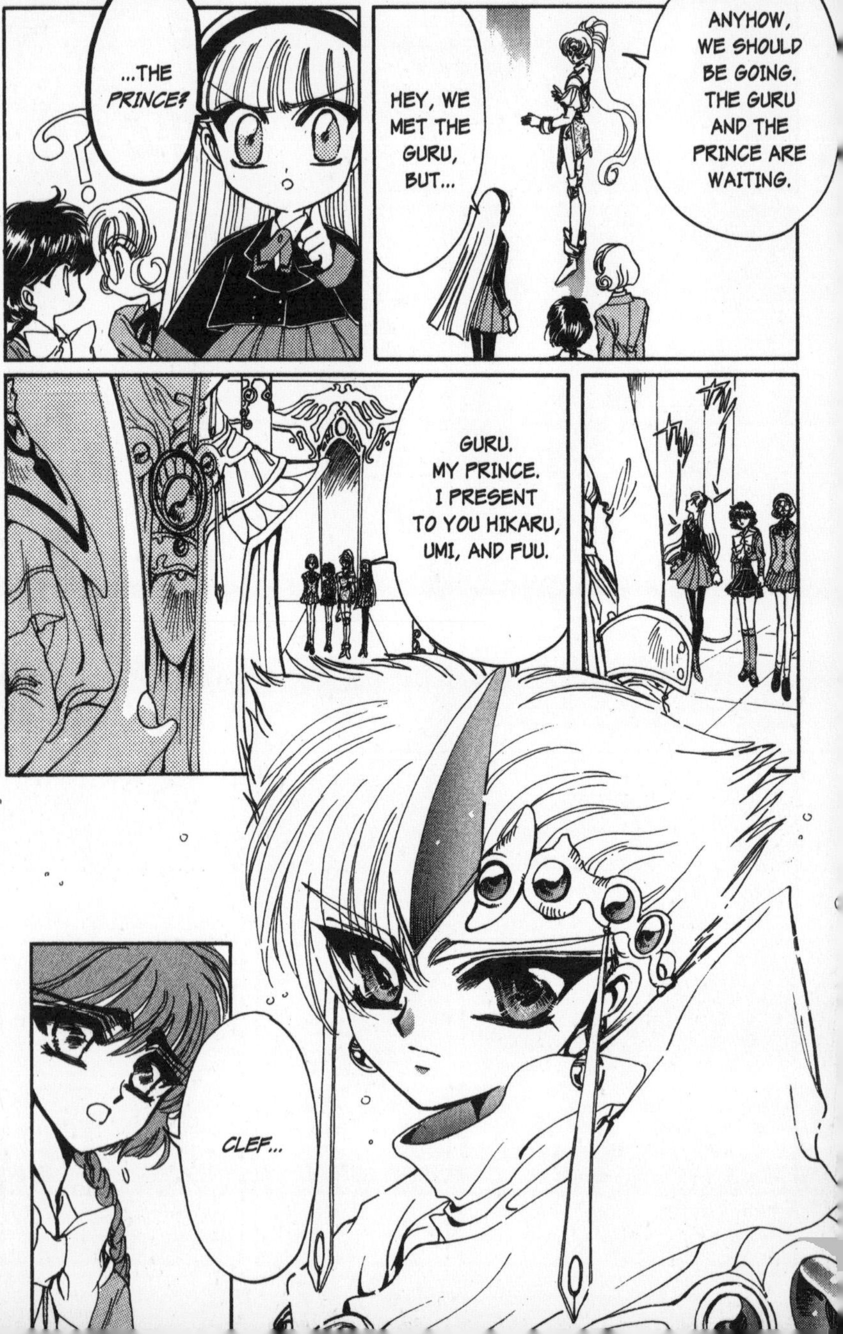
ANYHOW, WE SHOULD BE GOING. THE GURU AND THE PRINCE ARE WAITING.
HEY, WE MET THE GURU, BUT...
...THE *PRINCE?*
GURU. MY PRINCE. I PRESENT TO YOU HIKARU, UMI, AND FUU.
CLEF...

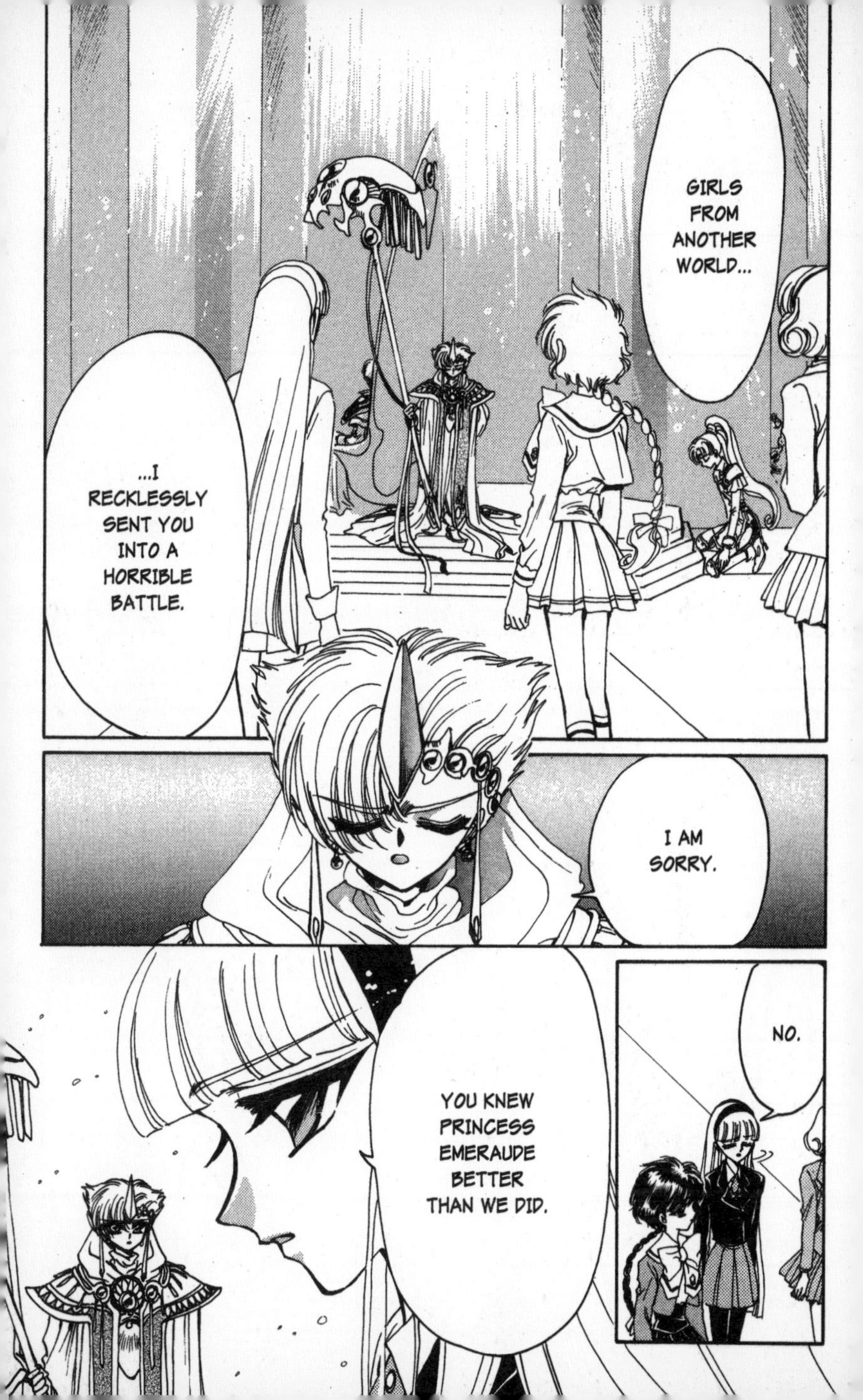
GIRLS FROM ANOTHER WORLD...
...I RECKLESSLY SENT YOU INTO A HORRIBLE BATTLE.
I AM SORRY.
NO.
YOU KNEW PRINCESS EMERAUDE BETTER THAN WE DID.

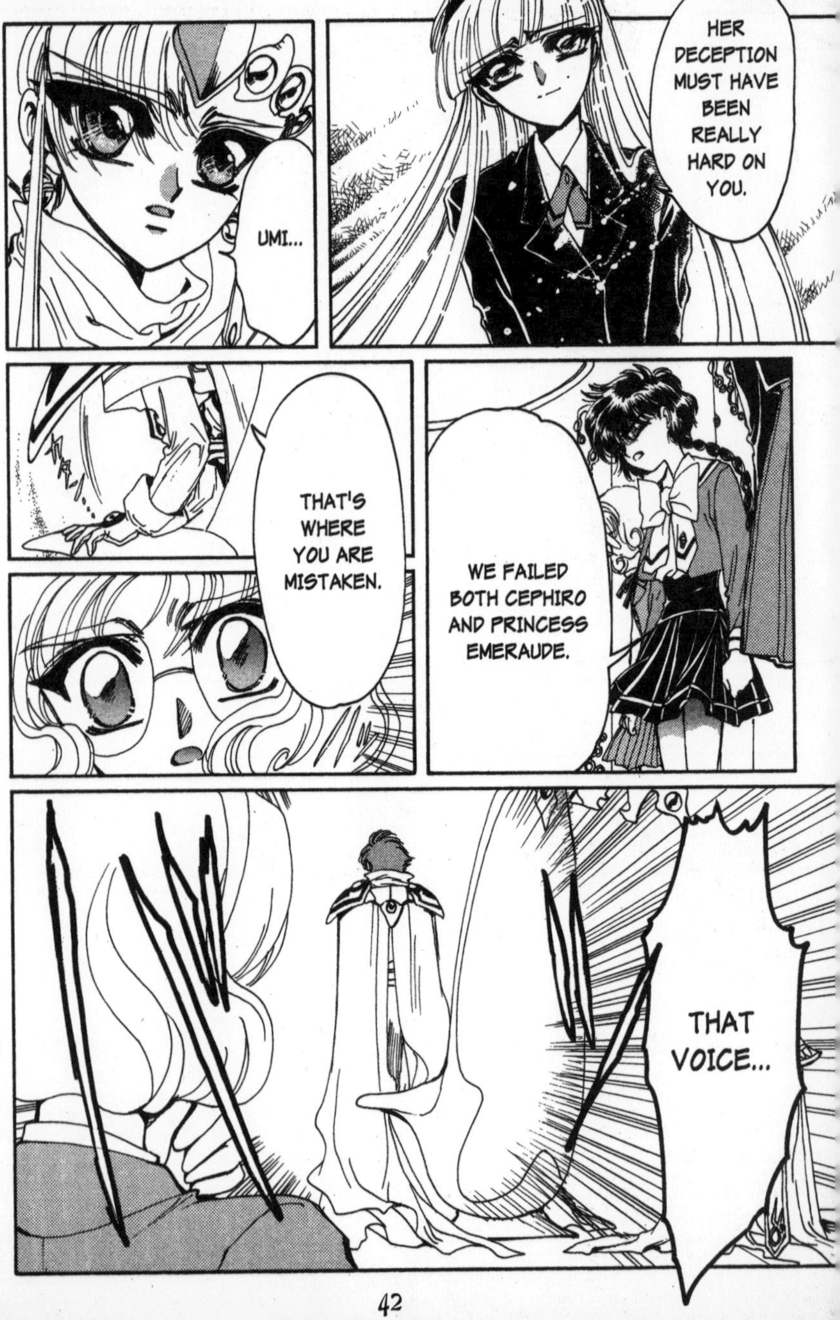
HER DECEPTION MUST HAVE BEEN REALLY HARD ON YOU.
UMI...
WE FAILED BOTH CEPHIRO AND PRINCESS EMERAUDE.
THAT'S WHERE YOU ARE MISTAKEN.
THAT VOICE...

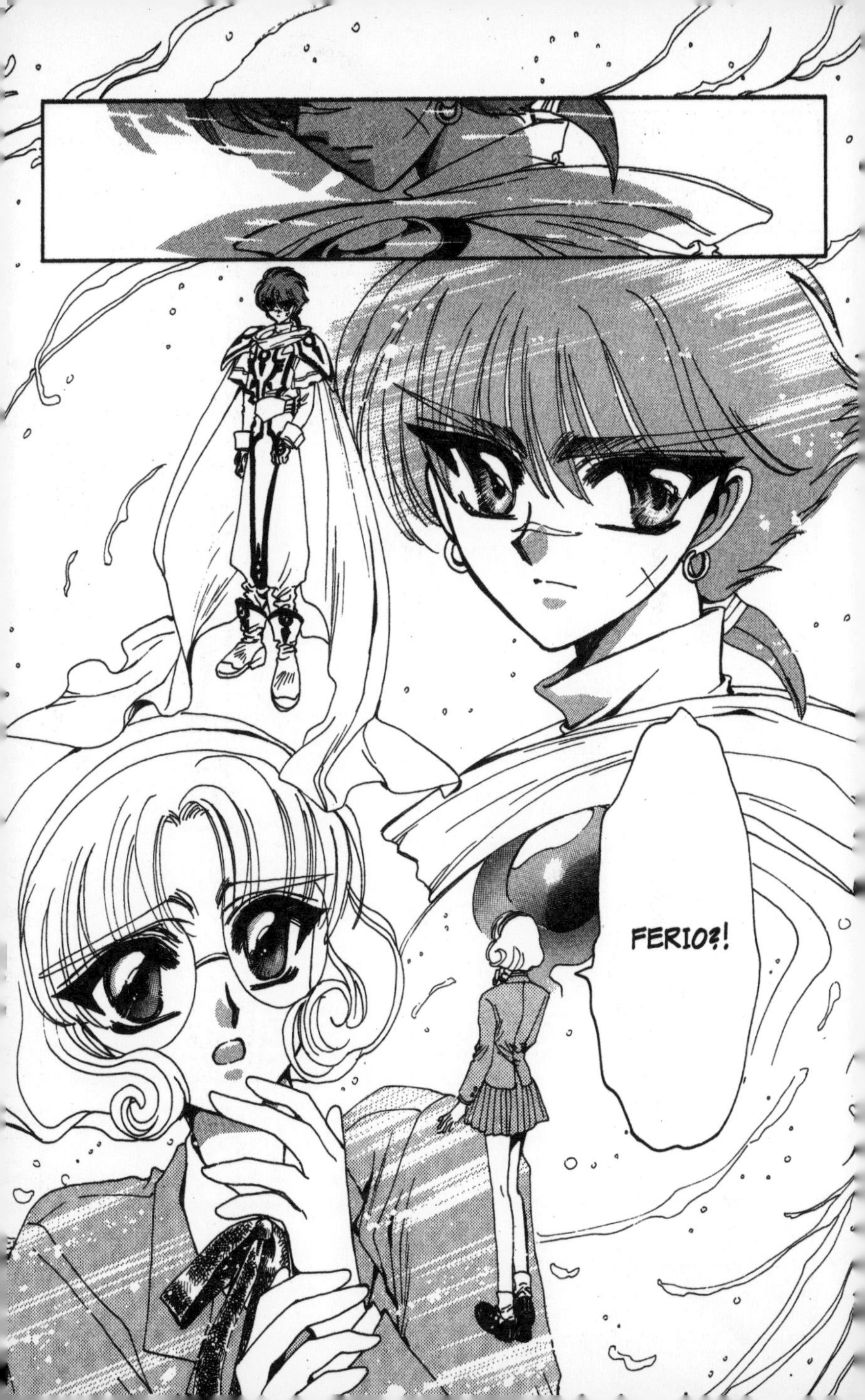
FERIO?!

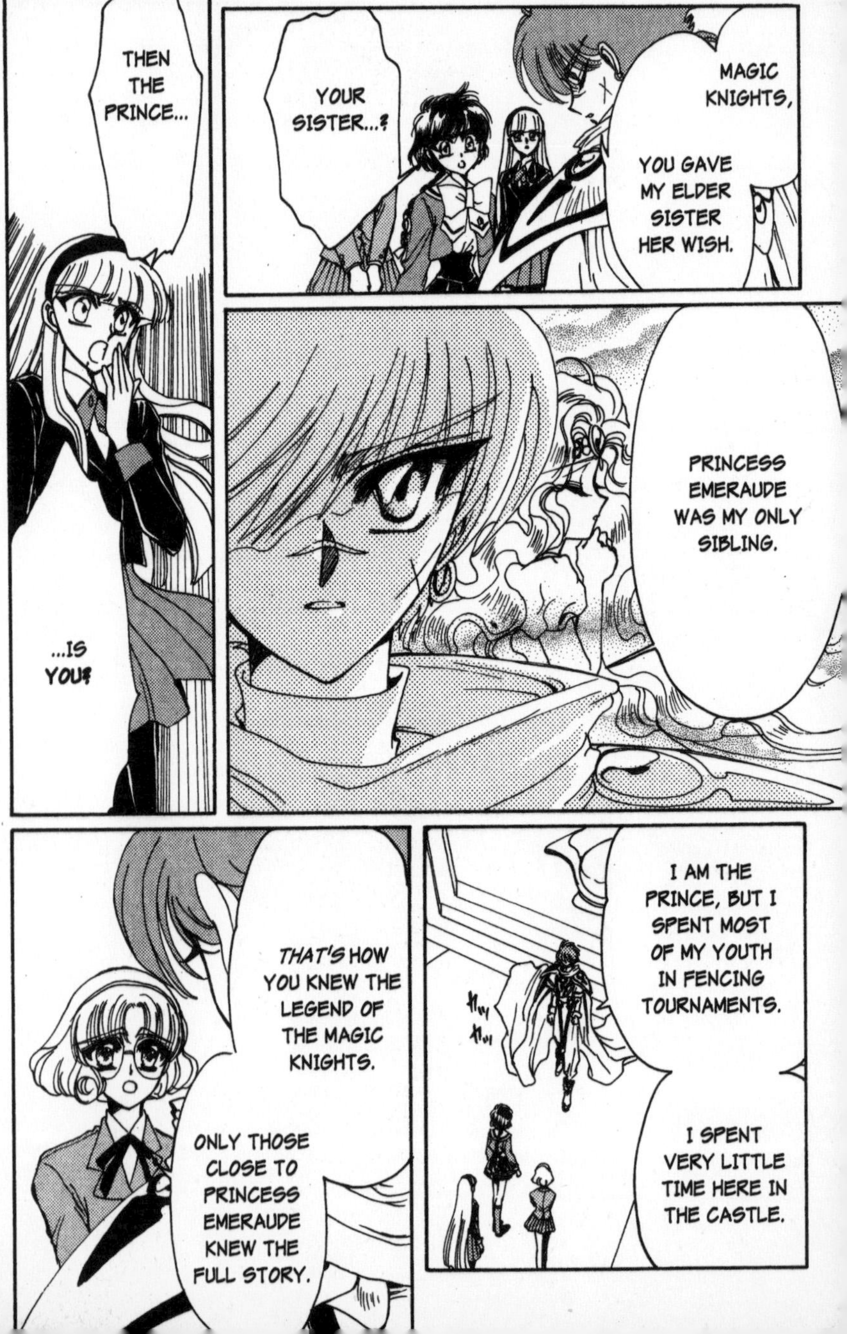

MAGIC KNIGHTS,
YOU GAVE MY ELDER SISTER HER WISH.
YOUR SISTER...?
PRINCESS EMERAUDE WAS MY ONLY SIBLING.
THEN THE PRINCE...
...IS YOU?
I AM THE PRINCE, BUT I SPENT MOST OF MY YOUTH IN FENCING TOURNAMENTS.
I SPENT VERY LITTLE TIME HERE IN THE CASTLE.
THAT'S HOW YOU KNEW THE LEGEND OF THE MAGIC KNIGHTS.
ONLY THOSE CLOSE TO PRINCESS EMERAUDE KNEW THE FULL STORY.

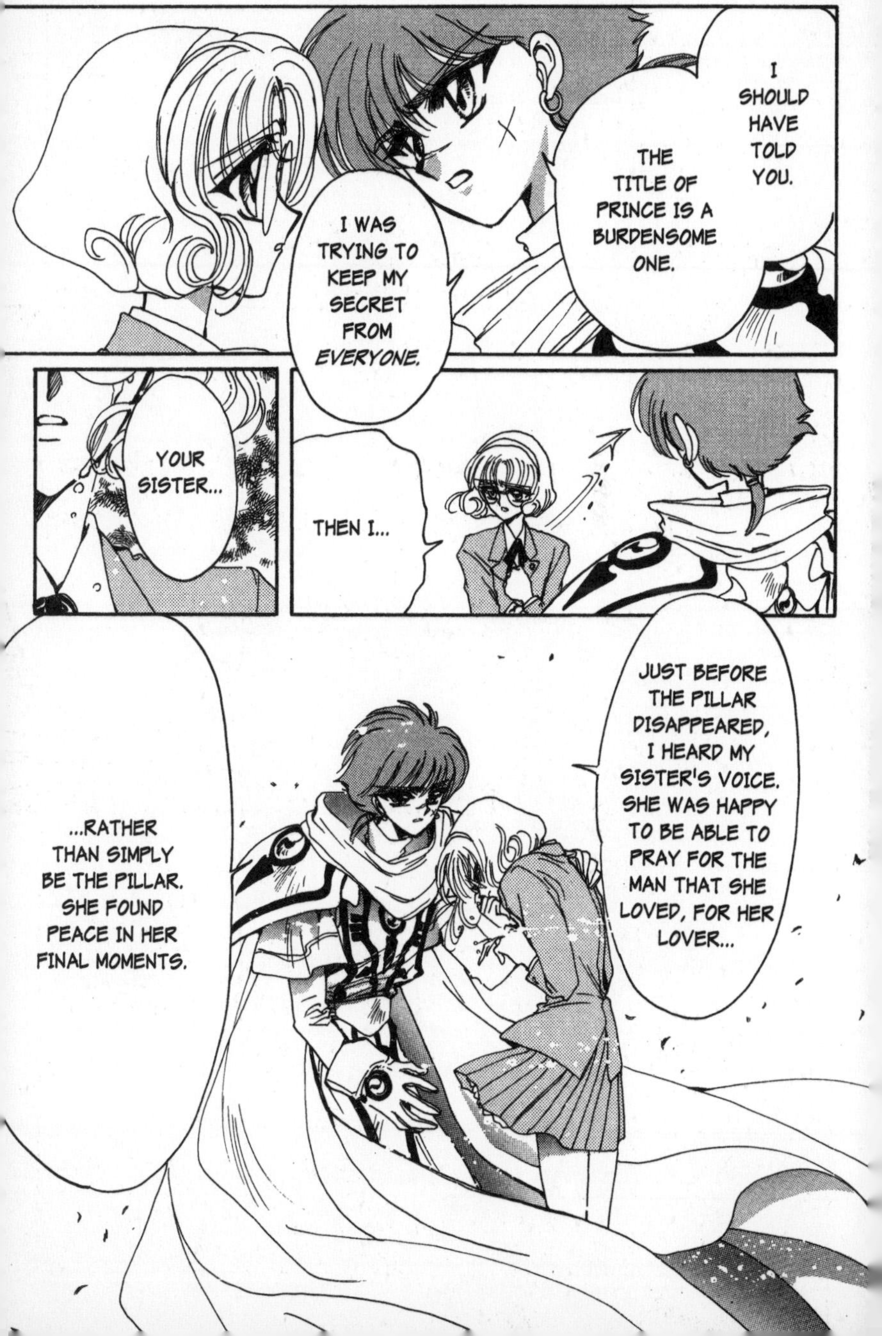

I SHOULD HAVE TOLD YOU.
THE TITLE OF PRINCE IS A BURDENSOME ONE.
I WAS TRYING TO KEEP MY SECRET FROM *EVERYONE.*
THEN I...
YOUR SISTER...
JUST BEFORE THE PILLAR DISAPPEARED, I HEARD MY SISTER'S VOICE. SHE WAS HAPPY TO BE ABLE TO PRAY FOR THE MAN THAT SHE LOVED, FOR HER LOVER...
...RATHER THAN SIMPLY BE THE PILLAR. SHE FOUND PEACE IN HER FINAL MOMENTS.

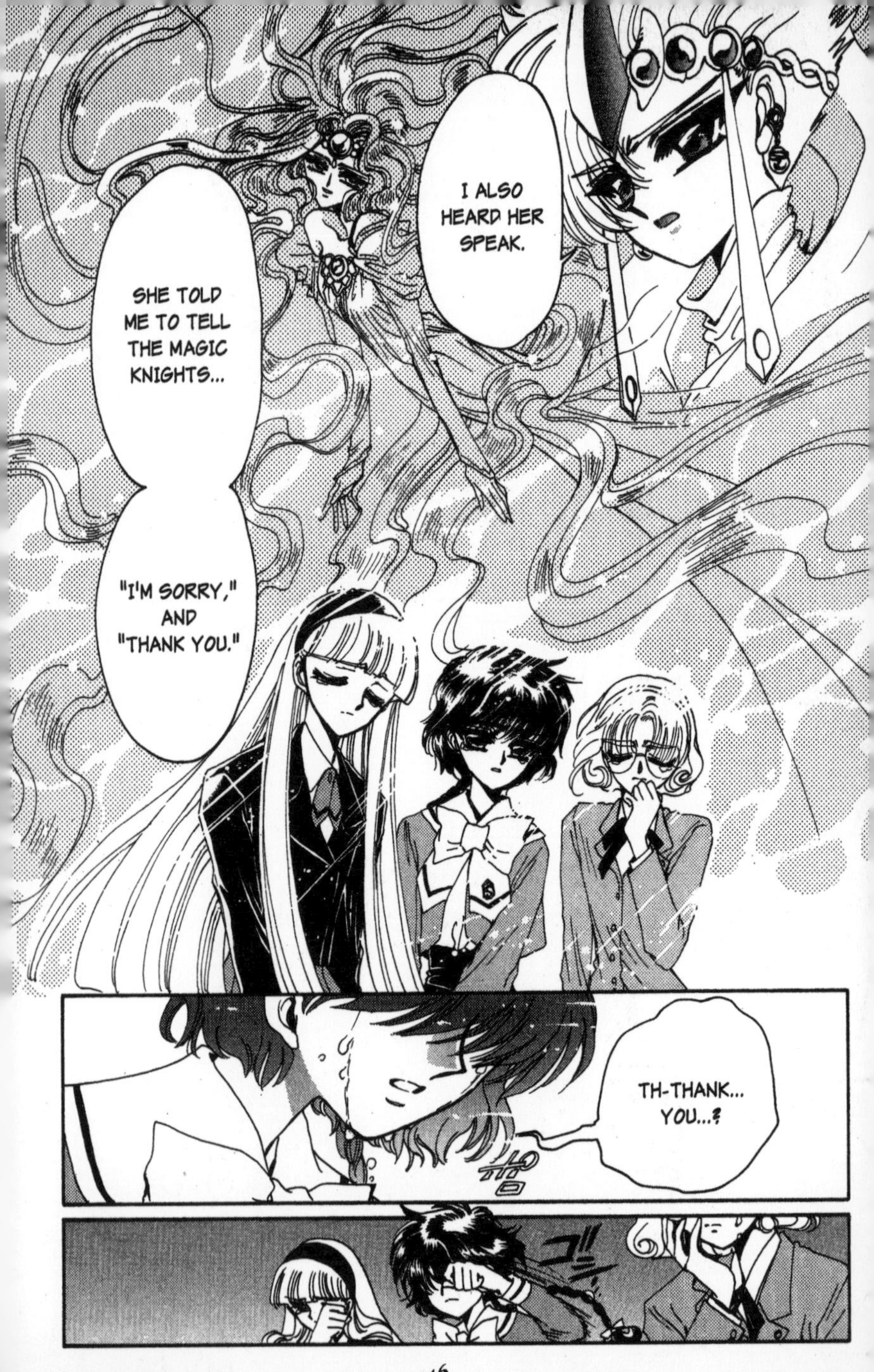
I ALSO HEARD HER SPEAK.
SHE TOLD ME TO TELL THE MAGIC KNIGHTS...
"I'M SORRY," AND "THANK YOU."
TH-THANK... YOU...?

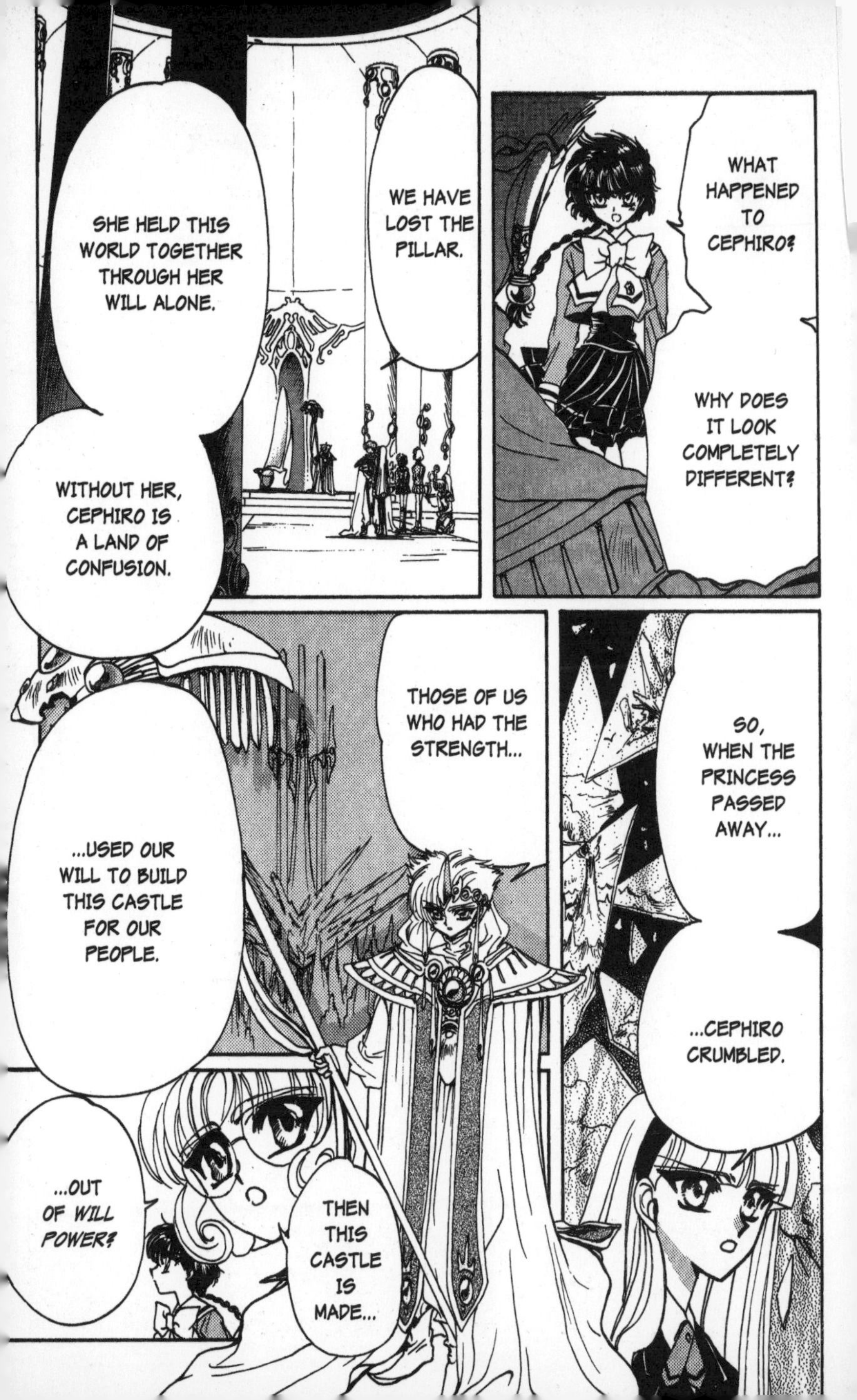
WHAT HAPPENED TO CEPHIRO?
WHY DOES IT LOOK COMPLETELY DIFFERENT?
WE HAVE LOST THE PILLAR.
SHE HELD THIS WORLD TOGETHER THROUGH HER WILL ALONE.
WITHOUT HER, CEPHIRO IS A LAND OF CONFUSION.
SO, WHEN THE PRINCESS PASSED AWAY...
...CEPHIRO CRUMBLED.
THOSE OF US WHO HAD THE STRENGTH...
...USED OUR WILL TO BUILD THIS CASTLE FOR OUR PEOPLE.
THEN THIS CASTLE IS MADE...
...OUT OF WILL POWER?

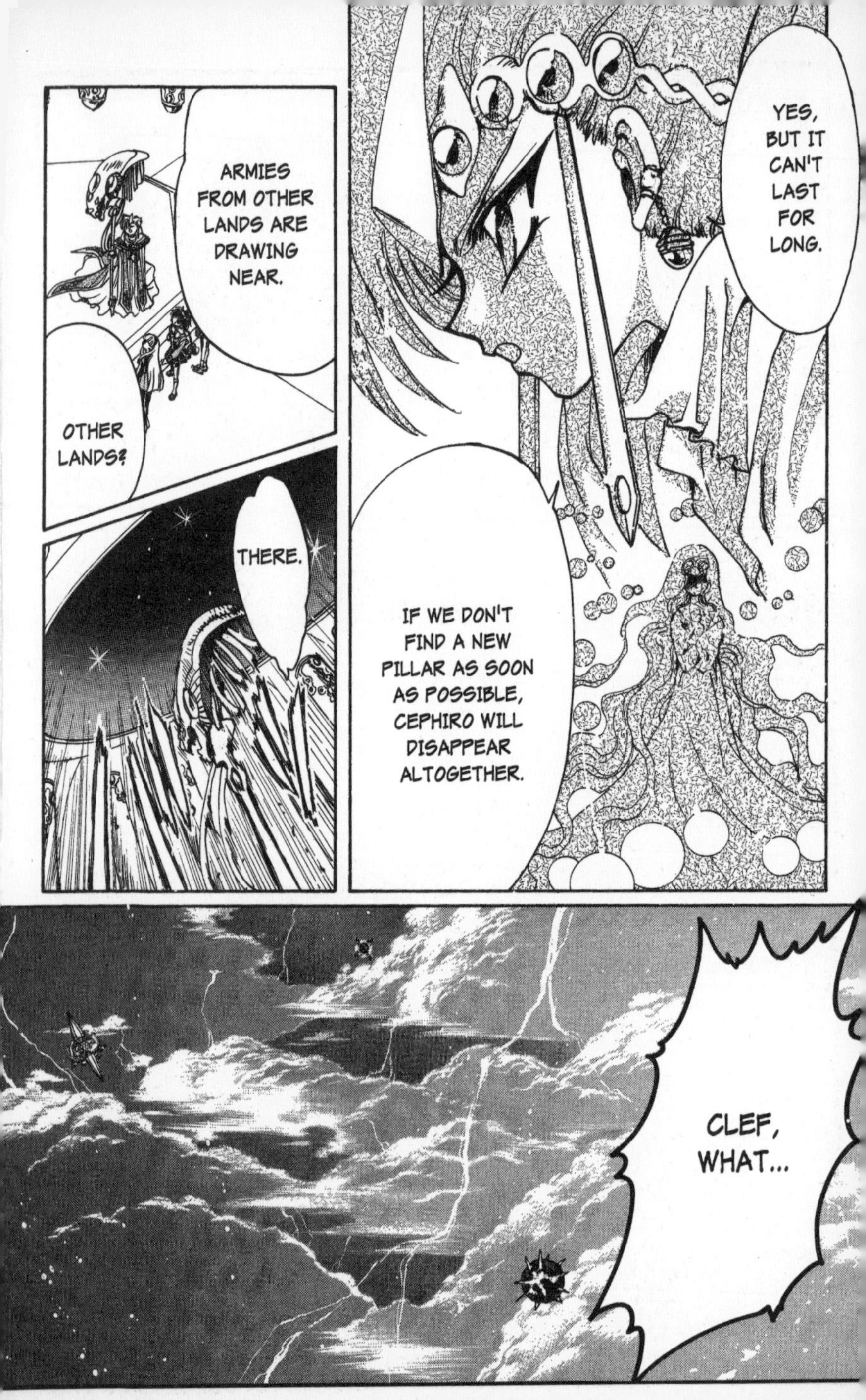
YES, BUT IT CAN'T LAST FOR LONG.
IF WE DON'T FIND A NEW PILLAR AS SOON AS POSSIBLE, CEPHIRO WILL DISAPPEAR ALTOGETHER.
ARMIES FROM OTHER LANDS ARE DRAWING NEAR.
OTHER LANDS?
THERE.
CLEF, WHAT...

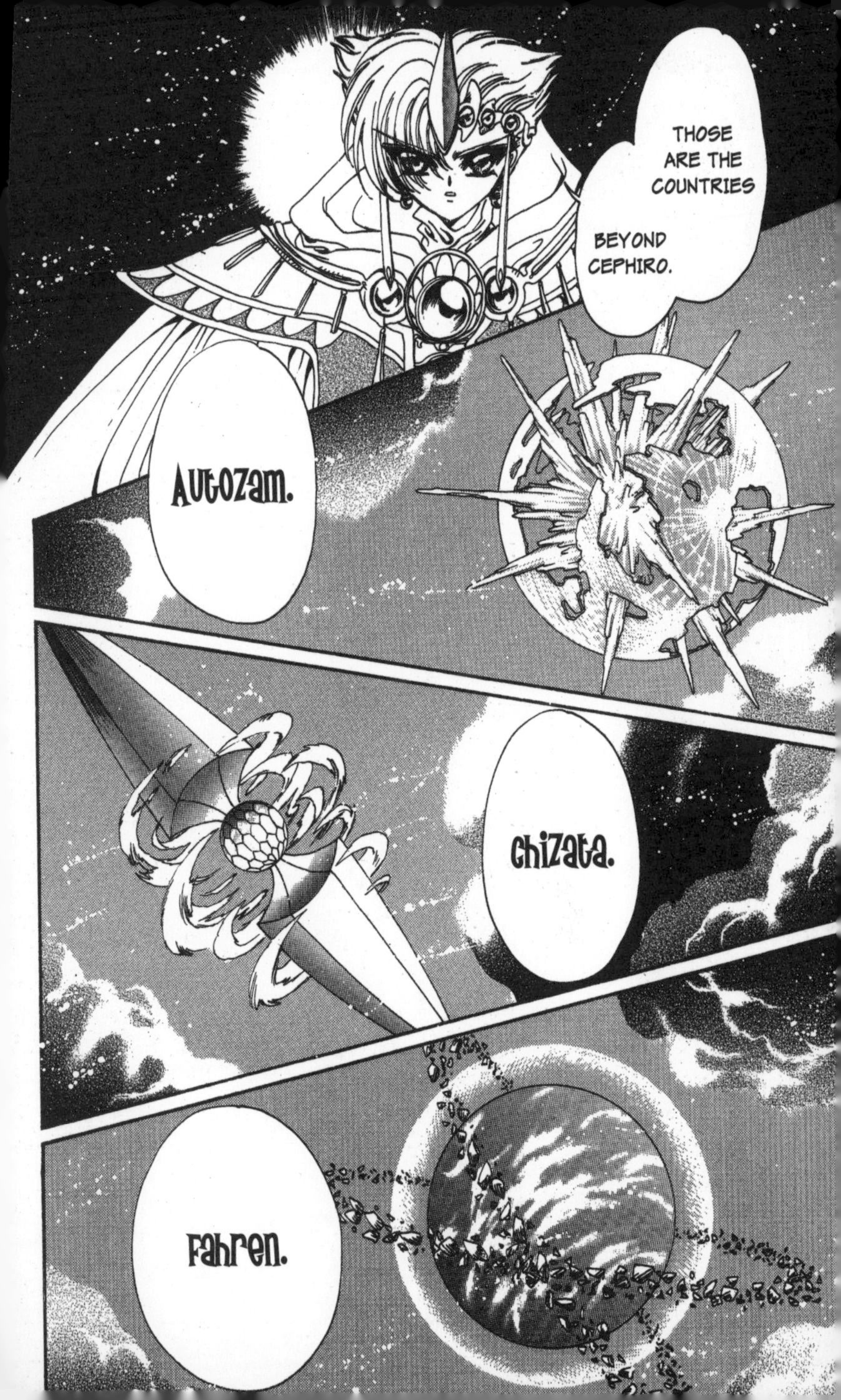
THOSE ARE THE COUNTRIES
BEYOND CEPHIRO.
Autozam.
Chizata.
Fahren.

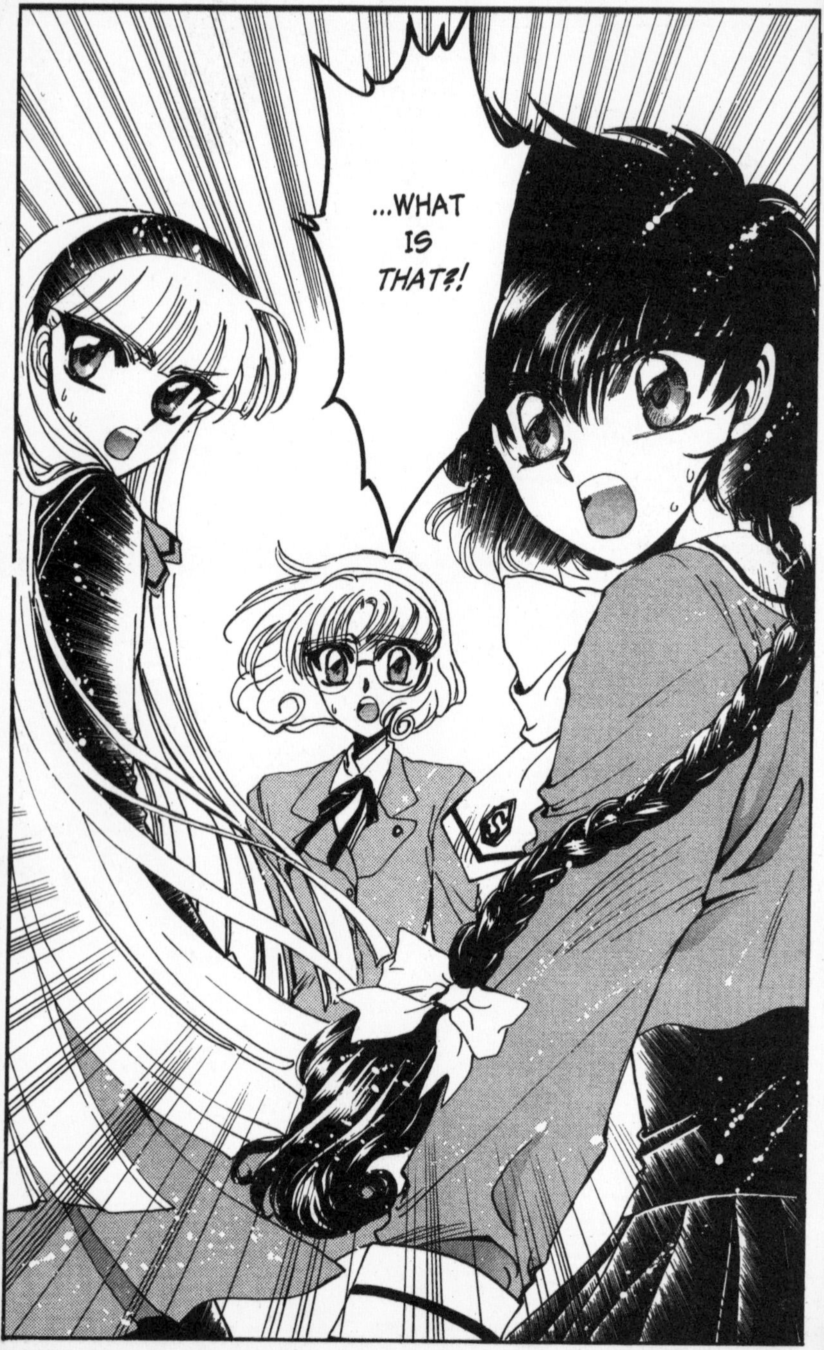
...WHAT IS THAT?!

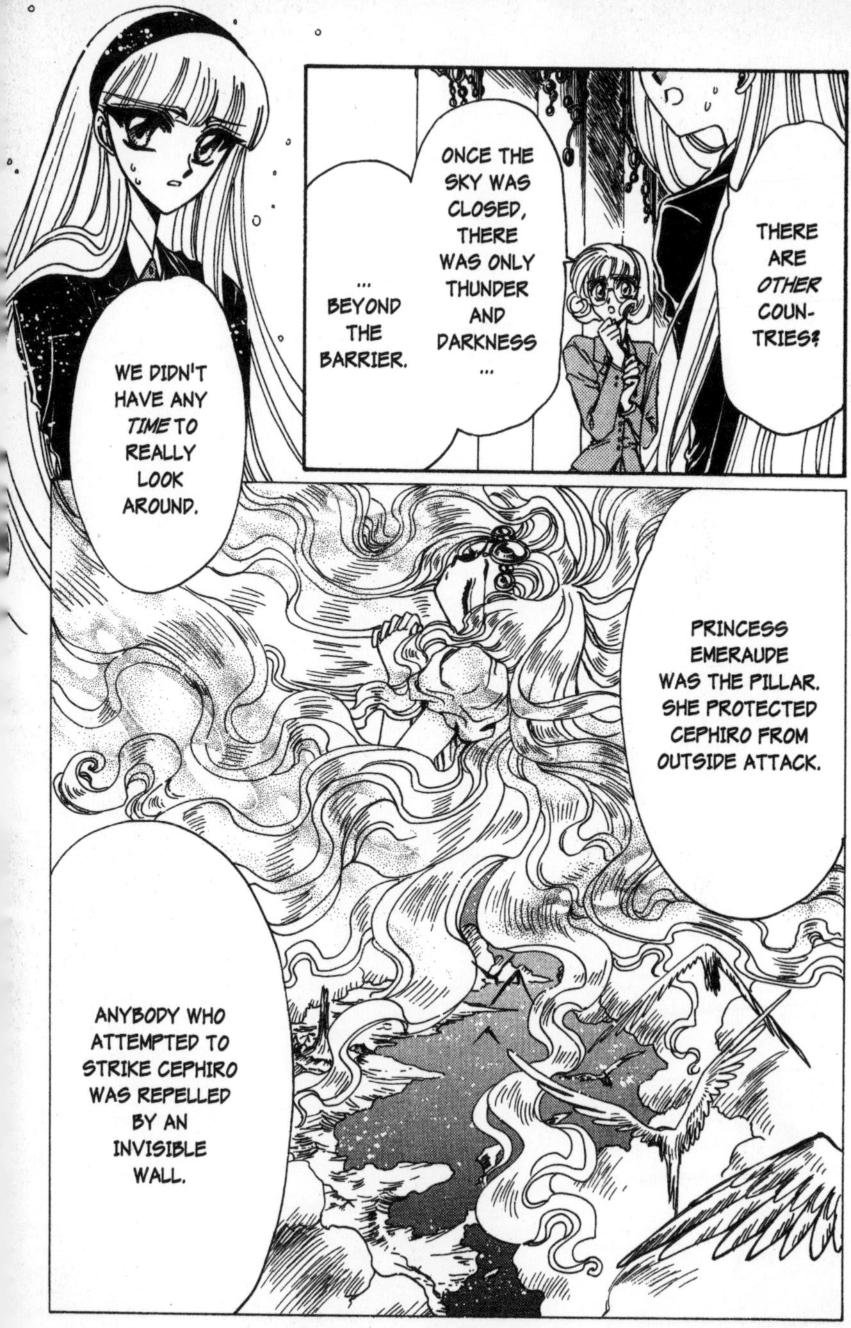
THERE ARE *OTHER* COUN-TRIES?
ONCE THE SKY WAS CLOSED, THERE WAS ONLY THUNDER AND DARKNESS ...
... BEYOND THE BARRIER.
WE DIDN'T HAVE ANY *TIME* TO REALLY LOOK AROUND.
PRINCESS EMERAUDE WAS THE PILLAR. SHE PROTECTED CEPHIRO FROM OUTSIDE ATTACK.
ANYBODY WHO ATTEMPTED TO STRIKE CEPHIRO WAS REPELLED BY AN INVISIBLE WALL.

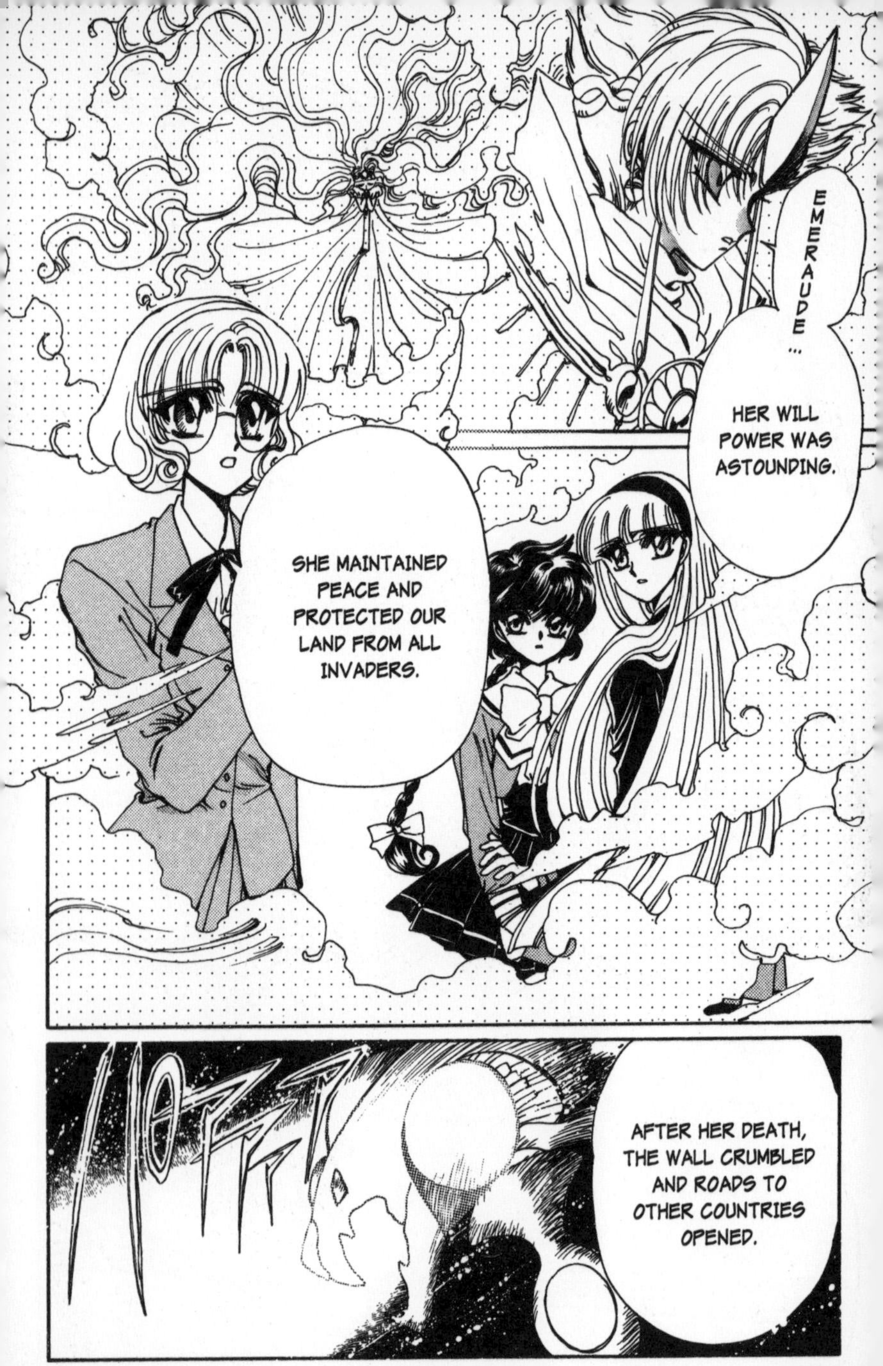
EMERAUDE...
HER WILL POWER WAS ASTOUNDING.
SHE MAINTAINED PEACE AND PROTECTED OUR LAND FROM ALL INVADERS.
AFTER HER DEATH, THE WALL CRUMBLED AND ROADS TO OTHER COUNTRIES OPENED.

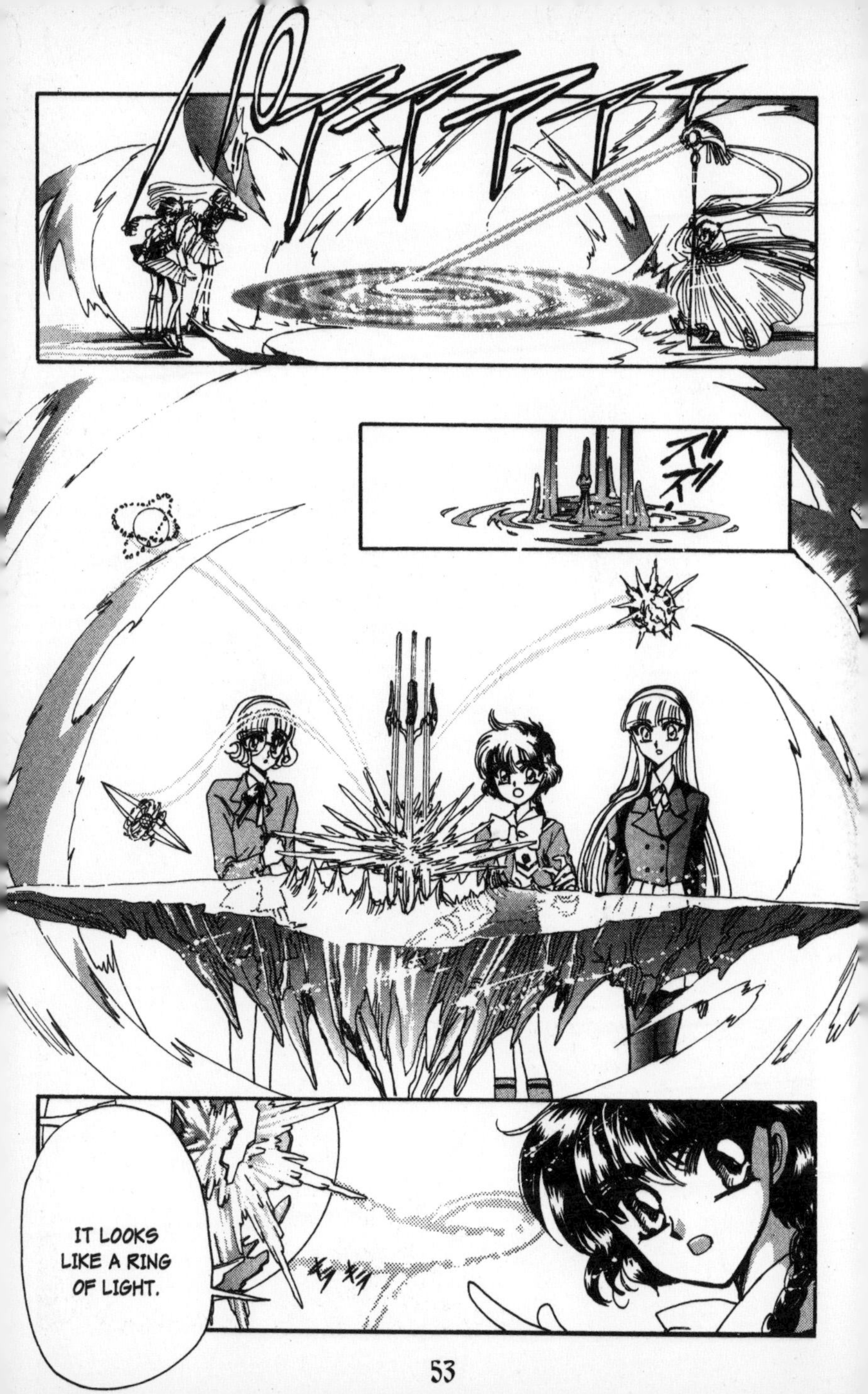

IT LOOKS LIKE A RING OF LIGHT.

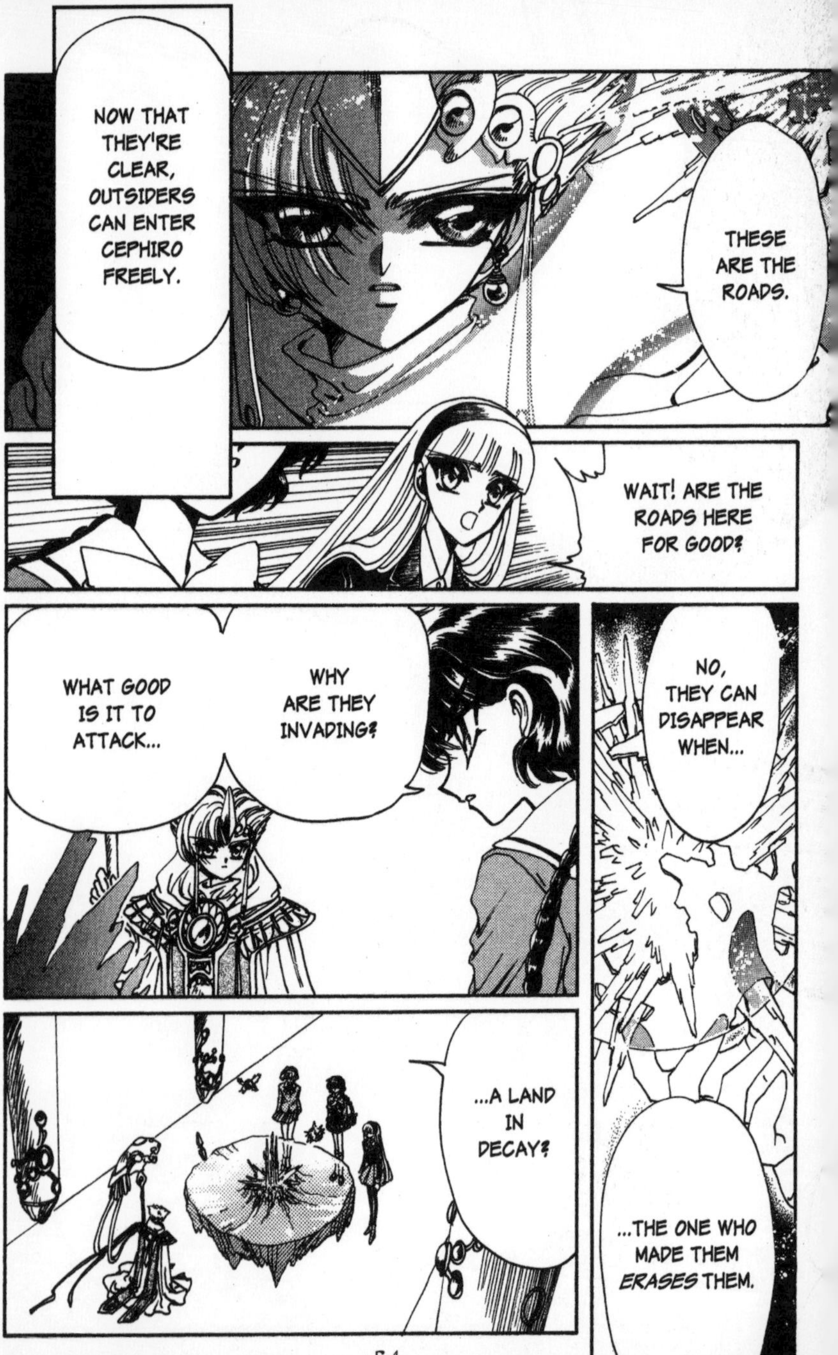
THESE ARE THE ROADS.
NOW THAT THEY'RE CLEAR, OUTSIDERS CAN ENTER CEPHIRO FREELY.
WAIT! ARE THE ROADS HERE FOR GOOD?
NO, THEY CAN DISAPPEAR WHEN...
...THE ONE WHO MADE THEM *ERASES* THEM.
WHY ARE THEY INVADING?
WHAT GOOD IS IT TO ATTACK...
...A LAND IN DECAY?

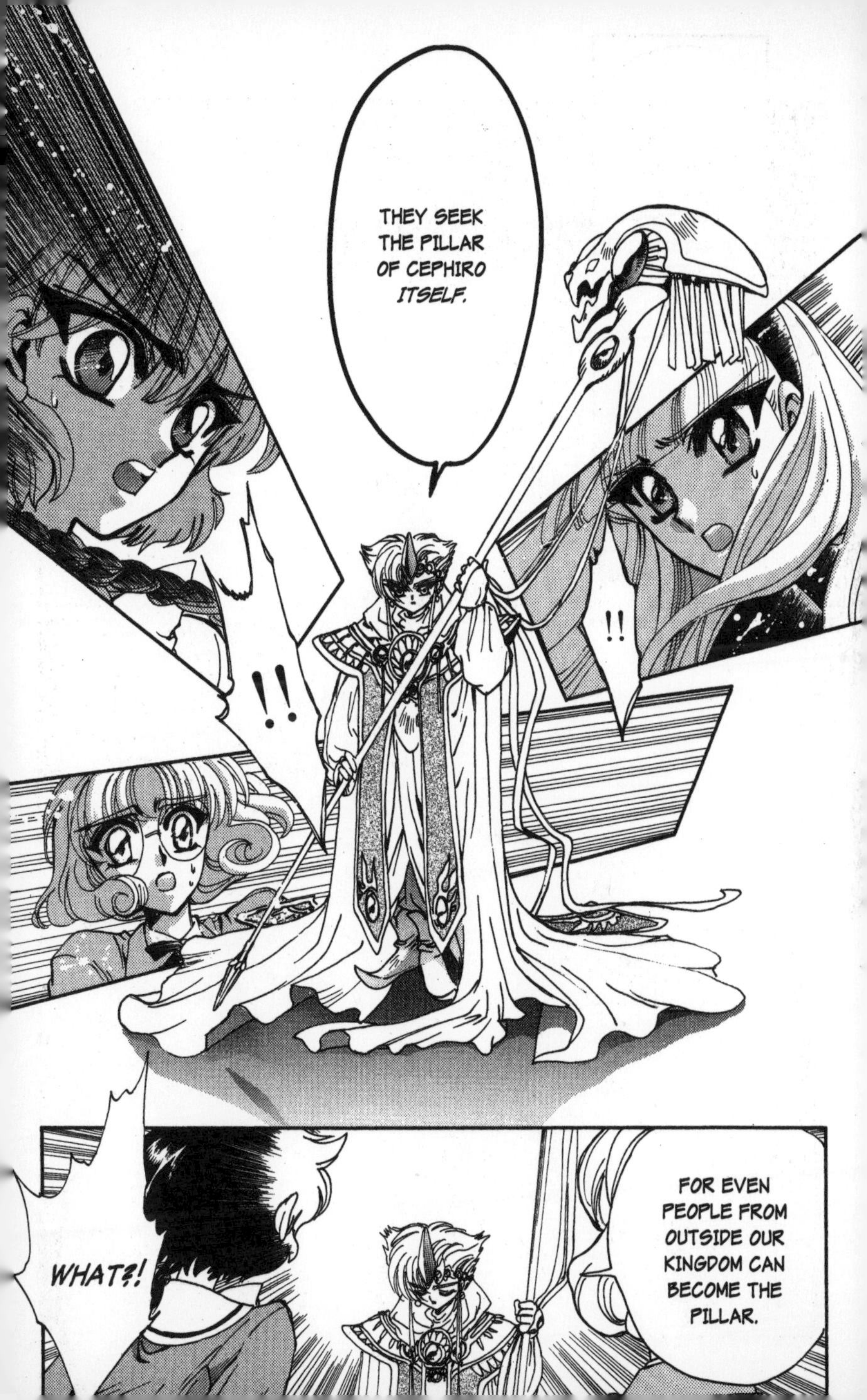
THEY SEEK THE PILLAR OF CEPHIRO *ITSELF.*
!!
!!
FOR EVEN PEOPLE FROM OUTSIDE OUR KINGDOM CAN BECOME THE PILLAR.
WHAT?!

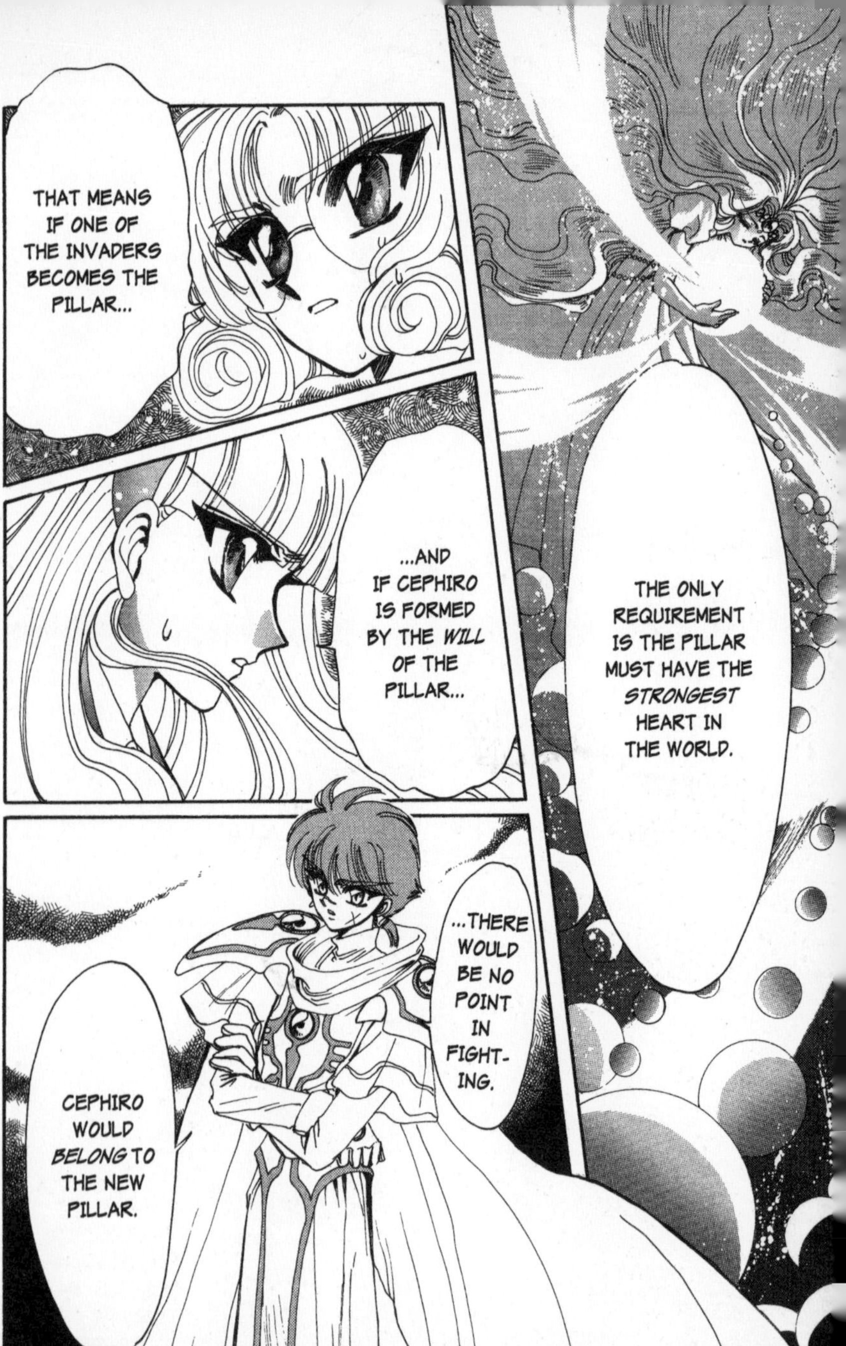
THE ONLY REQUIREMENT IS THE PILLAR MUST HAVE THE *STRONGEST* HEART IN THE WORLD.
THAT MEANS IF ONE OF THE INVADERS BECOMES THE PILLAR...
...AND IF CEPHIRO IS FORMED BY THE *WILL* OF THE PILLAR...
...THERE WOULD BE NO POINT IN FIGHT-ING.
CEPHIRO WOULD *BELONG* TO THE NEW PILLAR.

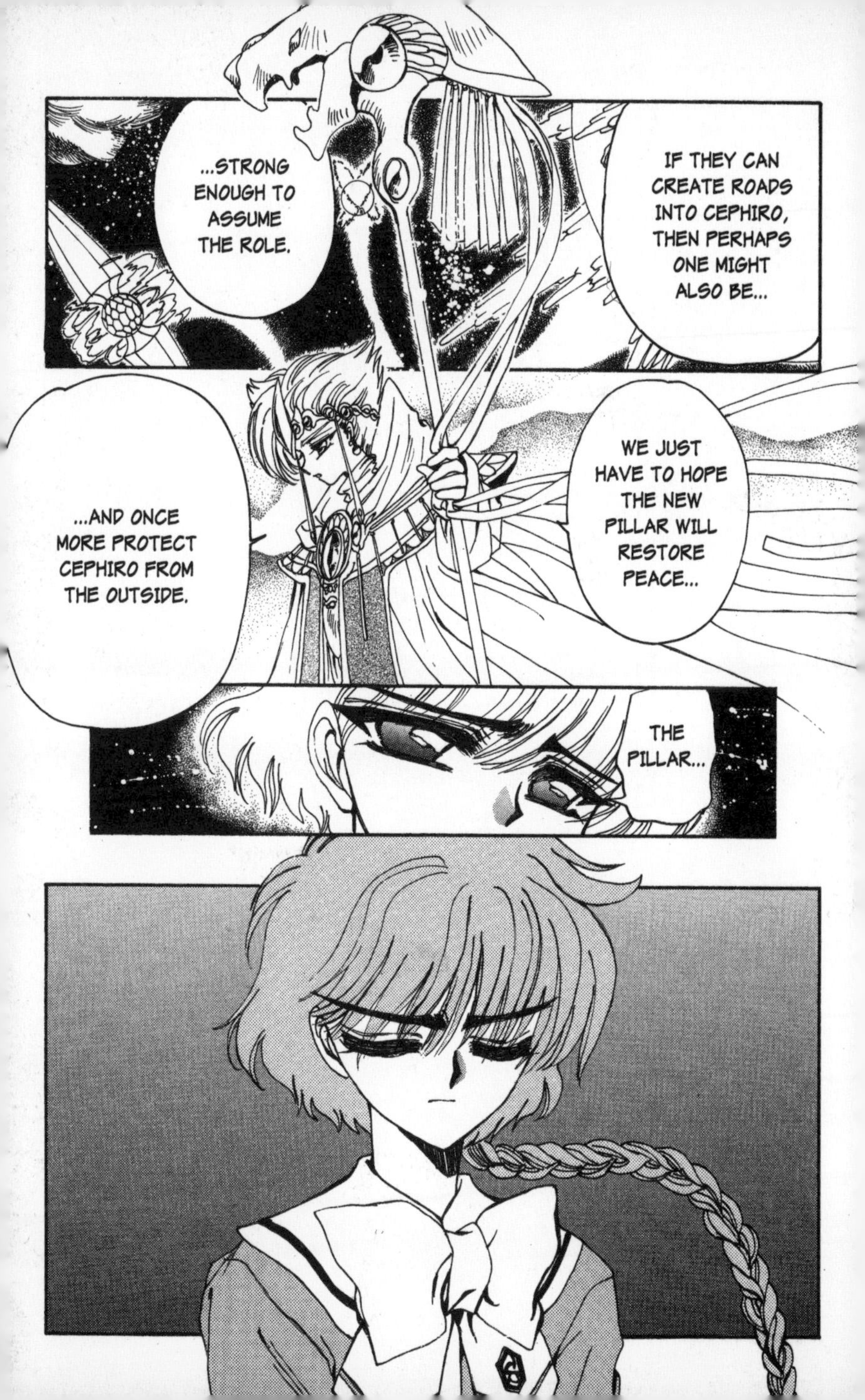
IF THEY CAN CREATE ROADS INTO CEPHIRO, THEN PERHAPS ONE MIGHT ALSO BE...
...STRONG ENOUGH TO ASSUME THE ROLE.
WE JUST HAVE TO HOPE THE NEW PILLAR WILL RESTORE PEACE...
...AND ONCE MORE PROTECT CEPHIRO FROM THE OUTSIDE.
THE PILLAR...

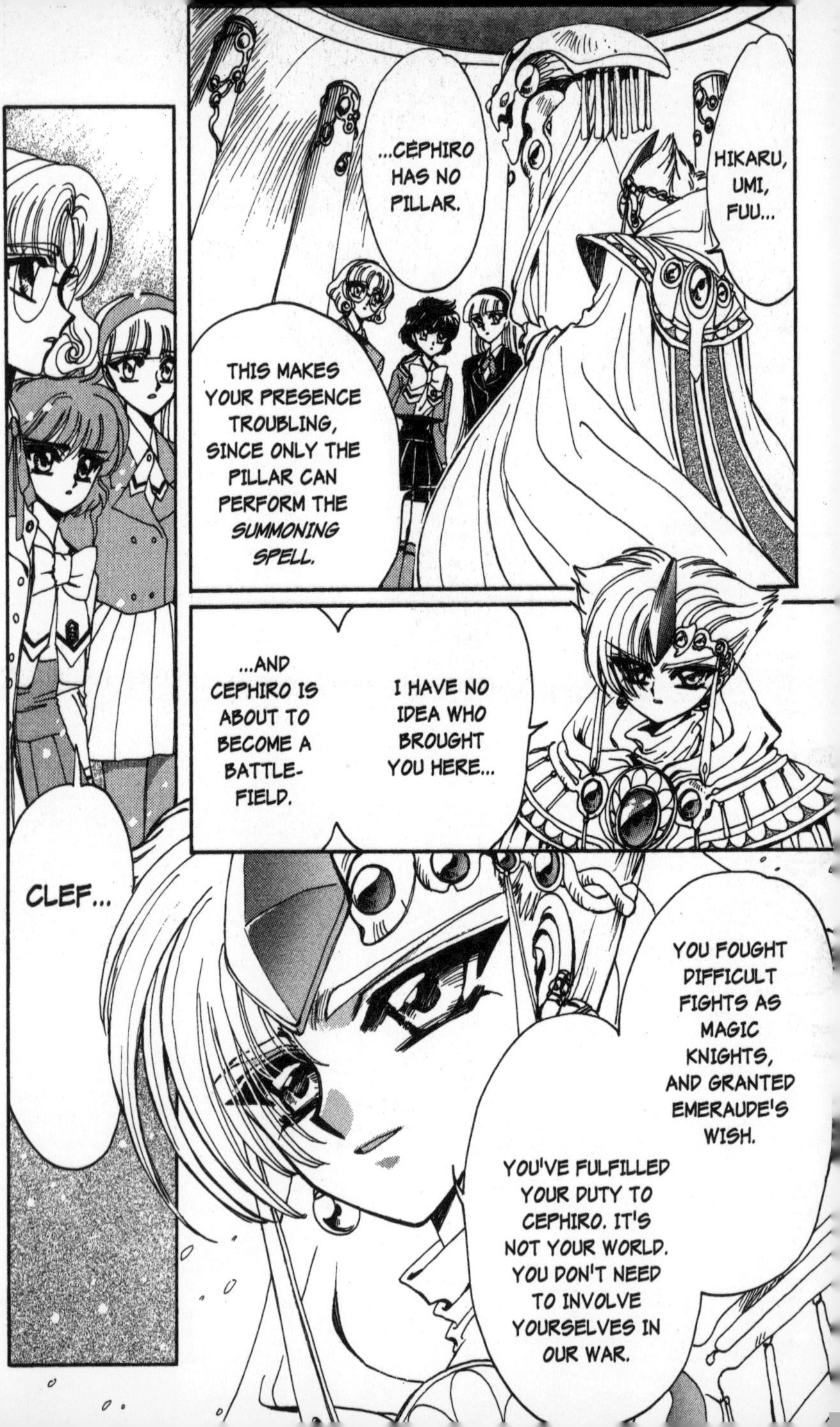
HIKARU, UMI, FUU...
...CEPHIRO HAS NO PILLAR.
THIS MAKES YOUR PRESENCE TROUBLING, SINCE ONLY THE PILLAR CAN PERFORM THE *SUMMONING SPELL.*
I HAVE NO IDEA WHO BROUGHT YOU HERE...
...AND CEPHIRO IS ABOUT TO BECOME A BATTLE-FIELD.
YOU FOUGHT DIFFICULT FIGHTS AS MAGIC KNIGHTS, AND GRANTED EMERAUDE'S WISH.
YOU'VE FULFILLED YOUR DUTY TO CEPHIRO. IT'S NOT YOUR WORLD. YOU DON'T NEED TO INVOLVE YOURSELVES IN OUR WAR.
CLEF...

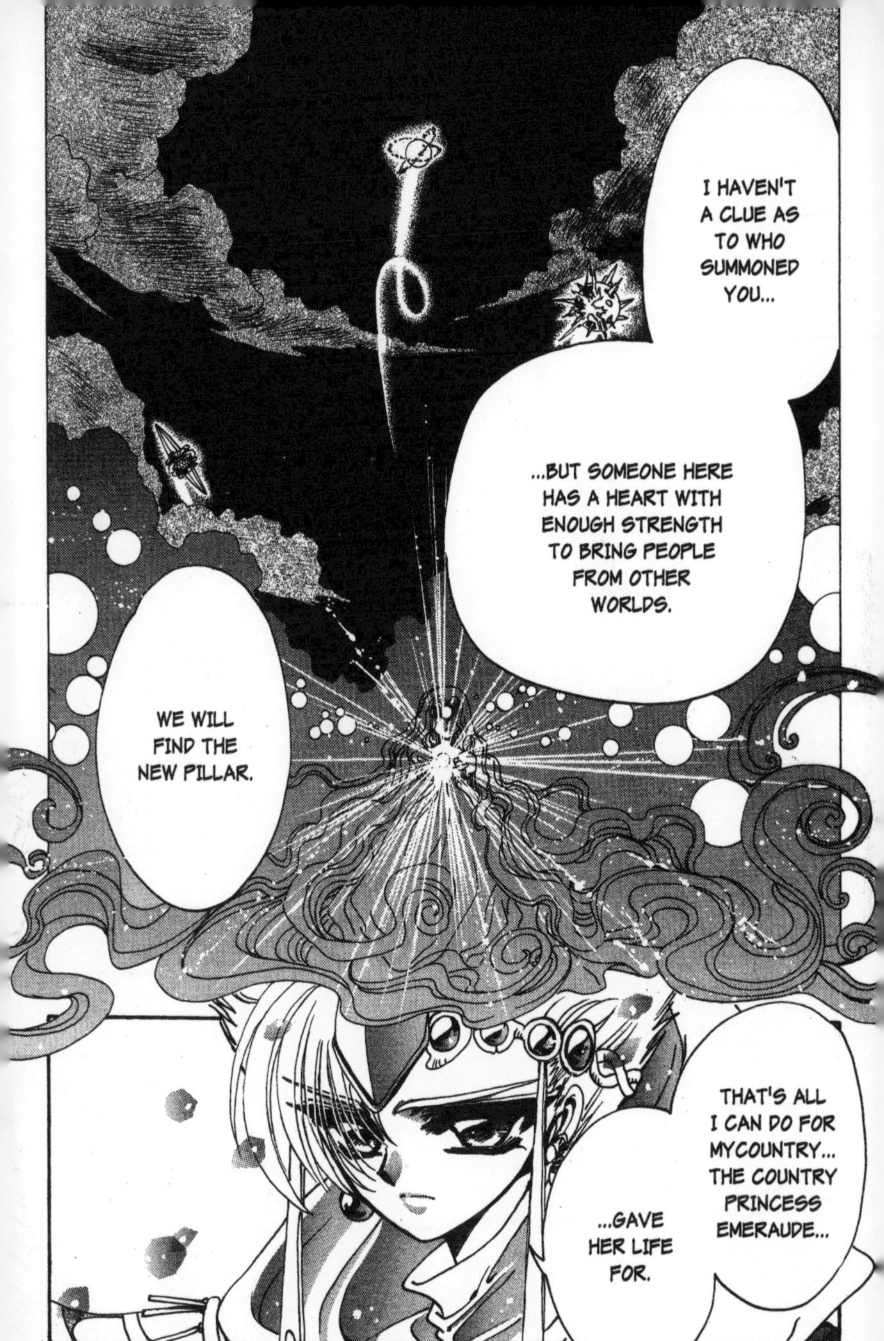
I HAVEN'T A CLUE AS TO WHO SUMMONED YOU...
...BUT SOMEONE HERE HAS A HEART WITH ENOUGH STRENGTH TO BRING PEOPLE FROM OTHER WORLDS.
WE WILL FIND THE NEW PILLAR.
THAT'S ALL I CAN DO FOR MYCOUNTRY... THE COUNTRY PRINCESS EMERAUDE...
...GAVE HER LIFE FOR.

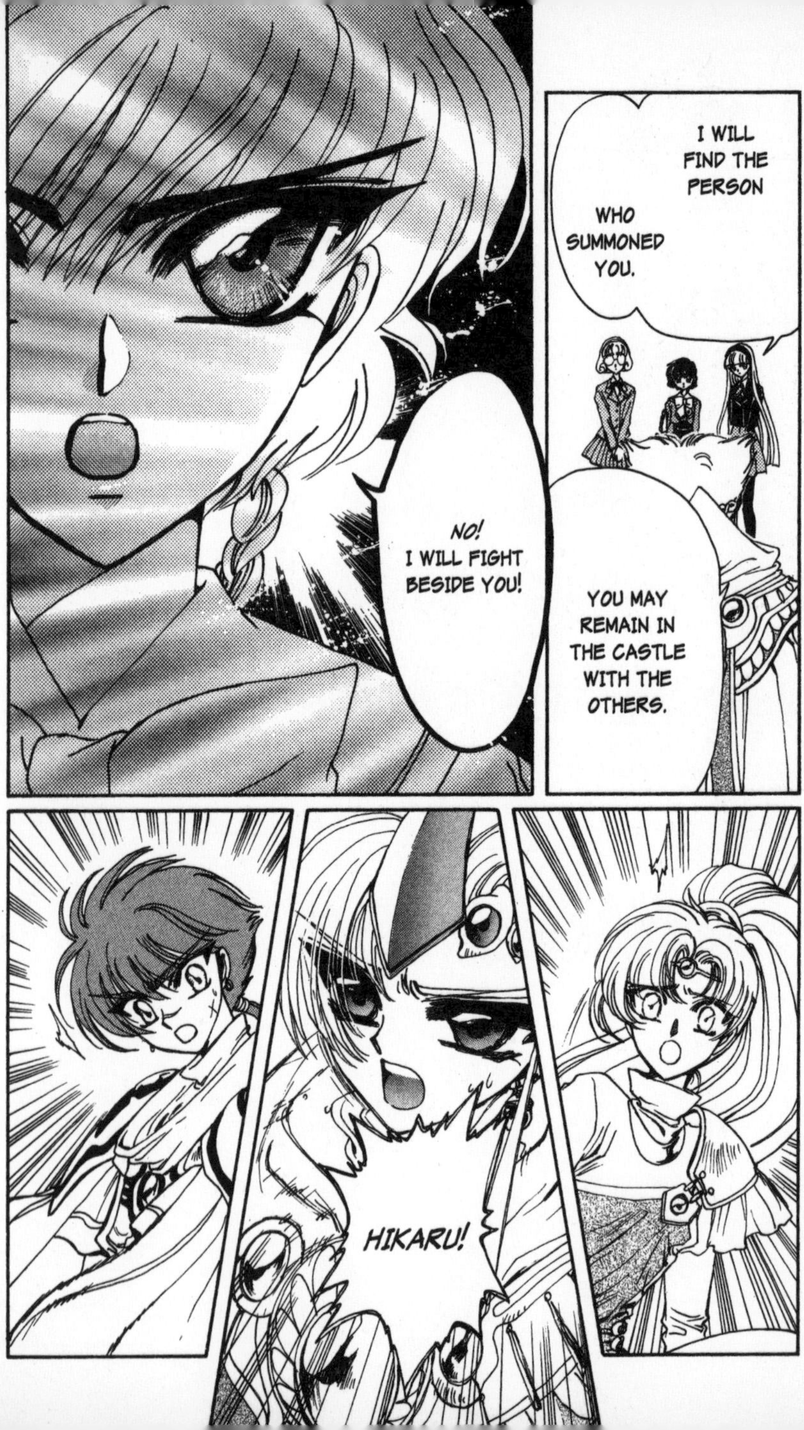
I WILL FIND THE PERSON WHO SUMMONED YOU.
YOU MAY REMAIN IN THE CASTLE WITH THE OTHERS.
NO! I WILL FIGHT BESIDE YOU!
HIKARU!

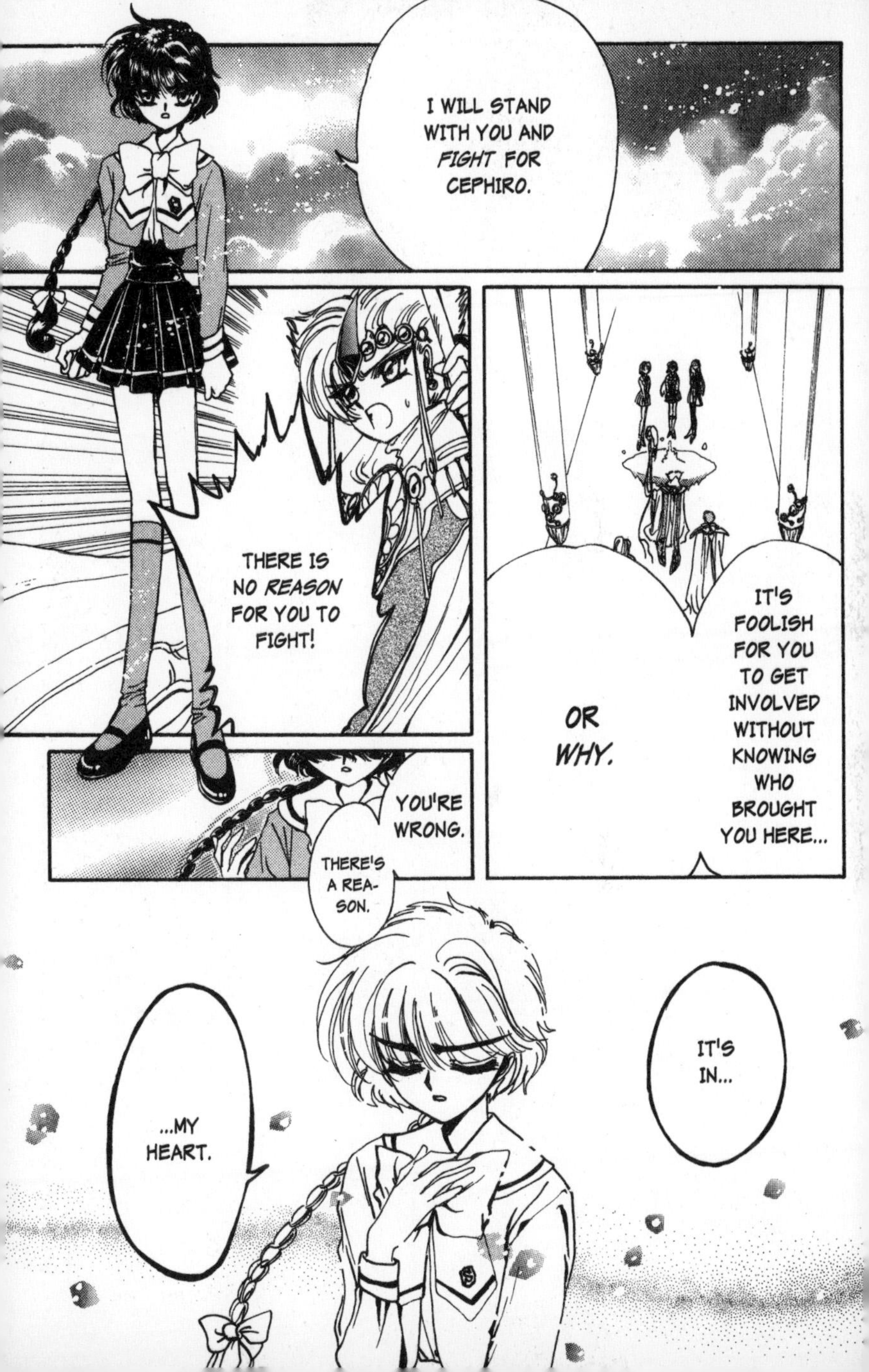
I WILL STAND WITH YOU AND *FIGHT* FOR CEPHIRO.
IT'S FOOLISH FOR YOU TO GET INVOLVED WITHOUT KNOWING WHO BROUGHT YOU HERE...
OR *WHY.*
THERE IS NO *REASON* FOR YOU TO FIGHT!
YOU'RE WRONG.
THERE'S A REA-SON.
IT'S IN...
...MY HEART.

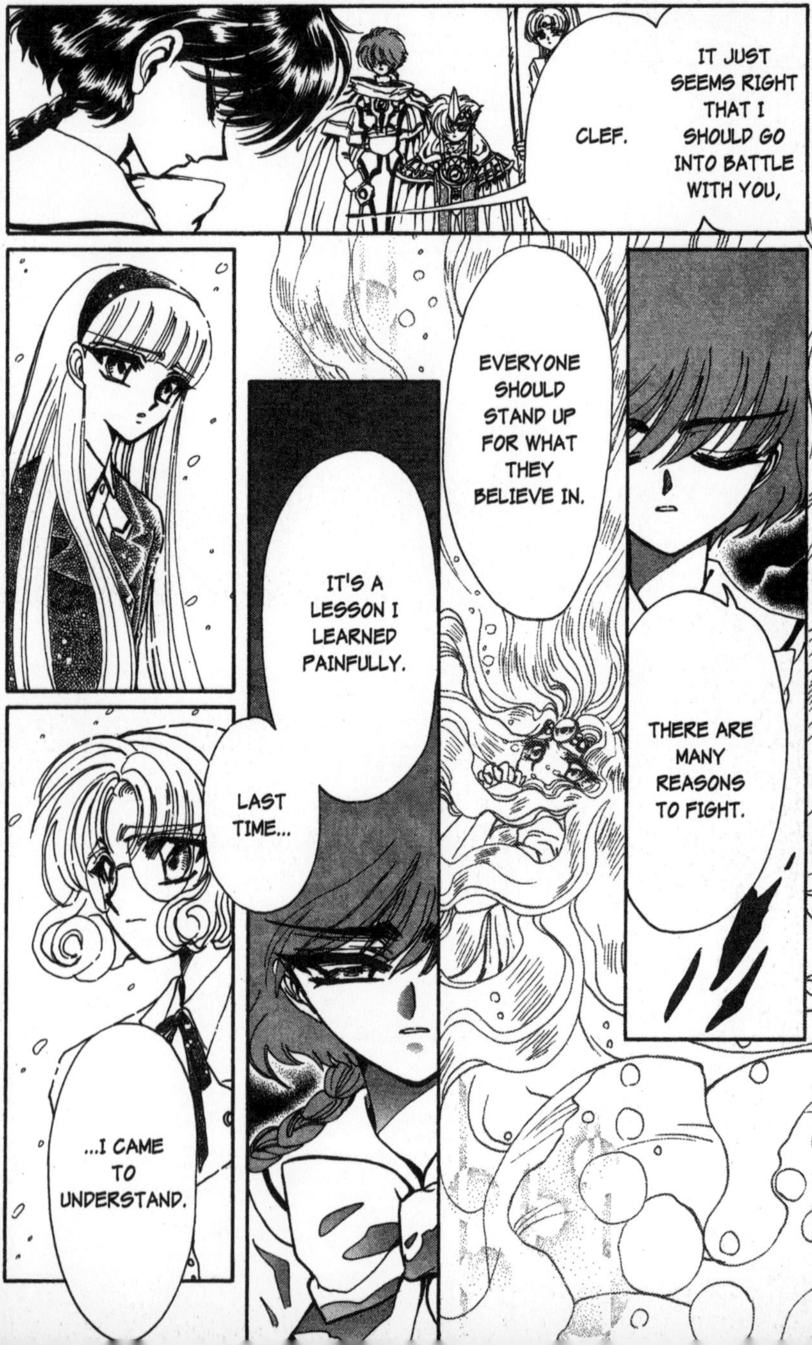
IT JUST SEEMS RIGHT THAT I SHOULD GO INTO BATTLE WITH YOU,
CLEF.
THERE ARE MANY REASONS TO FIGHT.
EVERYONE SHOULD STAND UP FOR WHAT THEY BELIEVE IN.
IT'S A LESSON I LEARNED PAINFULLY.
LAST TIME...
...I CAME TO UNDERSTAND.

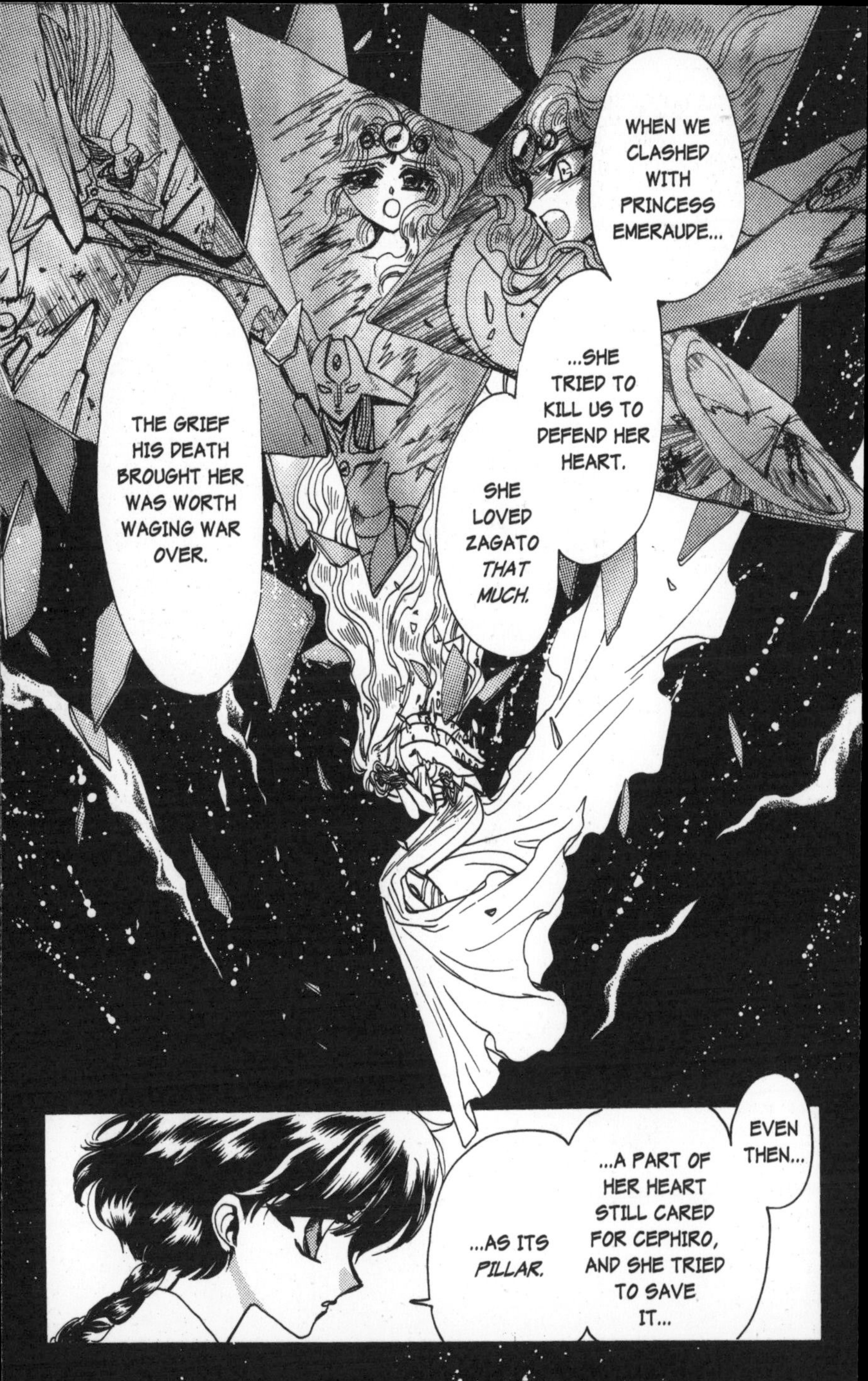
WHEN WE CLASHED WITH PRINCESS EMERAUDE...
...SHE TRIED TO KILL US TO DEFEND HER HEART.
SHE LOVED ZAGATO *THAT* MUCH.
THE GRIEF HIS DEATH BROUGHT HER WAS WORTH WAGING WAR OVER.
EVEN THEN...
...A PART OF HER HEART STILL CARED FOR CEPHIRO, AND SHE TRIED TO SAVE IT...
...AS ITS *PILLAR.*

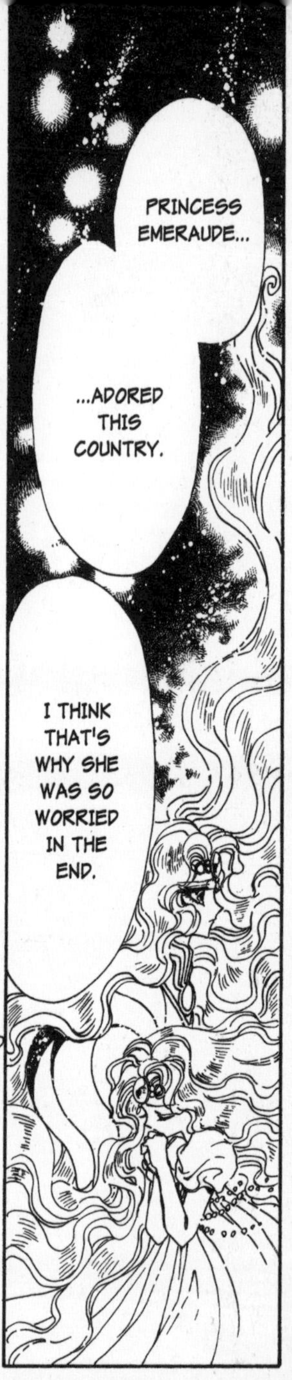
PRINCESS EMERAUDE...
...ADORED THIS COUNTRY.
I THINK THAT'S WHY SHE WAS SO WORRIED IN THE END.

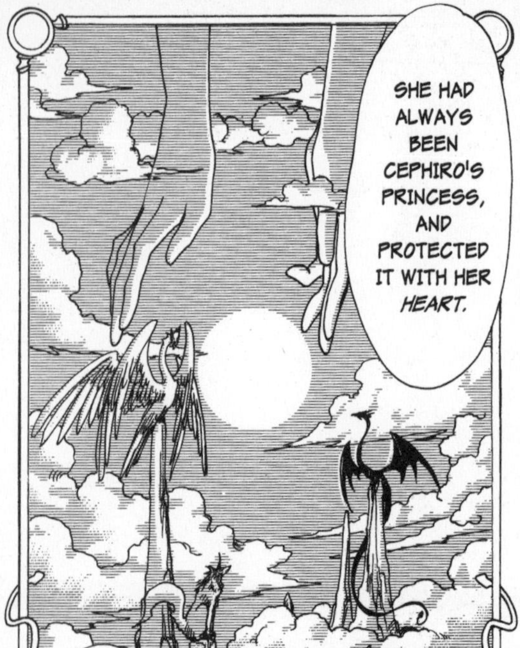
SHE HAD ALWAYS BEEN CEPHIRO'S PRINCESS, AND PROTECTED IT WITH HER *HEART.*
CLEF HAD TAUGHT US WHAT A BEAUTIFUL AND PEACEFUL COUNTRY IT HAD BEEN.

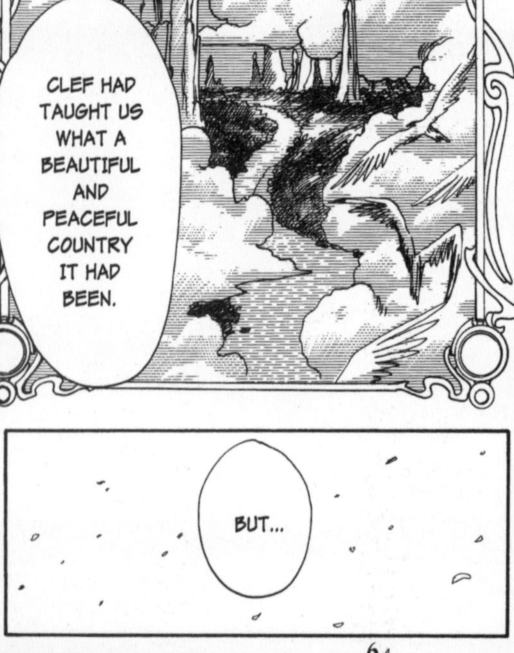
BUT...

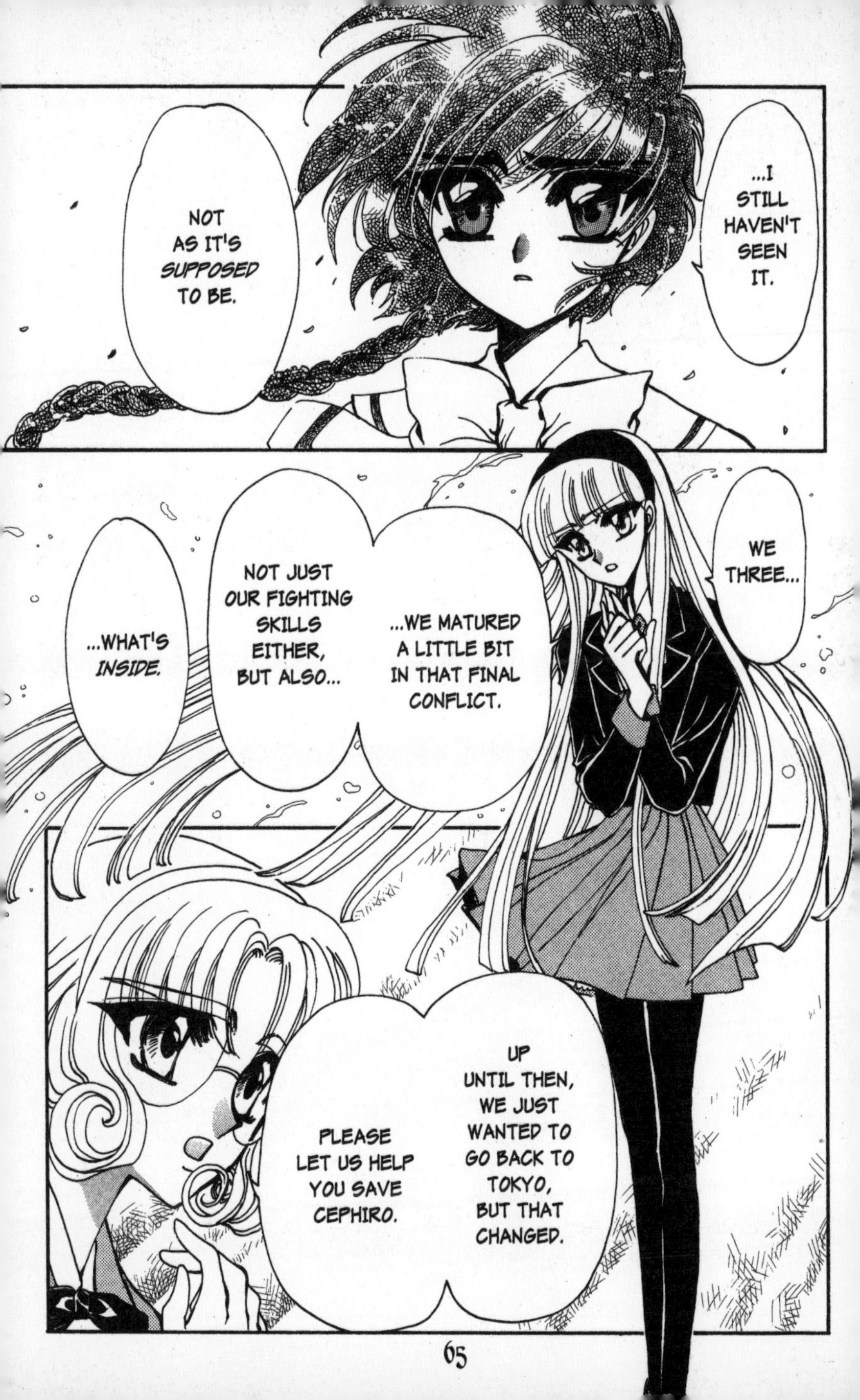
...I STILL HAVEN'T SEEN IT.
NOT AS IT'S *SUPPOSED* TO BE.
WE THREE...
...WE MATURED A LITTLE BIT IN THAT FINAL CONFLICT.
NOT JUST OUR FIGHTING SKILLS EITHER, BUT ALSO...
...WHAT'S *INSIDE.*
UP UNTIL THEN, WE JUST WANTED TO GO BACK TO TOKYO, BUT THAT CHANGED.
PLEASE LET US HELP YOU SAVE CEPHIRO.

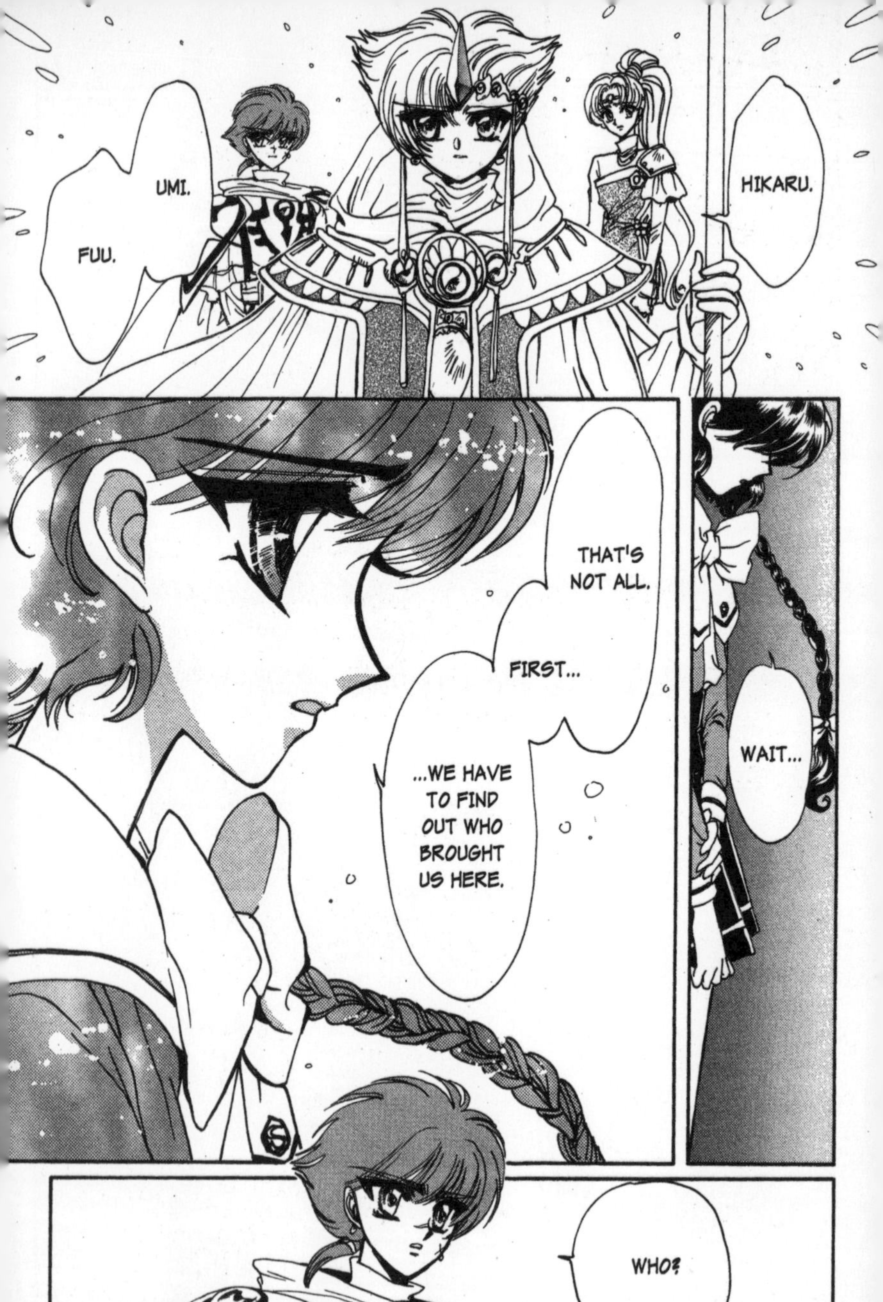
HIKARU.
UMI.
FUU.
WAIT...
THAT'S NOT ALL.
FIRST...
...WE HAVE TO FIND OUT WHO BROUGHT US HERE.
WHO?

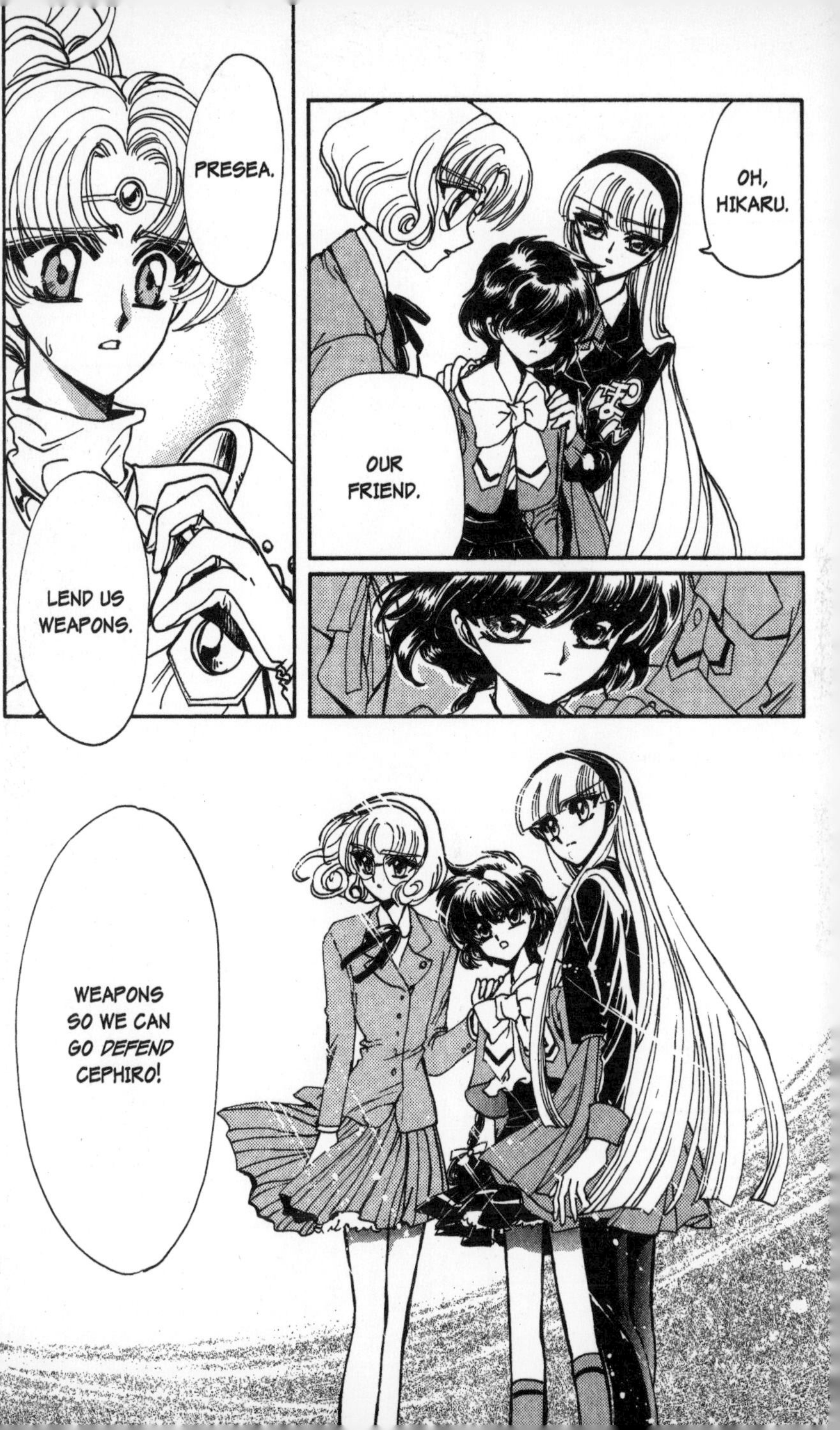
OH, HIKARU.
OUR FRIEND.
PRESEA.
LEND US WEAPONS.
WEAPONS SO WE CAN GO *DEFEND* CEPHIRO!

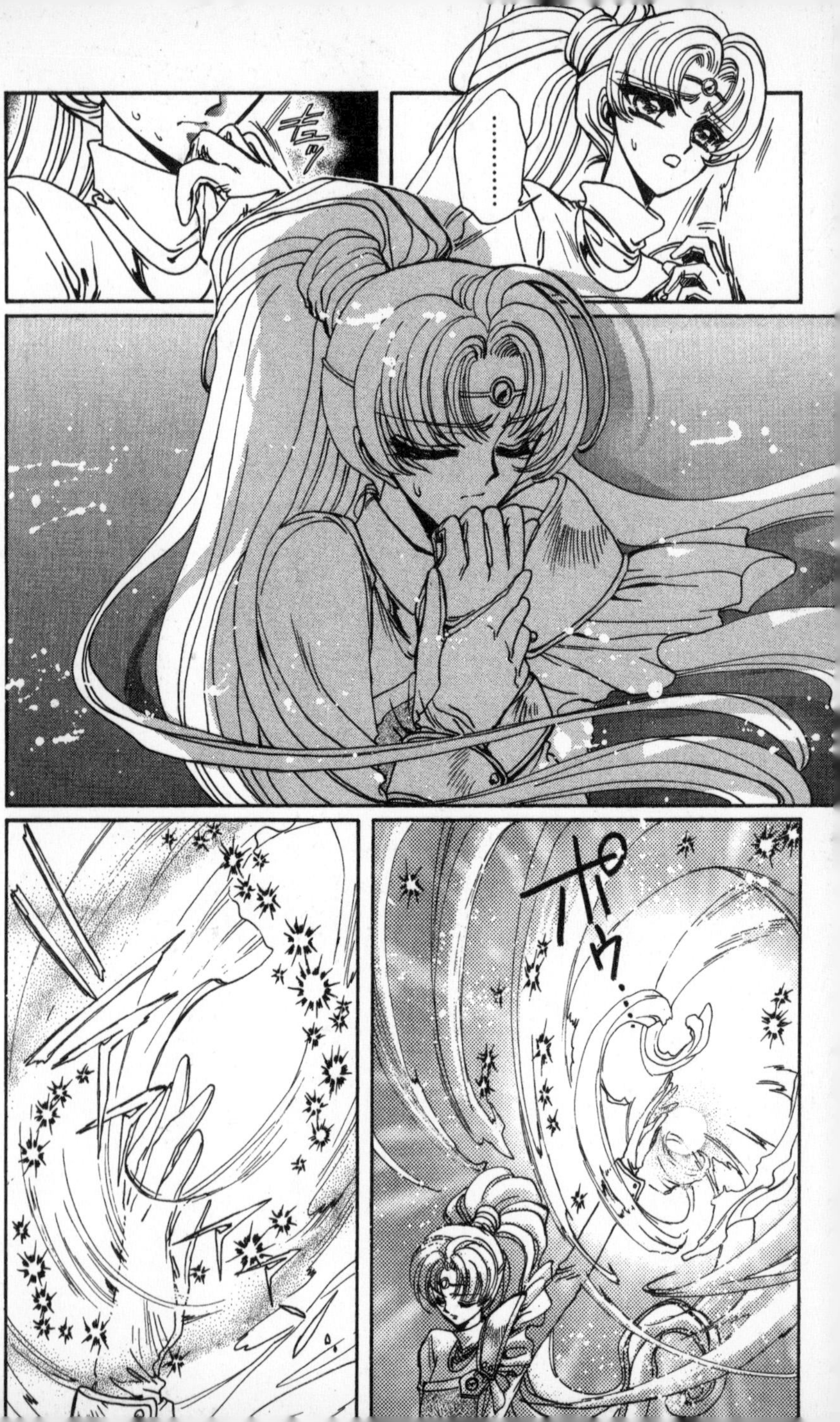
……
キュッ
ポウ…

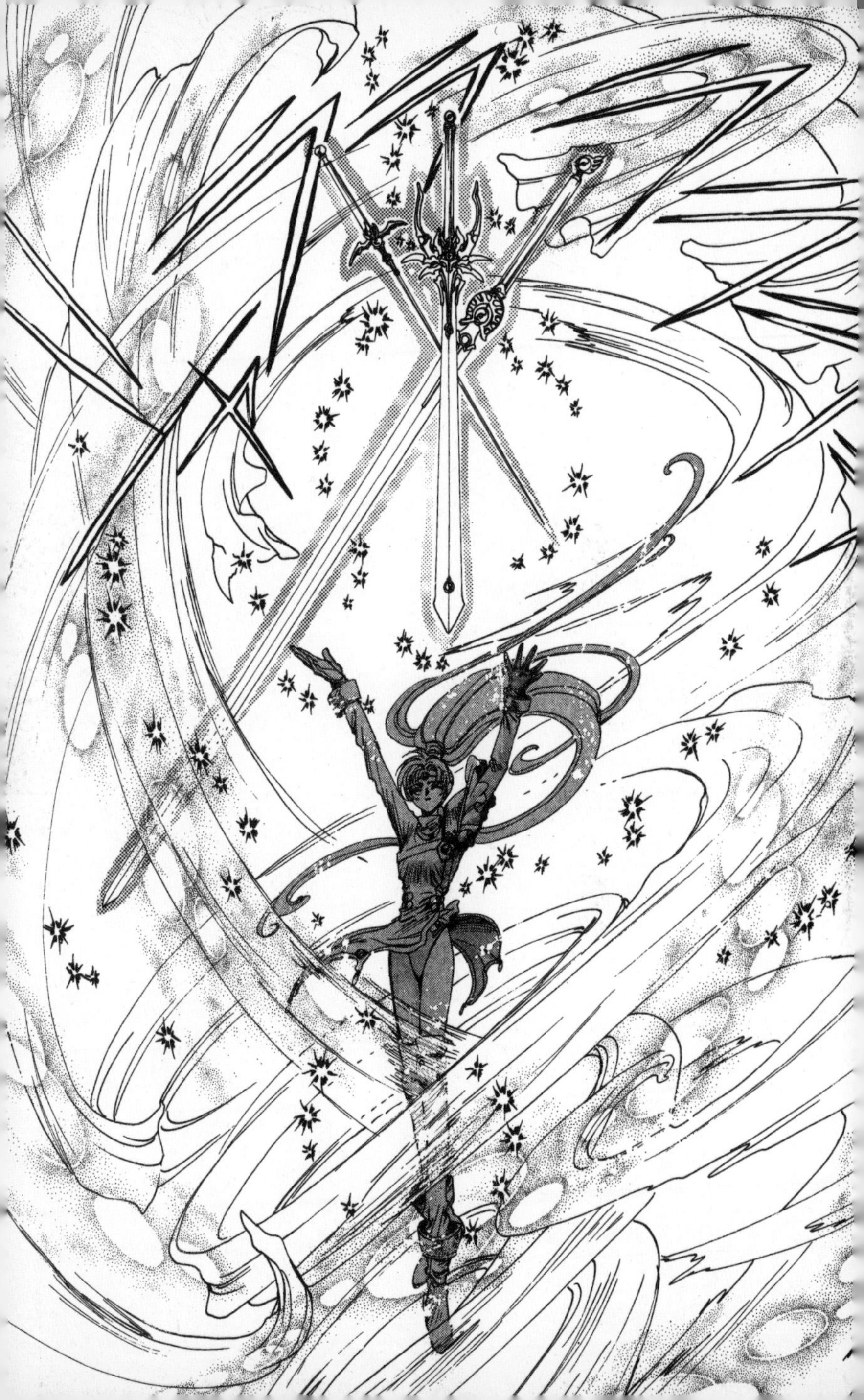

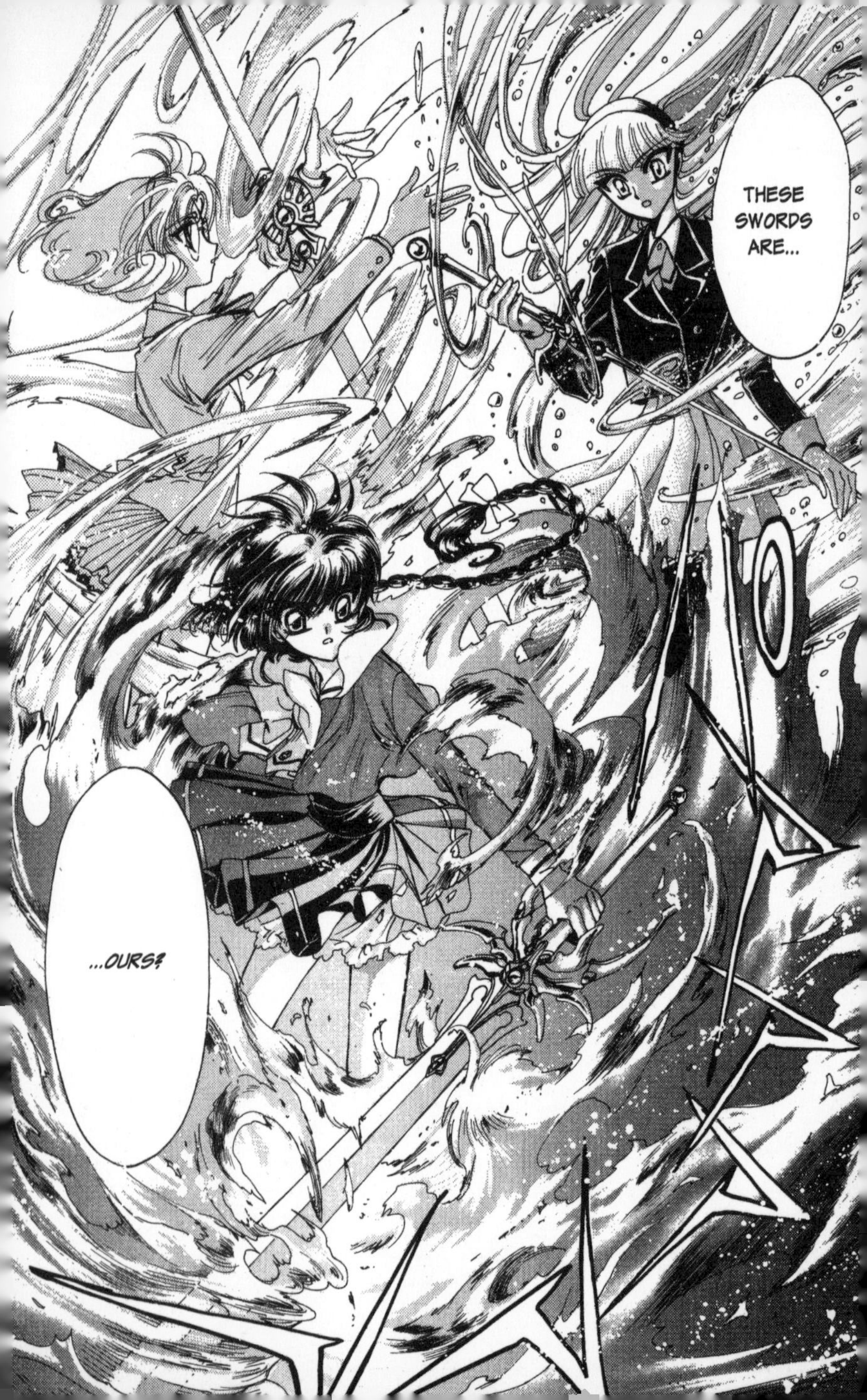
THESE SWORDS ARE...
...OURS?

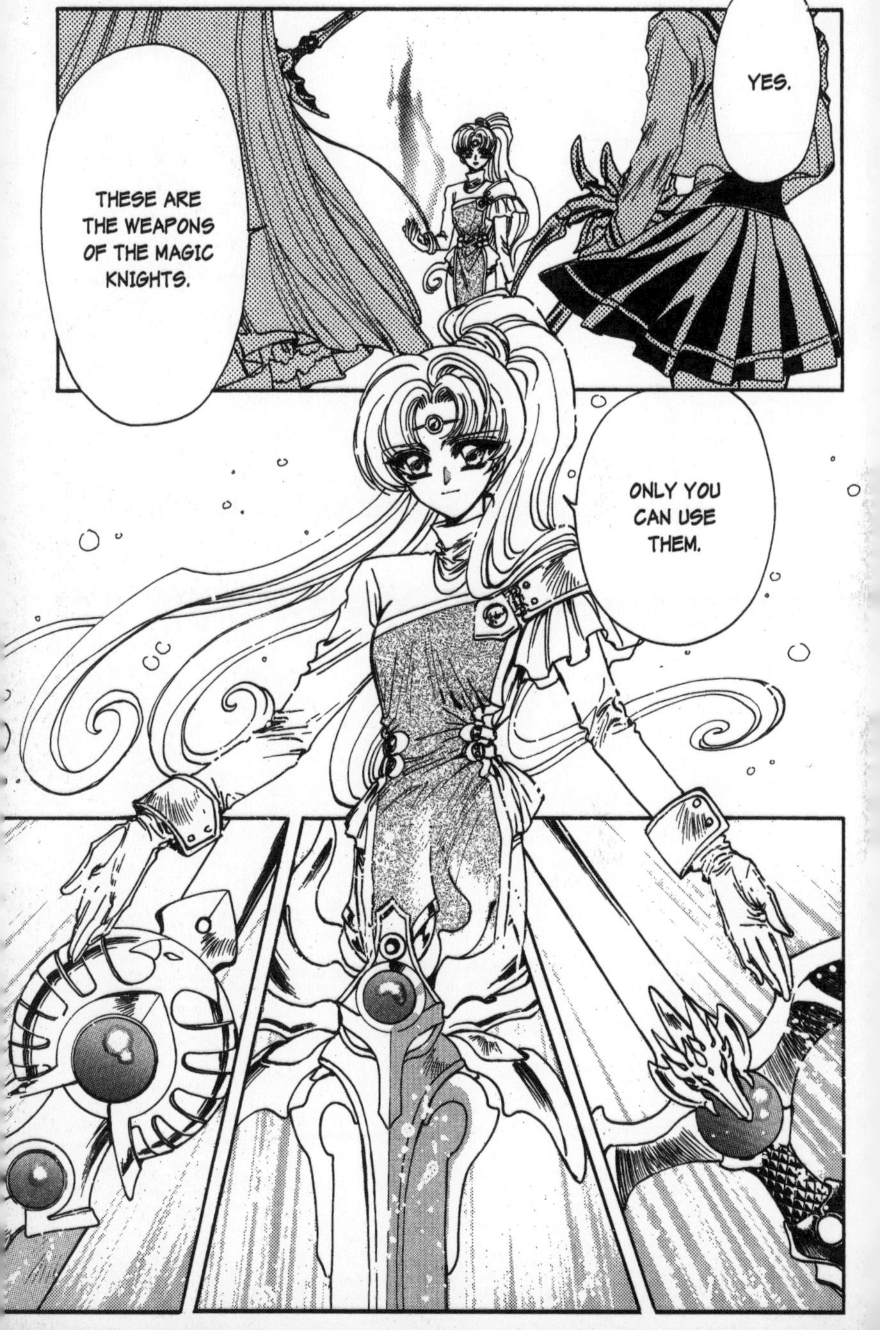
YES.
THESE ARE THE WEAPONS OF THE MAGIC KNIGHTS.
ONLY YOU CAN USE THEM.

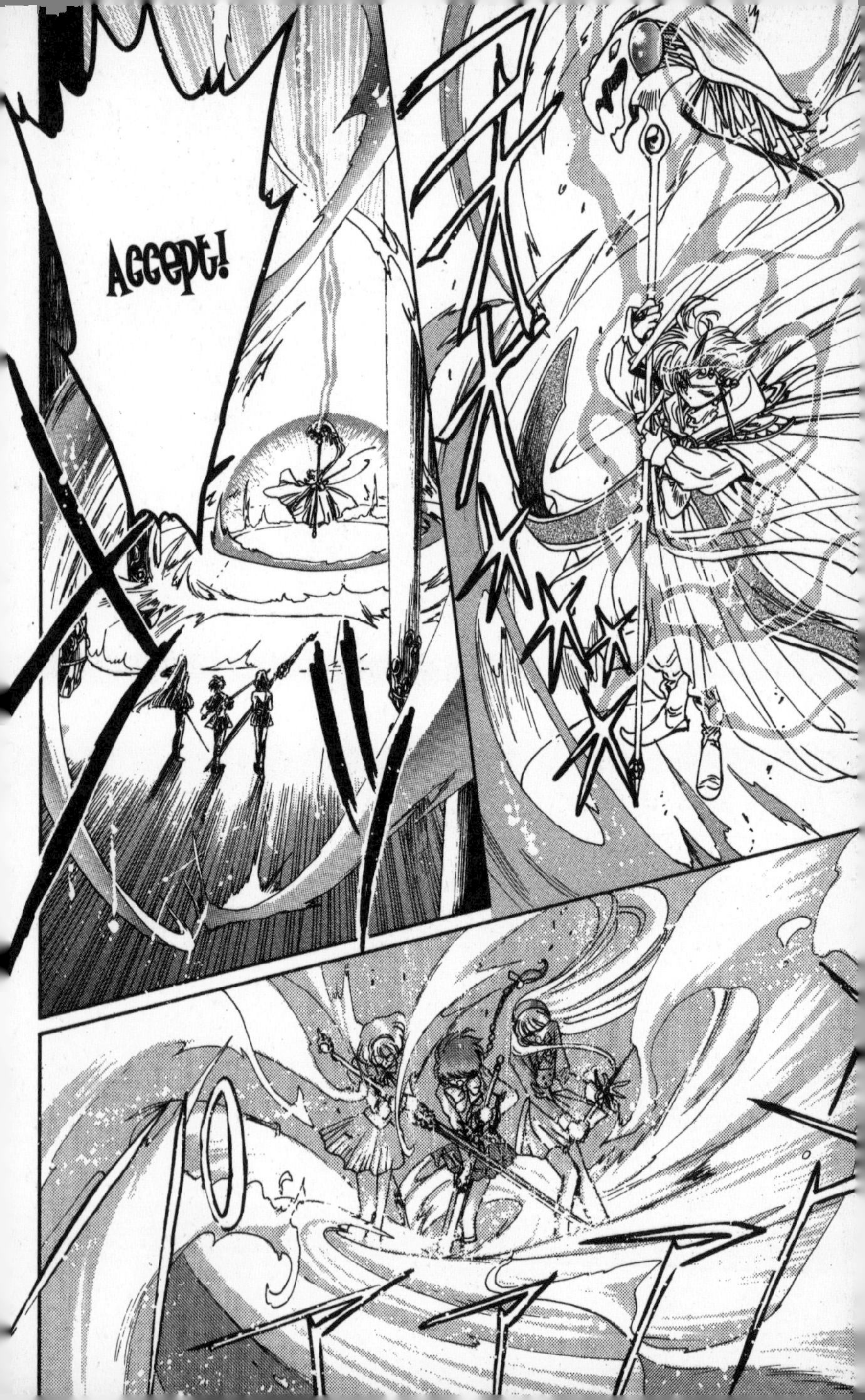
Accept!

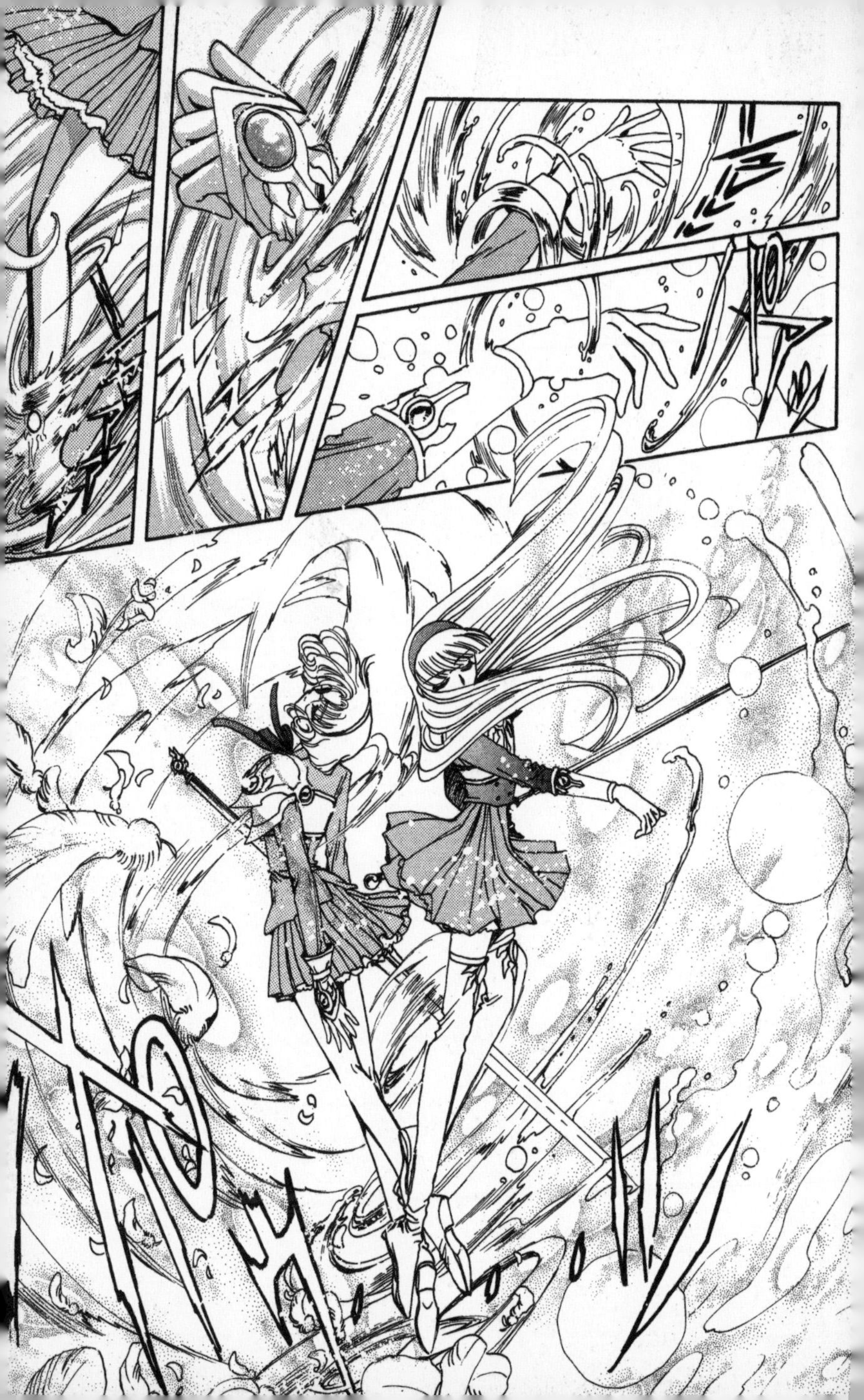

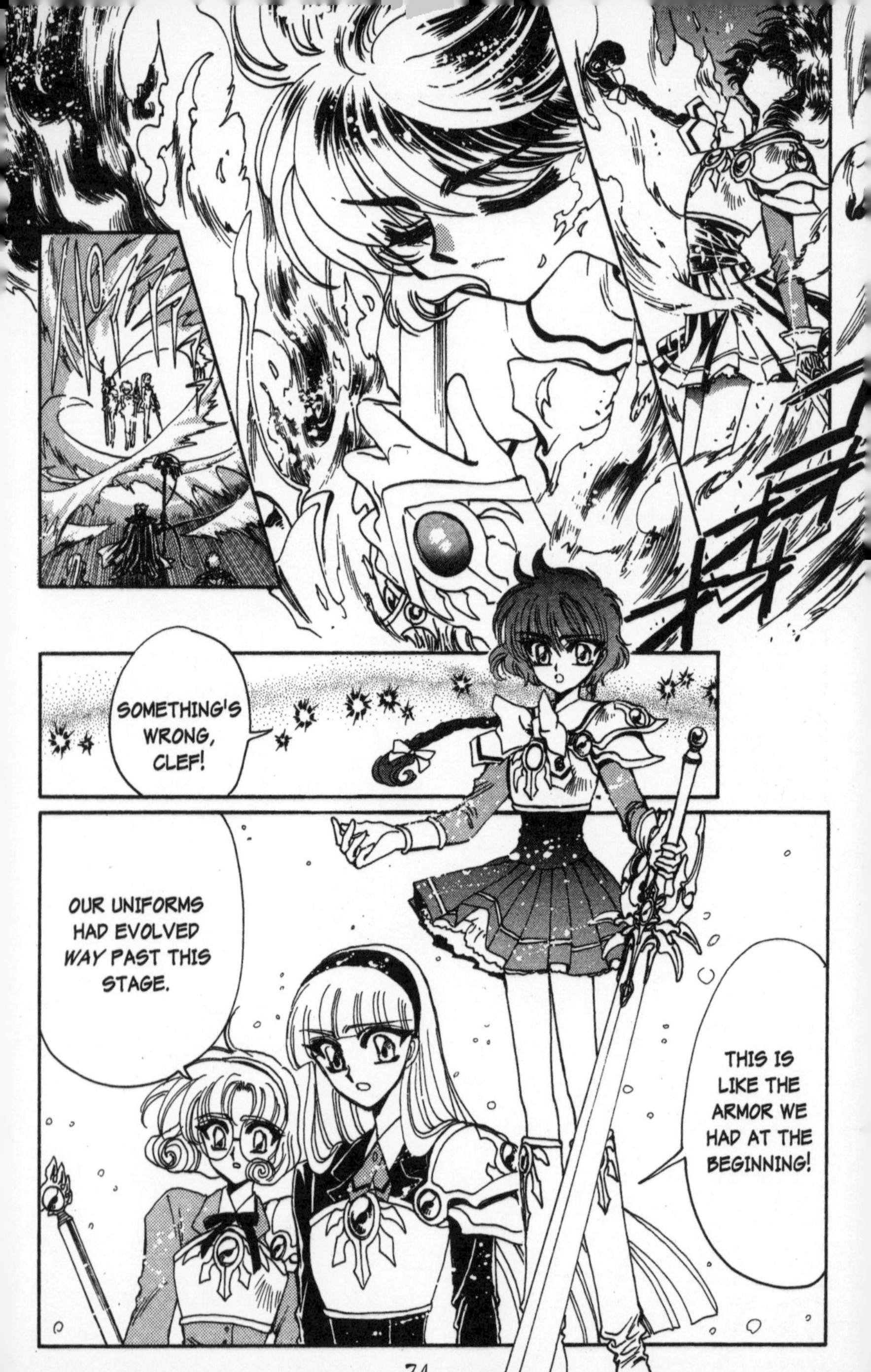
SOMETHING'S WRONG, CLEF!
THIS IS LIKE THE ARMOR WE HAD AT THE BEGINNING!
OUR UNIFORMS HAD EVOLVED *WAY* PAST THIS STAGE.

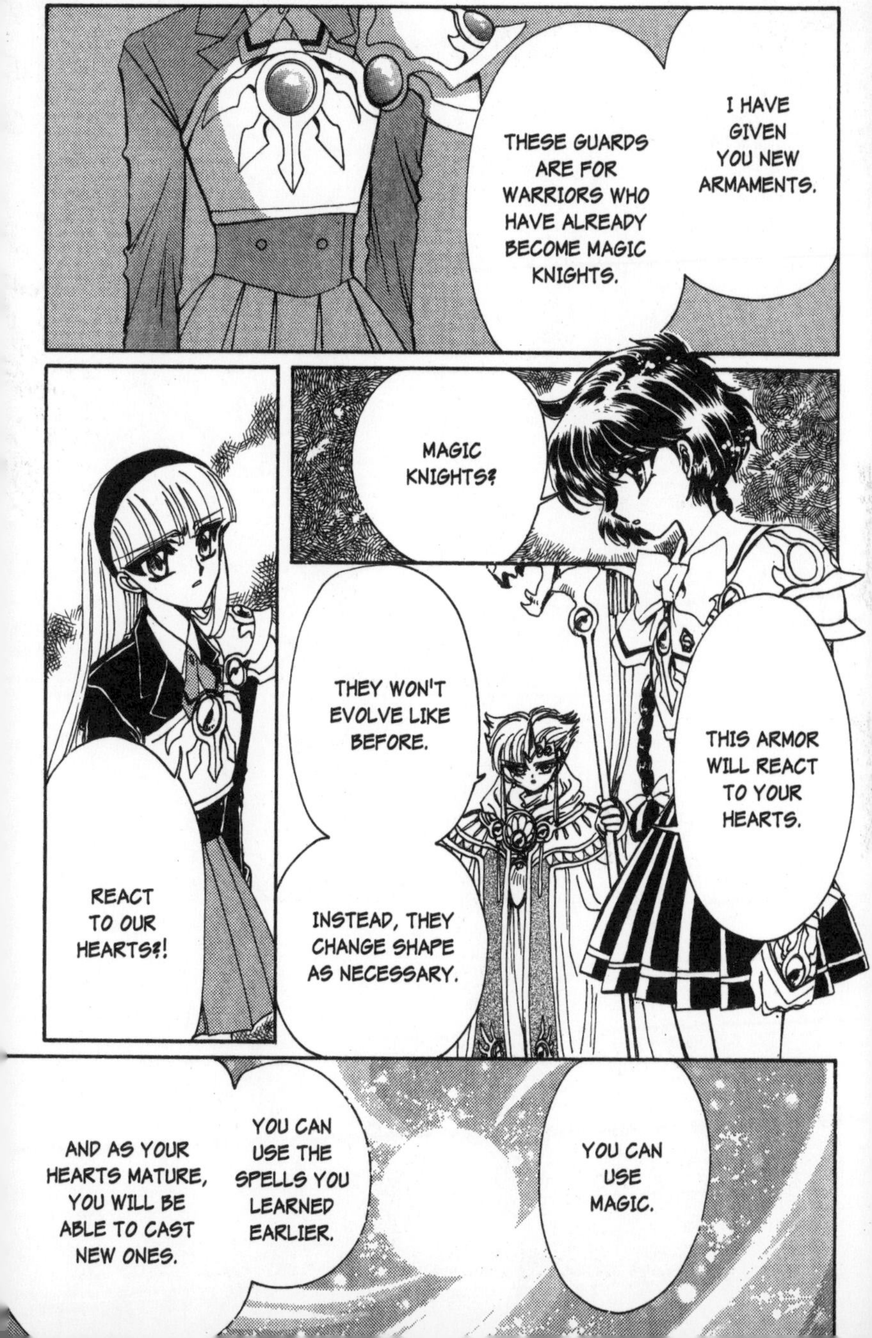
I HAVE GIVEN YOU NEW ARMAMENTS.
THESE GUARDS ARE FOR WARRIORS WHO HAVE ALREADY BECOME MAGIC KNIGHTS.
MAGIC KNIGHTS?
THIS ARMOR WILL REACT TO YOUR HEARTS.
THEY WON'T EVOLVE LIKE BEFORE.
INSTEAD, THEY CHANGE SHAPE AS NECESSARY.
REACT TO OUR HEARTS?!
YOU CAN USE MAGIC.
YOU CAN USE THE SPELLS YOU LEARNED EARLIER.
AND AS YOUR HEARTS MATURE, YOU WILL BE ABLE TO CAST NEW ONES.

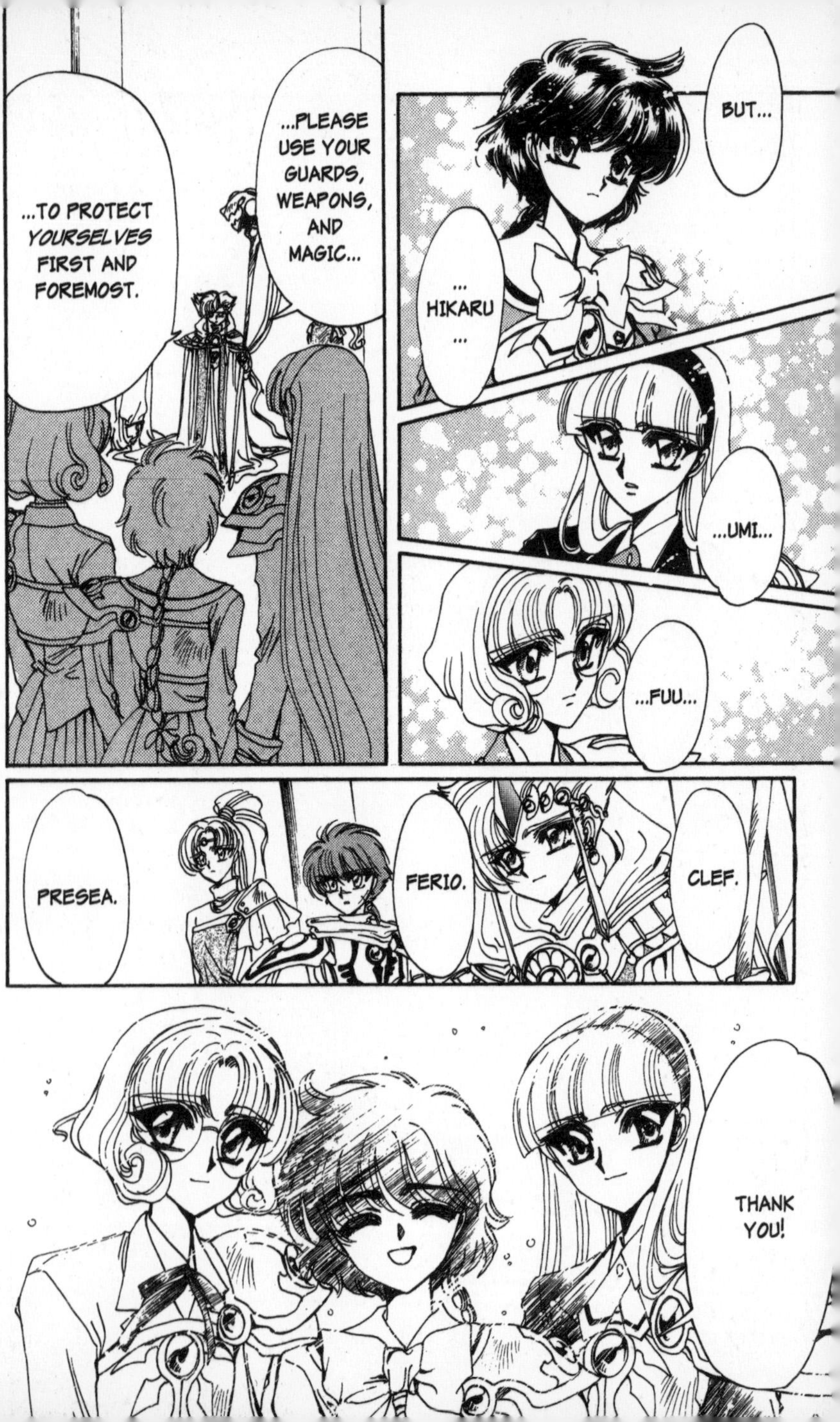
BUT...
... HIKARU ...
...UMI...
...FUU...
...PLEASE USE YOUR GUARDS, WEAPONS, AND MAGIC...
...TO PROTECT *YOURSELVES* FIRST AND FOREMOST.
CLEF.
FERIO.
PRESEA.
THANK YOU!

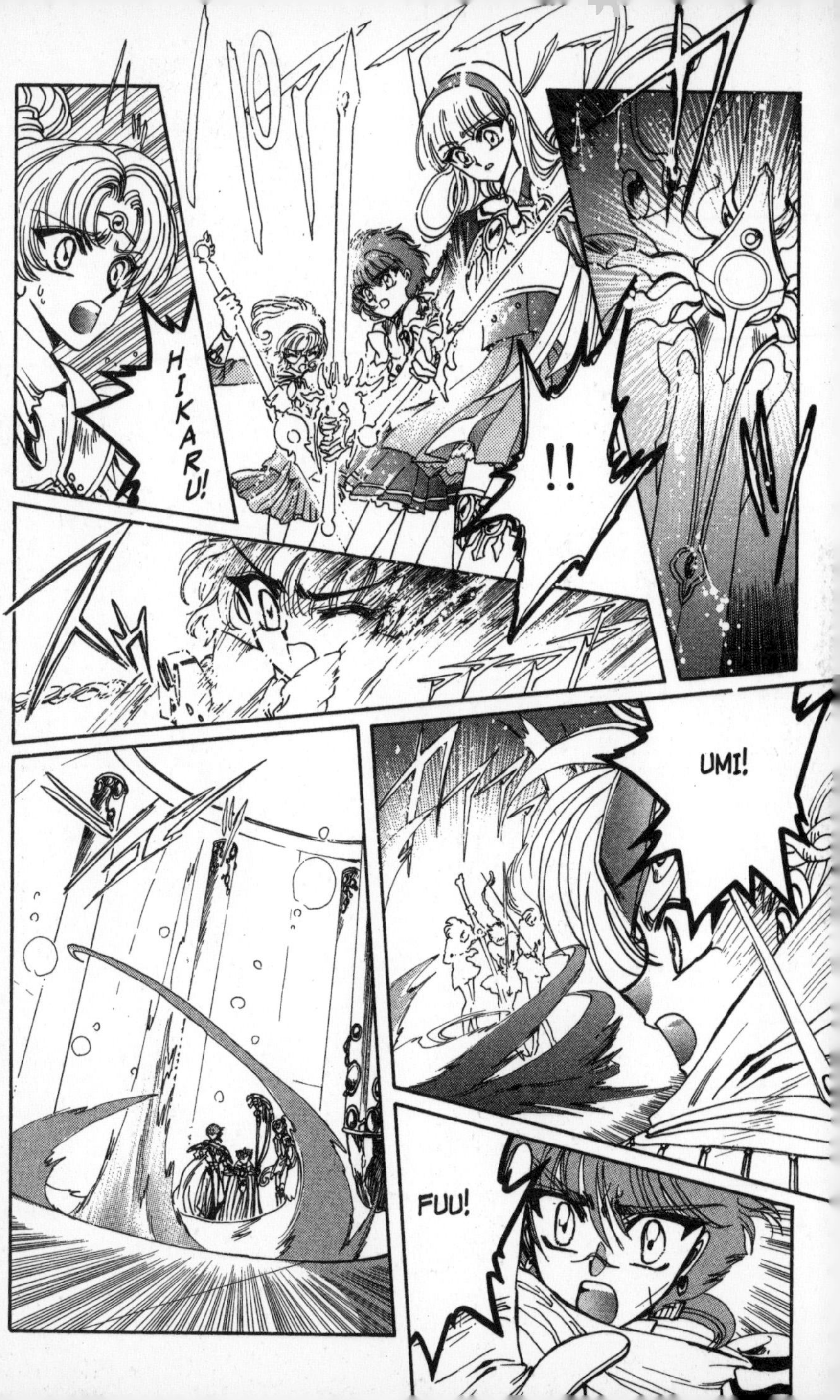
!!
HIKARU!
UMI!
FUU!

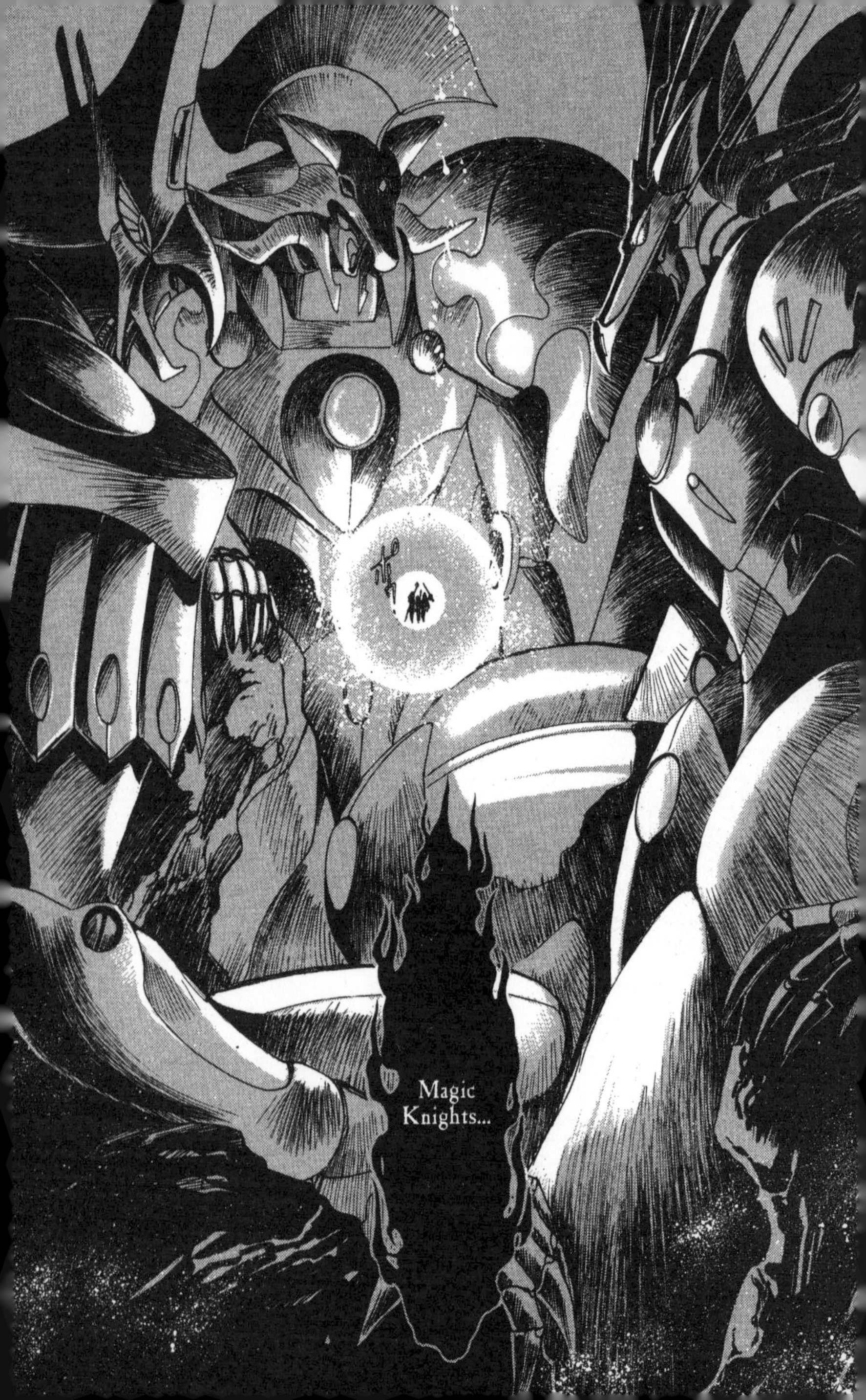
Magic Knights...

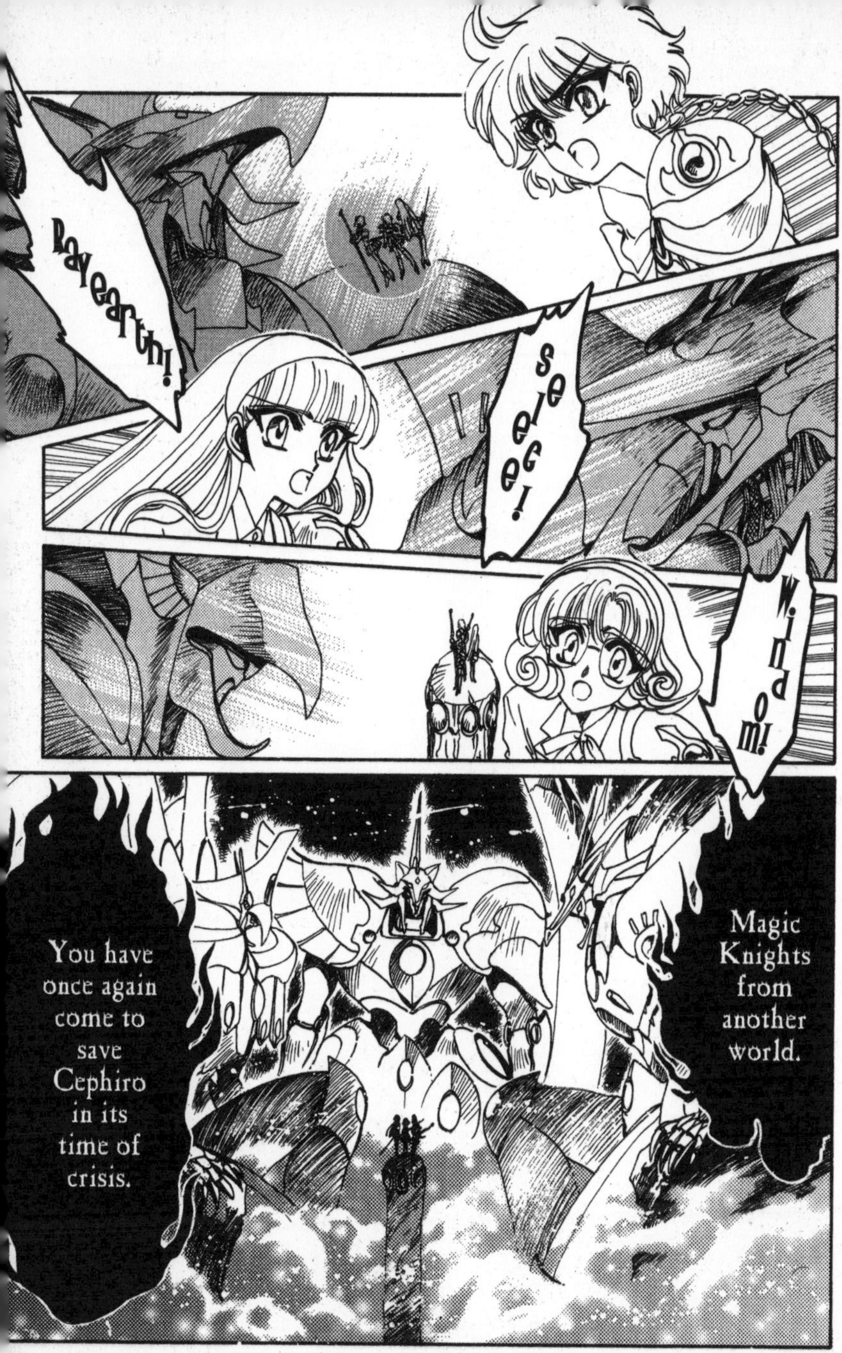
Rayearth!
Selece!
Windom!
Magic Knights from another world.
You have once again come to save Cephiro in its time of crisis.

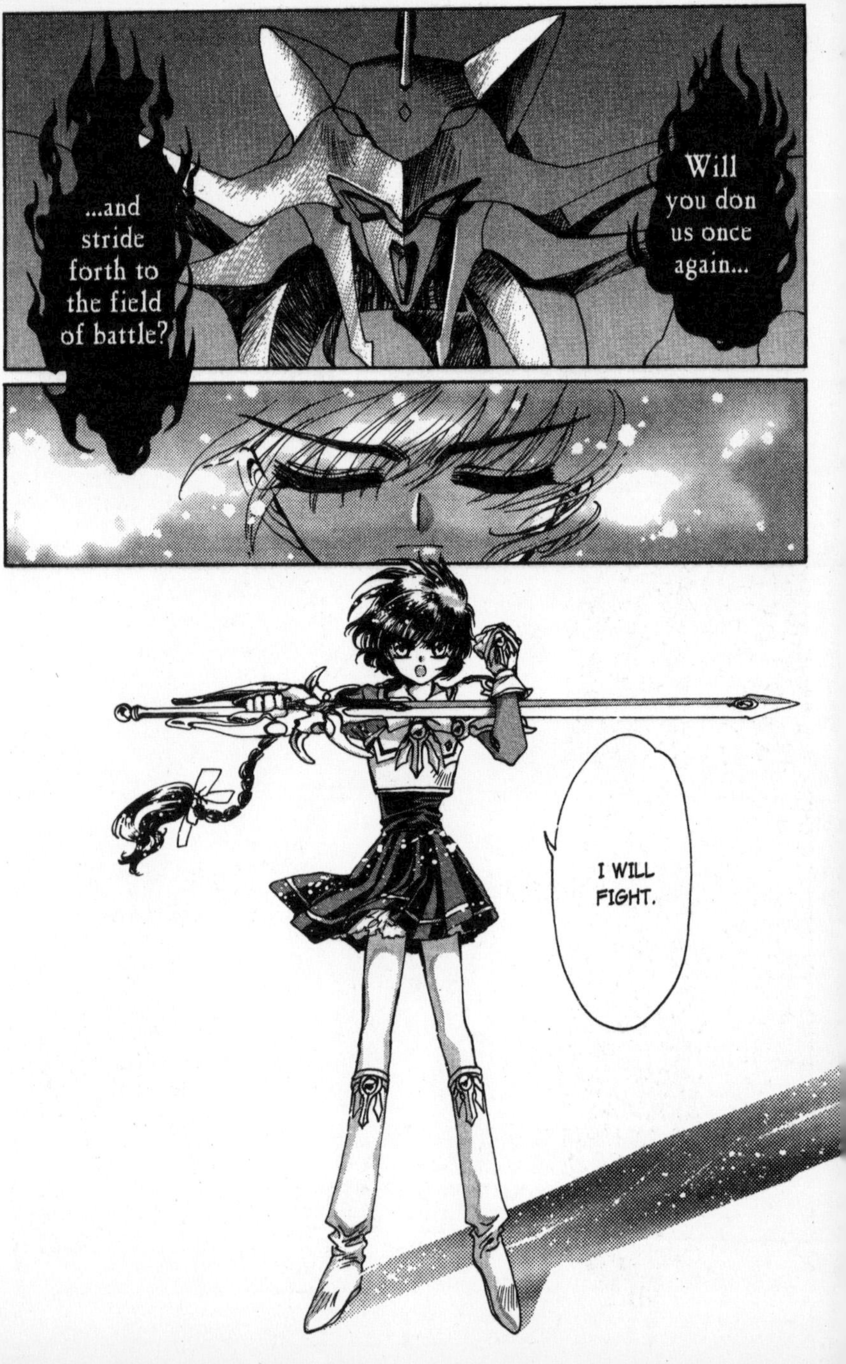
Will you don us once again...
...and stride forth to the field of battle?
I WILL FIGHT.

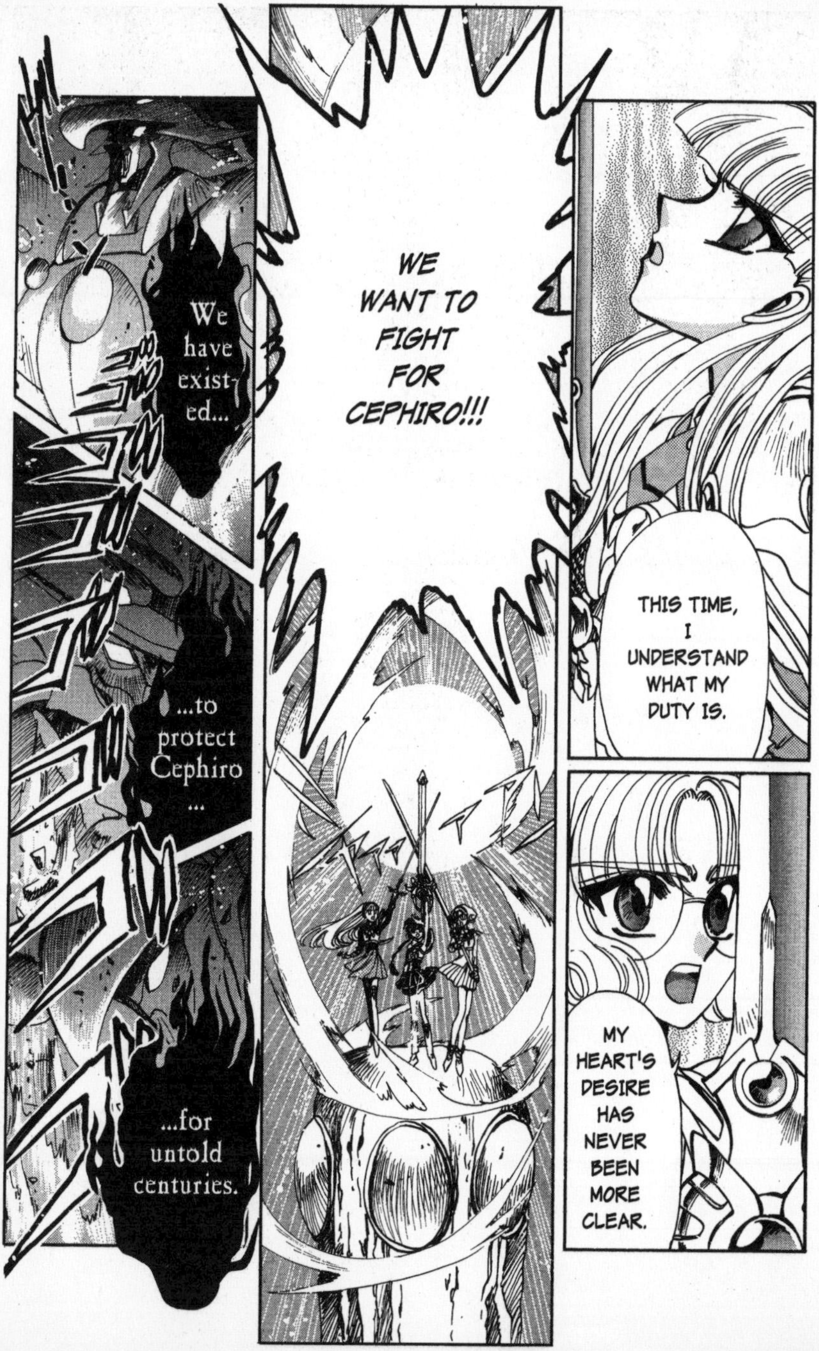
THIS TIME, I UNDERSTAND WHAT MY DUTY IS.
MY HEART'S DESIRE HAS NEVER BEEN MORE CLEAR.
WE WANT TO FIGHT FOR CEPHIRO!!!
We have exist-ed...
...to protect Cephiro...
...for untold centuries.

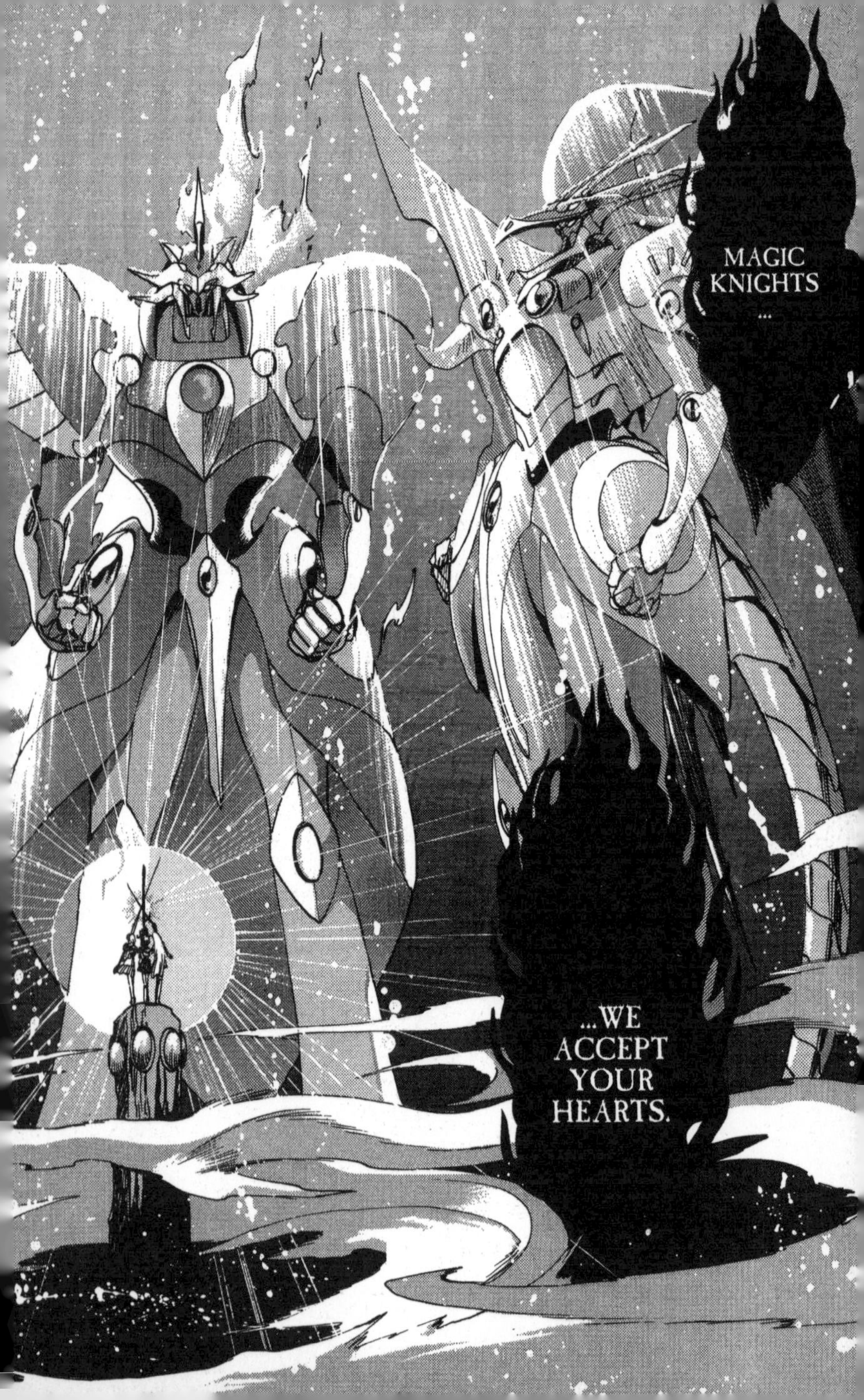
MAGIC KNIGHTS ...
...WE ACCEPT YOUR HEARTS.

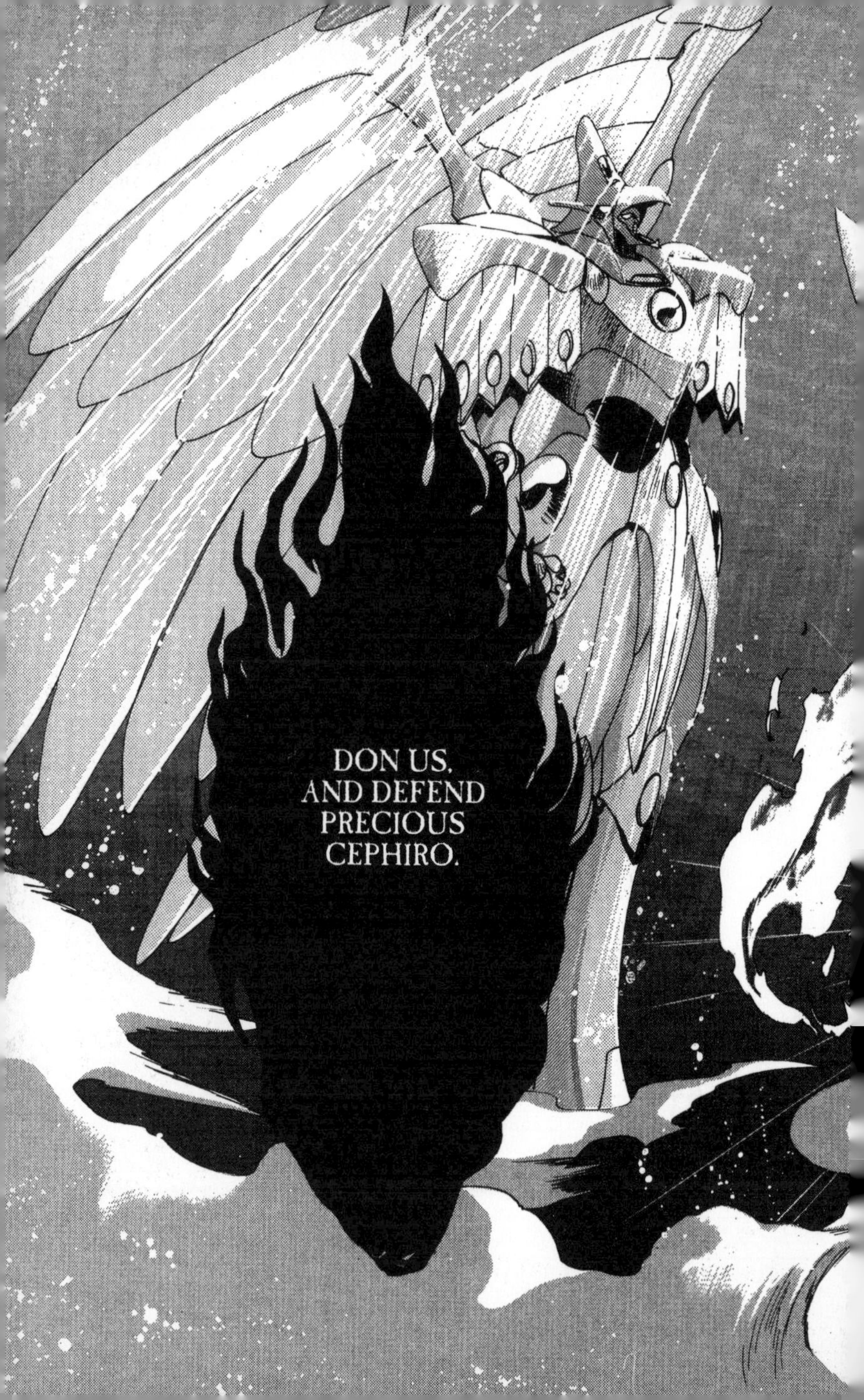
DON US, AND DEFEND PRECIOUS CEPHIRO.

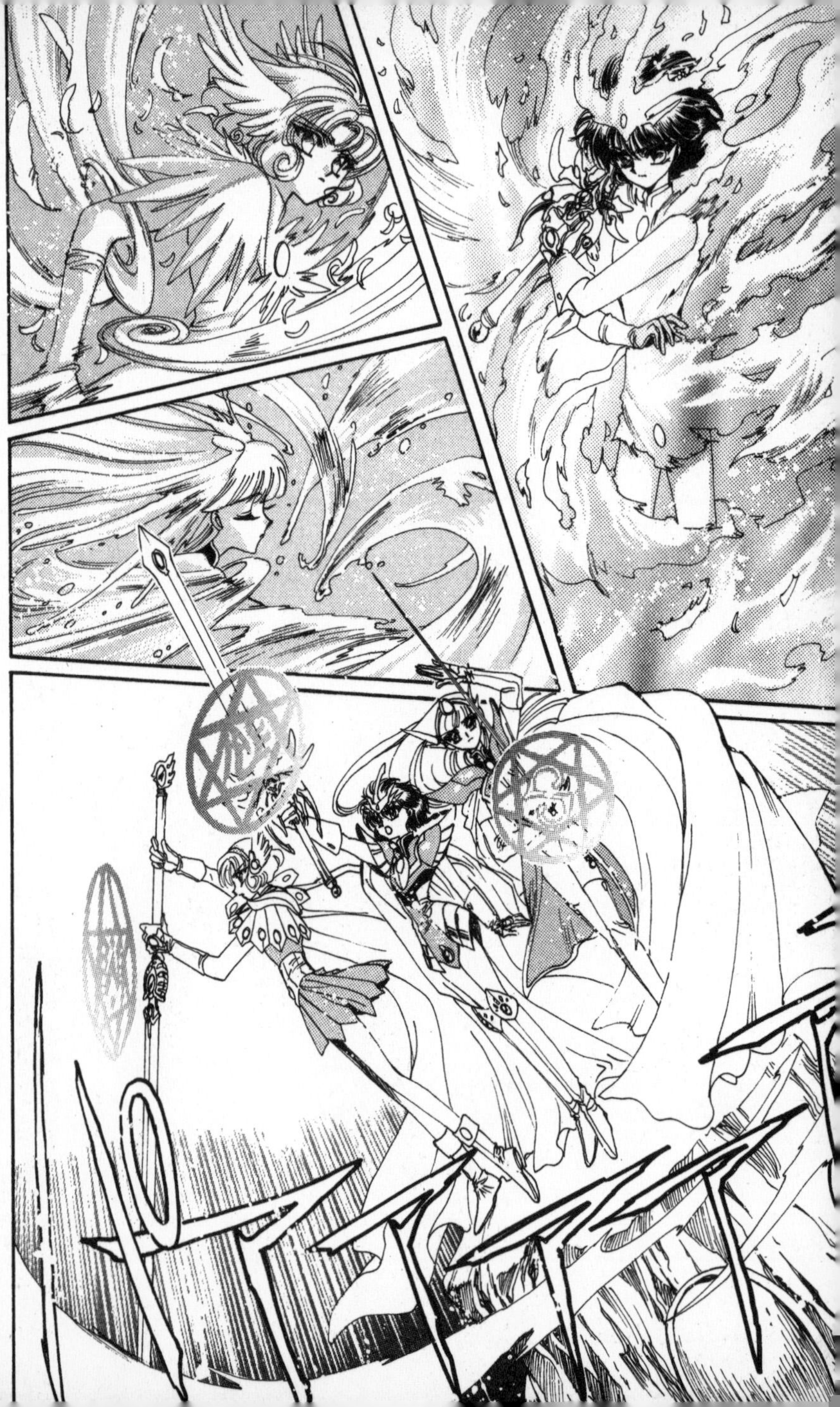

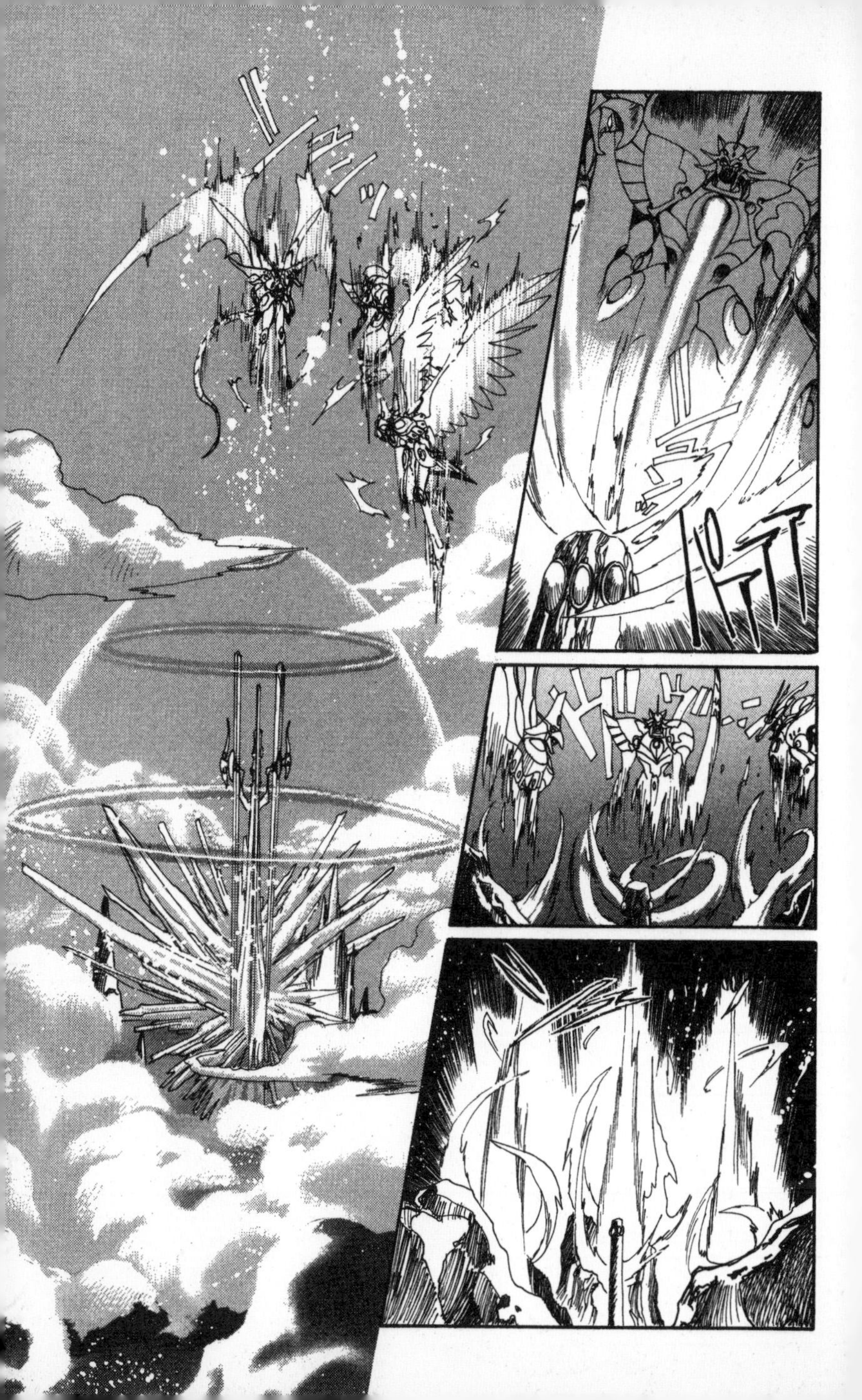
パァァァ

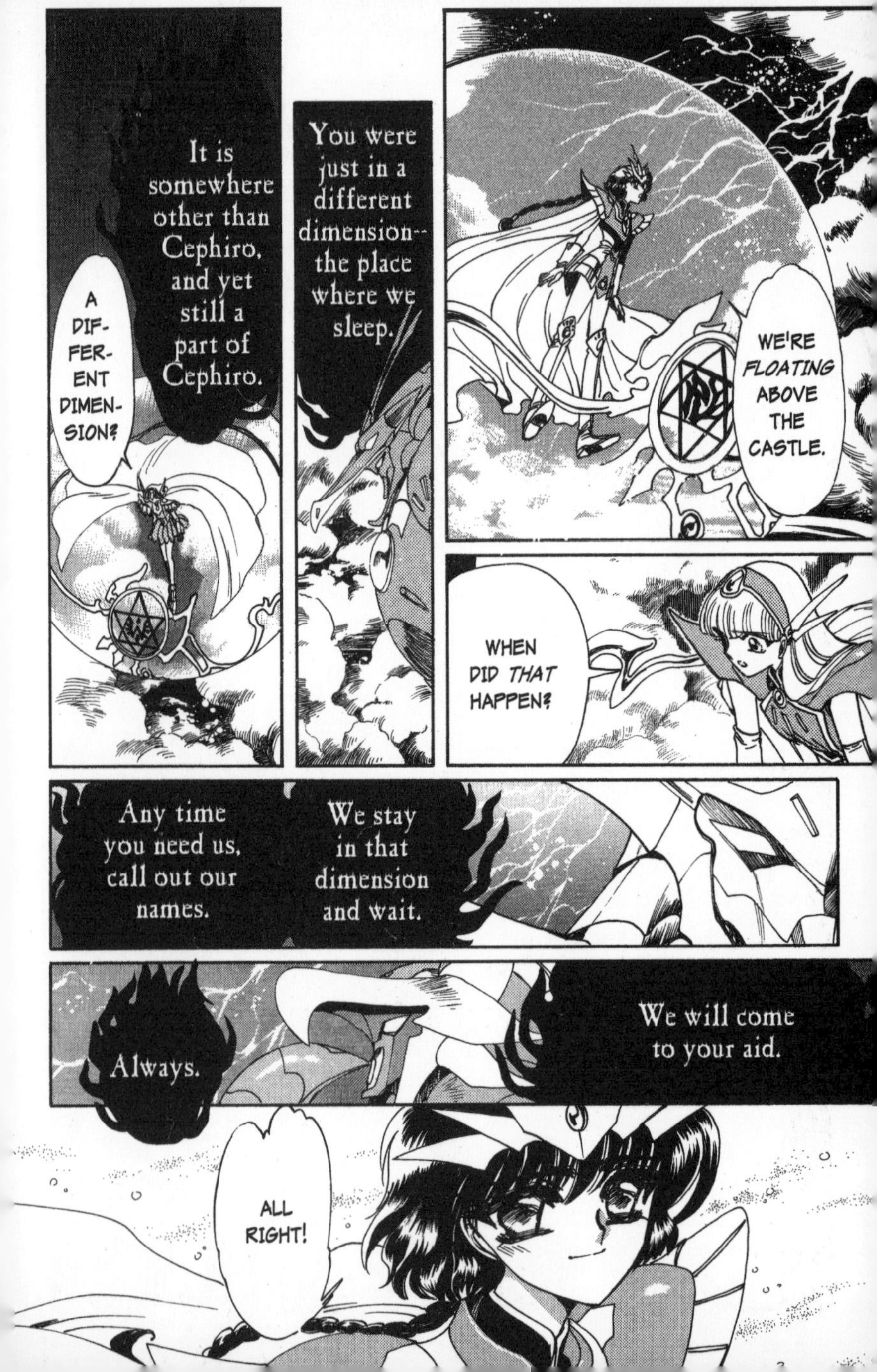
WE'RE *FLOATING* ABOVE THE CASTLE.
WHEN DID *THAT* HAPPEN?
You were just in a different dimension-- the place where we sleep.
A DIF-FER-ENT DIMEN-SION?
It is somewhere other than Cephiro, and yet still a part of Cephiro.
We stay in that dimension and wait.
Any time you need us, call out our names.
We will come to your aid.
Always.
ALL RIGHT!

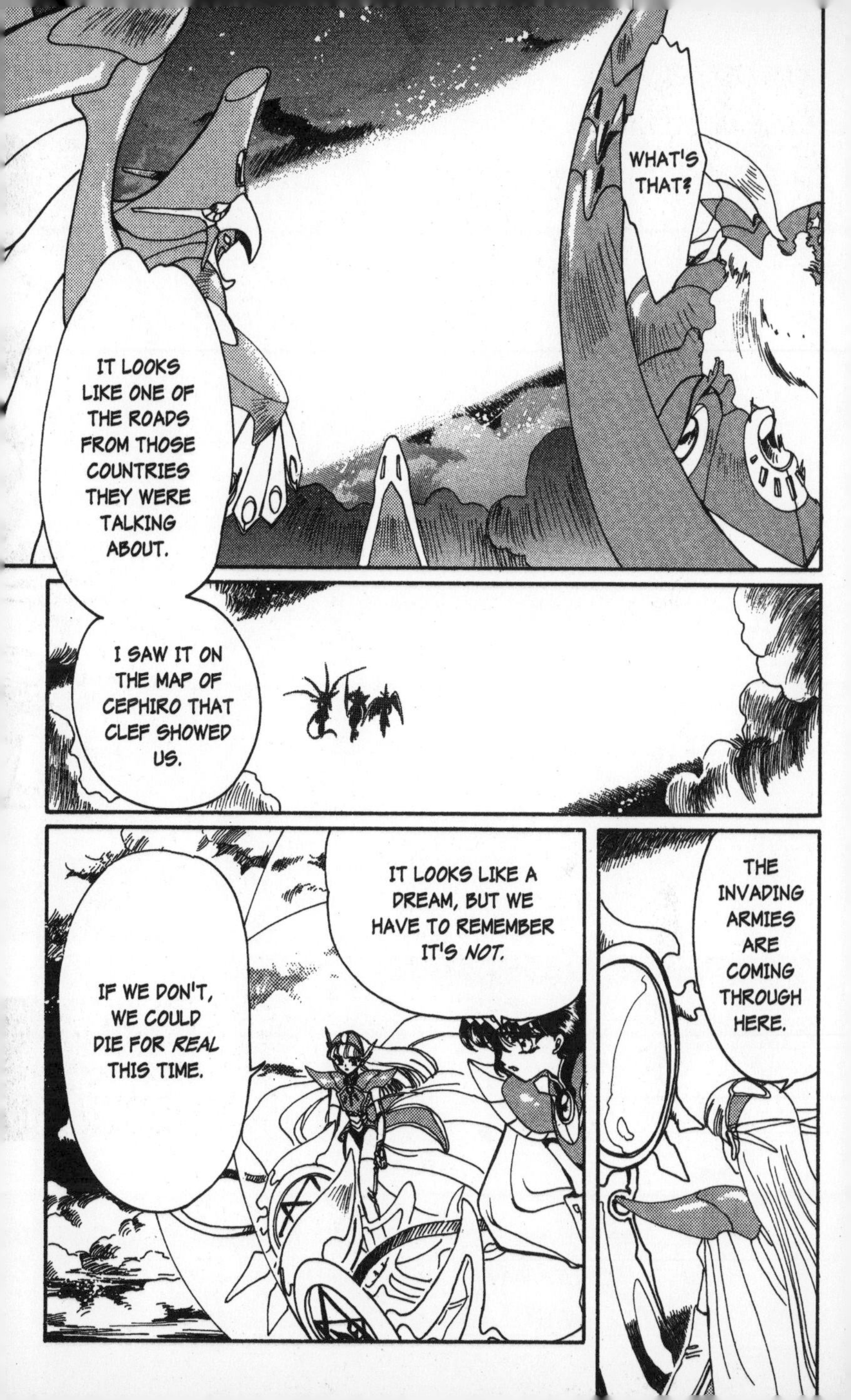
WHAT'S THAT?
IT LOOKS LIKE ONE OF THE ROADS FROM THOSE COUNTRIES THEY WERE TALKING ABOUT.
I SAW IT ON THE MAP OF CEPHIRO THAT CLEF SHOWED US.
THE INVADING ARMIES ARE COMING THROUGH HERE.
IT LOOKS LIKE A DREAM, BUT WE HAVE TO REMEMBER IT'S *NOT*.
IF WE DON'T, WE COULD DIE FOR *REAL* THIS TIME.

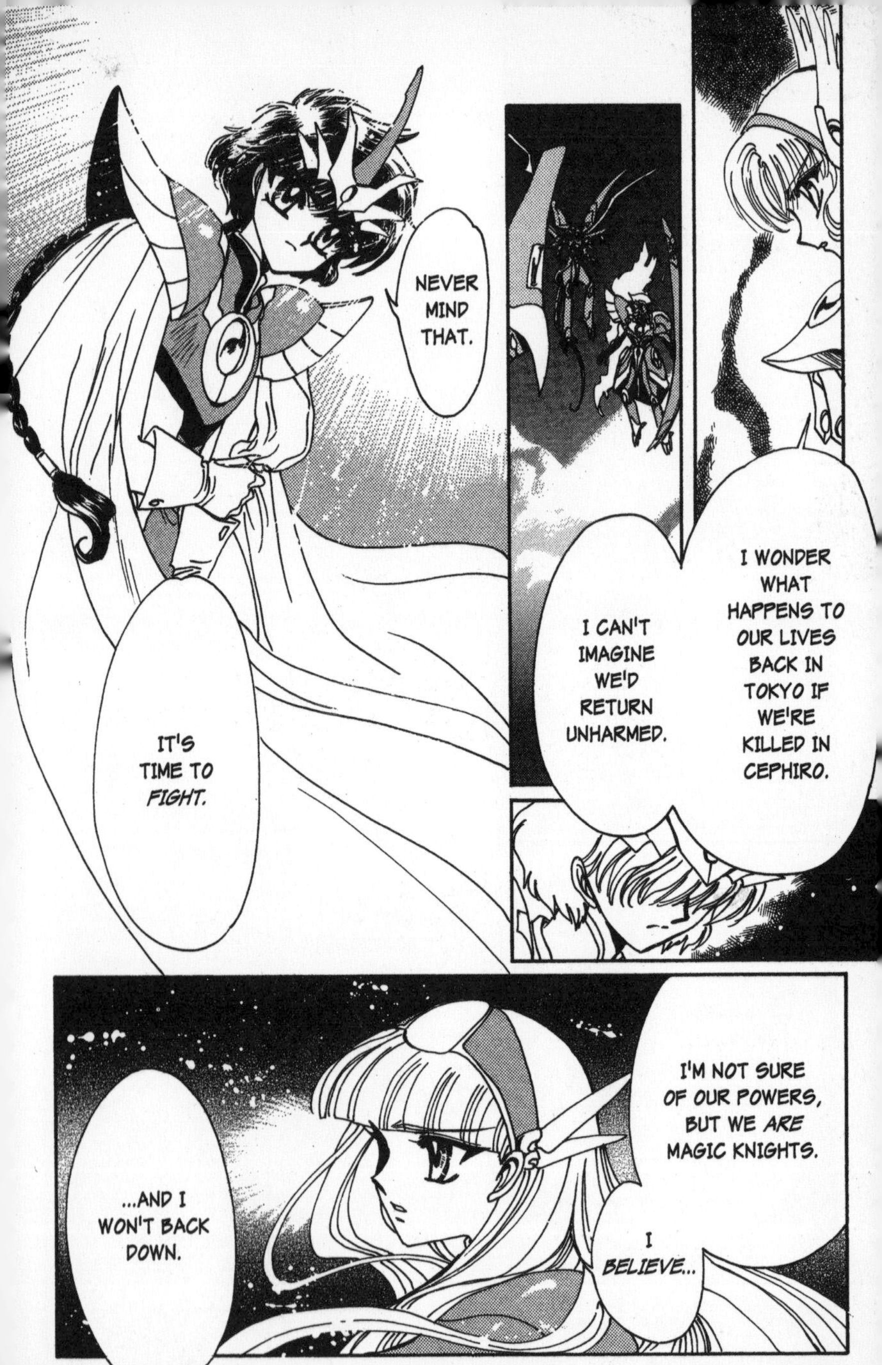
I WONDER WHAT HAPPENS TO OUR LIVES BACK IN TOKYO IF WE'RE KILLED IN CEPHIRO.
I CAN'T IMAGINE WE'D RETURN UNHARMED.
NEVER MIND THAT.
IT'S TIME TO *FIGHT.*
I'M NOT SURE OF OUR POWERS, BUT WE *ARE* MAGIC KNIGHTS.
I *BELIEVE...*
...AND I WON'T BACK DOWN.

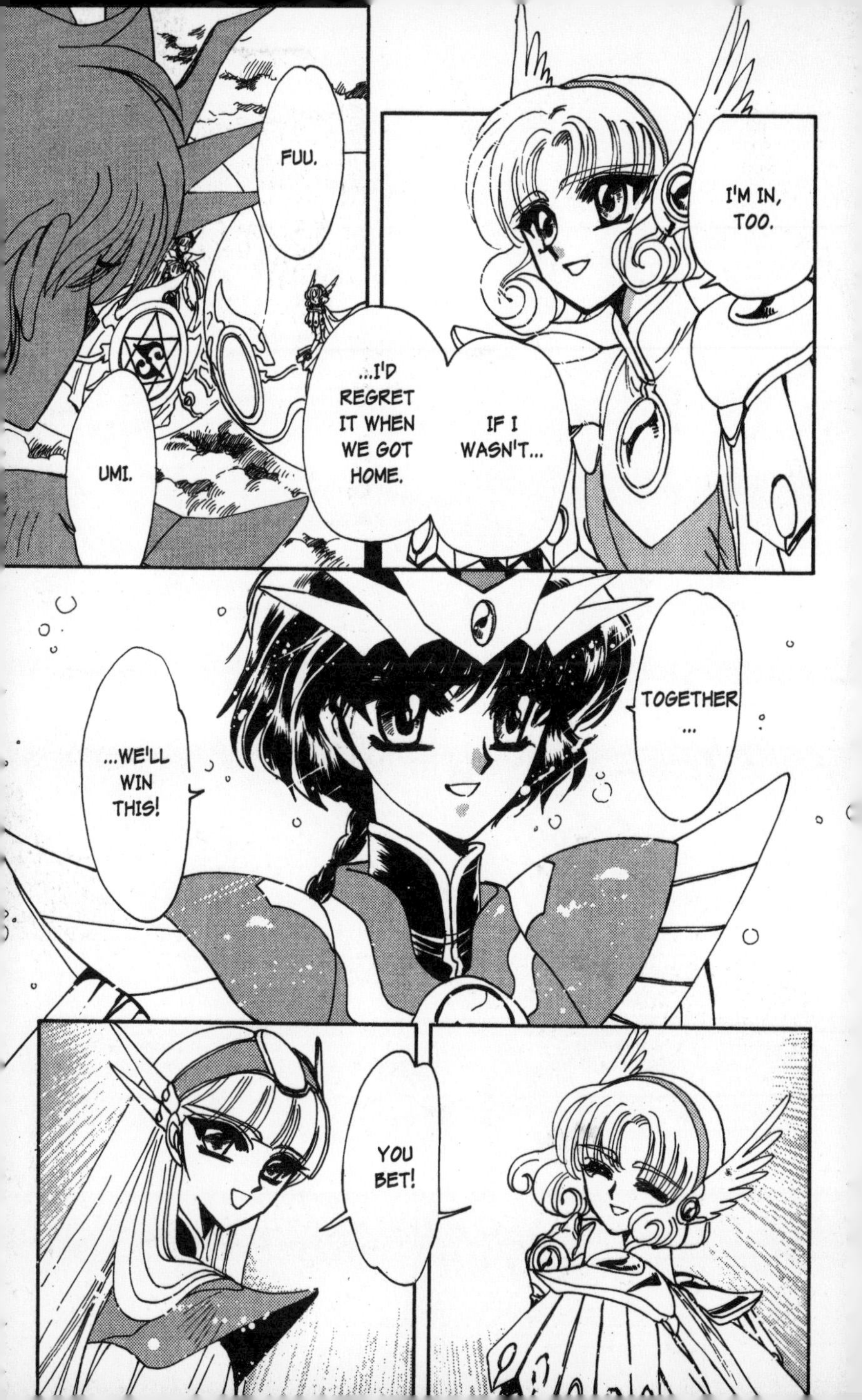
I'M IN, TOO.
IF I WASN'T...
...I'D REGRET IT WHEN WE GOT HOME.
FUU.
UMI.
TOGETHER...
...WE'LL WIN THIS!
YOU BET!

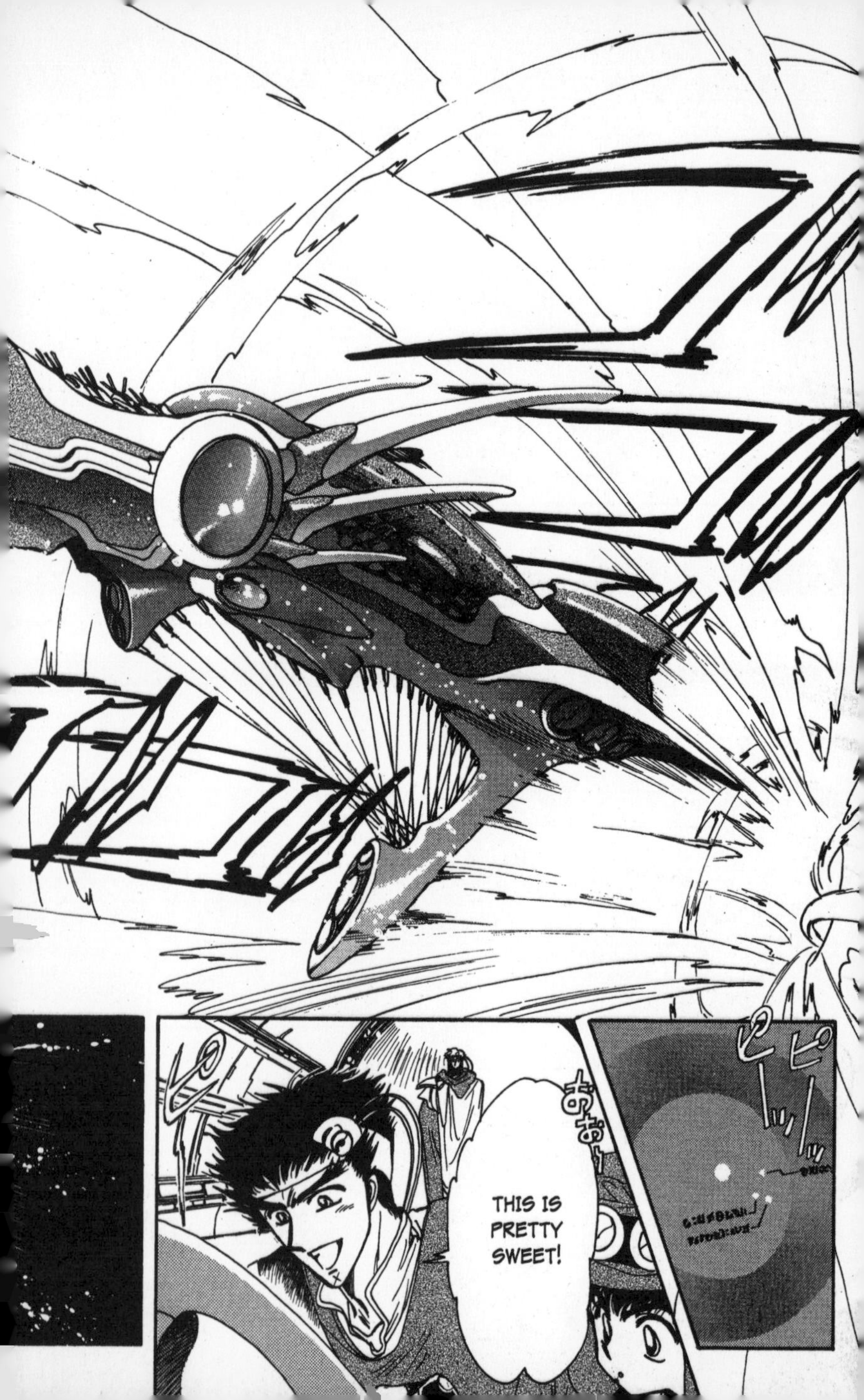

ピーッ ピーッ
おぉ
THIS IS PRETTY SWEET!

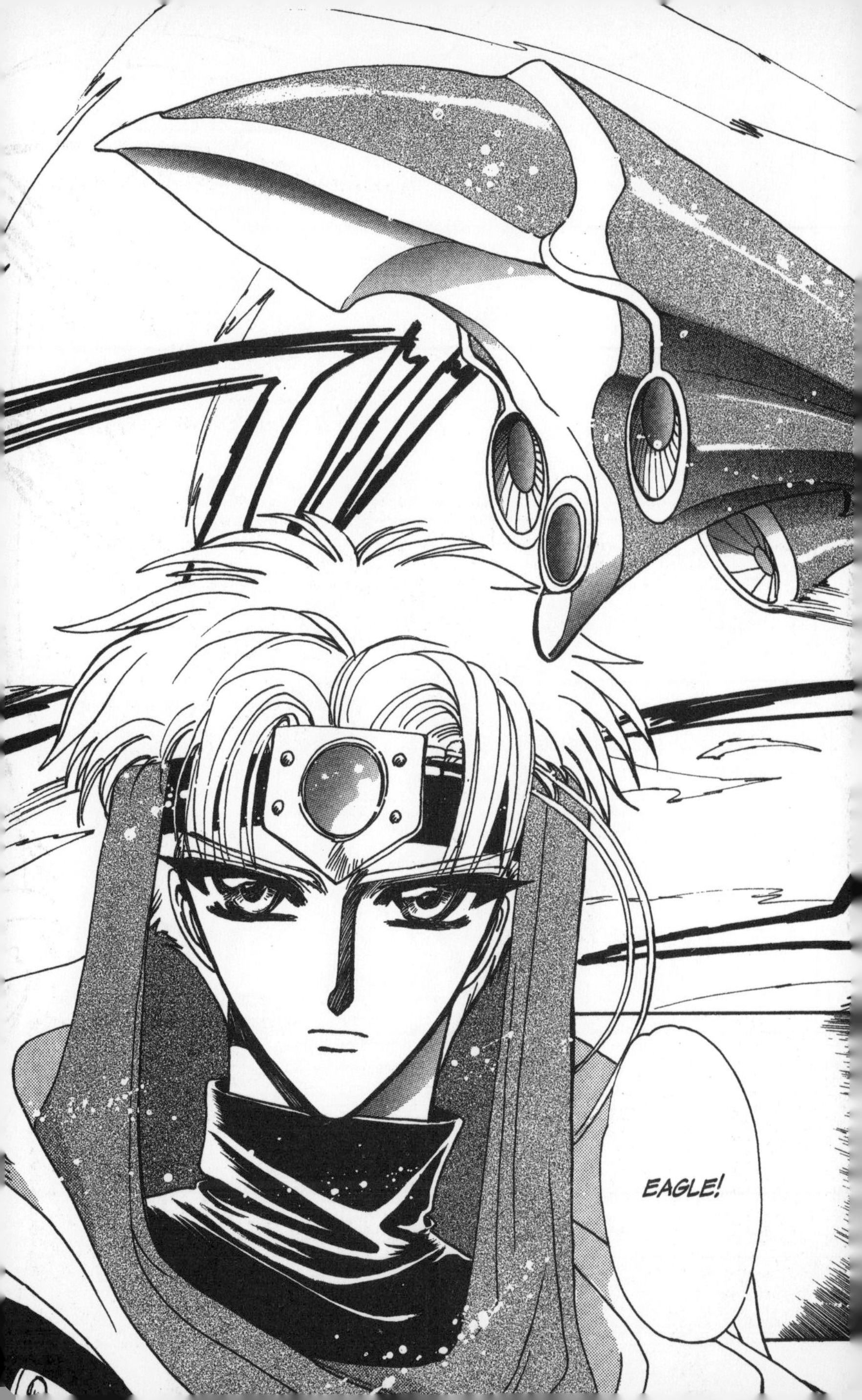
EAGLE!

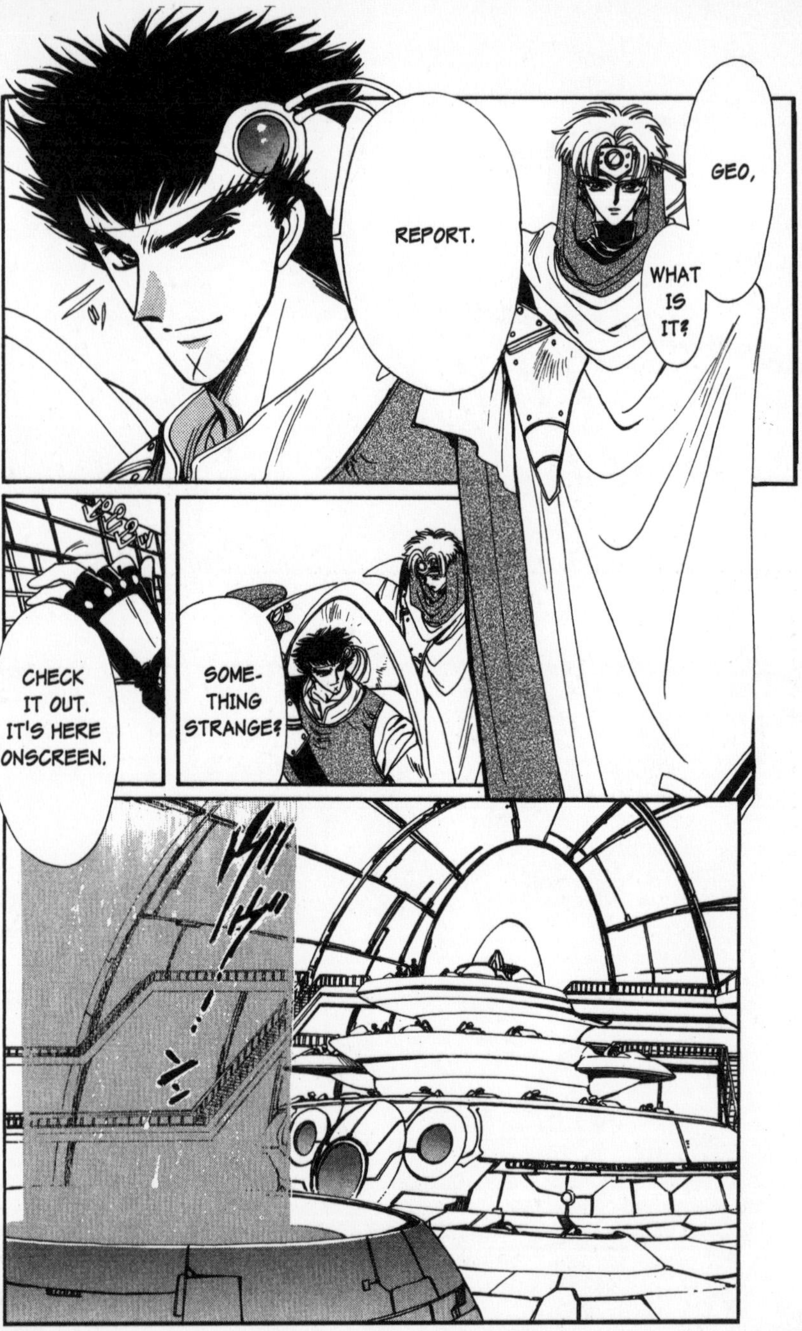
GEO,
WHAT IS IT?
REPORT.
SOME-THING STRANGE?
CHECK IT OUT. IT'S HERE ONSCREEN.

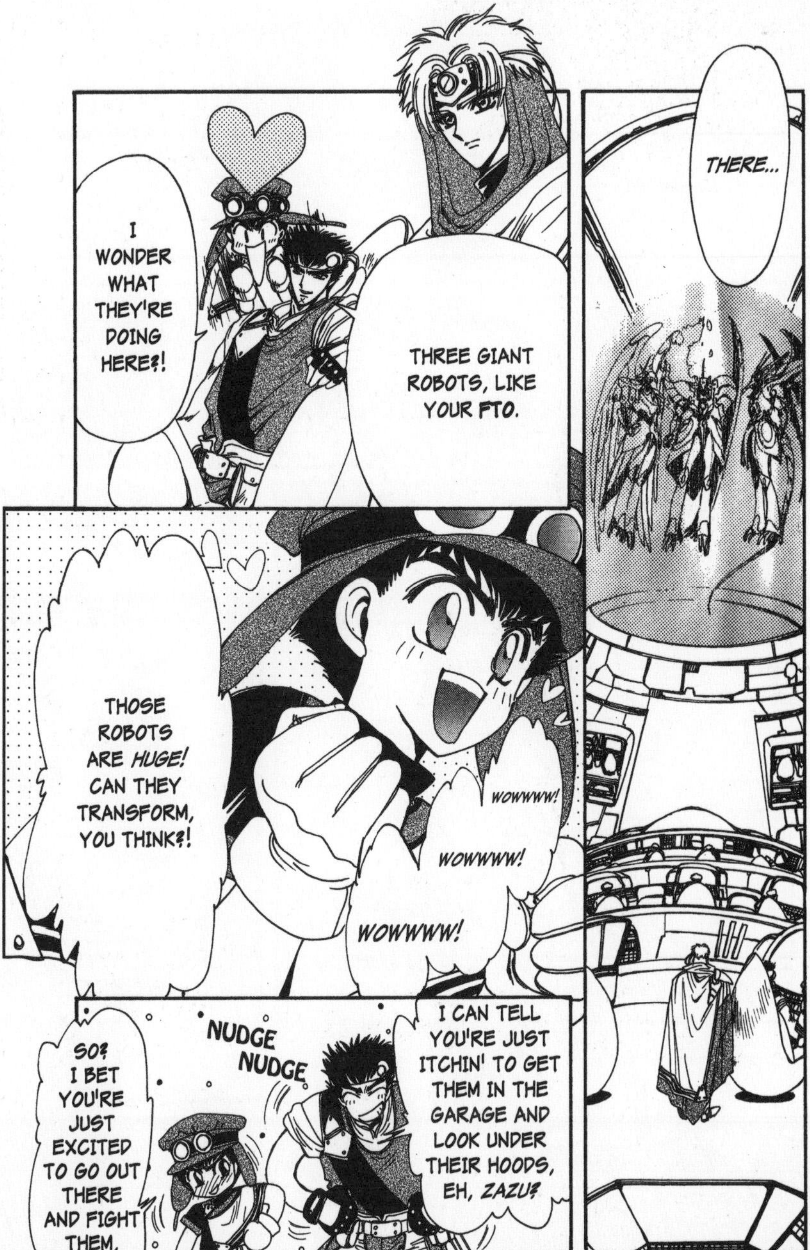
THERE...
THREE GIANT ROBOTS, LIKE YOUR FTO.
I WONDER WHAT THEY'RE DOING HERE?!
WOWWWW!
WOWWWW!
WOWWWW!
THOSE ROBOTS ARE *HUGE!* CAN THEY TRANSFORM, YOU THINK?!
I CAN TELL YOU'RE JUST ITCHIN' TO GET THEM IN THE GARAGE AND LOOK UNDER THEIR HOODS, EH, *ZAZU?*
NUDGE NUDGE
SO? I BET YOU'RE JUST EXCITED TO GO OUT THERE AND FIGHT THEM, RIGHT?

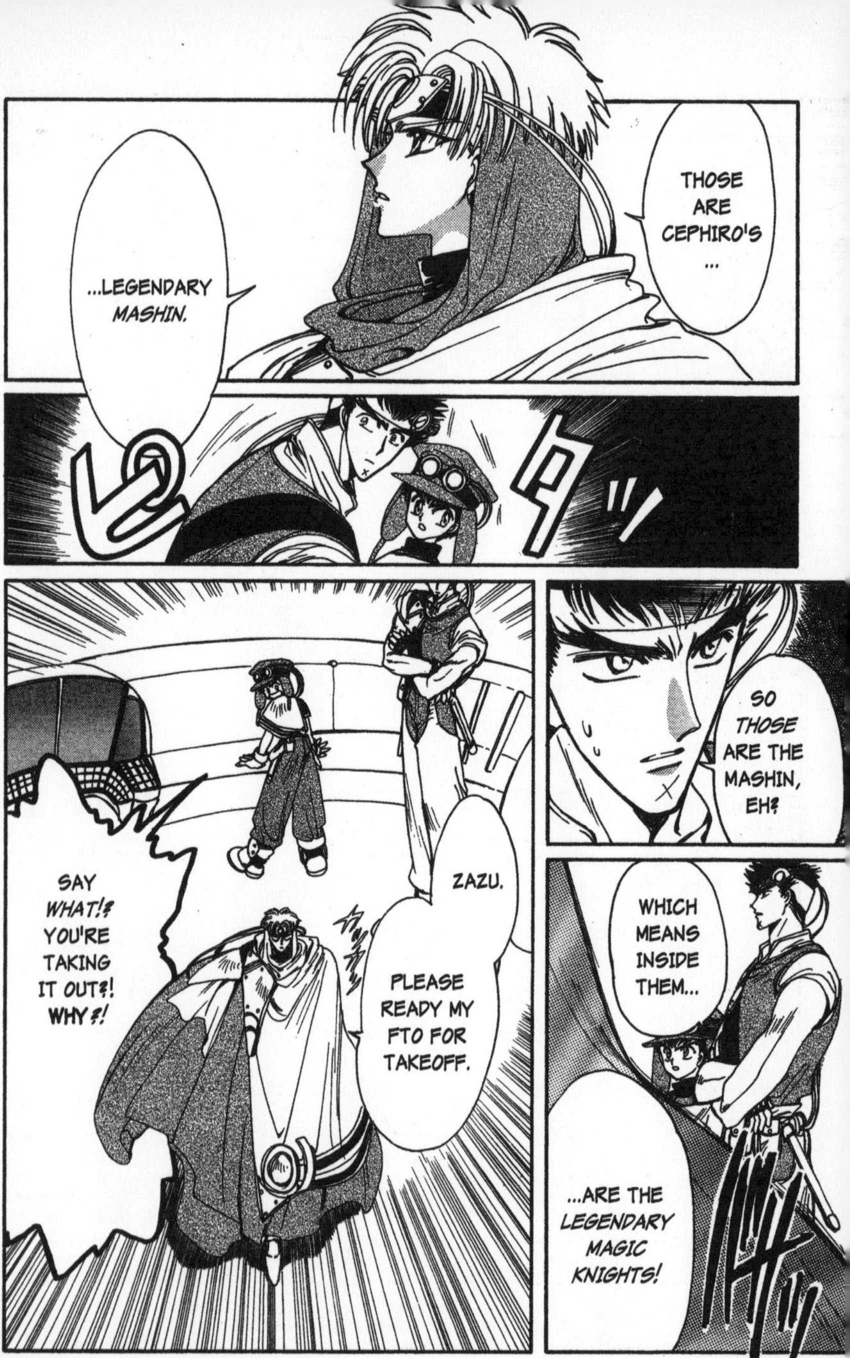
THOSE ARE CEPHIRO'S ...
...LEGENDARY *MASHIN.*
ピクッ
SO *THOSE* ARE THE MASHIN, EH?
WHICH MEANS INSIDE THEM...
...ARE THE *LEGENDARY MAGIC KNIGHTS!*
ZAZU.
PLEASE READY MY FTO FOR TAKEOFF.
SAY *WHAT!?* YOU'RE TAKING IT OUT?! WHY?!

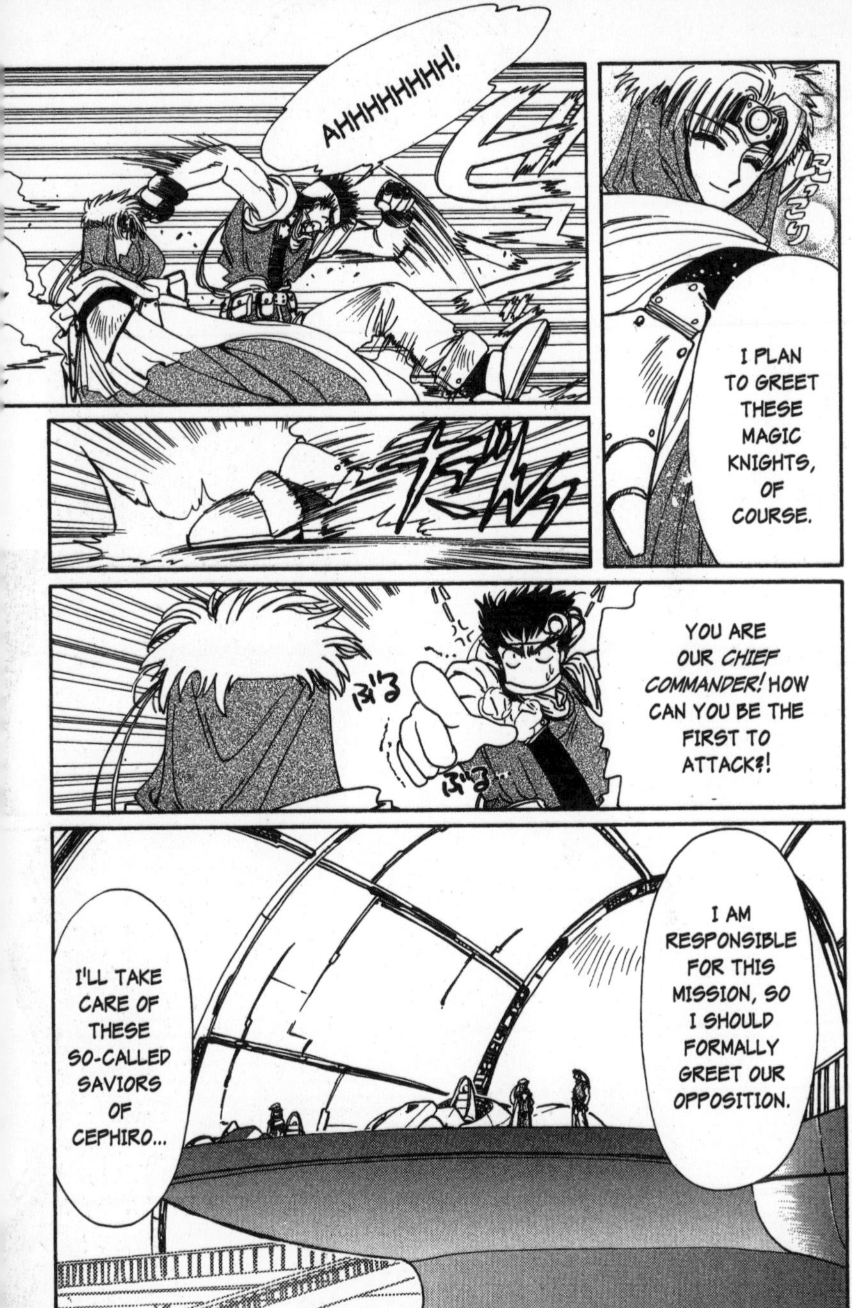
I PLAN TO GREET THESE MAGIC KNIGHTS, OF COURSE.
AHHHHHHHH!
YOU ARE OUR *CHIEF COMMANDER!* HOW CAN YOU BE THE FIRST TO ATTACK?!
I AM RESPONSIBLE FOR THIS MISSION, SO I SHOULD FORMALLY GREET OUR OPPOSITION.
I'LL TAKE CARE OF THESE SO-CALLED SAVIORS OF CEPHIRO...

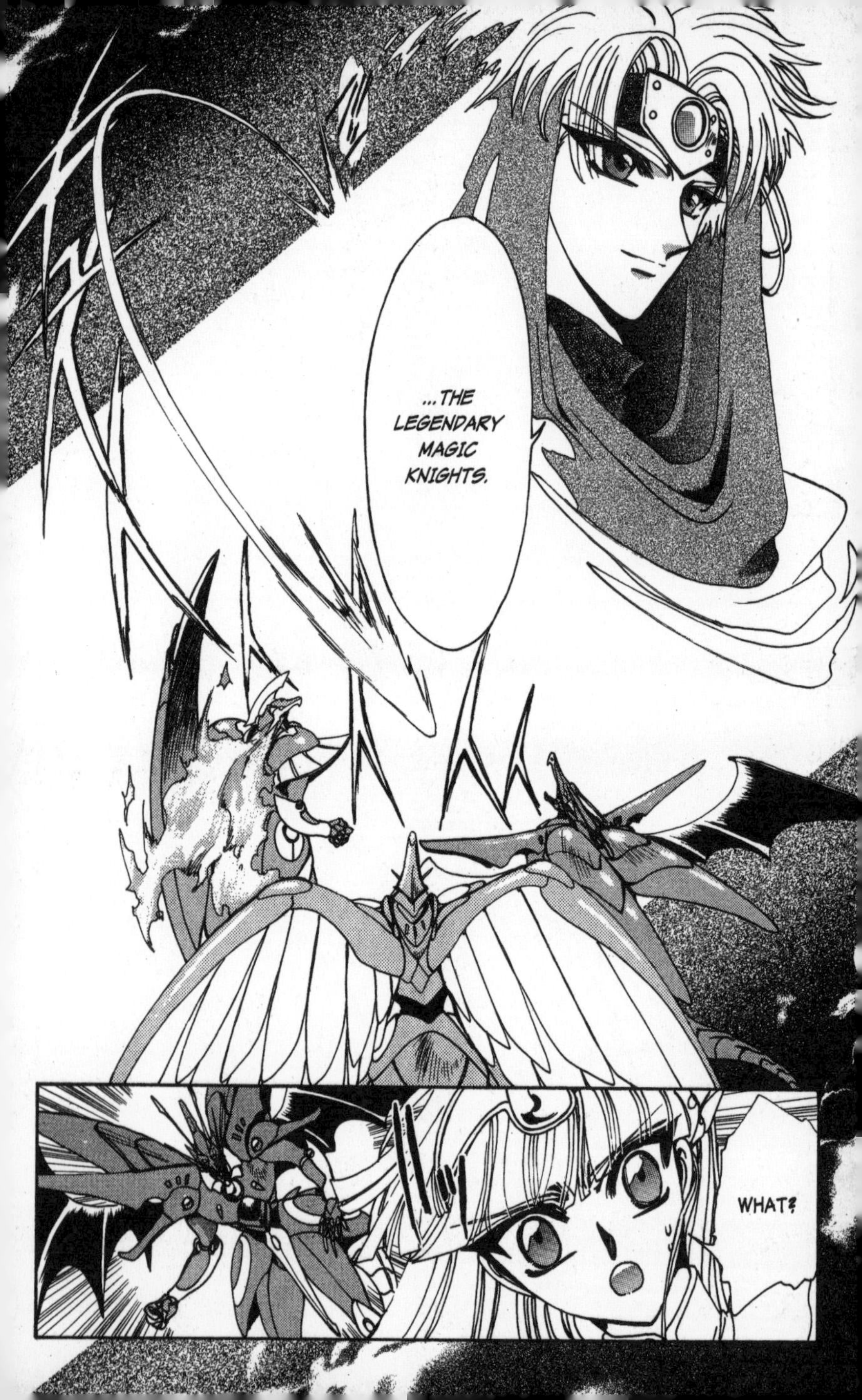
...THE LEGENDARY MAGIC KNIGHTS.
WHAT?

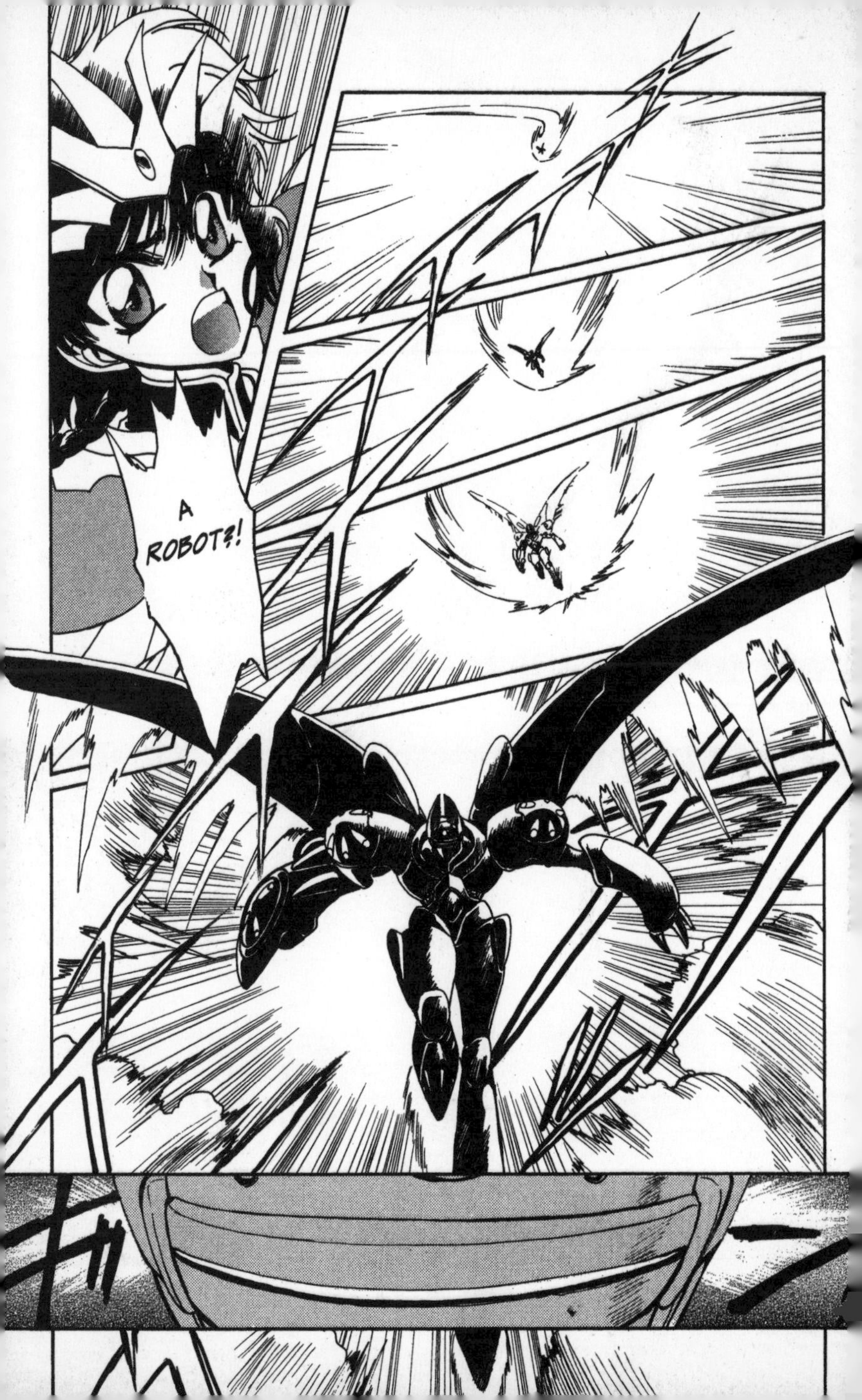
A ROBOT?!

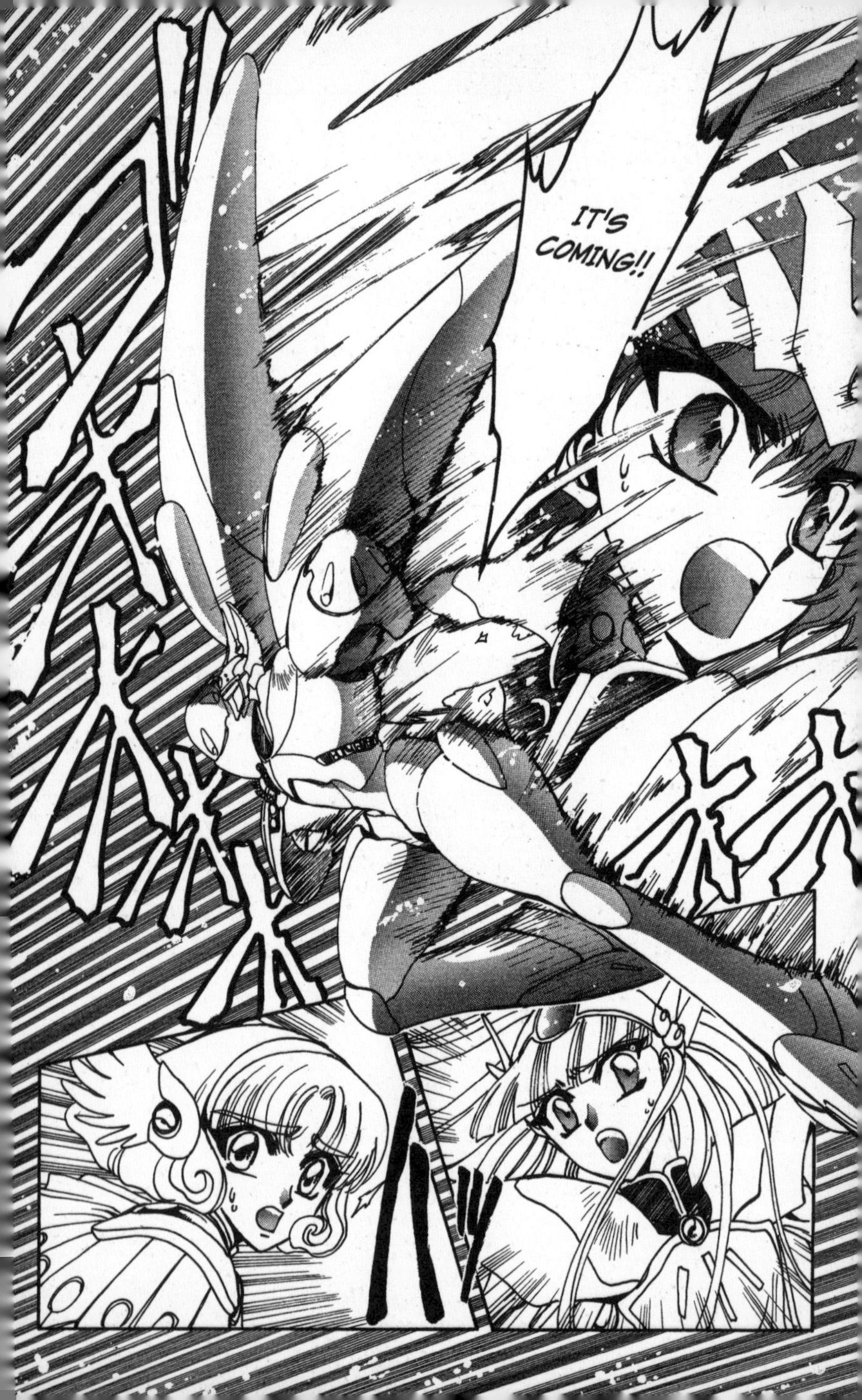
IT'S COMING!!

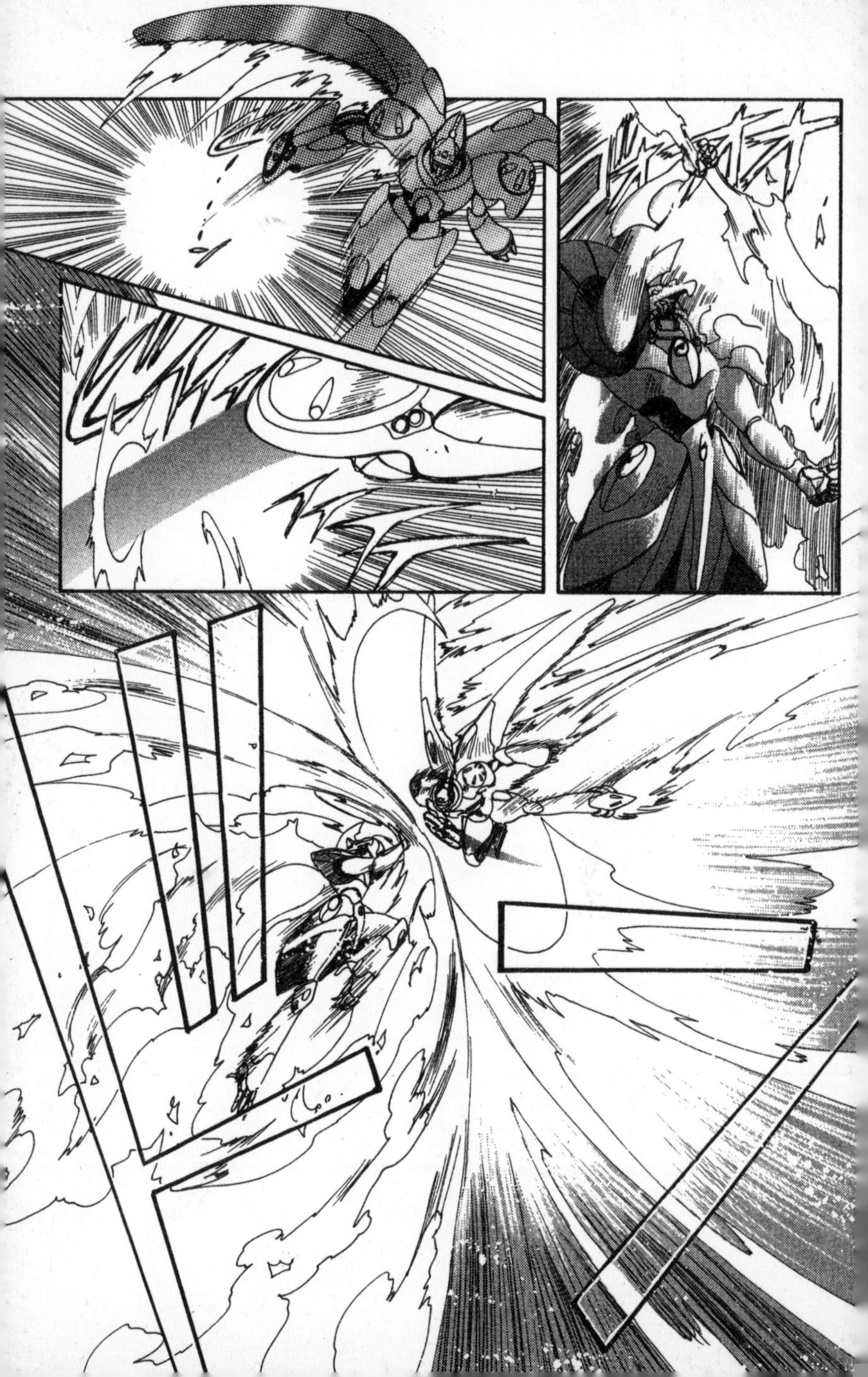

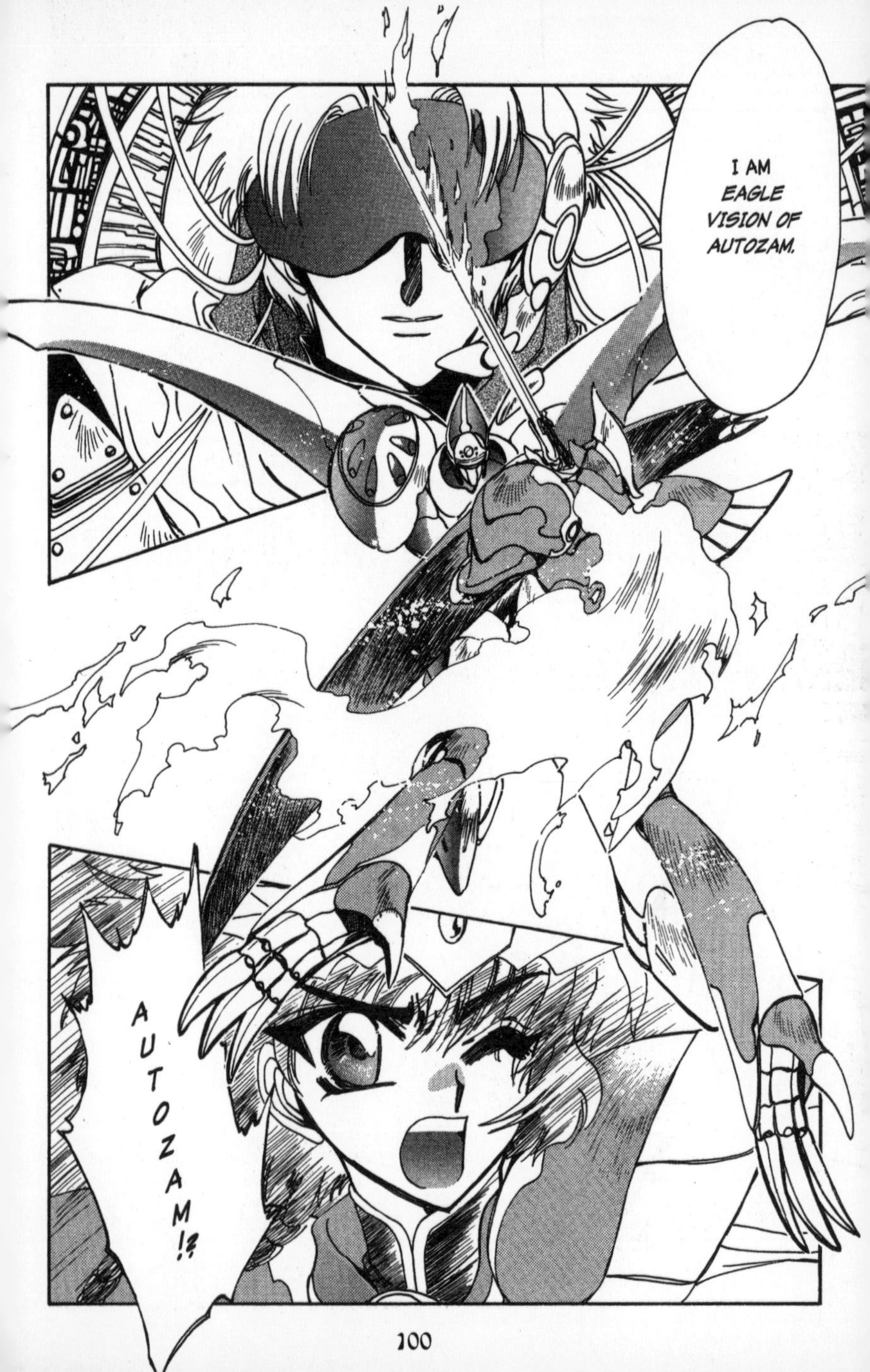
I AM EAGLE VISION OF AUTOZAM.
AUTOZAM!?

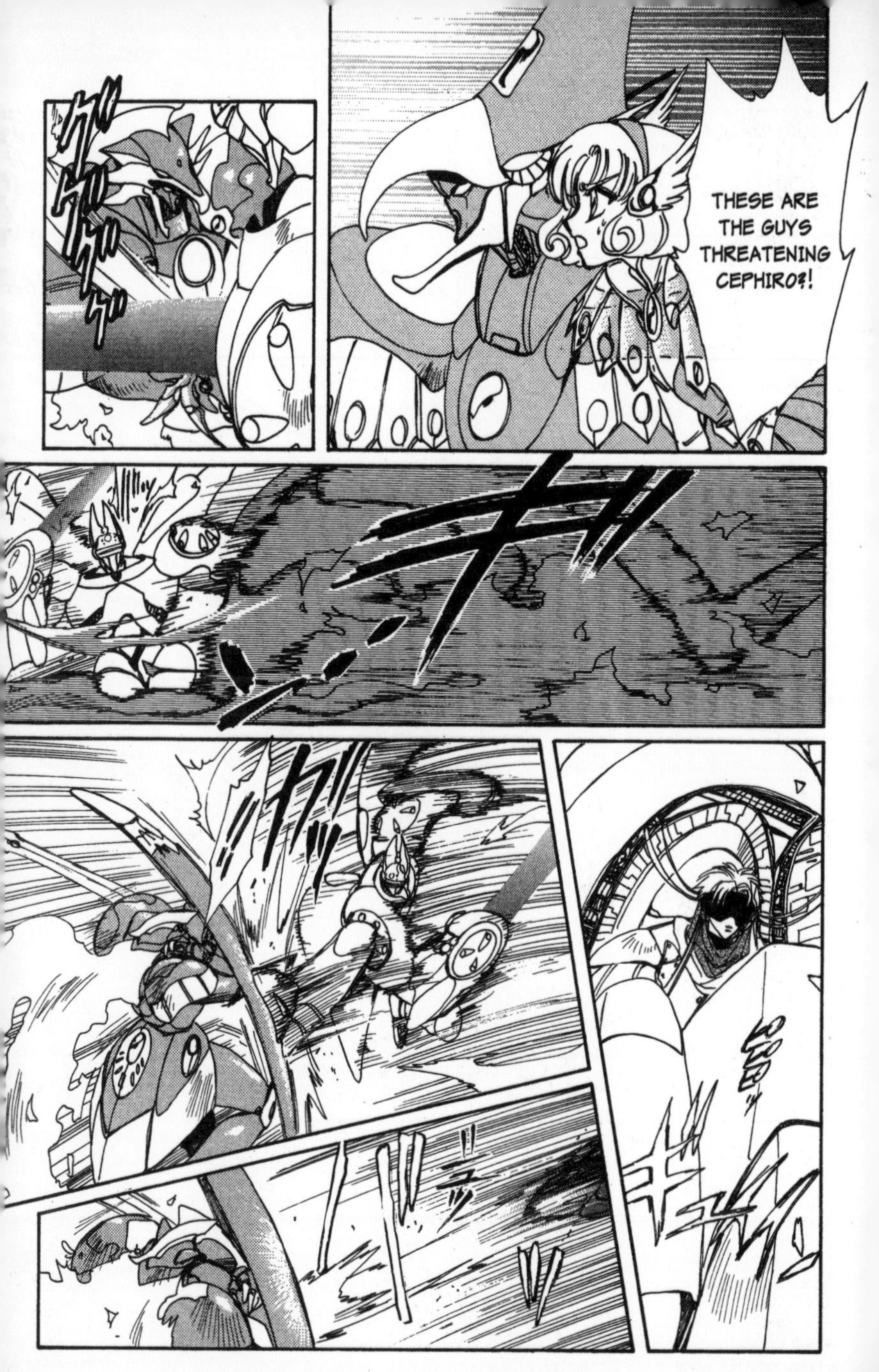
THESE ARE THE GUYS THREATENING CEPHIRO?!

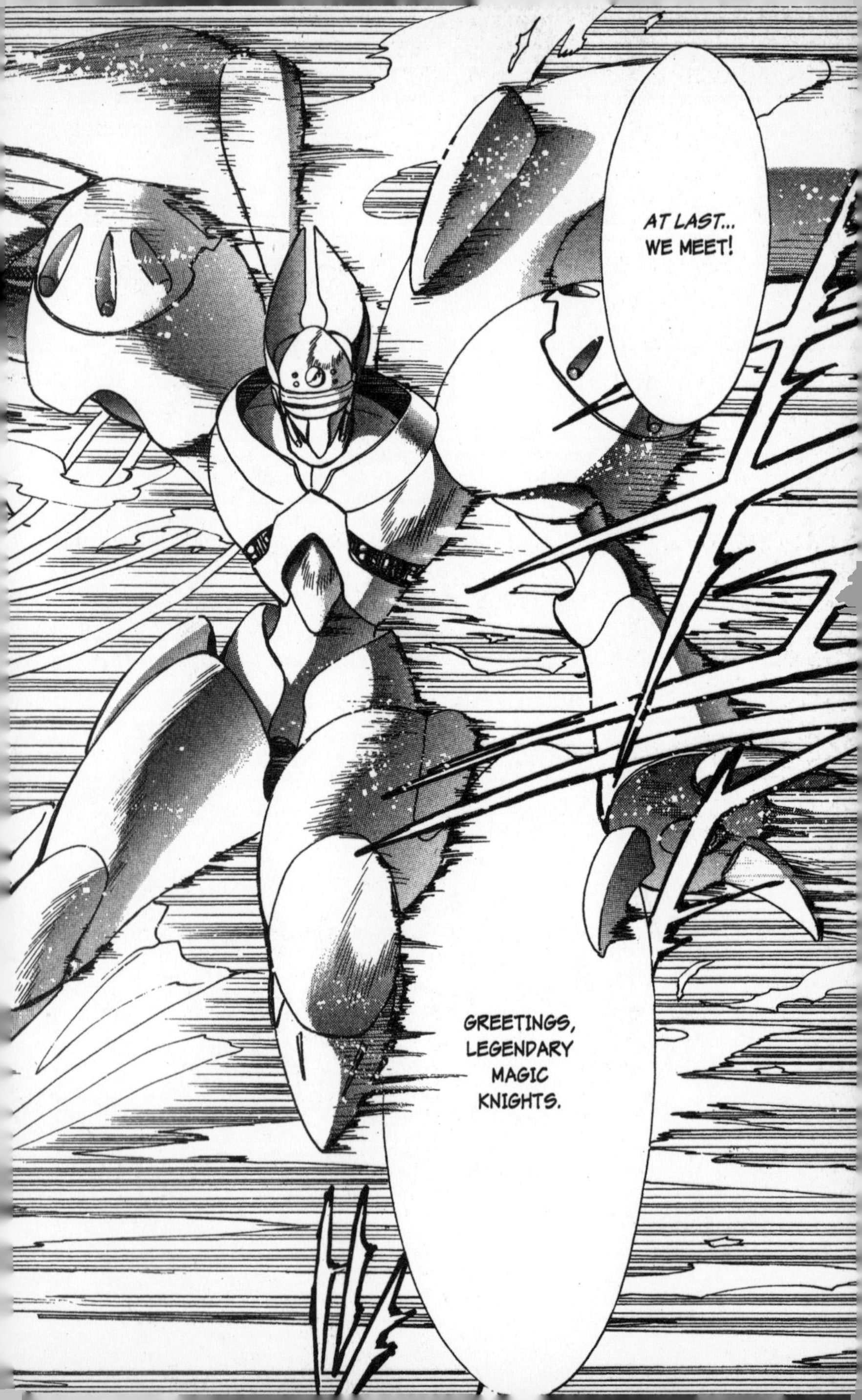
AT LAST... WE MEET!
GREETINGS, LEGENDARY MAGIC KNIGHTS.

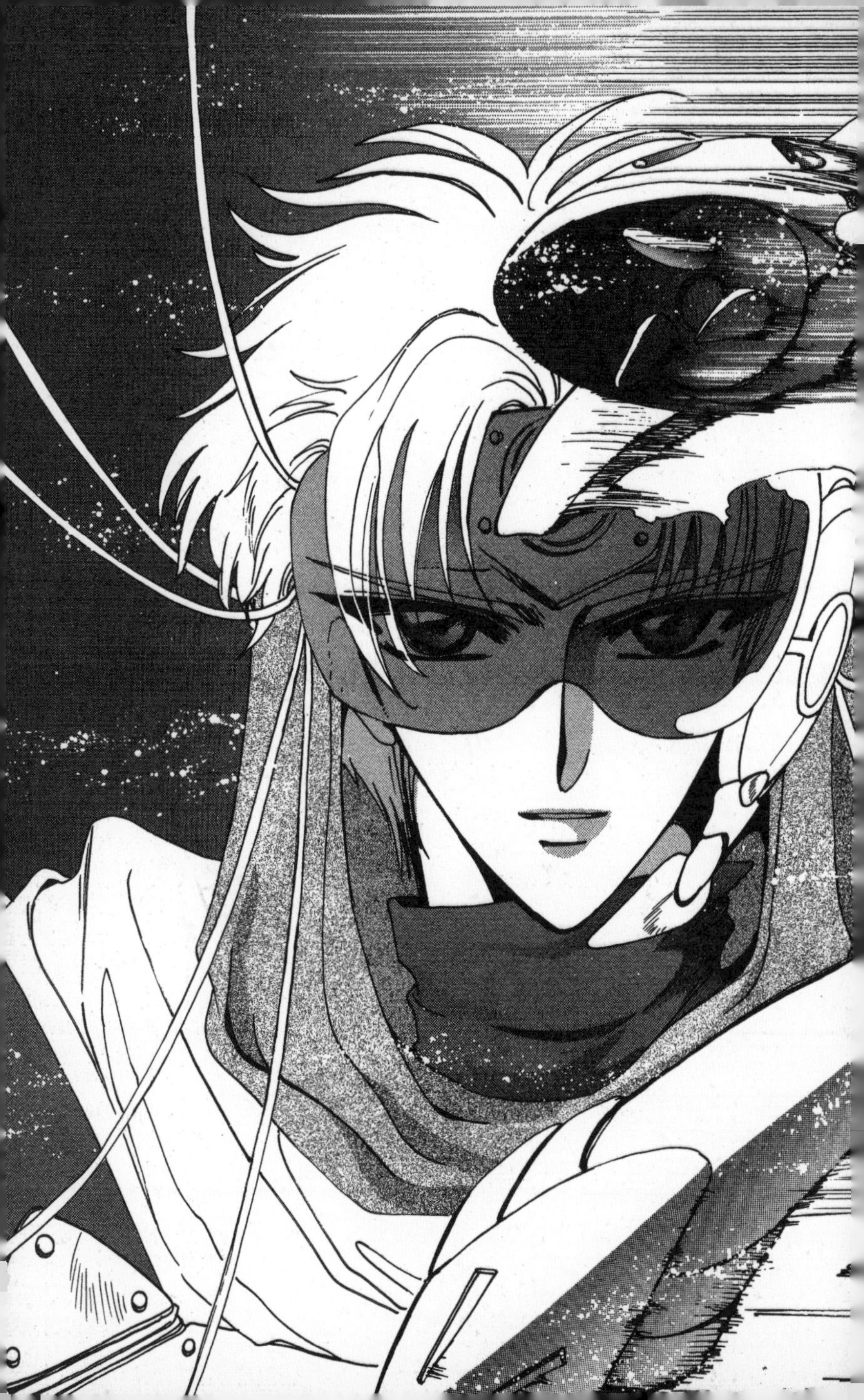

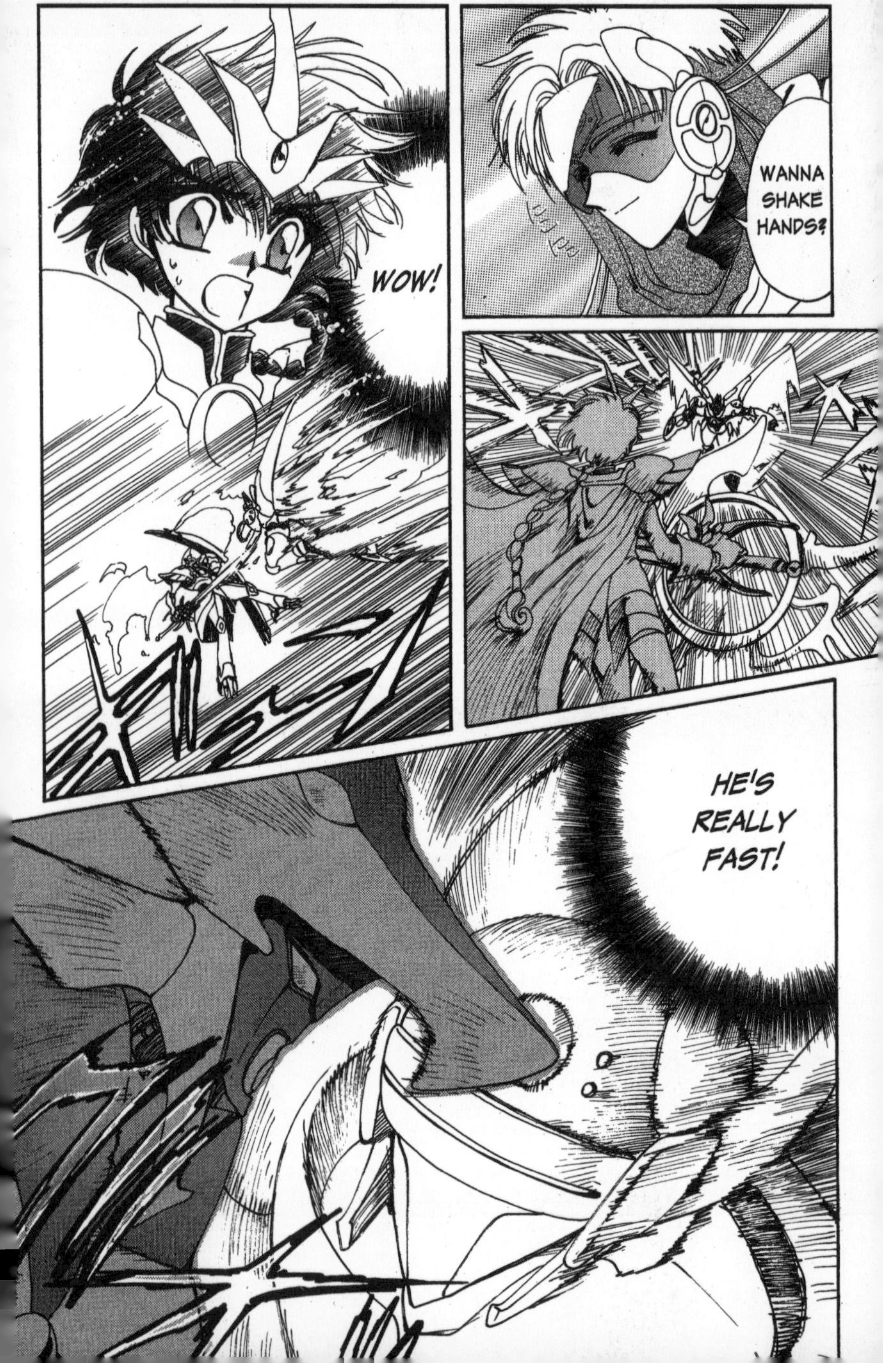
WANNA SHAKE HANDS?
WOW!
HE'S REALLY FAST!

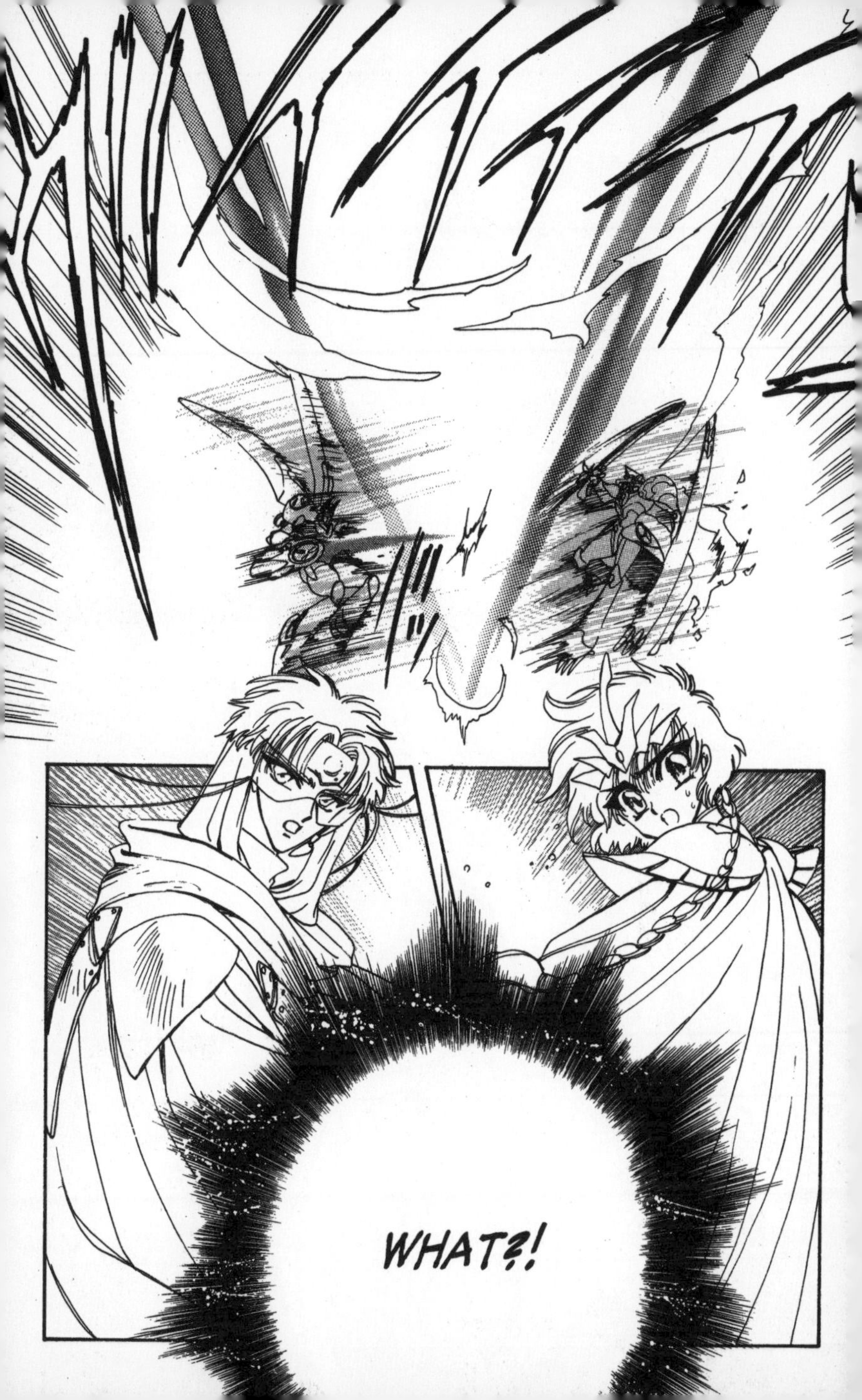
WHAT?!

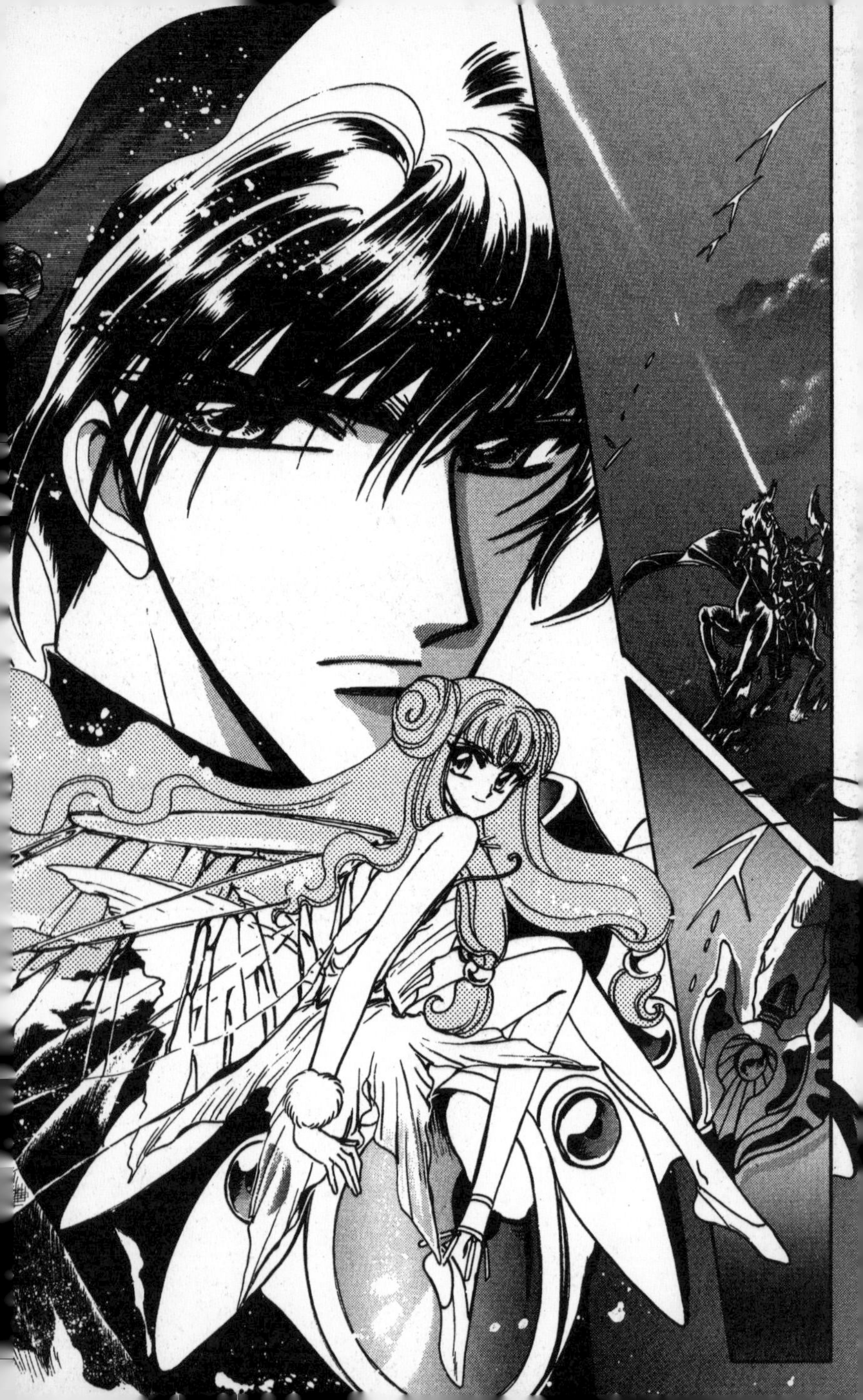

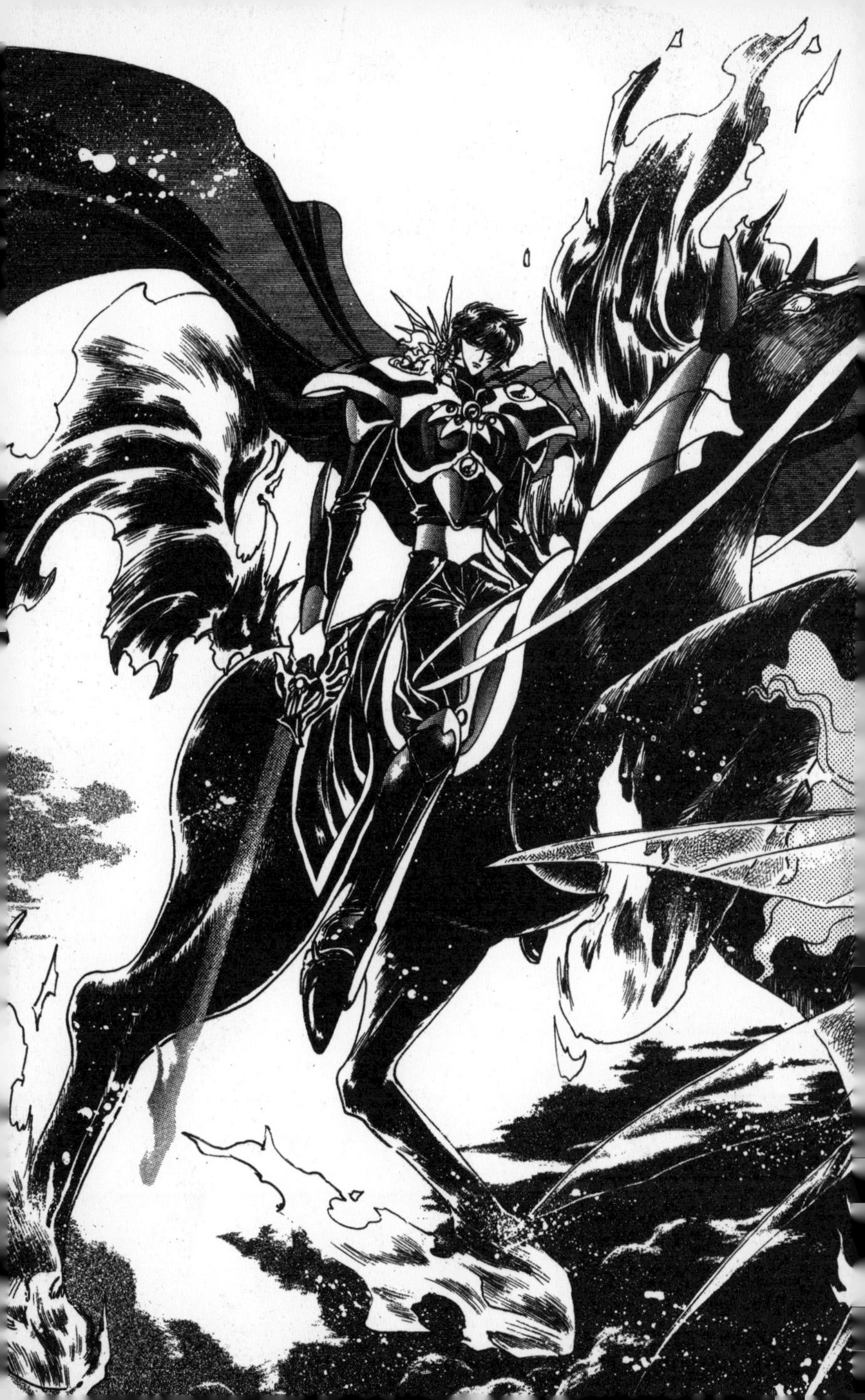

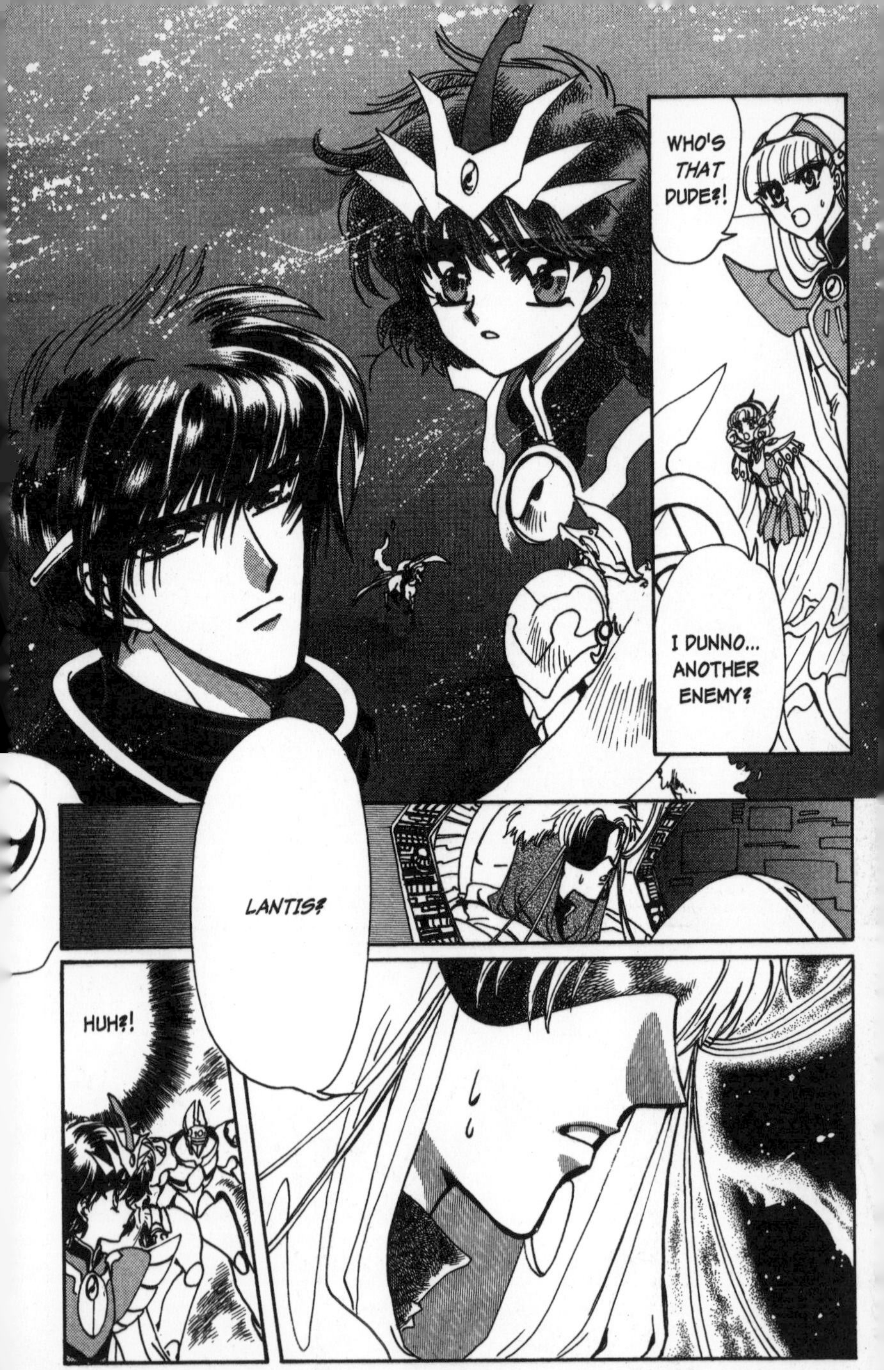
WHO'S THAT DUDE?!
I DUNNO... ANOTHER ENEMY?
LANTIS?
HUH?!

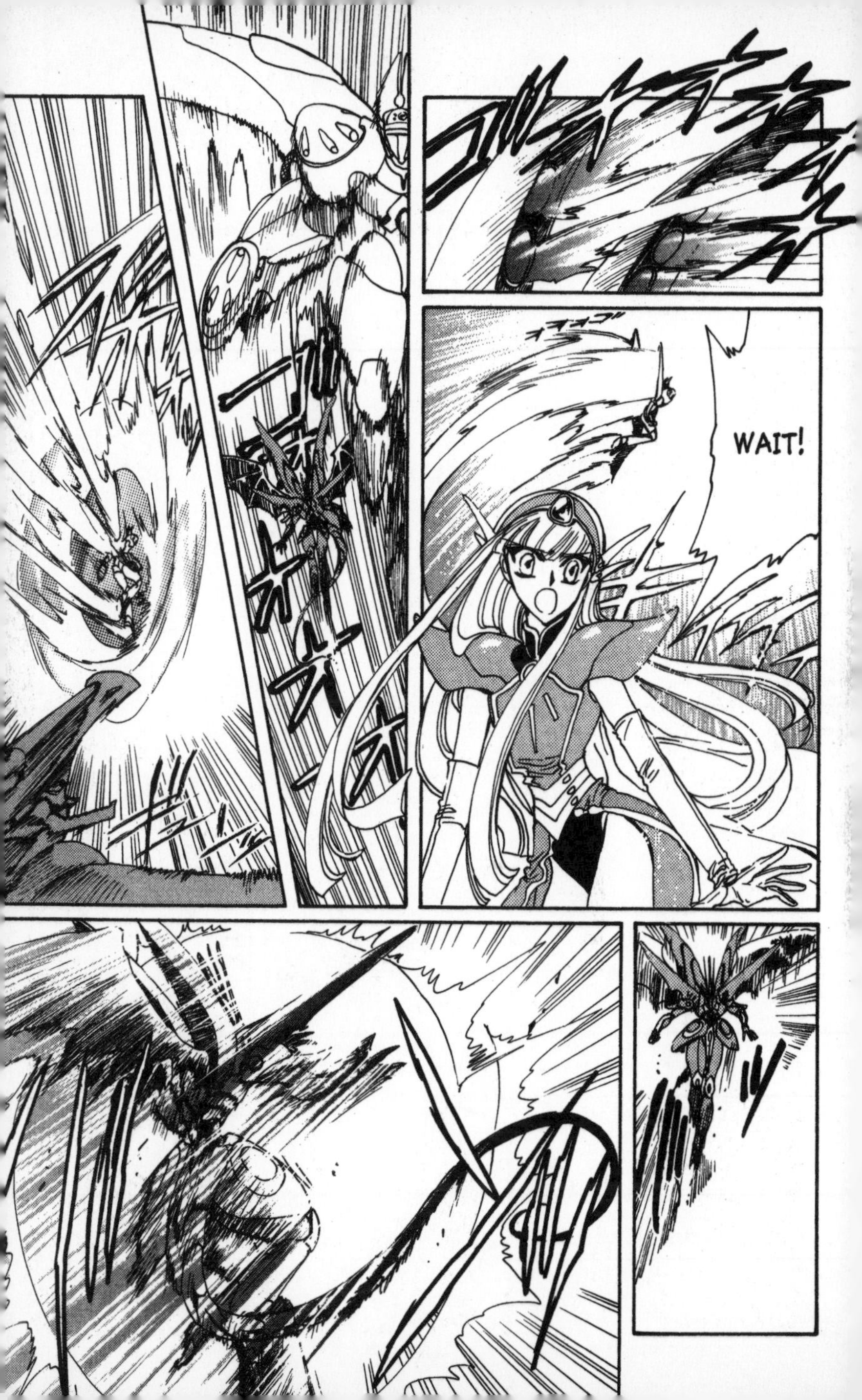
WAIT!

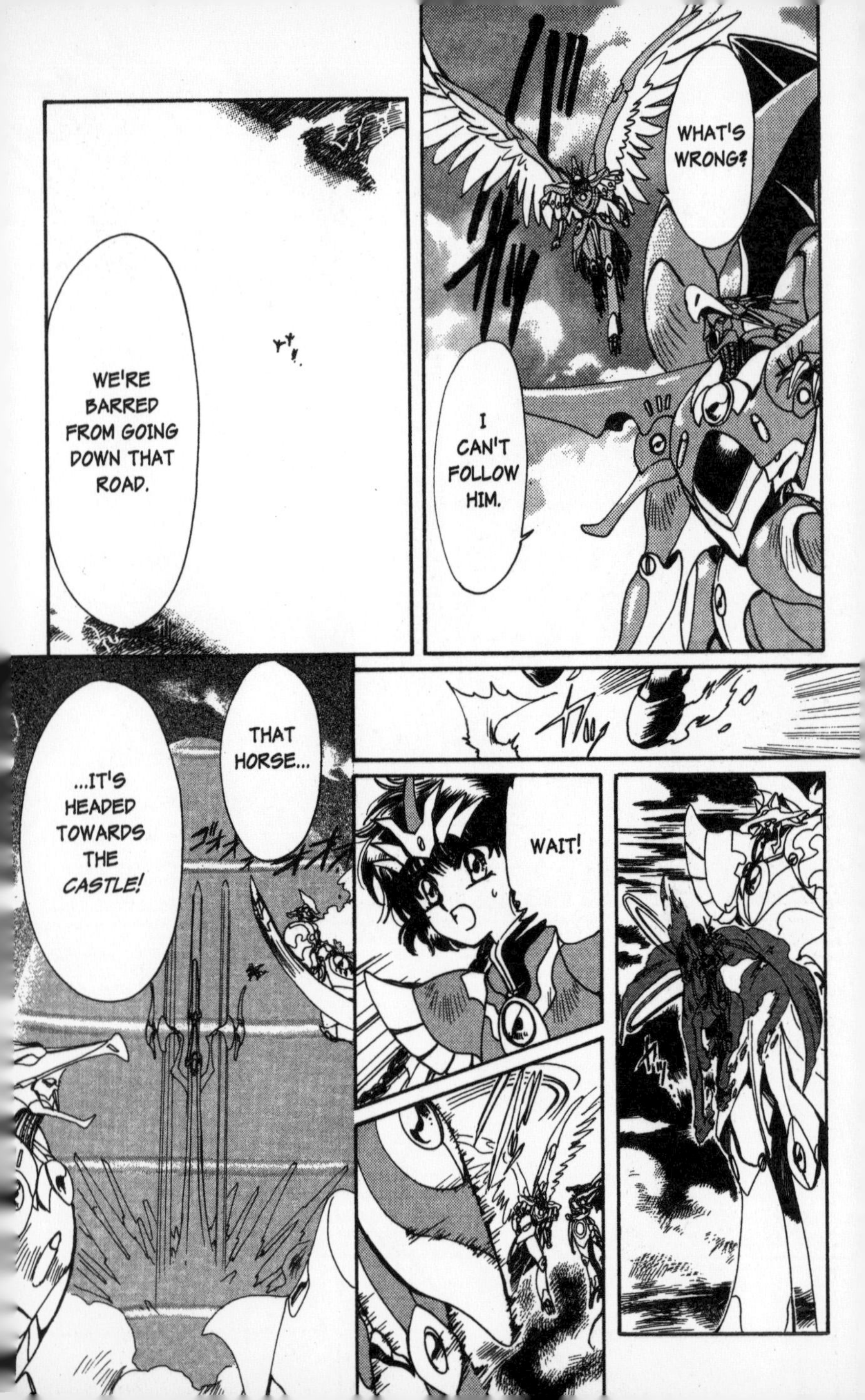
WHAT'S WRONG?
I CAN'T FOLLOW HIM.
WE'RE BARRED FROM GOING DOWN THAT ROAD.
WAIT!
THAT HORSE...
...IT'S HEADED TOWARDS THE *CASTLE!*

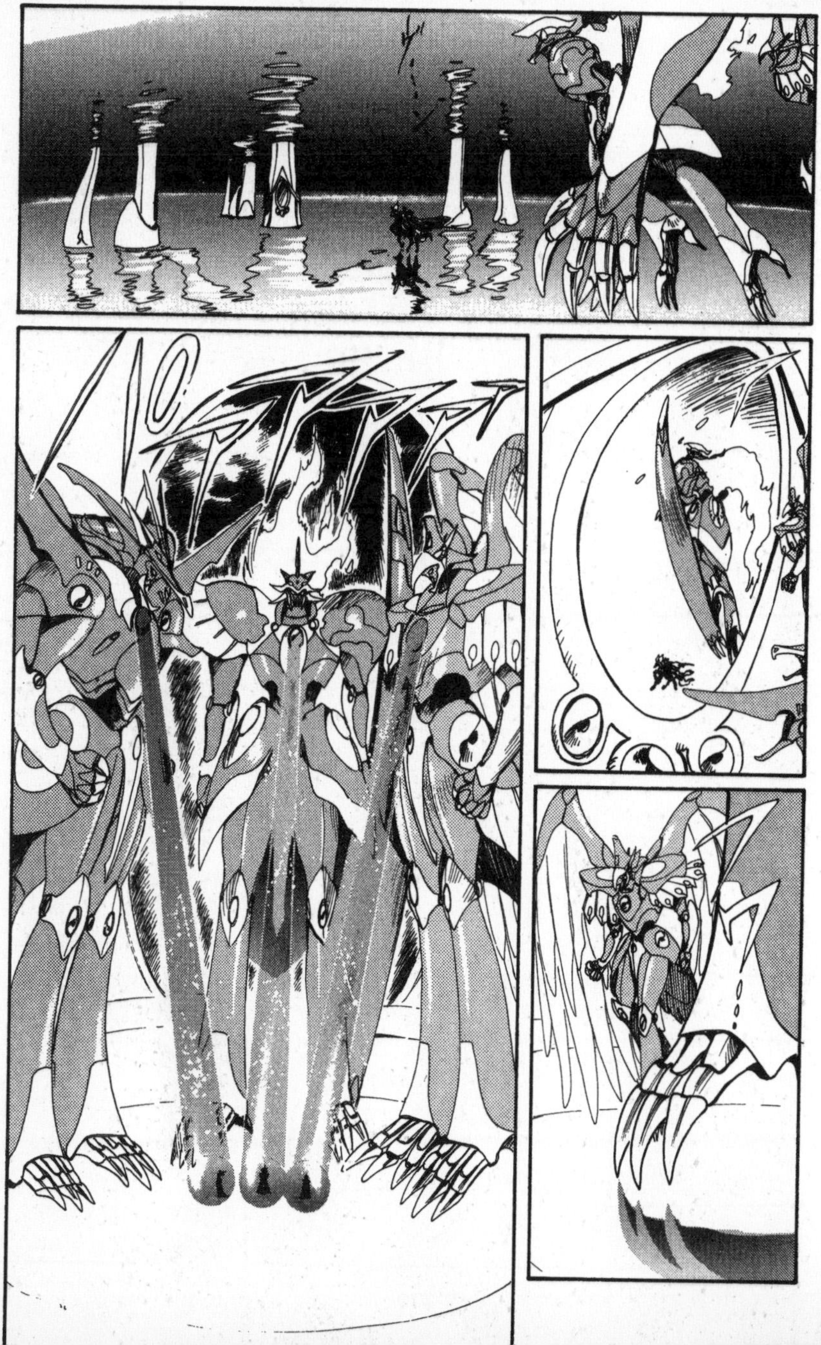

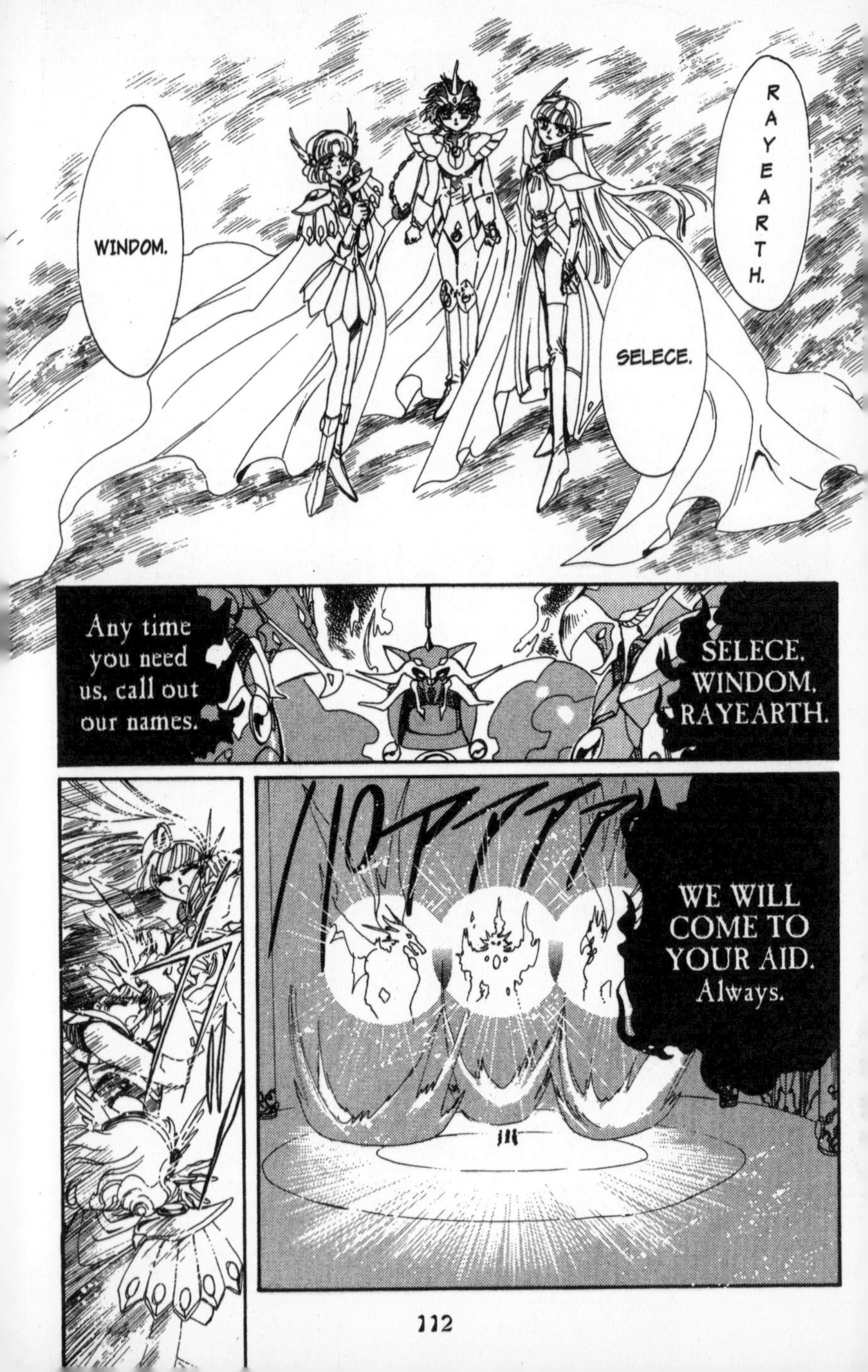
RAYEARTH.
SELECE.
WINDOM.
SELECE. WINDOM. RAYEARTH.
Any time you need us, call out our names.
WE WILL COME TO YOUR AID. Always.

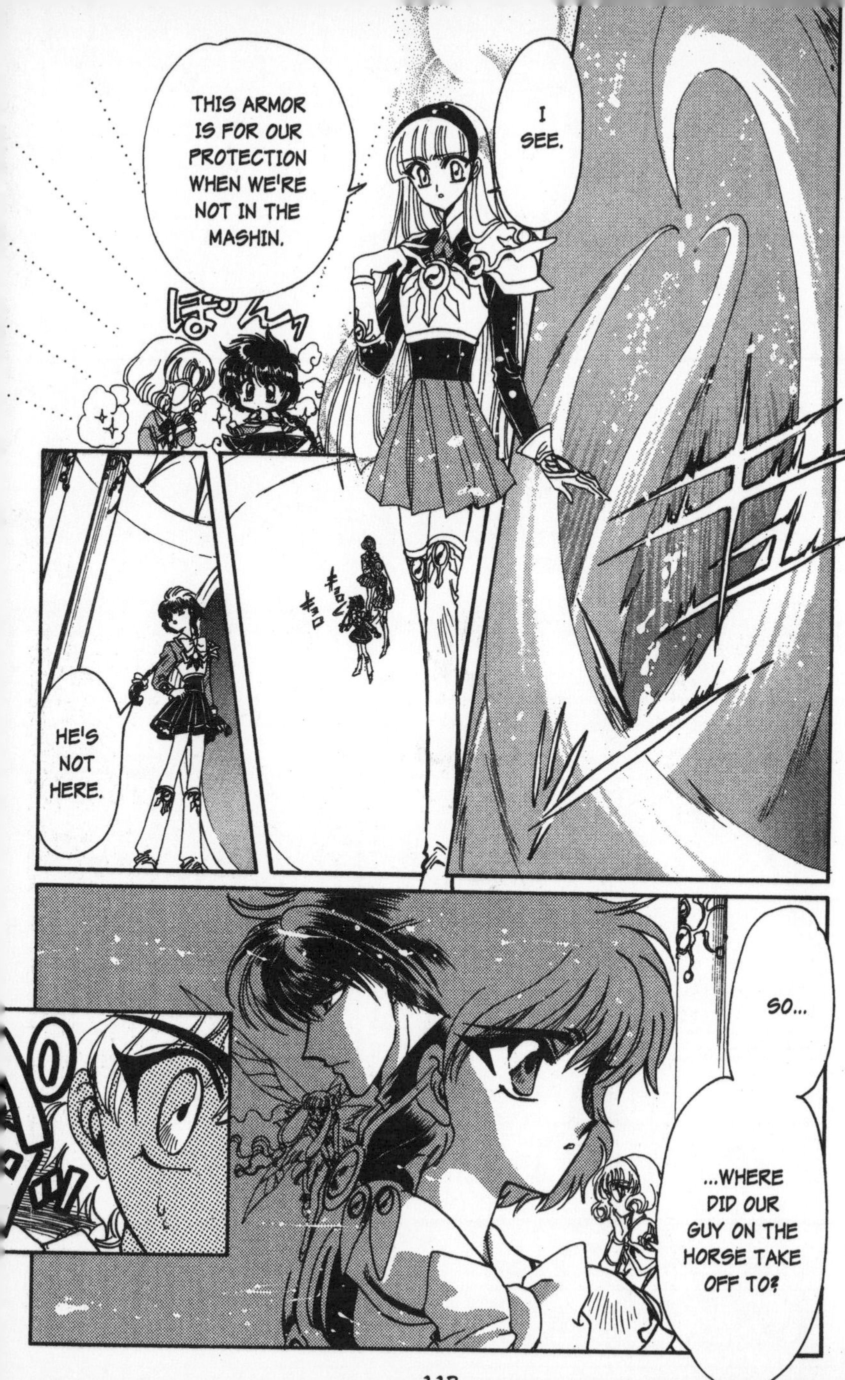
THIS ARMOR IS FOR OUR PROTECTION WHEN WE'RE NOT IN THE MASHIN.
I SEE.
HE'S NOT HERE.
SO...
...WHERE DID OUR GUY ON THE HORSE TAKE OFF TO?

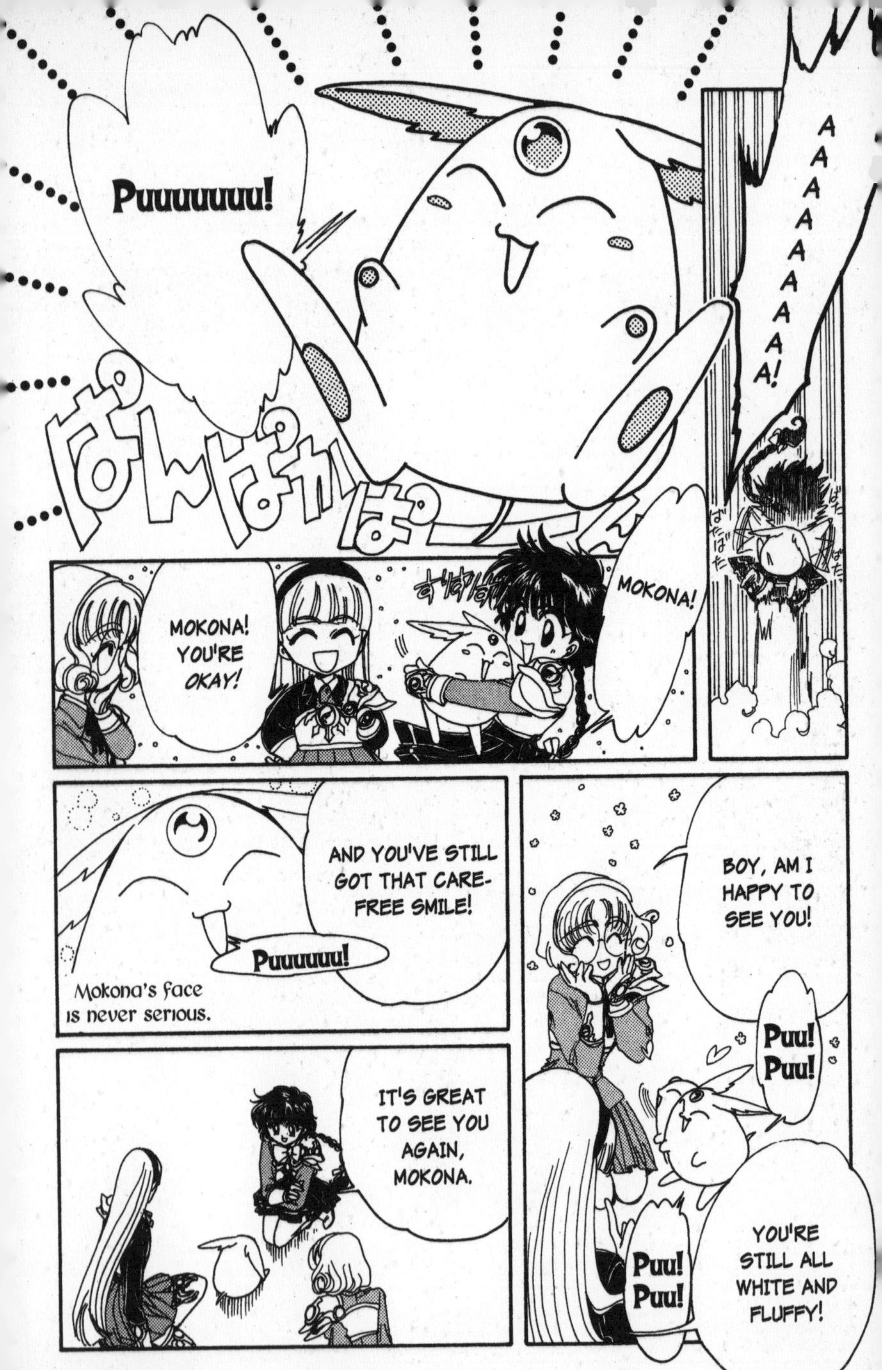
AAAAAAAAAA!
ばたばた
ばたばた
Puuuuuuu!
ぱんぱかぱっ
MOKONA!
MOKONA! YOU'RE OKAY!
BOY, AM I HAPPY TO SEE YOU!
Puu! Puu!
YOU'RE STILL ALL WHITE AND FLUFFY!
Puu! Puu!
AND YOU'VE STILL GOT THAT CARE-FREE SMILE!
Puuuuuu!
Mokona's face is never serious.
IT'S GREAT TO SEE YOU AGAIN, MOKONA.

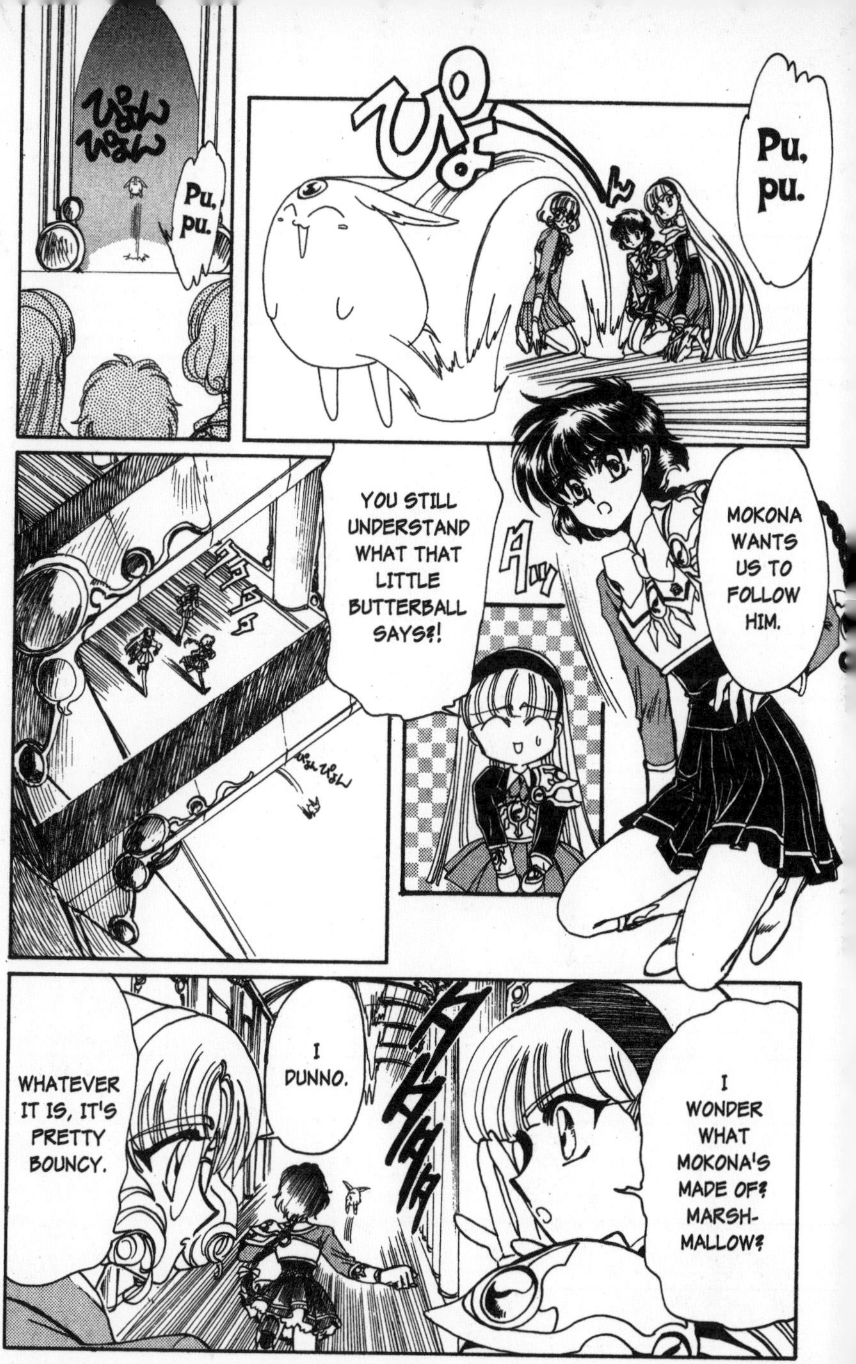
Pu, pu.
ぴょんぴょん
Pu, pu.
MOKONA WANTS US TO FOLLOW HIM.
YOU STILL UNDERSTAND WHAT THAT LITTLE BUTTERBALL SAYS?!
I WONDER WHAT MOKONA'S MADE OF? MARSH-MALLOW?
I DUNNO.
WHATEVER IT IS, IT'S PRETTY BOUNCY.

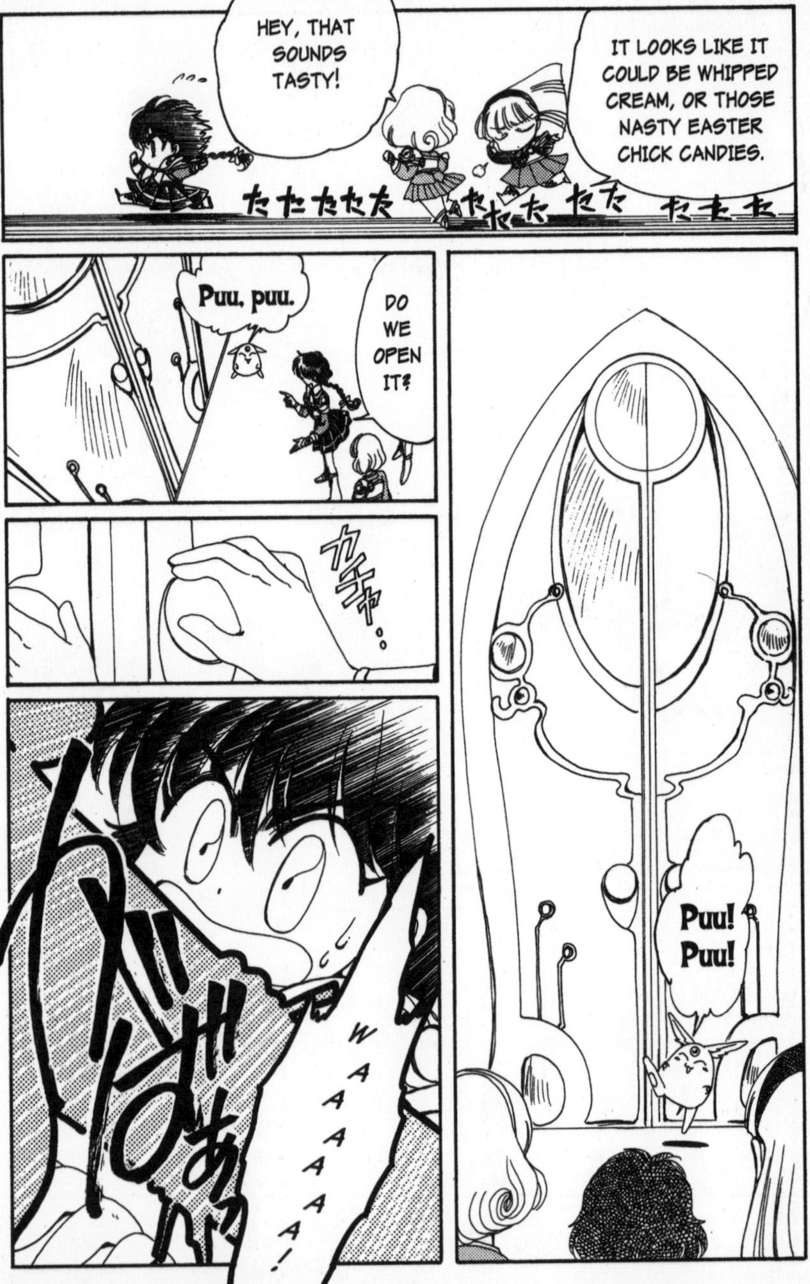
IT LOOKS LIKE IT COULD BE WHIPPED CREAM, OR THOSE NASTY EASTER CHICK CANDIES.
HEY, THAT SOUNDS TASTY!
Puu! Puu!
Puu, puu.
DO WE OPEN IT?
カチャ。。
WAAAAAAAAA!

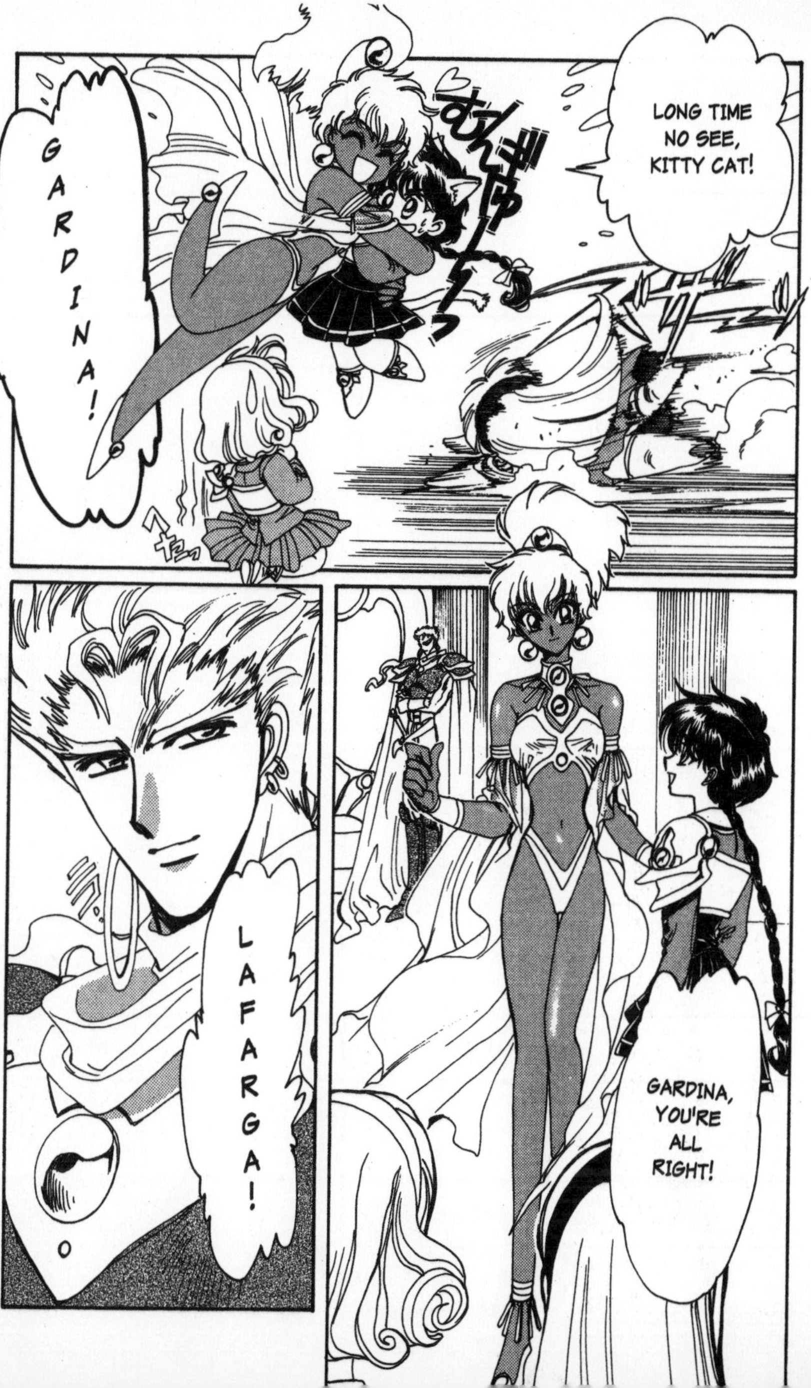
LONG TIME NO SEE, KITTY CAT!
GARDINA!
GARDINA, YOU'RE ALL RIGHT!
LAFARGA!

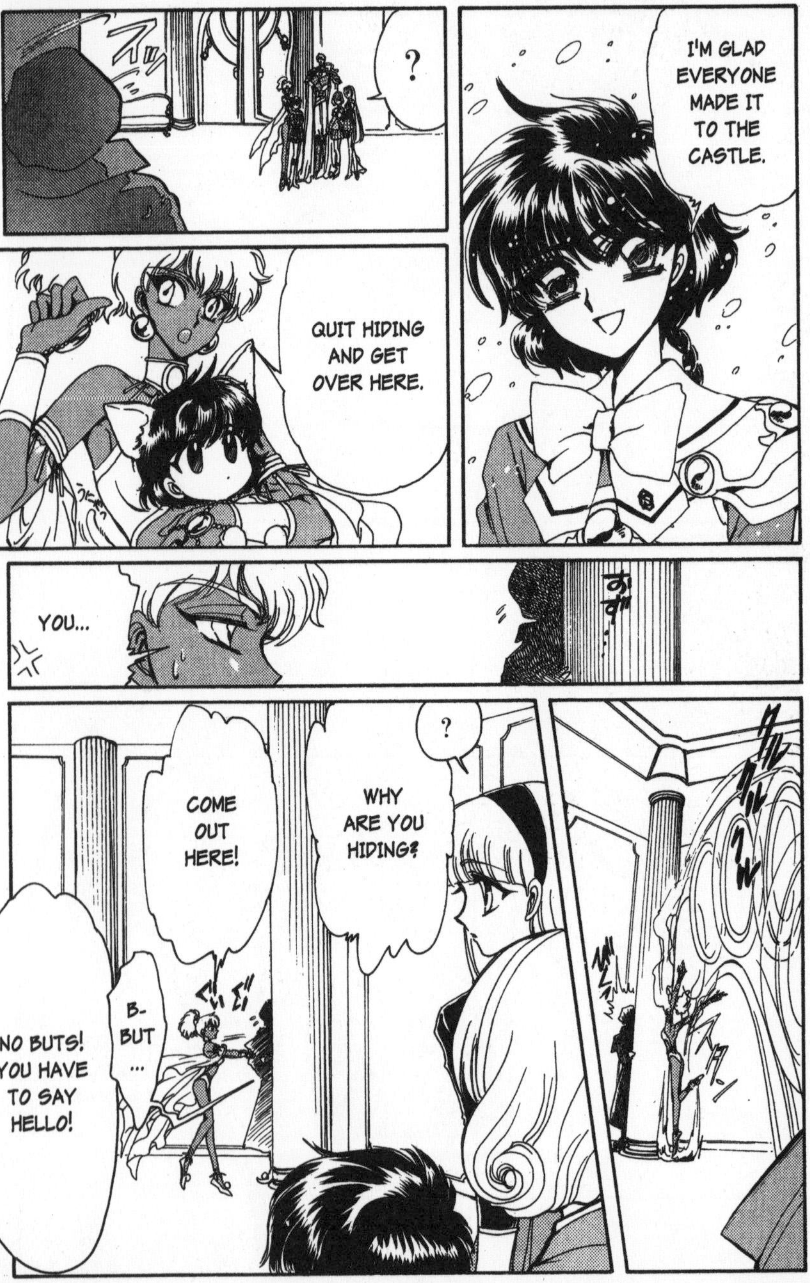
I'M GLAD EVERYONE MADE IT TO THE CASTLE.
?
QUIT HIDING AND GET OVER HERE.
YOU...
?
WHY ARE YOU HIDING?
COME OUT HERE!
B- BUT ...
NO BUTS! YOU HAVE TO SAY HELLO!

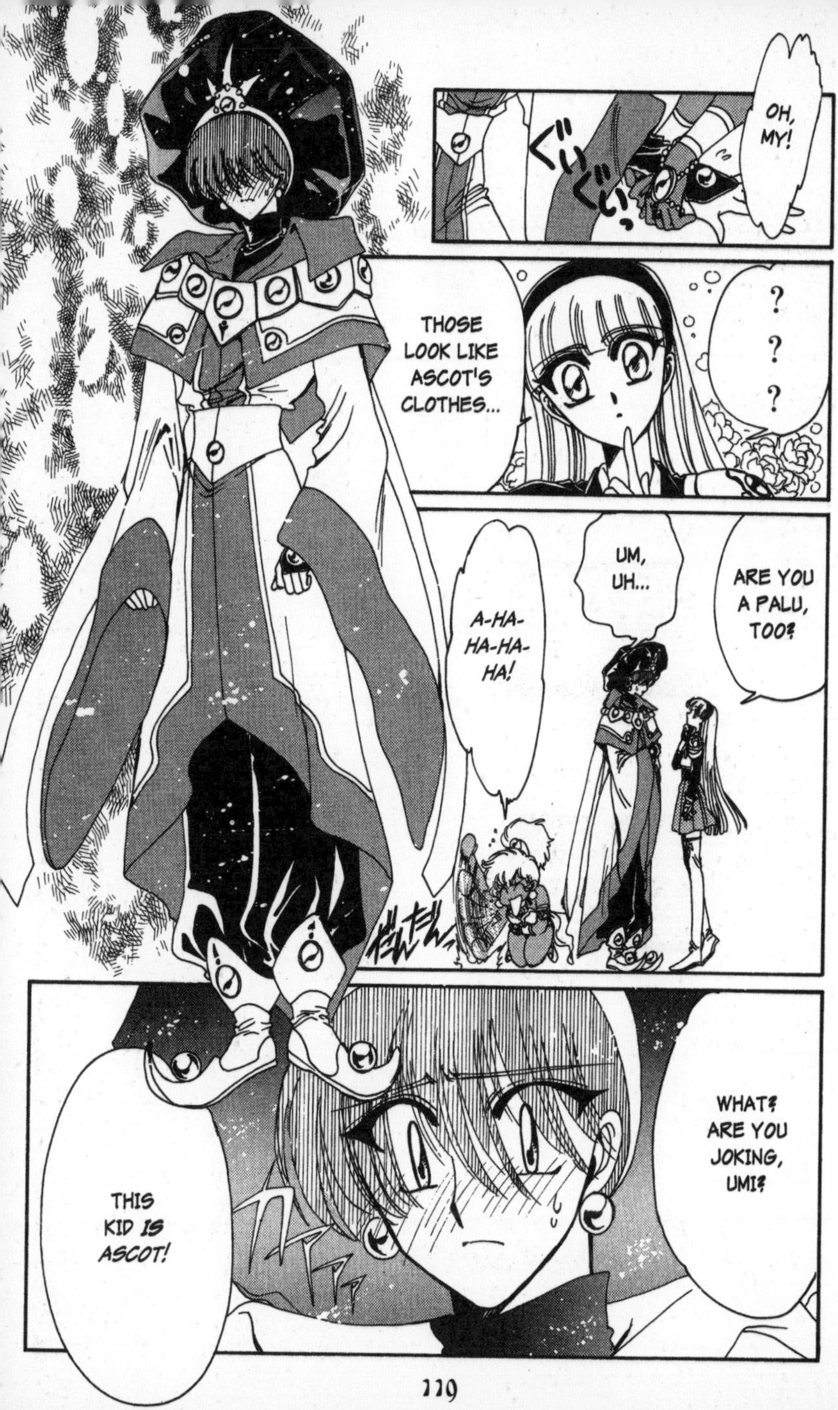
OH, MY!
ぐいぐいっ
? ? ?
THOSE LOOK LIKE ASCOT'S CLOTHES...
ARE YOU A PALU, TOO?
UM, UH...
A-HA-HA-HA-HA!
WHAT? ARE YOU JOKING, UMI?
THIS KID *IS* ASCOT!

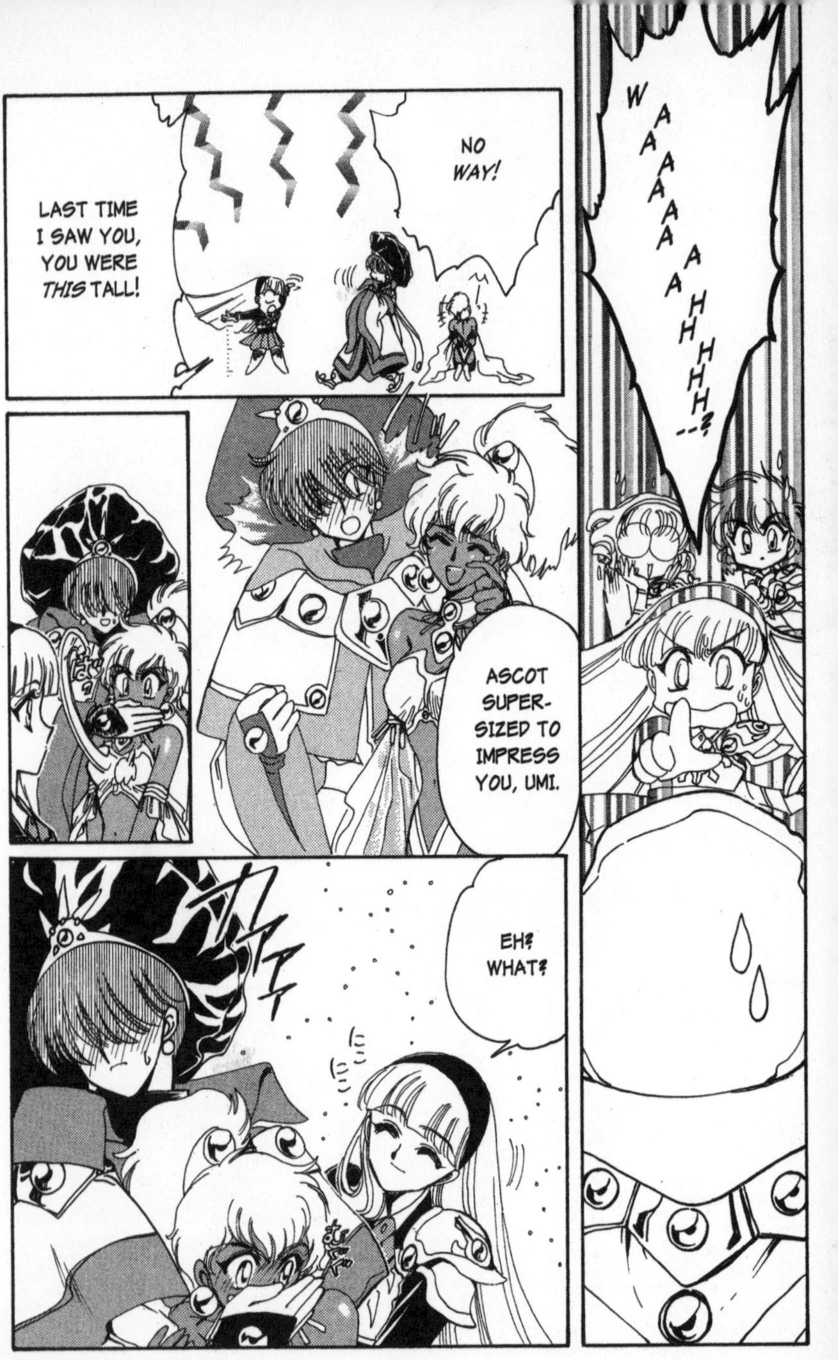
WAAAAAAAAHHHHH--?
NO WAY!
LAST TIME I SAW YOU, YOU WERE *THIS* TALL!
ASCOT SUPER-SIZED TO IMPRESS YOU, UMI.
EH? WHAT?

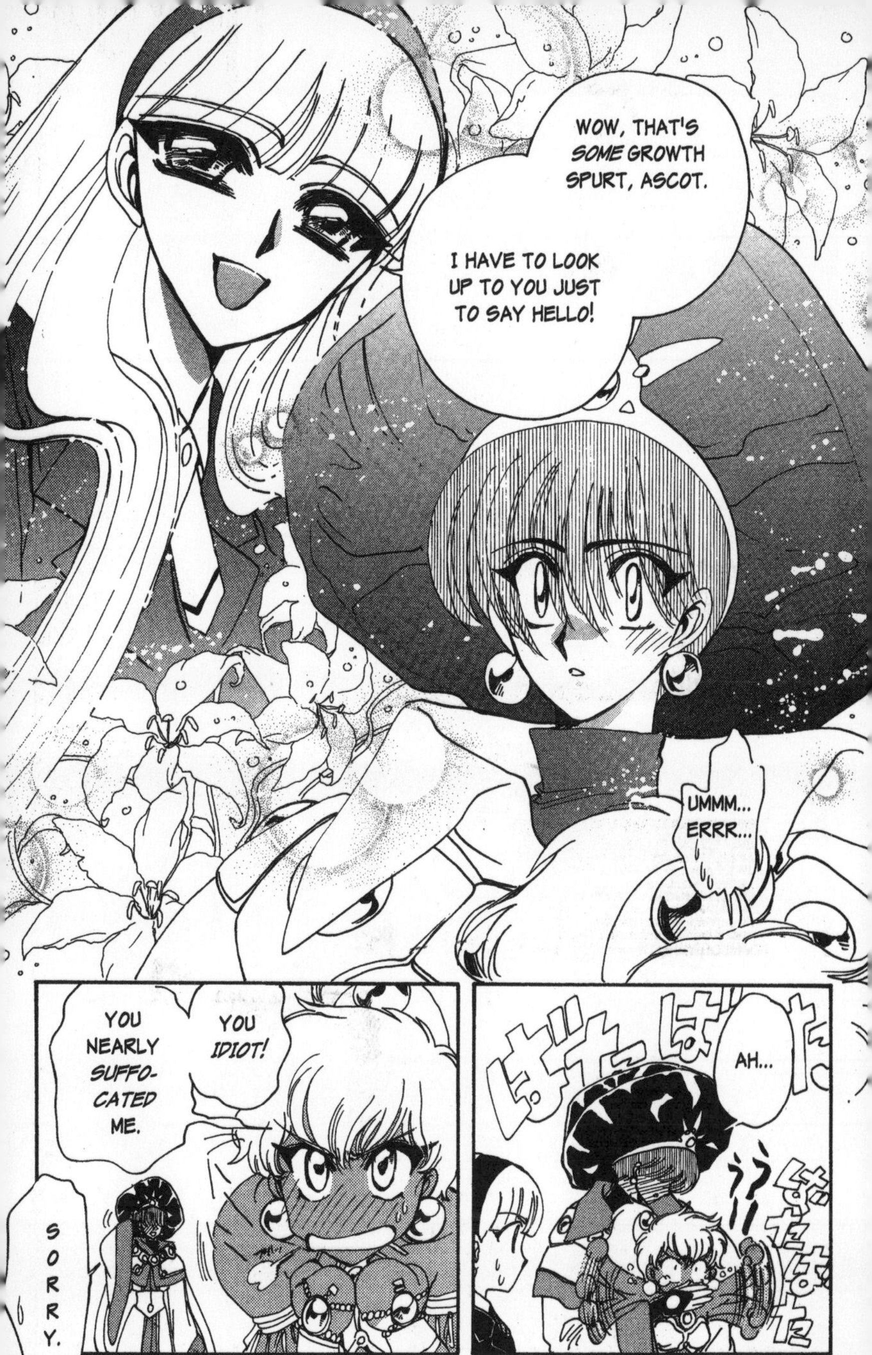

WOW, THAT'S SOME GROWTH SPURT, ASCOT.
I HAVE TO LOOK UP TO YOU JUST TO SAY HELLO!
UMMM... ERRR...
AH...
YOU IDIOT!
YOU NEARLY SUFFO-CATED ME.
SORRY.

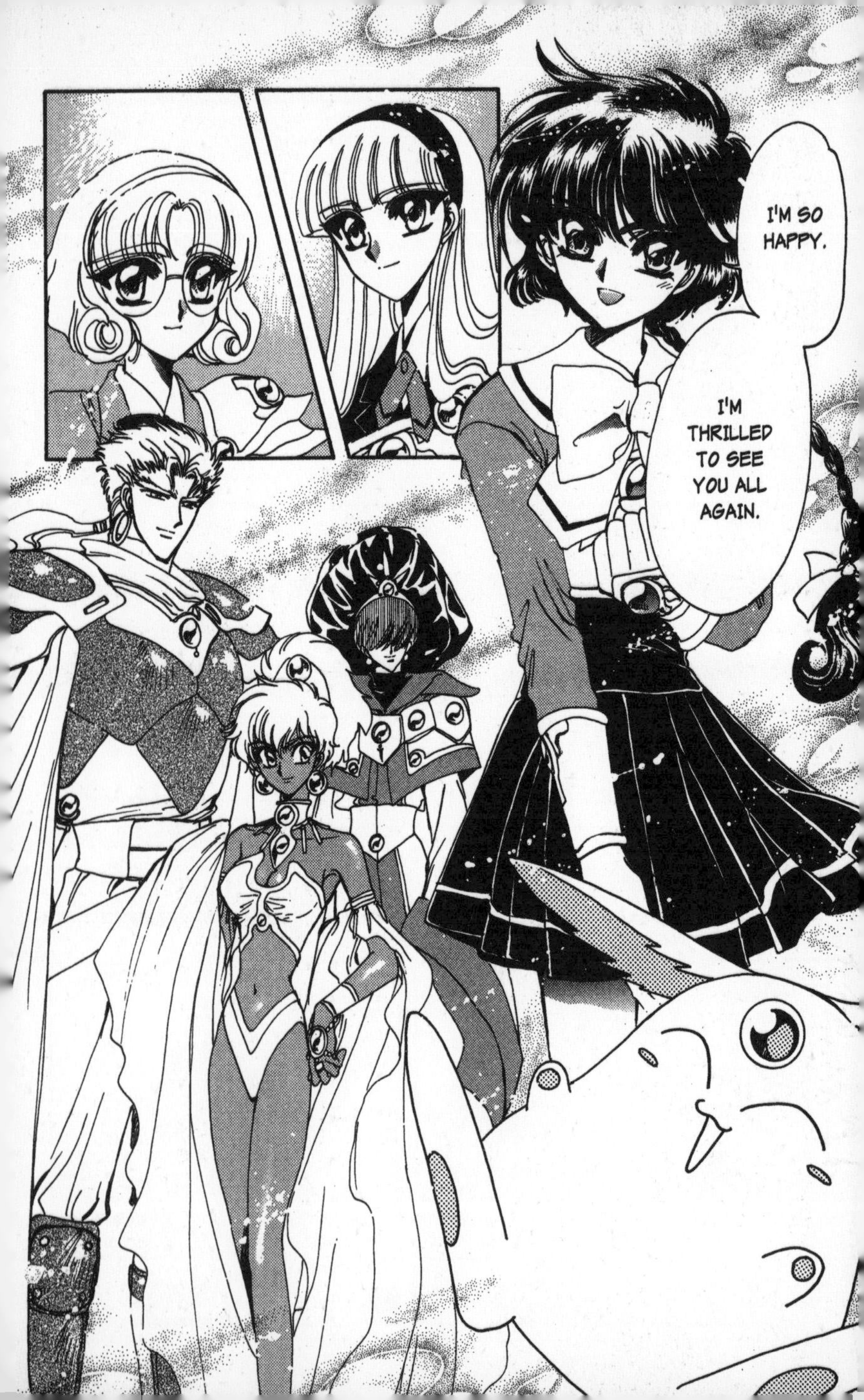
I'M SO HAPPY.
I'M THRILLED TO SEE YOU ALL AGAIN.

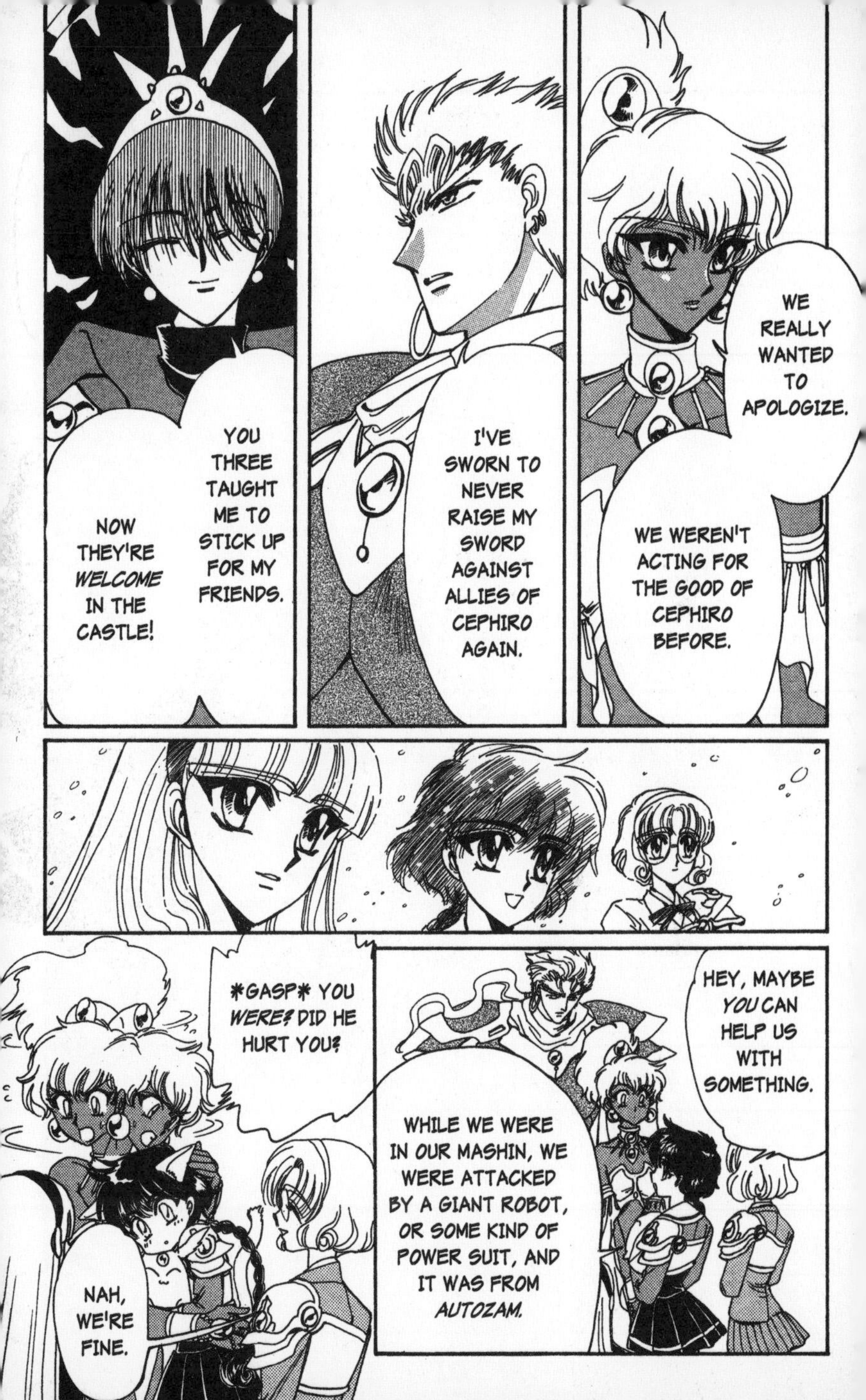
WE REALLY WANTED TO APOLOGIZE.
WE WEREN'T ACTING FOR THE GOOD OF CEPHIRO BEFORE.
I'VE SWORN TO NEVER RAISE MY SWORD AGAINST ALLIES OF CEPHIRO AGAIN.
YOU THREE TAUGHT ME TO STICK UP FOR MY FRIENDS.
NOW THEY'RE *WELCOME* IN THE CASTLE!
HEY, MAYBE *YOU* CAN HELP US WITH SOMETHING.
WHILE WE WERE IN OUR MASHIN, WE WERE ATTACKED BY A GIANT ROBOT, OR SOME KIND OF POWER SUIT, AND IT WAS FROM *AUTOZAM.*
GASP YOU *WERE?* DID HE HURT YOU?
NAH, WE'RE FINE.

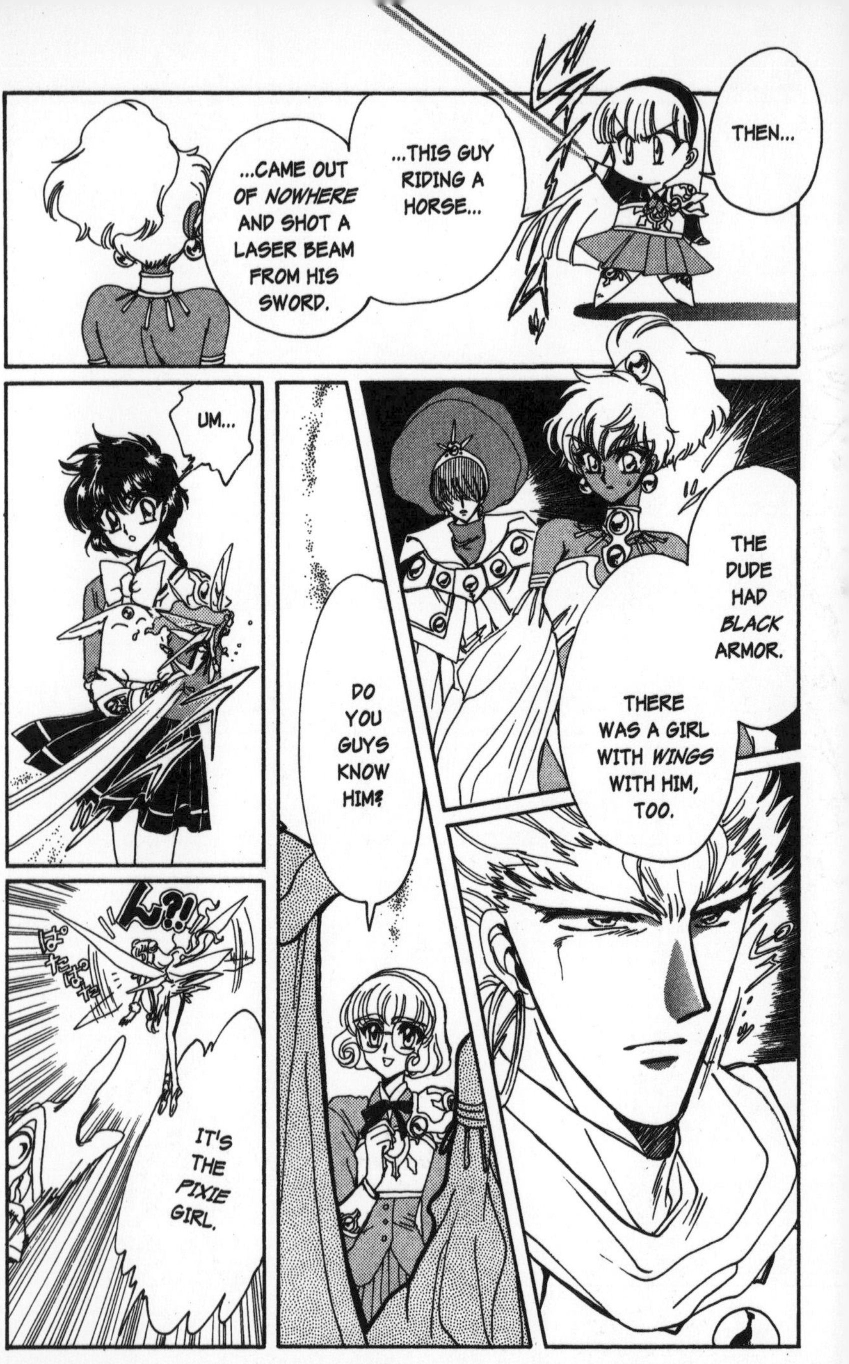
THEN...
...THIS GUY RIDING A HORSE...
...CAME OUT OF *NOWHERE* AND SHOT A LASER BEAM FROM HIS SWORD.
THE DUDE HAD *BLACK* ARMOR.
THERE WAS A GIRL WITH *WINGS* WITH HIM, TOO.
DO YOU GUYS KNOW HIM?
UM...
ん?!
ぱたぱた
IT'S THE *PIXIE* GIRL.

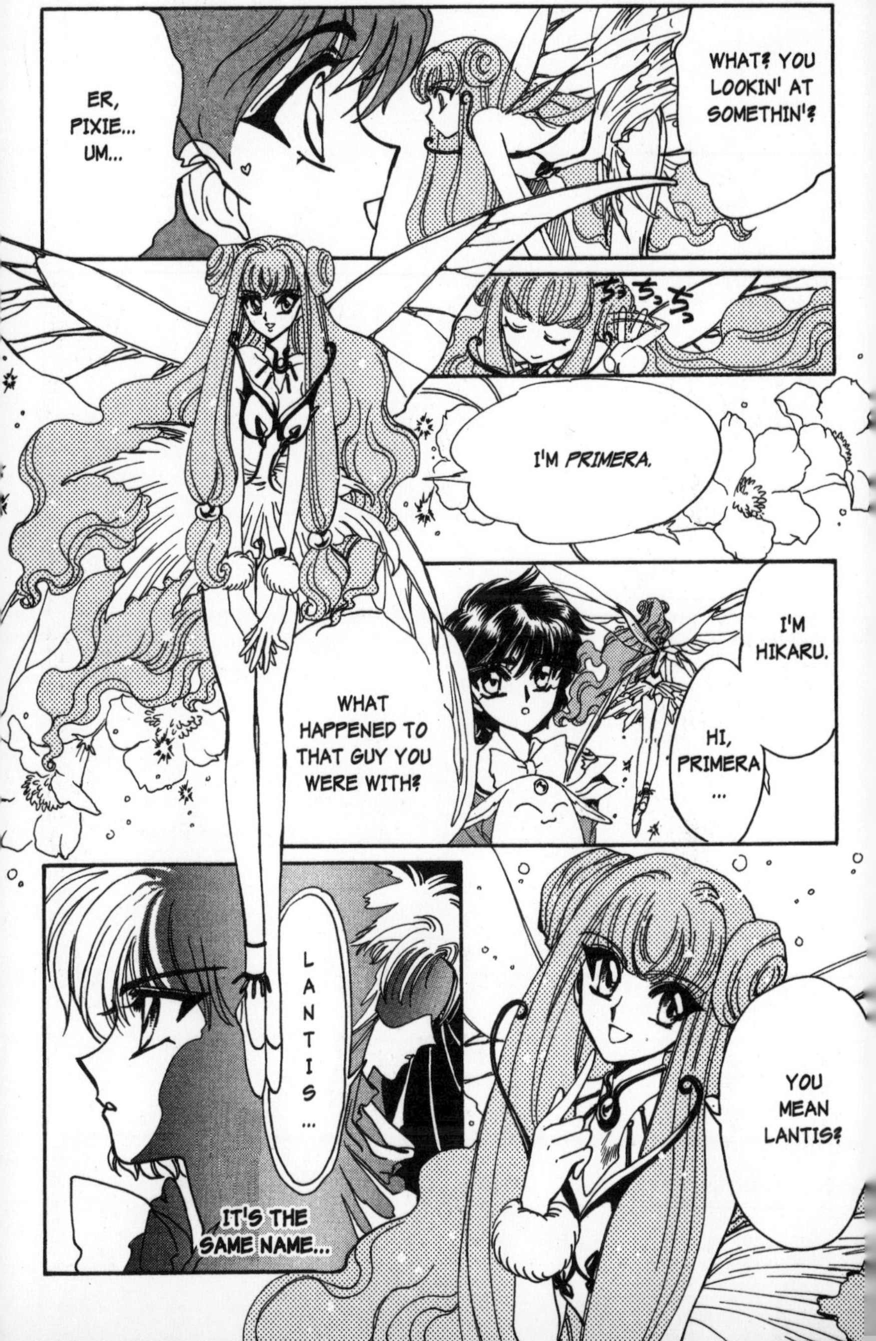
WHAT? YOU LOOKIN' AT SOMETHIN'?
ER, PIXIE... UM...
ちっちっちっ
I'M PRIMERA.
I'M HIKARU.
HI, PRIMERA...
WHAT HAPPENED TO THAT GUY YOU WERE WITH?
YOU MEAN LANTIS?
LANTIS...
IT'S THE SAME NAME...

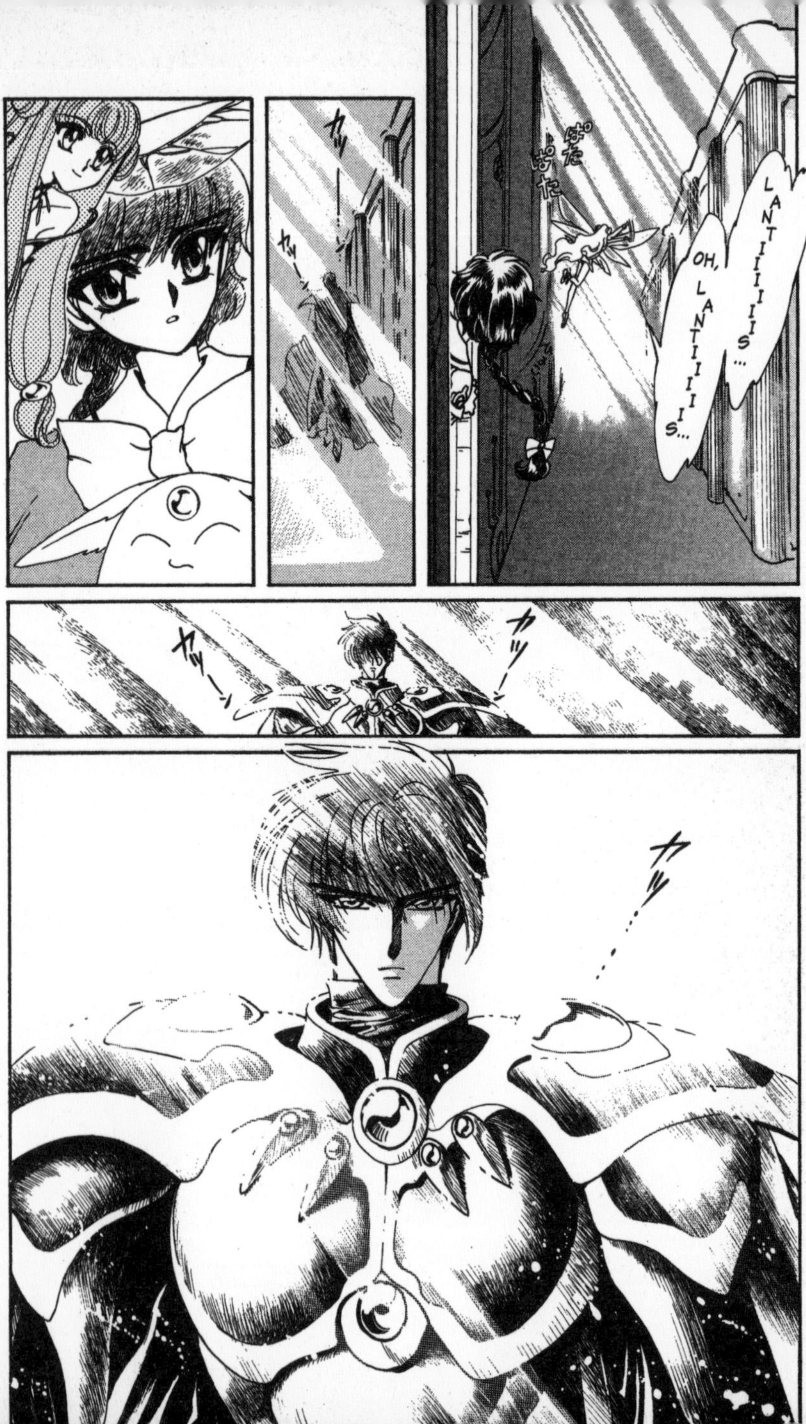
LANTIIIIIIS...
OH, LANTIIIIIIS...
ぱた ぱた

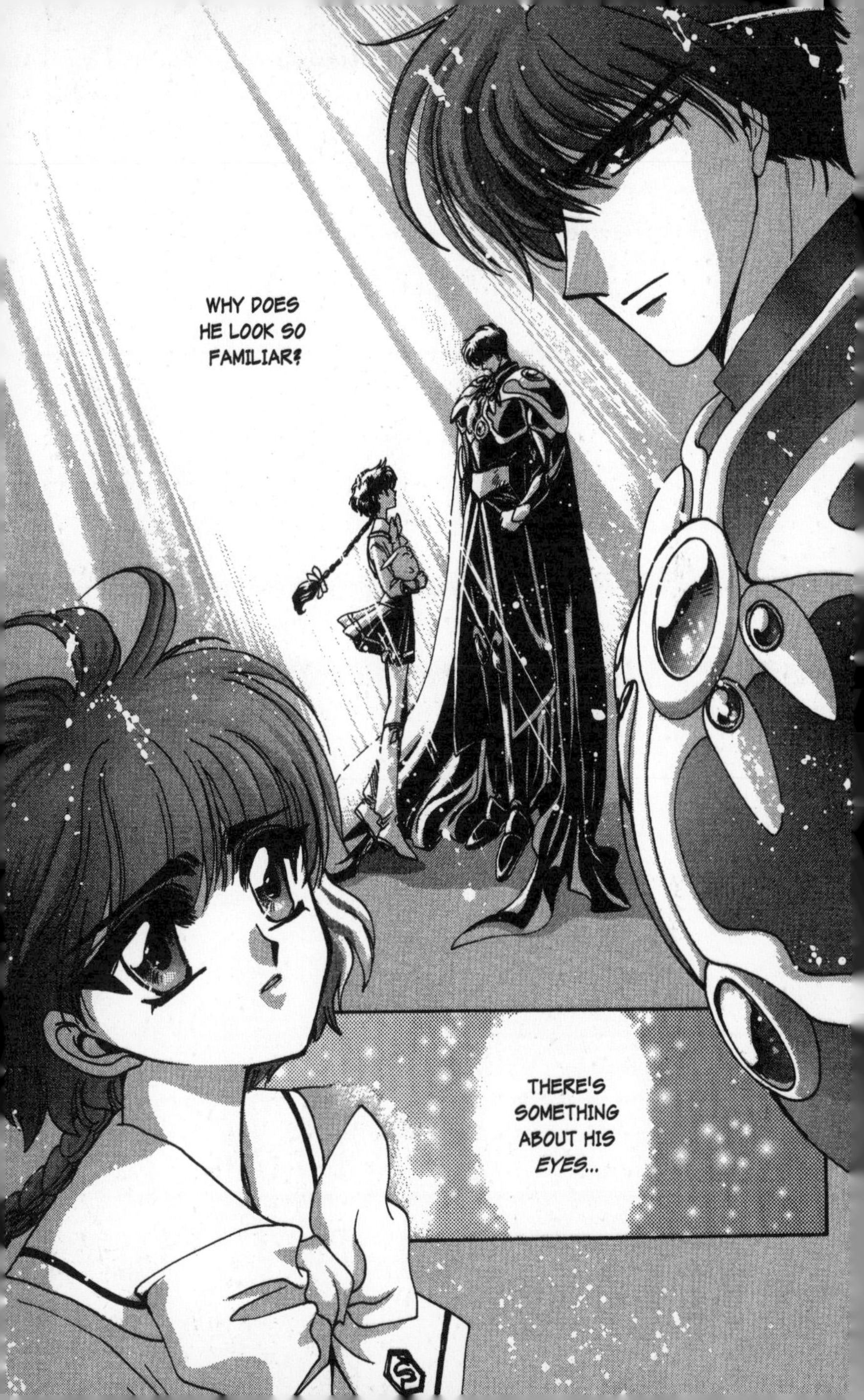
WHY DOES HE LOOK SO FAMILIAR?
THERE'S SOMETHING ABOUT HIS *EYES*...

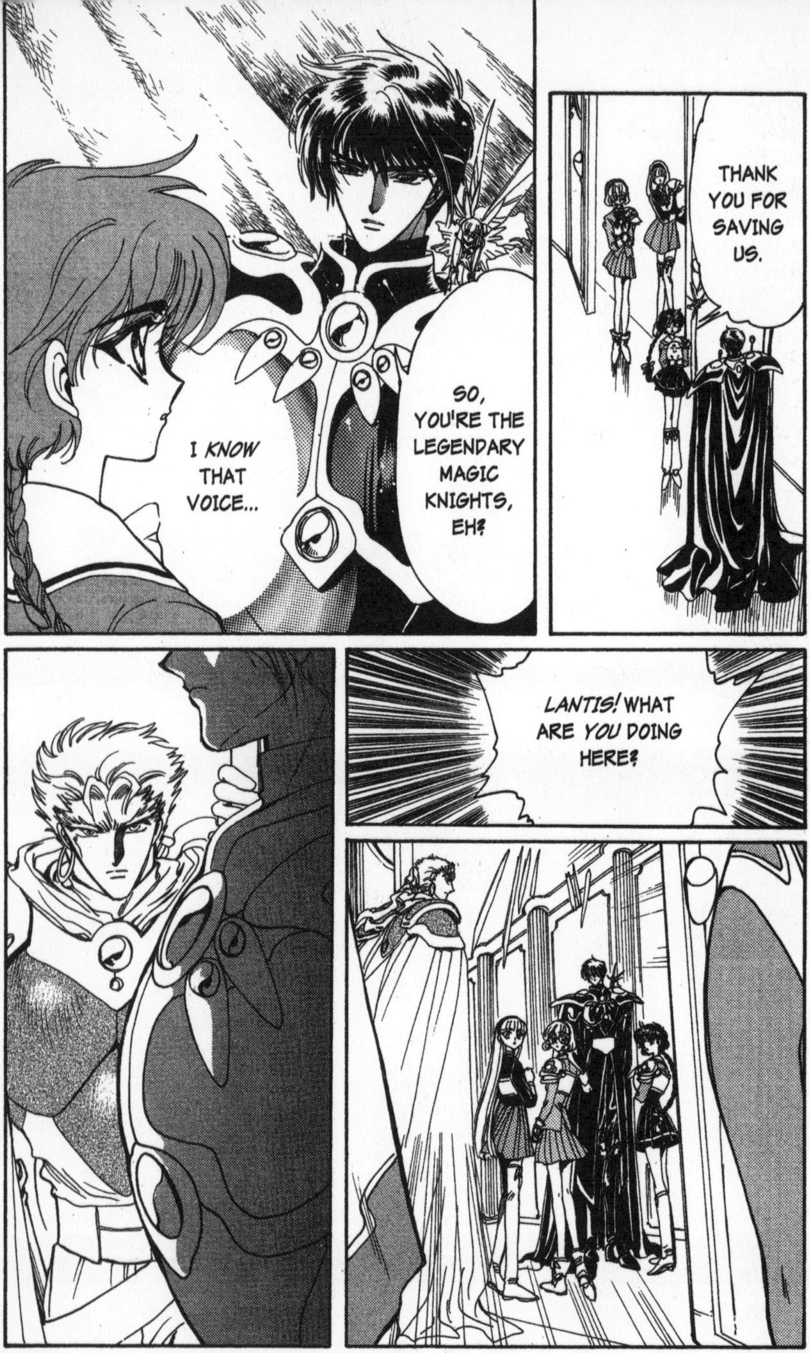
THANK YOU FOR SAVING US.
SO, YOU'RE THE LEGENDARY MAGIC KNIGHTS, EH?
I *KNOW* THAT VOICE...
LANTIS! WHAT ARE *YOU* DOING HERE?

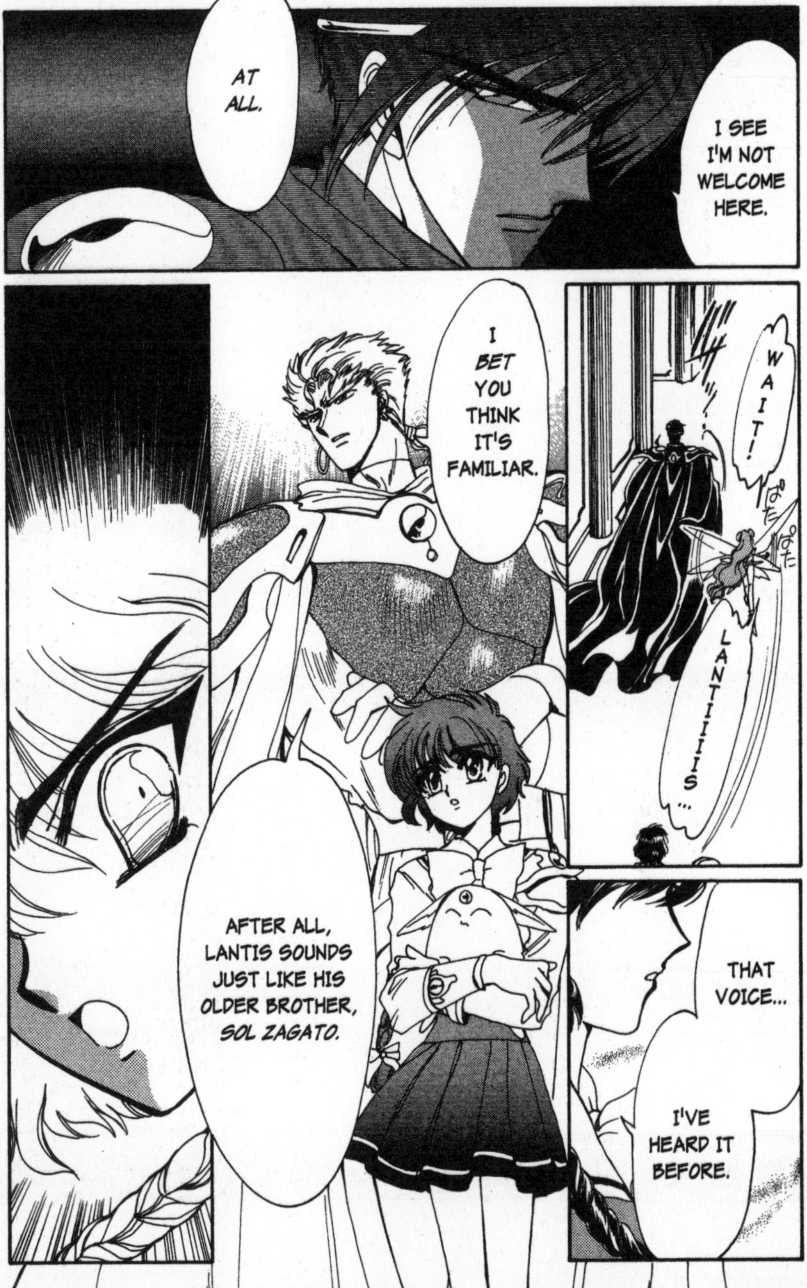
I SEE I'M NOT WELCOME HERE.
AT ALL.
WAIT!
ぱたぱた
LANTIIIIIS...
THAT VOICE...
I'VE HEARD IT BEFORE.
I BET YOU THINK IT'S FAMILIAR.
AFTER ALL, LANTIS SOUNDS JUST LIKE HIS OLDER BROTHER, SOL ZAGATO.

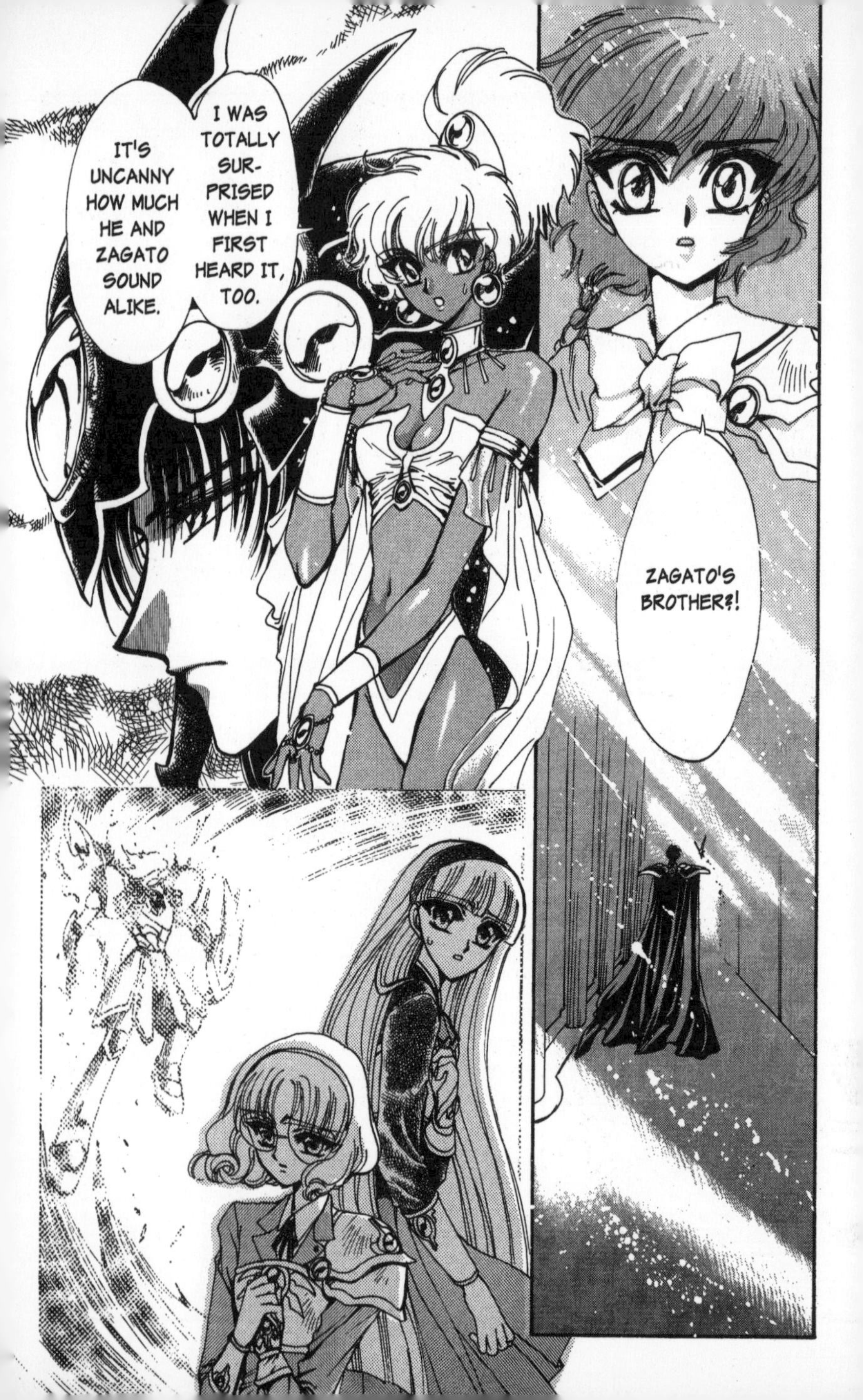
ZAGATO'S BROTHER?!
I WAS TOTALLY SUR-PRISED WHEN I FIRST HEARD IT, TOO.
IT'S UNCANNY HOW MUCH HE AND ZAGATO SOUND ALIKE.

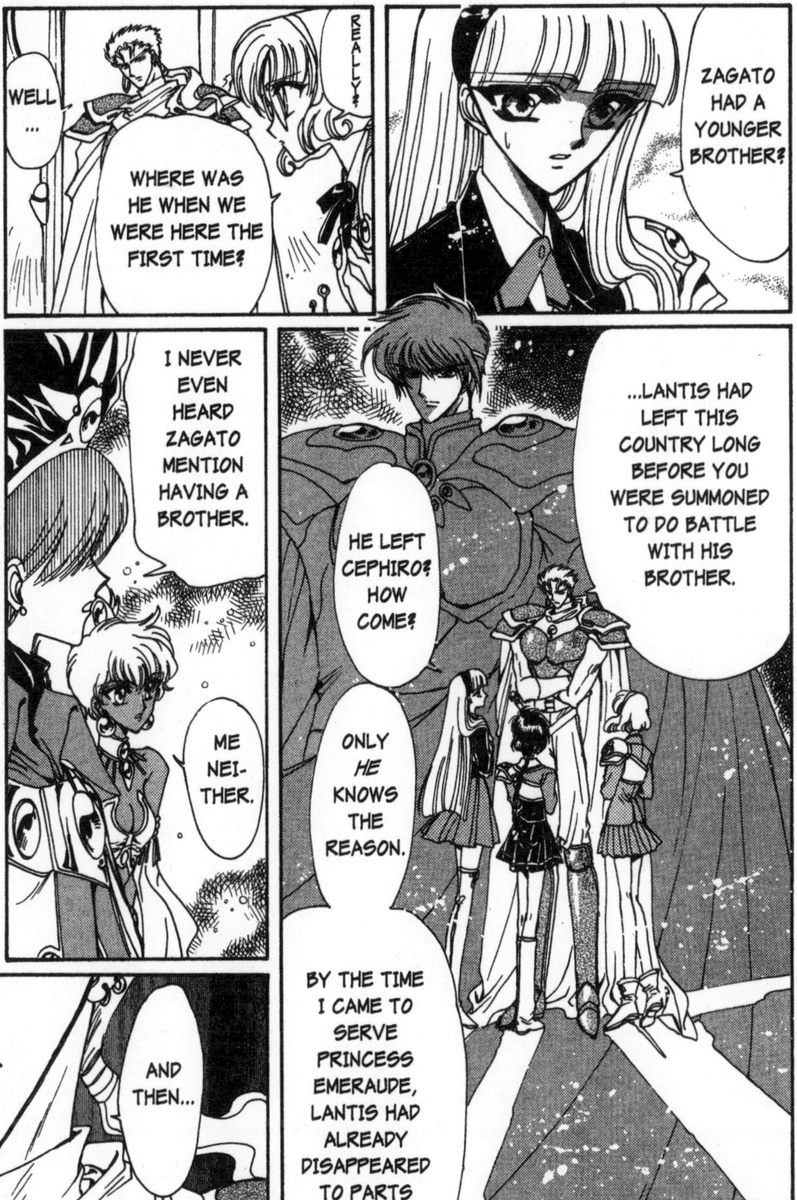
ZAGATO HAD A YOUNGER BROTHER?
REALLY?
WHERE WAS HE WHEN WE WERE HERE THE FIRST TIME?
WELL ...
...LANTIS HAD LEFT THIS COUNTRY LONG BEFORE YOU WERE SUMMONED TO DO BATTLE WITH HIS BROTHER.
HE LEFT CEPHIRO? HOW COME?
ONLY *HE* KNOWS THE REASON.
BY THE TIME I CAME TO SERVE PRINCESS EMERAUDE, LANTIS HAD ALREADY DISAPPEARED TO PARTS UNKNOWN.
I NEVER EVEN HEARD ZAGATO MENTION HAVING A BROTHER.
ME NEI-THER.
AND THEN...

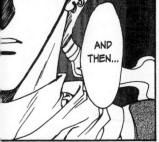

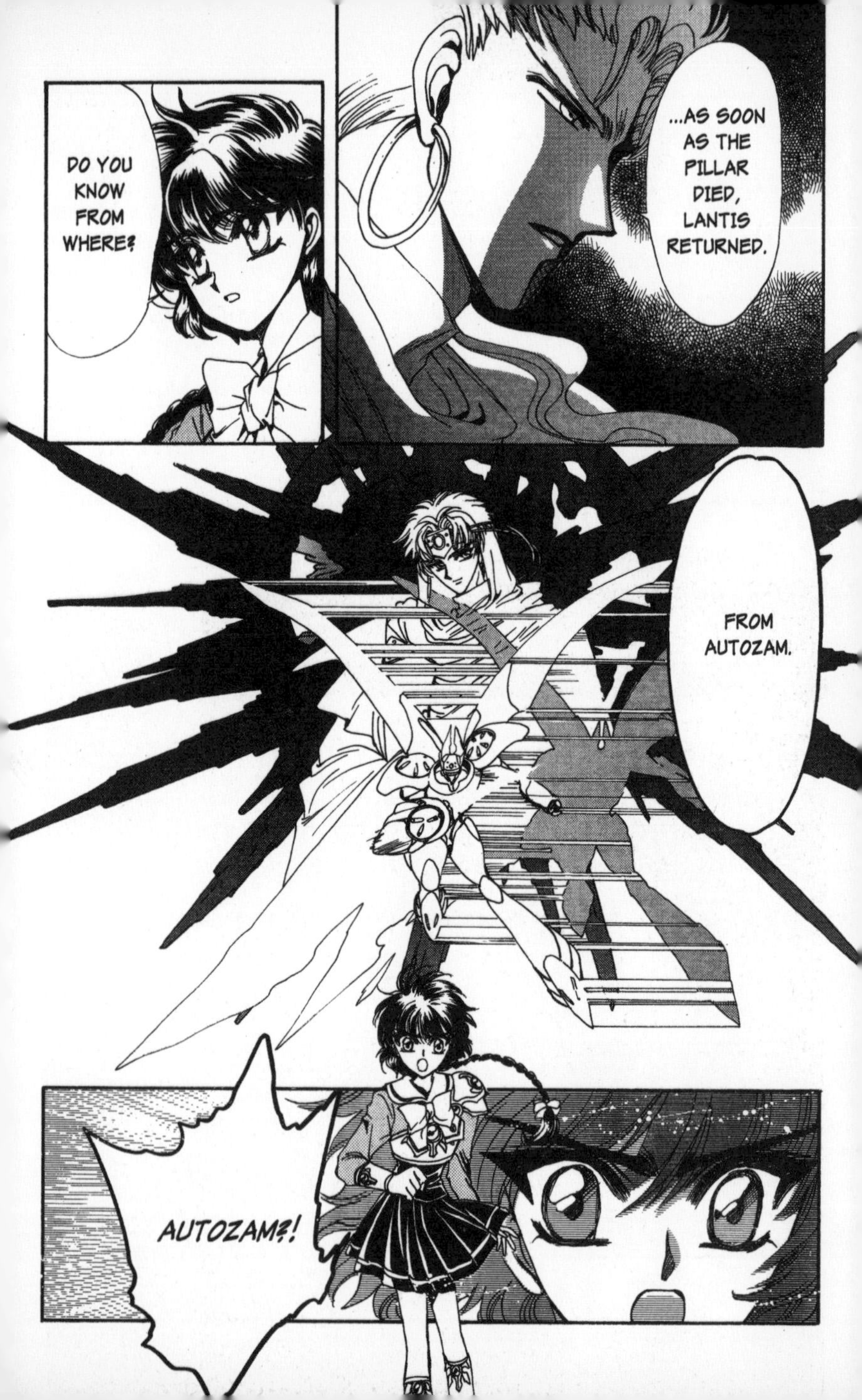
...AS SOON AS THE PILLAR DIED, LANTIS RETURNED.
DO YOU KNOW FROM WHERE?
FROM AUTOZAM.
AUTOZAM?!

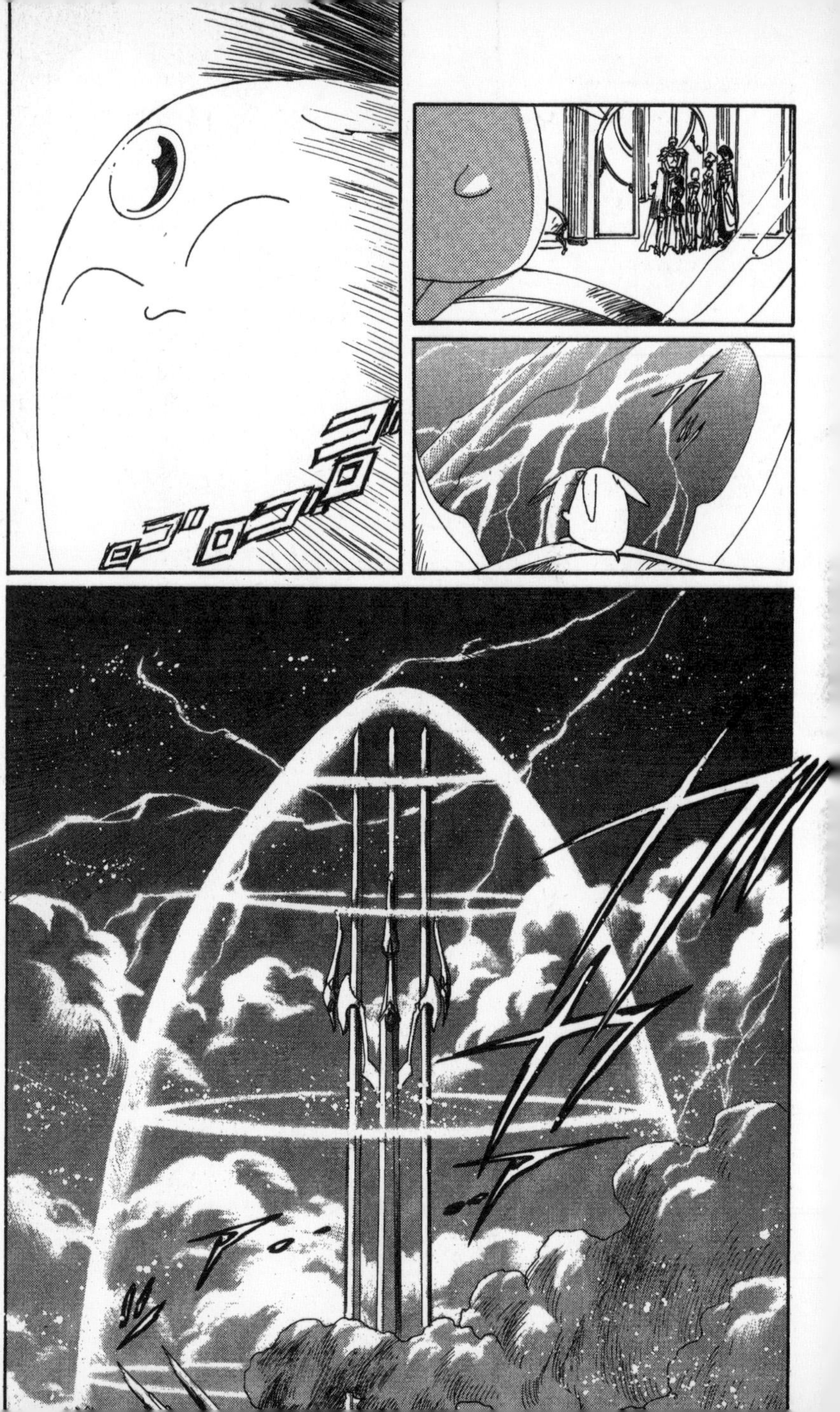
ゴロゴロゴロ

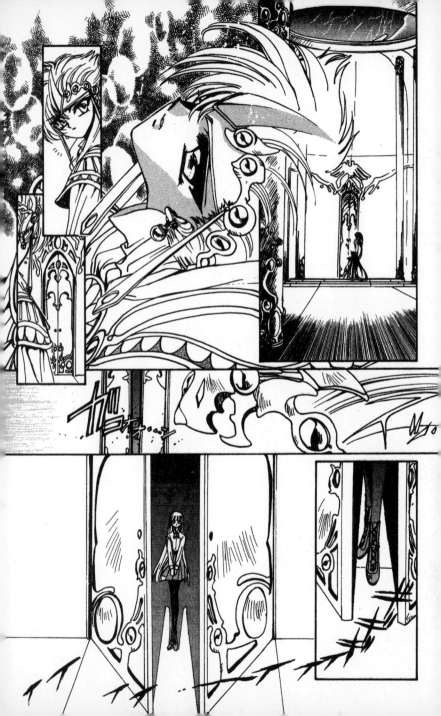

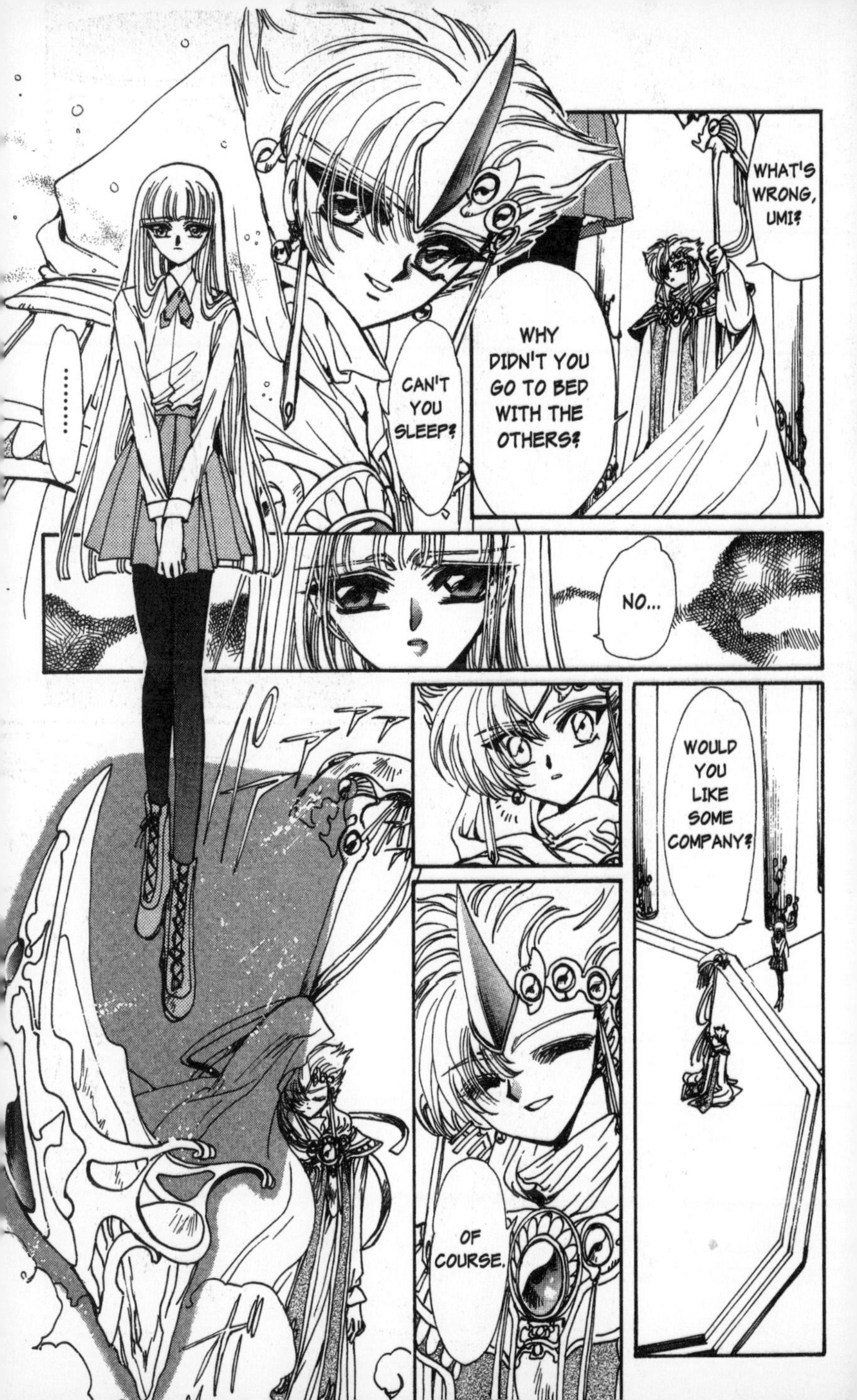
WHAT'S WRONG, UMI?
WHY DIDN'T YOU GO TO BED WITH THE OTHERS?
CAN'T YOU SLEEP?
....
NO...
WOULD YOU LIKE SOME COMPANY?
OF COURSE.

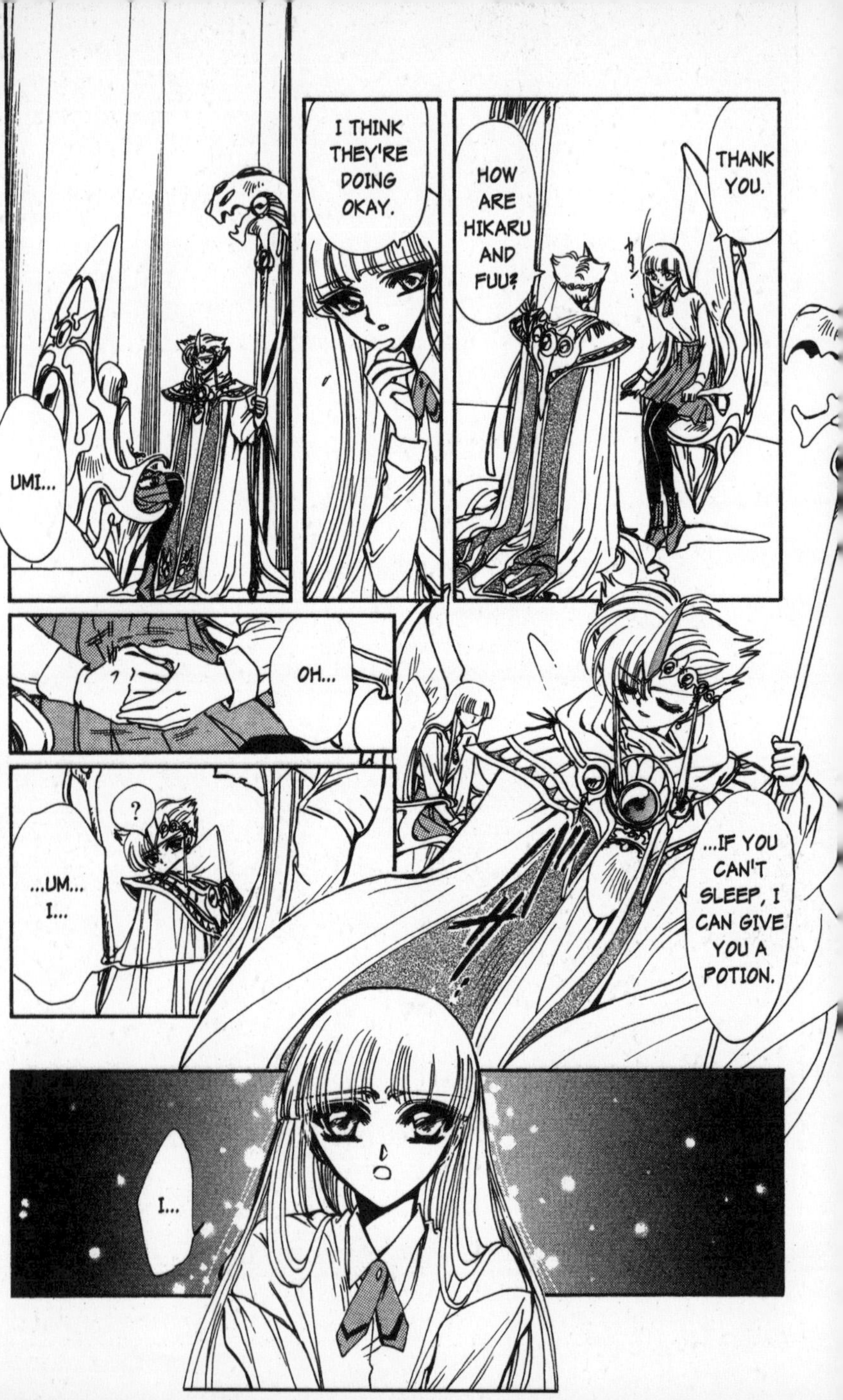
THANK YOU.
HOW ARE HIKARU AND FUU?
I THINK THEY'RE DOING OKAY.
UMI...
...IF YOU CAN'T SLEEP, I CAN GIVE YOU A POTION.
OH...
?
...UM... I...
I...

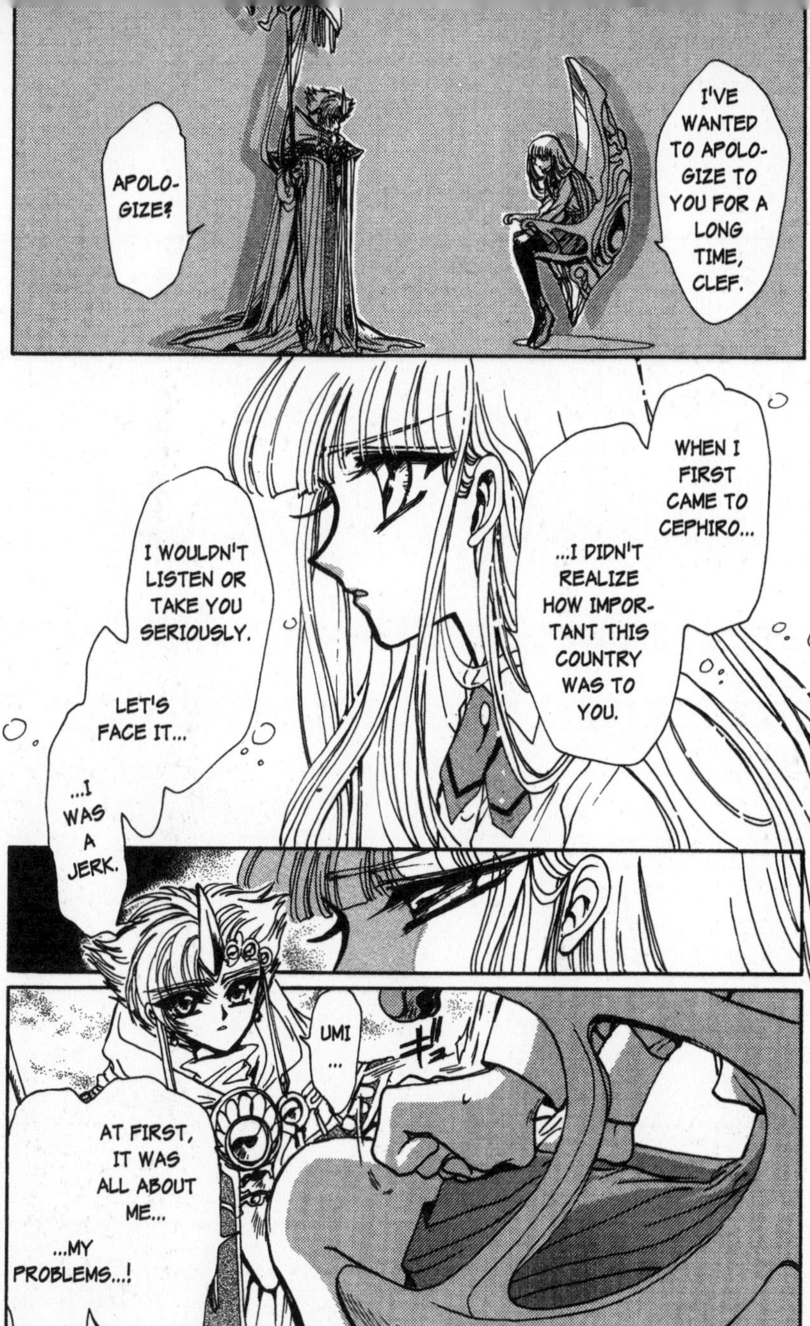
I'VE WANTED TO APOLOGIZE TO YOU FOR A LONG TIME, CLEF.
APOLOGIZE?
WHEN I FIRST CAME TO CEPHIRO...
...I DIDN'T REALIZE HOW IMPORTANT THIS COUNTRY WAS TO YOU.
I WOULDN'T LISTEN OR TAKE YOU SERIOUSLY.
LET'S FACE IT...
...I WAS A JERK.
ギュ
UMI ...
AT FIRST, IT WAS ALL ABOUT ME...
...MY PROBLEMS...!

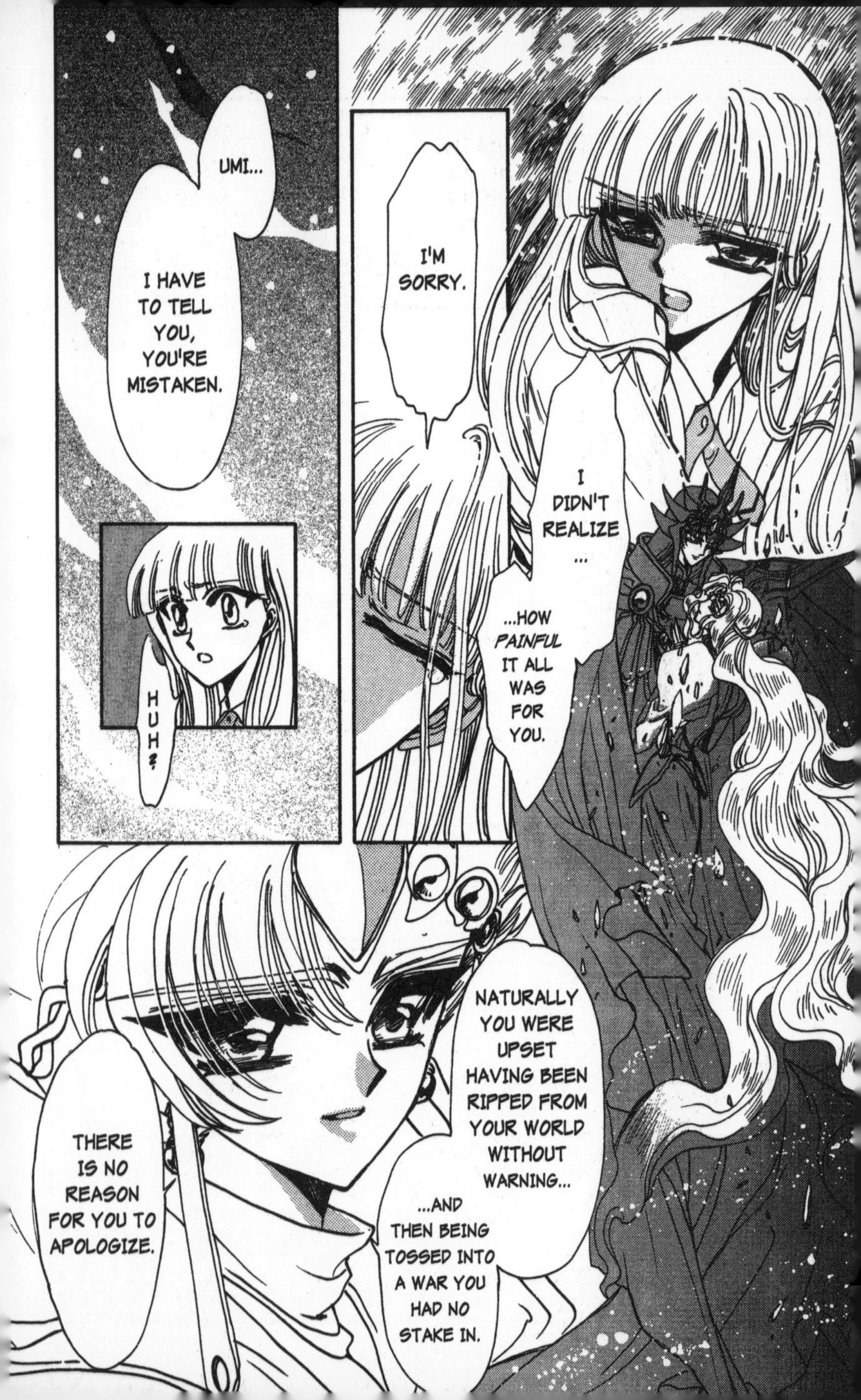

I'M SORRY.
I DIDN'T REALIZE ...
...HOW *PAINFUL* IT ALL WAS FOR YOU.
UMI...
I HAVE TO TELL YOU, YOU'RE MISTAKEN.
HUH?
NATURALLY YOU WERE UPSET HAVING BEEN RIPPED FROM YOUR WORLD WITHOUT WARNING...
...AND THEN BEING TOSSED INTO A WAR YOU HAD NO STAKE IN.
THERE IS NO REASON FOR YOU TO APOLOGIZE.

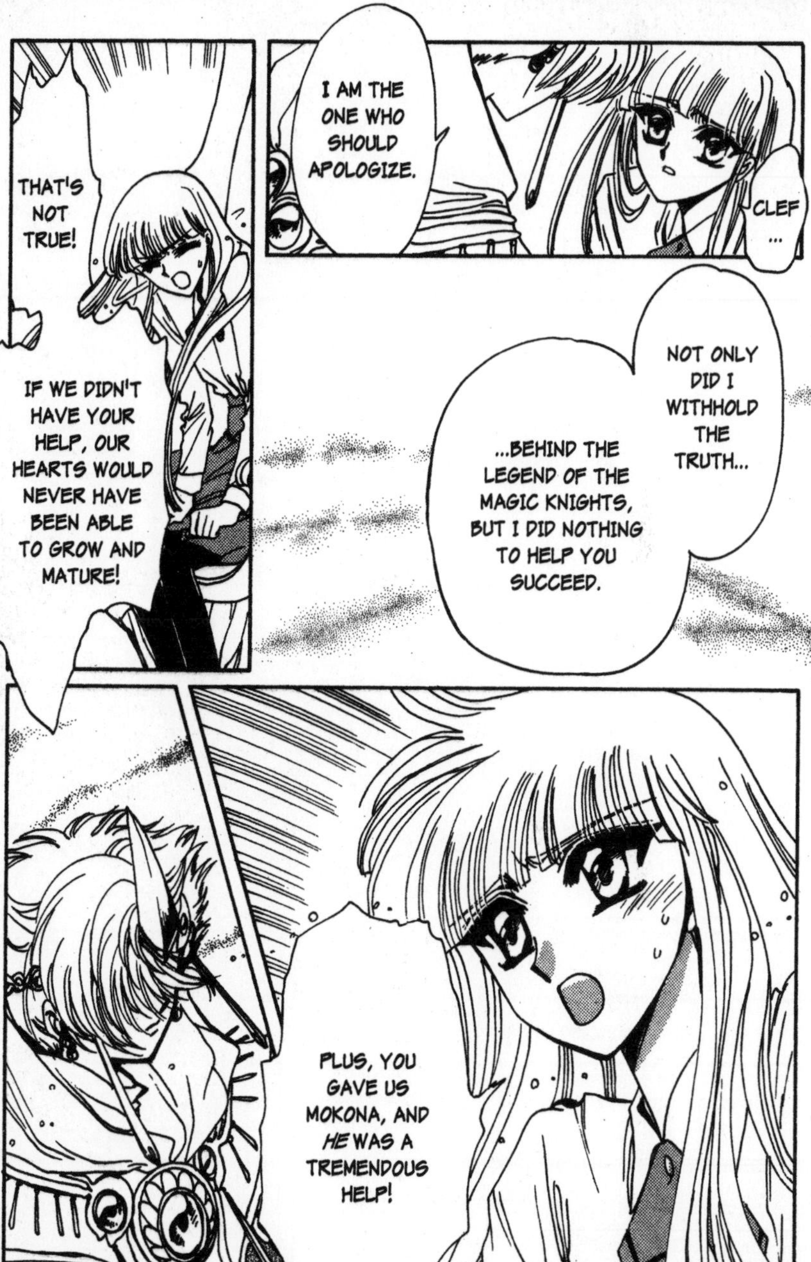
CLEF ...
I AM THE ONE WHO SHOULD APOLOGIZE.
NOT ONLY DID I WITHHOLD THE TRUTH...
...BEHIND THE LEGEND OF THE MAGIC KNIGHTS, BUT I DID NOTHING TO HELP YOU SUCCEED.
THAT'S NOT TRUE!
IF WE DIDN'T HAVE YOUR HELP, OUR HEARTS WOULD NEVER HAVE BEEN ABLE TO GROW AND MATURE!
PLUS, YOU GAVE US MOKONA, AND *HE* WAS A TREMENDOUS HELP!

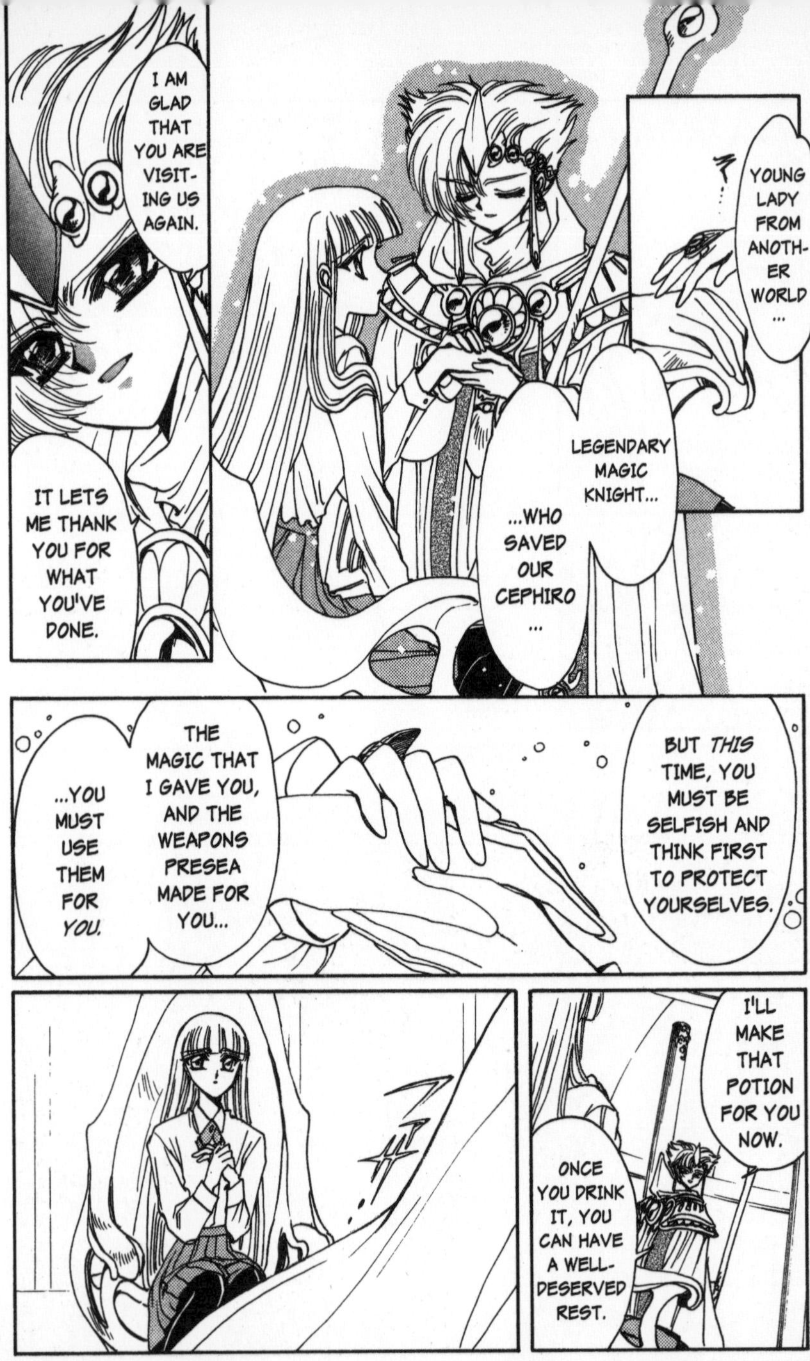
YOUNG LADY FROM ANOTHER WORLD...
LEGENDARY MAGIC KNIGHT...
...WHO SAVED OUR CEPHIRO...
I AM GLAD THAT YOU ARE VISITING US AGAIN.
IT LETS ME THANK YOU FOR WHAT YOU'VE DONE.
BUT *THIS* TIME, YOU MUST BE SELFISH AND THINK FIRST TO PROTECT YOURSELVES.
THE MAGIC THAT I GAVE YOU, AND THE WEAPONS PRESEA MADE FOR YOU...
...YOU MUST USE THEM FOR *YOU.*
I'LL MAKE THAT POTION FOR YOU NOW.
ONCE YOU DRINK IT, YOU CAN HAVE A WELL-DESERVED REST.

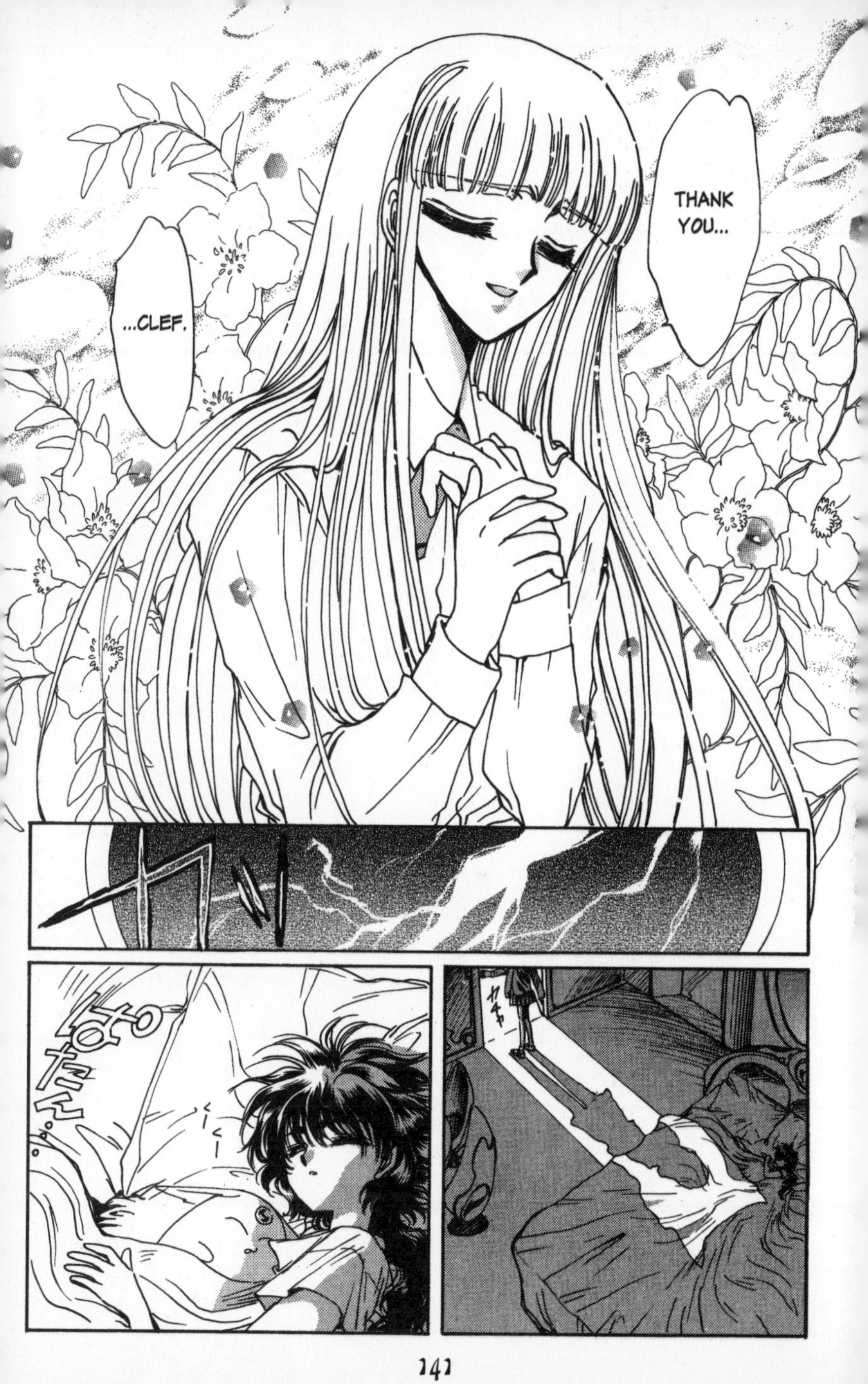
THANK YOU...
...CLEF.

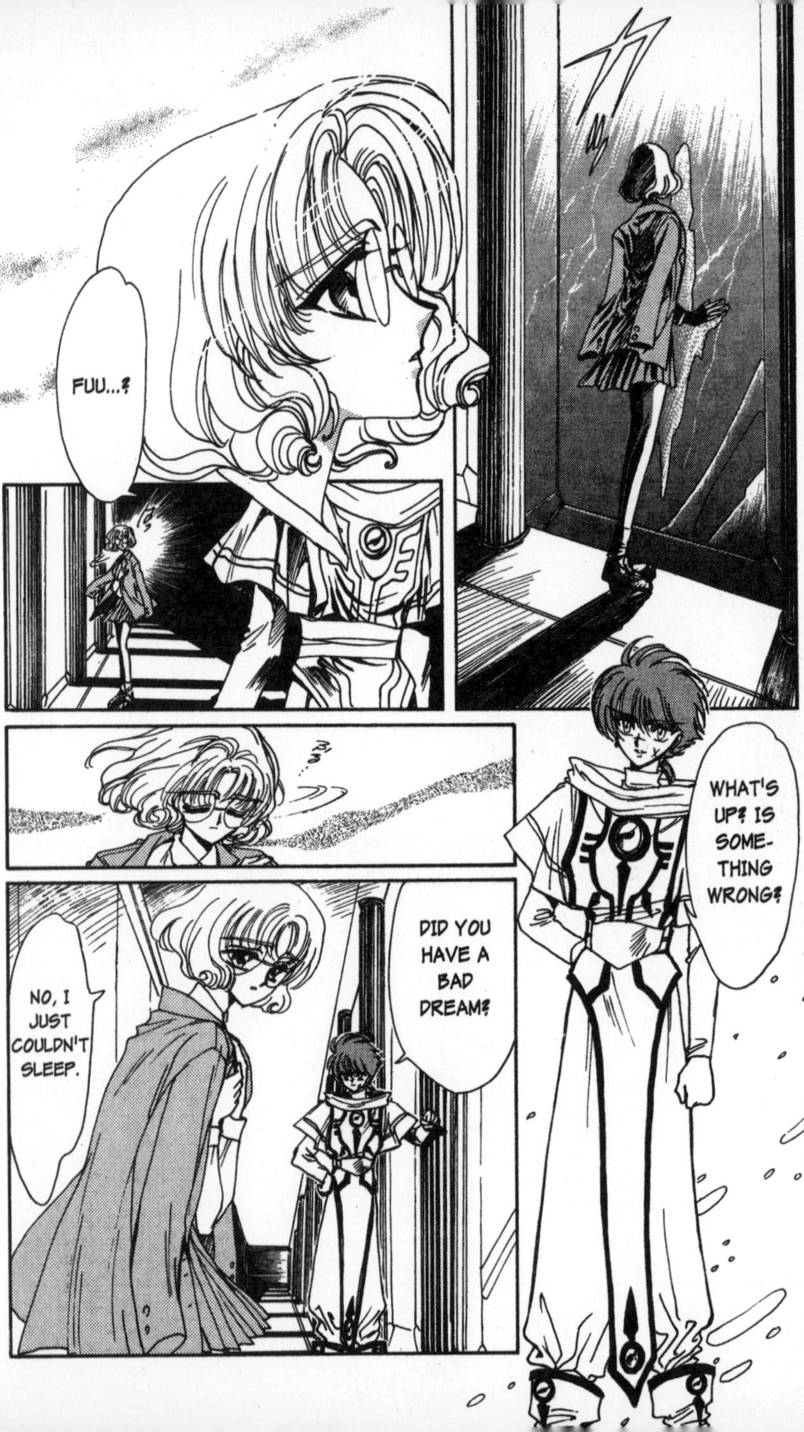
FUU...?
WHAT'S UP? IS SOMETHING WRONG?
DID YOU HAVE A BAD DREAM?
NO, I JUST COULDN'T SLEEP.

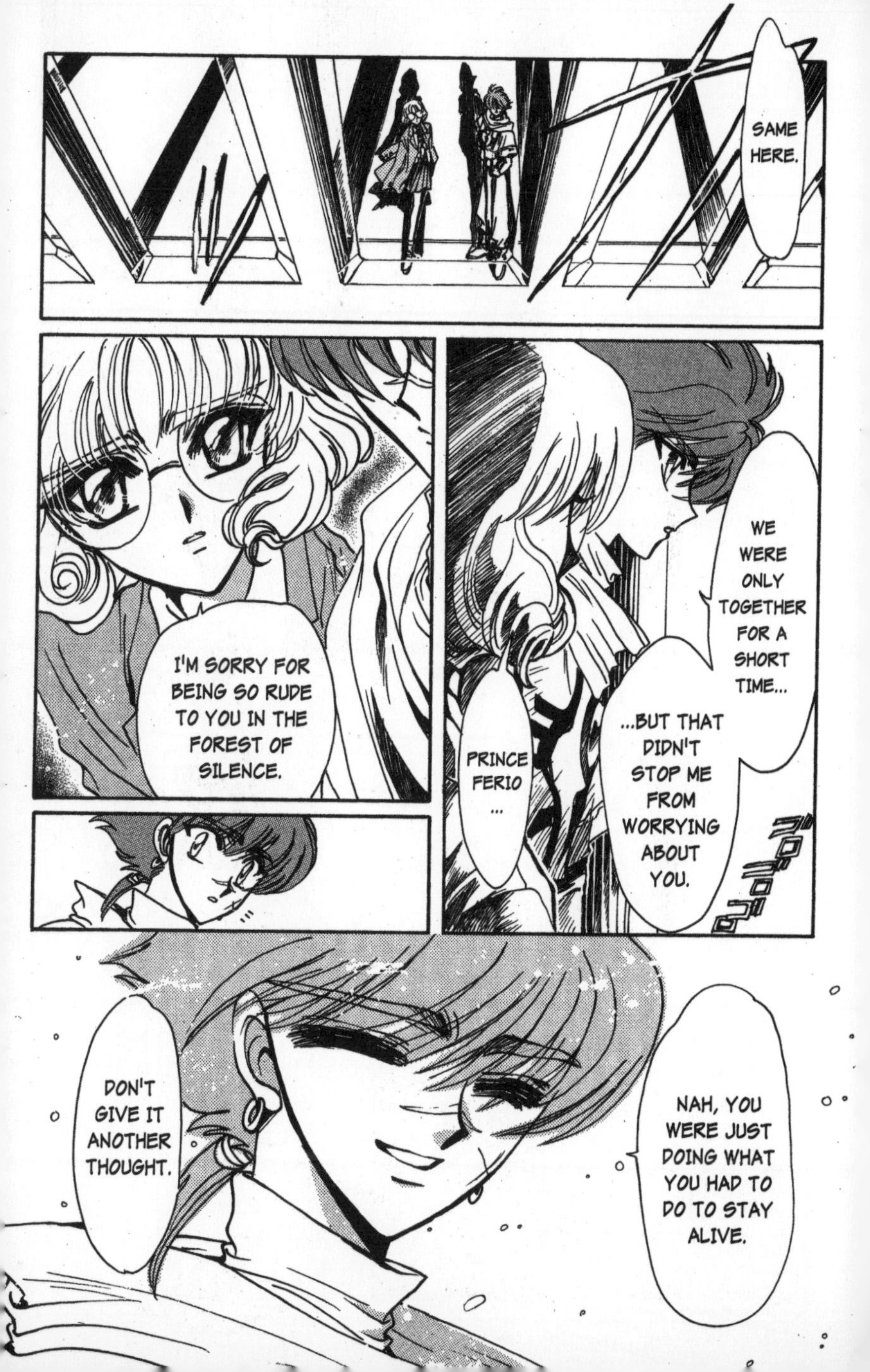
SAME HERE.
WE WERE ONLY TOGETHER FOR A SHORT TIME...
...BUT THAT DIDN'T STOP ME FROM WORRYING ABOUT YOU.
PRINCE FERIO ...
I'M SORRY FOR BEING SO RUDE TO YOU IN THE FOREST OF SILENCE.
NAH, YOU WERE JUST DOING WHAT YOU HAD TO DO TO STAY ALIVE.
DON'T GIVE IT ANOTHER THOUGHT.

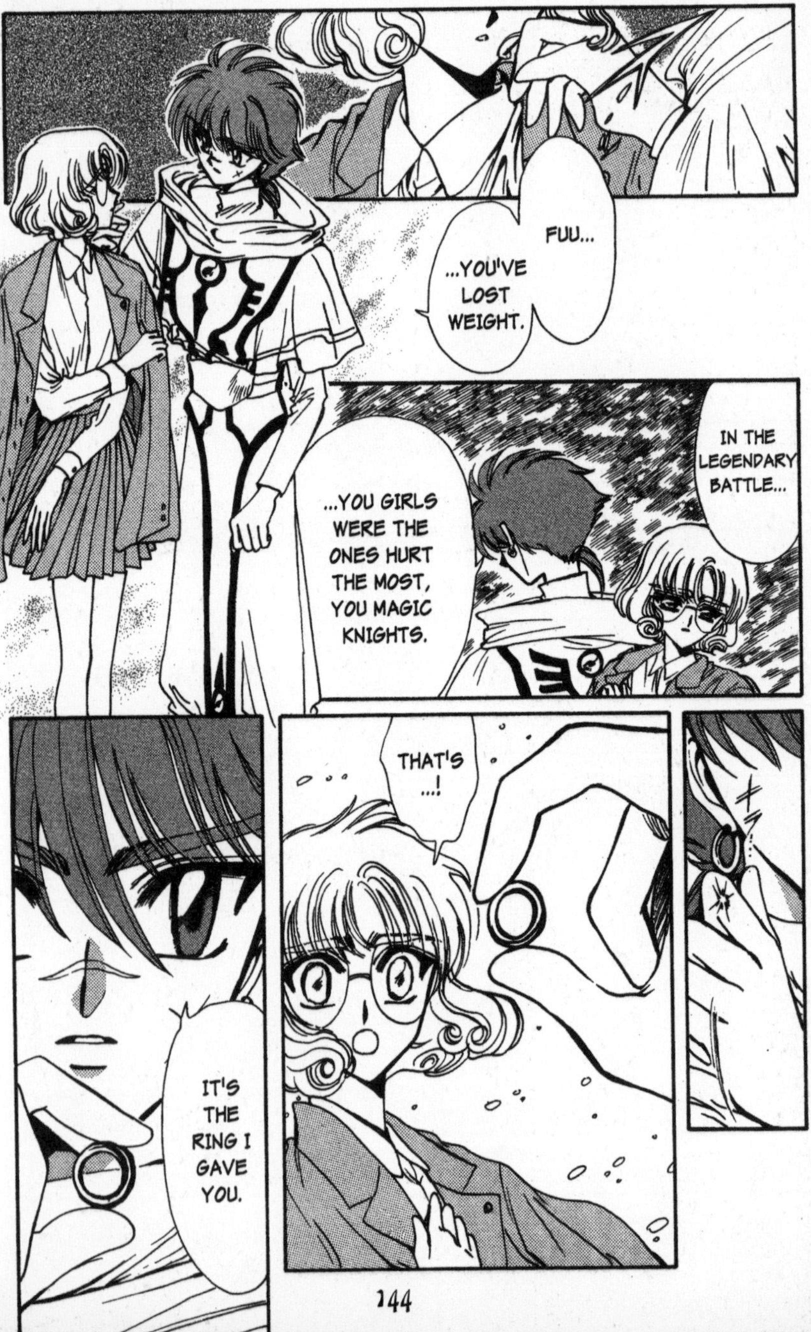
FUU... ...YOU'VE LOST WEIGHT.
IN THE LEGENDARY BATTLE...
...YOU GIRLS WERE THE ONES HURT THE MOST, YOU MAGIC KNIGHTS.
THAT'S ...!
IT'S THE RING I GAVE YOU.

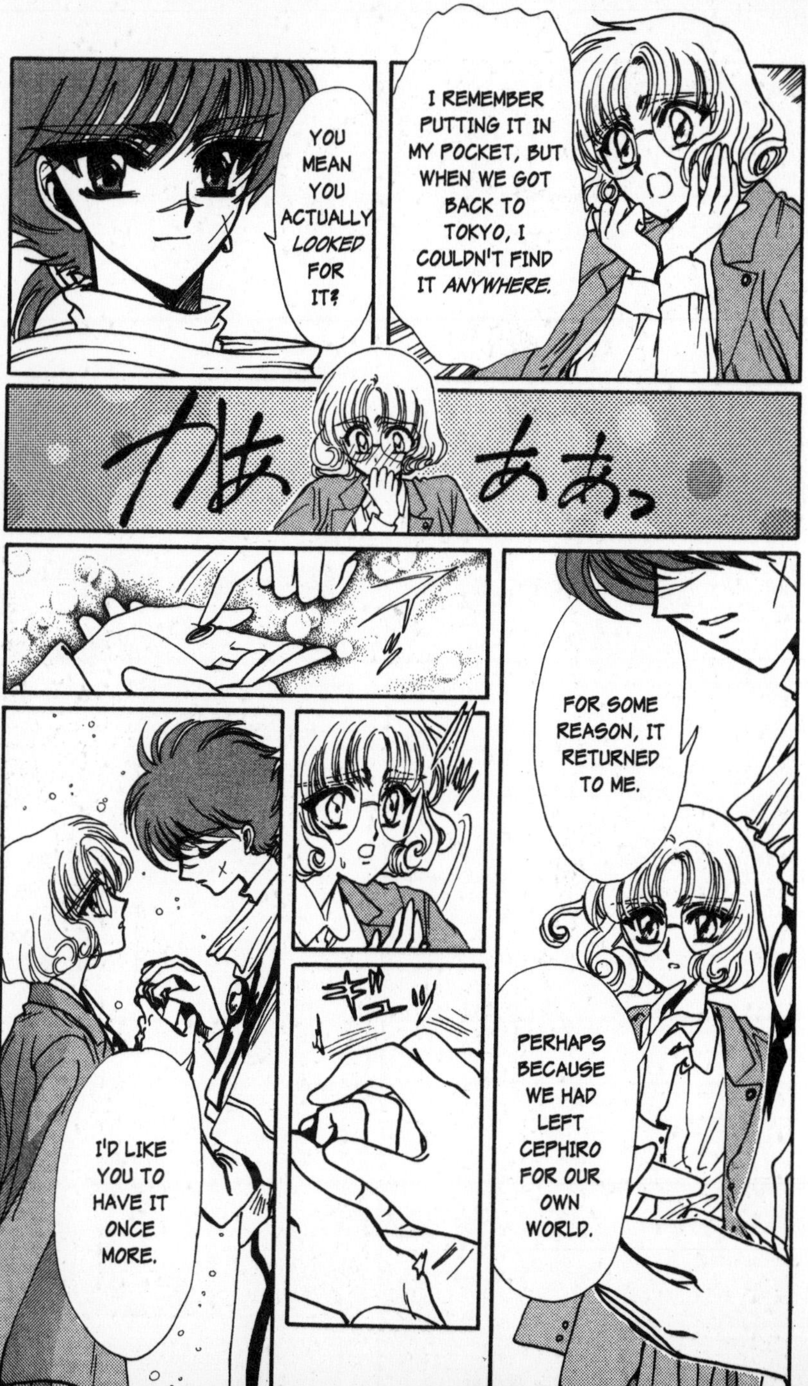
I REMEMBER PUTTING IT IN MY POCKET, BUT WHEN WE GOT BACK TO TOKYO, I COULDN'T FIND IT ANYWHERE.
YOU MEAN YOU ACTUALLY LOOKED FOR IT?
FOR SOME REASON, IT RETURNED TO ME.
PERHAPS BECAUSE WE HAD LEFT CEPHIRO FOR OUR OWN WORLD.
I'D LIKE YOU TO HAVE IT ONCE MORE.

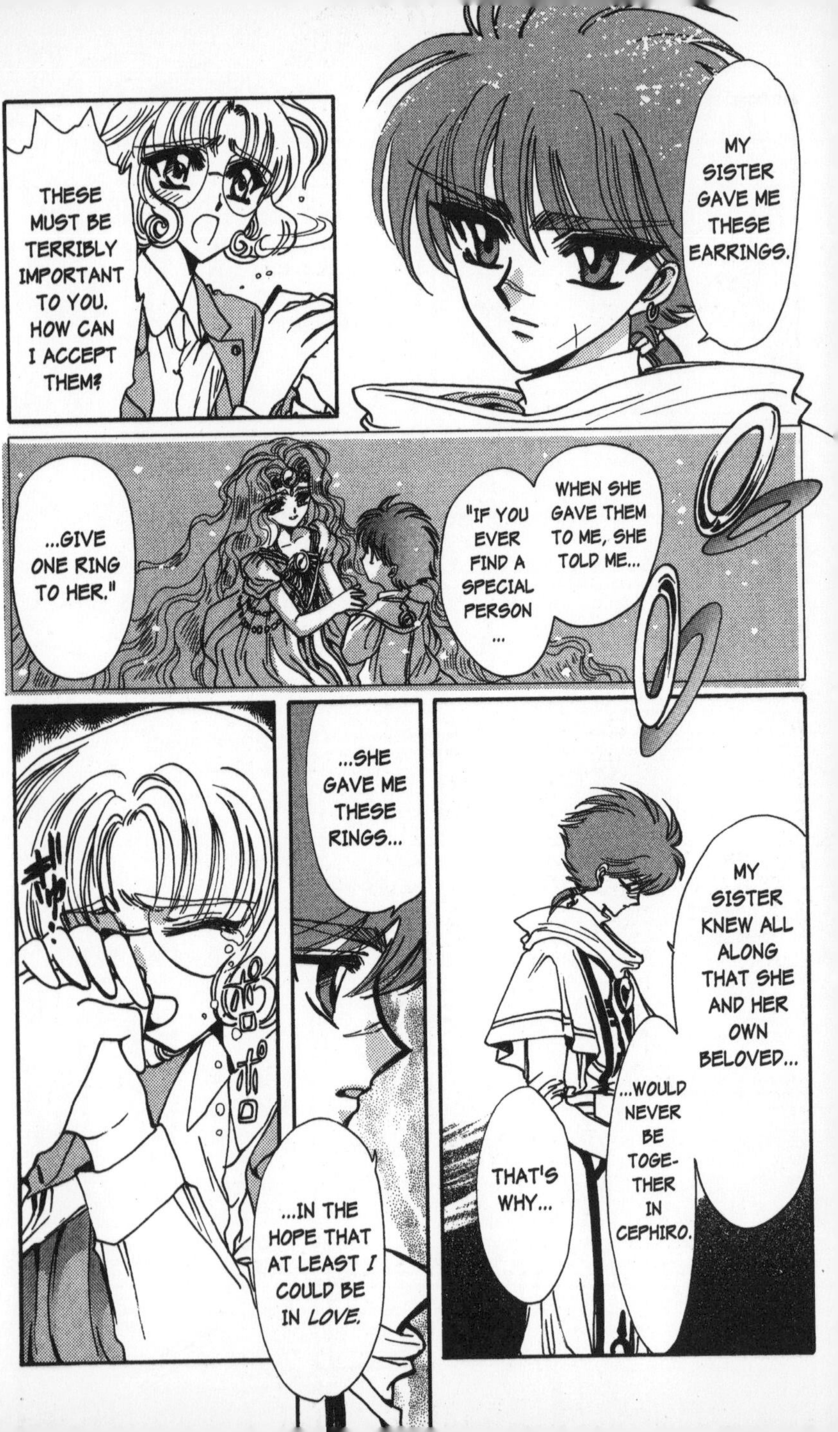
MY SISTER GAVE ME THESE EARRINGS.
THESE MUST BE TERRIBLY IMPORTANT TO YOU. HOW CAN I ACCEPT THEM?
WHEN SHE GAVE THEM TO ME, SHE TOLD ME...
"IF YOU EVER FIND A SPECIAL PERSON ...
...GIVE ONE RING TO HER."
MY SISTER KNEW ALL ALONG THAT SHE AND HER OWN BELOVED...
...WOULD NEVER BE TOGE-THER IN CEPHIRO.
THAT'S WHY...
...SHE GAVE ME THESE RINGS...
...IN THE HOPE THAT AT LEAST *I* COULD BE IN *LOVE.*

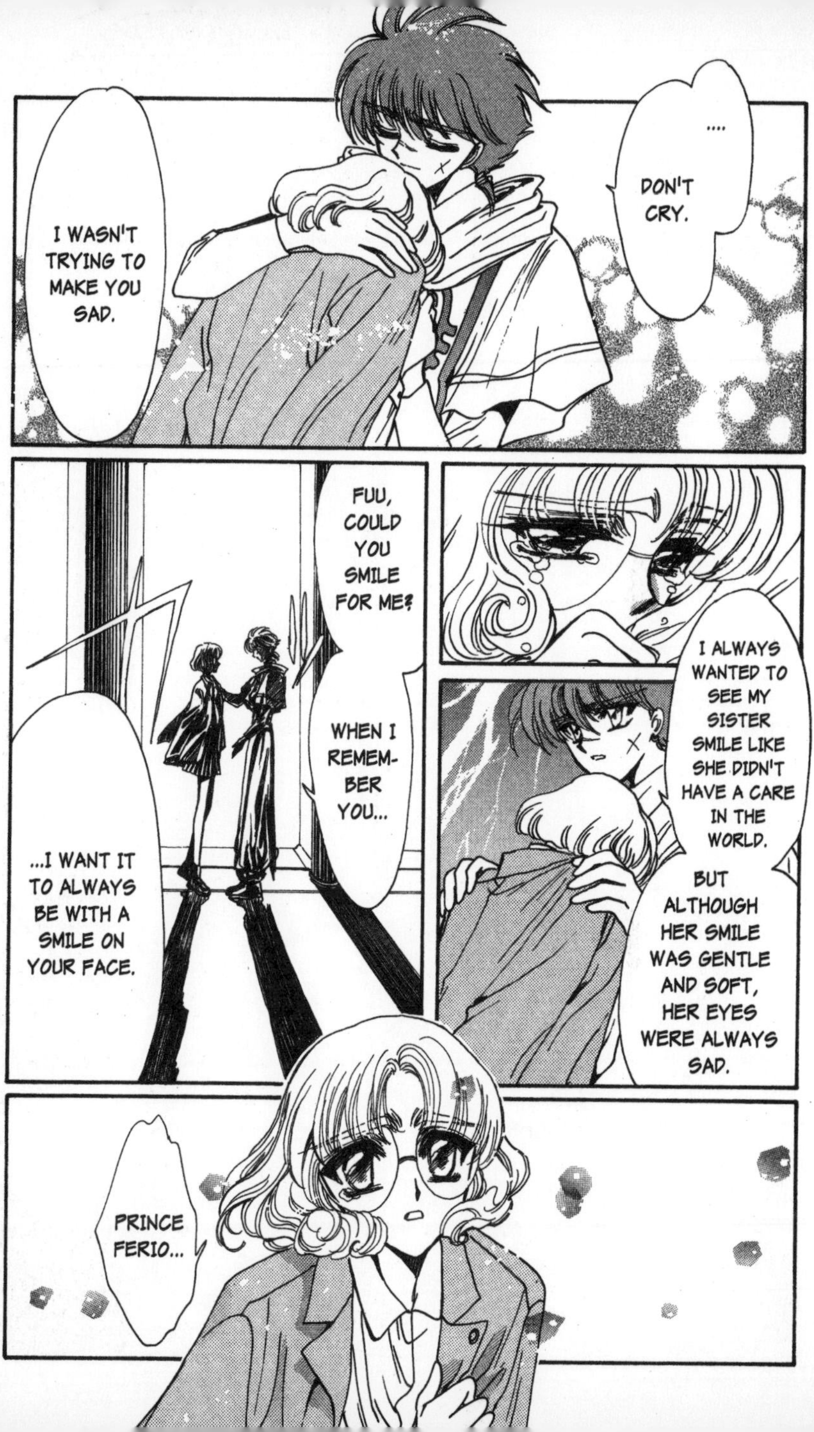
....
DON'T CRY.
I WASN'T TRYING TO MAKE YOU SAD.
I ALWAYS WANTED TO SEE MY SISTER SMILE LIKE SHE DIDN'T HAVE A CARE IN THE WORLD.
BUT ALTHOUGH HER SMILE WAS GENTLE AND SOFT, HER EYES WERE ALWAYS SAD.
FUU, COULD YOU SMILE FOR ME?
WHEN I REMEM-BER YOU...
...I WANT IT TO ALWAYS BE WITH A SMILE ON YOUR FACE.
PRINCE FERIO...

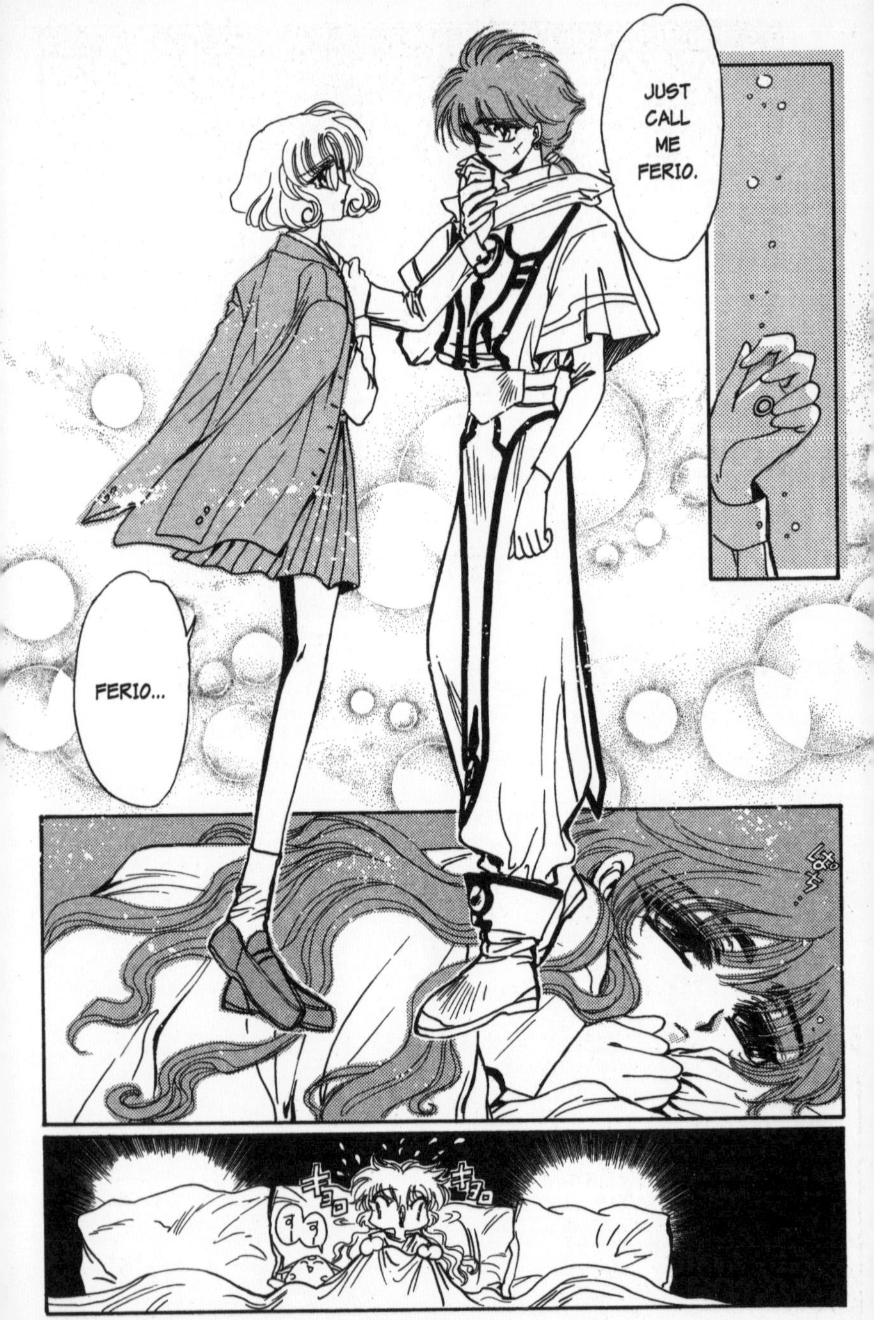
JUST CALL ME FERIO.
FERIO...

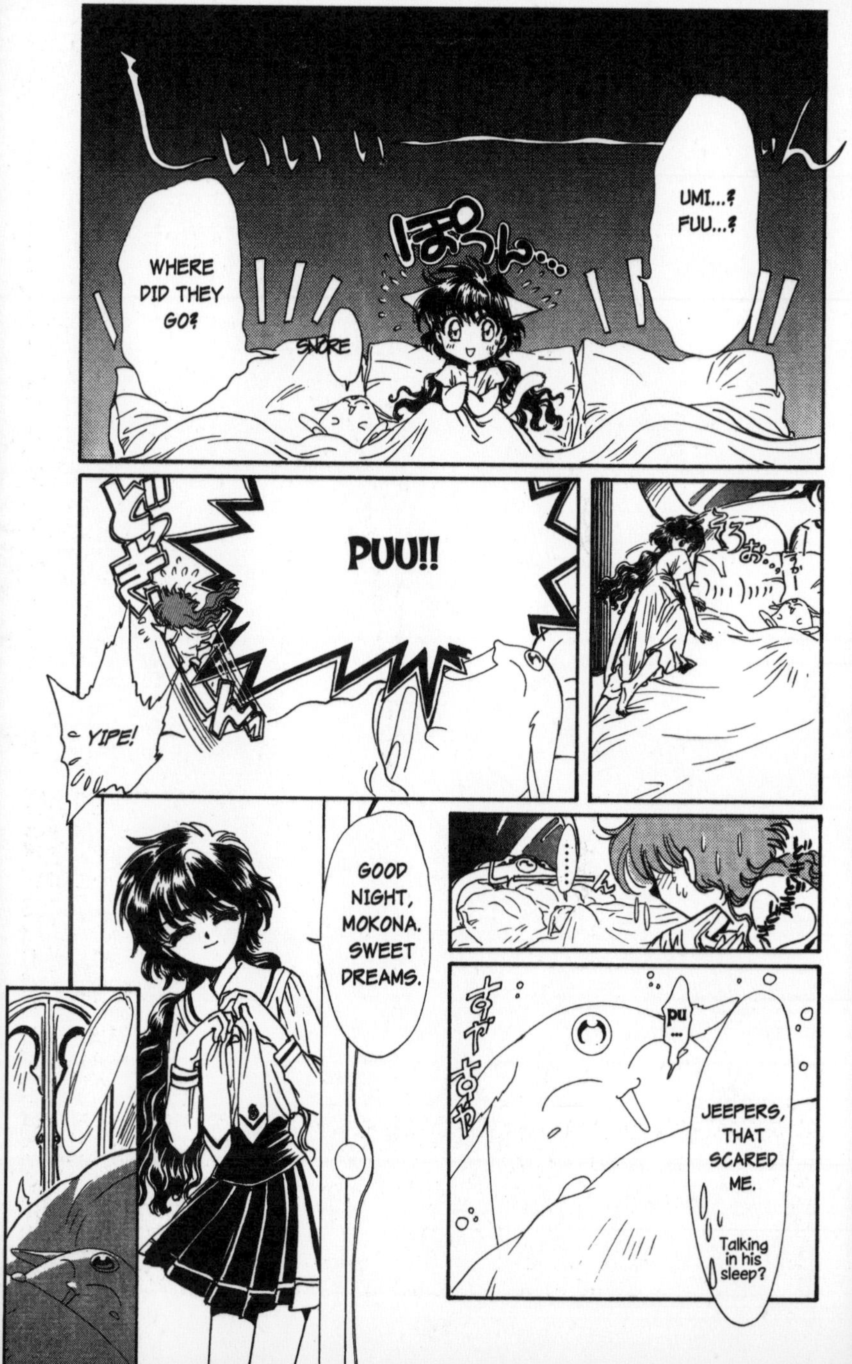

UMI...?
FUU...?
WHERE DID THEY GO?
SNORE
PUU!!
YIPE!
GOOD NIGHT, MOKONA. SWEET DREAMS.
pu...
JEEPERS, THAT SCARED ME.
Talking in his sleep?

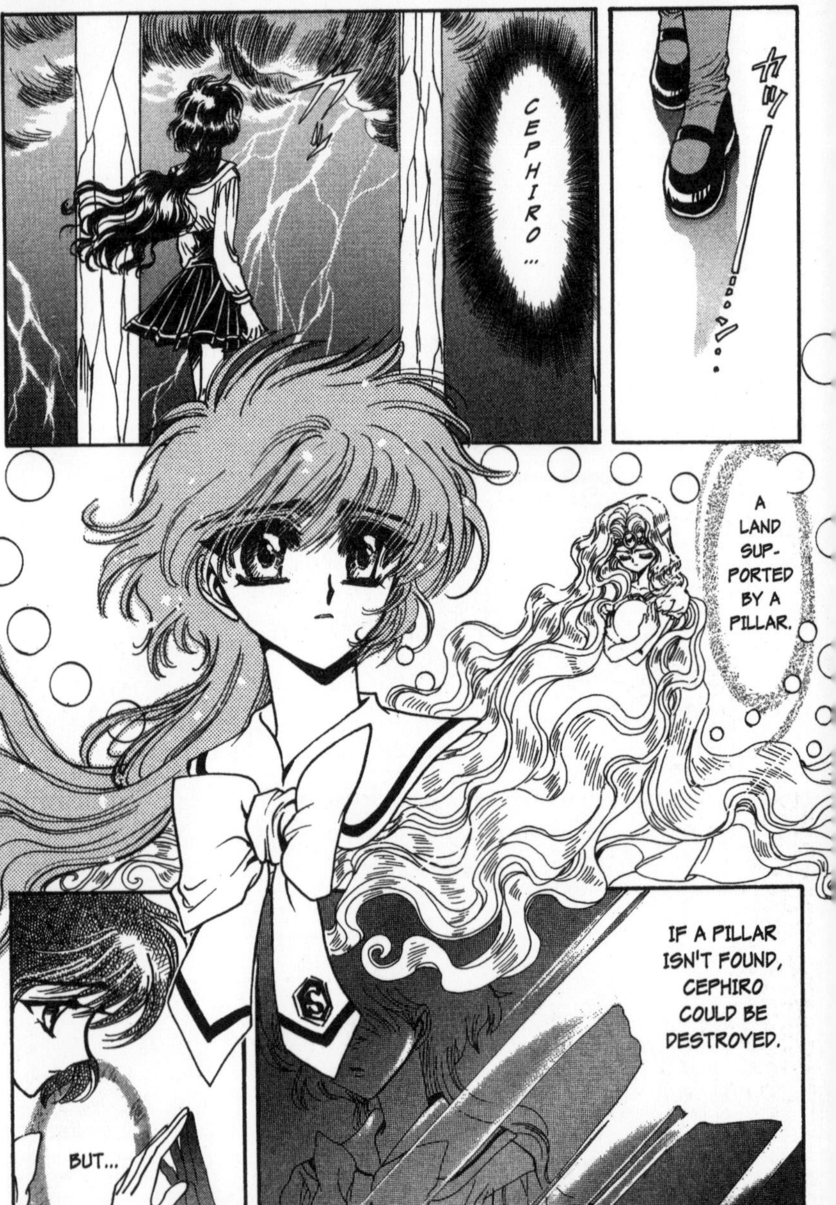
カッ
CEPHIRO...
A LAND SUP-PORTED BY A PILLAR.
IF A PILLAR ISN'T FOUND, CEPHIRO COULD BE DESTROYED.
BUT...

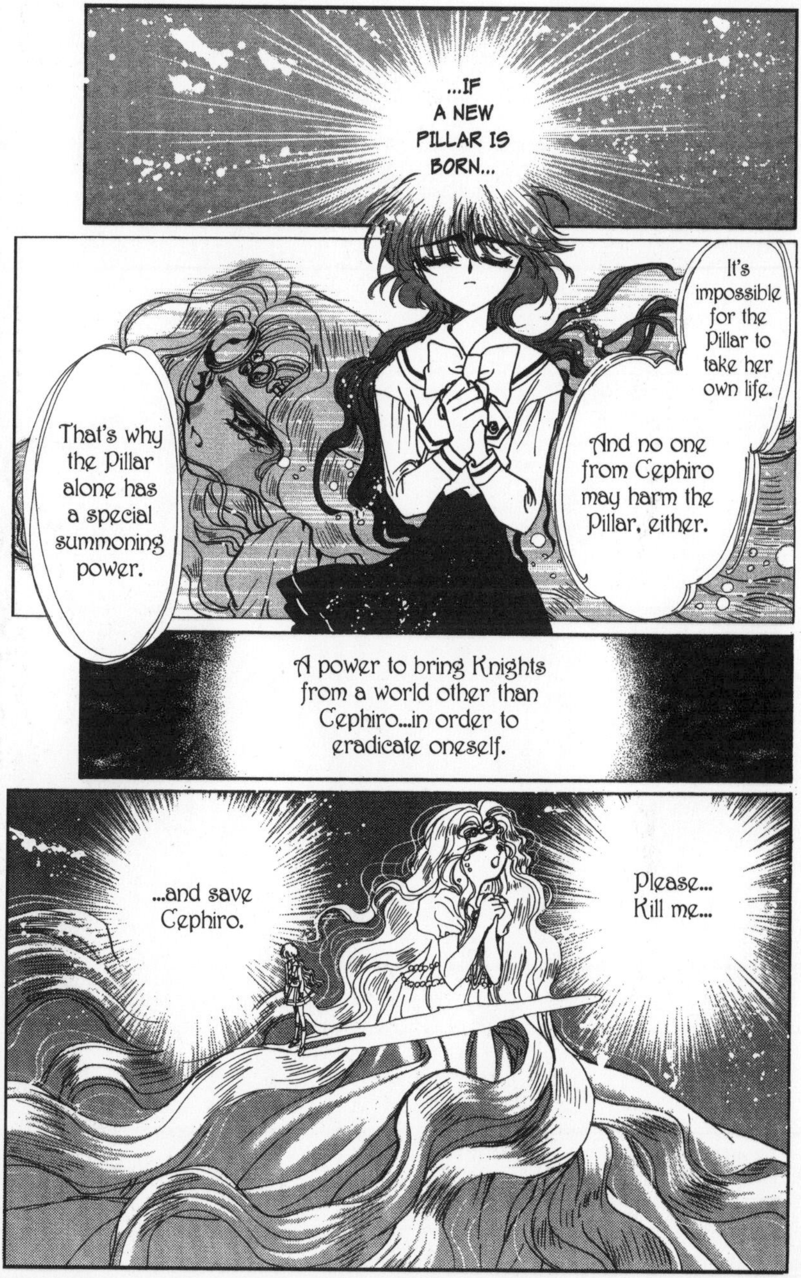
...IF A NEW PILLAR IS BORN...
It's impossible for the Pillar to take her own life.
And no one from Cephiro may harm the Pillar, either.
That's why the Pillar alone has a special summoning power.
A power to bring Knights from a world other than Cephiro...in order to eradicate oneself.
Please... Kill me...
...and save Cephiro.

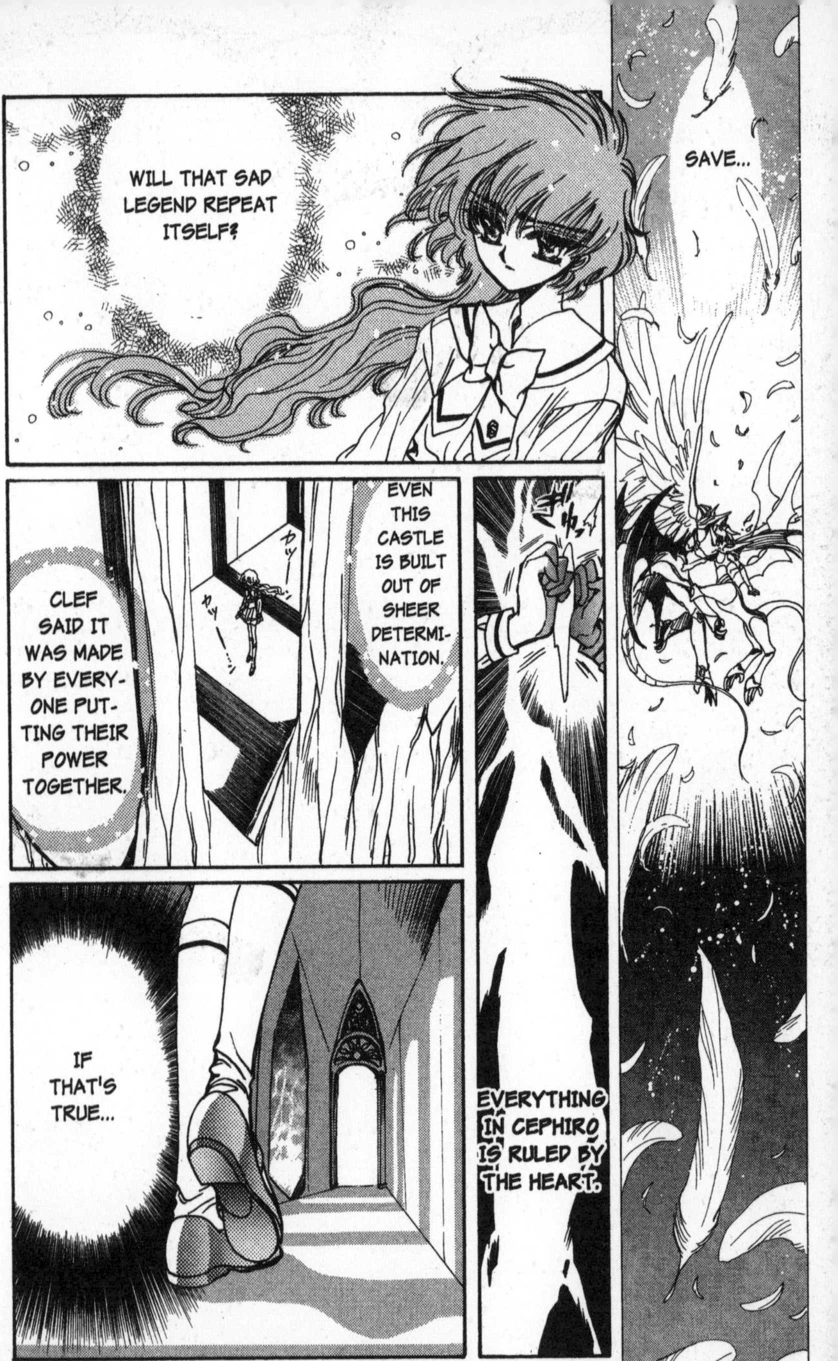
SAVE...
WILL THAT SAD LEGEND REPEAT ITSELF?
EVERYTHING IN CEPHIRO IS RULED BY THE HEART.
EVEN THIS CASTLE IS BUILT OUT OF SHEER DETERMINATION.
CLEF SAID IT WAS MADE BY EVERYONE PUTTING THEIR POWER TOGETHER.
IF THAT'S TRUE...

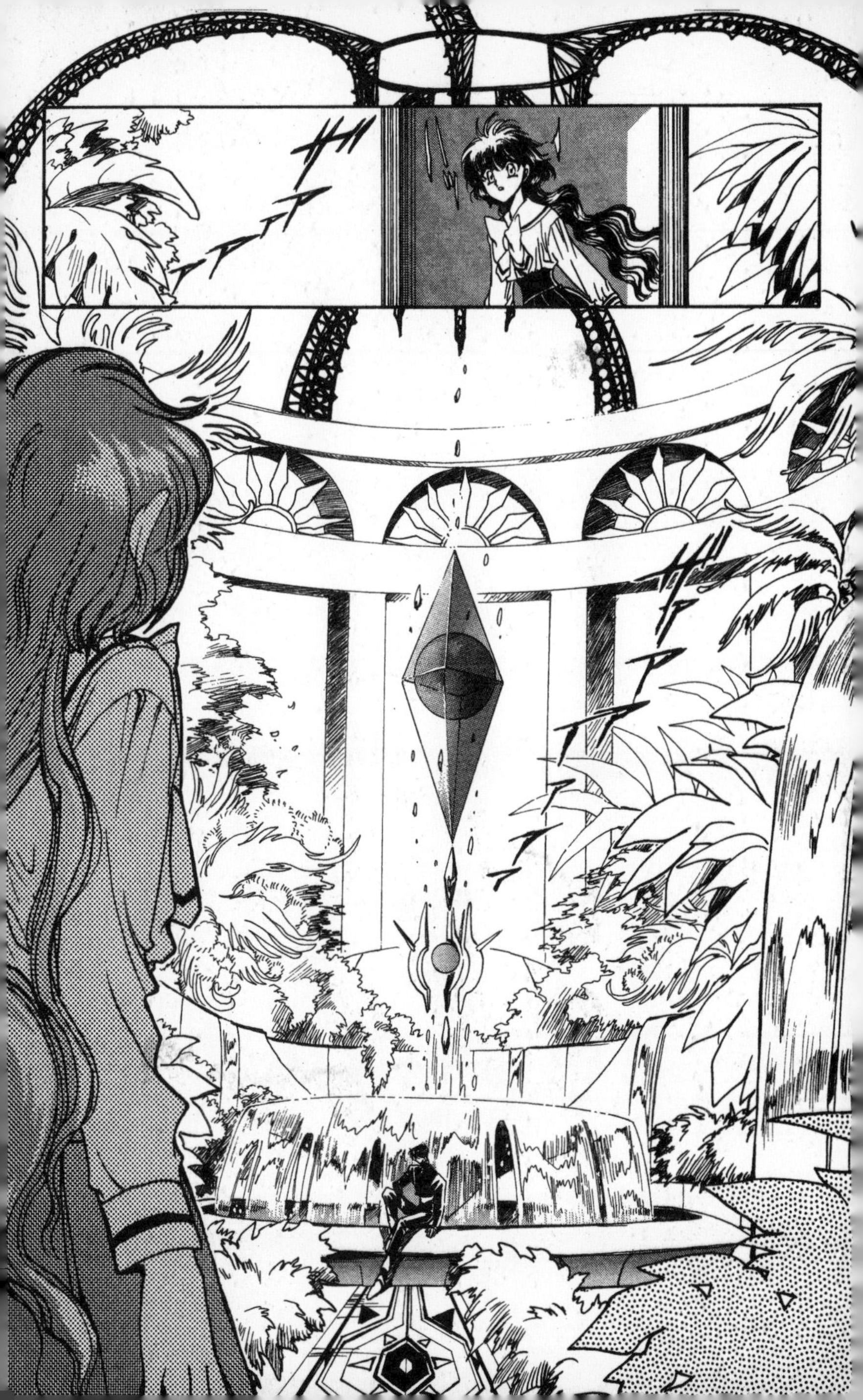

ザアアアア
ザアアアア

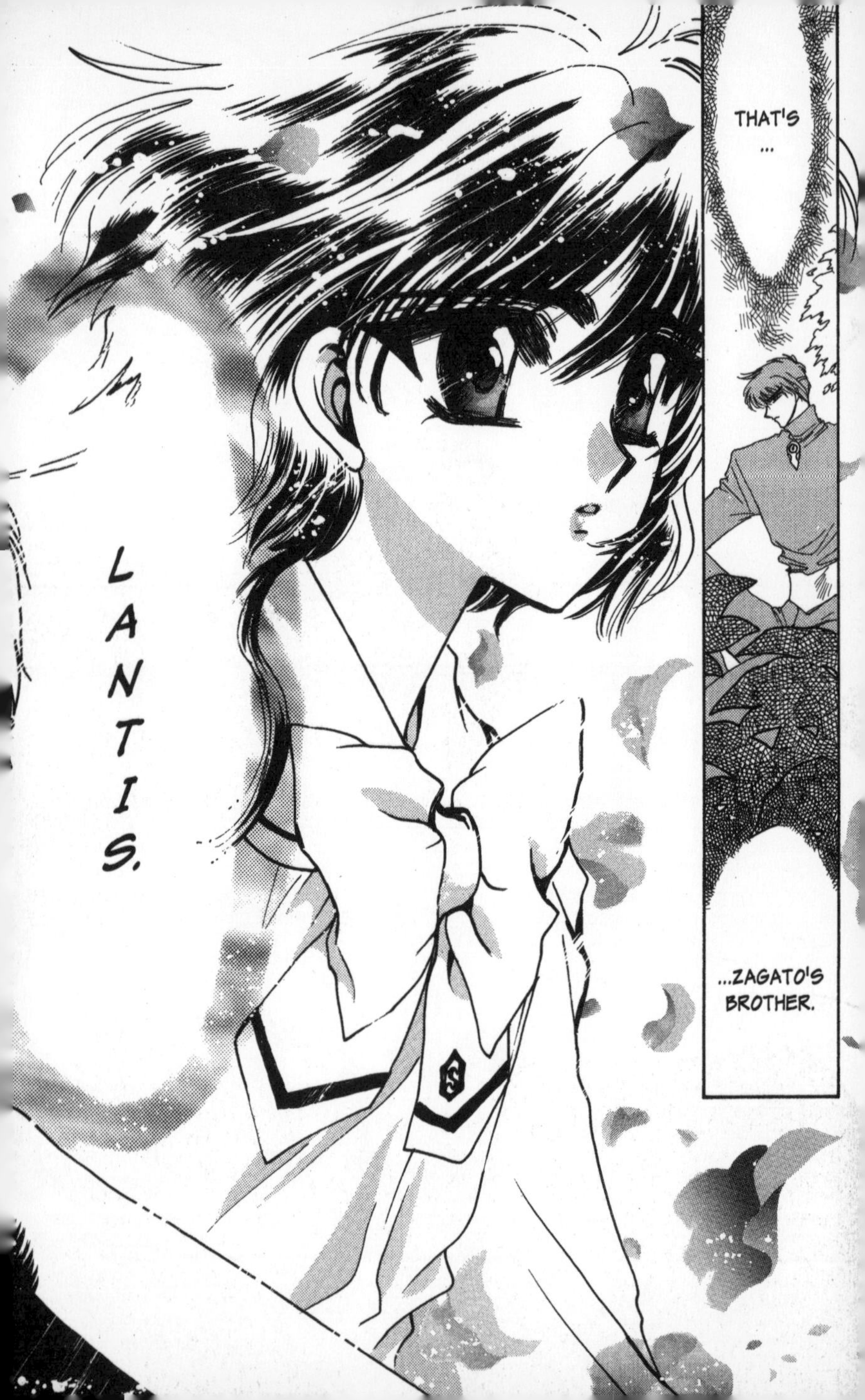
THAT'S ...
...ZAGATO'S BROTHER.
LANTIS.

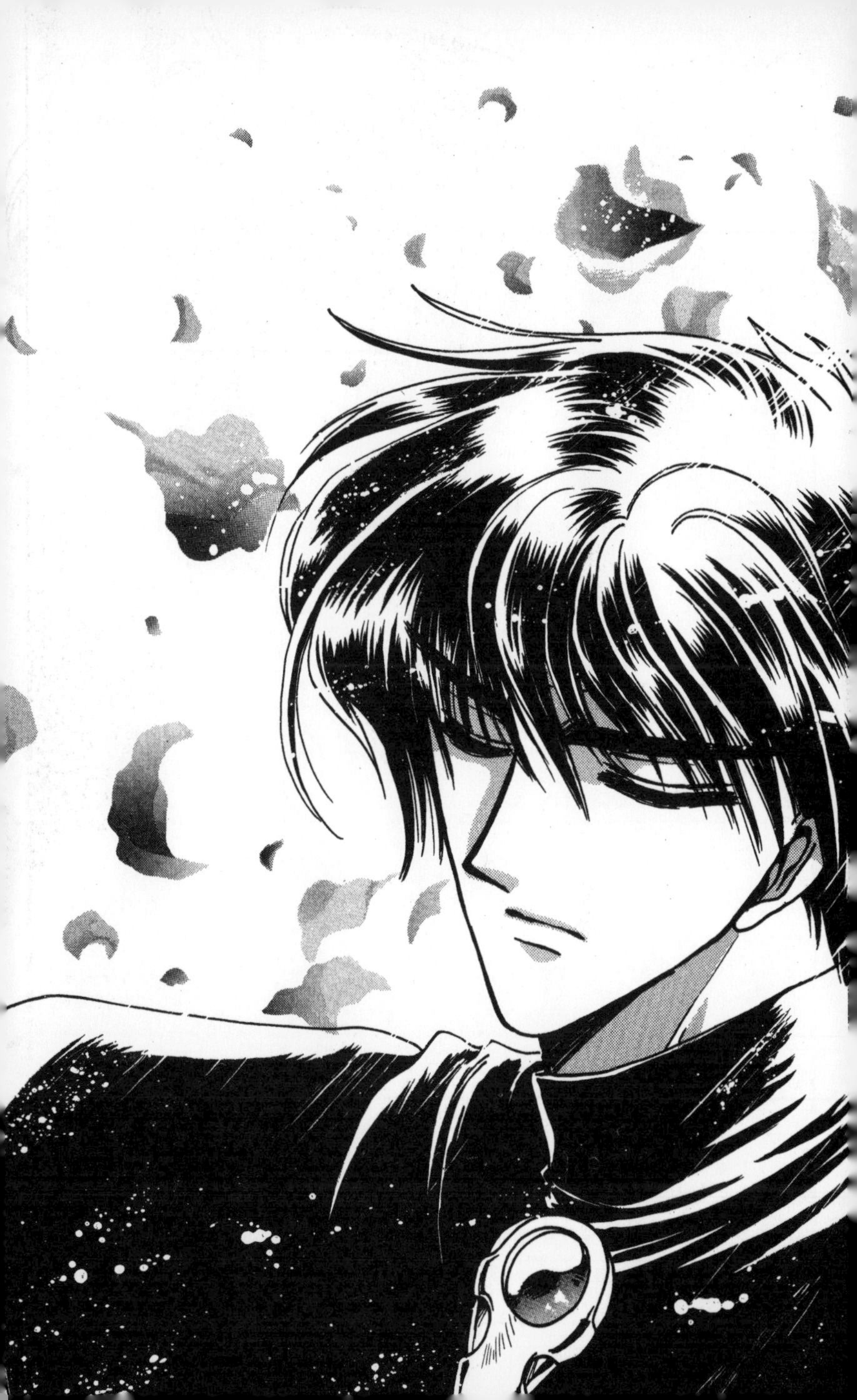

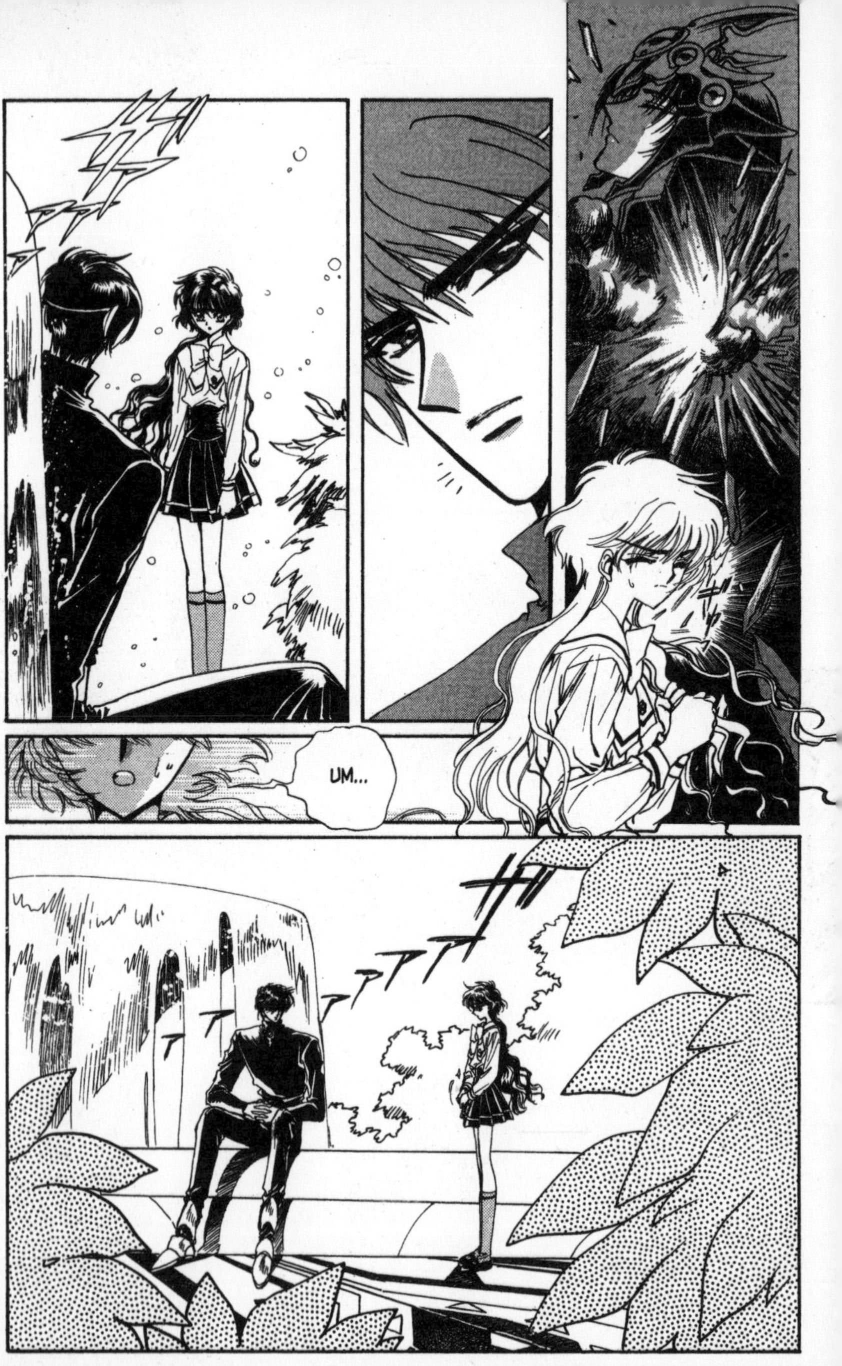
UM...

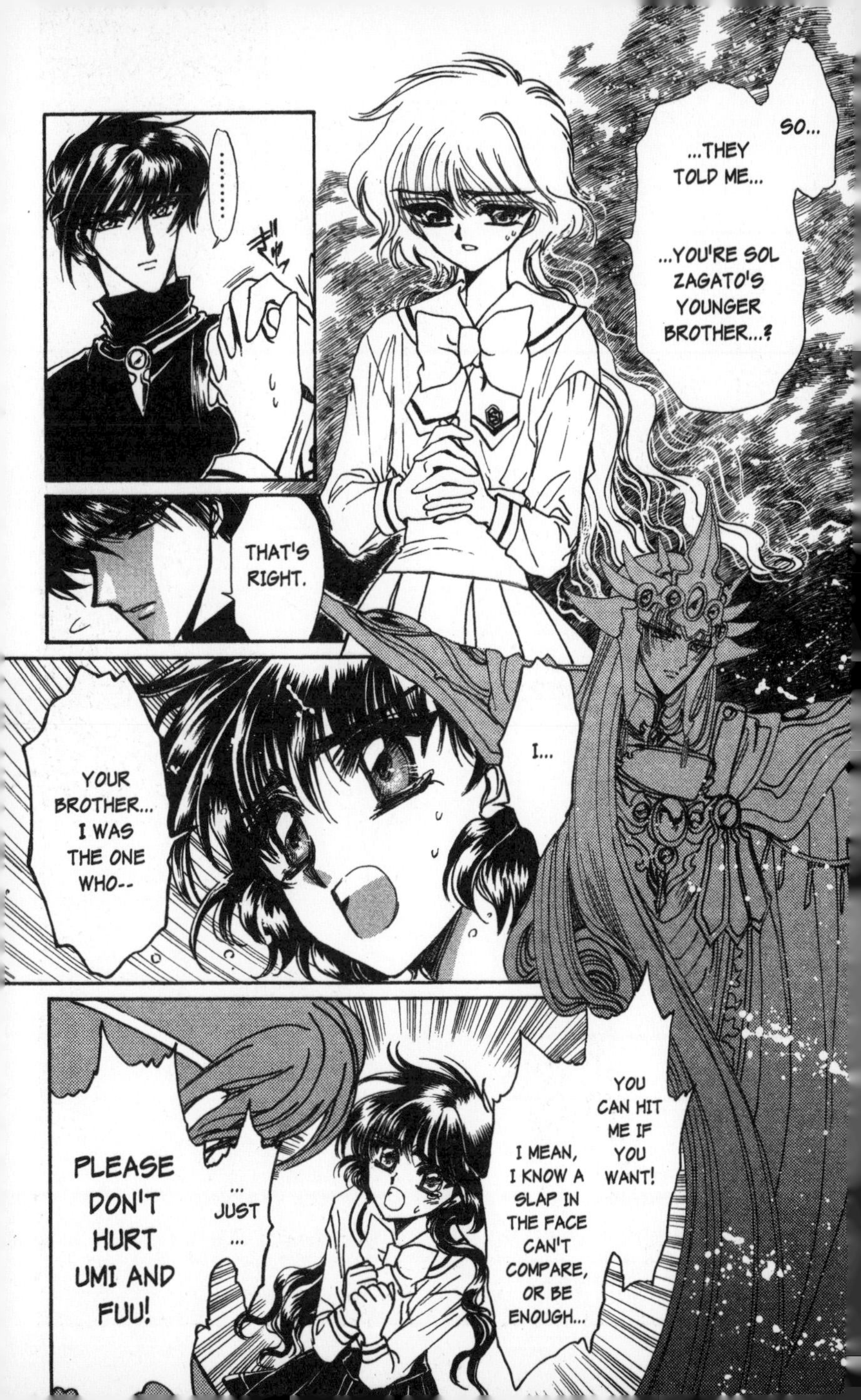
SO... ...THEY TOLD ME... ...YOU'RE SOL ZAGATO'S YOUNGER BROTHER...?
......
THAT'S RIGHT.
I...
YOUR BROTHER... I WAS THE ONE WHO--
YOU CAN HIT ME IF YOU WANT!
I MEAN, I KNOW A SLAP IN THE FACE CAN'T COMPARE, OR BE ENOUGH...
... JUST ...
PLEASE DON'T HURT UMI AND FUU!

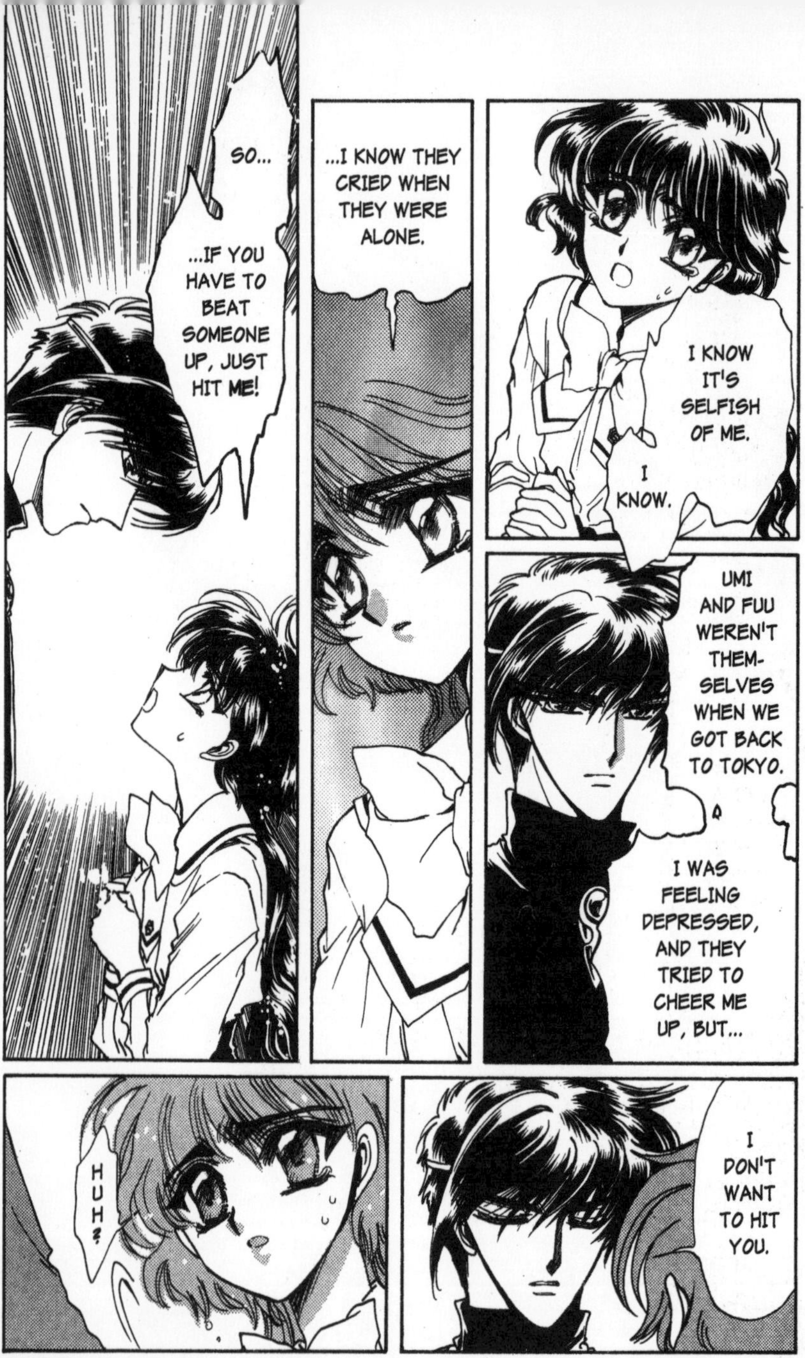
I KNOW IT'S SELFISH OF ME.
I KNOW.
UMI AND FUU WEREN'T THEM-SELVES WHEN WE GOT BACK TO TOKYO.
I WAS FEELING DEPRESSED, AND THEY TRIED TO CHEER ME UP, BUT...
...I KNOW THEY CRIED WHEN THEY WERE ALONE.
SO...
...IF YOU HAVE TO BEAT SOMEONE UP, JUST HIT ME!
I DON'T WANT TO HIT YOU.
HUH?

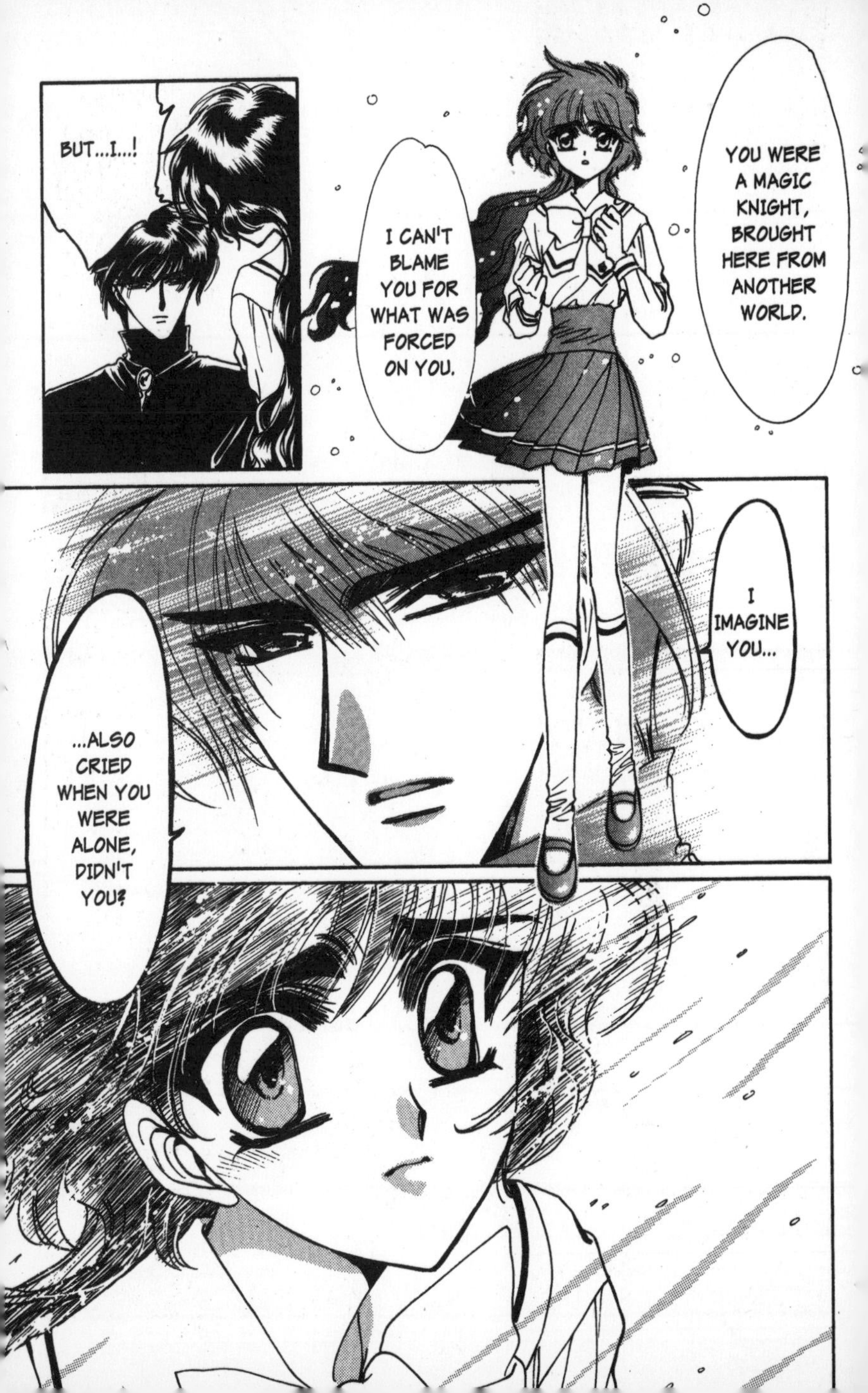
YOU WERE A MAGIC KNIGHT, BROUGHT HERE FROM ANOTHER WORLD.
I CAN'T BLAME YOU FOR WHAT WAS FORCED ON YOU.
BUT...I...!
I IMAGINE YOU...
...ALSO CRIED WHEN YOU WERE ALONE, DIDN'T YOU?

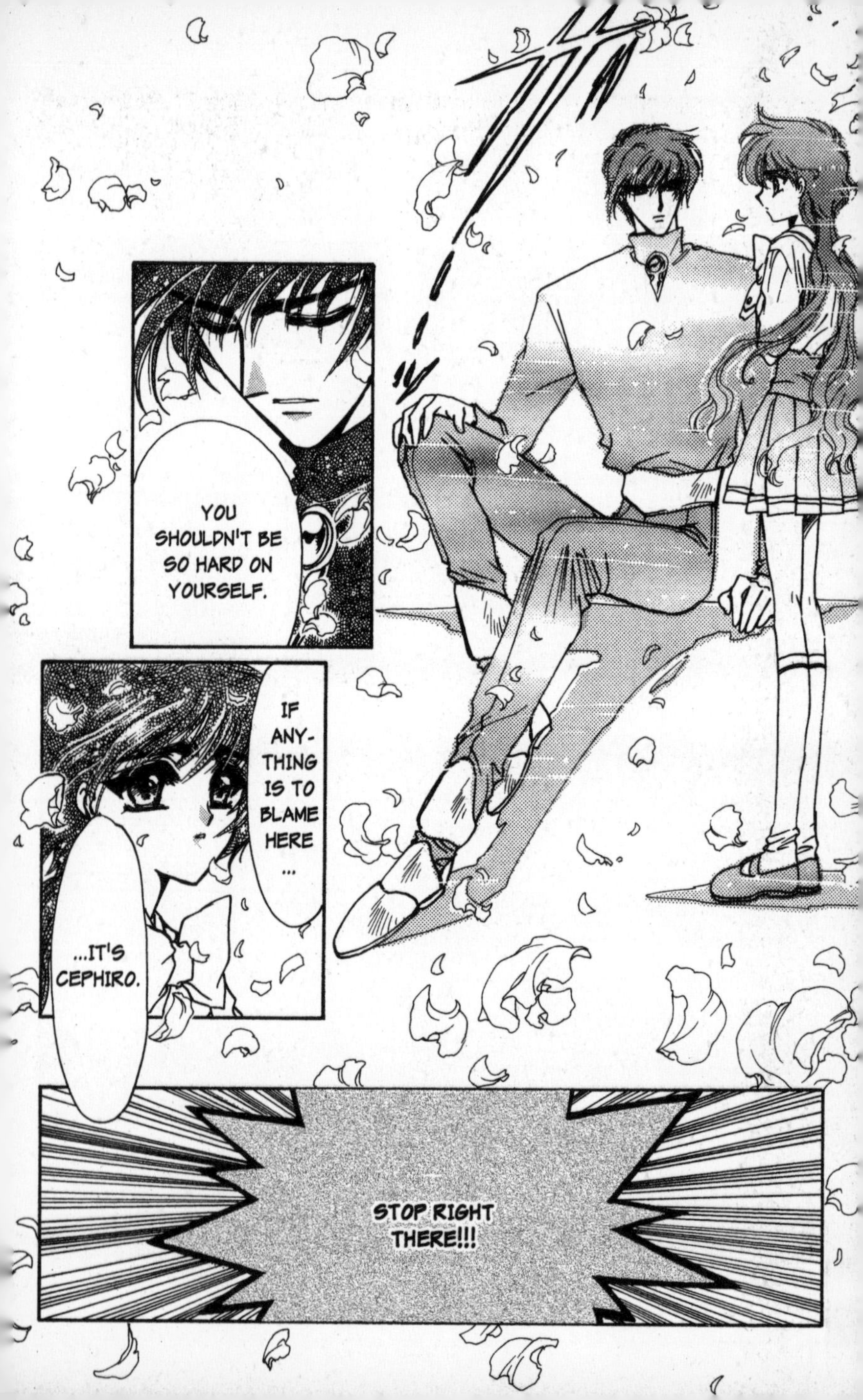
YOU SHOULDN'T BE SO HARD ON YOURSELF.
IF ANYTHING IS TO BLAME HERE...
...IT'S CEPHIRO.
STOP RIGHT THERE!!!

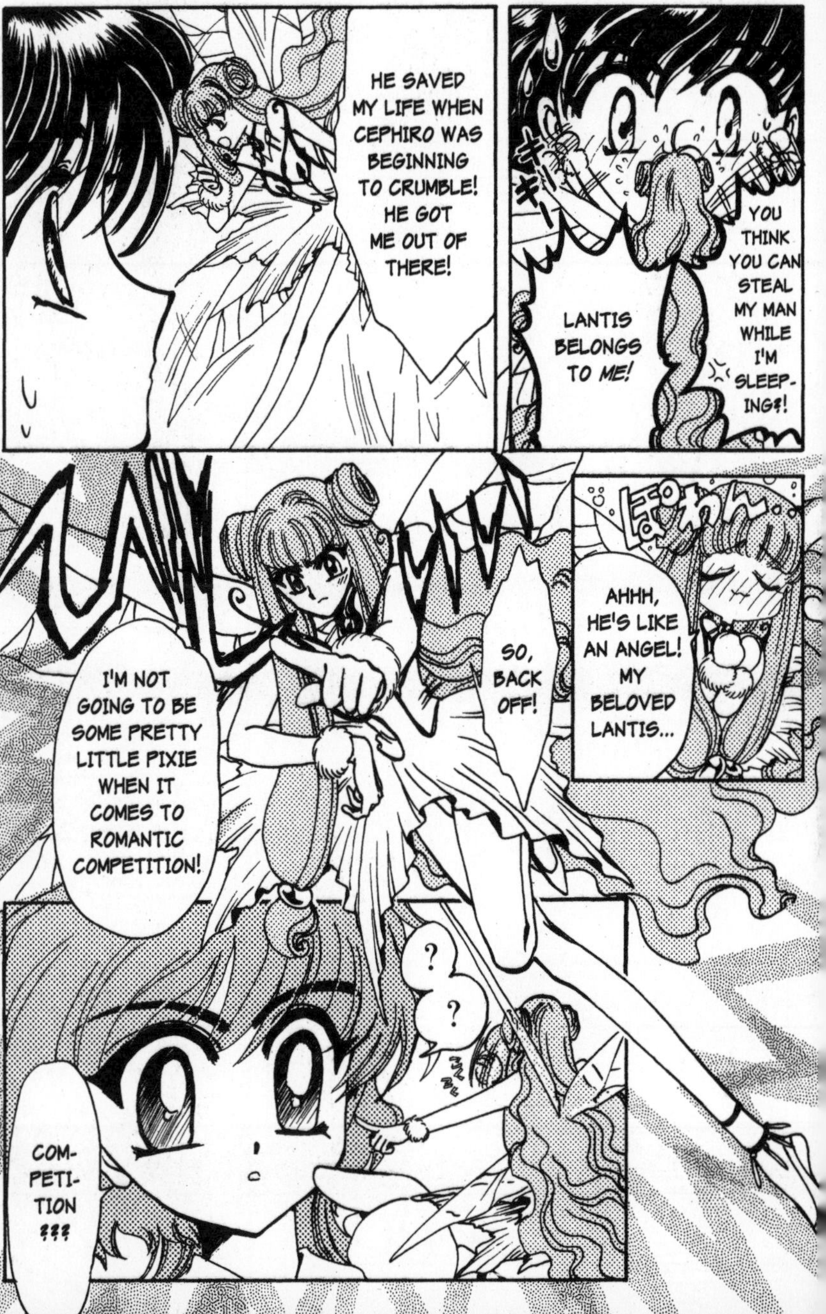
YOU THINK YOU CAN STEAL MY MAN WHILE I'M SLEEPING?!
LANTIS BELONGS TO ME!
HE SAVED MY LIFE WHEN CEPHIRO WAS BEGINNING TO CRUMBLE! HE GOT ME OUT OF THERE!
ぽわん
AHHH, HE'S LIKE AN ANGEL! MY BELOVED LANTIS...
SO, BACK OFF!
I'M NOT GOING TO BE SOME PRETTY LITTLE PIXIE WHEN IT COMES TO ROMANTIC COMPETITION!
?
?
COM-PETI-TION ???

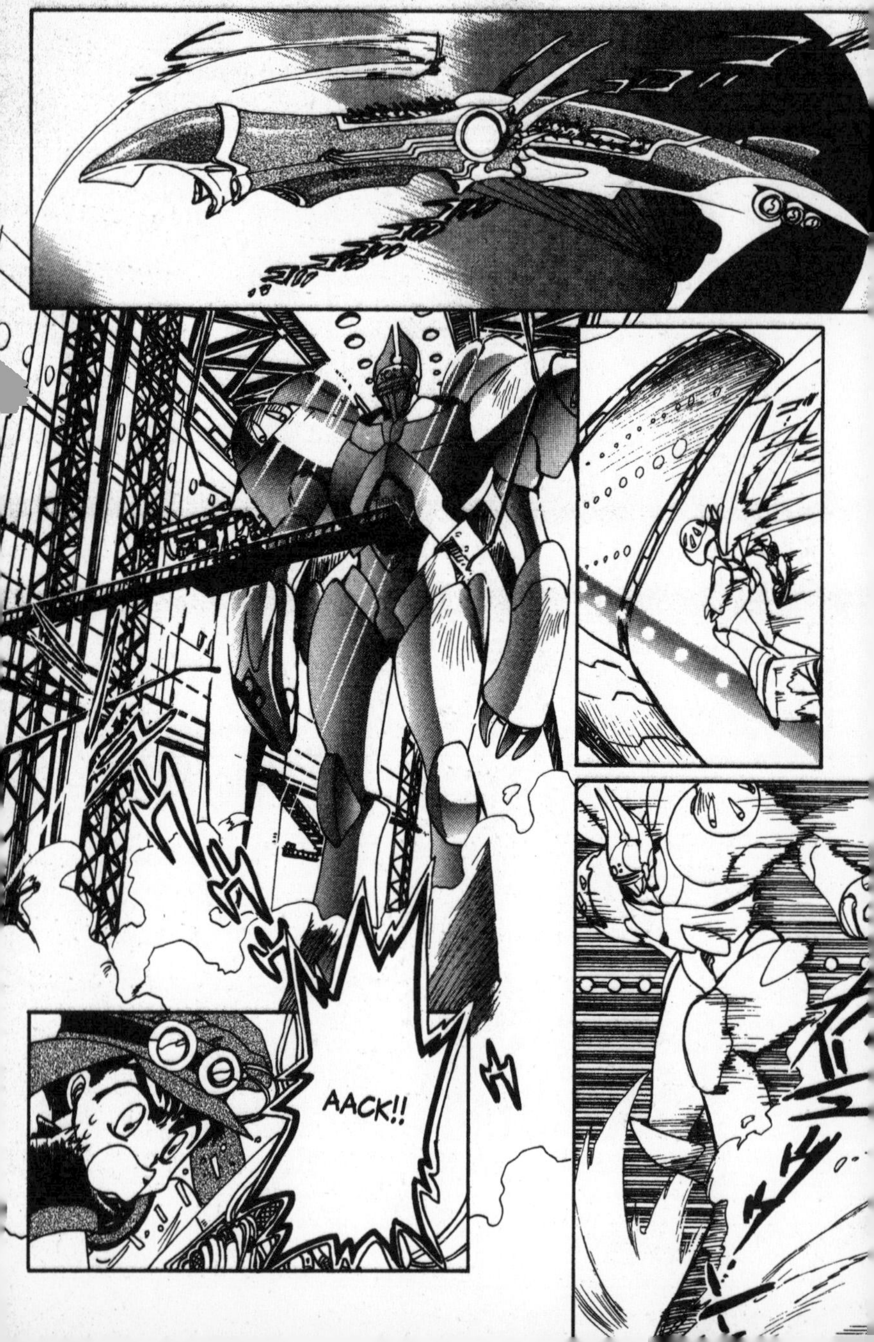
AACK!!

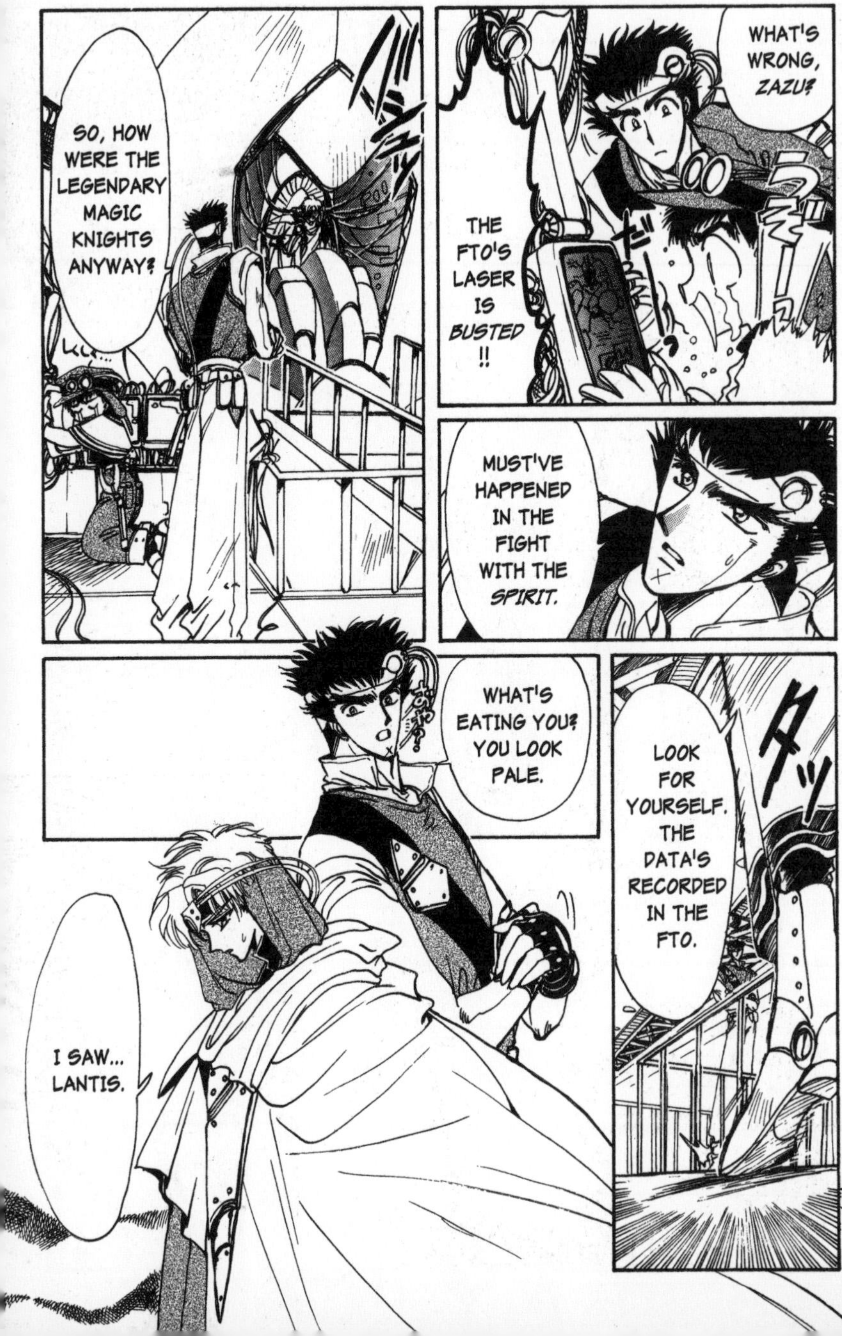
WHAT'S WRONG, ZAZU?
THE FTO'S LASER IS *BUSTED* !!
MUST'VE HAPPENED IN THE FIGHT WITH THE *SPIRIT.*
SO, HOW WERE THE LEGENDARY MAGIC KNIGHTS ANYWAY?
LOOK FOR YOURSELF. THE DATA'S RECORDED IN THE FTO.
WHAT'S EATING YOU? YOU LOOK PALE.
I SAW... LANTIS.

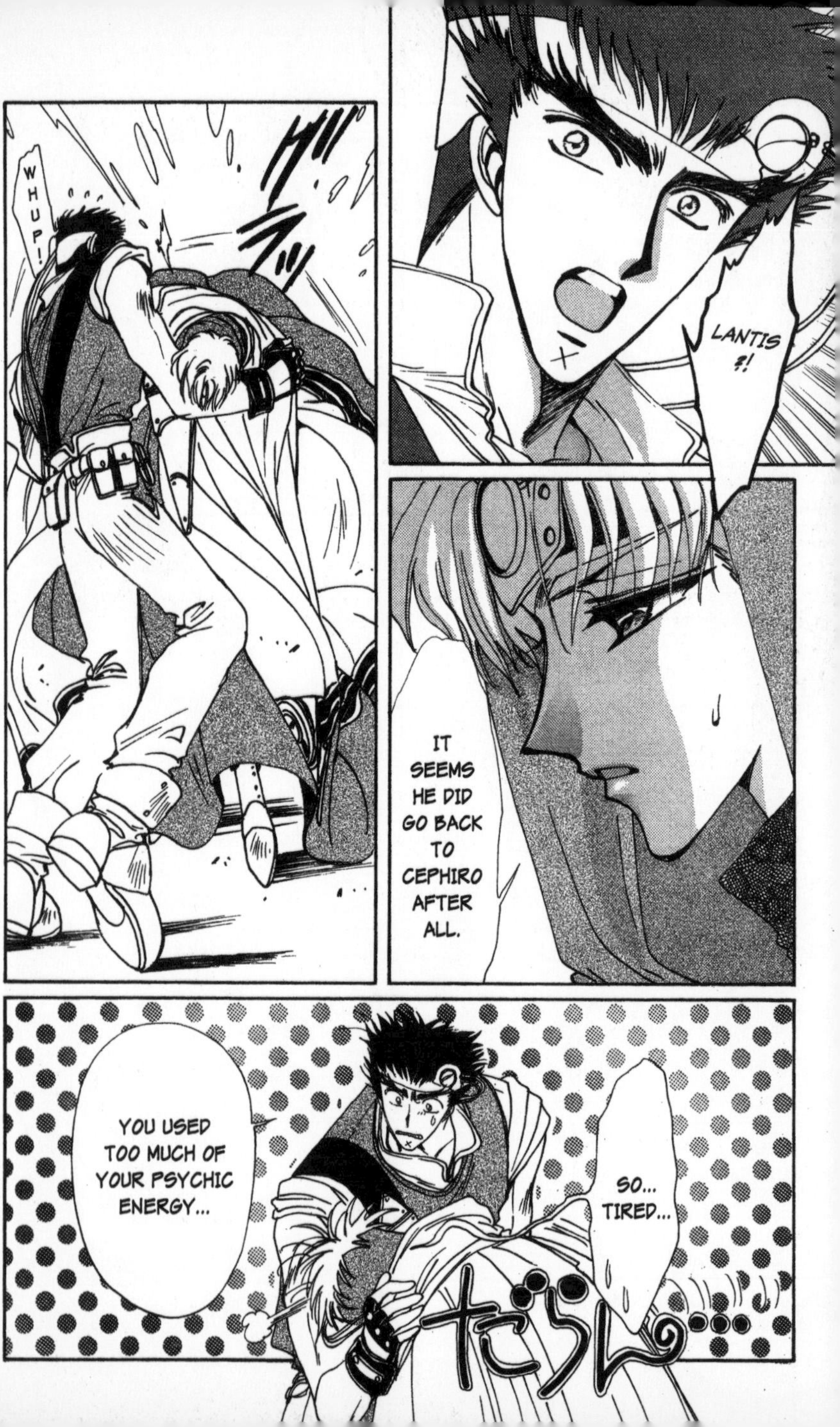
LANTIS ?!
IT SEEMS HE DID GO BACK TO CEPHIRO AFTER ALL.
WHUP!
SO... TIRED...
YOU USED TOO MUCH OF YOUR PSYCHIC ENERGY...

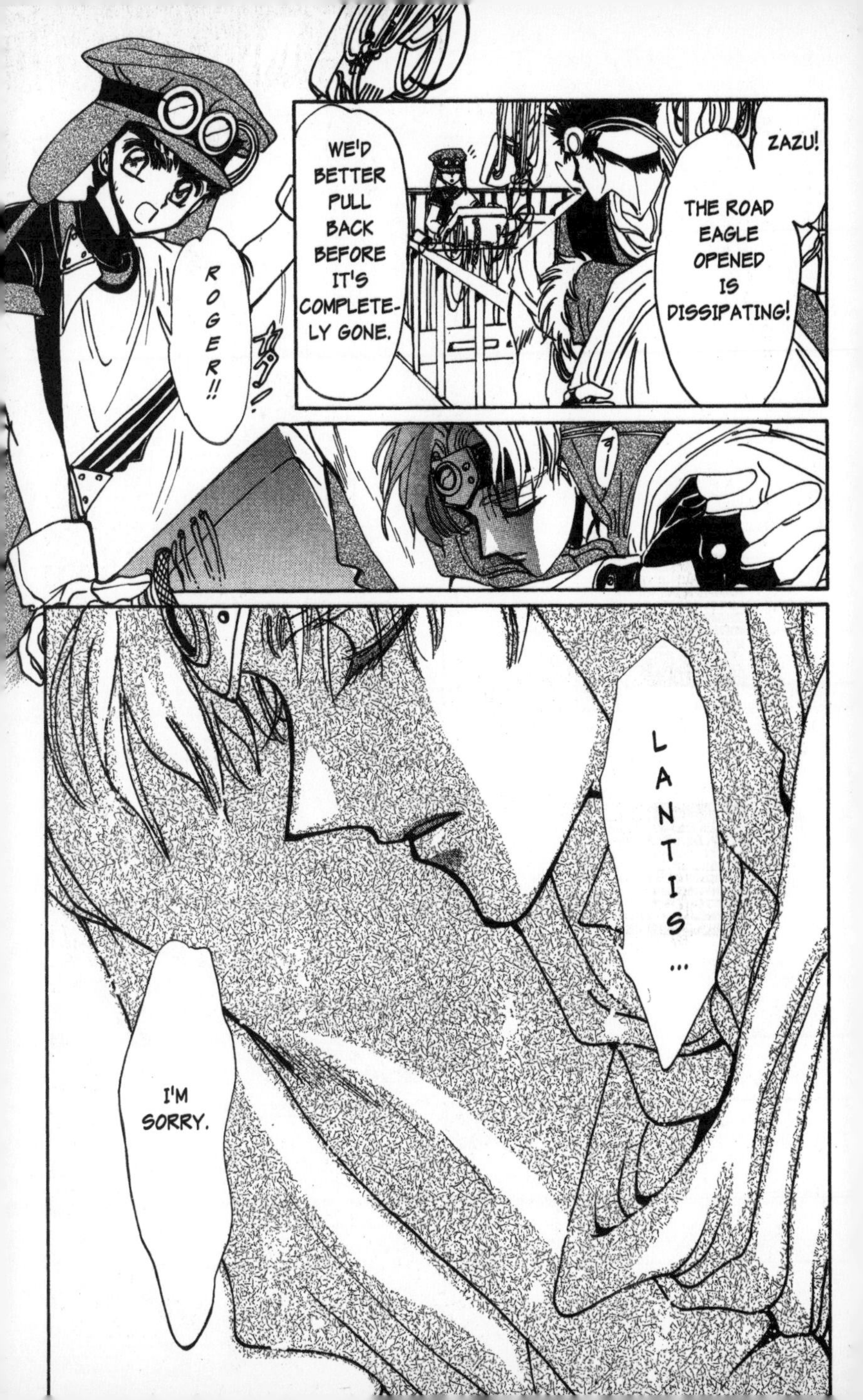
ZAZU!
THE ROAD EAGLE OPENED IS DISSIPATING!
WE'D BETTER PULL BACK BEFORE IT'S COMPLETELY GONE.
ROGER!!
LANTIS...
I'M SORRY.

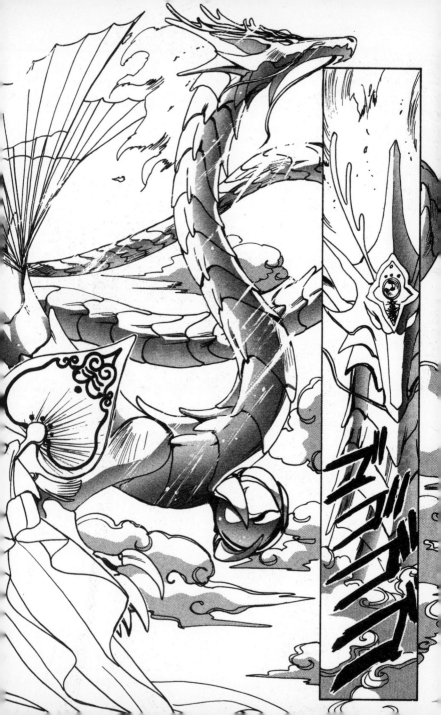

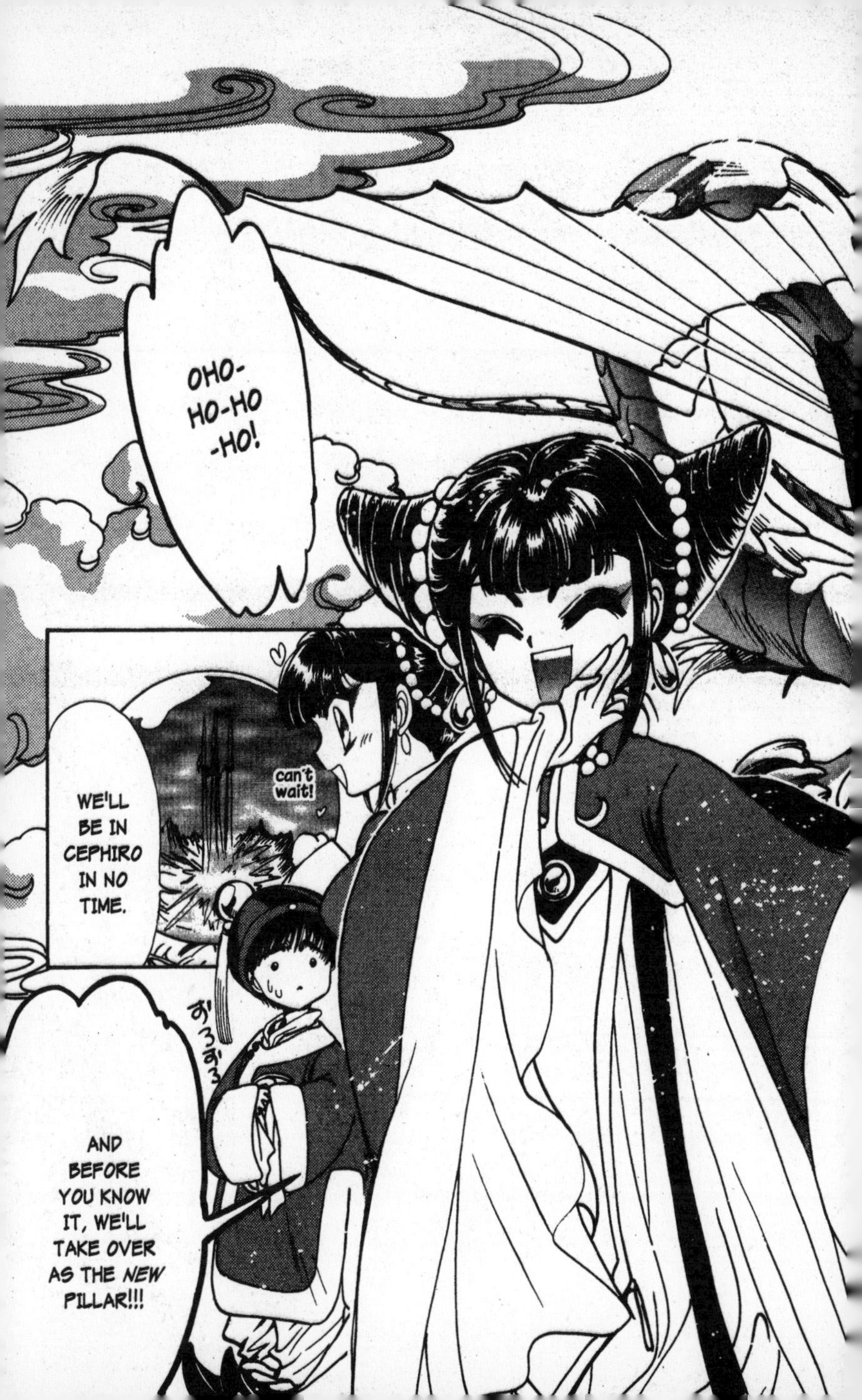
OHO-HO-HO-HO!
can't wait!
WE'LL BE IN CEPHIRO IN NO TIME.
ずるずる
AND BEFORE YOU KNOW IT, WE'LL TAKE OVER AS THE *NEW* PILLAR!!!

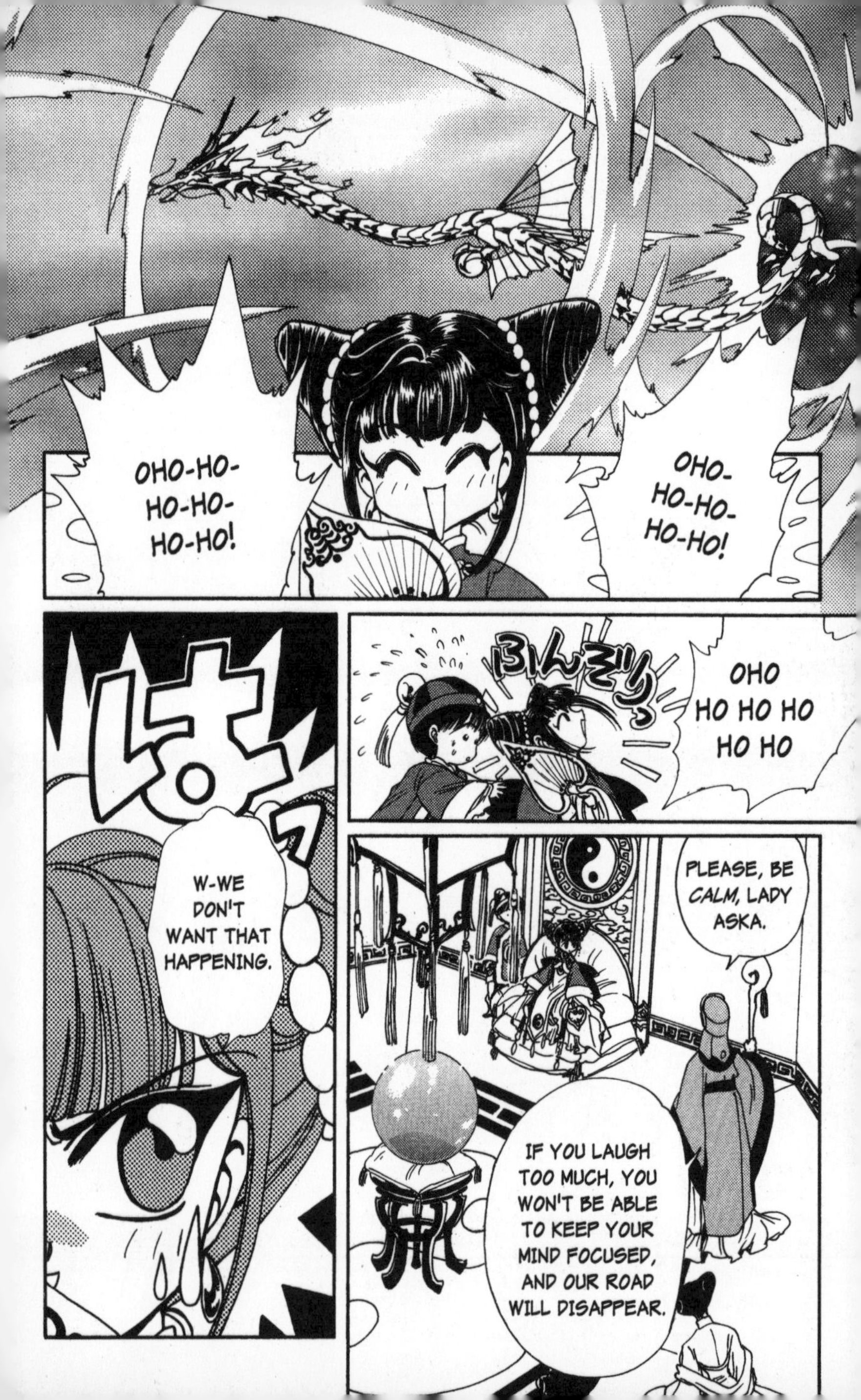
OHO-HO-HO-HO-HO!
OHO-HO-HO-HO-HO!
ふんぞりっ
OHO HO HO HO HO HO
PLEASE, BE CALM, LADY ASKA.
IF YOU LAUGH TOO MUCH, YOU WON'T BE ABLE TO KEEP YOUR MIND FOCUSED, AND OUR ROAD WILL DISAPPEAR.
はっ
W-WE DON'T WANT THAT HAPPENING.

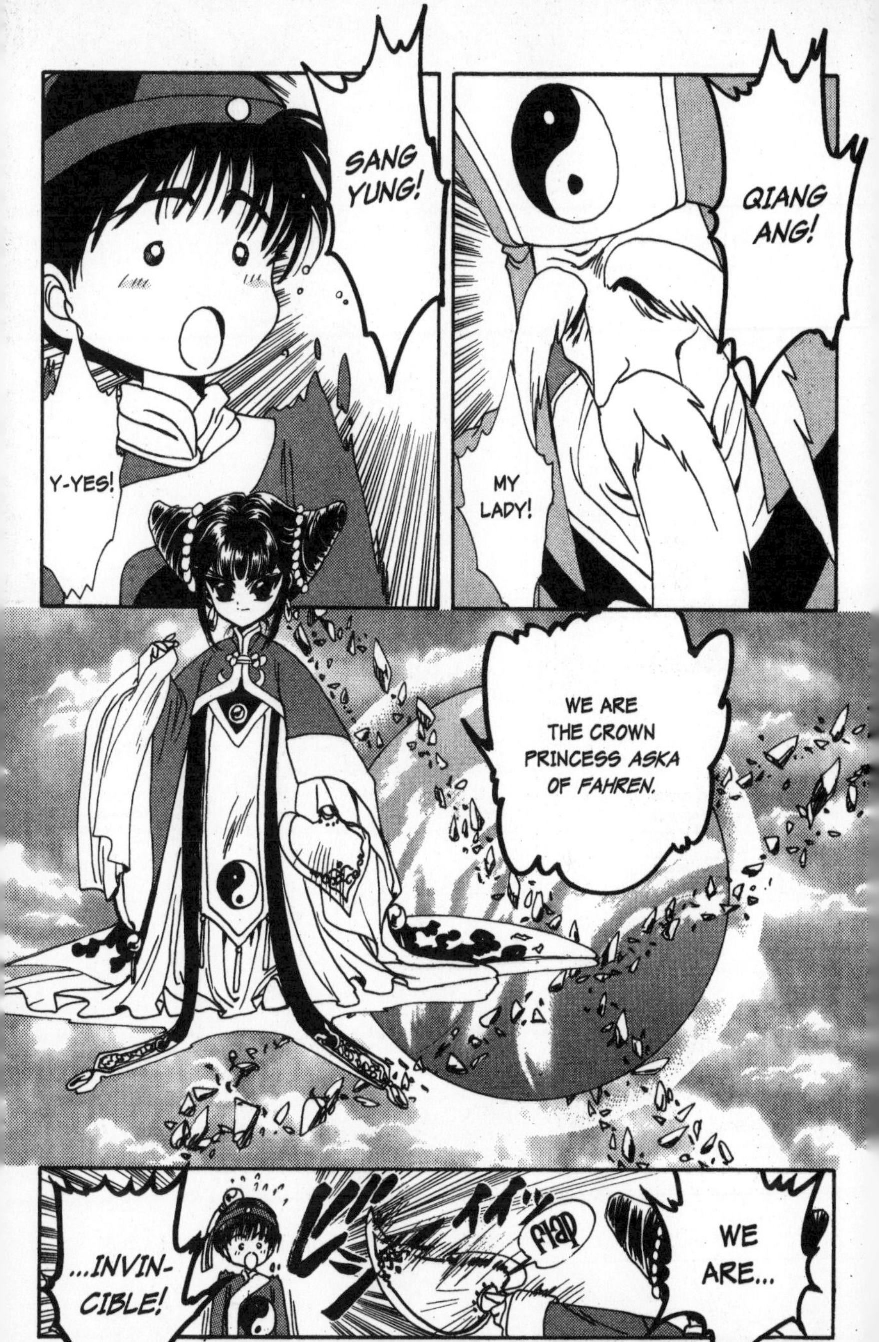
QIANG ANG!
MY LADY!
SANG YUNG!
Y-YES!
WE ARE THE CROWN PRINCESS ASKA OF FAHREN.
WE ARE...
flap
...INVIN-CIBLE!

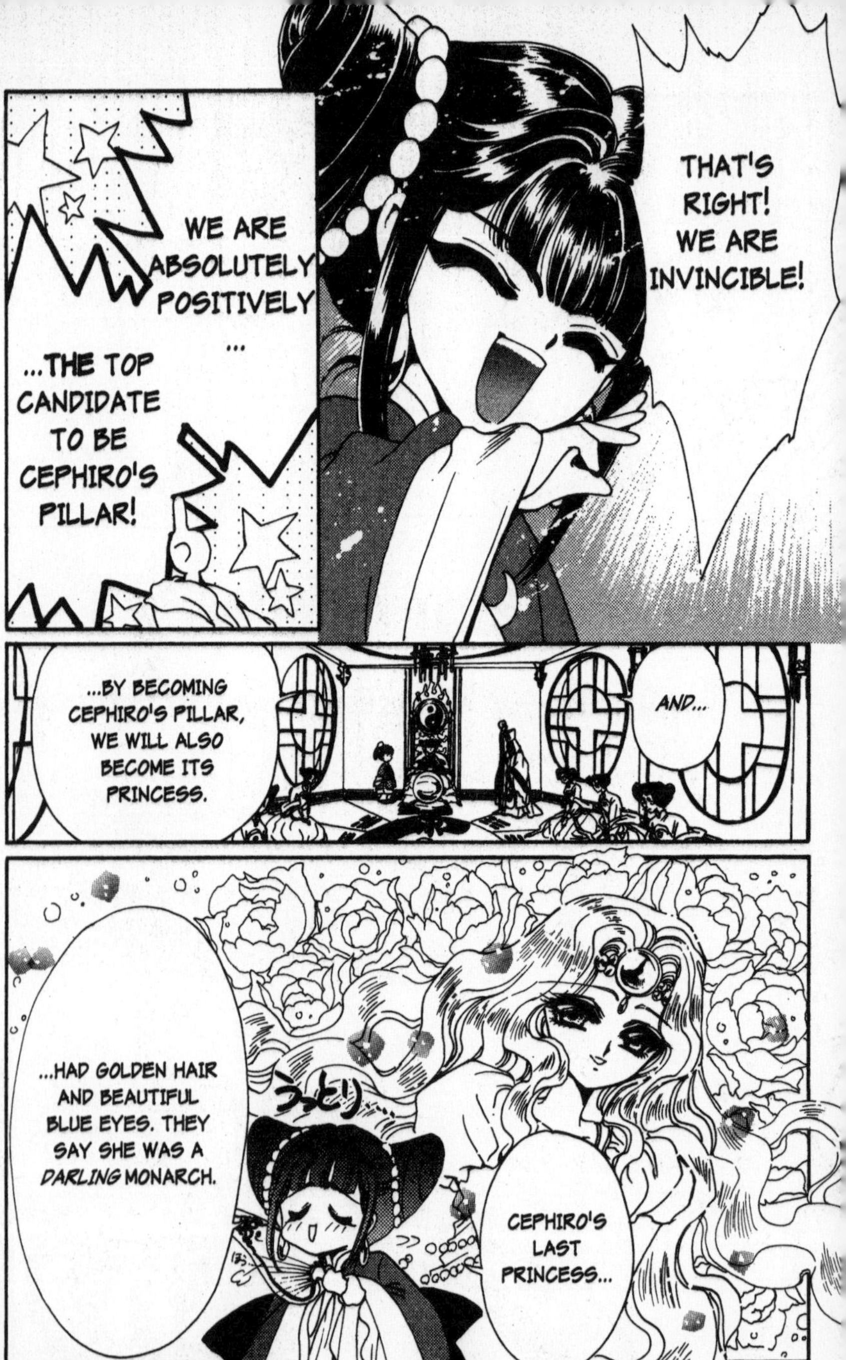
THAT'S RIGHT! WE ARE INVINCIBLE!
WE ARE ABSOLUTELY POSITIVELY ...
...THE TOP CANDIDATE TO BE CEPHIRO'S PILLAR!
AND...
...BY BECOMING CEPHIRO'S PILLAR, WE WILL ALSO BECOME ITS PRINCESS.
CEPHIRO'S LAST PRINCESS...
うっとり
...HAD GOLDEN HAIR AND BEAUTIFUL BLUE EYES. THEY SAY SHE WAS A *DARLING* MONARCH.

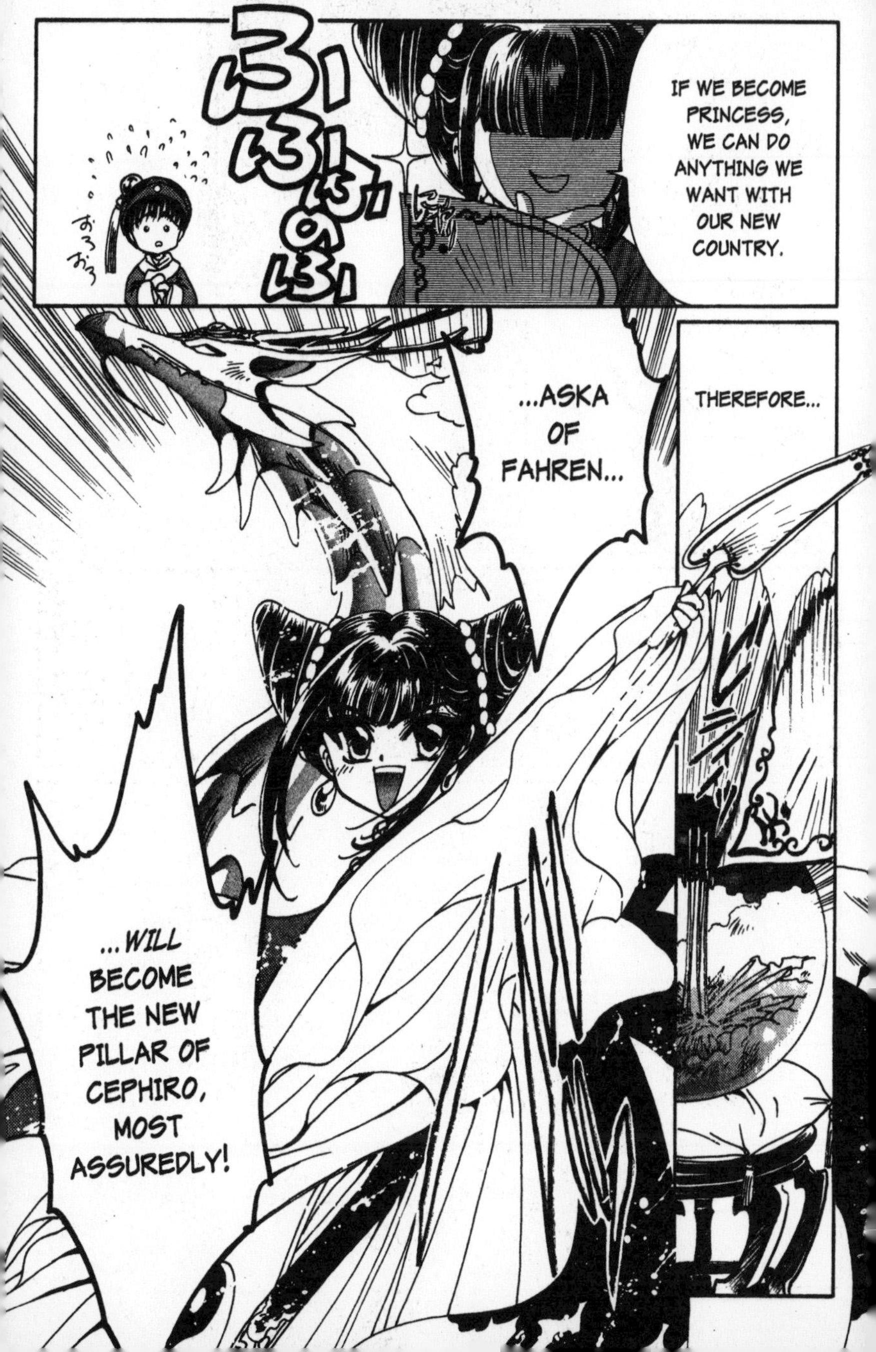
IF WE BECOME PRINCESS, WE CAN DO ANYTHING WE WANT WITH OUR NEW COUNTRY.
ふふふのふ
おろおろ
THEREFORE...
...ASKA OF FAHREN...
...WILL BECOME THE NEW PILLAR OF CEPHIRO, MOST ASSUREDLY!

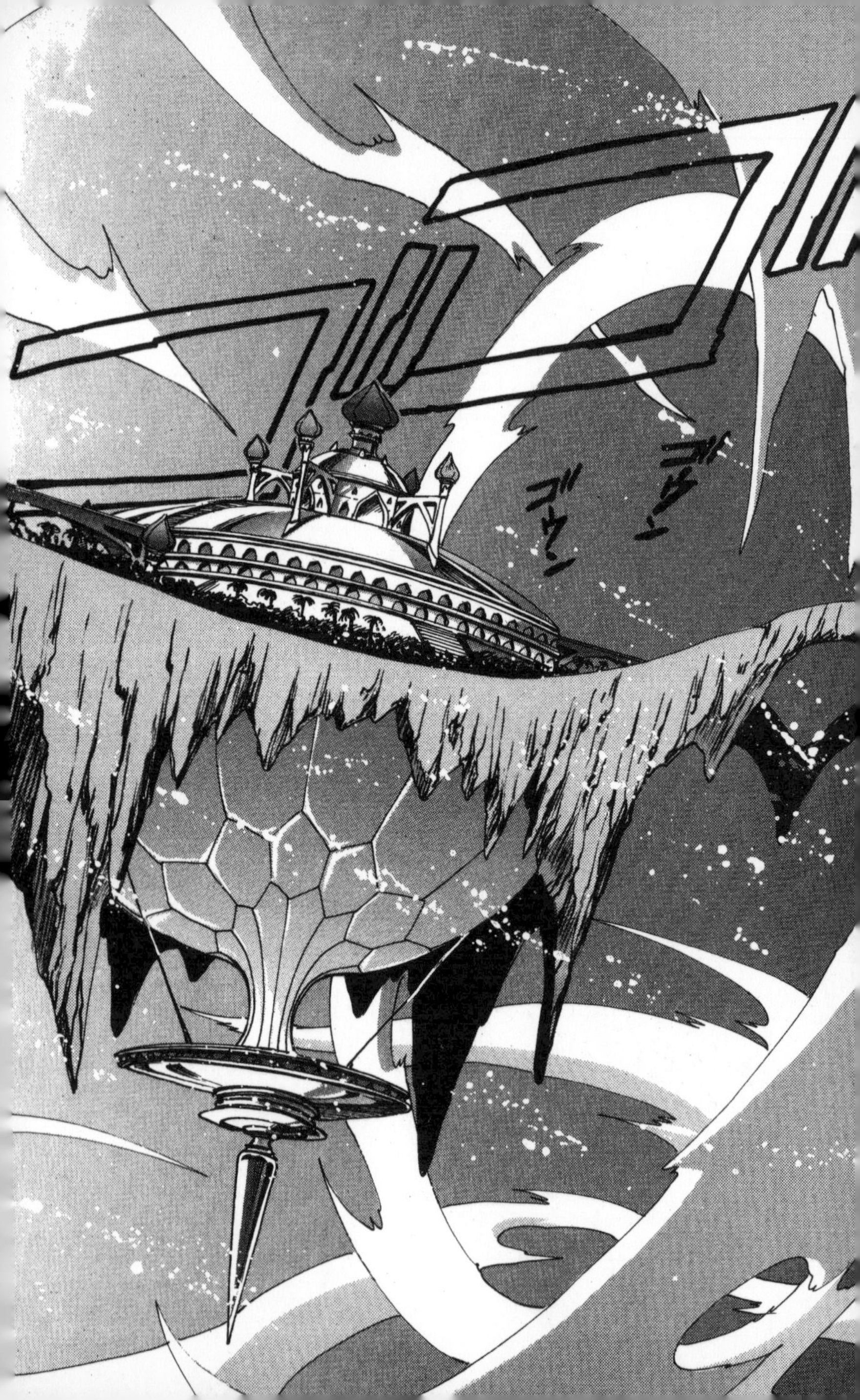
ゴウン
ゴウン

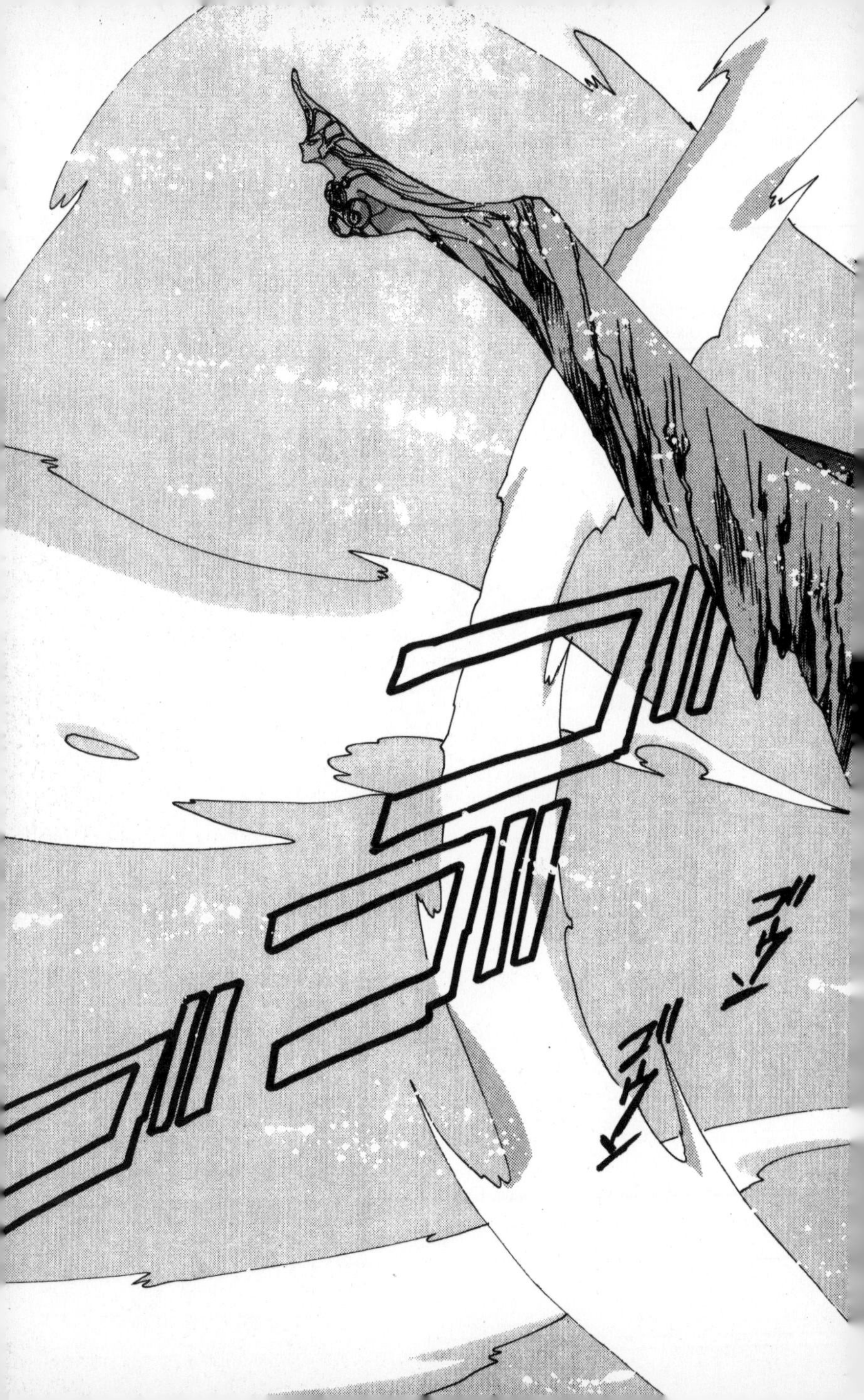
ゴゴゴ

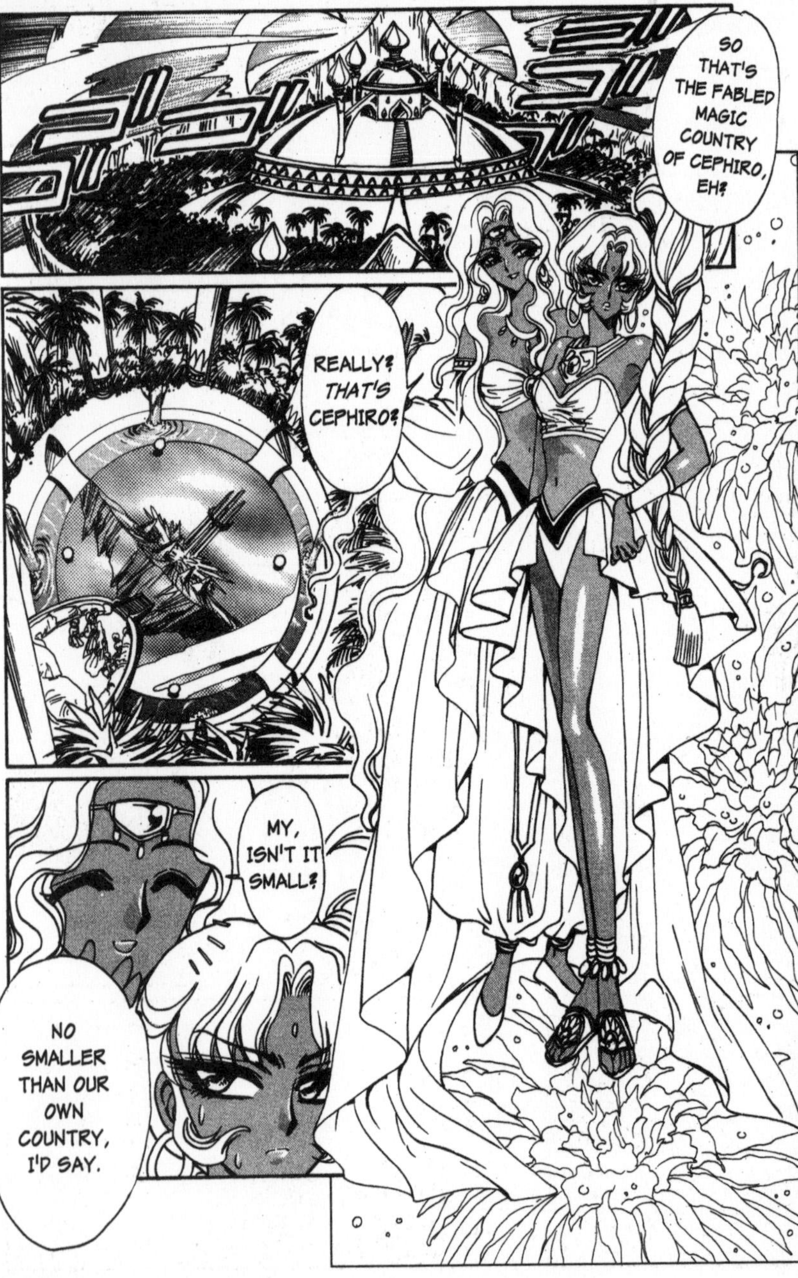
SO THAT'S THE FABLED MAGIC COUNTRY OF CEPHIRO, EH?
REALLY? THAT'S CEPHIRO?
MY, ISN'T IT SMALL?
NO SMALLER THAN OUR OWN COUNTRY, I'D SAY.

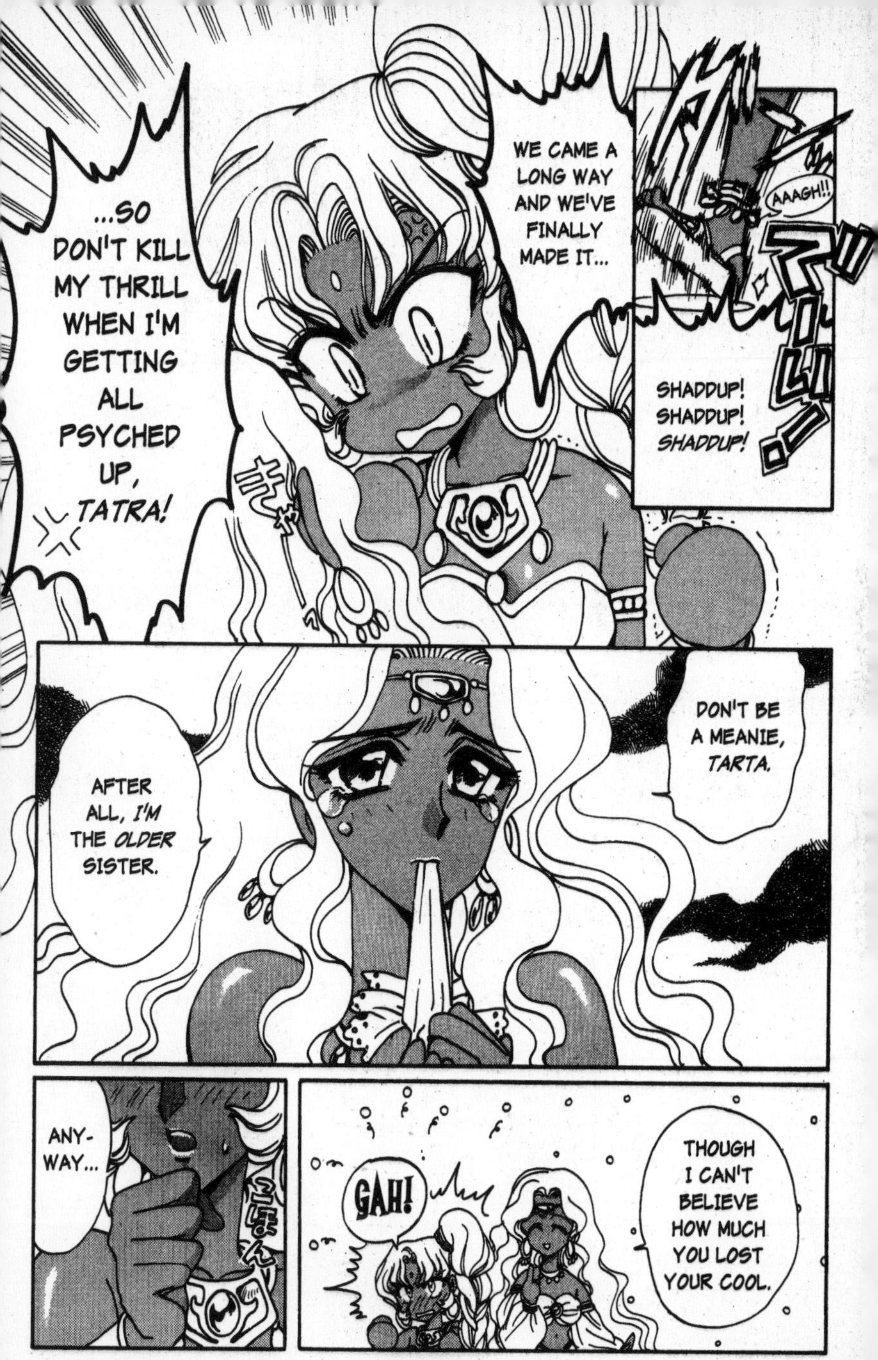
AAAGH!!
SHADDUP! SHADDUP! *SHADDUP!*
WE CAME A LONG WAY AND WE'VE FINALLY MADE IT...
...SO DON'T KILL MY THRILL WHEN I'M GETTING ALL PSYCHED UP, *TATRA!*
DON'T BE A MEANIE, *TARTA.*
AFTER ALL, *I'M* THE *OLDER* SISTER.
THOUGH I CAN'T BELIEVE HOW MUCH YOU LOST YOUR COOL.
GAH!
ANY-WAY...

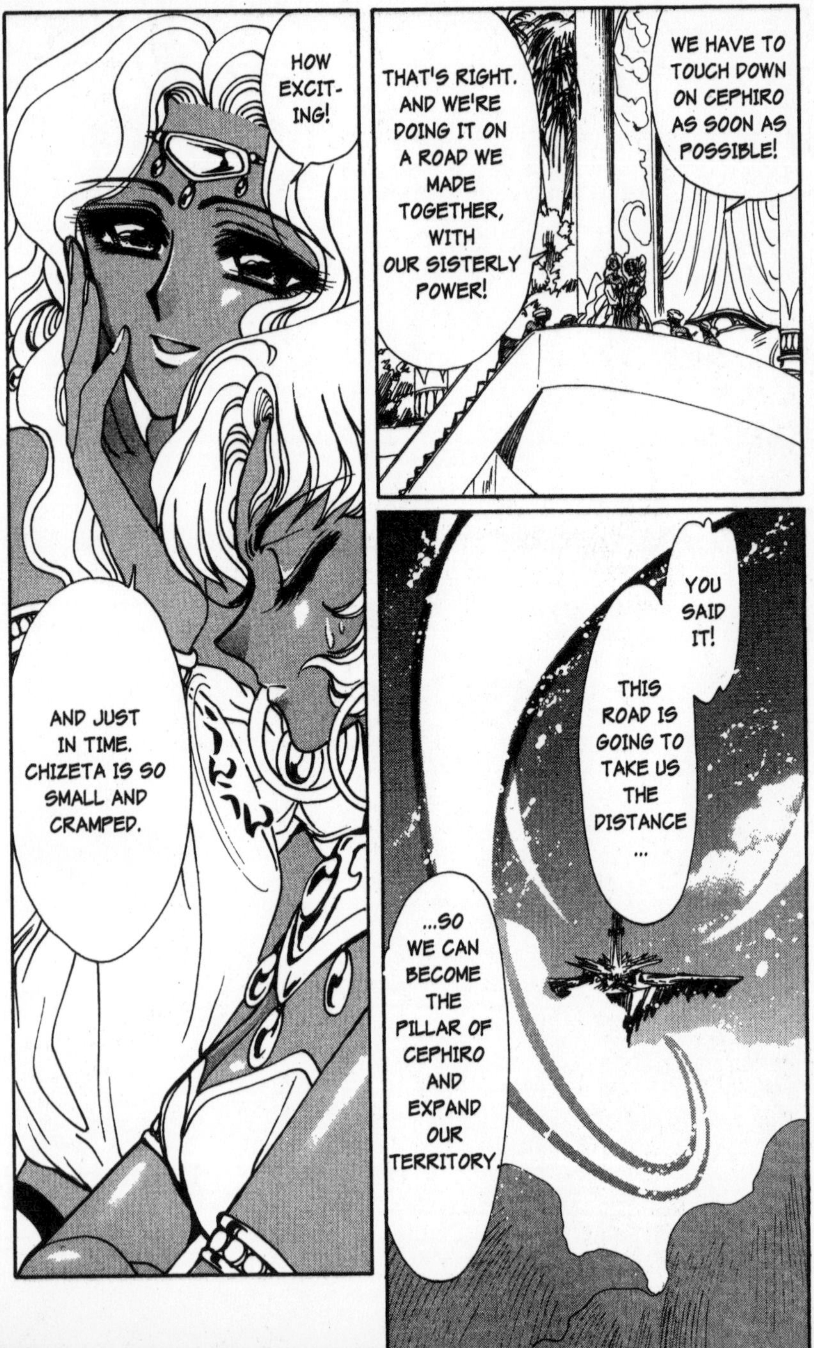
WE HAVE TO TOUCH DOWN ON CEPHIRO AS SOON AS POSSIBLE!
THAT'S RIGHT. AND WE'RE DOING IT ON A ROAD WE MADE TOGETHER, WITH OUR SISTERLY POWER!
YOU SAID IT!
THIS ROAD IS GOING TO TAKE US THE DISTANCE ...
...SO WE CAN BECOME THE PILLAR OF CEPHIRO AND EXPAND OUR TERRITORY.
HOW EXCITING!
AND JUST IN TIME. CHIZETA IS SO SMALL AND CRAMPED.

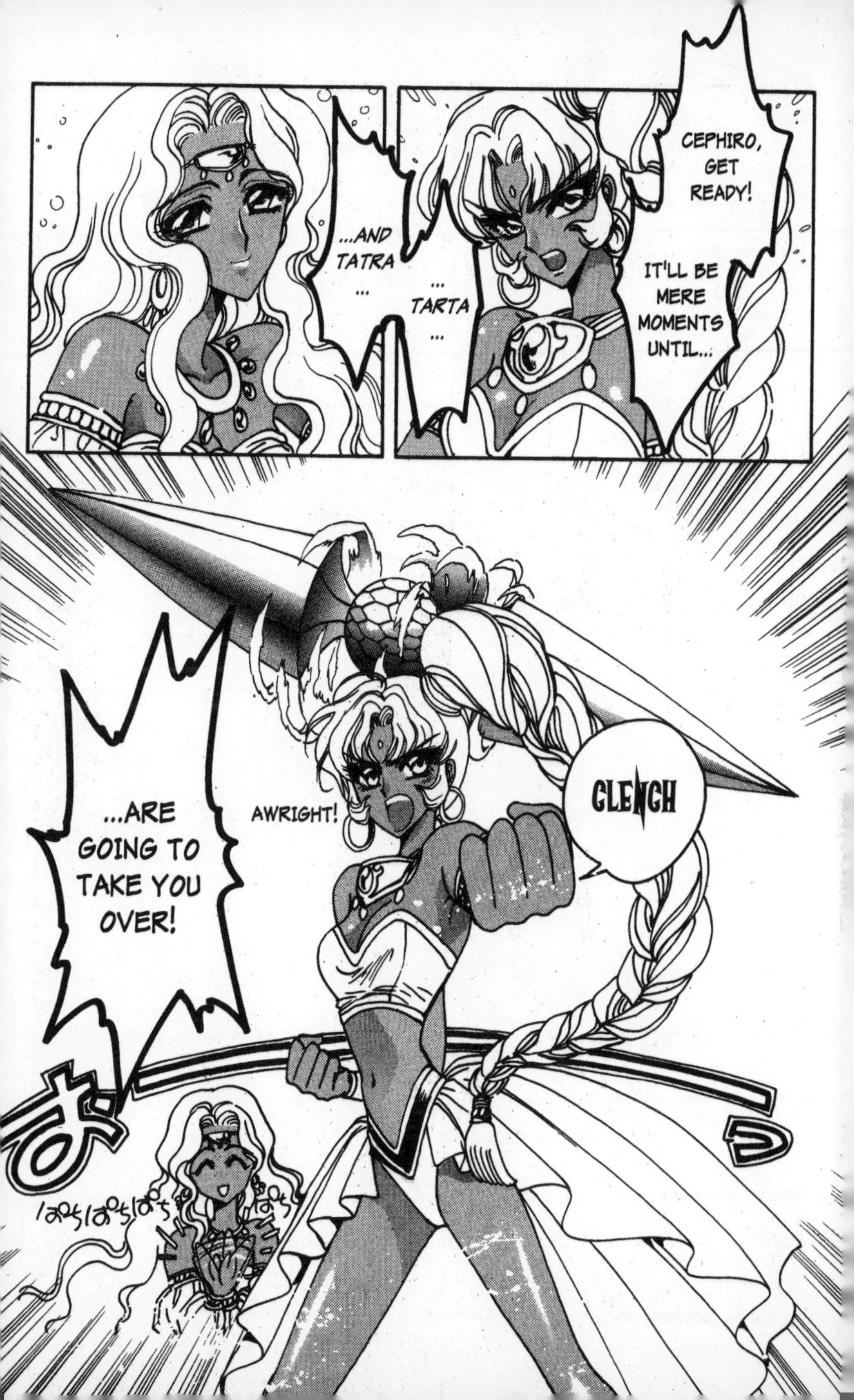
CEPHIRO, GET READY!
IT'LL BE MERE MOMENTS UNTIL...
...TARTA...
...AND TATRA...
CLENCH
AWRIGHT!
...ARE GOING TO TAKE YOU OVER!
よっ
ぱちぱちぱち
ぱち

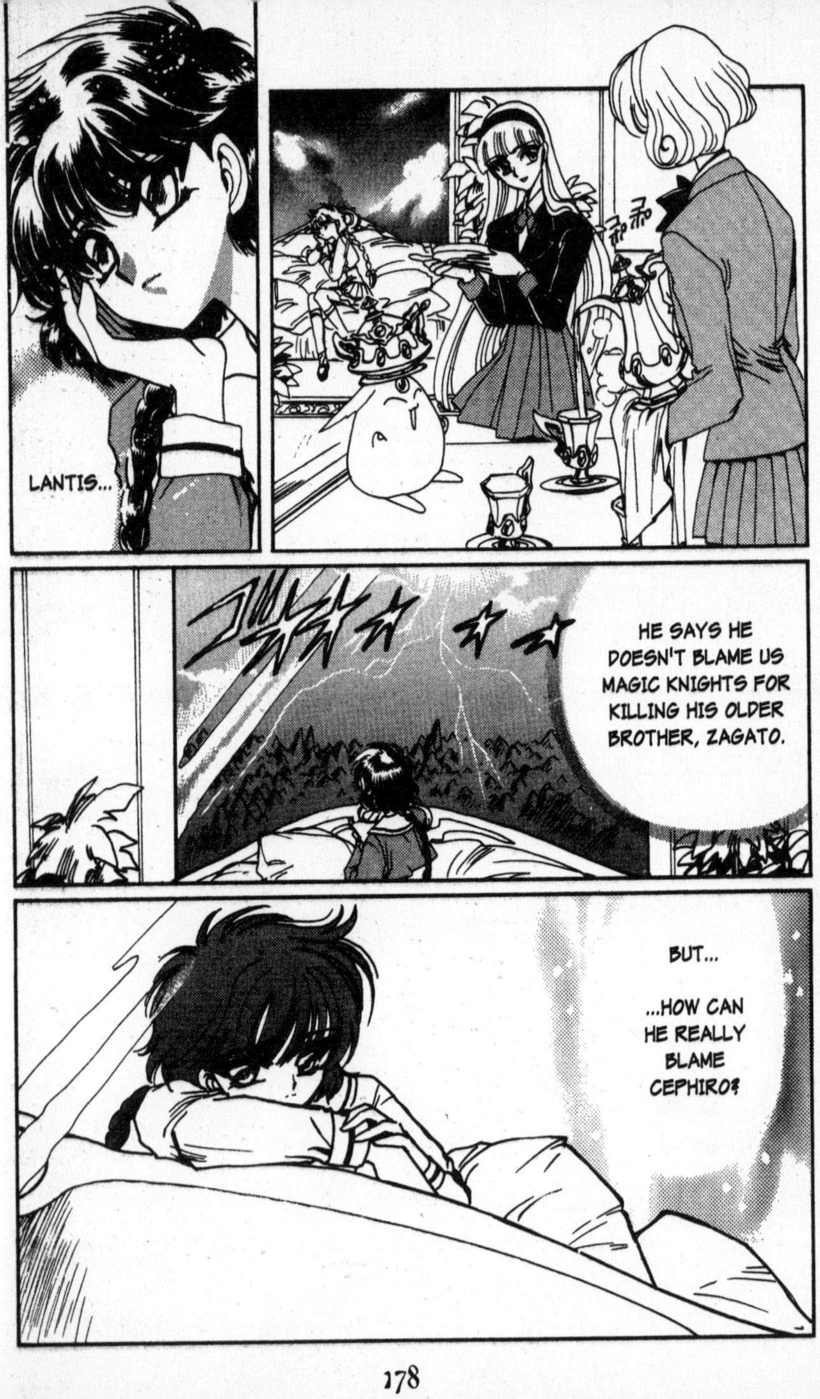
LANTIS...
HE SAYS HE DOESN'T BLAME US MAGIC KNIGHTS FOR KILLING HIS OLDER BROTHER, ZAGATO.
BUT...
...HOW CAN HE REALLY BLAME CEPHIRO?

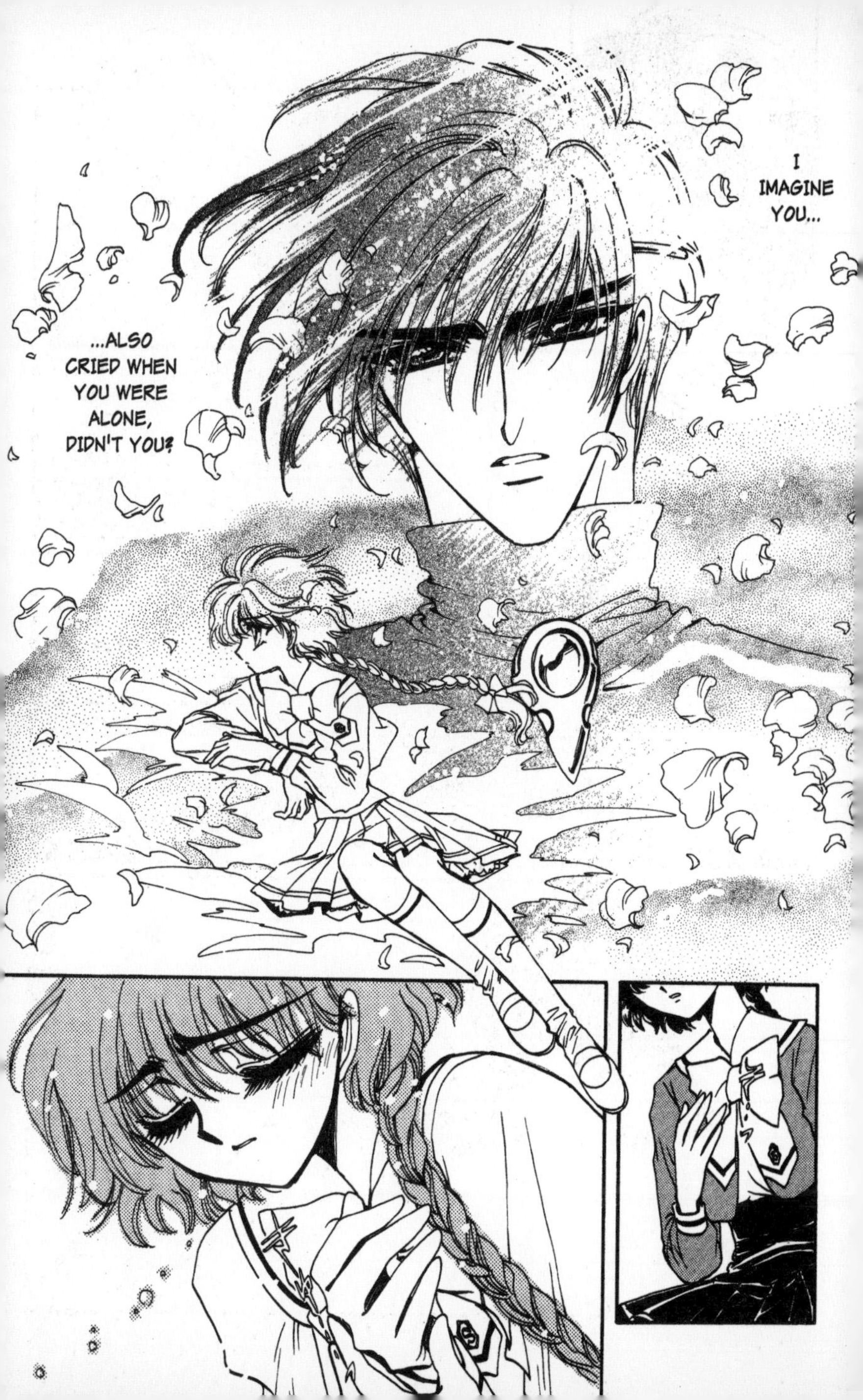
I IMAGINE YOU...
...ALSO CRIED WHEN YOU WERE ALONE, DIDN'T YOU?

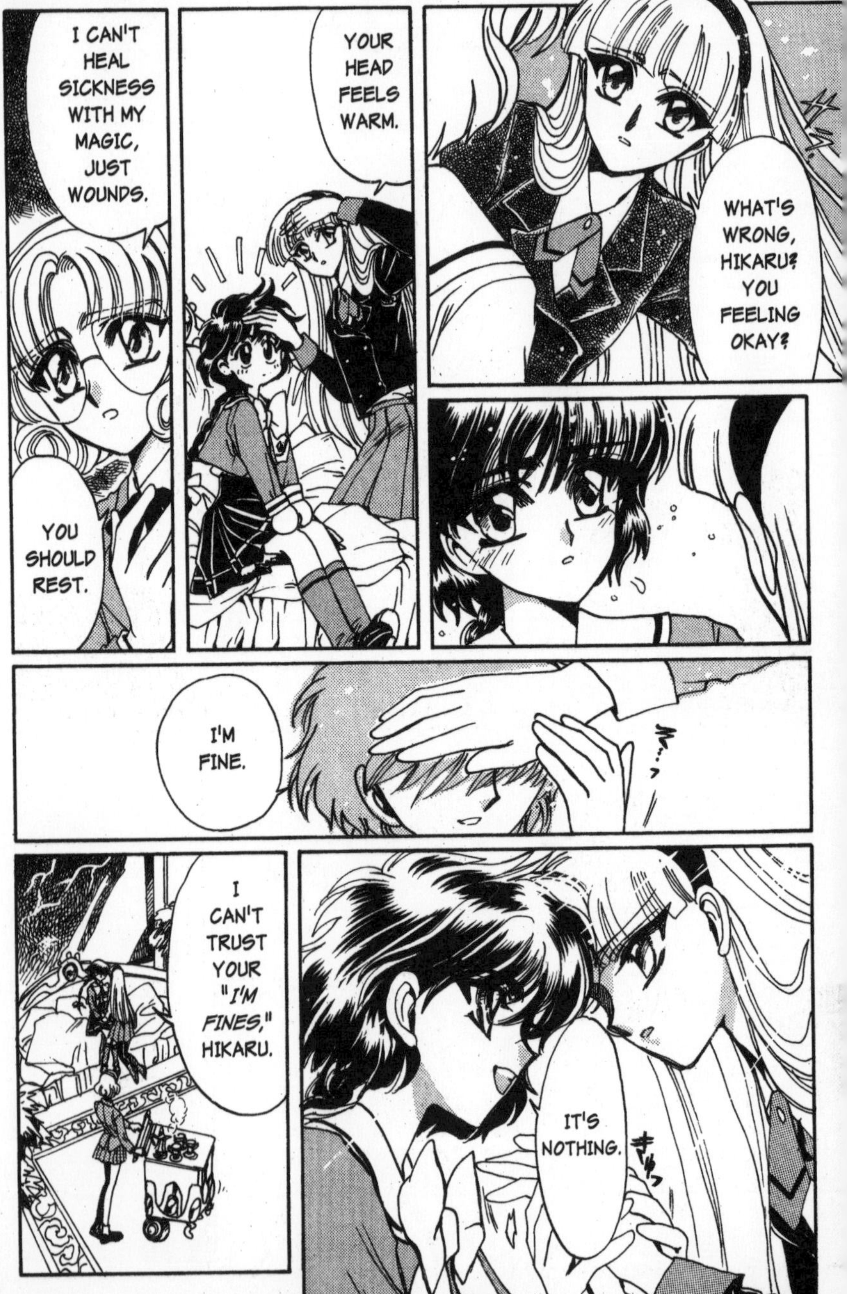
WHAT'S WRONG, HIKARU? YOU FEELING OKAY?
YOUR HEAD FEELS WARM.
I CAN'T HEAL SICKNESS WITH MY MAGIC, JUST WOUNDS.
YOU SHOULD REST.
I'M FINE.
IT'S NOTHING.
I CAN'T TRUST YOUR "*I'M FINES*," HIKARU.

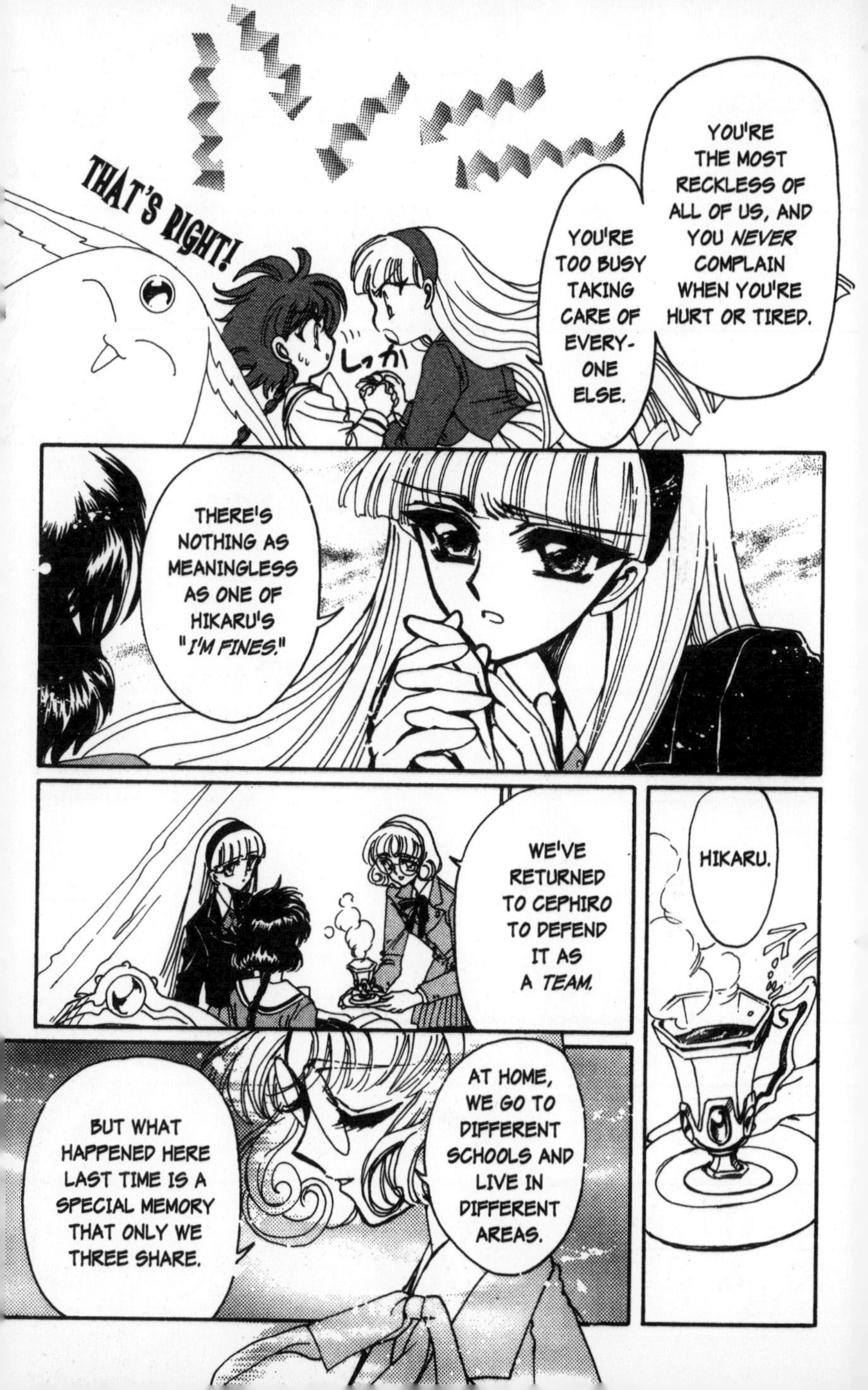
YOU'RE THE MOST RECKLESS OF ALL OF US, AND YOU *NEVER* COMPLAIN WHEN YOU'RE HURT OR TIRED.
YOU'RE TOO BUSY TAKING CARE OF EVERY-ONE ELSE.
THAT'S RIGHT!
しっか
THERE'S NOTHING AS MEANINGLESS AS ONE OF HIKARU'S "*I'M FINES.*"
HIKARU.
WE'VE RETURNED TO CEPHIRO TO DEFEND IT AS A *TEAM.*
AT HOME, WE GO TO DIFFERENT SCHOOLS AND LIVE IN DIFFERENT AREAS.
BUT WHAT HAPPENED HERE LAST TIME IS A SPECIAL MEMORY THAT ONLY WE THREE SHARE.

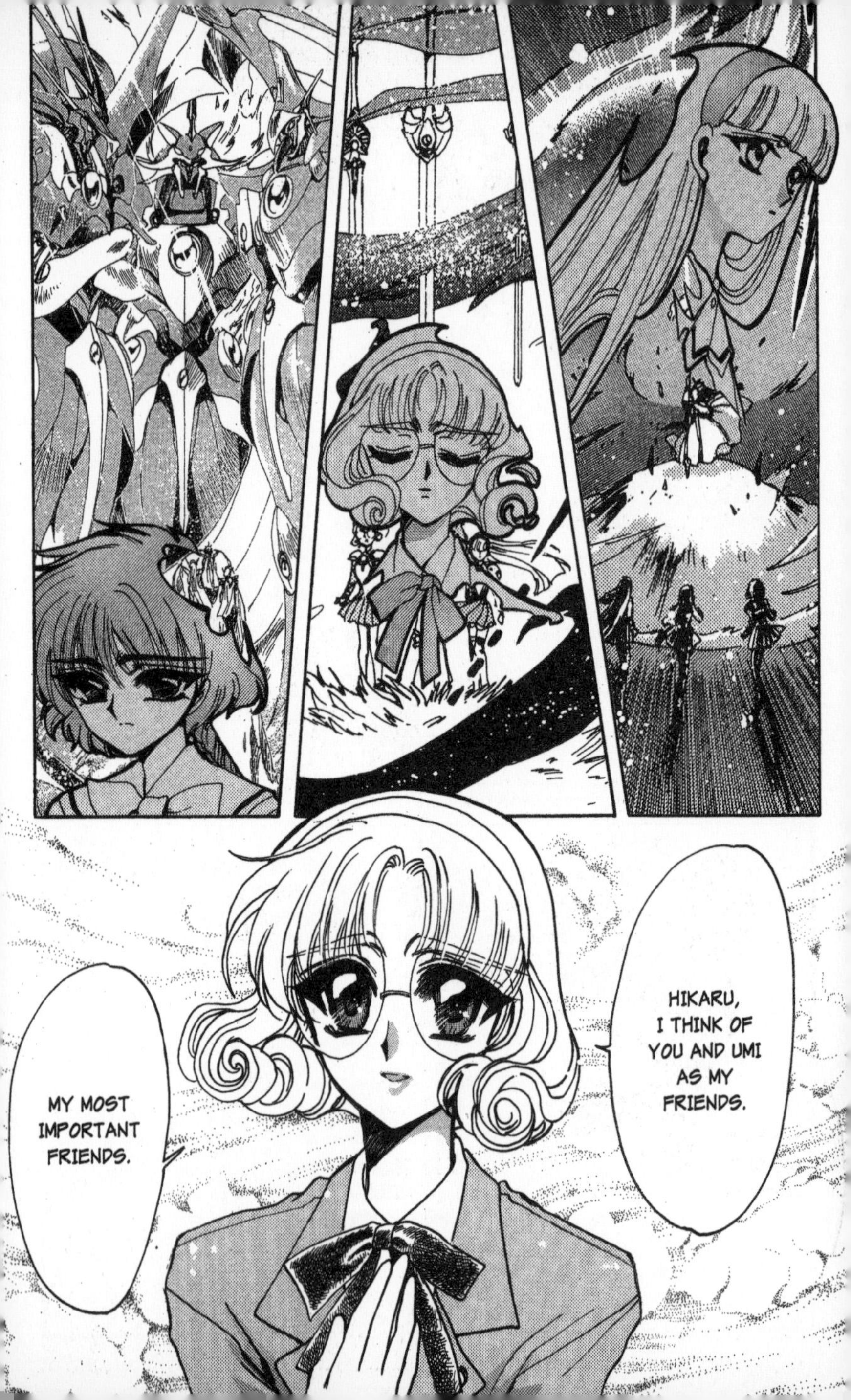
HIKARU, I THINK OF YOU AND UMI AS MY FRIENDS.
MY MOST IMPORTANT FRIENDS.

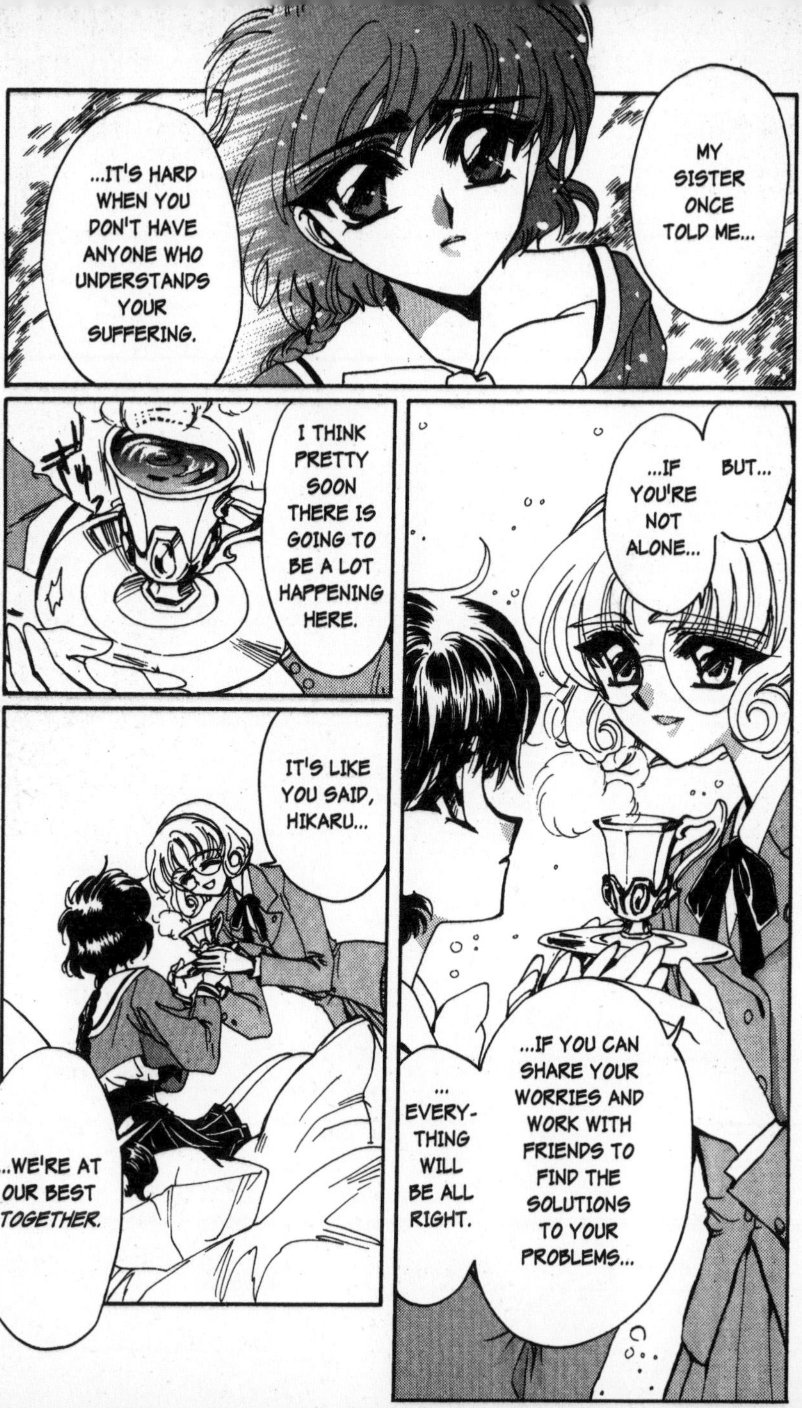
MY SISTER ONCE TOLD ME...
...IT'S HARD WHEN YOU DON'T HAVE ANYONE WHO UNDERSTANDS YOUR SUFFERING.
BUT...
...IF YOU'RE NOT ALONE...
...IF YOU CAN SHARE YOUR WORRIES AND WORK WITH FRIENDS TO FIND THE SOLUTIONS TO YOUR PROBLEMS...
...EVERY-THING WILL BE ALL RIGHT.
I THINK PRETTY SOON THERE IS GOING TO BE A LOT HAPPENING HERE.
IT'S LIKE YOU SAID, HIKARU...
...WE'RE AT OUR BEST *TOGETHER.*

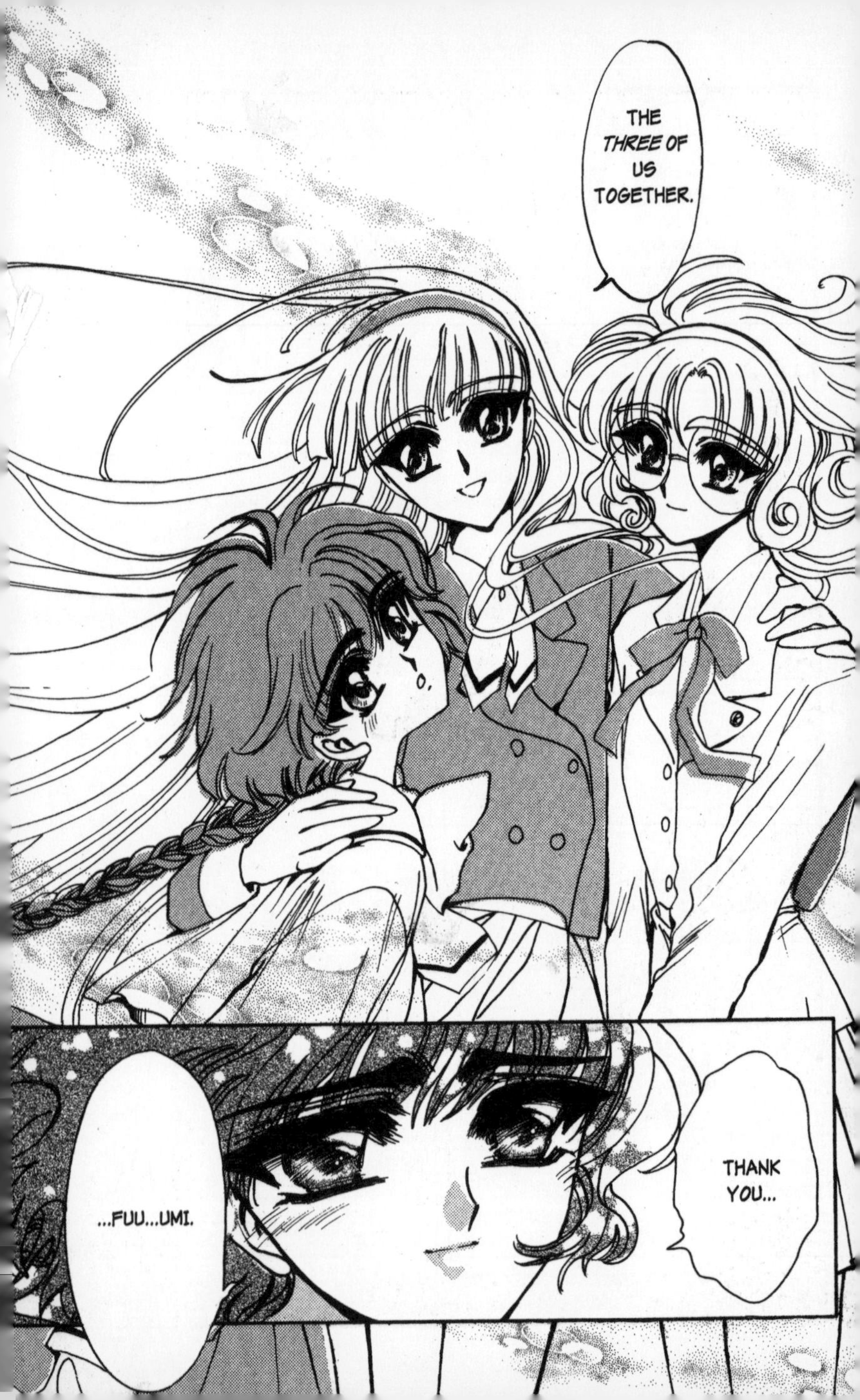
THE THREE OF US TOGETHER.
THANK YOU...
...FUU...UMI.

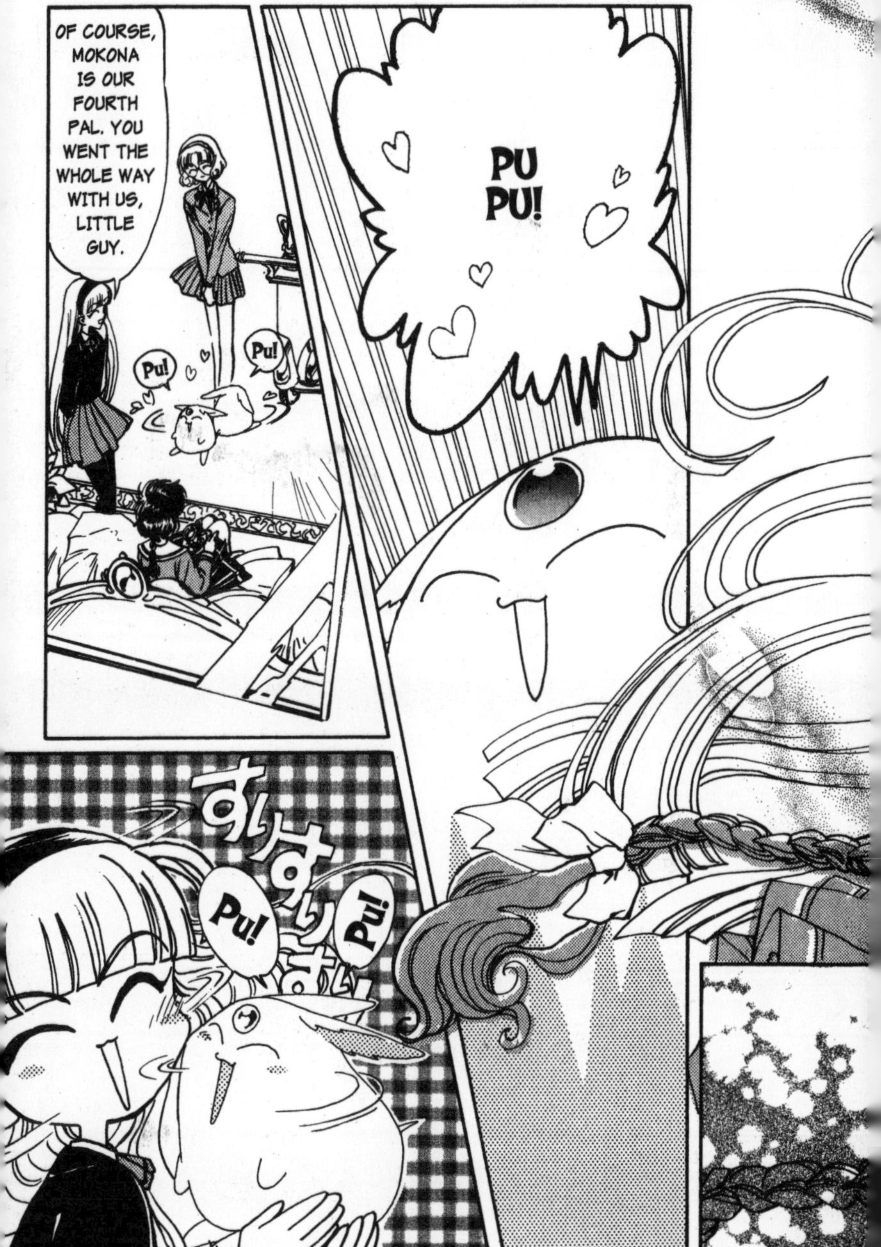
PU PU!
OF COURSE, MOKONA IS OUR FOURTH PAL. YOU WENT THE WHOLE WAY WITH US, LITTLE GUY.
Pu!
Pu!
すいすいすい
Pu!
Pu!

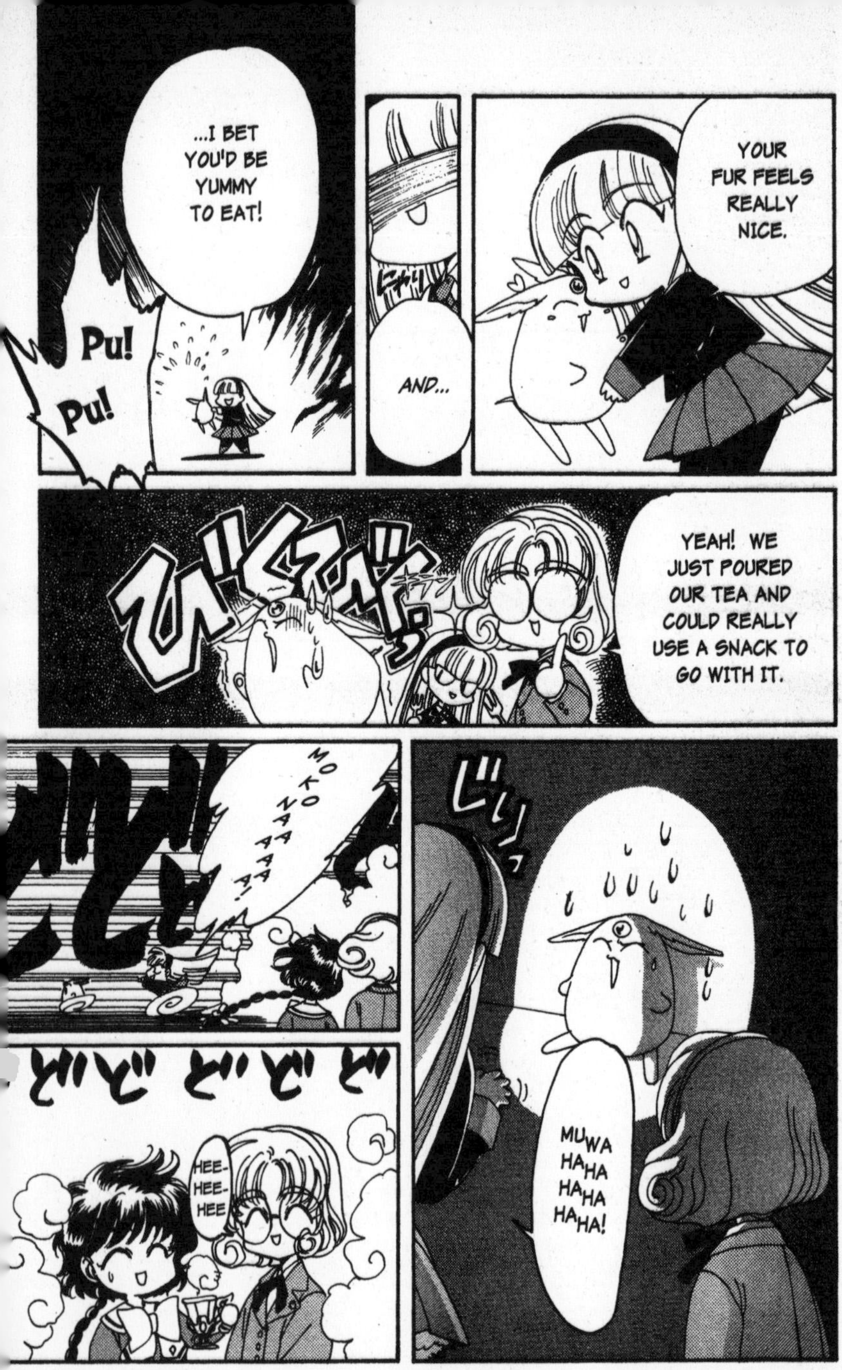
YOUR FUR FEELS REALLY NICE.
AND...
...I BET YOU'D BE YUMMY TO EAT!
Pu!
Pu!
YEAH! WE JUST POURED OUR TEA AND COULD REALLY USE A SNACK TO GO WITH IT.
MUWAHAHAHAHAHAHA!
MOKONAAAAAAA!
HEE-HEE-HEE

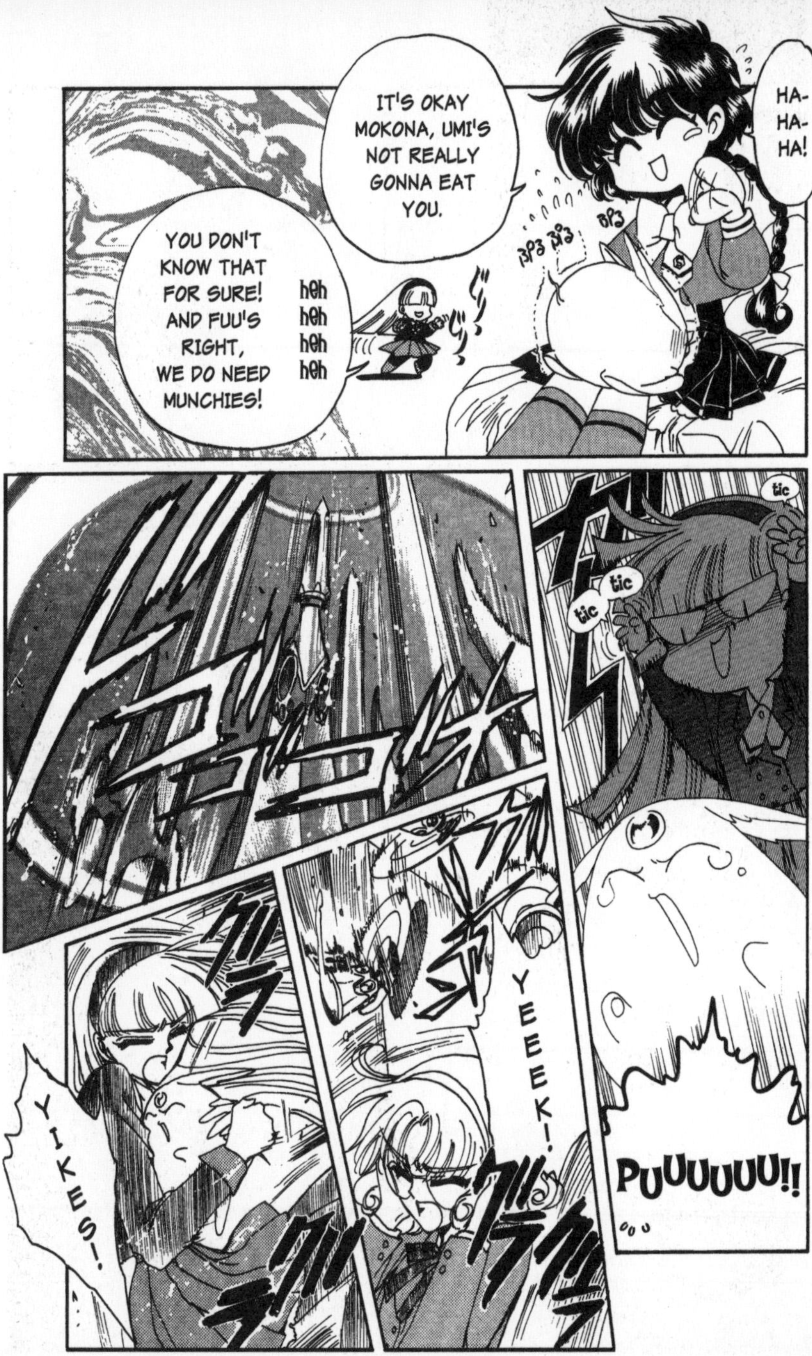
HA-HA-HA!
IT'S OKAY MOKONA, UMI'S NOT REALLY GONNA EAT YOU.
YOU DON'T KNOW THAT FOR SURE! AND FUU'S RIGHT, WE DO NEED MUNCHIES!
heh heh heh heh
tic
tic
tic
PUUUUUU!!
YEEEK!
YIKES!

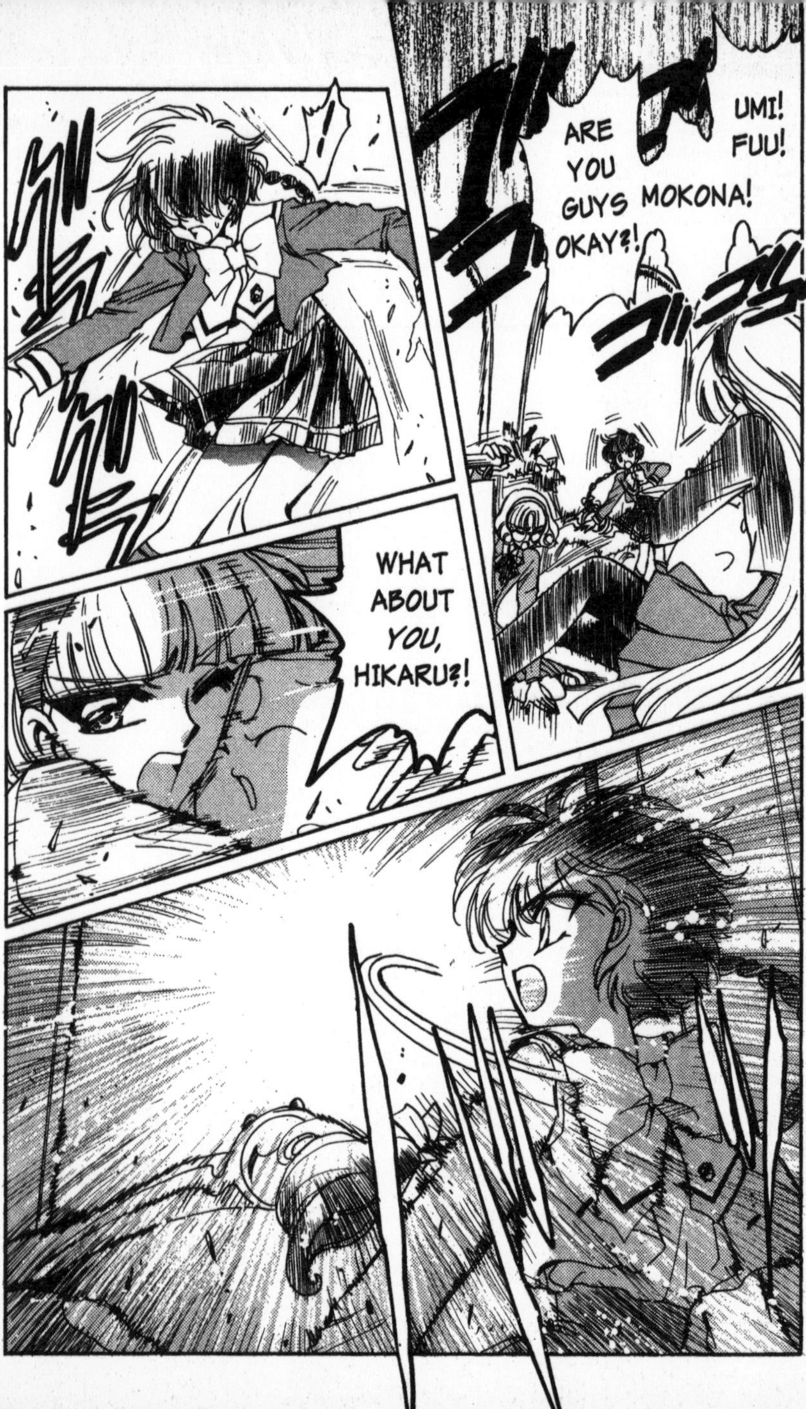
UMI! FUU! MOKONA!
ARE YOU GUYS OKAY?!
WHAT ABOUT YOU, HIKARU?!

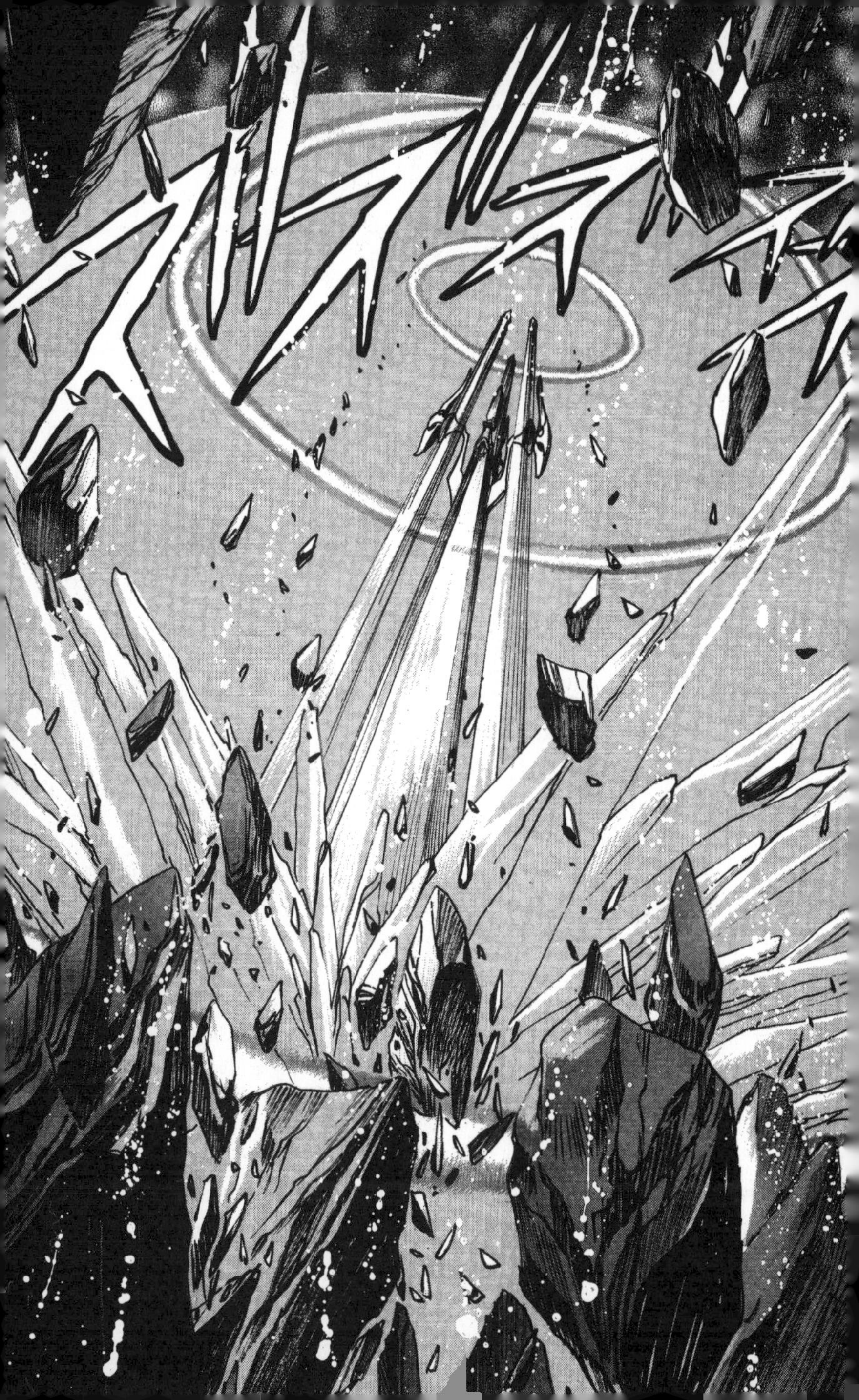

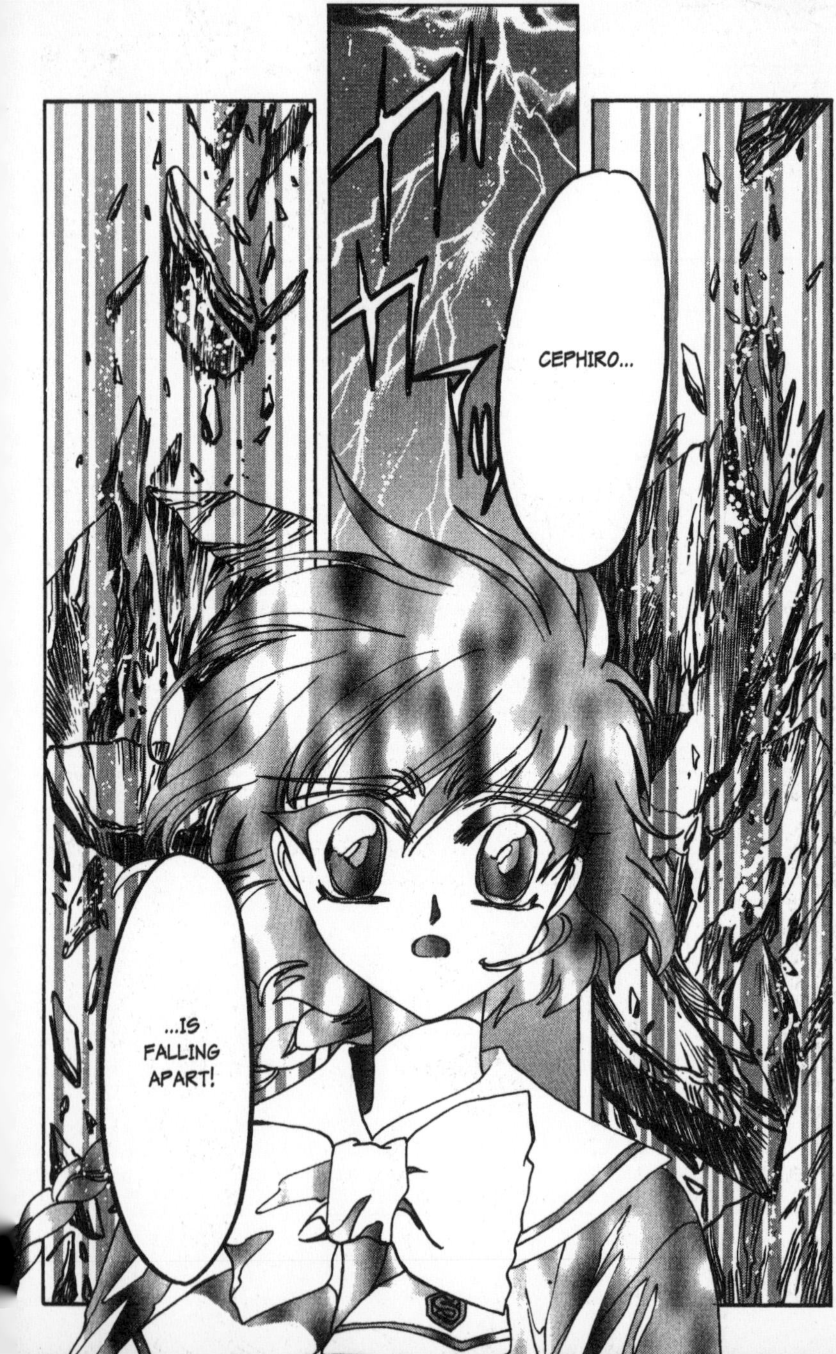
CEPHIRO...
...IS FALLING APART!

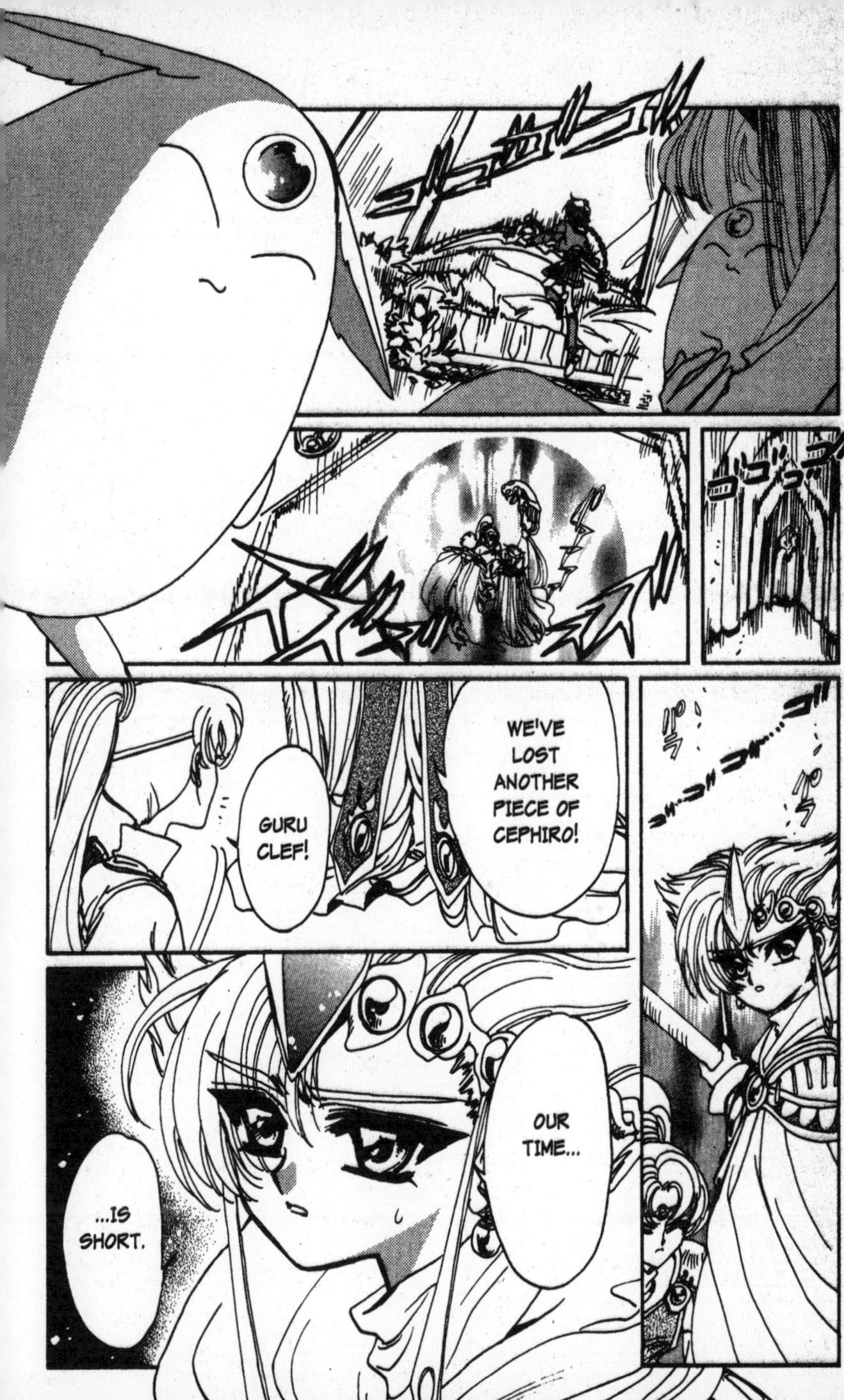
WE'VE LOST ANOTHER PIECE OF CEPHIRO!
GURU CLEF!
OUR TIME...
...IS SHORT.

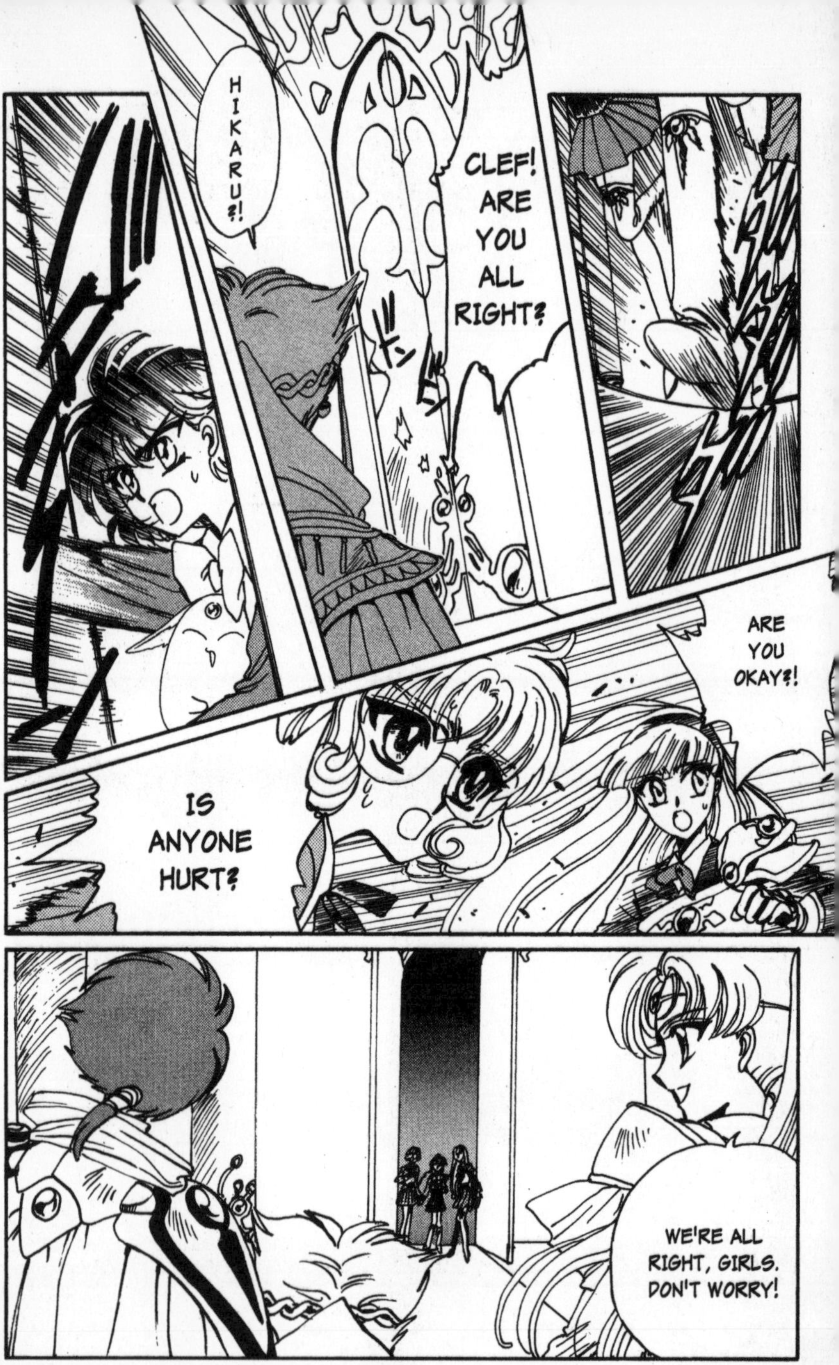
HIKARU?!
CLEF! ARE YOU ALL RIGHT?
ARE YOU OKAY?!
IS ANYONE HURT?
WE'RE ALL RIGHT, GIRLS. DON'T WORRY!

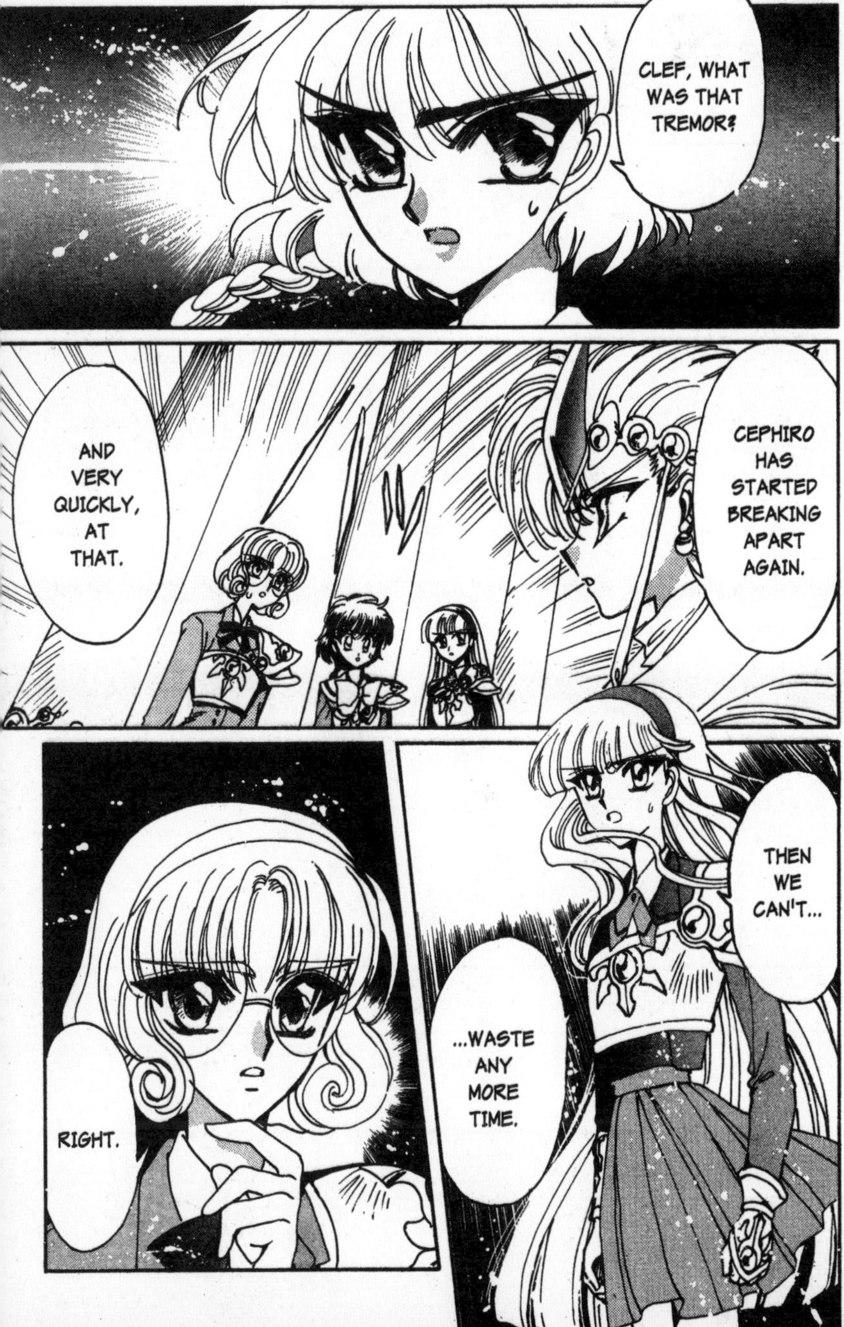
CLEF, WHAT WAS THAT TREMOR?
CEPHIRO HAS STARTED BREAKING APART AGAIN.
AND VERY QUICKLY, AT THAT.
THEN WE CAN'T...
...WASTE ANY MORE TIME.
RIGHT.

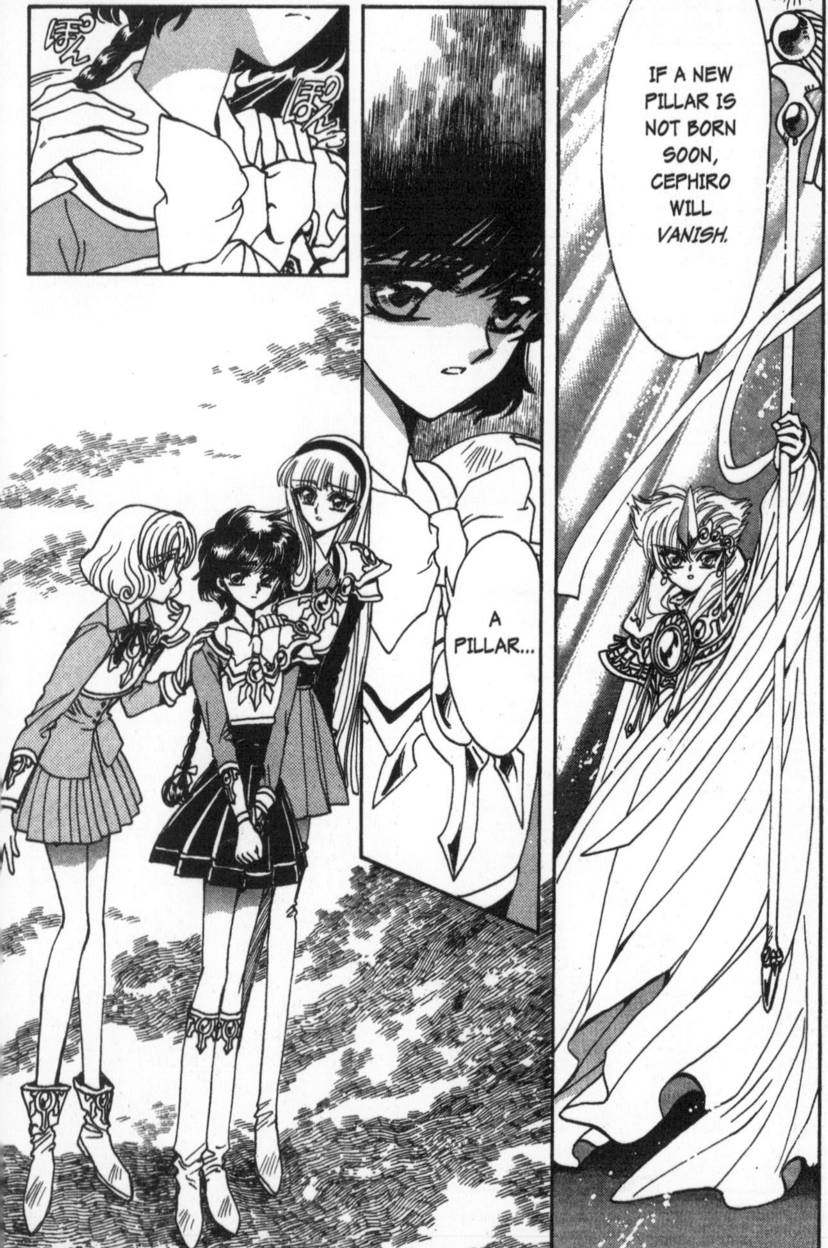
IF A NEW PILLAR IS NOT BORN SOON, CEPHIRO WILL *VANISH.*
A PILLAR...
ぽん
ぽん

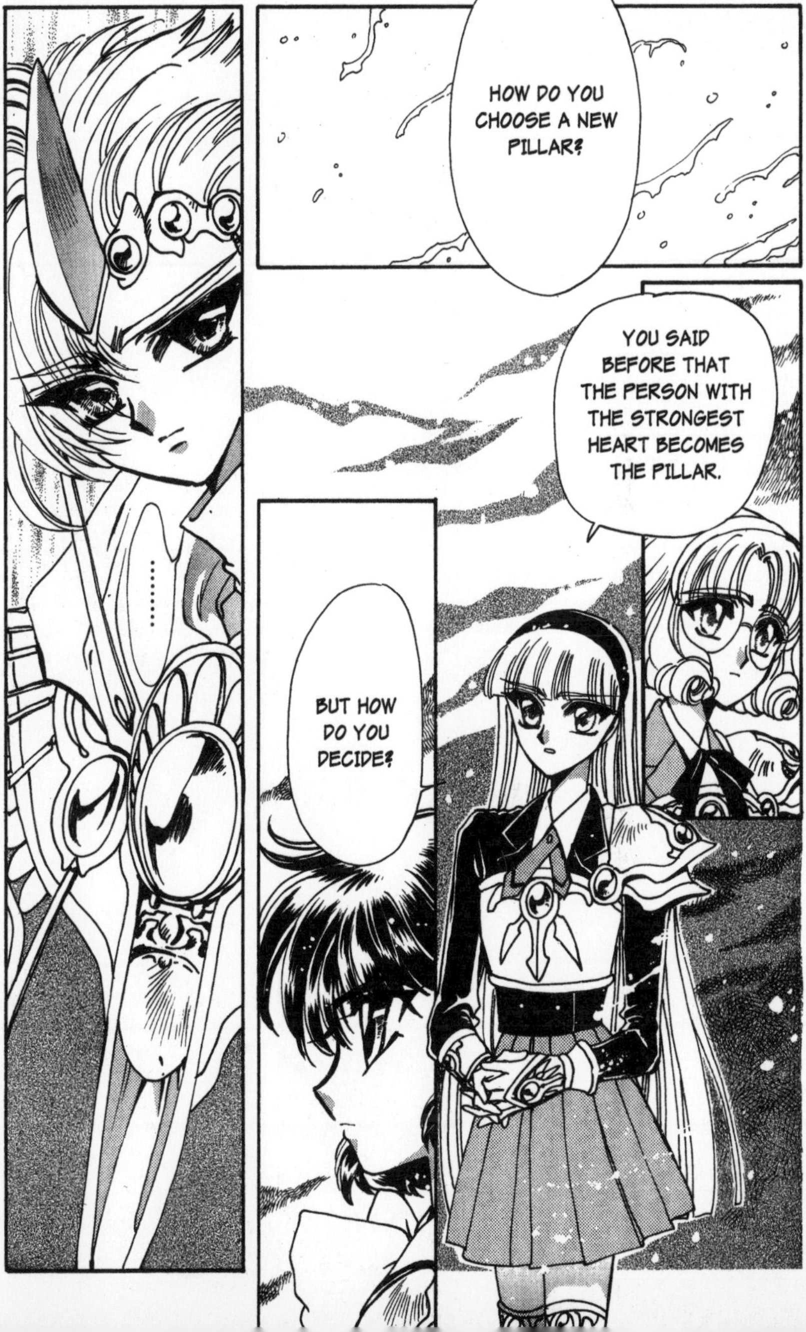
HOW DO YOU CHOOSE A NEW PILLAR?
YOU SAID BEFORE THAT THE PERSON WITH THE STRONGEST HEART BECOMES THE PILLAR.
BUT HOW DO YOU DECIDE?
......

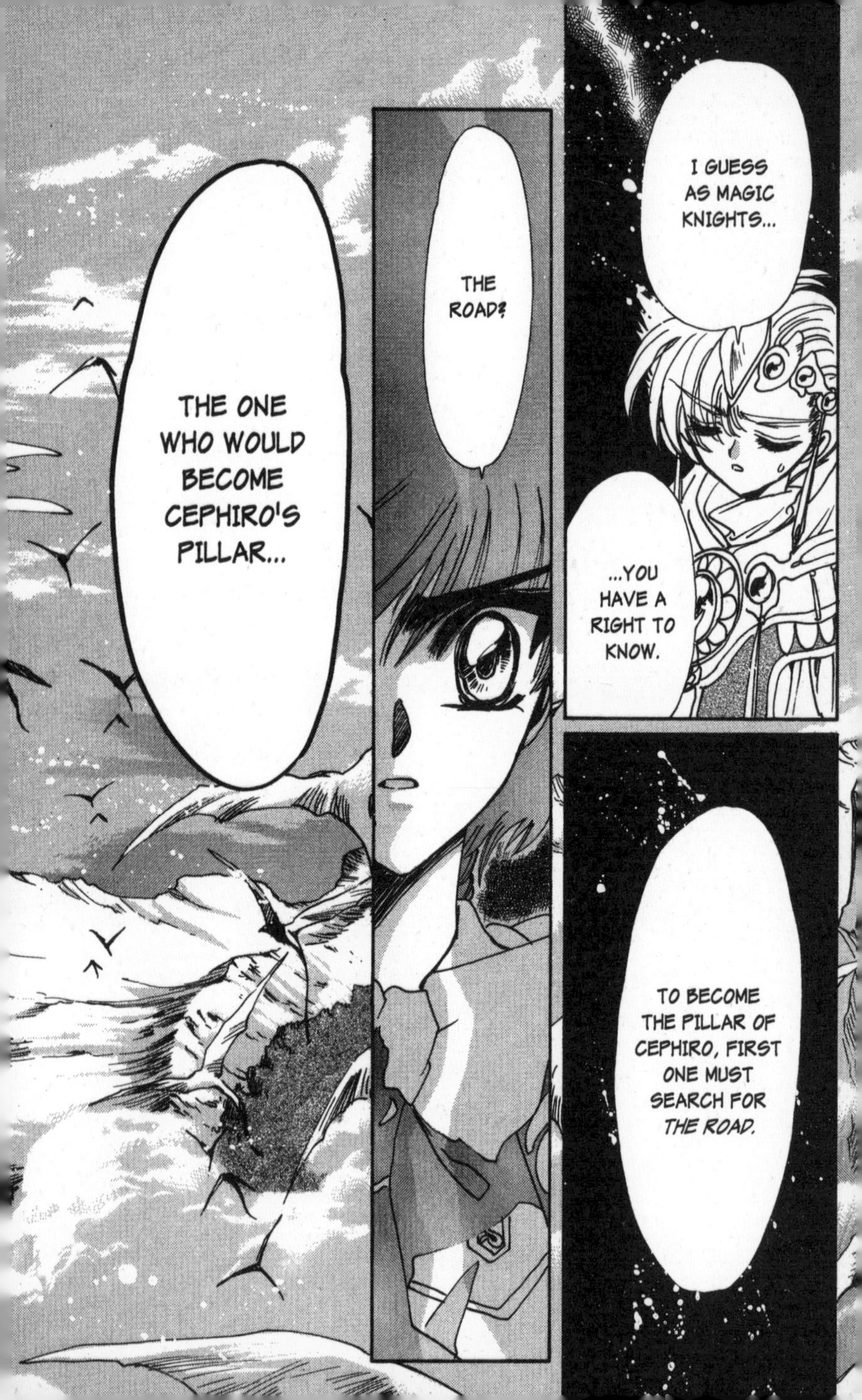
I GUESS AS MAGIC KNIGHTS...
...YOU HAVE A RIGHT TO KNOW.
TO BECOME THE PILLAR OF CEPHIRO, FIRST ONE MUST SEARCH FOR *THE ROAD.*
THE ROAD?
THE ONE WHO WOULD BECOME CEPHIRO'S PILLAR...

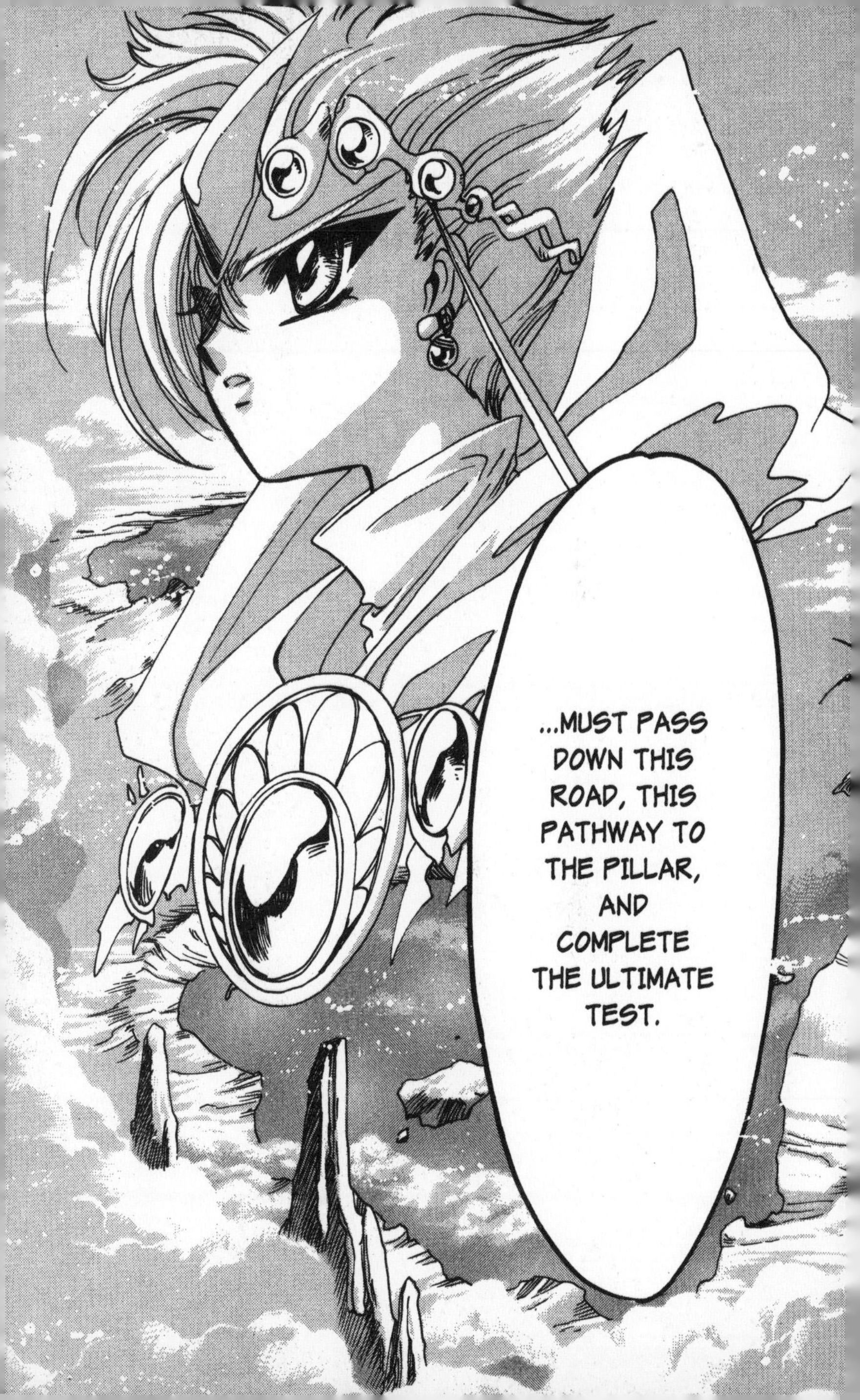
...MUST PASS DOWN THIS ROAD, THIS PATHWAY TO THE PILLAR, AND COMPLETE THE ULTIMATE TEST.

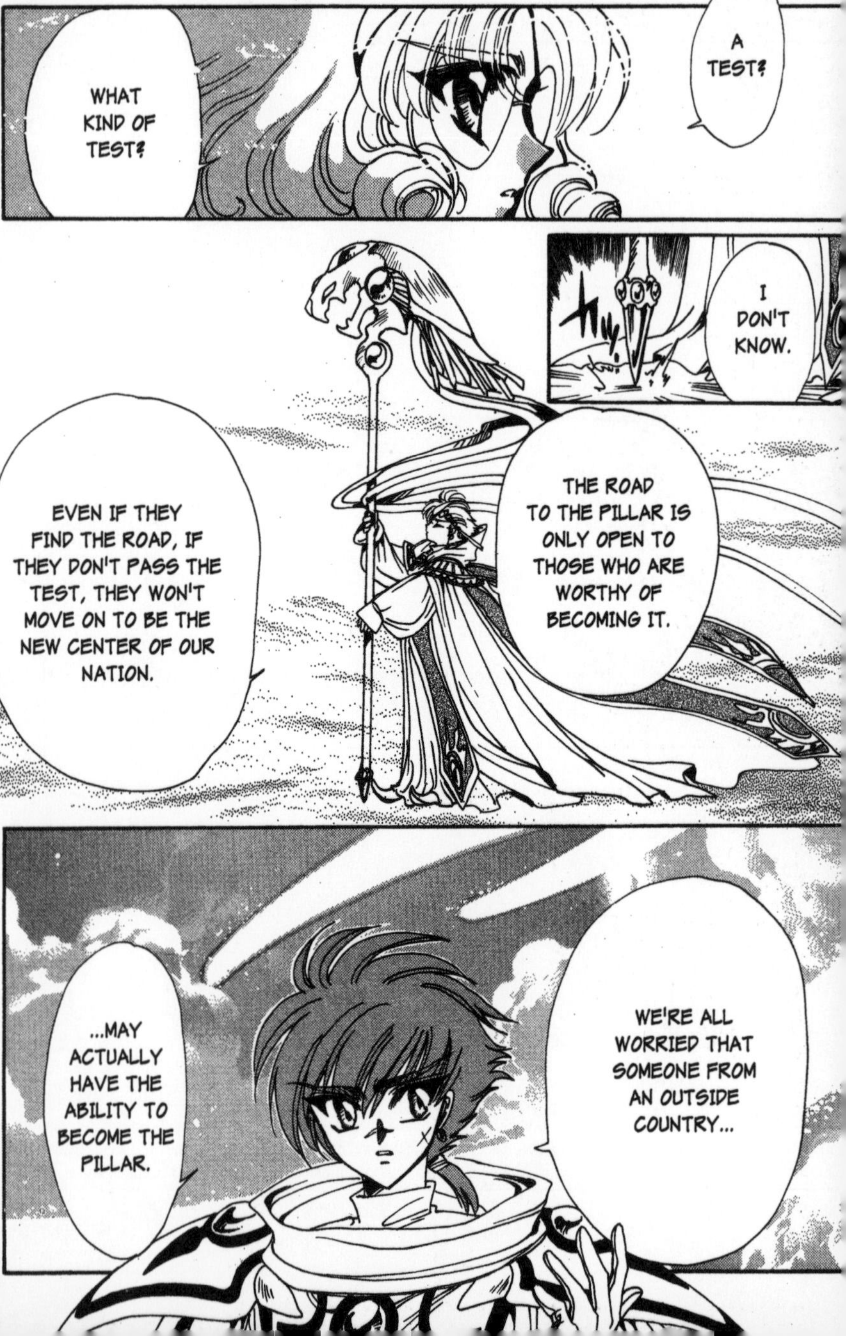
A TEST?
WHAT KIND OF TEST?
I DON'T KNOW.
THE ROAD TO THE PILLAR IS ONLY OPEN TO THOSE WHO ARE WORTHY OF BECOMING IT.
EVEN IF THEY FIND THE ROAD, IF THEY DON'T PASS THE TEST, THEY WON'T MOVE ON TO BE THE NEW CENTER OF OUR NATION.
WE'RE ALL WORRIED THAT SOMEONE FROM AN OUTSIDE COUNTRY...
...MAY ACTUALLY HAVE THE ABILITY TO BECOME THE PILLAR.

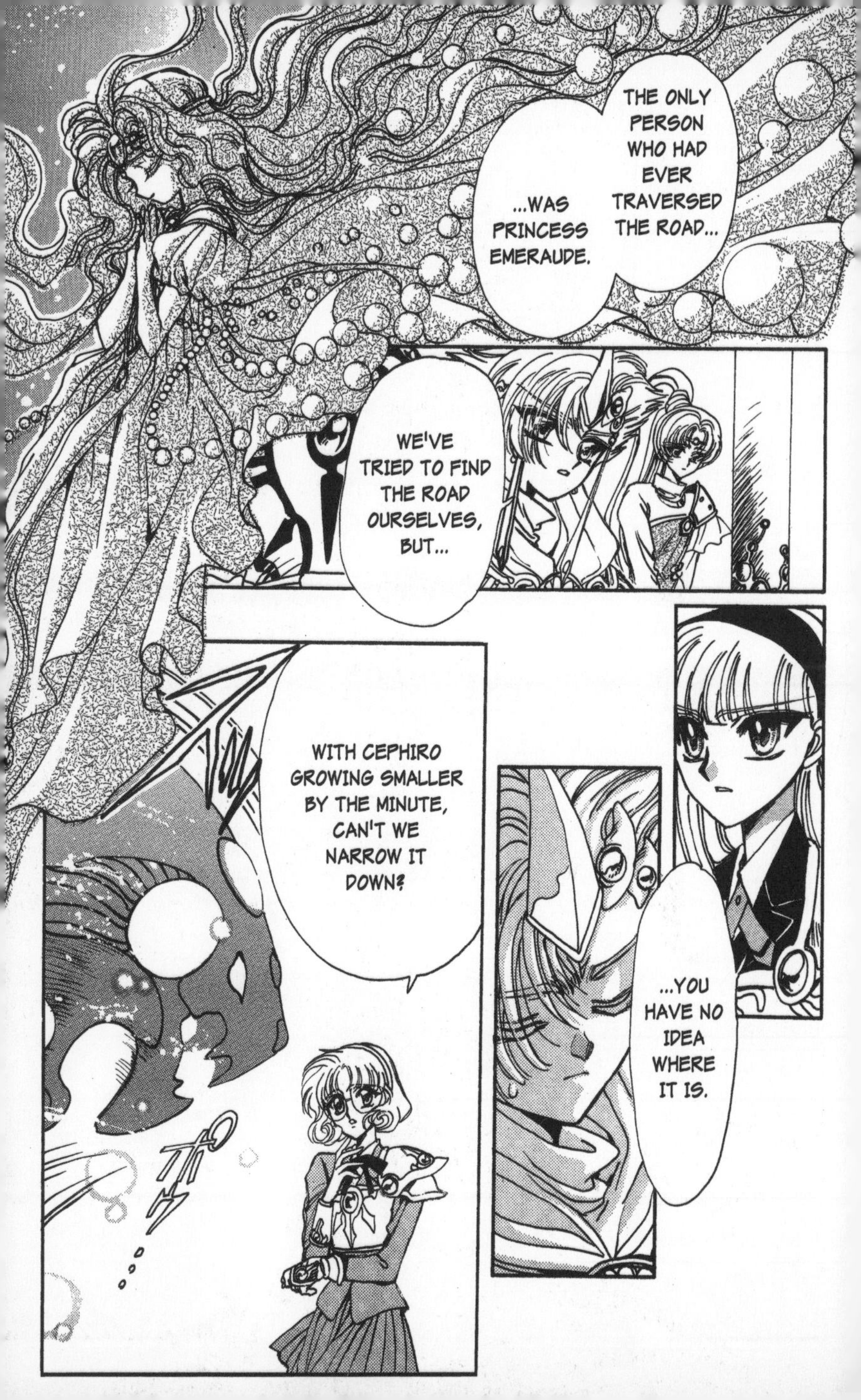
THE ONLY PERSON WHO HAD EVER TRAVERSED THE ROAD...
...WAS PRINCESS EMERAUDE.
WE'VE TRIED TO FIND THE ROAD OURSELVES, BUT...
...YOU HAVE NO IDEA WHERE IT IS.
WITH CEPHIRO GROWING SMALLER BY THE MINUTE, CAN'T WE NARROW IT DOWN?

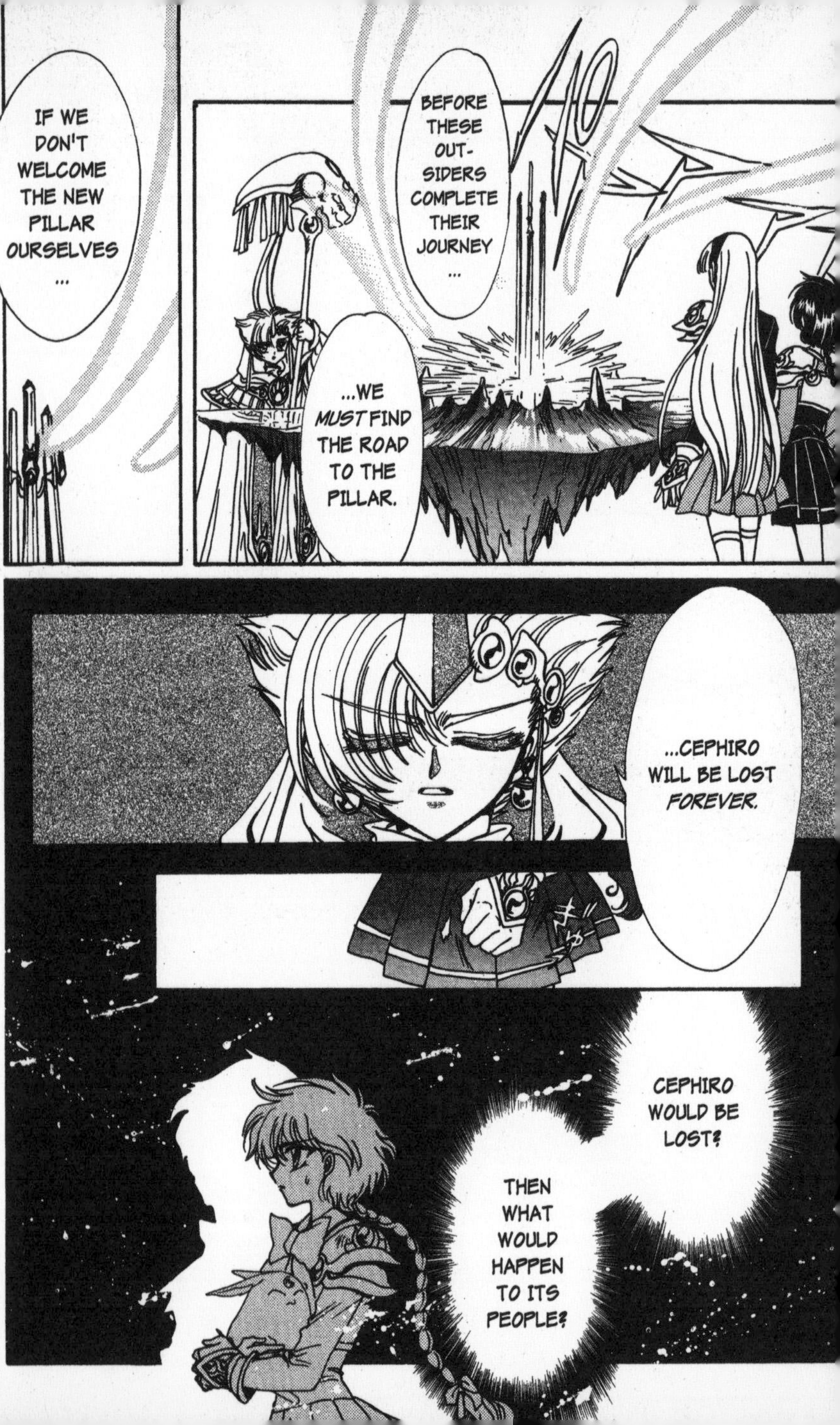
BEFORE THESE OUT-SIDERS COMPLETE THEIR JOURNEY ...
...WE *MUST* FIND THE ROAD TO THE PILLAR.
IF WE DON'T WELCOME THE NEW PILLAR OURSELVES ...
...CEPHIRO WILL BE LOST *FOREVER.*
CEPHIRO WOULD BE LOST?
THEN WHAT WOULD HAPPEN TO ITS PEOPLE?

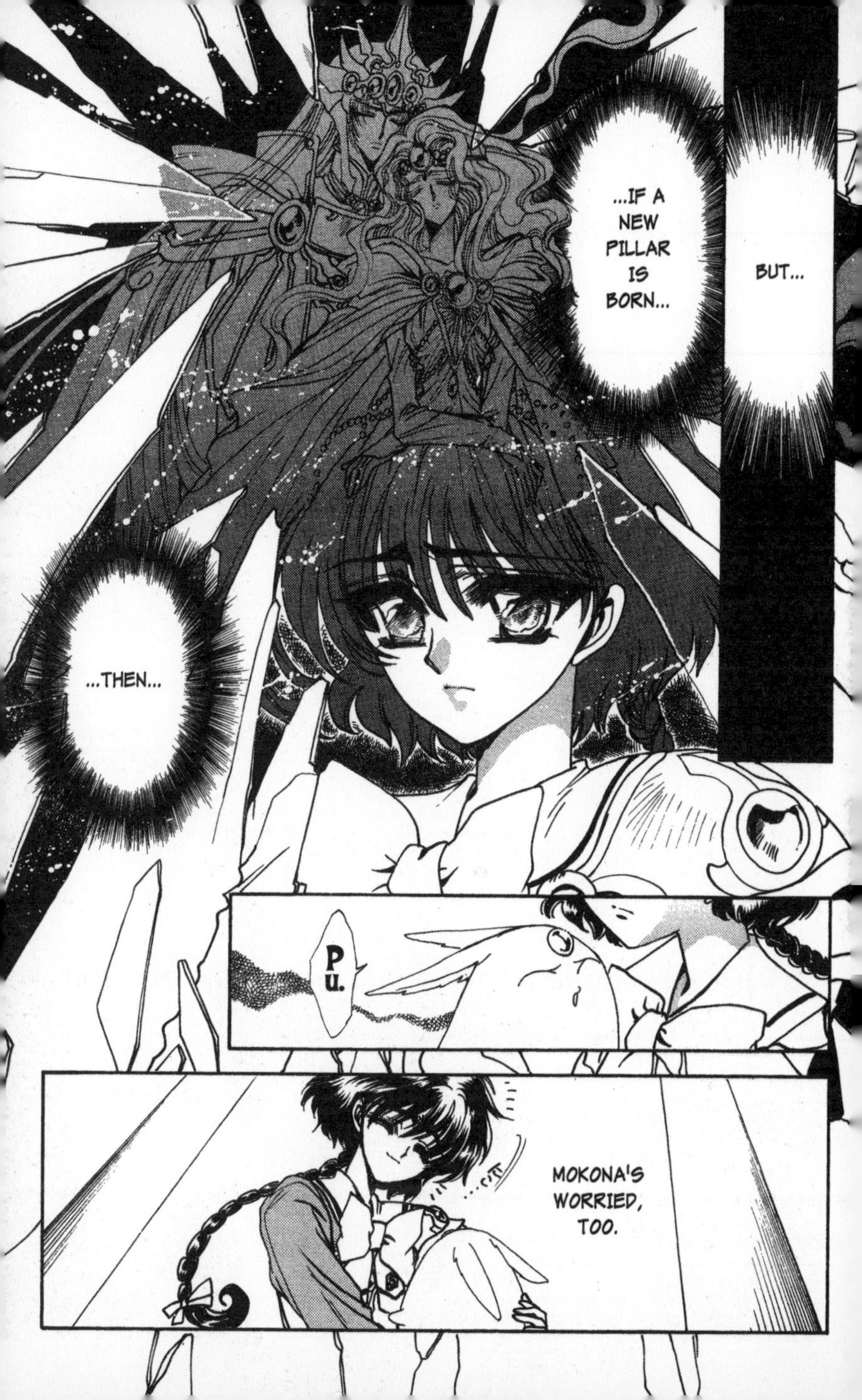
BUT...
...IF A NEW PILLAR IS BORN...
...THEN...
Pu.
MOKONA'S WORRIED, TOO.

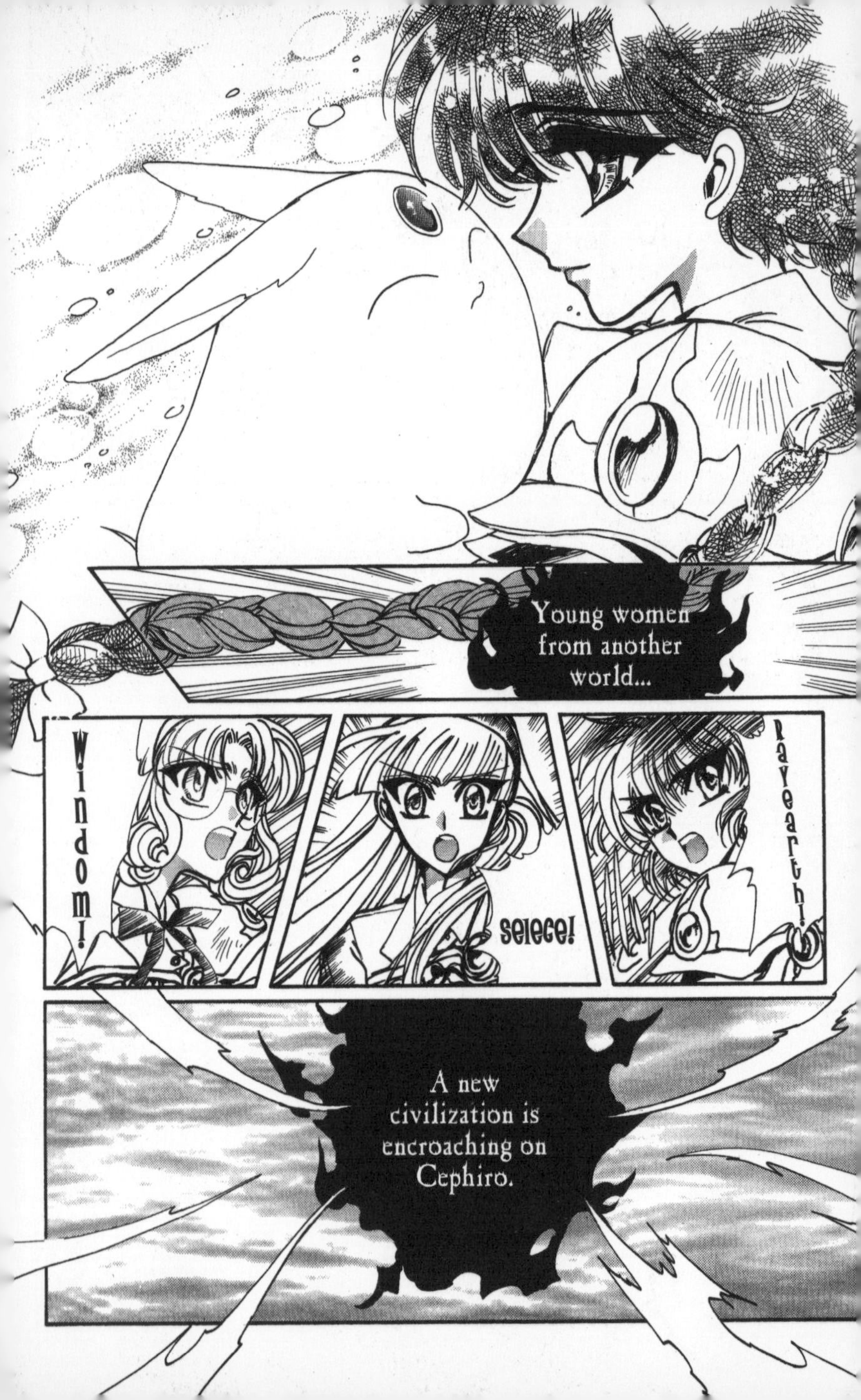
Young women from another world...
Rayearth!
Selece!
Windom!
A new civilization is encroaching on Cephiro.

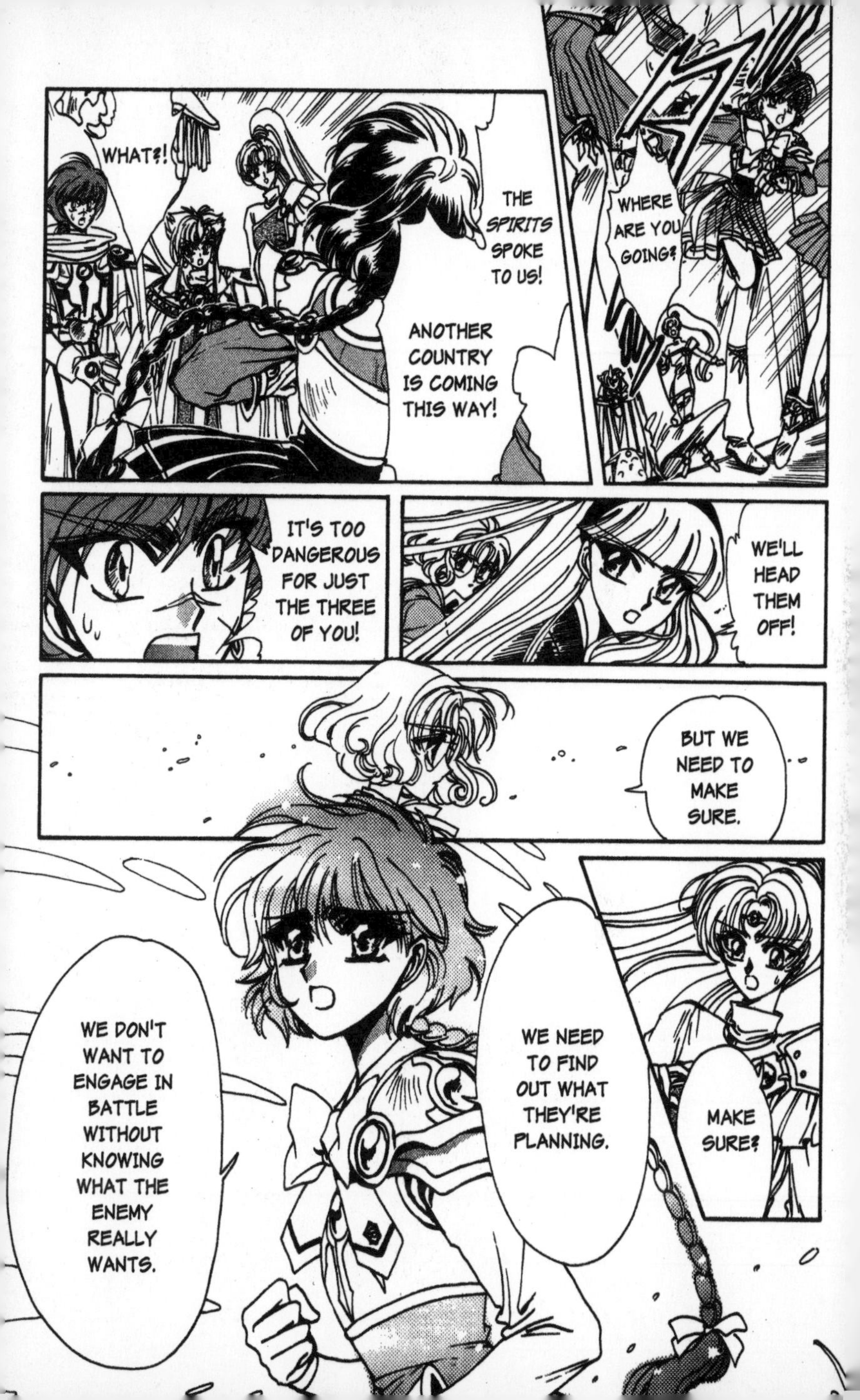
WHERE ARE YOU GOING?
THE SPIRITS SPOKE TO US!
ANOTHER COUNTRY IS COMING THIS WAY!
WHAT?!
WE'LL HEAD THEM OFF!
IT'S TOO DANGEROUS FOR JUST THE THREE OF YOU!
BUT WE NEED TO MAKE SURE.
MAKE SURE?
WE NEED TO FIND OUT WHAT THEY'RE PLANNING.
WE DON'T WANT TO ENGAGE IN BATTLE WITHOUT KNOWING WHAT THE ENEMY REALLY WANTS.

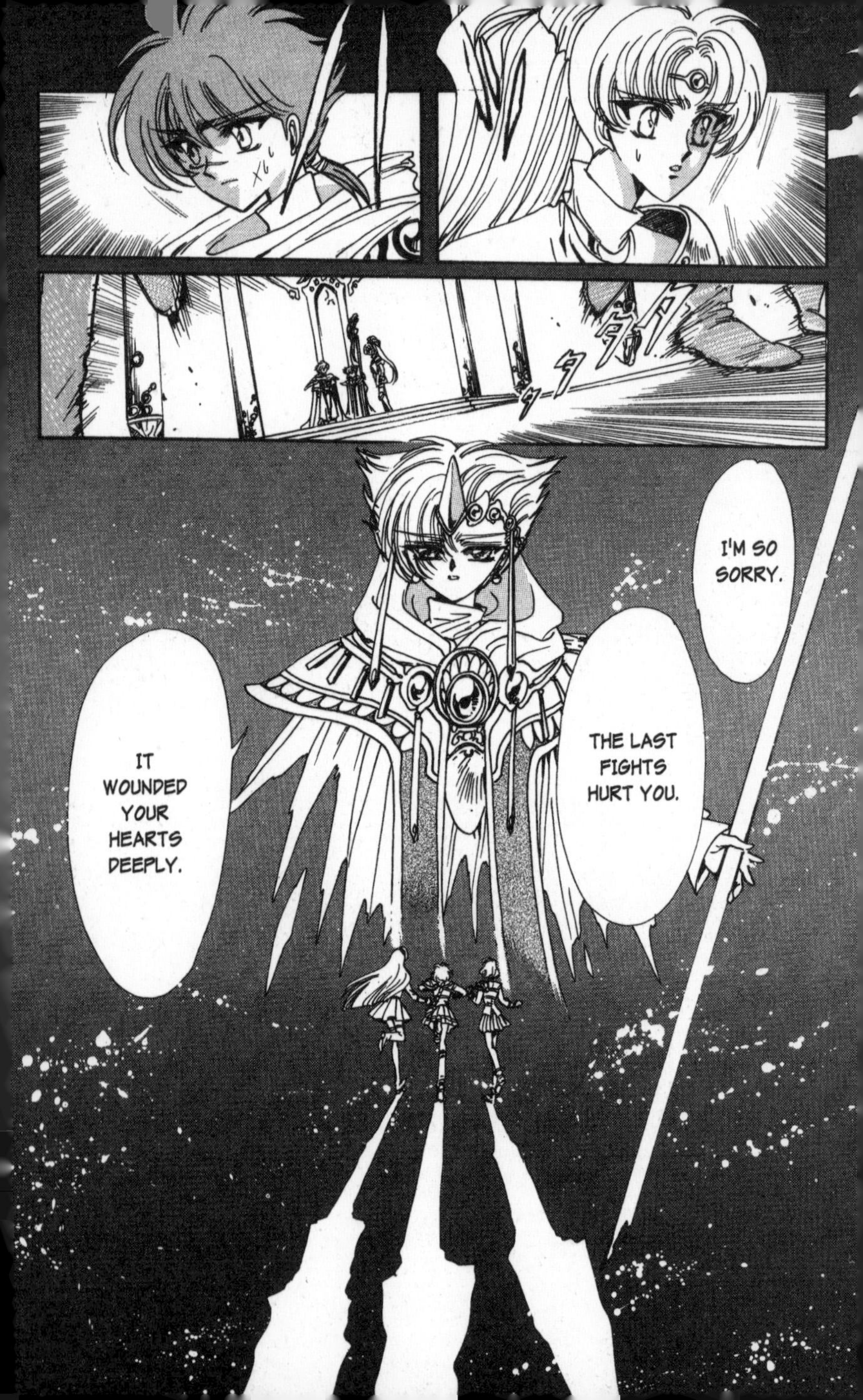
I'M SO SORRY.
THE LAST FIGHTS HURT YOU.
IT WOUNDED YOUR HEARTS DEEPLY.

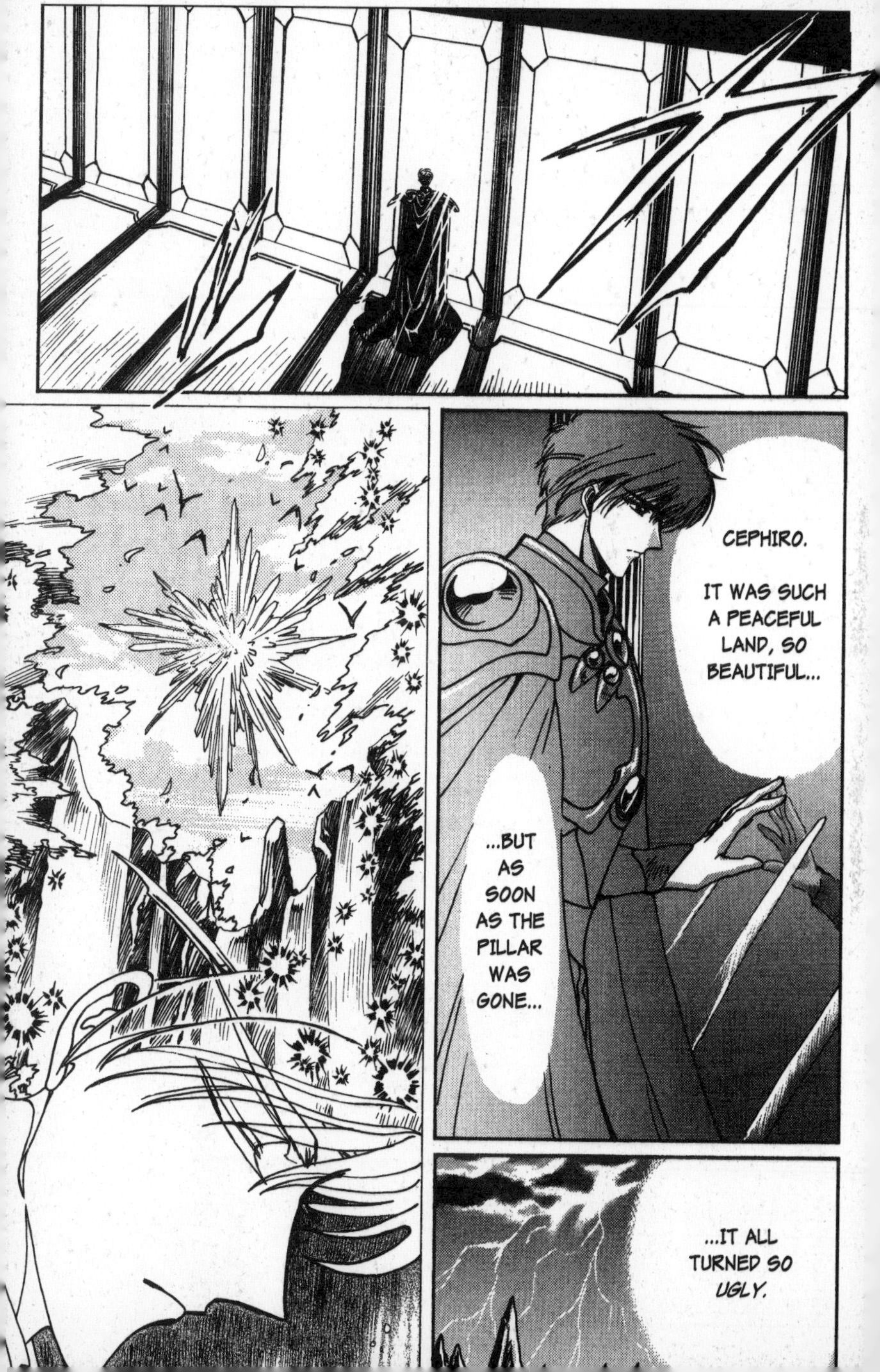
CEPHIRO.
IT WAS SUCH A PEACEFUL LAND, SO BEAUTIFUL...
...BUT AS SOON AS THE PILLAR WAS GONE...
...IT ALL TURNED SO *UGLY.*

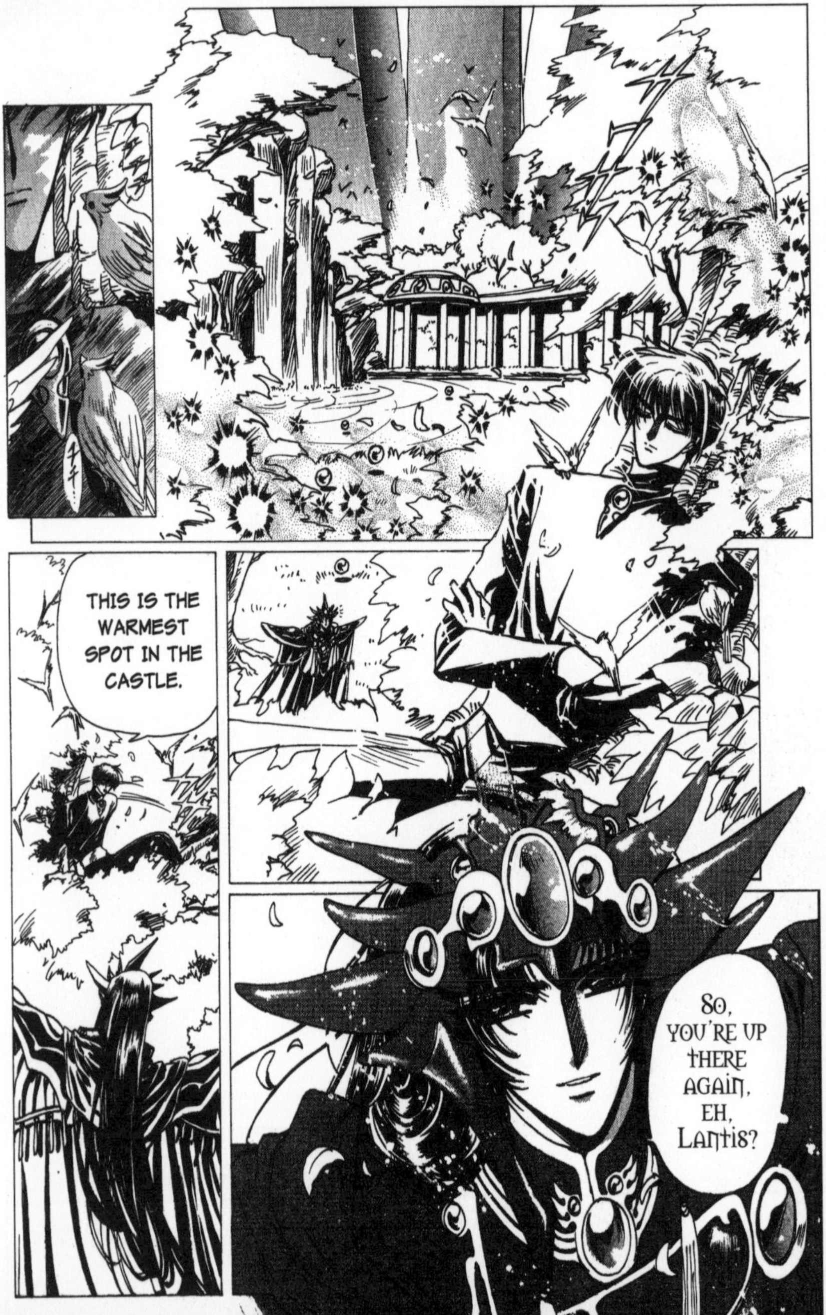
チチ
THIS IS THE WARMEST SPOT IN THE CASTLE.
SO, YOU'RE UP THERE AGAIN, EH, LANTIS?

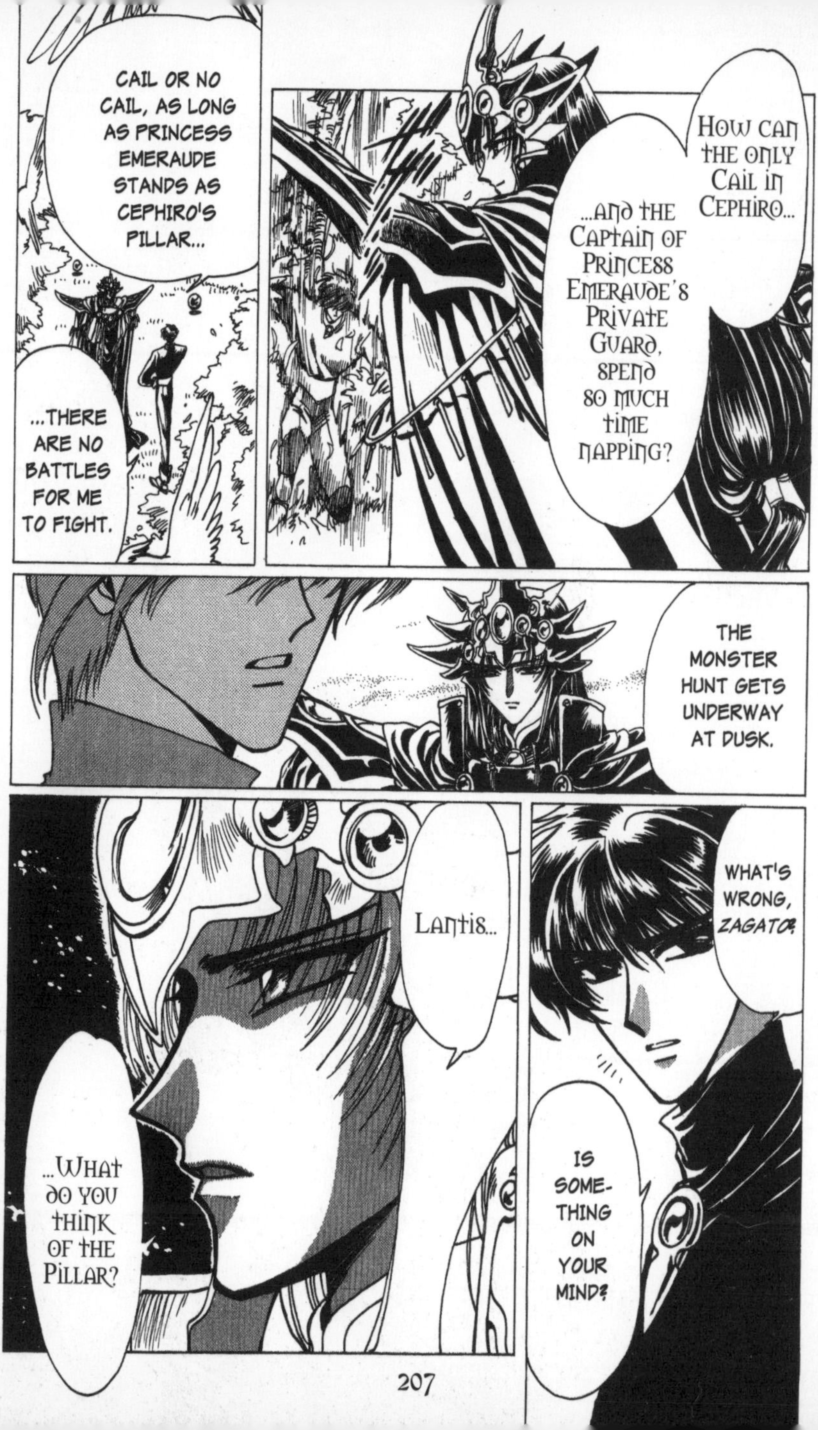
How can the only Cail in Cephiro...
...and the Captain of Princess Emeraude's Private Guard, spend so much time napping?
CAIL OR NO CAIL, AS LONG AS PRINCESS EMERAUDE STANDS AS CEPHIRO'S PILLAR...
...THERE ARE NO BATTLES FOR ME TO FIGHT.
THE MONSTER HUNT GETS UNDERWAY AT DUSK.
WHAT'S WRONG, ZAGATO?
IS SOME-THING ON YOUR MIND?
Lantis...
...What do you think of the Pillar?

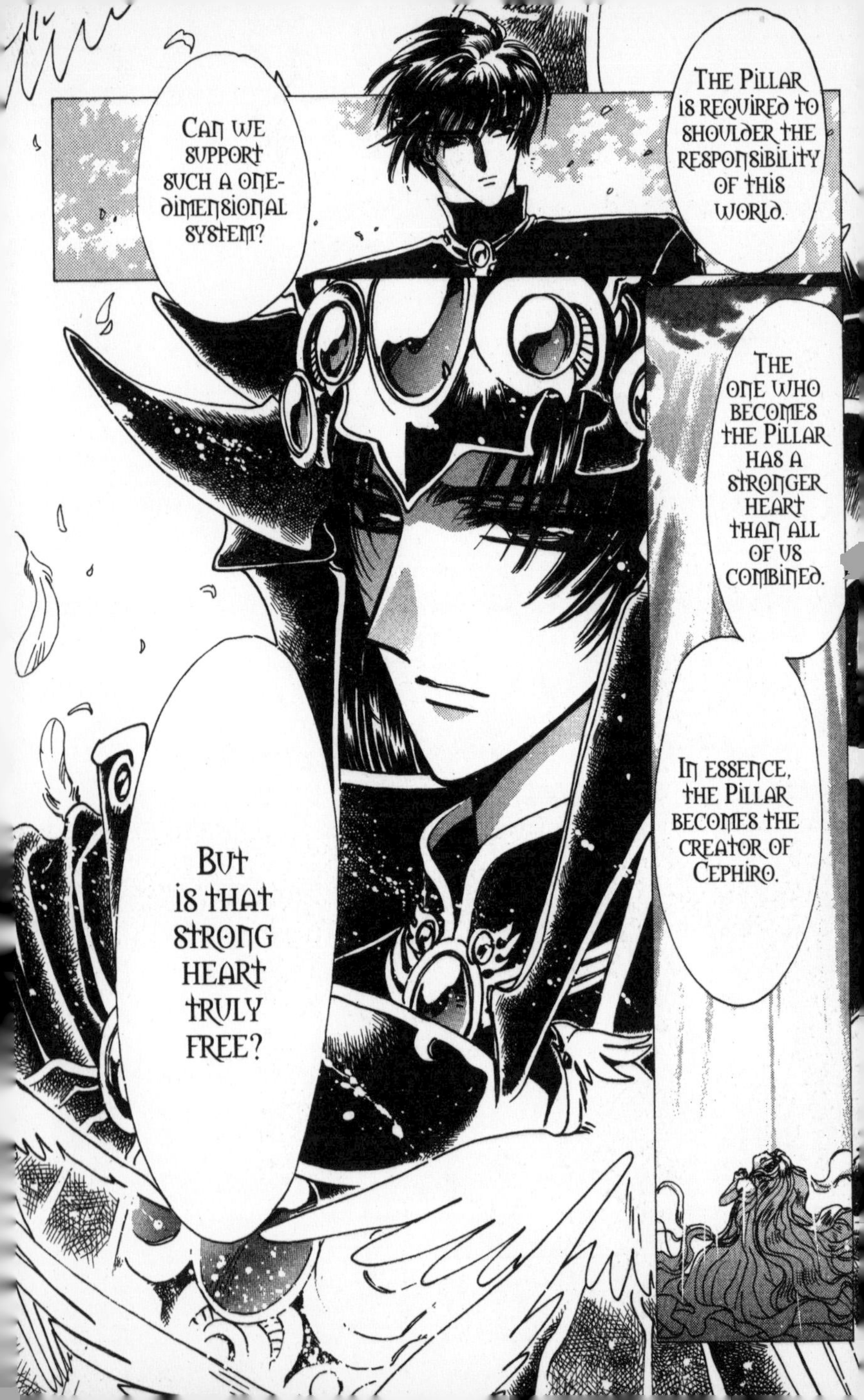
The Pillar is required to shoulder the responsibility of this world.
Can we support such a one-dimensional system?
The one who becomes the Pillar has a stronger heart than all of us combined.
In essence, the Pillar becomes the creator of Cephiro.
But is that strong heart truly free?

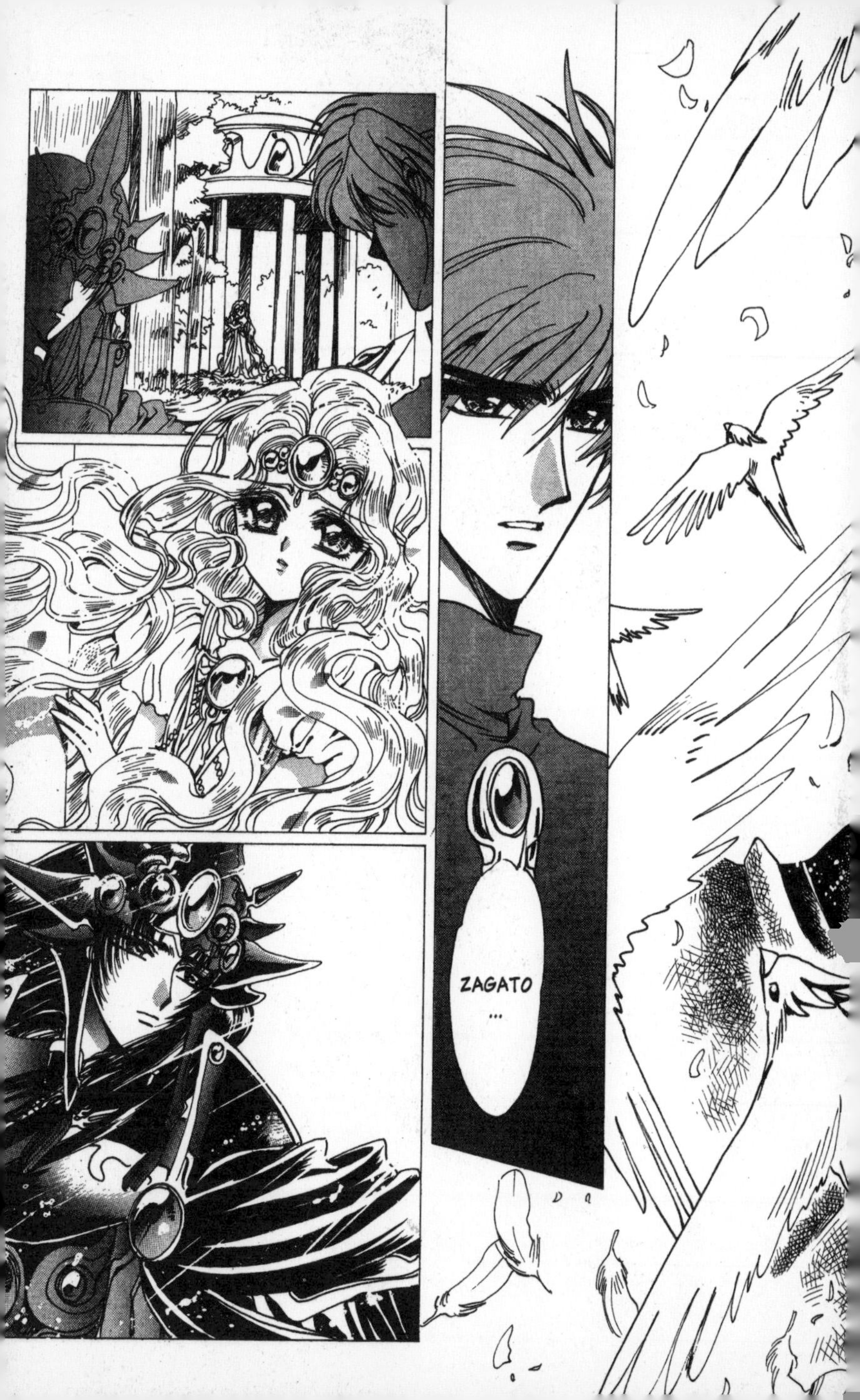
ZAGATO
...

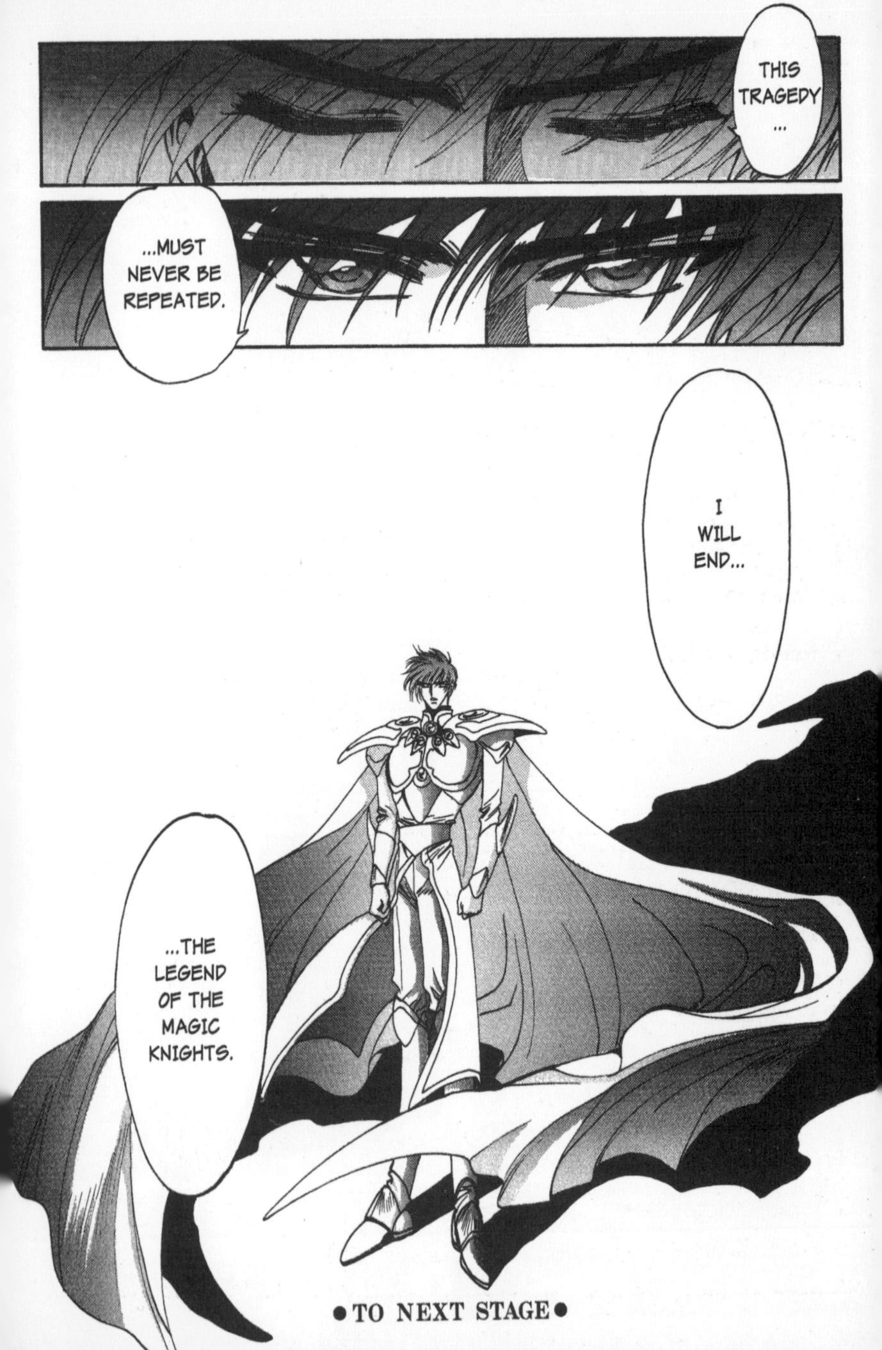
THIS TRAGEDY ...
...MUST NEVER BE REPEATED.
I WILL END...
...THE LEGEND OF THE MAGIC KNIGHTS.

•TO NEXT STAGE•

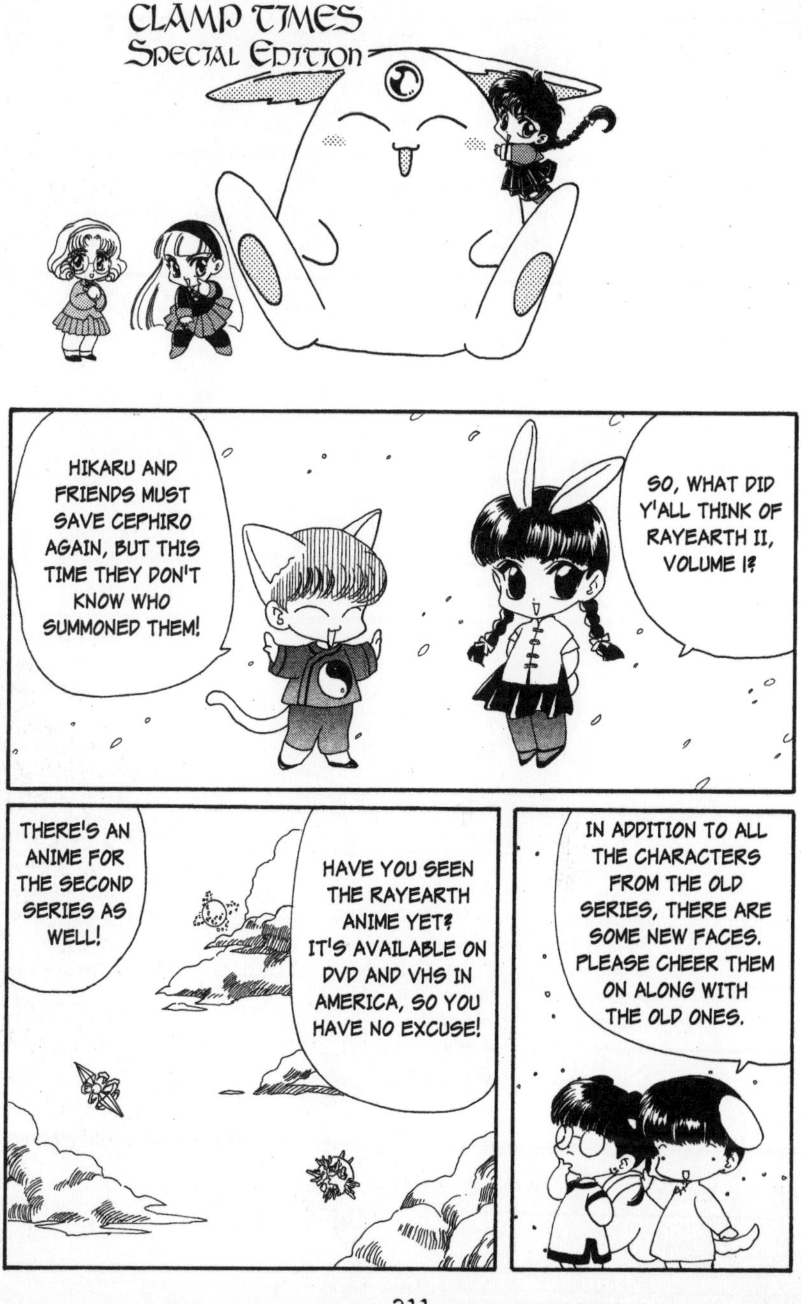
CLAMP TIMES
SPECIAL EDITION
SO, WHAT DID Y'ALL THINK OF RAYEARTH II, VOLUME 1?
HIKARU AND FRIENDS MUST SAVE CEPHIRO AGAIN, BUT THIS TIME THEY DON'T KNOW WHO SUMMONED THEM!
IN ADDITION TO ALL THE CHARACTERS FROM THE OLD SERIES, THERE ARE SOME NEW FACES. PLEASE CHEER THEM ON ALONG WITH THE OLD ONES.
HAVE YOU SEEN THE RAYEARTH ANIME YET? IT'S AVAILABLE ON DVD AND VHS IN AMERICA, SO YOU HAVE NO EXCUSE!
THERE'S AN ANIME FOR THE SECOND SERIES AS WELL!

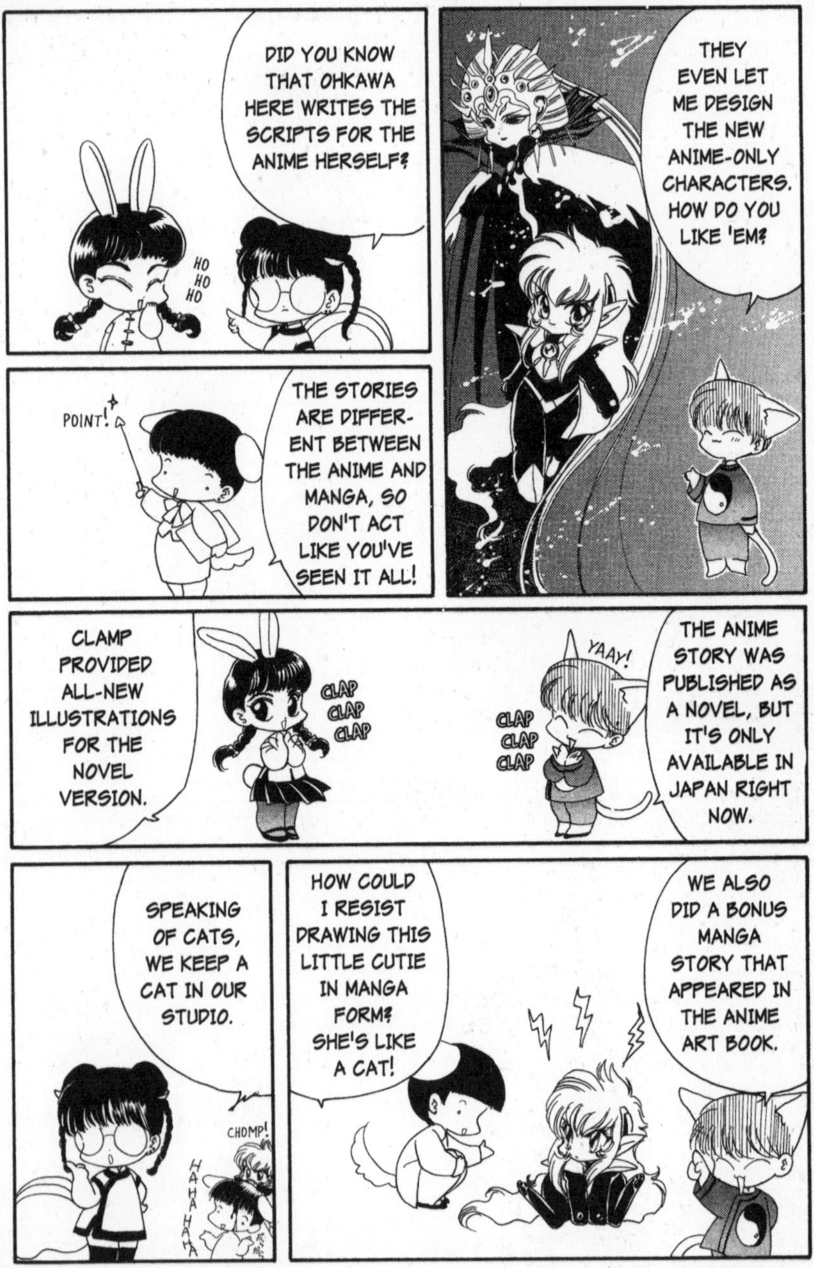
THEY EVEN LET ME DESIGN THE NEW ANIME-ONLY CHARACTERS. HOW DO YOU LIKE 'EM?
DID YOU KNOW THAT OHKAWA HERE WRITES THE SCRIPTS FOR THE ANIME HERSELF?
HO HO HO
THE STORIES ARE DIFFER-ENT BETWEEN THE ANIME AND MANGA, SO DON'T ACT LIKE YOU'VE SEEN IT ALL!
POINT!
THE ANIME STORY WAS PUBLISHED AS A NOVEL, BUT IT'S ONLY AVAILABLE IN JAPAN RIGHT NOW.
YAAY!
CLAP CLAP CLAP
CLAP CLAP CLAP
CLAMP PROVIDED ALL-NEW ILLUSTRATIONS FOR THE NOVEL VERSION.
WE ALSO DID A BONUS MANGA STORY THAT APPEARED IN THE ANIME ART BOOK.
HOW COULD I RESIST DRAWING THIS LITTLE CUTIE IN MANGA FORM? SHE'S LIKE A CAT!
SPEAKING OF CATS, WE KEEP A CAT IN OUR STUDIO.
CHOMP!
HAHAHAHA

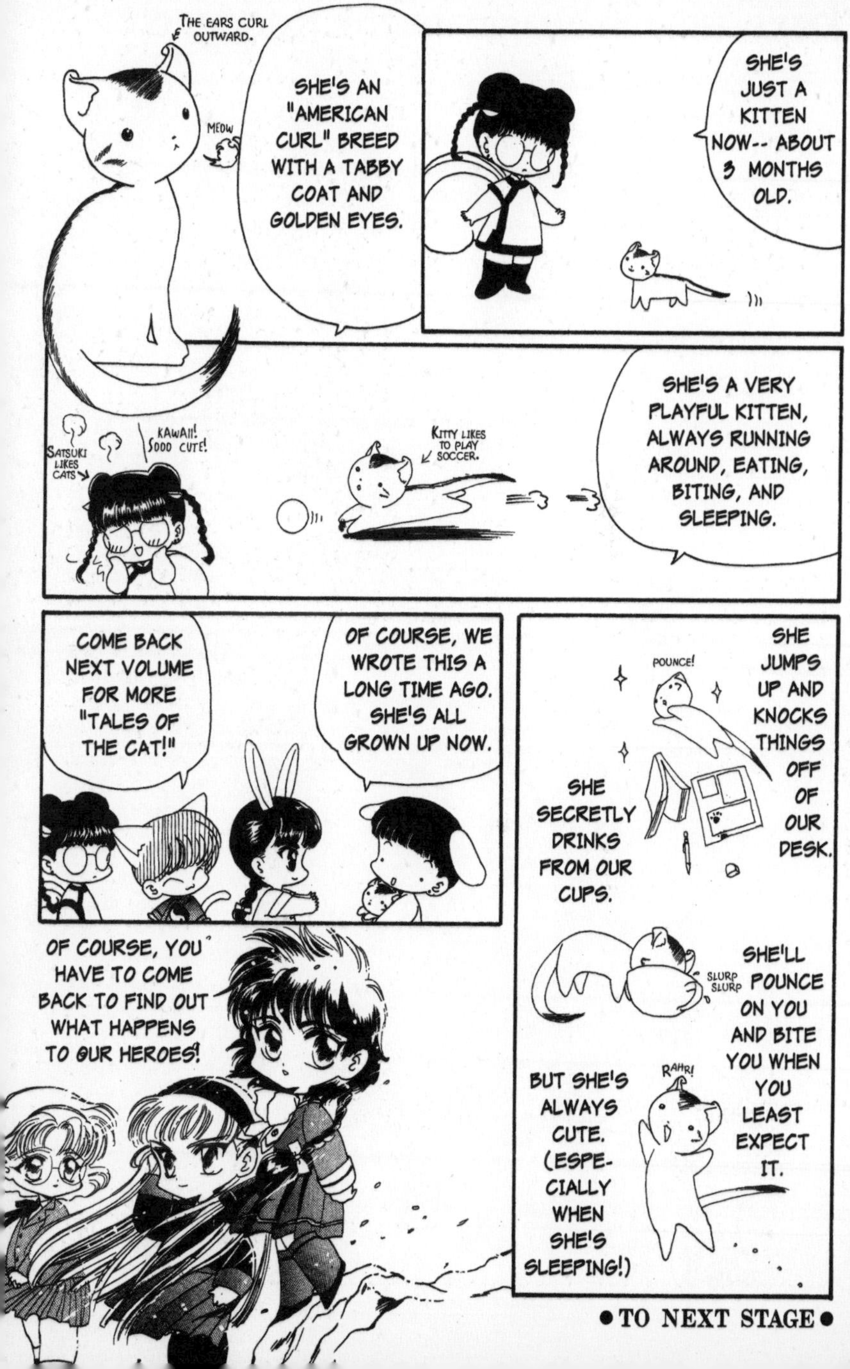

SHE'S JUST A KITTEN NOW-- ABOUT 3 MONTHS OLD.
THE EARS CURL OUTWARD.
SHE'S AN "AMERICAN CURL" BREED WITH A TABBY COAT AND GOLDEN EYES.
MEOW
SHE'S A VERY PLAYFUL KITTEN, ALWAYS RUNNING AROUND, EATING, BITING, AND SLEEPING.
KITTY LIKES TO PLAY SOCCER.
KAWAII! SOOO CUTE!
SATSUKI LIKES CATS
SHE JUMPS UP AND KNOCKS THINGS OFF OF OUR DESK.
POUNCE!
SHE SECRETLY DRINKS FROM OUR CUPS.
SLURP SLURP
SHE'LL POUNCE ON YOU AND BITE YOU WHEN YOU LEAST EXPECT IT.
RAHR!
BUT SHE'S ALWAYS CUTE. (ESPE-CIALLY WHEN SHE'S SLEEPING!)
OF COURSE, WE WROTE THIS A LONG TIME AGO. SHE'S ALL GROWN UP NOW.
COME BACK NEXT VOLUME FOR MORE "TALES OF THE CAT!"
OF COURSE, YOU HAVE TO COME BACK TO FIND OUT WHAT HAPPENS TO OUR HEROES!

• TO NEXT STAGE •

Next time in Magic Knight Rayearth 11...

To control Cephiro means to sacrifice oneself to keep it safe. This is a lesson the Magic Knights know only too well, however, the invading countries are not aware of this and continue the assault with greater force. When powerful Djinns, deadly dragons, and menacing mechs attack the peaceful nation, Hikaru, Umi and Fuu don their sacred armor once more to defend the land as Magic Knights!

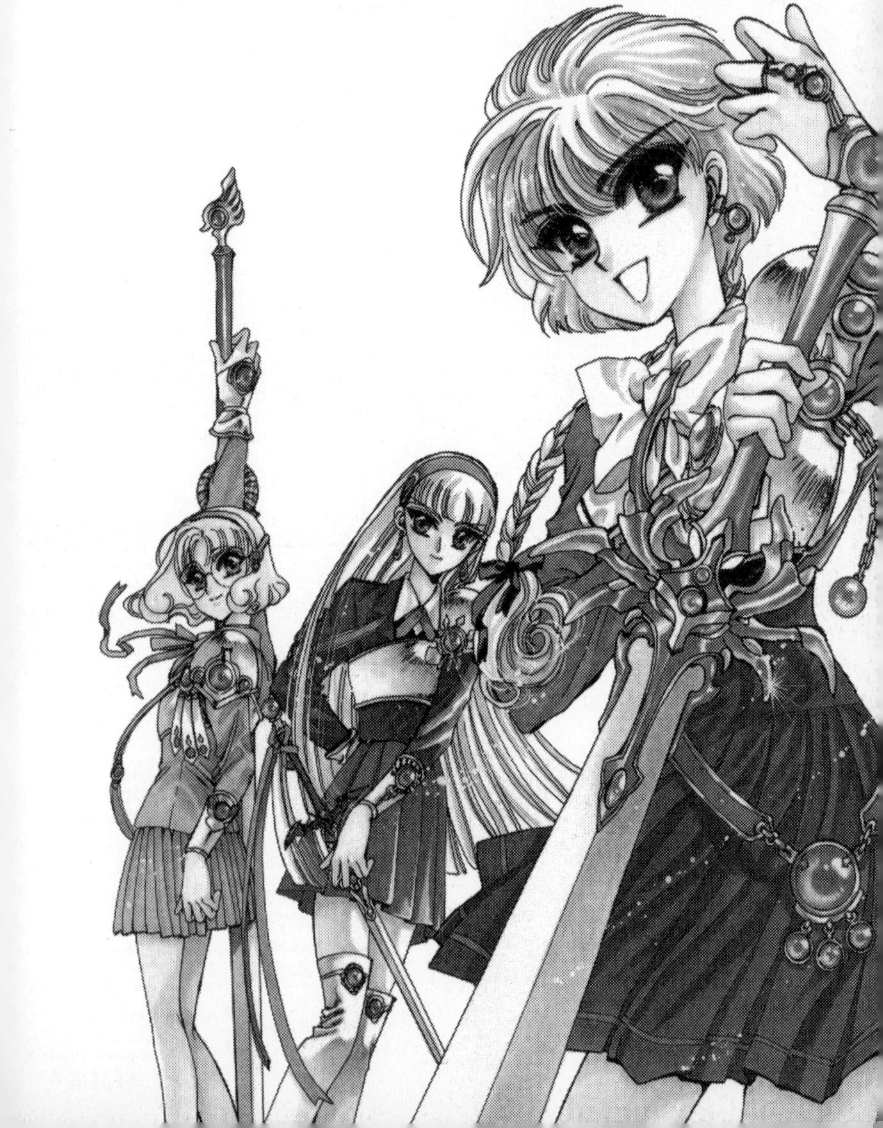

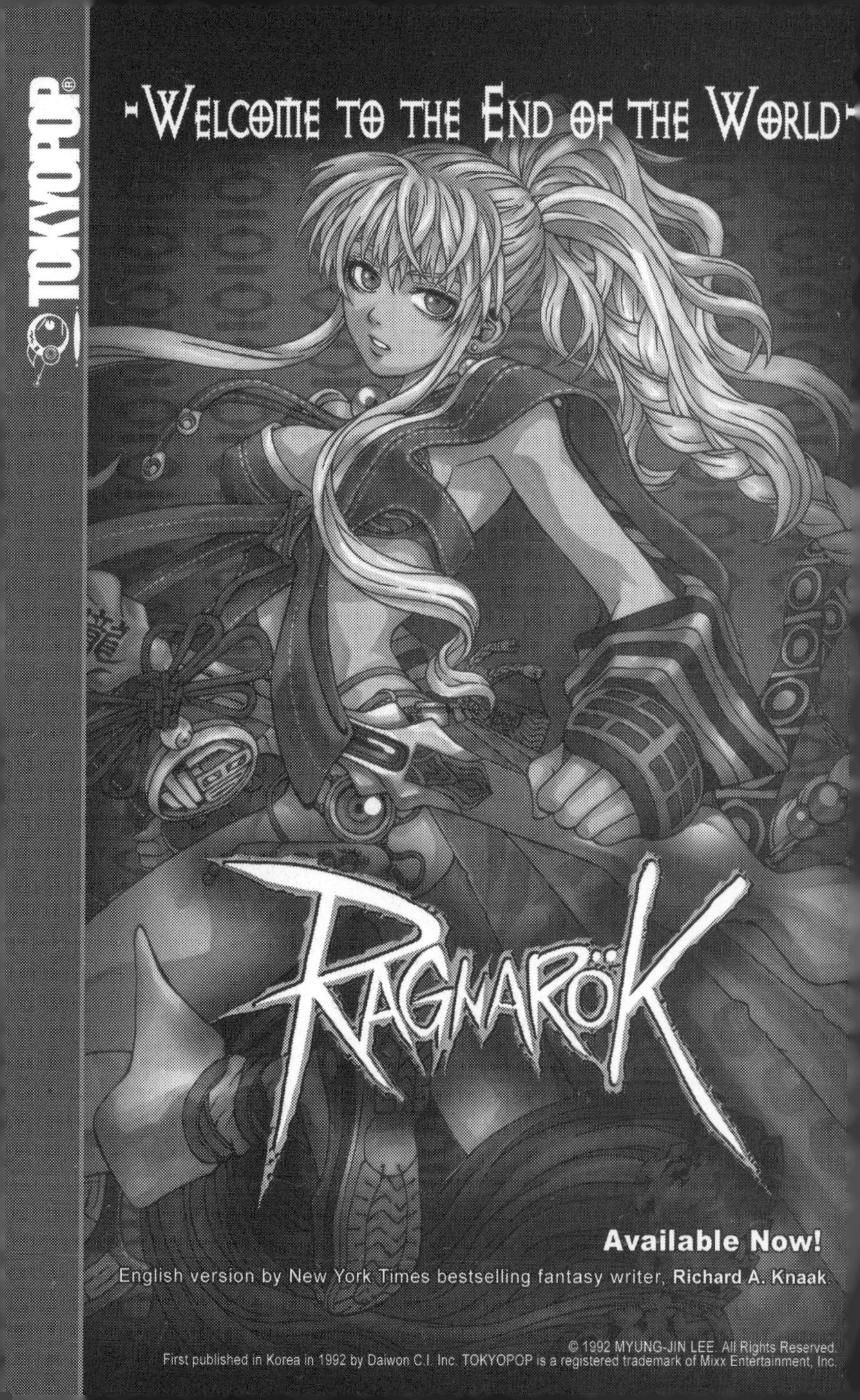

WELCOME TO THE END OF THE WORLD

RAGNARÖK

Available Now!

English version by New York Times bestselling fantasy writer, **Richard A. Knaak**.

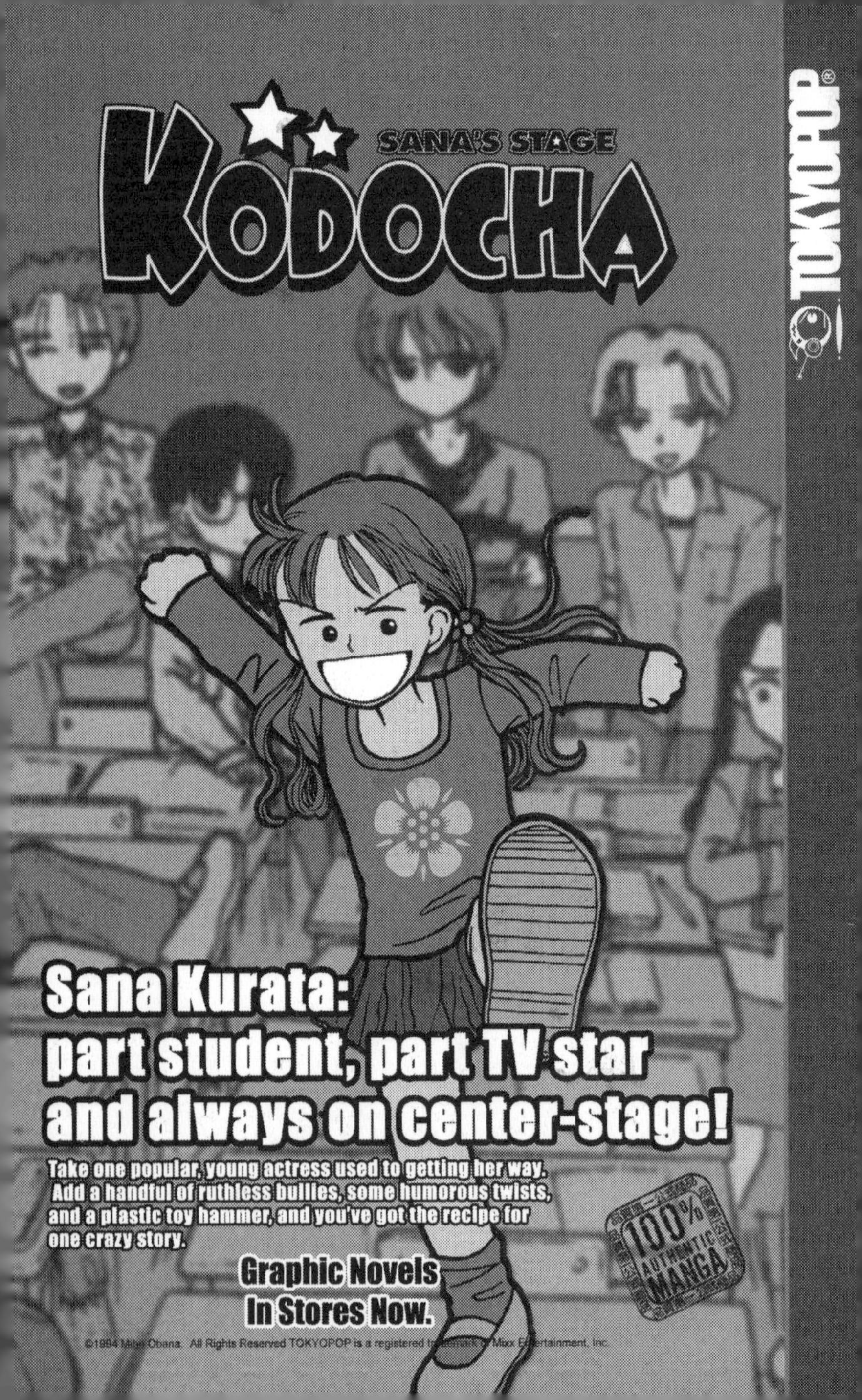
TOKYOPOP
KODOCHA
SANA'S STAGE
Sana Kurata:
part student, part TV star
and always on center-stage!
Take one popular, young actress used to getting her way.
Add a handful of ruthless bullies, some humorous twists,
and a plastic toy hammer, and you've got the recipe for
one crazy story.
Graphic Novels
In Stores Now.
100% AUTHENTIC MANGA
©1994 Miho Obana. All Rights Reserved TOKYOPOP is a registered trademark of Mixx Entertainment, Inc.

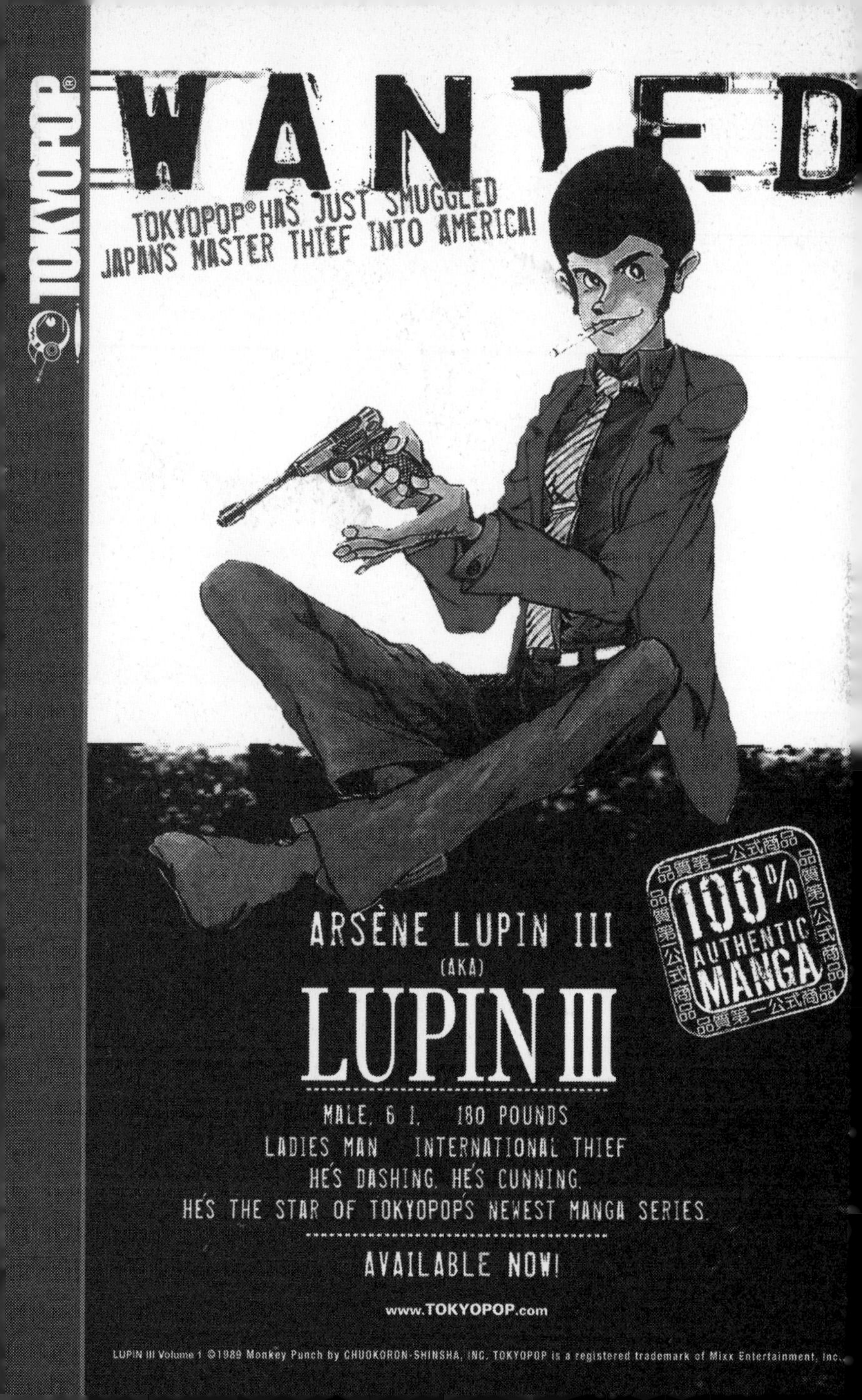
TOKYOPOP®
WANTED
TOKYOPOP® HAS JUST SMUGGLED JAPAN'S MASTER THIEF INTO AMERICA!
品質第一公式商品 100% AUTHENTIC MANGA
ARSÈNE LUPIN III
(AKA)
LUPIN III
MALE, 6 1, 180 POUNDS
LADIES MAN INTERNATIONAL THIEF
HE'S DASHING. HE'S CUNNING.
HE'S THE STAR OF TOKYOPOP'S NEWEST MANGA SERIES.
AVAILABLE NOW!
www.TOKYOPOP.com
LUPIN III Volume 1 ©1989 Monkey Punch by CHUOKORON-SHINSHA, INC. TOKYOPOP is a registered trademark of Mixx Entertainment, Inc.

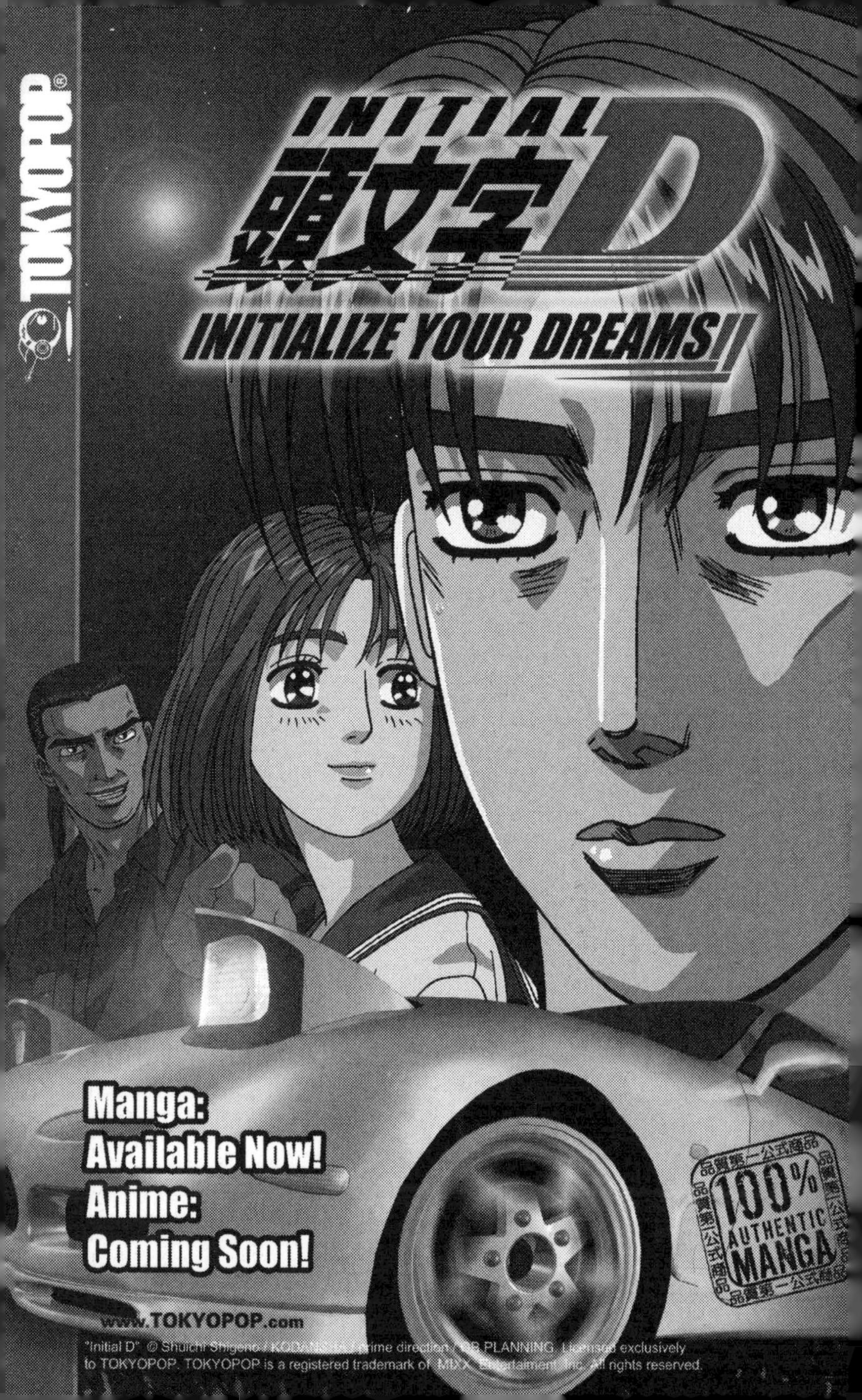
TOKYOPOP
INITIAL 頭文字 D
INITIALIZE YOUR DREAMS!!
Manga:
Available Now!
Anime:
Coming Soon!
100% AUTHENTIC MANGA
品質第一公式商品
www.TOKYOPOP.com
"Initial D" © Shuichi Shigeno / KODANSHA / Anime direction: OB PLANNING. Licensed exclusively to TOKYOPOP. TOKYOPOP is a registered trademark of Mixx Entertainment, Inc. All rights reserved.

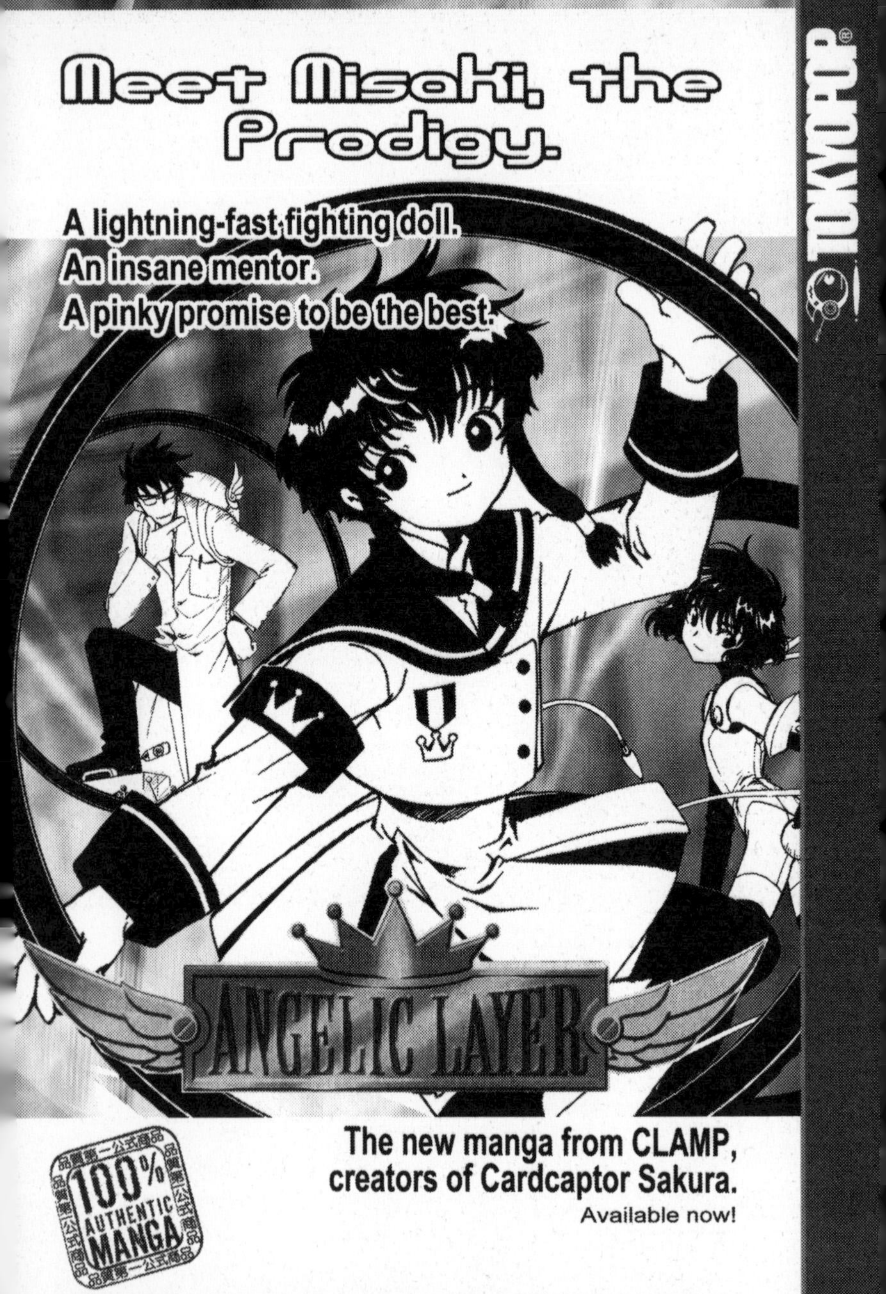

TOKYOPOP
Meet Misaki, the Prodigy.
A lightning-fast fighting doll.
An insane mentor.
A pinky promise to be the best.
ANGELIC LAYER
The new manga from CLAMP, creators of Cardcaptor Sakura.
Available now!
100% AUTHENTIC MANGA

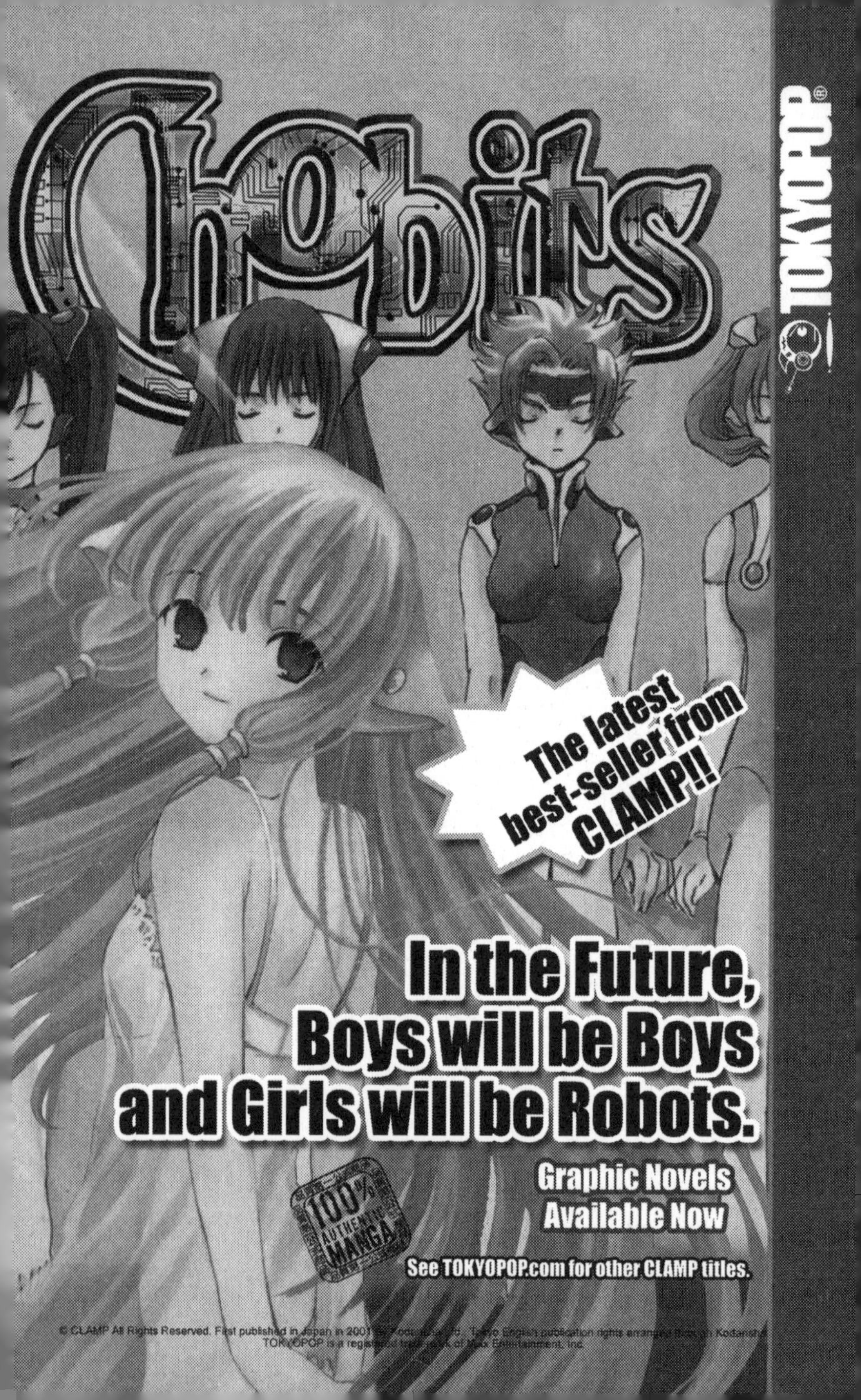
Chobits
TOKYOPOP®
The latest best-seller from CLAMP!!
In the Future, Boys will be Boys and Girls will be Robots.
Graphic Novels Available Now
100% AUTHENTIC MANGA
See TOKYOPOP.com for other CLAMP titles.
© CLAMP All Rights Reserved. First published in Japan in 2001

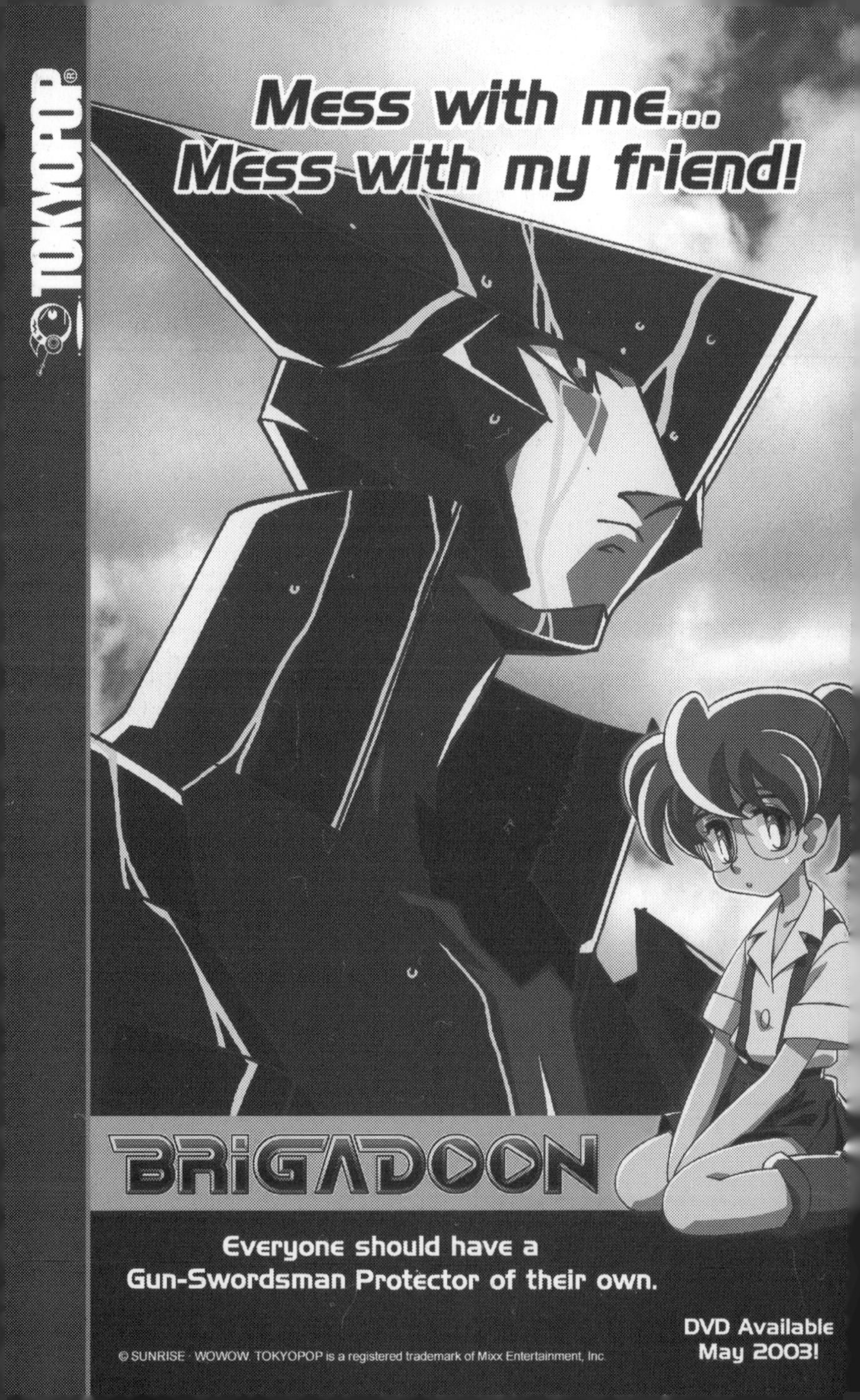

STOP!

This is the back of the book.
You wouldn't want to spoil a great ending!

This book is printed "manga-style," in the authentic Japanese right-to-left format. Since none of the artwork has been flipped or altered, readers get to experience the story just as the creator intended. You've been asking for it, so TOKYOPOP® delivered: authentic, hot-off-the-press, and far more fun!

DIRECTIONS

If this is your first time reading manga-style, here's a quick guide to help you understand how it works.

It's easy... just start in the top right panel and follow the numbers. Have fun, and look for more 100% authentic manga from TOKYOPOP®!

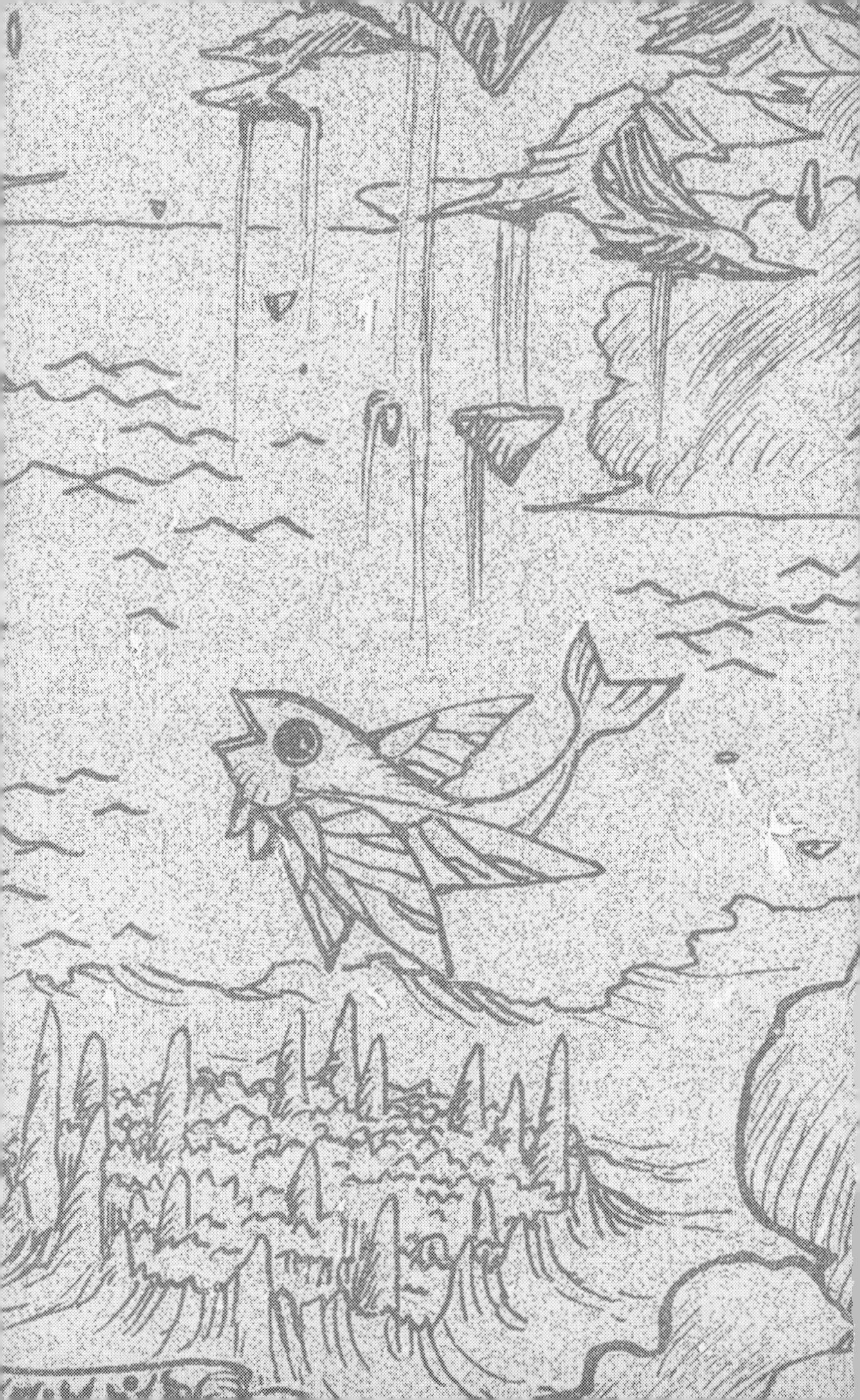

ALSO AVAILABLE FROM ⊙■TOKYOPOP®

MANGA

*INDICATES 100% AUTHENTIC MANGA (RIGHT-TO-LEFT FORMAT)

ANGELIC LAYER*
BABY BIRTH* (September 2003)
BATTLE ROYALE*
BRAIN POWERED* (June 2003)
BRIGADOON* (August 2003)
CARDCAPTOR SAKURA
CARDCAPTOR SAKURA: MASTER OF THE CLOW*
CLAMP SCHOOL DETECTIVES*
CHOBITS*
CHRONICLES OF THE CURSED SWORD (July 2003)
CLOVER
CONFIDENTIAL CONFESSIONS* (July 2003)
CORRECTOR YUI
COWBOY BEBOP*
COWBOY BEBOP: SHOOTING STAR* (June 2003)
DEMON DIARY (May 2003)
DIGIMON
DRAGON HUNTER (June 2003)
DRAGON KNIGHTS*
DUKLYON: CLAMP SCHOOL DEFENDERS* (September 2003)
ERICA SAKURAZAWA* (May 2003)
ESCAFLOWNE* (July 2003)
FAKE* (May 2003)
FLCL* (September 2003)
FORBIDDEN DANCE* (August 2003)
GATE KEEPERS*
G-GUNDAM* (June 2003)
GRAVITATION* (June 2003)
GTO*
GUNDAM WING
GUNDAM WING: ENDLESS WALTZ*
GUNDAM: THE LAST OUTPOST*
HAPPY MANIA*
HARLEM BEAT
INITIAL D*
I.N.V.U.
ISLAND
JING: KING OF BANDITS* (June 2003)
JULINE
KARE KANO*
KINDAICHI CASE FILES* (June 2003)
KING OF HELL (June 2003)

KODOCHA*
LOVE HINA*
LUPIN III*
MAGIC KNIGHT RAYEARTH* (August 2003)
MAN OF MANY FACES* (May 2003)
MARMALADE BOY*
MARS*
MIRACLE GIRLS
MIYUKI-CHAN IN WONDERLAND* (October 2003)
MONSTERS, INC.
NIEA_7* (August 2003)
PARADISE KISS*
PARASYTE
PEACH GIRL
PEACH GIRL: CHANGE OF HEART*
PET SHOP OF HORRORS* (June 2003)
PLANET LADDER
PLANETS* (October 2003)
PRIEST
RAGNAROK
RAVE MASTER*
REAL BOUT HIGH SCHOOL*
REALITY CHECK
REBIRTH
REBOUND*
SABER MARIONETTE J* (July 2003)
SAILOR MOON
SAINT TAIL
SAMURAI DEEPER KYO* (June 2003)
SCRYED*
SHAOLIN SISTERS*
SHIRAHIME-SYO* (December 2003)
THE SKULL MAN*
SORCERER HUNTERS
TOKYO MEW MEW*
UNDER THE GLASS MOON (June 2003)
VAMPIRE GAME* (June 2003)
WILD ACT* (July 2003)
WISH*
X-DAY* (August 2003)
ZODIAC P.I.* (July 2003)

CINE-MANGA™

AKIRA*
CARDCAPTORS
JIMMY NEUTRON (COMING SOON)
KIM POSSIBLE
LIZZIE McGUIRE
SPONGEBOB SQUAREPANTS (COMING SOON)
SPY KIDS 2

NOVELS

SAILOR MOON
KARMA CLUB (COMING SOON)

TOKYOPOP KIDS

STRAY SHEEP (September 2003)

ART BOOKS

CARDCAPTOR SAKURA*
MAGIC KNIGHT RAYEARTH*

ANIME GUIDES

GUNDAM TECHNICAL MANUALS
COWBOY BEBOP
SAILOR MOON SCOUT GUIDES

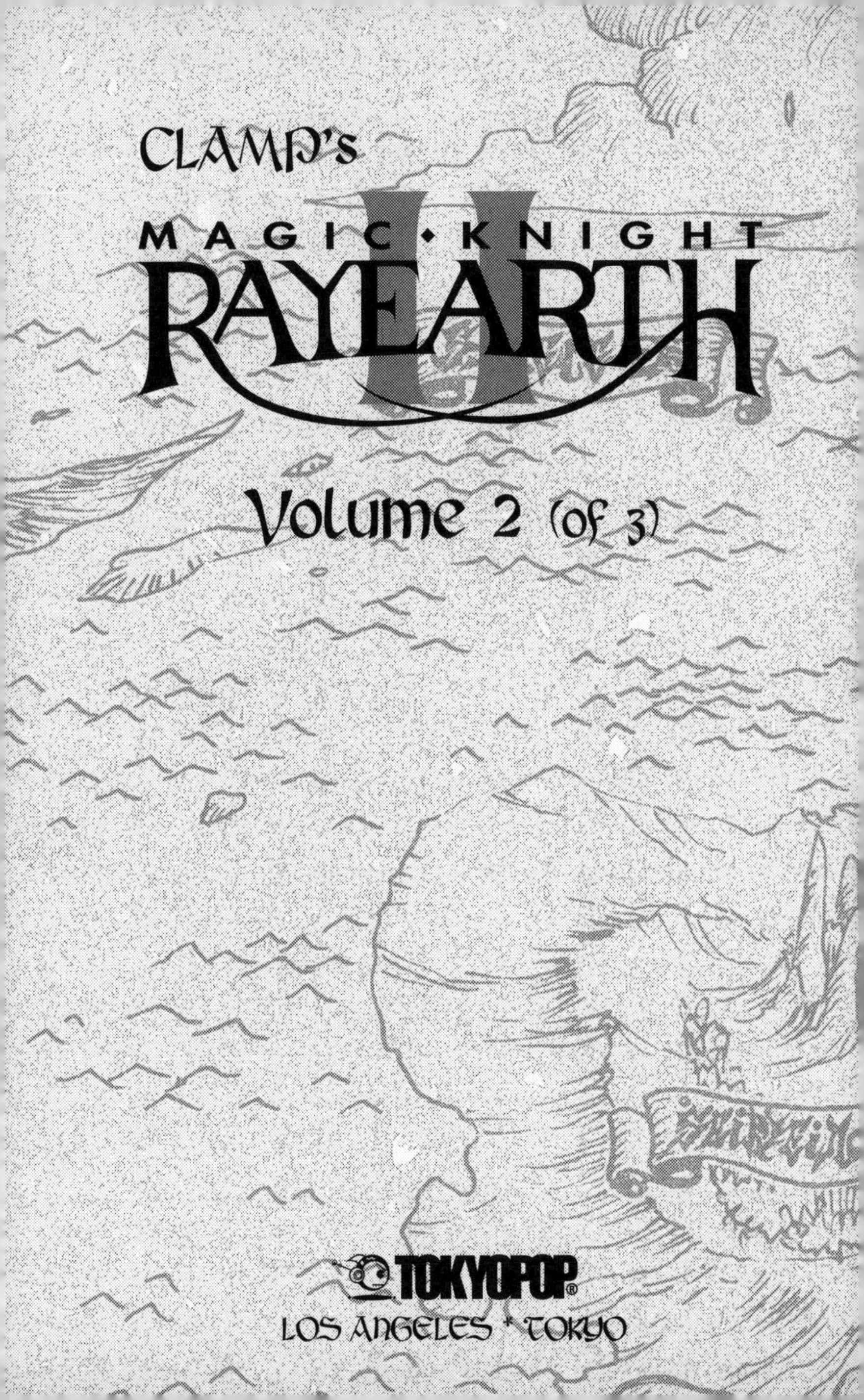

CLAMP's

MAGIC•KNIGHT RAYEARTH II

Volume 2 (of 3)

TOKYOPOP®
LOS ANGELES * TOKYO

Translator - Anita Sengupta
English Adaption - Jamie S. Rich
Copy Editors - Bryce Coleman, Carol Fox
Retouch - Paul Morrissey
Lettering - Monalisa de Asis
Cover Layout - Patrick Hook

Editor - Jake Forbes
Managing Editor - Jill Freshney
Production Coordinator - Antonio DePietro
Production Manager - Jennifer Miller
Art Director - Matthew Alford
Director of Editorial - Jeremy Ross
VP of Production & Manufacturing - Ron Klamert
President & C.O.O. - John Parker
Publisher & C.E.O. - Stuart Levy

Email: editor@TOKYOPOP.com
Come visit us online at www.TOKYOPOP.com

A  Manga

TOKYOPOP® is an imprint of Mixx Entertainment, Inc.
5900 Wilshire Blvd. Suite 2000, Los Angeles, CA 90036

ISBN: 1-59182-267-X

First TOKYOPOP® printing: April 2003

10 9 8 7 6 5 4 3 2 1

Printed in Canada

The Story So Far...

The magical land of Cephiro is under attack! After the Magic Knights eliminated Princess Emeraude, they left the land without its "Pillar." Now the land is crumbling and three foreign nations lead invasion forces to claim Cephiro as their own. Each of the three countries has sent out an enchanted "road" in order to penetrate Cephiro's border. In order to become the new Pillar, however, they must find the one hidden road which leads to Cephiro's heart.

Hikaru, Umi and Fuu, three ordinary Tokyo schoolgirls who became the Magic Knights, are summoned back to Cephiro, just in time. What's strange is that no one knows who summoned them. The people of Cephiro are happy to see the girls, nonetheless. All of their old friends are there: Presea the blacksmith, Clef the magician and Ferio the swordsman, who reveals himself to be the prince! Oh, and we can't forget Mokona, the little white puffball. The girls meet a few new citizens of Cephiro as well: Lantis, Zagato's brother and a powerful warrior, and Primera, the pixie who's infatuated with him.

There isn't much time for introductions, however, as the first of the three countries begins its assault. Autozam, a land of machines, sends a giant "mech" to attack. It's piloted by the noble Eagle Vision, a former friend of Lantis, and Autozam's leader. The three girls don the "Mashin," or Spirits, in order to fight off Eagle's mech, but you can be sure he will return.

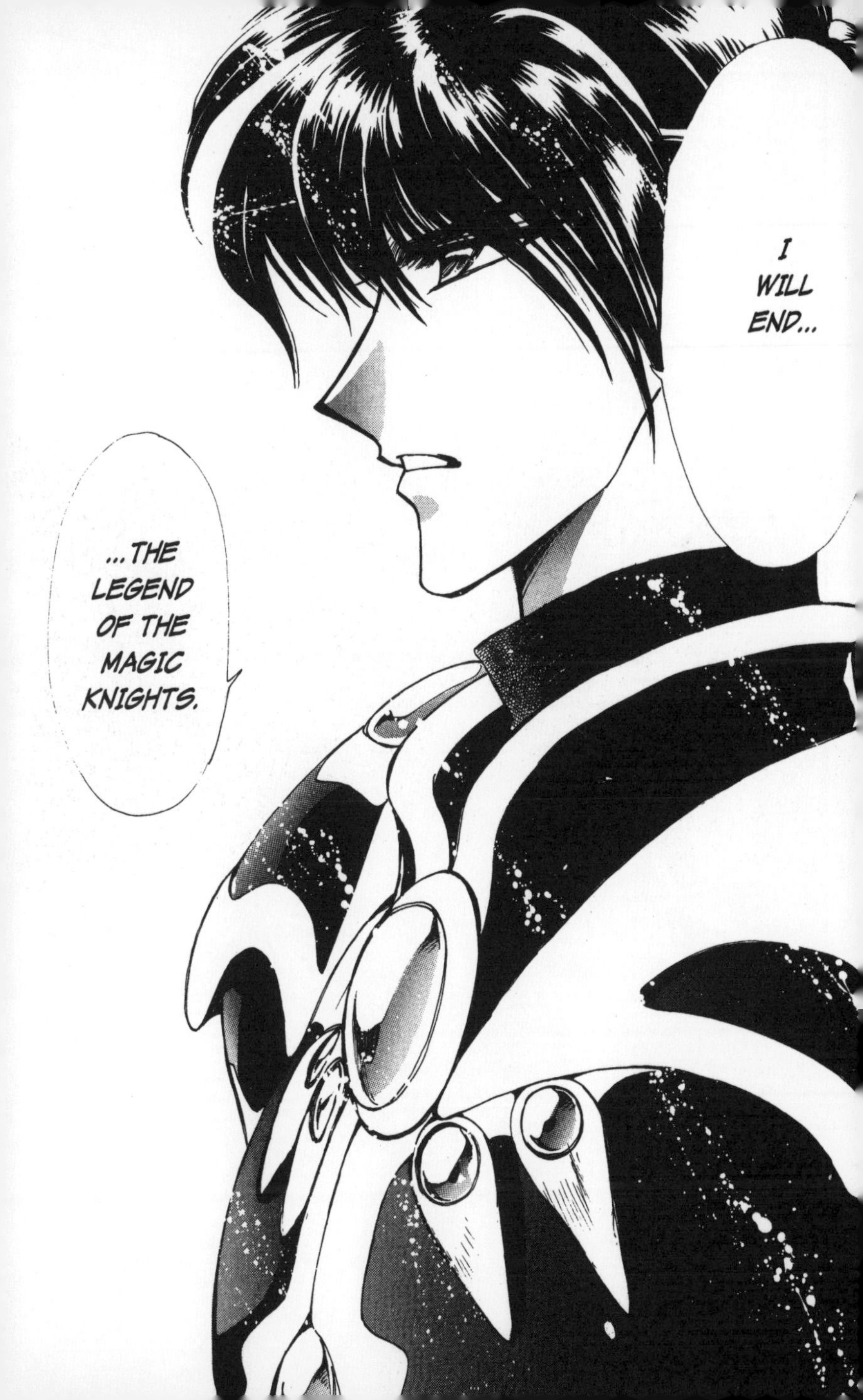
I WILL END...
...THE LEGEND OF THE MAGIC KNIGHTS.

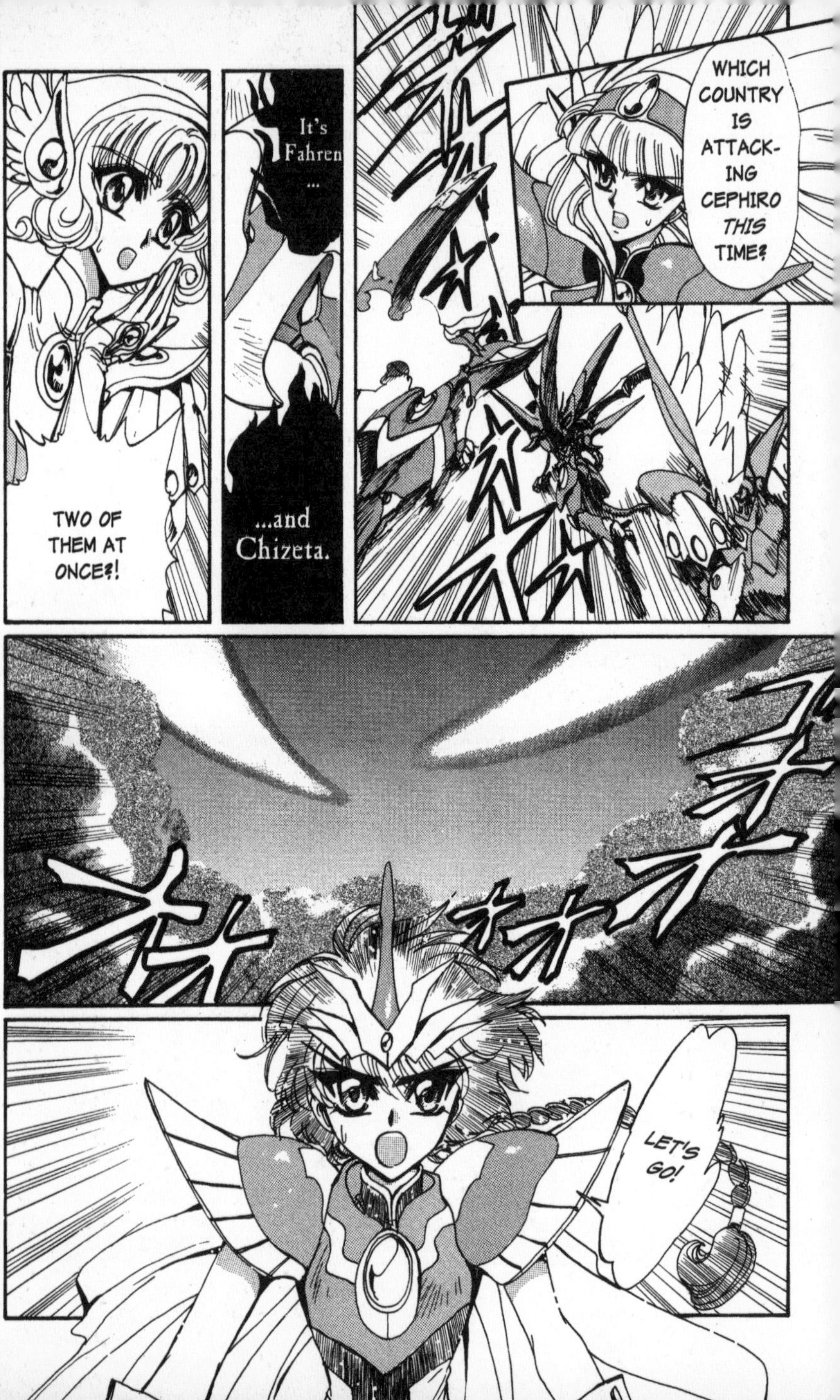
WHICH COUNTRY IS ATTACKING CEPHIRO THIS TIME?
It's Fahren ...
...and Chizeta.
TWO OF THEM AT ONCE?!
LET'S GO!

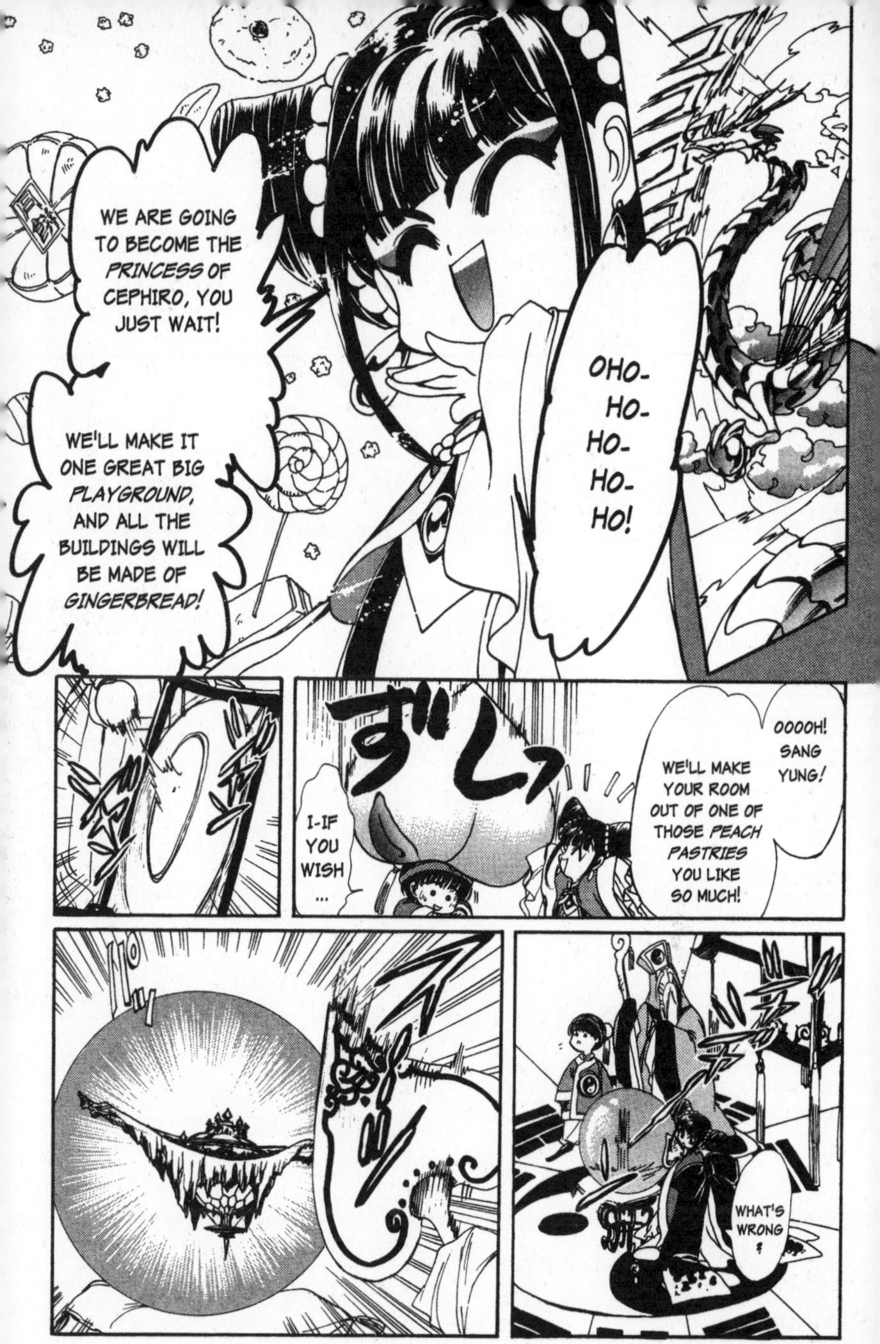
OHO-HO-HO-HO-HO!
WE ARE GOING TO BECOME THE *PRINCESS* OF CEPHIRO, YOU JUST WAIT!
WE'LL MAKE IT ONE GREAT BIG *PLAYGROUND*, AND ALL THE BUILDINGS WILL BE MADE OF *GINGERBREAD!*
OOOOH! SANG YUNG!
WE'LL MAKE YOUR ROOM OUT OF ONE OF THOSE *PEACH PASTRIES* YOU LIKE SO MUCH!
ずしっ
I-IF YOU WISH ...
WHAT'S WRONG?

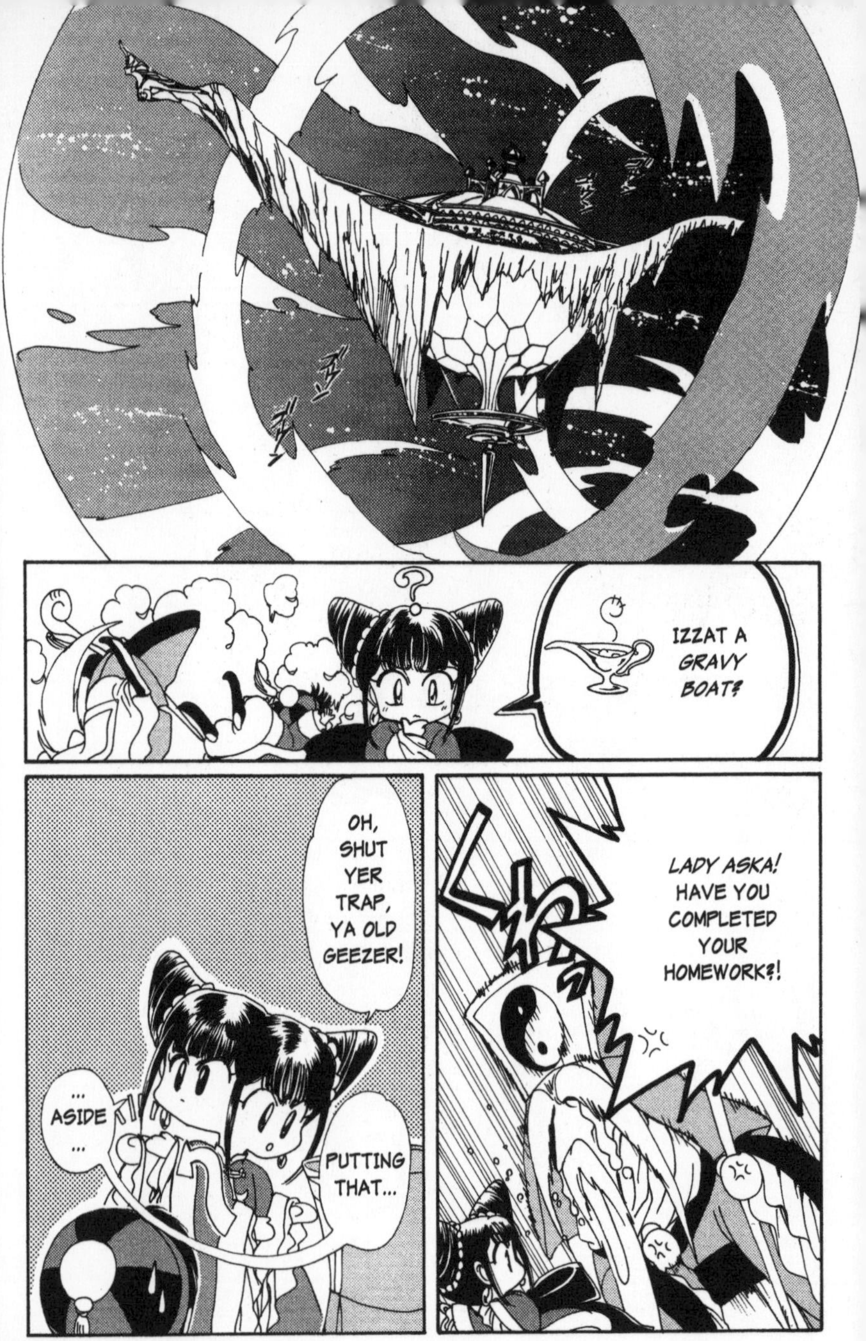
IZZAT A GRAVY BOAT?
LADY ASKA! HAVE YOU COMPLETED YOUR HOMEWORK?!
OH, SHUT YER TRAP, YA OLD GEEZER!
PUTTING THAT...
... ASIDE ...

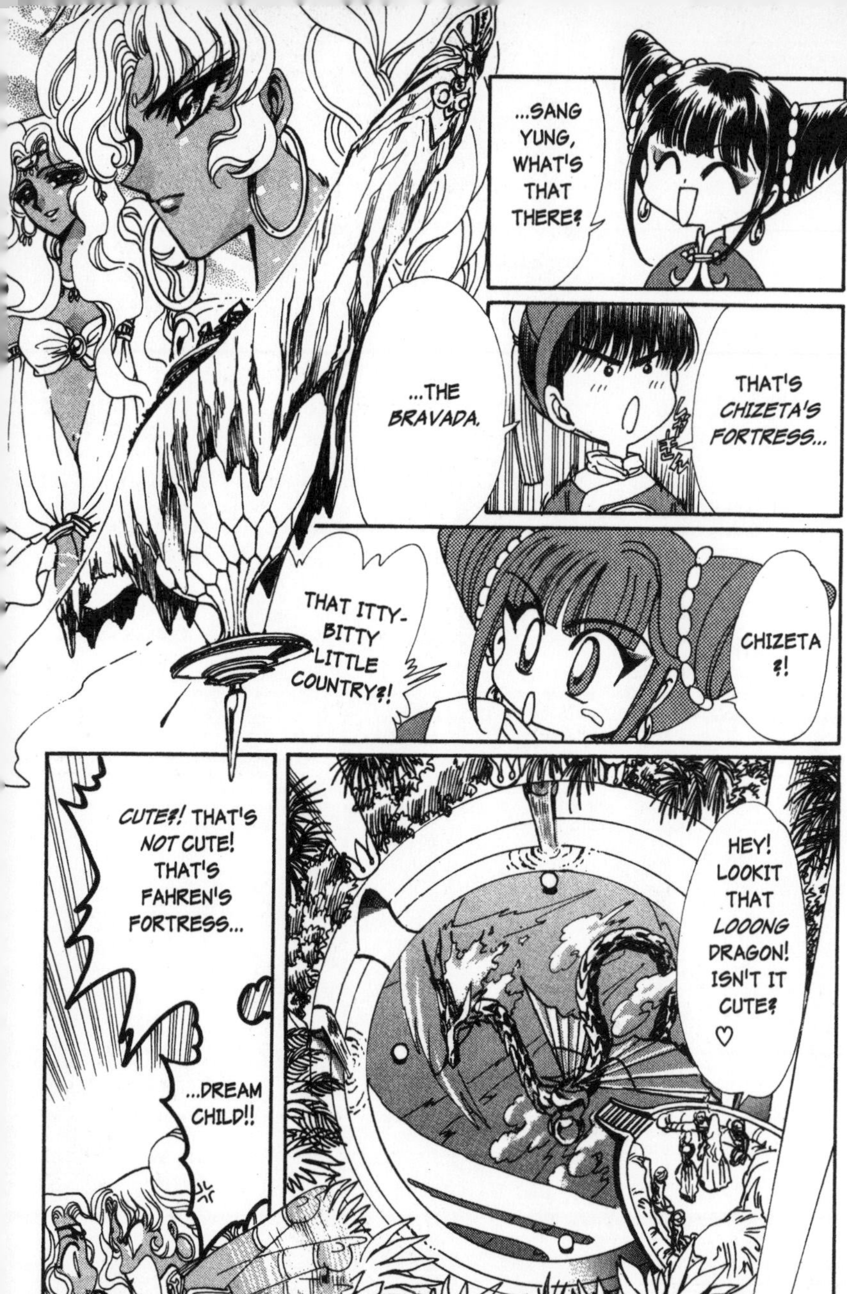
...SANG YUNG, WHAT'S THAT THERE?
THAT'S CHIZETA'S FORTRESS...
...THE BRAVADA.
CHIZETA?!
THAT ITTY-BITTY LITTLE COUNTRY?!
HEY! LOOKIT THAT LOOONG DRAGON! ISN'T IT CUTE? ♡
CUTE?! THAT'S NOT CUTE! THAT'S FAHREN'S FORTRESS...
...DREAM CHILD!!

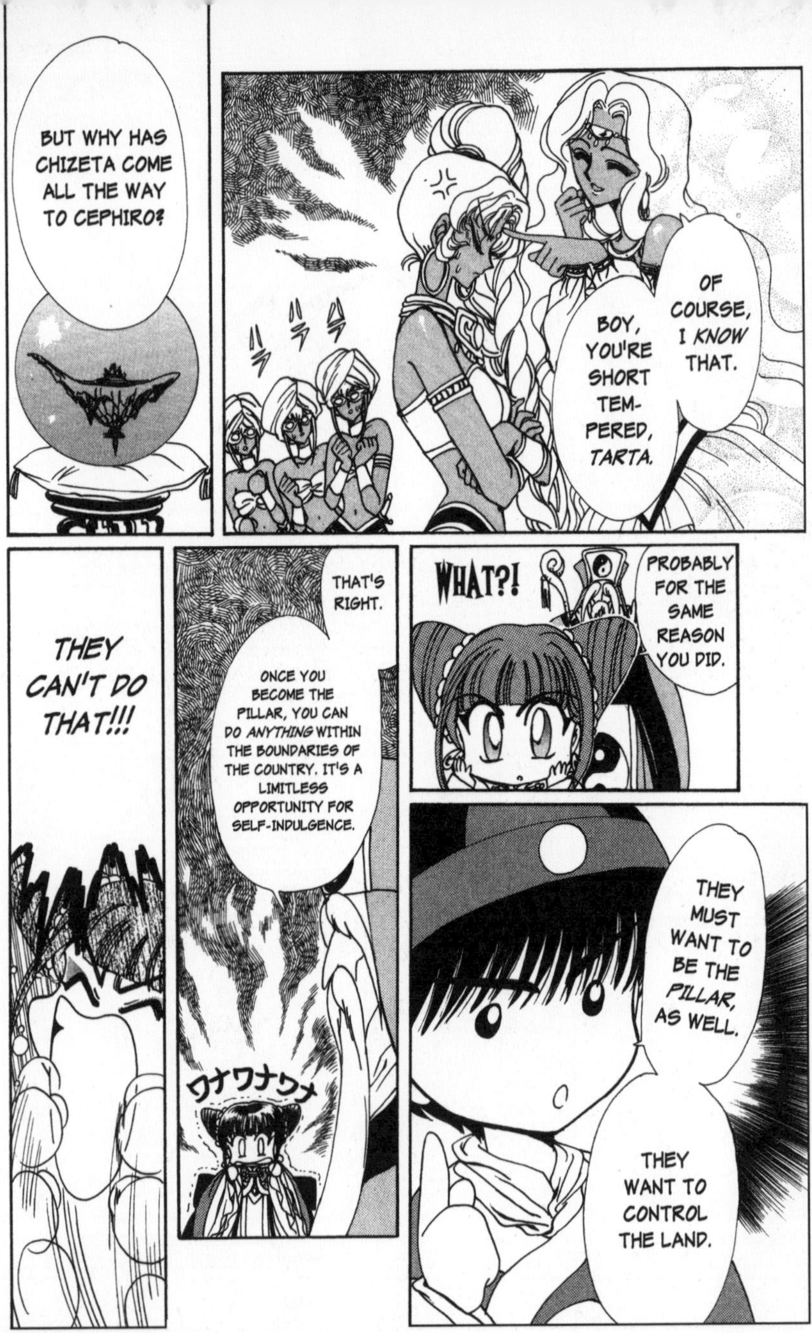
OF COURSE, I *KNOW* THAT.
BOY, YOU'RE SHORT TEMPERED, *TARTA.*
BUT WHY HAS CHIZETA COME ALL THE WAY TO CEPHIRO?
PROBABLY FOR THE SAME REASON YOU DID.
WHAT?!
THEY MUST WANT TO BE THE *PILLAR,* AS WELL.
THEY WANT TO CONTROL THE LAND.
THAT'S RIGHT.
ONCE YOU BECOME THE PILLAR, YOU CAN DO *ANYTHING* WITHIN THE BOUNDARIES OF THE COUNTRY. IT'S A LIMITLESS OPPORTUNITY FOR SELF-INDULGENCE.
ワナワナワナ
THEY CAN'T DO THAT!!!

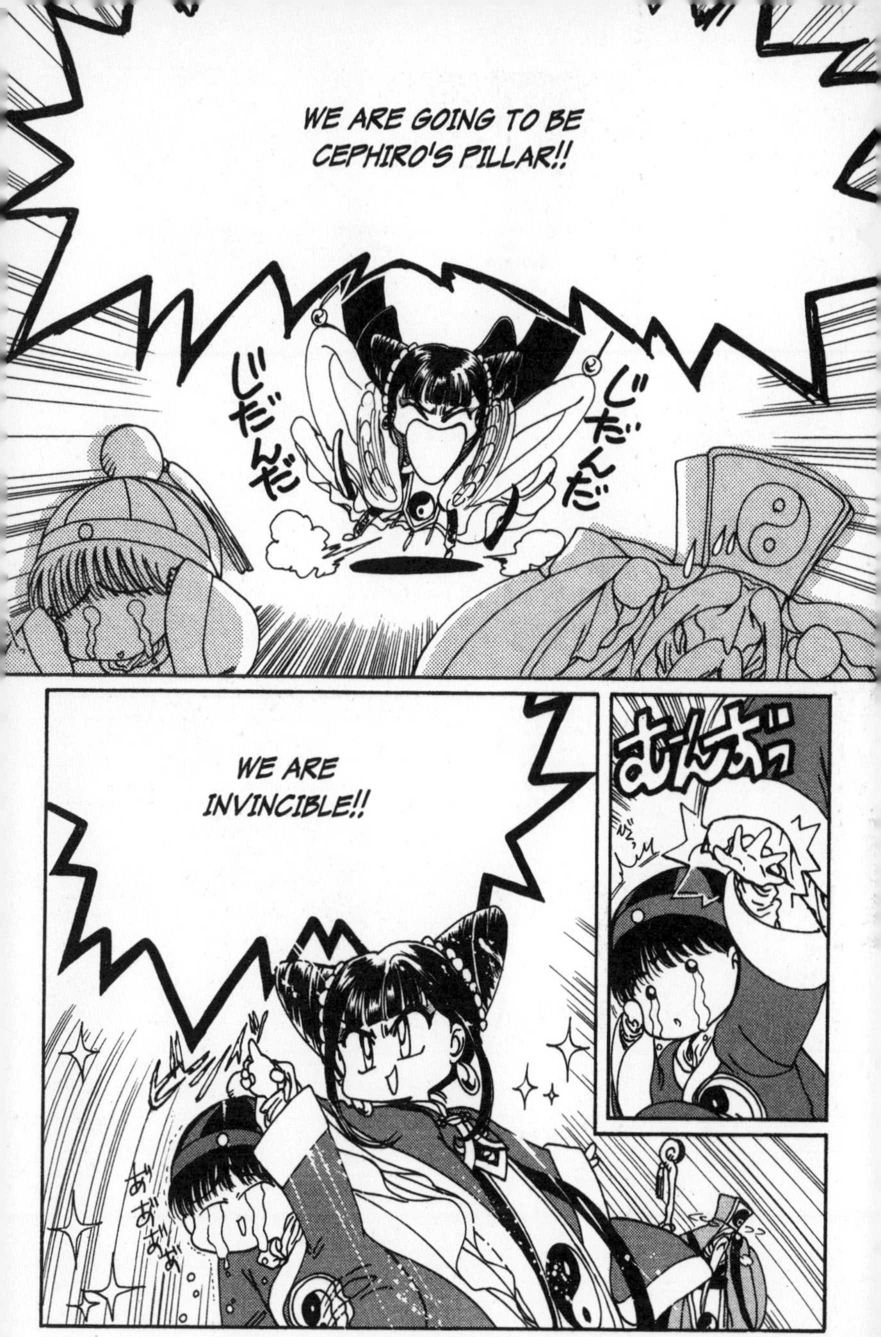
WE ARE GOING TO BE CEPHIRO'S PILLAR!!
じだんだ
じだんだ
WE ARE INVINCIBLE!!

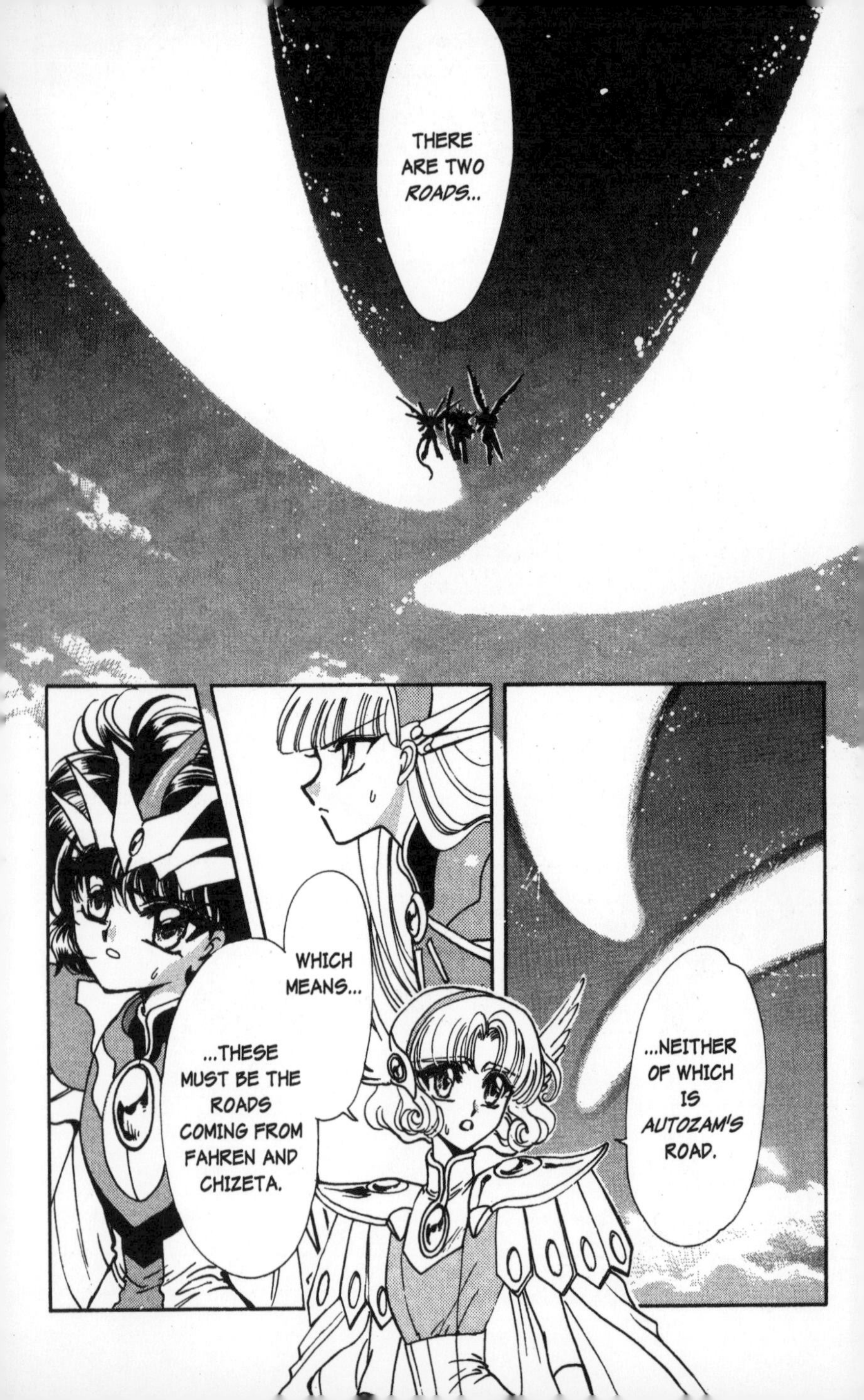
THERE ARE TWO *ROADS*...
WHICH MEANS...
...THESE MUST BE THE ROADS COMING FROM FAHREN AND CHIZETA.
...NEITHER OF WHICH IS *AUTOZAM'S* ROAD.

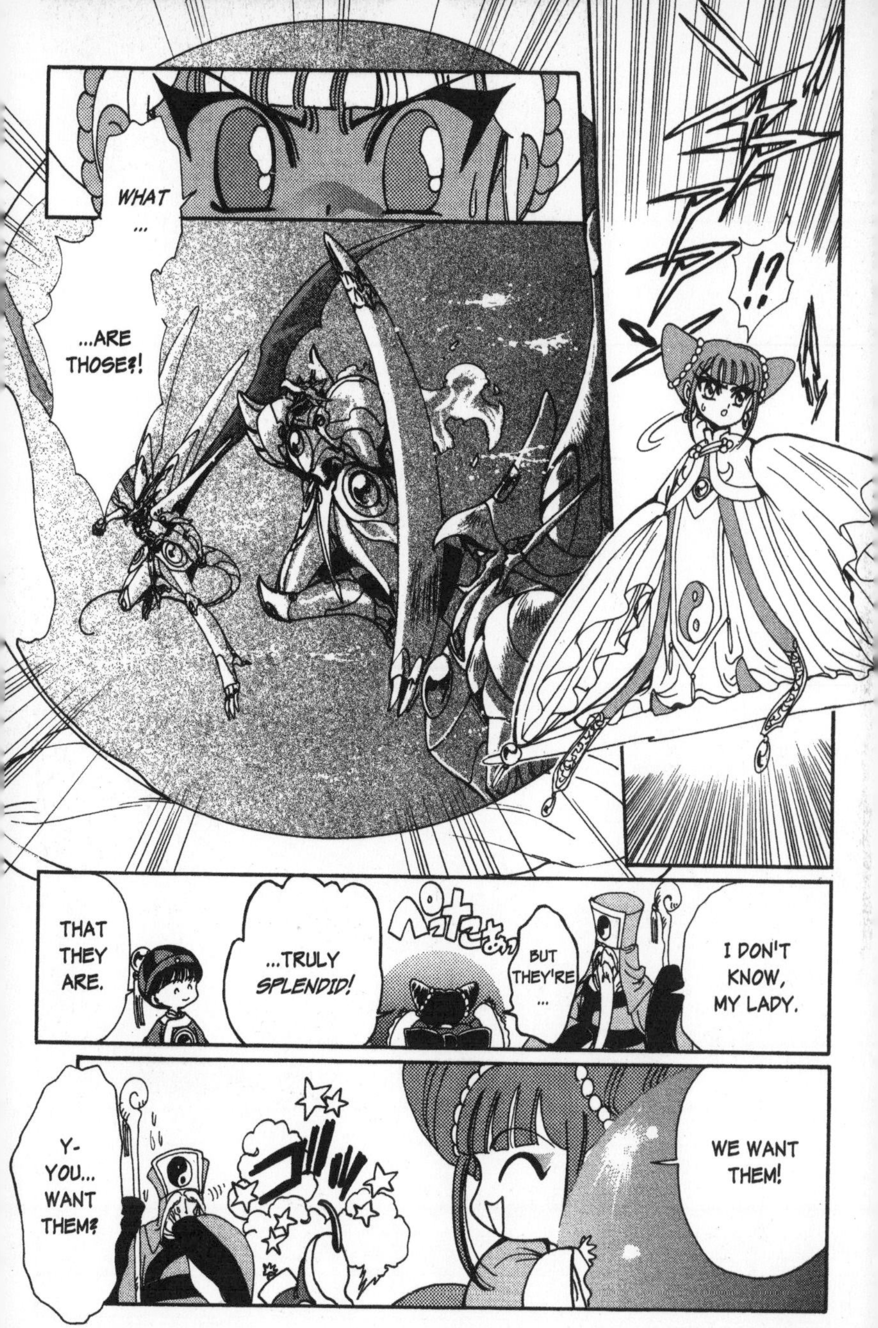
!?
WHAT ...
...ARE THOSE?!
I DON'T KNOW, MY LADY.
BUT THEY'RE ...
...TRULY SPLENDID!
THAT THEY ARE.
WE WANT THEM!
Y- YOU... WANT THEM?

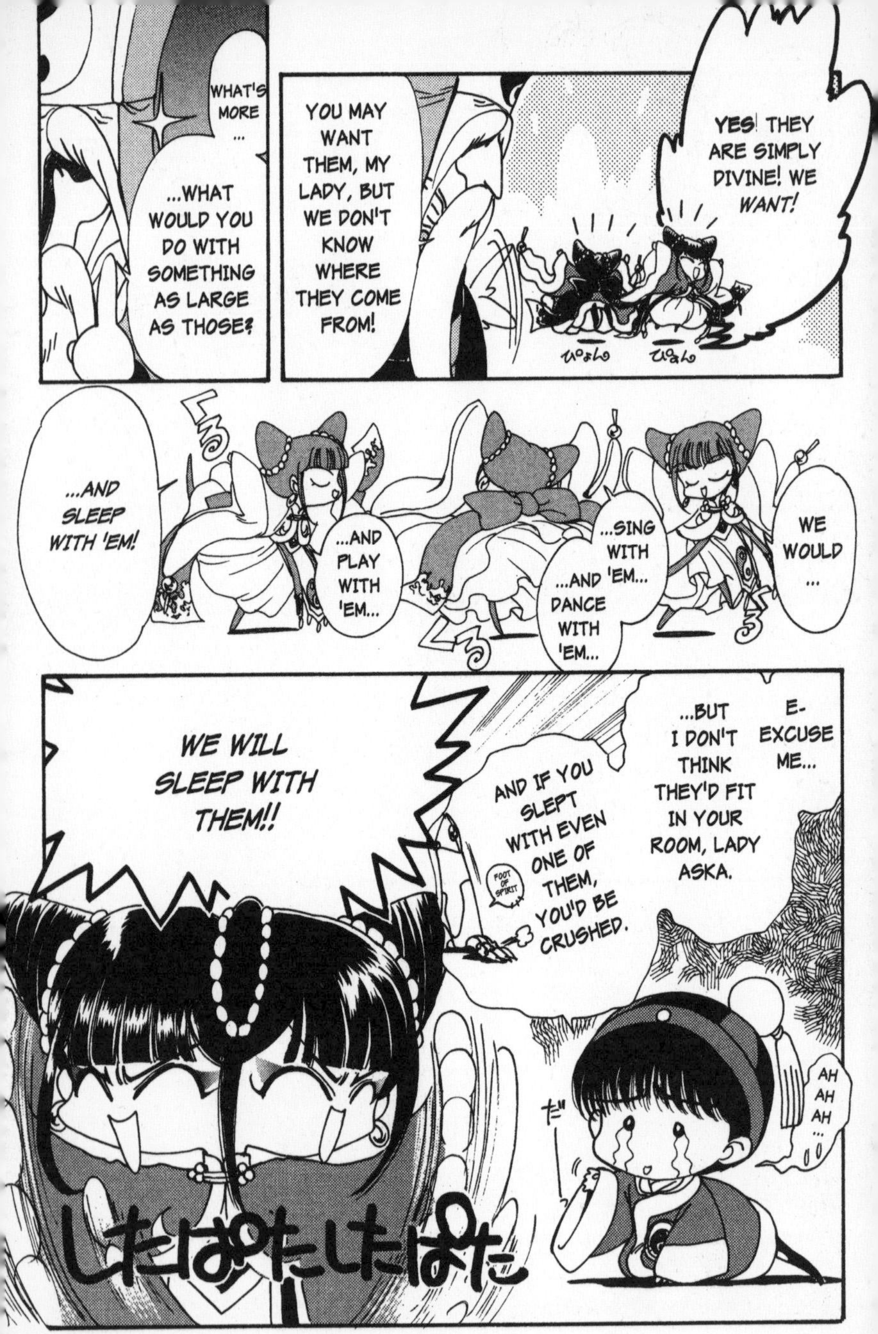
YES! THEY ARE SIMPLY DIVINE! WE WANT!
ぴょん
ぴょん
YOU MAY WANT THEM, MY LADY, BUT WE DON'T KNOW WHERE THEY COME FROM!
WHAT'S MORE ...
...WHAT WOULD YOU DO WITH SOMETHING AS LARGE AS THOSE?
WE WOULD ...
...SING WITH 'EM...
...AND DANCE WITH 'EM...
...AND PLAY WITH 'EM...
...AND SLEEP WITH 'EM!
E- EXCUSE ME...
...BUT I DON'T THINK THEY'D FIT IN YOUR ROOM, LADY ASKA.
AND IF YOU SLEPT WITH EVEN ONE OF THEM, YOU'D BE CRUSHED.
FOOT OF SPIRIT
WE WILL SLEEP WITH THEM!!
AH AH AH ...
したぱたしたぱた

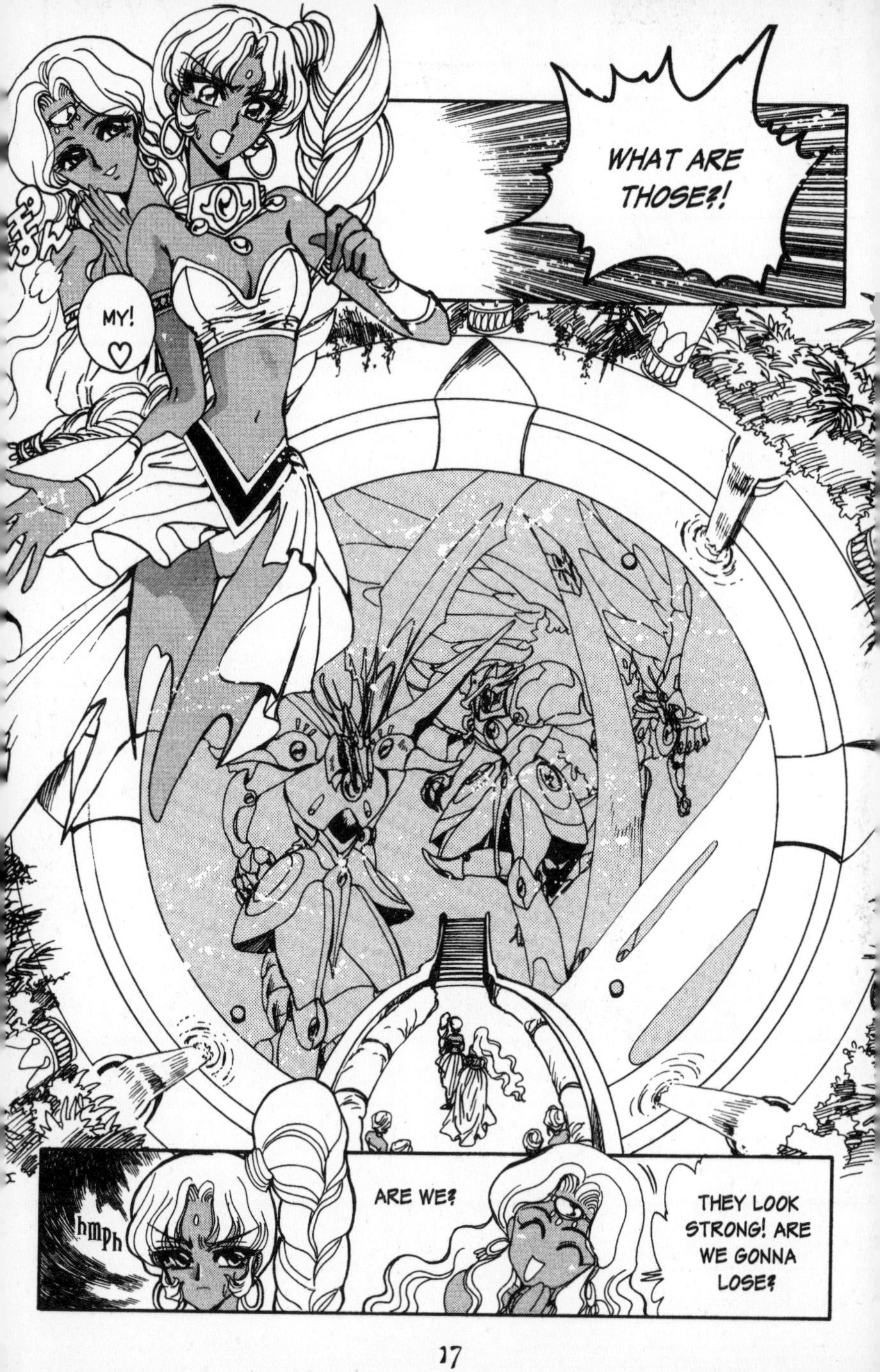
WHAT ARE THOSE?!
MY! ♡
THEY LOOK STRONG! ARE WE GONNA LOSE?
ARE WE?
hmph

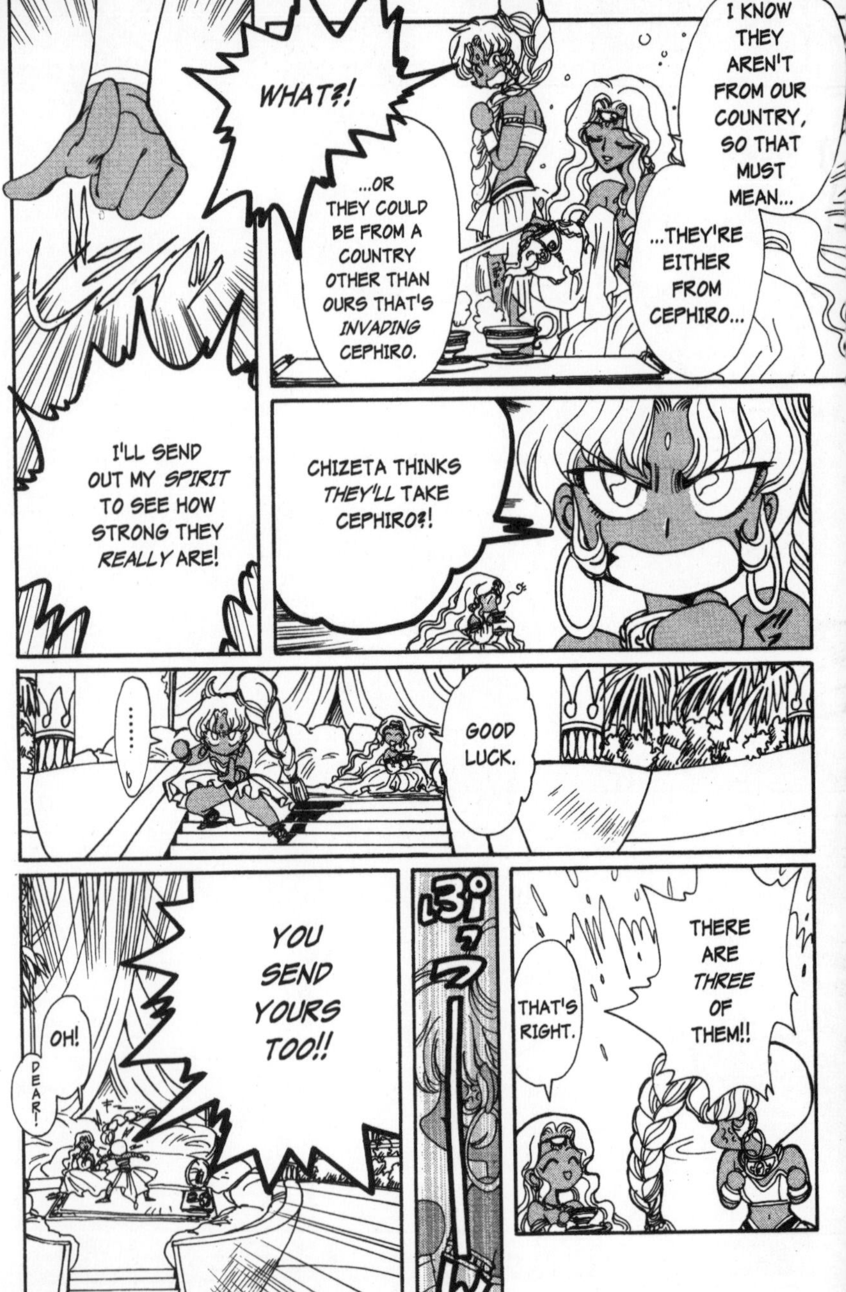
I KNOW THEY AREN'T FROM OUR COUNTRY, SO THAT MUST MEAN...
...THEY'RE EITHER FROM CEPHIRO...
...OR THEY COULD BE FROM A COUNTRY OTHER THAN OURS THAT'S *INVADING* CEPHIRO.
WHAT?!
CHIZETA THINKS *THEY'LL* TAKE CEPHIRO?!
I'LL SEND OUT MY *SPIRIT* TO SEE HOW STRONG THEY *REALLY* ARE!
GOOD LUCK.
......
THERE ARE *THREE* OF THEM!!
THAT'S RIGHT.
YOU SEND YOURS TOO!!
OH!
DEAR!

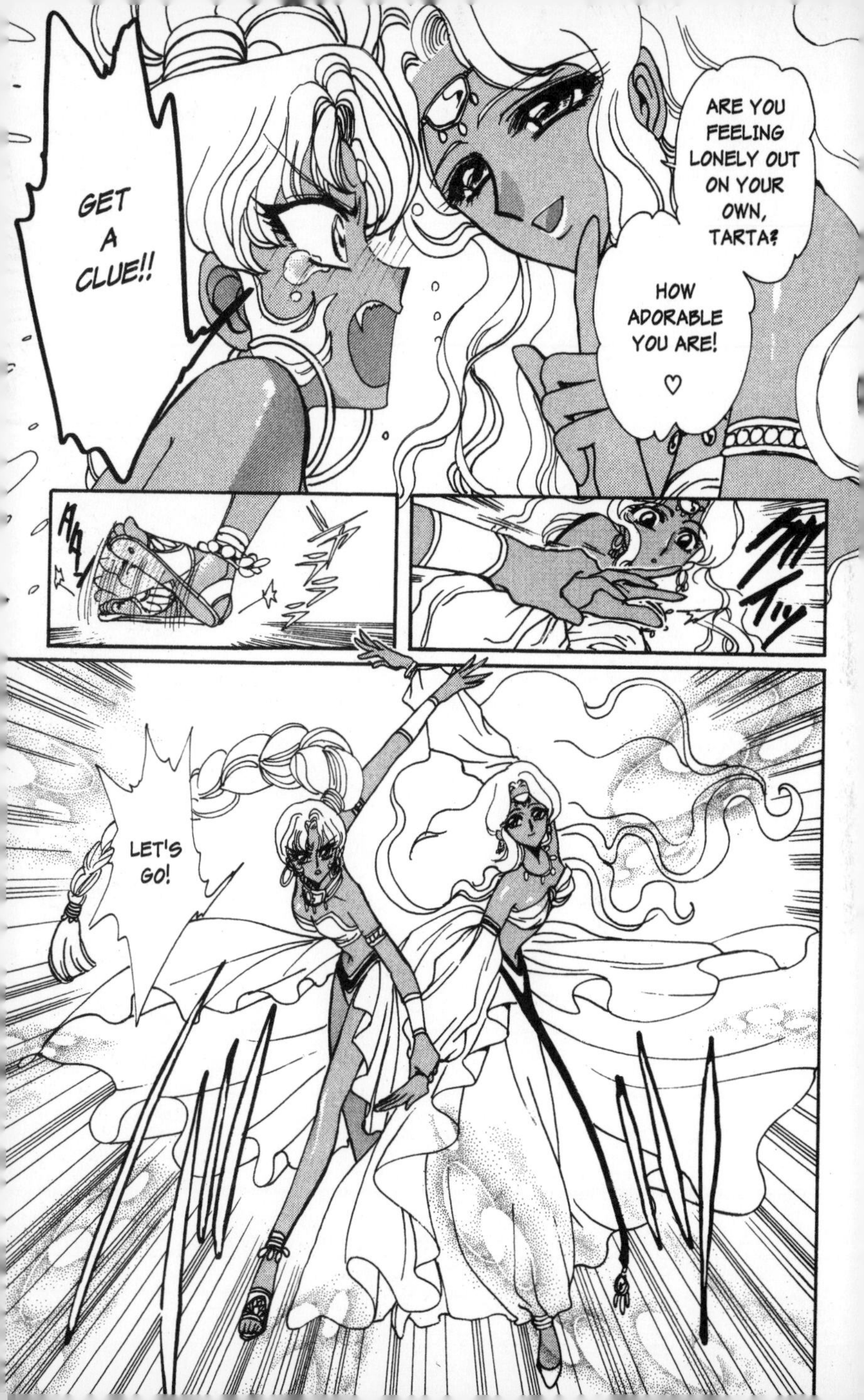
ARE YOU FEELING LONELY OUT ON YOUR OWN, TARTA?
HOW ADORABLE YOU ARE! ♡
GET A CLUE!!
LET'S GO!

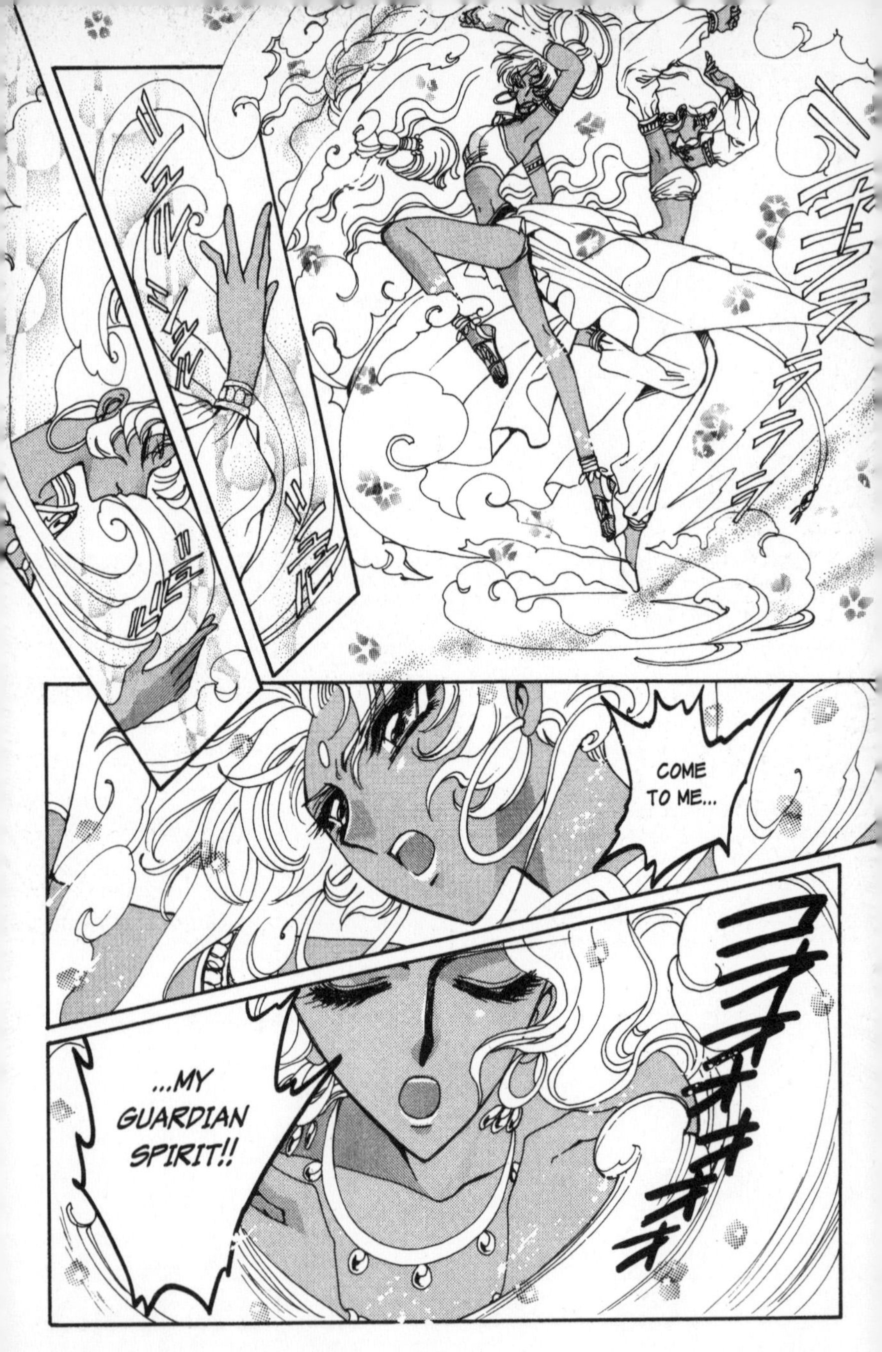
COME TO ME...
...MY GUARDIAN SPIRIT!!

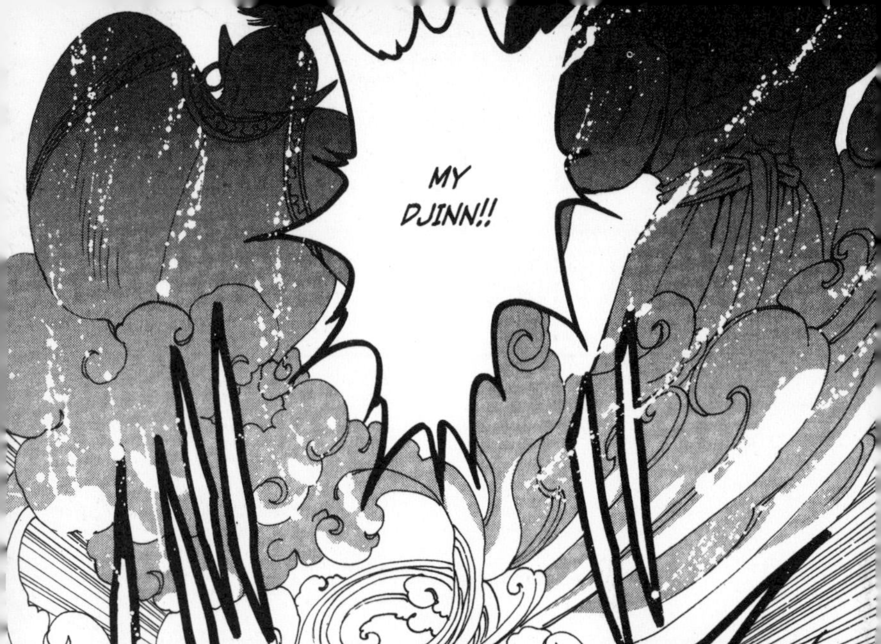
MY DJINN!!
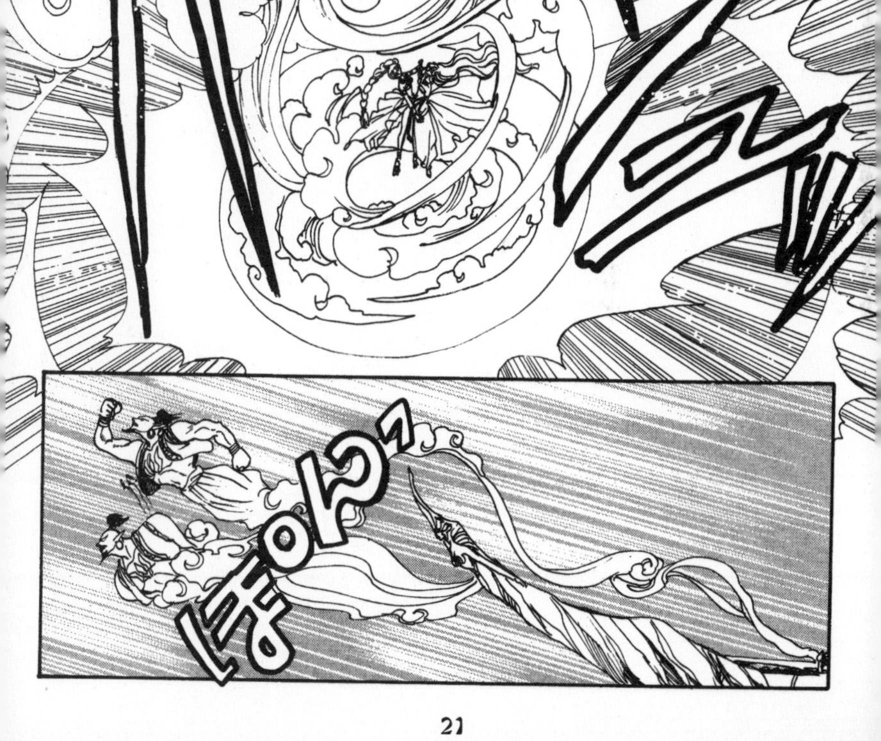

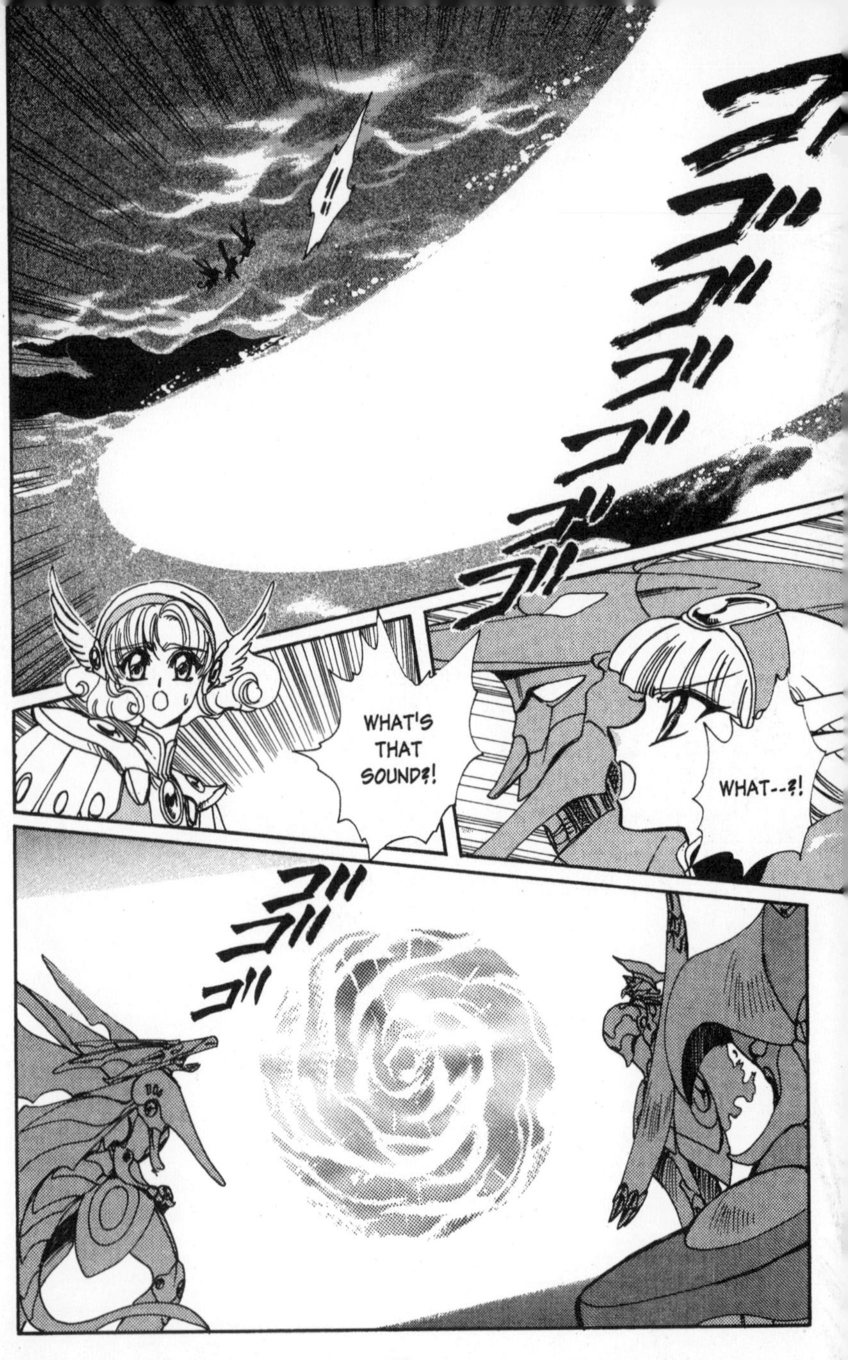
WHAT--?!
WHAT'S THAT SOUND?!
ゴゴゴ

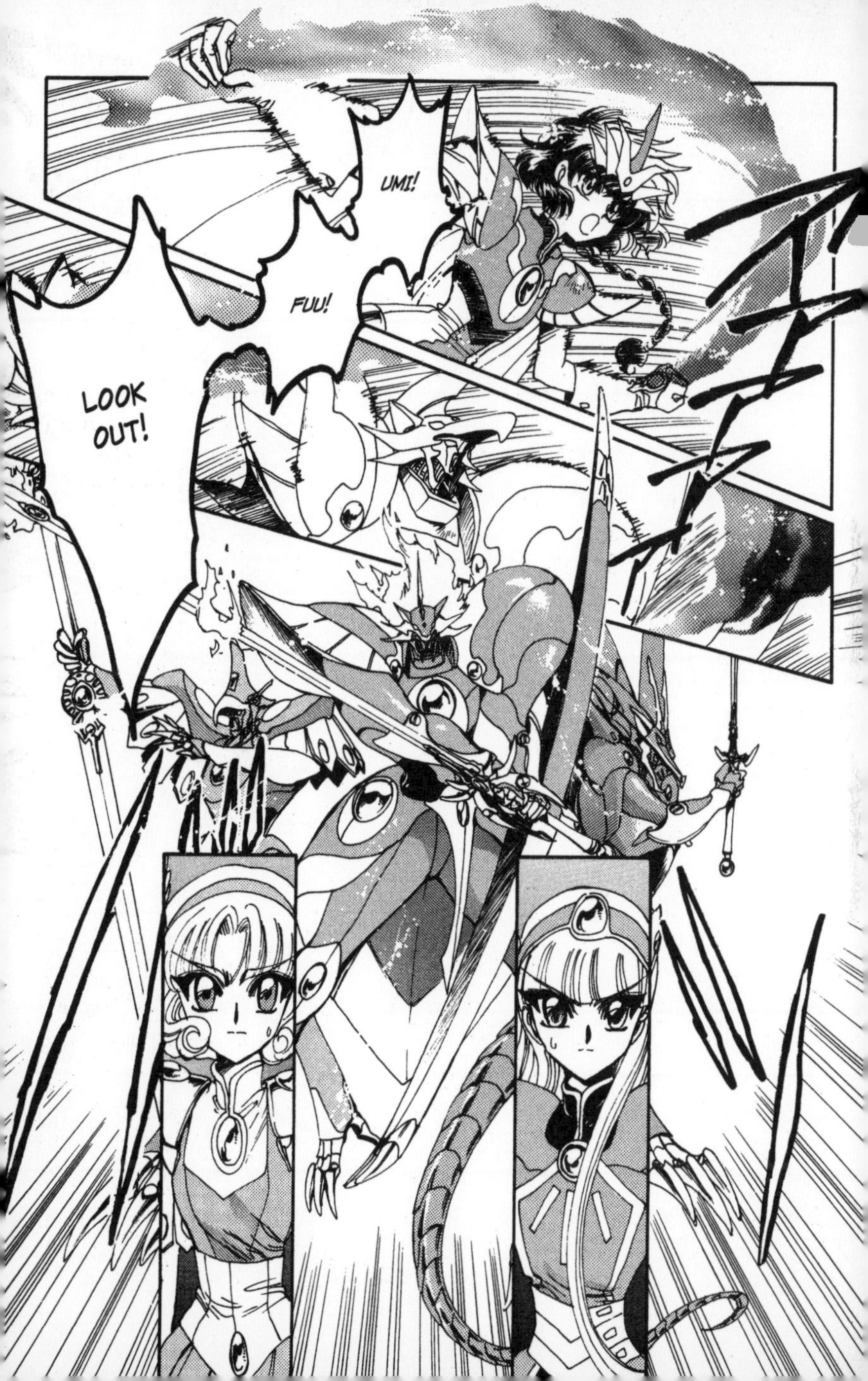
UMI!
FUU!
LOOK OUT!

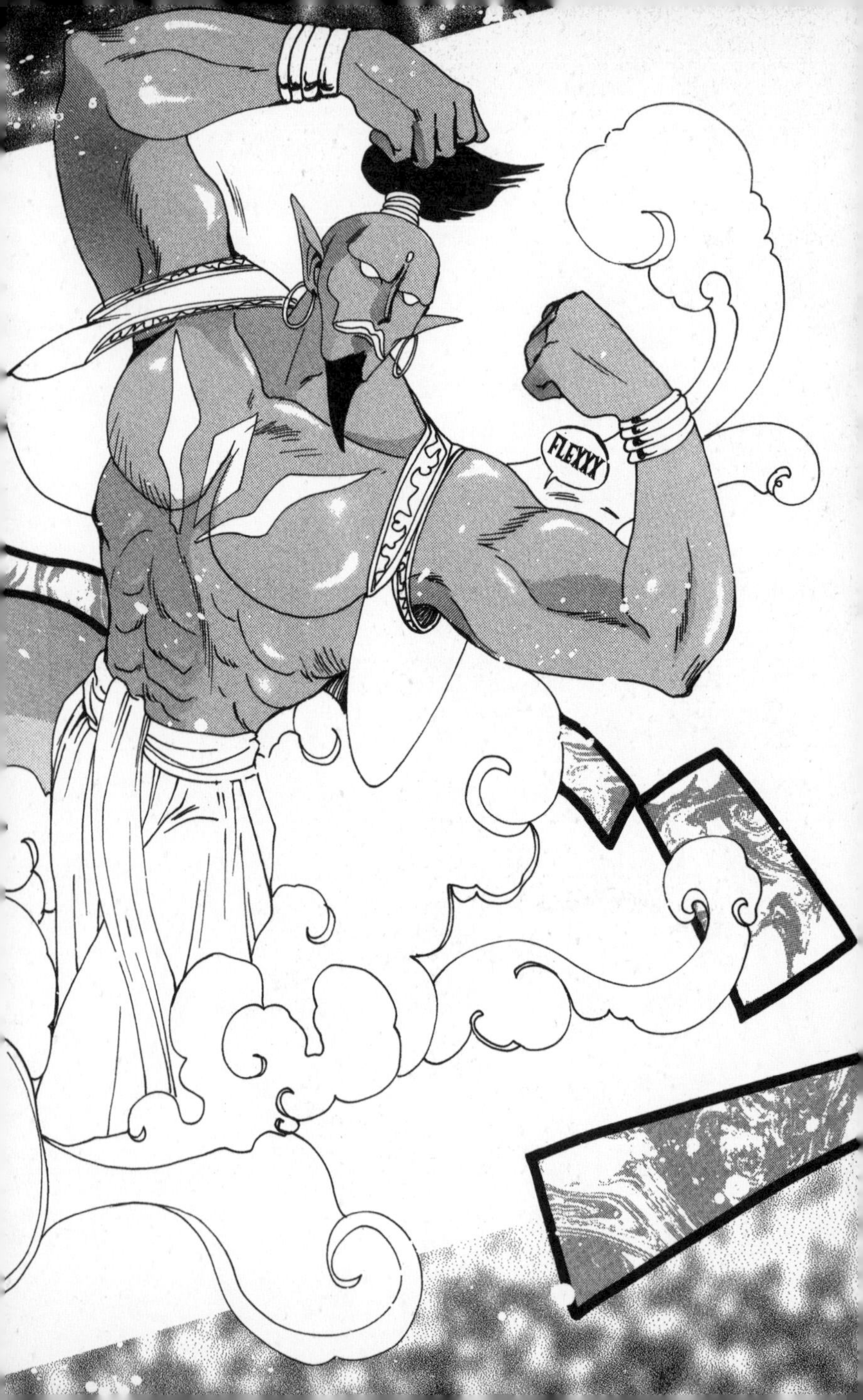
FLEXXX

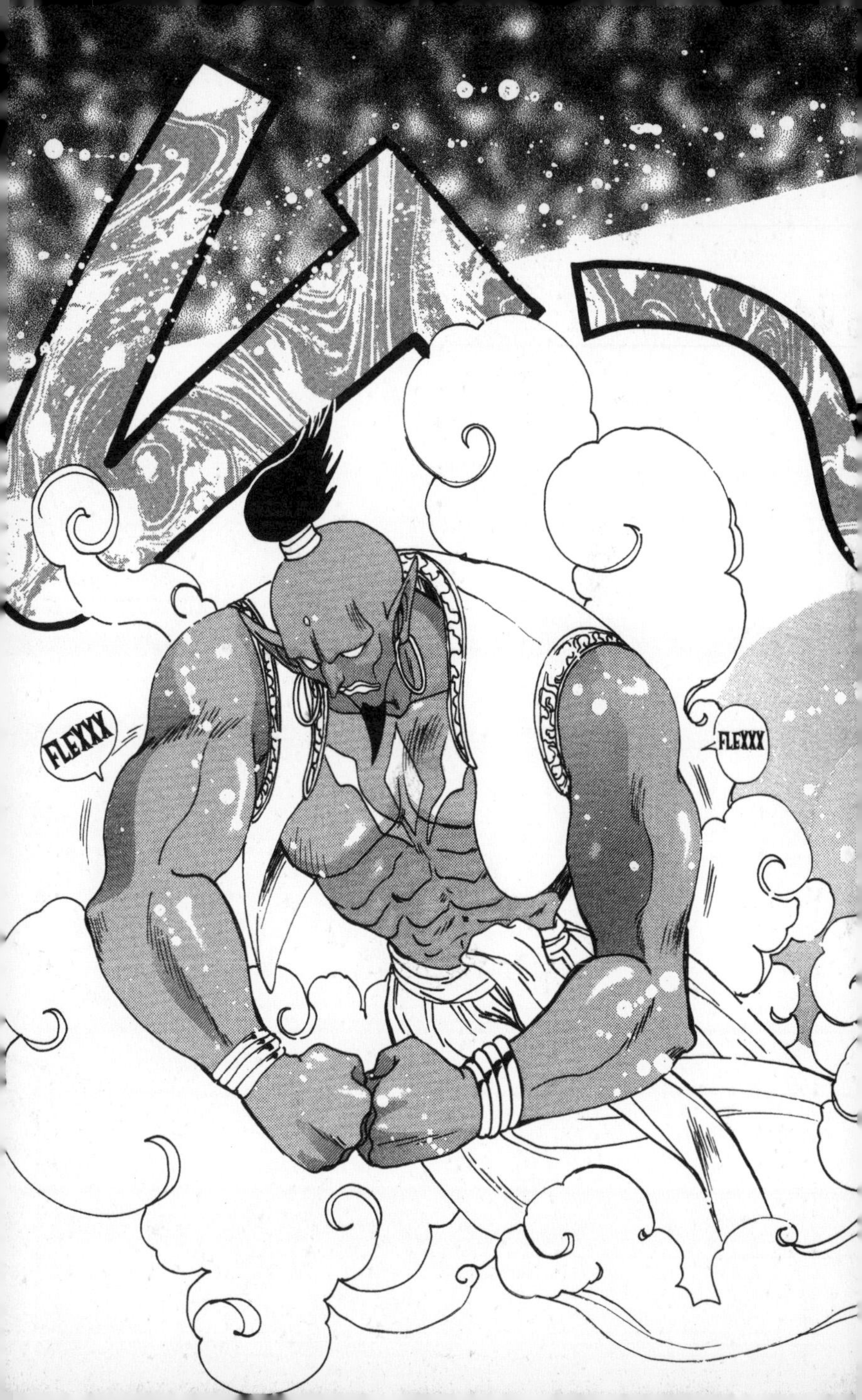
FLEXXX
FLEXXX

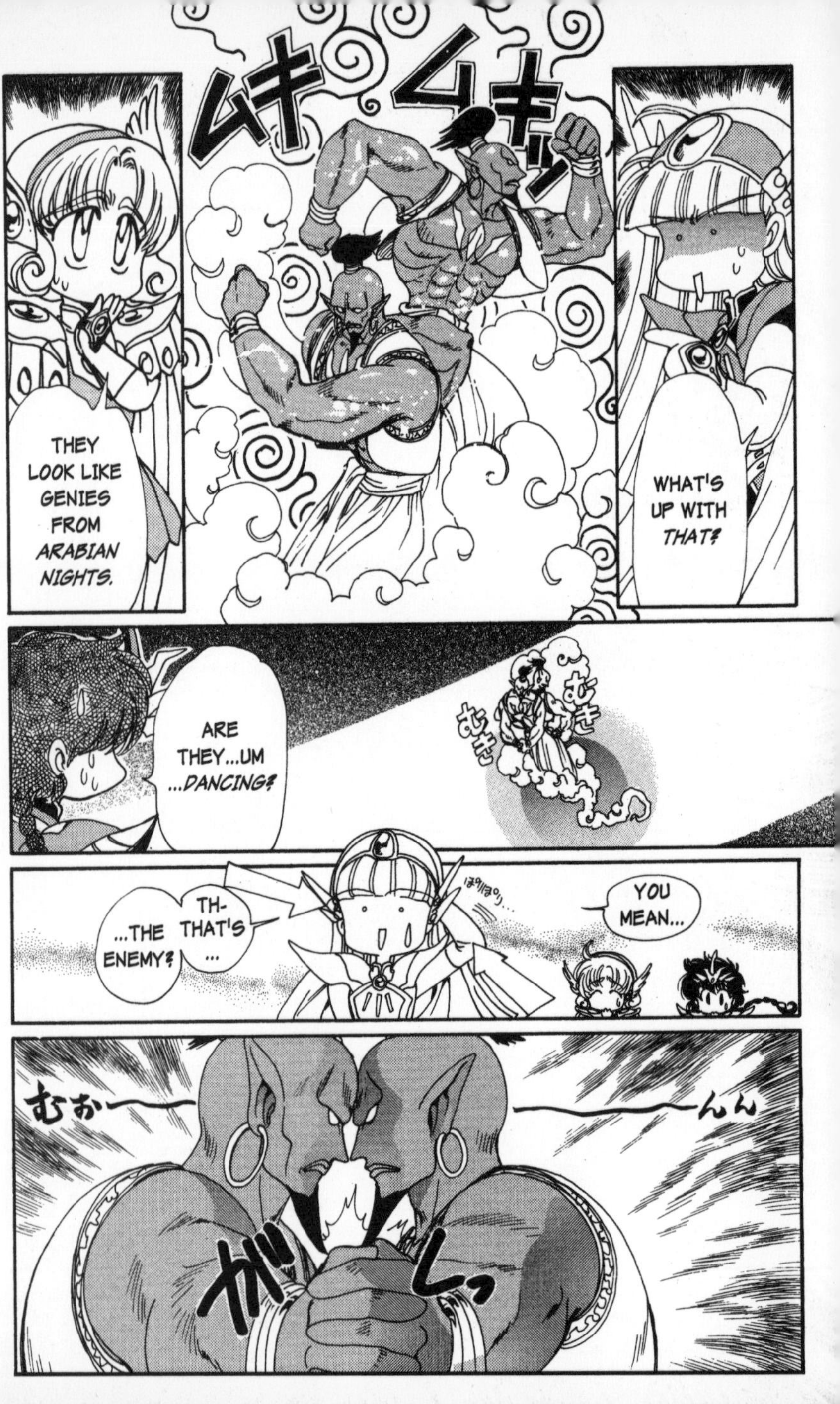
ムキムキッ
WHAT'S UP WITH THAT?
THEY LOOK LIKE GENIES FROM ARABIAN NIGHTS.
むきむき
ARE THEY...UM ...DANCING?
YOU MEAN...
ぽりぽり...
TH- THAT'S ...
...THE ENEMY?
むぉーーーんん
がしっ

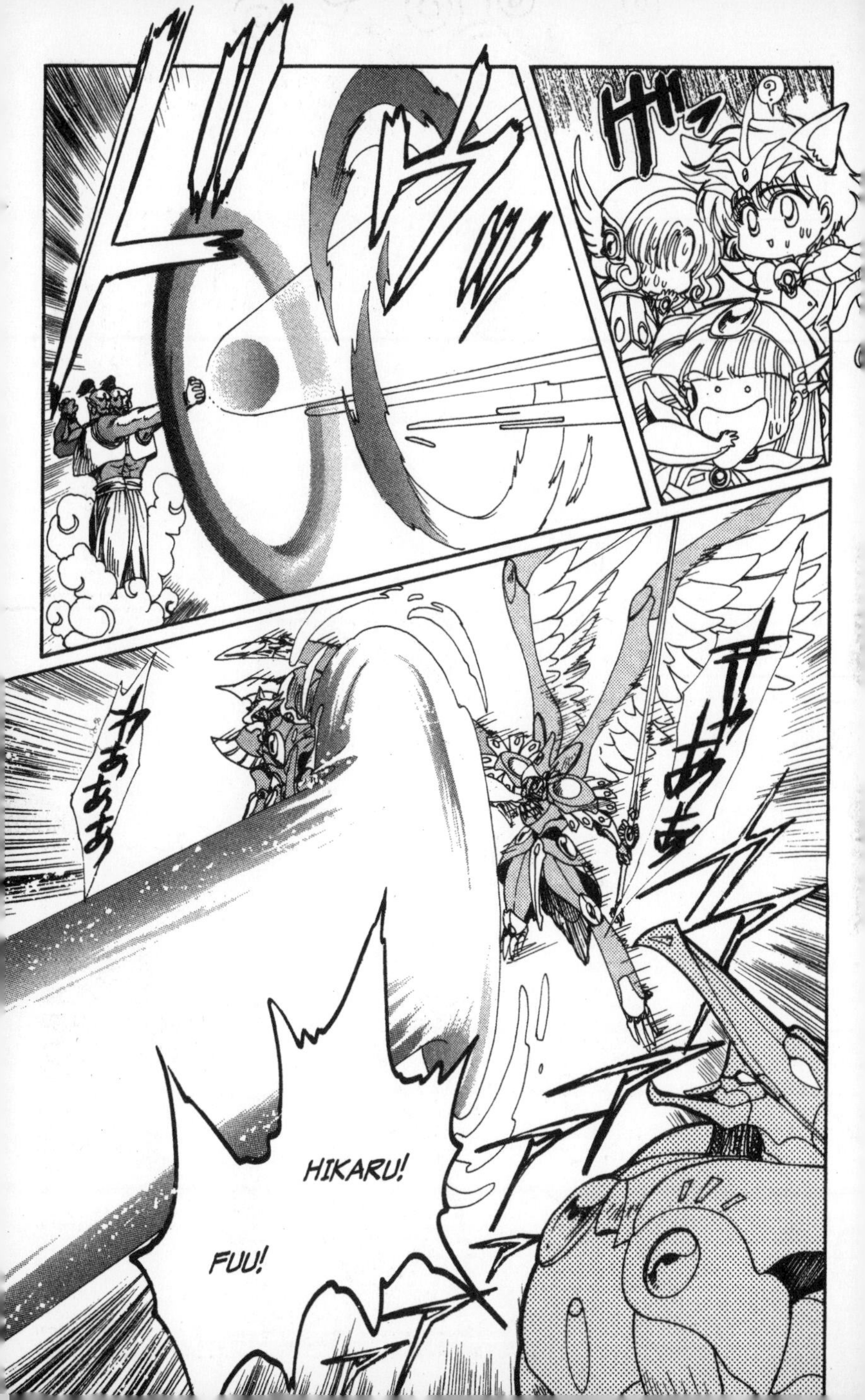
わあああ
HIKARU!
FUU!

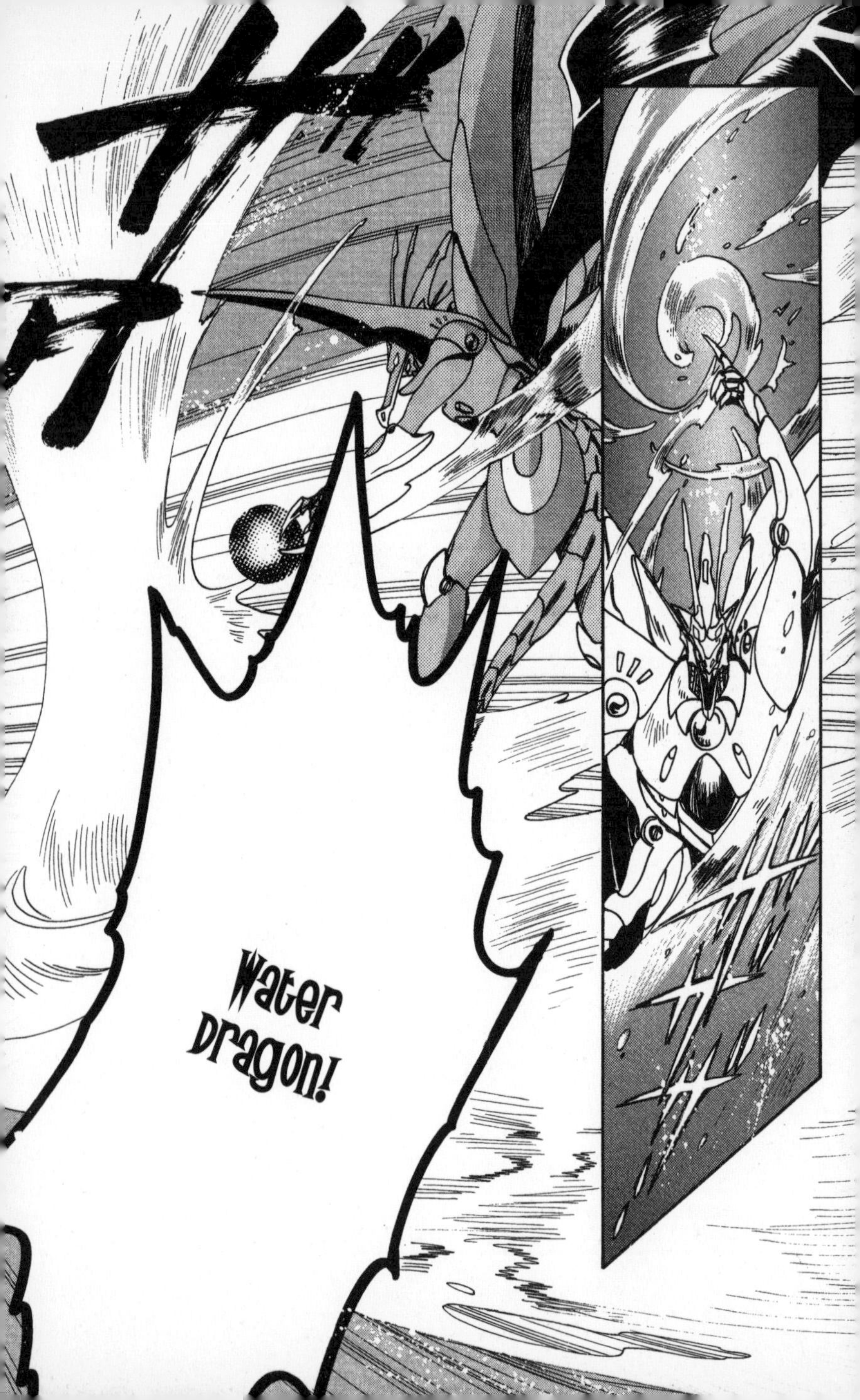
Water Dragon!

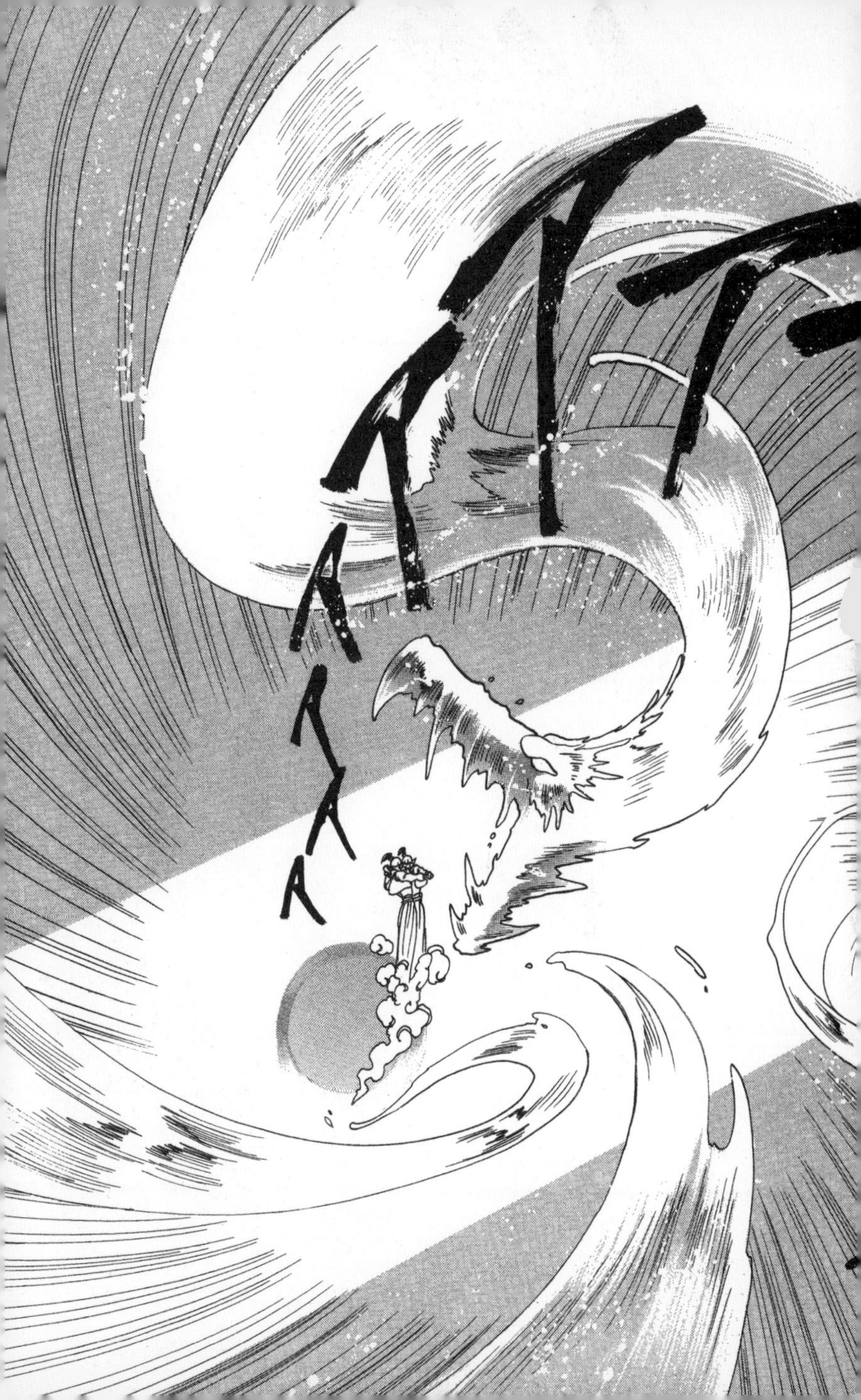
AAAAAAAA

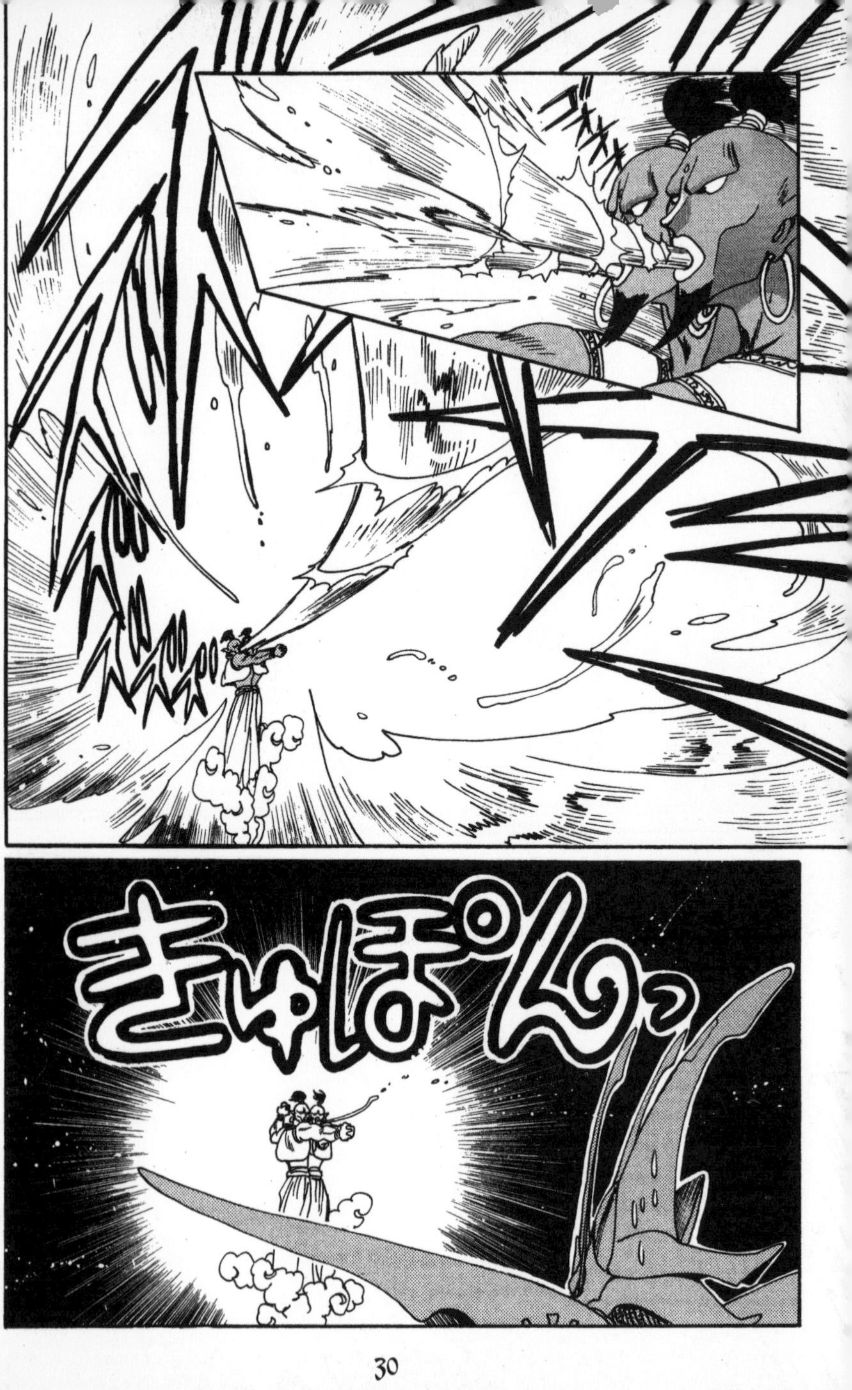
ゴオォォ
きゅぽんっ

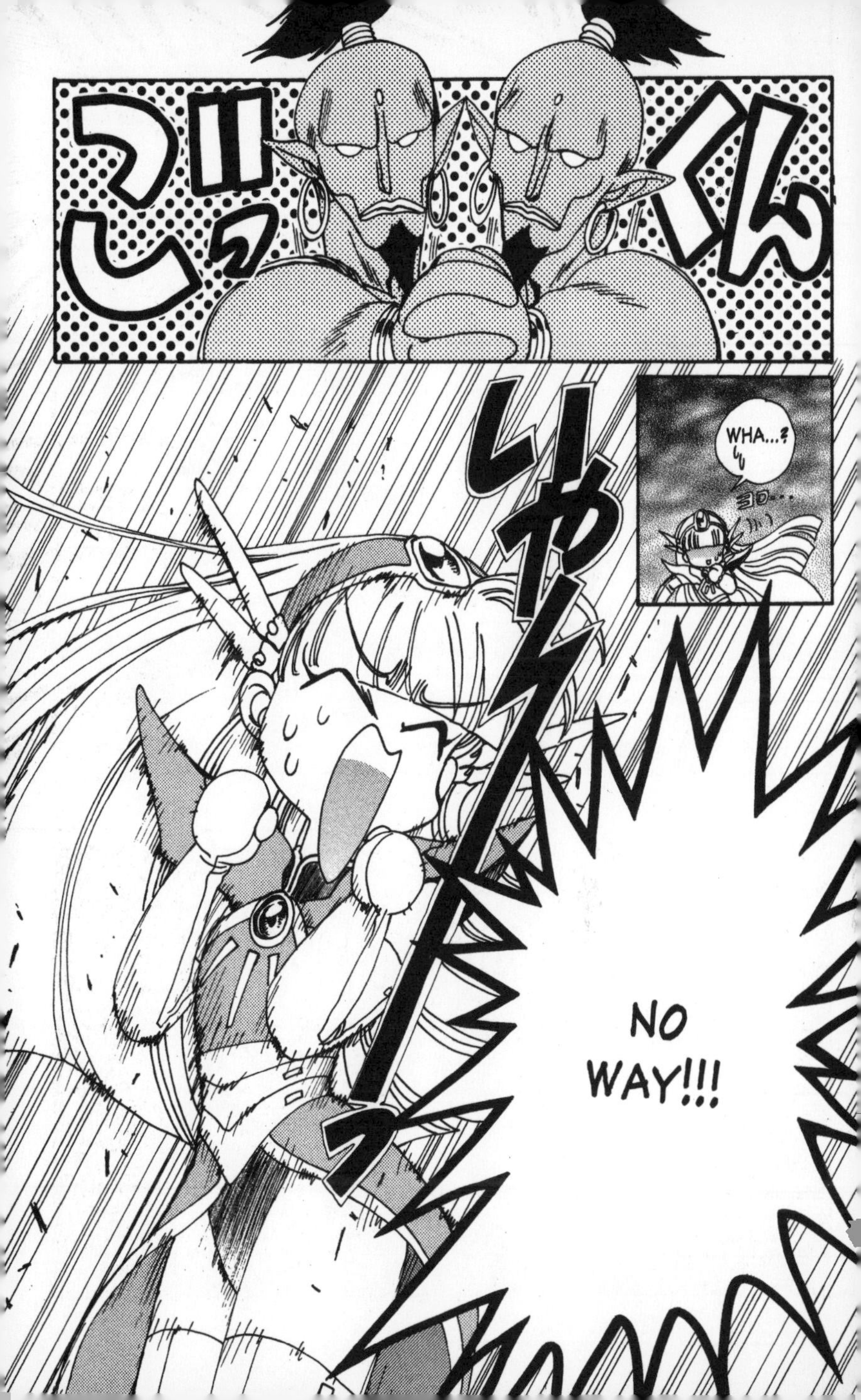
ごっくん
WHA...?
ヨロ...
しゃーっ
NO WAY!!!

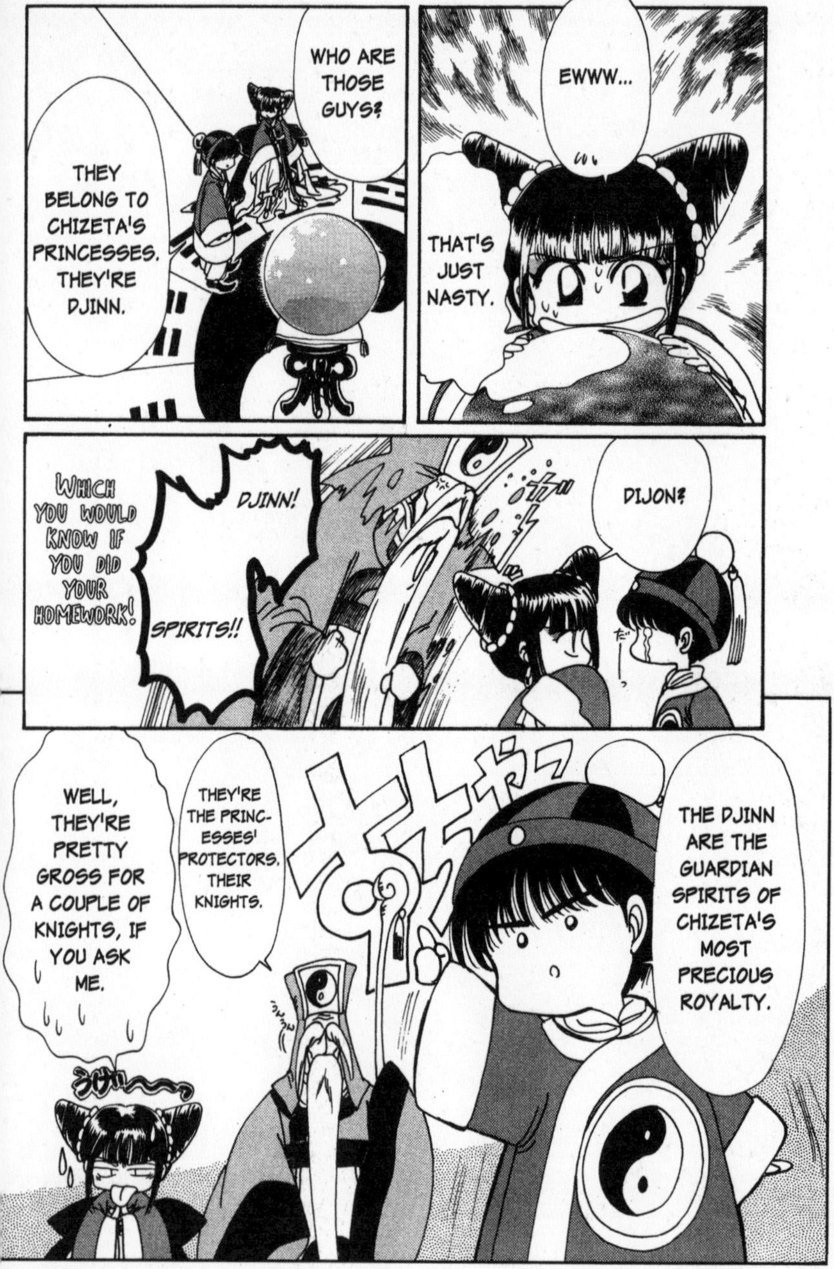
EWWW...
THAT'S JUST NASTY.
WHO ARE THOSE GUYS?
THEY BELONG TO CHIZETA'S PRINCESSES. THEY'RE DJINN.
DIJON?
DJINN!
SPIRITS!!
WHICH YOU WOULD KNOW IF YOU DID YOUR HOMEWORK!
THE DJINN ARE THE GUARDIAN SPIRITS OF CHIZETA'S MOST PRECIOUS ROYALTY.
THEY'RE THE PRINCESSES' PROTECTORS. THEIR KNIGHTS.
WELL, THEY'RE PRETTY GROSS FOR A COUPLE OF KNIGHTS, IF YOU ASK ME.

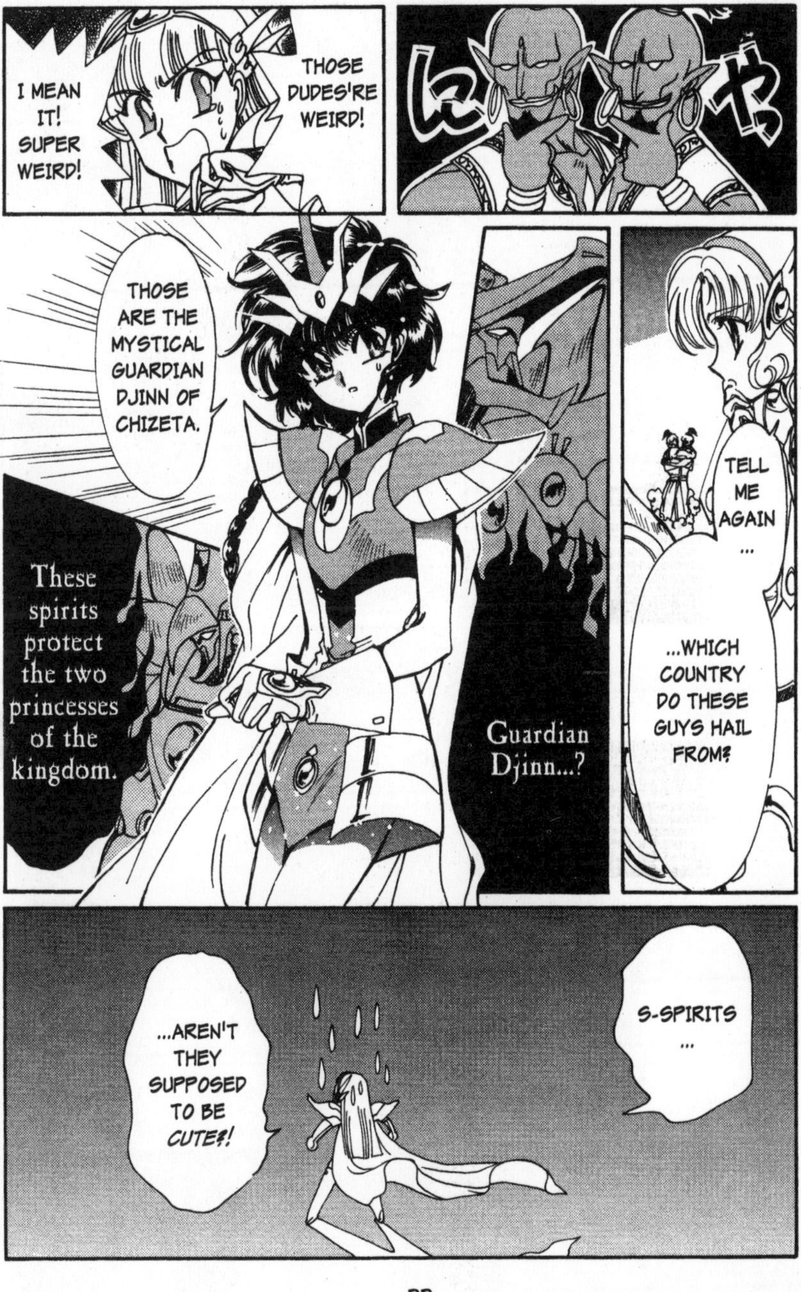
にや
THOSE DUDES'RE WEIRD!
I MEAN IT! SUPER WEIRD!
TELL ME AGAIN...
...WHICH COUNTRY DO THESE GUYS HAIL FROM?
Guardian Djinn...?
THOSE ARE THE MYSTICAL GUARDIAN DJINN OF CHIZETA.
These spirits protect the two princesses of the kingdom.
S-SPIRITS...
...AREN'T THEY SUPPOSED TO BE *CUTE*?!

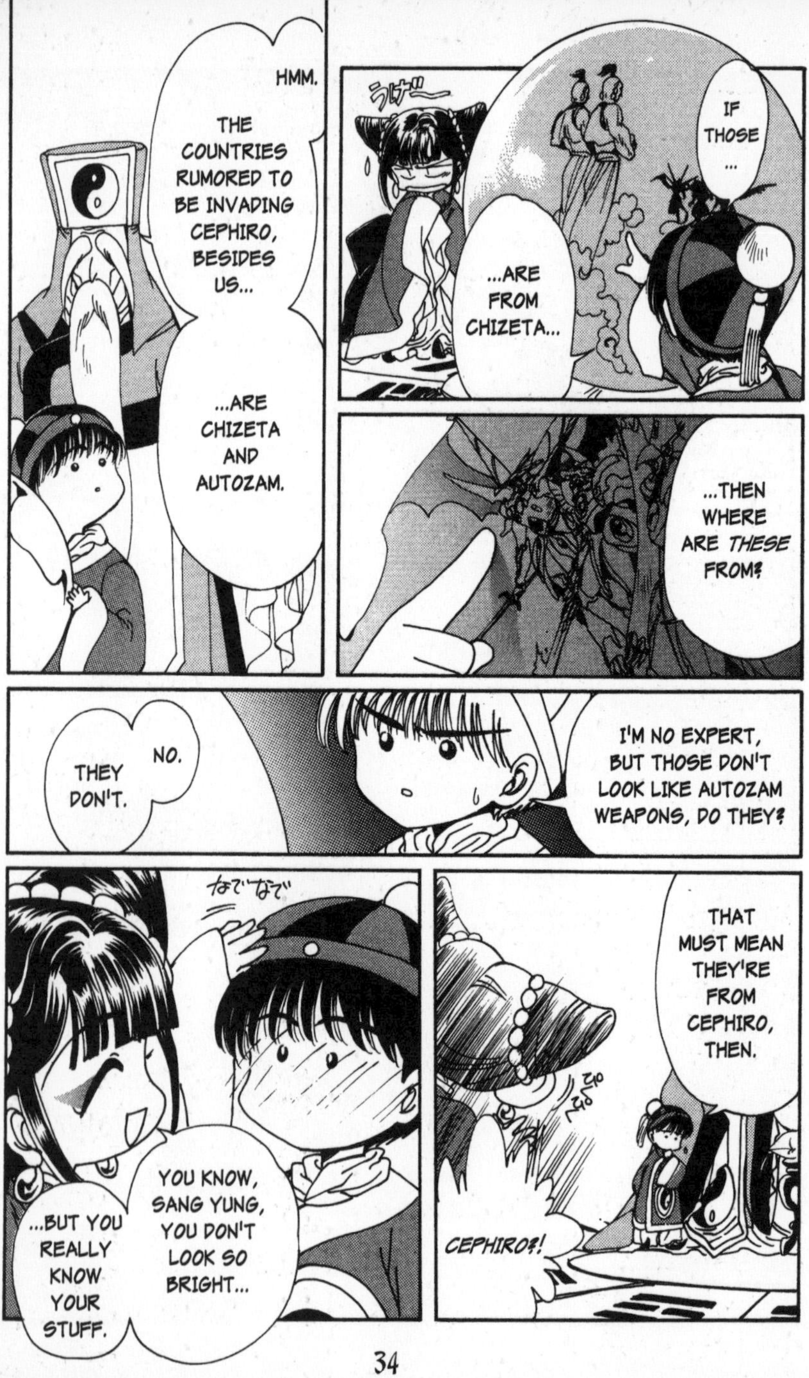
IF THOSE ...
...ARE FROM CHIZETA...
うげ〜
...THEN WHERE ARE *THESE* FROM?
HMM.
THE COUNTRIES RUMORED TO BE INVADING CEPHIRO, BESIDES US...
...ARE CHIZETA AND AUTOZAM.
I'M NO EXPERT, BUT THOSE DON'T LOOK LIKE AUTOZAM WEAPONS, DO THEY?
NO.
THEY DON'T.
THAT MUST MEAN THEY'RE FROM CEPHIRO, THEN.
CEPHIRO?!
なでなで
YOU KNOW, SANG YUNG, YOU DON'T LOOK SO BRIGHT...
...BUT YOU REALLY KNOW YOUR STUFF.

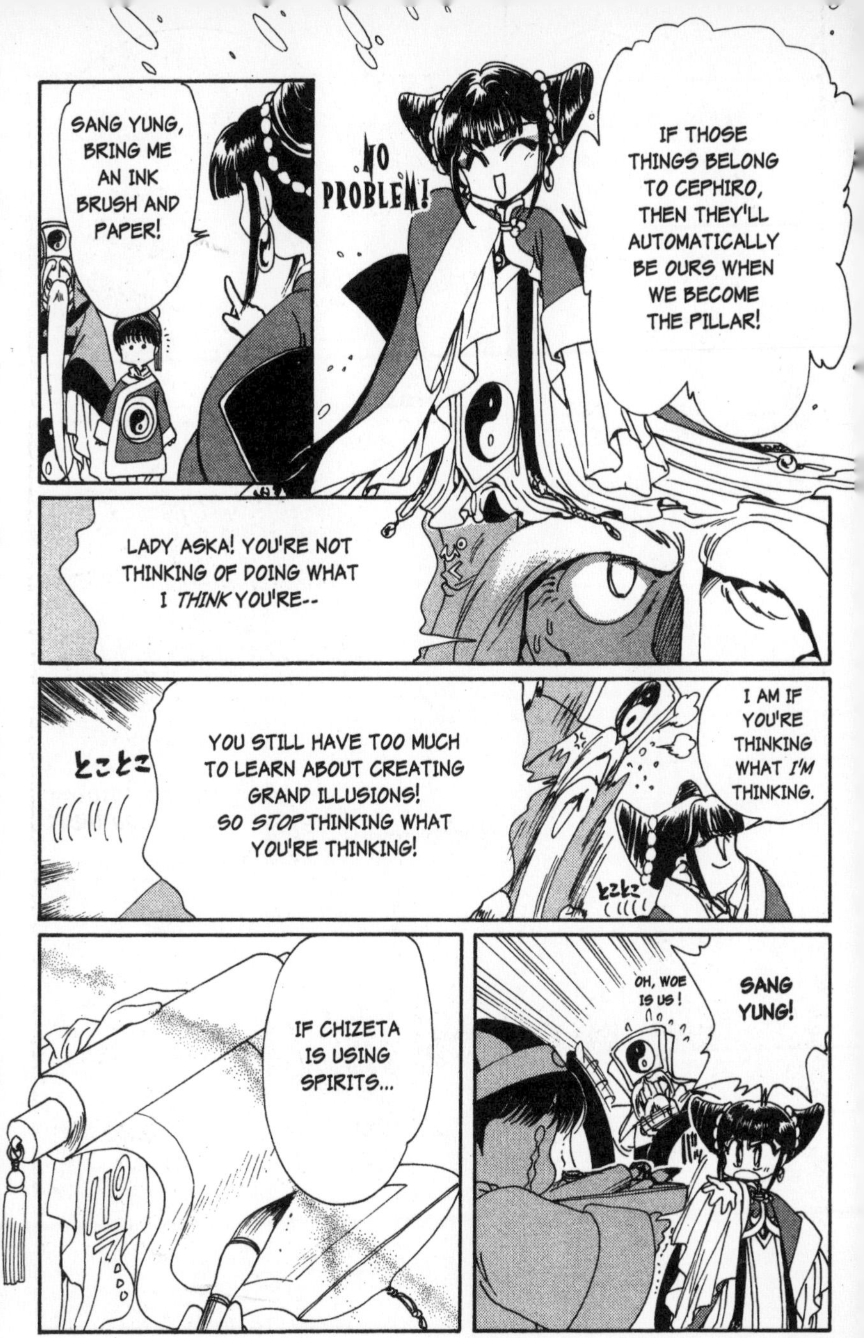
IF THOSE THINGS BELONG TO CEPHIRO, THEN THEY'LL AUTOMATICALLY BE OURS WHEN WE BECOME THE PILLAR!
NO PROBLEM!
SANG YUNG, BRING ME AN INK BRUSH AND PAPER!
LADY ASKA! YOU'RE NOT THINKING OF DOING WHAT I THINK YOU'RE--
I AM IF YOU'RE THINKING WHAT I'M THINKING.
とことこ
YOU STILL HAVE TOO MUCH TO LEARN ABOUT CREATING GRAND ILLUSIONS! SO STOP THINKING WHAT YOU'RE THINKING!
とことこ
SANG YUNG!
OH, WOE IS US!
IF CHIZETA IS USING SPIRITS...

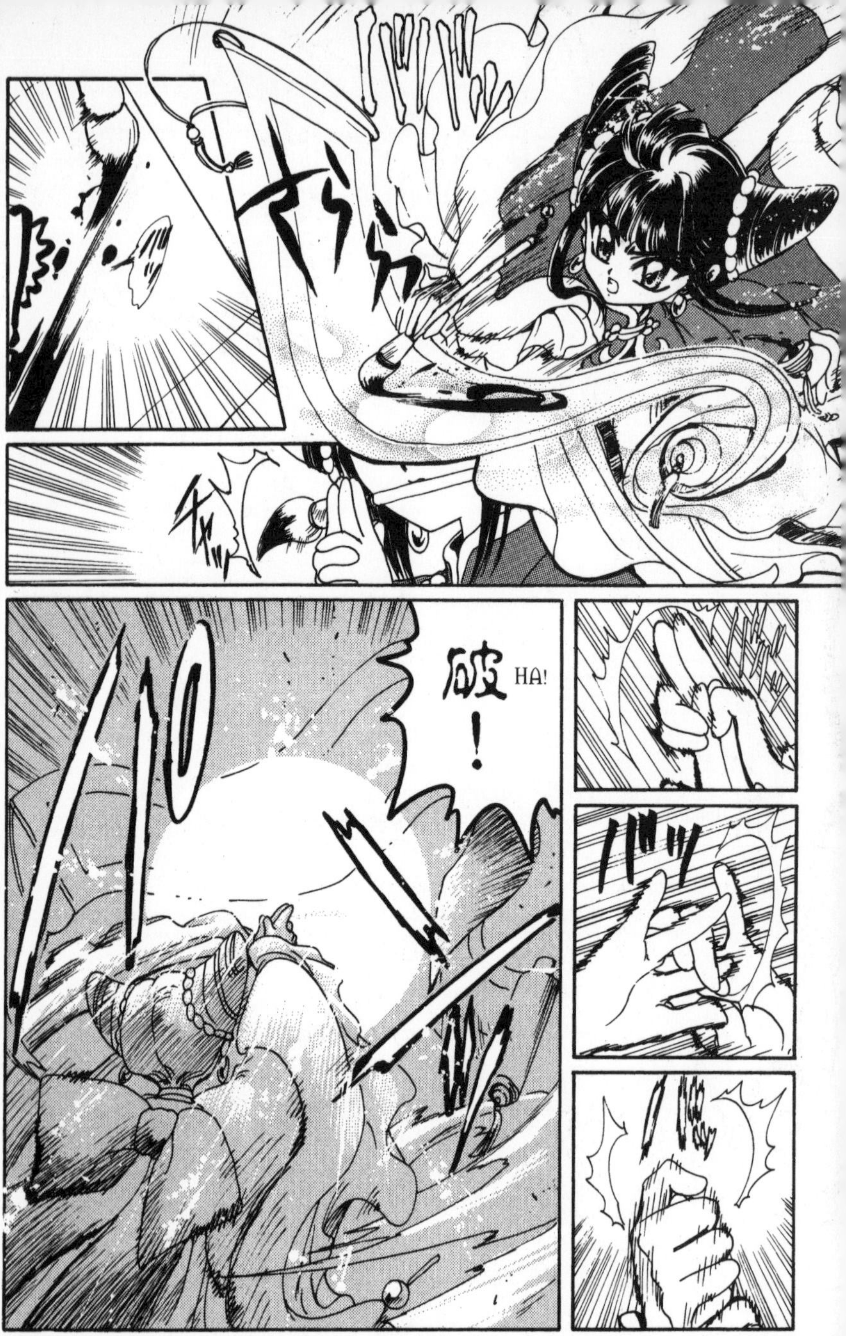
破！ HA!

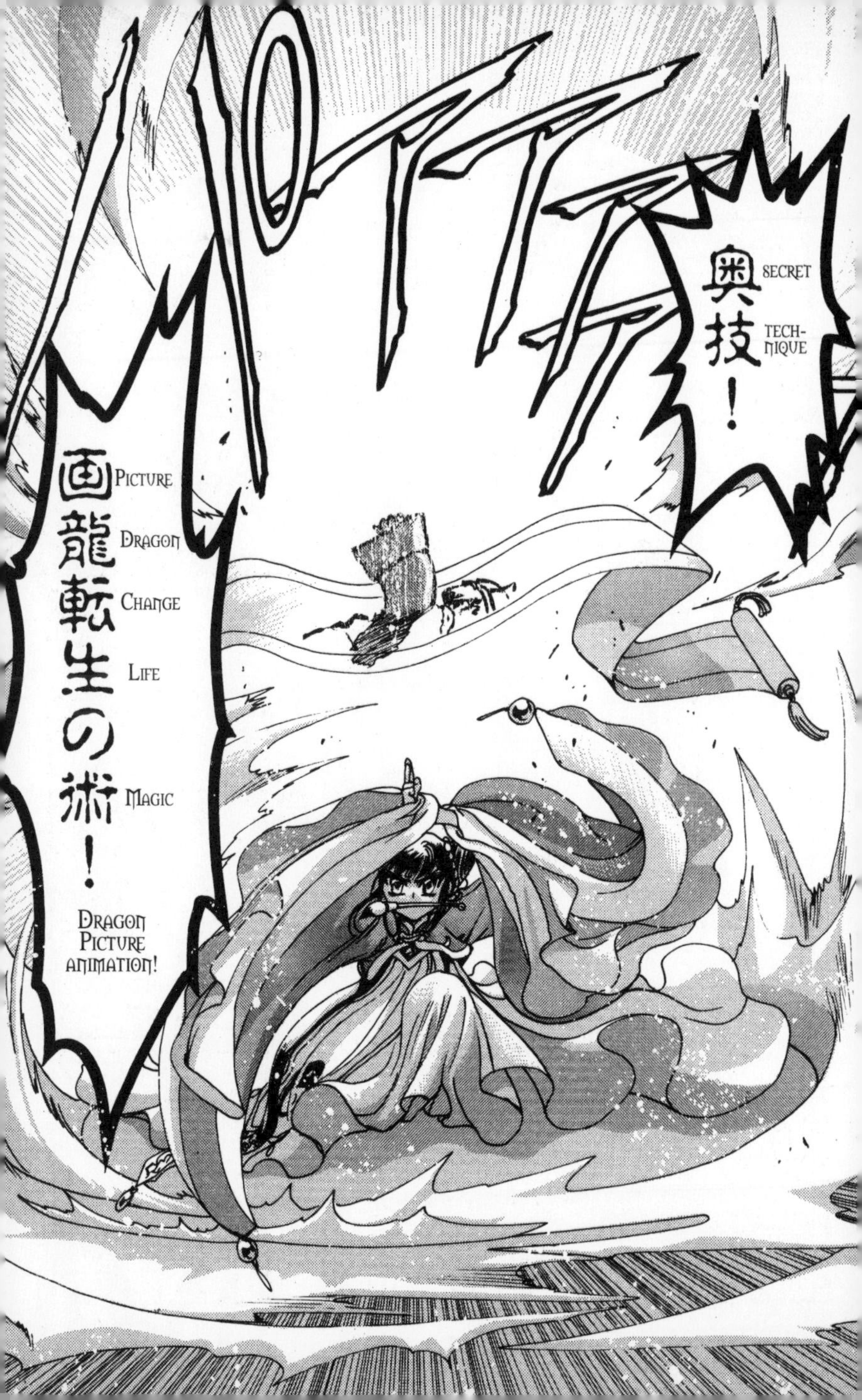
奥技！
SECRET TECH-NIQUE
画龍転生の術！
PICTURE DRAGON CHANGE LIFE MAGIC
DRAGON PICTURE ANIMATION!

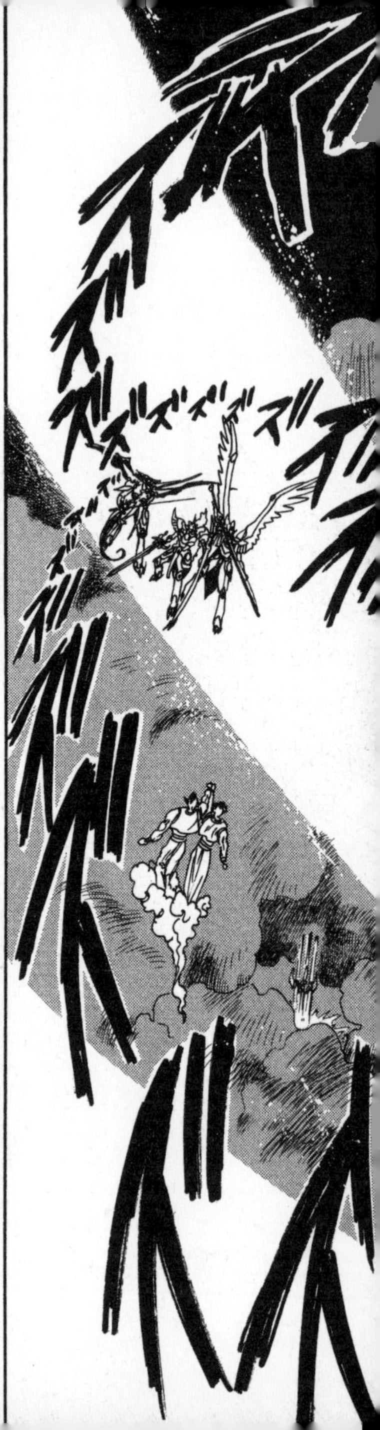

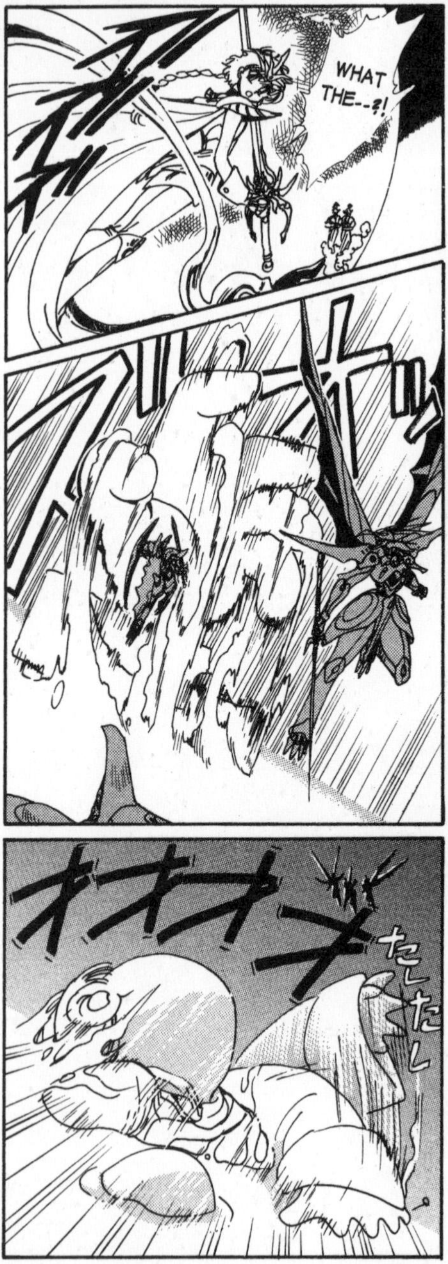
WHAT THE--?!
オオオオ
たしたし

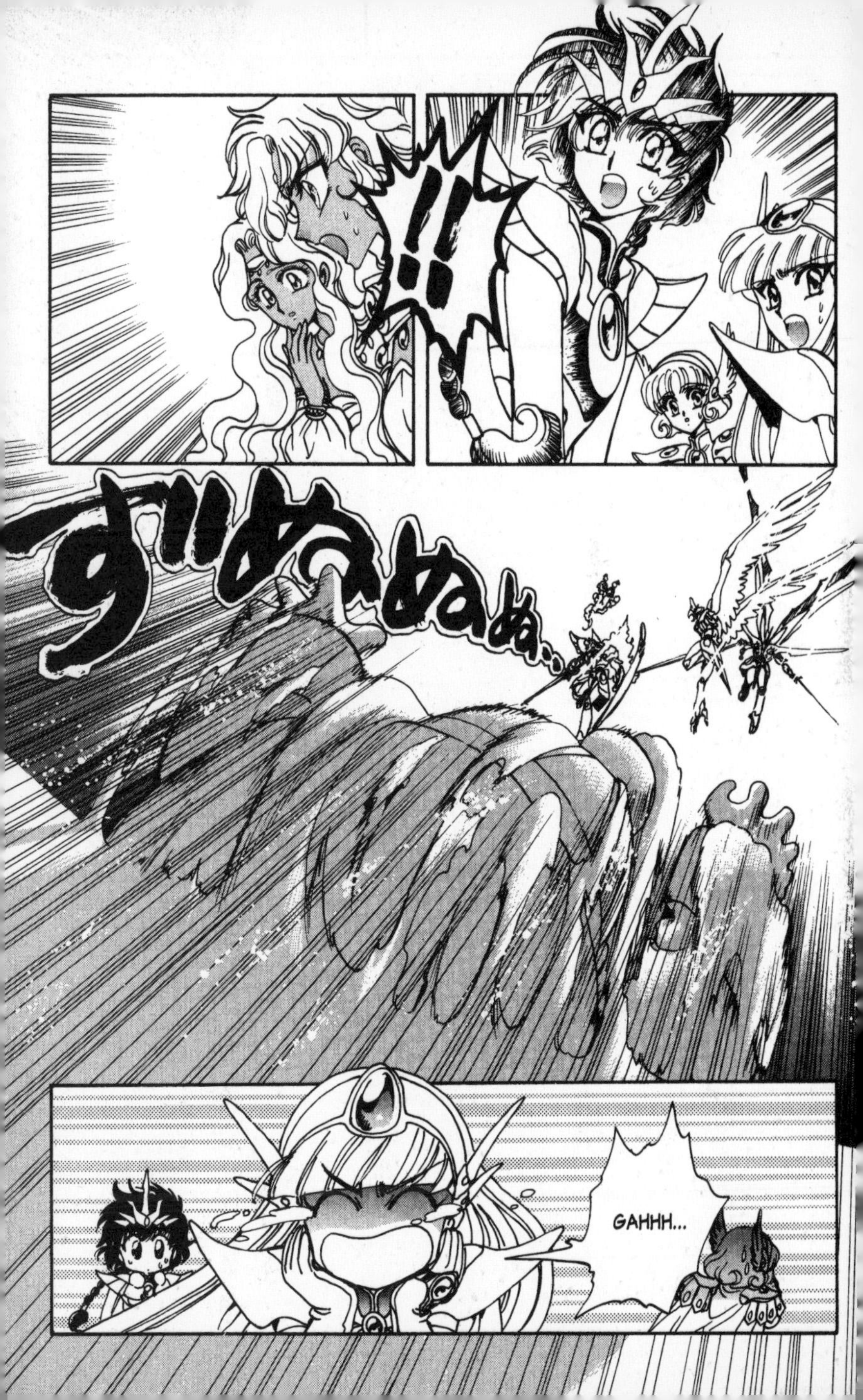
!!
GAHHH...

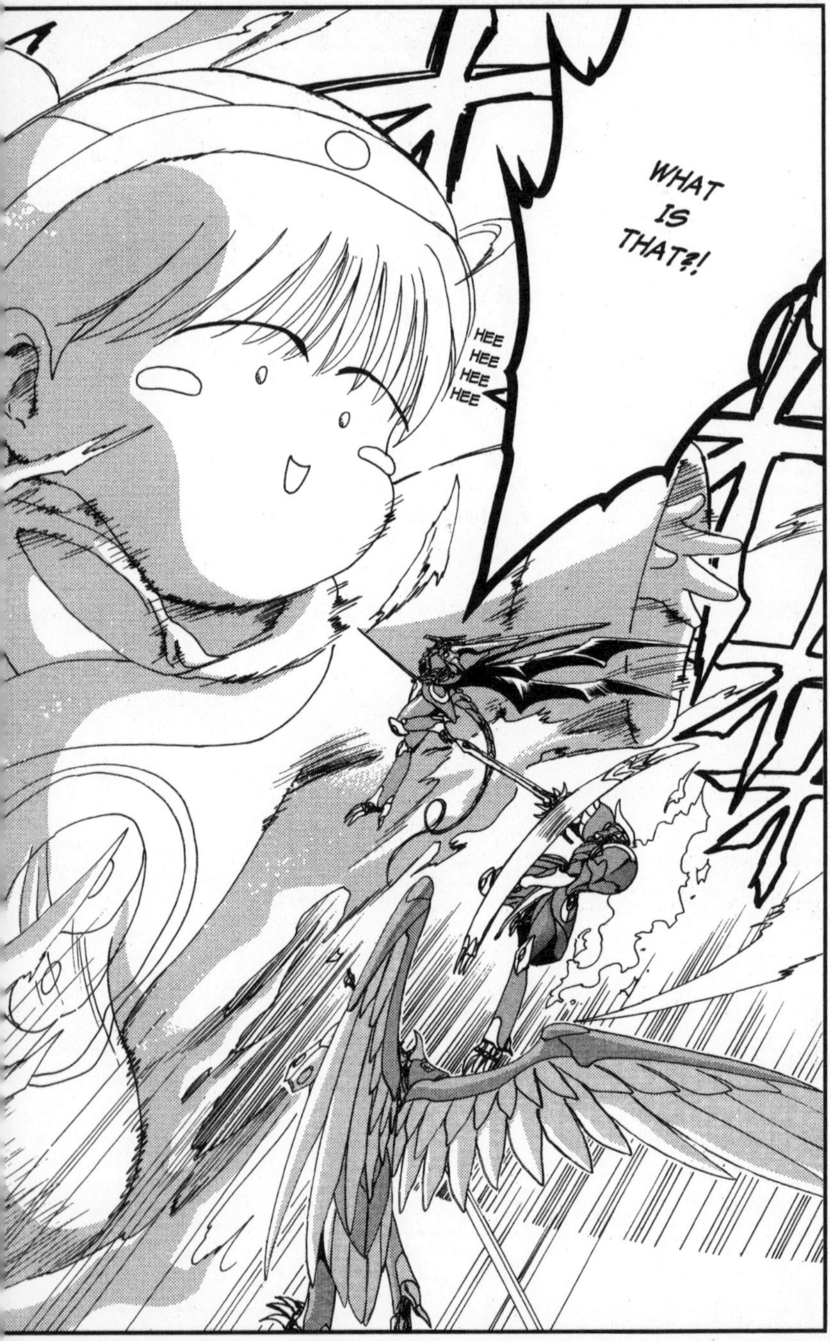
WHAT IS THAT?!
HEE HEE HEE HEE

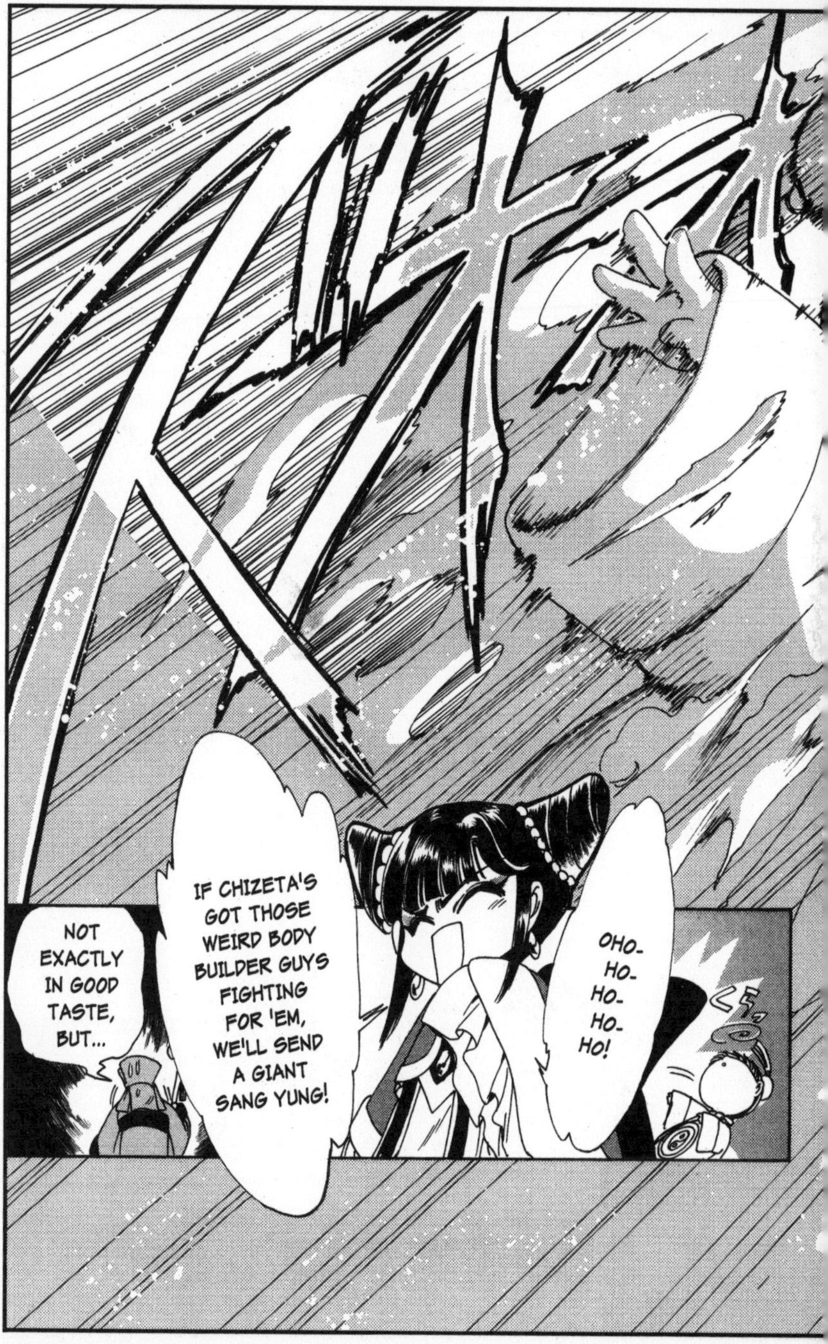
OHO-HO-HO-HO-HO!
IF CHIZETA'S GOT THOSE WEIRD BODY BUILDER GUYS FIGHTING FOR 'EM, WE'LL SEND A GIANT SANG YUNG!
NOT EXACTLY IN GOOD TASTE, BUT...

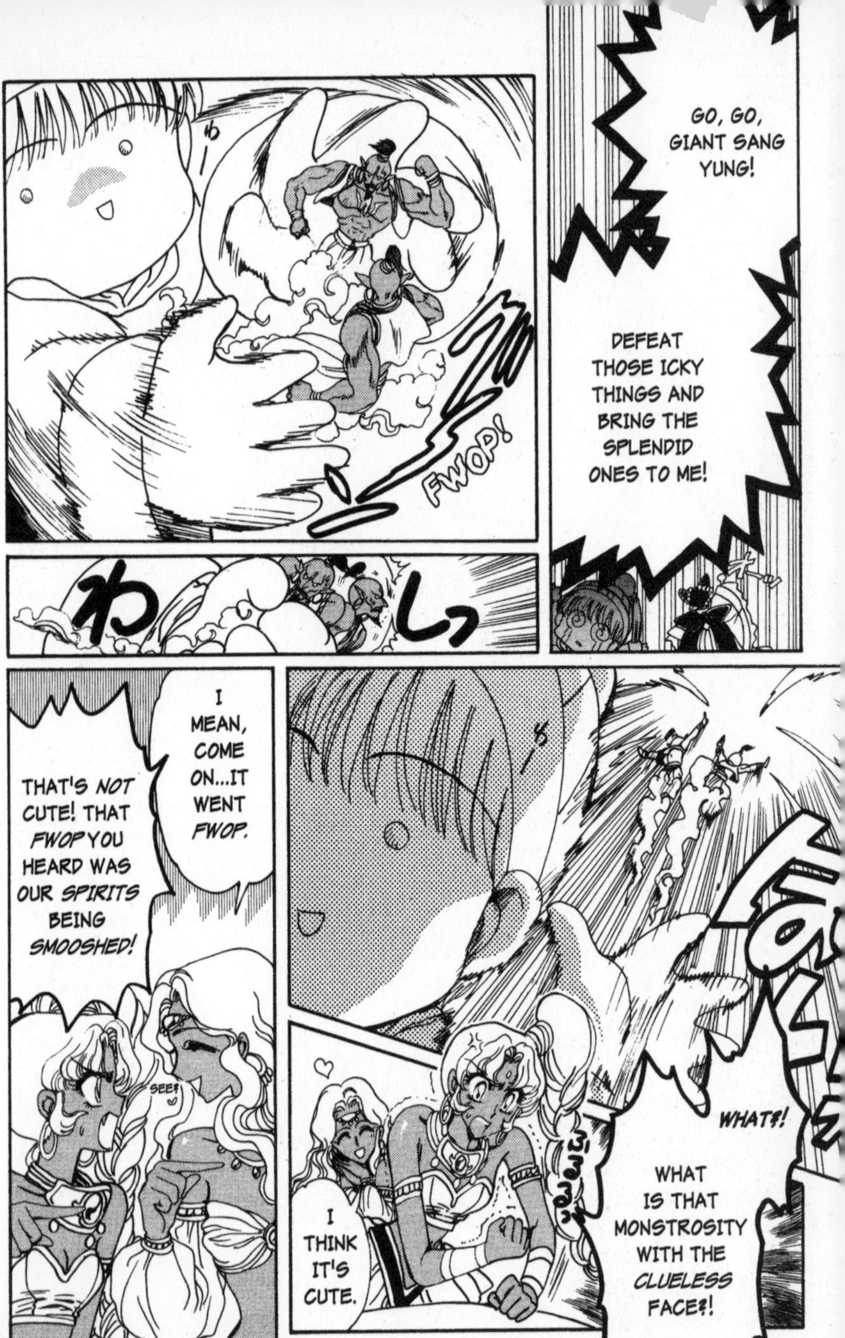
GO, GO, GIANT SANG YUNG!
DEFEAT THOSE ICKY THINGS AND BRING THE SPLENDID ONES TO ME!
FWOP!
わしっ
WHAT?!
WHAT IS THAT MONSTROSITY WITH THE CLUELESS FACE?!
I THINK IT'S CUTE.
I MEAN, COME ON...IT WENT FWOP.
THAT'S NOT CUTE! THAT FWOP YOU HEARD WAS OUR SPIRITS BEING SMOOSHED!
SEE?

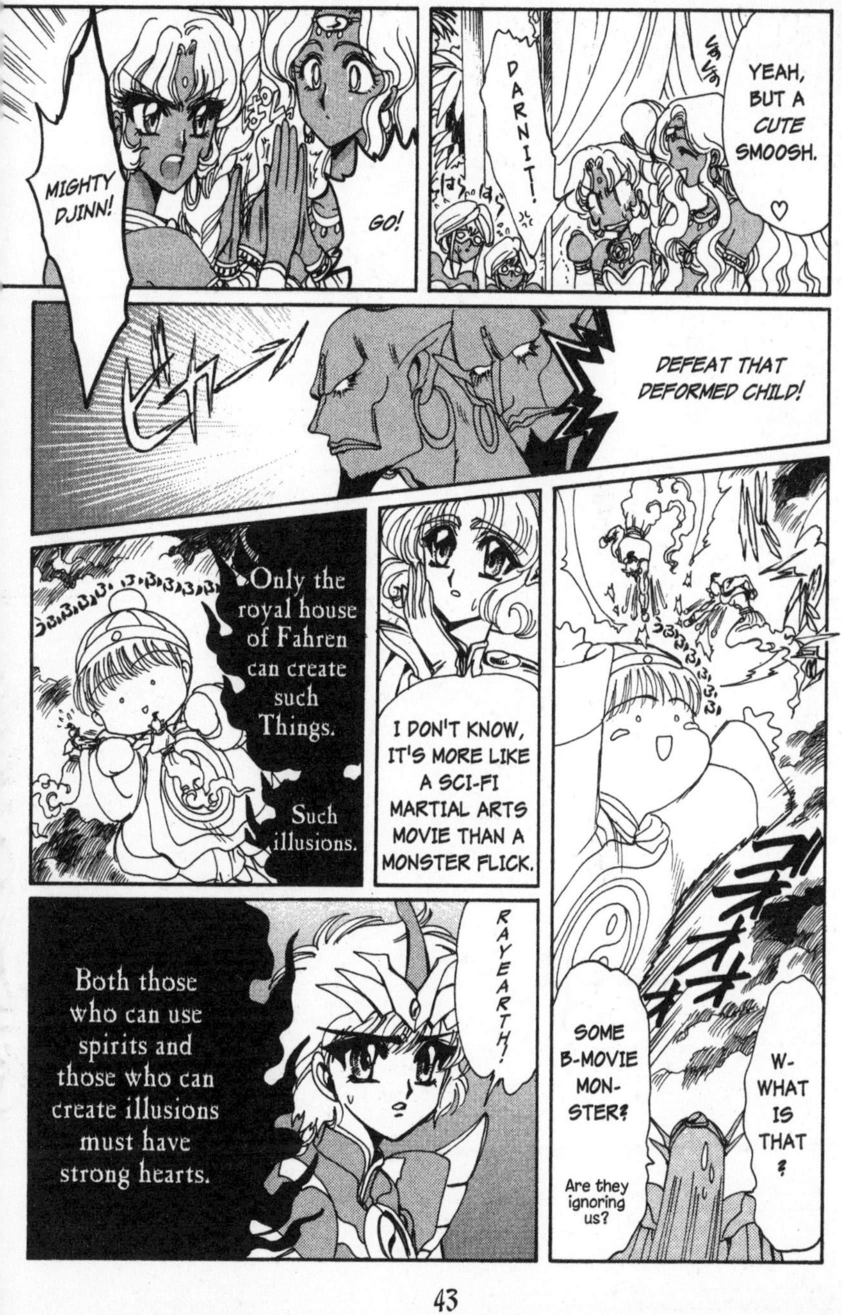

YEAH, BUT A CUTE SMOOSH. ♥
DARNIT!
MIGHTY DJINN!
GO!
DEFEAT THAT DEFORMED CHILD!
W-WHAT IS THAT?
SOME B-MOVIE MONSTER?
Are they ignoring us?
I DON'T KNOW, IT'S MORE LIKE A SCI-FI MARTIAL ARTS MOVIE THAN A MONSTER FLICK.
Only the royal house of Fahren can create such Things.
Such illusions.
RAYEARTH!
Both those who can use spirits and those who can create illusions must have strong hearts.

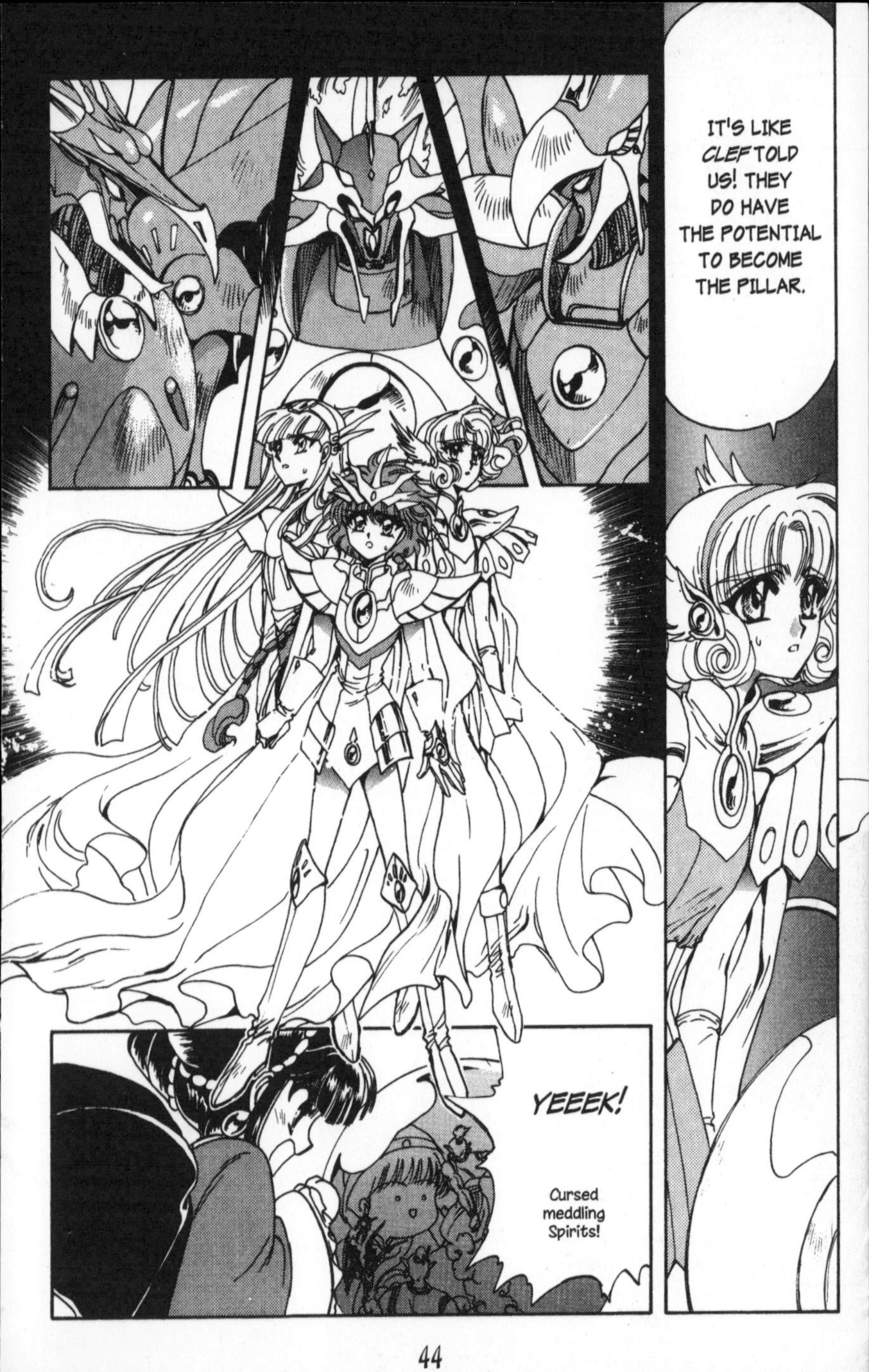
IT'S LIKE *CLEF* TOLD US! THEY DO HAVE THE POTENTIAL TO BECOME THE PILLAR.
YEEEK!
Cursed meddling Spirits!

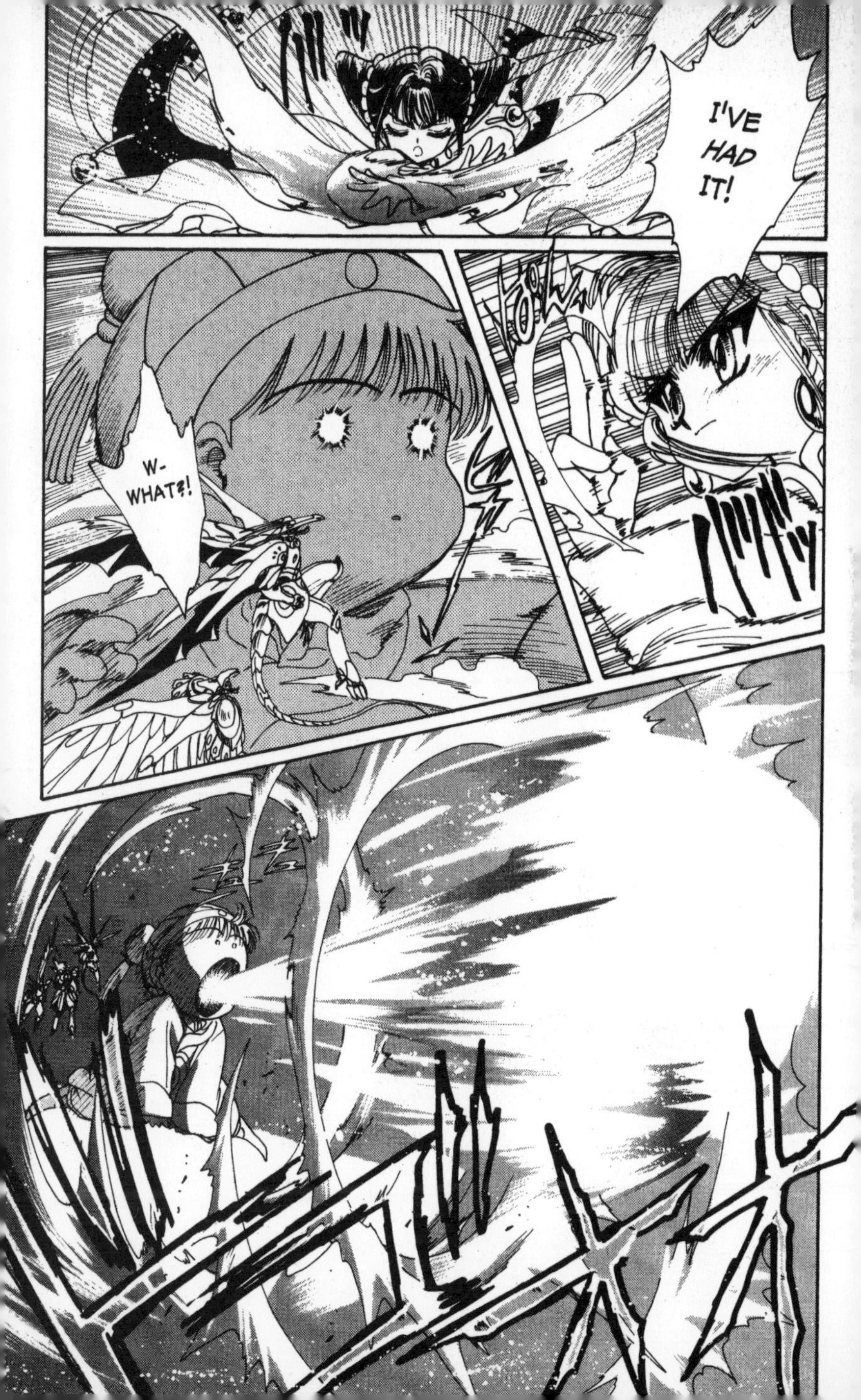
I'VE HAD IT!
W-WHAT?!

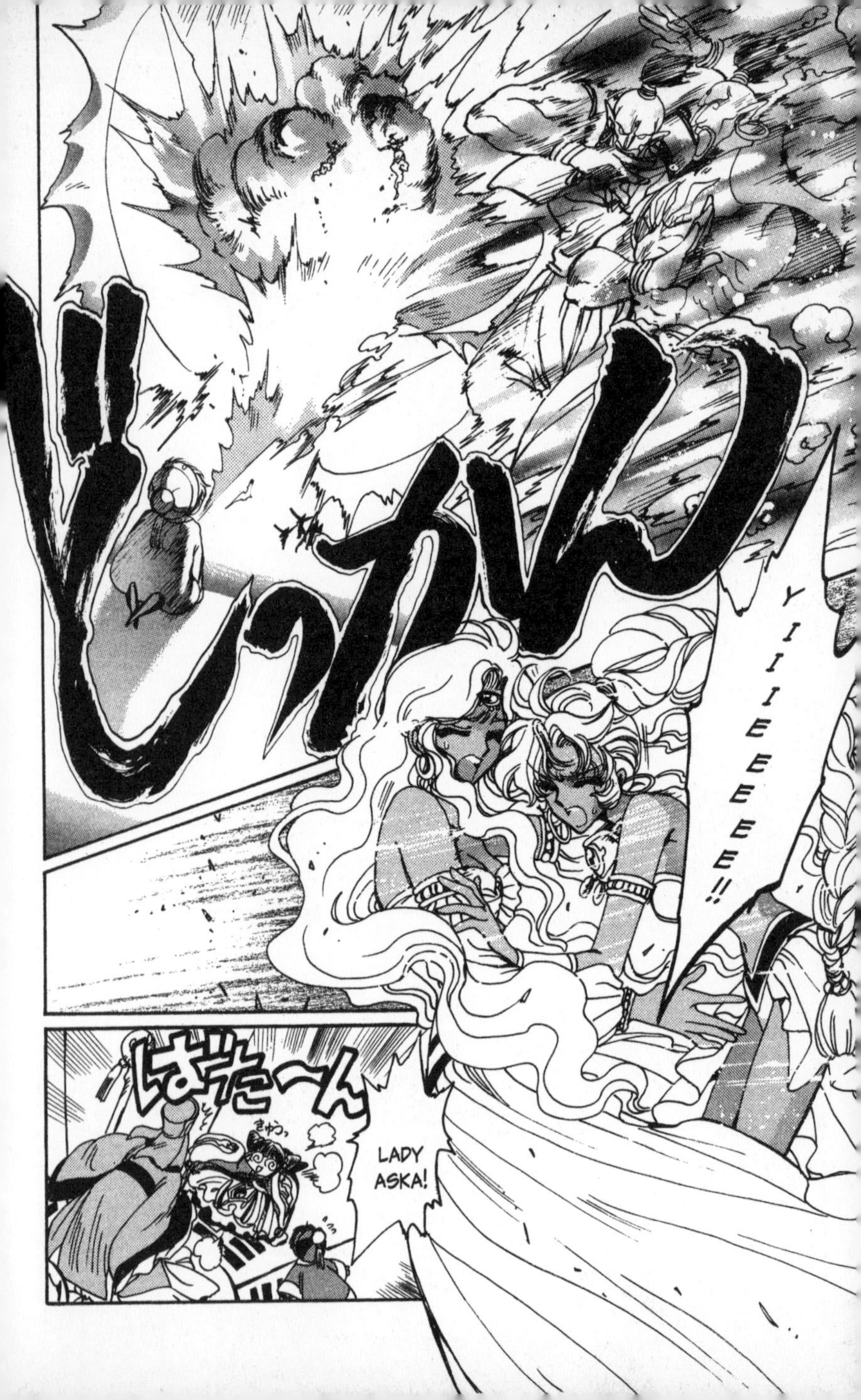
YIIIEEEEEE!!
ばた〜ん
LADY ASKA!

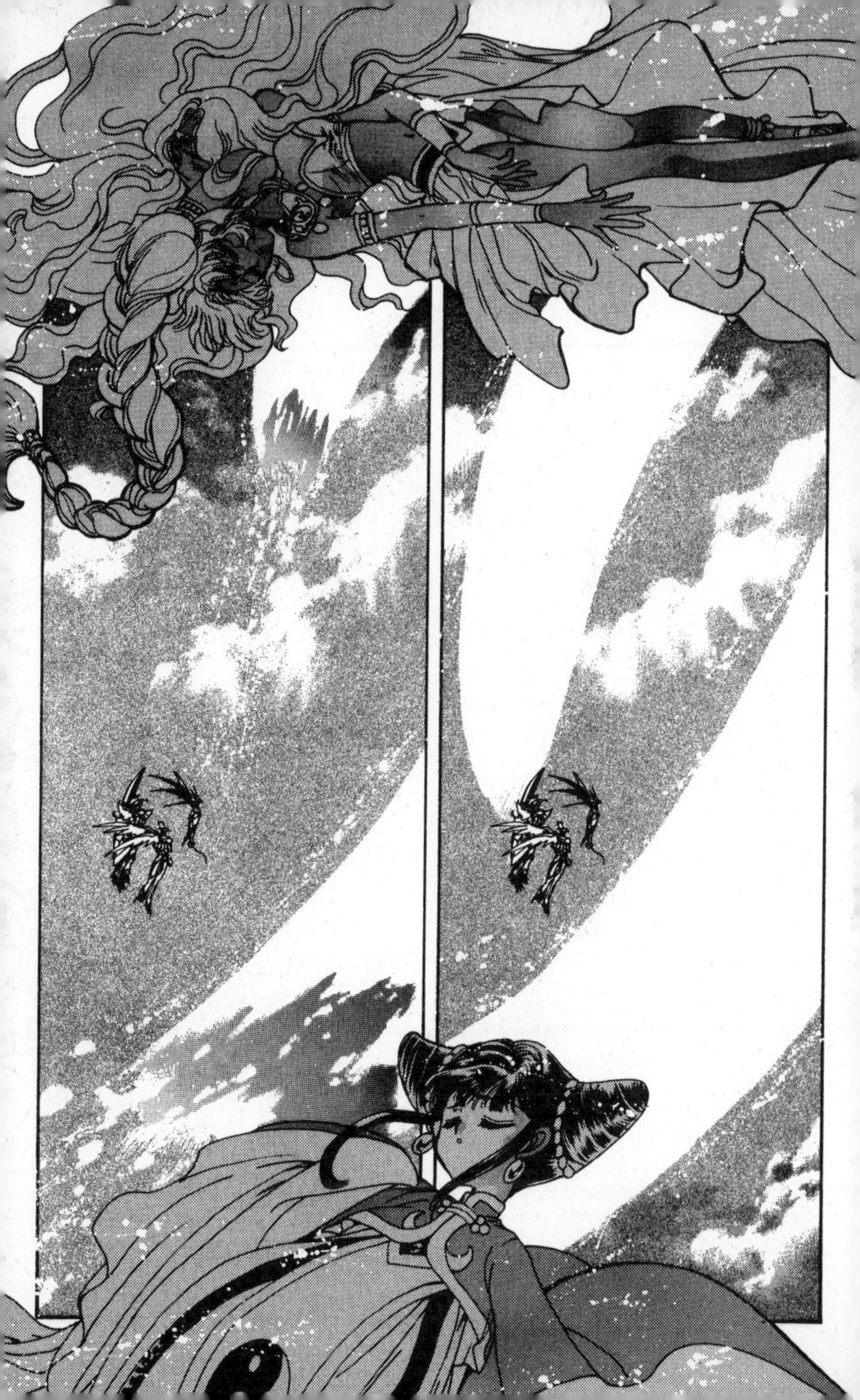

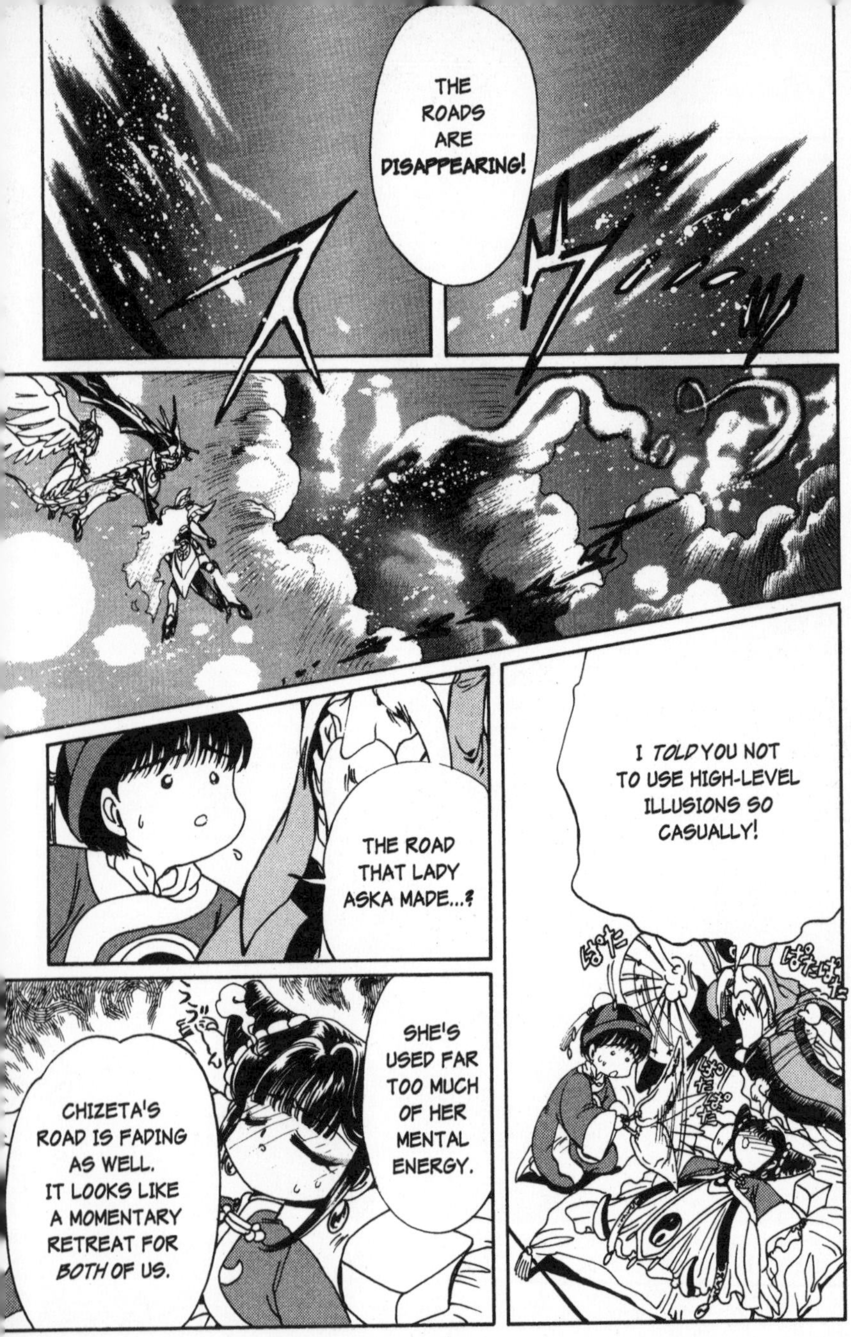
THE ROADS ARE DISAPPEARING!
I *TOLD* YOU NOT TO USE HIGH-LEVEL ILLUSIONS SO CASUALLY!
THE ROAD THAT LADY ASKA MADE...?
SHE'S USED FAR TOO MUCH OF HER MENTAL ENERGY.
CHIZETA'S ROAD IS FADING AS WELL. IT LOOKS LIKE A MOMENTARY RETREAT FOR *BOTH* OF US.

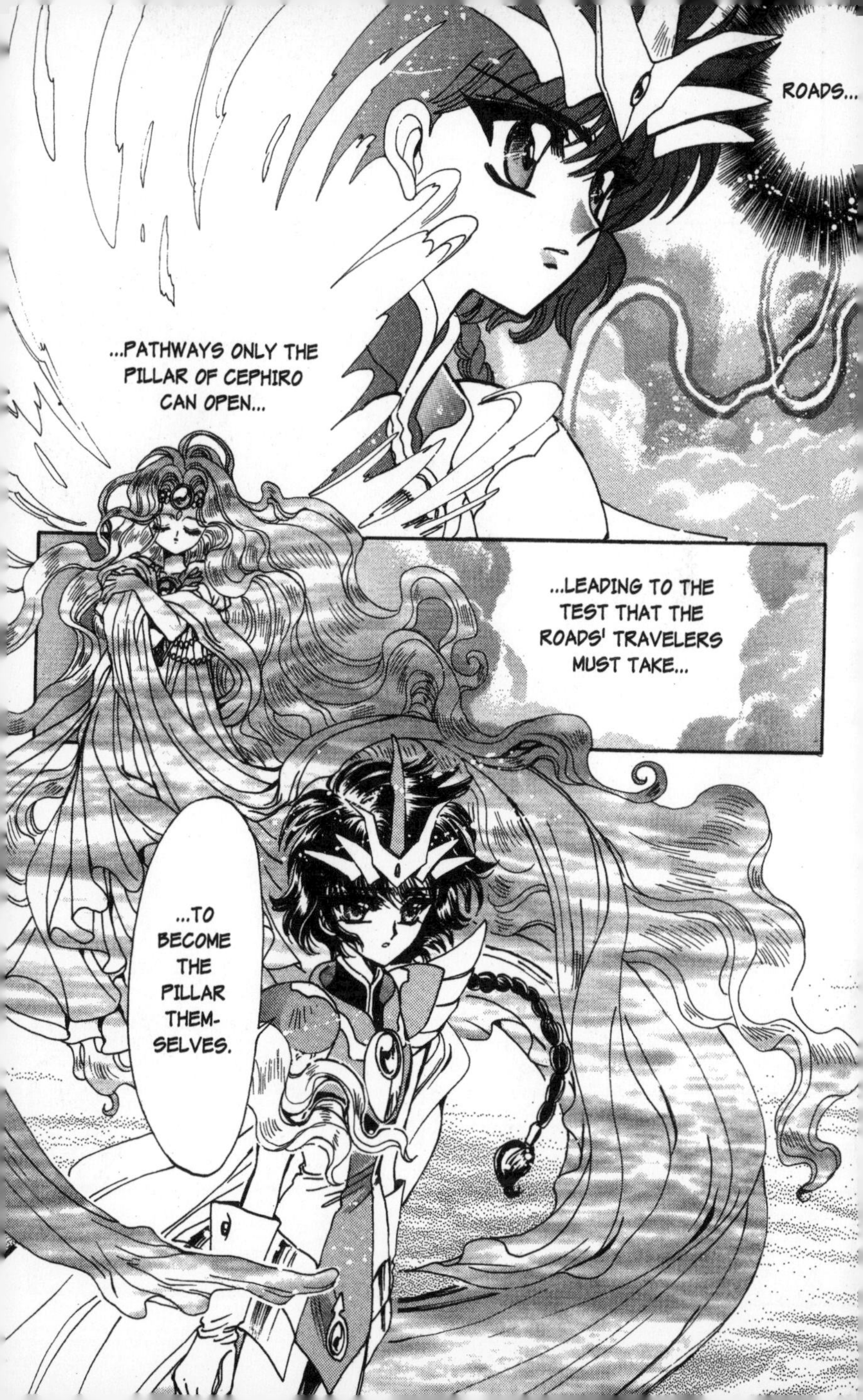
ROADS...
...PATHWAYS ONLY THE PILLAR OF CEPHIRO CAN OPEN...
...LEADING TO THE TEST THAT THE ROADS' TRAVELERS MUST TAKE...
...TO BECOME THE PILLAR THEM-SELVES.

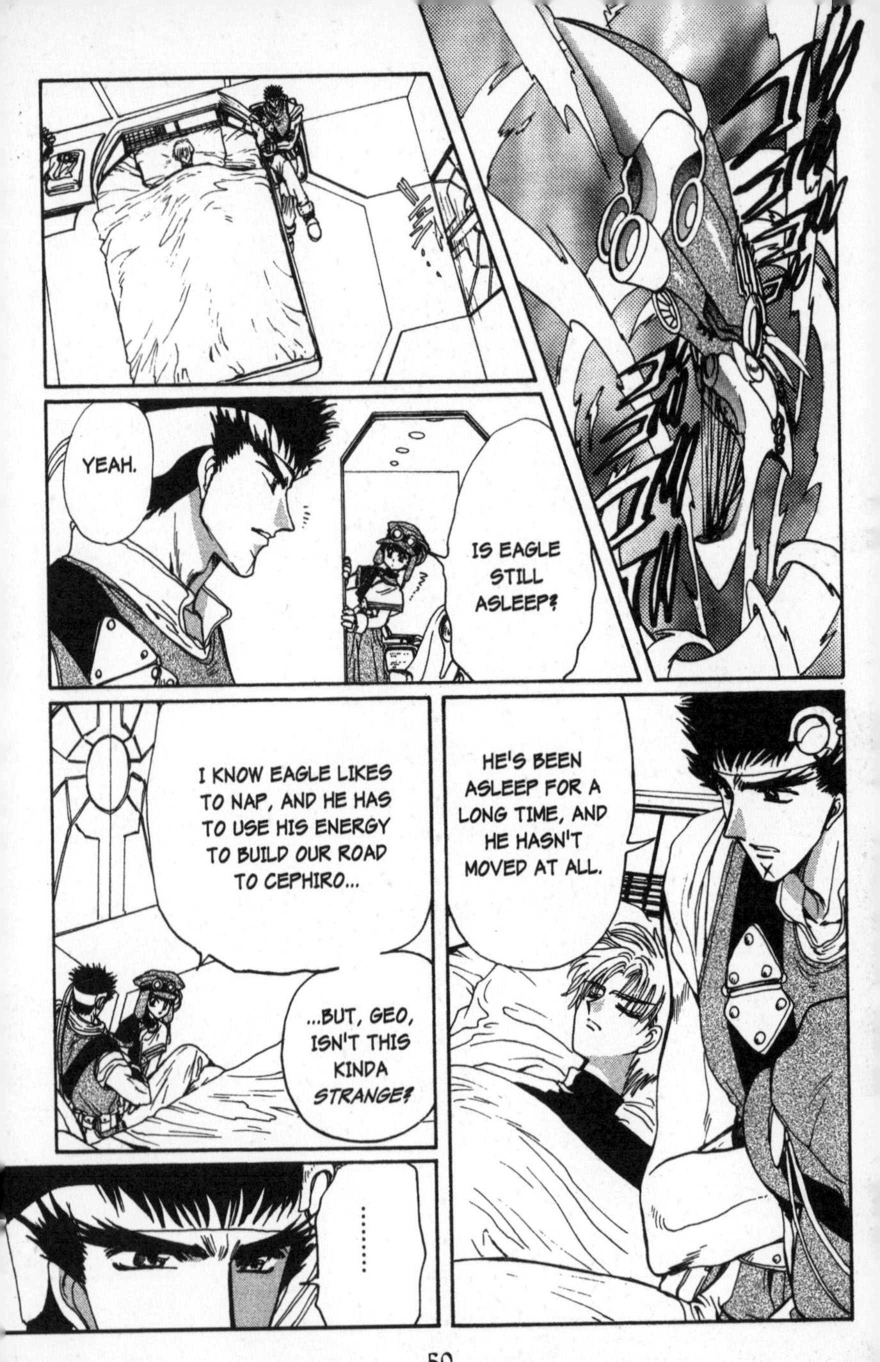
IS EAGLE STILL ASLEEP?
YEAH.
HE'S BEEN ASLEEP FOR A LONG TIME, AND HE HASN'T MOVED AT ALL.
I KNOW EAGLE LIKES TO NAP, AND HE HAS TO USE HIS ENERGY TO BUILD OUR ROAD TO CEPHIRO...
...BUT, GEO, ISN'T THIS KINDA *STRANGE?*
......

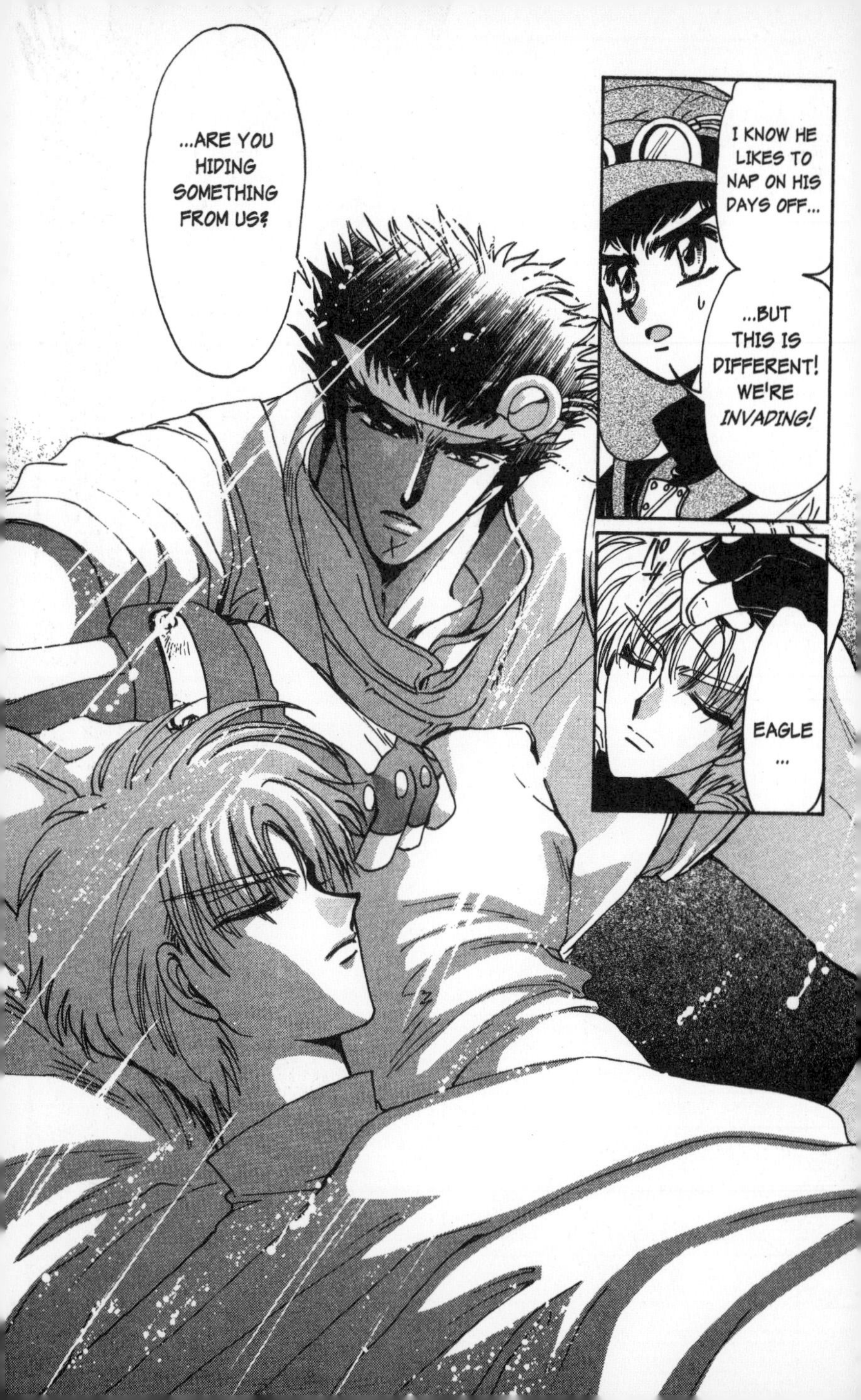
I KNOW HE LIKES TO NAP ON HIS DAYS OFF...
...BUT THIS IS DIFFERENT! WE'RE *INVADING!*
EAGLE ...
...ARE YOU HIDING SOMETHING FROM US?

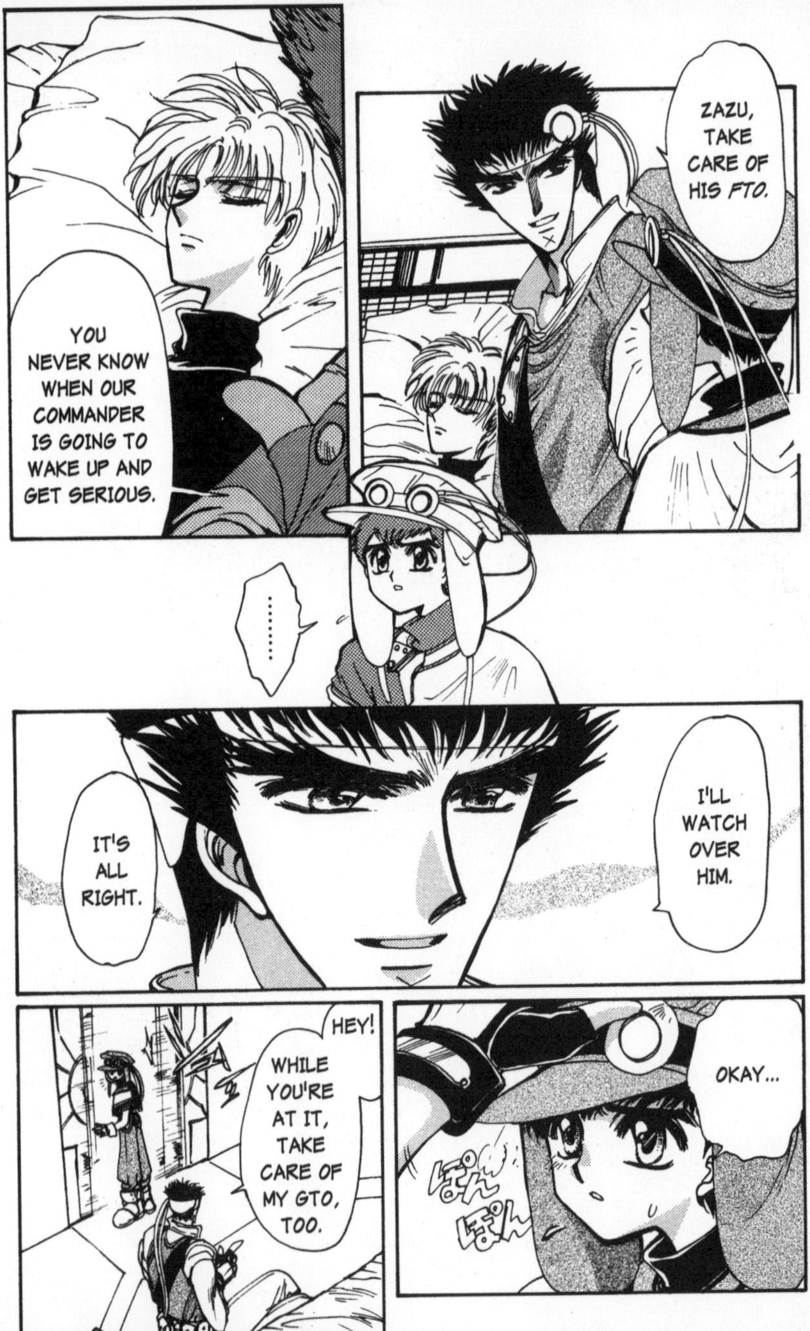
ZAZU, TAKE CARE OF HIS *FTO.*
YOU NEVER KNOW WHEN OUR COMMANDER IS GOING TO WAKE UP AND GET SERIOUS.
......
I'LL WATCH OVER HIM.
IT'S ALL RIGHT.
OKAY...
ぽん ぽん
HEY!
WHILE YOU'RE AT IT, TAKE CARE OF MY GTO, TOO.

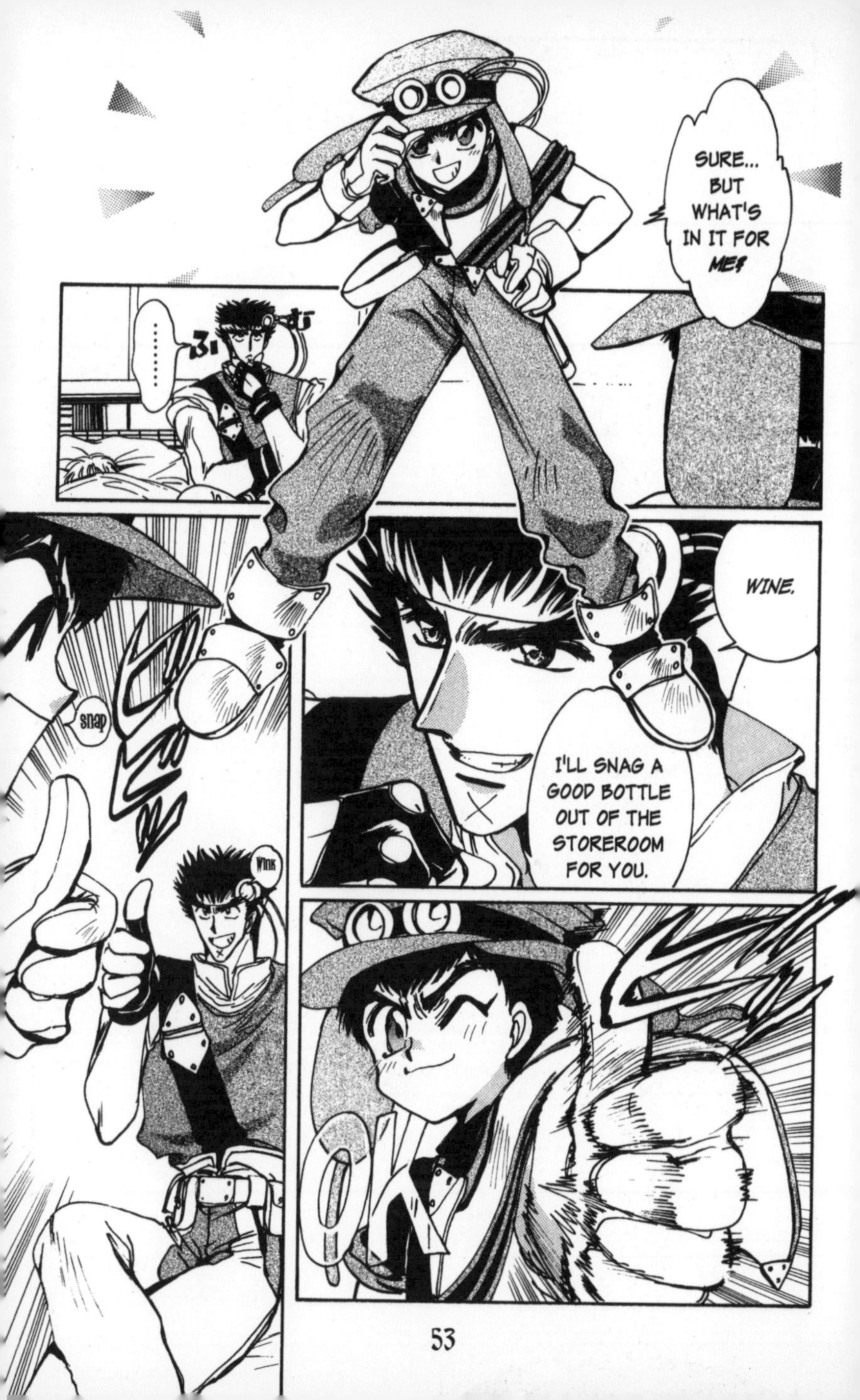
SURE... BUT WHAT'S IN IT FOR *ME?*
......
WINE.
I'LL SNAG A GOOD BOTTLE OUT OF THE STOREROOM FOR YOU.
snap
Wink

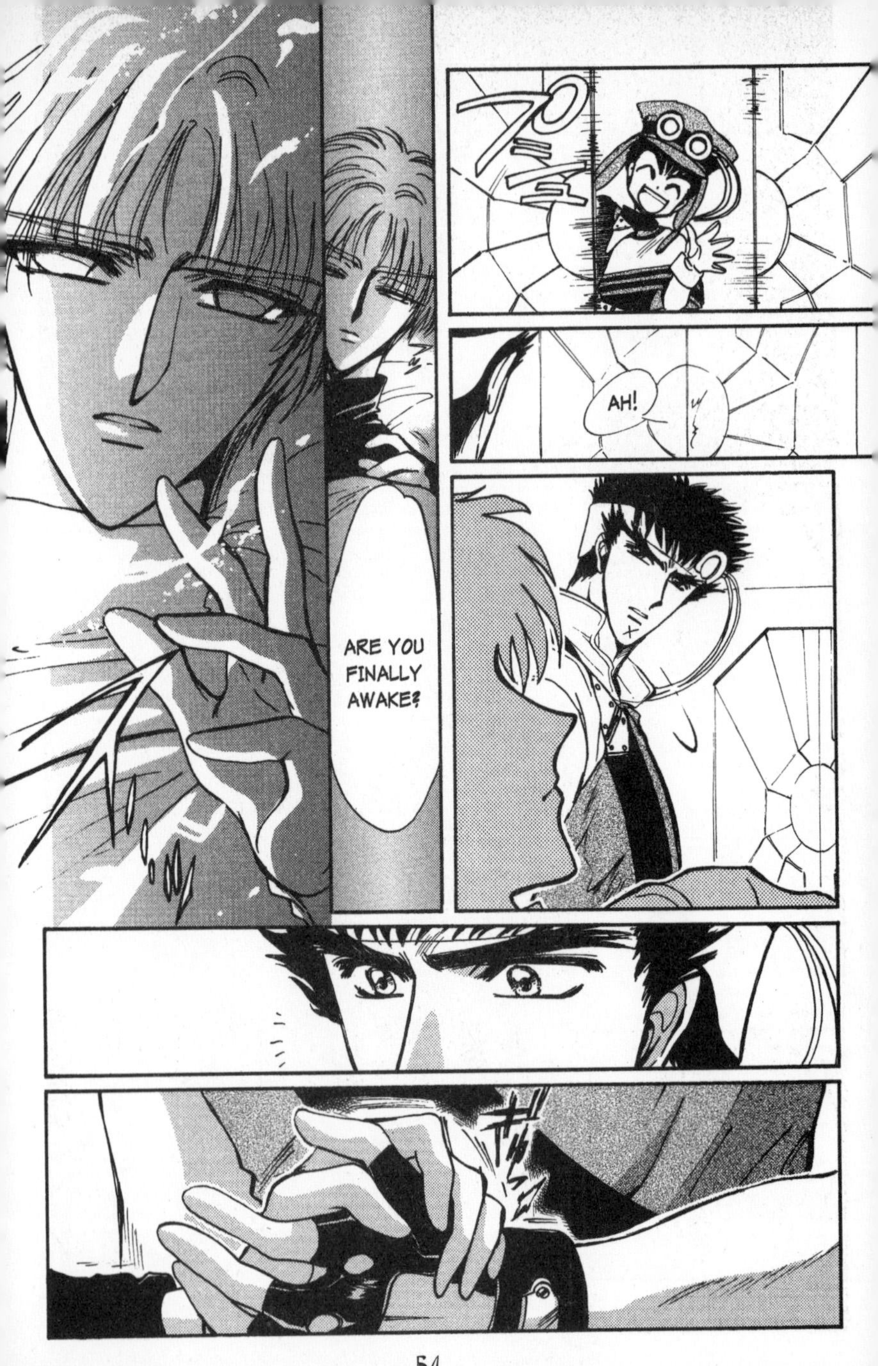
AH!
ARE YOU FINALLY AWAKE?

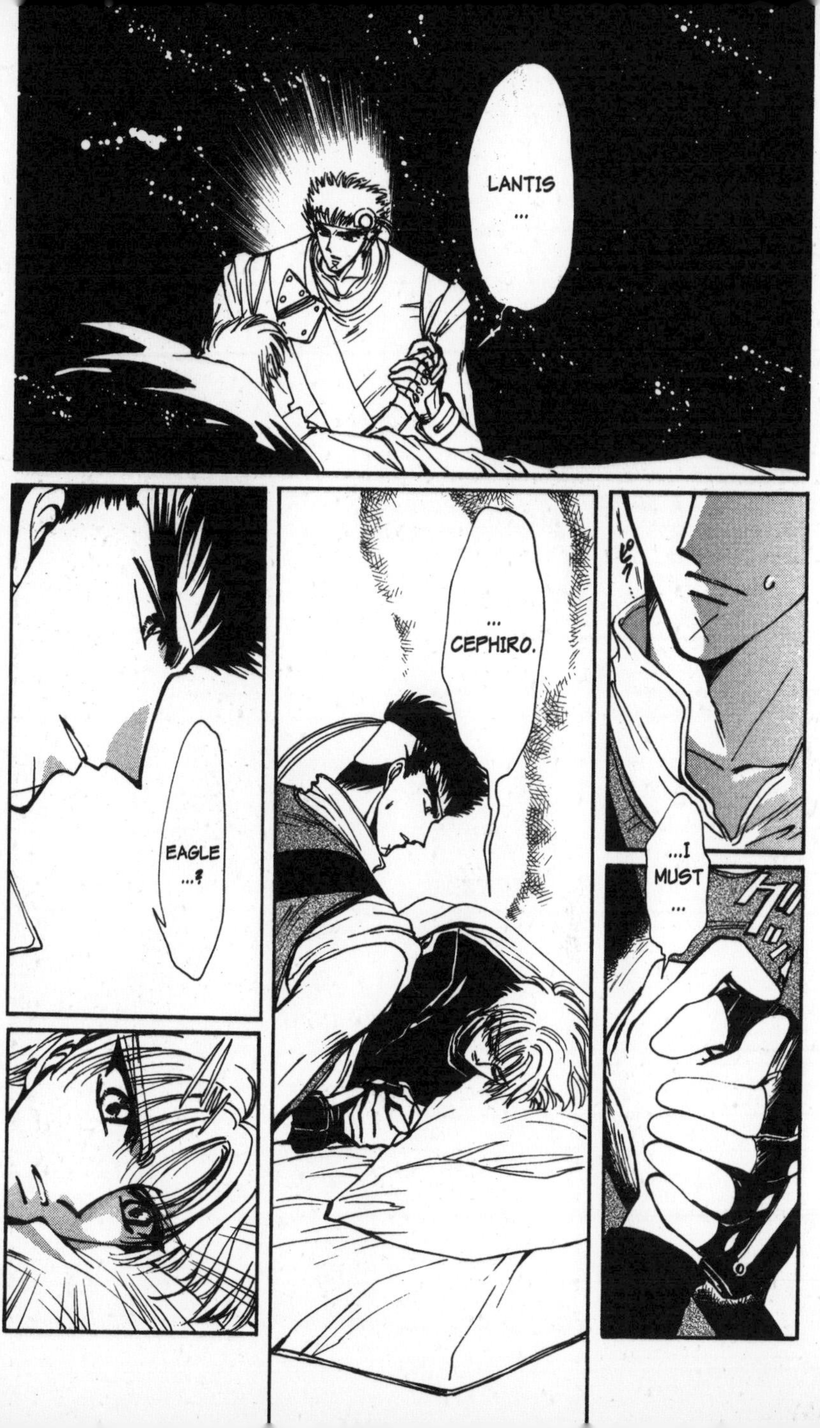
LANTIS ...
...I MUST ...
... CEPHIRO.
EAGLE ...?

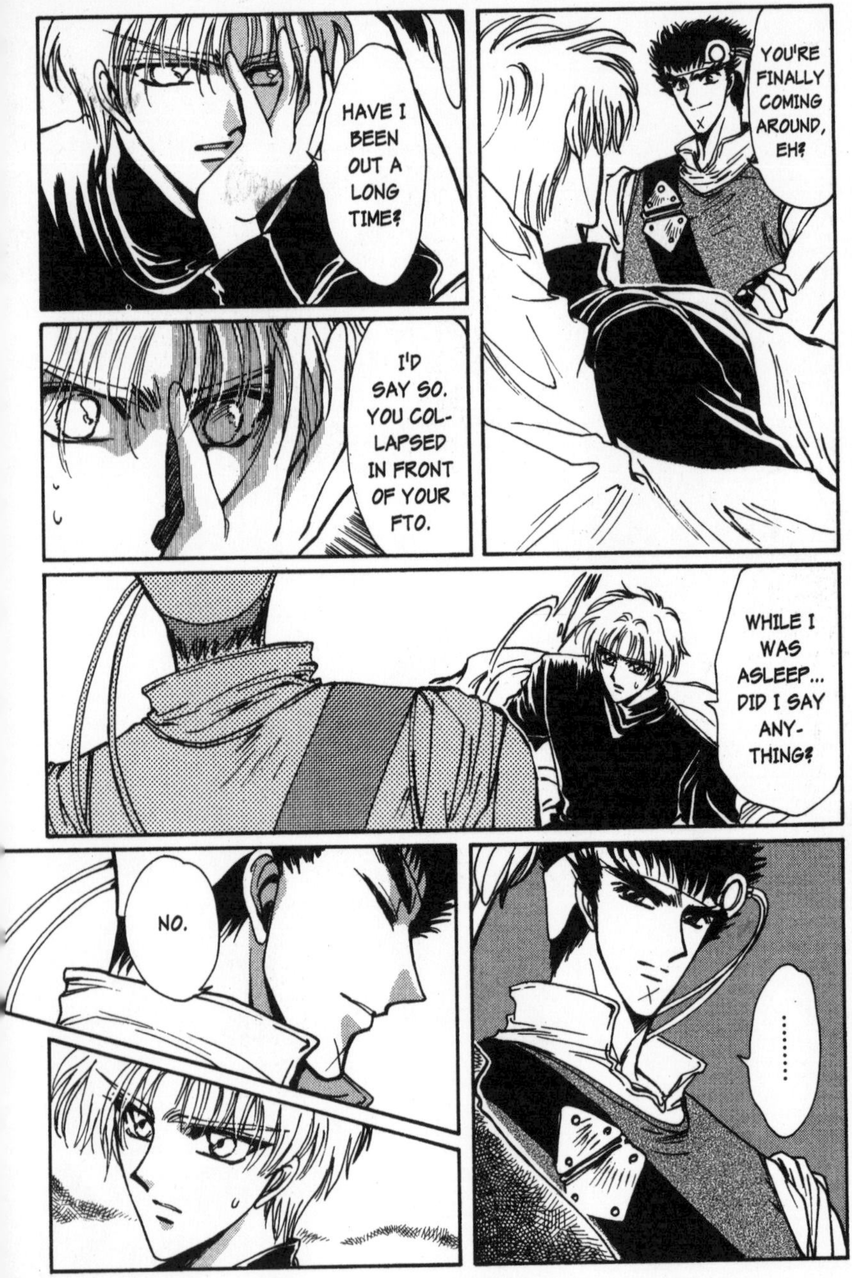
YOU'RE FINALLY COMING AROUND, EH?
HAVE I BEEN OUT A LONG TIME?
I'D SAY SO. YOU COL-LAPSED IN FRONT OF YOUR FTO.
WHILE I WAS ASLEEP... DID I SAY ANY-THING?
....
NO.

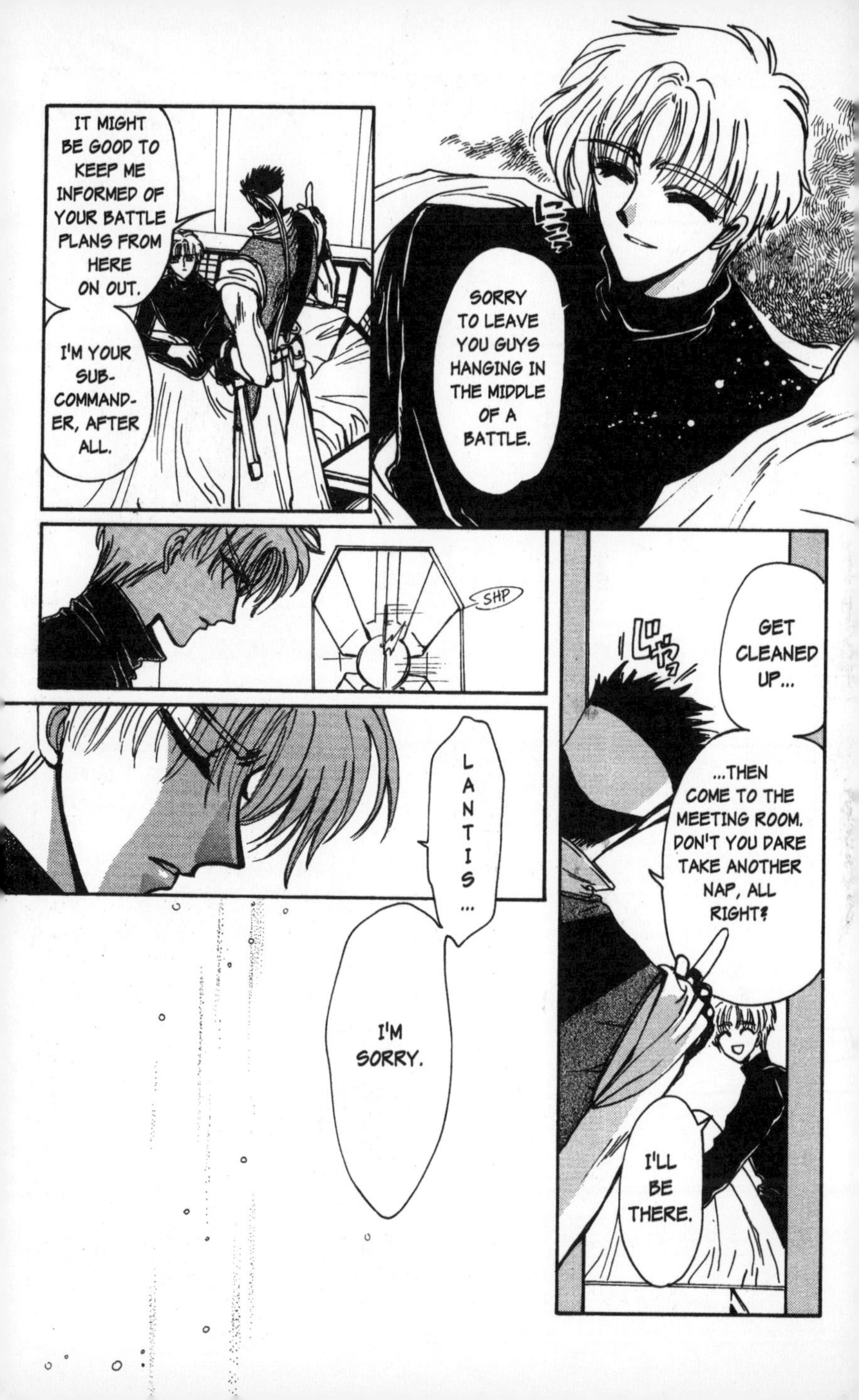
SORRY TO LEAVE YOU GUYS HANGING IN THE MIDDLE OF A BATTLE.
IT MIGHT BE GOOD TO KEEP ME INFORMED OF YOUR BATTLE PLANS FROM HERE ON OUT.
I'M YOUR SUB-COMMANDER, AFTER ALL.
GET CLEANED UP...
...THEN COME TO THE MEETING ROOM. DON'T YOU DARE TAKE ANOTHER NAP, ALL RIGHT?
I'LL BE THERE.
SHP
LANTIS...
I'M SORRY.

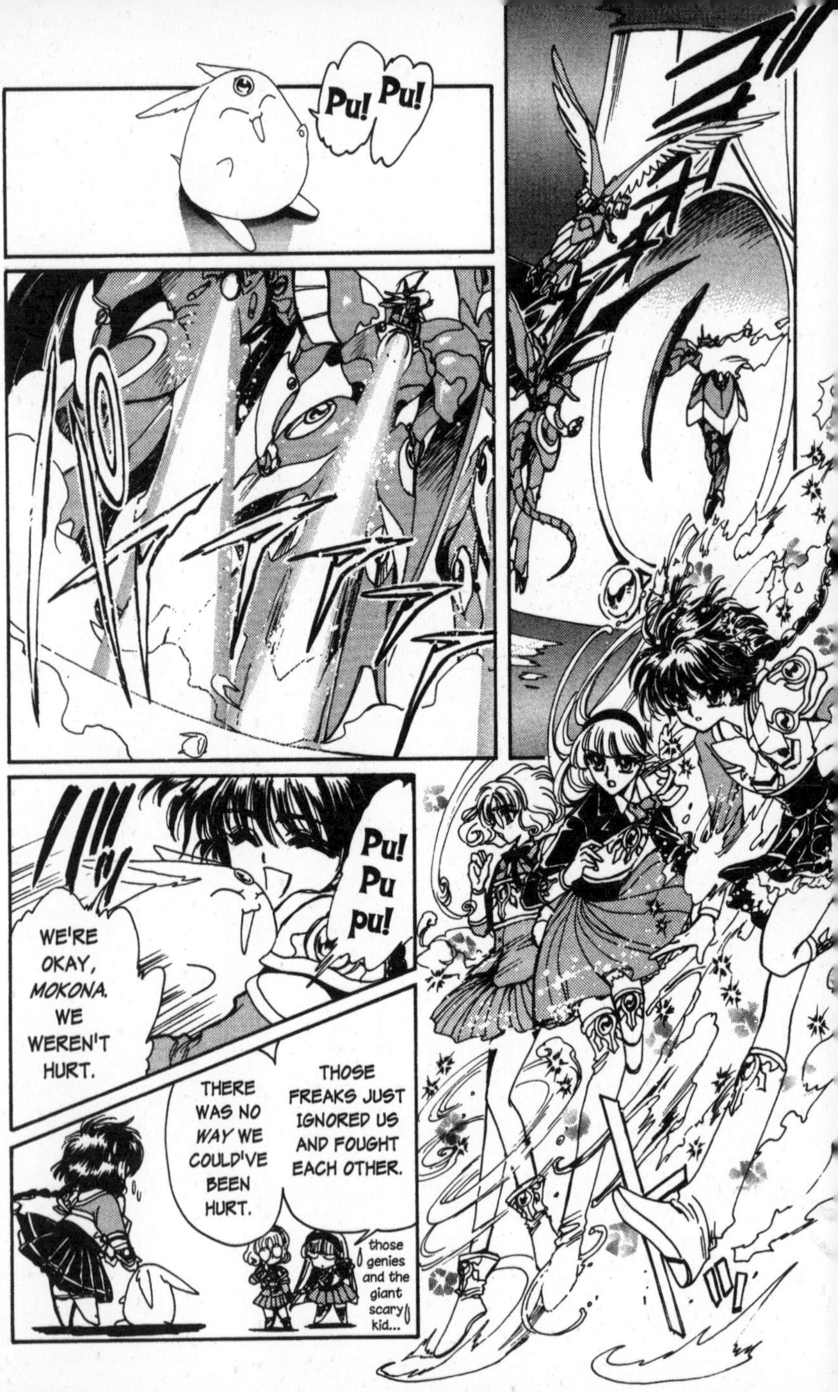
Pu! Pu!
Pu! Pu pu!
WE'RE OKAY, *MOKONA.* WE WEREN'T HURT.
THOSE FREAKS JUST IGNORED US AND FOUGHT EACH OTHER.
THERE WAS NO *WAY* WE COULD'VE BEEN HURT.
those genies and the giant scary kid...

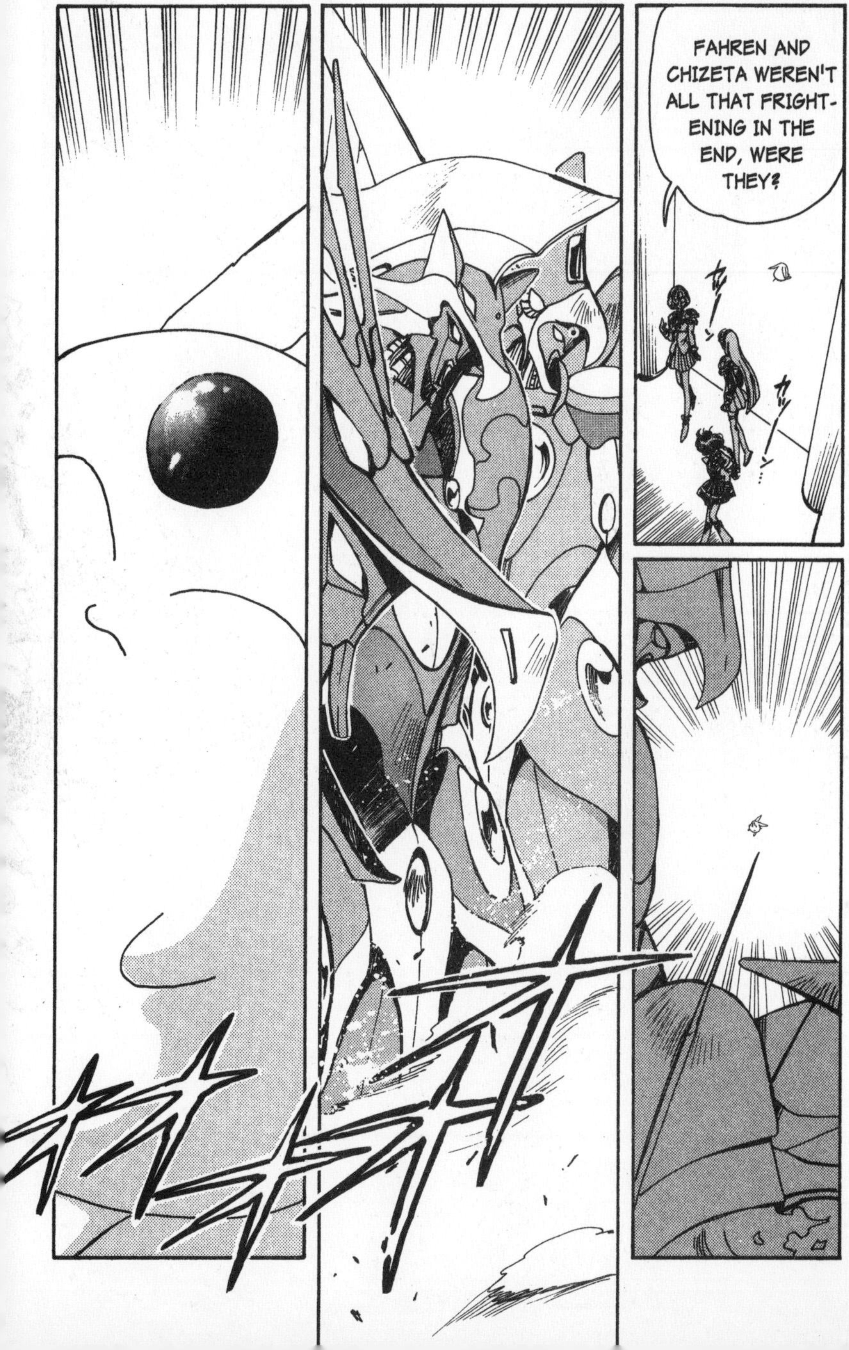
FAHREN AND CHIZETA WEREN'T ALL THAT FRIGHTENING IN THE END, WERE THEY?

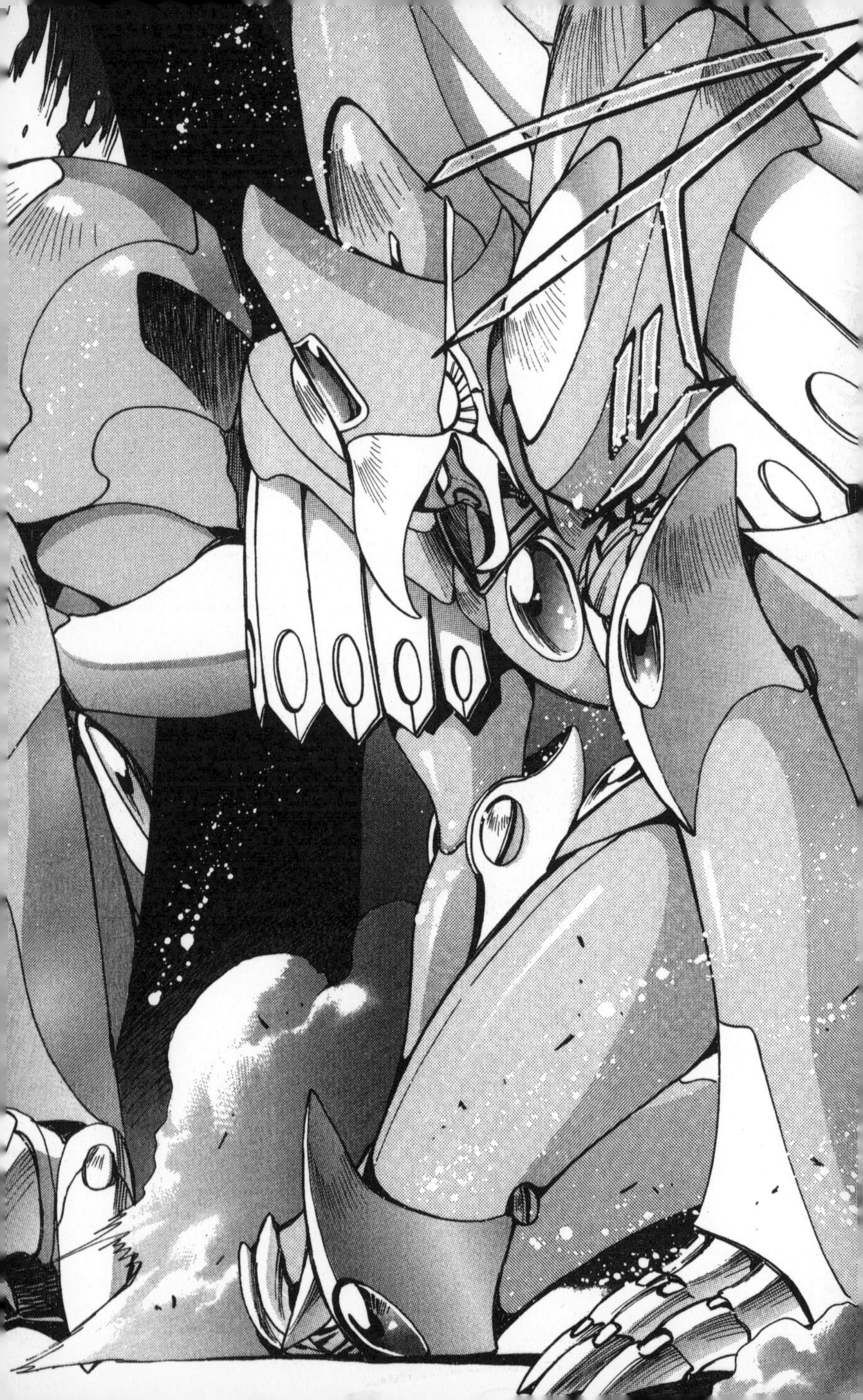

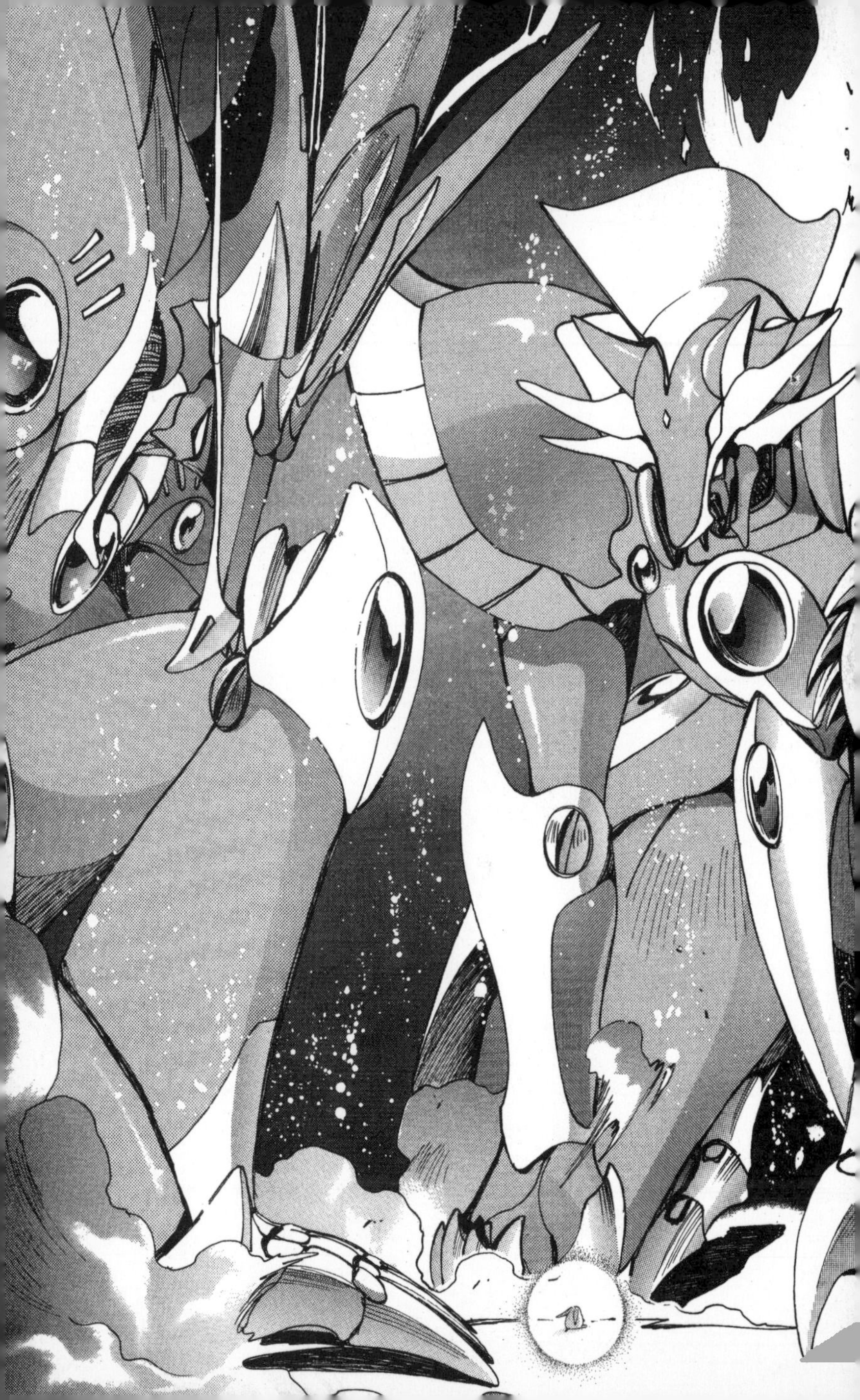

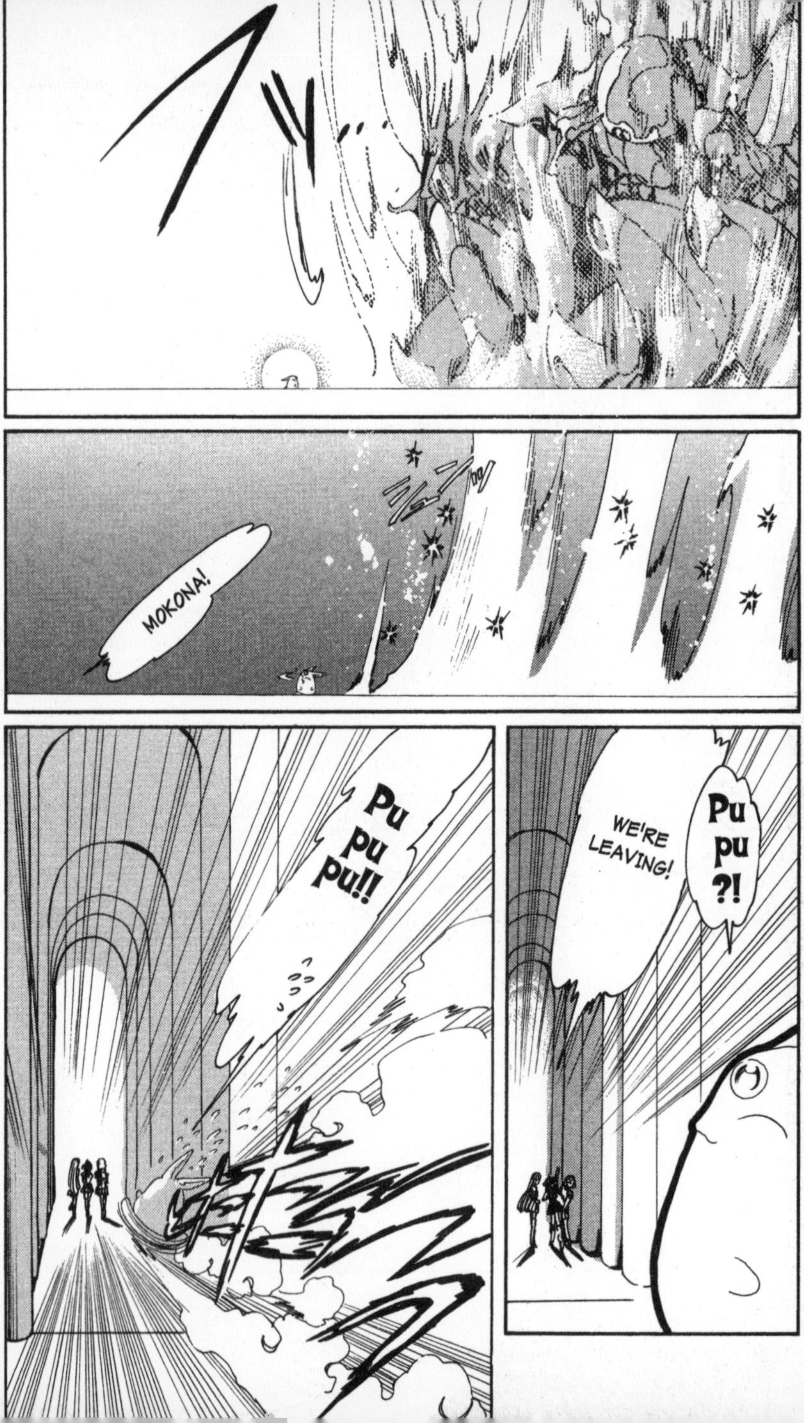
MOKONA!
Pu pu ?!
WE'RE LEAVING!
Pu pu pu!!

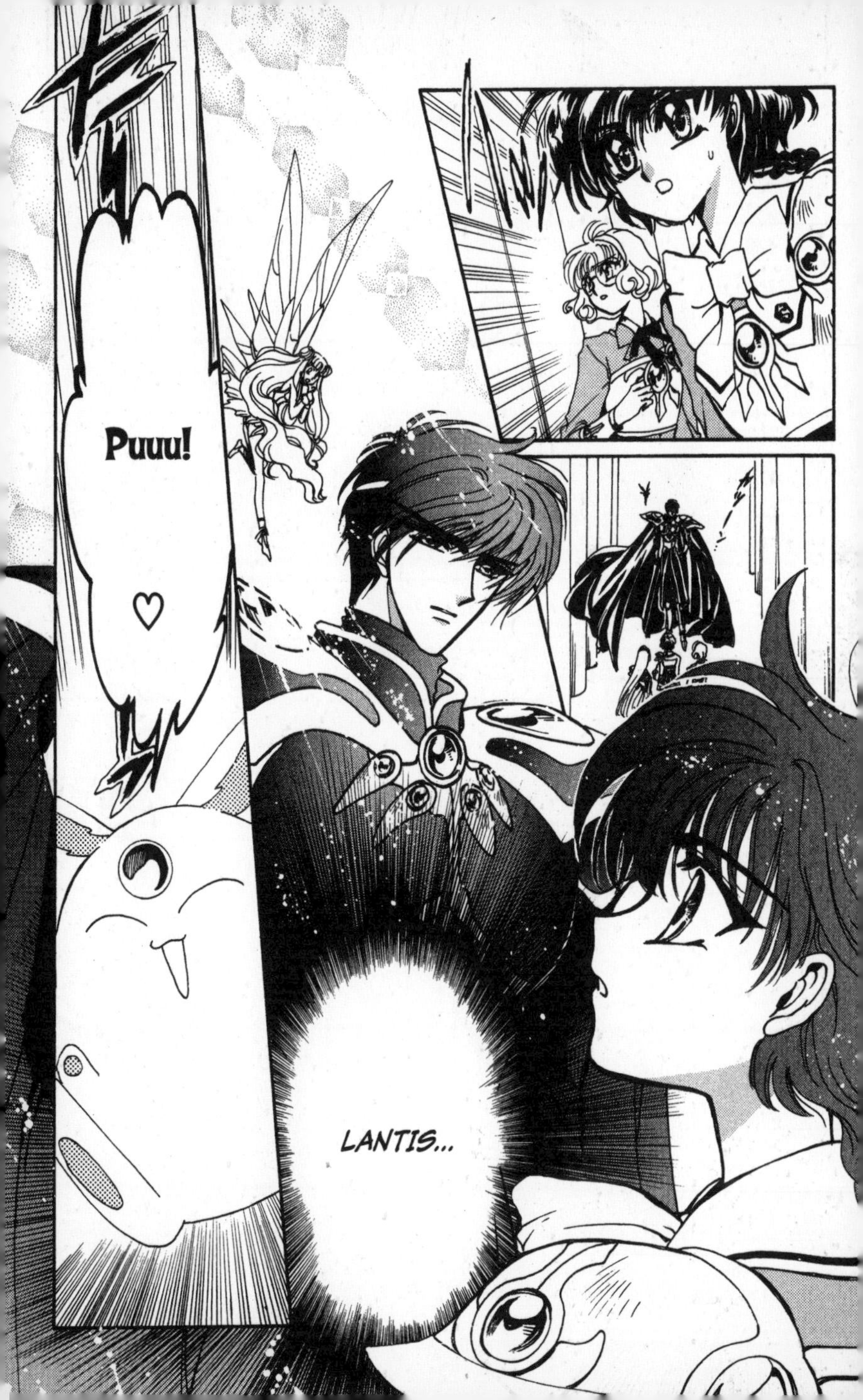
Puuu!
♡
LANTIS...

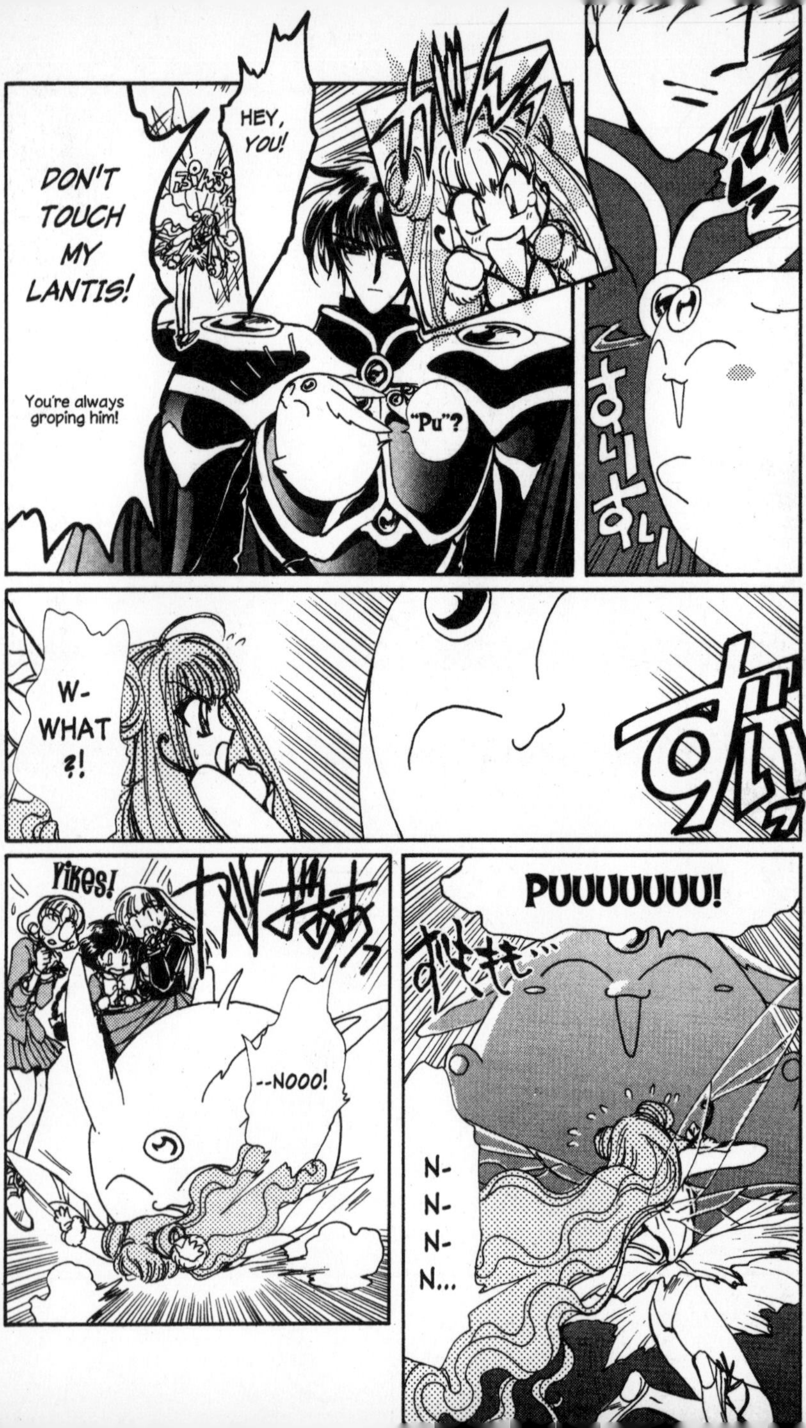
HEY, YOU!
DON'T TOUCH MY LANTIS!
"Pu"?
You're always groping him!
W-WHAT?!
PUUUUUUU!
N-N-N-N...
Yikes!
--NOOO!

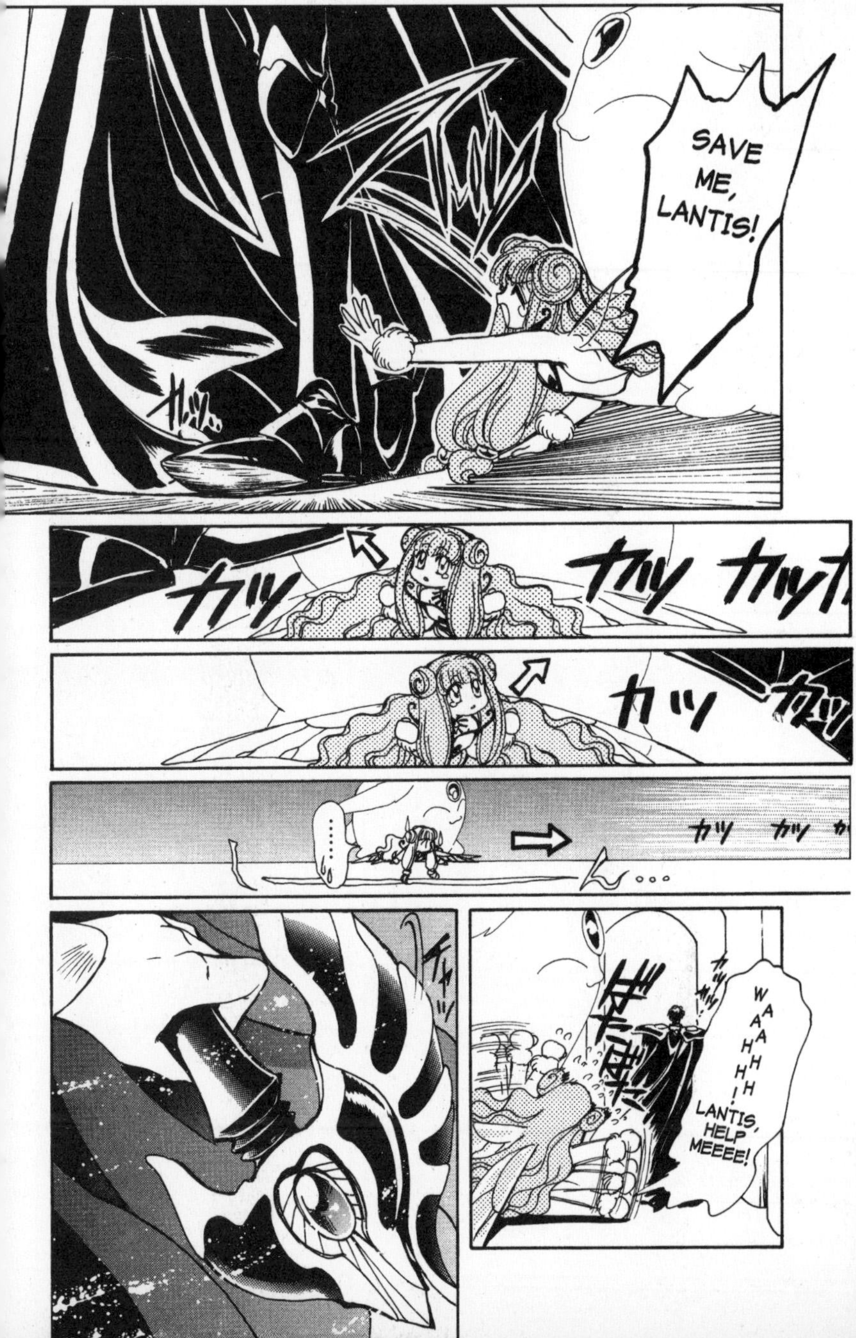
SAVE ME, LANTIS!
カツ カツ
カツ
カツ
カツ
......
カツ カツ
ん...
WAAAHHHH! LANTIS, HELP MEEEE!

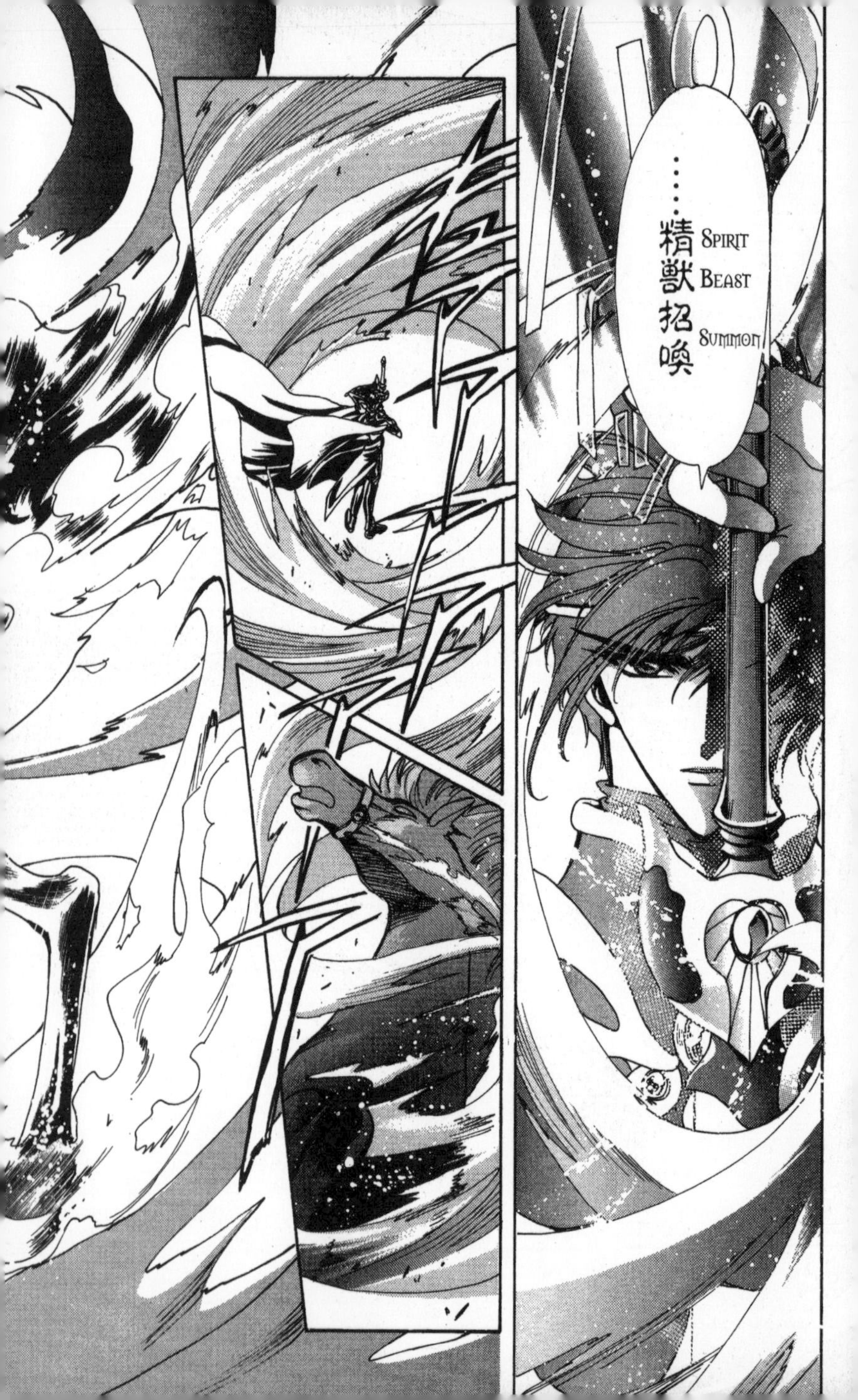
……精獣招喚 Spirit Beast Summon

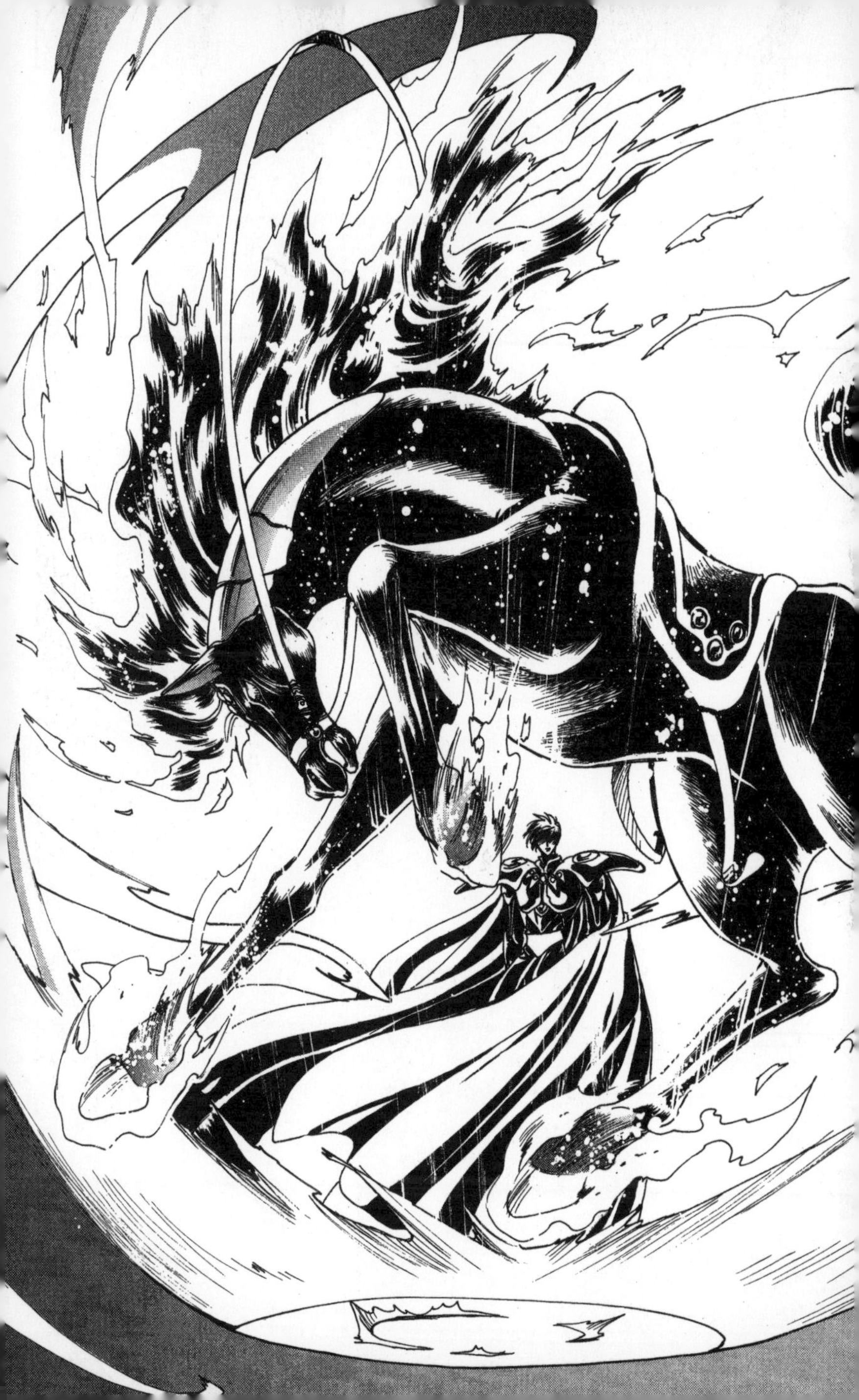

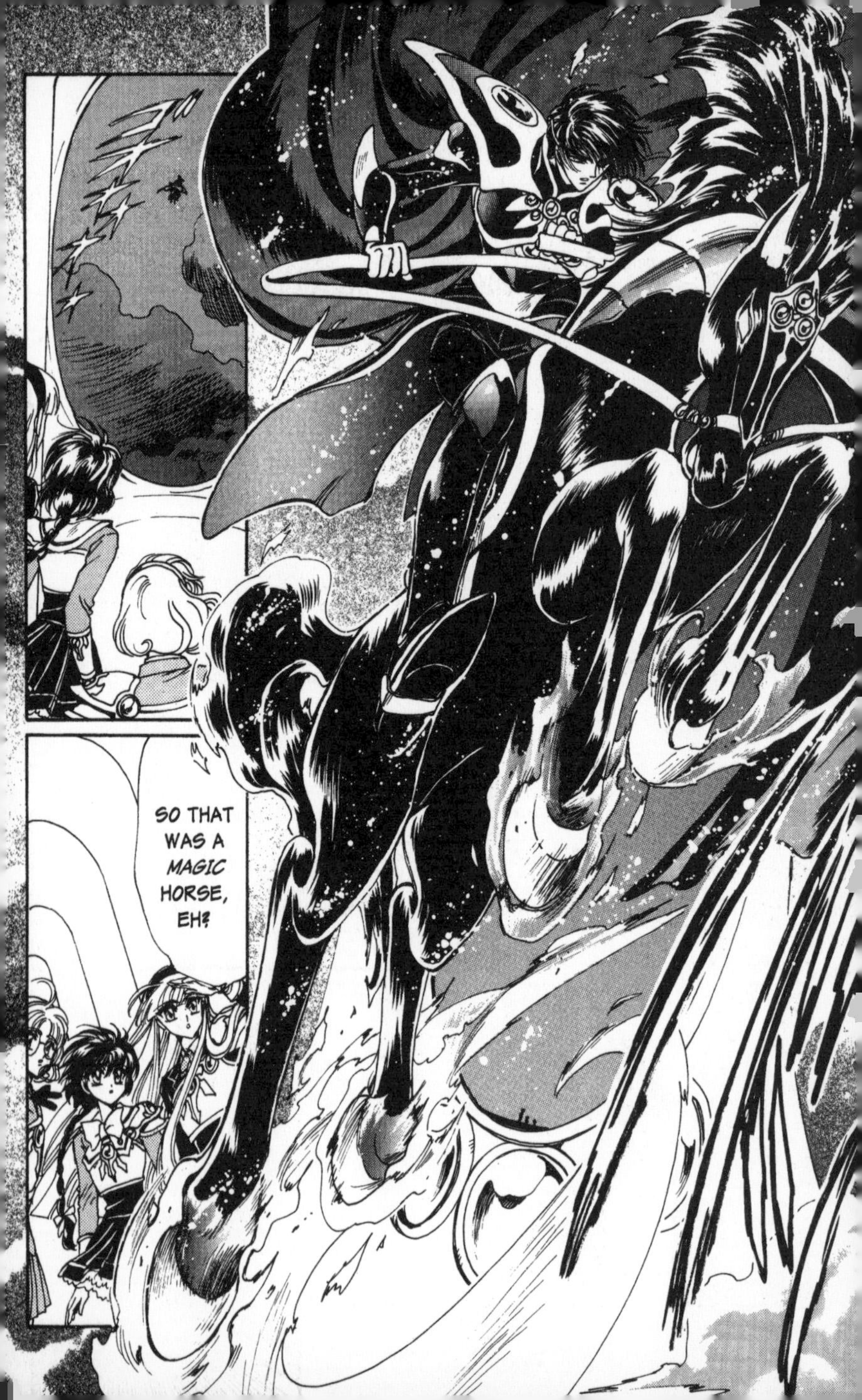
SO THAT WAS A *MAGIC* HORSE, EH?

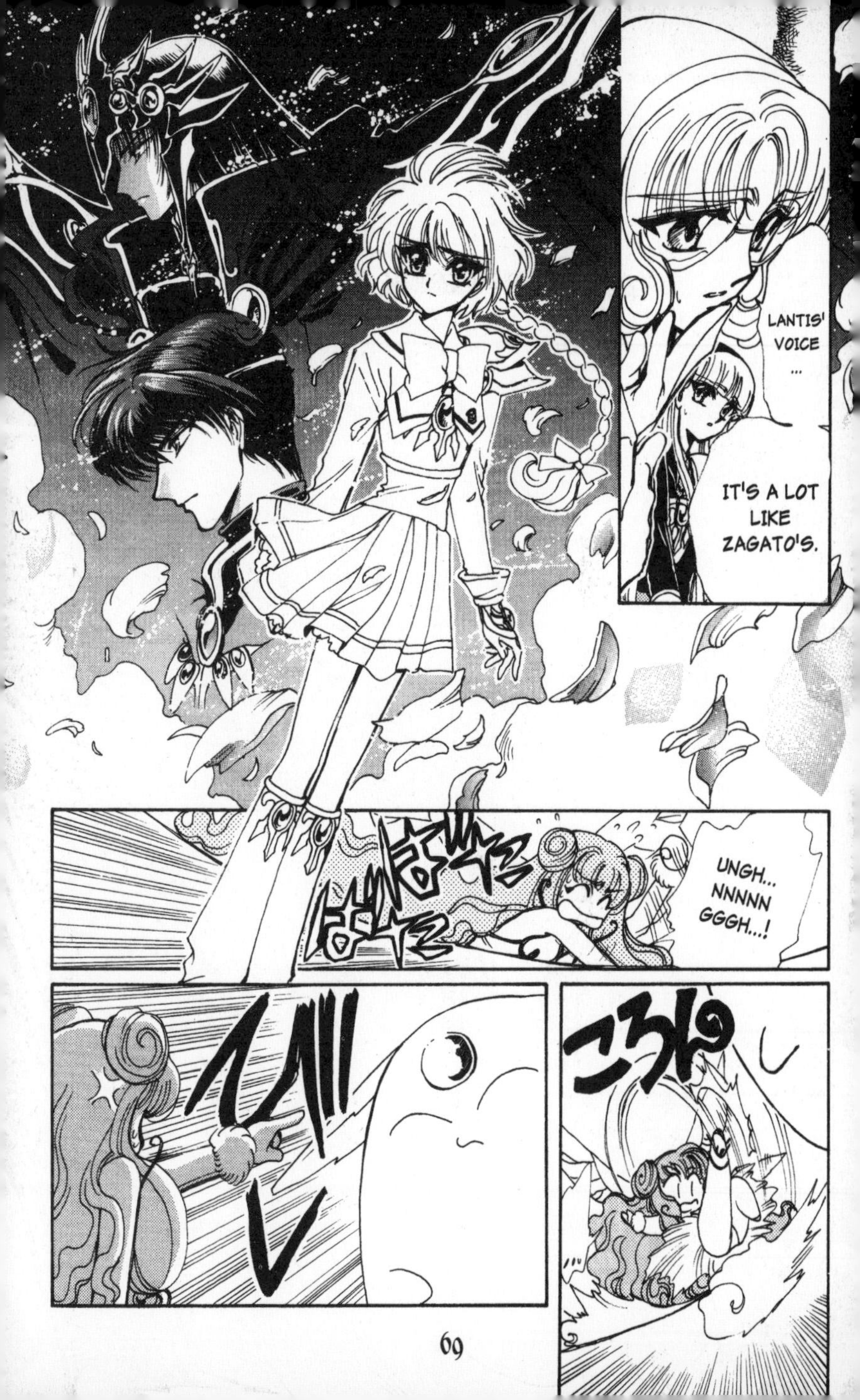
LANTIS' VOICE ...
IT'S A LOT LIKE ZAGATO'S.
UNGH... NNNNN GGGH...!

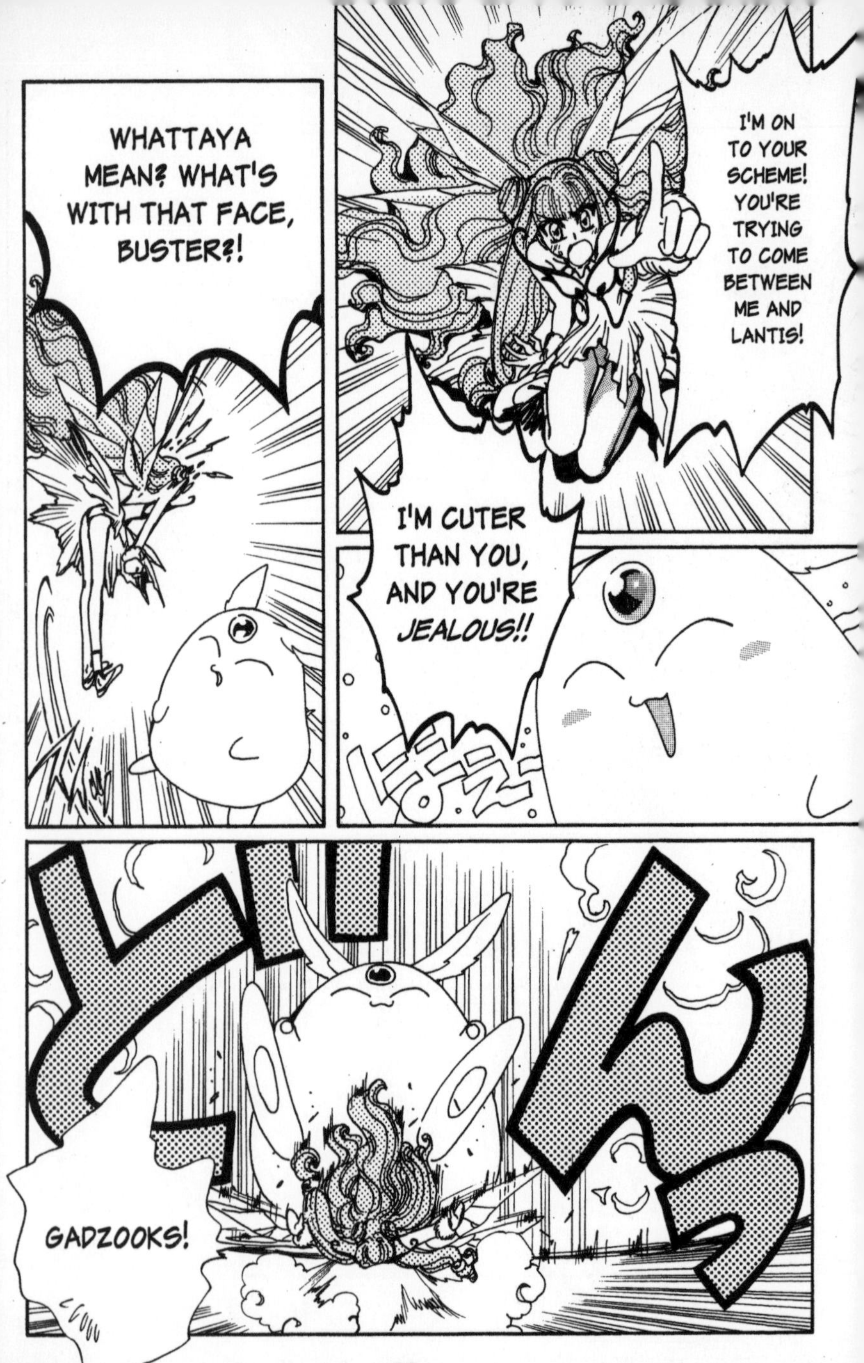
I'M ON TO YOUR SCHEME! YOU'RE TRYING TO COME BETWEEN ME AND LANTIS!
I'M CUTER THAN YOU, AND YOU'RE *JEALOUS*!!
WHATTAYA MEAN? WHAT'S WITH THAT FACE, BUSTER?!
GADZOOKS!

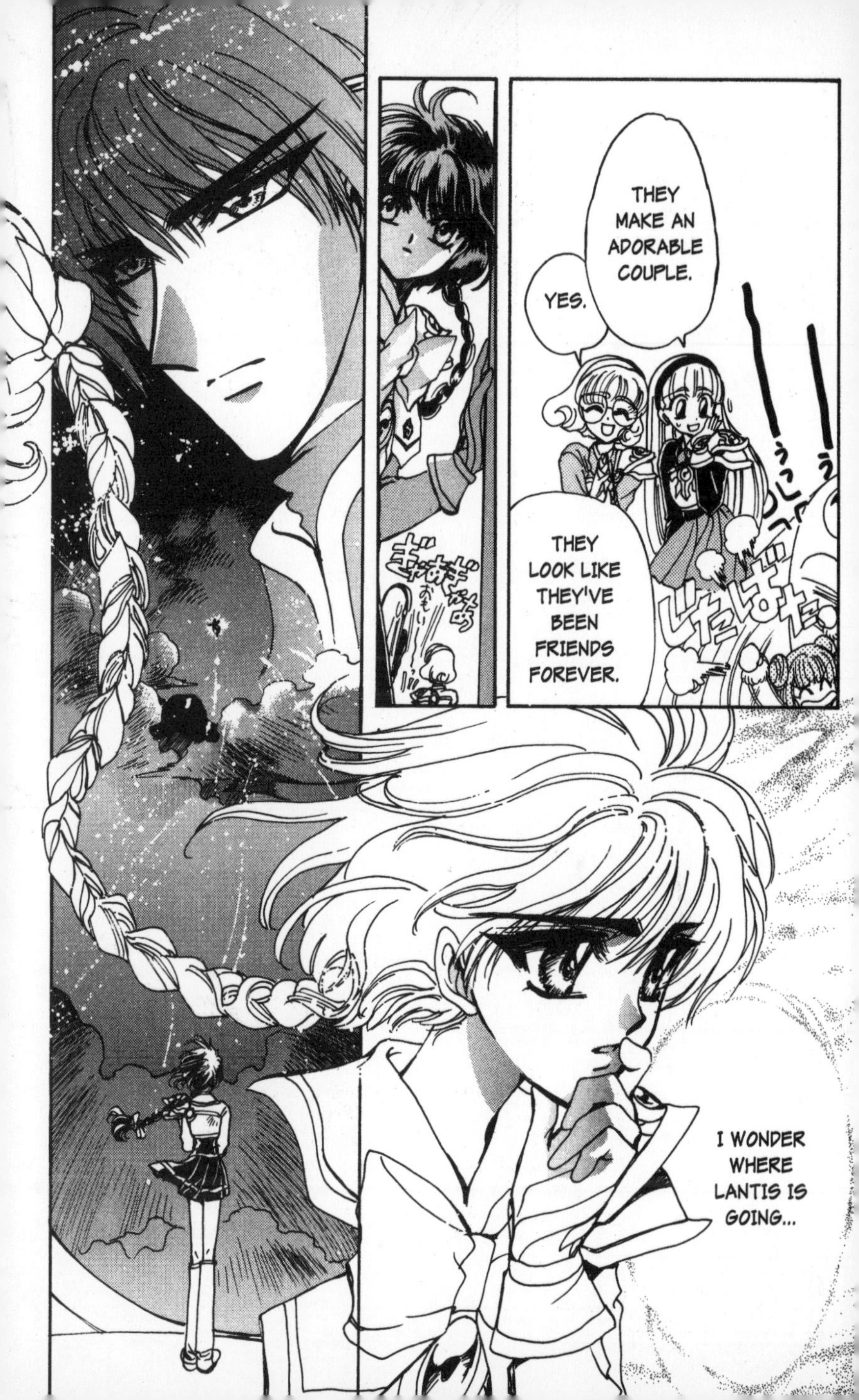
THEY MAKE AN ADORABLE COUPLE.
YES.
THEY LOOK LIKE THEY'VE BEEN FRIENDS FOREVER.
I WONDER WHERE LANTIS IS GOING...

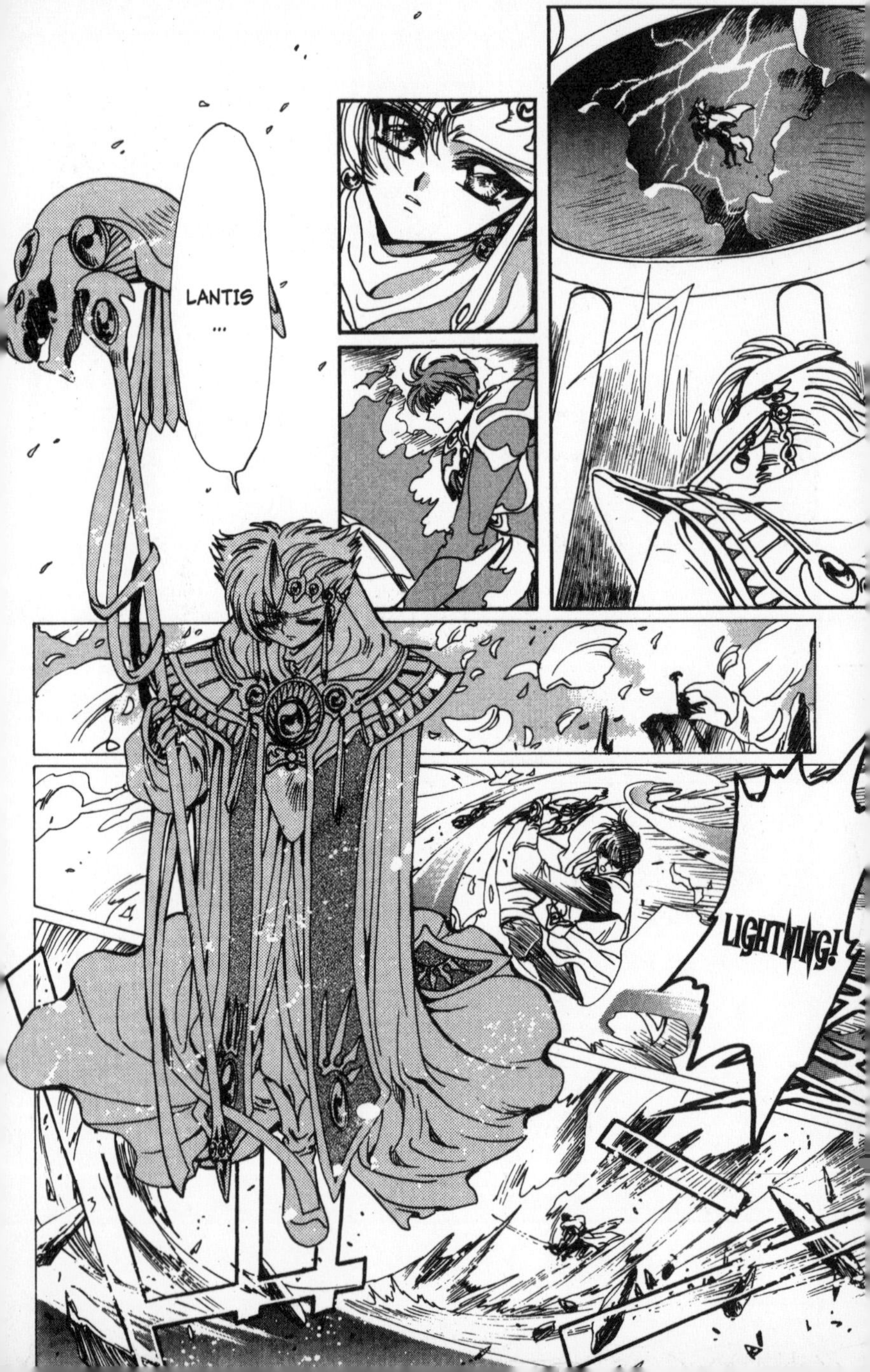
LANTIS ...
LIGHTNING!

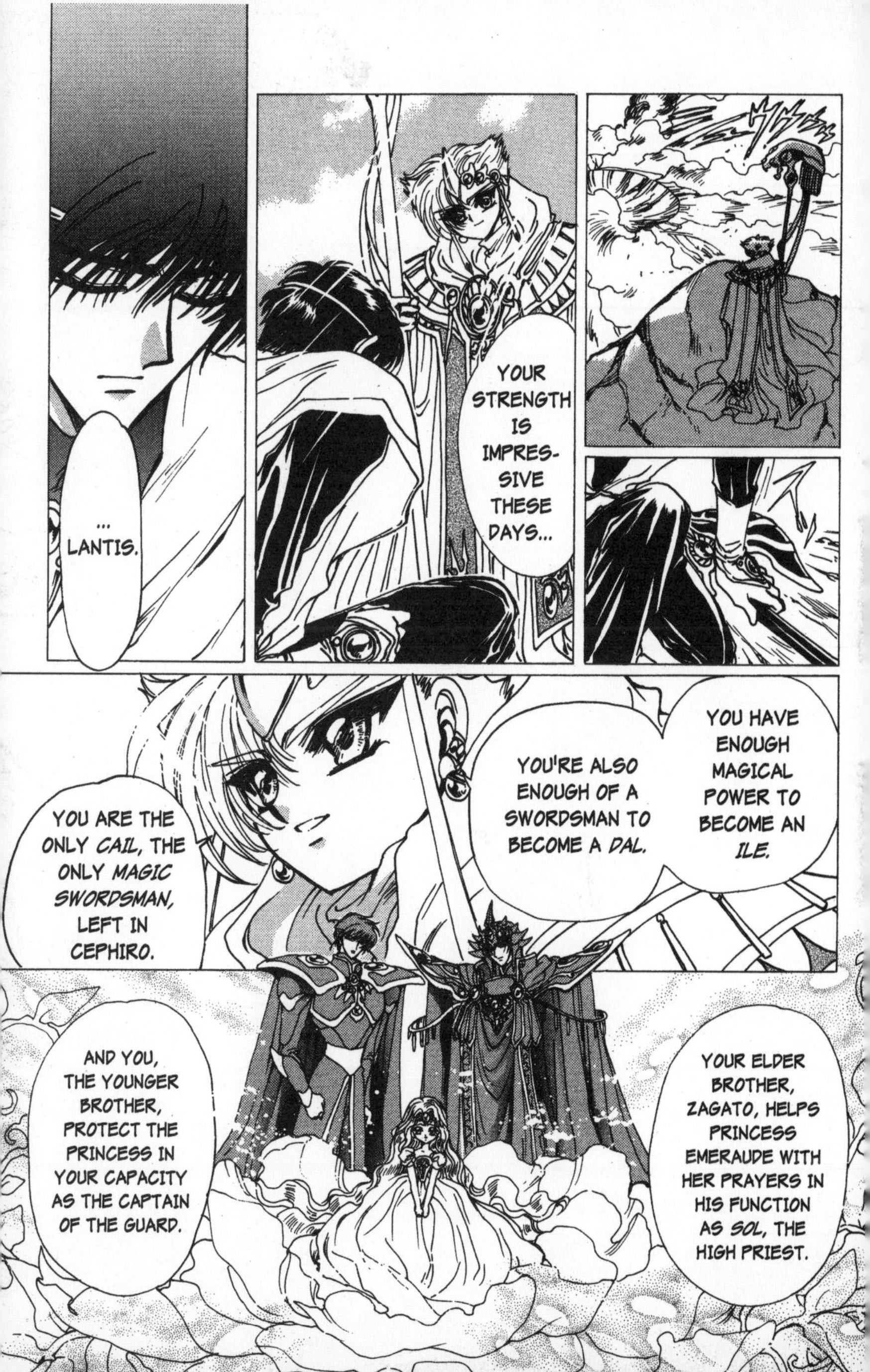
YOUR STRENGTH IS IMPRES- SIVE THESE DAYS...
... LANTIS.
YOU HAVE ENOUGH MAGICAL POWER TO BECOME AN *ILE*.
YOU'RE ALSO ENOUGH OF A SWORDSMAN TO BECOME A *DAL*.
YOU ARE THE ONLY *CAIL*, THE ONLY *MAGIC SWORDSMAN*, LEFT IN CEPHIRO.
YOUR ELDER BROTHER, ZAGATO, HELPS PRINCESS EMERAUDE WITH HER PRAYERS IN HIS FUNCTION AS *SOL*, THE HIGH PRIEST.
AND YOU, THE YOUNGER BROTHER, PROTECT THE PRINCESS IN YOUR CAPACITY AS THE CAPTAIN OF THE GUARD.

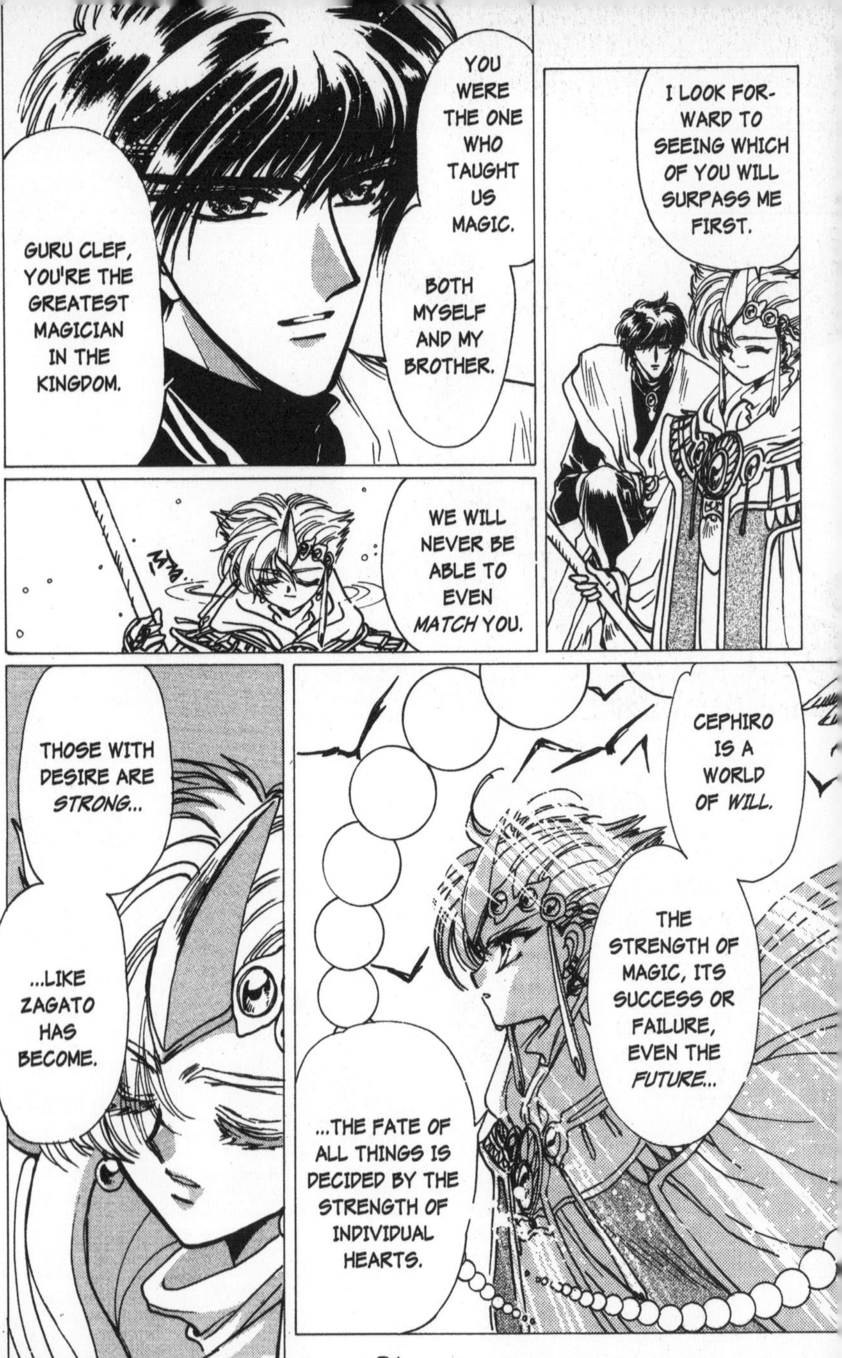
I LOOK FOR-WARD TO SEEING WHICH OF YOU WILL SURPASS ME FIRST.
YOU WERE THE ONE WHO TAUGHT US MAGIC.
BOTH MYSELF AND MY BROTHER.
GURU CLEF, YOU'RE THE GREATEST MAGICIAN IN THE KINGDOM.
WE WILL NEVER BE ABLE TO EVEN *MATCH* YOU.
CEPHIRO IS A WORLD OF *WILL*.
THE STRENGTH OF MAGIC, ITS SUCCESS OR FAILURE, EVEN THE *FUTURE*...
...THE FATE OF ALL THINGS IS DECIDED BY THE STRENGTH OF INDIVIDUAL HEARTS.
THOSE WITH DESIRE ARE *STRONG*...
...LIKE ZAGATO HAS BECOME.

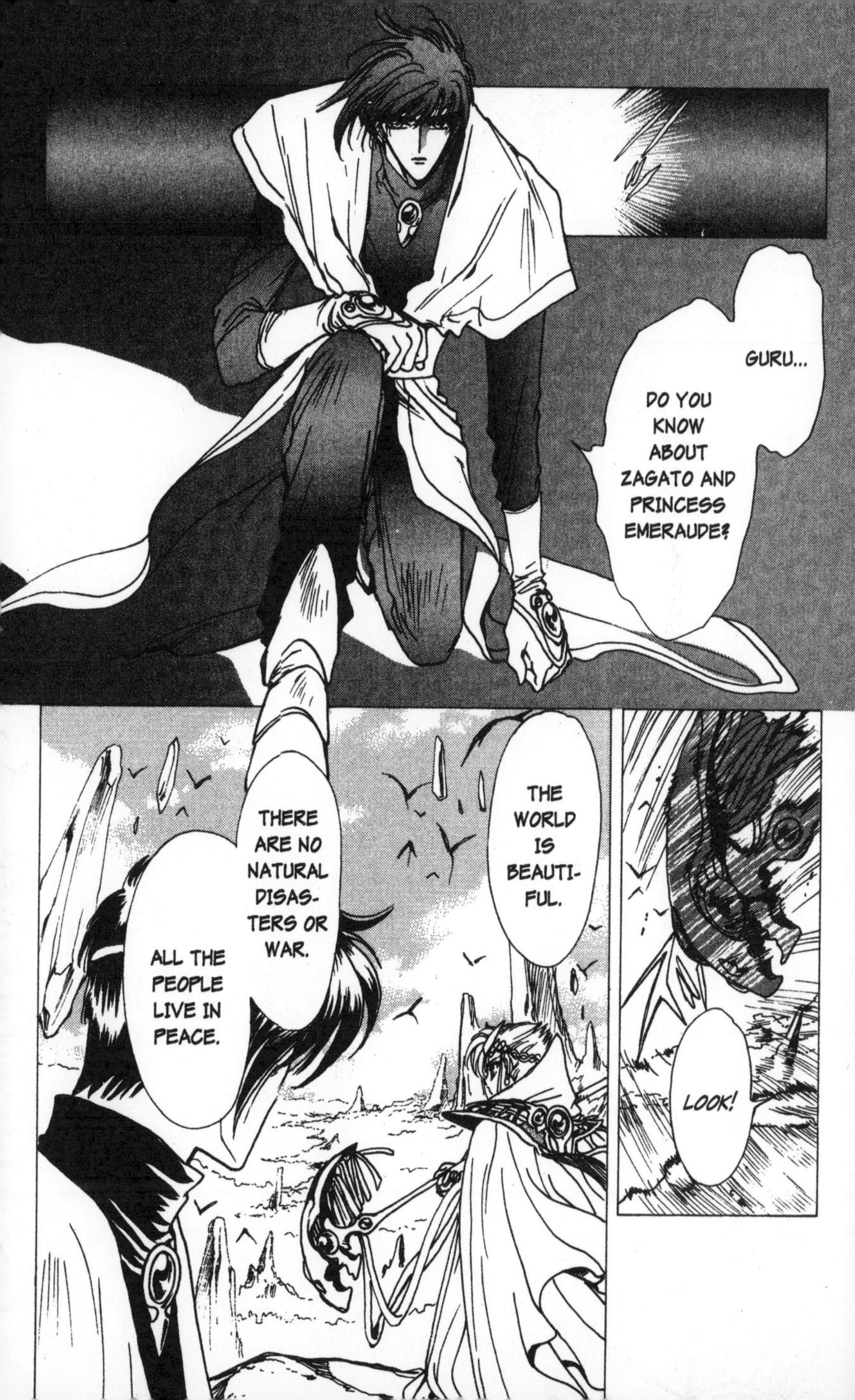
GURU...
DO YOU KNOW ABOUT ZAGATO AND PRINCESS EMERAUDE?
LOOK!
THE WORLD IS BEAUTI-FUL.
THERE ARE NO NATURAL DISAS-TERS OR WAR.
ALL THE PEOPLE LIVE IN PEACE.

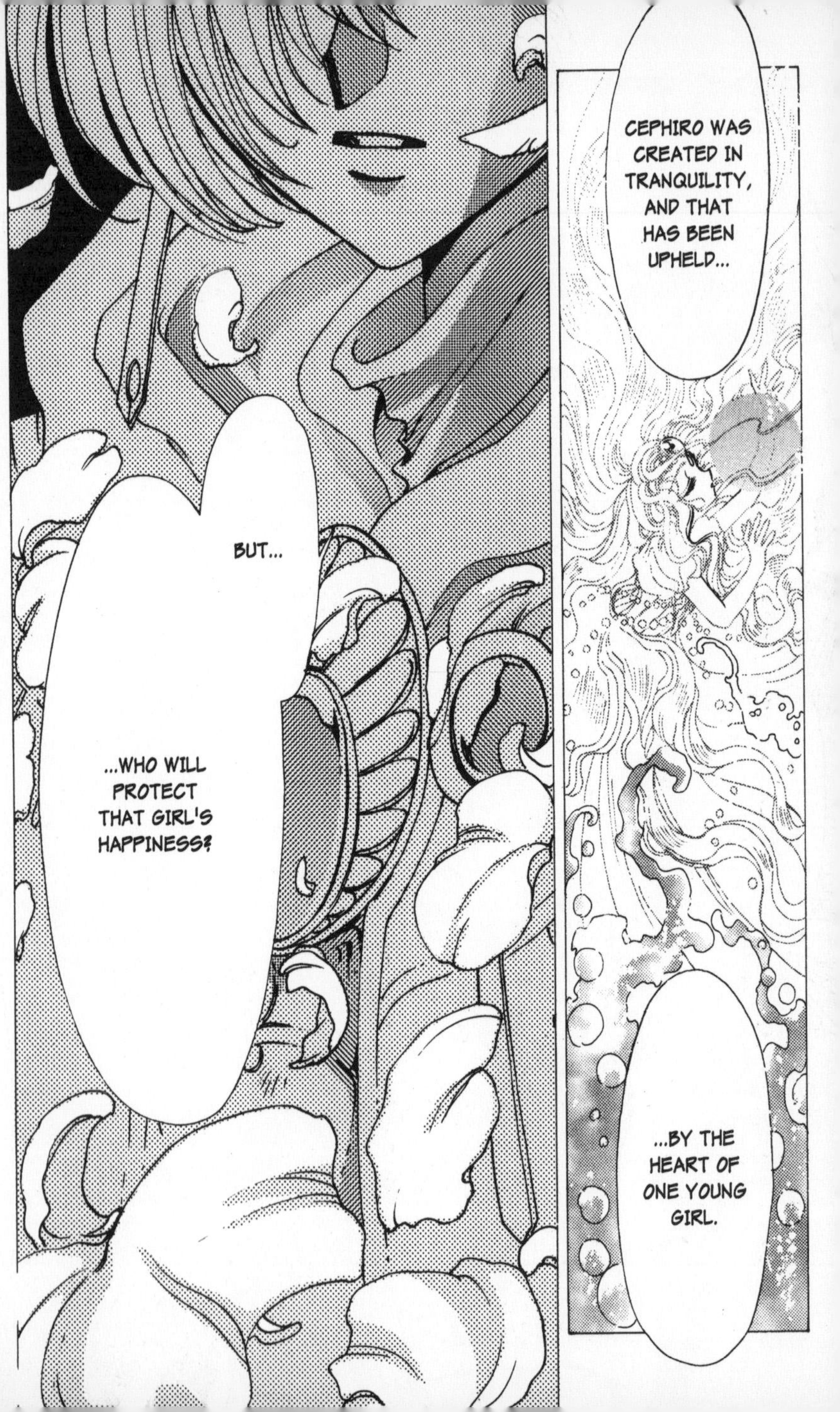
CEPHIRO WAS CREATED IN TRANQUILITY, AND THAT HAS BEEN UPHELD...
...BY THE HEART OF ONE YOUNG GIRL.
BUT...
...WHO WILL PROTECT THAT GIRL'S HAPPINESS?

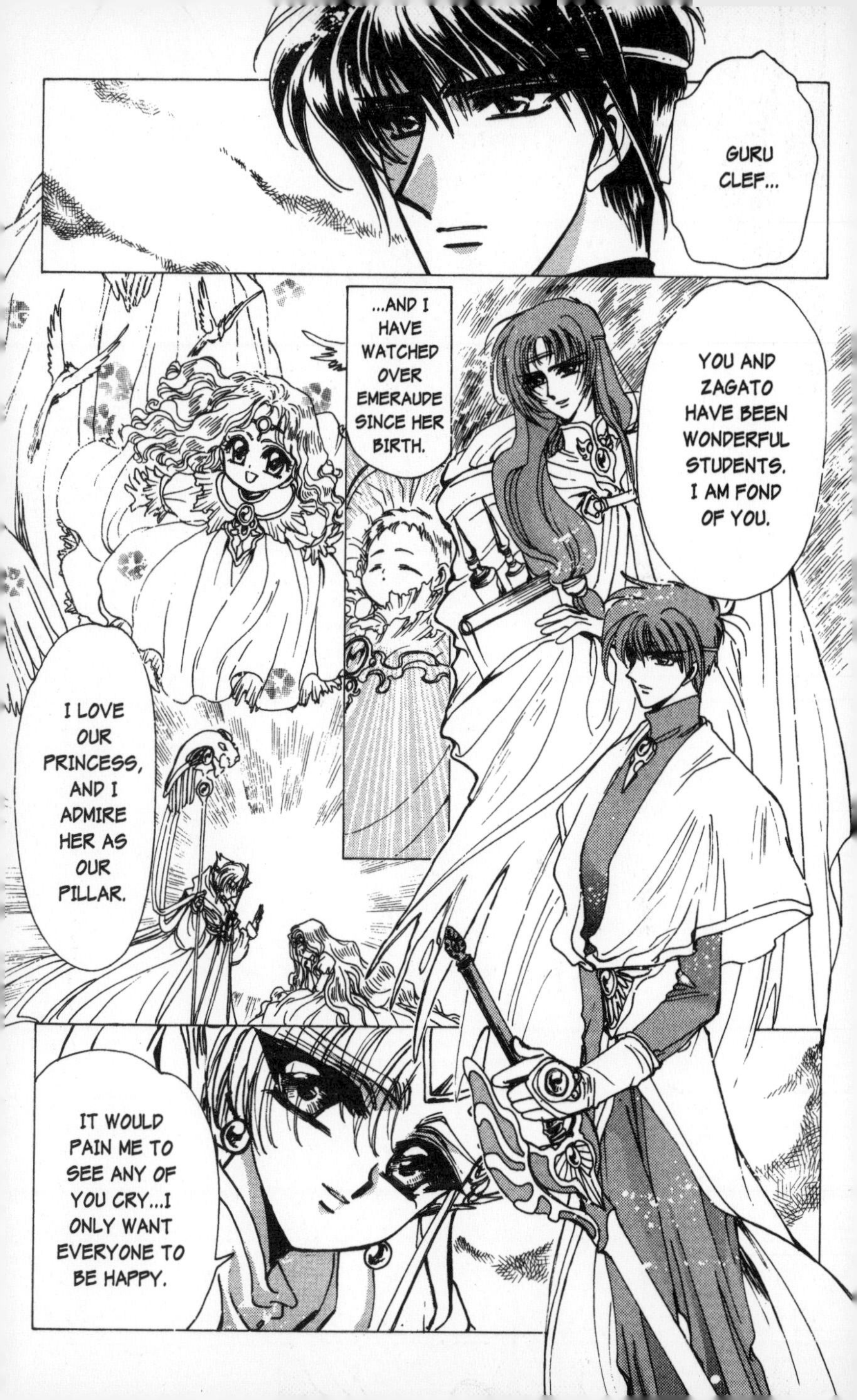
GURU CLEF...
YOU AND ZAGATO HAVE BEEN WONDERFUL STUDENTS. I AM FOND OF YOU.
...AND I HAVE WATCHED OVER EMERAUDE SINCE HER BIRTH.
I LOVE OUR PRINCESS, AND I ADMIRE HER AS OUR PILLAR.
IT WOULD PAIN ME TO SEE ANY OF YOU CRY...I ONLY WANT EVERYONE TO BE HAPPY.

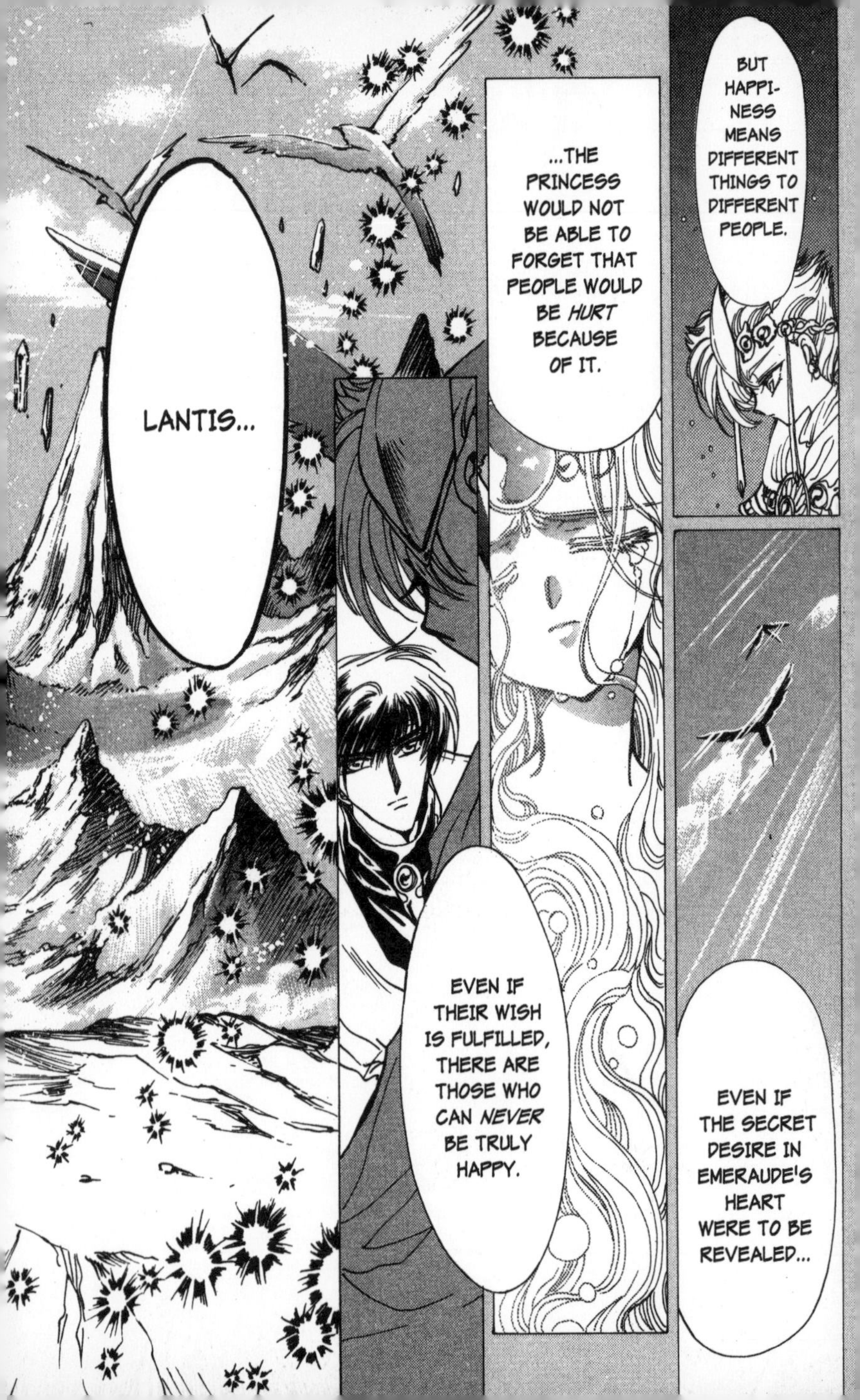
BUT HAPPINESS MEANS DIFFERENT THINGS TO DIFFERENT PEOPLE.
EVEN IF THEIR WISH IS FULFILLED, THERE ARE THOSE WHO CAN *NEVER* BE TRULY HAPPY.
EVEN IF THE SECRET DESIRE IN EMERAUDE'S HEART WERE TO BE REVEALED...
...THE PRINCESS WOULD NOT BE ABLE TO FORGET THAT PEOPLE WOULD BE *HURT* BECAUSE OF IT.
LANTIS...

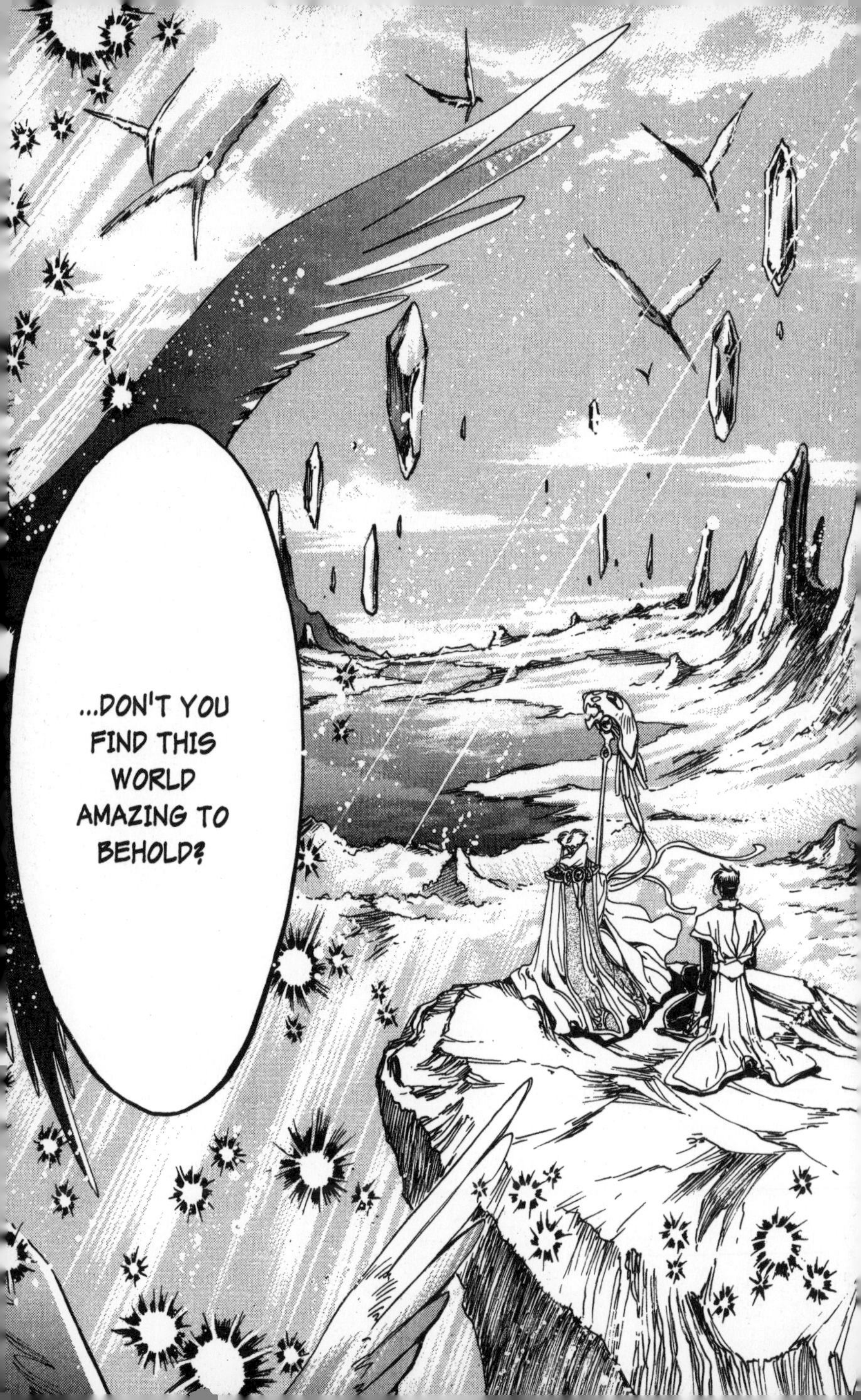
...DON'T YOU FIND THIS WORLD AMAZING TO BEHOLD?

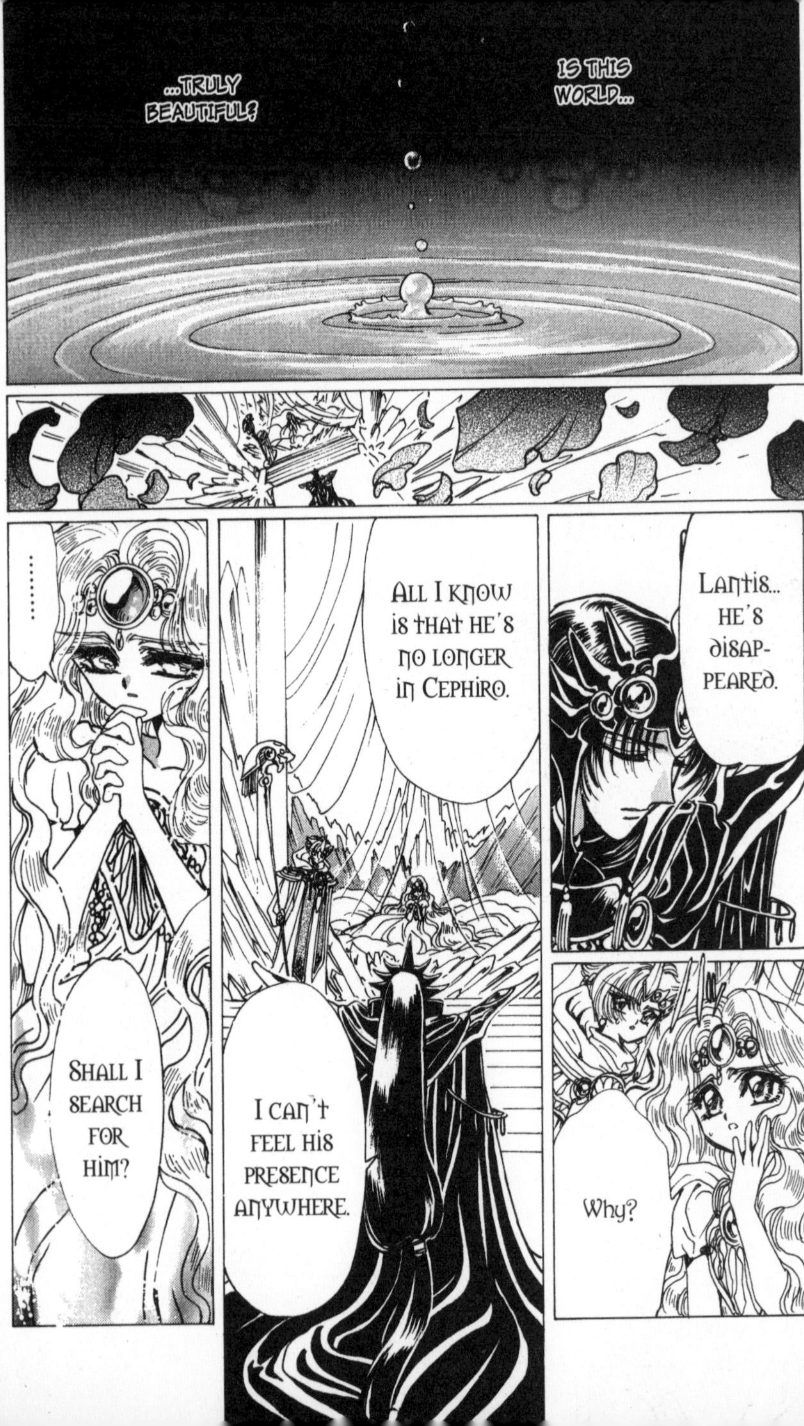
IS THIS WORLD...
...TRULY BEAUTIFUL?
Lantis... he's disappeared.
Why?
All I know is that he's no longer in Cephiro.
I can't feel his presence anywhere.
......
Shall I search for him?

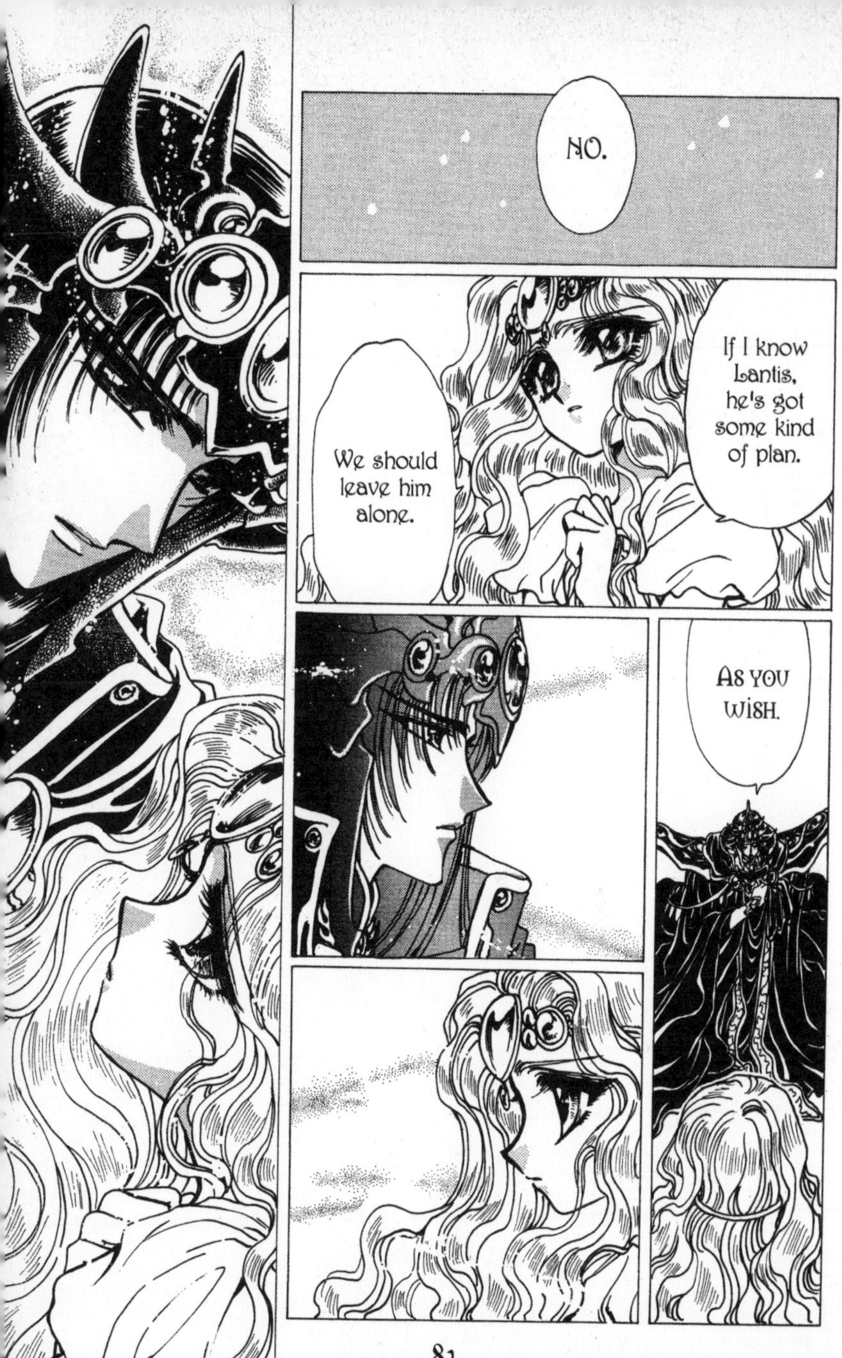
NO.
If I know Lantis, he's got some kind of plan.
We should leave him alone.
AS YOU WISH.

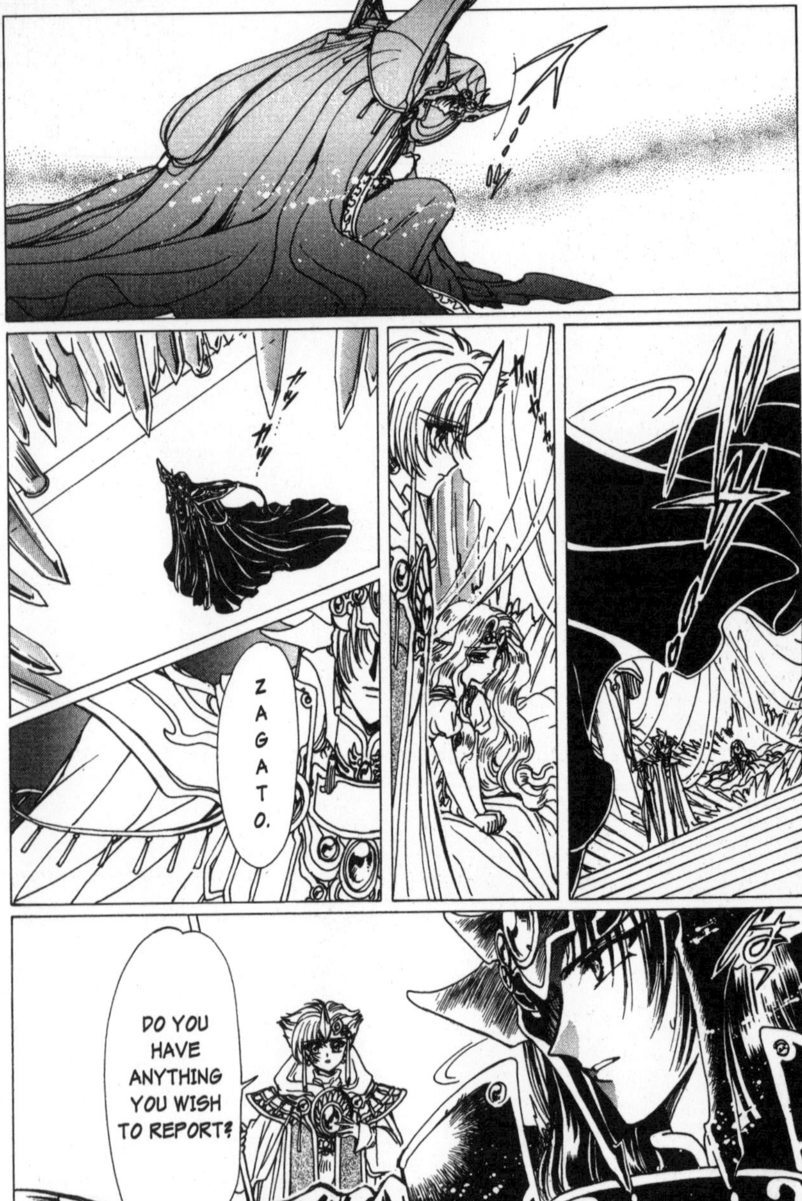
ZAGATO.
DO YOU HAVE ANYTHING YOU WISH TO REPORT?

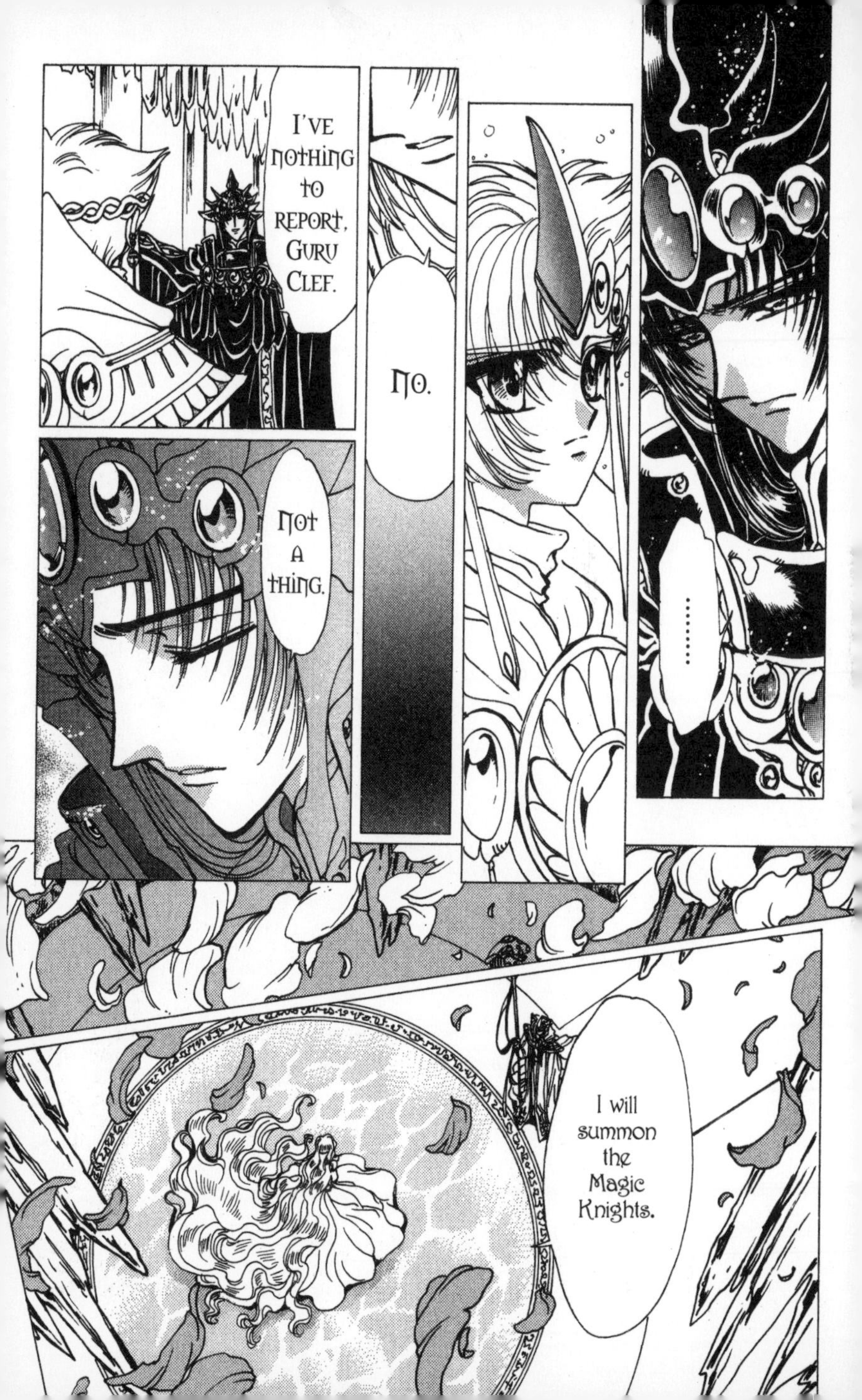
......
No.
I'VE NOTHING TO REPORT, GURU CLEF.
NOT A THING.
I will summon the Magic Knights.

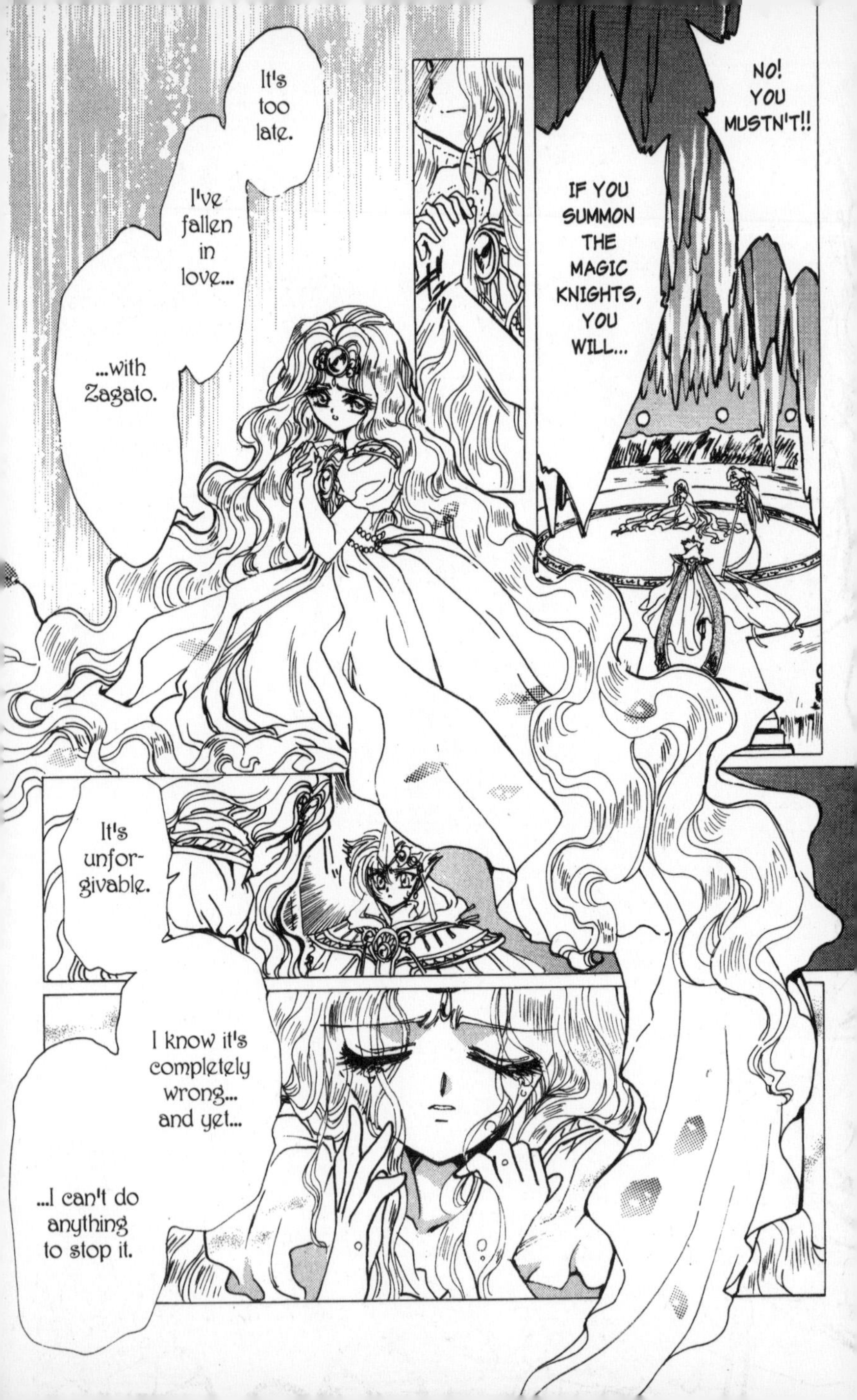
NO! YOU MUSTN'T!!
IF YOU SUMMON THE MAGIC KNIGHTS, YOU WILL...
It's too late.
I've fallen in love...
...with Zagato.
It's unforgivable.
I know it's completely wrong... and yet...
...I can't do anything to stop it.

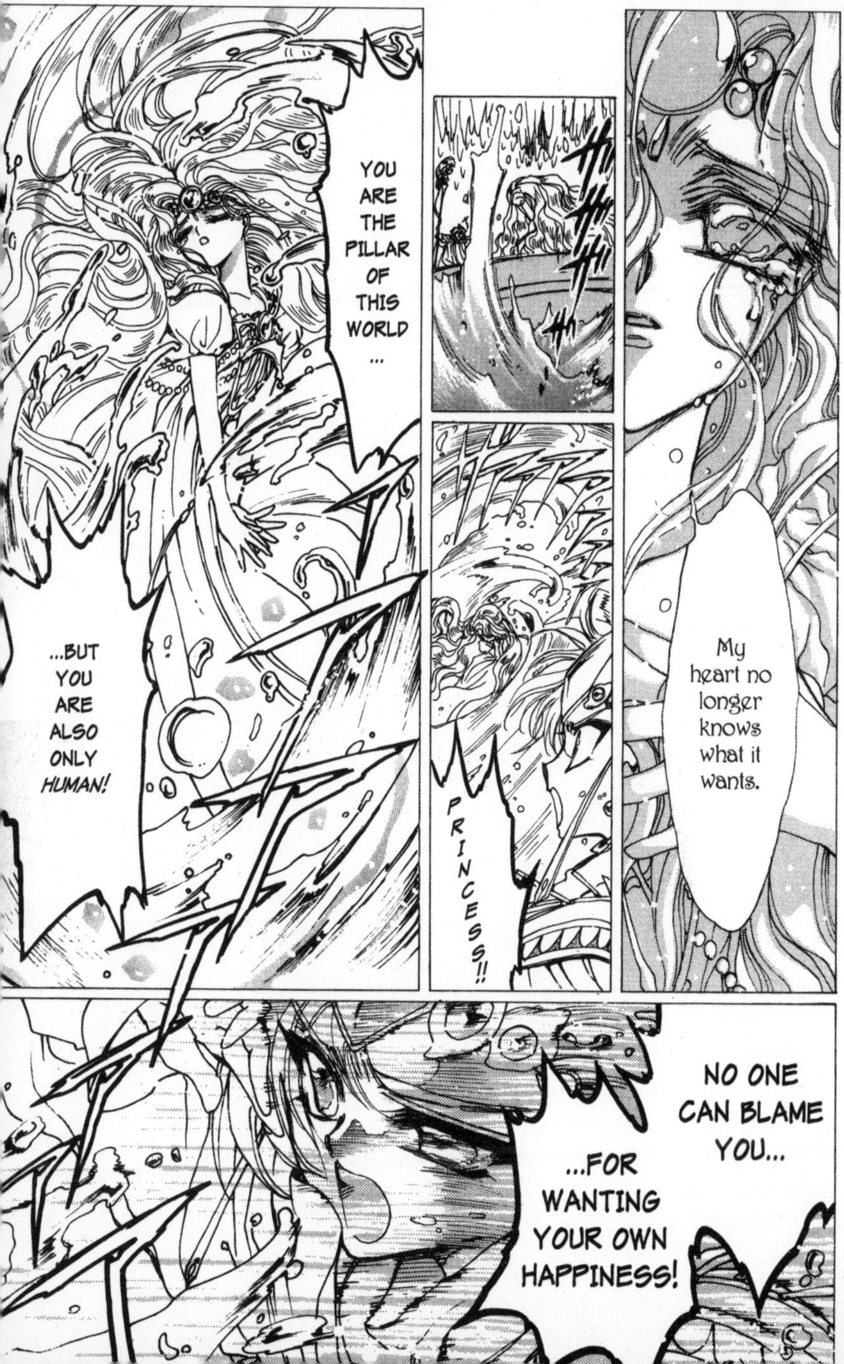
My heart no longer knows what it wants.
PRINCESS!!
YOU ARE THE PILLAR OF THIS WORLD...
...BUT YOU ARE ALSO ONLY HUMAN!
NO ONE CAN BLAME YOU...
...FOR WANTING YOUR OWN HAPPINESS!

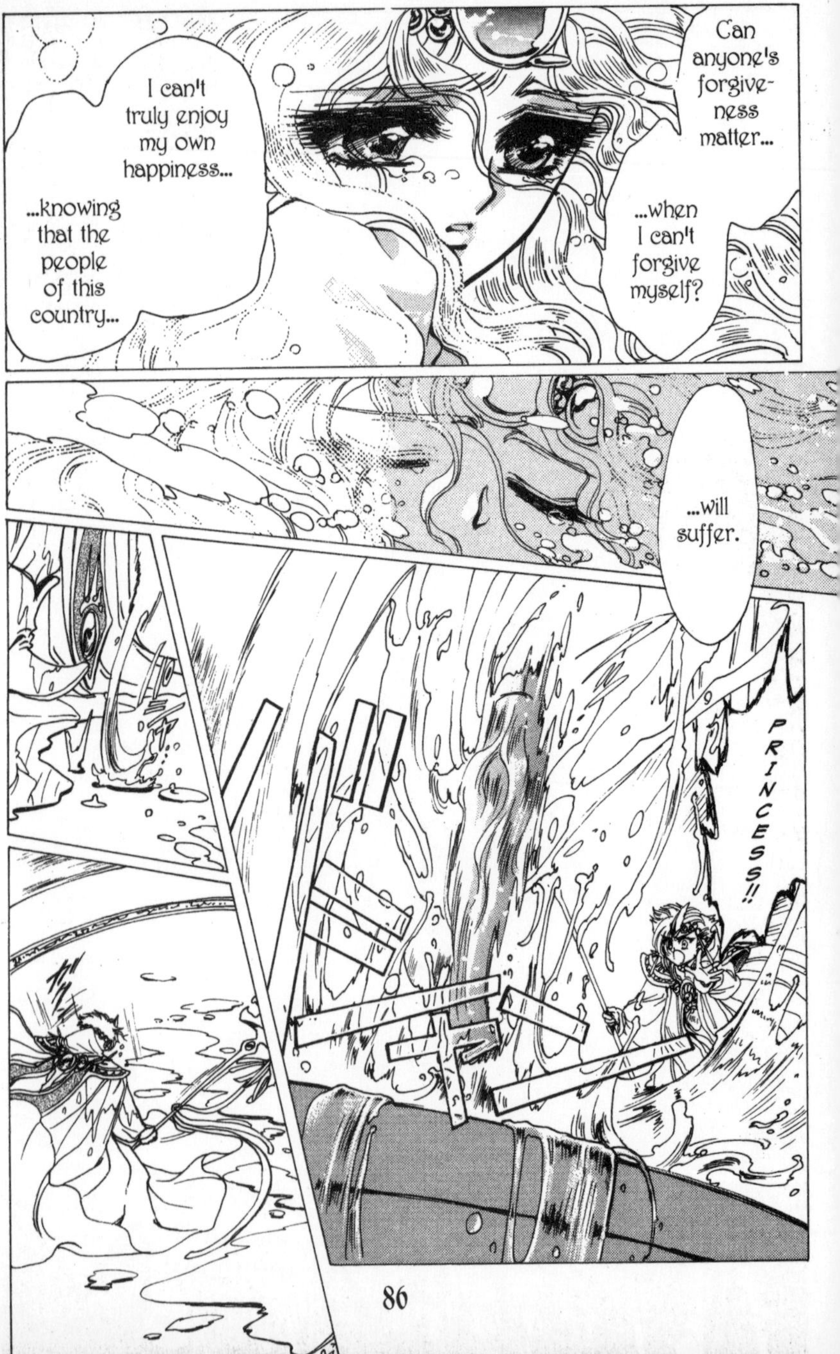
Can anyone's forgiveness matter...
...when I can't forgive myself?
I can't truly enjoy my own happiness...
...knowing that the people of this country...
...will suffer.
PRINCESS!!

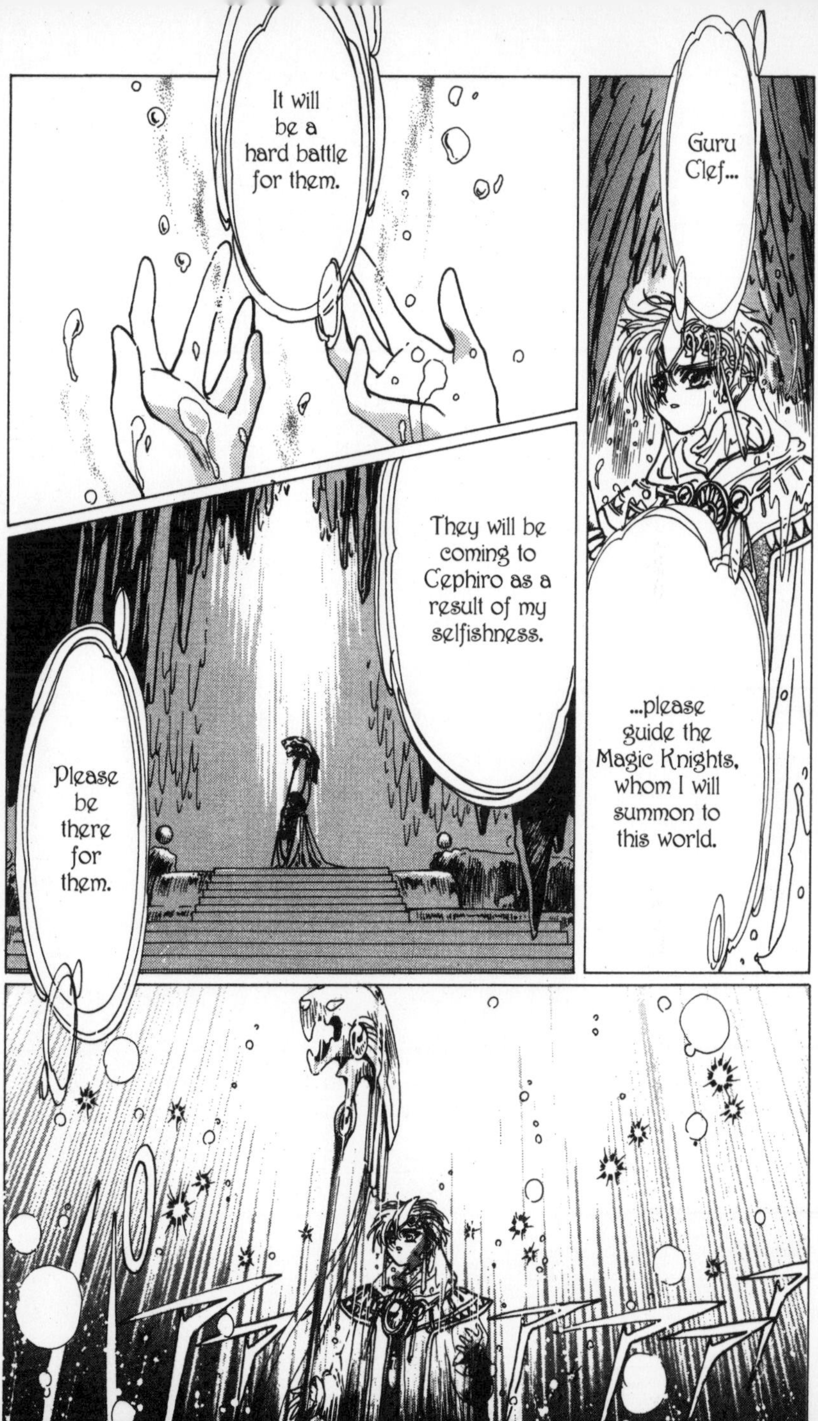
Guru Clef...
...please guide the Magic Knights, whom I will summon to this world.
It will be a hard battle for them.
They will be coming to Cephiro as a result of my selfishness.
Please be there for them.

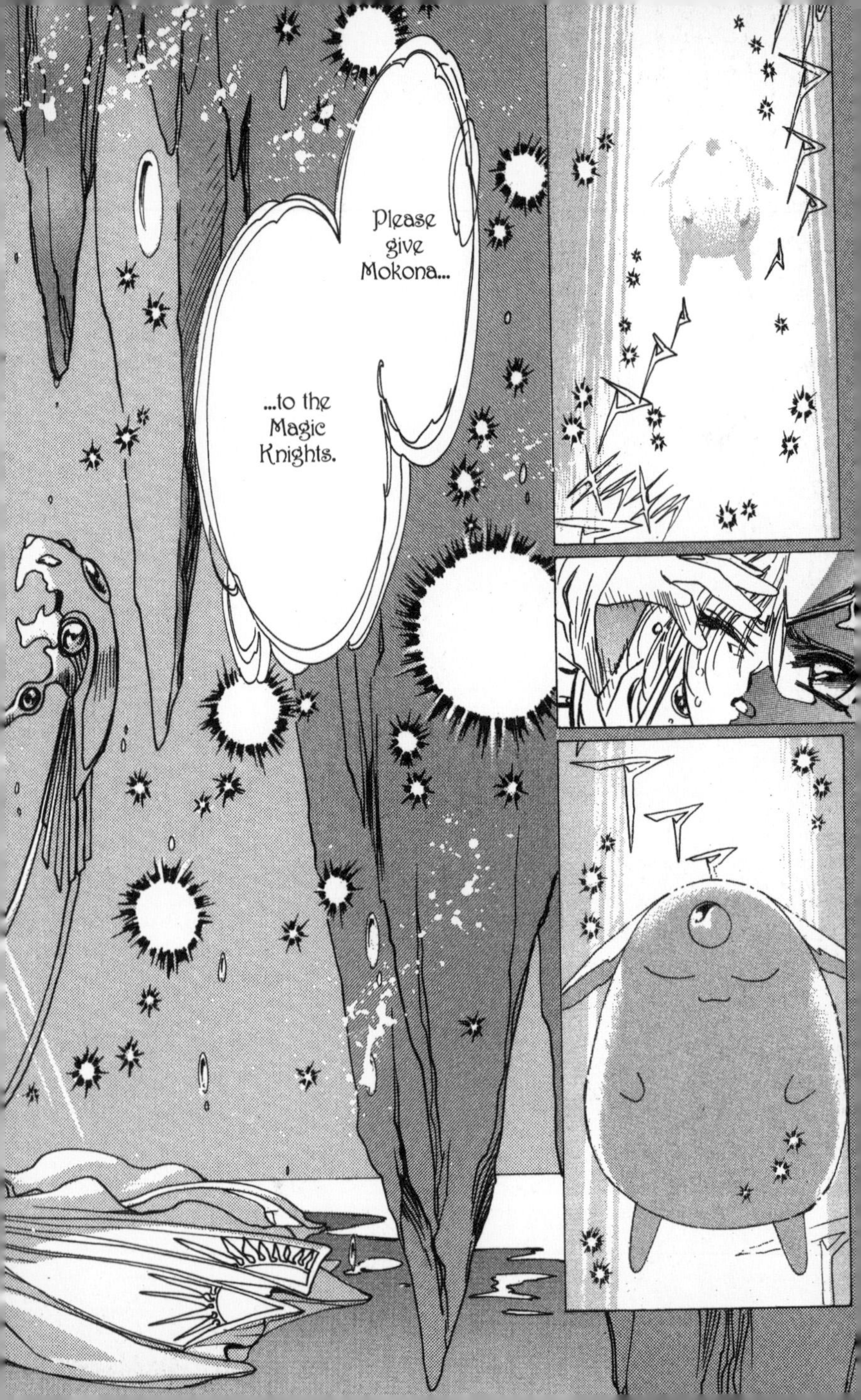
Please give Mokona...
...to the Magic Knights.

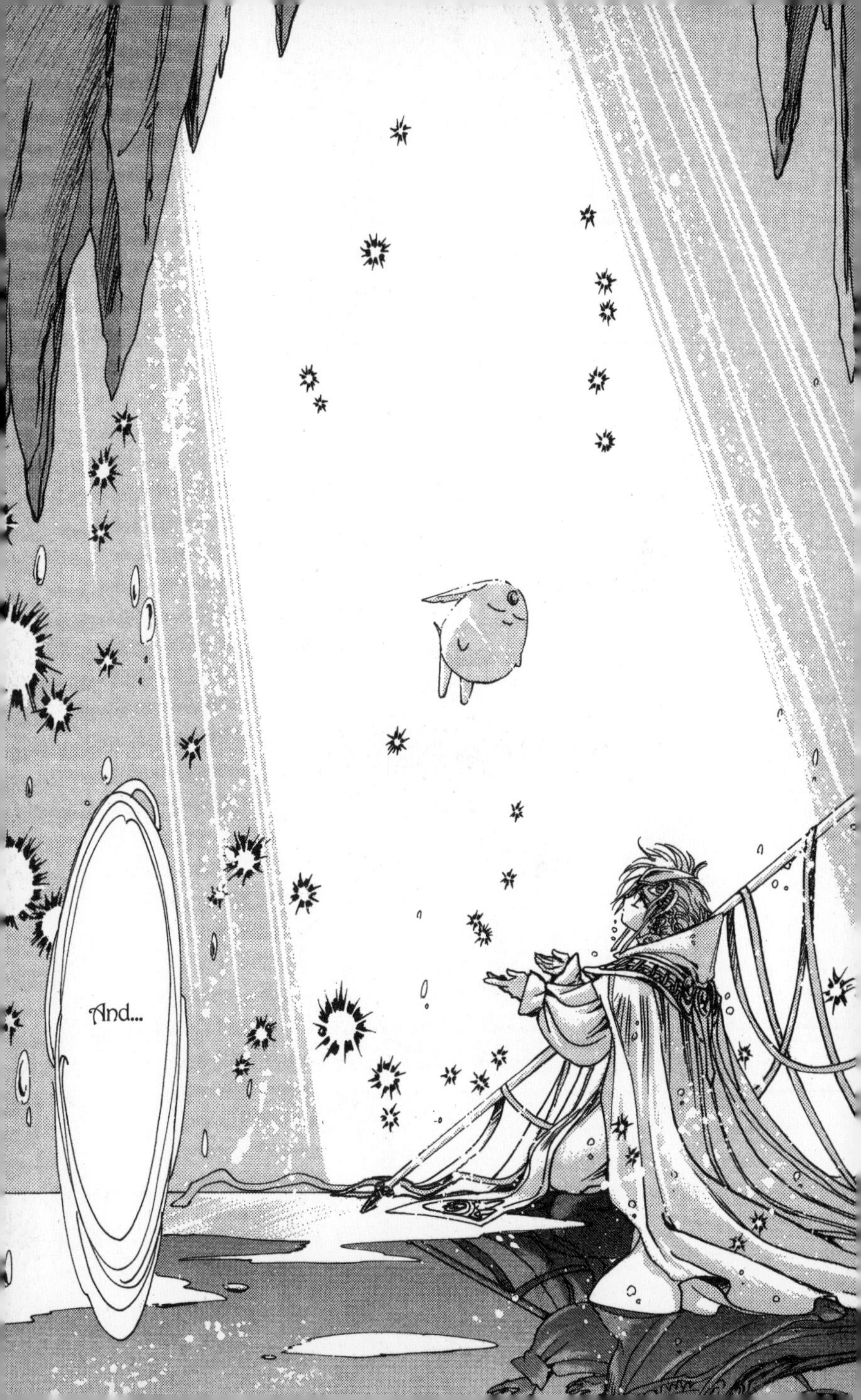
And...

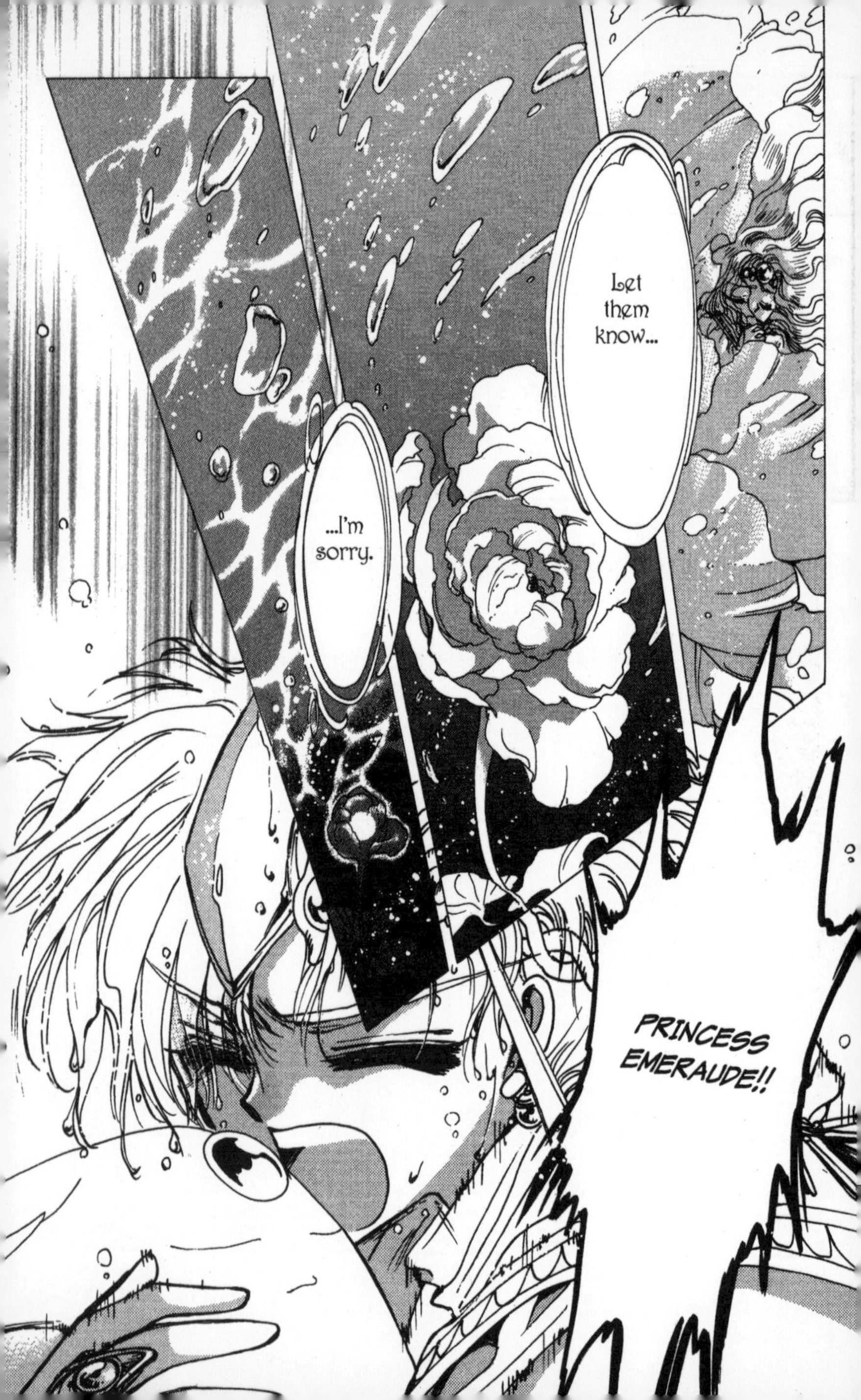
Let them know...
...I'm sorry.
PRINCESS EMERAUDE!!

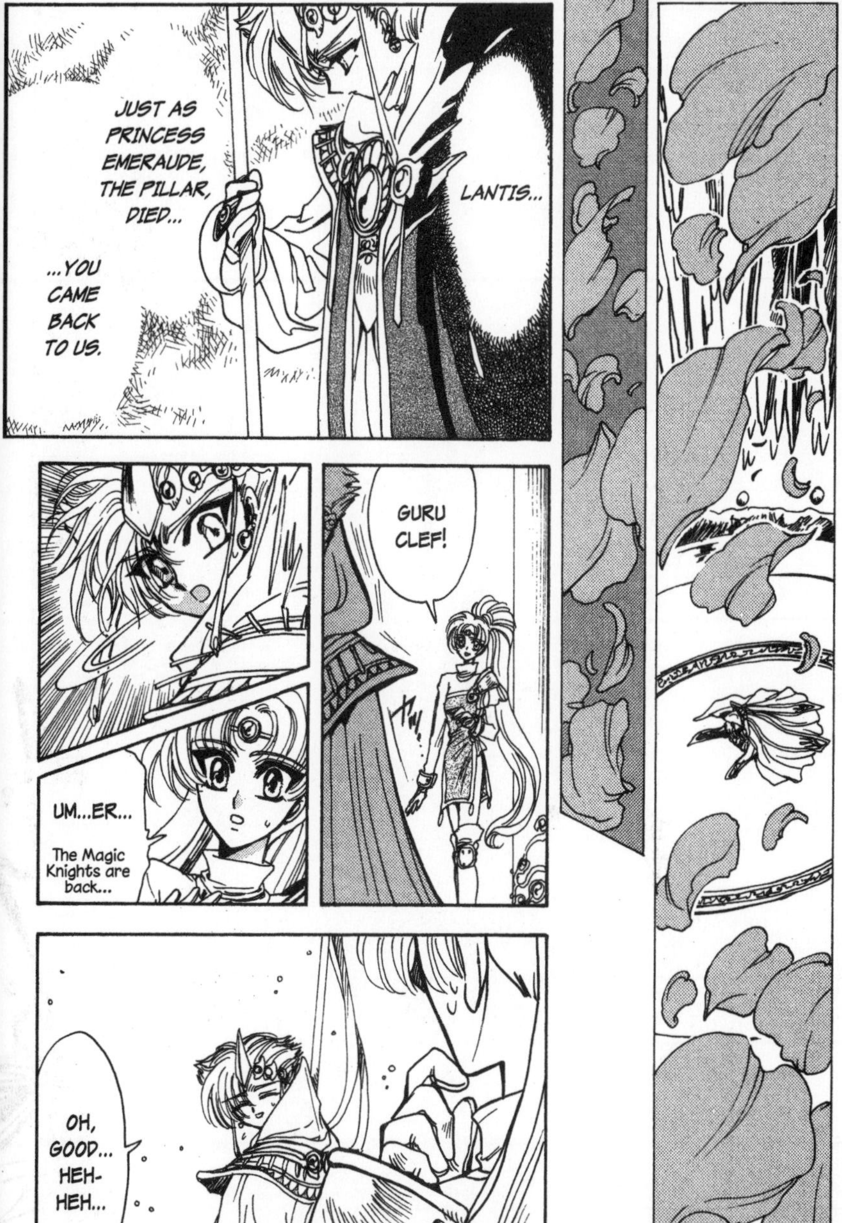
LANTIS...
JUST AS PRINCESS EMERAUDE, THE PILLAR, DIED...
...YOU CAME BACK TO US.
GURU CLEF!
UM...ER...
The Magic Knights are back...
OH, GOOD... HEH-HEH...

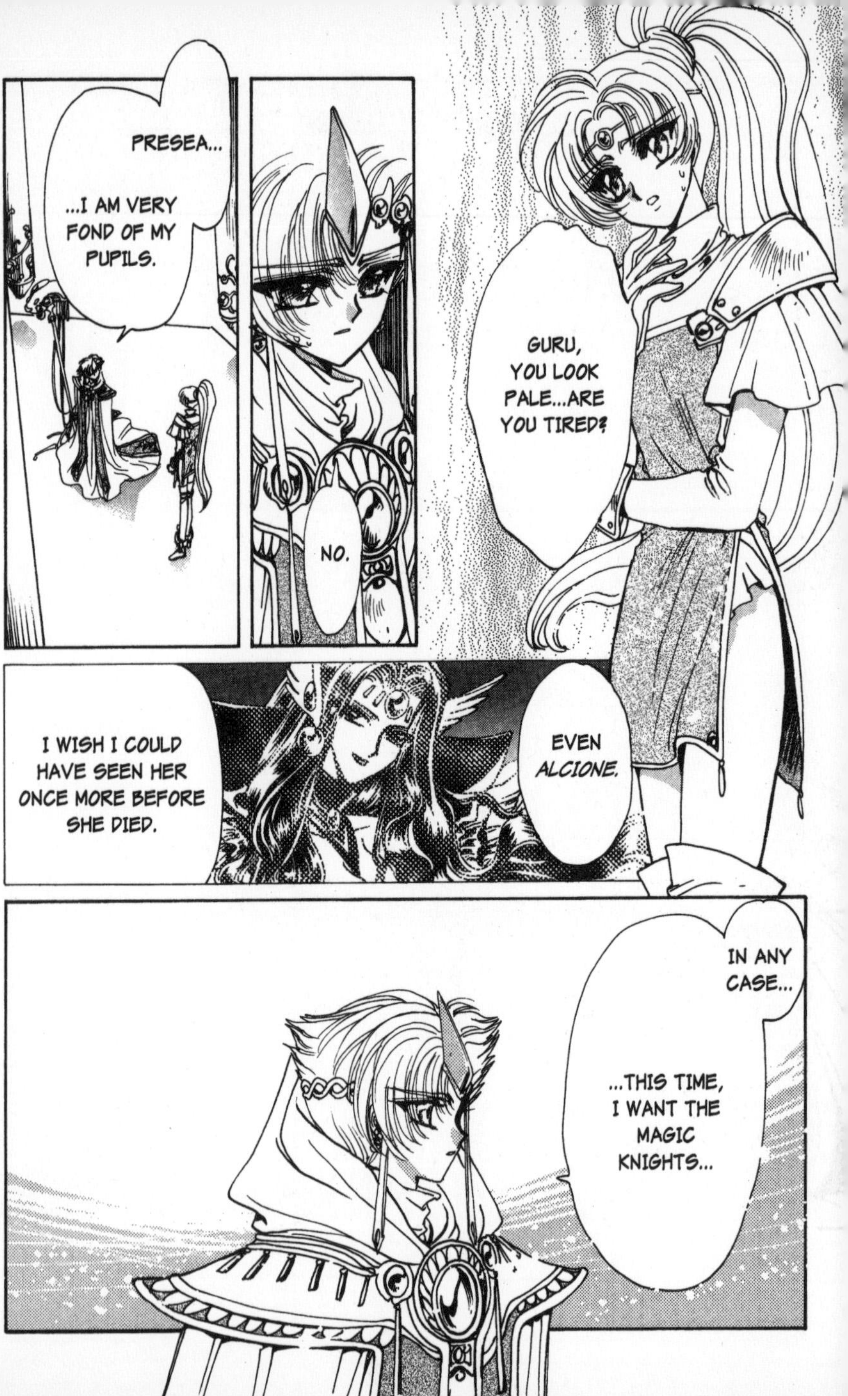
GURU, YOU LOOK PALE...ARE YOU TIRED?
NO.
PRESEA...
...I AM VERY FOND OF MY PUPILS.
EVEN ALCIONE.
I WISH I COULD HAVE SEEN HER ONCE MORE BEFORE SHE DIED.
IN ANY CASE...
...THIS TIME, I WANT THE MAGIC KNIGHTS...

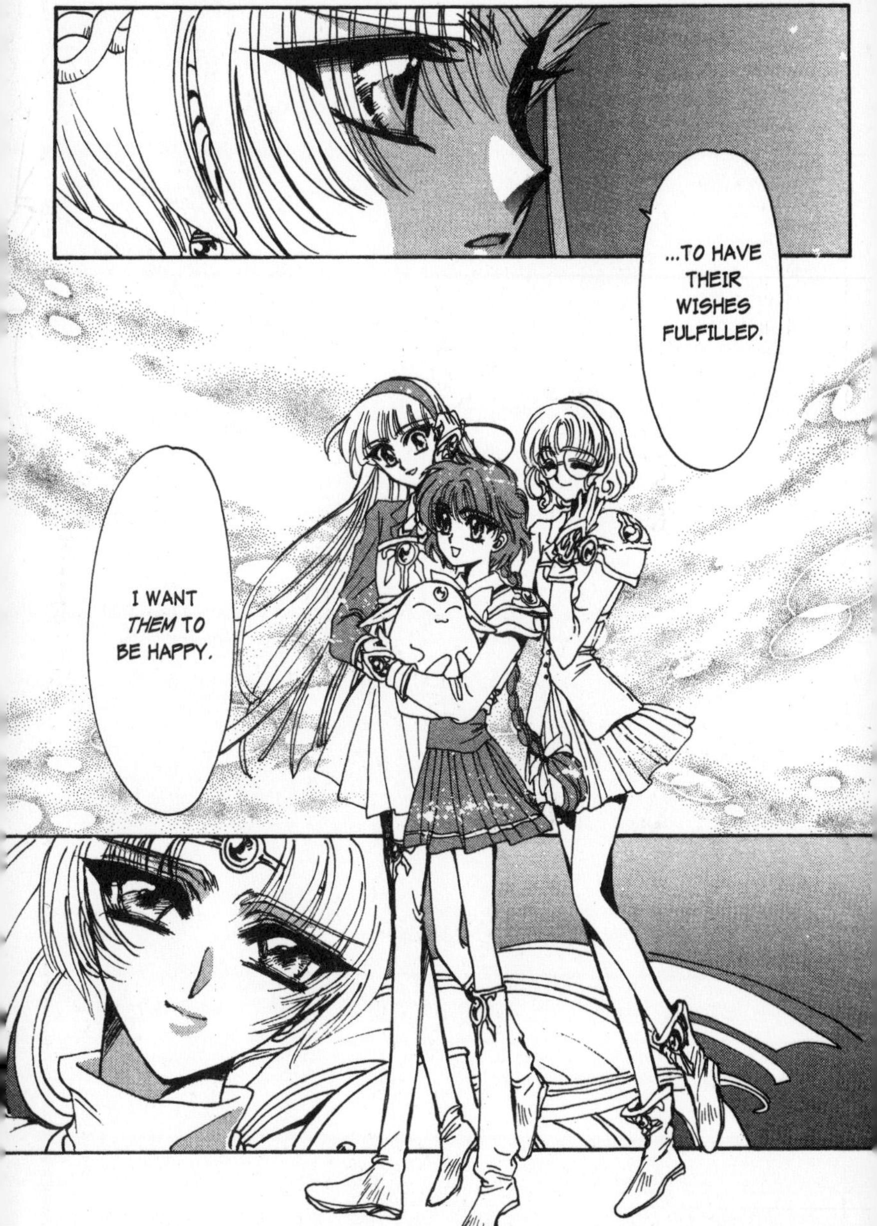
...TO HAVE THEIR WISHES FULFILLED.
I WANT *THEM* TO BE HAPPY.

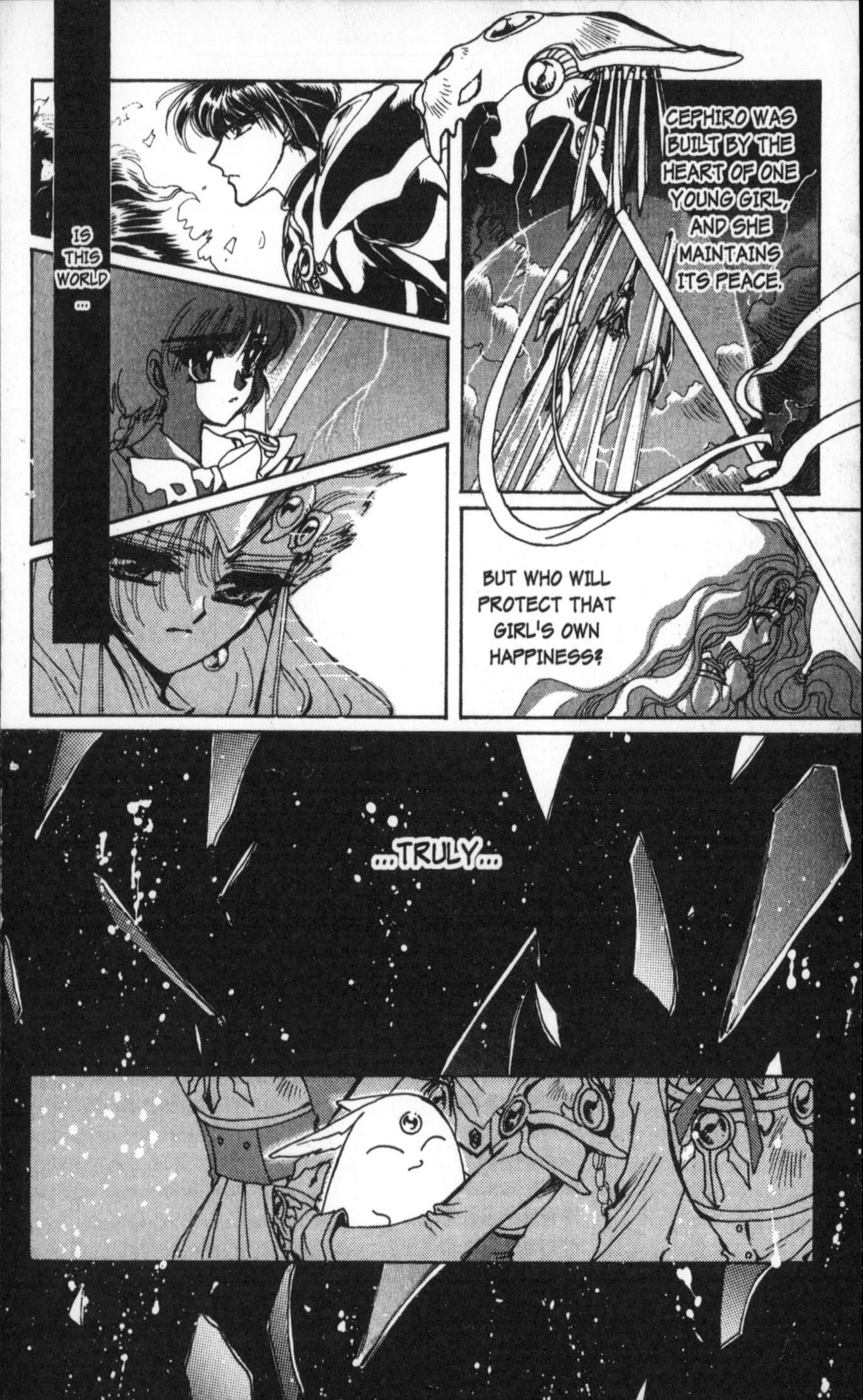
CEPHIRO WAS BUILT BY THE HEART OF ONE YOUNG GIRL, AND SHE MAINTAINS ITS PEACE.
BUT WHO WILL PROTECT THAT GIRL'S OWN HAPPINESS?
IS THIS WORLD ...
...TRULY...

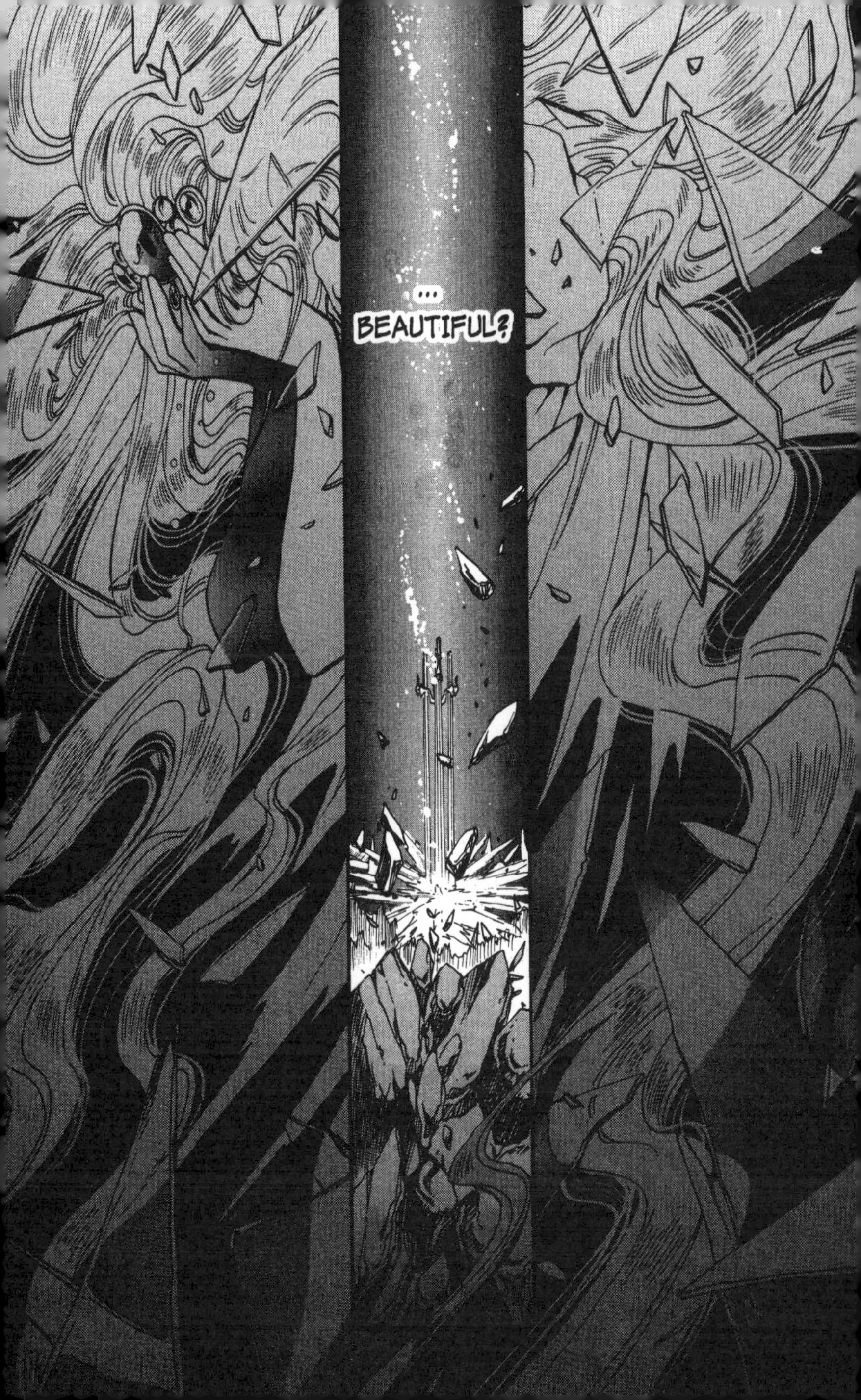
...
BEAUTIFUL?

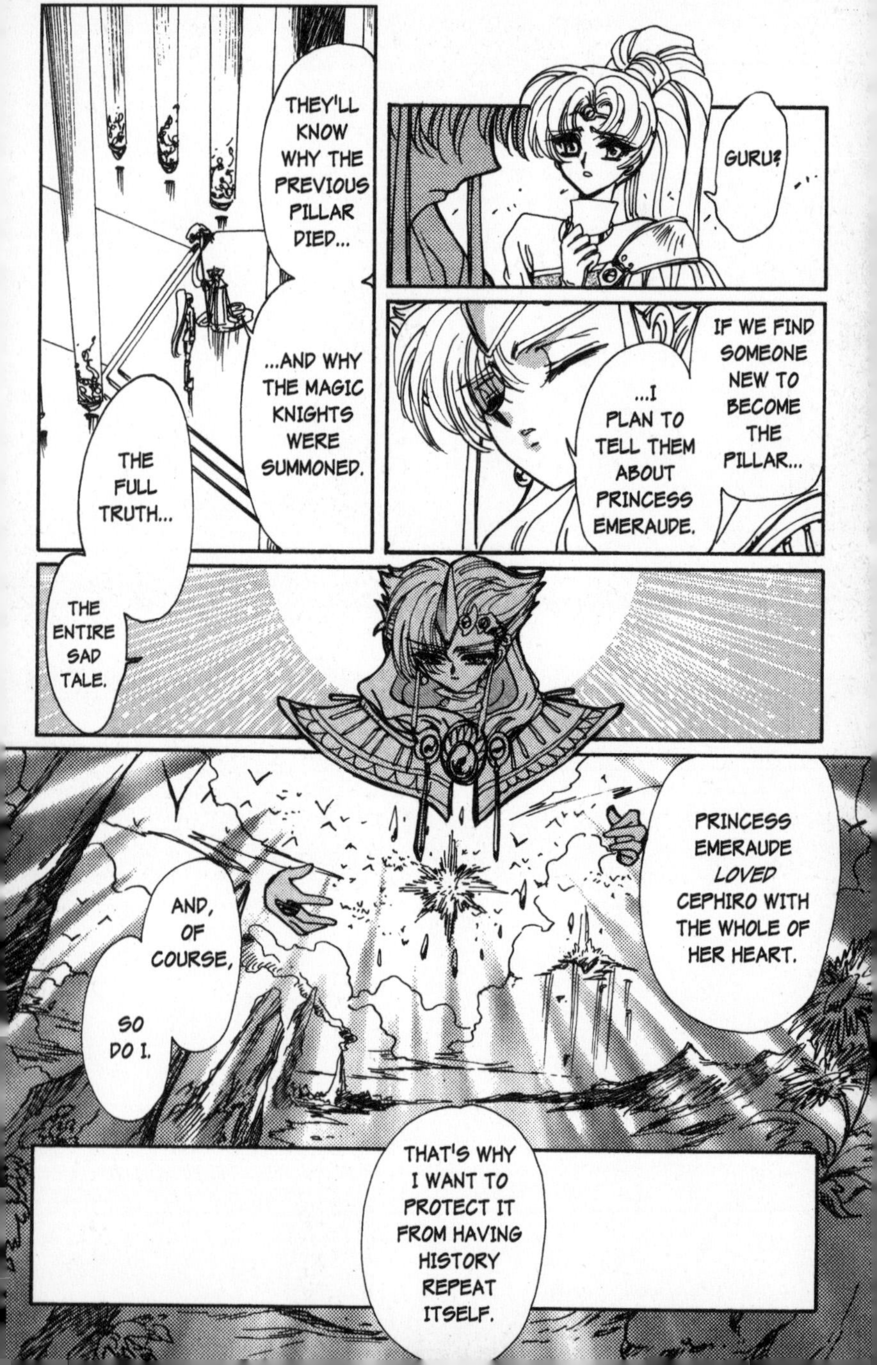
GURU?
IF WE FIND SOMEONE NEW TO BECOME THE PILLAR...
...I PLAN TO TELL THEM ABOUT PRINCESS EMERAUDE.
THEY'LL KNOW WHY THE PREVIOUS PILLAR DIED...
...AND WHY THE MAGIC KNIGHTS WERE SUMMONED.
THE FULL TRUTH...
THE ENTIRE SAD TALE.
PRINCESS EMERAUDE *LOVED* CEPHIRO WITH THE WHOLE OF HER HEART.
AND, OF COURSE,
SO DO I.
THAT'S WHY I WANT TO PROTECT IT FROM HAVING HISTORY REPEAT ITSELF.

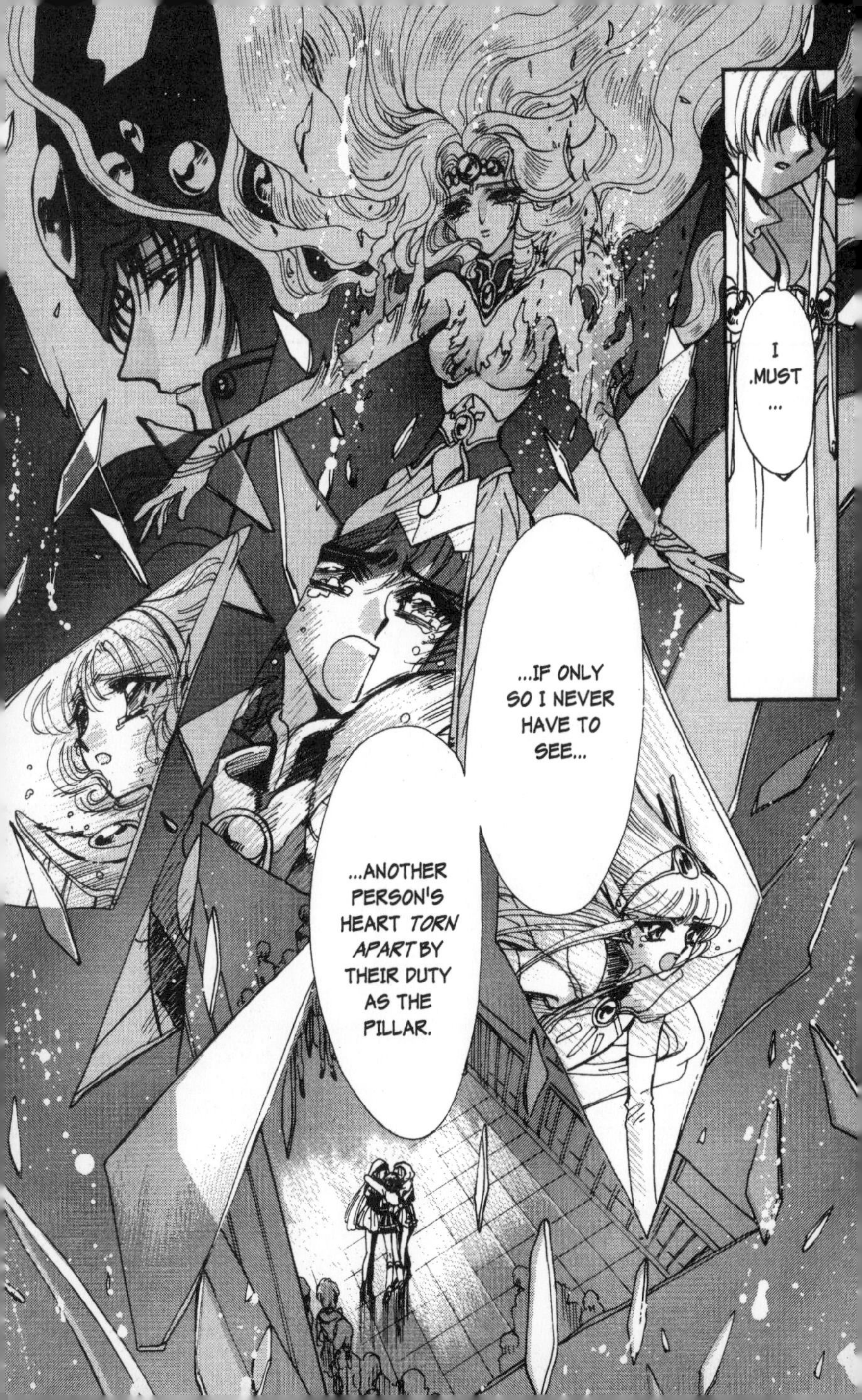
I .MUST ...
...IF ONLY SO I NEVER HAVE TO SEE...
...ANOTHER PERSON'S HEART TORN APART BY THEIR DUTY AS THE PILLAR.

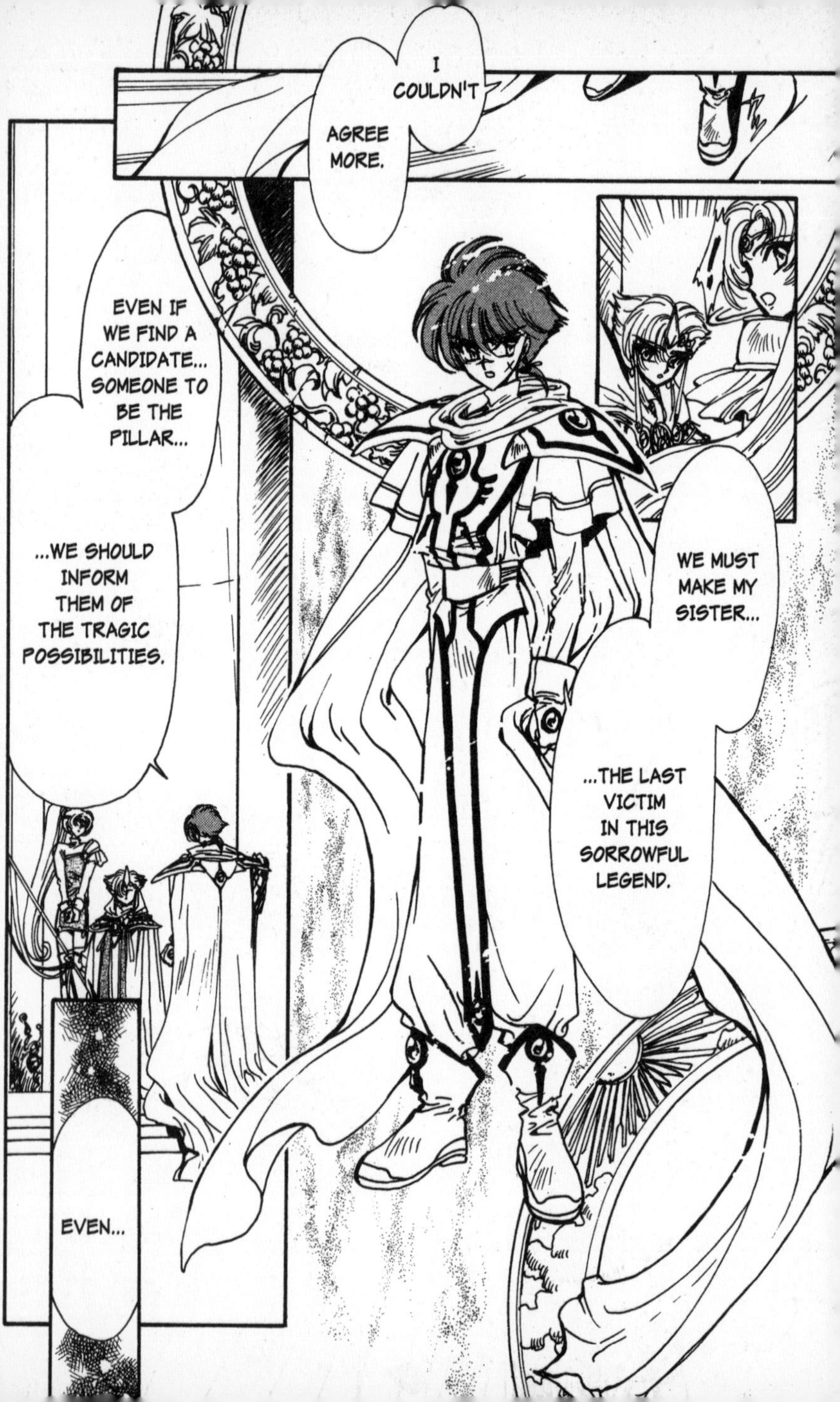
I COULDN'T
AGREE MORE.
WE MUST MAKE MY SISTER...
...THE LAST VICTIM IN THIS SORROWFUL LEGEND.
EVEN IF WE FIND A CANDIDATE... SOMEONE TO BE THE PILLAR...
...WE SHOULD INFORM THEM OF THE TRAGIC POSSIBILITIES.
EVEN...

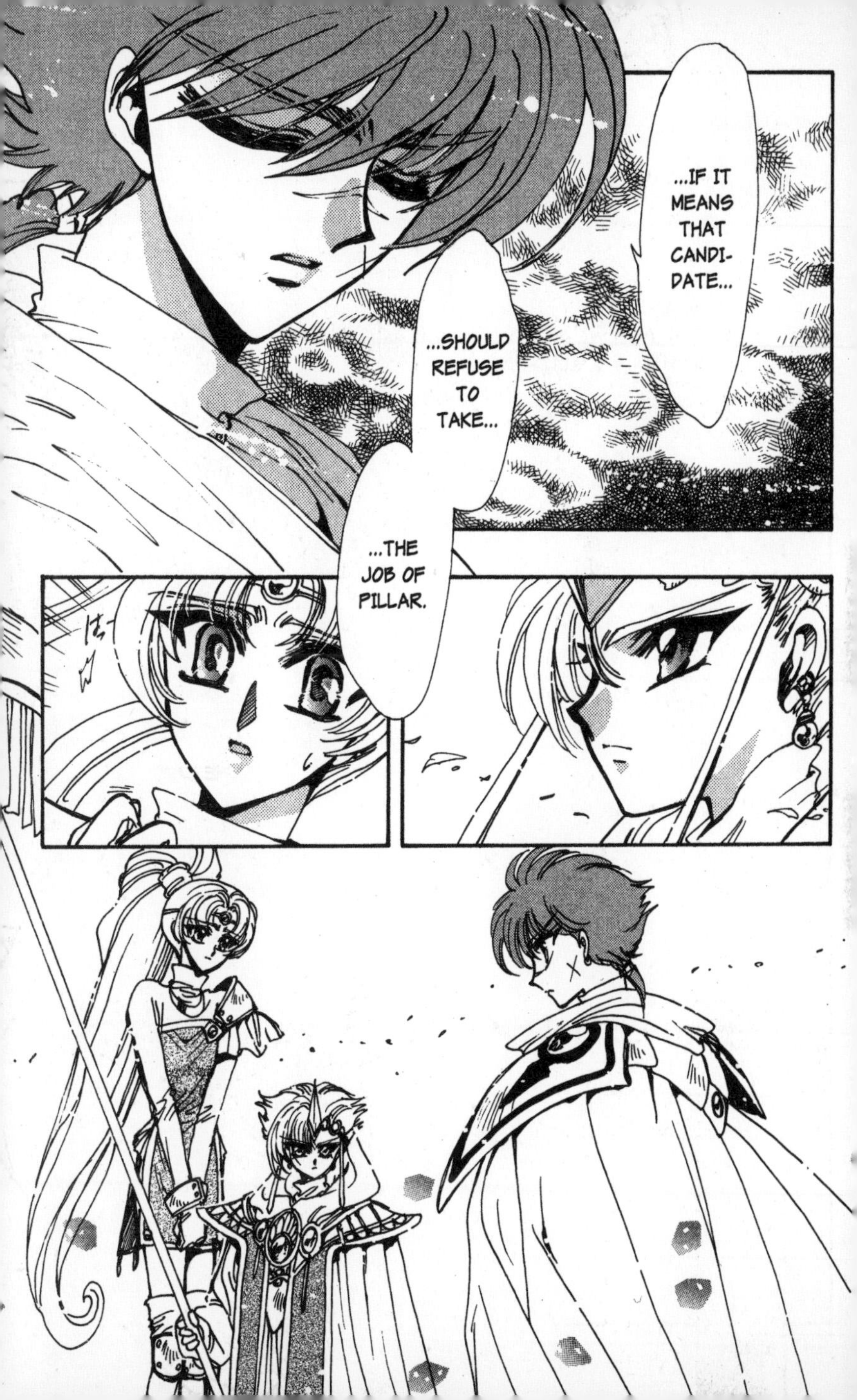
...IF IT MEANS THAT CANDI-DATE...
...SHOULD REFUSE TO TAKE...
...THE JOB OF PILLAR.

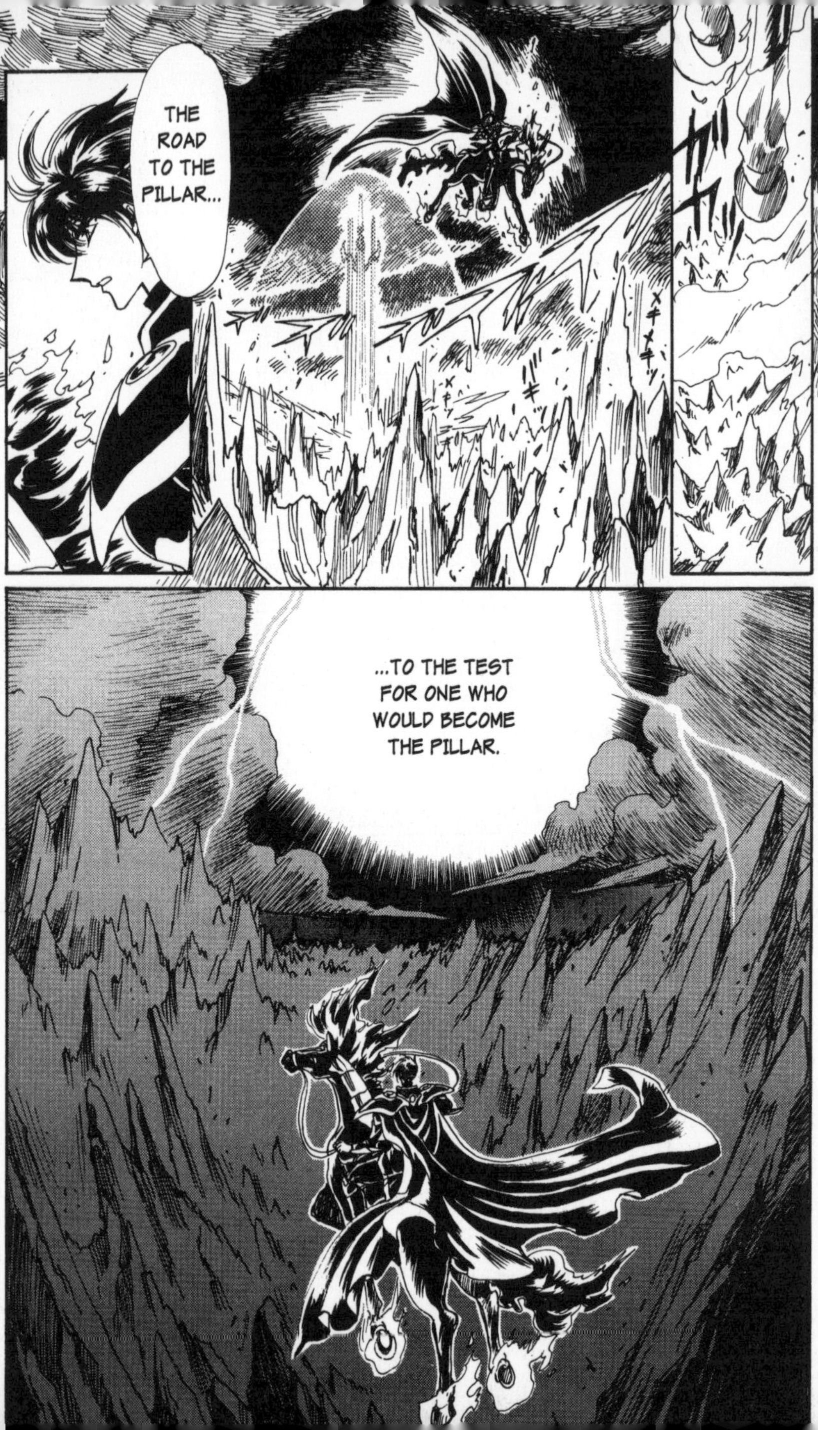
THE ROAD TO THE PILLAR...
...TO THE TEST FOR ONE WHO WOULD BECOME THE PILLAR.

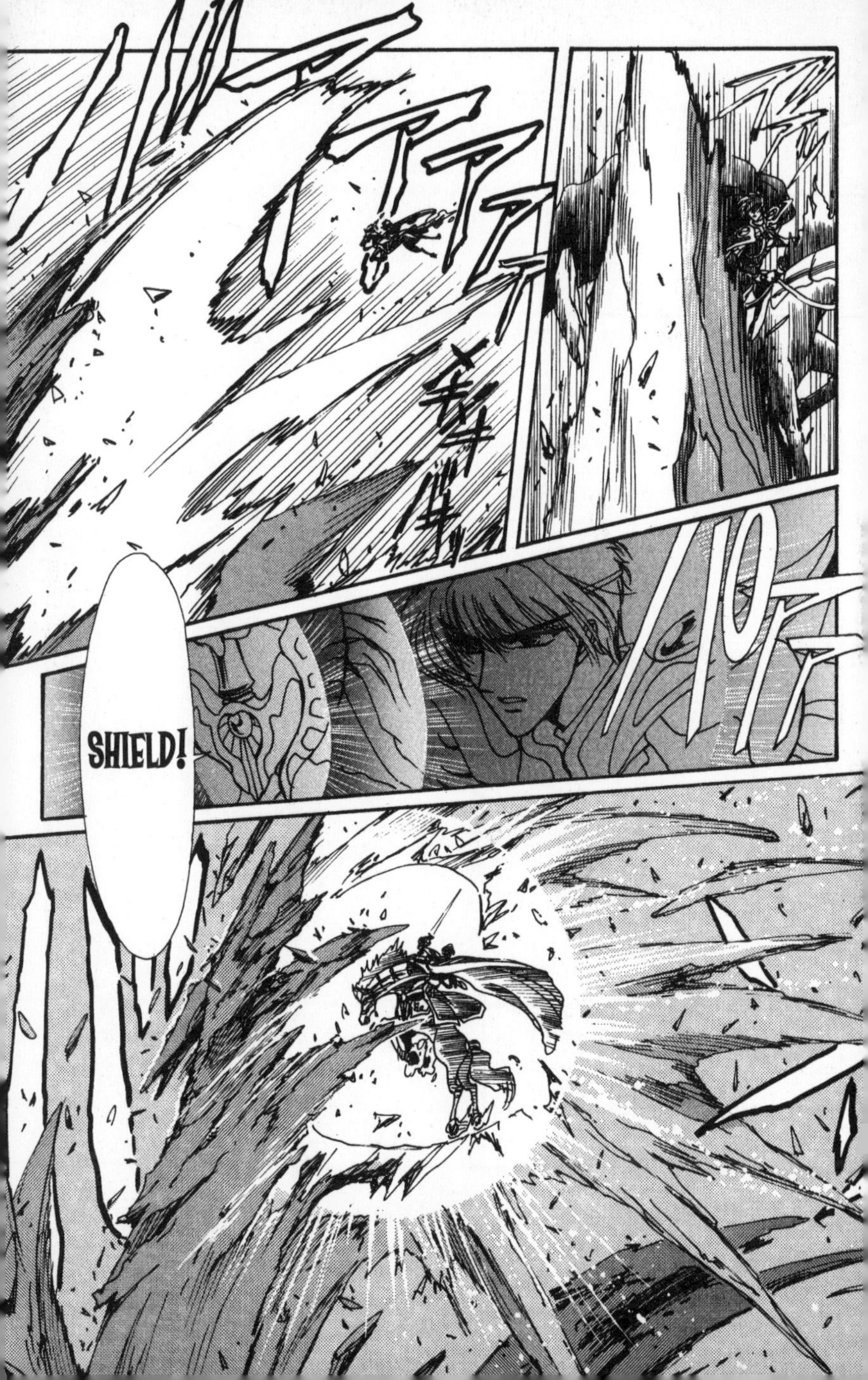
SHIELD!

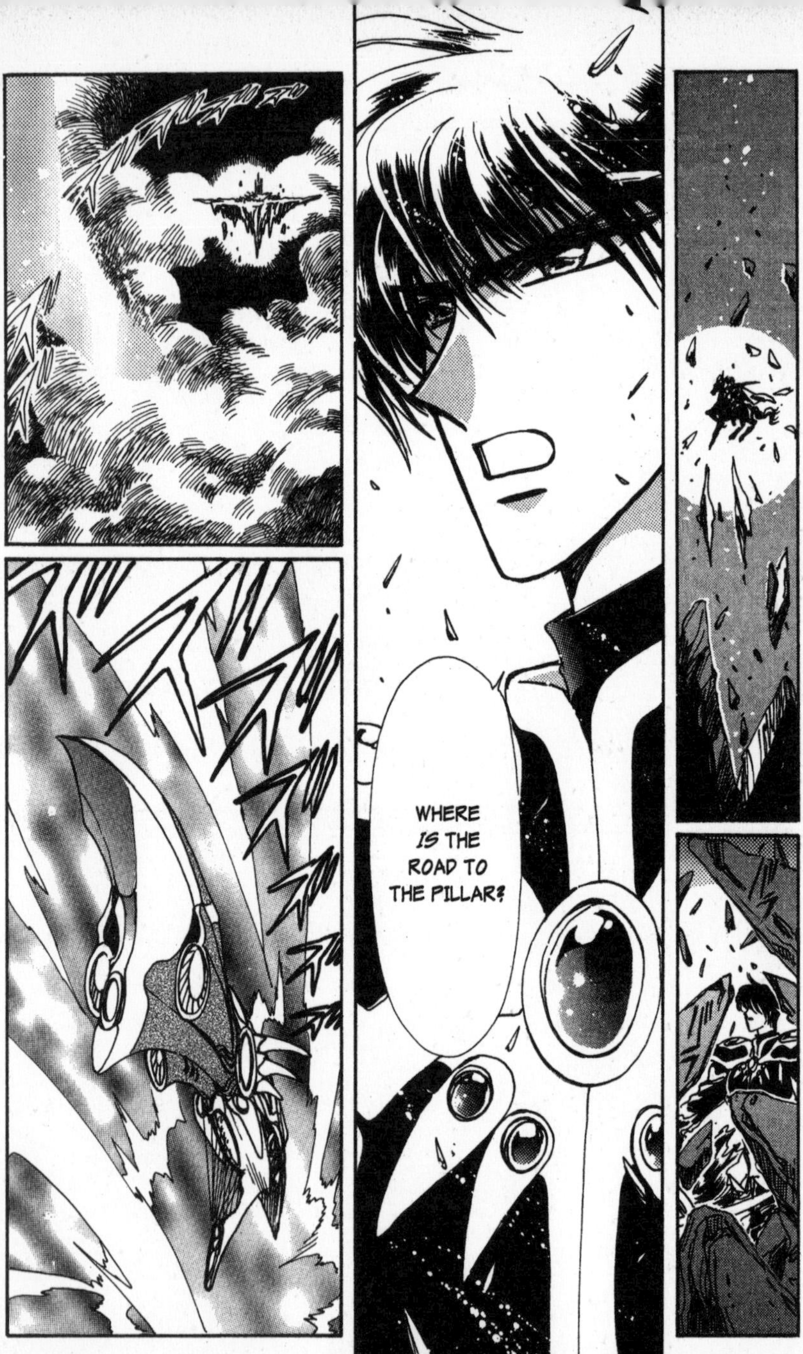
WHERE IS THE ROAD TO THE PILLAR?

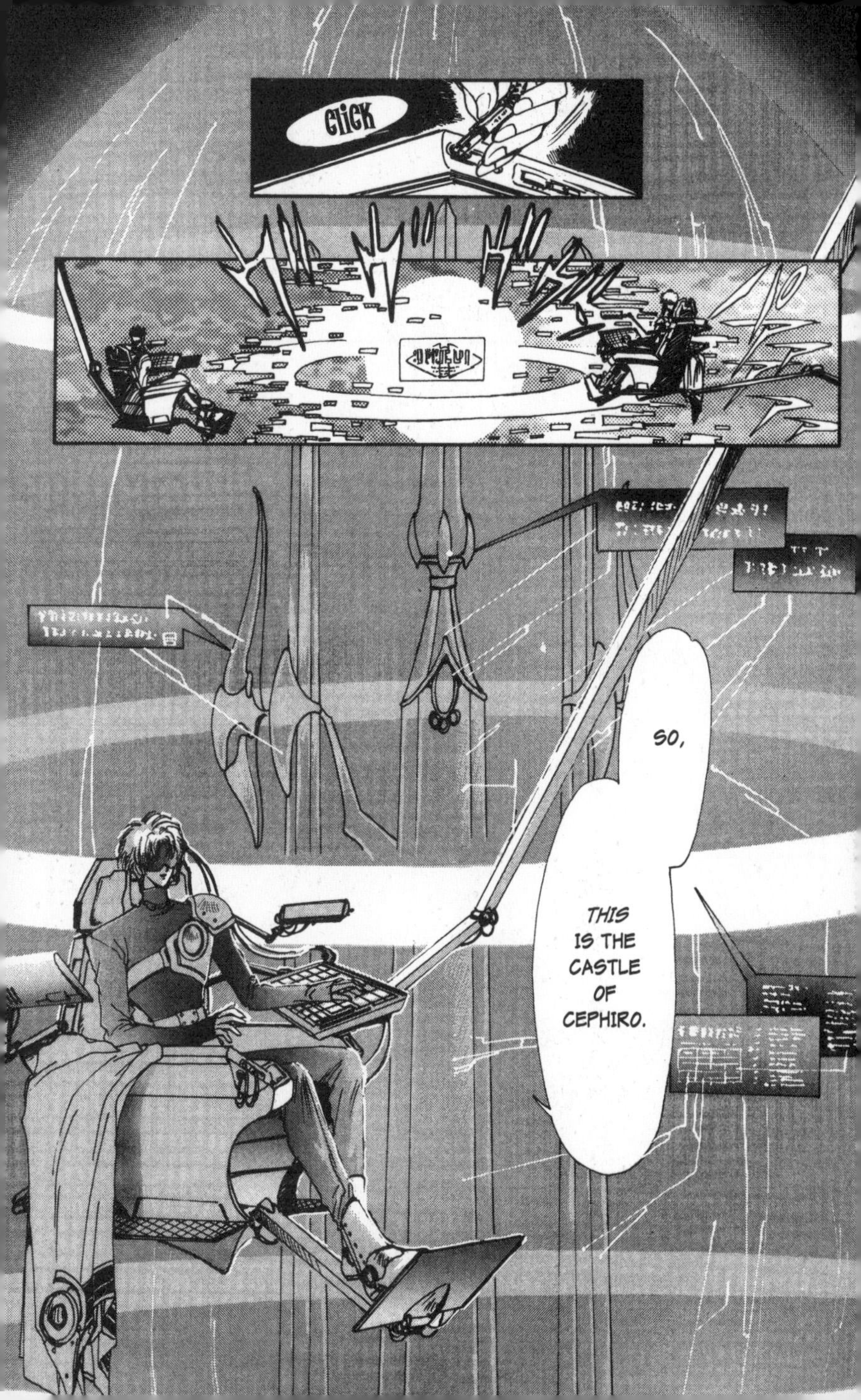

CLICK
SO,
THIS IS THE CASTLE OF CEPHIRO.

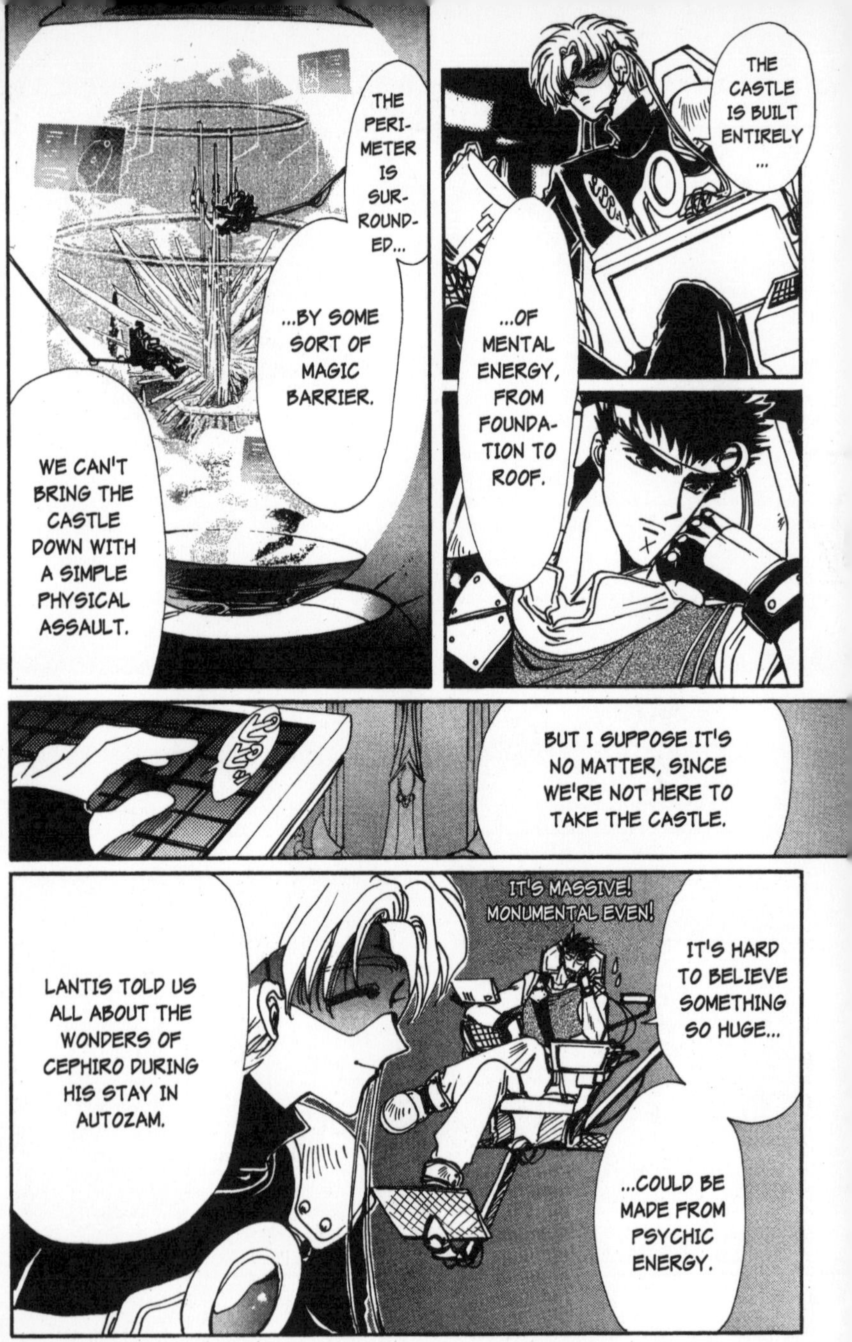
THE CASTLE IS BUILT ENTIRELY ...
...OF MENTAL ENERGY, FROM FOUNDATION TO ROOF.
THE PERIMETER IS SURROUNDED...
...BY SOME SORT OF MAGIC BARRIER.
WE CAN'T BRING THE CASTLE DOWN WITH A SIMPLE PHYSICAL ASSAULT.
BUT I SUPPOSE IT'S NO MATTER, SINCE WE'RE NOT HERE TO TAKE THE CASTLE.
IT'S HARD TO BELIEVE SOMETHING SO HUGE...
...COULD BE MADE FROM PSYCHIC ENERGY.
IT'S MASSIVE! MONUMENTAL EVEN!
LANTIS TOLD US ALL ABOUT THE WONDERS OF CEPHIRO DURING HIS STAY IN AUTOZAM.

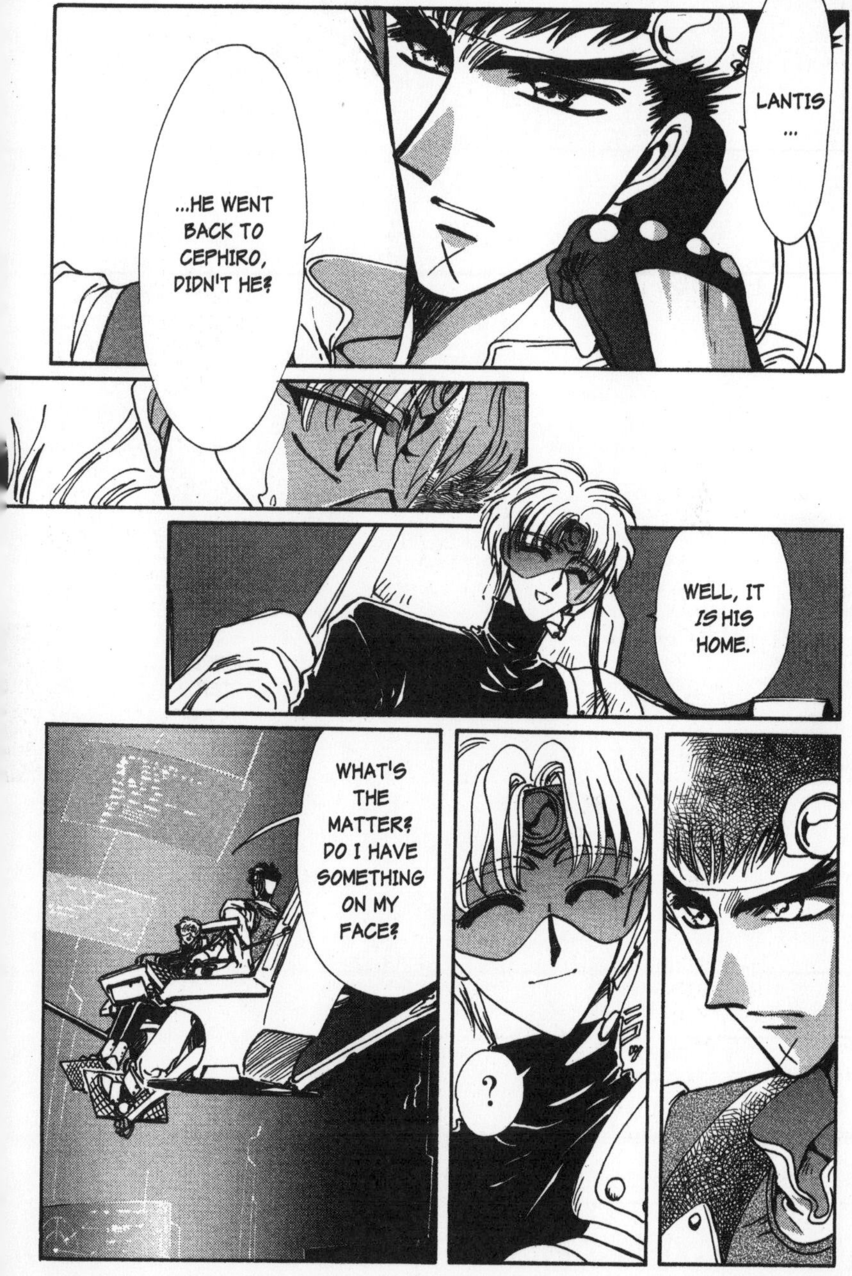
LANTIS ...
...HE WENT BACK TO CEPHIRO, DIDN'T HE?
WELL, IT *IS* HIS HOME.
?
WHAT'S THE MATTER? DO I HAVE SOMETHING ON MY FACE?

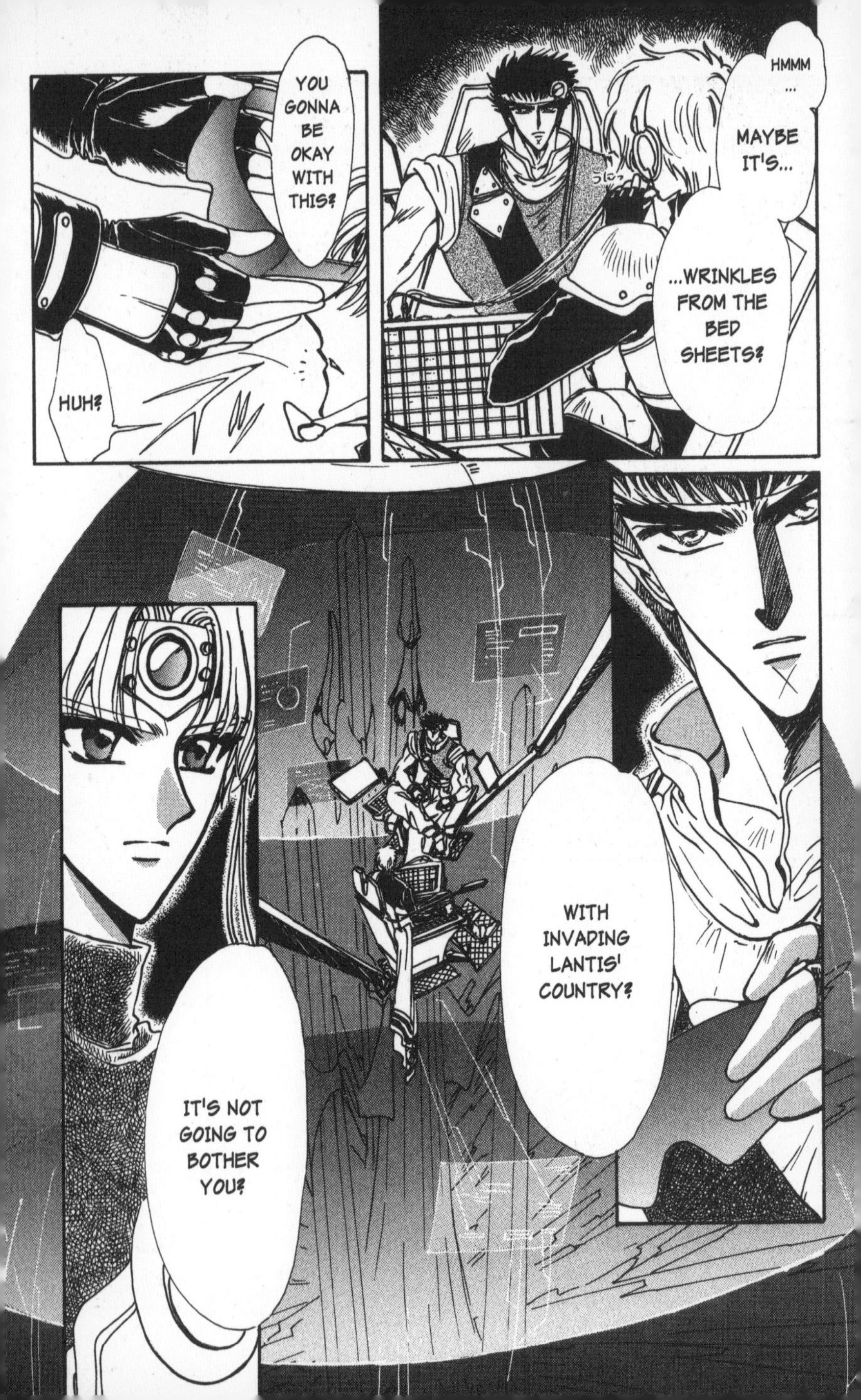
HMMM ...
MAYBE IT'S...
...WRINKLES FROM THE BED SHEETS?
YOU GONNA BE OKAY WITH THIS?
HUH?
WITH INVADING LANTIS' COUNTRY?
IT'S NOT GOING TO BOTHER YOU?

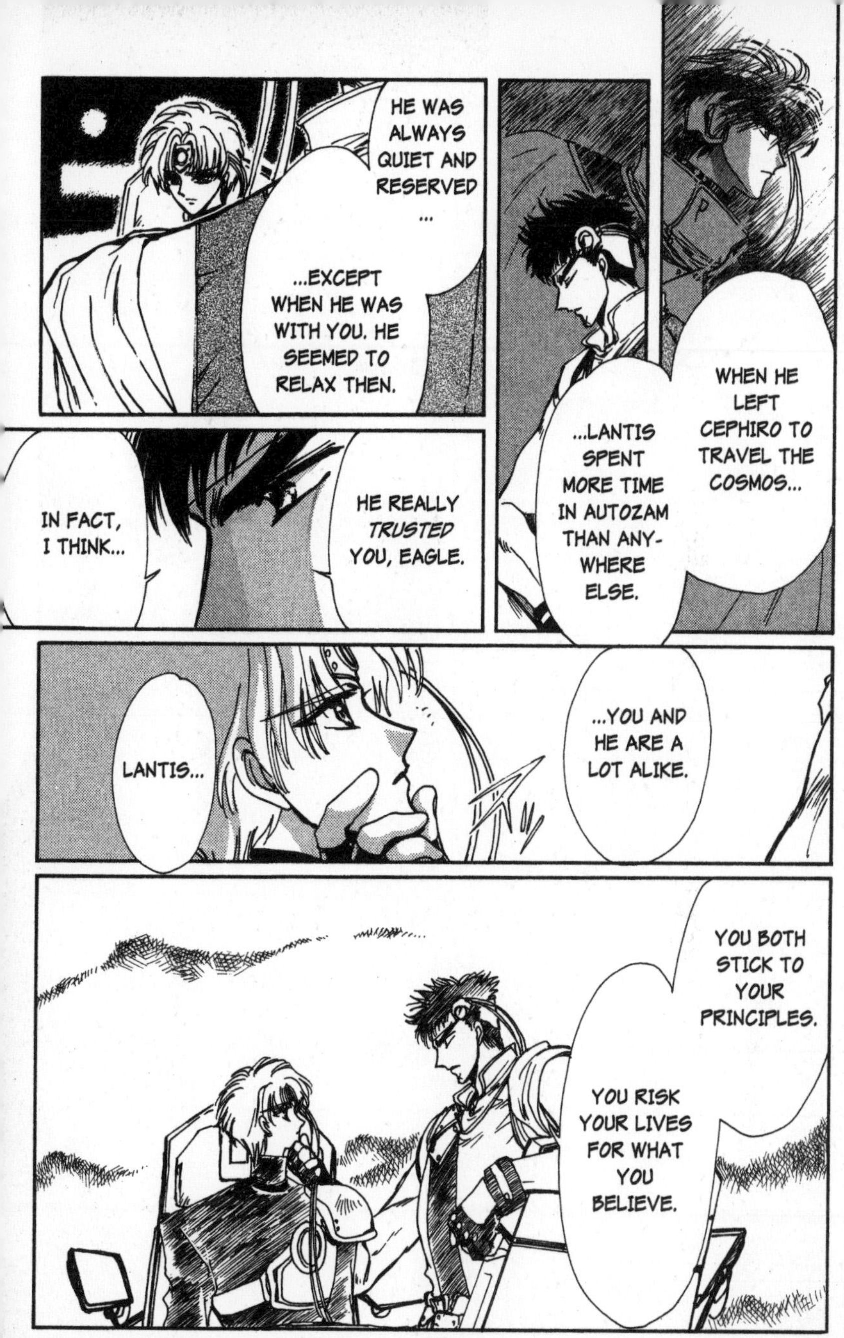
WHEN HE LEFT CEPHIRO TO TRAVEL THE COSMOS...
...LANTIS SPENT MORE TIME IN AUTOZAM THAN ANY-WHERE ELSE.
HE WAS ALWAYS QUIET AND RESERVED ...
...EXCEPT WHEN HE WAS WITH YOU. HE SEEMED TO RELAX THEN.
HE REALLY *TRUSTED* YOU, EAGLE.
IN FACT, I THINK...
...YOU AND HE ARE A LOT ALIKE.
LANTIS...
YOU BOTH STICK TO YOUR PRINCIPLES.
YOU RISK YOUR LIVES FOR WHAT YOU BELIEVE.

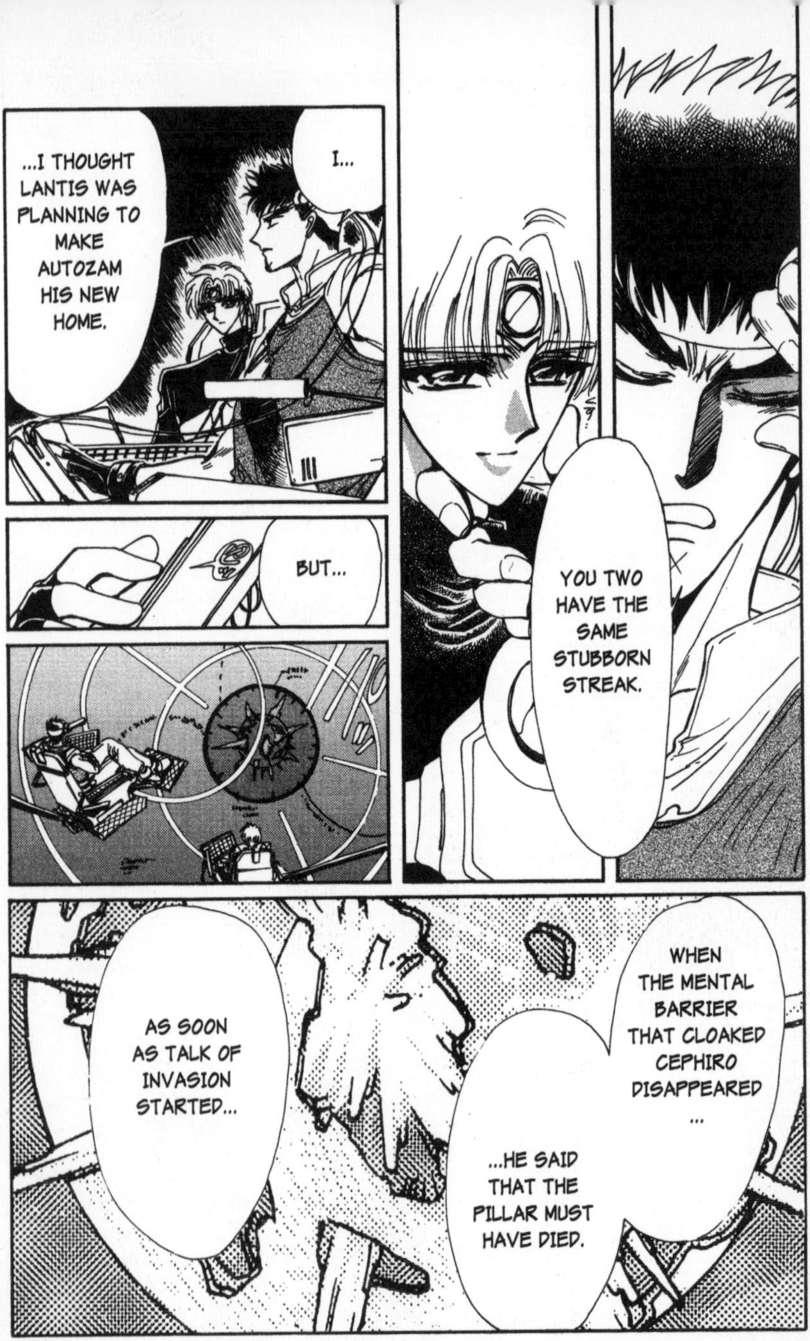
YOU TWO HAVE THE SAME STUBBORN STREAK.
I...
...I THOUGHT LANTIS WAS PLANNING TO MAKE AUTOZAM HIS NEW HOME.
BUT...
WHEN THE MENTAL BARRIER THAT CLOAKED CEPHIRO DISAPPEARED...
...HE SAID THAT THE PILLAR MUST HAVE DIED.
AS SOON AS TALK OF INVASION STARTED...

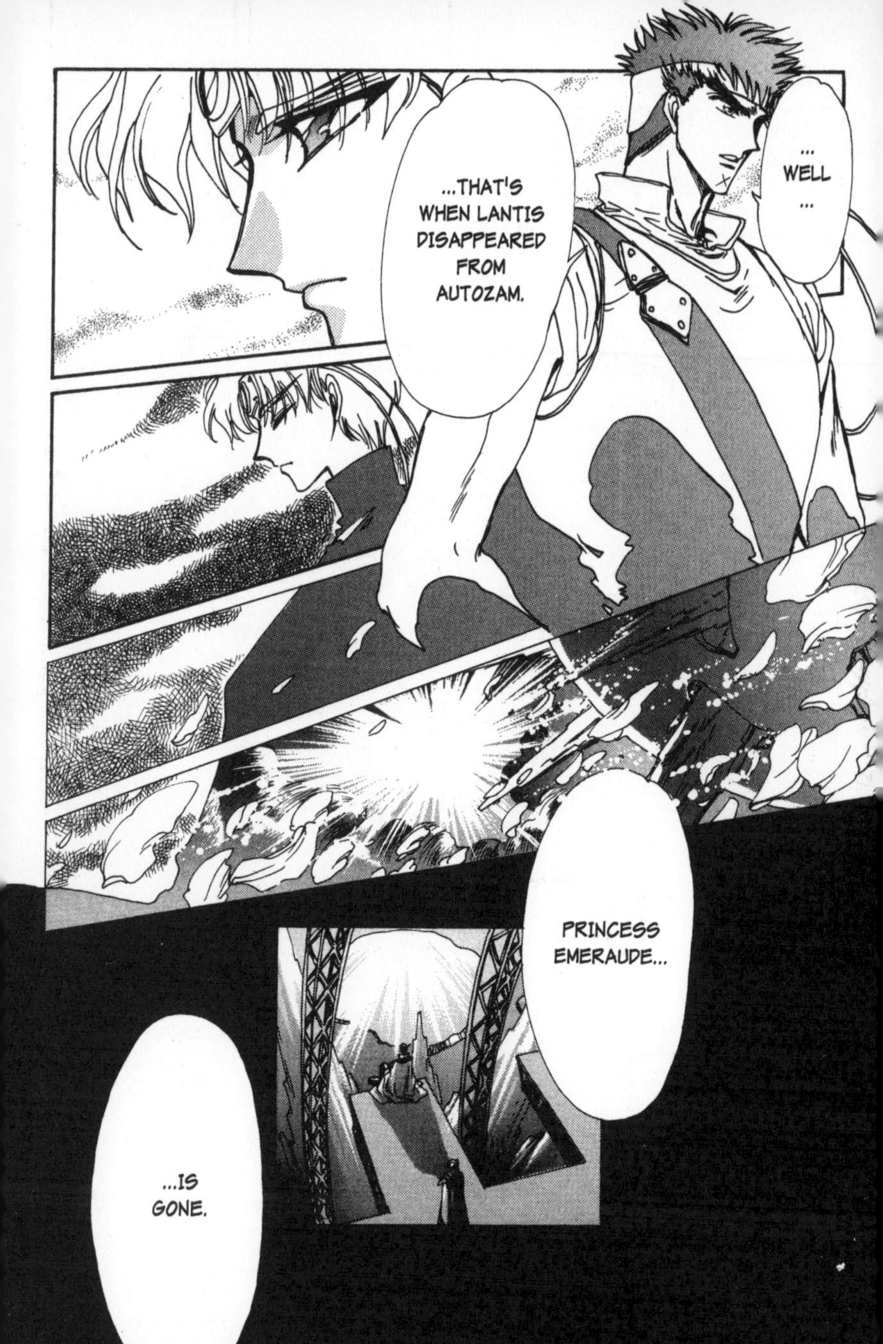
... WELL ...
...THAT'S WHEN LANTIS DISAPPEARED FROM AUTOZAM.
PRINCESS EMERAUDE...
...IS GONE.

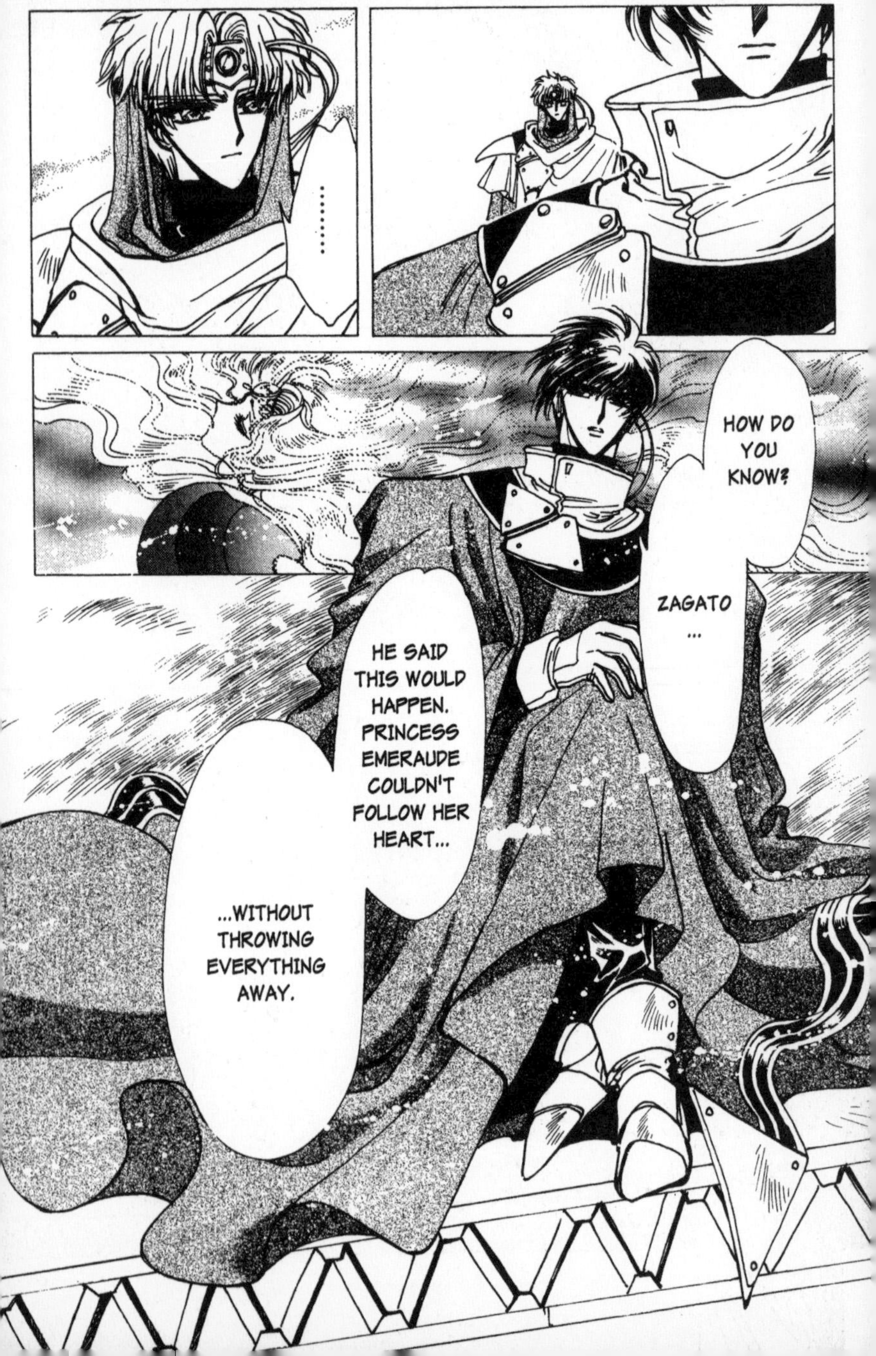
HOW DO YOU KNOW?
ZAGATO ...
HE SAID THIS WOULD HAPPEN. PRINCESS EMERAUDE COULDN'T FOLLOW HER HEART...
...WITHOUT THROWING EVERYTHING AWAY.

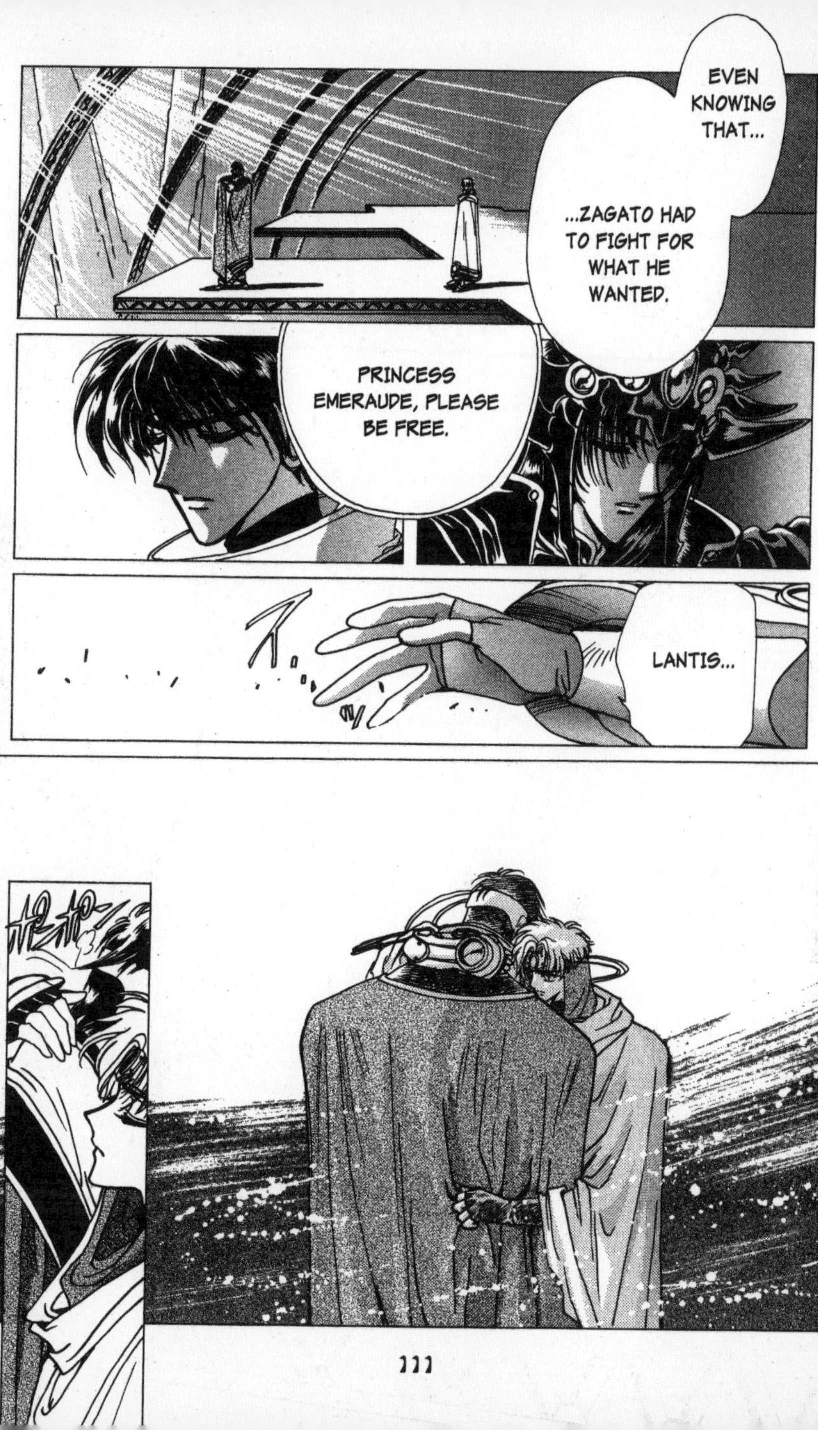
EVEN KNOWING THAT...
...ZAGATO HAD TO FIGHT FOR WHAT HE WANTED.
PRINCESS EMERAUDE, PLEASE BE FREE.
LANTIS...

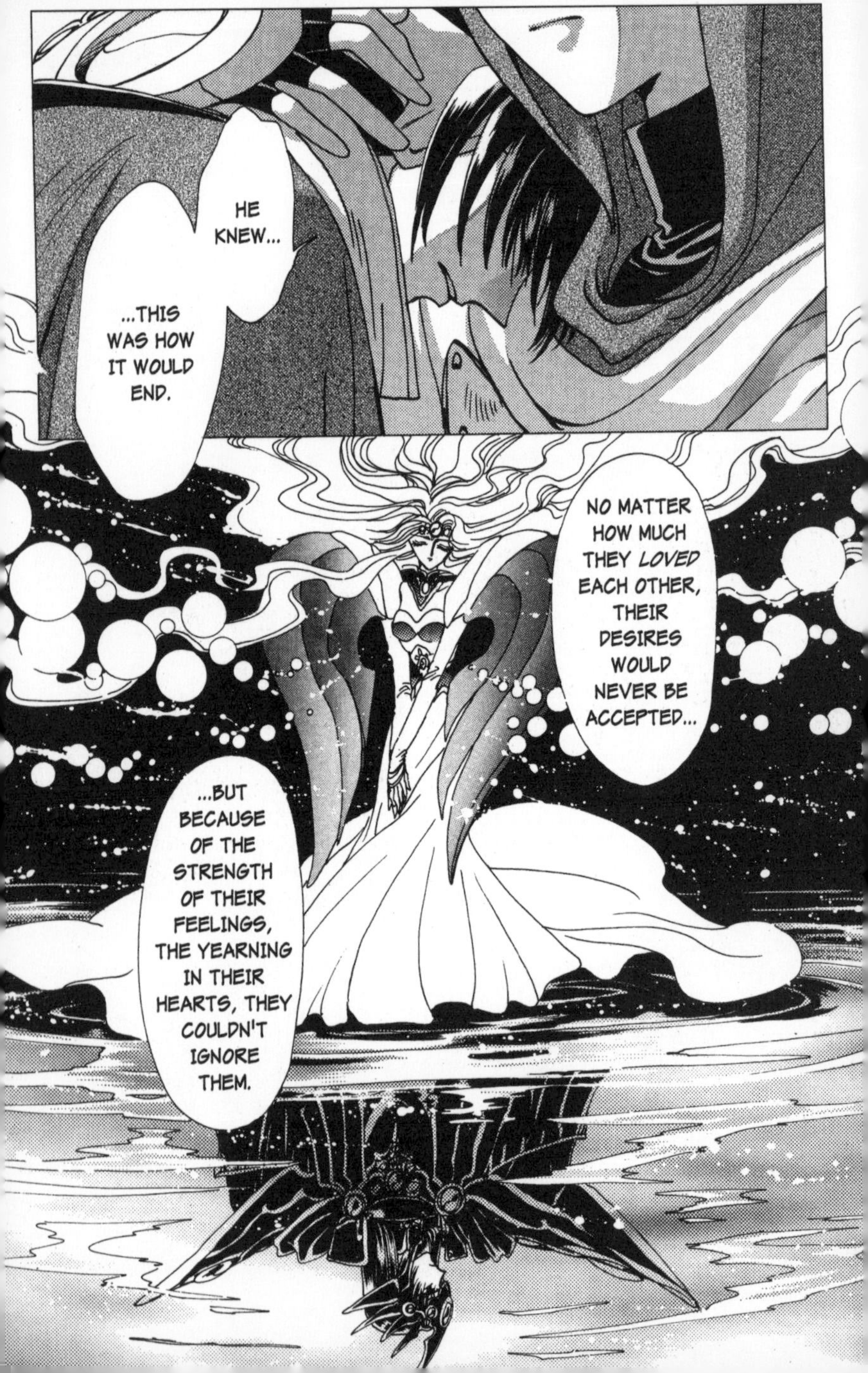
HE KNEW...
...THIS WAS HOW IT WOULD END.
NO MATTER HOW MUCH THEY *LOVED* EACH OTHER, THEIR DESIRES WOULD NEVER BE ACCEPTED...
...BUT BECAUSE OF THE STRENGTH OF THEIR FEELINGS, THE YEARNING IN THEIR HEARTS, THEY COULDN'T IGNORE THEM.

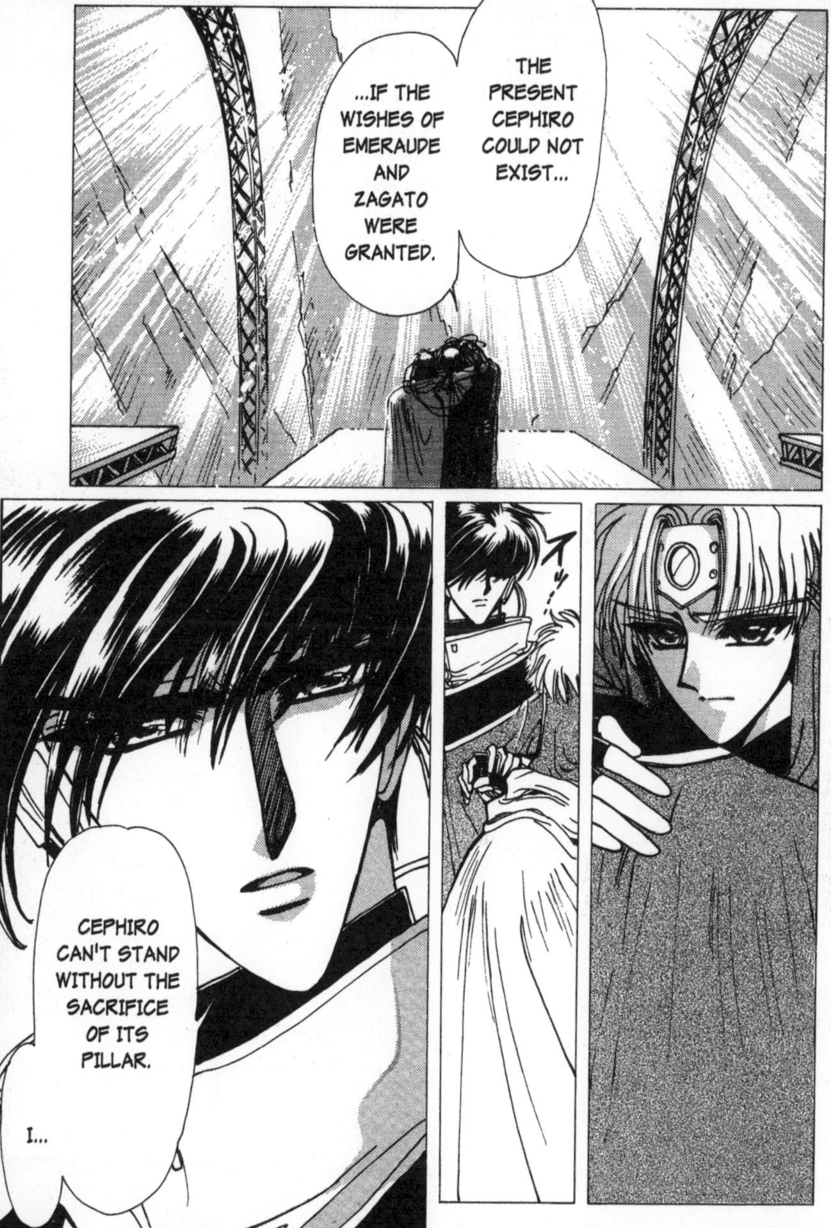
THE PRESENT CEPHIRO COULD NOT EXIST...
...IF THE WISHES OF EMERAUDE AND ZAGATO WERE GRANTED.
CEPHIRO CAN'T STAND WITHOUT THE SACRIFICE OF ITS PILLAR.
I...

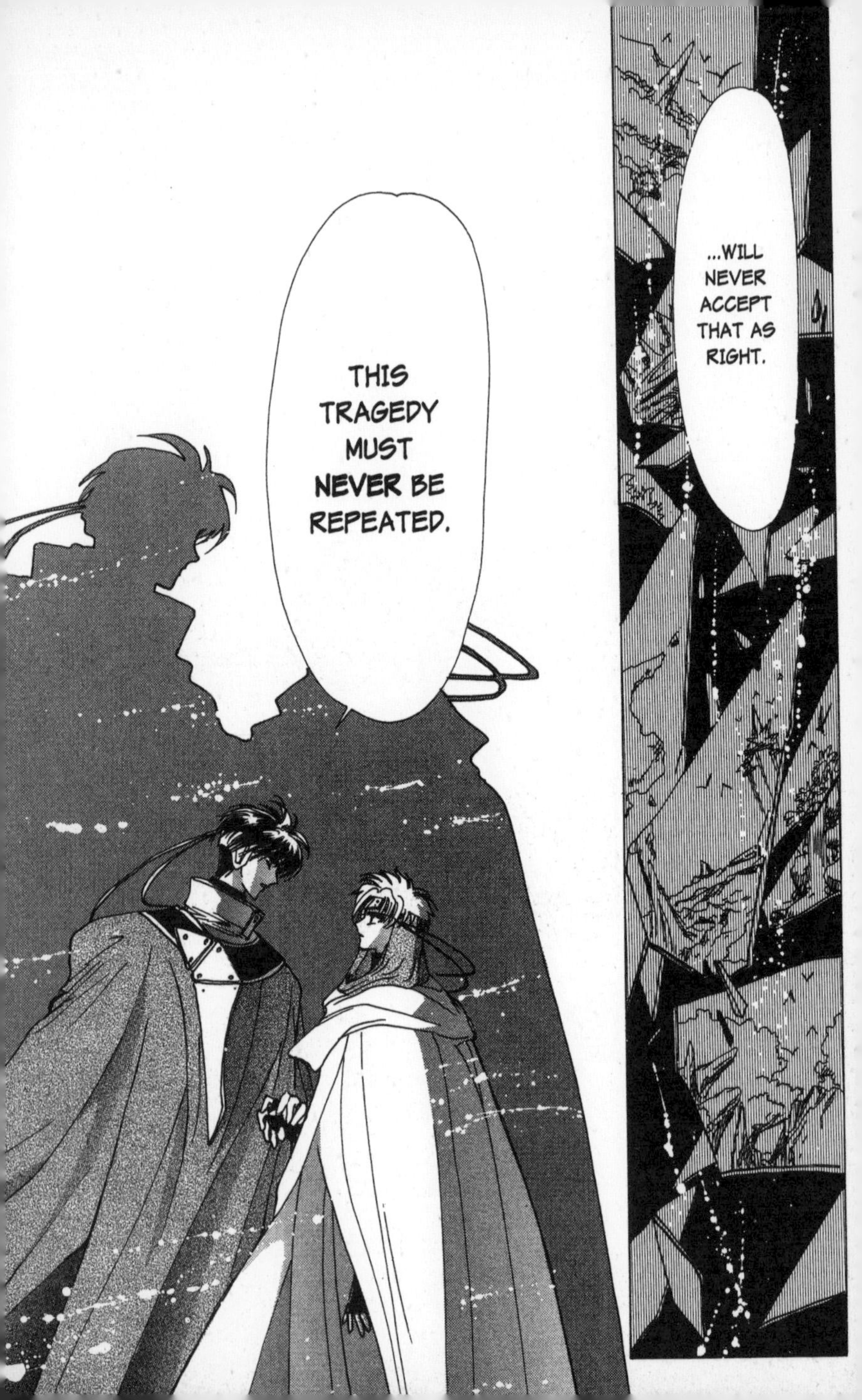
...WILL NEVER ACCEPT THAT AS RIGHT.
THIS TRAGEDY MUST **NEVER** BE REPEATED.

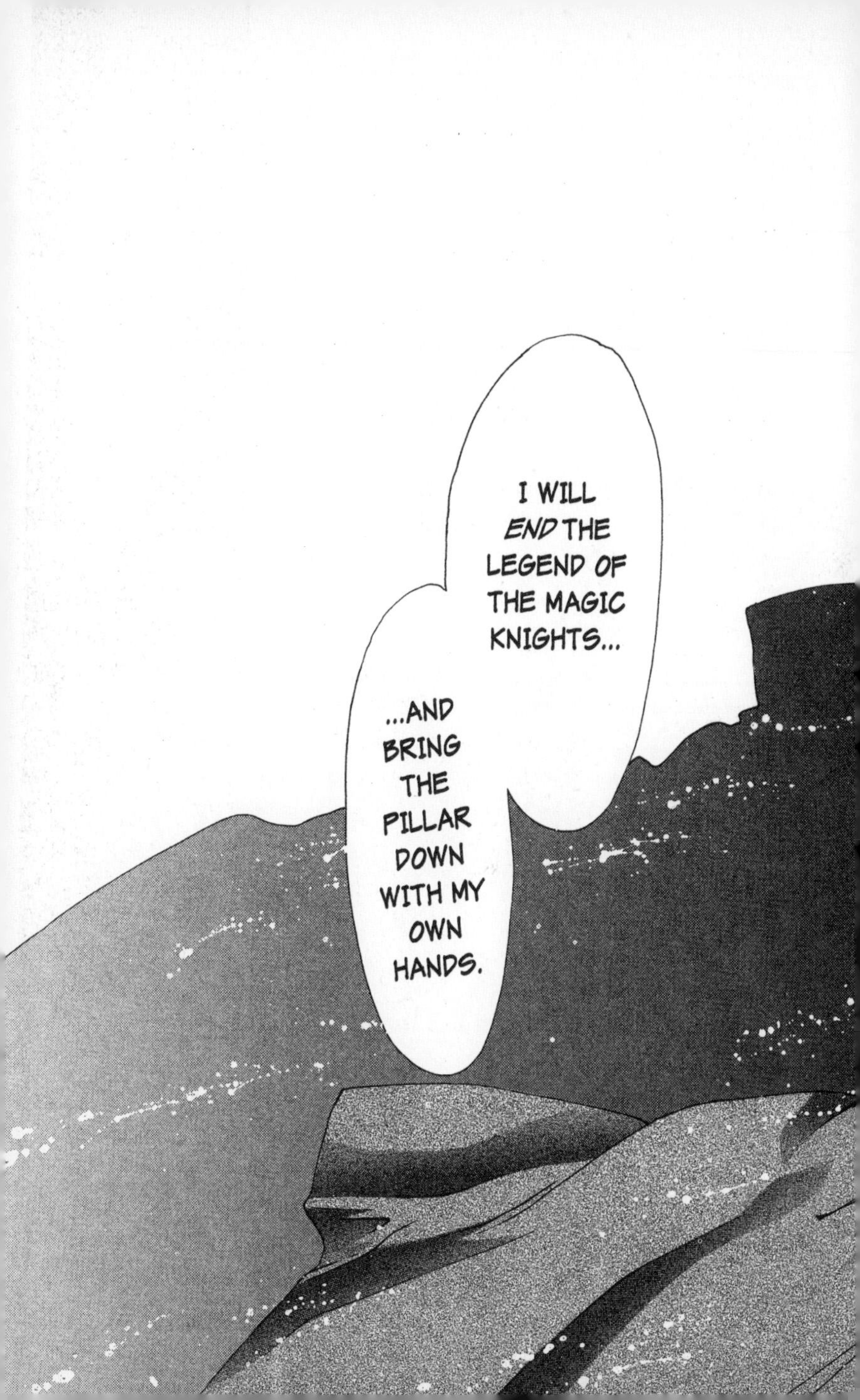
I WILL *END* THE LEGEND OF THE MAGIC KNIGHTS...
...AND BRING THE PILLAR DOWN WITH MY OWN HANDS.

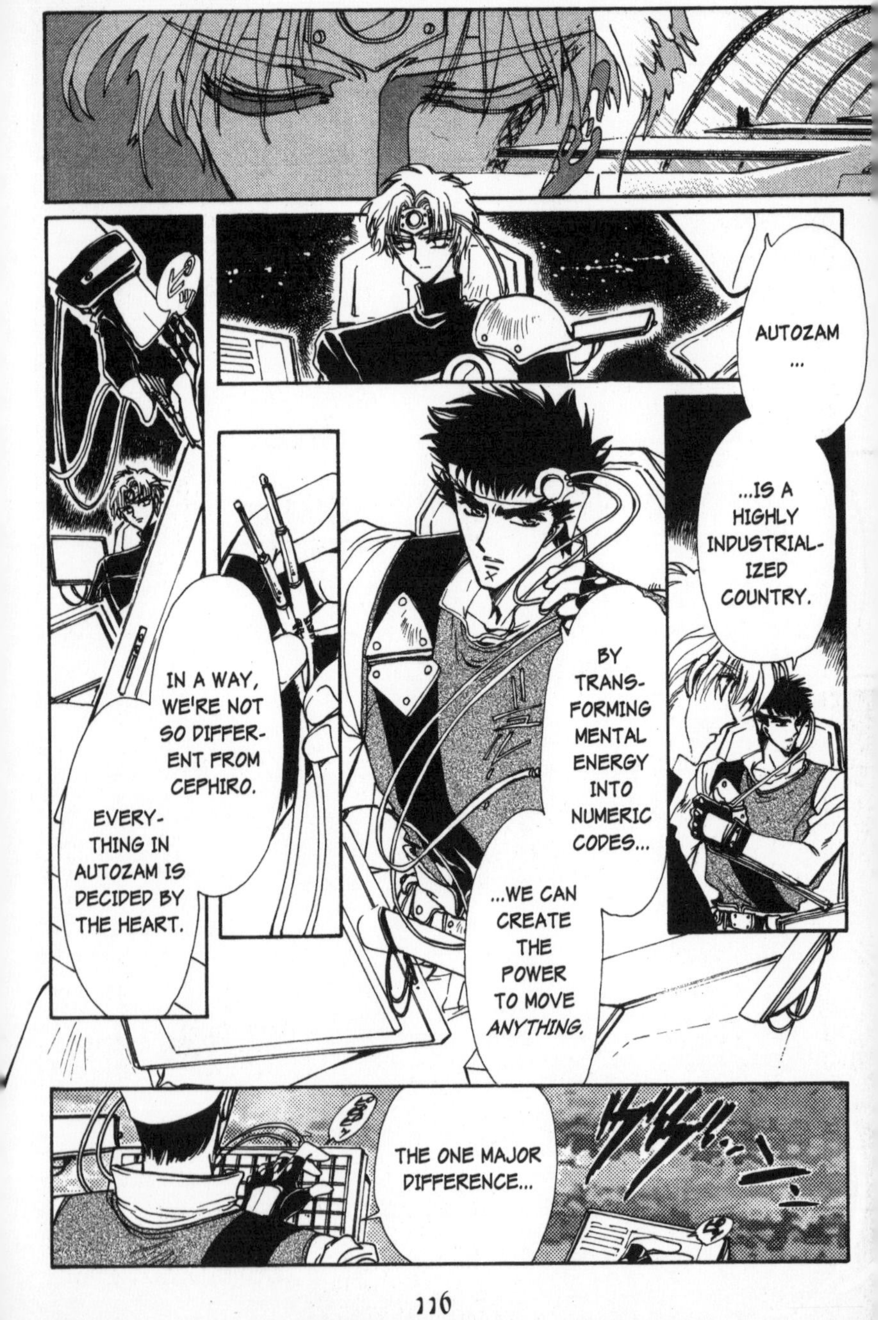
AUTOZAM ...
...IS A HIGHLY INDUSTRIAL-IZED COUNTRY.
BY TRANS-FORMING MENTAL ENERGY INTO NUMERIC CODES...
...WE CAN CREATE THE POWER TO MOVE *ANYTHING.*
IN A WAY, WE'RE NOT SO DIFFER-ENT FROM CEPHIRO.
EVERY-THING IN AUTOZAM IS DECIDED BY THE HEART.
THE ONE MAJOR DIFFERENCE...

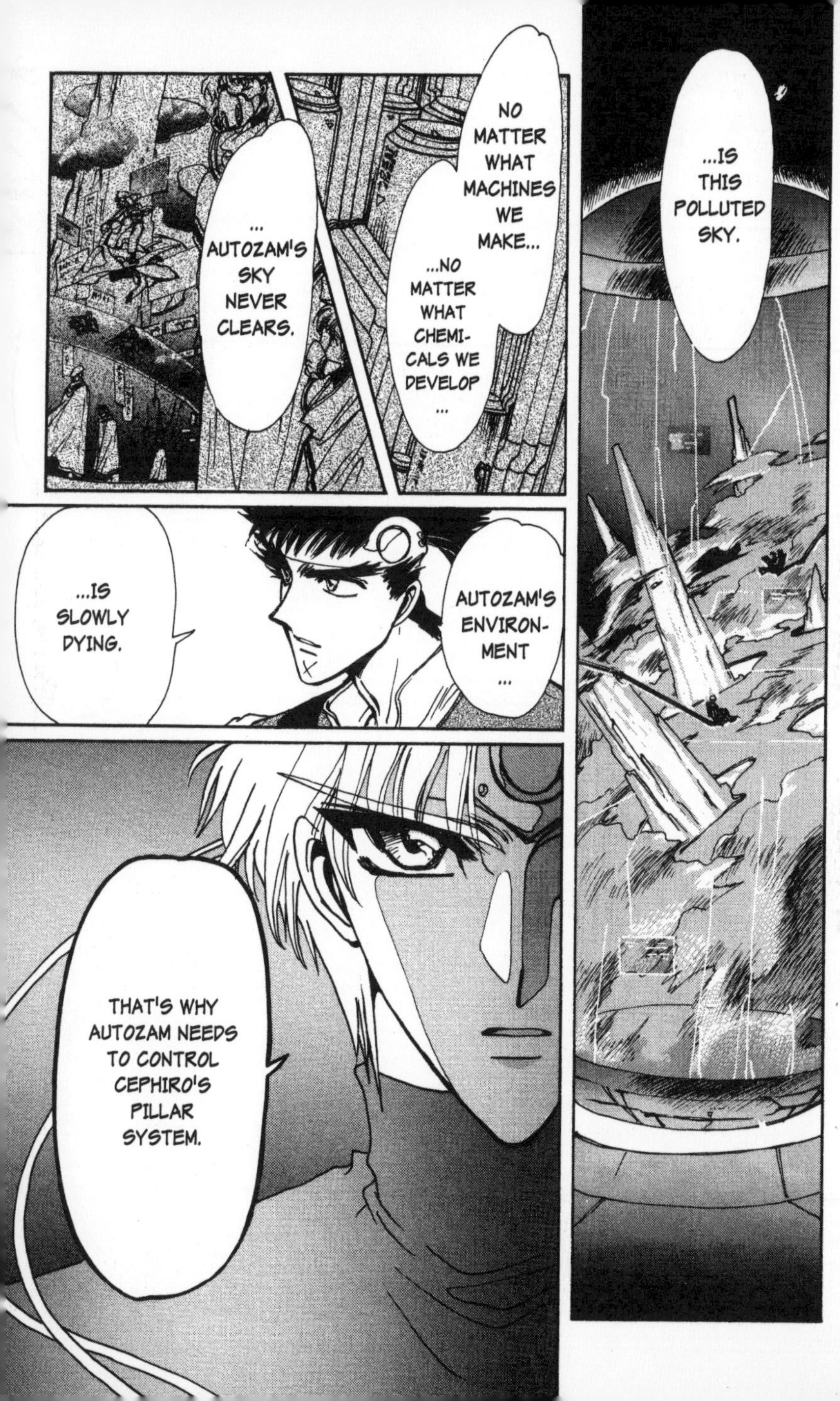
...IS THIS POLLUTED SKY.
NO MATTER WHAT MACHINES WE MAKE...
...NO MATTER WHAT CHEMICALS WE DEVELOP ...
... AUTOZAM'S SKY NEVER CLEARS.
AUTOZAM'S ENVIRONMENT ...
...IS SLOWLY DYING.
THAT'S WHY AUTOZAM NEEDS TO CONTROL CEPHIRO'S PILLAR SYSTEM.

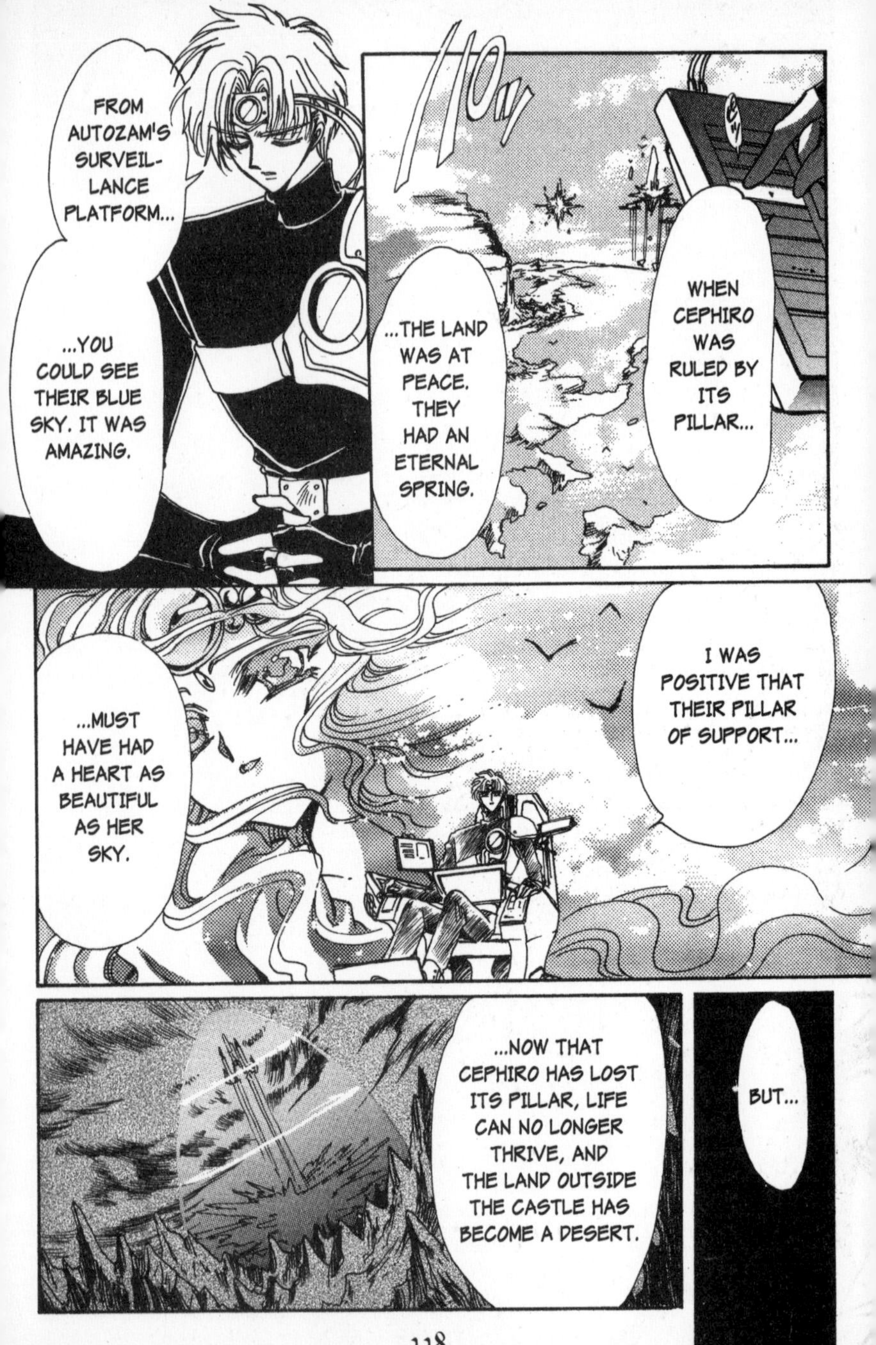
WHEN CEPHIRO WAS RULED BY ITS PILLAR...
...THE LAND WAS AT PEACE. THEY HAD AN ETERNAL SPRING.
FROM AUTOZAM'S SURVEIL-LANCE PLATFORM...
...YOU COULD SEE THEIR BLUE SKY. IT WAS AMAZING.
I WAS POSITIVE THAT THEIR PILLAR OF SUPPORT...
...MUST HAVE HAD A HEART AS BEAUTIFUL AS HER SKY.
BUT...
...NOW THAT CEPHIRO HAS LOST ITS PILLAR, LIFE CAN NO LONGER THRIVE, AND THE LAND OUTSIDE THE CASTLE HAS BECOME A DESERT.

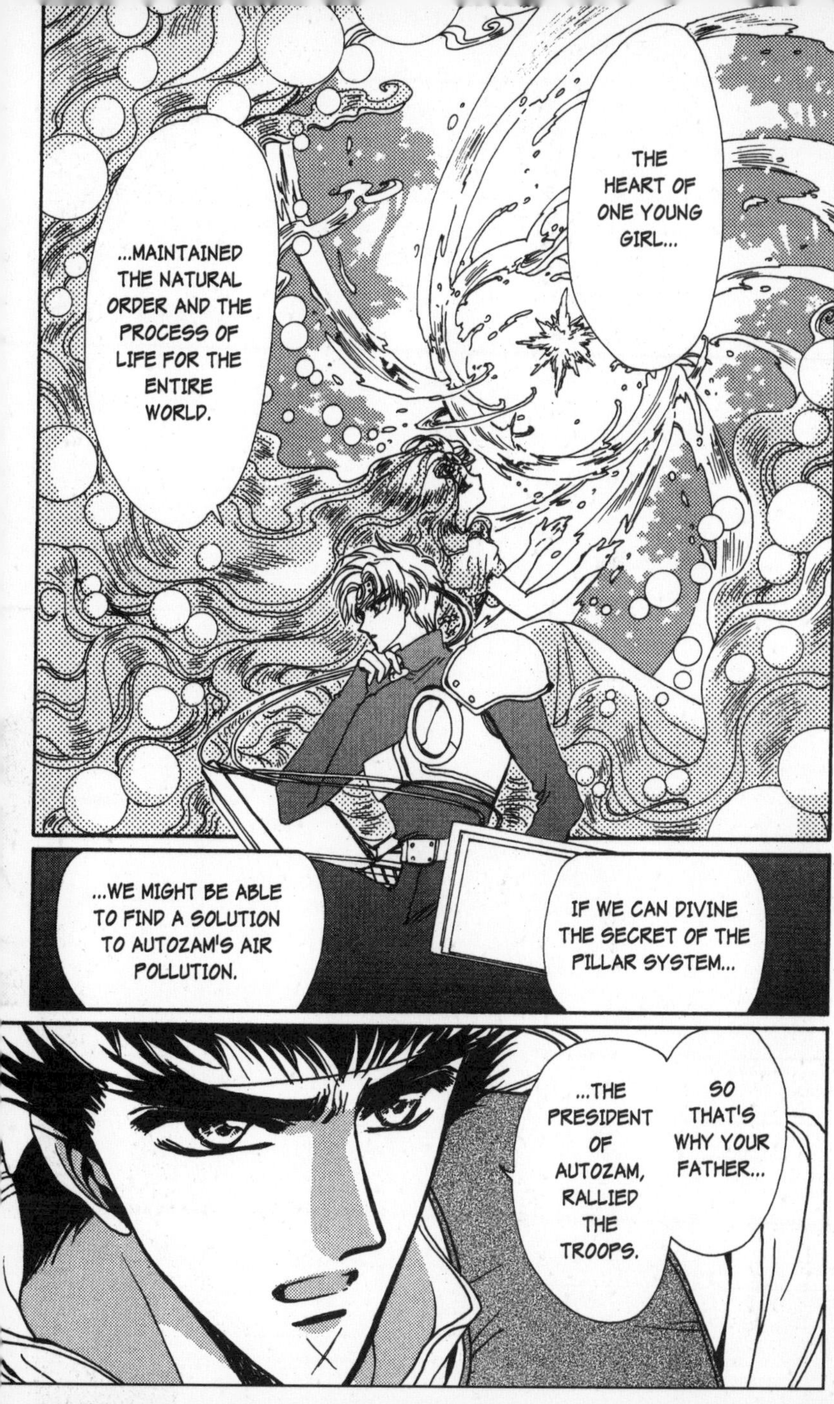
THE HEART OF ONE YOUNG GIRL...
...MAINTAINED THE NATURAL ORDER AND THE PROCESS OF LIFE FOR THE ENTIRE WORLD.
IF WE CAN DIVINE THE SECRET OF THE PILLAR SYSTEM...
...WE MIGHT BE ABLE TO FIND A SOLUTION TO AUTOZAM'S AIR POLLUTION.
SO THAT'S WHY YOUR FATHER...
...THE PRESIDENT OF AUTOZAM, RALLIED THE TROOPS.

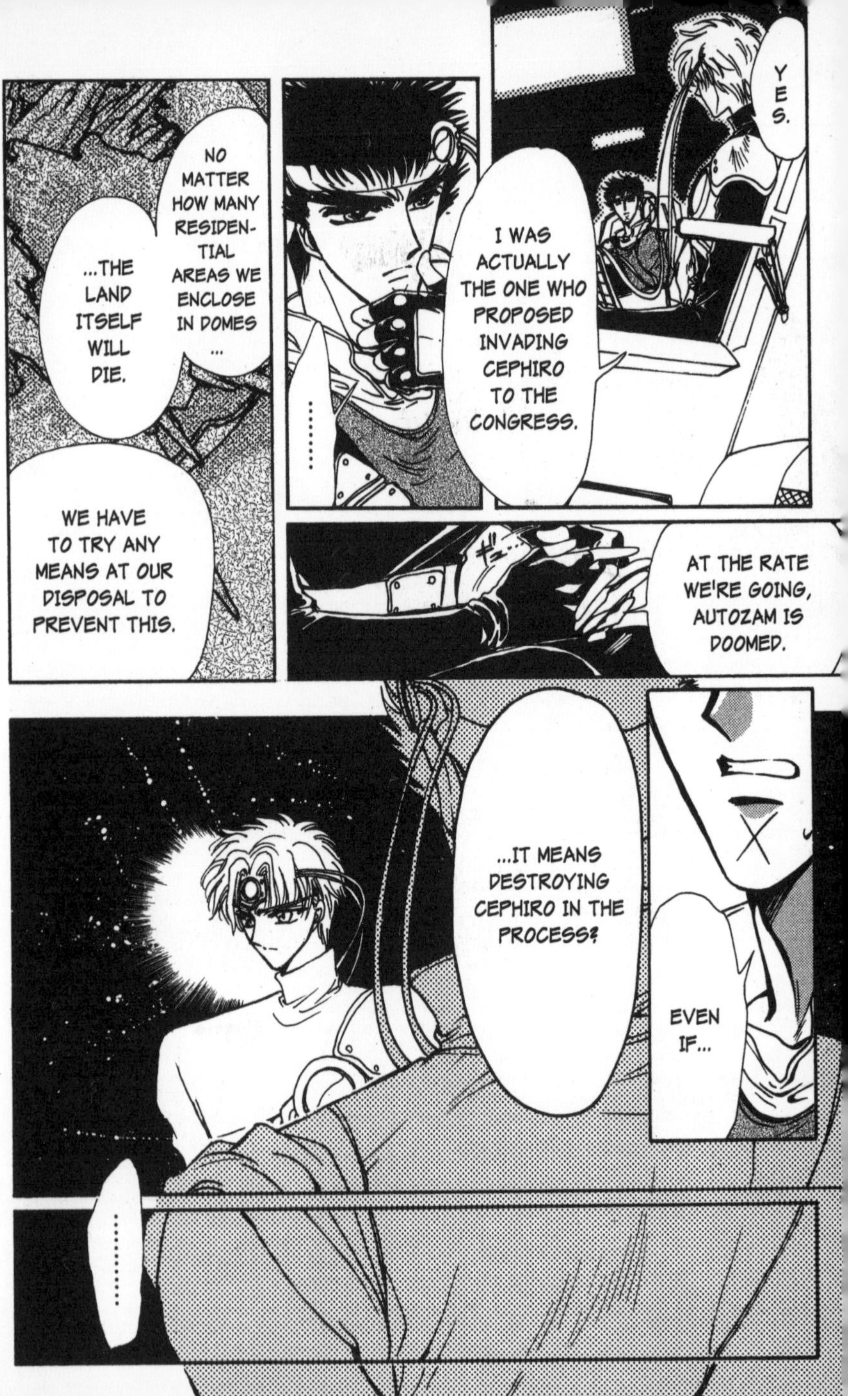
YES.
I WAS ACTUALLY THE ONE WHO PROPOSED INVADING CEPHIRO TO THE CONGRESS.
......
AT THE RATE WE'RE GOING, AUTOZAM IS DOOMED.
NO MATTER HOW MANY RESIDEN-TIAL AREAS WE ENCLOSE IN DOMES...
...THE LAND ITSELF WILL DIE.
WE HAVE TO TRY ANY MEANS AT OUR DISPOSAL TO PREVENT THIS.
EVEN IF...
...IT MEANS DESTROYING CEPHIRO IN THE PROCESS?
......

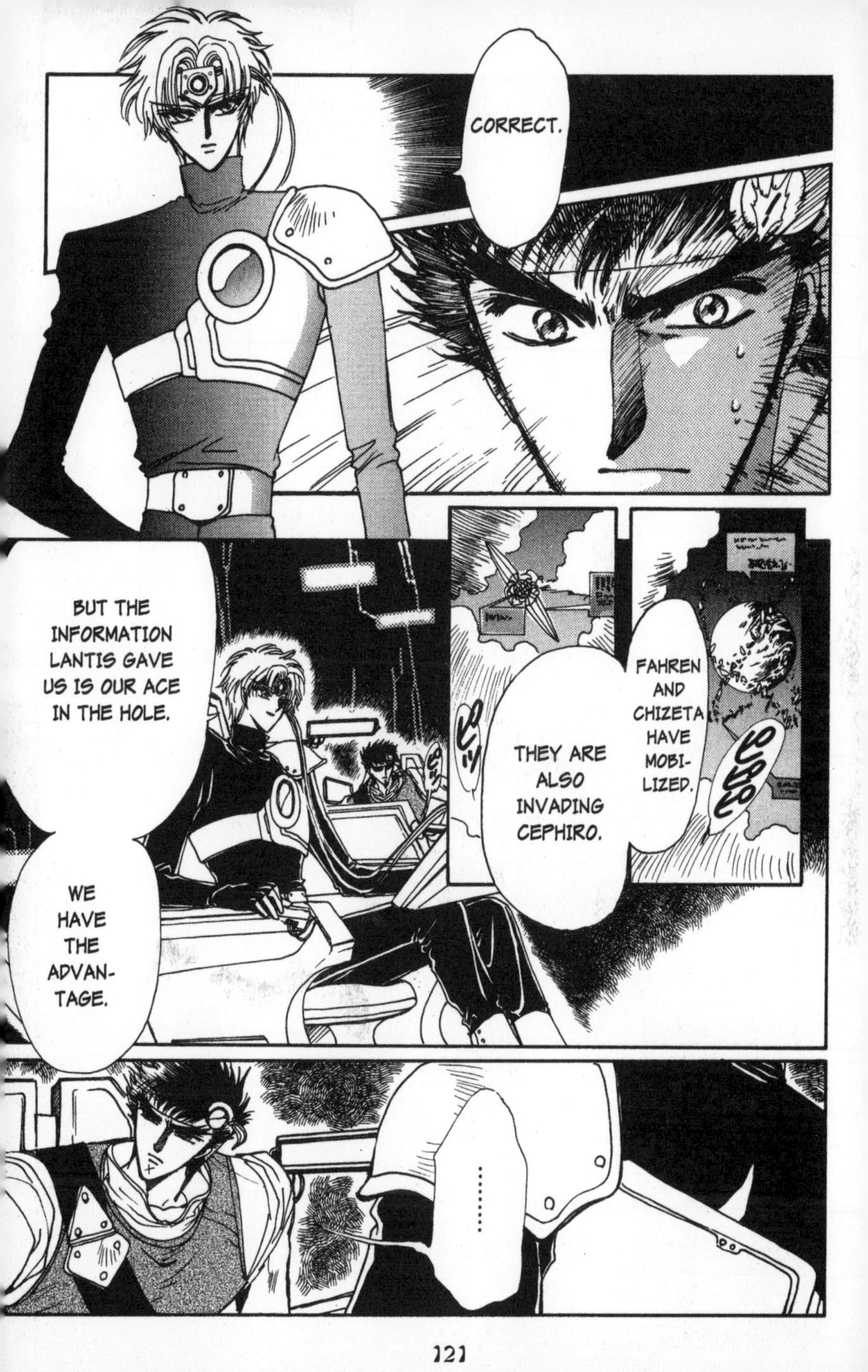
CORRECT.
FAHREN AND CHIZETA HAVE MOBI-LIZED.
THEY ARE ALSO INVADING CEPHIRO.
BUT THE INFORMATION LANTIS GAVE US IS OUR ACE IN THE HOLE.
WE HAVE THE ADVAN-TAGE.
......

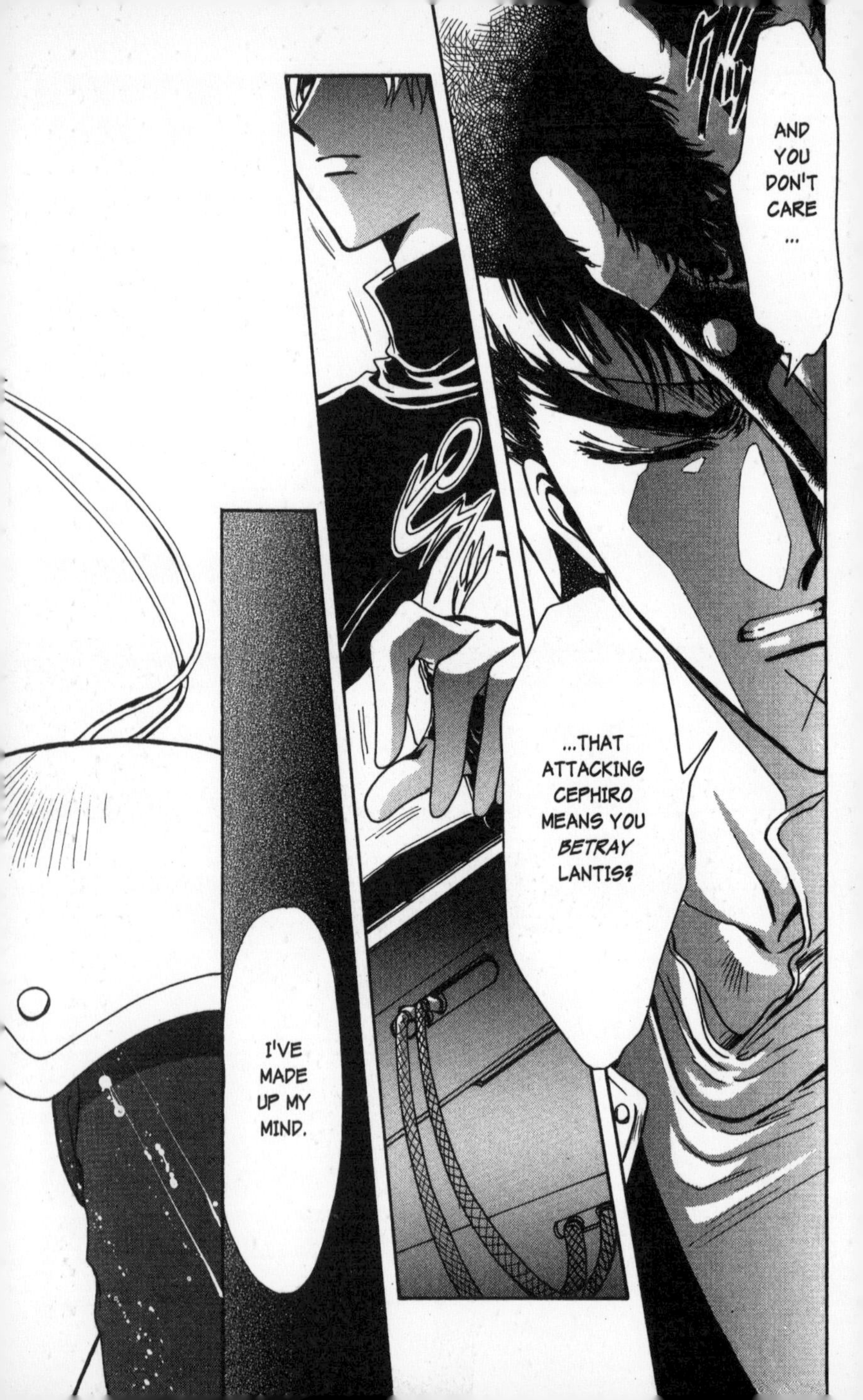
AND YOU DON'T CARE ...
...THAT ATTACKING CEPHIRO MEANS YOU *BETRAY* LANTIS?
I'VE MADE UP MY MIND.

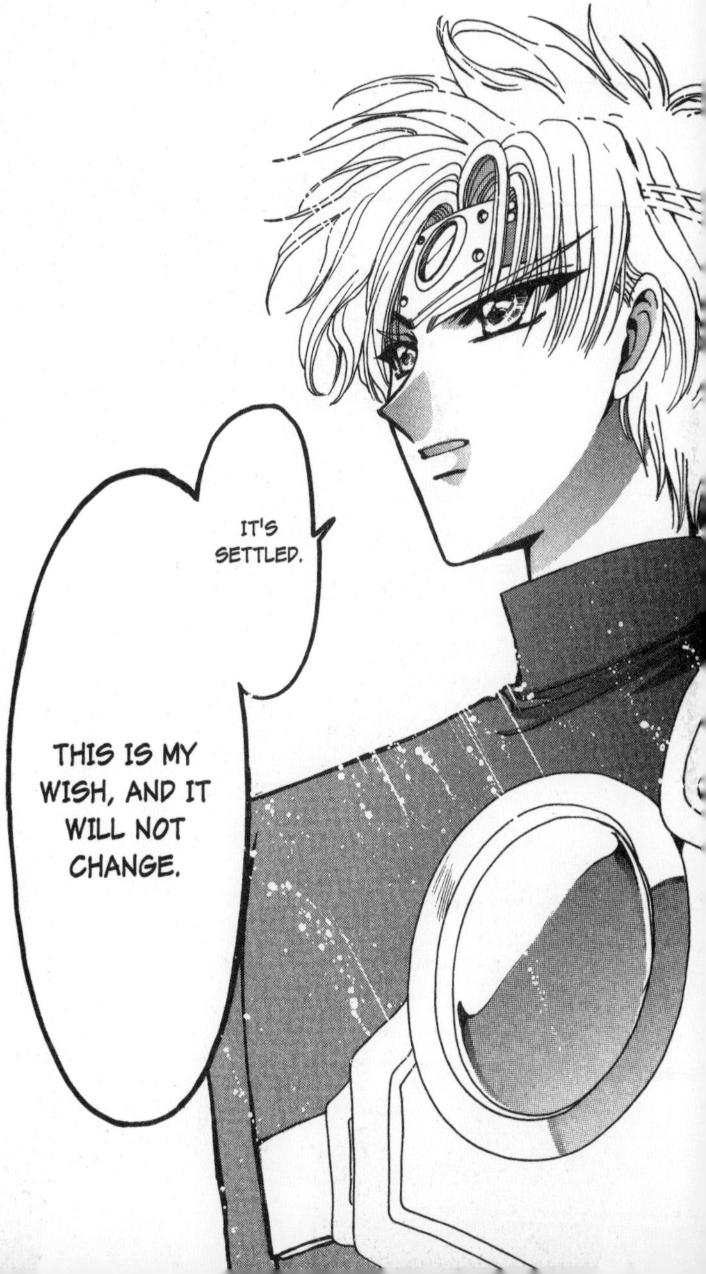
IT'S SETTLED.
THIS IS MY WISH, AND IT WILL NOT CHANGE.

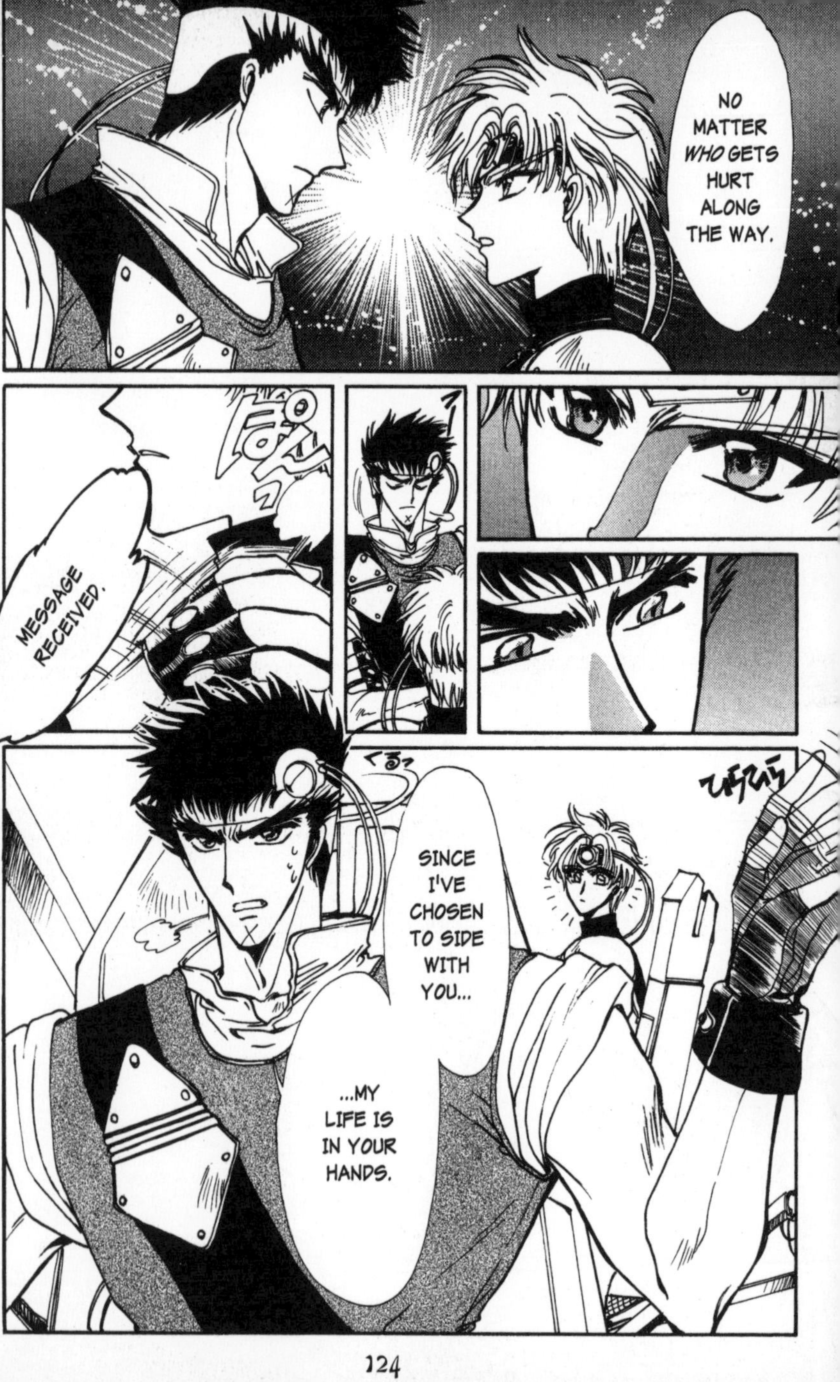
NO MATTER *WHO* GETS HURT ALONG THE WAY.
MESSAGE RECEIVED.
ひらひら
くるっ
SINCE I'VE CHOSEN TO SIDE WITH YOU...
...MY LIFE IS IN YOUR HANDS.

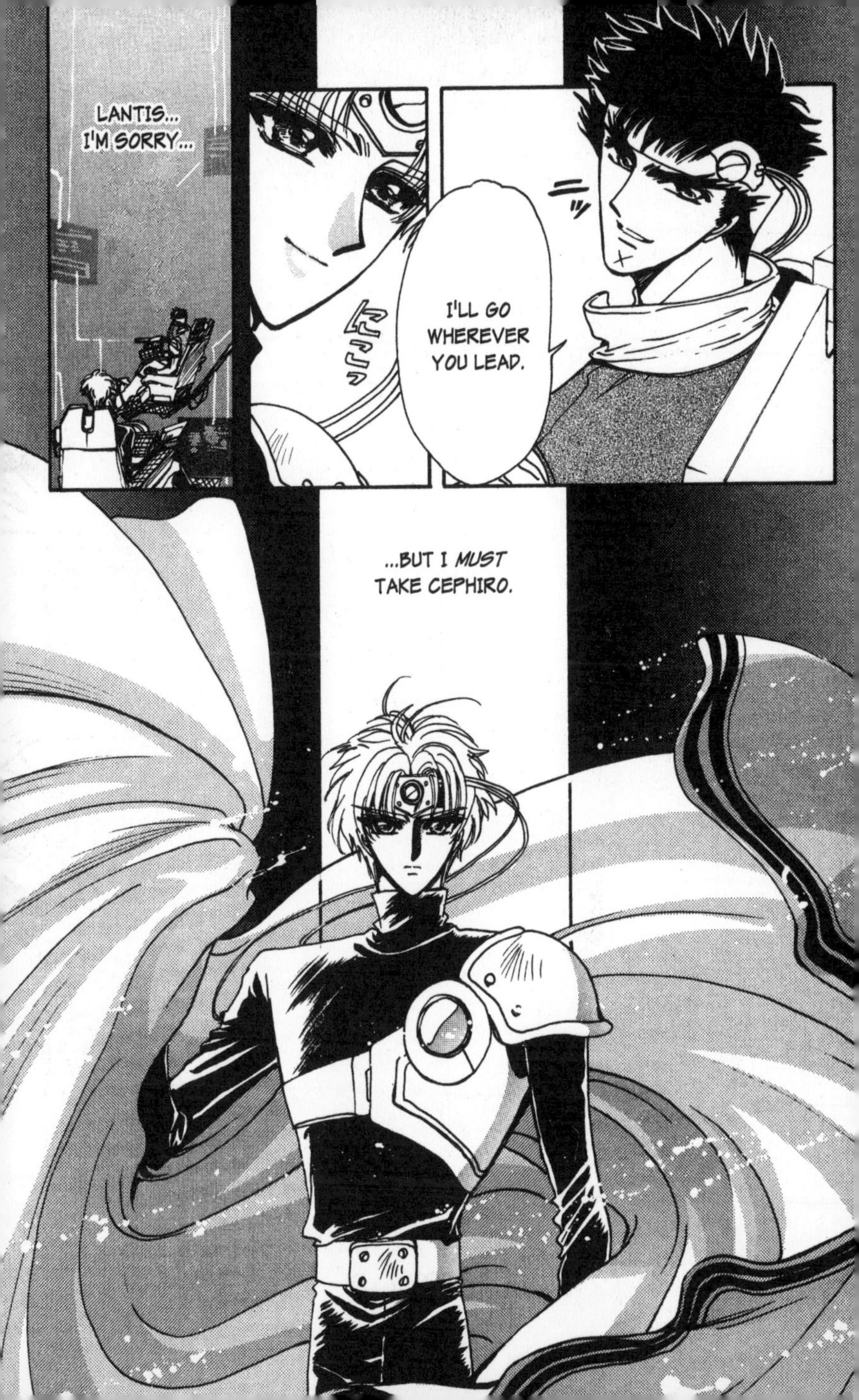
I'LL GO WHEREVER YOU LEAD.
LANTIS... I'M SORRY...
...BUT I MUST TAKE CEPHIRO.

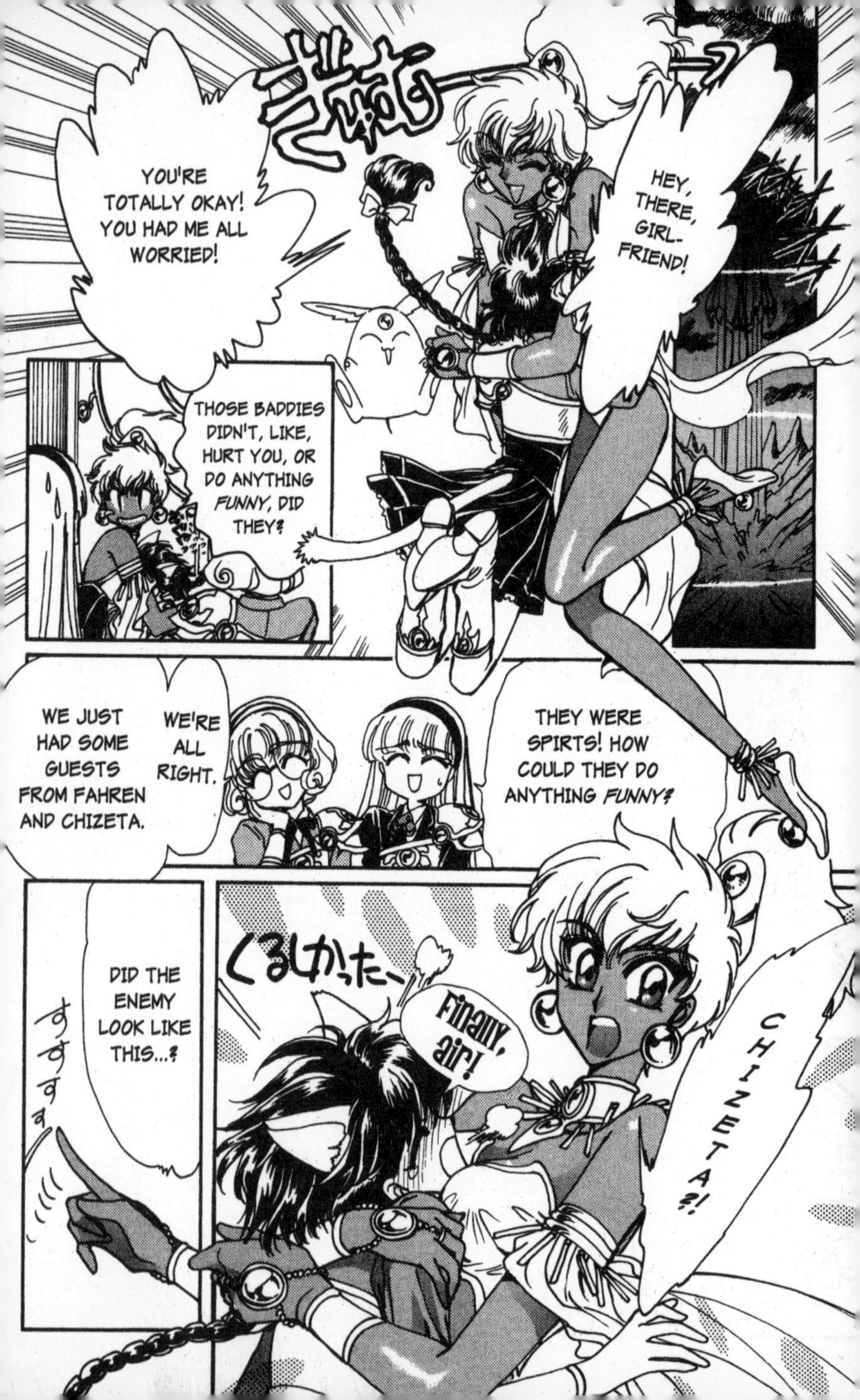
HEY, THERE, GIRL-FRIEND!
YOU'RE TOTALLY OKAY! YOU HAD ME ALL WORRIED!
THOSE BADDIES DIDN'T, LIKE, HURT YOU, OR DO ANYTHING *FUNNY*, DID THEY?
THEY WERE SPIRTS! HOW COULD THEY DO ANYTHING *FUNNY*?
WE'RE ALL RIGHT.
WE JUST HAD SOME GUESTS FROM FAHREN AND CHIZETA.
CHIZETA?!
くるしかったー
Finally, air!
DID THE ENEMY LOOK LIKE THIS...?
すすすす

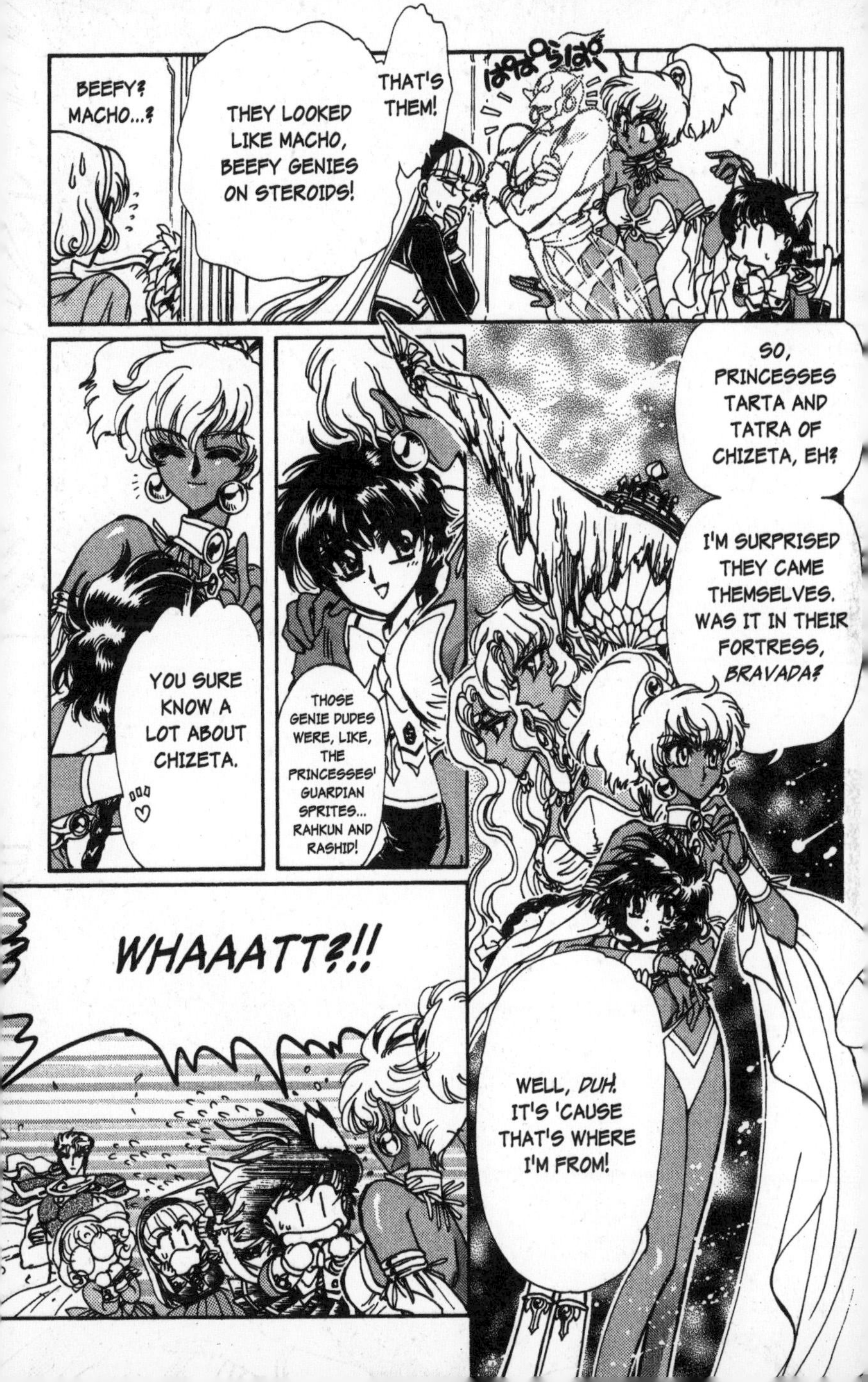
ぱぱぱらぱ
THEY LOOKED LIKE MACHO, BEEFY GENIES ON STEROIDS!
THAT'S THEM!
BEEFY? MACHO...?
SO, PRINCESSES TARTA AND TATRA OF CHIZETA, EH?
I'M SURPRISED THEY CAME THEMSELVES. WAS IT IN THEIR FORTRESS, *BRAVADA*?
THOSE GENIE DUDES WERE, LIKE, THE PRINCESSES' GUARDIAN SPRITES... RAHKUN AND RASHID!
YOU SURE KNOW A LOT ABOUT CHIZETA.
WELL, *DUH*. IT'S 'CAUSE THAT'S WHERE I'M FROM!
WHAAATT?!!

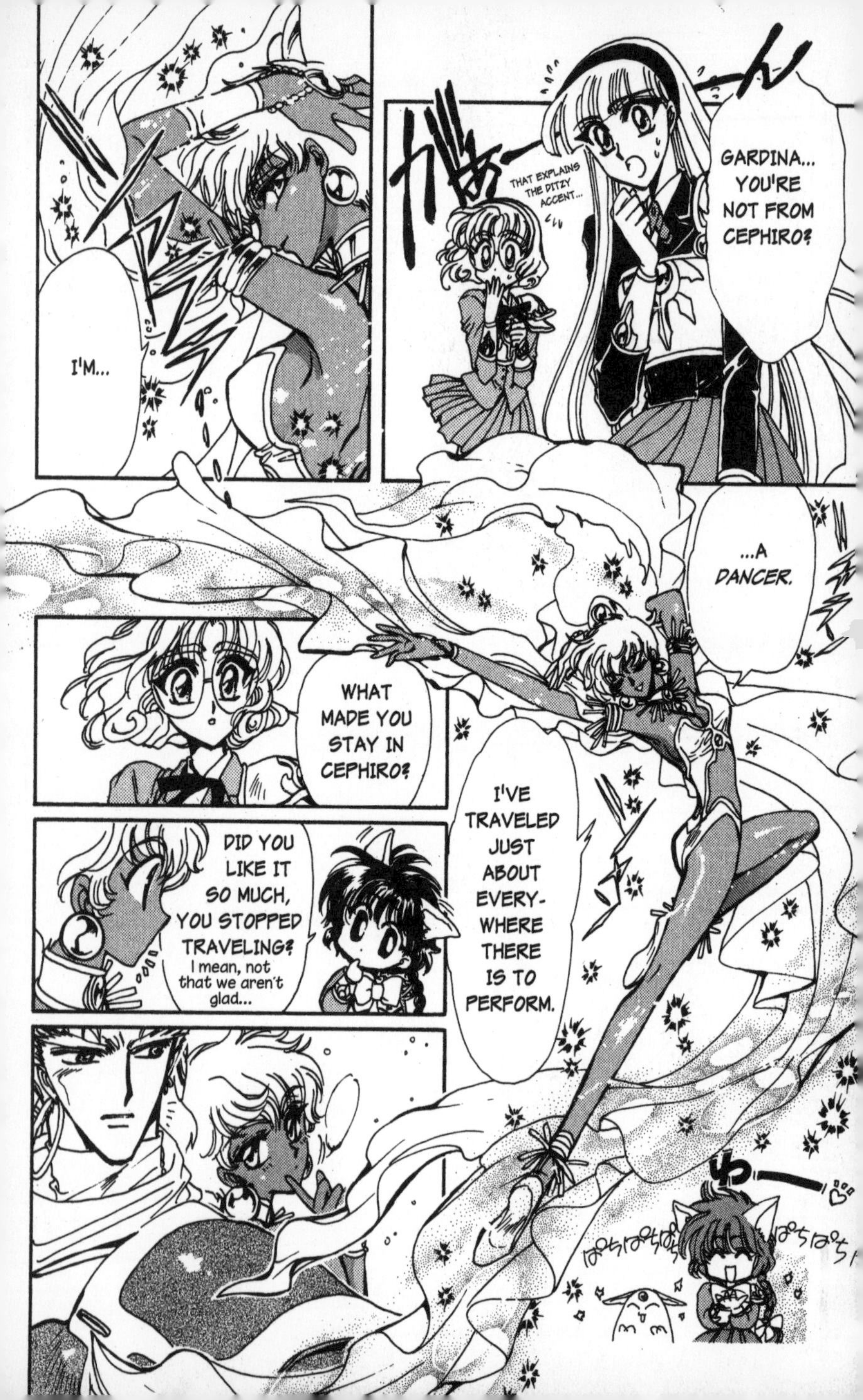
GARDINA... YOU'RE NOT FROM CEPHIRO?
THAT EXPLAINS THE DITZY ACCENT...
I'M...
...A DANCER.
I'VE TRAVELED JUST ABOUT EVERY-WHERE THERE IS TO PERFORM.
WHAT MADE YOU STAY IN CEPHIRO?
DID YOU LIKE IT SO MUCH, YOU STOPPED TRAVELING?
I mean, not that we aren't glad...
ぱちぱちぱち
ぱちぱち

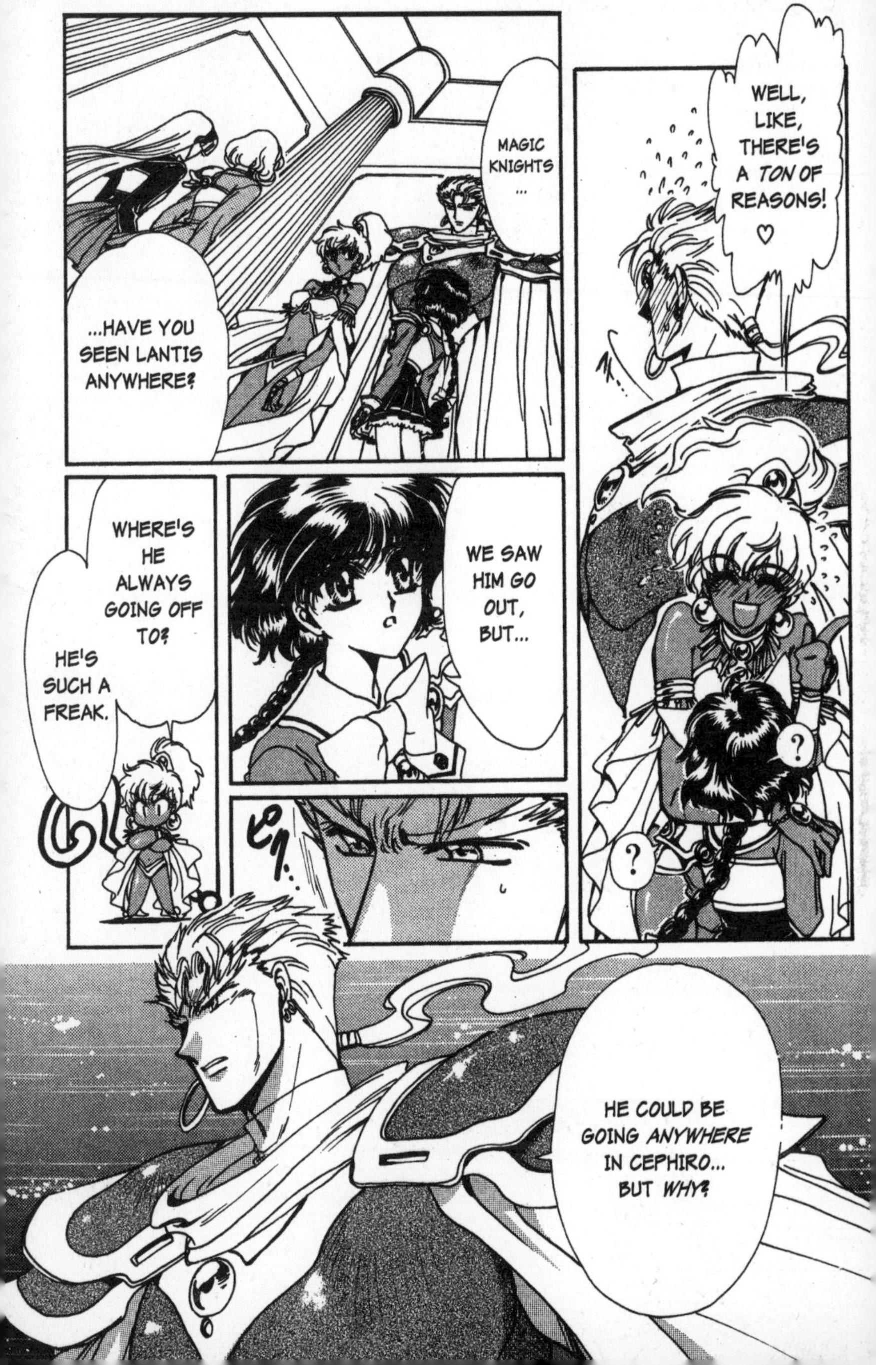
MAGIC KNIGHTS ...
...HAVE YOU SEEN LANTIS ANYWHERE?
WE SAW HIM GO OUT, BUT...
WHERE'S HE ALWAYS GOING OFF TO?
HE'S SUCH A FREAK.
WELL, LIKE, THERE'S A *TON* OF REASONS! ♥
?
?
HE COULD BE GOING *ANYWHERE* IN CEPHIRO... BUT *WHY*?

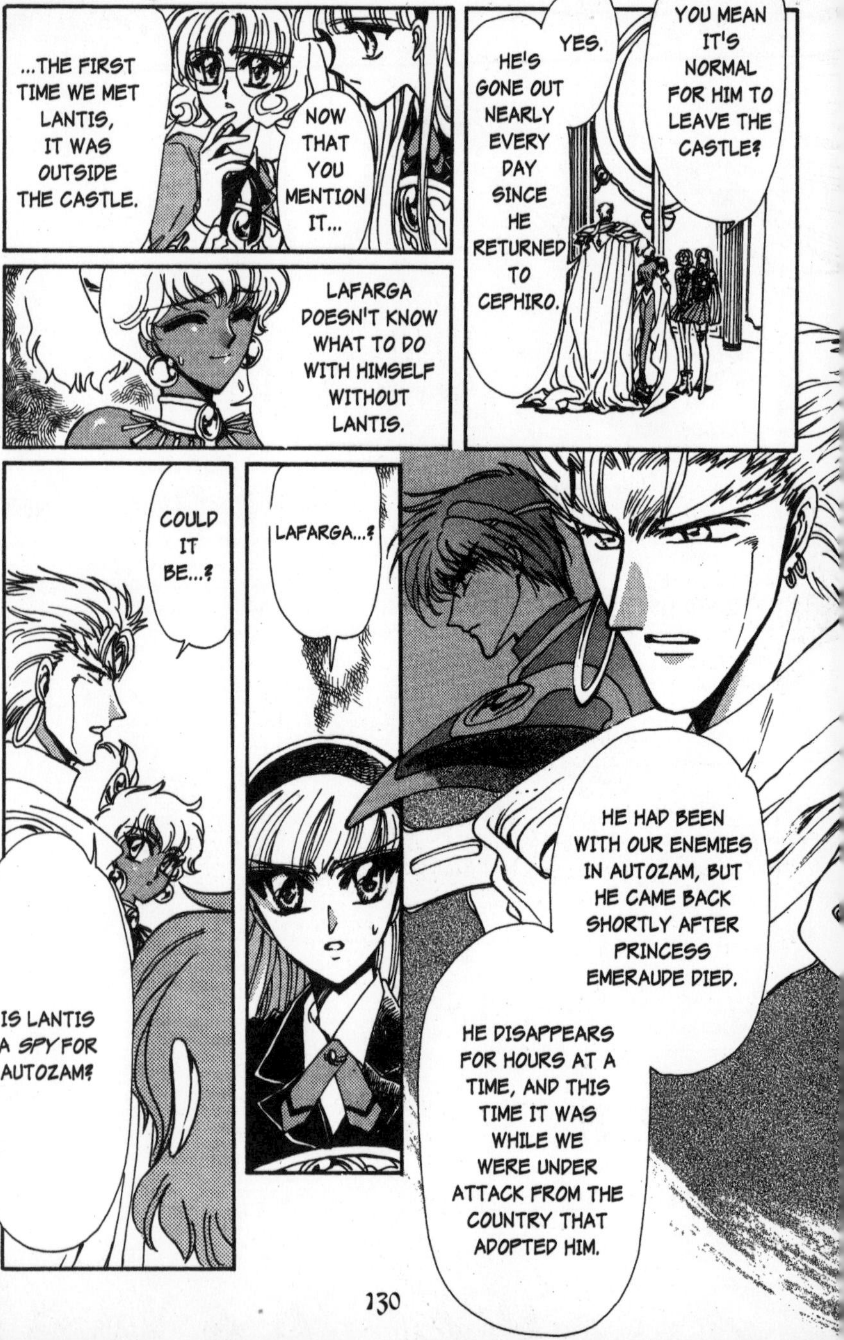
YOU MEAN IT'S NORMAL FOR HIM TO LEAVE THE CASTLE?
YES. HE'S GONE OUT NEARLY EVERY DAY SINCE HE RETURNED TO CEPHIRO.
NOW THAT YOU MENTION IT...
...THE FIRST TIME WE MET LANTIS, IT WAS OUTSIDE THE CASTLE.
LAFARGA DOESN'T KNOW WHAT TO DO WITH HIMSELF WITHOUT LANTIS.
HE HAD BEEN WITH OUR ENEMIES IN AUTOZAM, BUT HE CAME BACK SHORTLY AFTER PRINCESS EMERAUDE DIED.
HE DISAPPEARS FOR HOURS AT A TIME, AND THIS TIME IT WAS WHILE WE WERE UNDER ATTACK FROM THE COUNTRY THAT ADOPTED HIM.
LAFARGA...?
COULD IT BE...?
IS LANTIS A *SPY* FOR AUTOZAM?

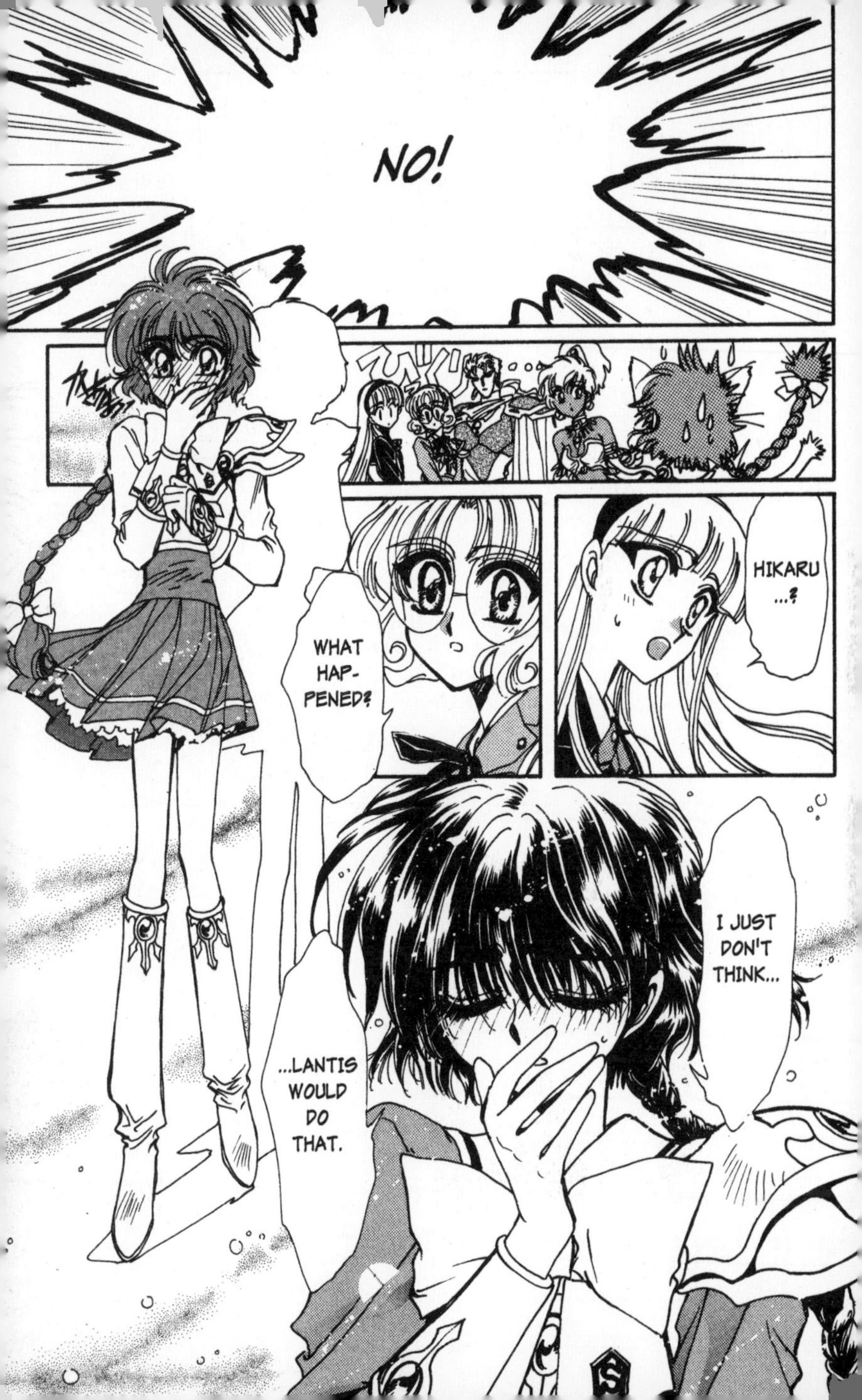
NO!
HIKARU ...?
WHAT HAP-PENED?
I JUST DON'T THINK...
...LANTIS WOULD DO THAT.

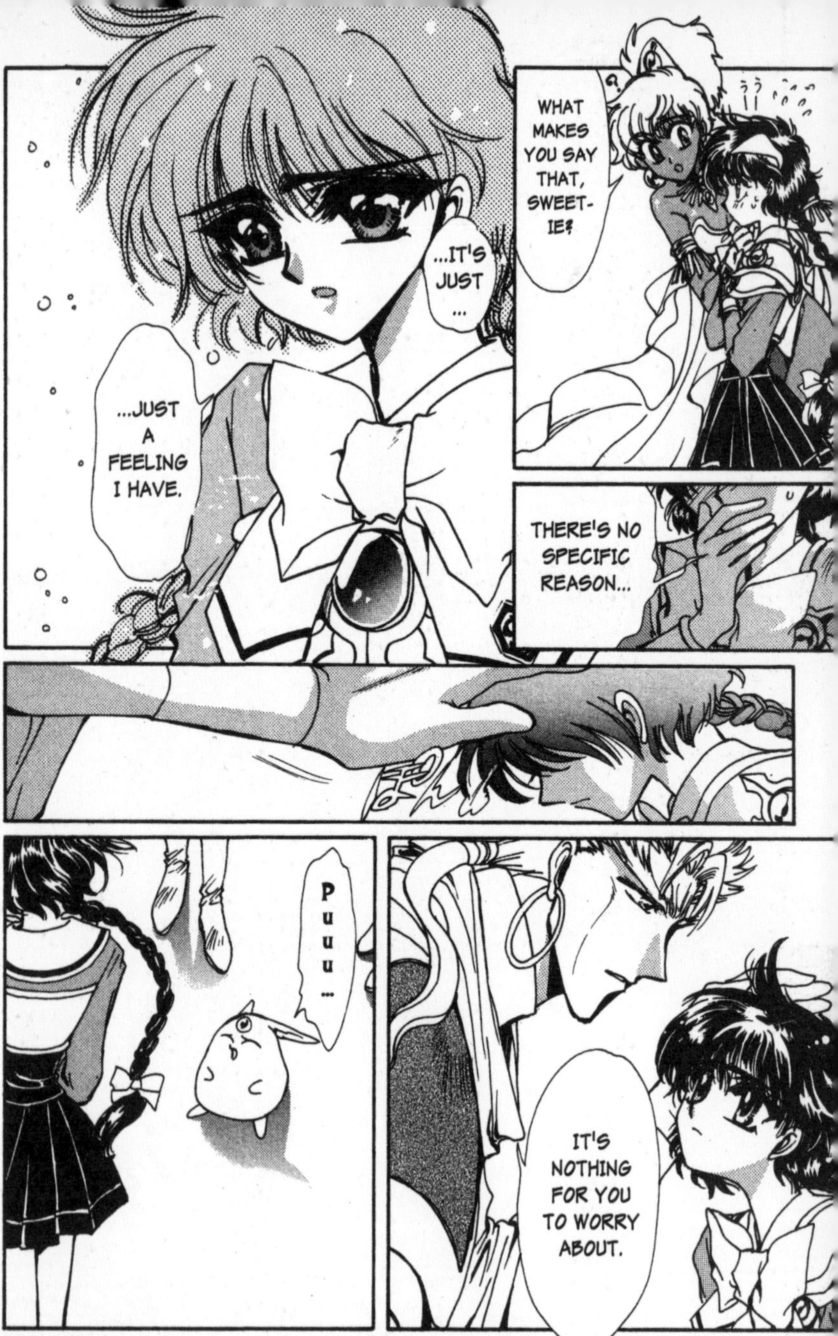
WHAT MAKES YOU SAY THAT, SWEET-IE?
THERE'S NO SPECIFIC REASON...
...IT'S JUST ...
...JUST A FEELING I HAVE.
IT'S NOTHING FOR YOU TO WORRY ABOUT.
Puuu...

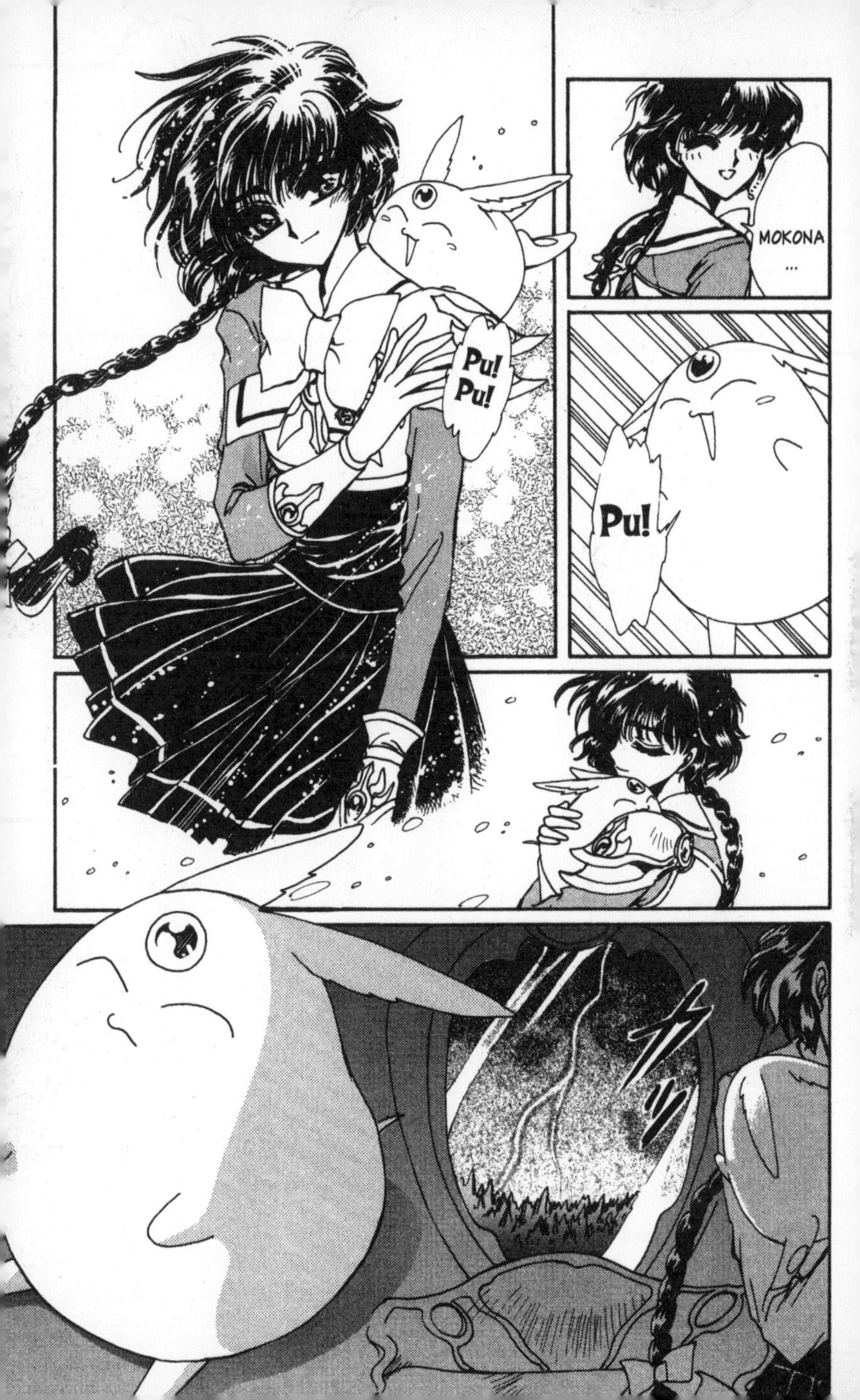
MOKONA
...
Pu!
Pu!
Pu!

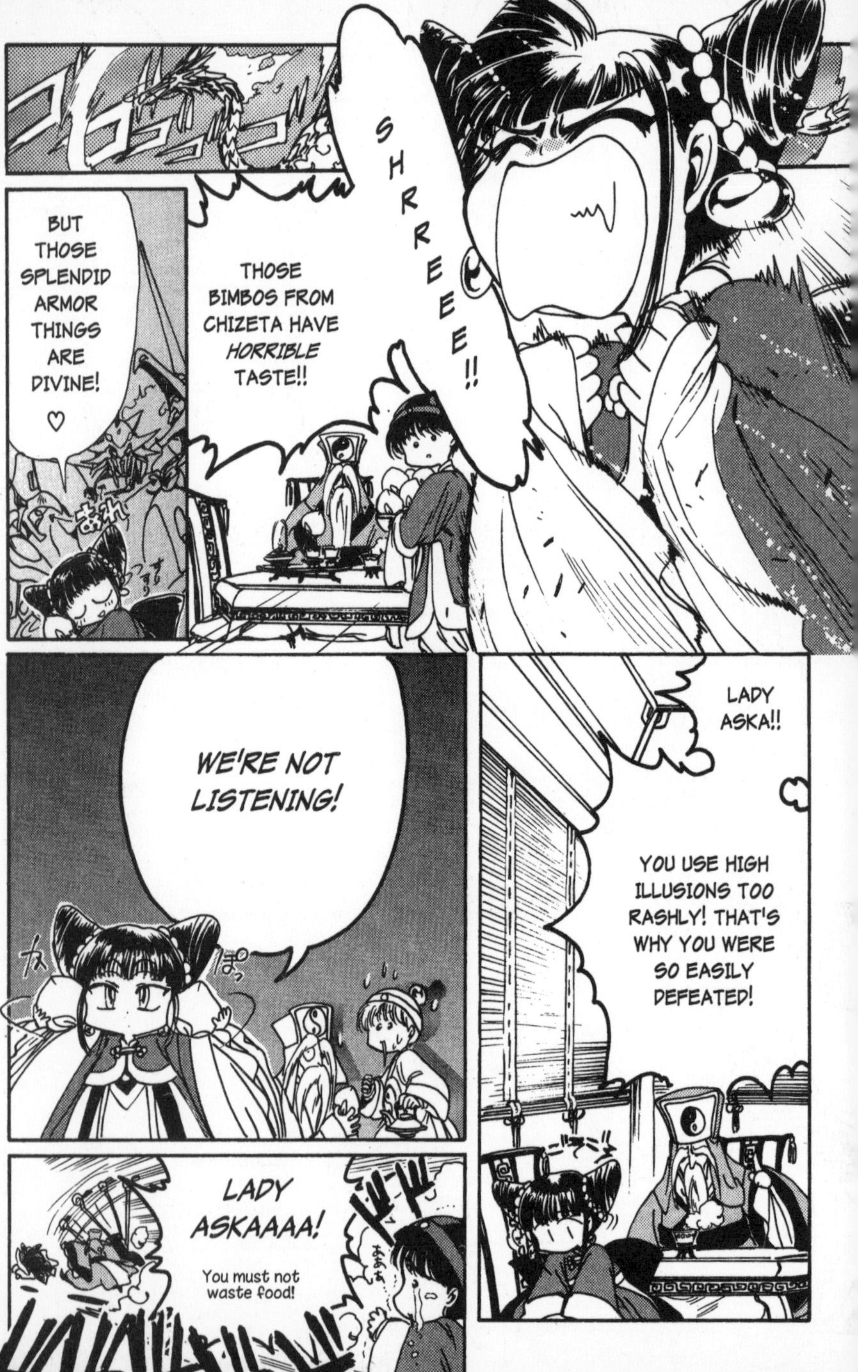

SHRREEEE!!
THOSE BIMBOS FROM CHIZETA HAVE *HORRIBLE* TASTE!!
BUT THOSE SPLENDID ARMOR THINGS ARE DIVINE! ♡
あれ
LADY ASKA!!
YOU USE HIGH ILLUSIONS TOO RASHLY! THAT'S WHY YOU WERE SO EASILY DEFEATED!
WE'RE NOT LISTENING!
LADY ASKAAAA!
You must not waste food!

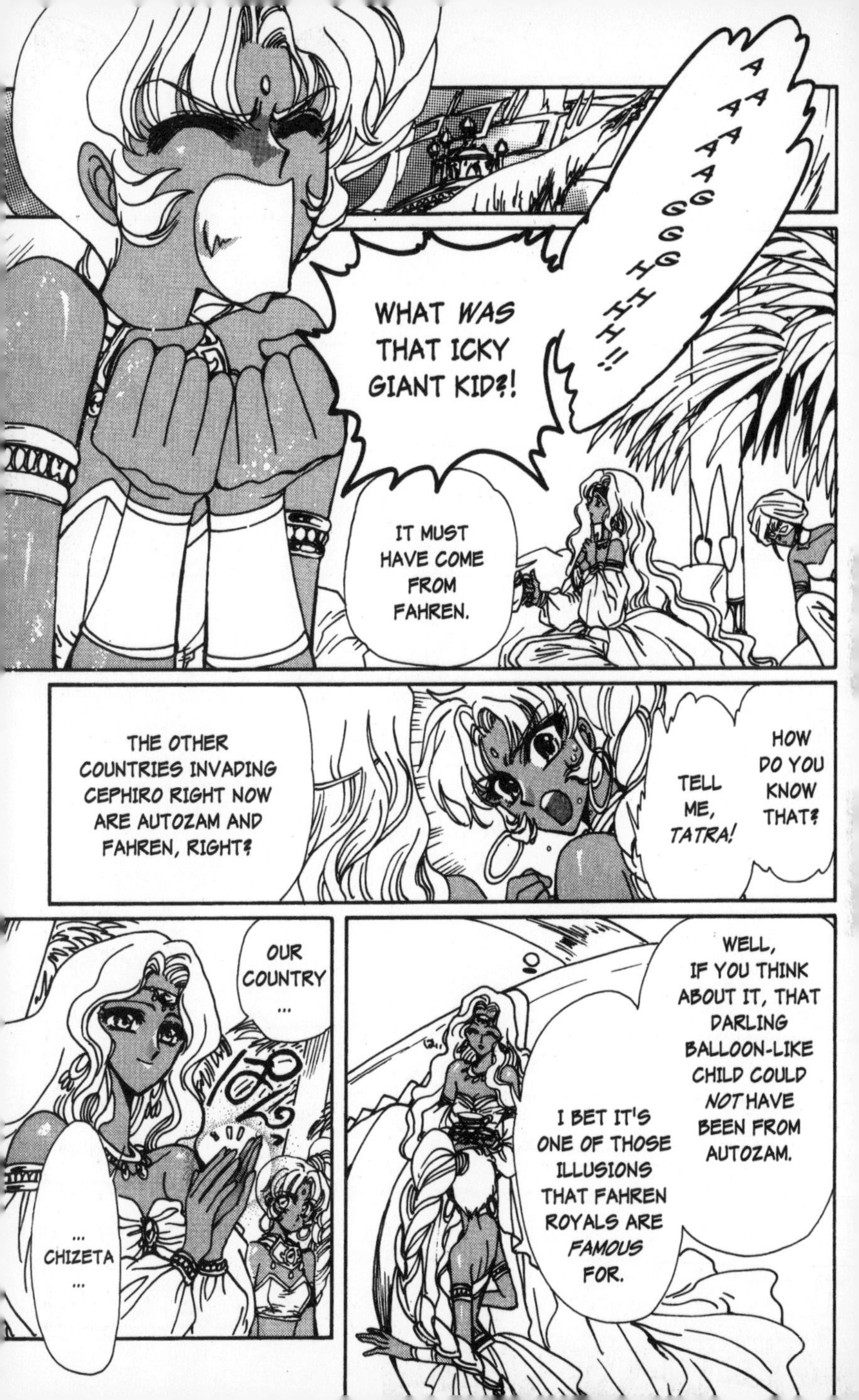
AAAAAAAGGGGHHHH!!!
WHAT *WAS* THAT ICKY GIANT KID?!
IT MUST HAVE COME FROM FAHREN.
HOW DO YOU KNOW THAT?
TELL ME, *TATRA!*
THE OTHER COUNTRIES INVADING CEPHIRO RIGHT NOW ARE AUTOZAM AND FAHREN, RIGHT?
WELL, IF YOU THINK ABOUT IT, THAT DARLING BALLOON-LIKE CHILD COULD *NOT* HAVE BEEN FROM AUTOZAM.
I BET IT'S ONE OF THOSE ILLUSIONS THAT FAHREN ROYALS ARE *FAMOUS* FOR.
OUR COUNTRY ...
... CHIZETA ...

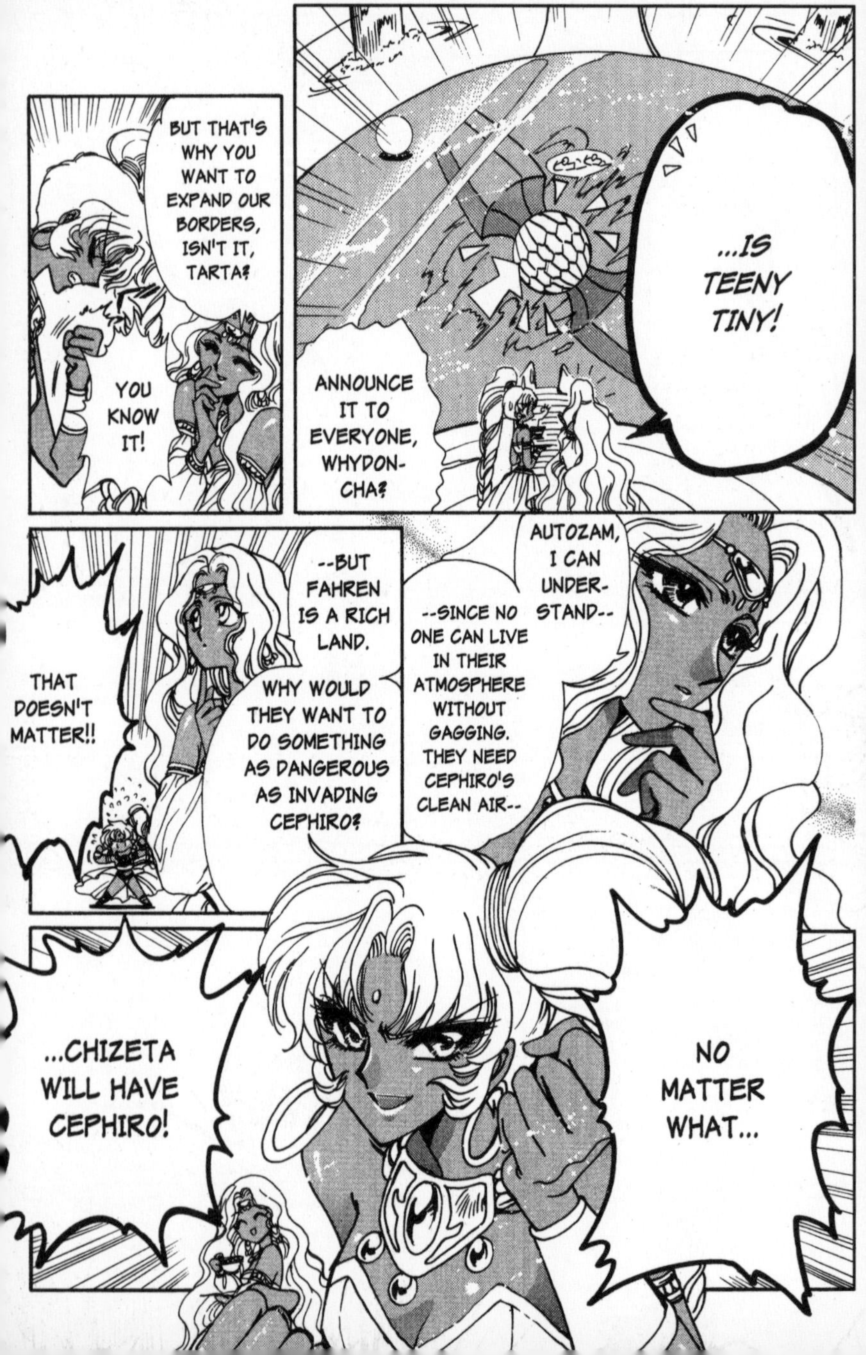

...IS TEENY TINY!
ANNOUNCE IT TO EVERYONE, WHYDON-CHA?
BUT THAT'S WHY YOU WANT TO EXPAND OUR BORDERS, ISN'T IT, TARTA?
YOU KNOW IT!
AUTOZAM, I CAN UNDER-STAND--
--SINCE NO ONE CAN LIVE IN THEIR ATMOSPHERE WITHOUT GAGGING. THEY NEED CEPHIRO'S CLEAN AIR--
--BUT FAHREN IS A RICH LAND.
WHY WOULD THEY WANT TO DO SOMETHING AS DANGEROUS AS INVADING CEPHIRO?
THAT DOESN'T MATTER!!
NO MATTER WHAT...
...CHIZETA WILL HAVE CEPHIRO!

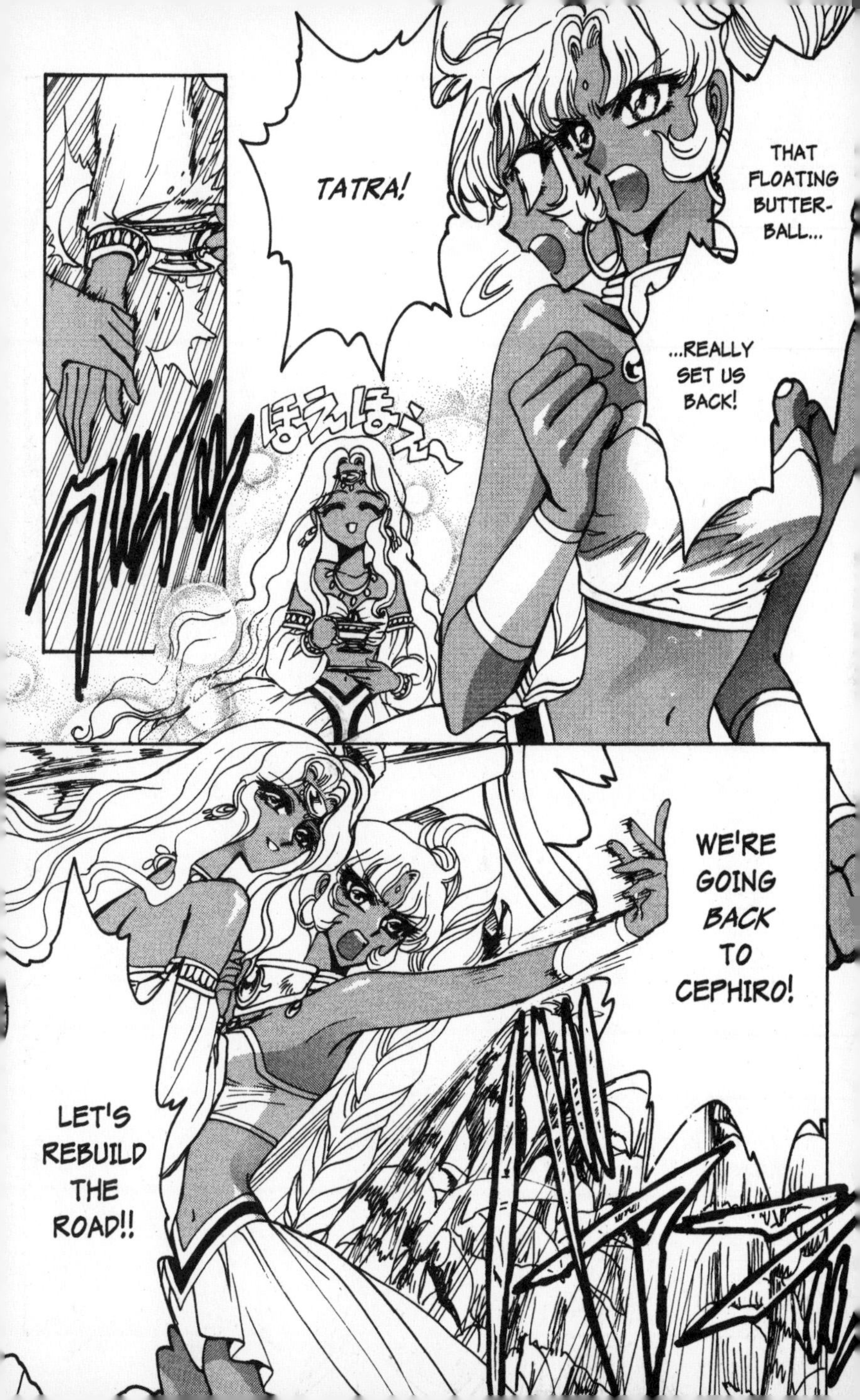
THAT FLOATING BUTTER-BALL...
...REALLY SET US BACK!
TATRA!
ほえほえ～
WE'RE GOING BACK TO CEPHIRO!
LET'S REBUILD THE ROAD!!

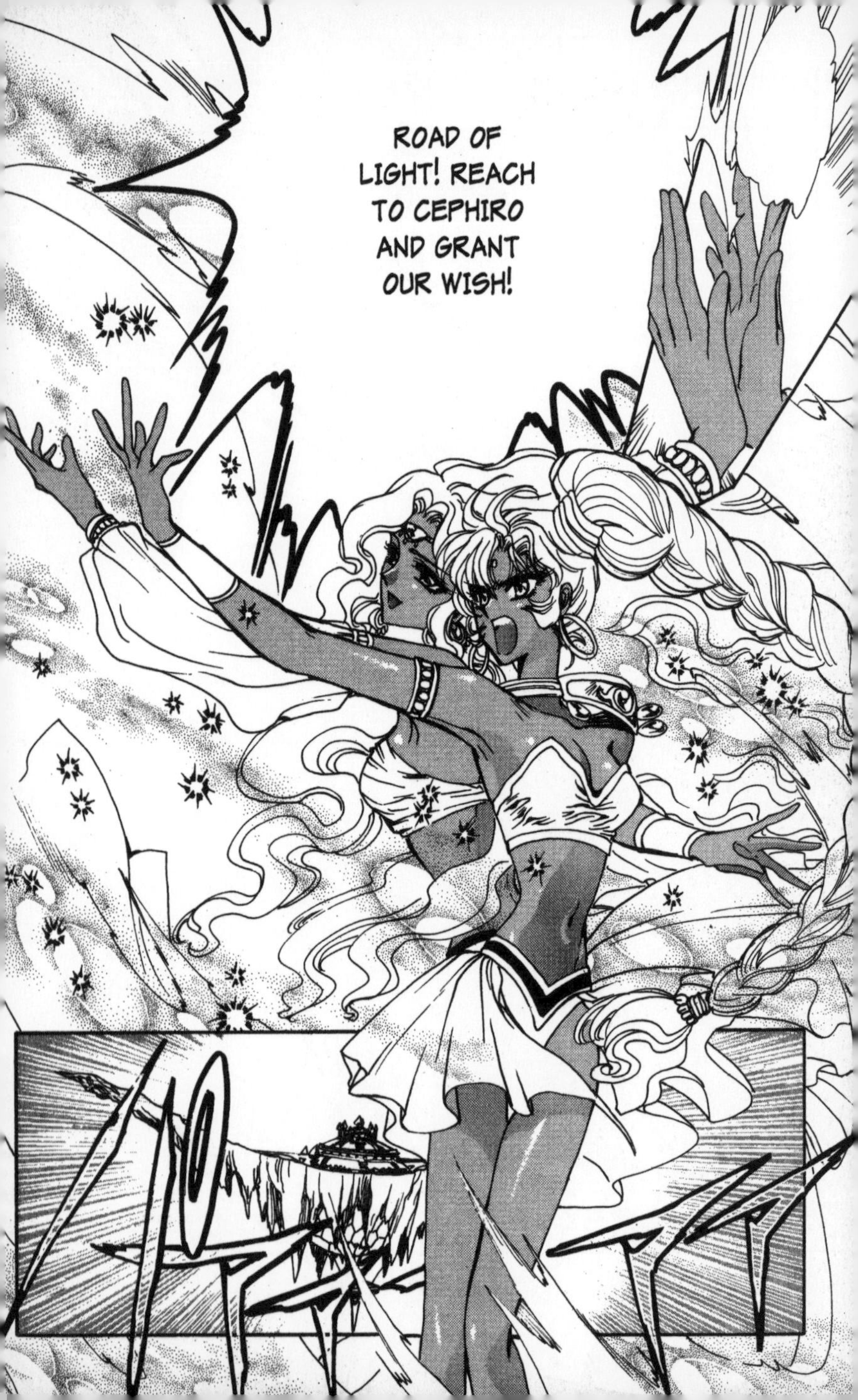
ROAD OF LIGHT! REACH TO CEPHIRO AND GRANT OUR WISH!

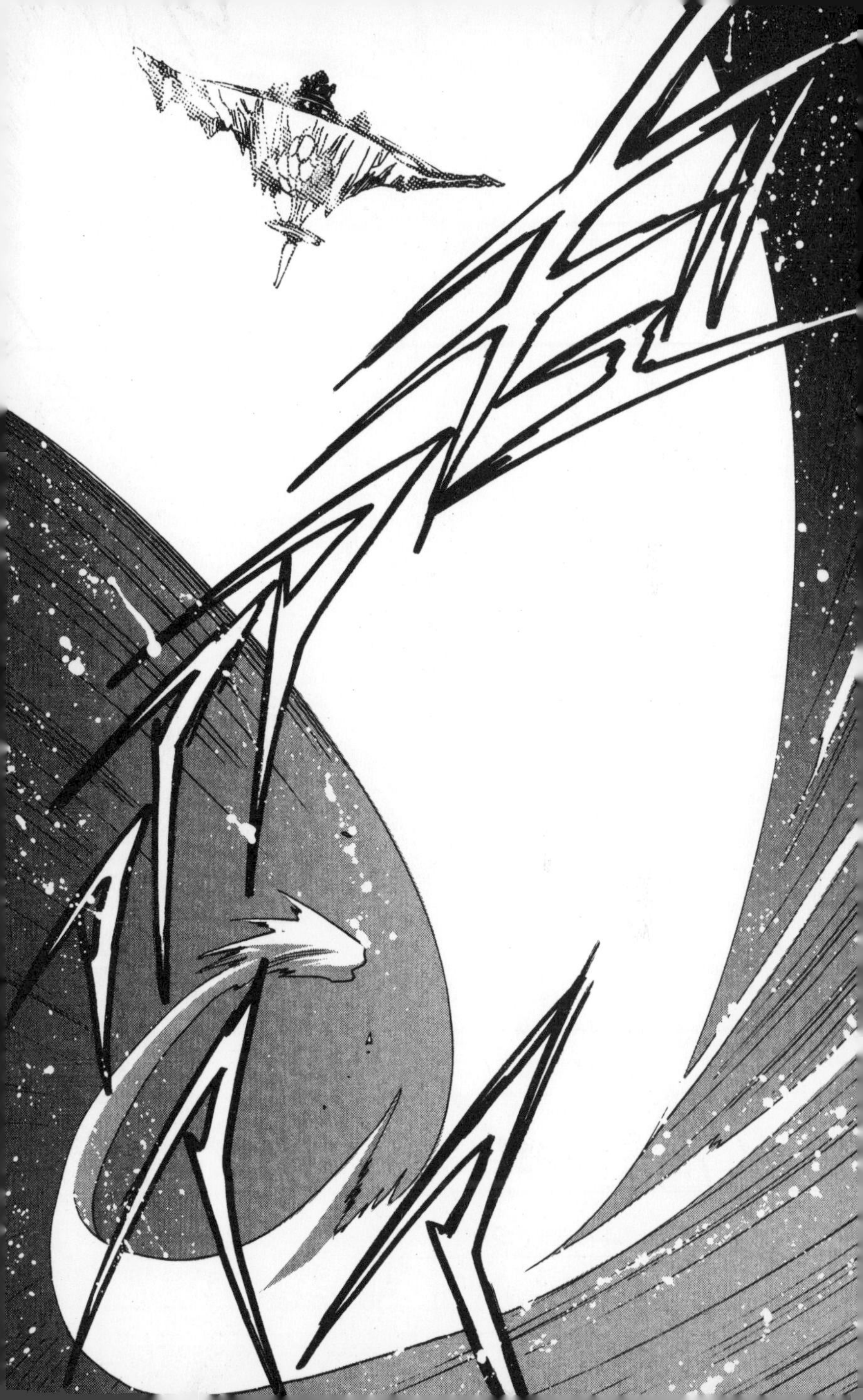

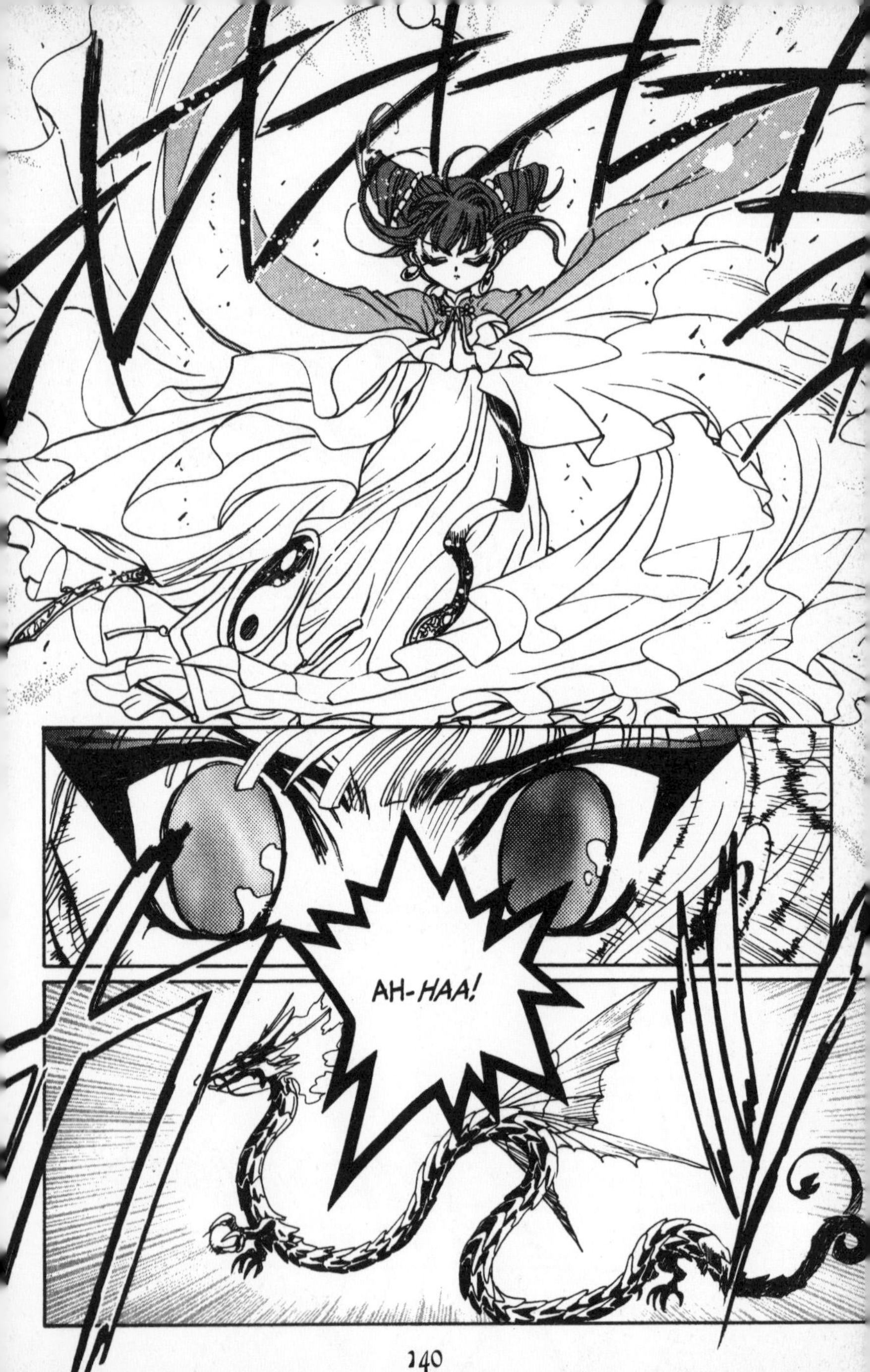
AH-HAA!

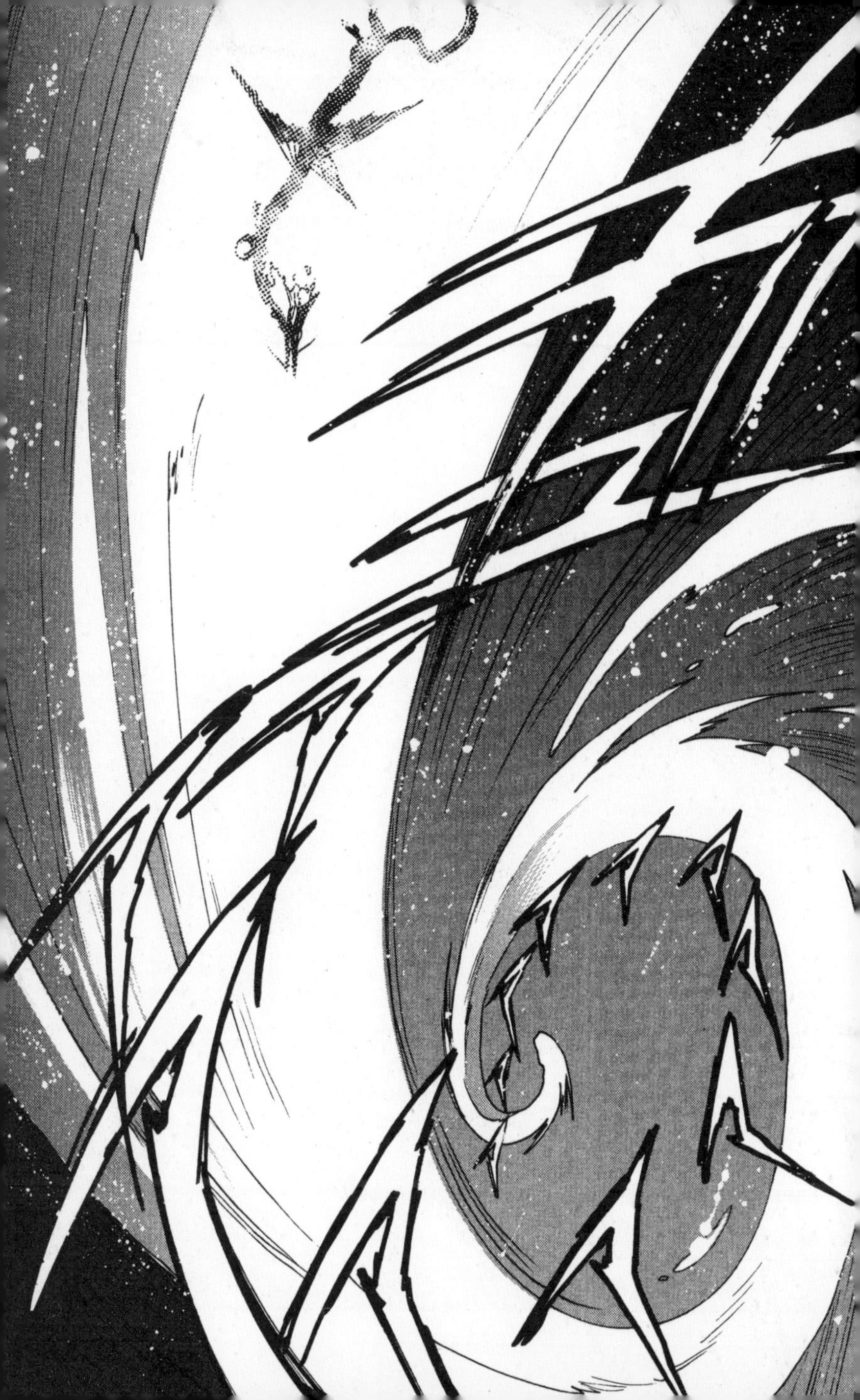

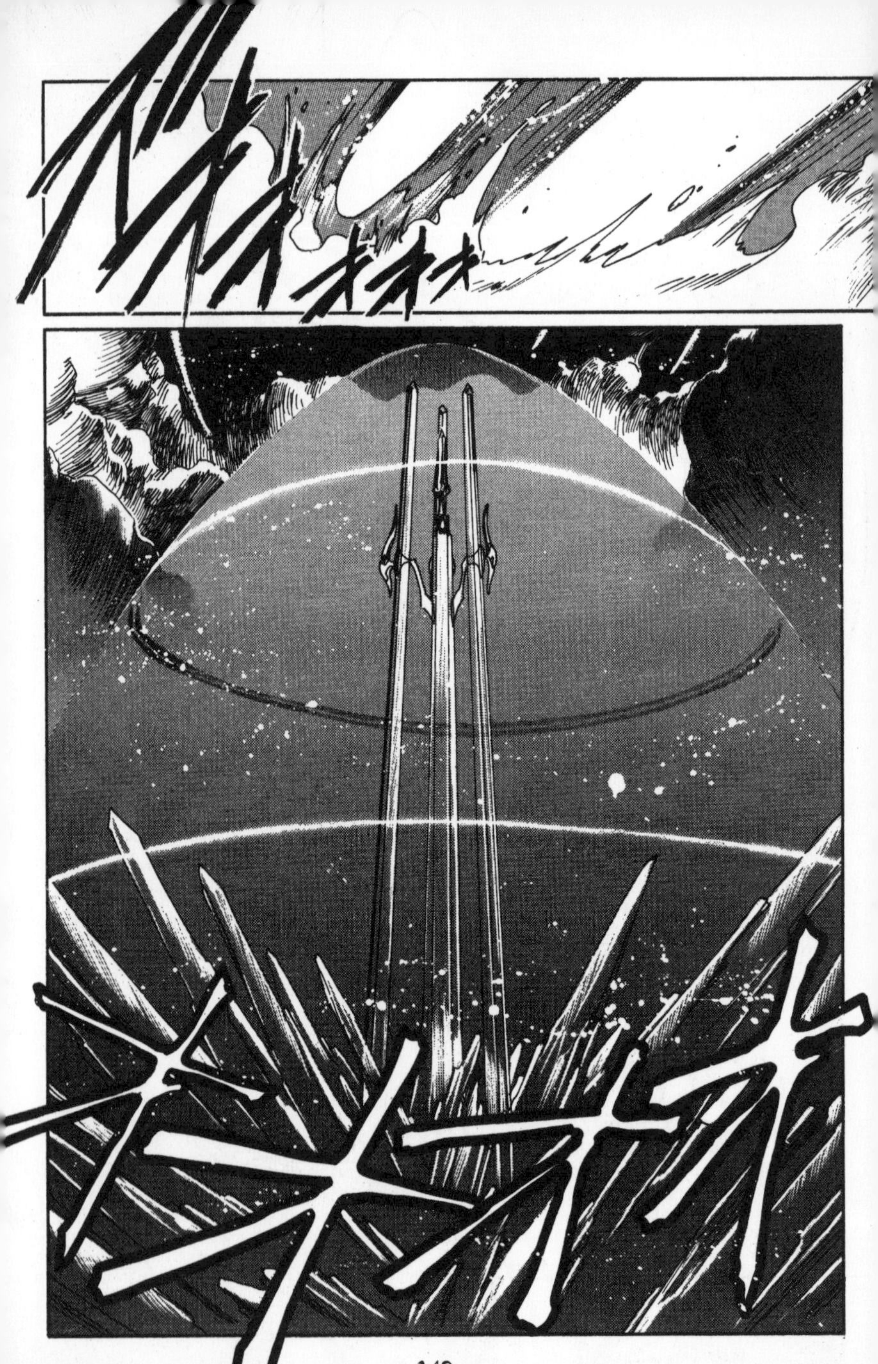

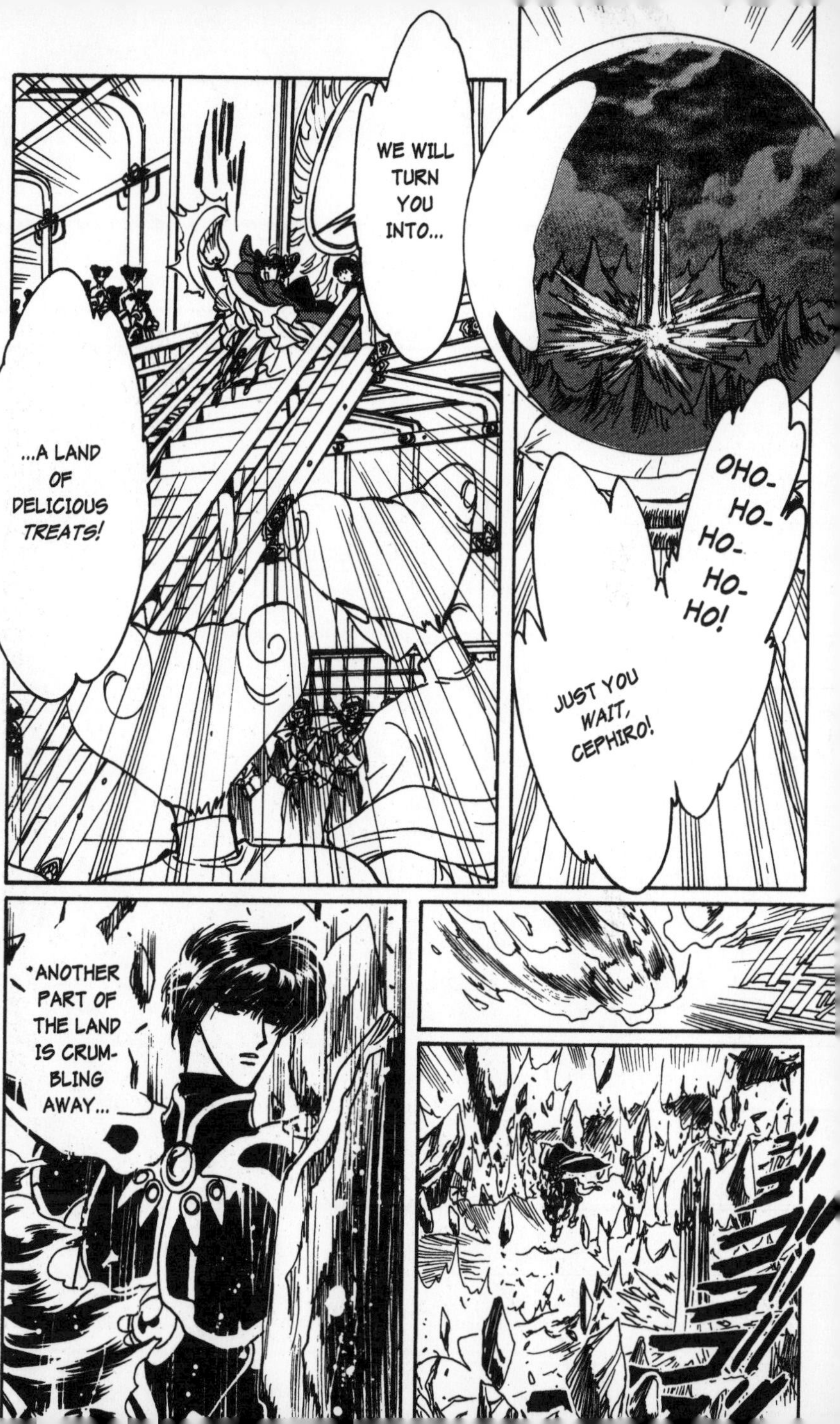
WE WILL TURN YOU INTO...
...A LAND OF DELICIOUS TREATS!
OHO-HO-HO-HO-HO!
JUST YOU WAIT, CEPHIRO!
ANOTHER PART OF THE LAND IS CRUM-BLING AWAY...

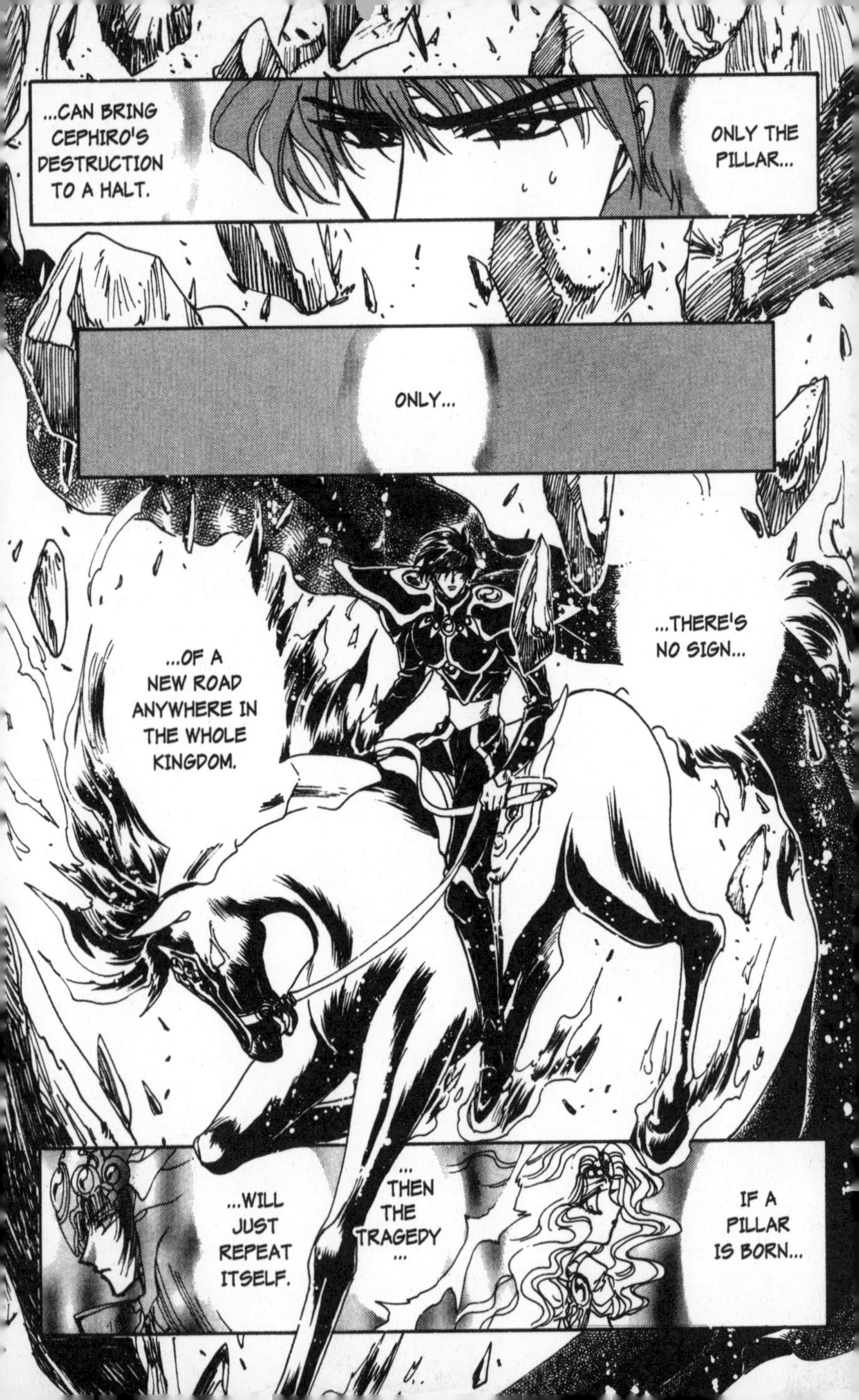
ONLY THE PILLAR...
...CAN BRING CEPHIRO'S DESTRUCTION TO A HALT.
ONLY...
...THERE'S NO SIGN...
...OF A NEW ROAD ANYWHERE IN THE WHOLE KINGDOM.
IF A PILLAR IS BORN...
...THEN THE TRAGEDY...
...WILL JUST REPEAT ITSELF.

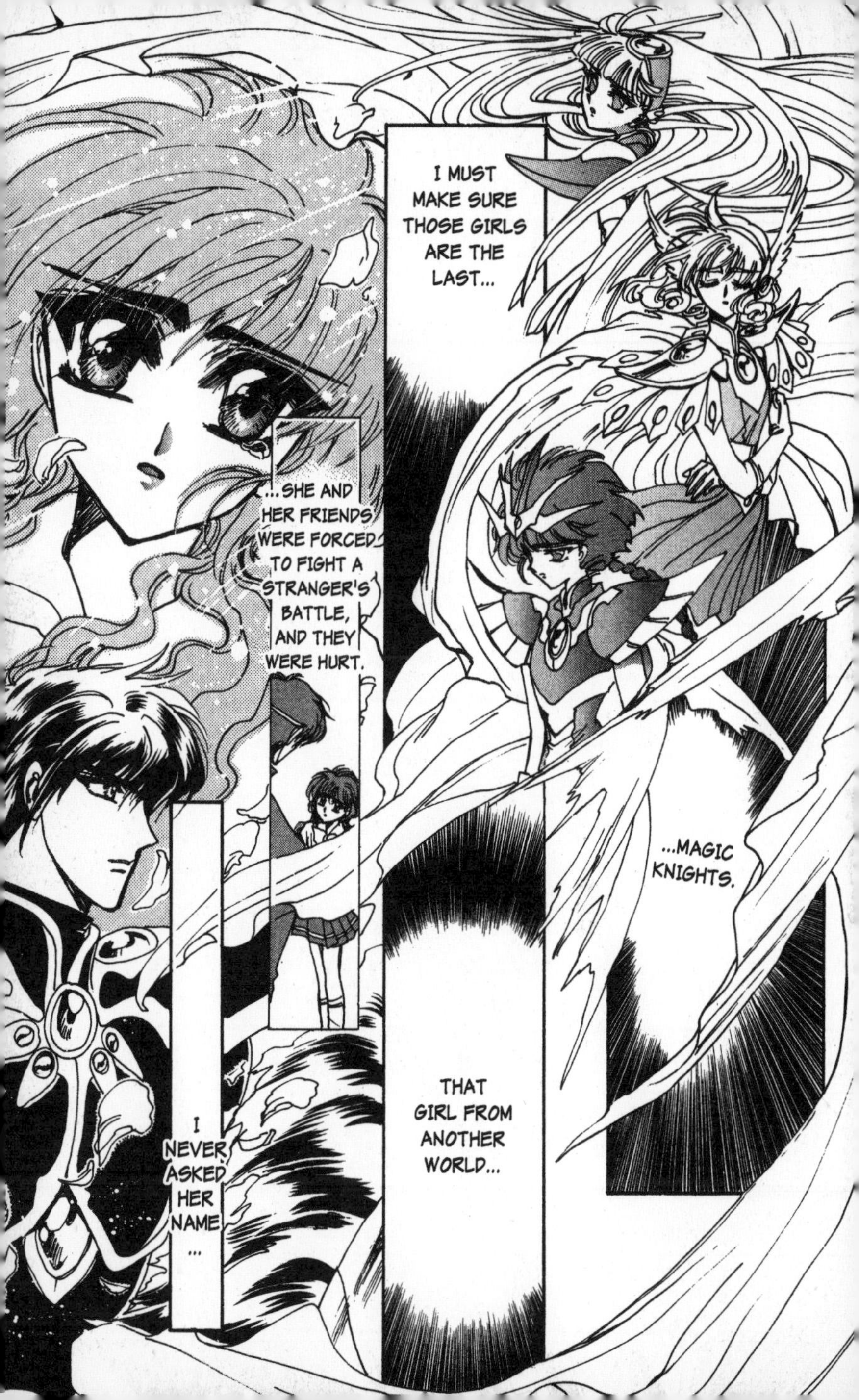
I MUST MAKE SURE THOSE GIRLS ARE THE LAST...
...MAGIC KNIGHTS.
THAT GIRL FROM ANOTHER WORLD...
...SHE AND HER FRIENDS WERE FORCED TO FIGHT A STRANGER'S BATTLE, AND THEY WERE HURT.
I NEVER ASKED HER NAME...

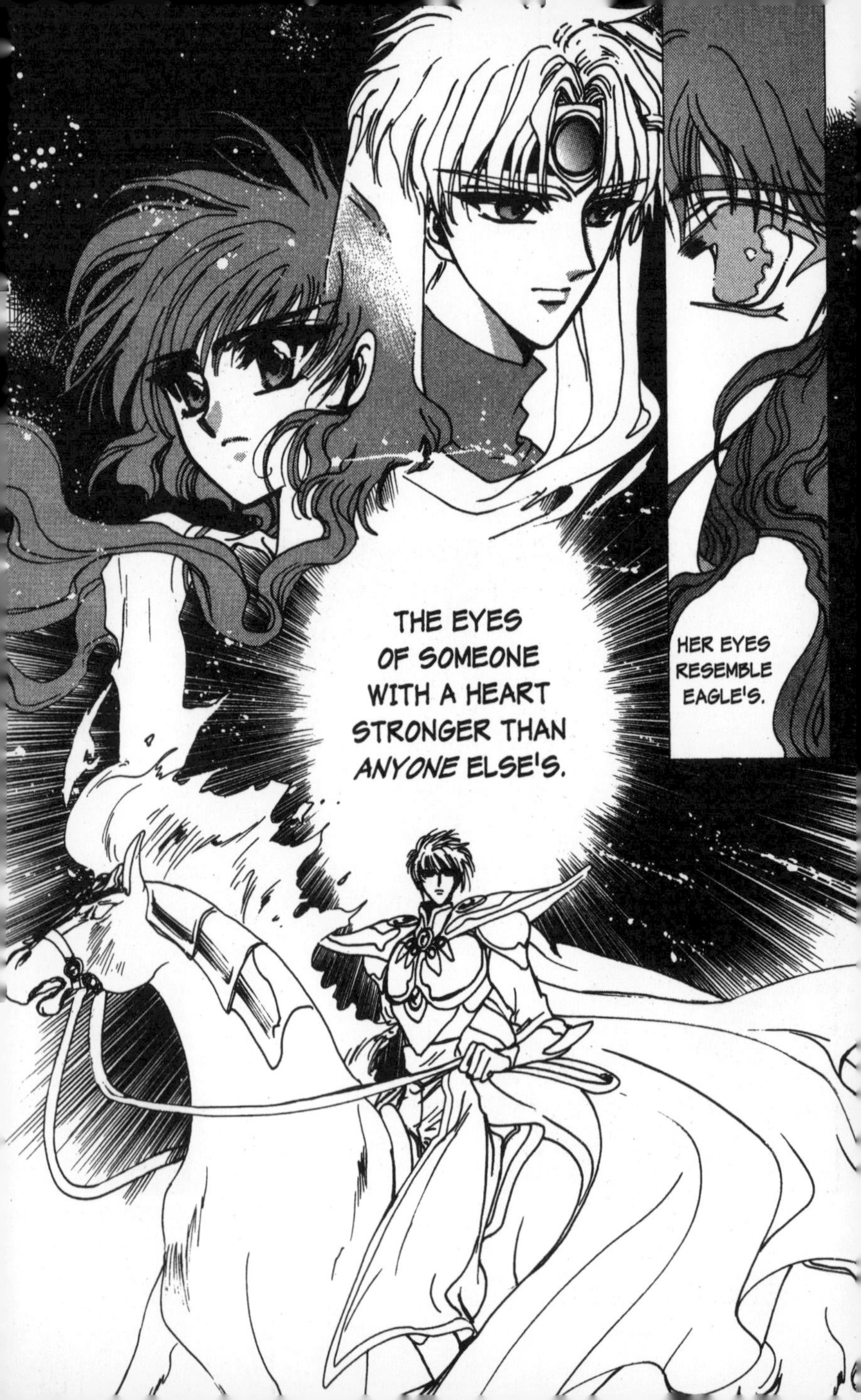
HER EYES RESEMBLE EAGLE'S.
THE EYES OF SOMEONE WITH A HEART STRONGER THAN *ANYONE* ELSE'S.

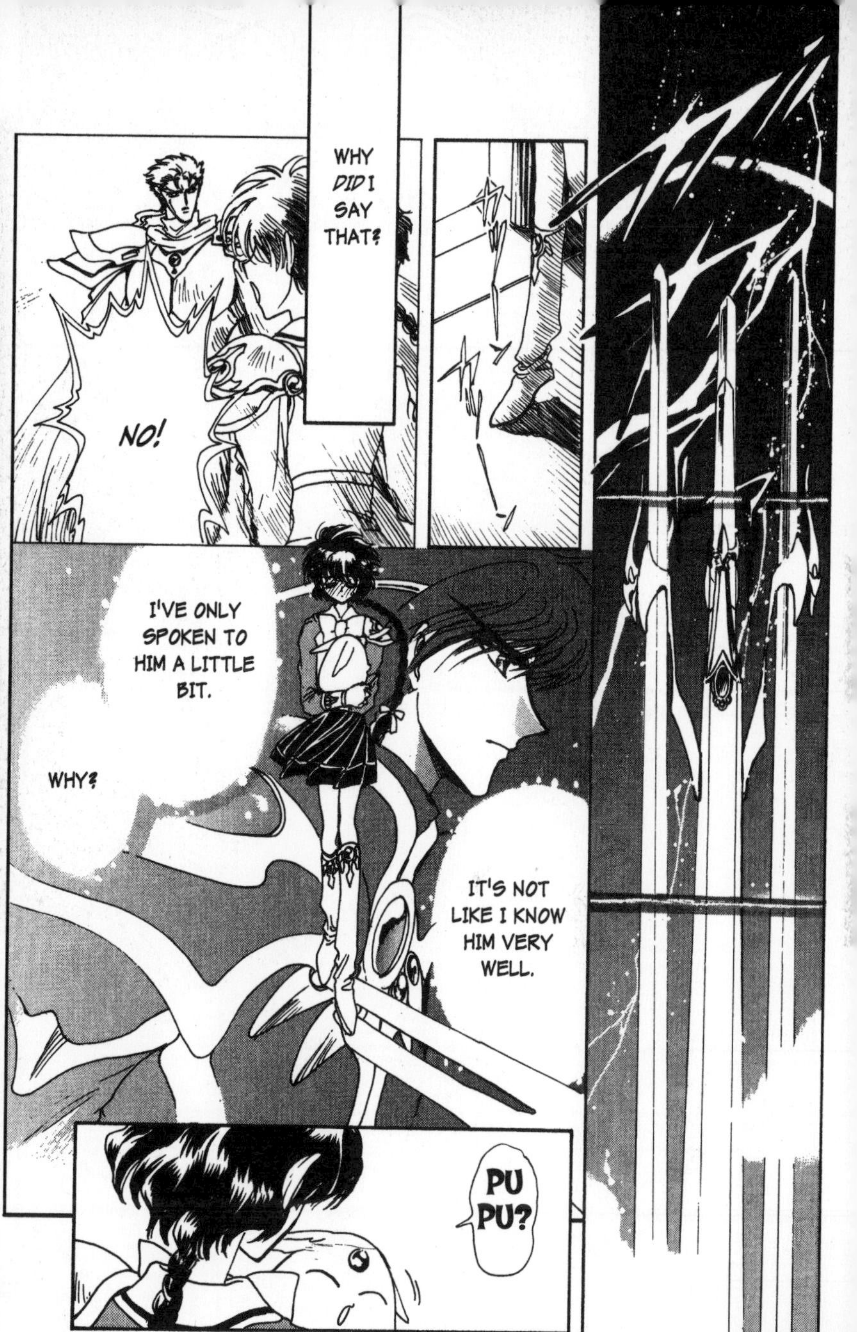
WHY *DID* I SAY THAT?
NO!
I'VE ONLY SPOKEN TO HIM A LITTLE BIT.
WHY?
IT'S NOT LIKE I KNOW HIM VERY WELL.
PU PU?

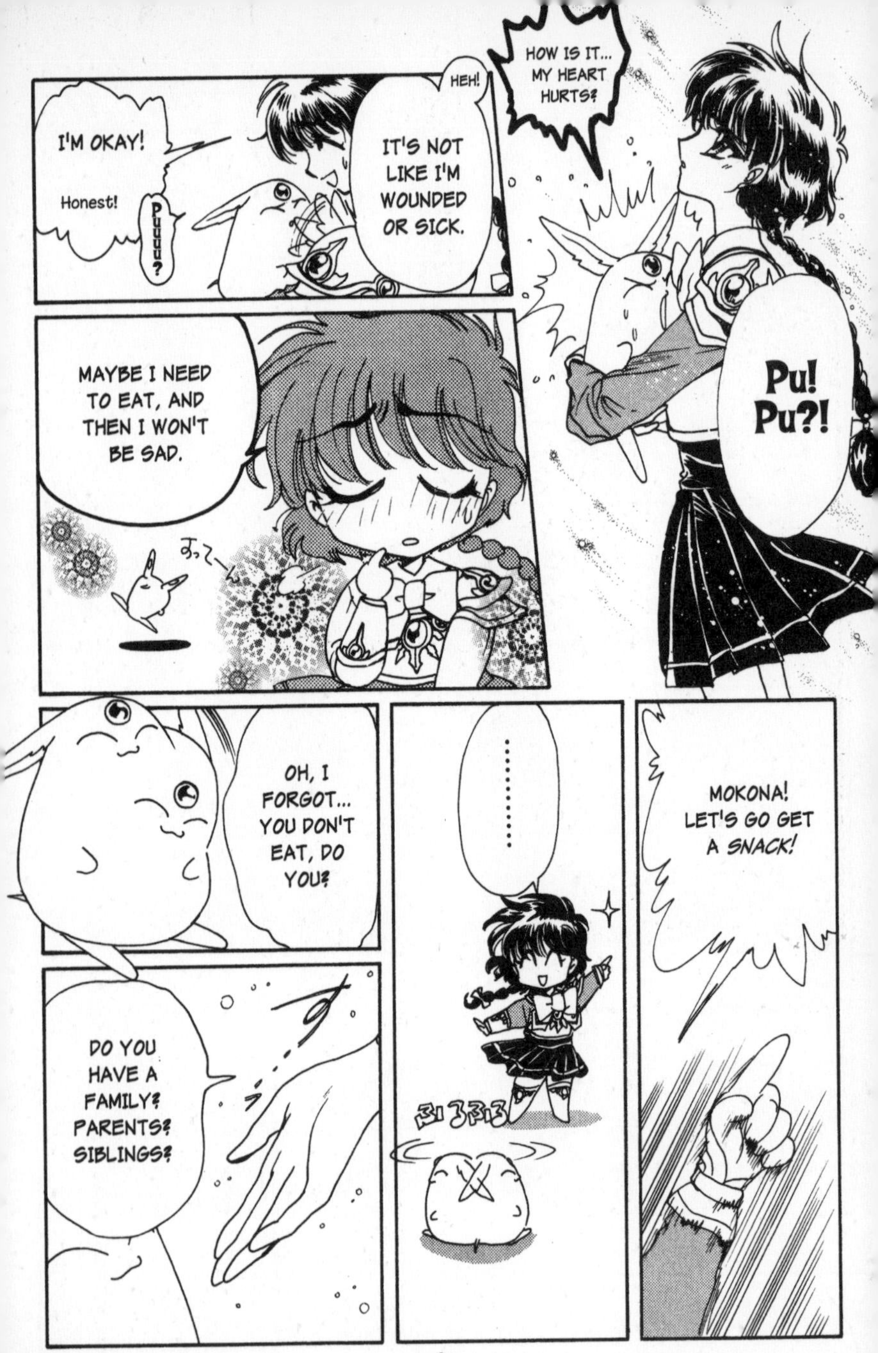
HOW IS IT... MY HEART HURTS?
Pu! Pu?!
HEH!
IT'S NOT LIKE I'M WOUNDED OR SICK.
Puuuu?
I'M OKAY!
Honest!
MAYBE I NEED TO EAT, AND THEN I WON'T BE SAD.
MOKONA! LET'S GO GET A SNACK!
......
OH, I FORGOT... YOU DON'T EAT, DO YOU?
DO YOU HAVE A FAMILY? PARENTS? SIBLINGS?

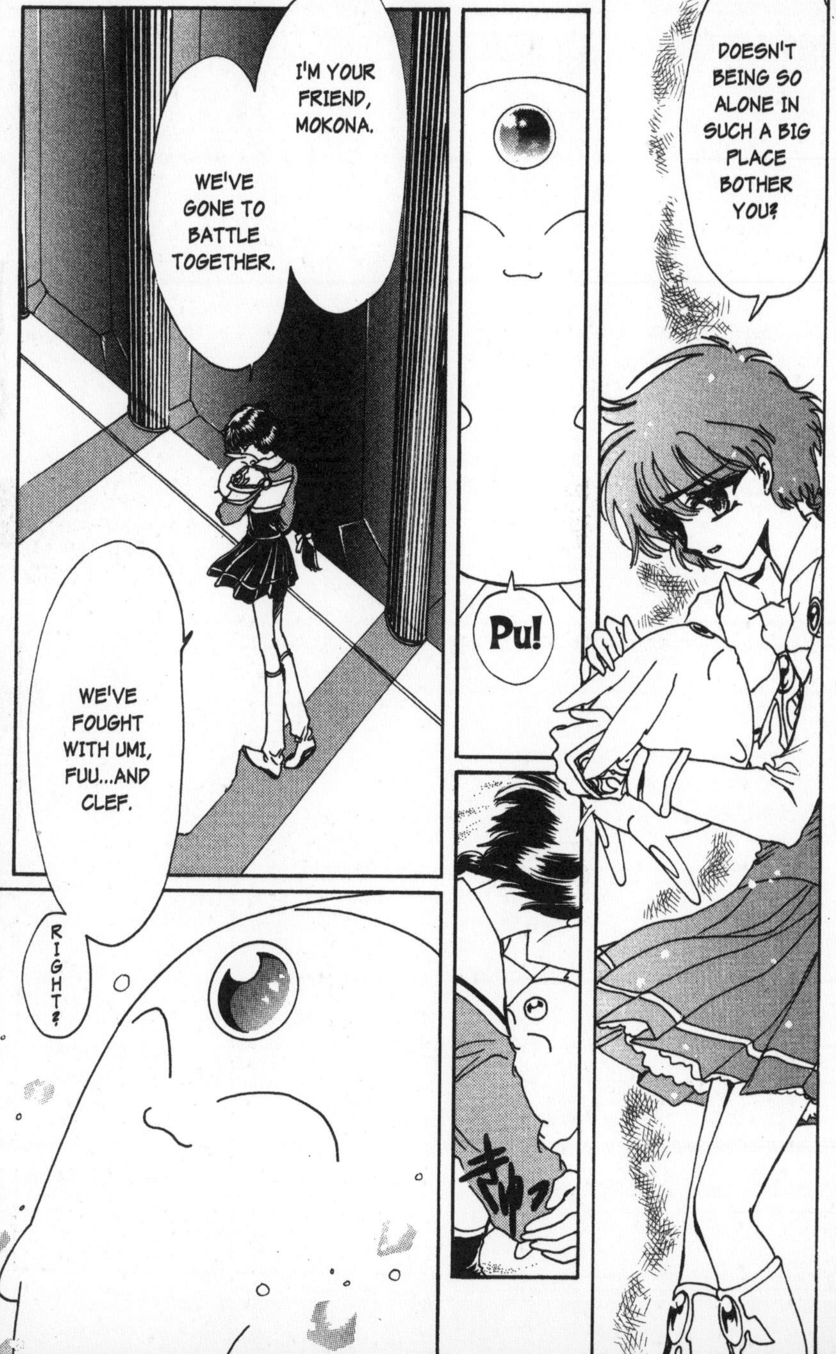
DOESN'T BEING SO ALONE IN SUCH A BIG PLACE BOTHER YOU?
Pu!
きゅっ
I'M YOUR FRIEND, MOKONA.
WE'VE GONE TO BATTLE TOGETHER.
WE'VE FOUGHT WITH UMI, FUU...AND CLEF.
RIGHT?

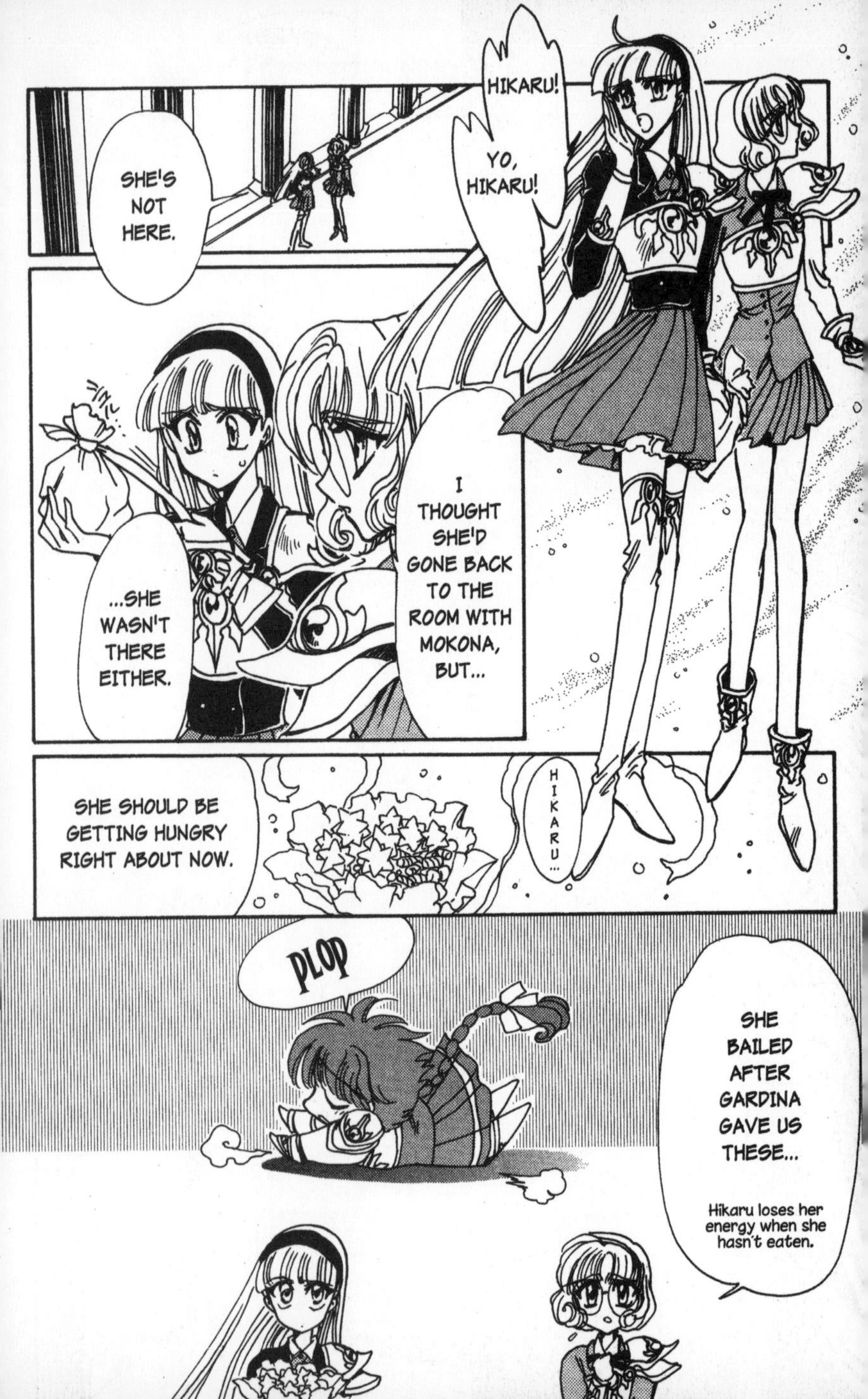
HIKARU!
YO, HIKARU!
SHE'S NOT HERE.
I THOUGHT SHE'D GONE BACK TO THE ROOM WITH MOKONA, BUT...
...SHE WASN'T THERE EITHER.
HIKARU...
SHE SHOULD BE GETTING HUNGRY RIGHT ABOUT NOW.
PLOP
SHE BAILED AFTER GARDINA GAVE US THESE...
Hikaru loses her energy when she hasn't eaten.

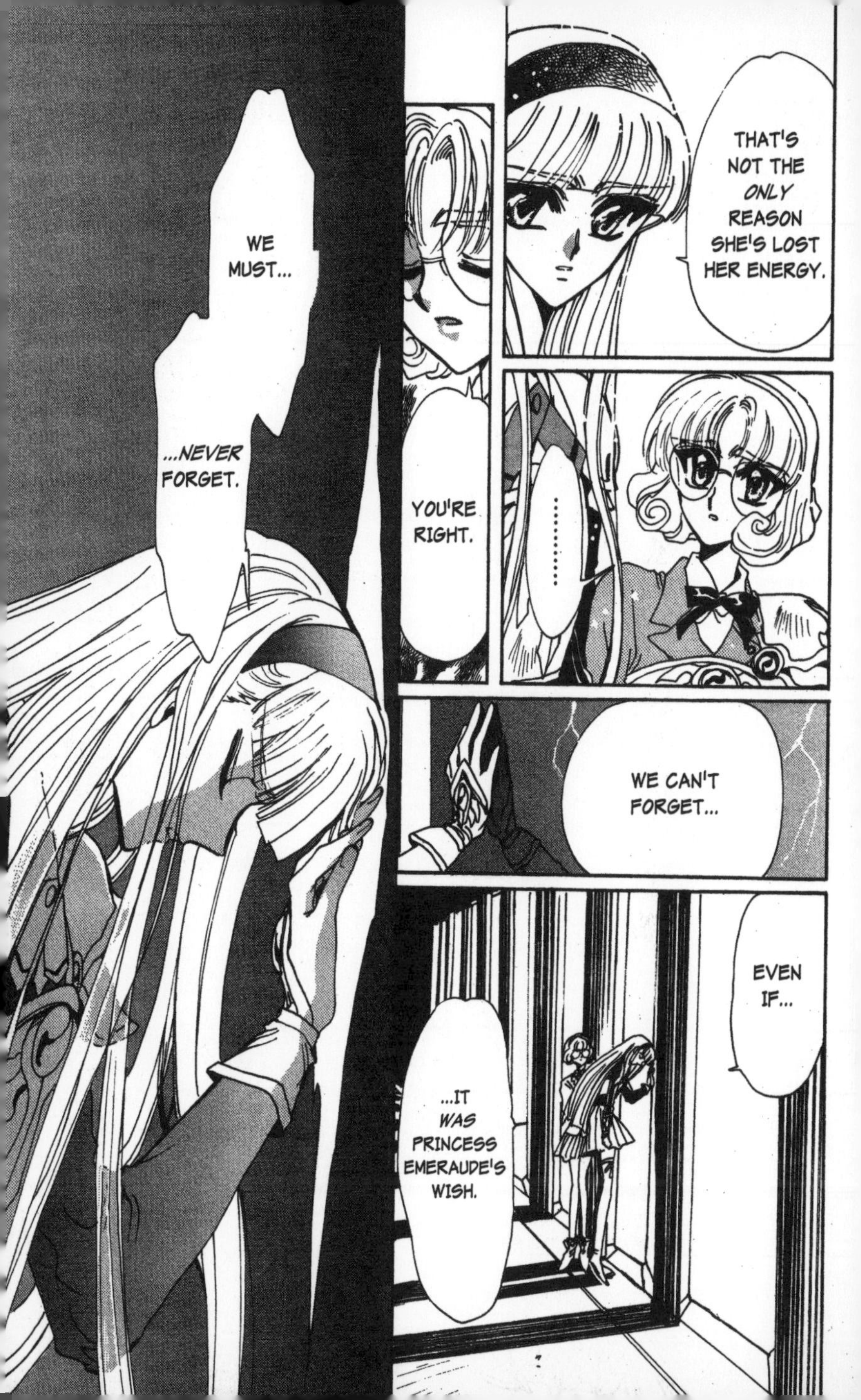
THAT'S NOT THE *ONLY* REASON SHE'S LOST HER ENERGY.
......
YOU'RE RIGHT.
WE CAN'T FORGET...
EVEN IF...
...IT *WAS* PRINCESS EMERAUDE'S WISH.
WE MUST...
...*NEVER* FORGET.

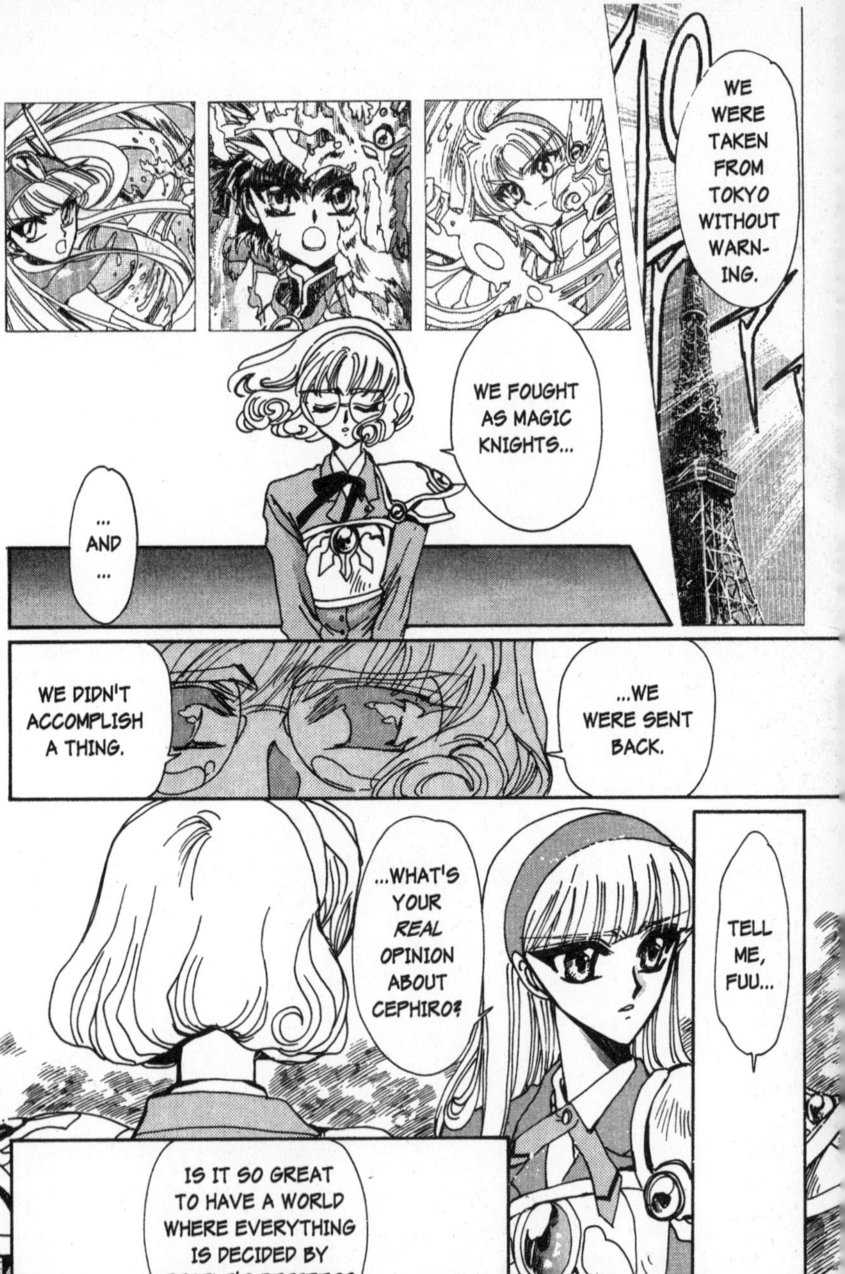
WE WERE TAKEN FROM TOKYO WITHOUT WARN-ING.
WE FOUGHT AS MAGIC KNIGHTS...
... AND ...
...WE WERE SENT BACK.
WE DIDN'T ACCOMPLISH A THING.
TELL ME, FUU...
...WHAT'S YOUR *REAL* OPINION ABOUT CEPHIRO?
IS IT SO GREAT TO HAVE A WORLD WHERE EVERYTHING IS DECIDED BY PEOPLE'S DESIRES?

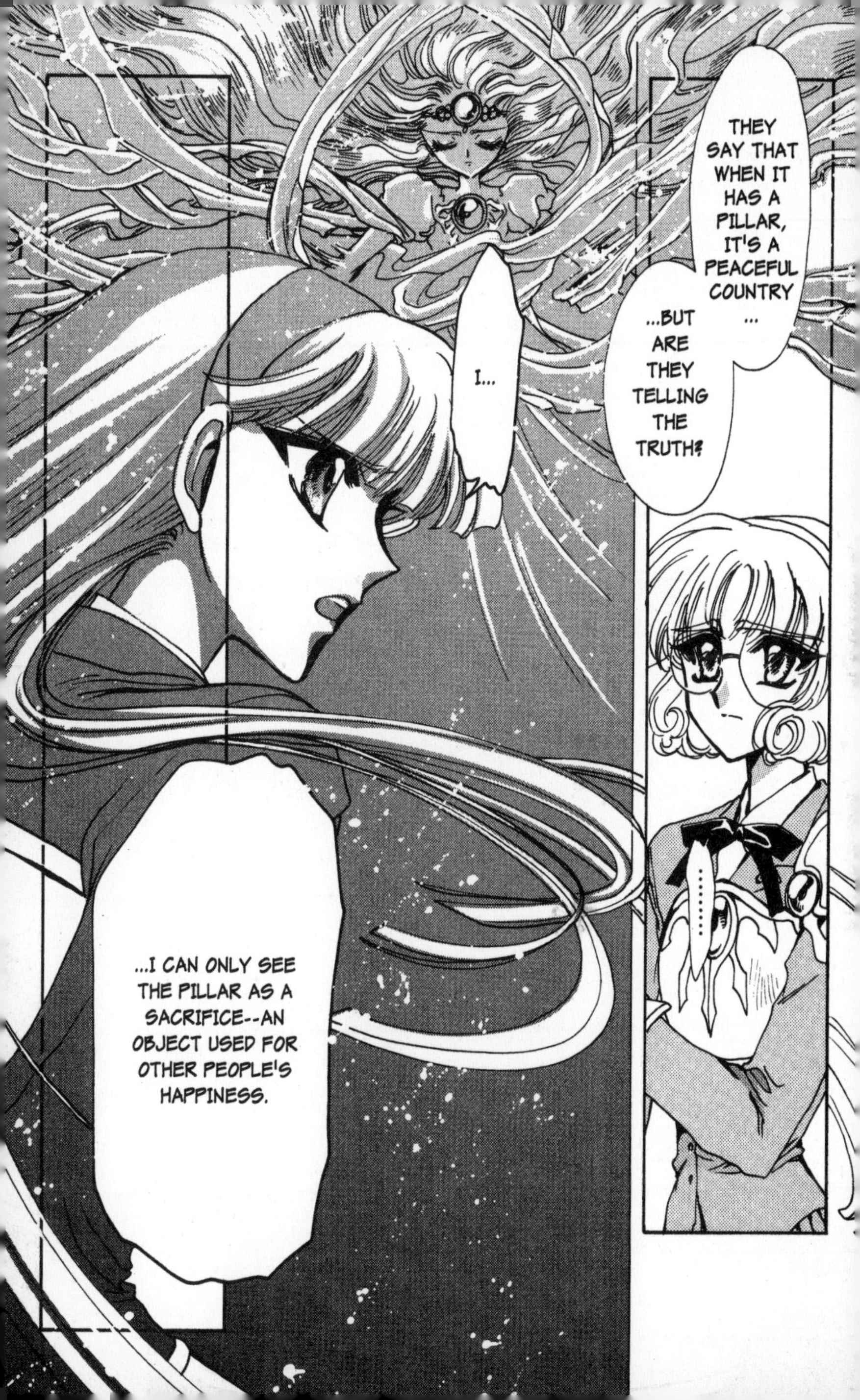
THEY SAY THAT WHEN IT HAS A PILLAR, IT'S A PEACEFUL COUNTRY...
...BUT ARE THEY TELLING THE TRUTH?
I...
......
...I CAN ONLY SEE THE PILLAR AS A SACRIFICE--AN OBJECT USED FOR OTHER PEOPLE'S HAPPINESS.

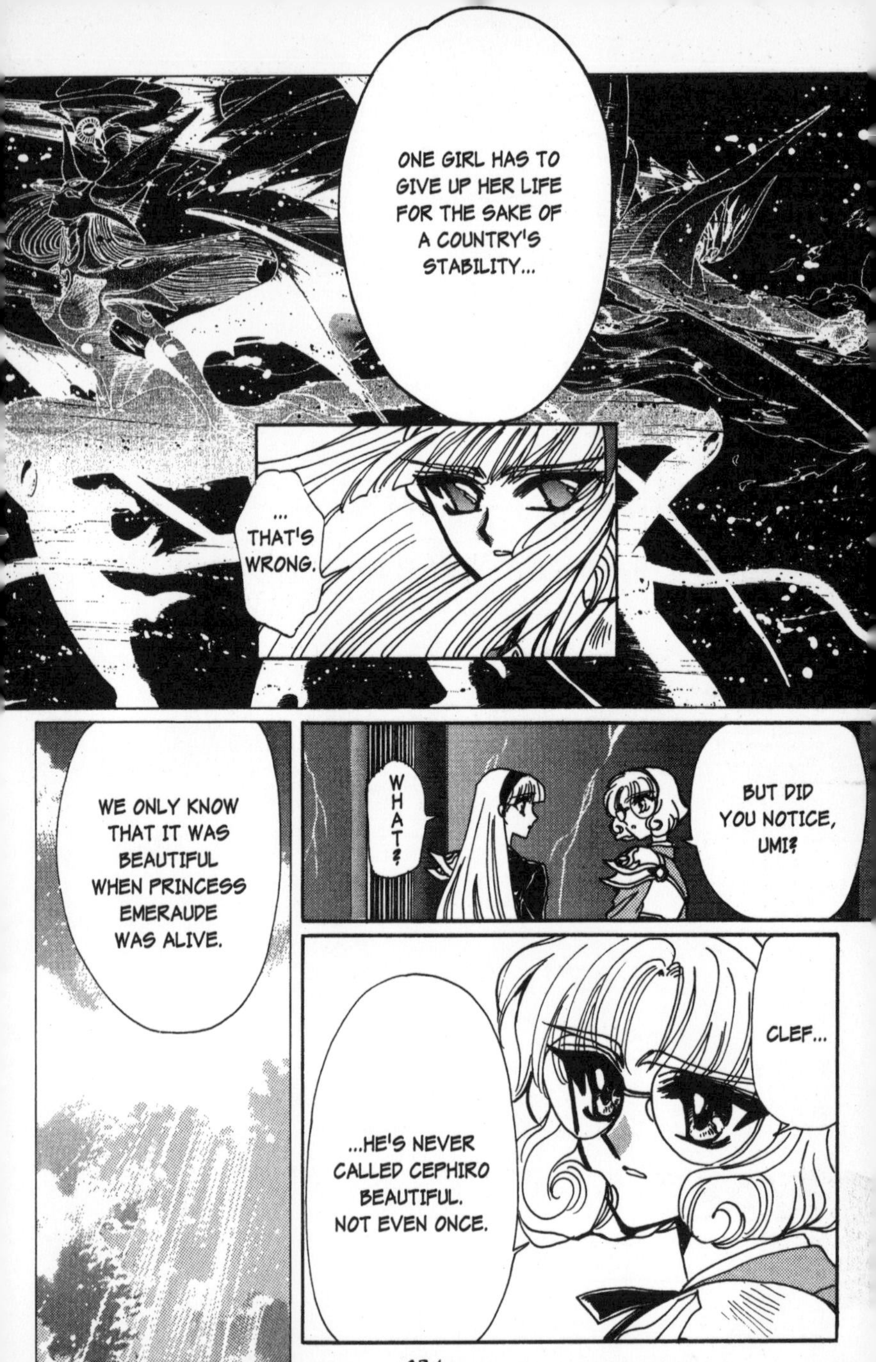
ONE GIRL HAS TO GIVE UP HER LIFE FOR THE SAKE OF A COUNTRY'S STABILITY...
... THAT'S WRONG.
BUT DID YOU NOTICE, UMI?
WHAT?
CLEF...
...HE'S NEVER CALLED CEPHIRO BEAUTIFUL. NOT EVEN ONCE.
WE ONLY KNOW THAT IT WAS BEAUTIFUL WHEN PRINCESS EMERAUDE WAS ALIVE.

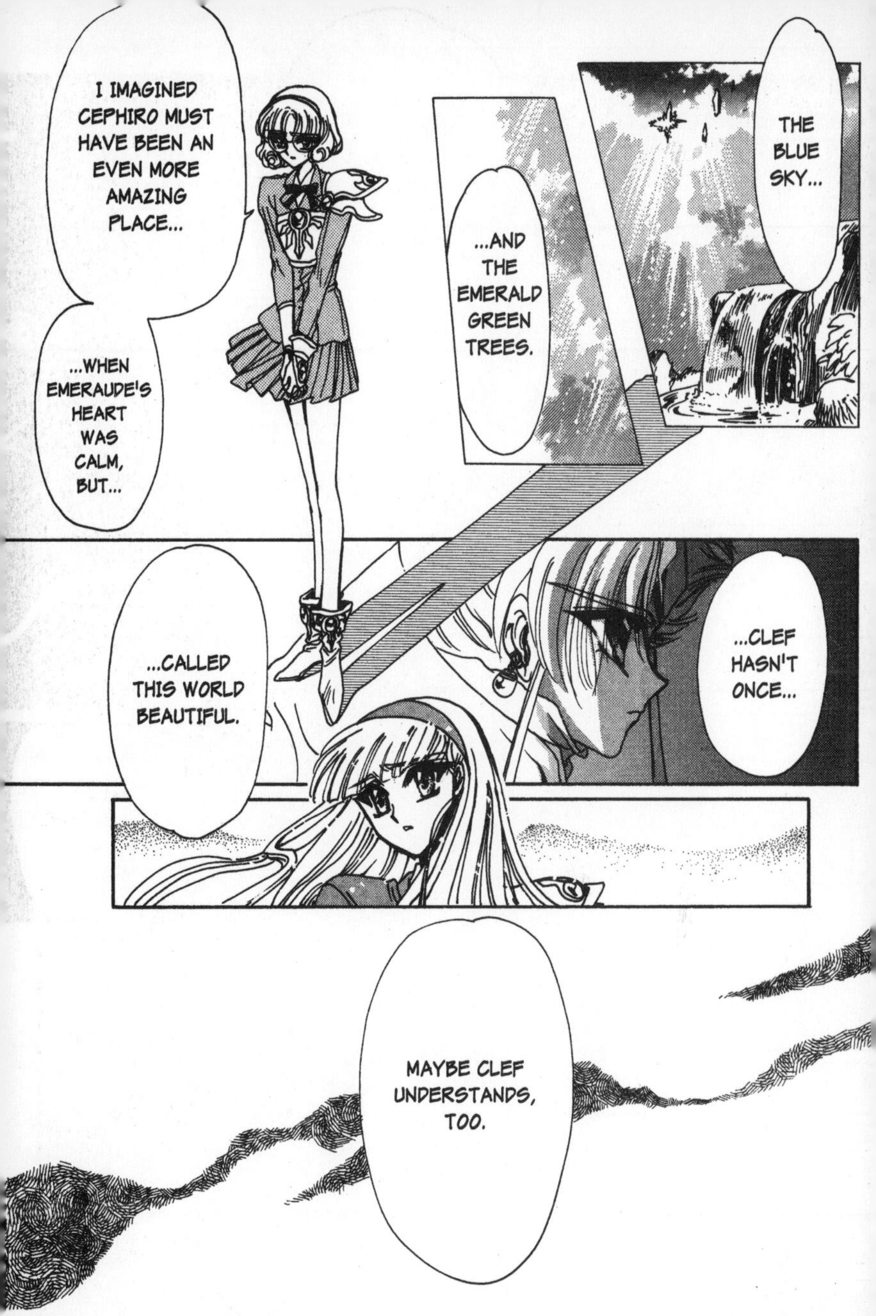
THE BLUE SKY...
...AND THE EMERALD GREEN TREES.
I IMAGINED CEPHIRO MUST HAVE BEEN AN EVEN MORE AMAZING PLACE...
...WHEN EMERAUDE'S HEART WAS CALM, BUT...
...CLEF HASN'T ONCE...
...CALLED THIS WORLD BEAUTIFUL.
MAYBE CLEF UNDERSTANDS, TOO.

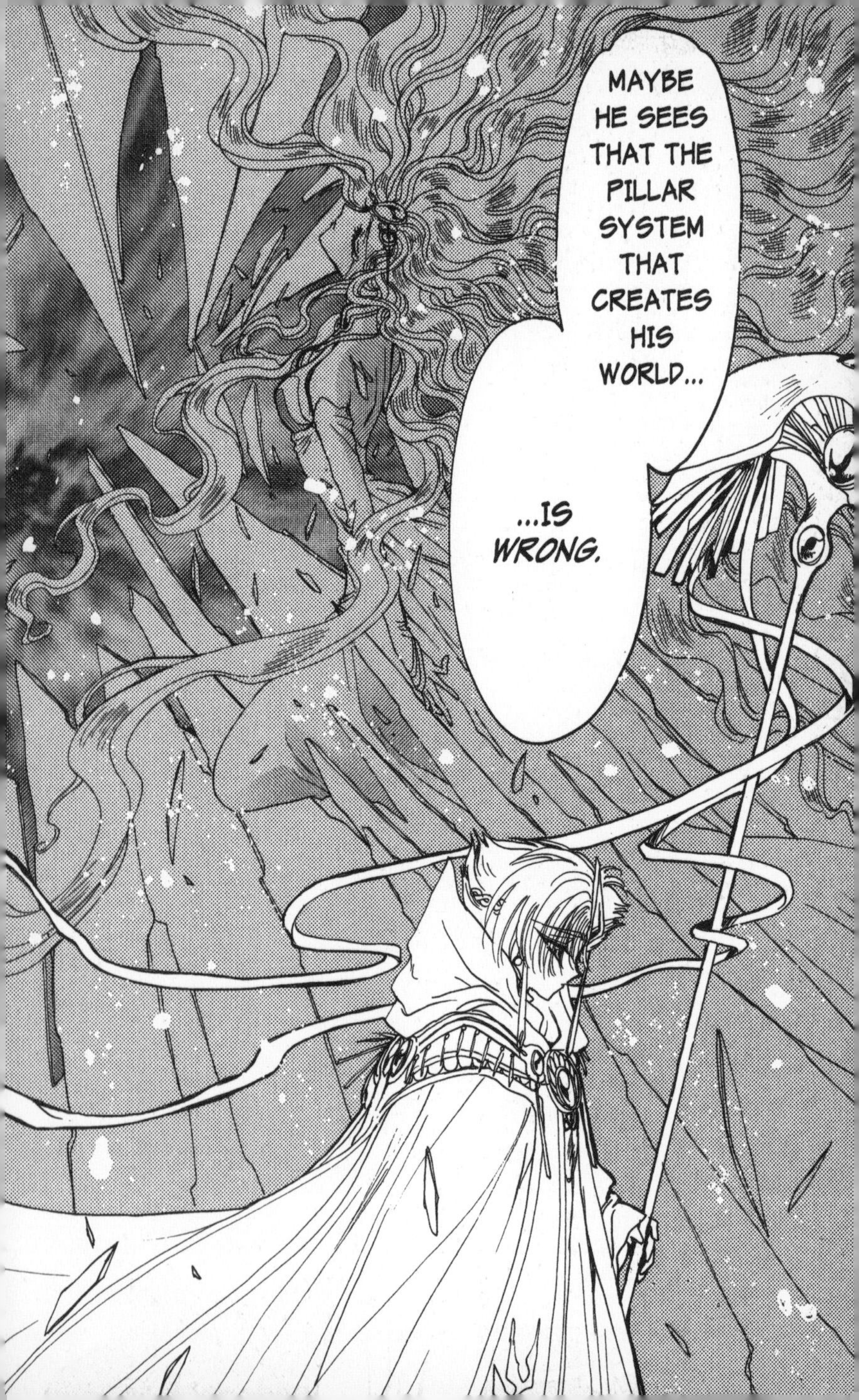
MAYBE HE SEES THAT THE PILLAR SYSTEM THAT CREATES HIS WORLD...
...IS *WRONG.*

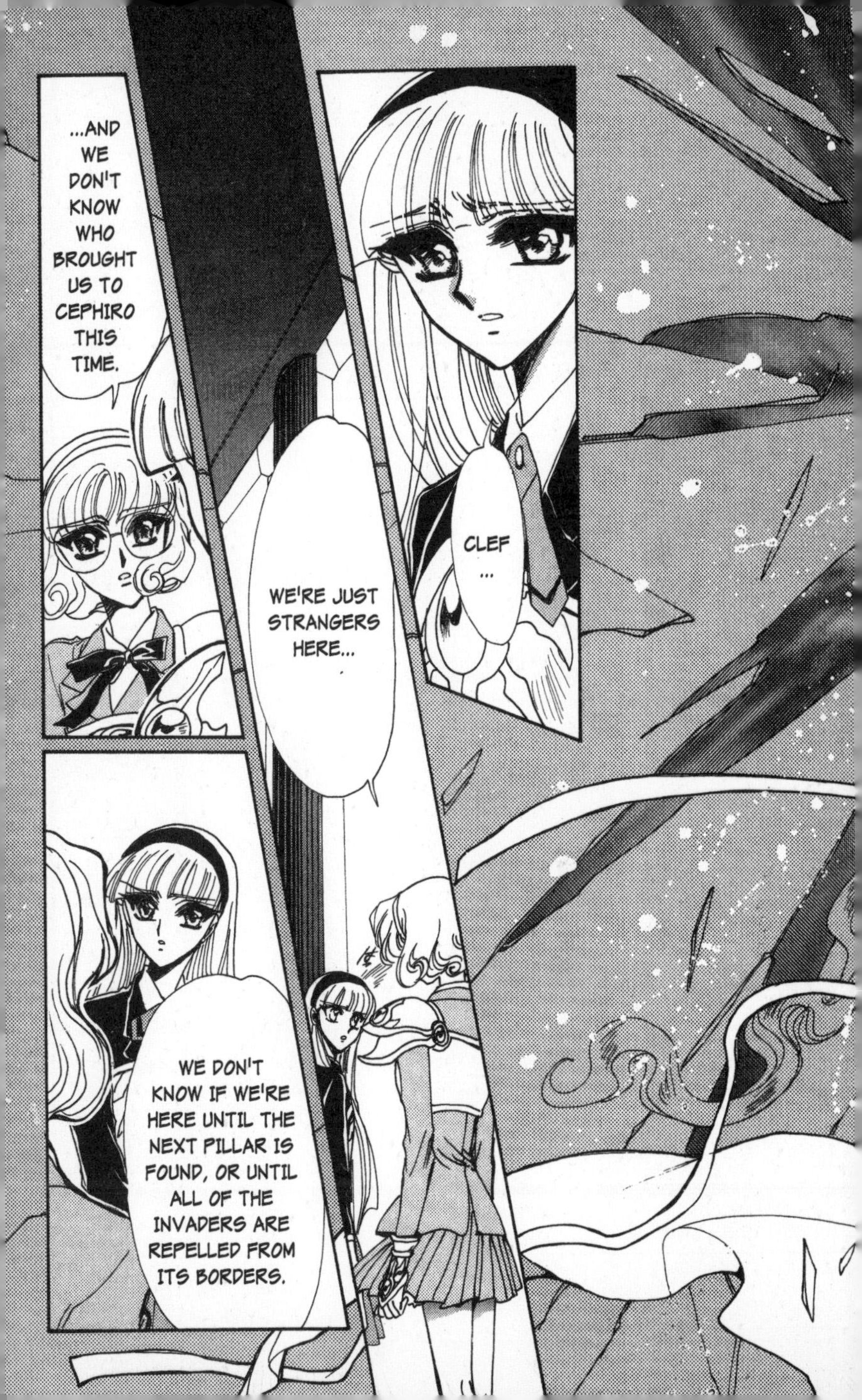

CLEF ...
WE'RE JUST STRANGERS HERE...
...AND WE DON'T KNOW WHO BROUGHT US TO CEPHIRO THIS TIME.
WE DON'T KNOW IF WE'RE HERE UNTIL THE NEXT PILLAR IS FOUND, OR UNTIL ALL OF THE INVADERS ARE REPELLED FROM ITS BORDERS.

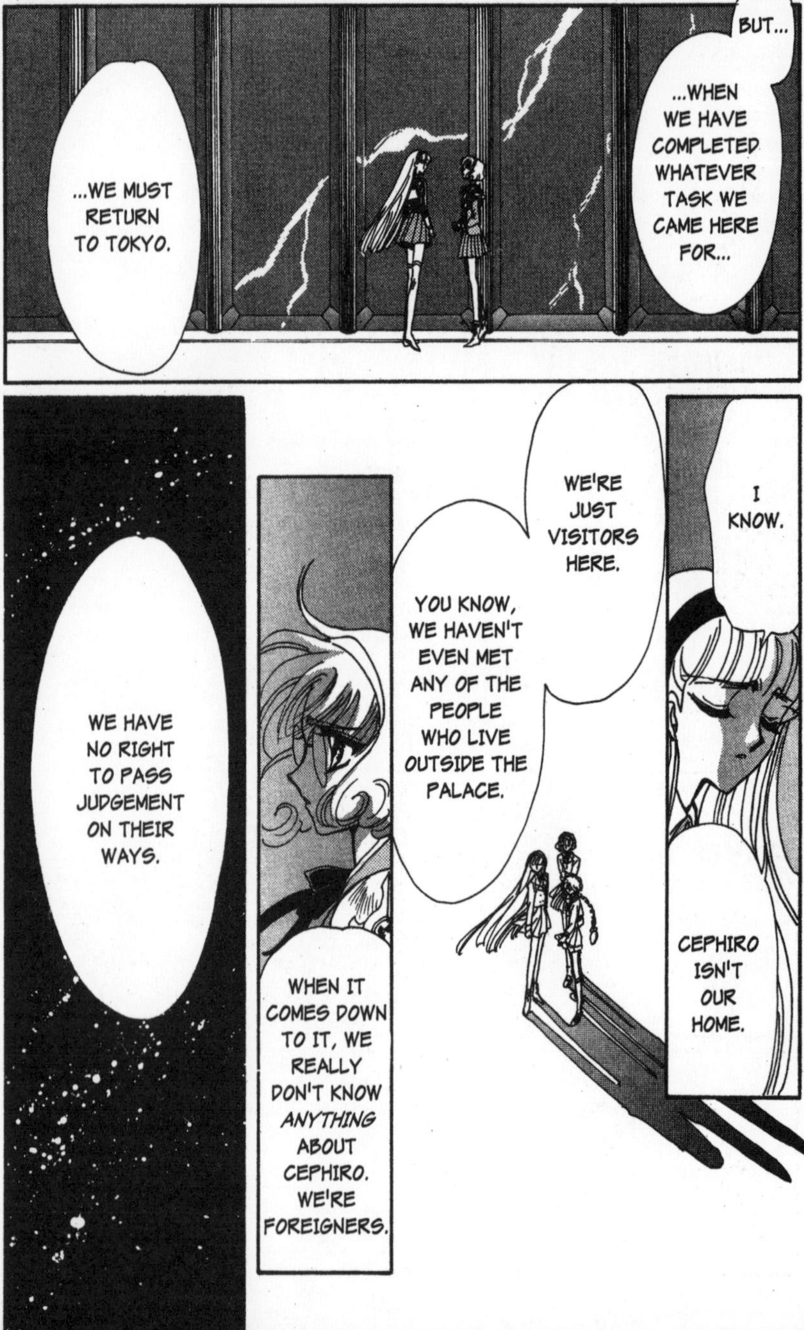
BUT...
...WHEN WE HAVE COMPLETED WHATEVER TASK WE CAME HERE FOR...
...WE MUST RETURN TO TOKYO.
I KNOW.
CEPHIRO ISN'T OUR HOME.
WE'RE JUST VISITORS HERE.
YOU KNOW, WE HAVEN'T EVEN MET ANY OF THE PEOPLE WHO LIVE OUTSIDE THE PALACE.
WHEN IT COMES DOWN TO IT, WE REALLY DON'T KNOW *ANYTHING* ABOUT CEPHIRO. WE'RE FOREIGNERS.
WE HAVE NO RIGHT TO PASS JUDGEMENT ON THEIR WAYS.

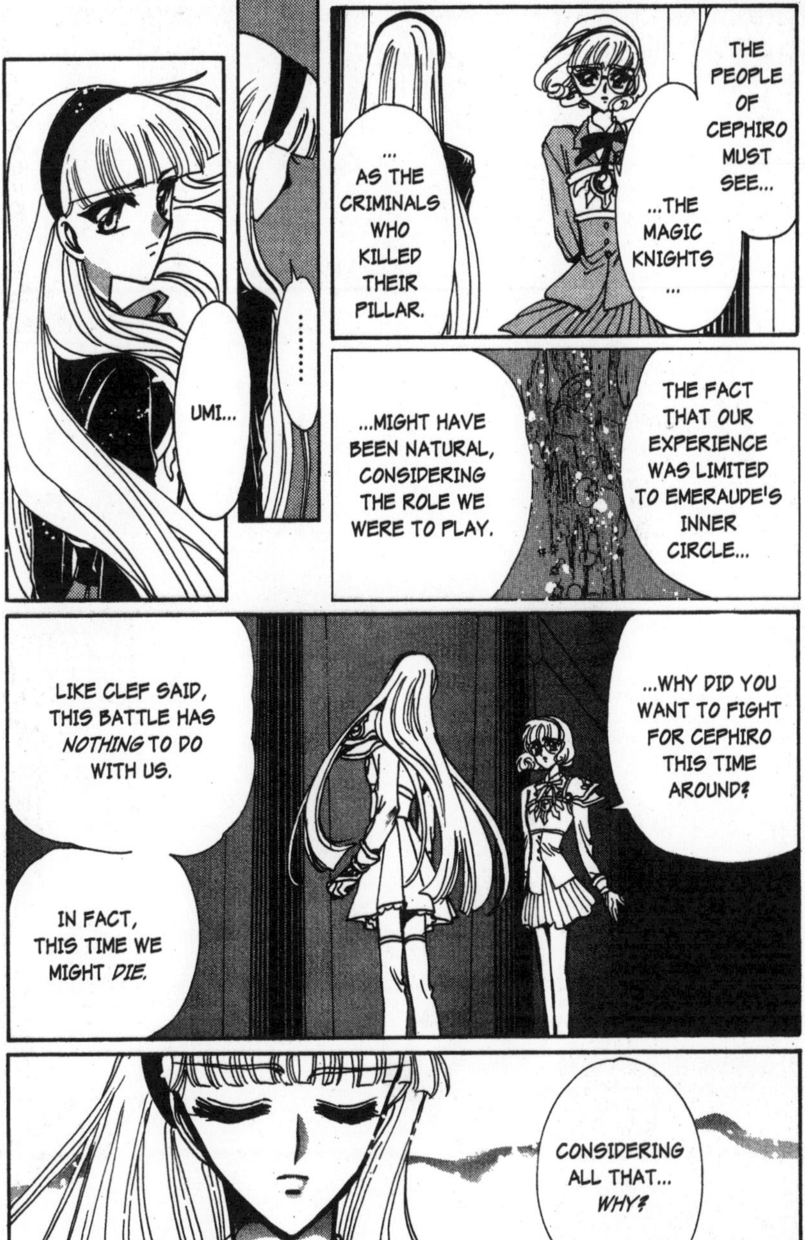
THE PEOPLE OF CEPHIRO MUST SEE...
...THE MAGIC KNIGHTS ...
... AS THE CRIMINALS WHO KILLED THEIR PILLAR.
THE FACT THAT OUR EXPERIENCE WAS LIMITED TO EMERAUDE'S INNER CIRCLE...
...MIGHT HAVE BEEN NATURAL, CONSIDERING THE ROLE WE WERE TO PLAY.
......
UMI...
...WHY DID YOU WANT TO FIGHT FOR CEPHIRO THIS TIME AROUND?
LIKE CLEF SAID, THIS BATTLE HAS *NOTHING* TO DO WITH US.
IN FACT, THIS TIME WE MIGHT *DIE.*
CONSIDERING ALL THAT... *WHY?*

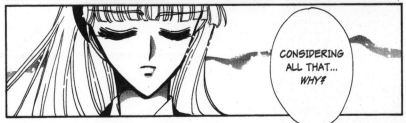

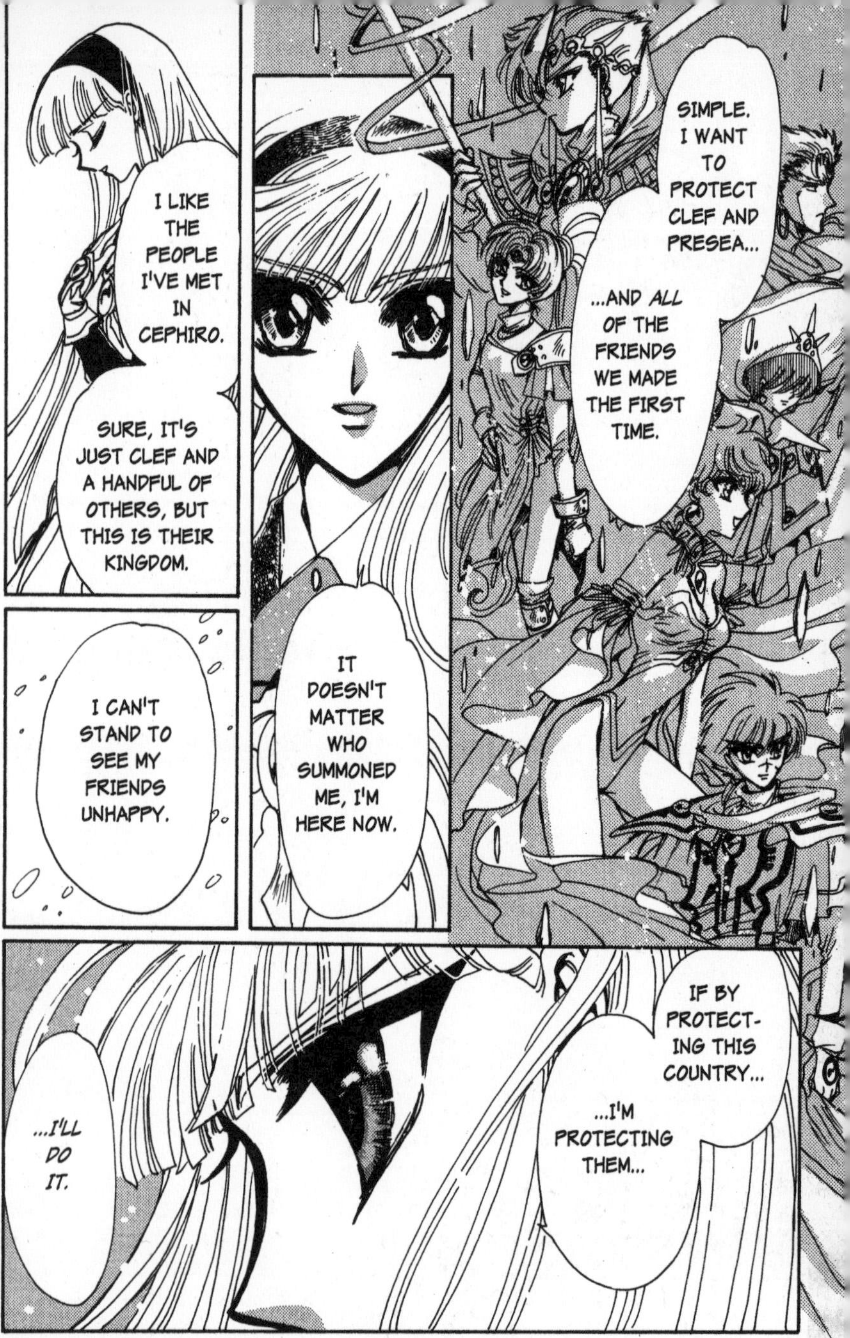
SIMPLE. I WANT TO PROTECT CLEF AND PRESEA...
...AND *ALL* OF THE FRIENDS WE MADE THE FIRST TIME.
IT DOESN'T MATTER WHO SUMMONED ME, I'M HERE NOW.
I LIKE THE PEOPLE I'VE MET IN CEPHIRO.
SURE, IT'S JUST CLEF AND A HANDFUL OF OTHERS, BUT THIS IS THEIR KINGDOM.
I CAN'T STAND TO SEE MY FRIENDS UNHAPPY.
IF BY PROTECTING THIS COUNTRY...
...I'M PROTECTING THEM...
...I'LL DO IT.

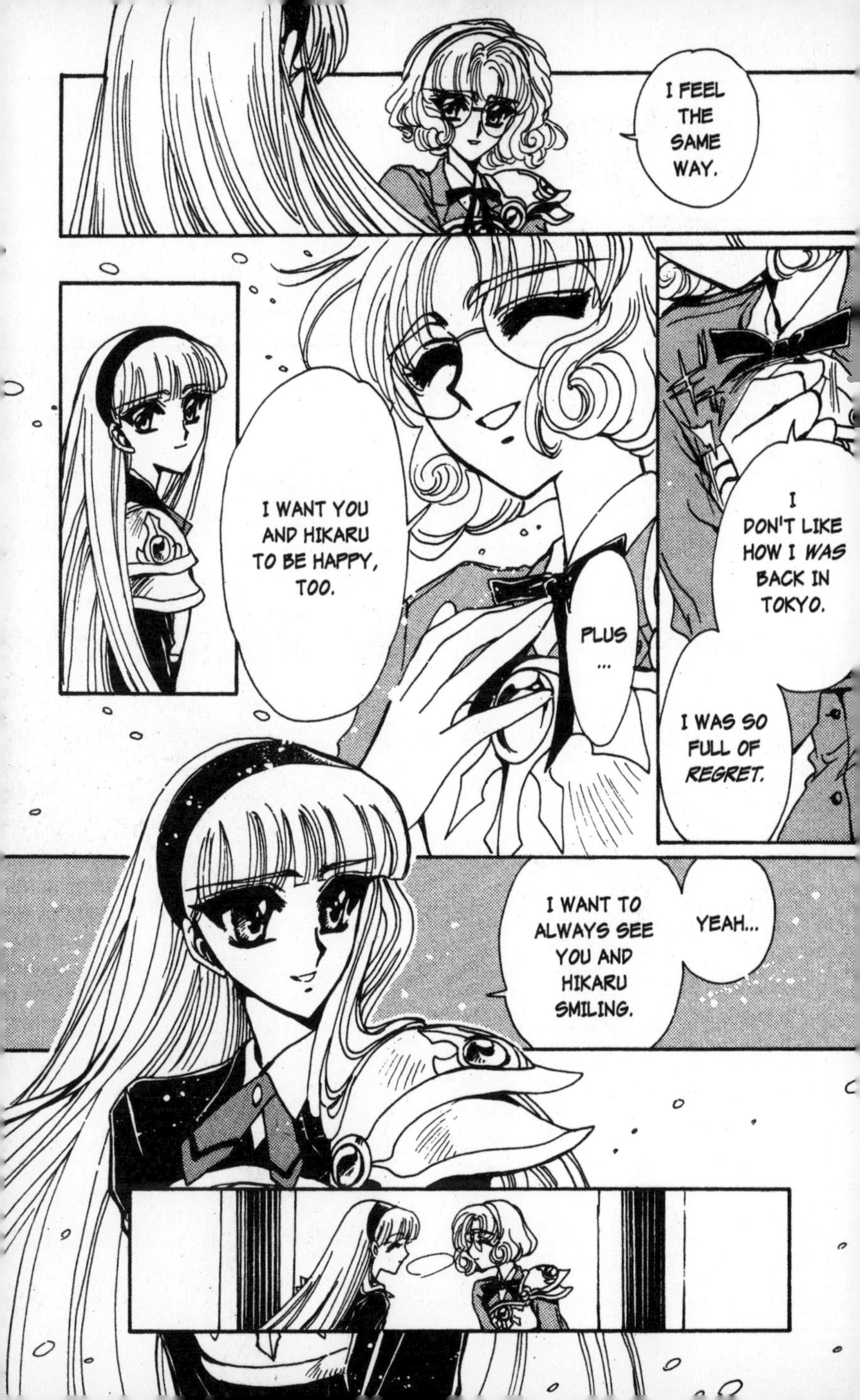
I FEEL THE SAME WAY.
I DON'T LIKE HOW I *WAS* BACK IN TOKYO.
I WAS SO FULL OF *REGRET*.
PLUS ...
I WANT YOU AND HIKARU TO BE HAPPY, TOO.
YEAH...
I WANT TO ALWAYS SEE YOU AND HIKARU SMILING.

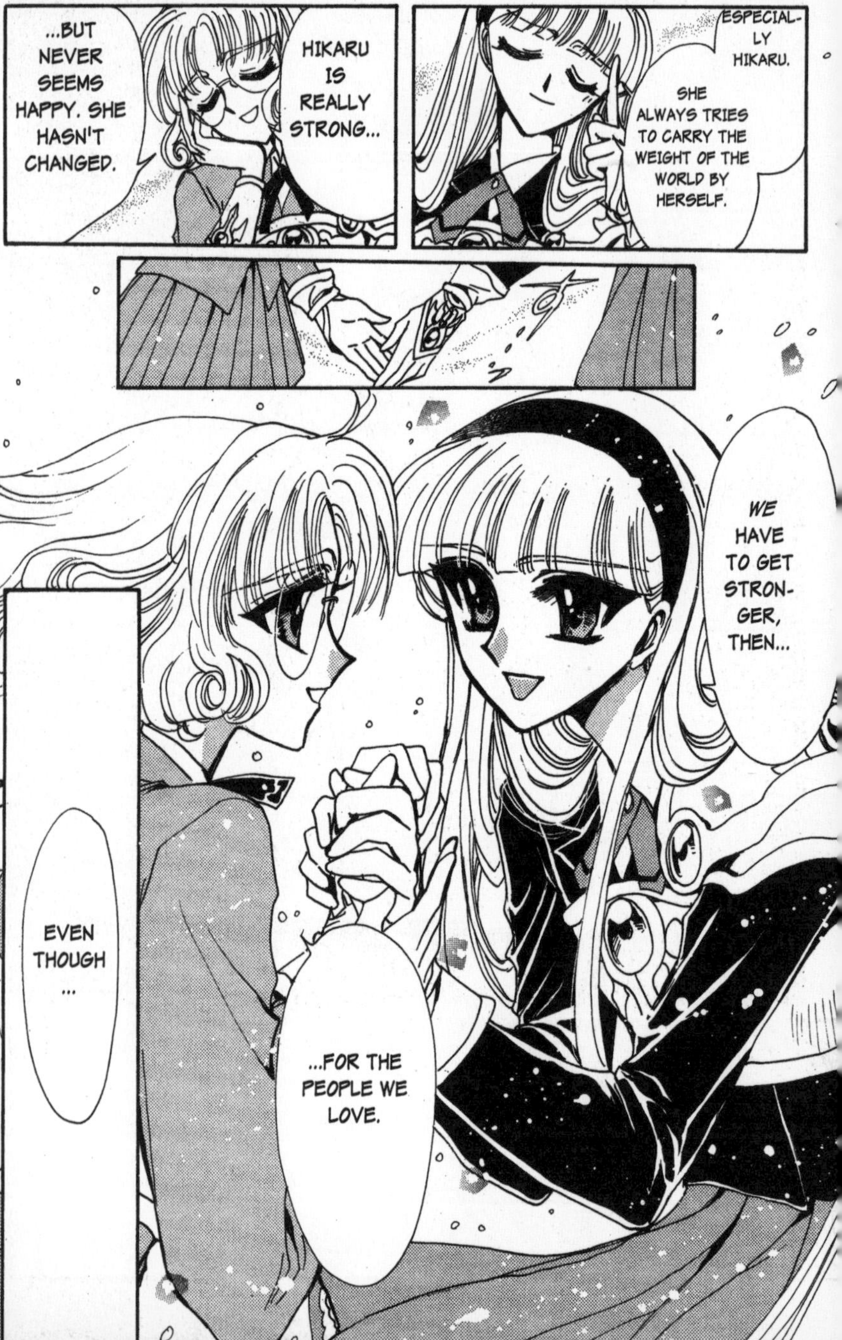
ESPECIALLY HIKARU.
SHE ALWAYS TRIES TO CARRY THE WEIGHT OF THE WORLD BY HERSELF.
HIKARU IS REALLY STRONG...
...BUT NEVER SEEMS HAPPY. SHE HASN'T CHANGED.
WE HAVE TO GET STRONGER, THEN...
EVEN THOUGH ...
...FOR THE PEOPLE WE LOVE.

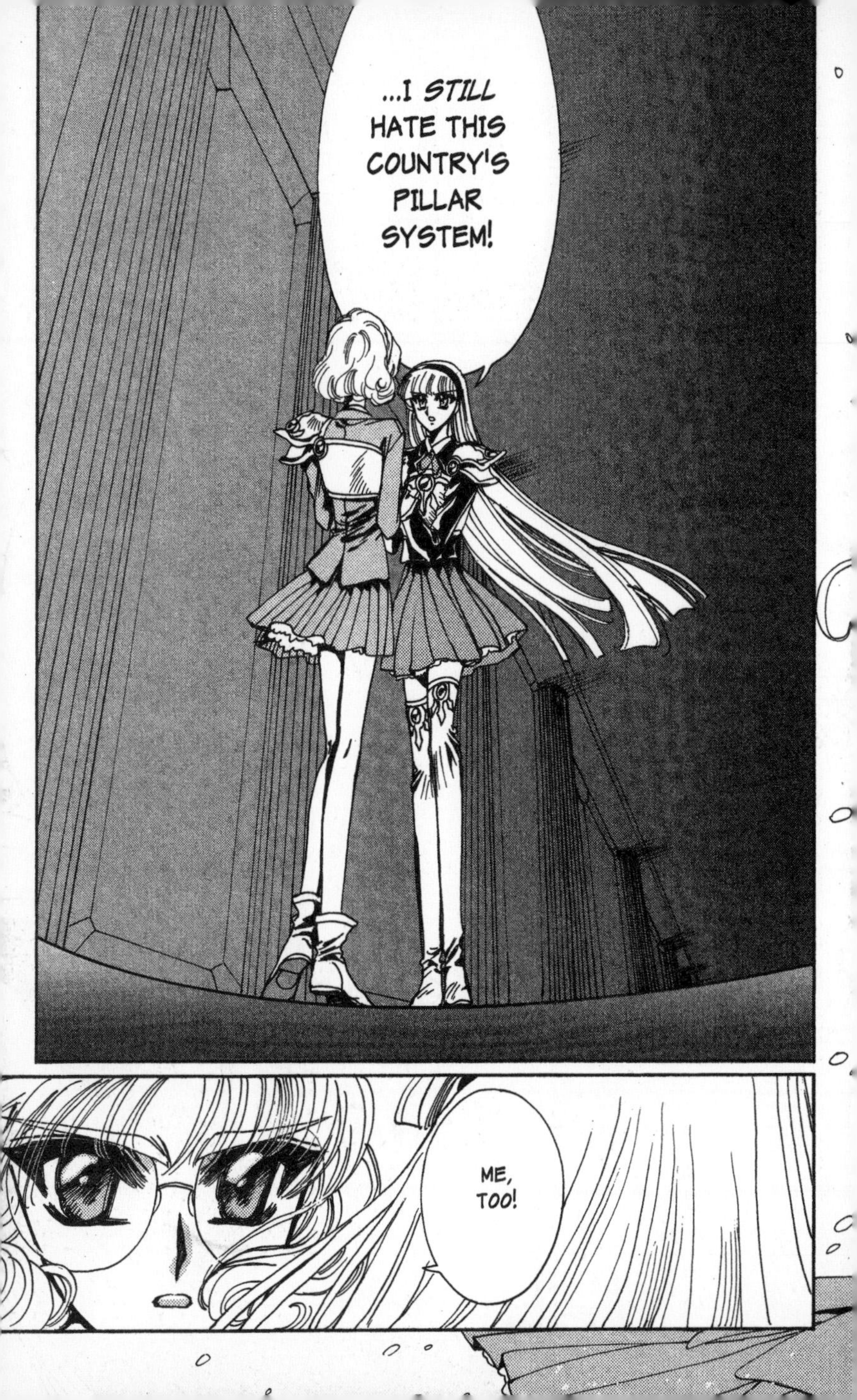
...I STILL HATE THIS COUNTRY'S PILLAR SYSTEM!
ME, TOO!

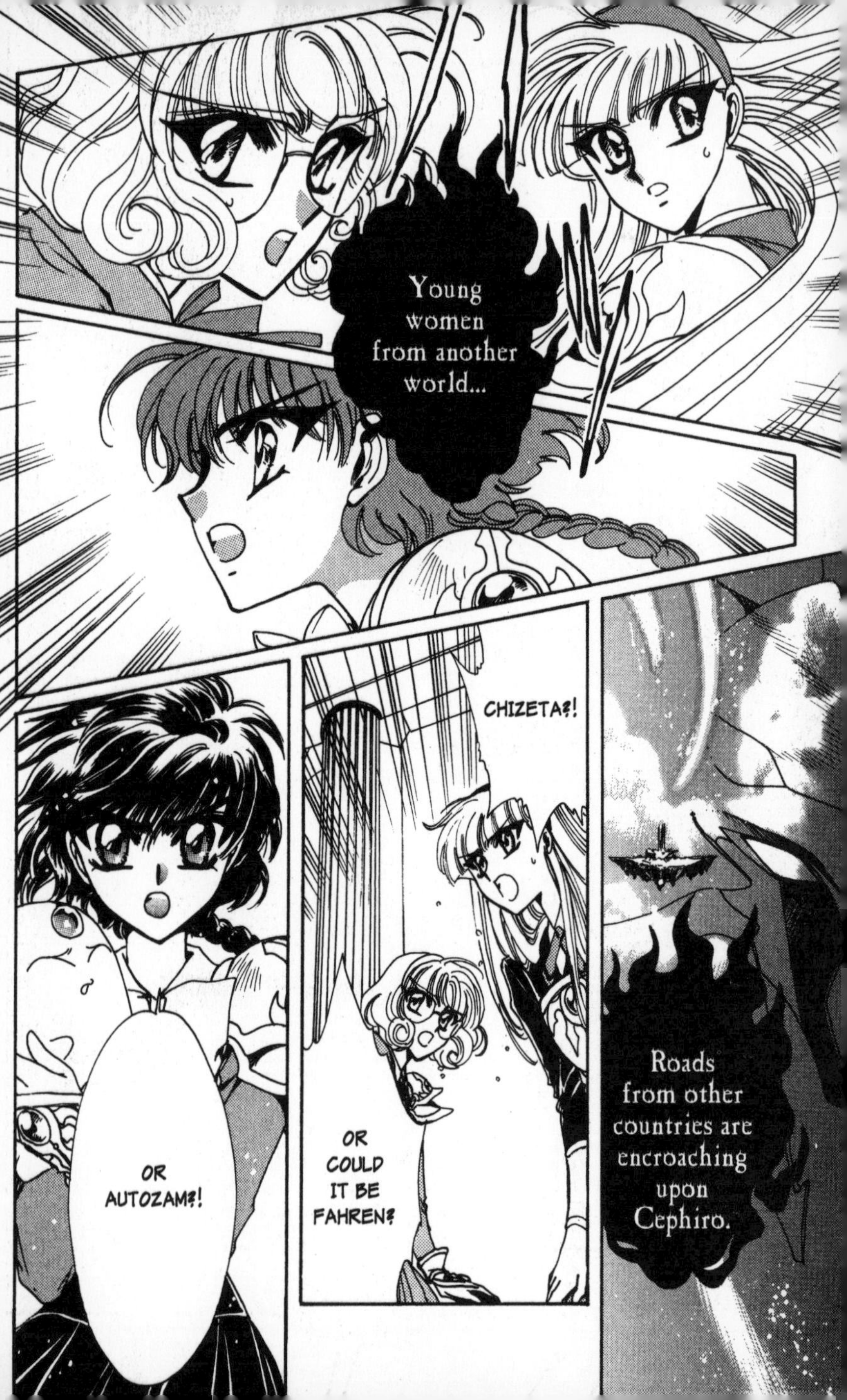
Young women from another world...
Roads from other countries are encroaching upon Cephiro.
CHIZETA?!
OR COULD IT BE FAHREN?
OR AUTOZAM?!

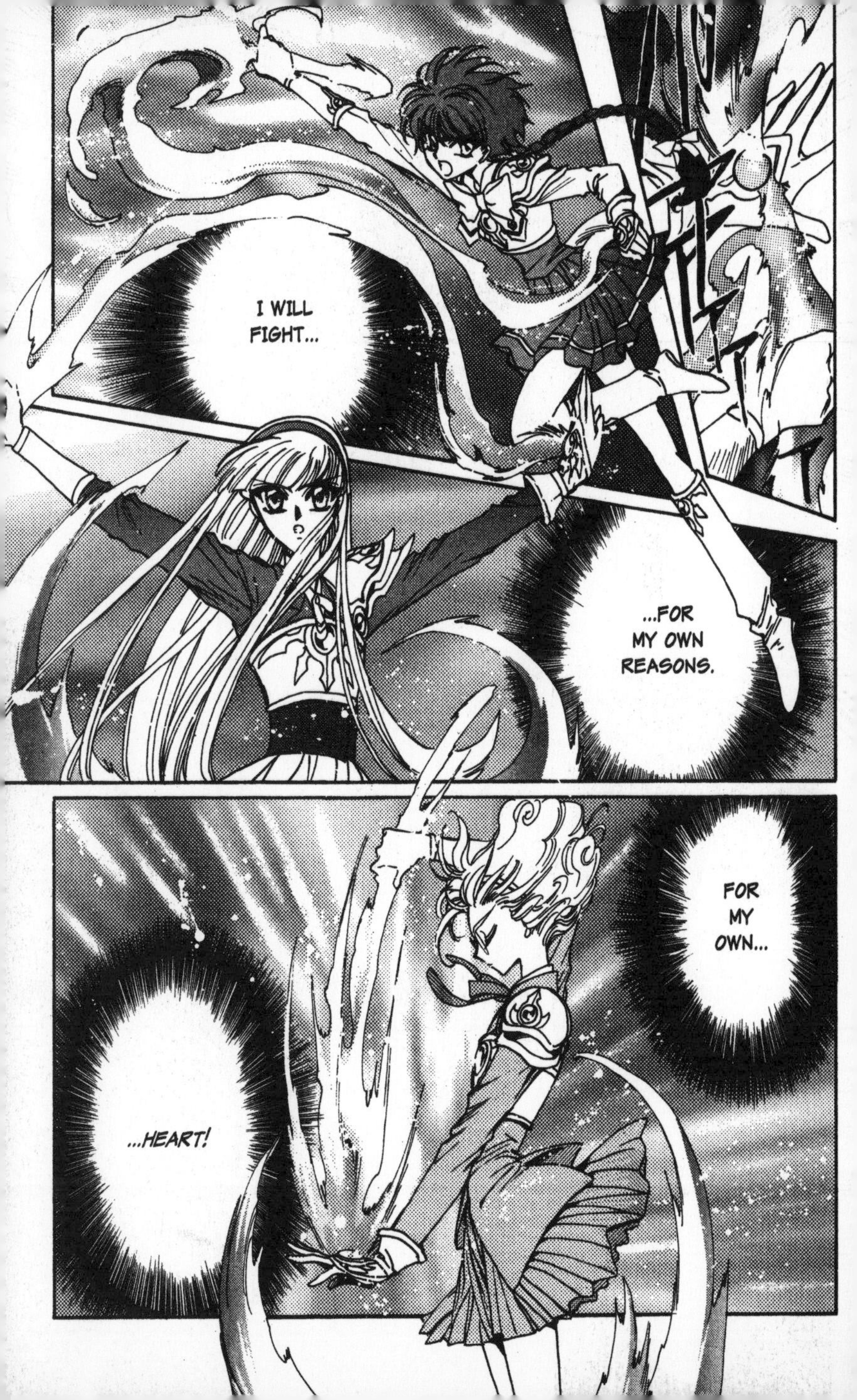
I WILL FIGHT...
...FOR MY OWN REASONS.
FOR MY OWN...
...HEART!

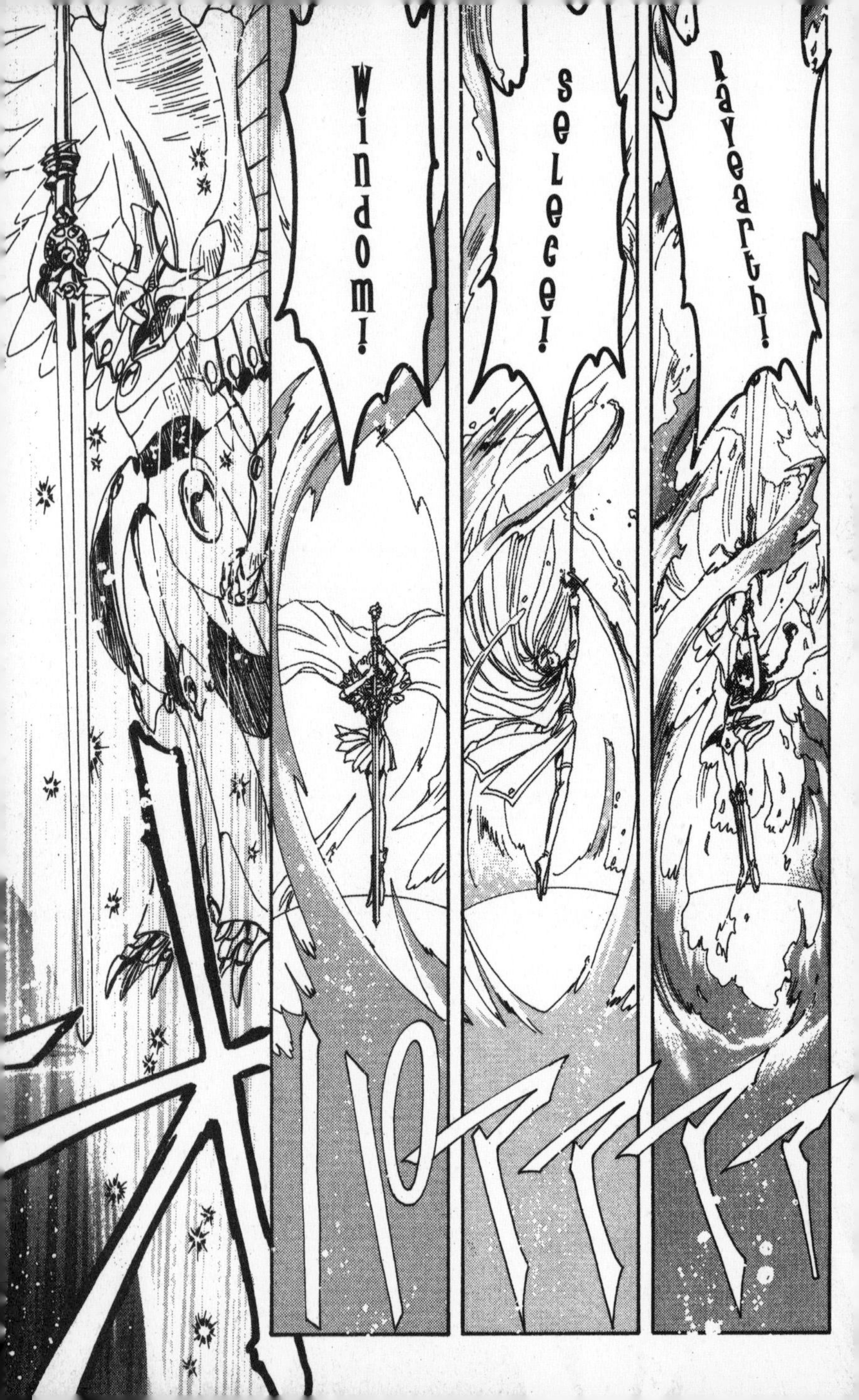
Rayearth!
Selece!
Windom!

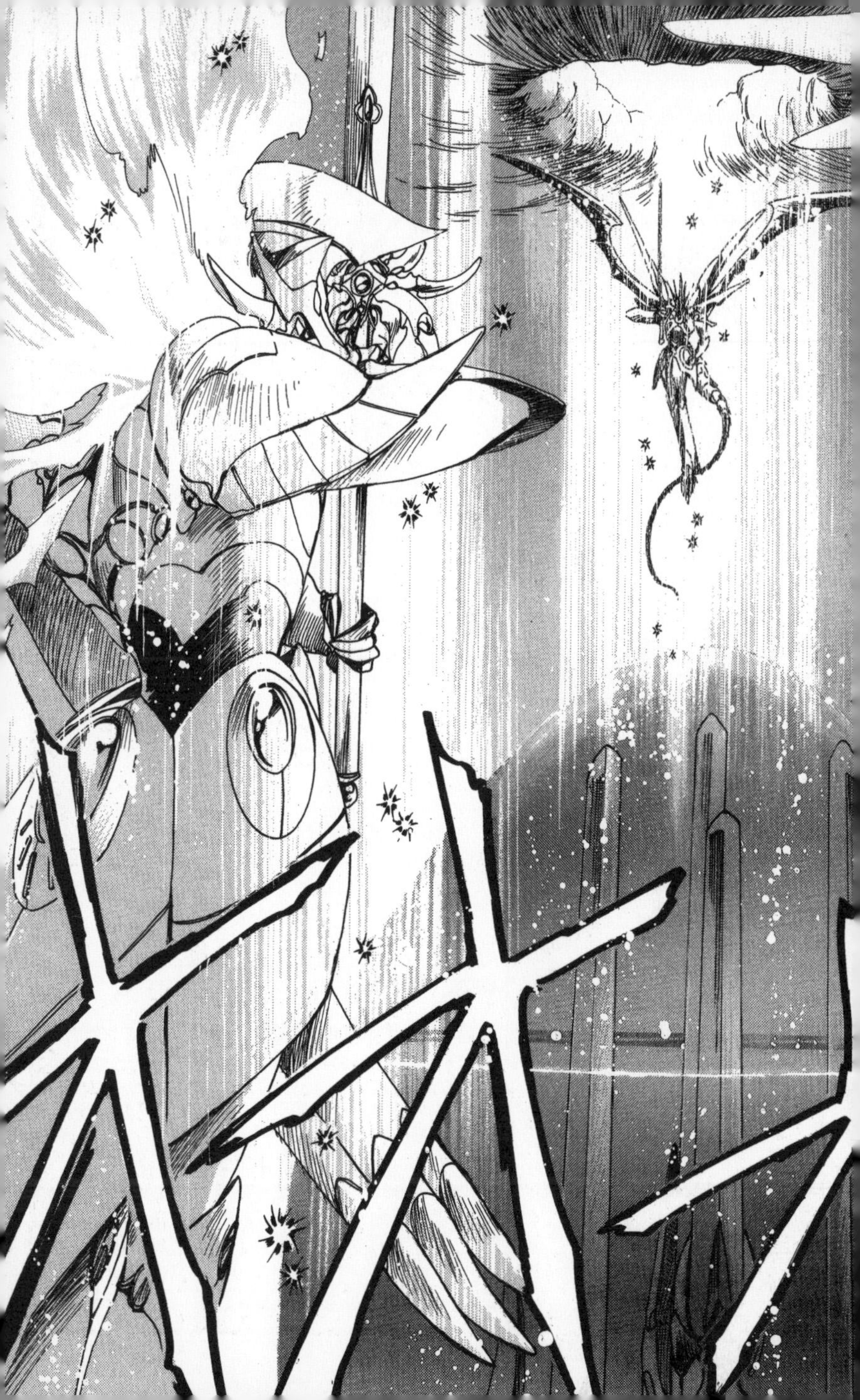

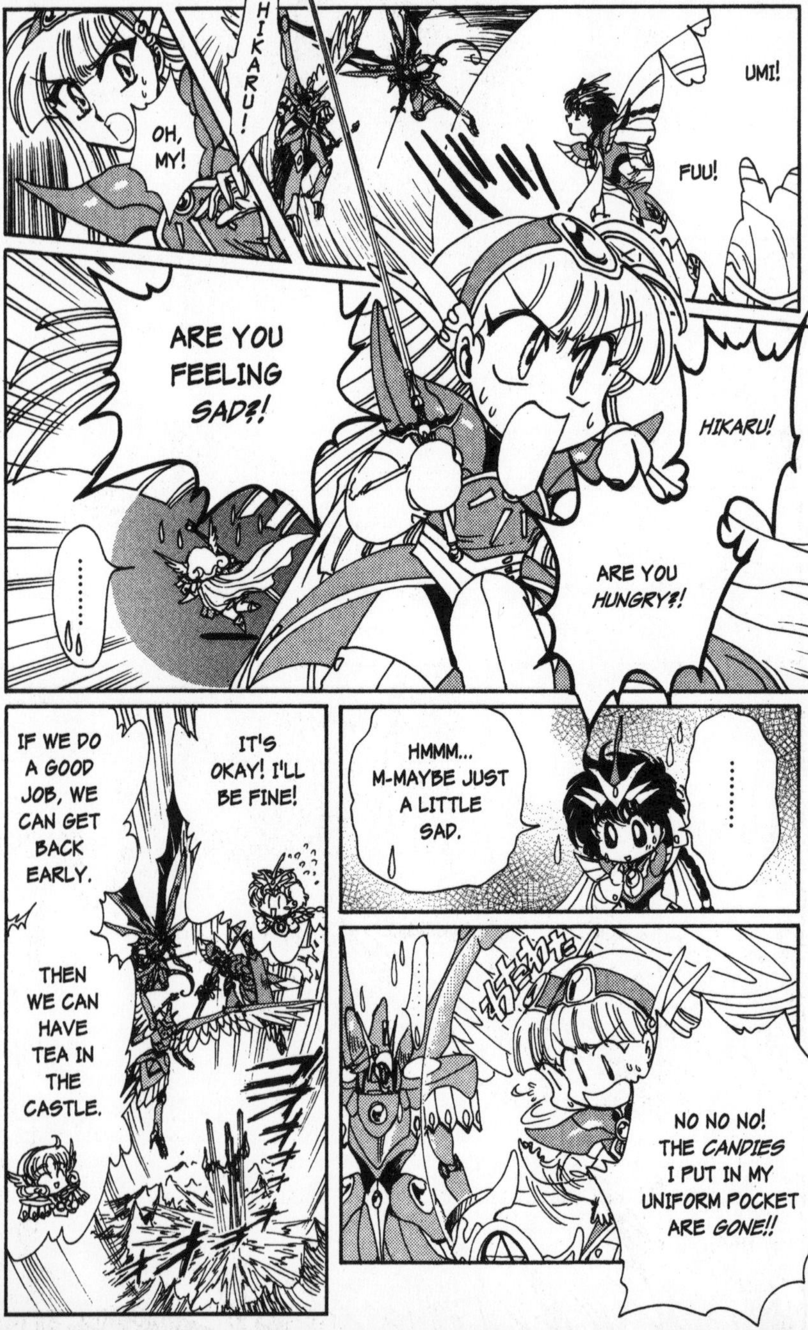
UMI!
FUU!
HIKARU!
OH, MY!
HIKARU!
ARE YOU FEELING *SAD*?!
ARE YOU *HUNGRY*?!
......
......
HMMM... M-MAYBE JUST A LITTLE SAD.
NO NO NO! THE *CANDIES* I PUT IN MY UNIFORM POCKET ARE *GONE*!!
IT'S OKAY! I'LL BE FINE!
IF WE DO A GOOD JOB, WE CAN GET BACK EARLY.
THEN WE CAN HAVE TEA IN THE CASTLE.

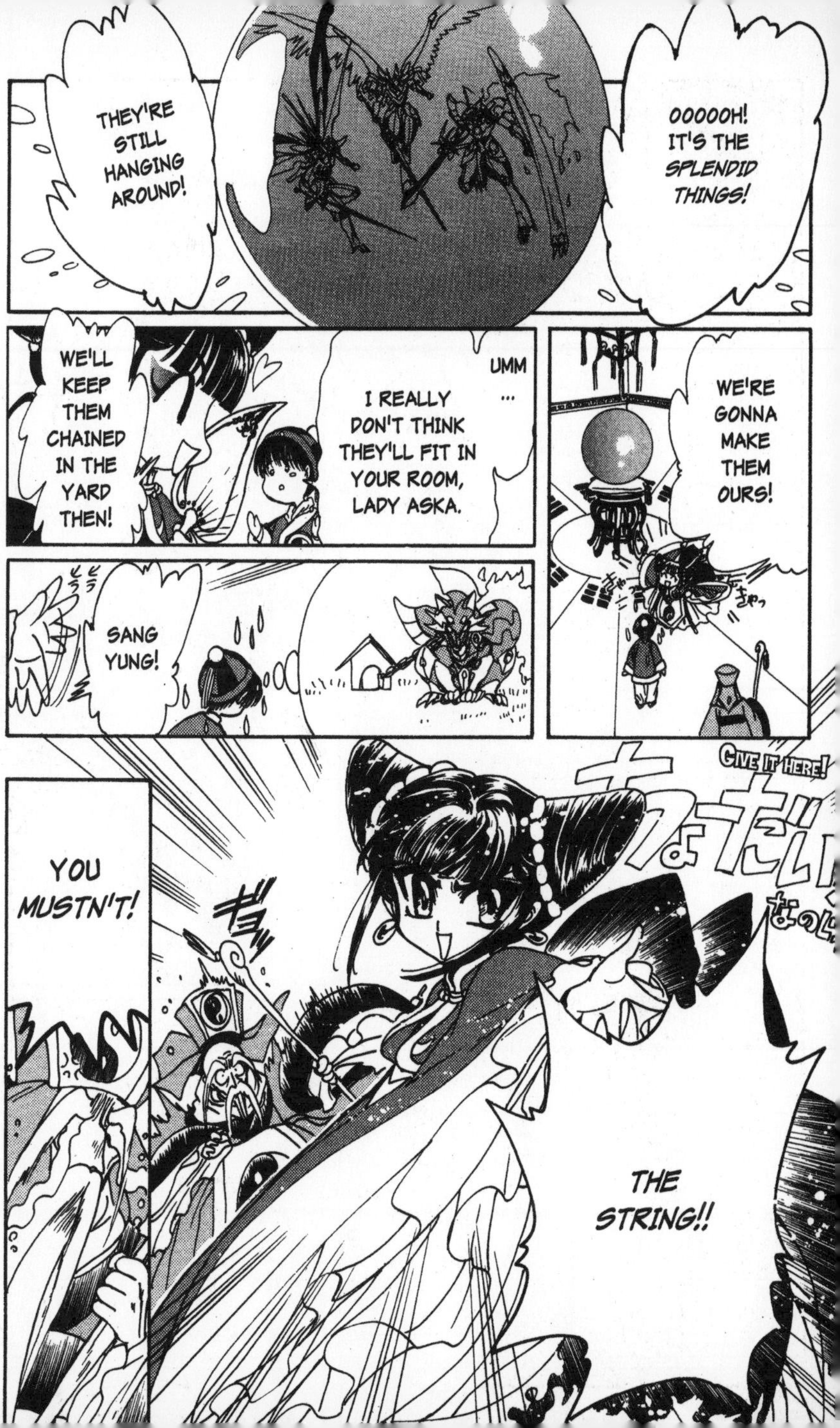
OOOOOH! IT'S THE SPLENDID THINGS!
THEY'RE STILL HANGING AROUND!
WE'RE GONNA MAKE THEM OURS!
UMM ...
I REALLY DON'T THINK THEY'LL FIT IN YOUR ROOM, LADY ASKA.
WE'LL KEEP THEM CHAINED IN THE YARD THEN!
SANG YUNG!
GIVE IT HERE!
THE STRING!!
YOU MUSTN'T!

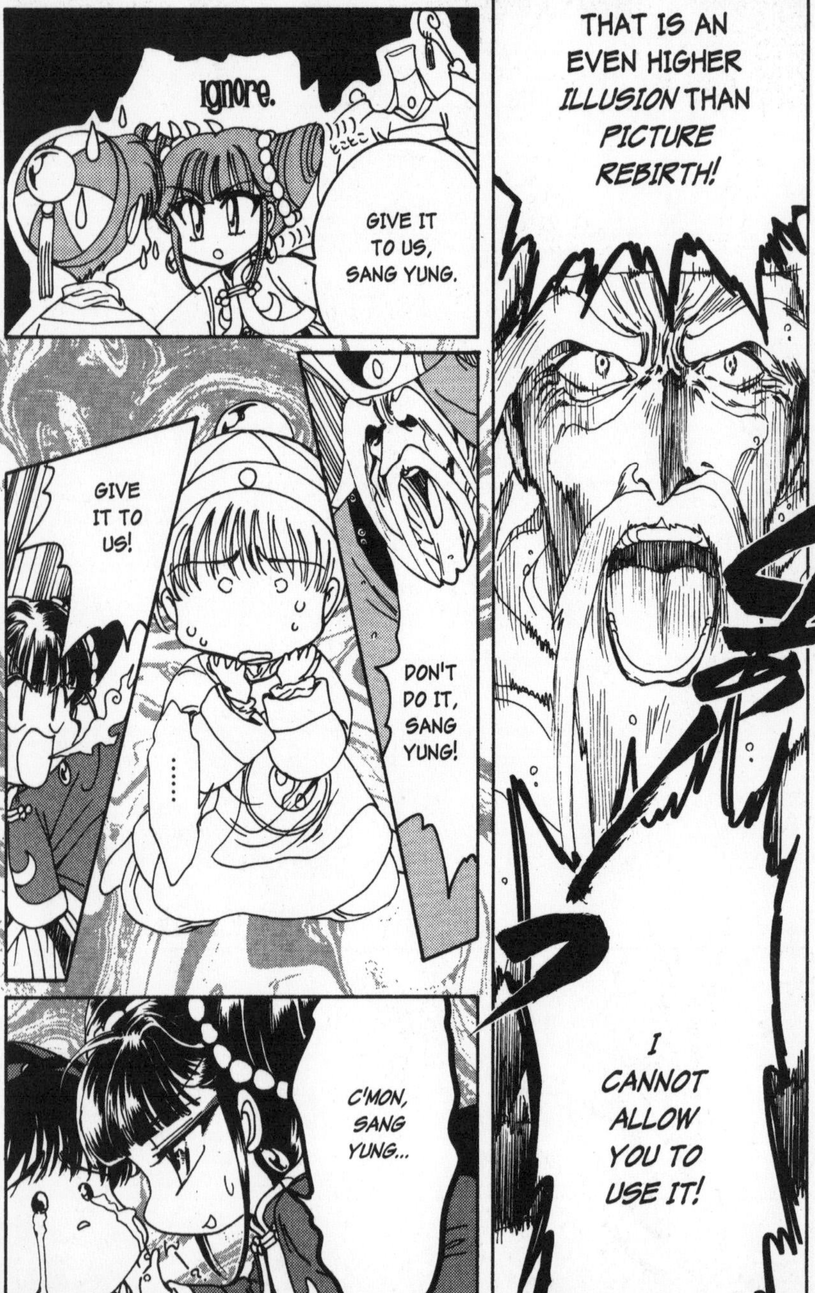
THAT IS AN EVEN HIGHER ILLUSION THAN PICTURE REBIRTH!
I CANNOT ALLOW YOU TO USE IT!
Ignore.
GIVE IT TO US, SANG YUNG.
GIVE IT TO US!
DON'T DO IT, SANG YUNG!
......
C'MON, SANG YUNG...

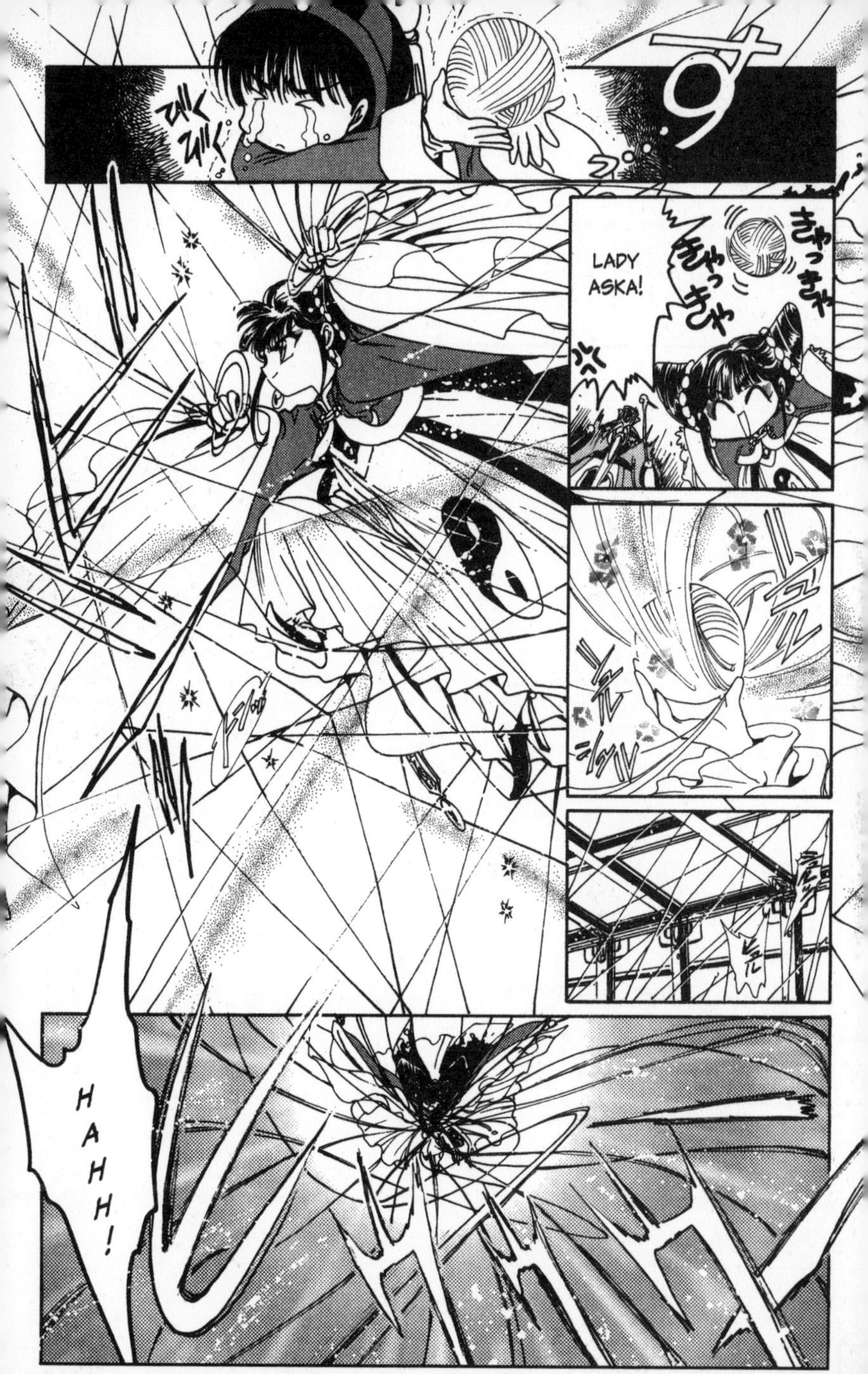
す
ぴくぴく
LADY ASKA!
きゃっきゃ きゃっきゃ
HAHHH!

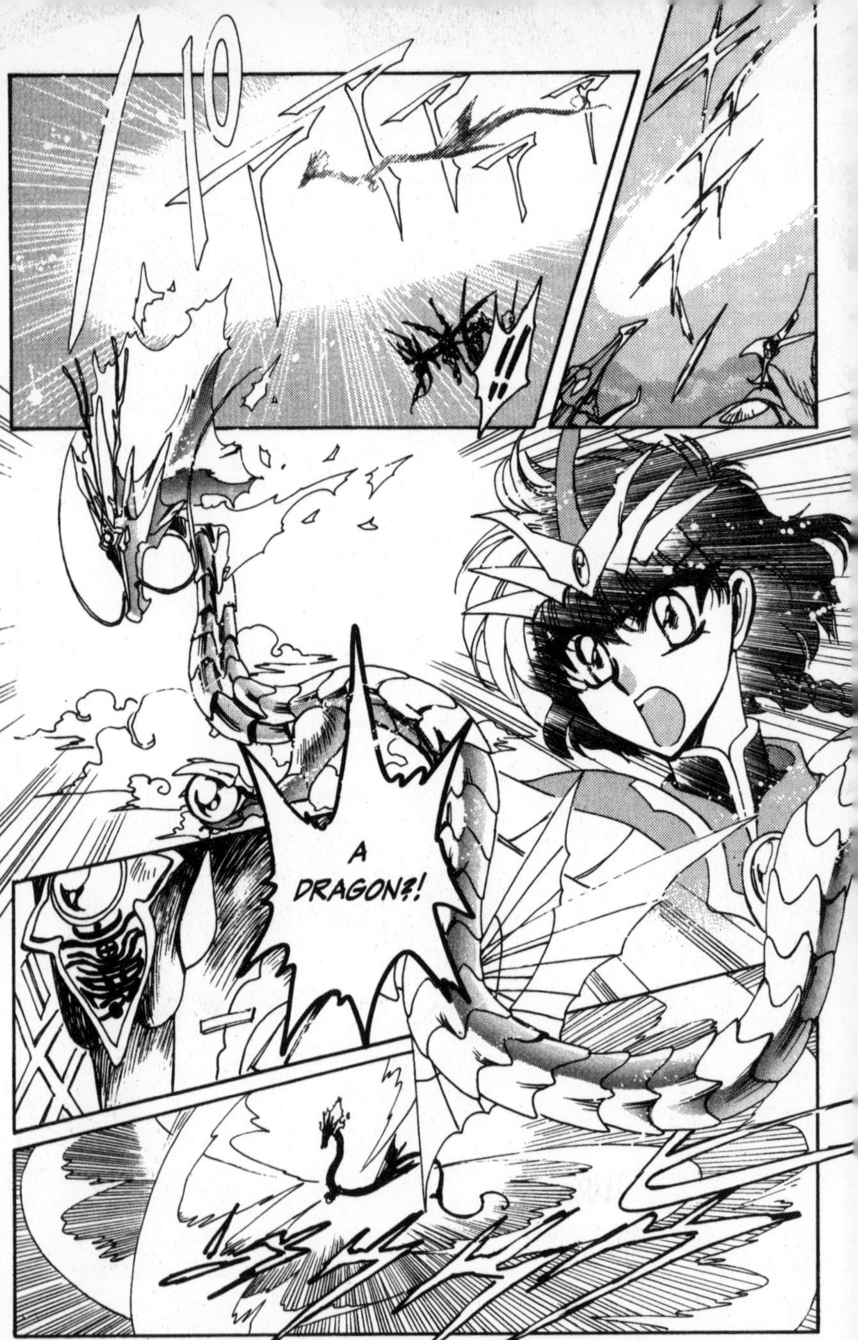
A DRAGON?!

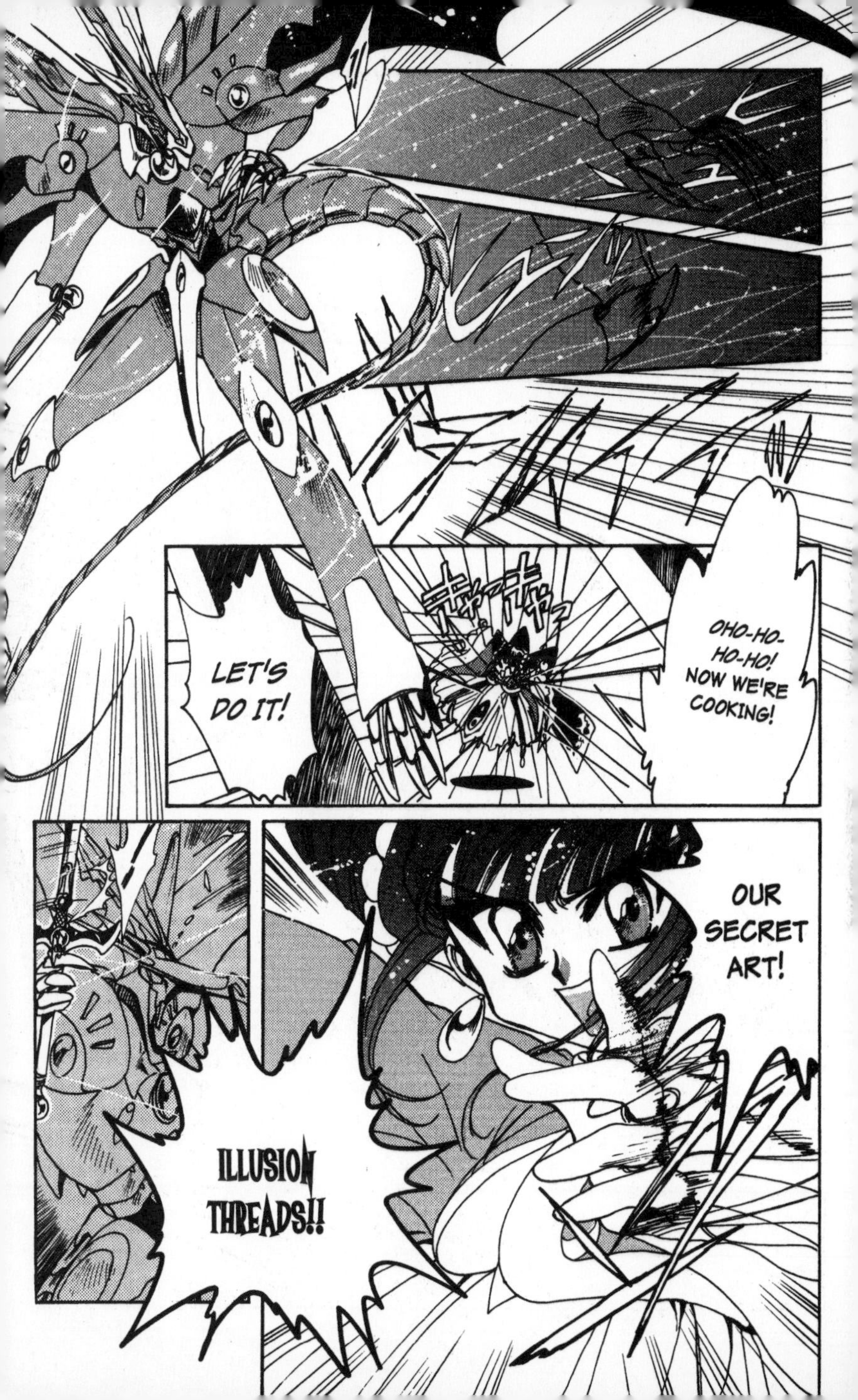
OHO-HO-HO-HO! NOW WE'RE COOKING!
LET'S DO IT!
OUR SECRET ART!
ILLUSION THREADS!!

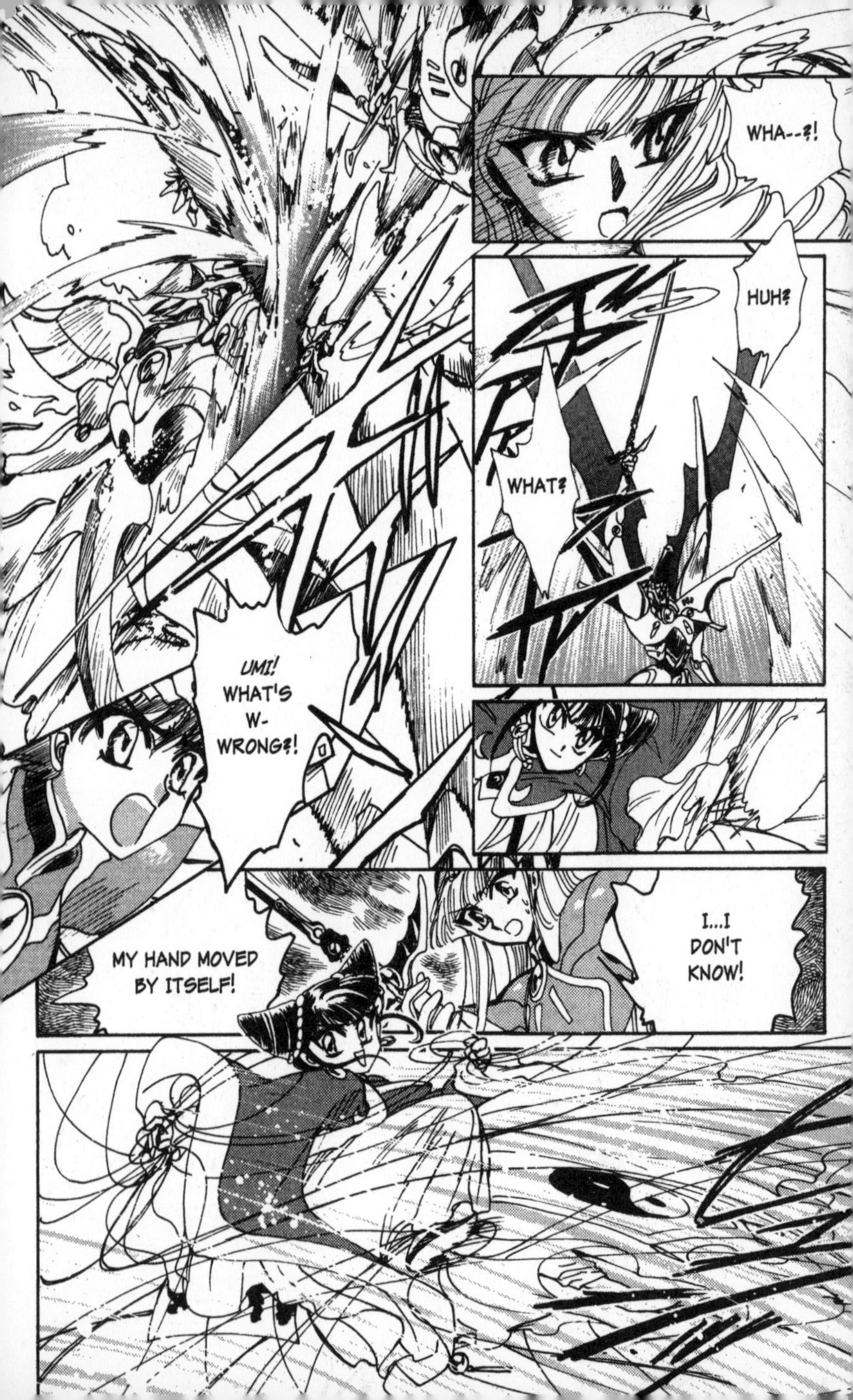
WHA--?!
HUH?
WHAT?
UMI! WHAT'S W-WRONG?!
I...I DON'T KNOW!
MY HAND MOVED BY ITSELF!

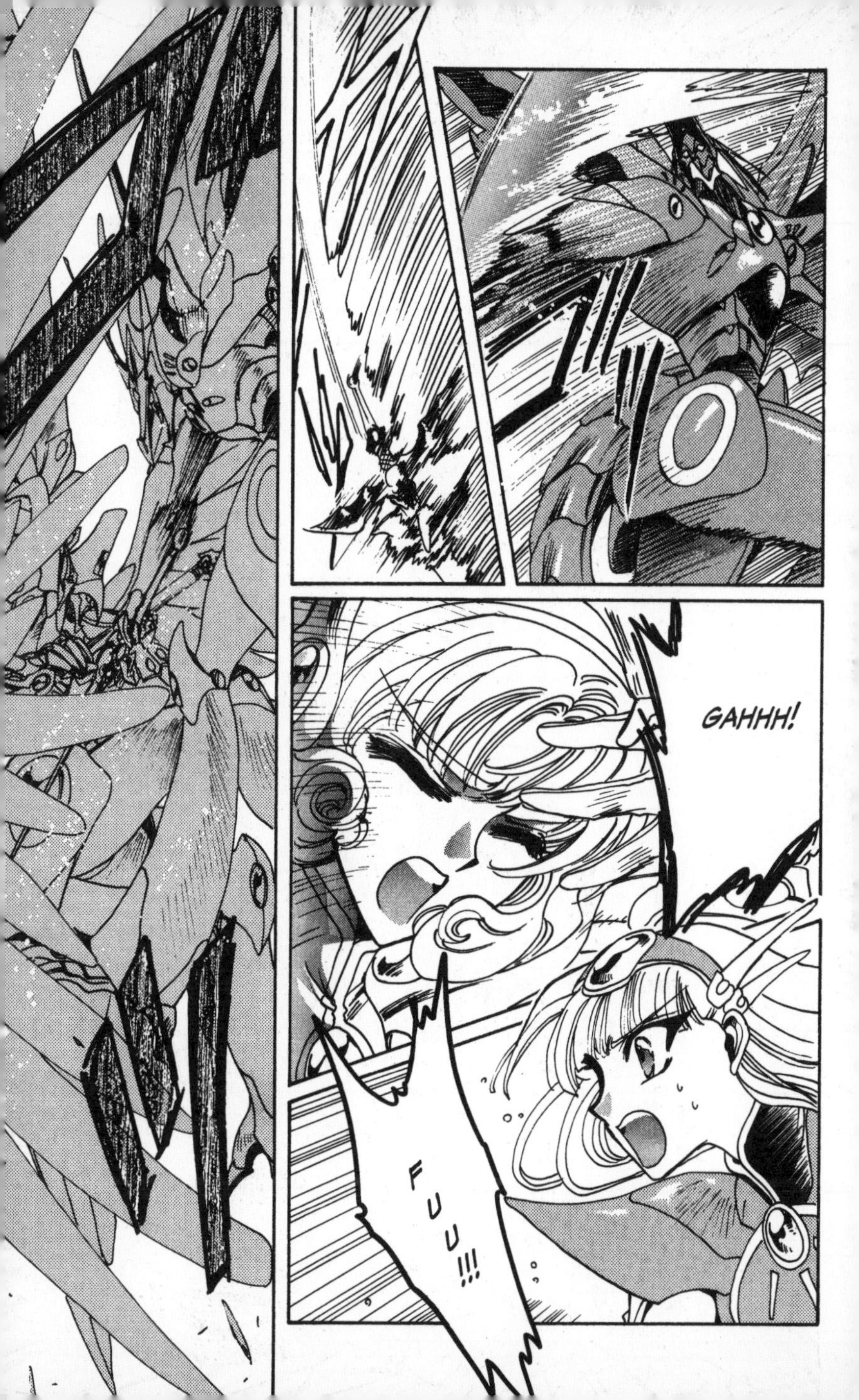
GAHHH!
FUUU!!!

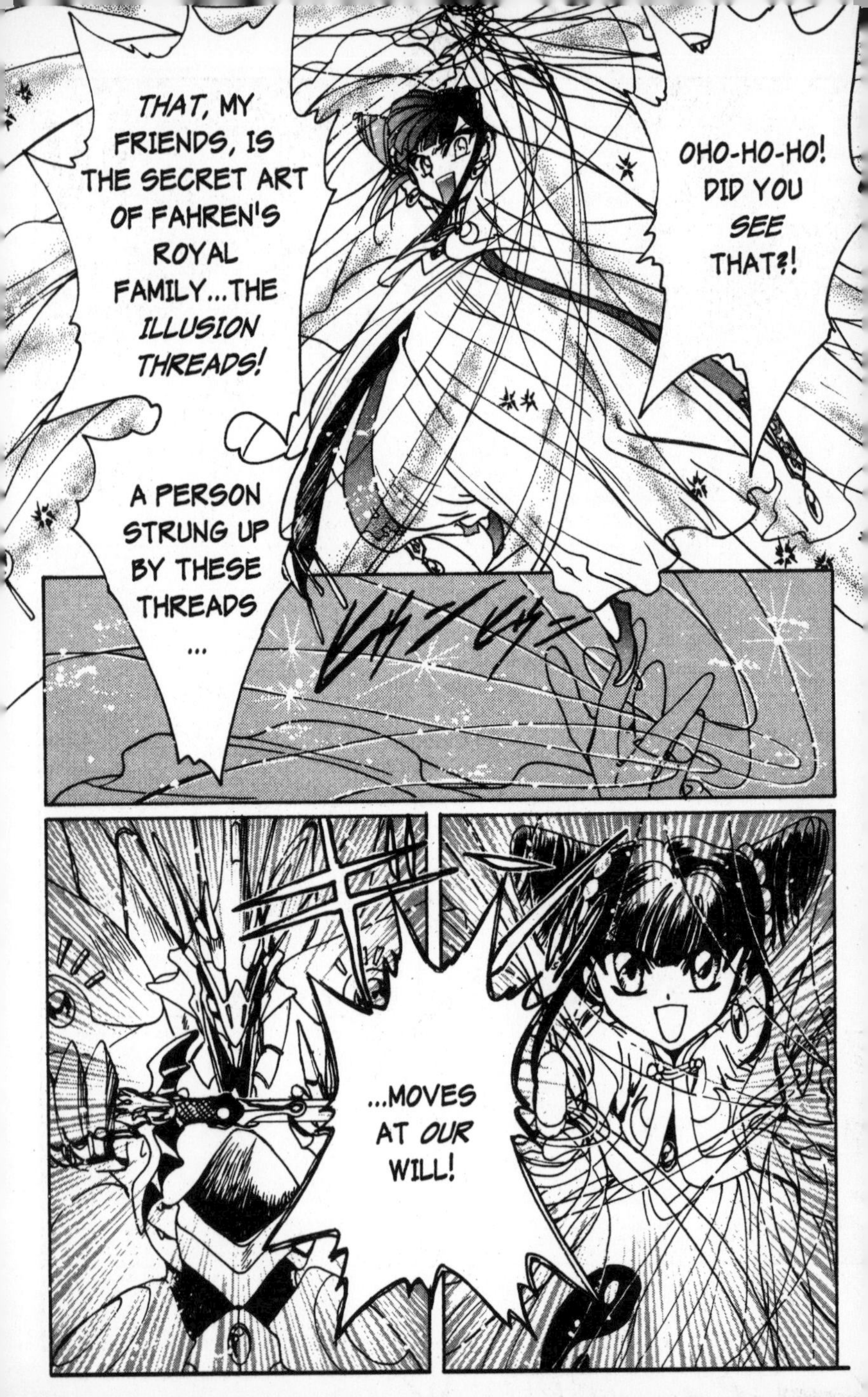
OHO-HO-HO! DID YOU SEE THAT?!
THAT, MY FRIENDS, IS THE SECRET ART OF FAHREN'S ROYAL FAMILY...THE ILLUSION THREADS!
A PERSON STRUNG UP BY THESE THREADS...
...MOVES AT OUR WILL!

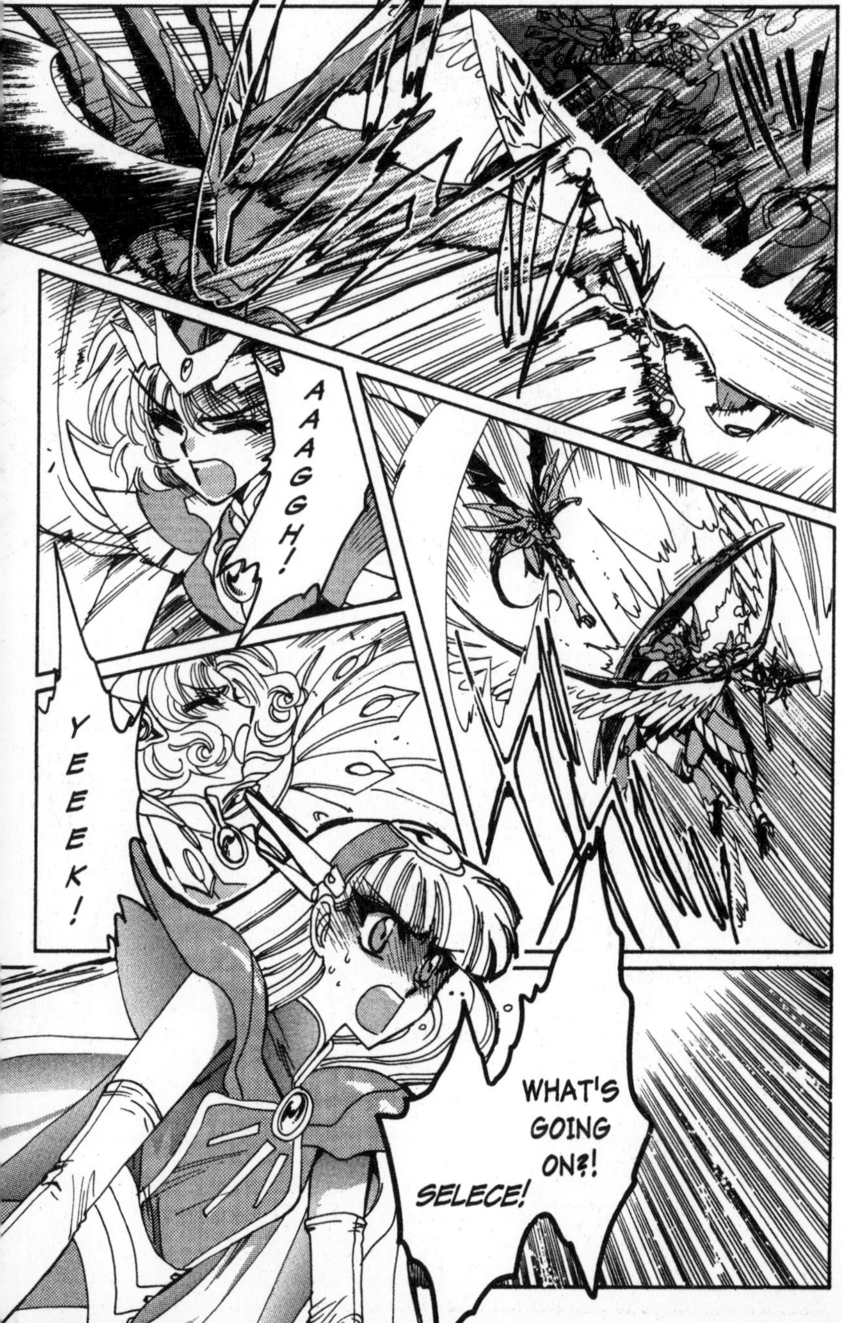
AAAGGH!
YEEEEK!
WHAT'S GOING ON?!
SELECE!

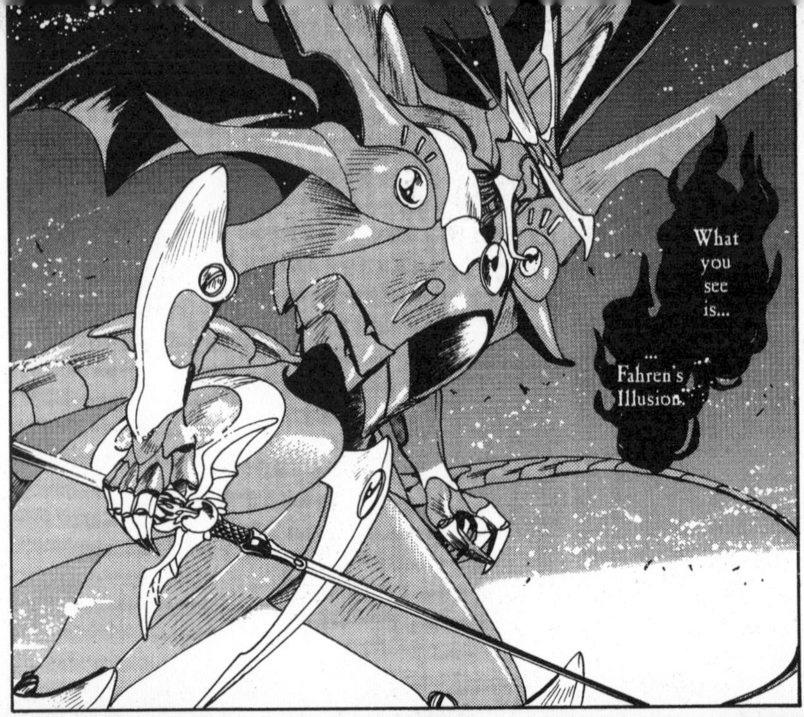
What you see is...
...Fahren's Illusion.
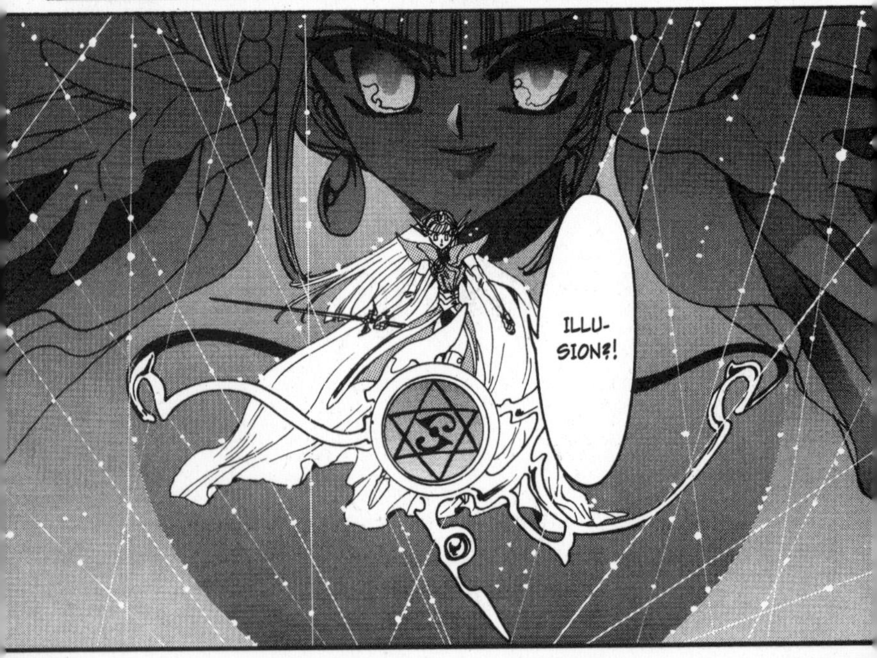
ILLUSION?!

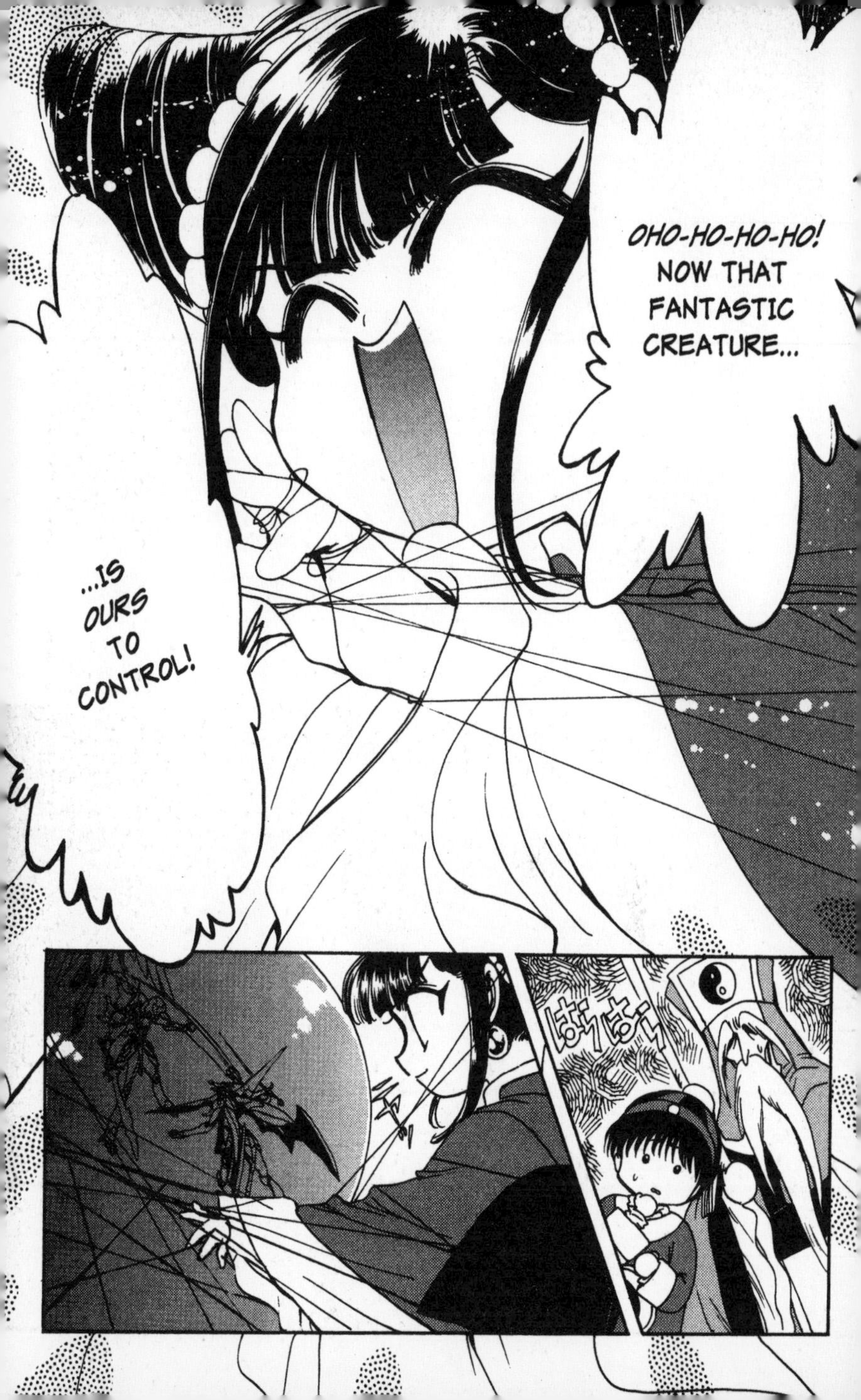
OHO-HO-HO-HO! NOW THAT FANTASTIC CREATURE...
...IS OURS TO CONTROL!

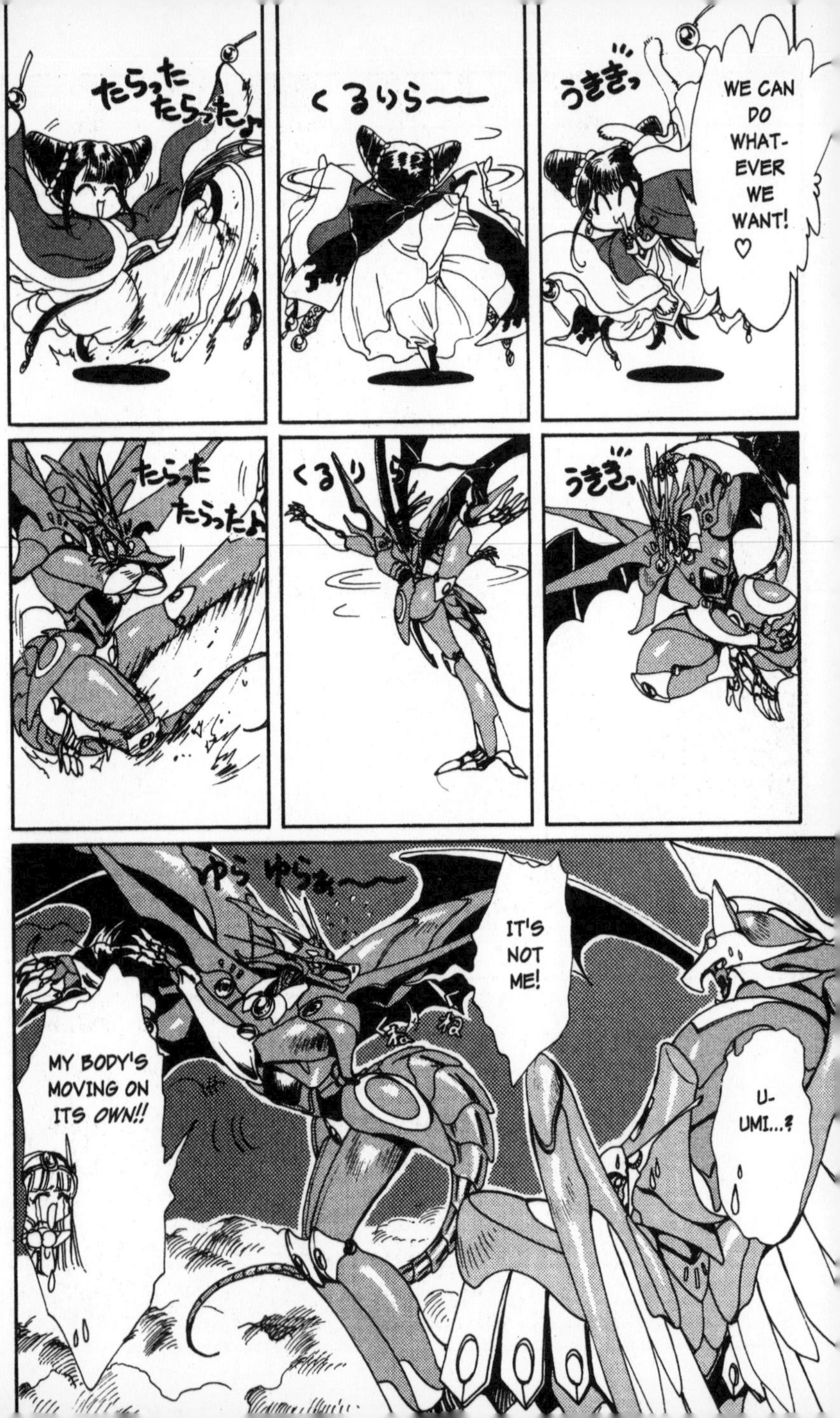
うききっ
WE CAN DO WHAT-EVER WE WANT! ♡
くるりら〜〜
たらったたらったた♪
うききっ
くるりら
たらったたらったた♪
ゆら ゆらぁ〜〜
U-UMI...?
IT'S NOT ME!
MY BODY'S MOVING ON ITS OWN!!

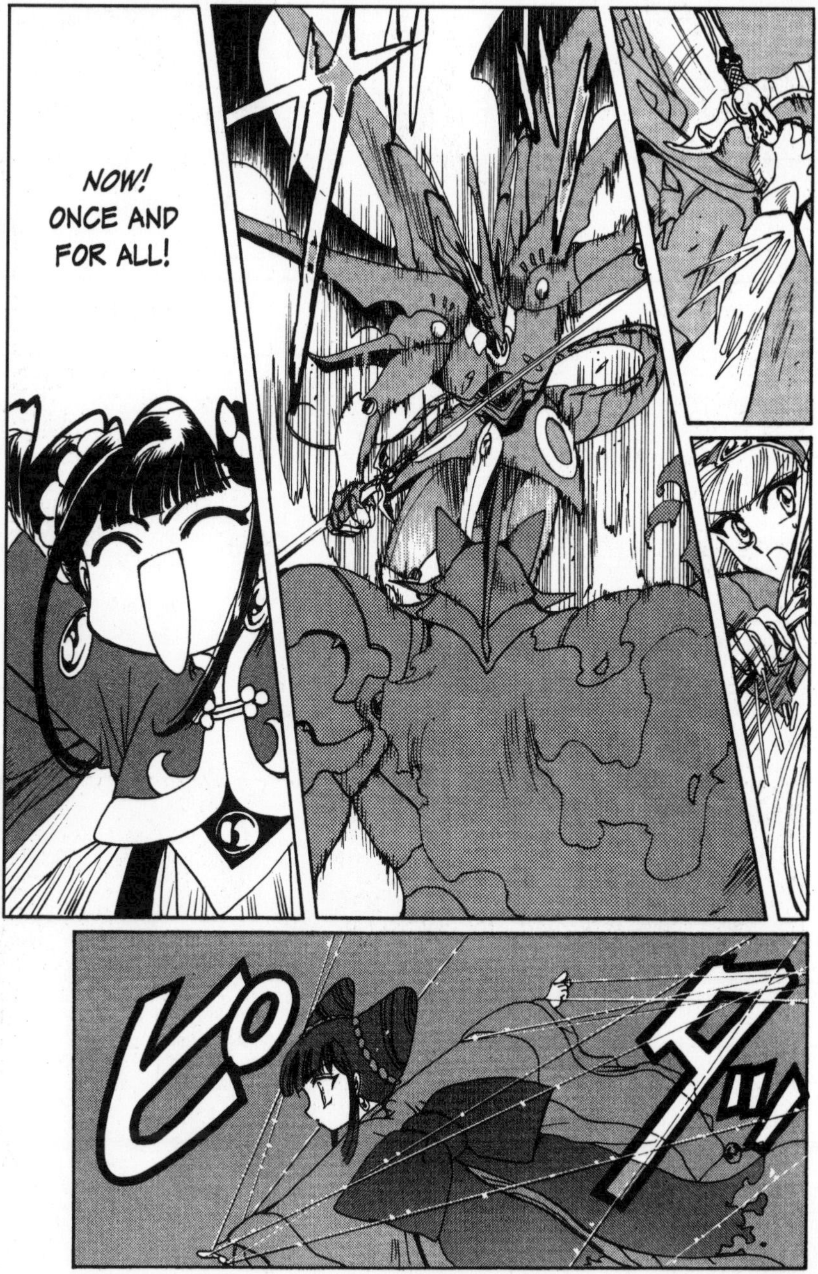
NOW! ONCE AND FOR ALL!
ピタッ

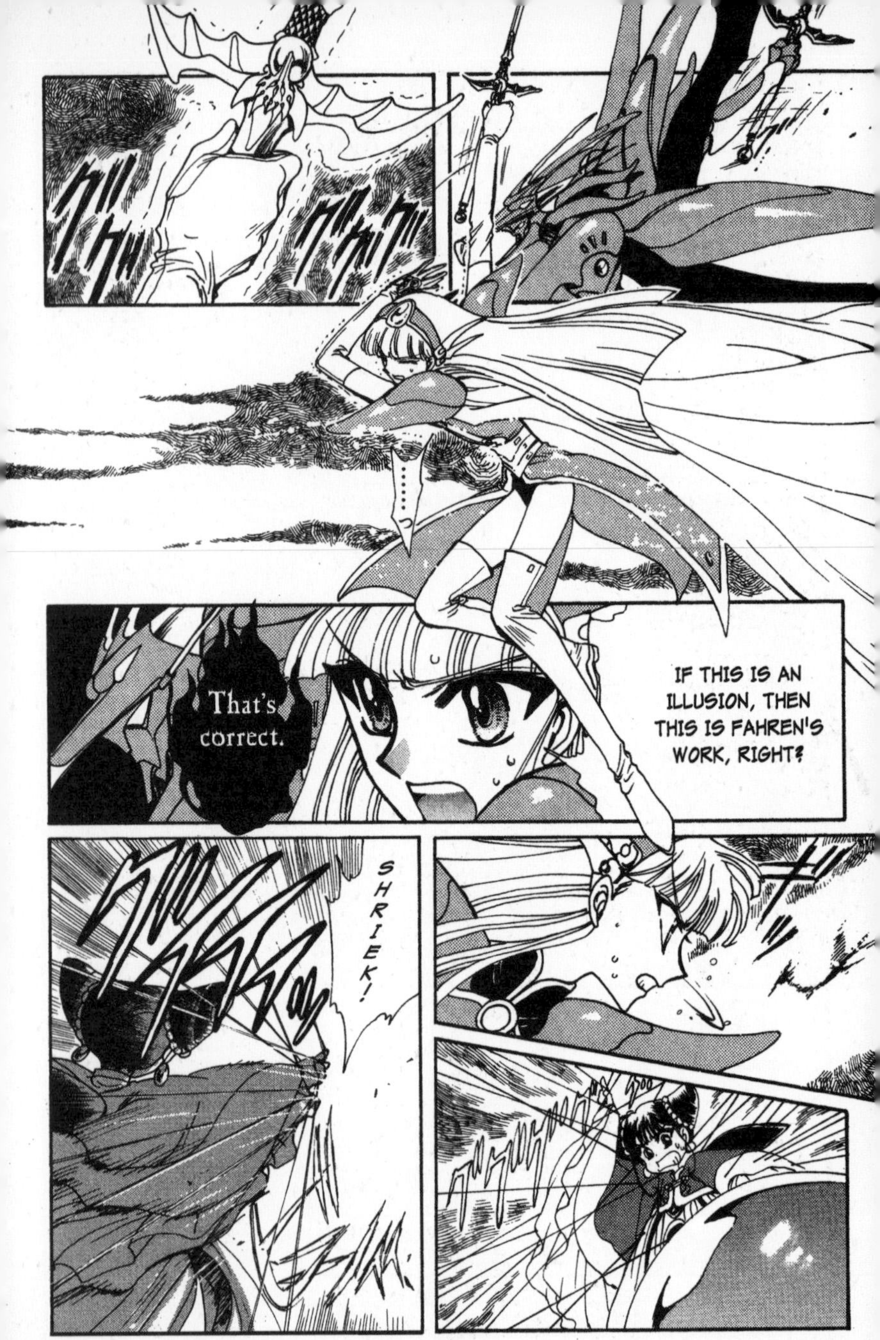
IF THIS IS AN ILLUSION, THEN THIS IS FAHREN'S WORK, RIGHT?
That's correct.
SHRIEK!

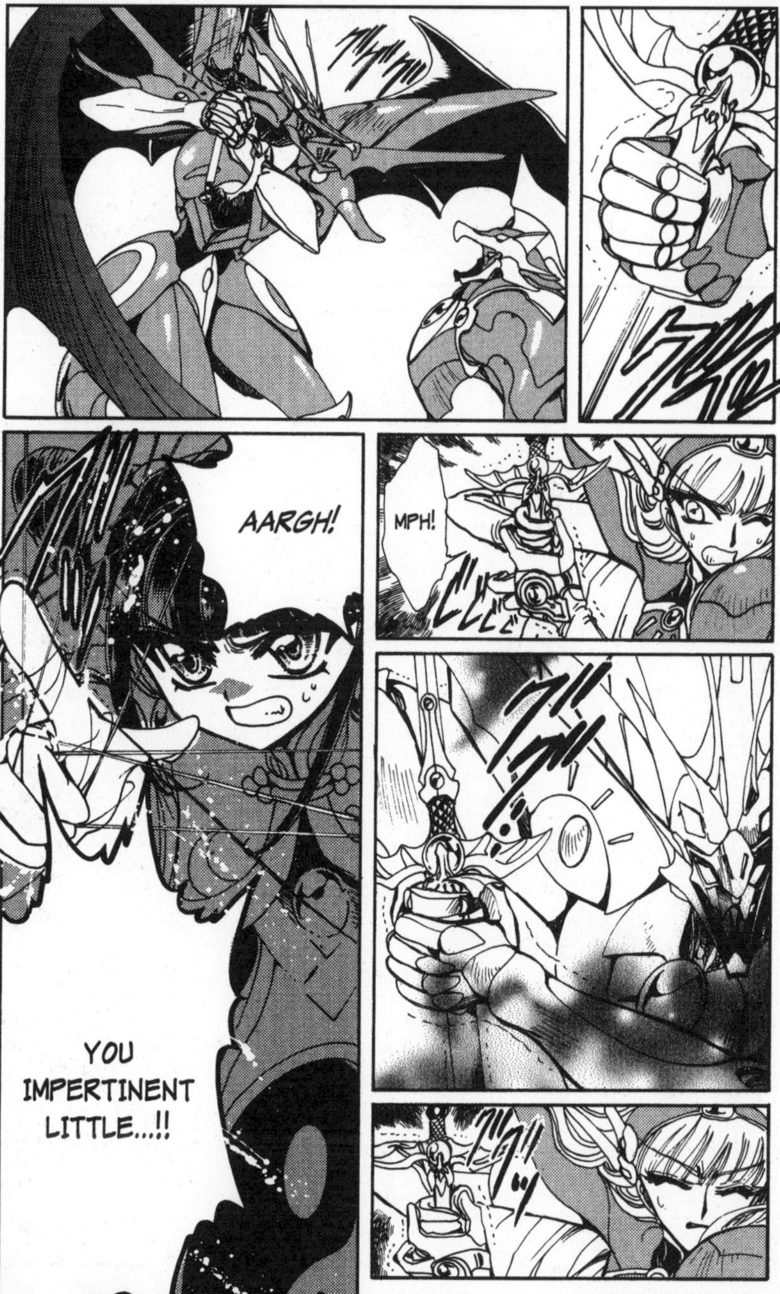
MPH!
AARGH!
YOU IMPERTINENT LITTLE...!!

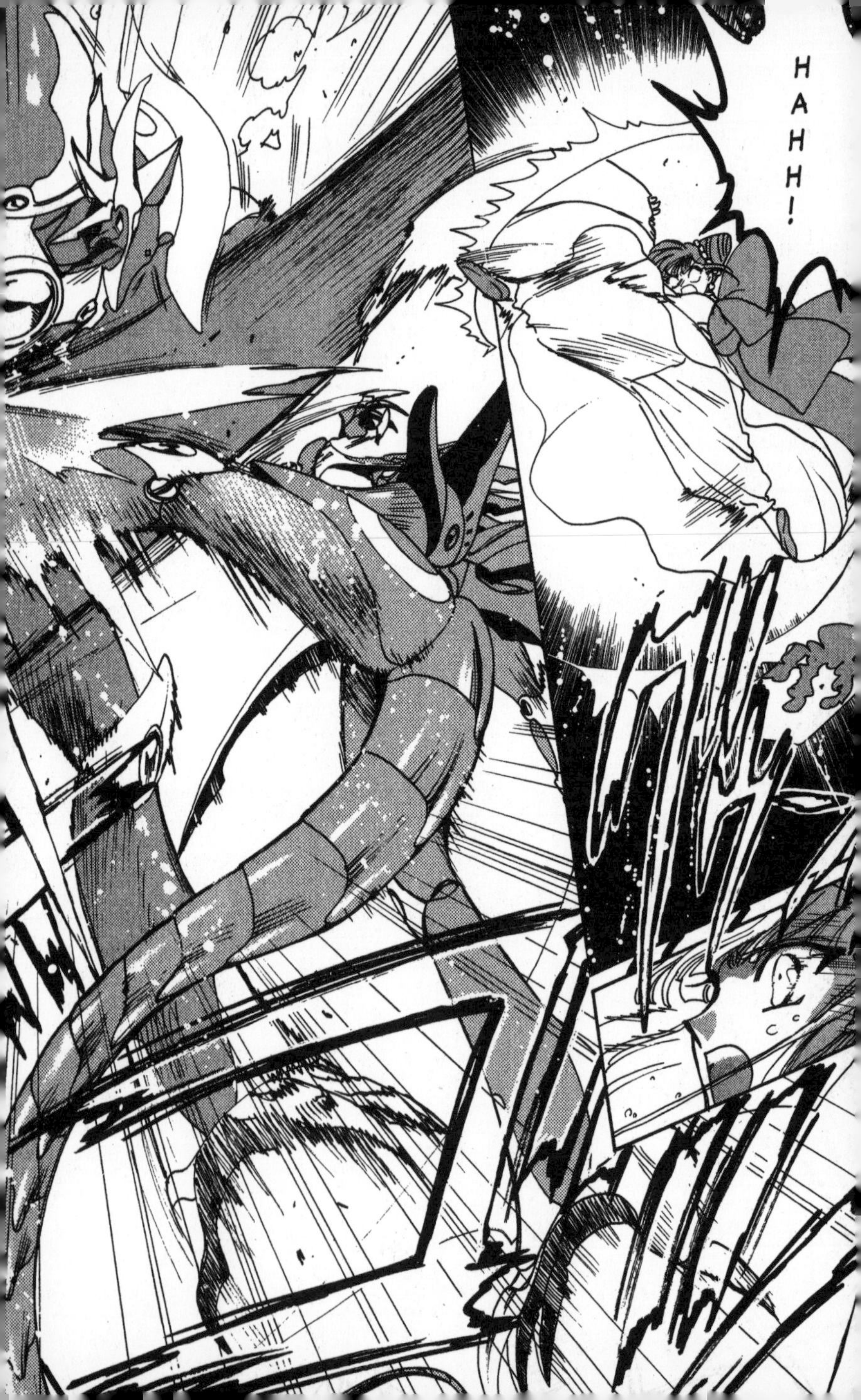
HAHHH!

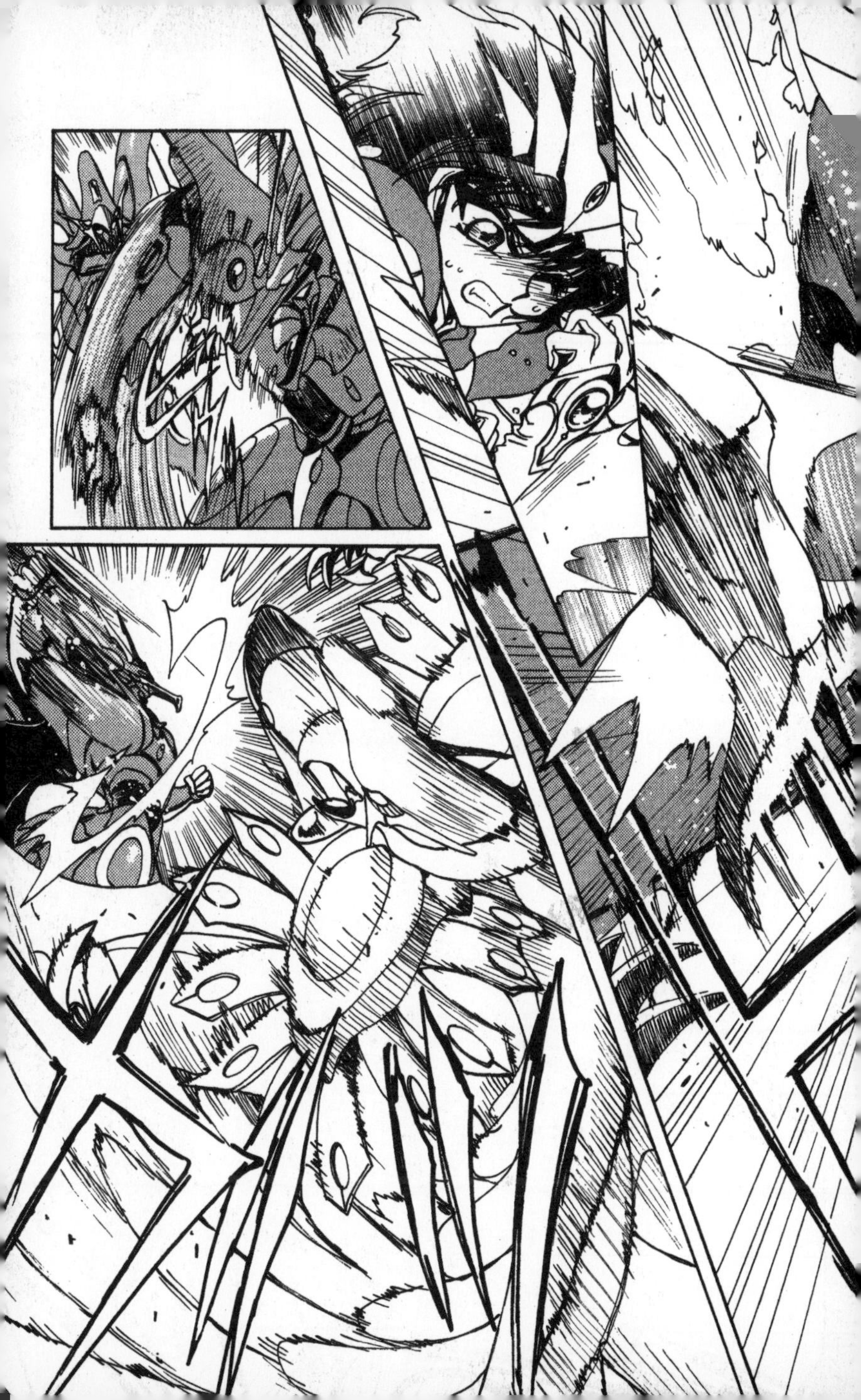

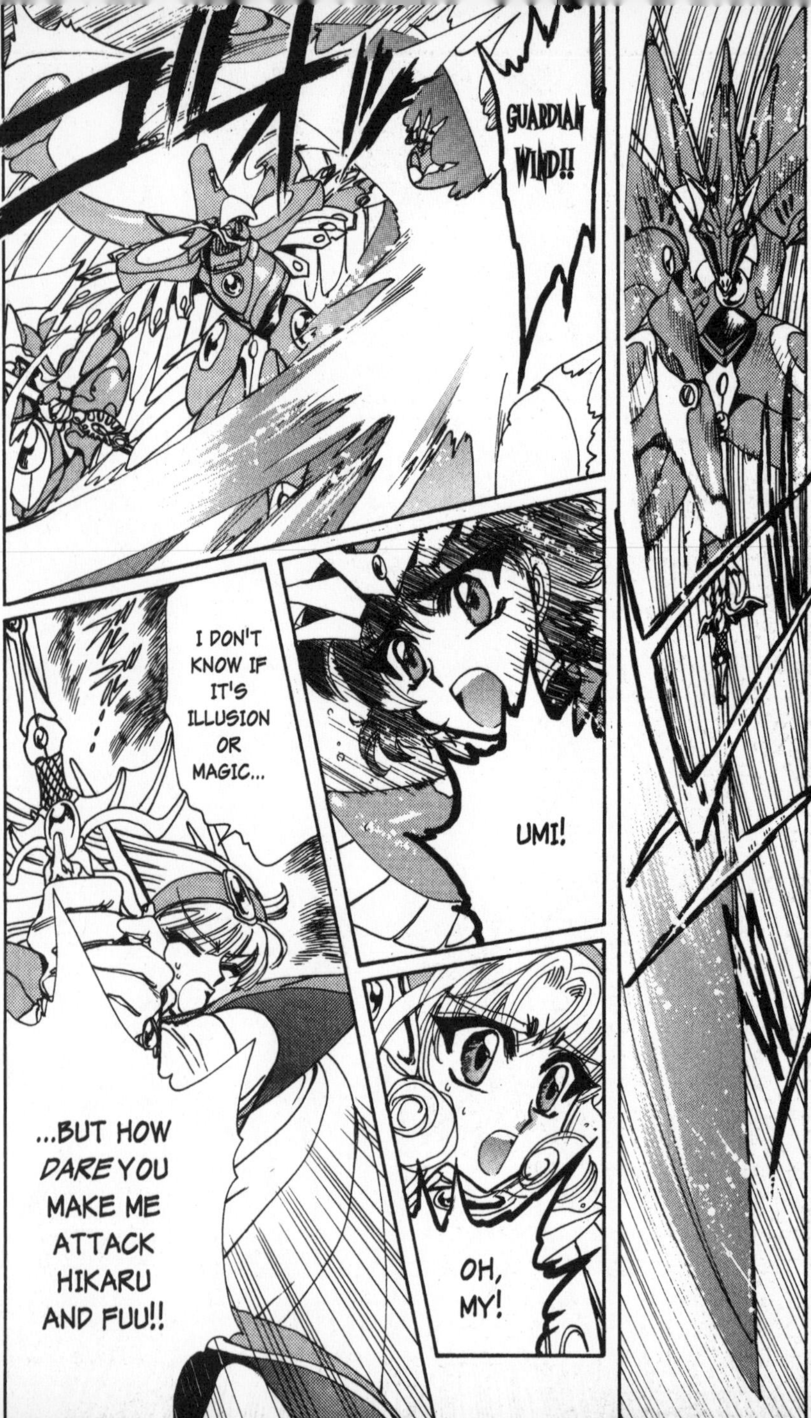
GUARDIAN WIND!!
UMI!
OH, MY!
I DON'T KNOW IF IT'S ILLUSION OR MAGIC...
...BUT HOW *DARE* YOU MAKE ME ATTACK HIKARU AND FUU!!

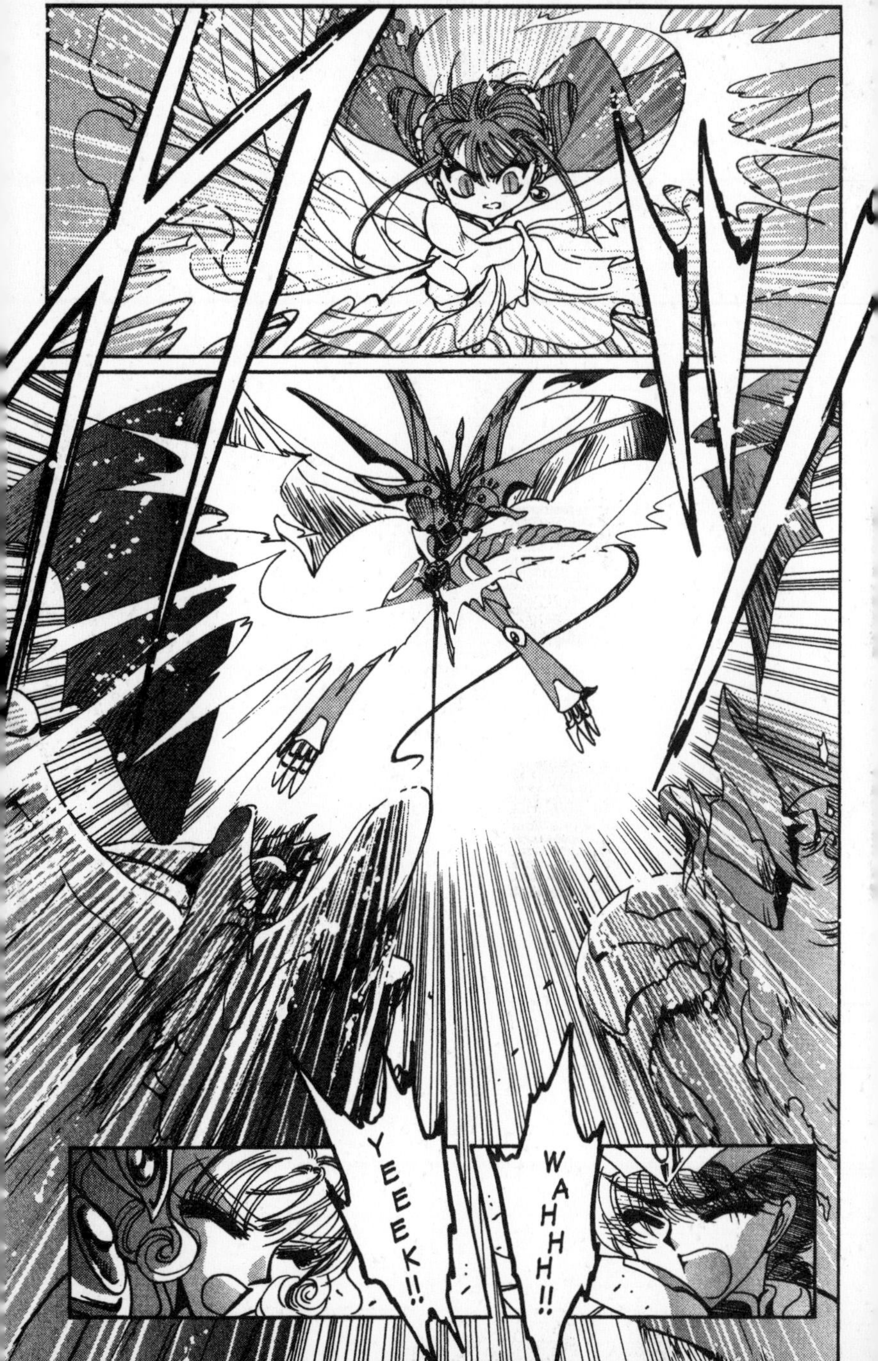
WAHHH!!
YEEEK!!

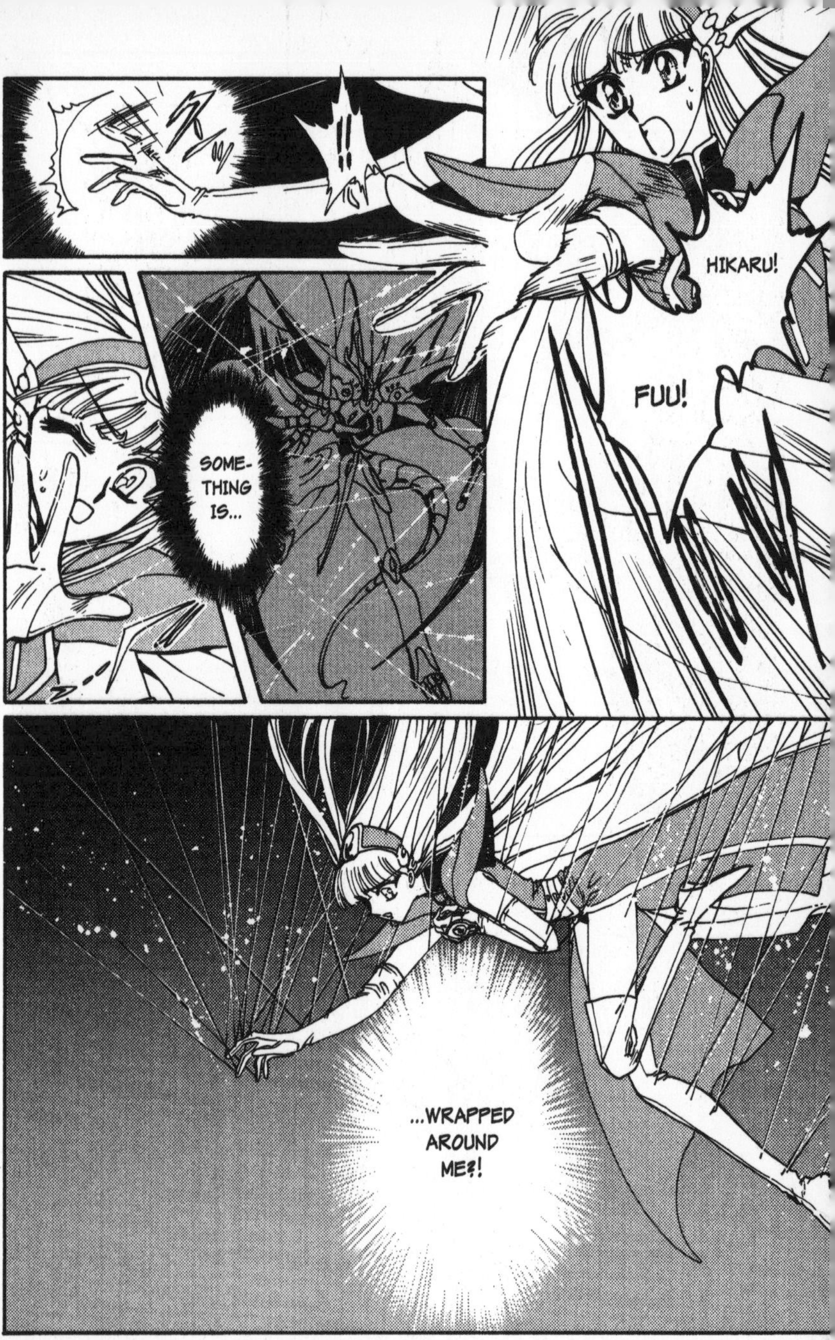
HIKARU!
FUU!
SOME-THING IS...
...WRAPPED AROUND ME?!

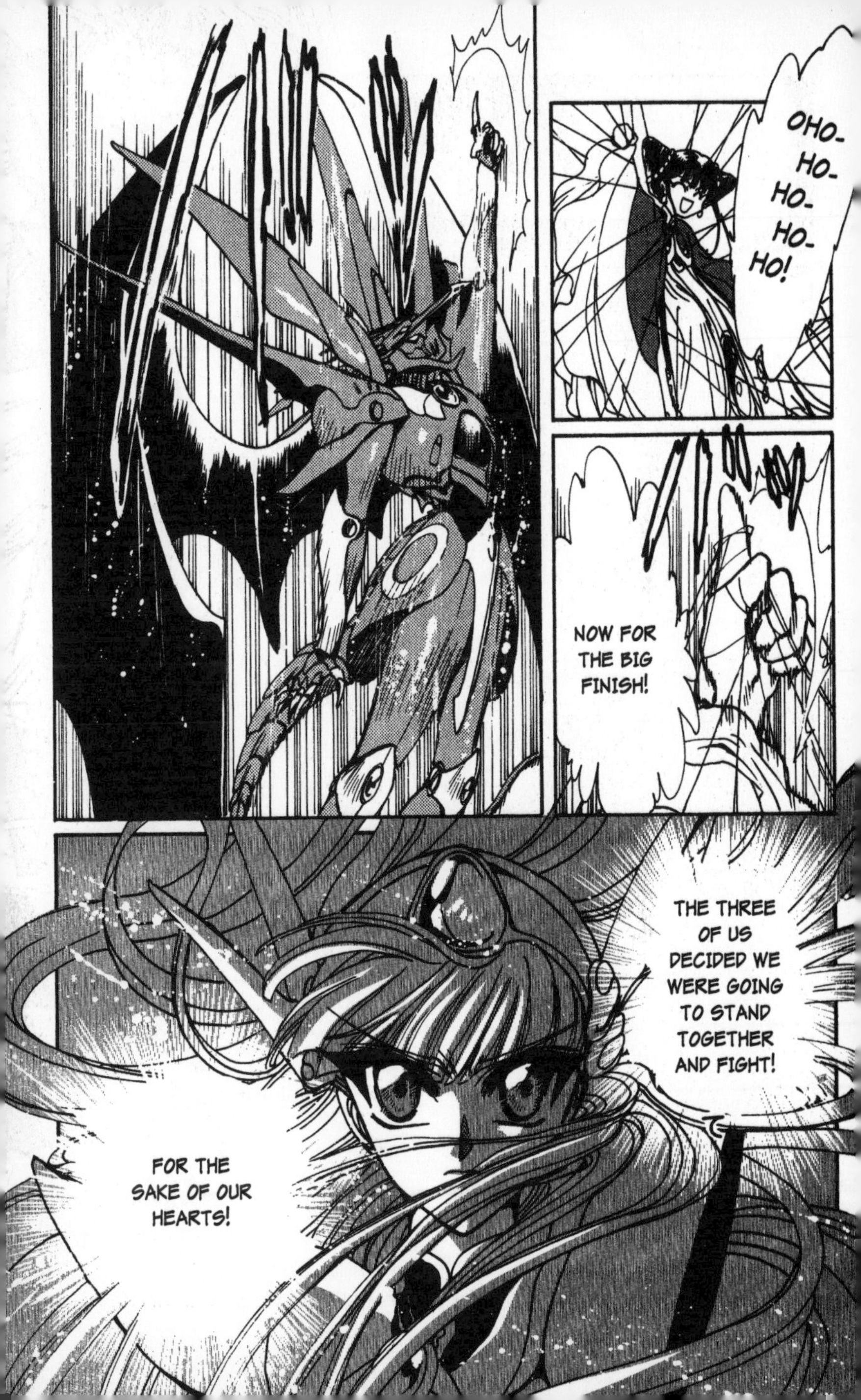
OHO-HO-HO-HO-HO!
NOW FOR THE BIG FINISH!
THE THREE OF US DECIDED WE WERE GOING TO STAND TOGETHER AND FIGHT!
FOR THE SAKE OF OUR HEARTS!

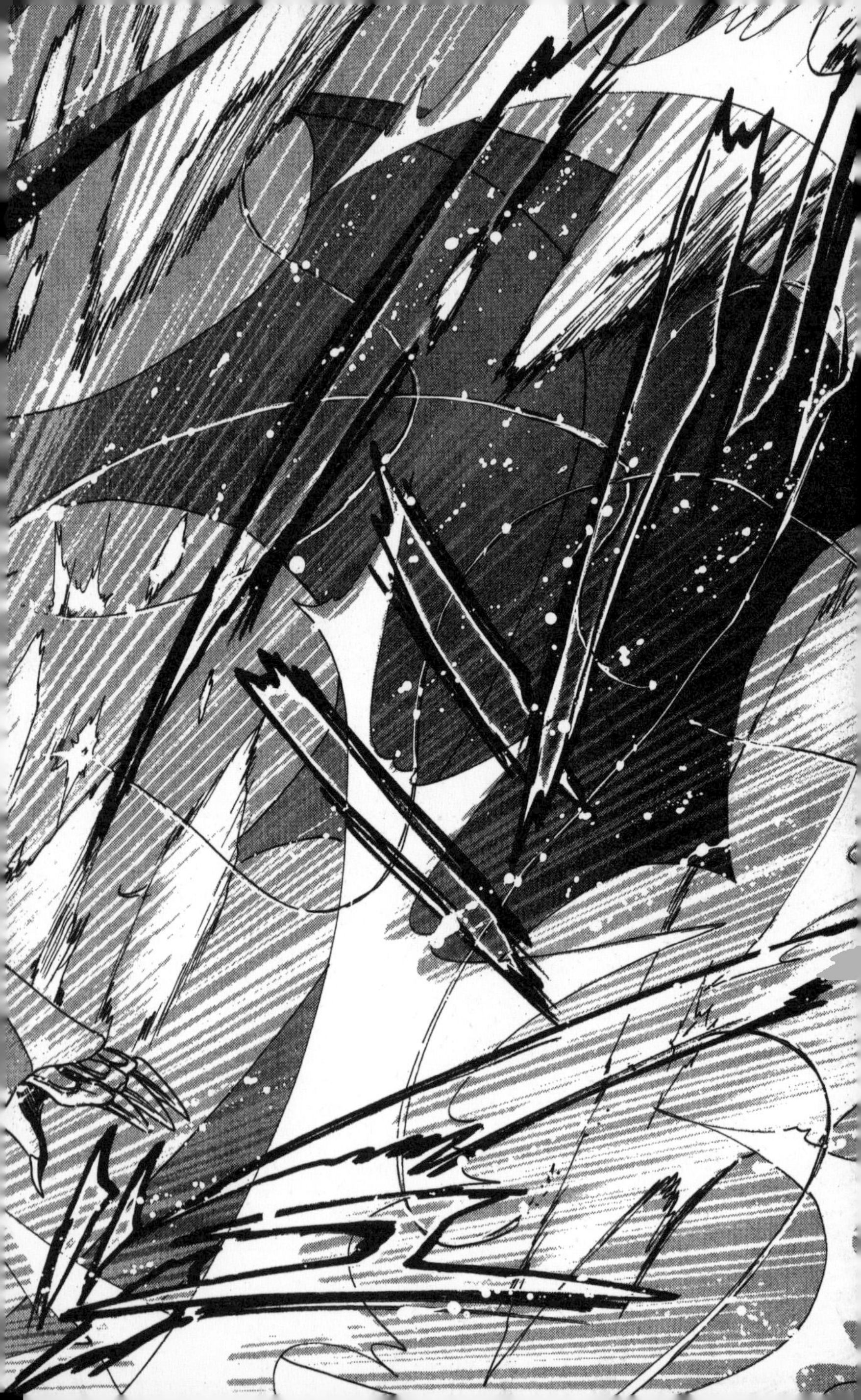

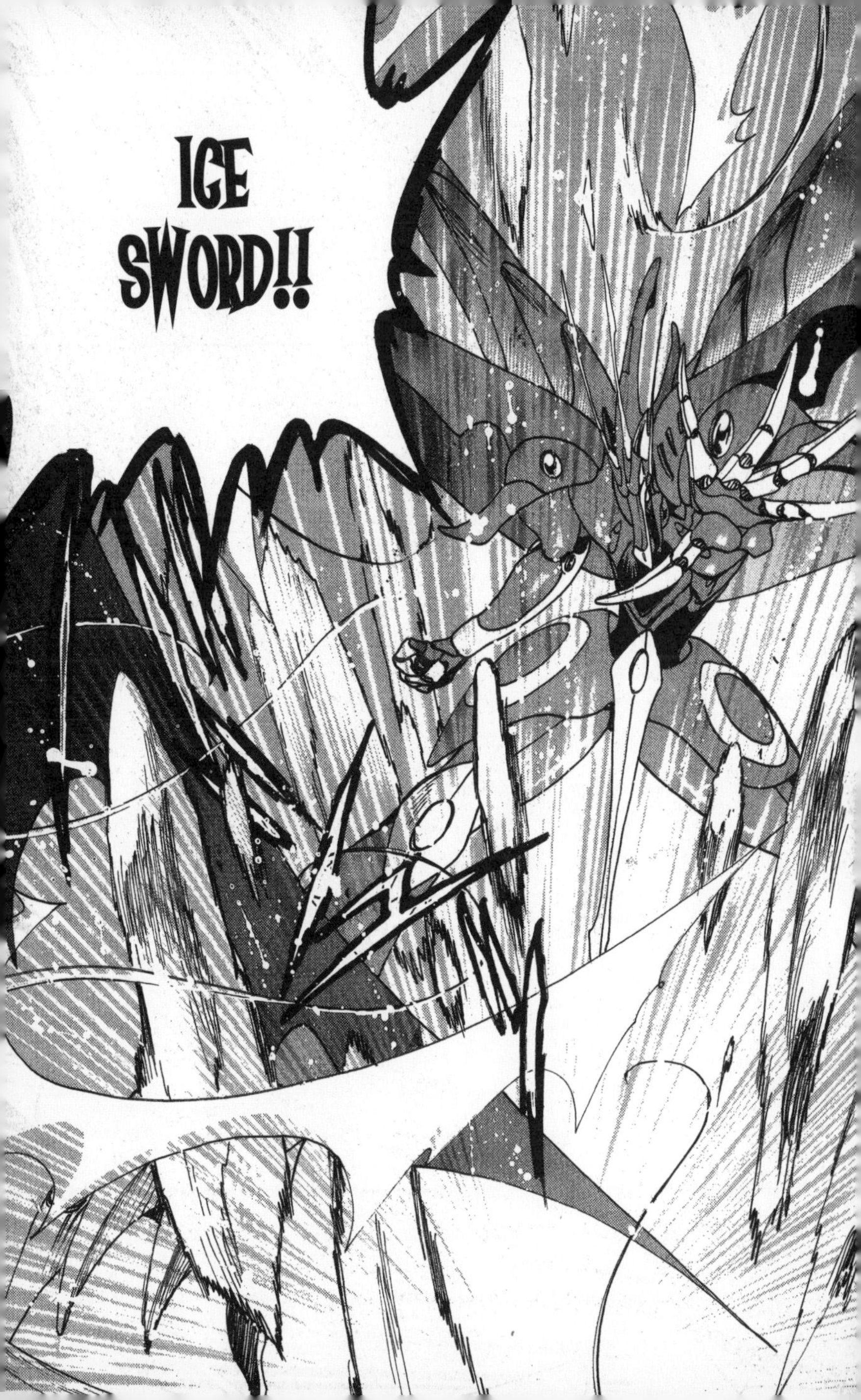
ICE SWORD!!

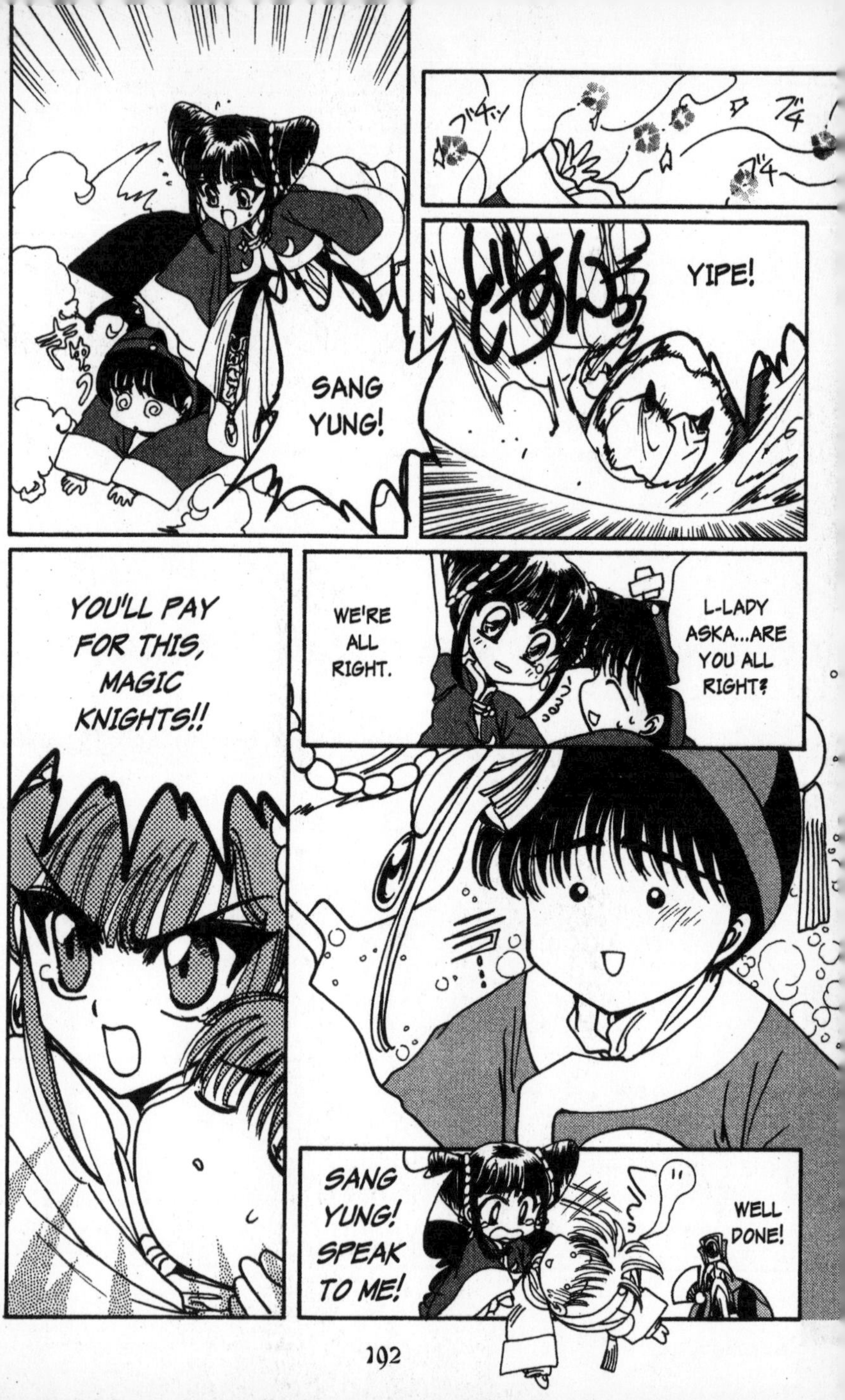
YIPE!
SANG YUNG!
L-LADY ASKA...ARE YOU ALL RIGHT?
WE'RE ALL RIGHT.
WELL DONE!
SANG YUNG! SPEAK TO ME!
YOU'LL PAY FOR THIS, MAGIC KNIGHTS!!

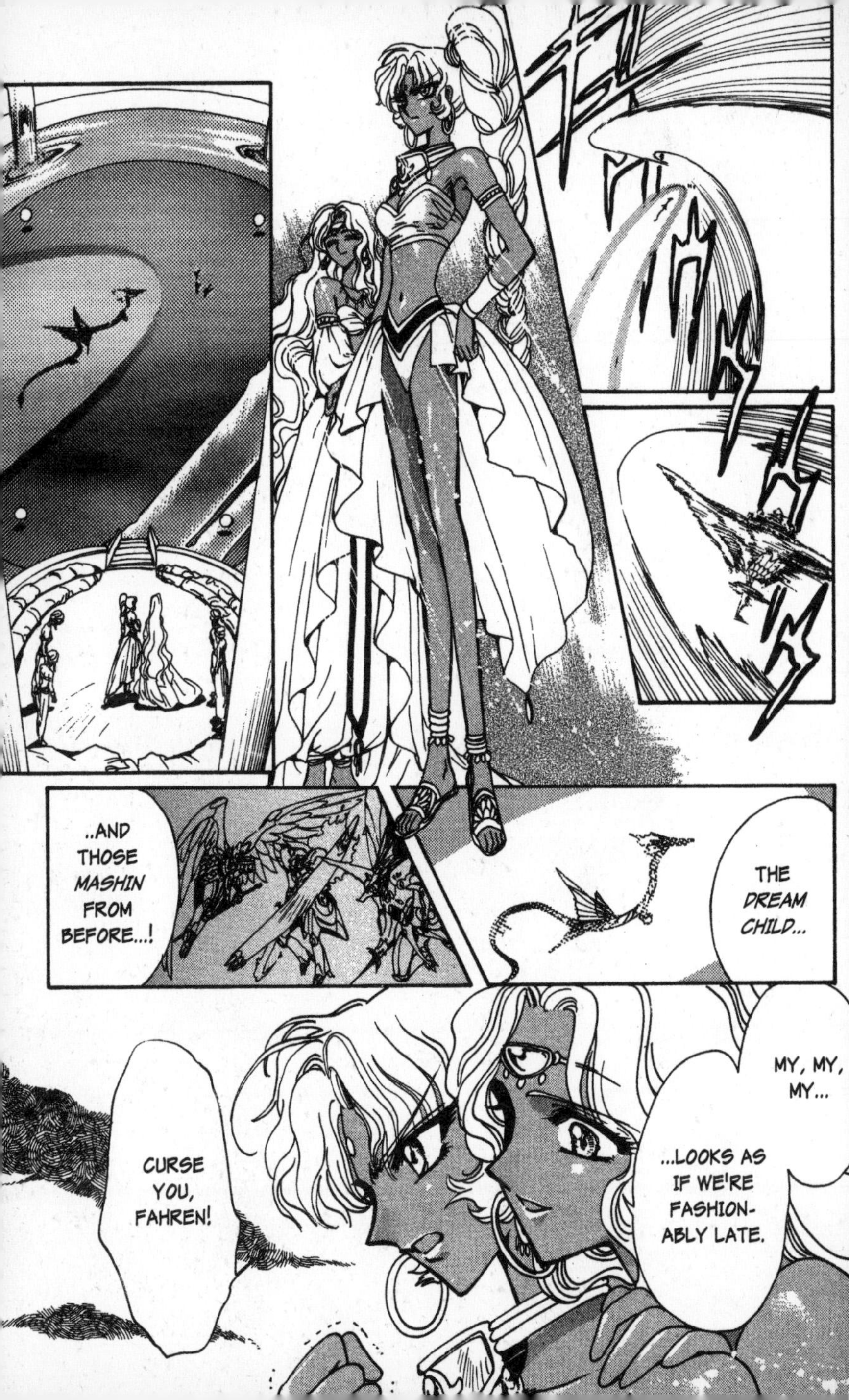
THE DREAM CHILD...
..AND THOSE MASHIN FROM BEFORE...!
MY, MY, MY...
...LOOKS AS IF WE'RE FASHION-ABLY LATE.
CURSE YOU, FAHREN!

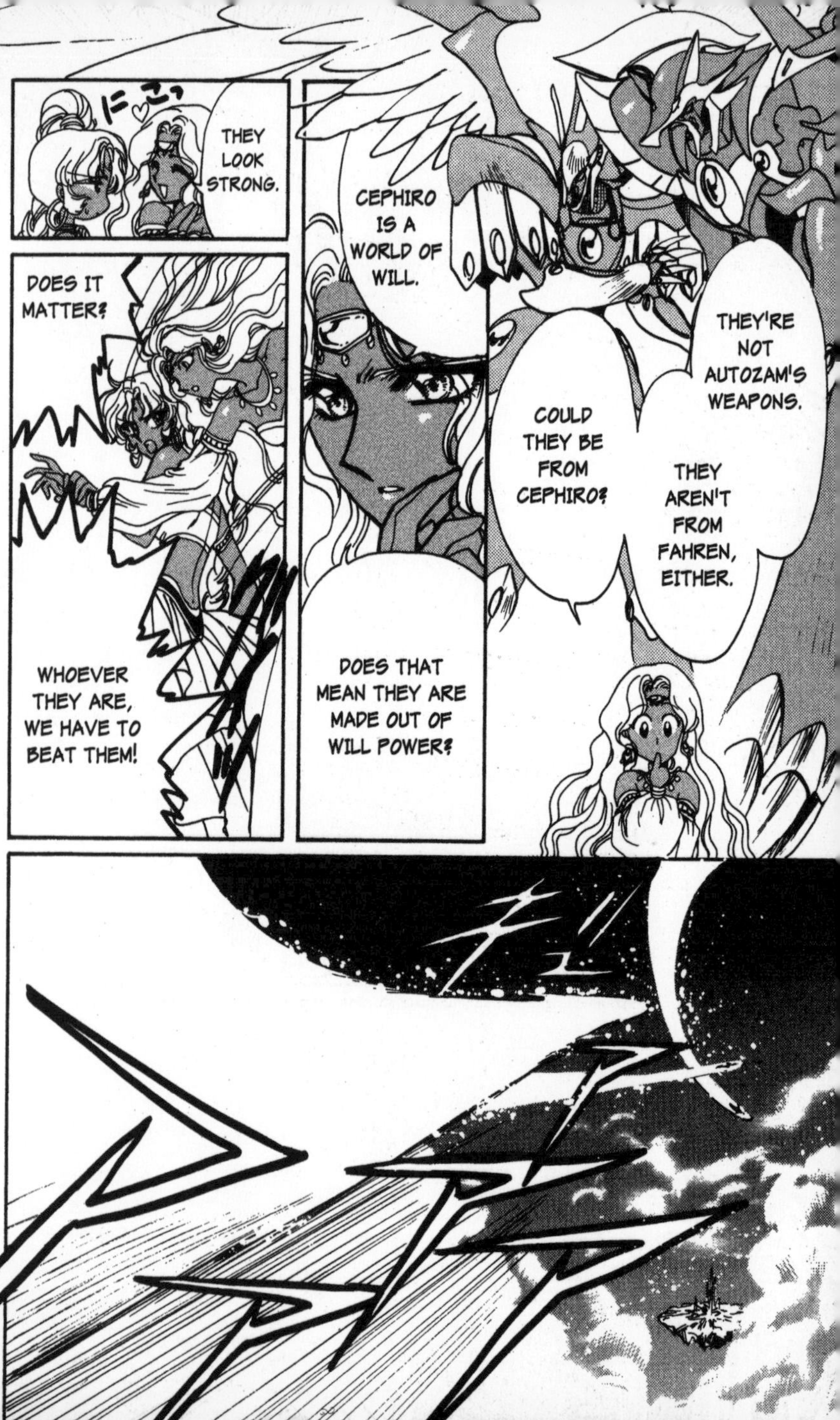
THEY'RE NOT AUTOZAM'S WEAPONS.
THEY AREN'T FROM FAHREN, EITHER.
COULD THEY BE FROM CEPHIRO?
CEPHIRO IS A WORLD OF WILL.
DOES THAT MEAN THEY ARE MADE OUT OF WILL POWER?
にこっ
THEY LOOK STRONG.
DOES IT MATTER?
WHOEVER THEY ARE, WE HAVE TO BEAT THEM!

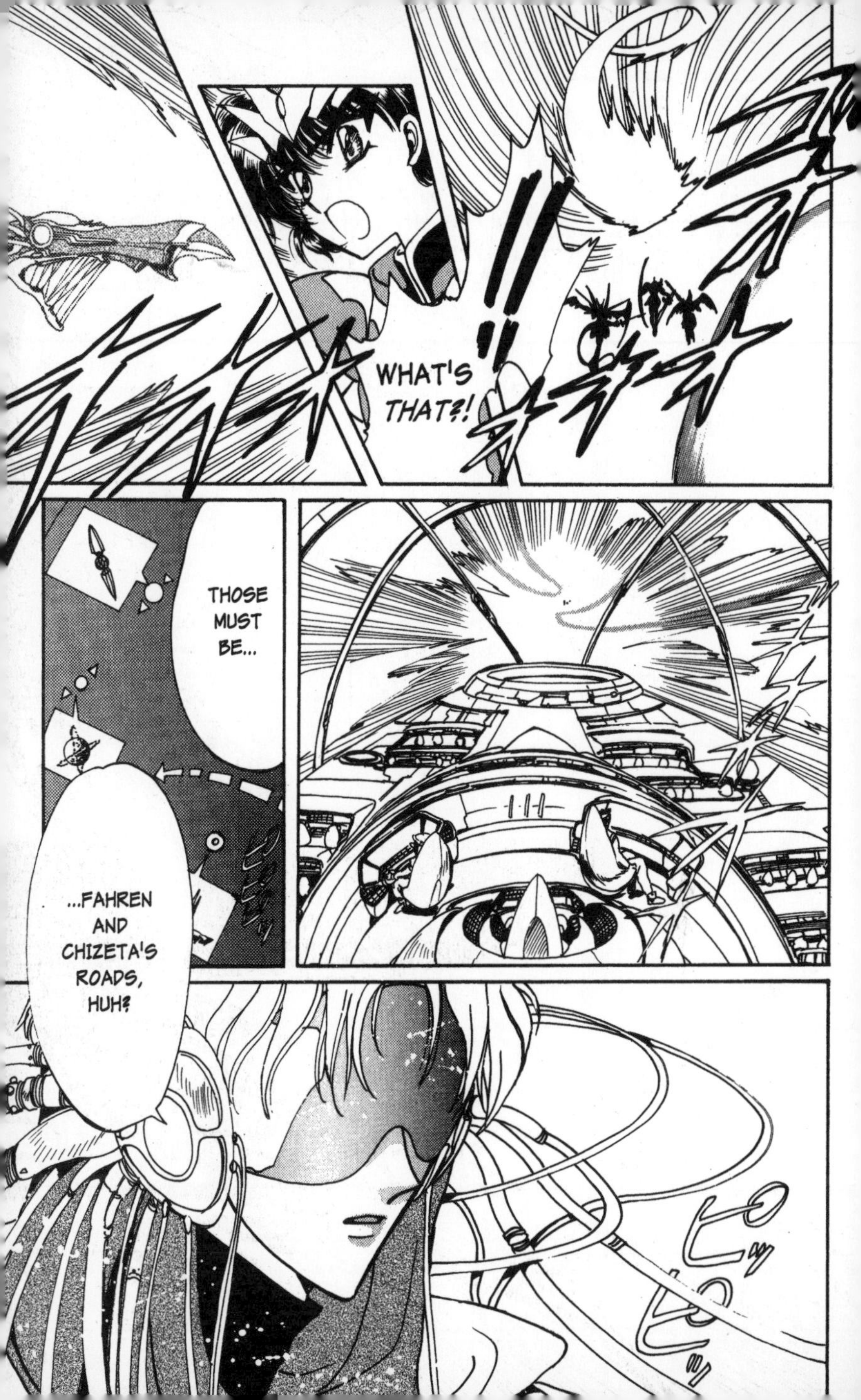
WHAT'S THAT?!
THOSE MUST BE...
...FAHREN AND CHIZETA'S ROADS, HUH?

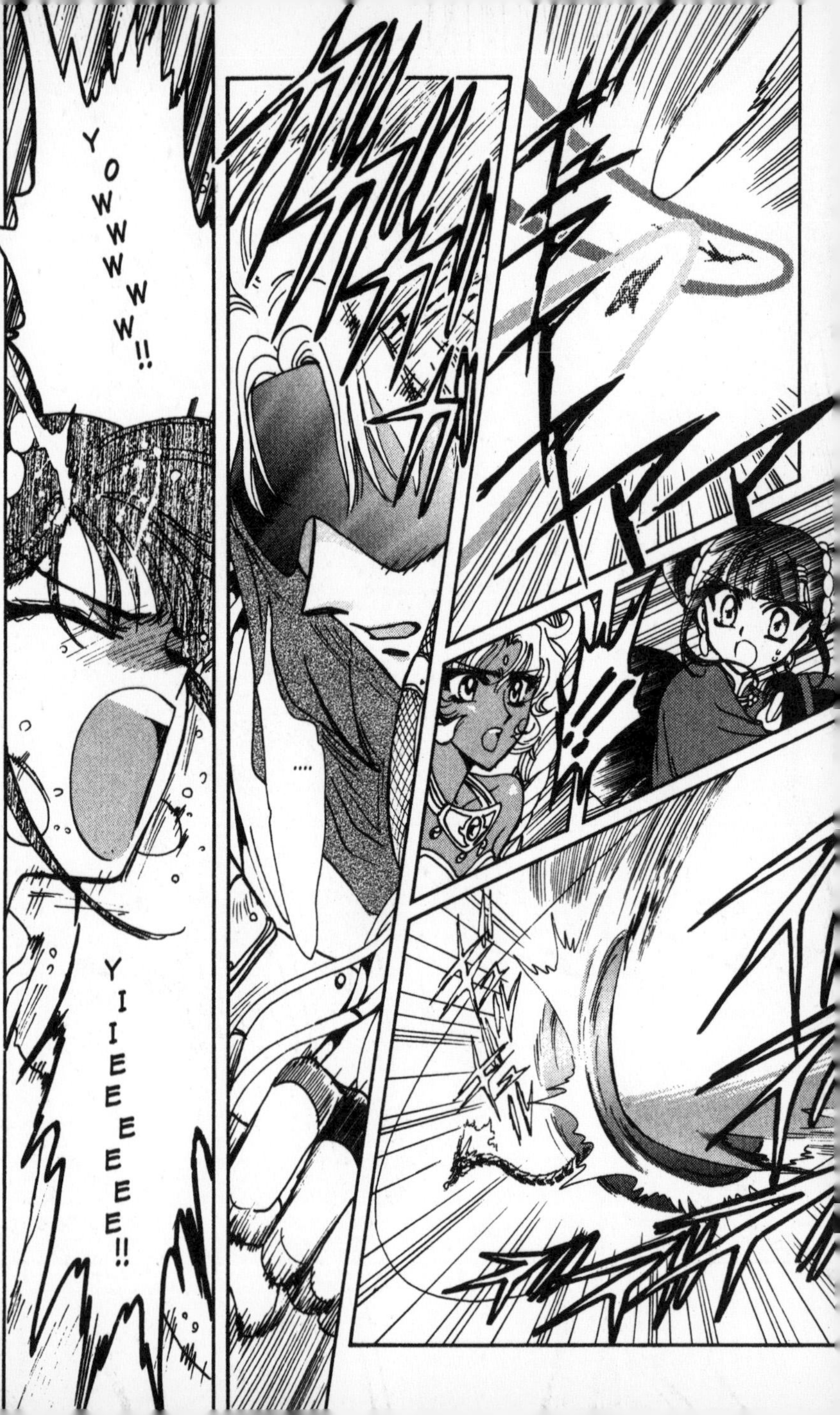
....
YOWWWWW!!
YIIEEEEEE!!

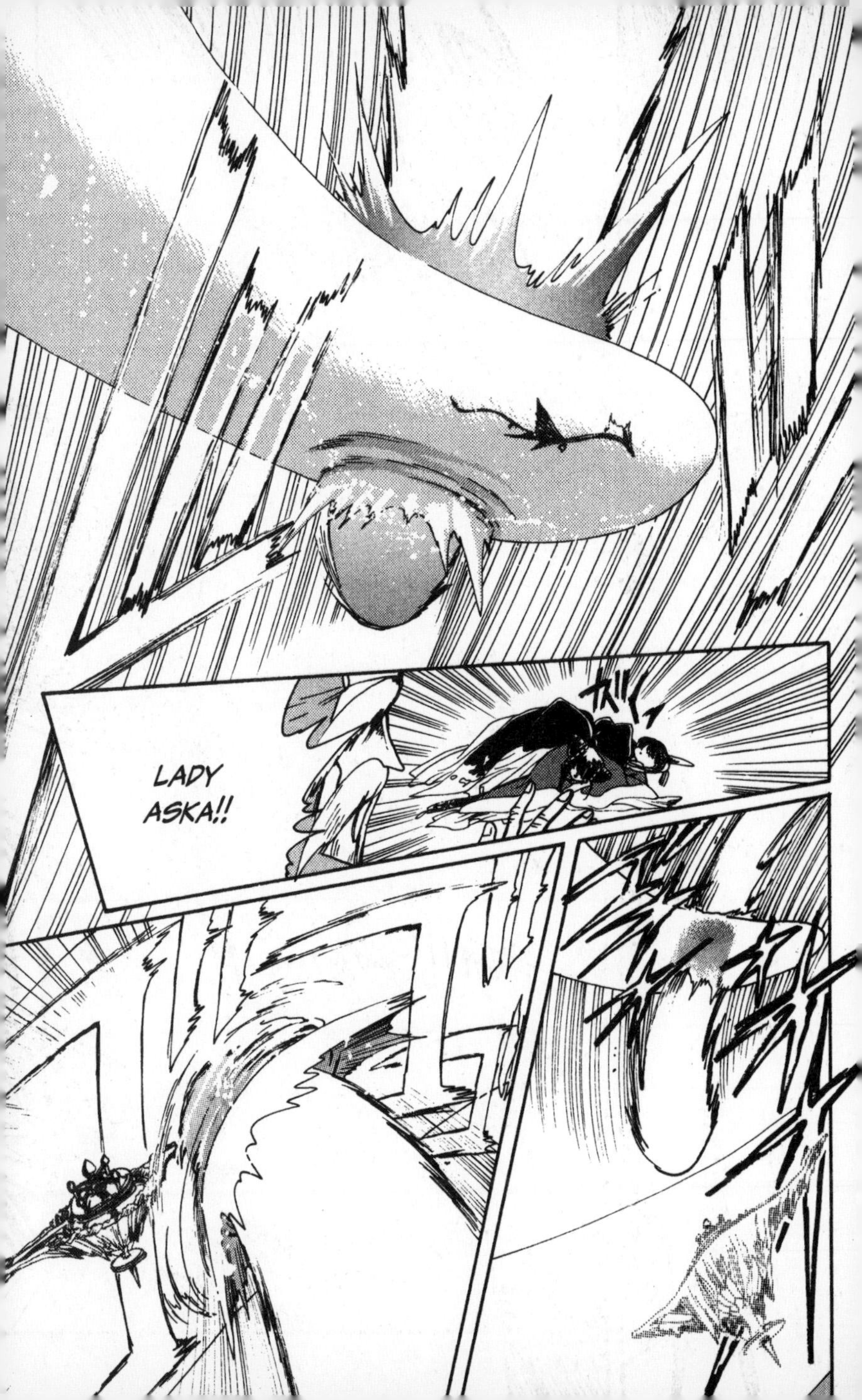
LADY ASKA!!

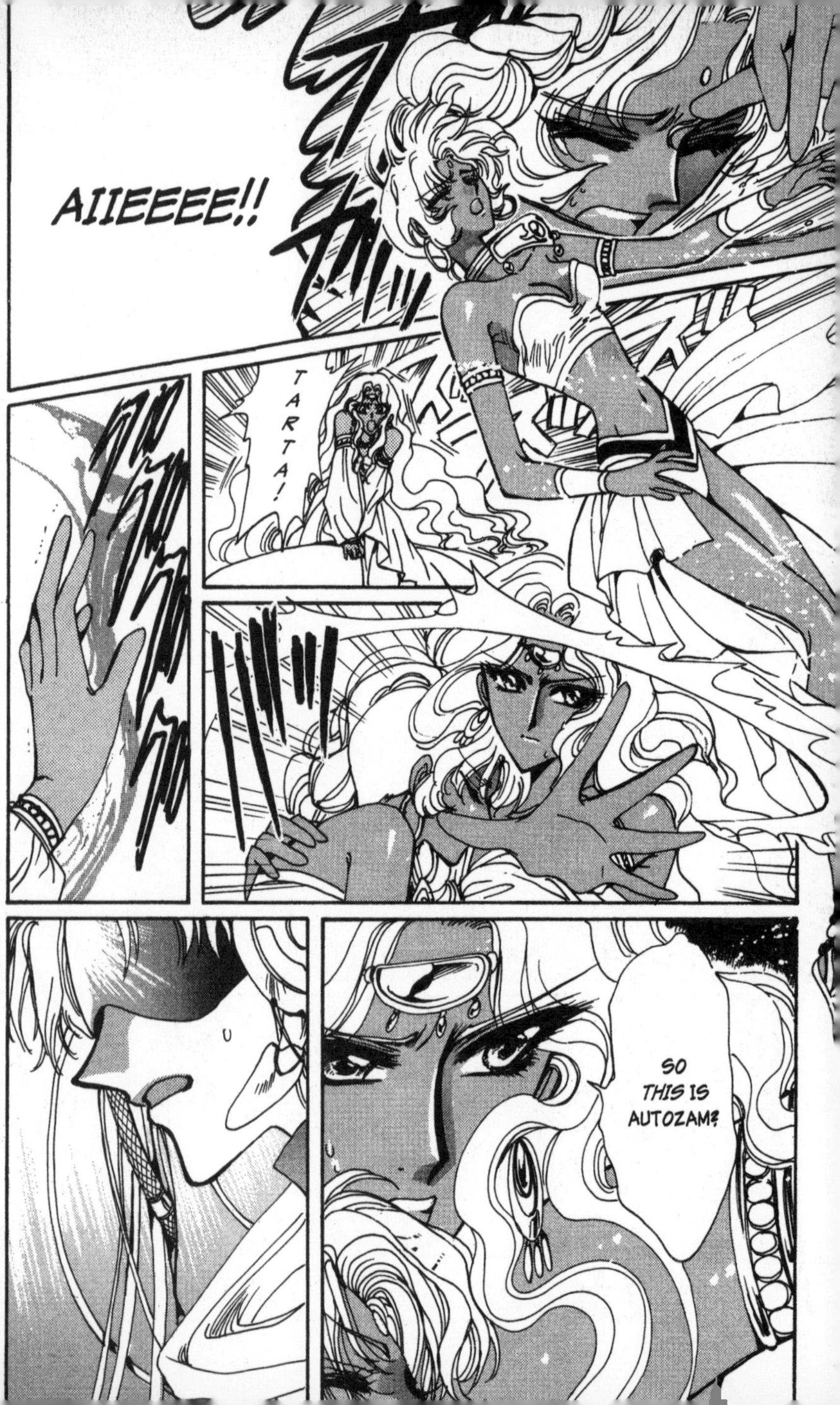
AIIEEEE!!
TARTA!
SO THIS IS AUTOZAM?

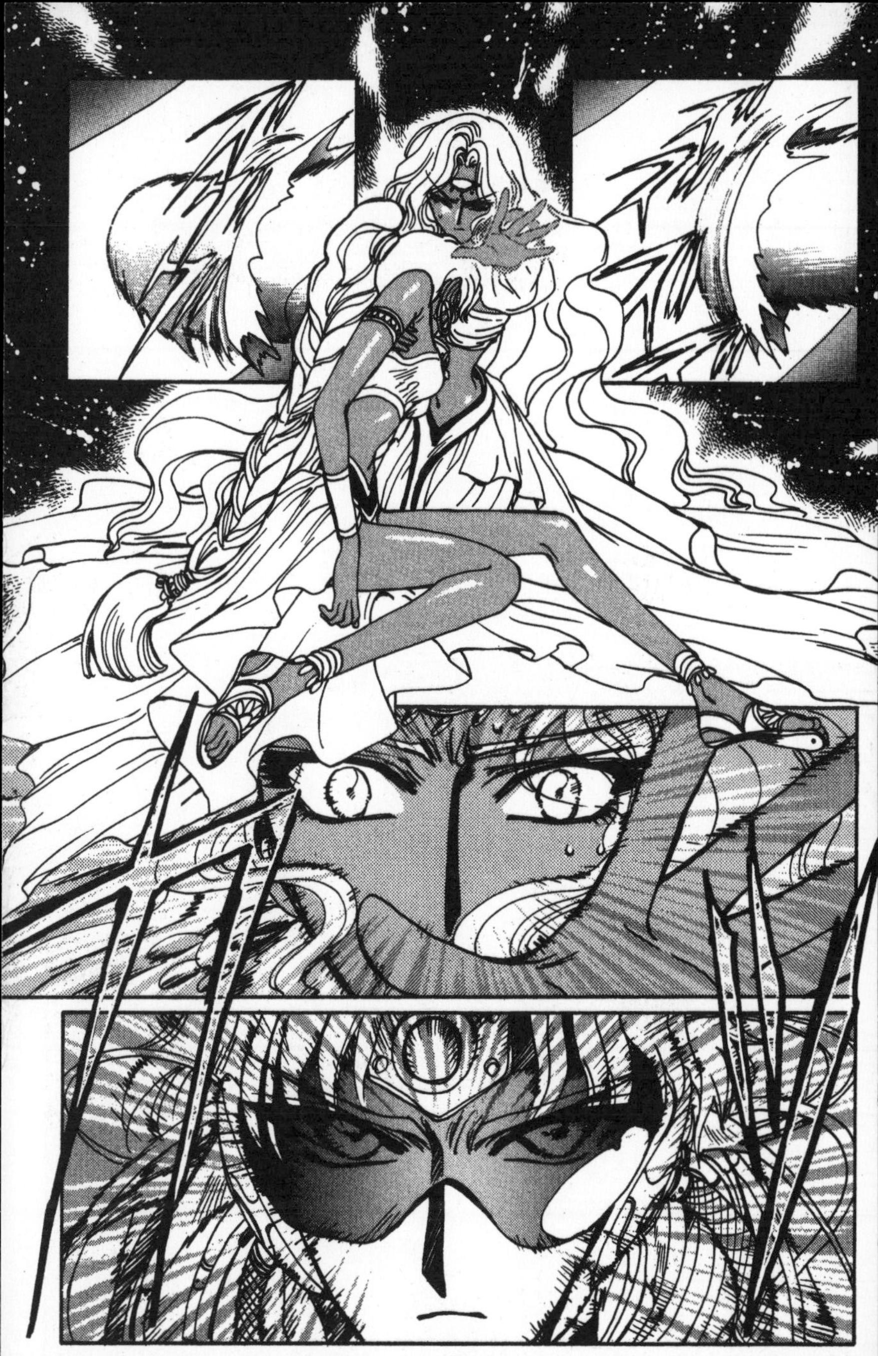

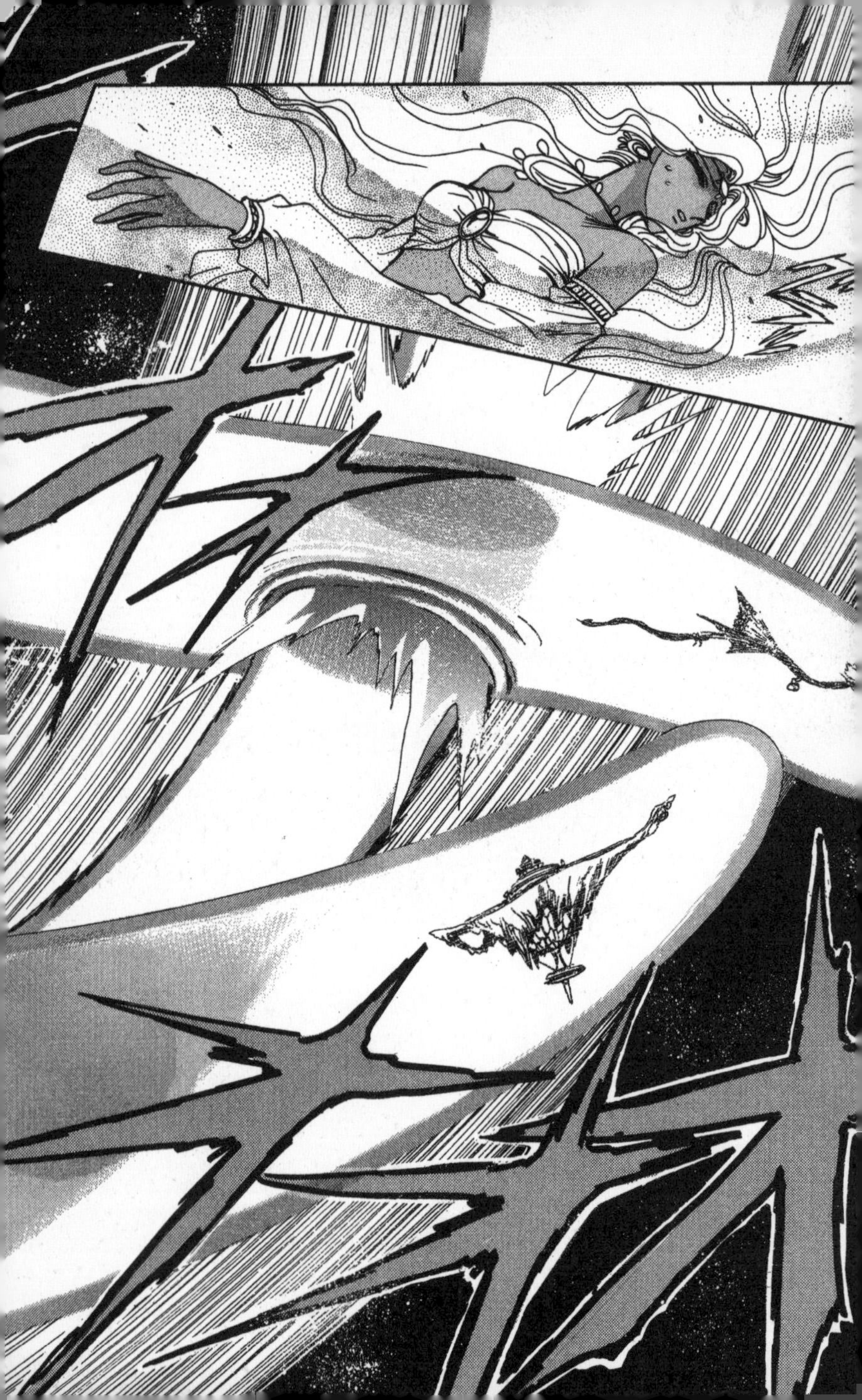

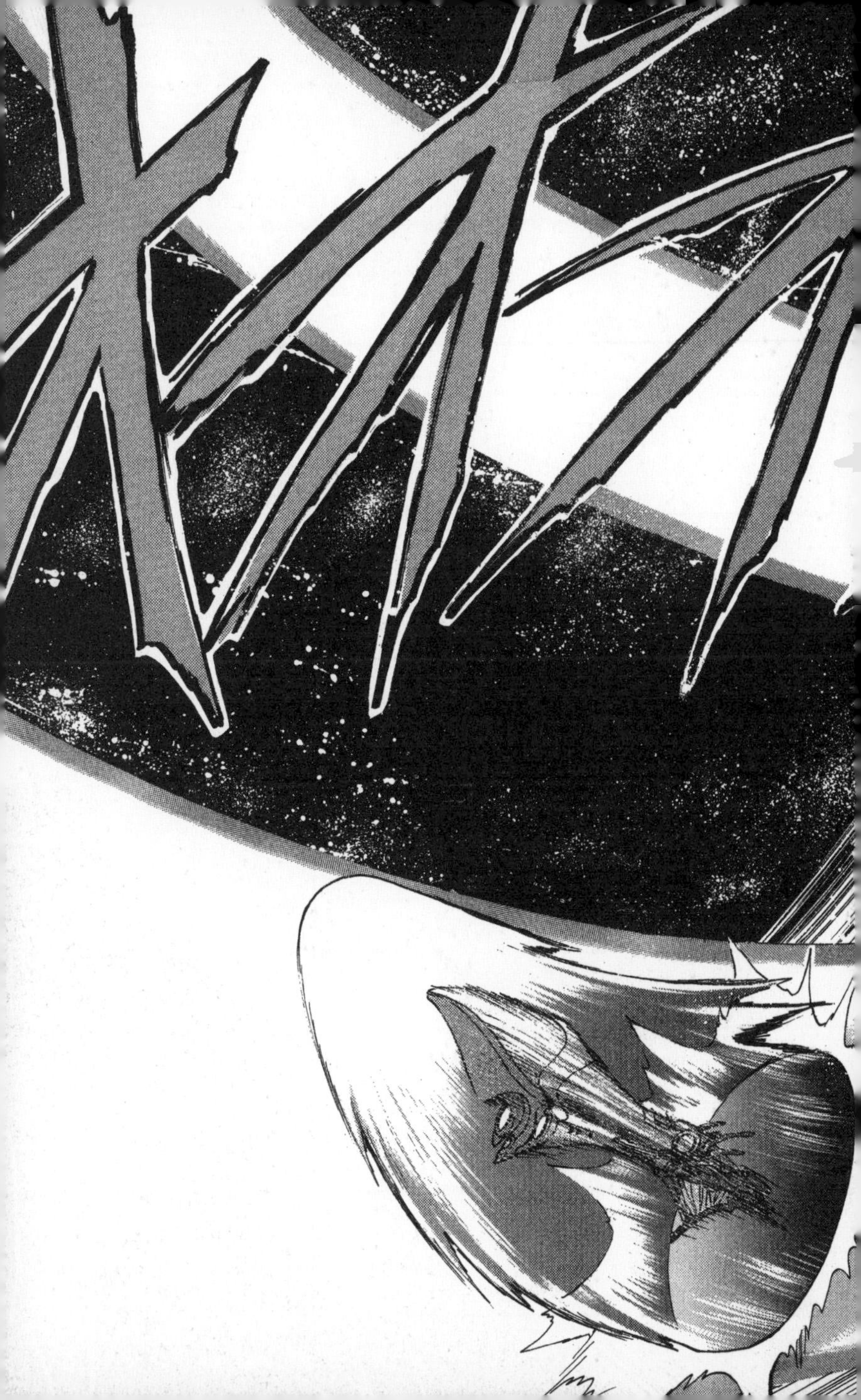

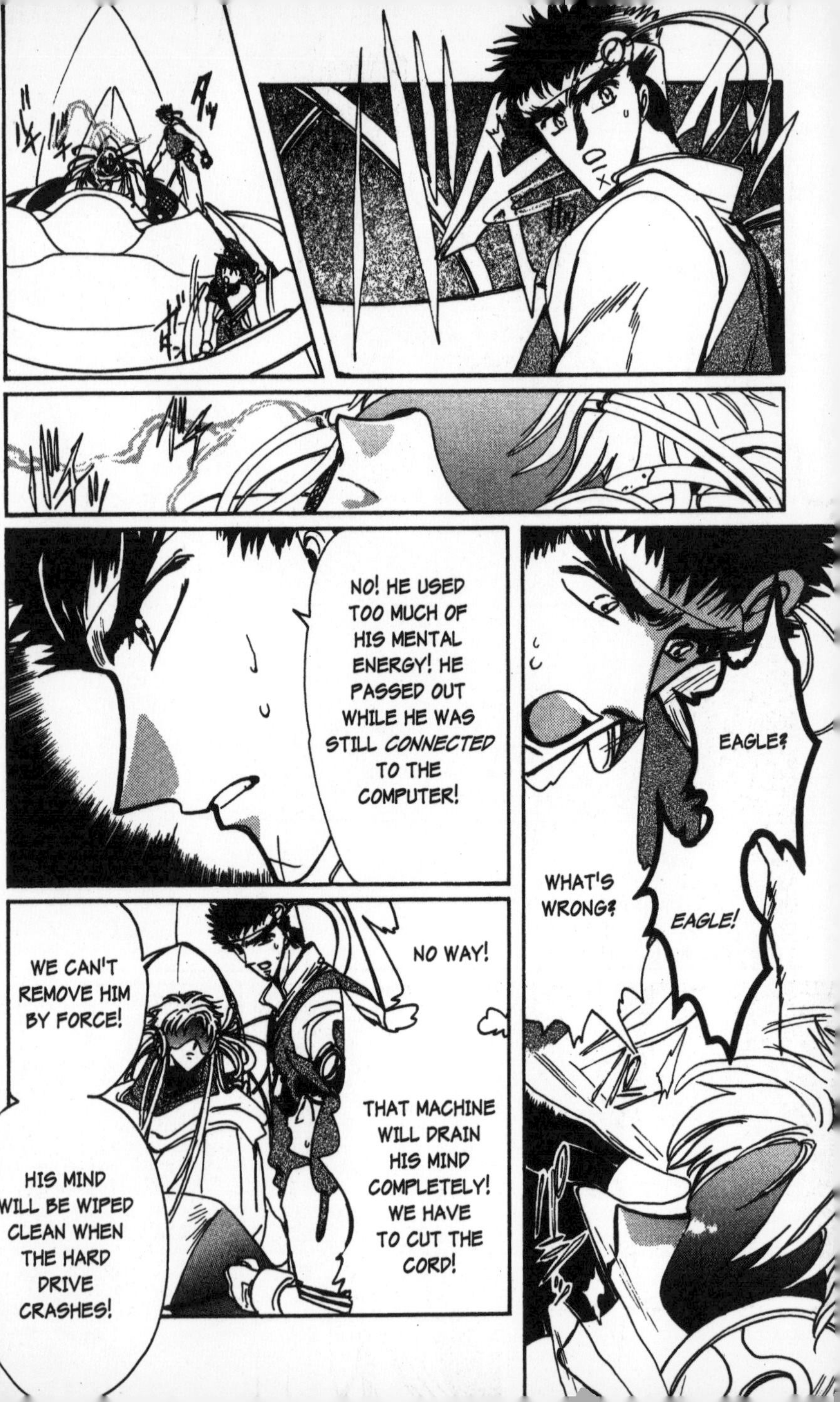
EAGLE?
WHAT'S WRONG?
EAGLE!
NO! HE USED TOO MUCH OF HIS MENTAL ENERGY! HE PASSED OUT WHILE HE WAS STILL *CONNECTED* TO THE COMPUTER!
NO WAY!
WE CAN'T REMOVE HIM BY FORCE!
THAT MACHINE WILL DRAIN HIS MIND COMPLETELY! WE HAVE TO CUT THE CORD!
HIS MIND WILL BE WIPED CLEAN WHEN THE HARD DRIVE CRASHES!

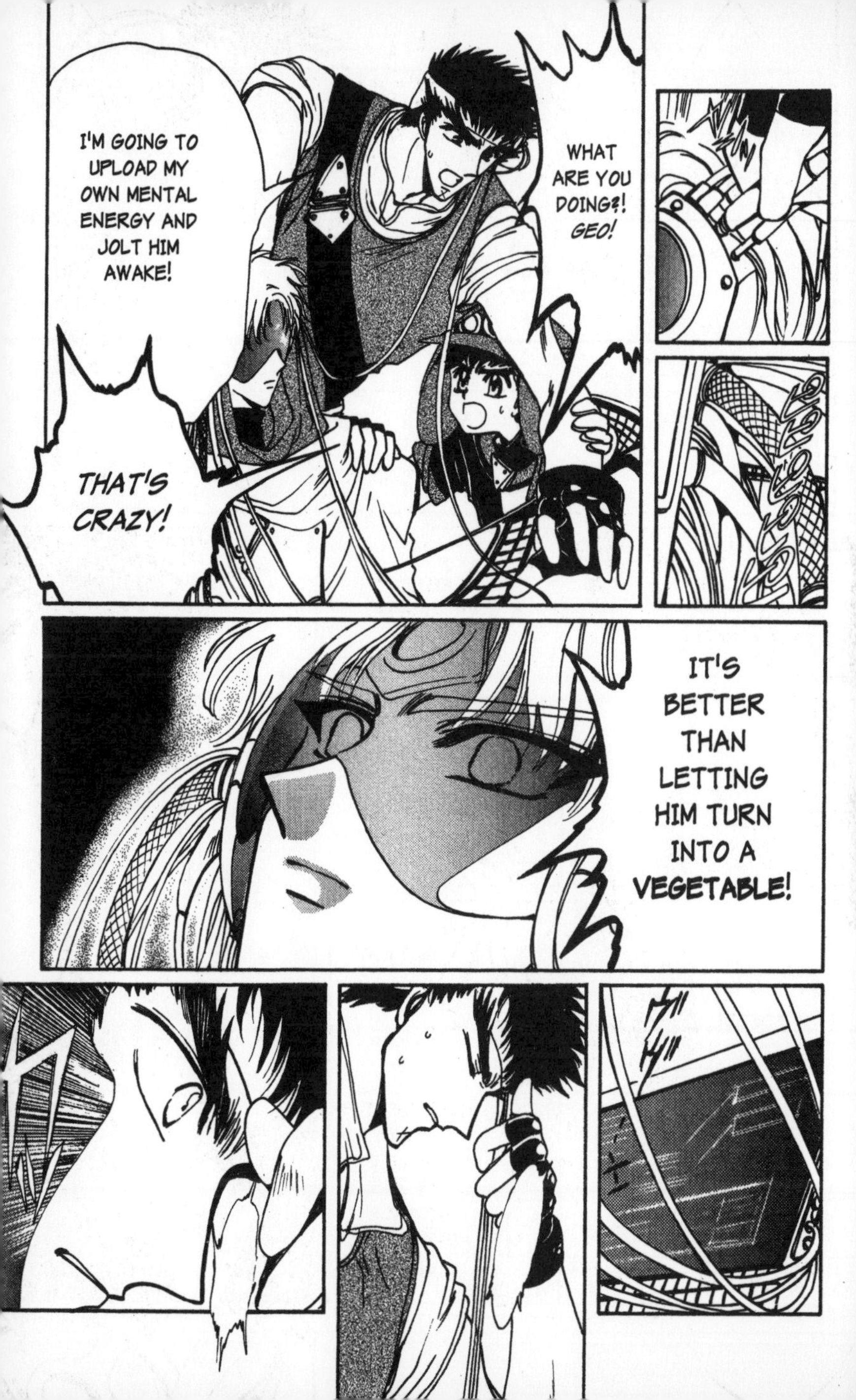
WHAT ARE YOU DOING?! GEO!
I'M GOING TO UPLOAD MY OWN MENTAL ENERGY AND JOLT HIM AWAKE!
THAT'S CRAZY!
IT'S BETTER THAN LETTING HIM TURN INTO A VEGETABLE!

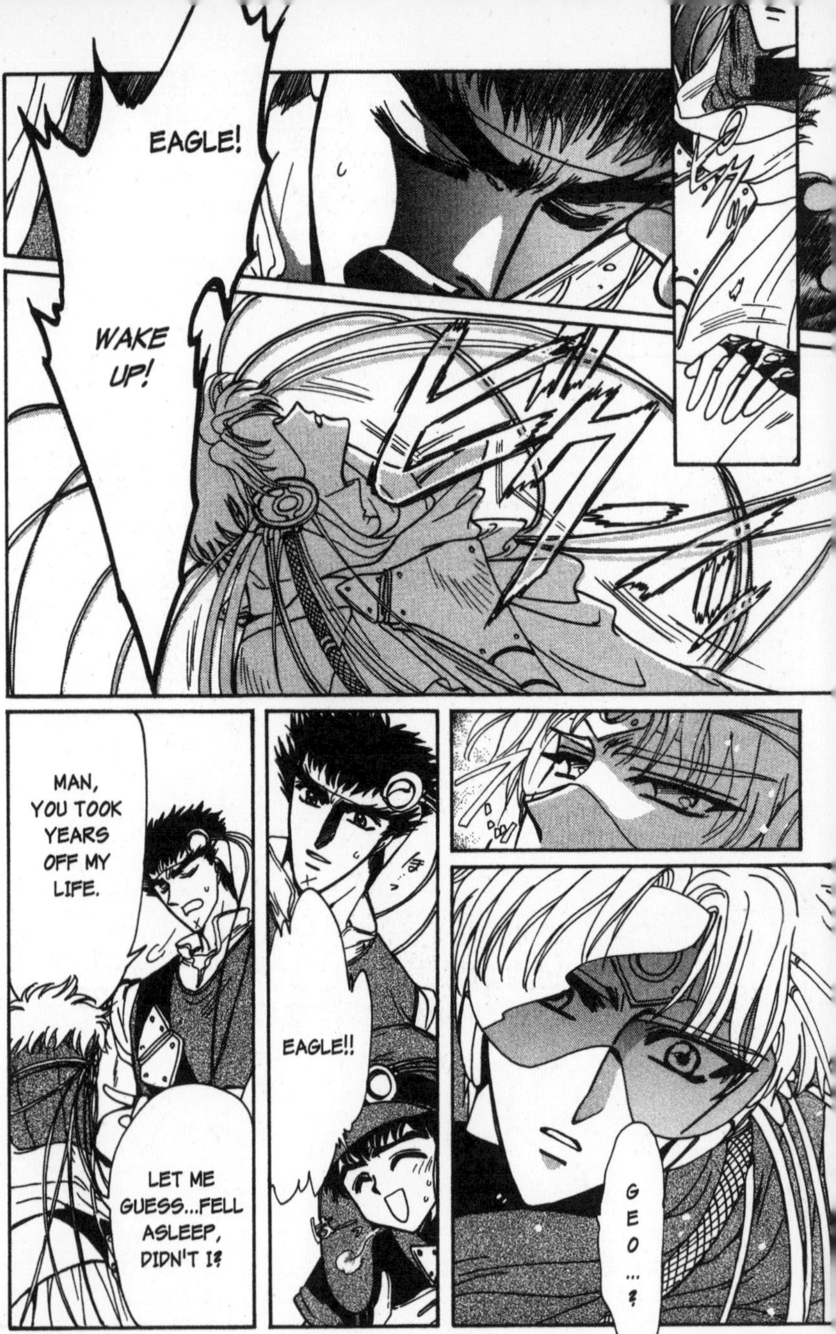
EAGLE!
WAKE UP!
GEO...?
EAGLE!!
MAN, YOU TOOK YEARS OFF MY LIFE.
LET ME GUESS...FELL ASLEEP, DIDN'T I?

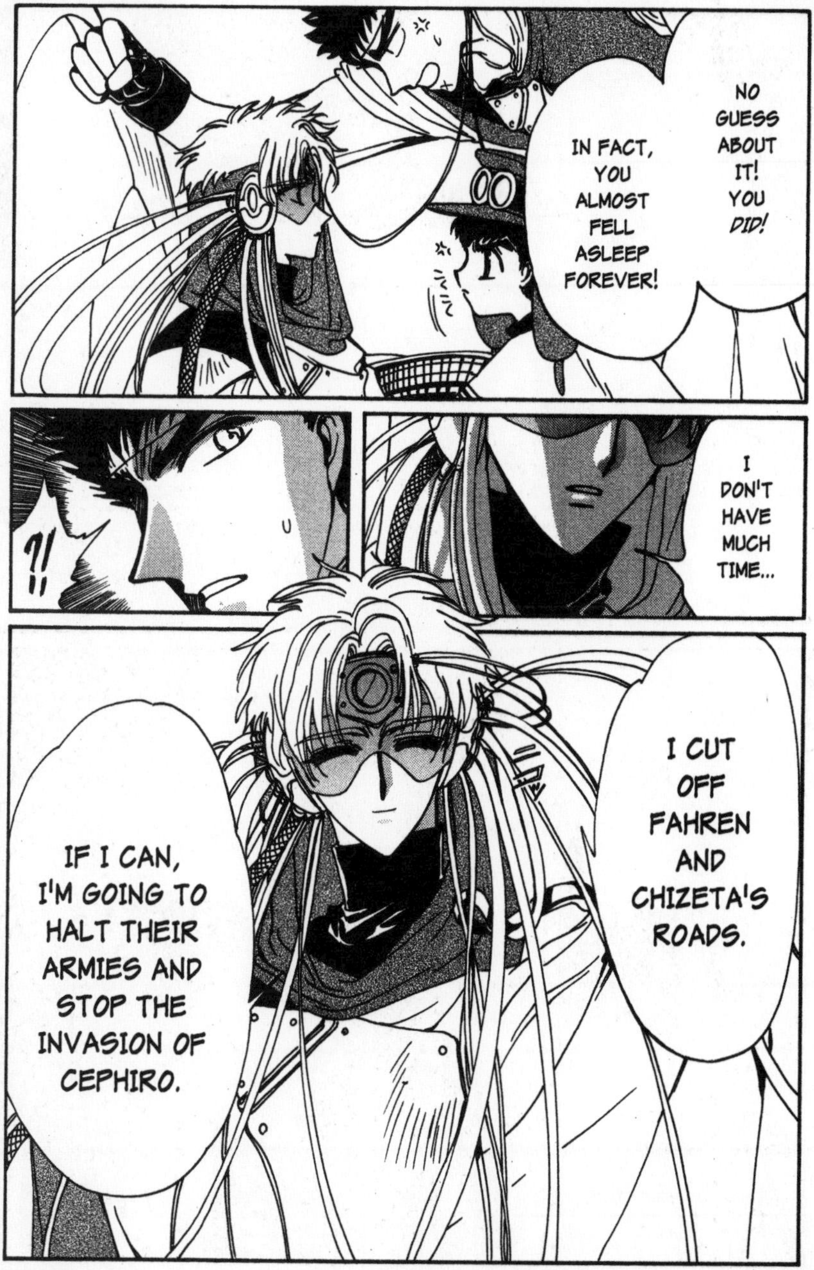

NO GUESS ABOUT IT! YOU *DID!*
IN FACT, YOU ALMOST FELL ASLEEP FOREVER!
I DON'T HAVE MUCH TIME...
?!
I CUT OFF FAHREN AND CHIZETA'S ROADS.
IF I CAN, I'M GOING TO HALT THEIR ARMIES AND STOP THE INVASION OF CEPHIRO.

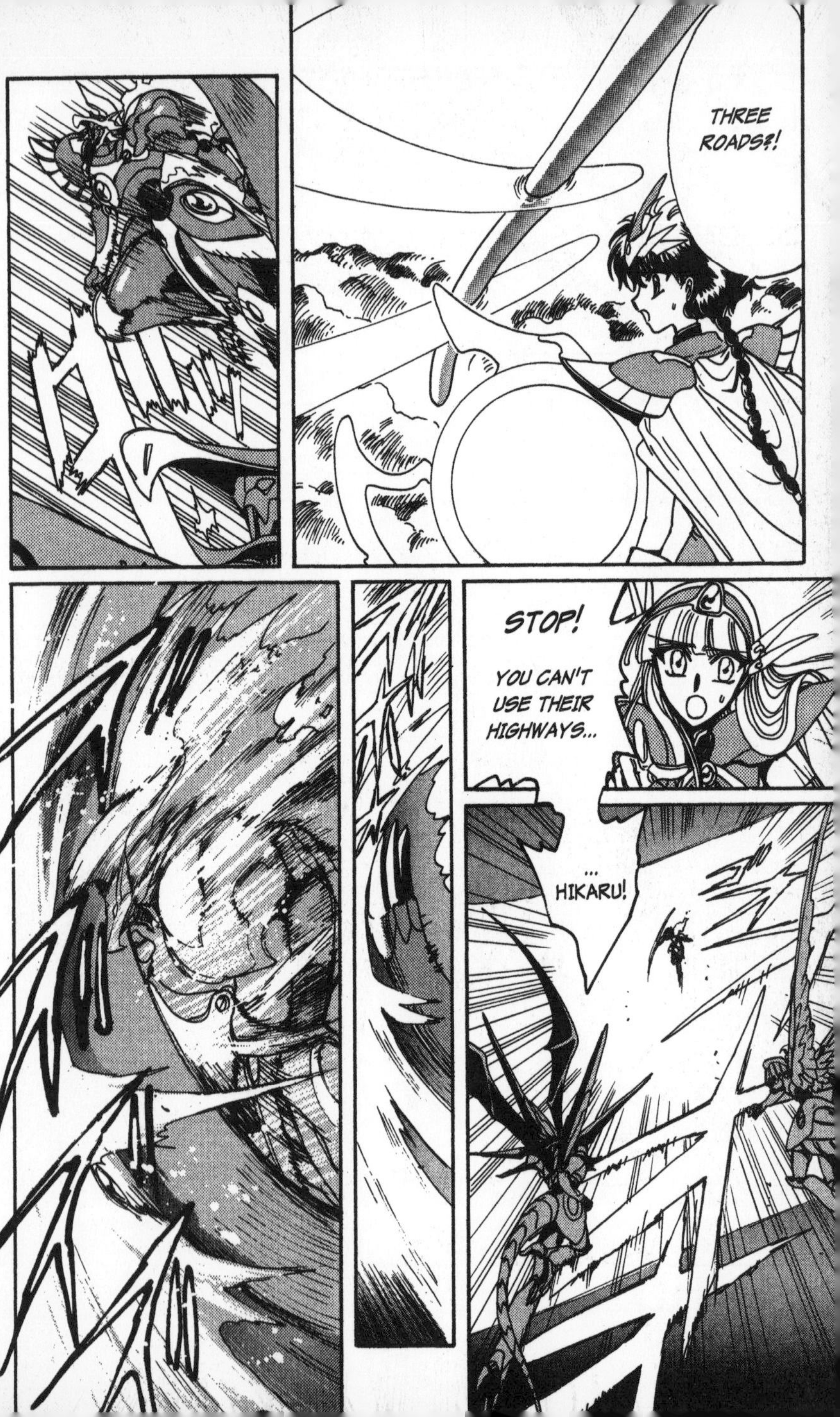
THREE ROADS?!
STOP!
YOU CAN'T USE THEIR HIGHWAYS...
... HIKARU!

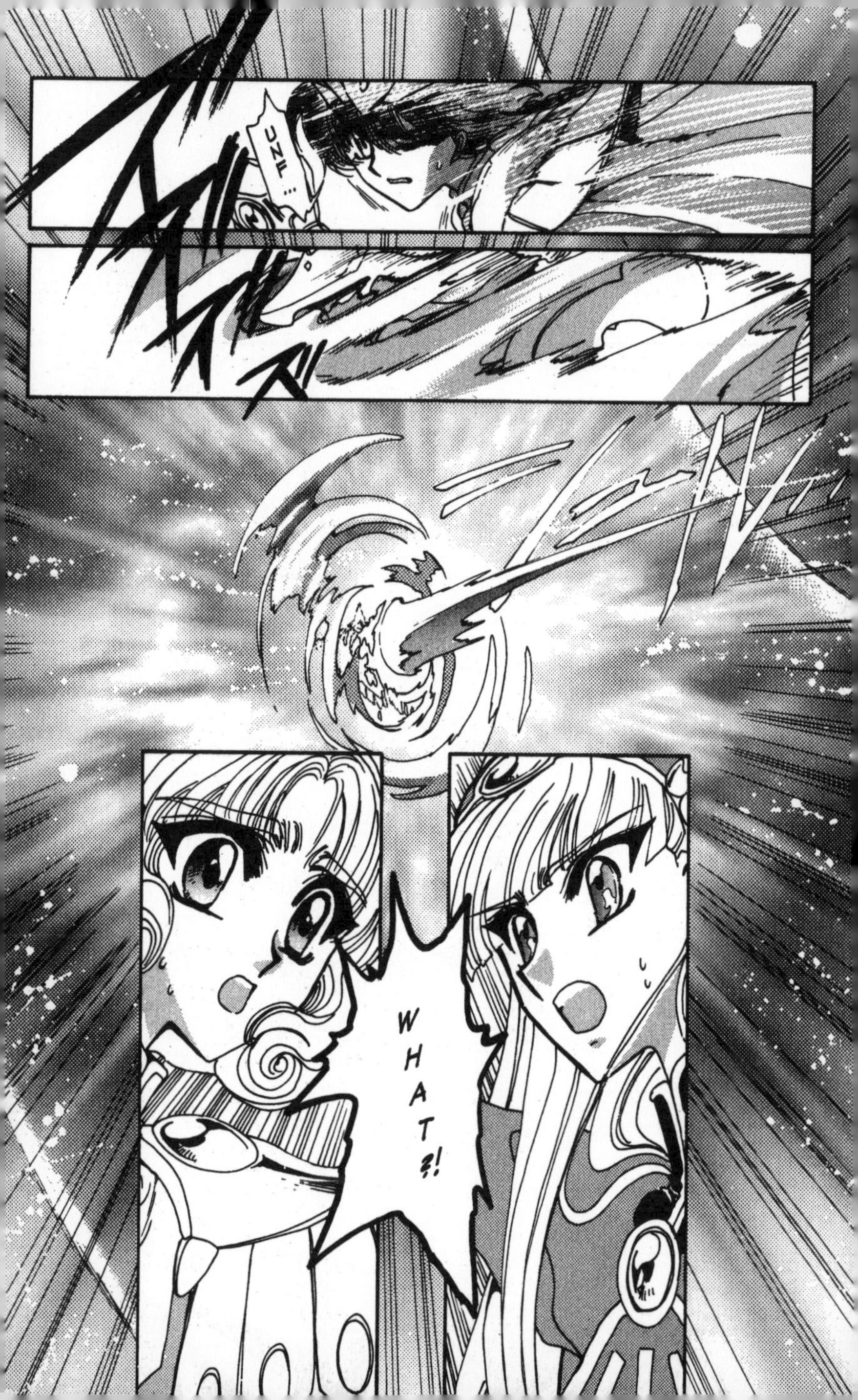
UNF...
WHAT?!

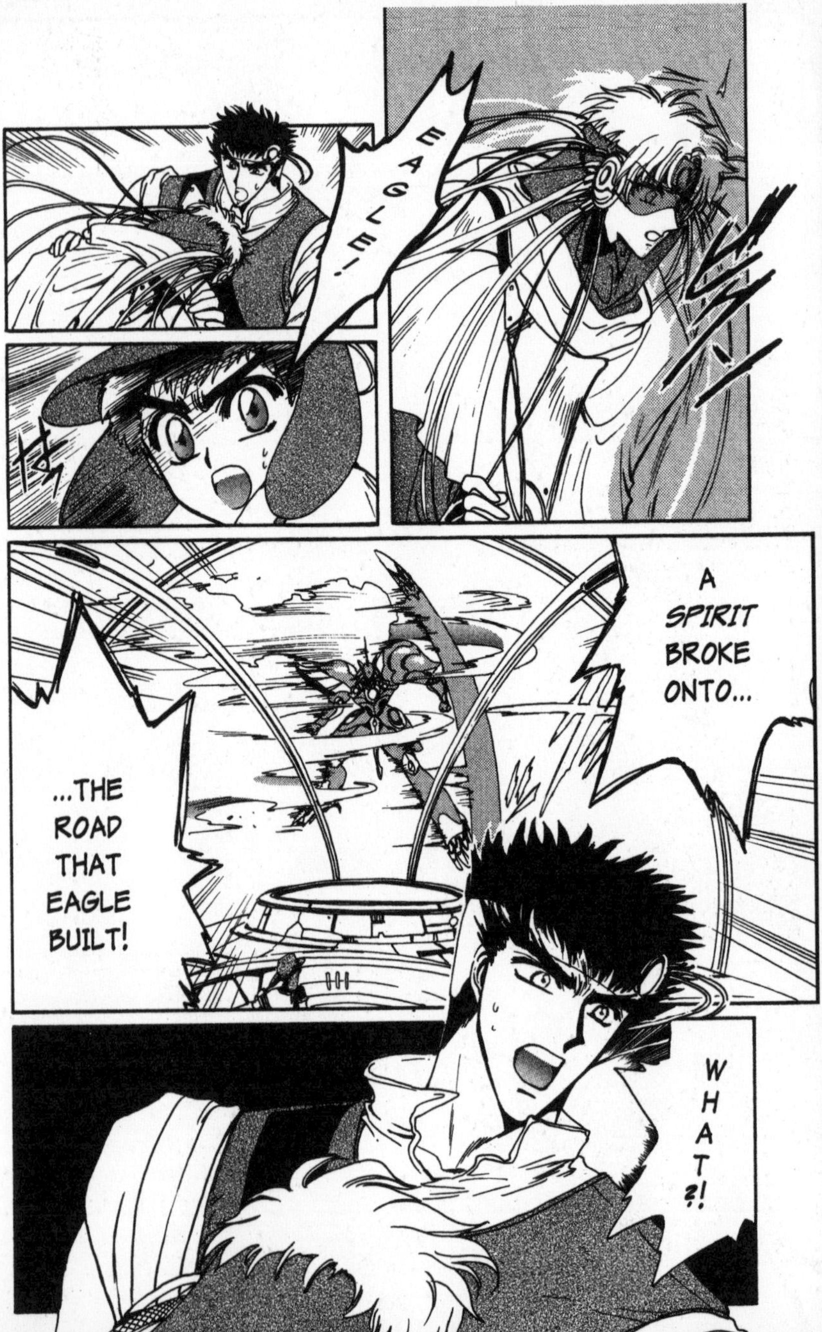
EAGLE!
A SPIRIT BROKE ONTO...
...THE ROAD THAT EAGLE BUILT!
WHAT?!

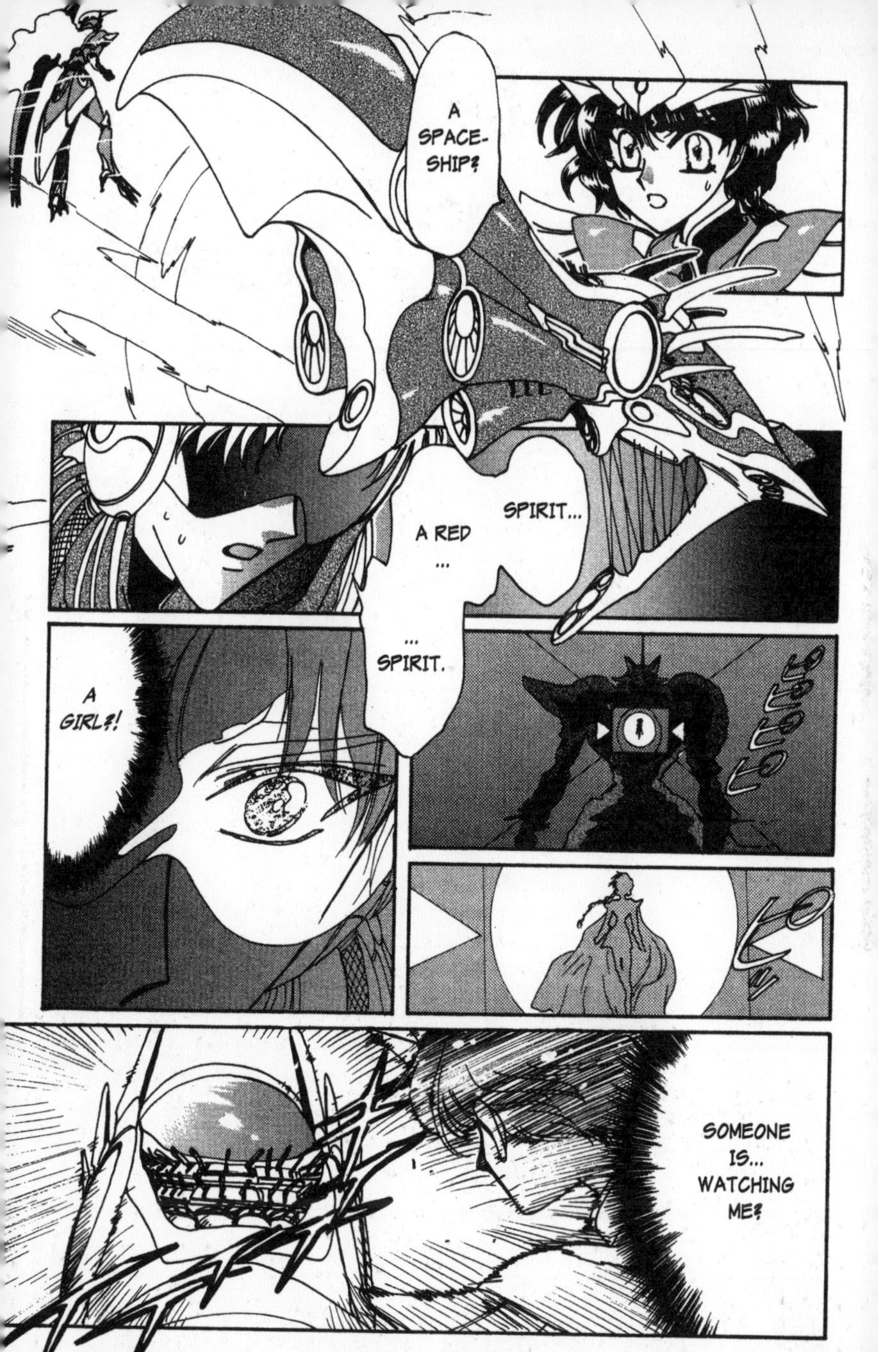
A SPACE-SHIP?
SPIRIT...
A RED ...
... SPIRIT.
A GIRL?!
SOMEONE IS... WATCHING ME?

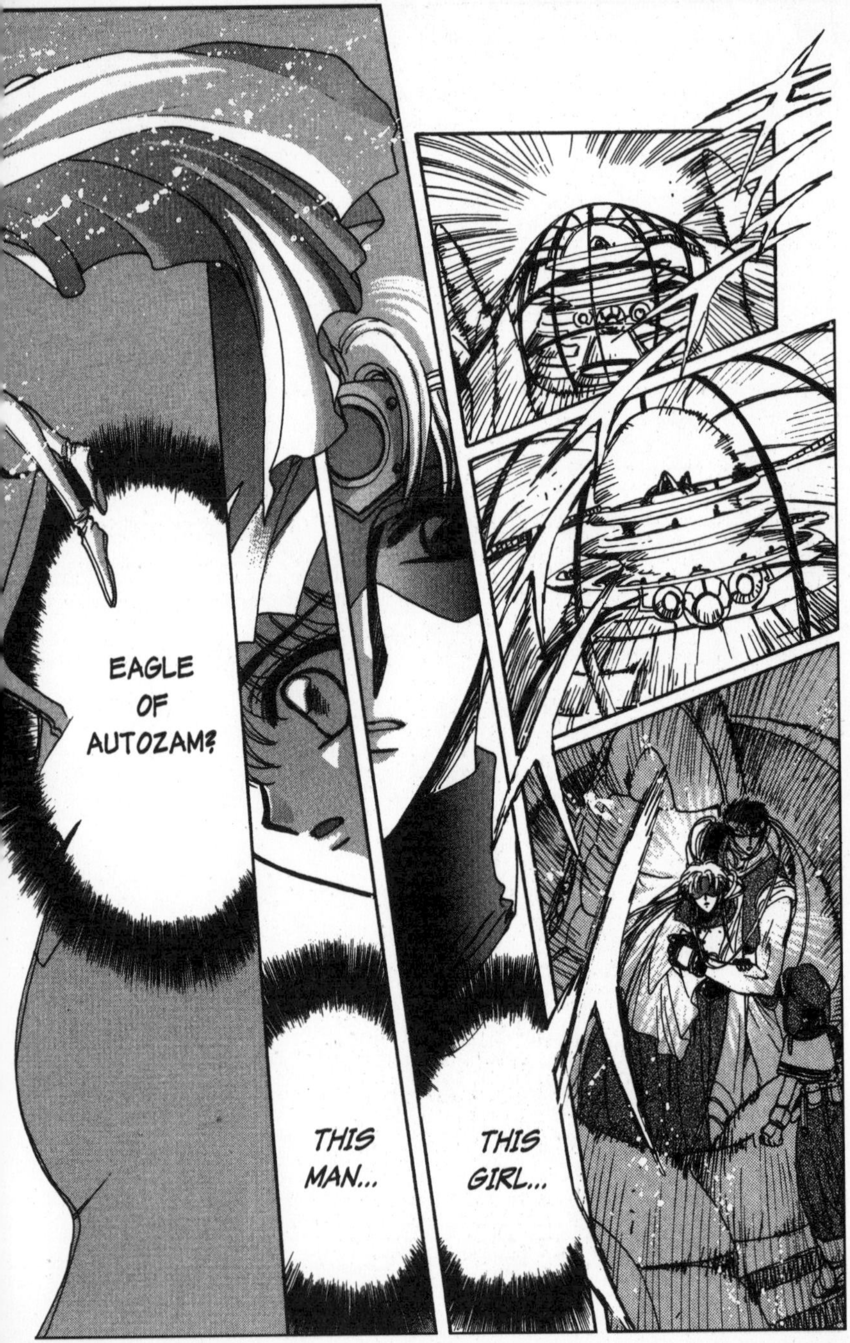
THIS GIRL...
THIS MAN...
EAGLE OF AUTOZAM?

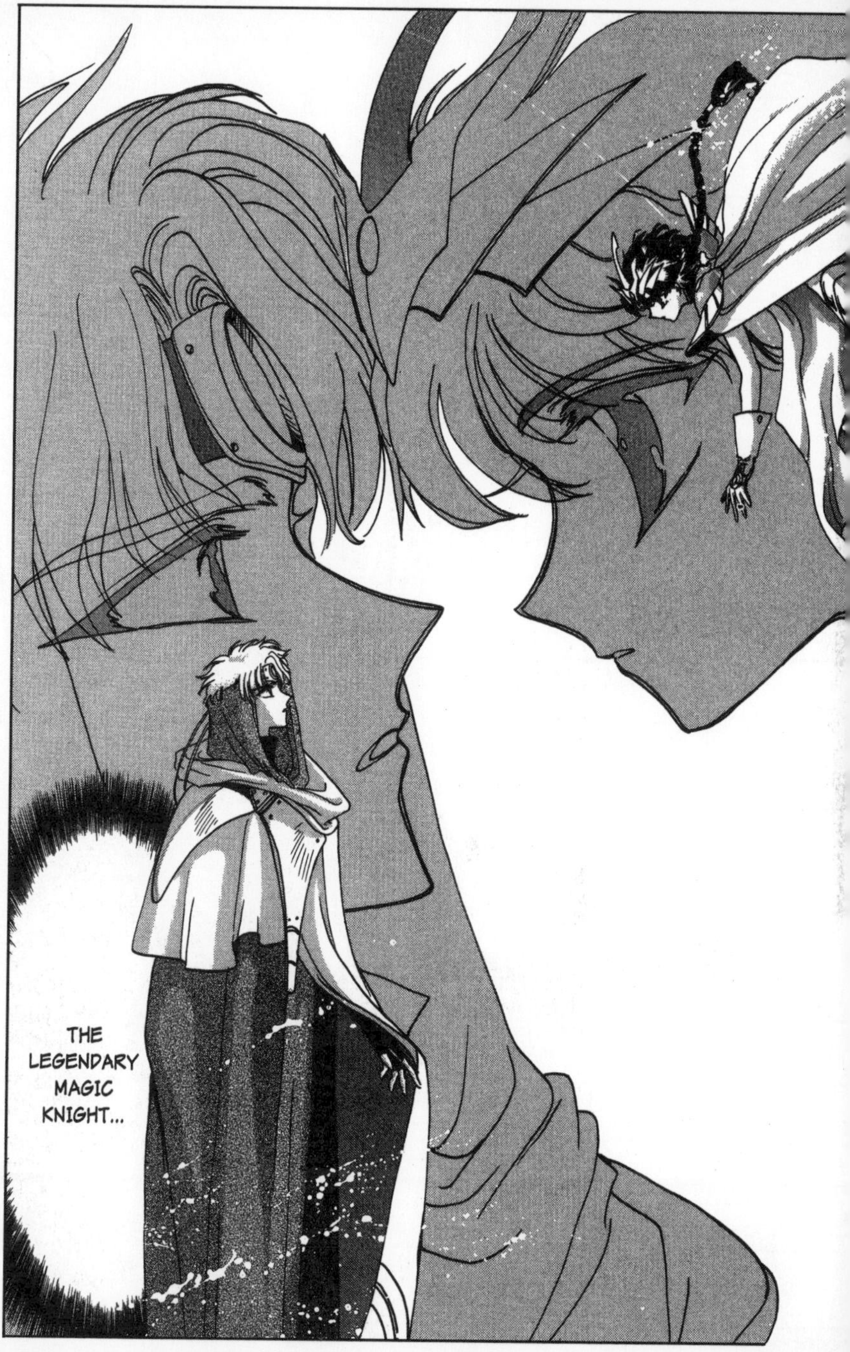
THE LEGENDARY MAGIC KNIGHT...

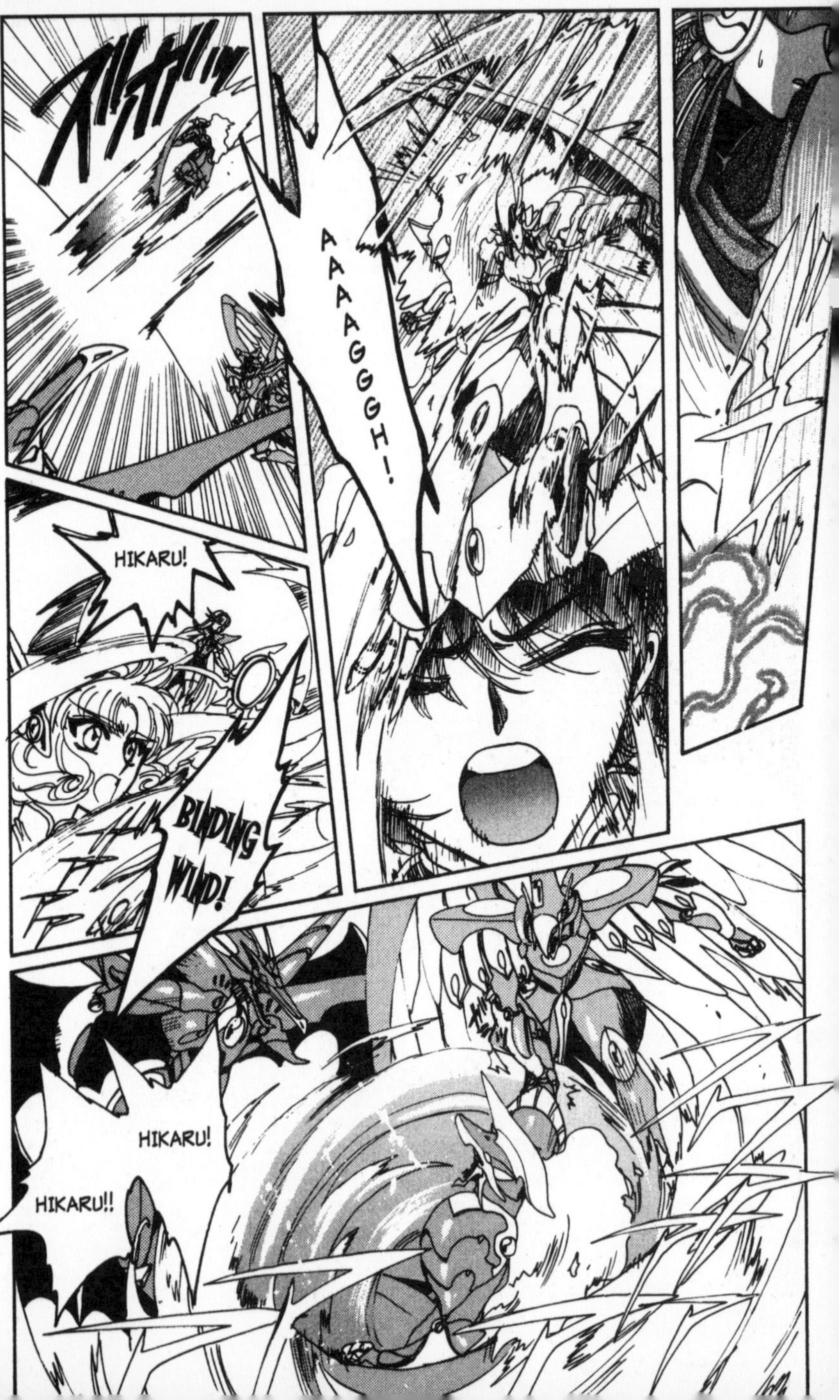
AAAAGGGH!
HIKARU!
BINDING WIND!
HIKARU!
HIKARU!!

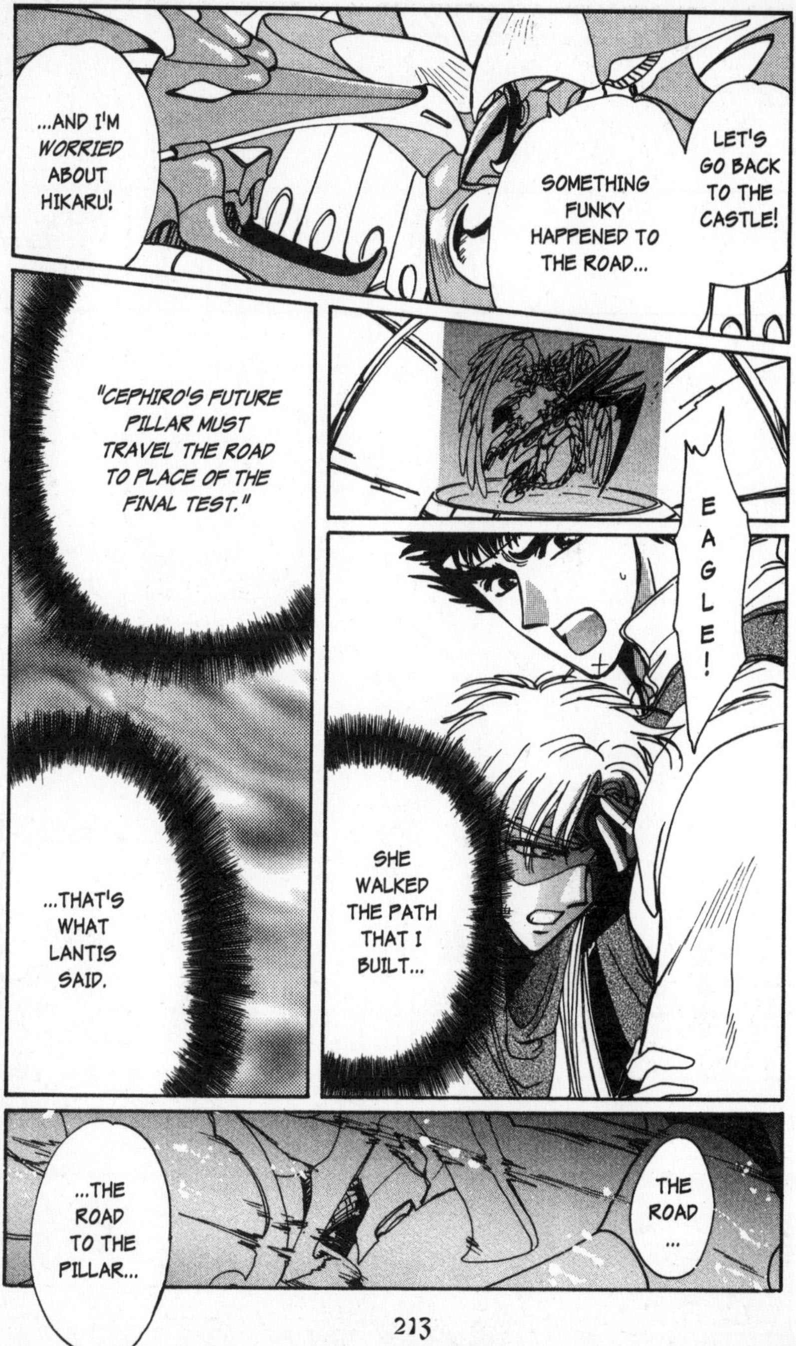
LET'S GO BACK TO THE CASTLE!
SOMETHING FUNKY HAPPENED TO THE ROAD...
...AND I'M *WORRIED* ABOUT HIKARU!
EAGLE!
SHE WALKED THE PATH THAT I BUILT...
"CEPHIRO'S FUTURE PILLAR MUST TRAVEL THE ROAD TO PLACE OF THE FINAL TEST."
...THAT'S WHAT LANTIS SAID.
THE ROAD ...
...THE ROAD TO THE PILLAR...

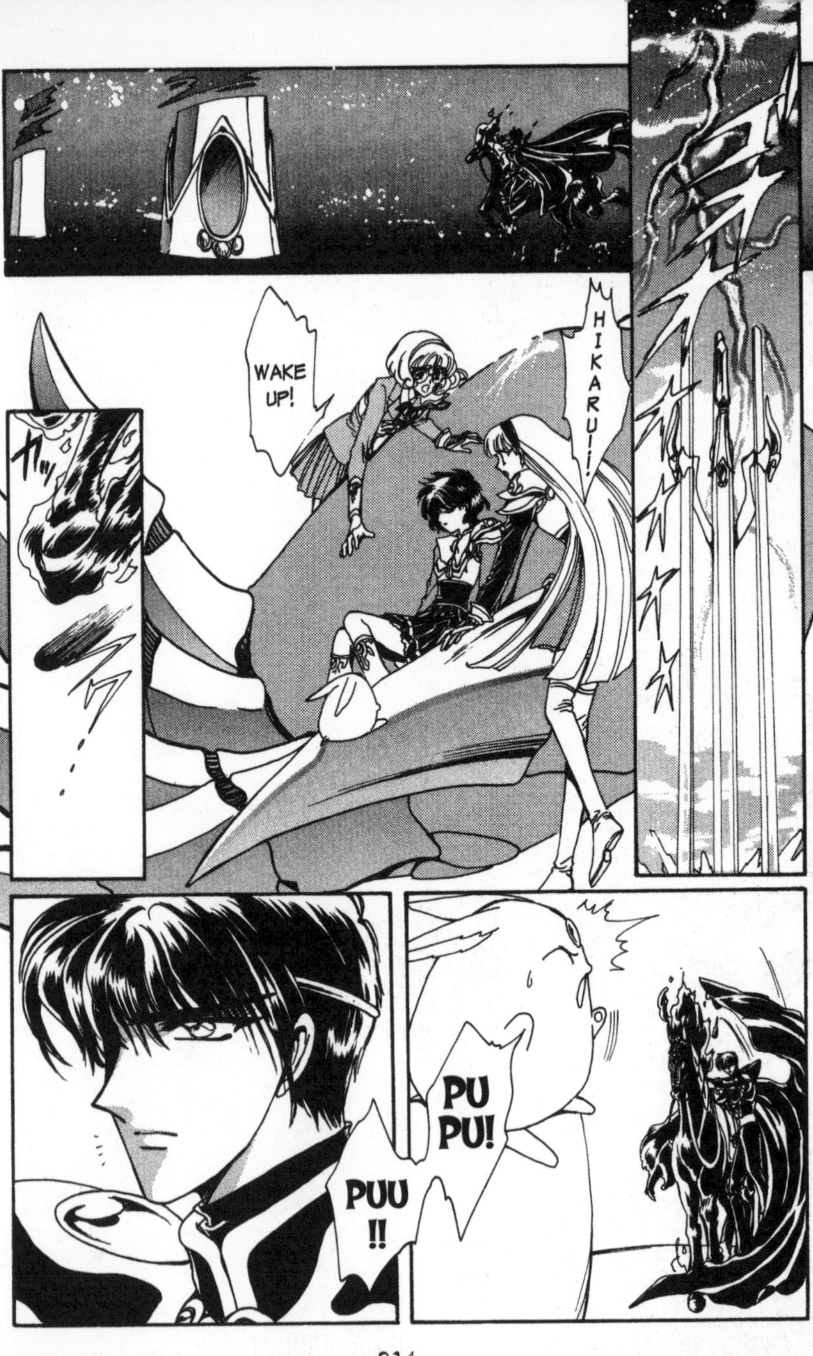
HIKARU!!
WAKE UP!
PU PU!
PUU !!

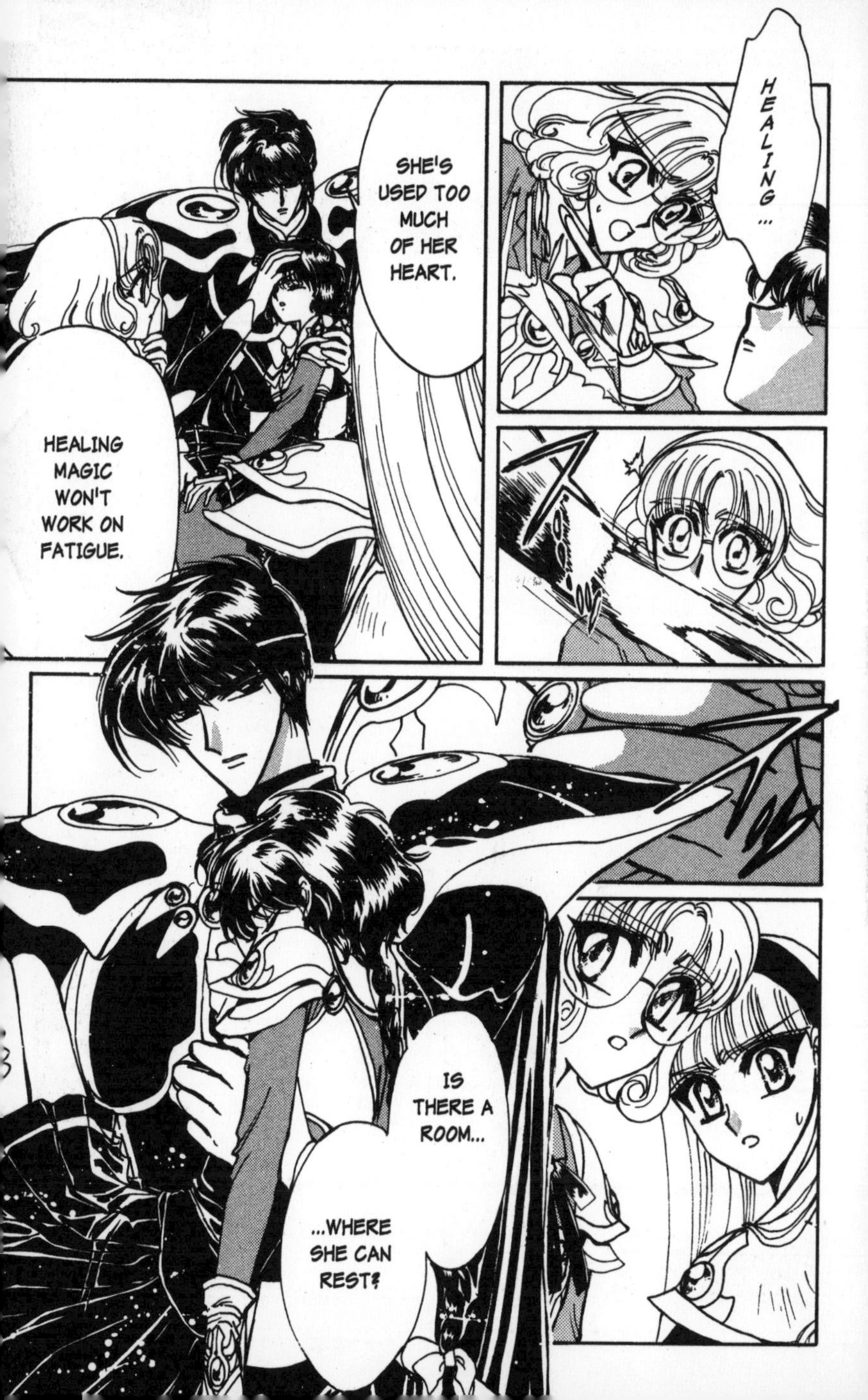
HEALING...
SHE'S USED TOO MUCH OF HER HEART.
HEALING MAGIC WON'T WORK ON FATIGUE.
IS THERE A ROOM...
...WHERE SHE CAN REST?

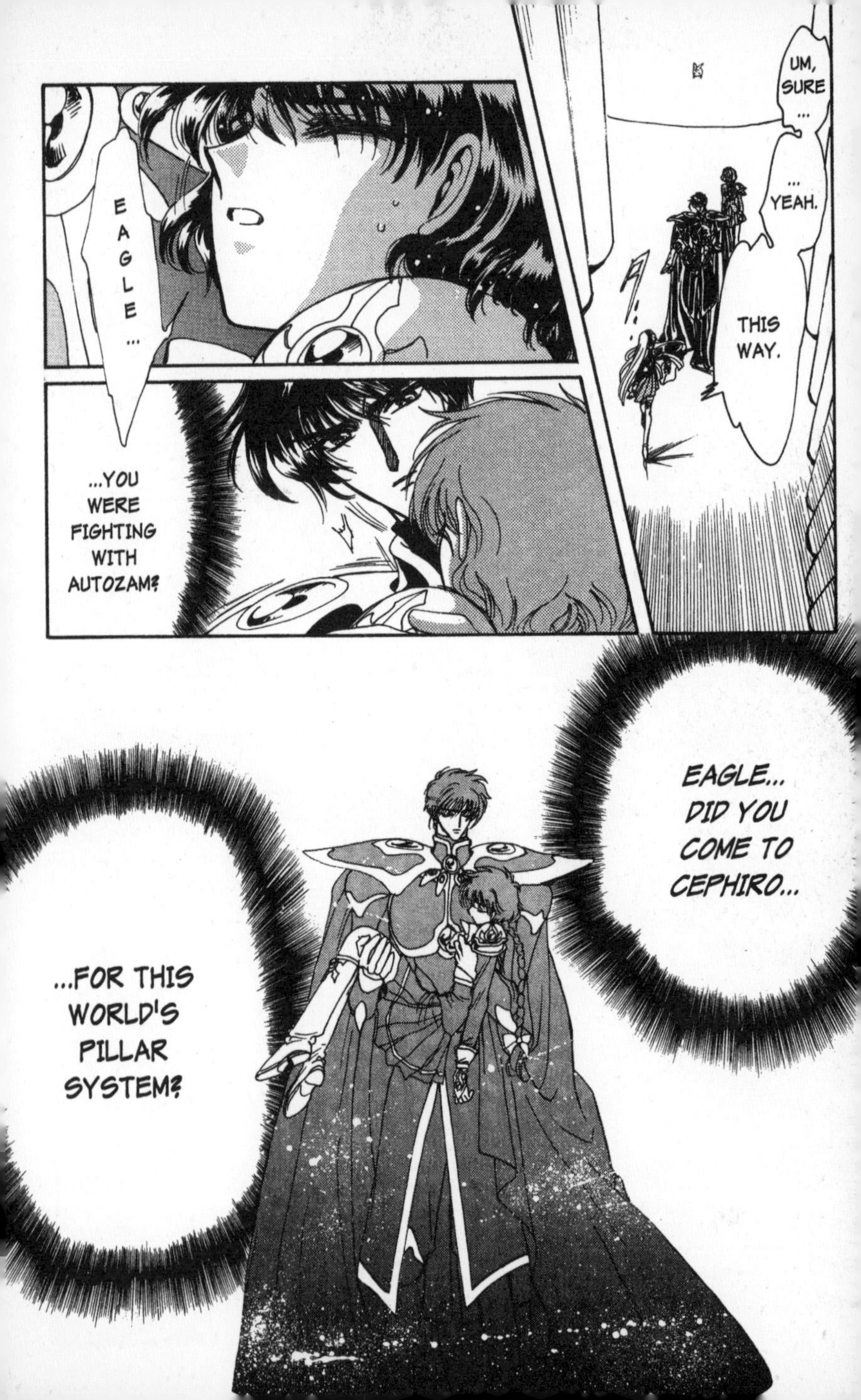
UM, SURE ...
... YEAH.
THIS WAY.
EAGLE ...
...YOU WERE FIGHTING WITH AUTOZAM?
EAGLE... DID YOU COME TO CEPHIRO...
...FOR THIS WORLD'S PILLAR SYSTEM?

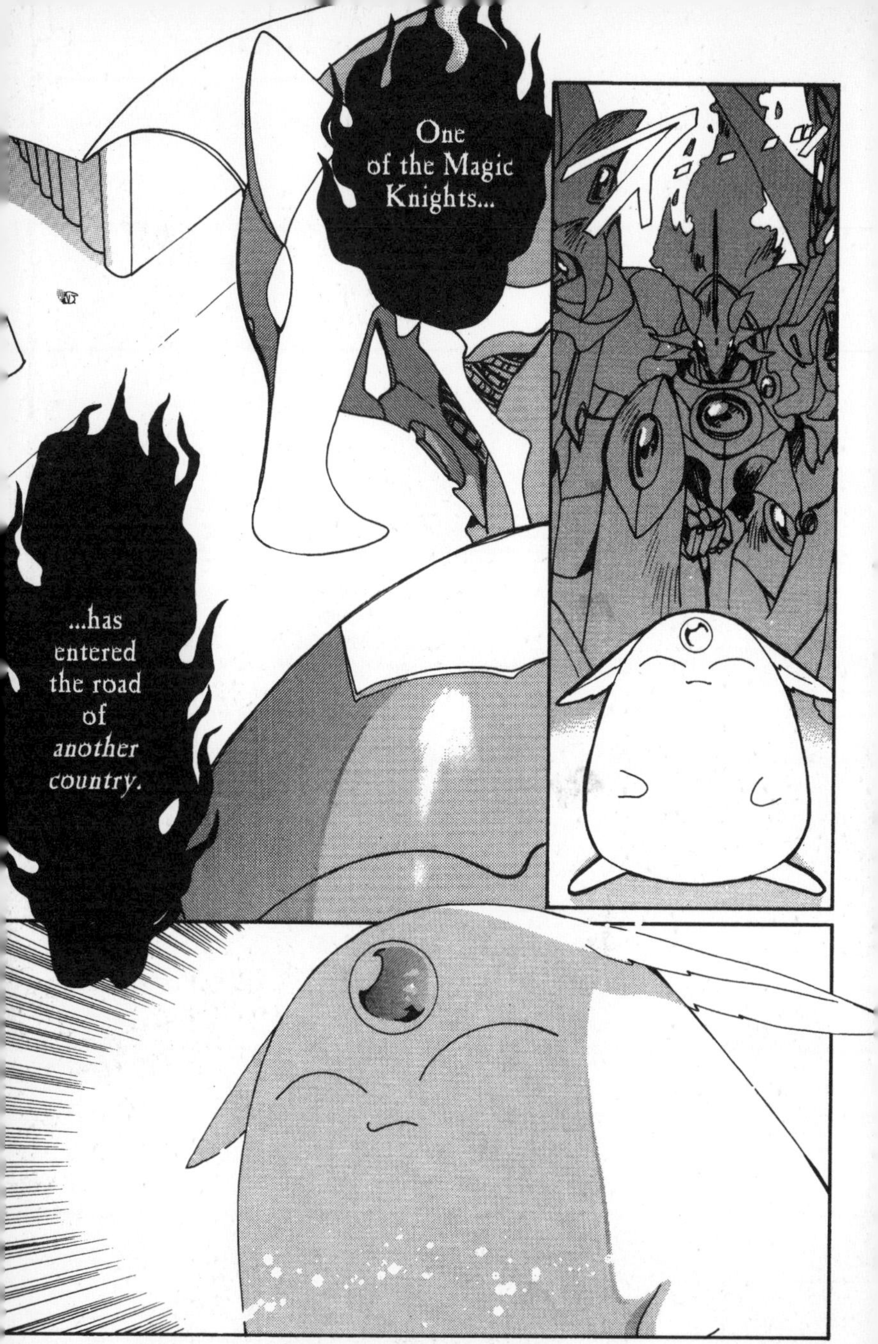
One of the Magic Knights...
...has entered the road of *another country.*

•TO NEXT STAGE•

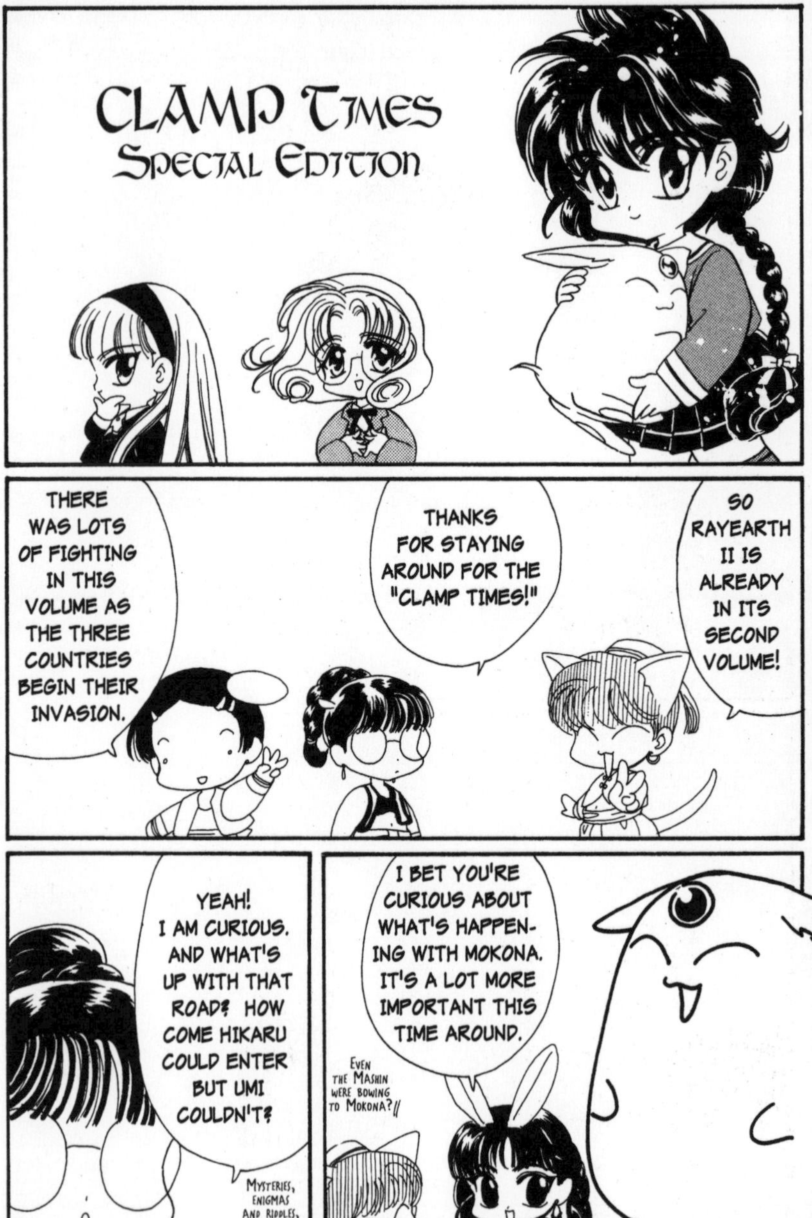
CLAMP TIMES
SPECIAL EDITION
SO RAYEARTH II IS ALREADY IN ITS SECOND VOLUME!
THANKS FOR STAYING AROUND FOR THE "CLAMP TIMES!"
THERE WAS LOTS OF FIGHTING IN THIS VOLUME AS THE THREE COUNTRIES BEGIN THEIR INVASION.
I BET YOU'RE CURIOUS ABOUT WHAT'S HAPPENING WITH MOKONA. IT'S A LOT MORE IMPORTANT THIS TIME AROUND.
EVEN THE MASHIN WERE BOWING TO MOKONA?!
YEAH! I AM CURIOUS. AND WHAT'S UP WITH THAT ROAD? HOW COME HIKARU COULD ENTER BUT UMI COULDN'T?
MYSTERIES, ENIGMAS AND RIDDLES, OH MY!

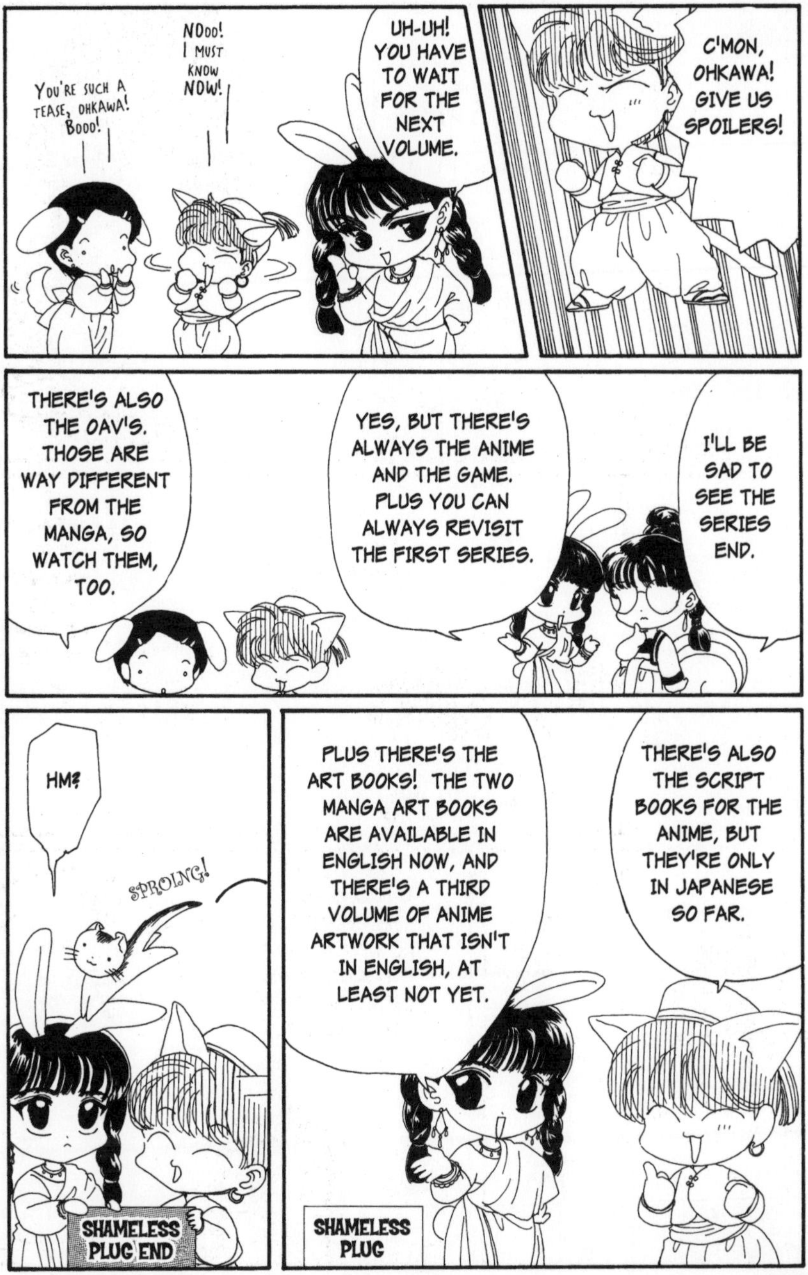
C'MON, OHKAWA! GIVE US SPOILERS!
UH-UH! YOU HAVE TO WAIT FOR THE NEXT VOLUME.
NOoo! I MUST KNOW NOW!
YOU'RE SUCH A TEASE, OHKAWA! BOOO!
I'LL BE SAD TO SEE THE SERIES END.
YES, BUT THERE'S ALWAYS THE ANIME AND THE GAME. PLUS YOU CAN ALWAYS REVISIT THE FIRST SERIES.
THERE'S ALSO THE OAV'S. THOSE ARE WAY DIFFERENT FROM THE MANGA, SO WATCH THEM, TOO.
THERE'S ALSO THE SCRIPT BOOKS FOR THE ANIME, BUT THEY'RE ONLY IN JAPANESE SO FAR.
PLUS THERE'S THE ART BOOKS! THE TWO MANGA ART BOOKS ARE AVAILABLE IN ENGLISH NOW, AND THERE'S A THIRD VOLUME OF ANIME ARTWORK THAT ISN'T IN ENGLISH, AT LEAST NOT YET.
SHAMELESS PLUG
HM?
SPROING!
SHAMELESS PLUG END

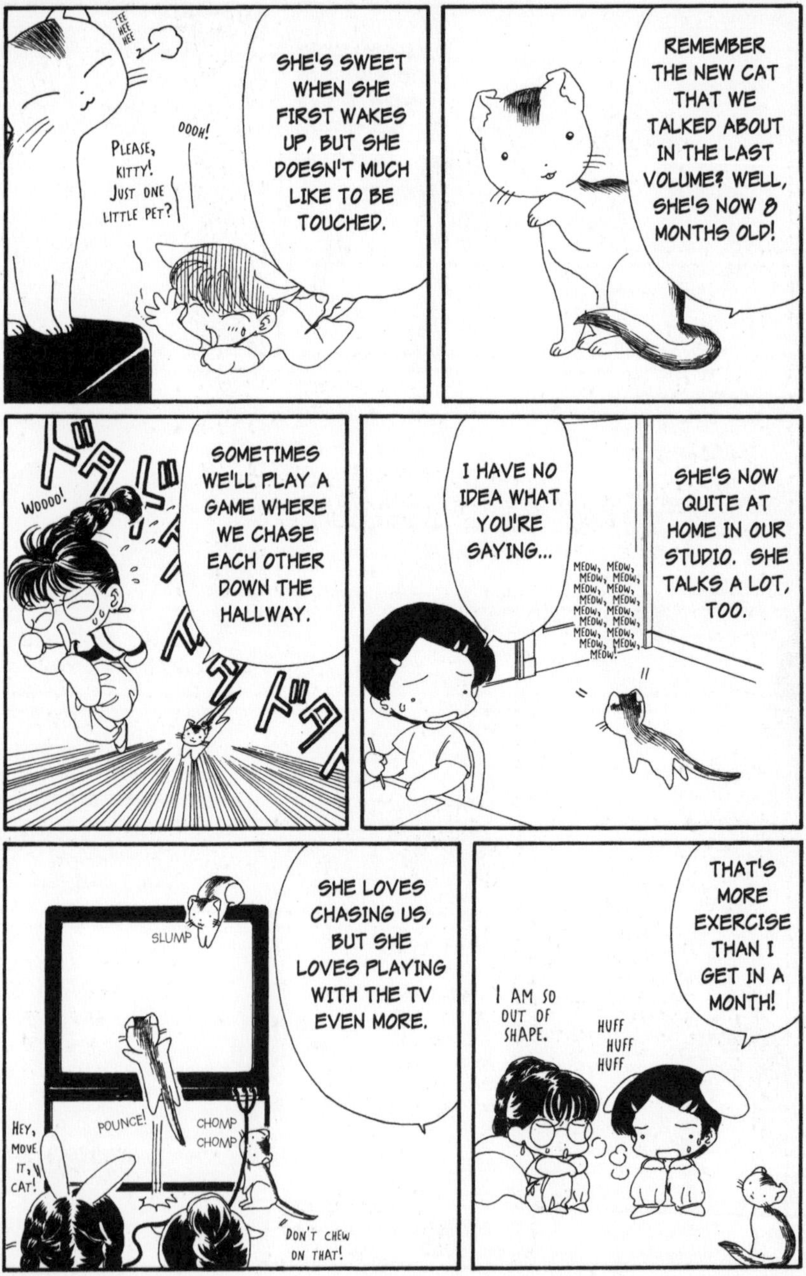
REMEMBER THE NEW CAT THAT WE TALKED ABOUT IN THE LAST VOLUME? WELL, SHE'S NOW 8 MONTHS OLD!
SHE'S SWEET WHEN SHE FIRST WAKES UP, BUT SHE DOESN'T MUCH LIKE TO BE TOUCHED.
TEE HEE HEE
OOOH!
PLEASE, KITTY! JUST ONE LITTLE PET?
SHE'S NOW QUITE AT HOME IN OUR STUDIO. SHE TALKS A LOT, TOO.
I HAVE NO IDEA WHAT YOU'RE SAYING...
MEOW, MEOW, MEOW, MEOW, MEOW, MEOW, MEOW, MEOW, MEOW, MEOW, MEOW, MEOW, MEOW, MEOW, MEOW, MEOW, MEOW!
SOMETIMES WE'LL PLAY A GAME WHERE WE CHASE EACH OTHER DOWN THE HALLWAY.
WOOOO!
THAT'S MORE EXERCISE THAN I GET IN A MONTH!
I AM SO OUT OF SHAPE.
HUFF HUFF HUFF
SHE LOVES CHASING US, BUT SHE LOVES PLAYING WITH THE TV EVEN MORE.
SLUMP
CHOMP CHOMP
POUNCE!
HEY, MOVE IT, CAT!
DON'T CHEW ON THAT!

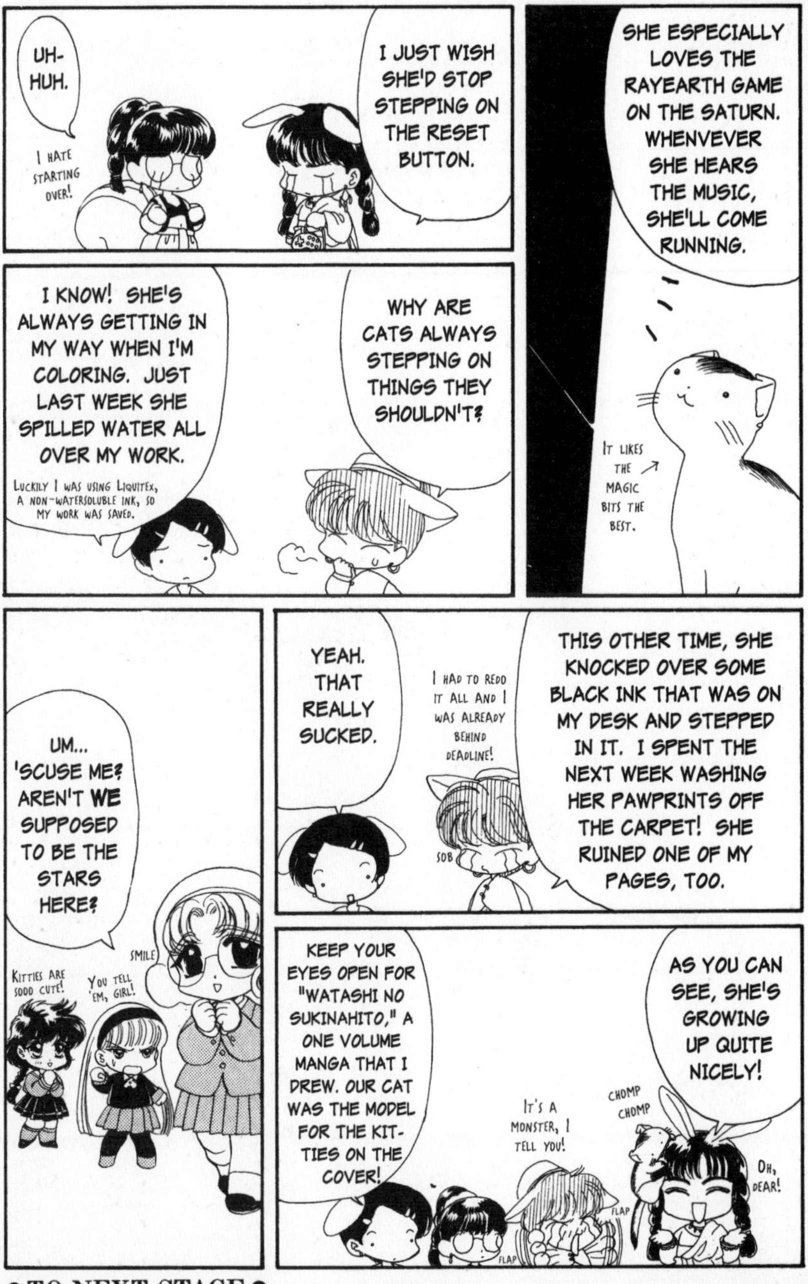
SHE ESPECIALLY LOVES THE RAYEARTH GAME ON THE SATURN. WHENVEVER SHE HEARS THE MUSIC, SHE'LL COME RUNNING.
IT LIKES THE MAGIC BITS THE BEST.
I JUST WISH SHE'D STOP STEPPING ON THE RESET BUTTON.
UH-HUH.
I HATE STARTING OVER!
WHY ARE CATS ALWAYS STEPPING ON THINGS THEY SHOULDN'T?
I KNOW! SHE'S ALWAYS GETTING IN MY WAY WHEN I'M COLORING. JUST LAST WEEK SHE SPILLED WATER ALL OVER MY WORK.
LUCKILY I WAS USING LIQUITEX, A NON-WATERSOLUBLE INK, SO MY WORK WAS SAVED.
THIS OTHER TIME, SHE KNOCKED OVER SOME BLACK INK THAT WAS ON MY DESK AND STEPPED IN IT. I SPENT THE NEXT WEEK WASHING HER PAWPRINTS OFF THE CARPET! SHE RUINED ONE OF MY PAGES, TOO.
I HAD TO REDO IT ALL AND I WAS ALREADY BEHIND DEADLINE!
SOB
YEAH. THAT REALLY SUCKED.
AS YOU CAN SEE, SHE'S GROWING UP QUITE NICELY!
OH, DEAR!
CHOMP CHOMP
IT'S A MONSTER, I TELL YOU!
FLAP
FLAP
KEEP YOUR EYES OPEN FOR "WATASHI NO SUKINAHITO," A ONE VOLUME MANGA THAT I DREW. OUR CAT WAS THE MODEL FOR THE KITTIES ON THE COVER!
UM... 'SCUSE ME? AREN'T WE SUPPOSED TO BE THE STARS HERE?
SMILE
YOU TELL 'EM, GIRL!
KITTIES ARE SOOO CUTE!

Next time in Magic Knight Rayearth II...

Many battle to become Cephiro's new Pillar, but only two will be allowed to enter the road and take the test. Who will those two be, what will happen to them, and what will become of Cephiro's citizens when a new Pillar is chosen? Can Cephiro become "truly beautiful"? Come back for the shocking conclusion of Rayearth II!

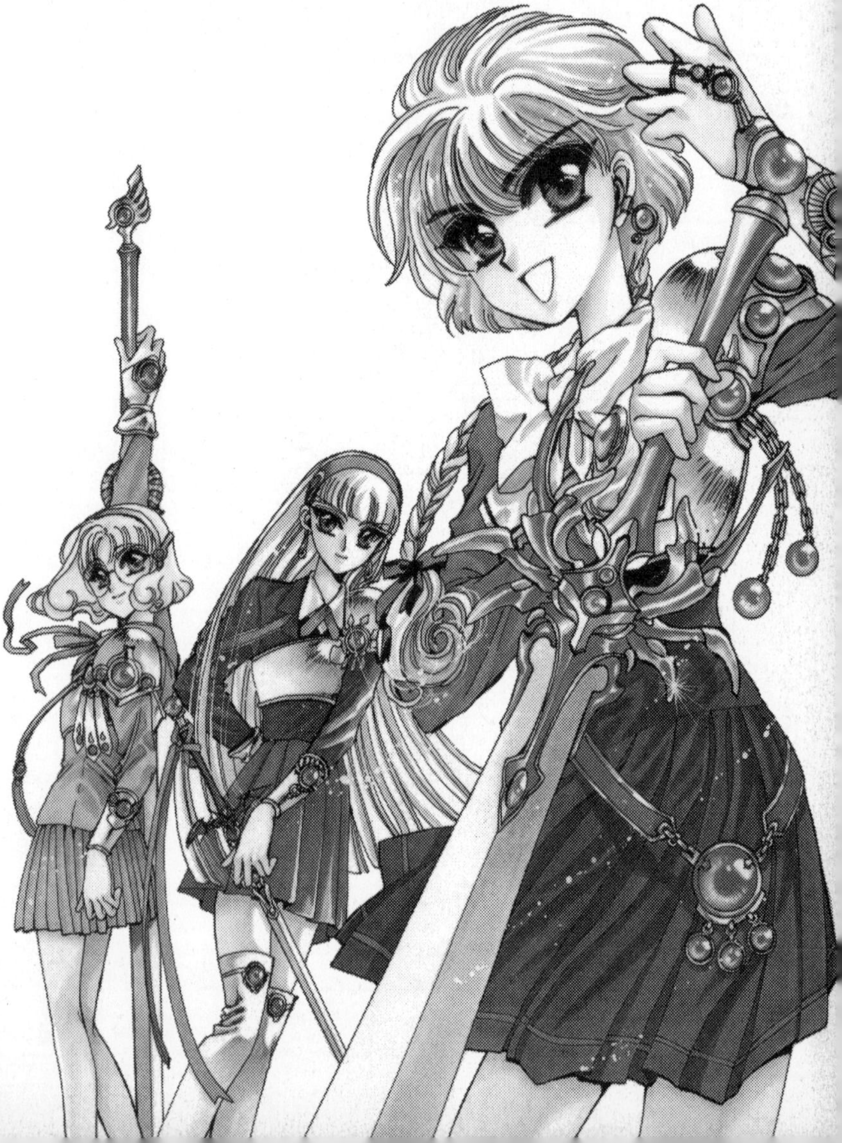

STOP!

This is the back of the book.
You wouldn't want to spoil a great ending!

This book is printed "manga-style," in the authentic Japanese right-to-left format. Since none of the artwork has been flipped or altered, readers get to experience the story just as the creator intended. You've been asking for it, so TOKYOPOP® delivered: authentic, hot-off-the-press, and far more fun!

DIRECTIONS

If this is your first time reading manga-style, here's a quick guide to help you understand how it works.

It's easy... just start in the top right panel and follow the numbers. Have fun, and look for more 100% authentic manga from TOKYOPOP®!

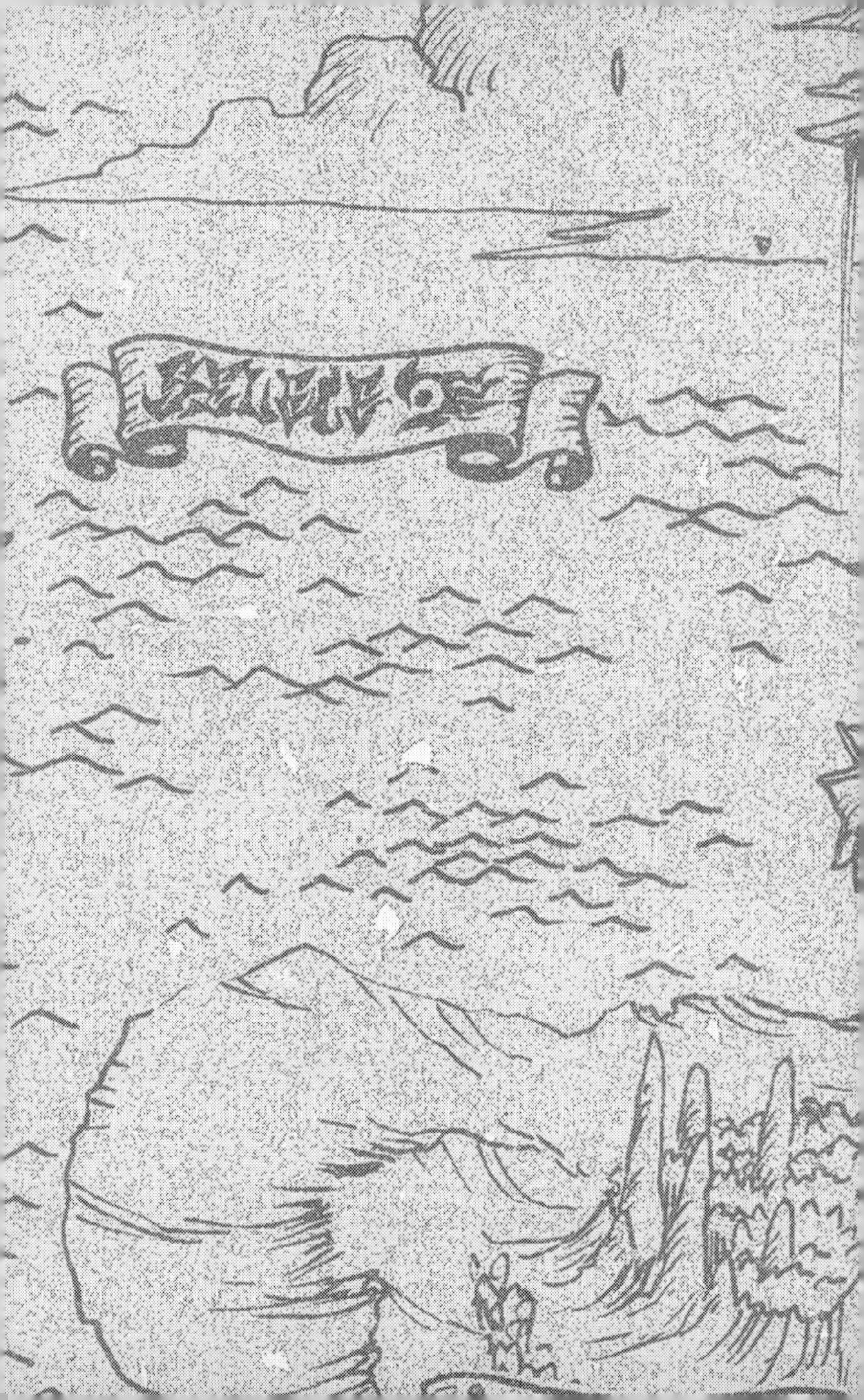

ALSO AVAILABLE FROM TOKYOPOP.

MANGA

*INDICATES 100% AUTHENTIC MANGA (RIGHT-TO-LEFT FORMAT)

ANGELIC LAYER*
BABY BIRTH* (September 2003)
BATTLE ROYALE*
BRAIN POWERED* (June 2003)
BRIGADOON* (August 2003)
CARDCAPTOR SAKURA
CARDCAPTOR SAKURA: MASTER OF THE CLOW*
CLAMP SCHOOL DETECTIVES*
CHOBITS*
CHRONICLES OF THE CURSED SWORD (July 2003)
CLOVER
CONFIDENTIAL CONFESSIONS* (July 2003)
CORRECTOR YUI
COWBOY BEBOP*
COWBOY BEBOP: SHOOTING STAR* (June 2003)
DEMON DIARY (May 2003)
DIGIMON
DRAGON HUNTER (June 2003)
DRAGON KNIGHTS*
DUKLYON: CLAMP SCHOOL DEFENDERS* (September 2003)
ERICA SAKURAZAWA* (May 2003)
ESCAFLOWNE* (July 2003)
FAKE* (May 2003)
FLCL* (September 2003)
FORBIDDEN DANCE* (August 2003)
GATE KEEPERS*
G-GUNDAM* (June 2003)
GRAVITATION* (June 2003)
GTO*
GUNDAM WING
GUNDAM WING: ENDLESS WALTZ*
GUNDAM: THE LAST OUTPOST*
HAPPY MANIA*
HARLEM BEAT
INITIAL D*
I.N.V.U.
ISLAND
JING: KING OF BANDITS* (June 2003)
JULINE
KARE KANO*
KINDAICHI CASE FILES* (June 2003)
KING OF HELL (June 2003)

KODOCHA*
LOVE HINA*
LUPIN III*
MAGIC KNIGHT RAYEARTH* (August 2003)
MAN OF MANY FACES* (May 2003)
MARMALADE BOY*
MARS*
MIRACLE GIRLS
MIYUKI-CHAN IN WONDERLAND* (October 2003)
MONSTERS, INC.
NIEA_7* (August 2003)
PARADISE KISS*
PARASYTE
PEACH GIRL
PEACH GIRL: CHANGE OF HEART*
PET SHOP OF HORRORS* (June 2003)
PLANET LADDER
PLANETS* (October 2003)
PRIEST
RAGNAROK
RAVE MASTER*
REAL BOUT HIGH SCHOOL*
REALITY CHECK
REBIRTH
REBOUND*
SABER MARIONETTE J* (July 2003)
SAILOR MOON
SAINT TAIL
SAMURAI DEEPER KYO* (June 2003)
SCRYED*
SHAOLIN SISTERS*
SHIRAHIME-SYO* (December 2003)
THE SKULL MAN*
SORCERER HUNTERS
TOKYO MEW MEW*
UNDER THE GLASS MOON (June 2003)
VAMPIRE GAME* (June 2003)
WILD ACT* (July 2003)
WISH*
X-DAY* (August 2003)
ZODIAC P.I.* (July 2003)

CINE-MANGA™

AKIRA*
CARDCAPTORS
JIMMY NEUTRON (COMING SOON)
KIM POSSIBLE
LIZZIE McGUIRE
SPONGEBOB SQUAREPANTS (COMING SOON)
SPY KIDS 2

NOVELS

SAILOR MOON
KARMA CLUB (COMING SOON)

TOKYOPOP KIDS

STRAY SHEEP (September 2003)

ART BOOKS

CARDCAPTOR SAKURA*
MAGIC KNIGHT RAYEARTH*

ANIME GUIDES

GUNDAM TECHNICAL MANUALS
COWBOY BEBOP
SAILOR MOON SCOUT GUIDES

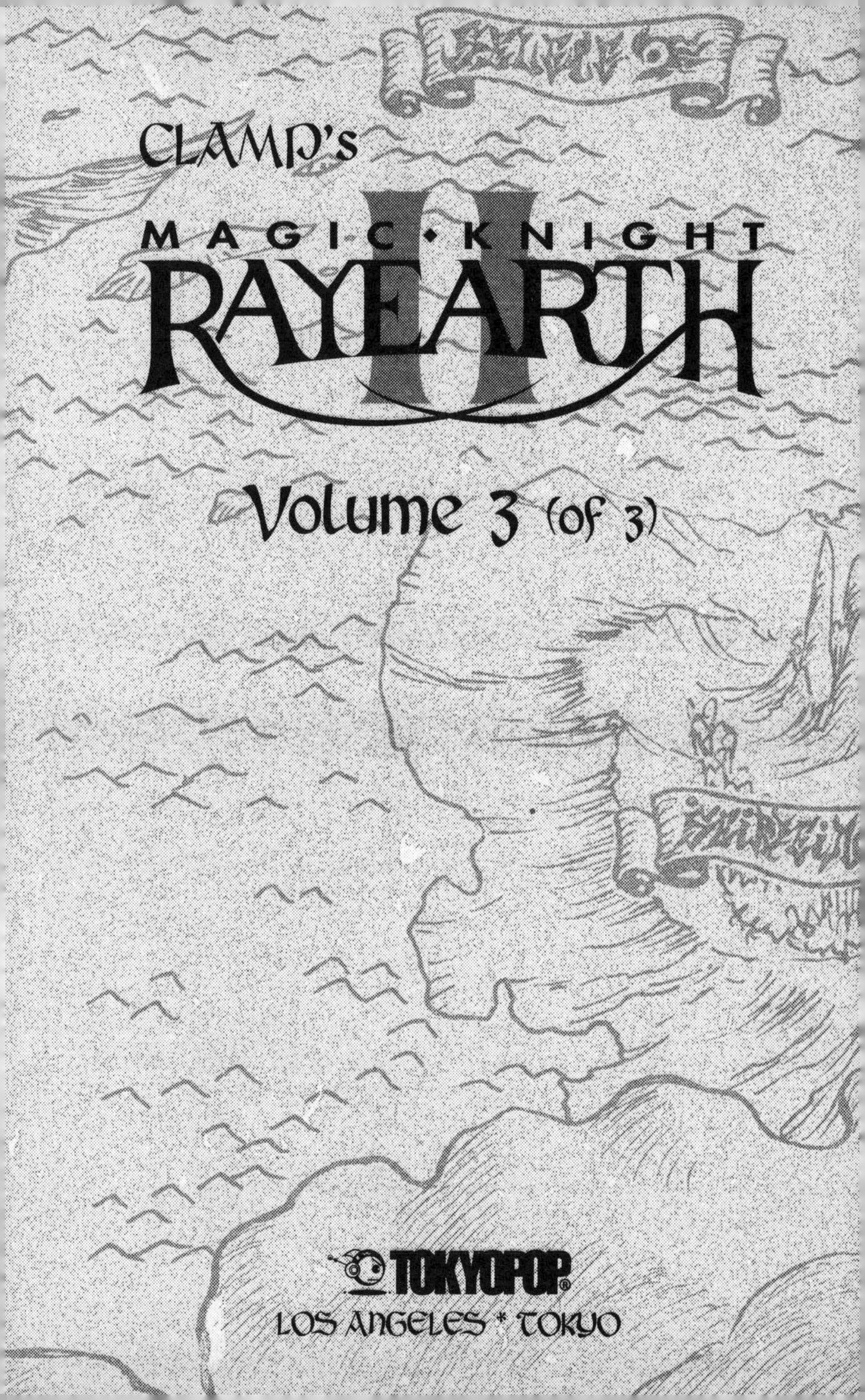

CLAMP's

MAGIC•KNIGHT RAYEARTH II

Volume 3 (of 3)

TOKYOPOP®
LOS ANGELES * TOKYO

Translator - Anita Sengupta
English Adaption - Jamie S. Rich
Copy Editor - Bryce P. Coleman
Retouch - Monalisa de Asis
Lettering - Paul Morrissey
Cover Layout - Patrick Hook

Editor - Jake Forbes
Managing Editor - Jill Freshney
Production Coordinator - Antonio DePietro
Production Manager - Jennifer Miller
Art Director - Matthew Alford
Director of Editorial - Jeremy Ross
VP of Production & Manufacturing - Ron Klamert
President & C.O.O. - John Parker
Publisher & C.E.O. - Stuart Levy

Email: editor@TOKYOPOP.com
Come visit us online at www.TOKYOPOP.com

A **TOKYOPOP** Manga

TOKYOPOP® is an imprint of Mixx Entertainment, Inc.
5900 Wilshire Blvd. Suite 2000, Los Angeles, CA 90036

Magic Knight Rayearth II Vol. 3 ©1996 CLAMP.
First published in 1996 by Kodansha Ltd., Tokyo.
English publication rights arranged through Kodansha Ltd.

English text © 2003 by Mixx Entertainment, Inc.
TOKYOPOP is a registered trademark of Mixx Entertainment, Inc.

ISBN: 1-59182-268-8

First TOKYOPOP® printing: April 2003

10 9 8 7 6 5 4 3 2 1

Printed in Canada

The Story So Far...

The future of Cephiro hangs in the balance. If a new Pillar is not found soon, the country will surely fall. To make things worse, three nations are warring to become the new Pillar. Each country has its reasons, but should they succeed, it would be at the expense of Cephiro's own people.

The Magic Knights, three schoolgirls summoned from Earth, are Cephiro's only defenders. Hikaru, Umi and Fuu have been working with their old friends to find the Road that leads to the Pillar, but even if they should find it, they are not sure if they even want a new Pillar. As Princess Emeraude, the last Pillar, showed, it is a tragic fate, for the Pillar must dedicate himself or herself entirely to the country and may harbor no selfish thoughts.

When last we left our young heroines, the battle for Cephiro took an unexpected turn. Autozam, country of machines, cut off the advances of the other two invaders, Fahren and Chizeta. During this maneuver, Hikaru actually enters the road of the other nation, an act which no one else could do. Eagle Vision, leader of the Autozam forces, collapses following the attack, revealing his growing weakness to his crew.

And now, the conclusion...

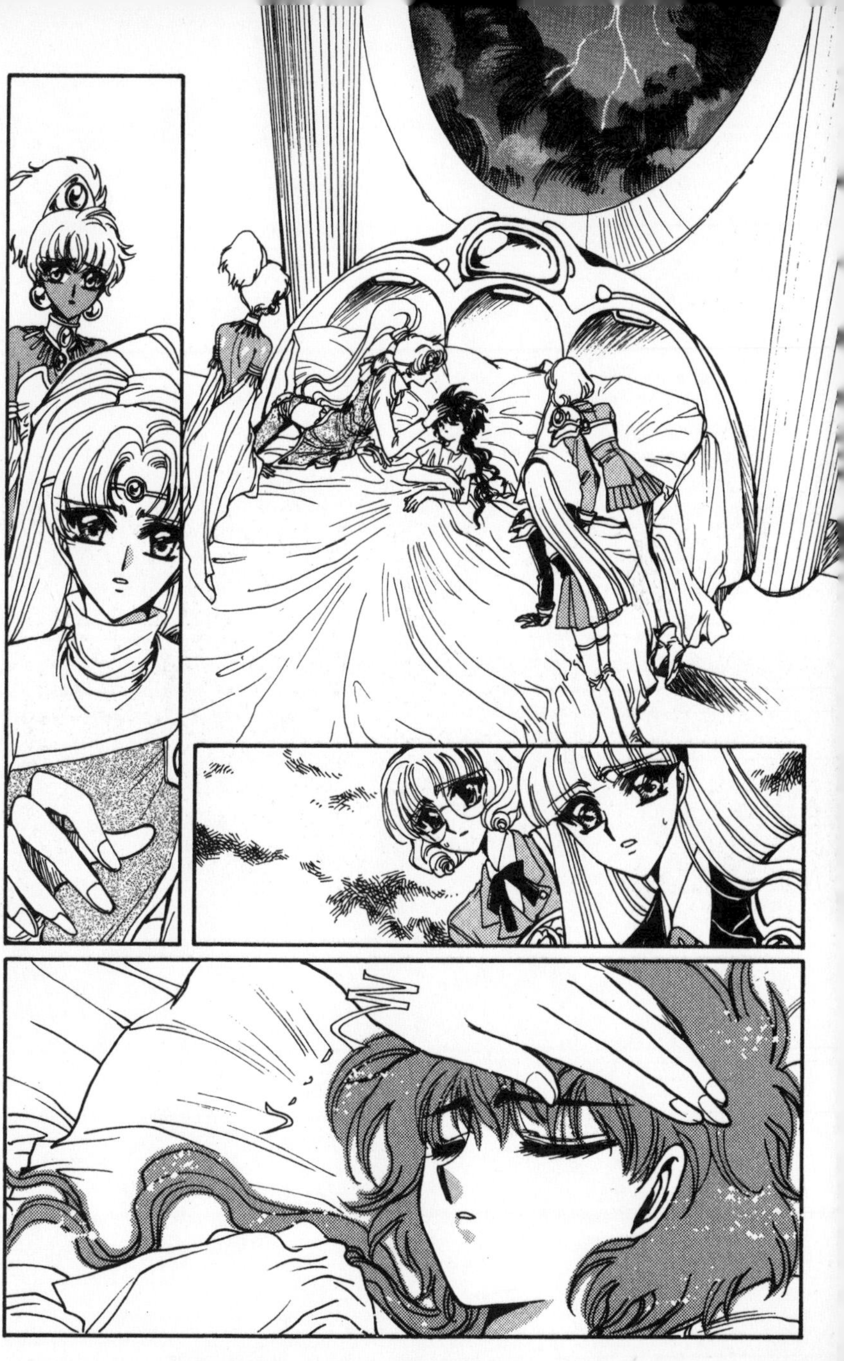

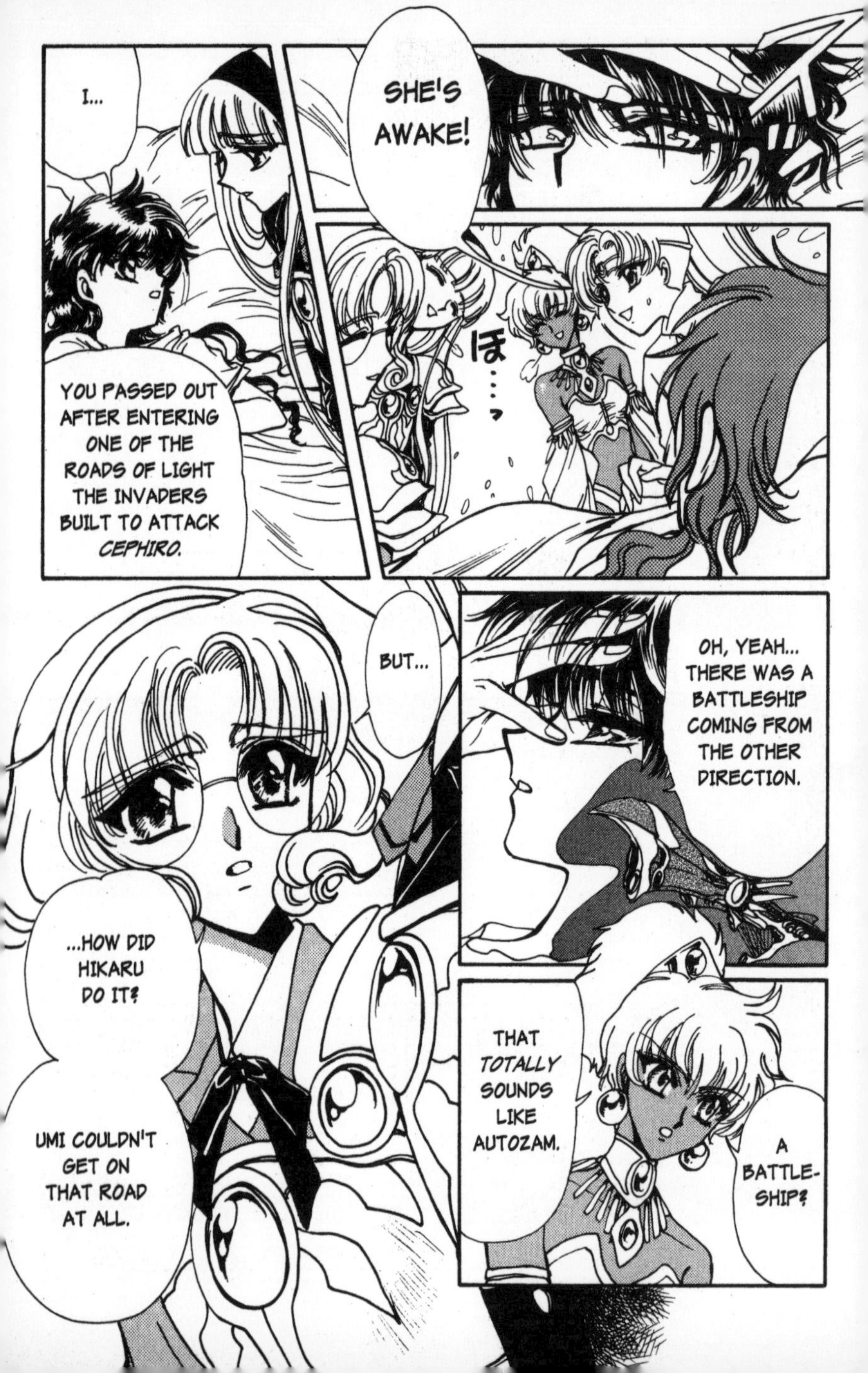
SHE'S AWAKE!
ほ…っ
I...
YOU PASSED OUT AFTER ENTERING ONE OF THE ROADS OF LIGHT THE INVADERS BUILT TO ATTACK *CEPHIRO*.
OH, YEAH... THERE WAS A BATTLESHIP COMING FROM THE OTHER DIRECTION.
A BATTLE-SHIP?
THAT *TOTALLY* SOUNDS LIKE AUTOZAM.
BUT...
...HOW DID HIKARU DO IT?
UMI COULDN'T GET ON THAT ROAD AT ALL.

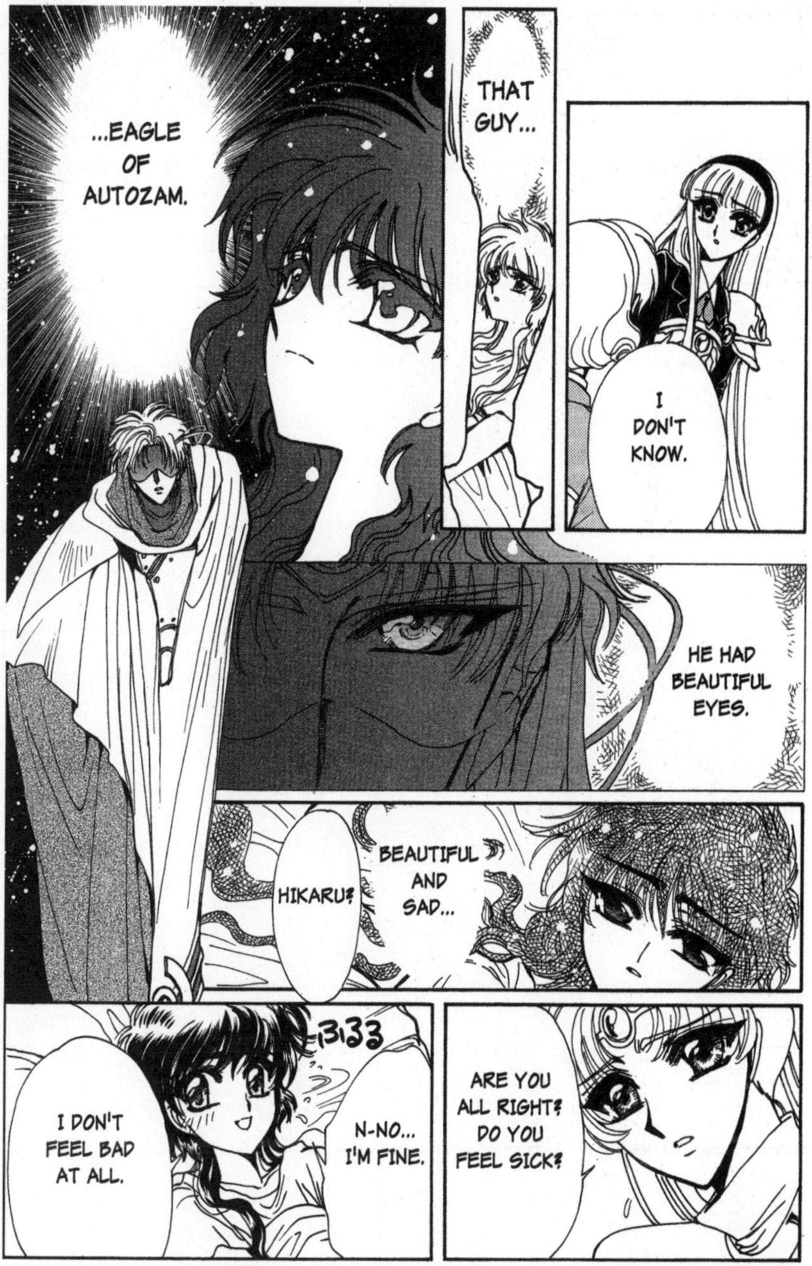
I DON'T KNOW.
THAT GUY...
HE HAD BEAUTIFUL EYES.
BEAUTIFUL AND SAD...
HIKARU?
...EAGLE OF AUTOZAM.
ARE YOU ALL RIGHT? DO YOU FEEL SICK?
ふるるる
N-NO... I'M FINE.
I DON'T FEEL BAD AT ALL.

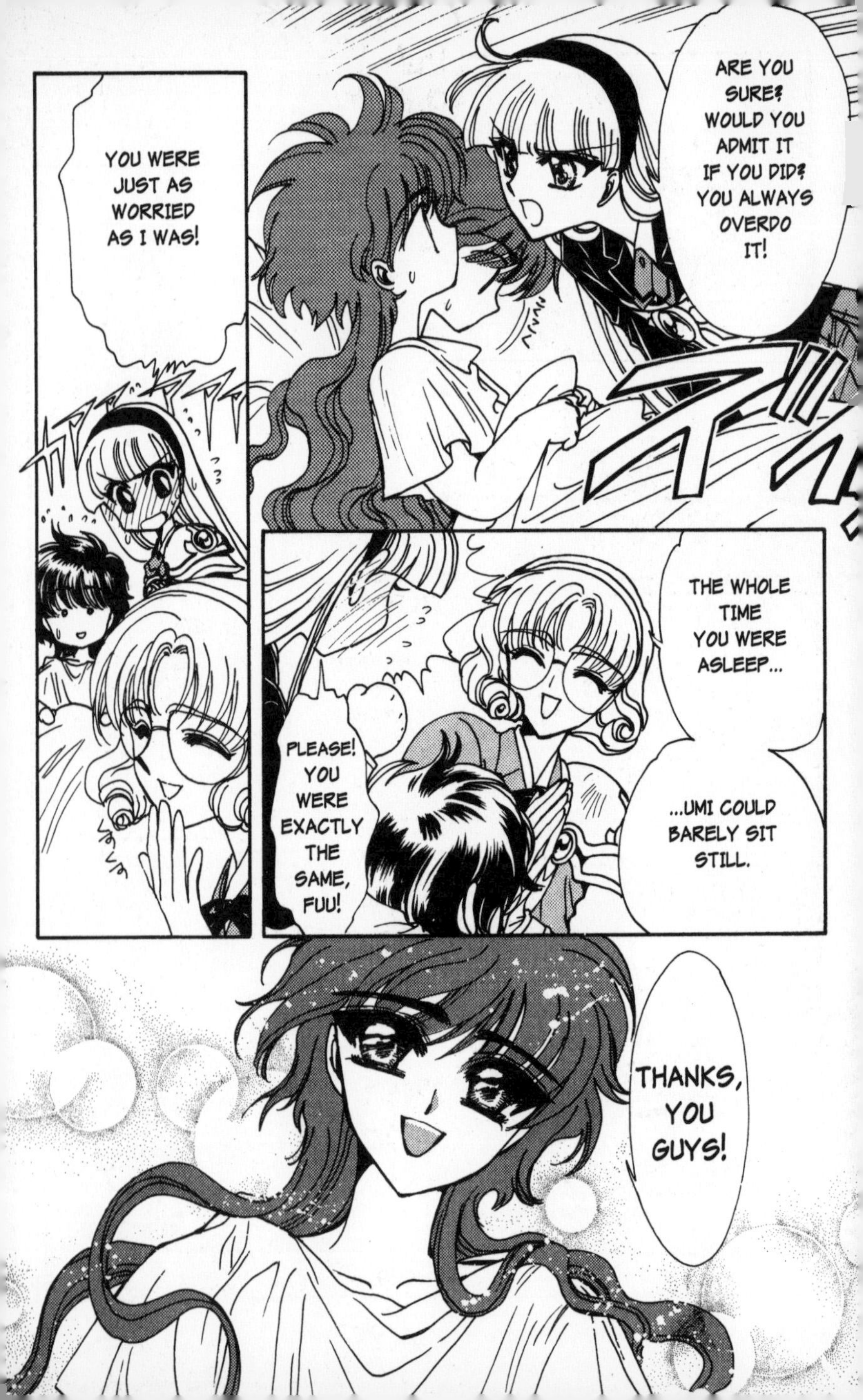
ARE YOU SURE? WOULD YOU ADMIT IT IF YOU DID? YOU ALWAYS OVERDO IT!
THE WHOLE TIME YOU WERE ASLEEP...
...UMI COULD BARELY SIT STILL.
PLEASE! YOU WERE EXACTLY THE SAME, FUU!
YOU WERE JUST AS WORRIED AS I WAS!
THANKS, YOU GUYS!

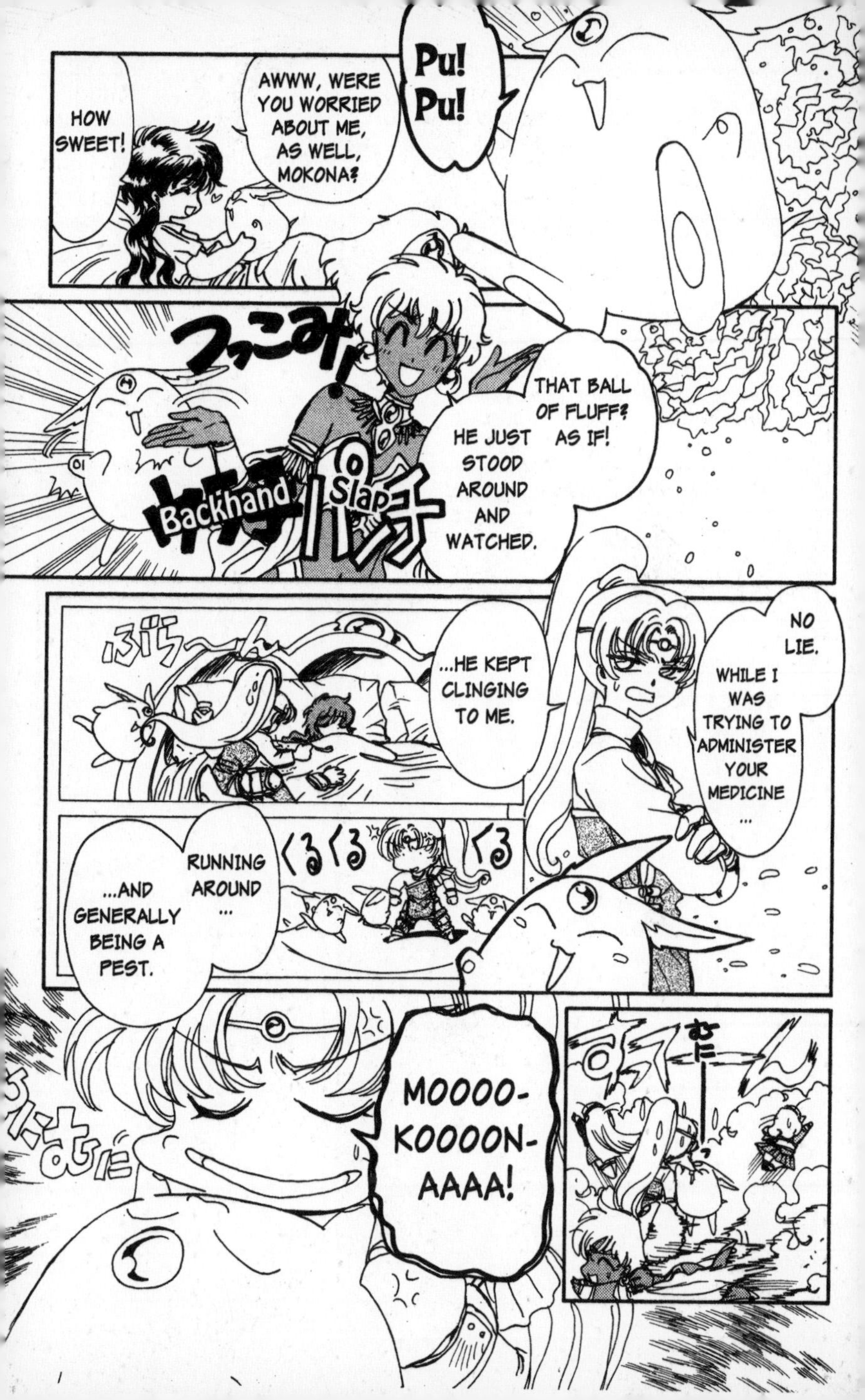
Pu! Pu!
AWWW, WERE YOU WORRIED ABOUT ME, AS WELL, MOKONA?
HOW SWEET!
THAT BALL OF FLUFF? AS IF!
HE JUST STOOD AROUND AND WATCHED.
Backhand Slap
NO LIE. WHILE I WAS TRYING TO ADMINISTER YOUR MEDICINE ...
...HE KEPT CLINGING TO ME.
RUNNING AROUND ...
...AND GENERALLY BEING A PEST.
くるくる くる
MOOOO-KOOOON-AAAA!

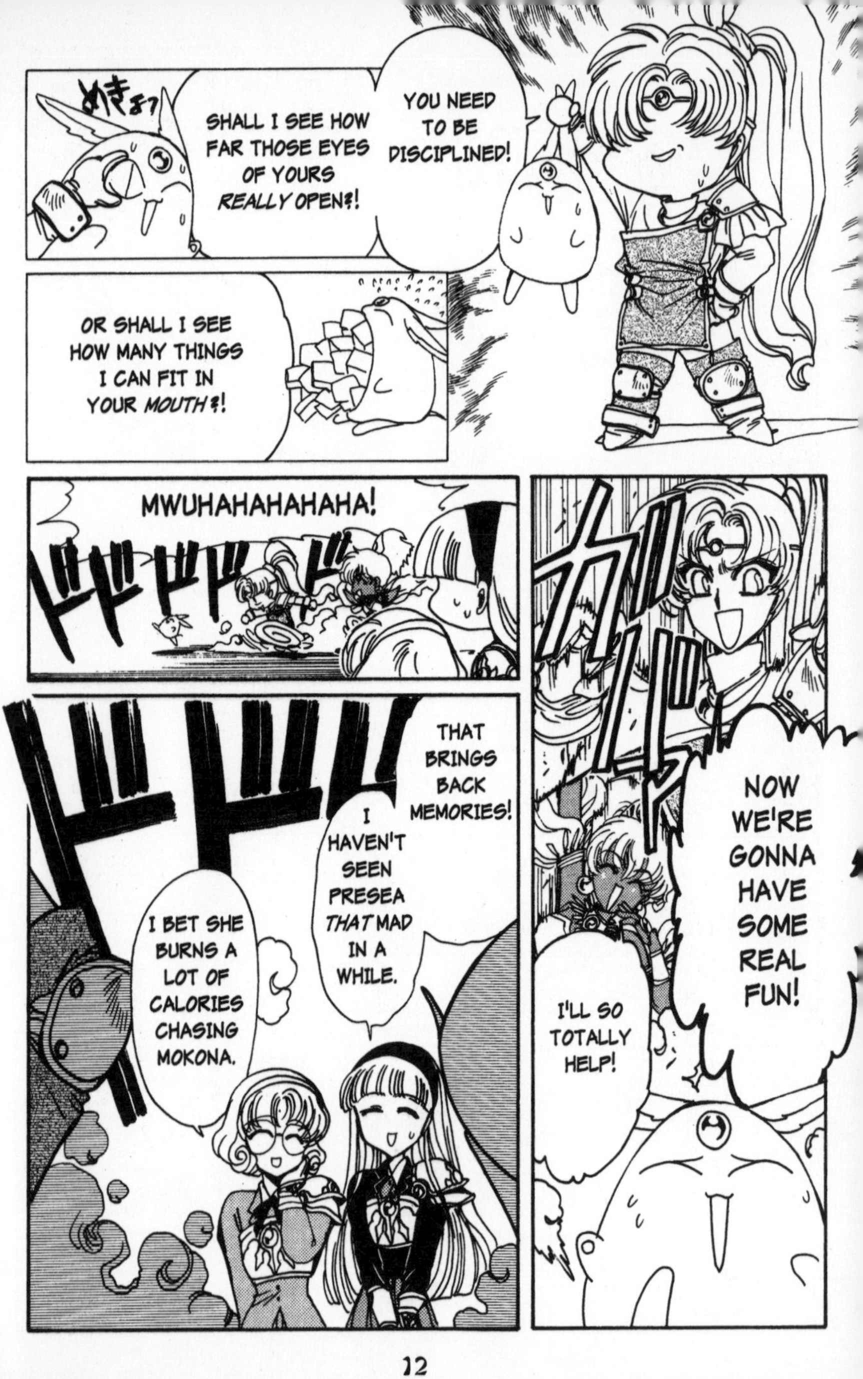
YOU NEED TO BE DISCIPLINED!
SHALL I SEE HOW FAR THOSE EYES OF YOURS *REALLY* OPEN?!
OR SHALL I SEE HOW MANY THINGS I CAN FIT IN YOUR *MOUTH*?!
NOW WE'RE GONNA HAVE SOME REAL FUN!
I'LL SO TOTALLY HELP!
MWUHAHAHAHAHA!
THAT BRINGS BACK MEMORIES!
I HAVEN'T SEEN PRESEA *THAT* MAD IN A WHILE.
I BET SHE BURNS A LOT OF CALORIES CHASING MOKONA.

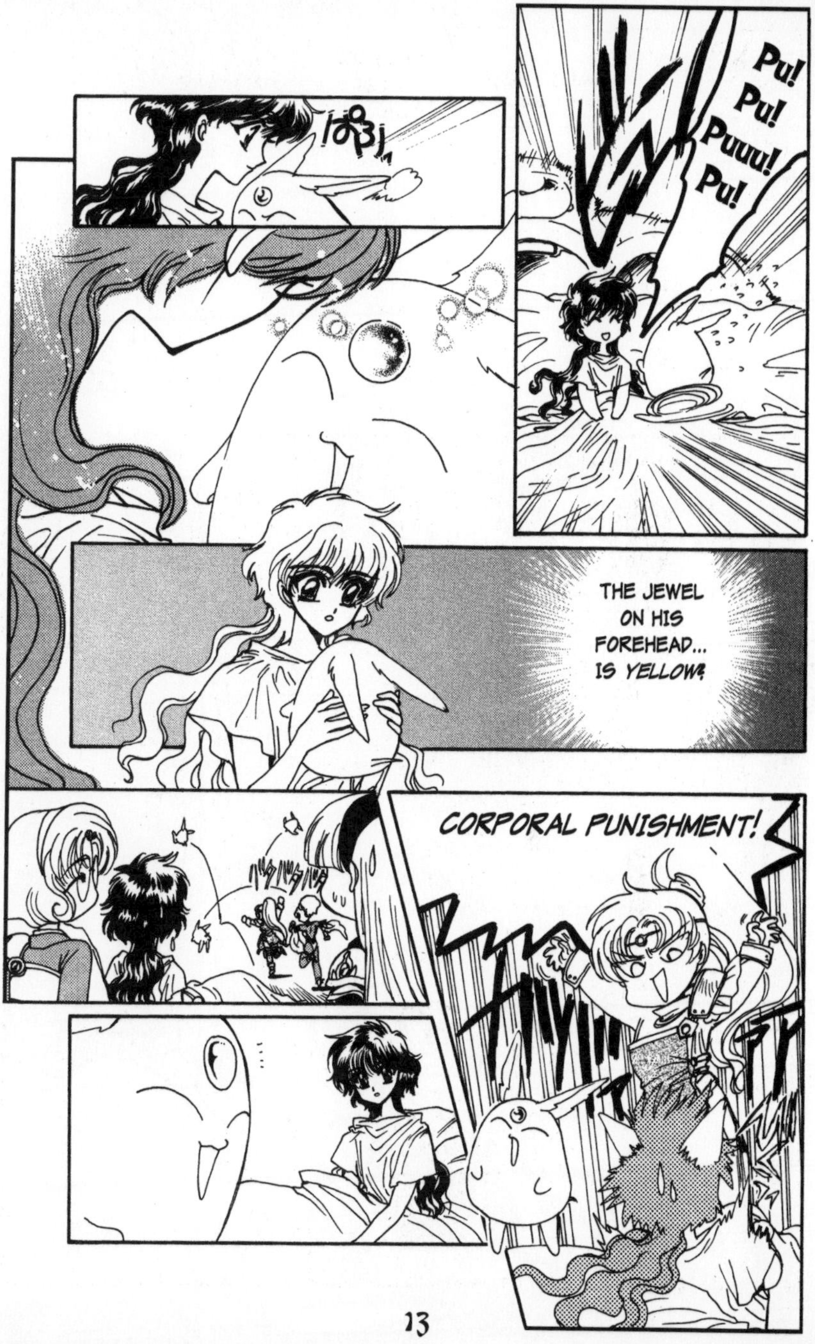
Pu! Pu! Puuu! Pu!
THE JEWEL ON HIS FOREHEAD... IS YELLOW?
CORPORAL PUNISHMENT!

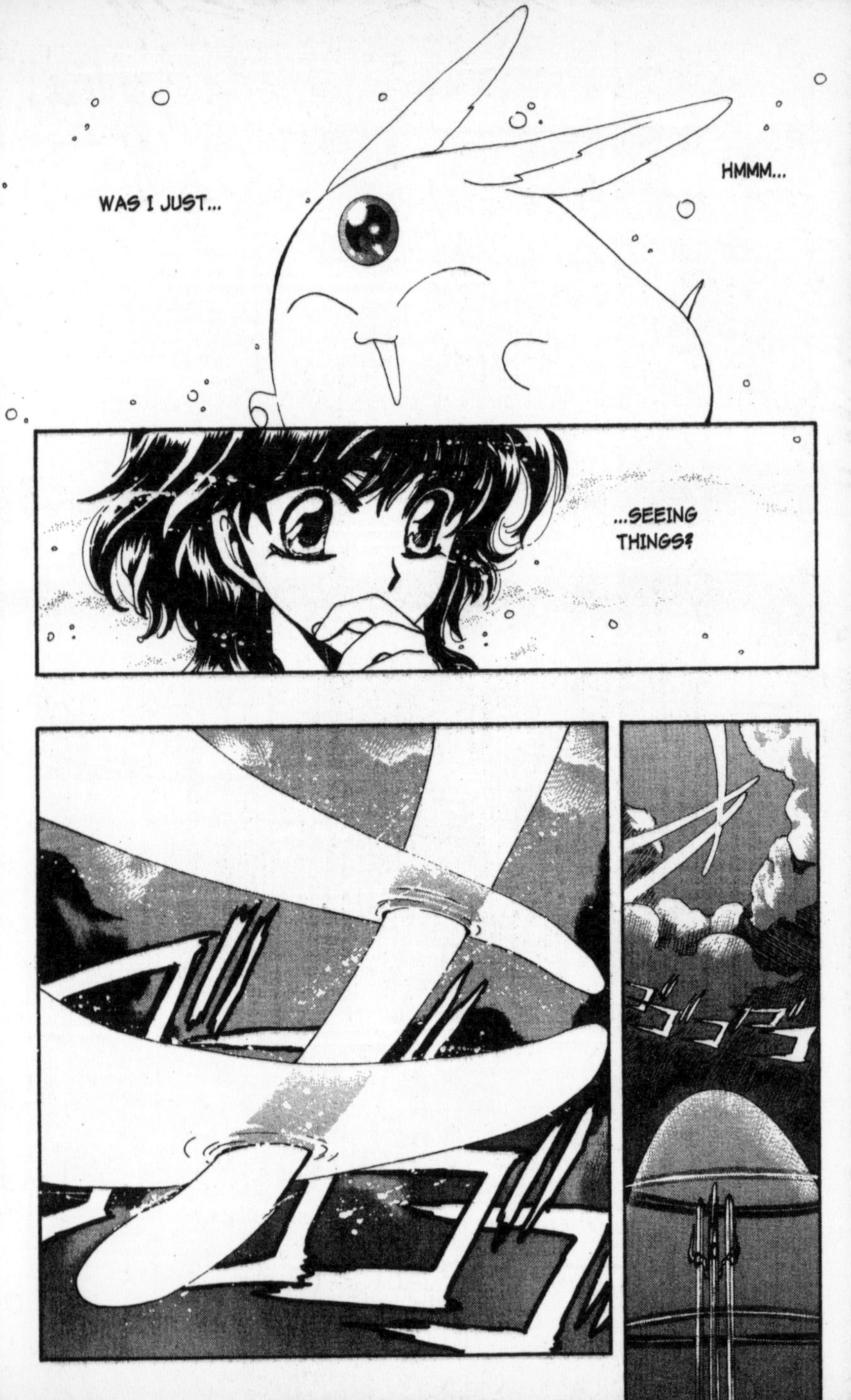
HMMM...
WAS I JUST...
...SEEING THINGS?

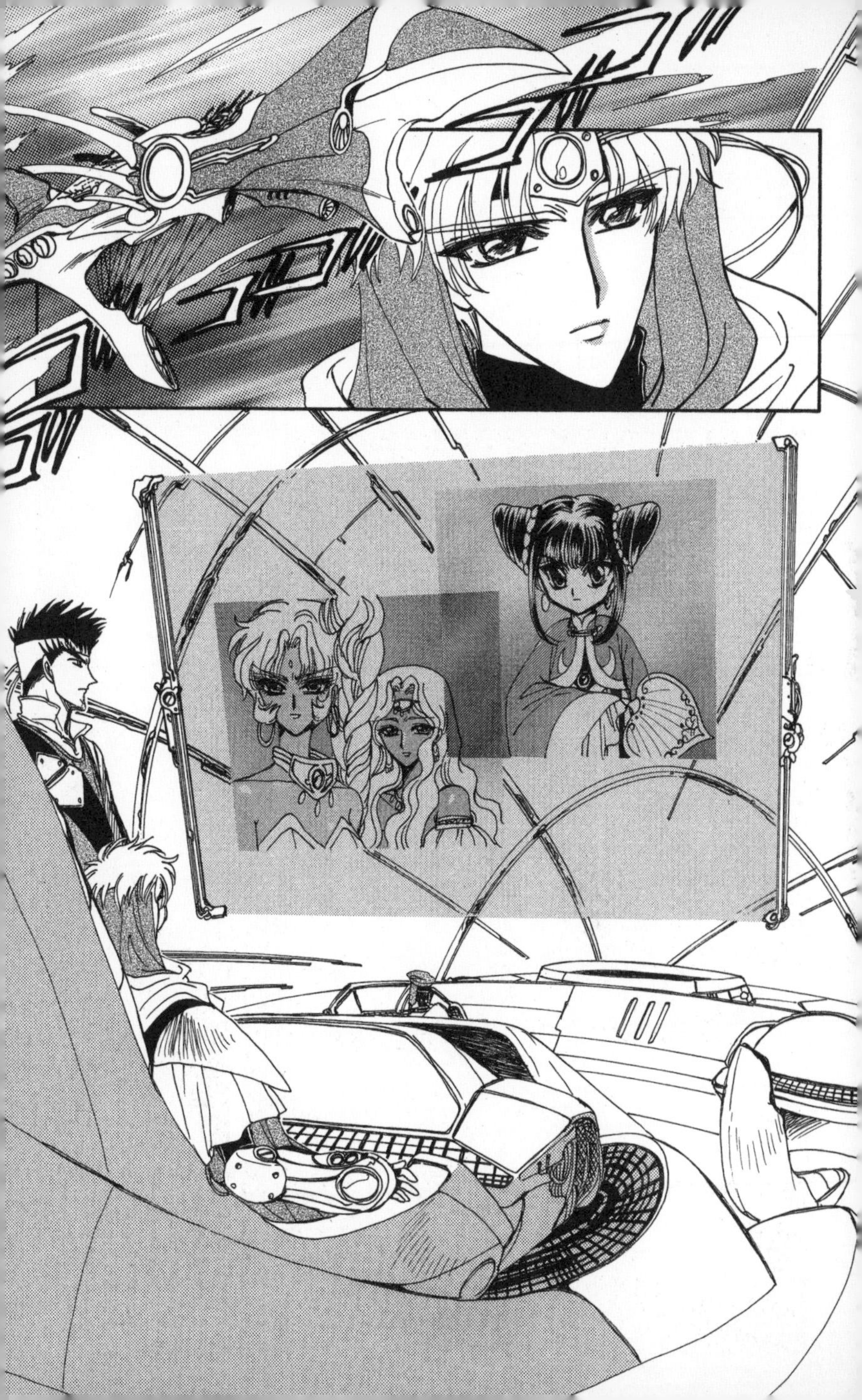

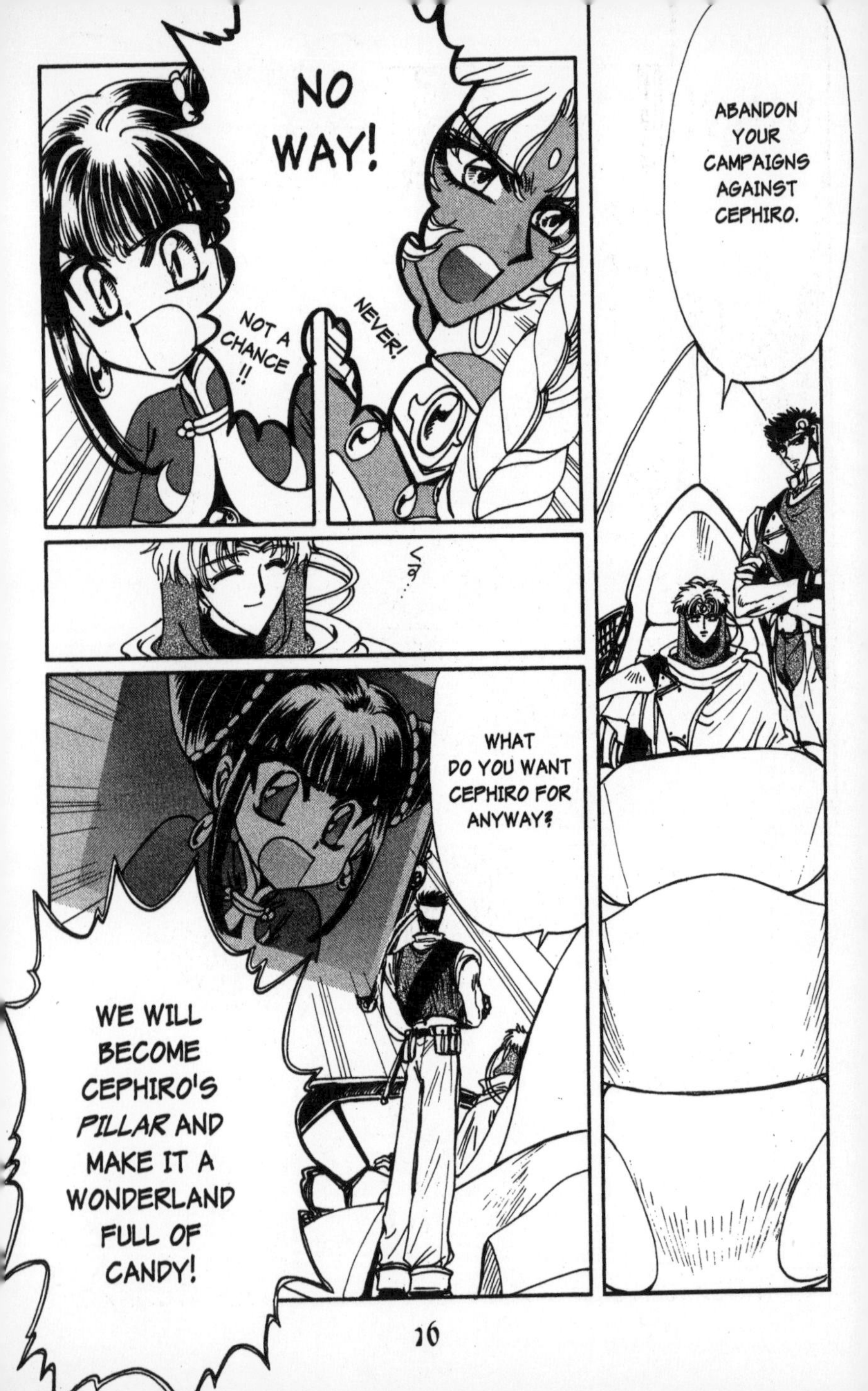

ABANDON YOUR CAMPAIGNS AGAINST CEPHIRO.
NO WAY!
NEVER!
NOT A CHANCE!!
くす…
WHAT DO YOU WANT CEPHIRO FOR ANYWAY?
WE WILL BECOME CEPHIRO'S *PILLAR* AND MAKE IT A WONDERLAND FULL OF CANDY!

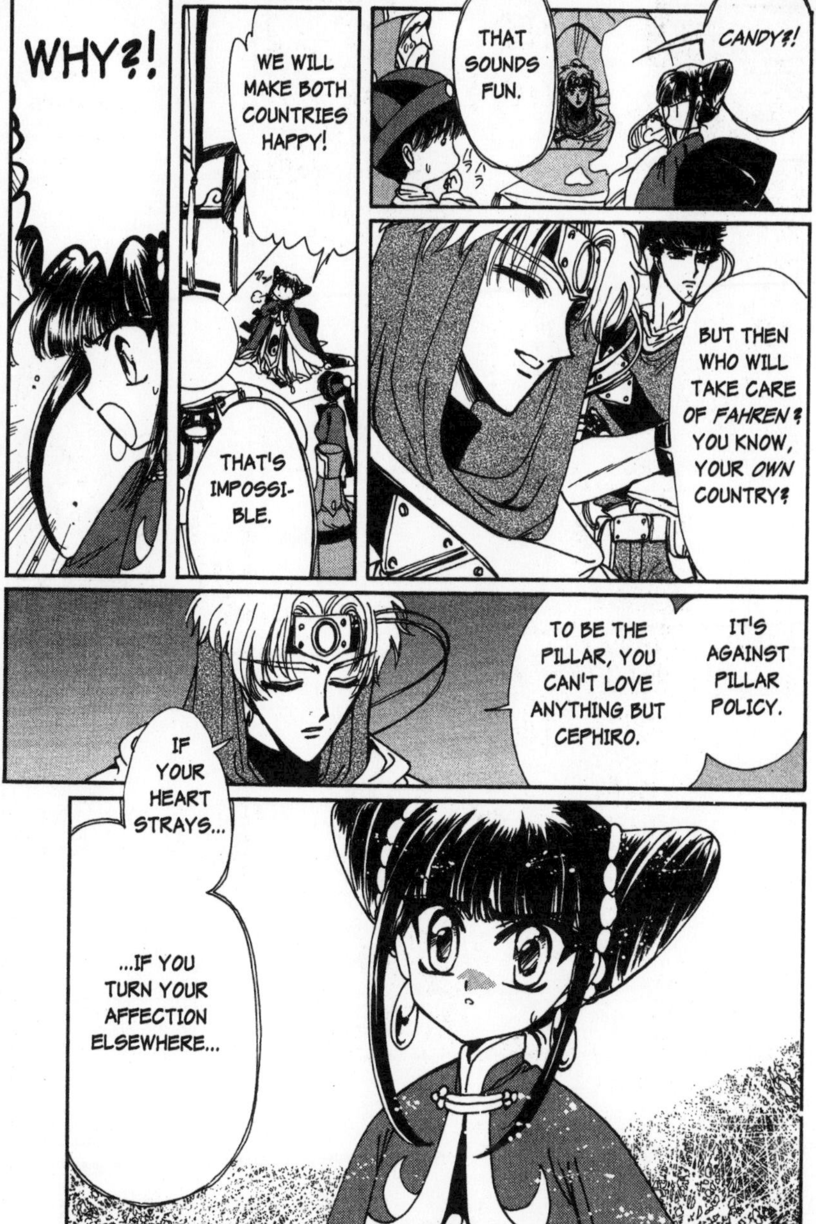
CANDY?!
THAT SOUNDS FUN.
BUT THEN WHO WILL TAKE CARE OF *FAHREN*? YOU KNOW, YOUR *OWN* COUNTRY?
WE WILL MAKE BOTH COUNTRIES HAPPY!
THAT'S IMPOSSI-BLE.
WHY?!
IT'S AGAINST PILLAR POLICY.
TO BE THE PILLAR, YOU CAN'T LOVE ANYTHING BUT CEPHIRO.
IF YOUR HEART STRAYS...
...IF YOU TURN YOUR AFFECTION ELSEWHERE...

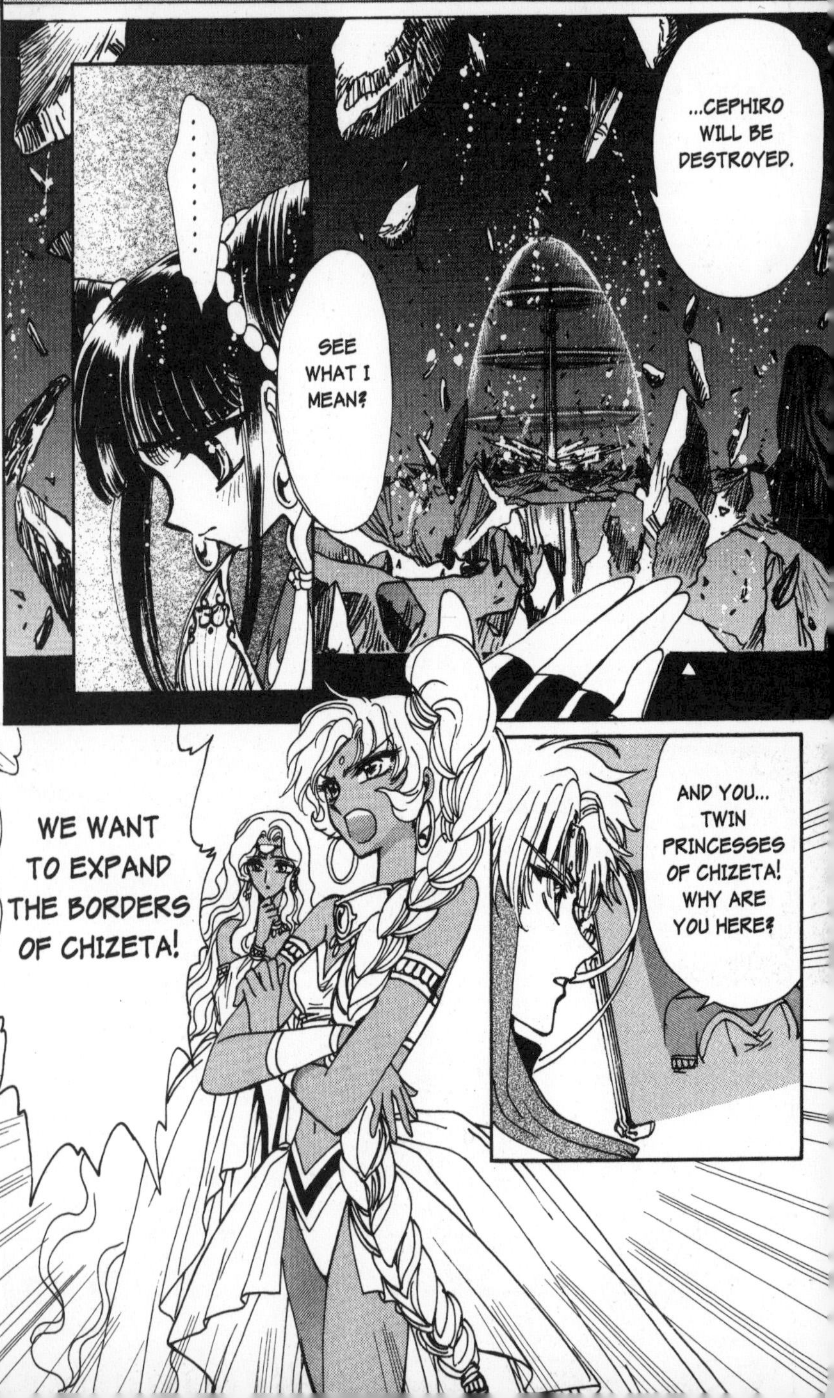
...CEPHIRO WILL BE DESTROYED.
SEE WHAT I MEAN?
......
AND YOU... TWIN PRINCESSES OF CHIZETA! WHY ARE YOU HERE?
WE WANT TO EXPAND THE BORDERS OF CHIZETA!

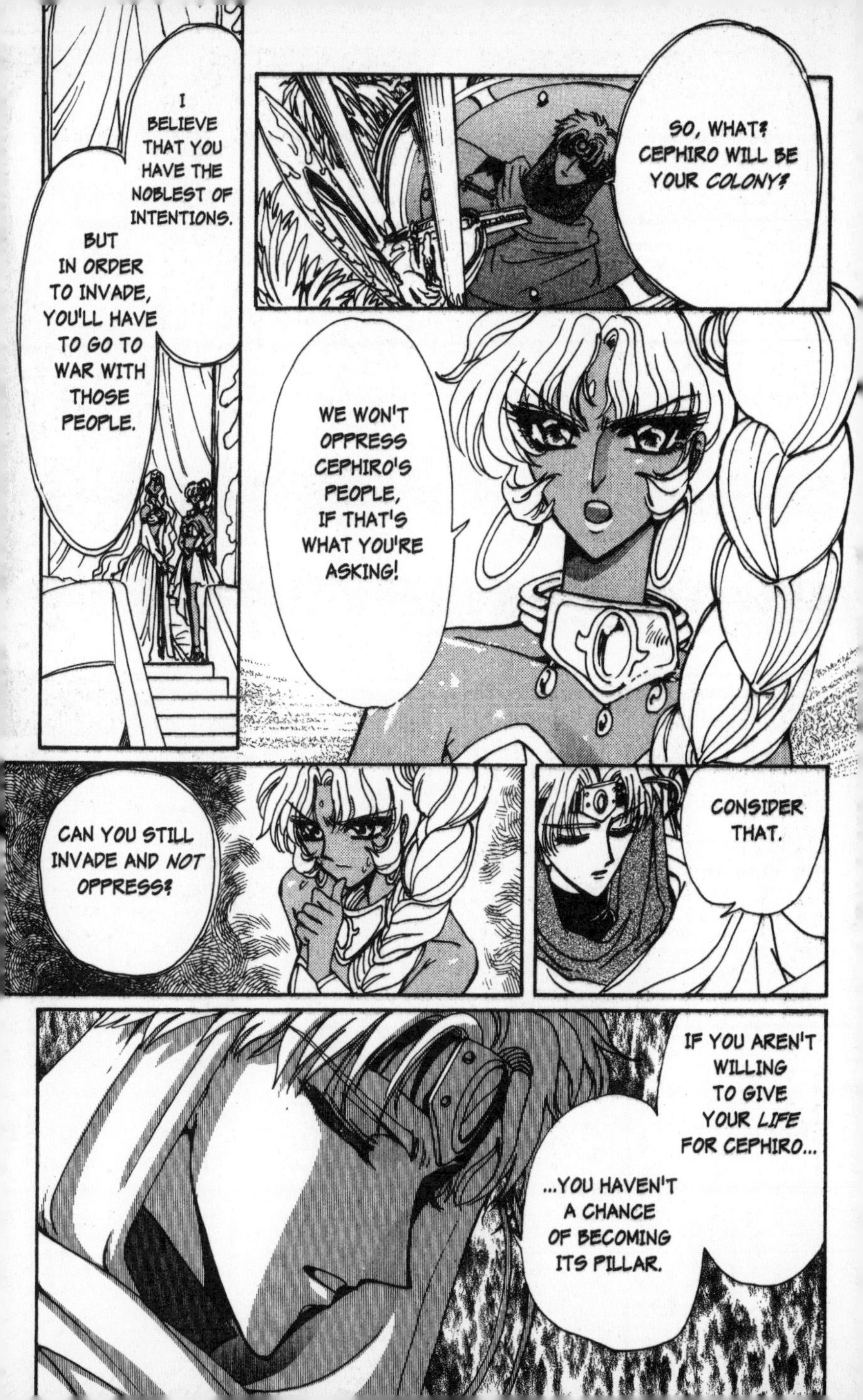
SO, WHAT? CEPHIRO WILL BE YOUR *COLONY*?
WE WON'T OPPRESS CEPHIRO'S PEOPLE, IF THAT'S WHAT YOU'RE ASKING!
I BELIEVE THAT YOU HAVE THE NOBLEST OF INTENTIONS.
BUT IN ORDER TO INVADE, YOU'LL HAVE TO GO TO WAR WITH THOSE PEOPLE.
CONSIDER THAT.
CAN YOU STILL INVADE AND *NOT* OPPRESS?
IF YOU AREN'T WILLING TO GIVE YOUR *LIFE* FOR CEPHIRO...
...YOU HAVEN'T A CHANCE OF BECOMING ITS PILLAR.

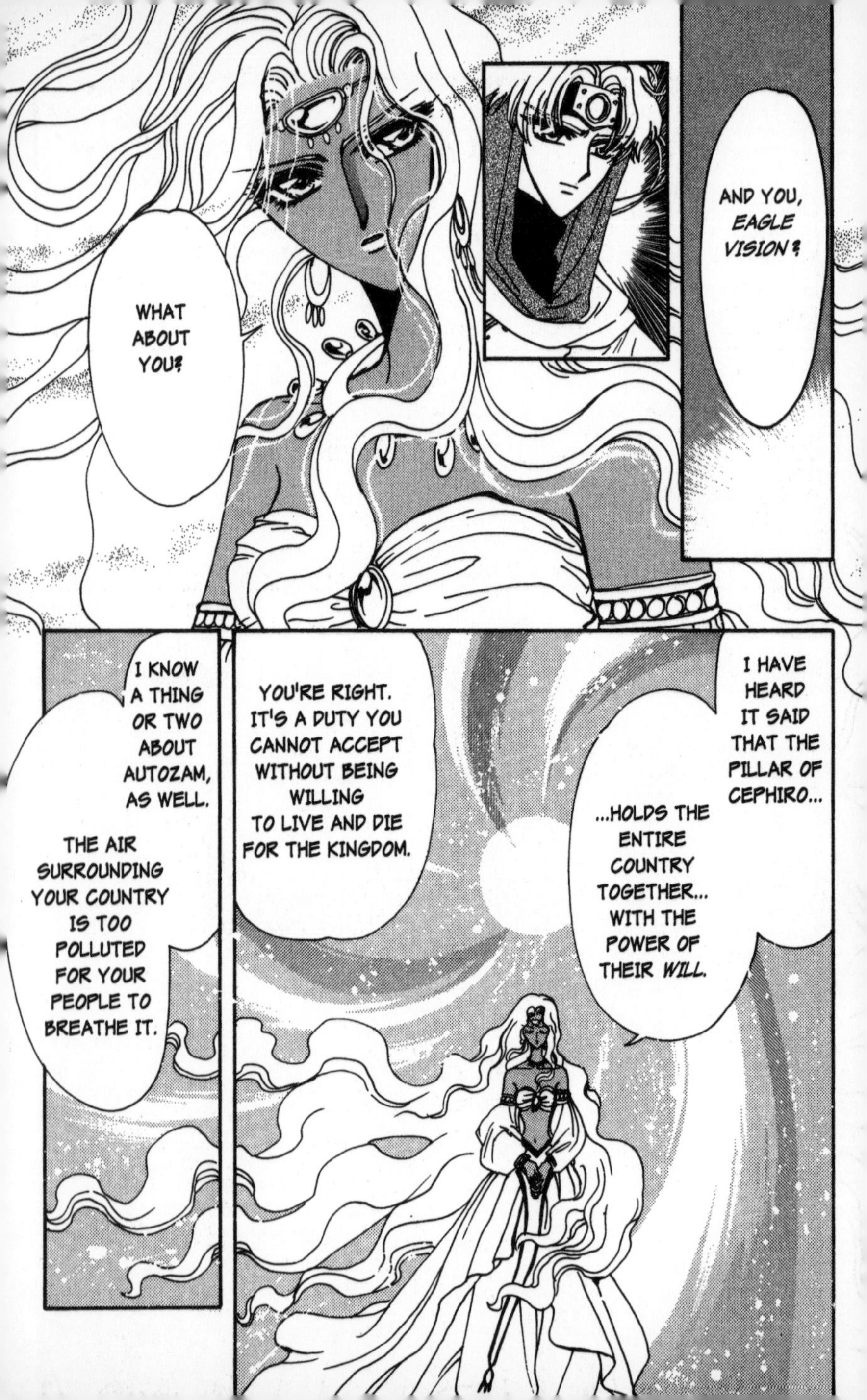
AND YOU, EAGLE VISION?
WHAT ABOUT YOU?
I HAVE HEARD IT SAID THAT THE PILLAR OF CEPHIRO...
...HOLDS THE ENTIRE COUNTRY TOGETHER... WITH THE POWER OF THEIR WILL.
YOU'RE RIGHT. IT'S A DUTY YOU CANNOT ACCEPT WITHOUT BEING WILLING TO LIVE AND DIE FOR THE KINGDOM.
I KNOW A THING OR TWO ABOUT AUTOZAM, AS WELL.
THE AIR SURROUNDING YOUR COUNTRY IS TOO POLLUTED FOR YOUR PEOPLE TO BREATHE IT.

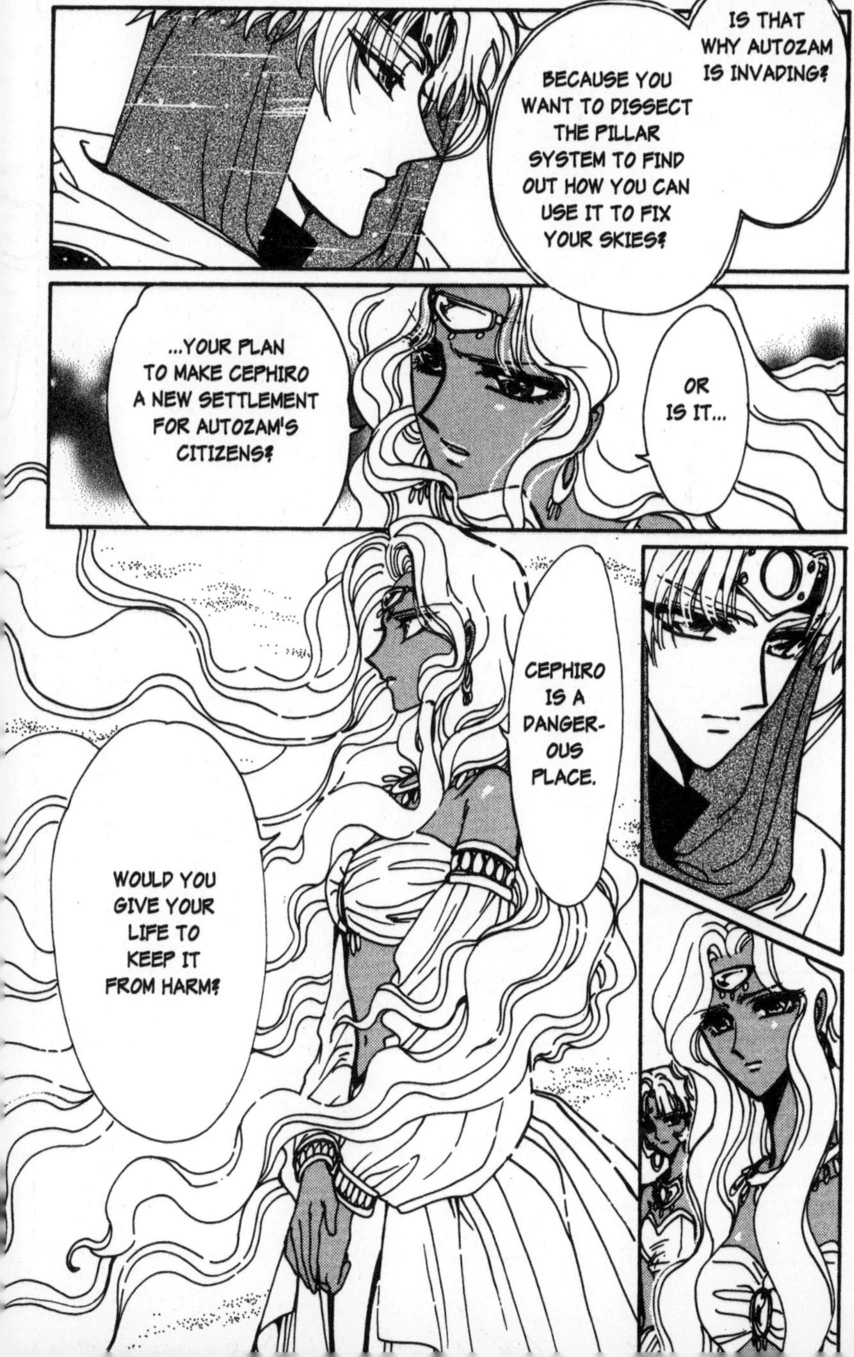
IS THAT WHY AUTOZAM IS INVADING?
BECAUSE YOU WANT TO DISSECT THE PILLAR SYSTEM TO FIND OUT HOW YOU CAN USE IT TO FIX YOUR SKIES?
OR IS IT...
...YOUR PLAN TO MAKE CEPHIRO A NEW SETTLEMENT FOR AUTOZAM'S CITIZENS?
CEPHIRO IS A DANGER-OUS PLACE.
WOULD YOU GIVE YOUR LIFE TO KEEP IT FROM HARM?

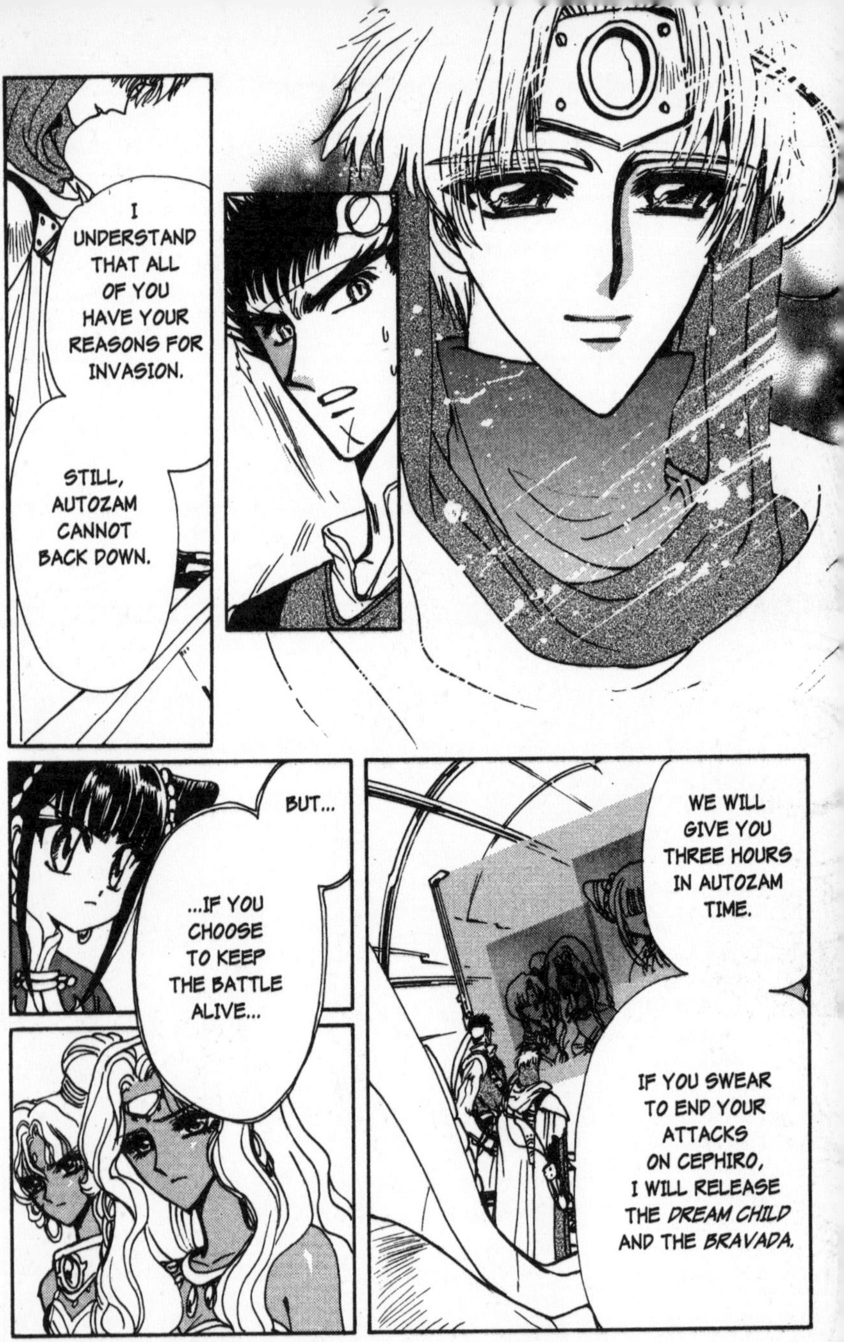
I UNDERSTAND THAT ALL OF YOU HAVE YOUR REASONS FOR INVASION.
STILL, AUTOZAM CANNOT BACK DOWN.
WE WILL GIVE YOU THREE HOURS IN AUTOZAM TIME.
IF YOU SWEAR TO END YOUR ATTACKS ON CEPHIRO, I WILL RELEASE THE *DREAM CHILD* AND THE *BRAVADA*.
BUT...
...IF YOU CHOOSE TO KEEP THE BATTLE ALIVE...

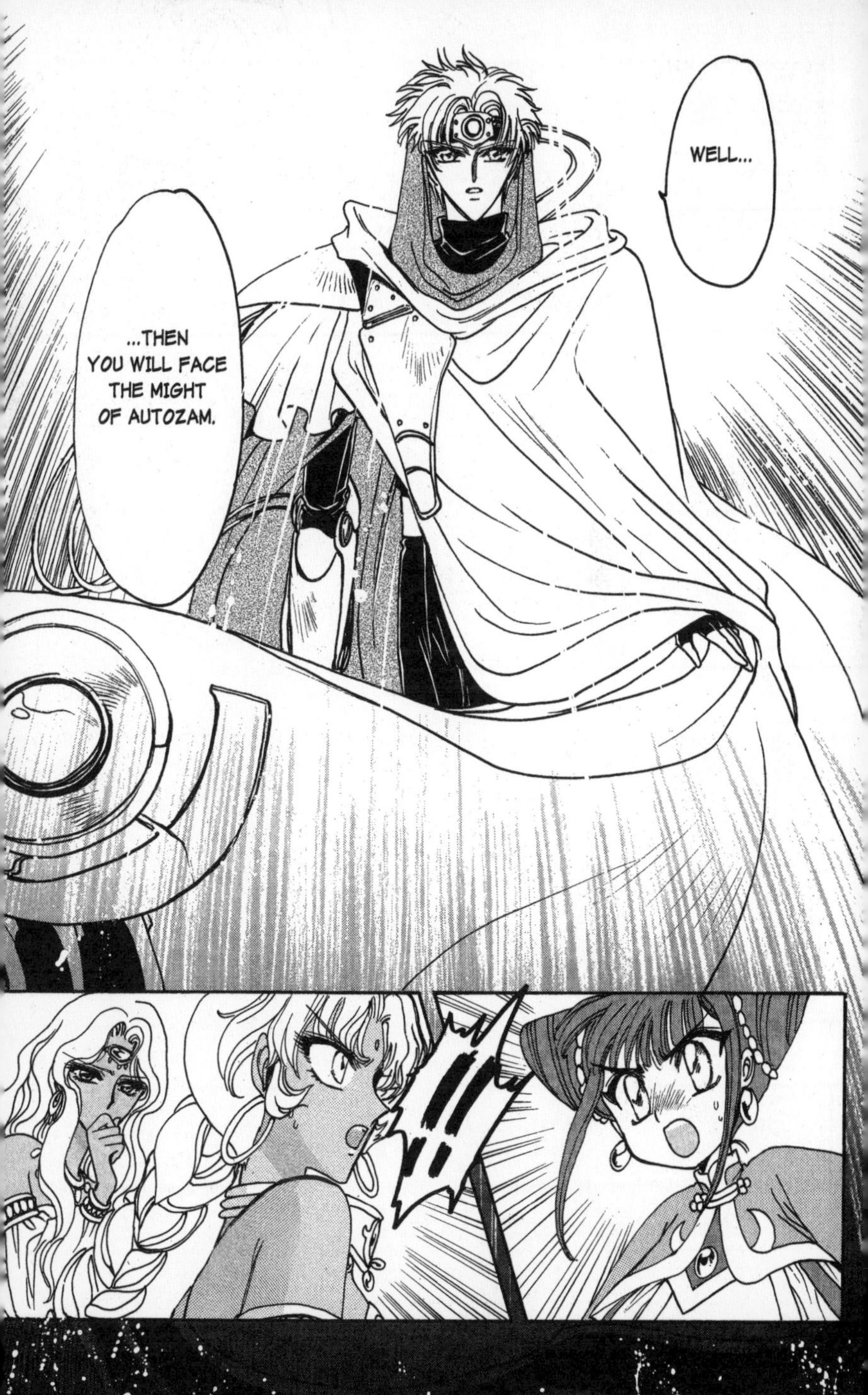
WELL...
...THEN YOU WILL FACE THE MIGHT OF AUTOZAM.
!!

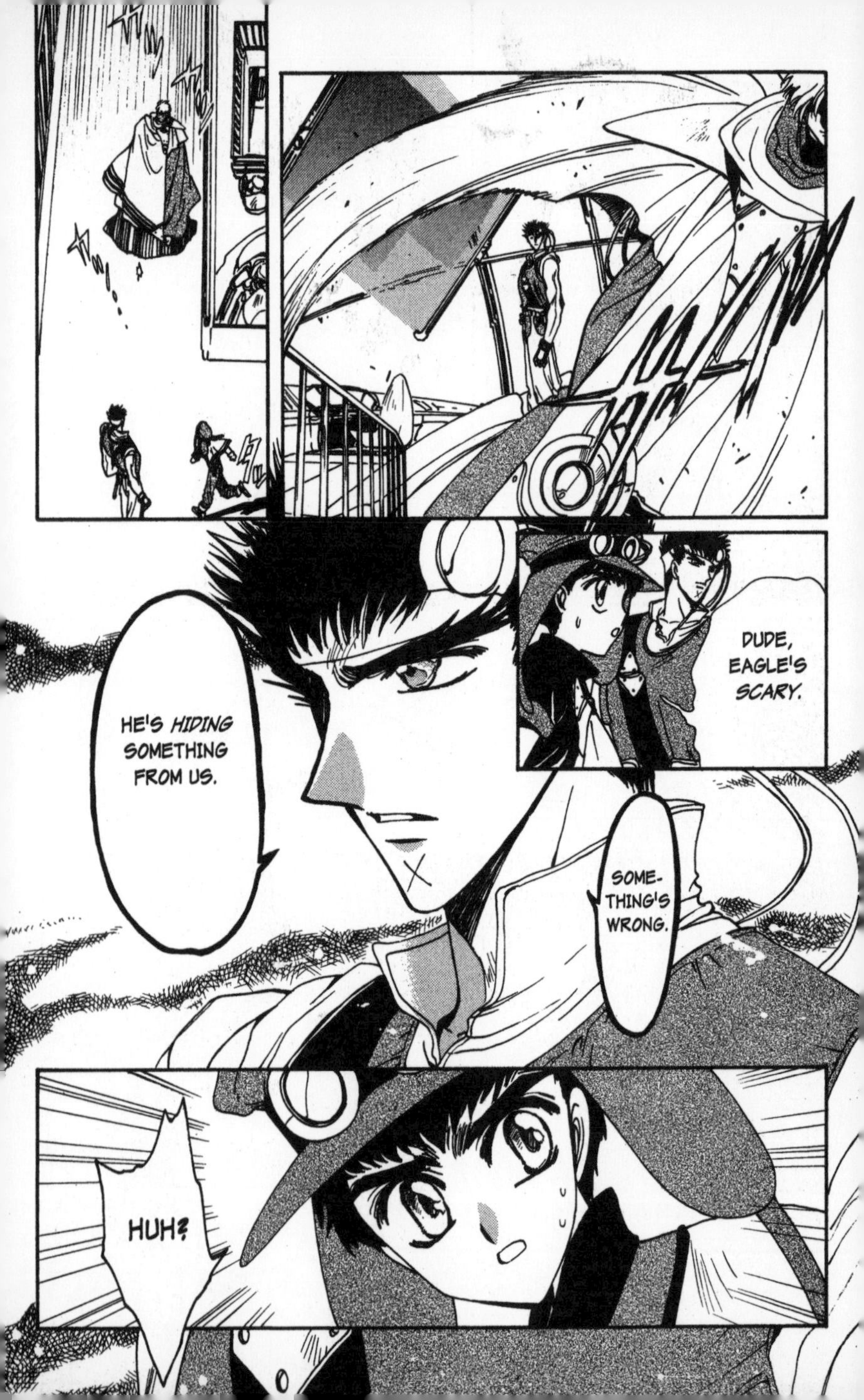
DUDE, EAGLE'S SCARY.
SOME-THING'S WRONG.
HE'S HIDING SOMETHING FROM US.
HUH?

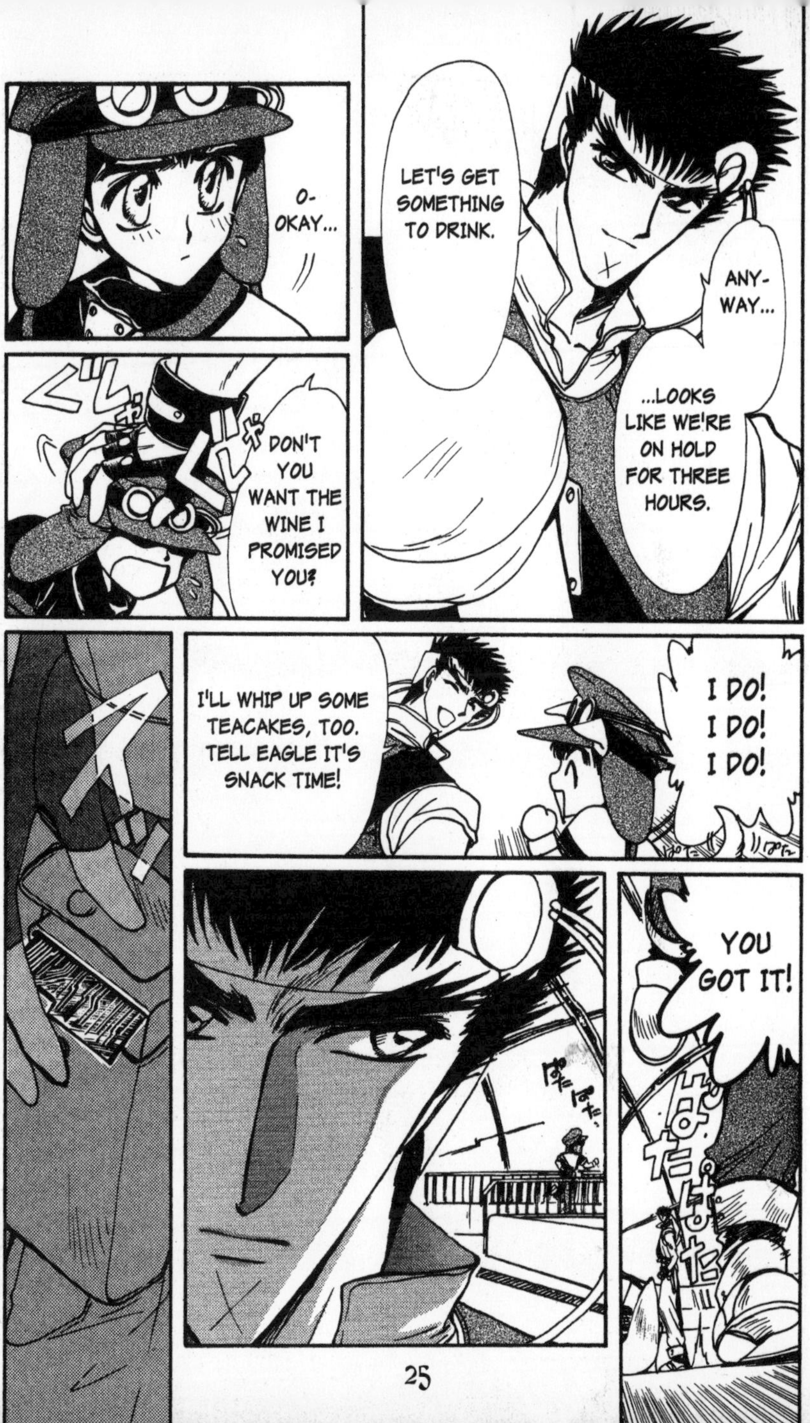
ANY-WAY...
...LOOKS LIKE WE'RE ON HOLD FOR THREE HOURS.
LET'S GET SOMETHING TO DRINK.
O-OKAY...
DON'T YOU WANT THE WINE I PROMISED YOU?
I DO! I DO! I DO!
I'LL WHIP UP SOME TEACAKES, TOO. TELL EAGLE IT'S SNACK TIME!
YOU GOT IT!

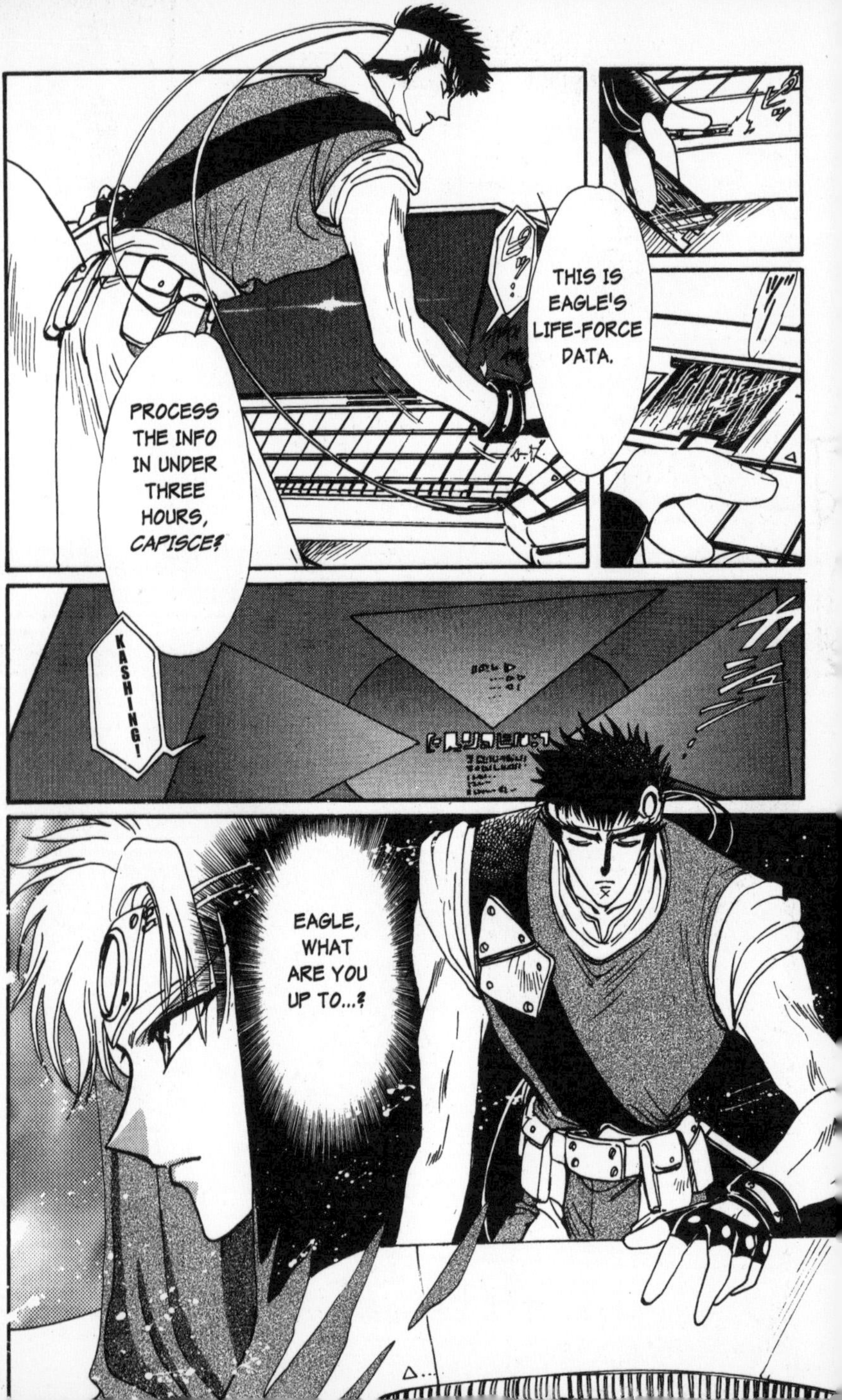
THIS IS EAGLE'S LIFE-FORCE DATA.
PROCESS THE INFO IN UNDER THREE HOURS, *CAPISCE?*
KASHING!
EAGLE, WHAT ARE YOU UP TO...?

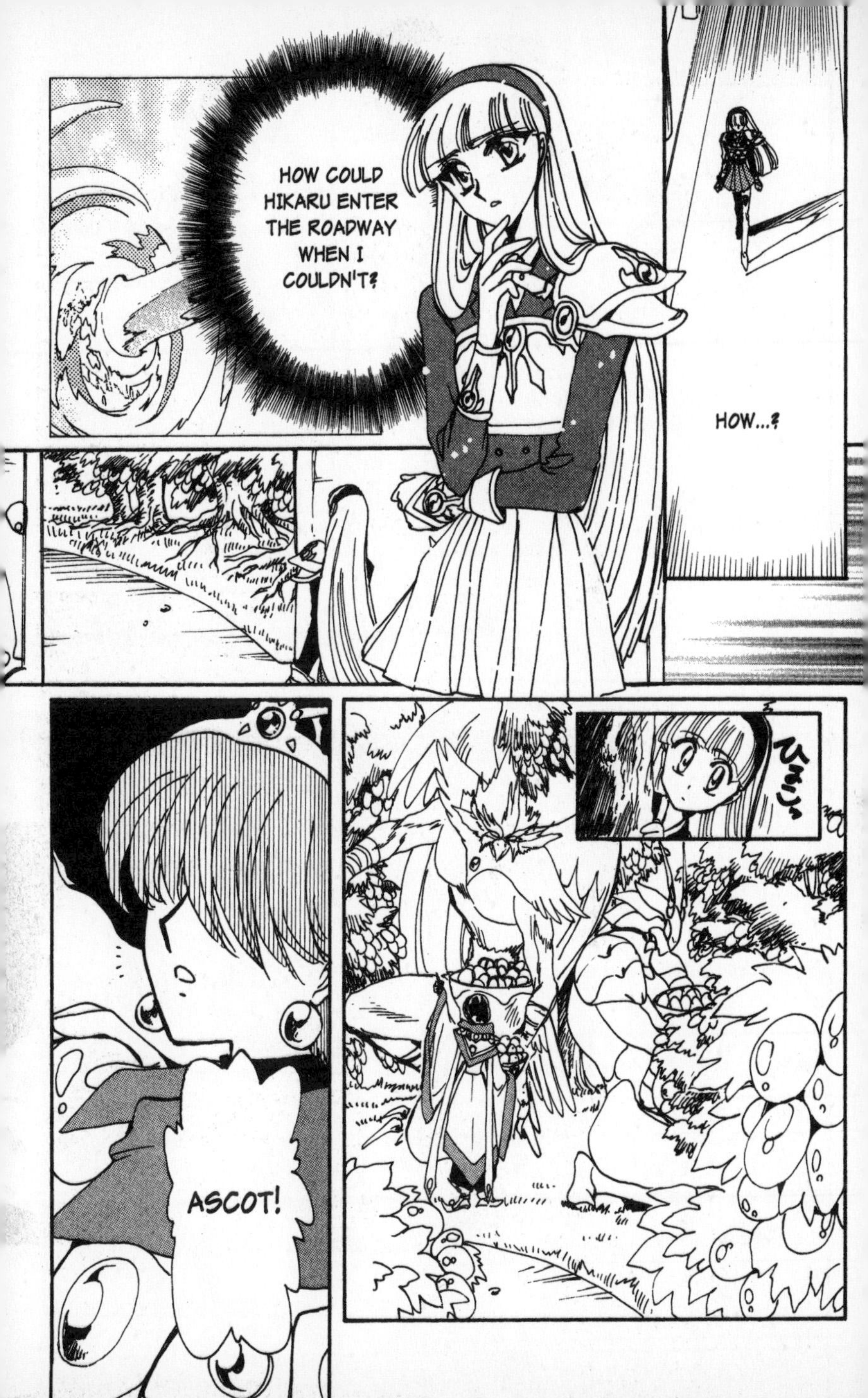
HOW...?
HOW COULD HIKARU ENTER THE ROADWAY WHEN I COULDN'T?
ひょこっ
ASCOT!

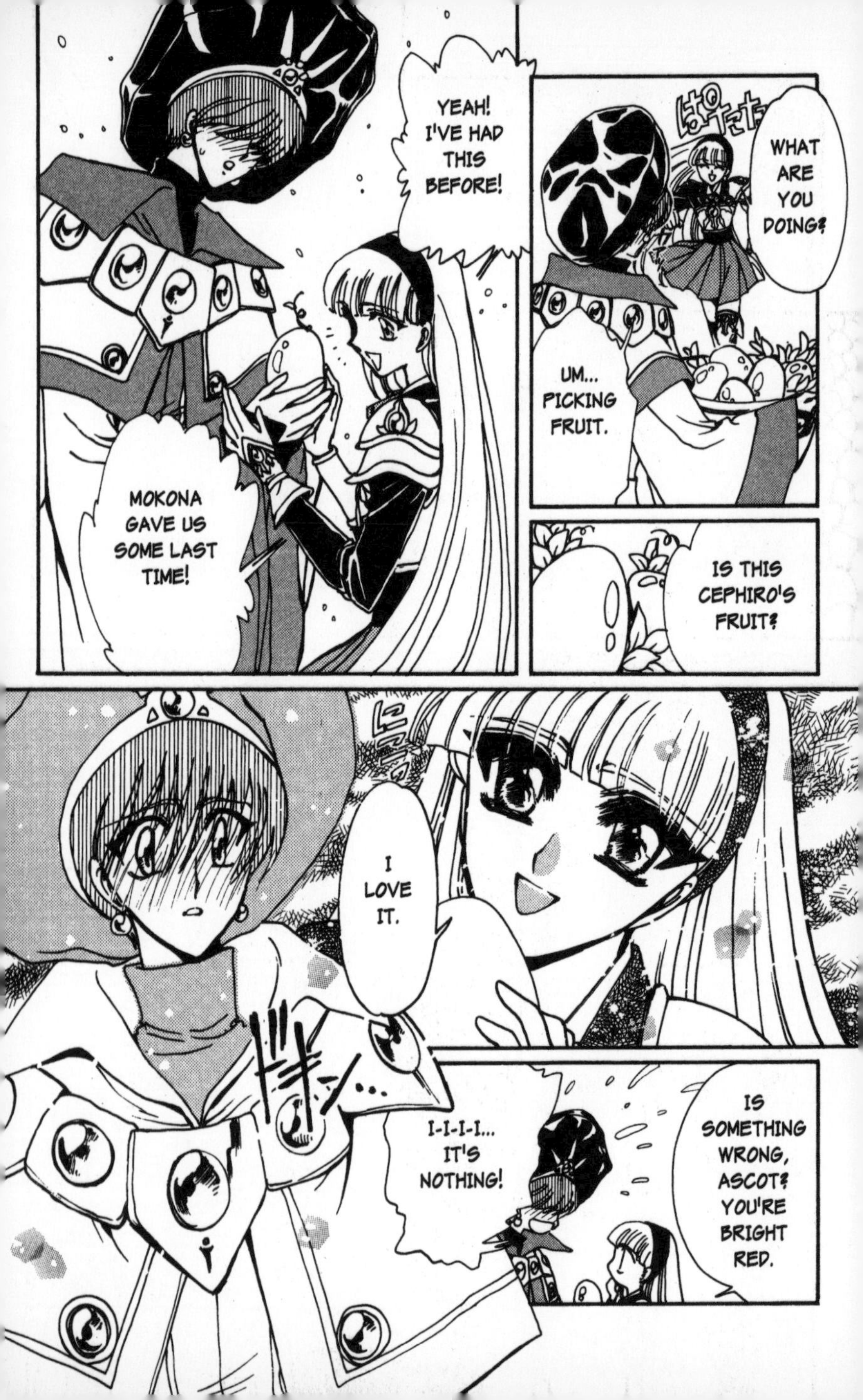
WHAT ARE YOU DOING?
UM... PICKING FRUIT.
IS THIS CEPHIRO'S FRUIT?
YEAH! I'VE HAD THIS BEFORE!
MOKONA GAVE US SOME LAST TIME!
I LOVE IT.
IS SOMETHING WRONG, ASCOT? YOU'RE BRIGHT RED.
I-I-I-I... IT'S NOTHING!

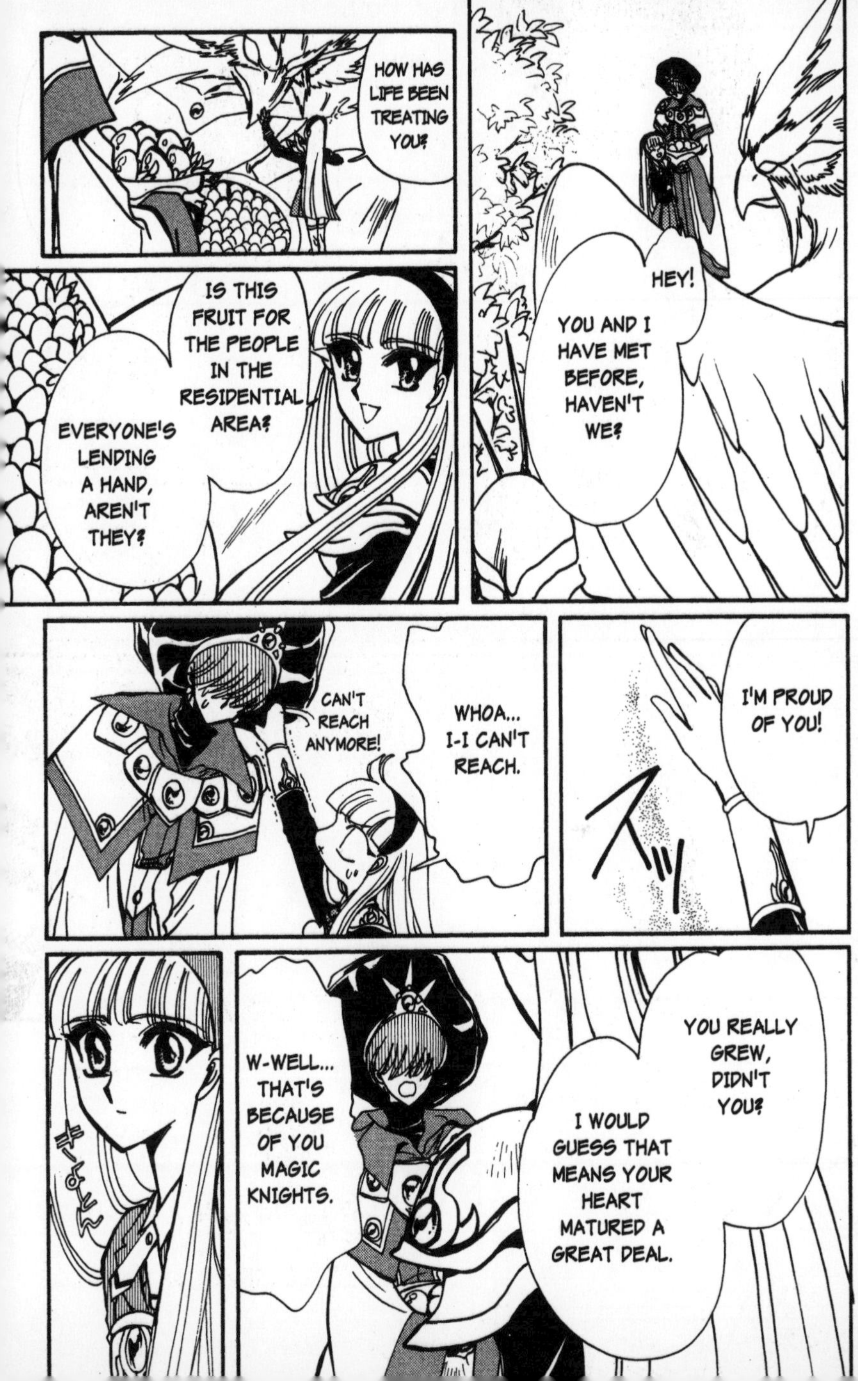
HEY!
YOU AND I HAVE MET BEFORE, HAVEN'T WE?
HOW HAS LIFE BEEN TREATING YOU?
IS THIS FRUIT FOR THE PEOPLE IN THE RESIDENTIAL AREA?
EVERYONE'S LENDING A HAND, AREN'T THEY?
I'M PROUD OF YOU!
WHOA... I-I CAN'T REACH.
CAN'T REACH ANYMORE!
YOU REALLY GREW, DIDN'T YOU?
I WOULD GUESS THAT MEANS YOUR HEART MATURED A GREAT DEAL.
W-WELL... THAT'S BECAUSE OF YOU MAGIC KNIGHTS.

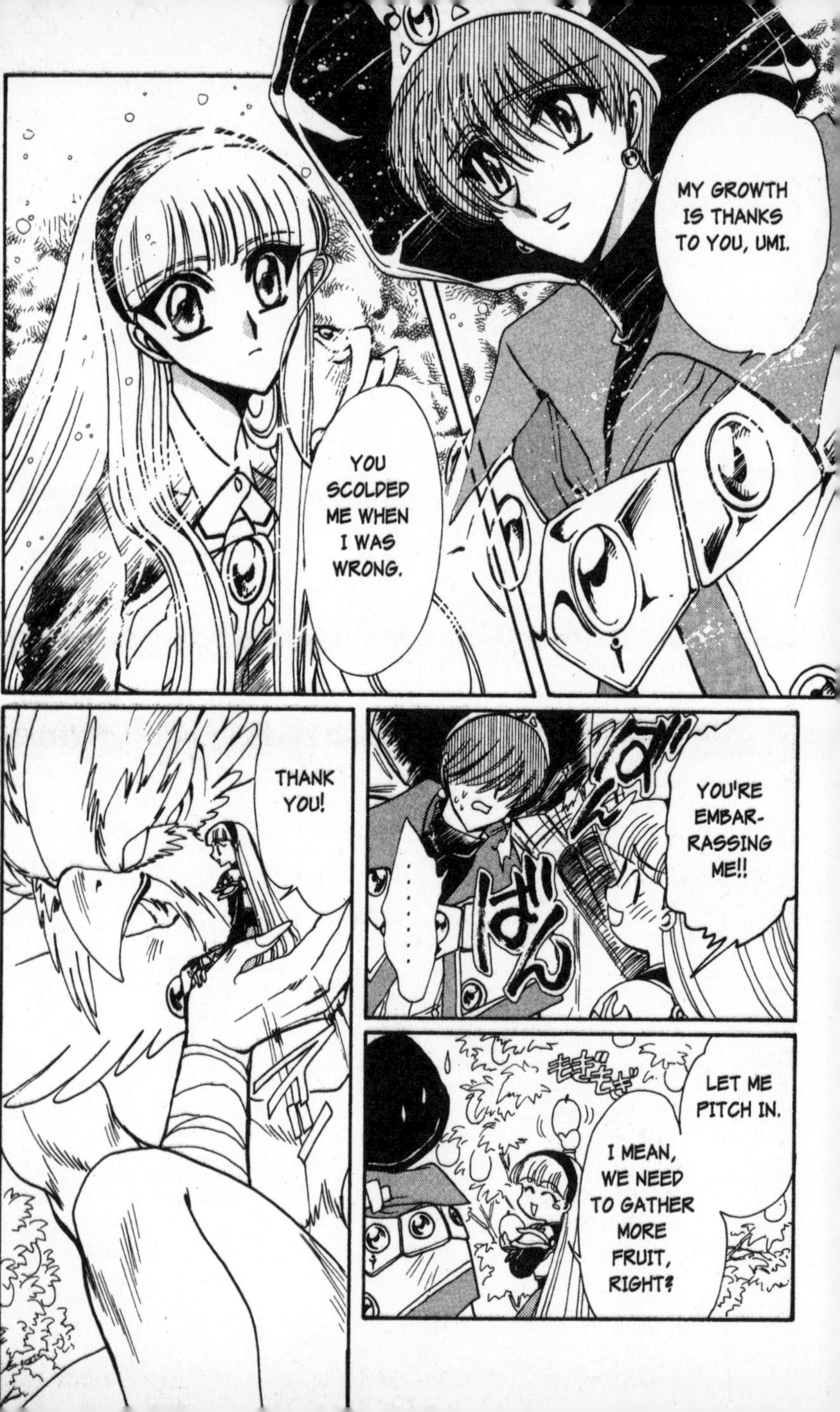
MY GROWTH IS THANKS TO YOU, UMI.
YOU SCOLDED ME WHEN I WAS WRONG.
YOU'RE EMBARRASSING ME!!
ばん
......
LET ME PITCH IN.
もぎもぎ
I MEAN, WE NEED TO GATHER MORE FRUIT, RIGHT?
THANK YOU!

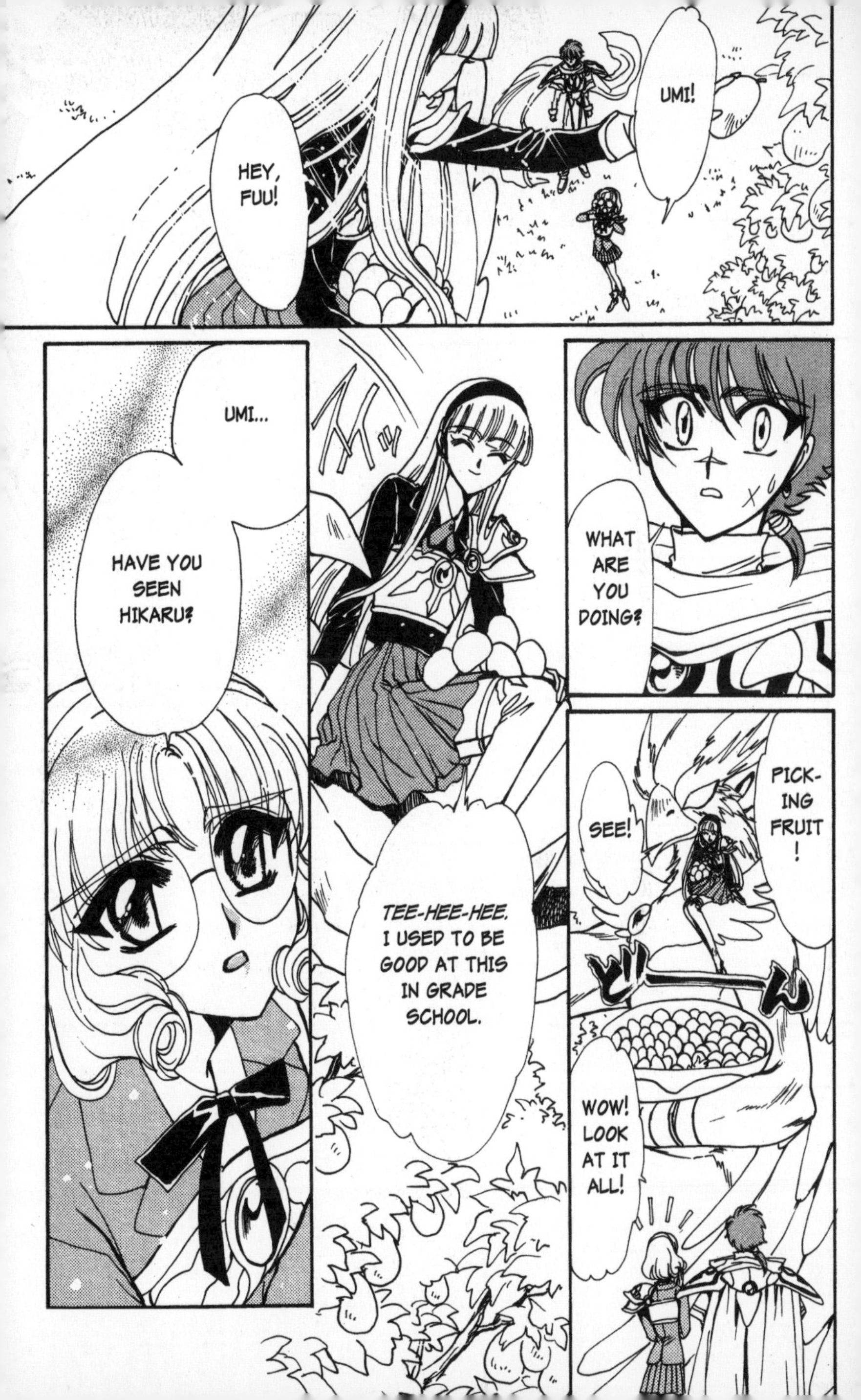
UMI!
HEY, FUU!
WHAT ARE YOU DOING?
PICK-ING FRUIT!
SEE!
WOW! LOOK AT IT ALL!
TEE-HEE-HEE. I USED TO BE GOOD AT THIS IN GRADE SCHOOL.
UMI...
HAVE YOU SEEN HIKARU?

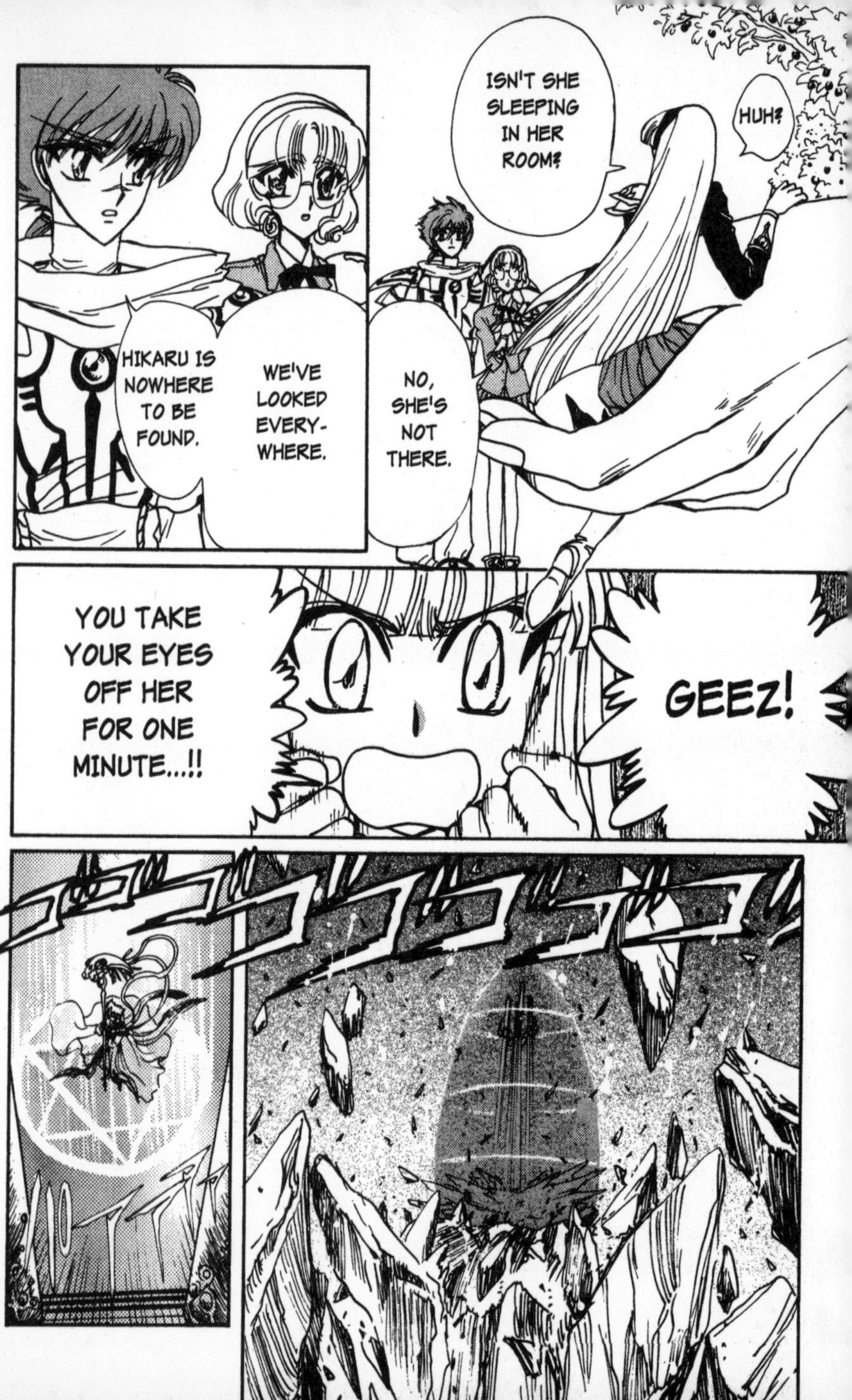
HUH?
ISN'T SHE SLEEPING IN HER ROOM?
NO, SHE'S NOT THERE.
WE'VE LOOKED EVERY-WHERE.
HIKARU IS NOWHERE TO BE FOUND.
YOU TAKE YOUR EYES OFF HER FOR ONE MINUTE...!!
GEEZ!

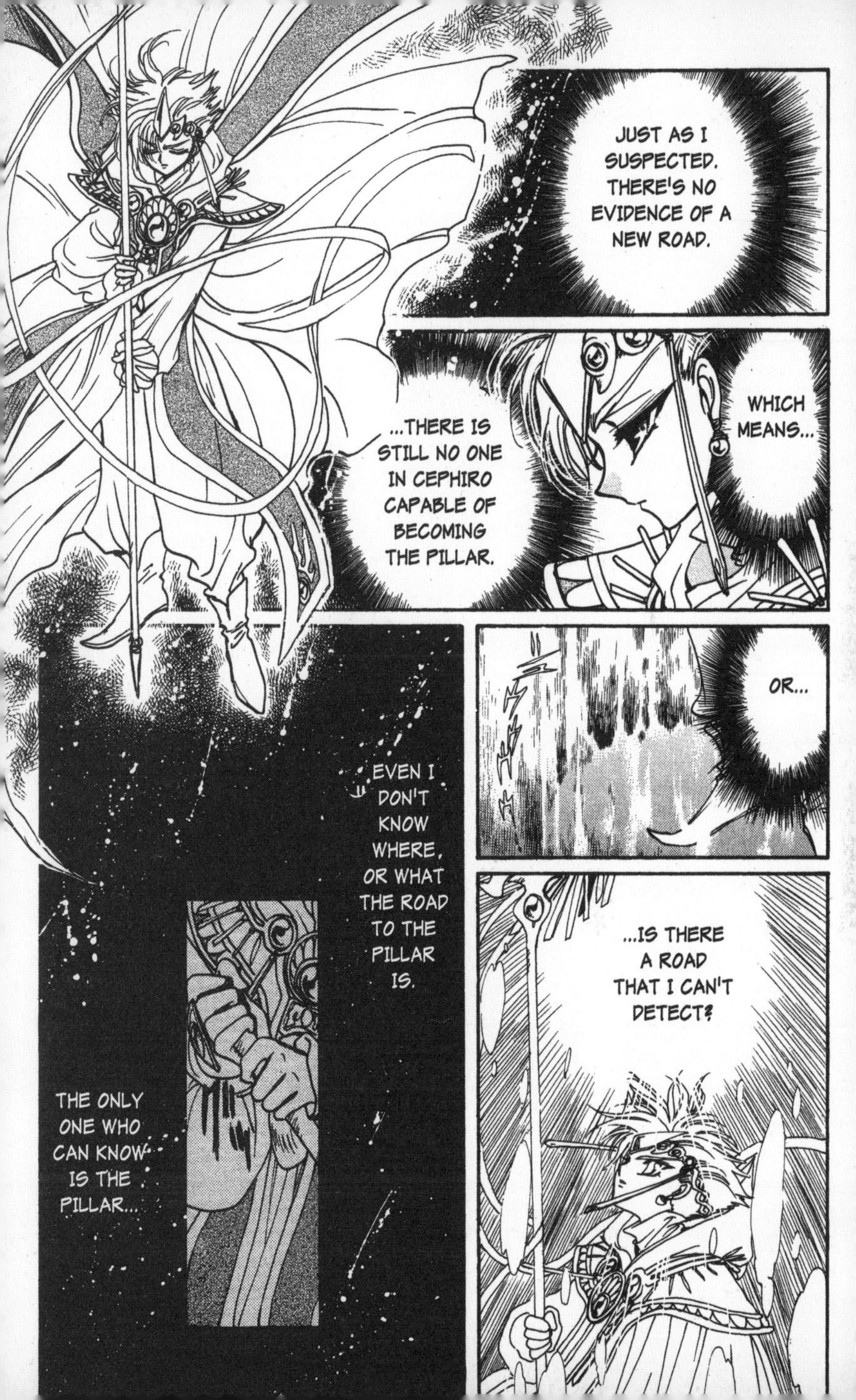
JUST AS I SUSPECTED. THERE'S NO EVIDENCE OF A NEW ROAD.
WHICH MEANS...
...THERE IS STILL NO ONE IN CEPHIRO CAPABLE OF BECOMING THE PILLAR.
OR...
...IS THERE A ROAD THAT I CAN'T DETECT?
EVEN I DON'T KNOW WHERE, OR WHAT THE ROAD TO THE PILLAR IS.
THE ONLY ONE WHO CAN KNOW IS THE PILLAR...

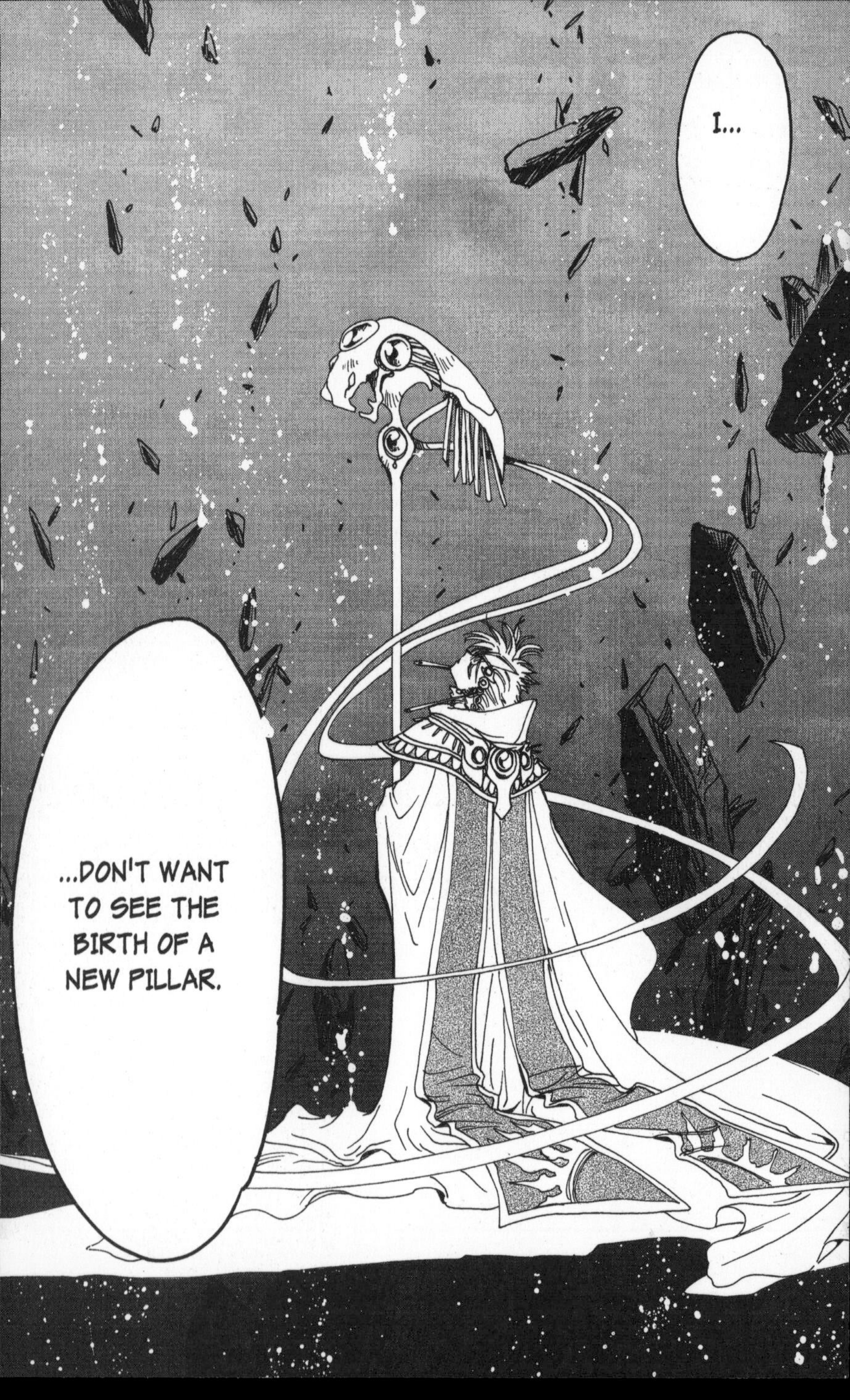
I...
...DON'T WANT TO SEE THE BIRTH OF A NEW PILLAR.

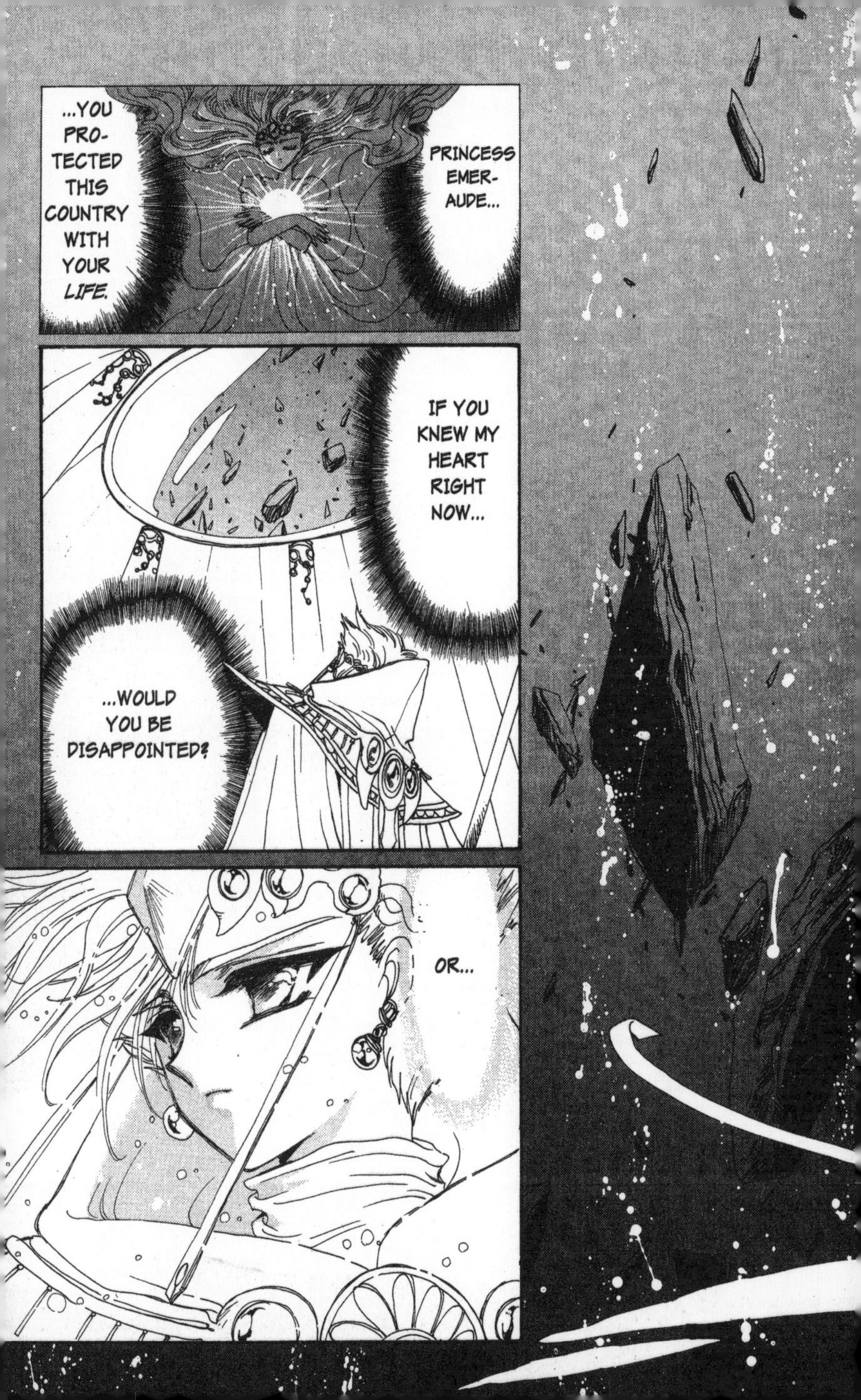
PRINCESS EMER-AUDE...
...YOU PRO-TECTED THIS COUNTRY WITH YOUR LIFE.
IF YOU KNEW MY HEART RIGHT NOW...
...WOULD YOU BE DISAPPOINTED?
OR...

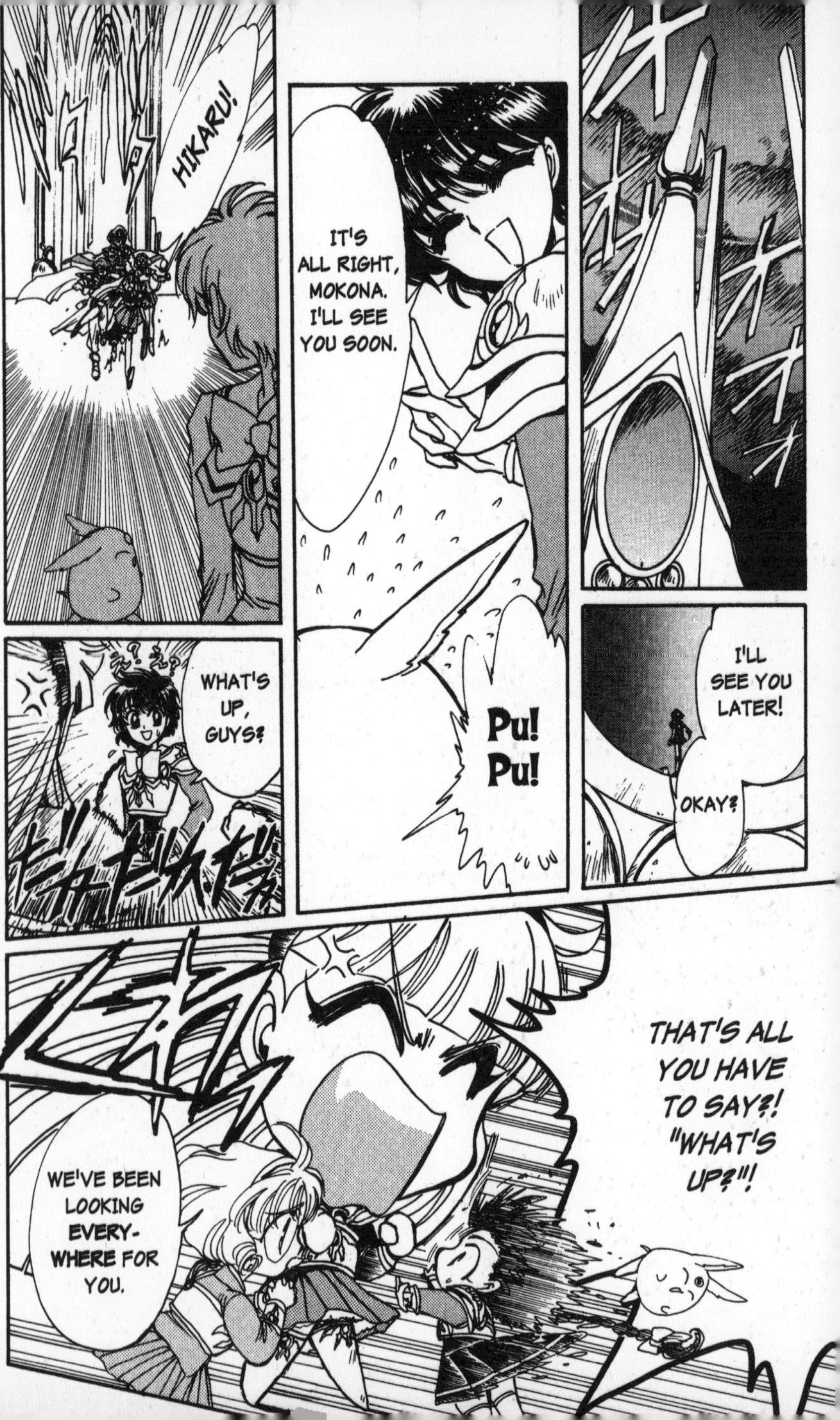
I'LL SEE YOU LATER!
OKAY?
IT'S ALL RIGHT, MOKONA. I'LL SEE YOU SOON.
Pu! Pu!
HIKARU!
WHAT'S UP, GUYS?
THAT'S ALL YOU HAVE TO SAY?! "WHAT'S UP?"!
WE'VE BEEN LOOKING EVERY-WHERE FOR YOU.

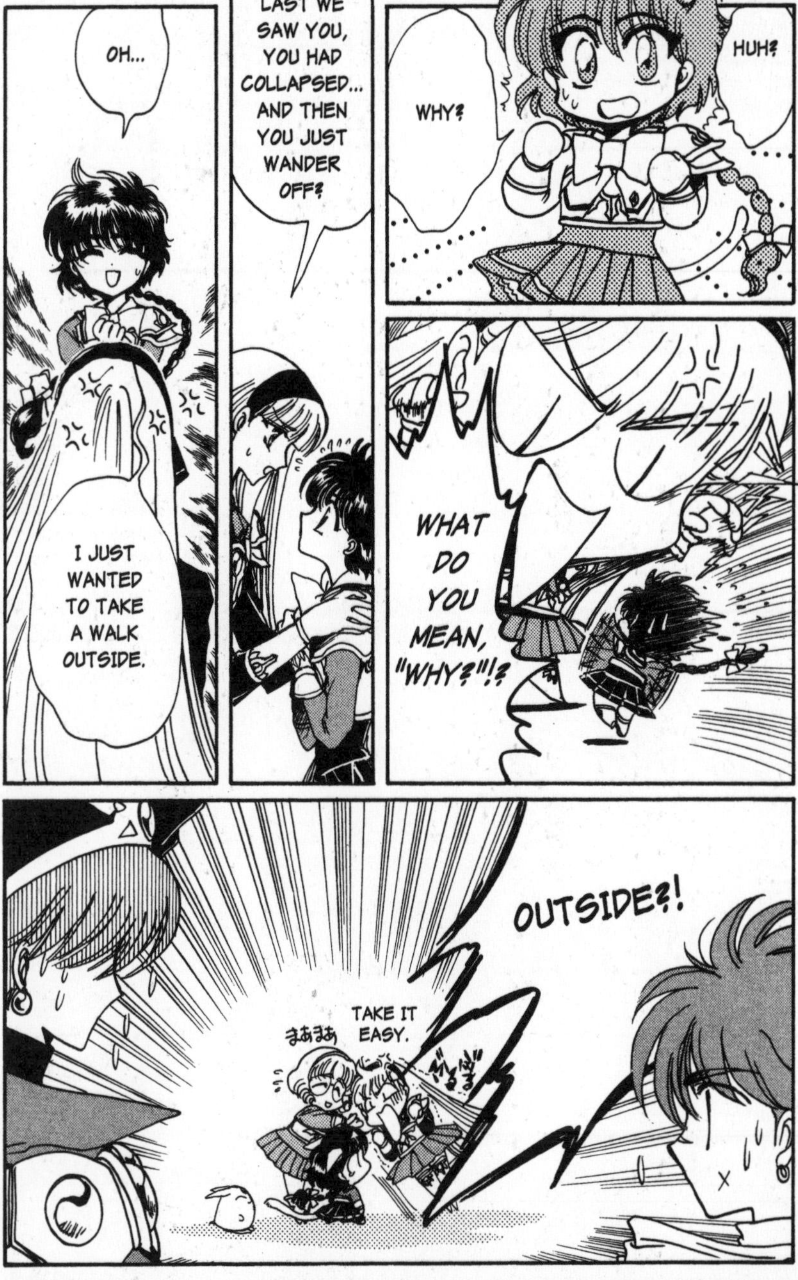
HUH?
WHY?
WHAT DO YOU MEAN, "WHY?"!?
LAST WE SAW YOU, YOU HAD COLLAPSED... AND THEN YOU JUST WANDER OFF?
OH...
I JUST WANTED TO TAKE A WALK OUTSIDE.
OUTSIDE?!
TAKE IT EASY.
まあまあ

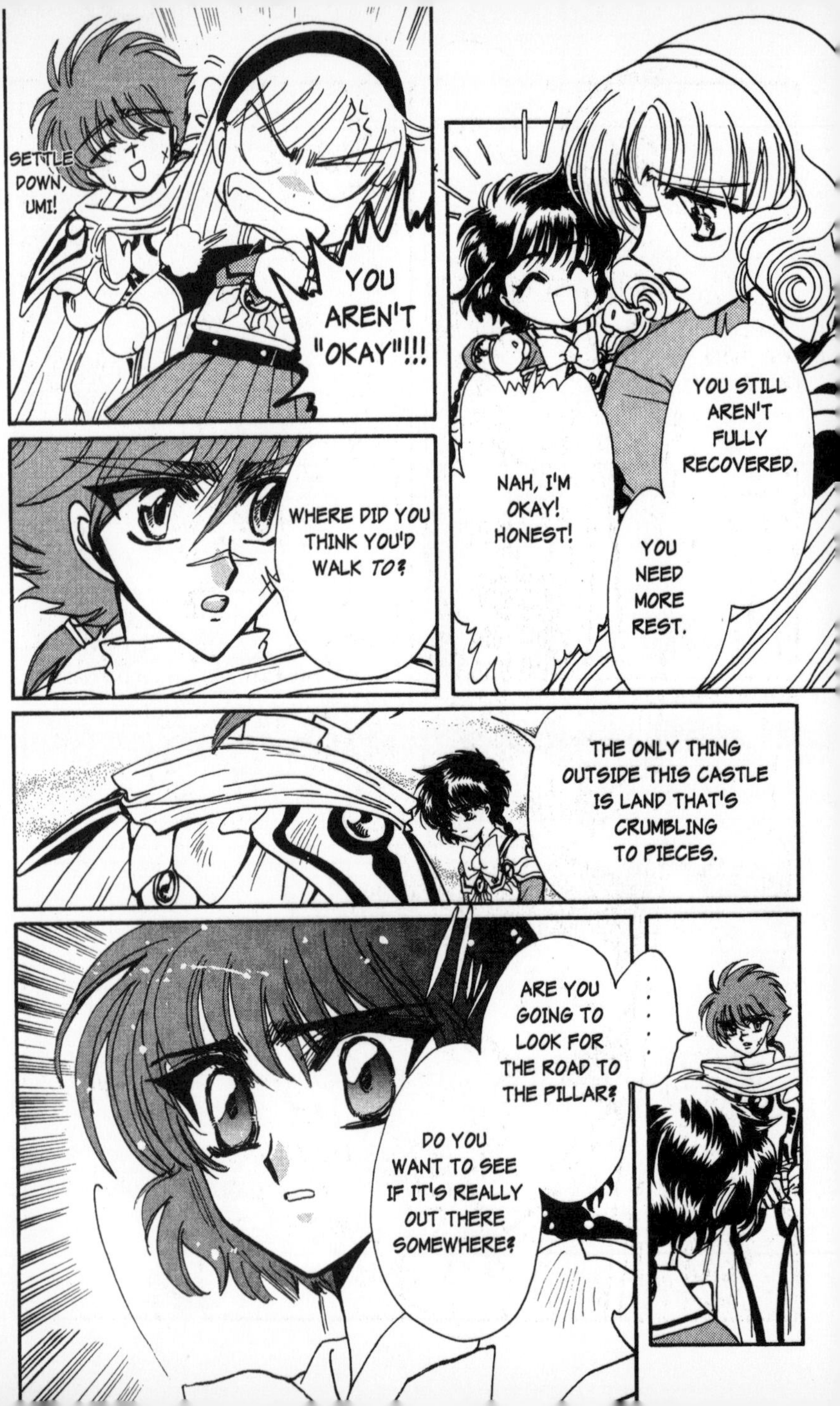

YOU STILL AREN'T FULLY RECOVERED.
YOU NEED MORE REST.
NAH, I'M OKAY! HONEST!
YOU AREN'T "OKAY"!!!
SETTLE DOWN, UMI!
WHERE DID YOU THINK YOU'D WALK *TO*?
THE ONLY THING OUTSIDE THIS CASTLE IS LAND THAT'S CRUMBLING TO PIECES.
....
ARE YOU GOING TO LOOK FOR THE ROAD TO THE PILLAR?
DO YOU WANT TO SEE IF IT'S REALLY OUT THERE SOMEWHERE?

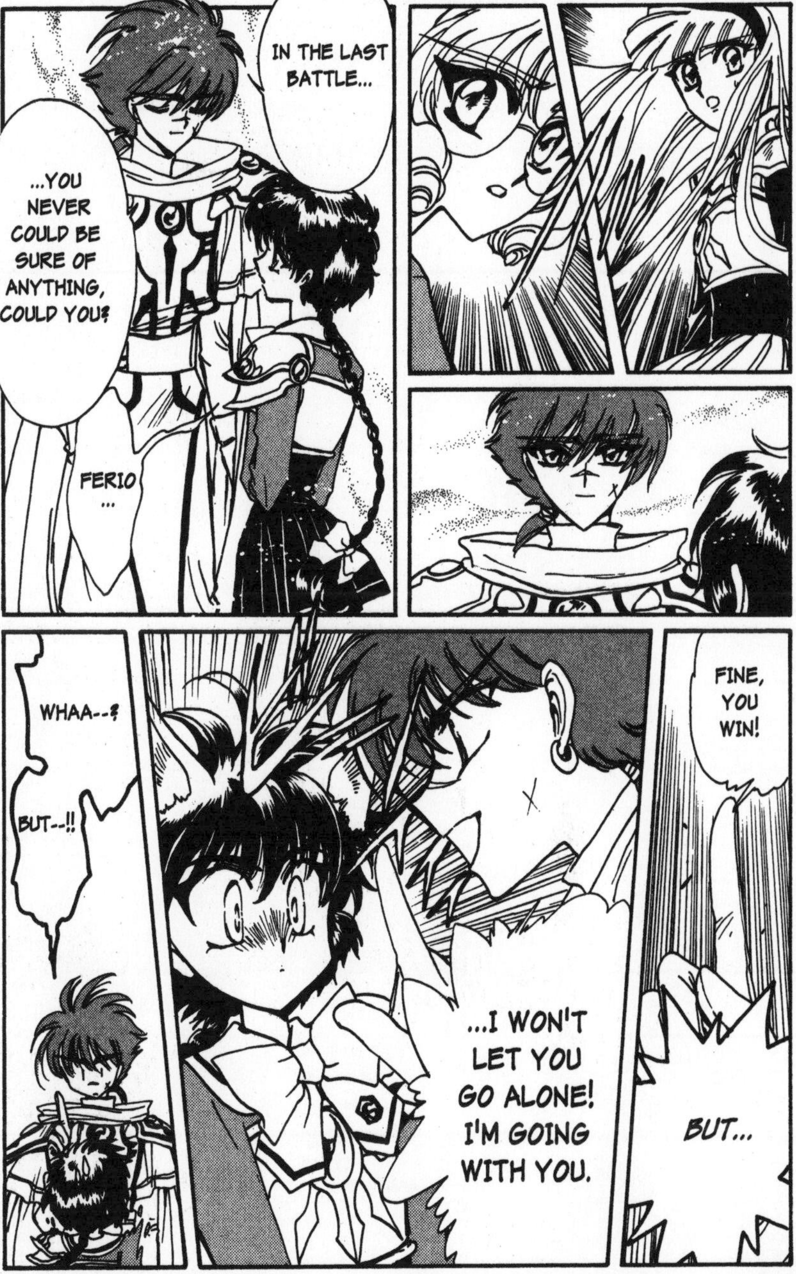
IN THE LAST BATTLE...
...YOU NEVER COULD BE SURE OF ANYTHING, COULD YOU?
FERIO ...
FINE, YOU WIN!
BUT...
...I WON'T LET YOU GO ALONE! I'M GOING WITH YOU.
WHAA--?
BUT--!!

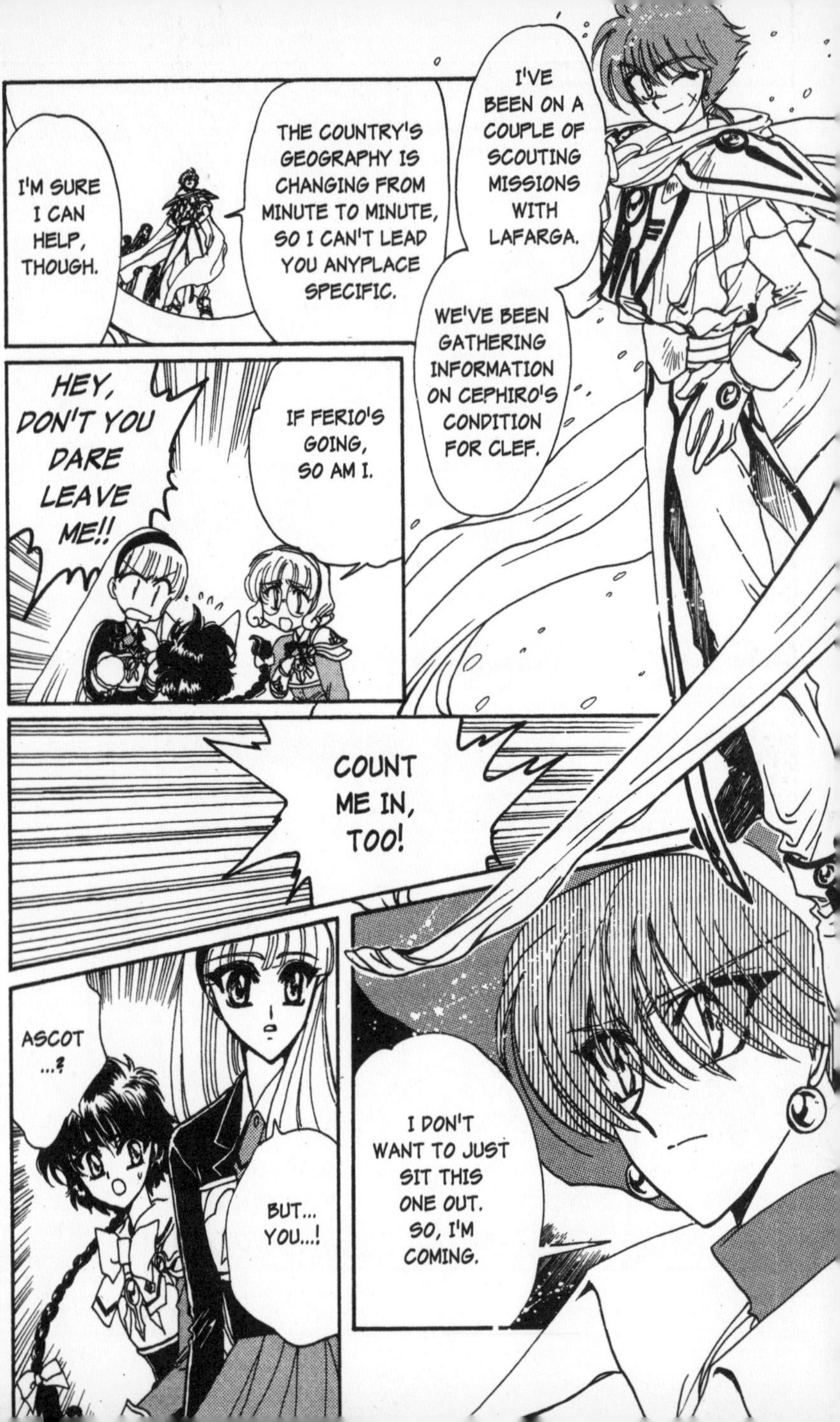
I'VE BEEN ON A COUPLE OF SCOUTING MISSIONS WITH LAFARGA.
WE'VE BEEN GATHERING INFORMATION ON CEPHIRO'S CONDITION FOR CLEF.
THE COUNTRY'S GEOGRAPHY IS CHANGING FROM MINUTE TO MINUTE, SO I CAN'T LEAD YOU ANYPLACE SPECIFIC.
I'M SURE I CAN HELP, THOUGH.
IF FERIO'S GOING, SO AM I.
HEY, DON'T YOU DARE LEAVE ME!!
COUNT ME IN, TOO!
I DON'T WANT TO JUST SIT THIS ONE OUT. SO, I'M COMING.
ASCOT ...?
BUT... YOU...!

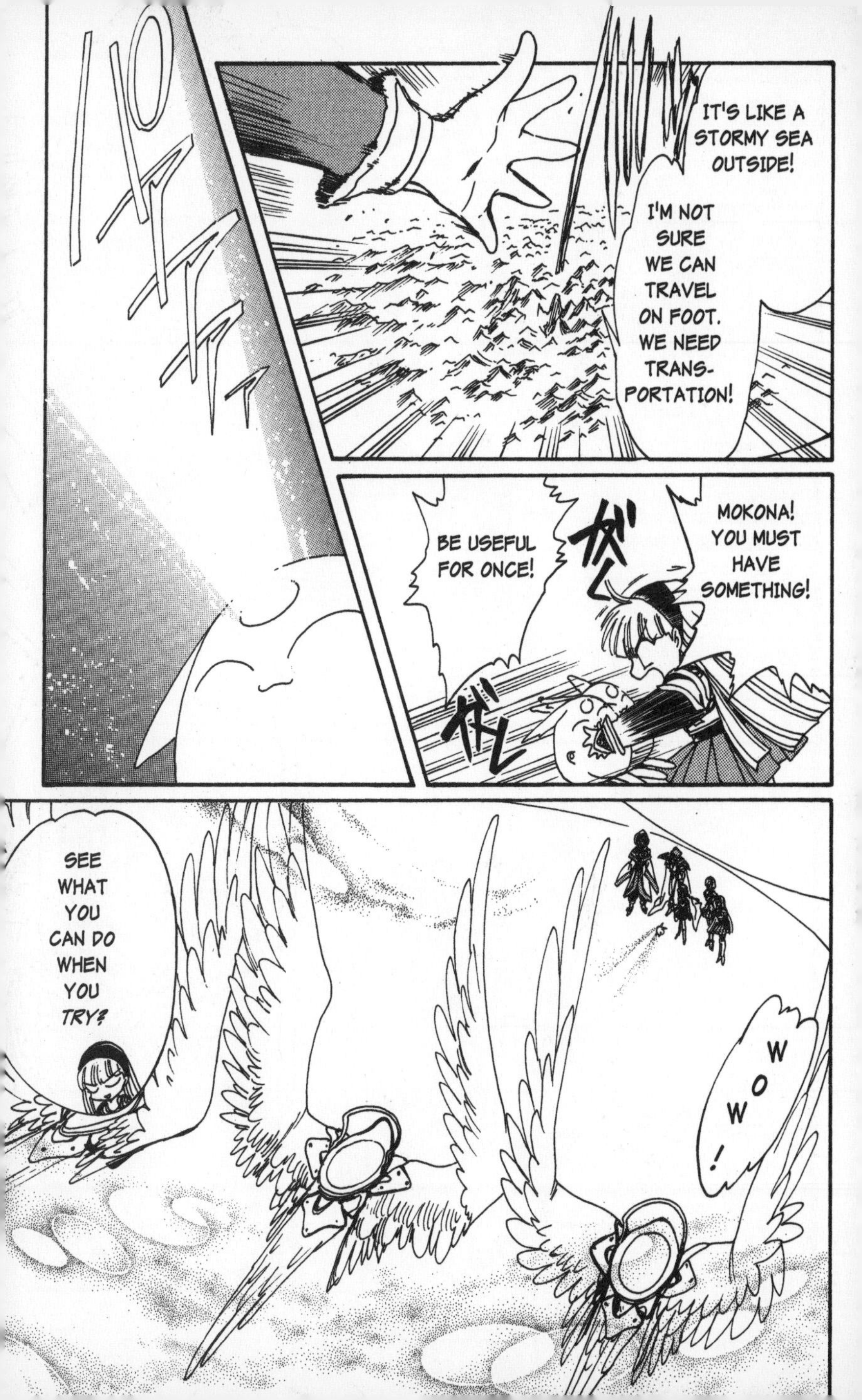
IT'S LIKE A STORMY SEA OUTSIDE!
I'M NOT SURE WE CAN TRAVEL ON FOOT. WE NEED TRANSPORTATION!
MOKONA! YOU MUST HAVE SOMETHING!
BE USEFUL FOR ONCE!
WOW!
SEE WHAT YOU CAN DO WHEN YOU *TRY*?

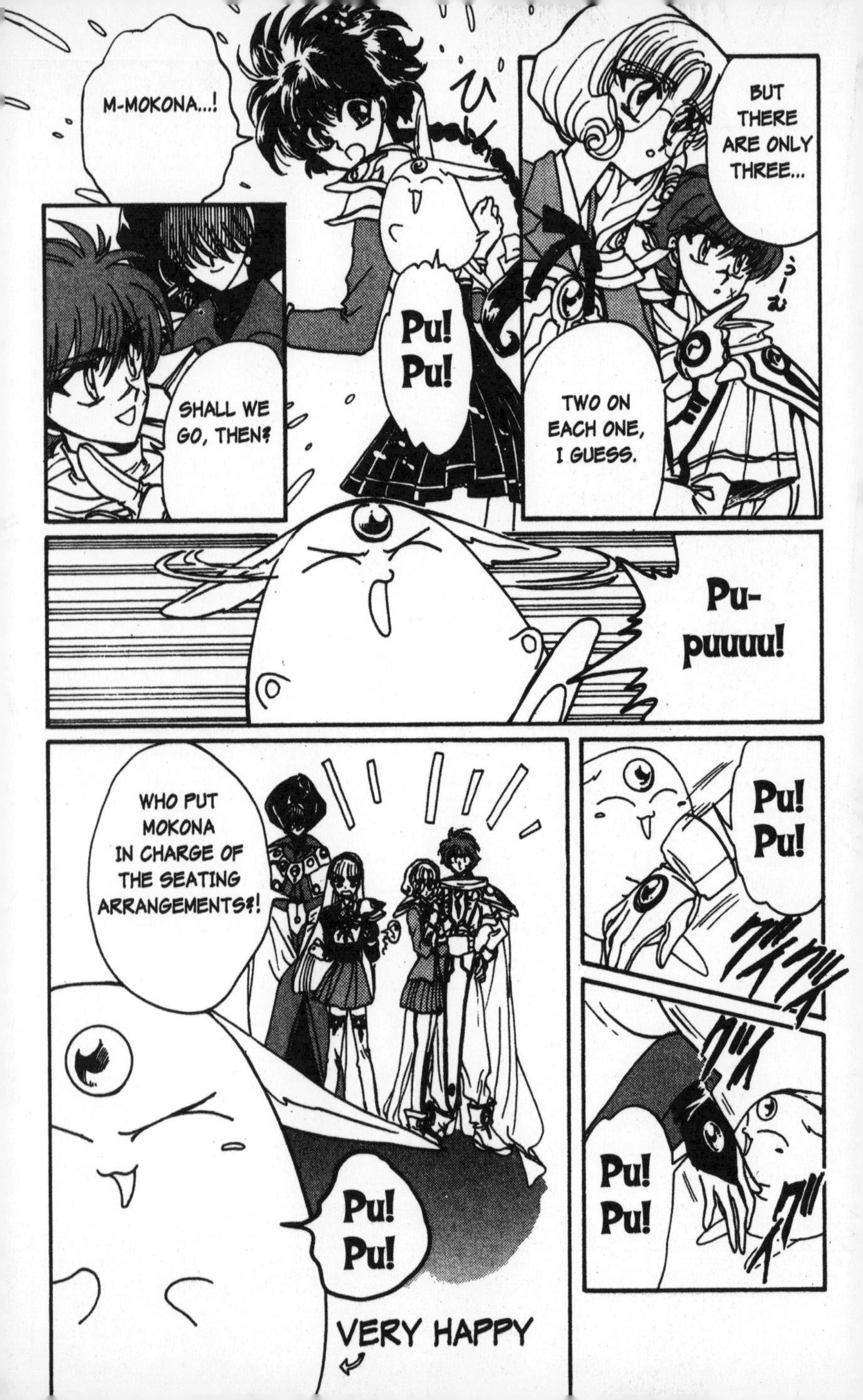
BUT THERE ARE ONLY THREE...
TWO ON EACH ONE, I GUESS.
M-MOKONA...!
Pu! Pu!
SHALL WE GO, THEN?
Pu-puuuu!
Pu! Pu!
Pu! Pu!
WHO PUT MOKONA IN CHARGE OF THE SEATING ARRANGEMENTS?!
Pu! Pu!
VERY HAPPY

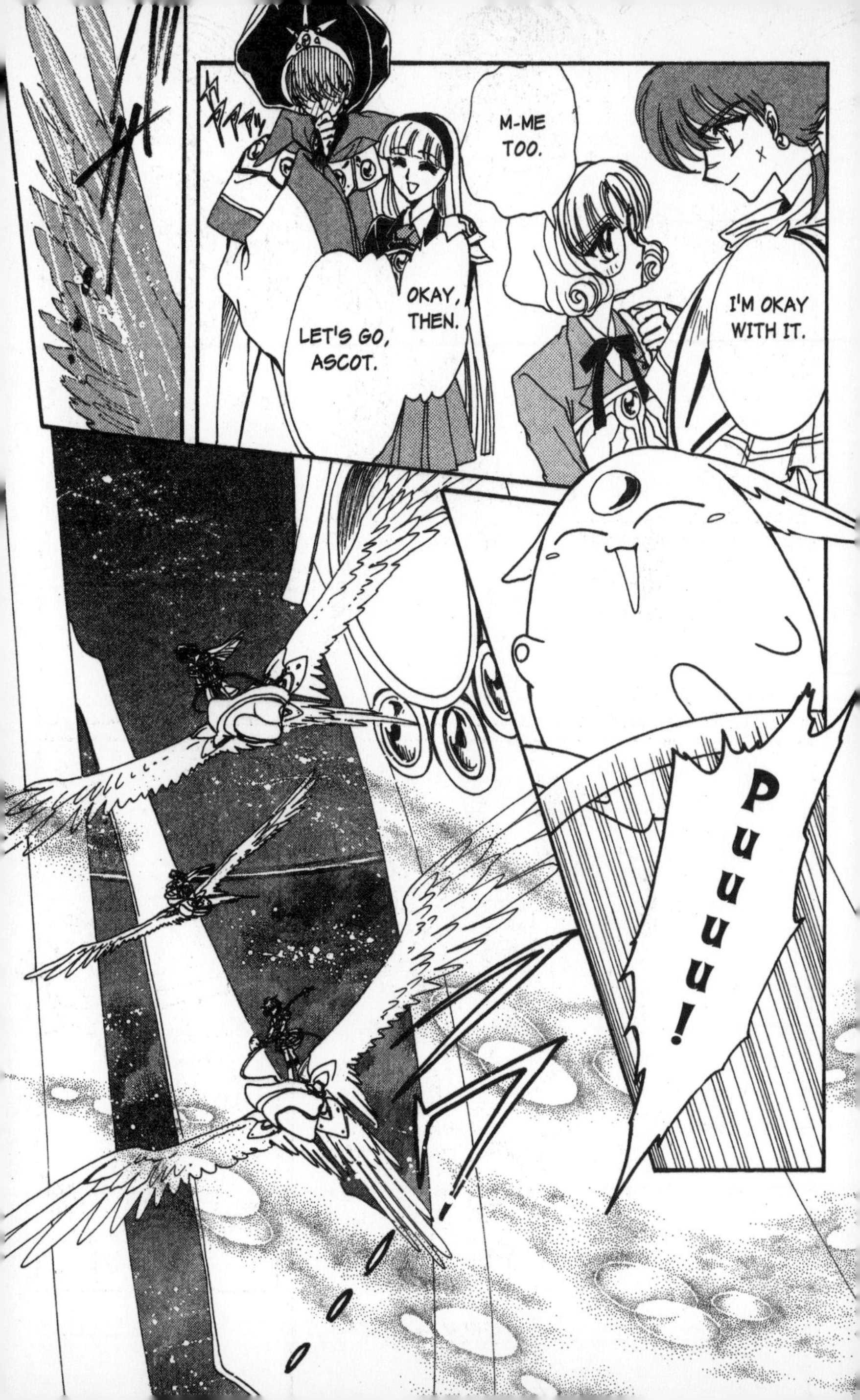
I'M OKAY WITH IT.
M-ME TOO.
OKAY, THEN.
LET'S GO, ASCOT.
Puuuu!

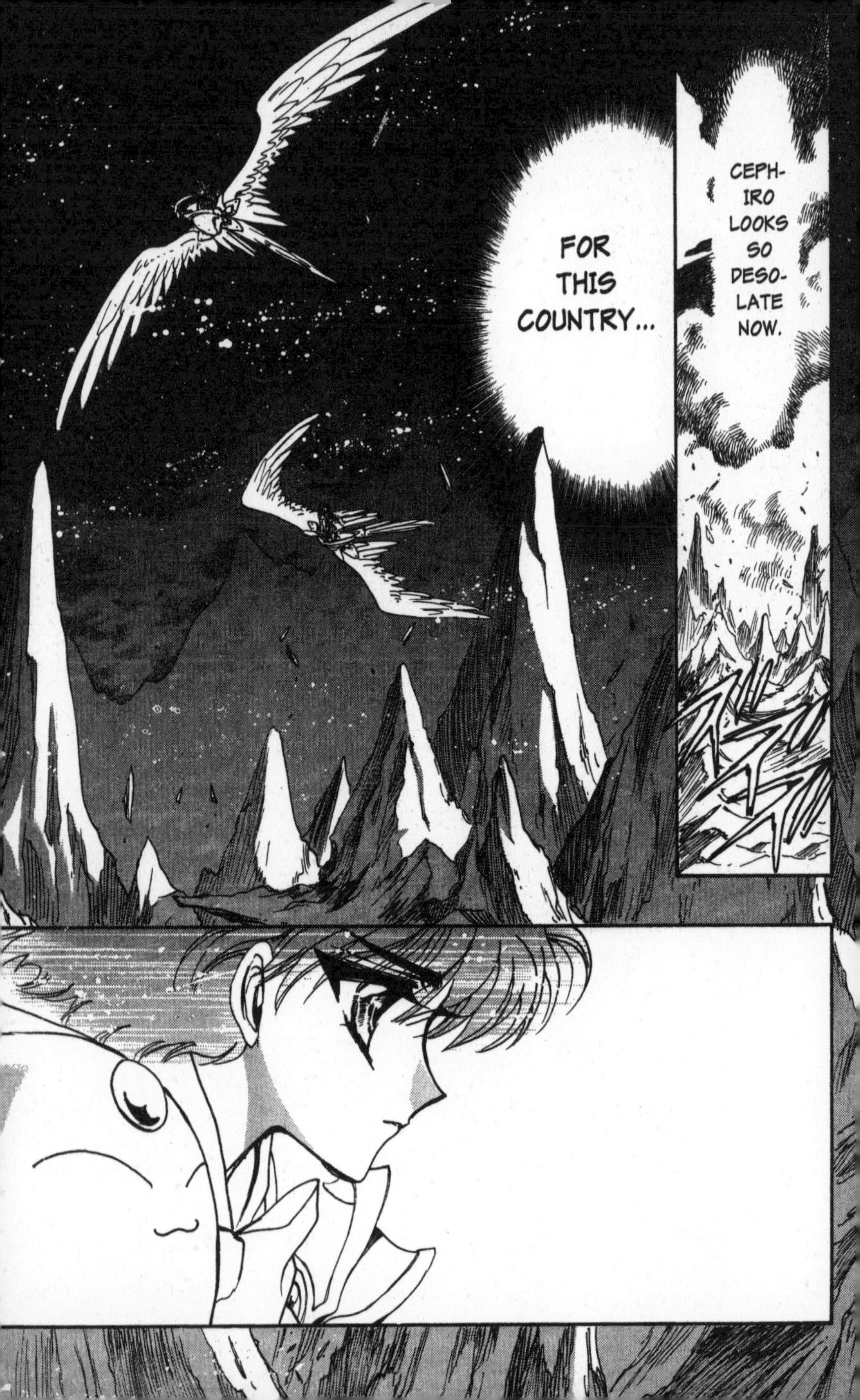
CEPH-IRO LOOKS SO DESO-LATE NOW.
FOR THIS COUNTRY...

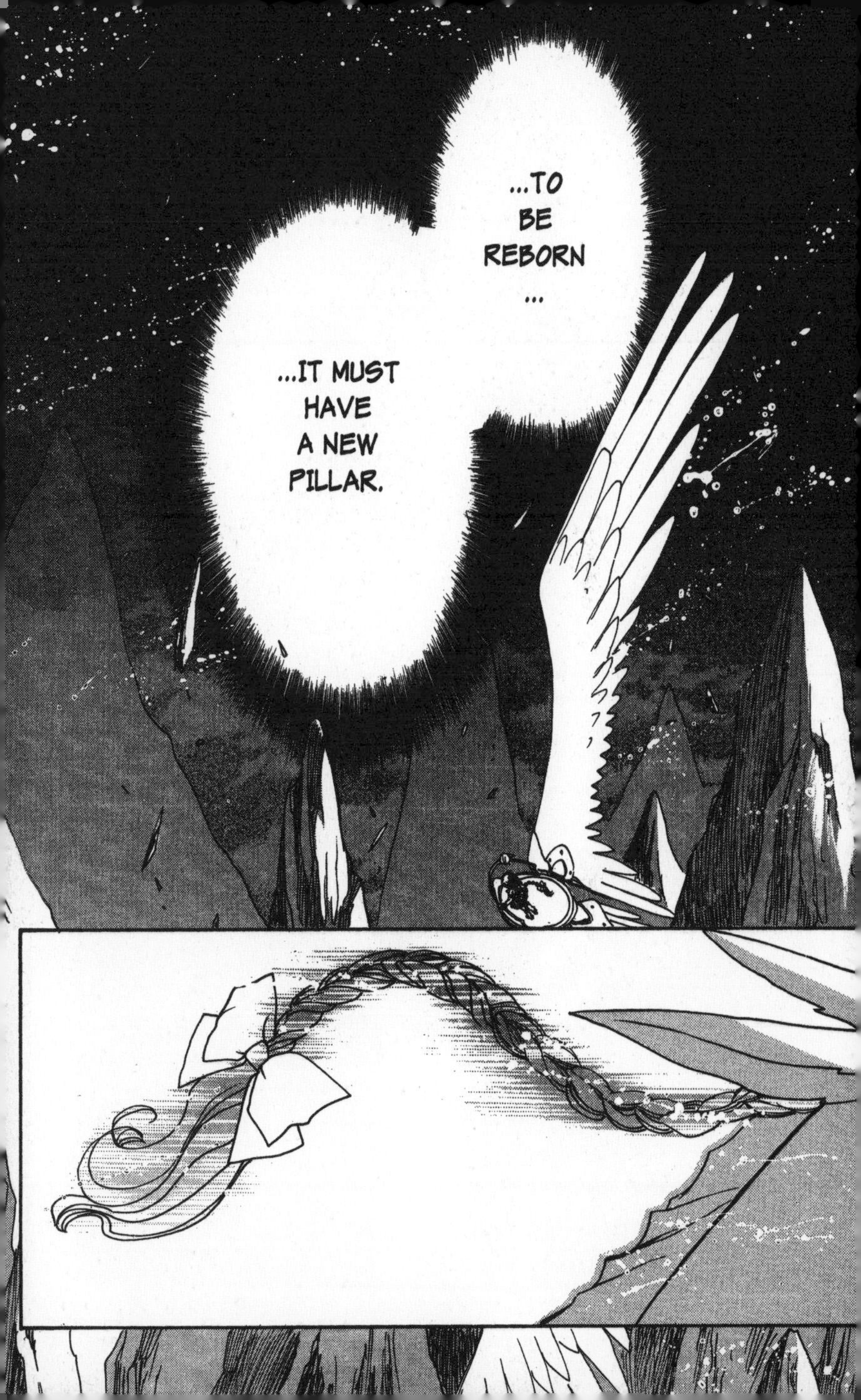
...TO BE REBORN ...
...IT MUST HAVE A NEW PILLAR.

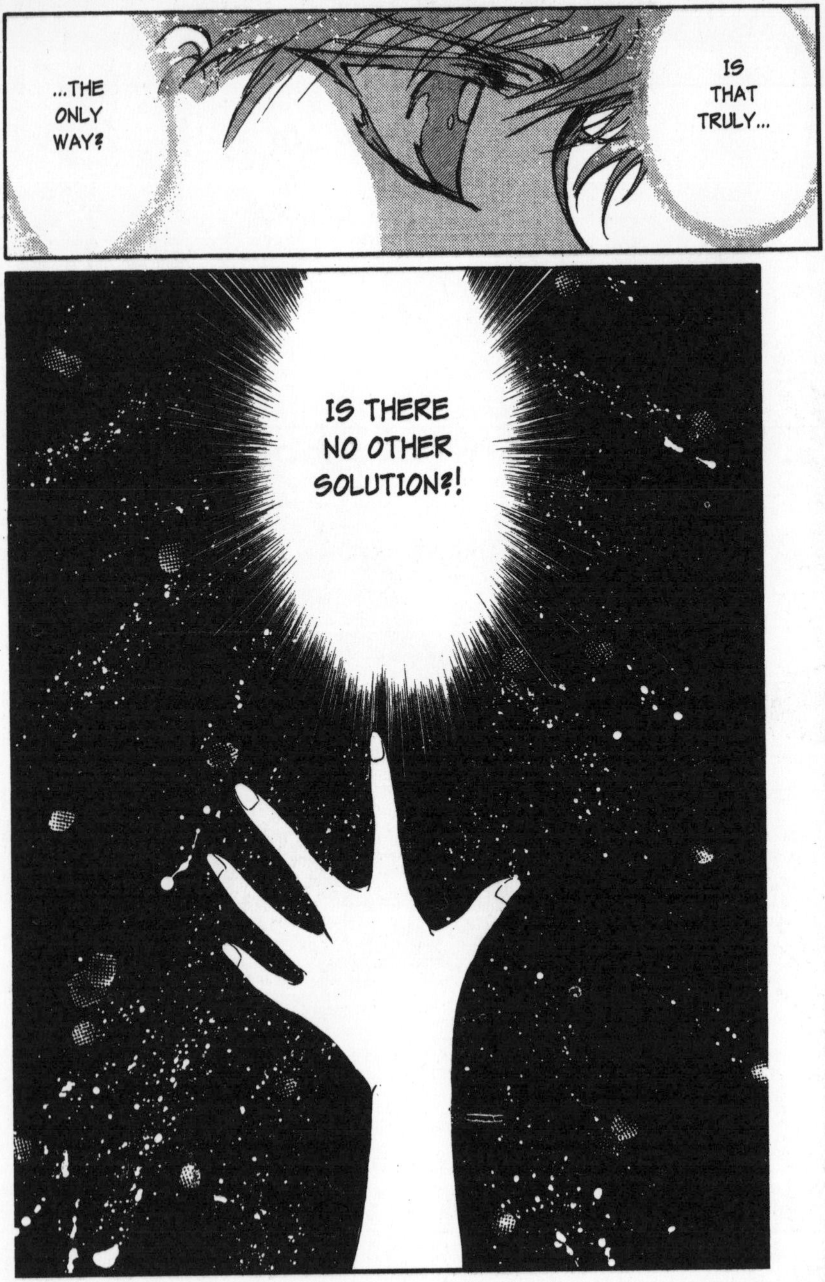
IS THAT TRULY...
...THE ONLY WAY?
IS THERE NO OTHER SOLUTION?!

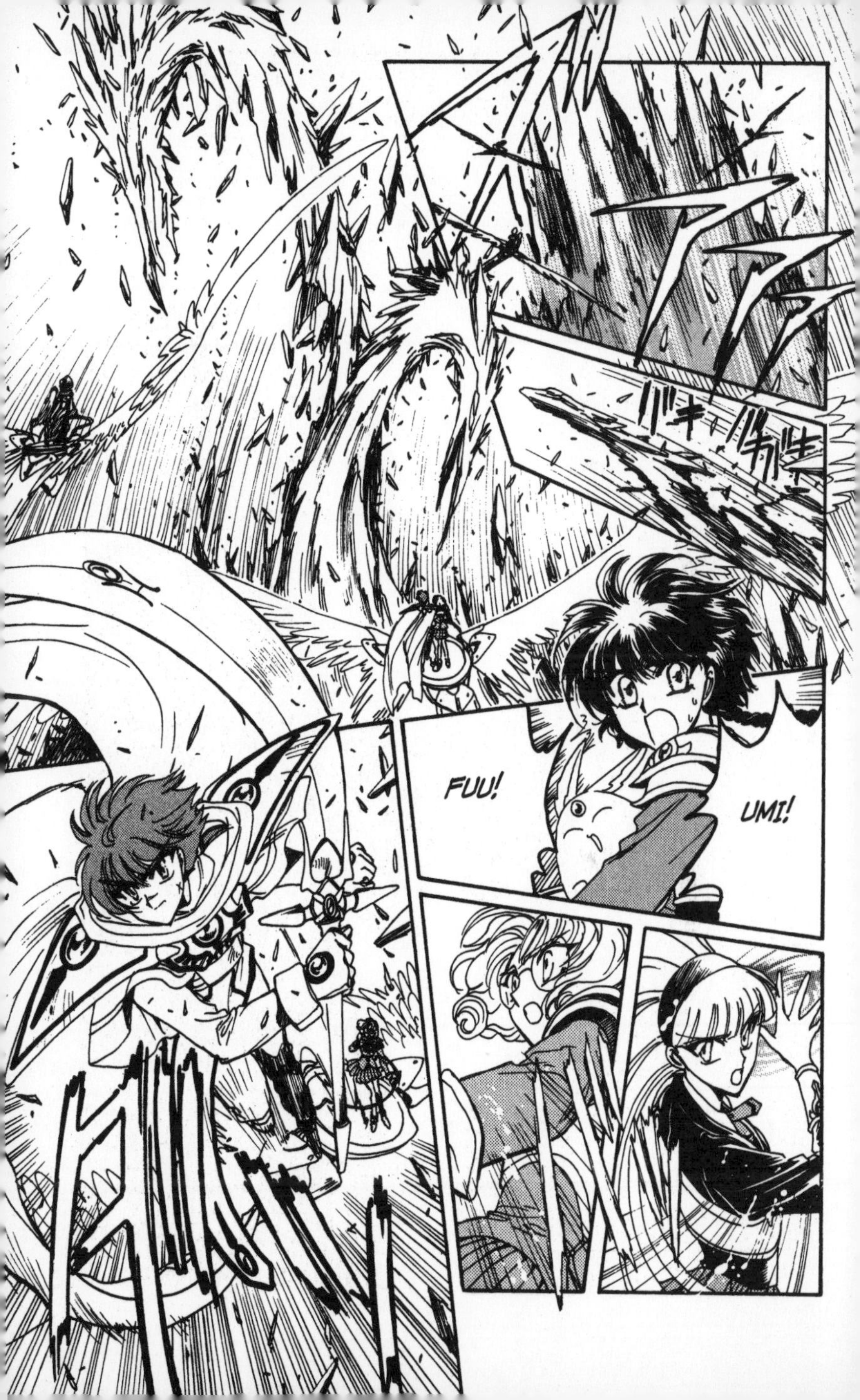
UMI!
FUU!

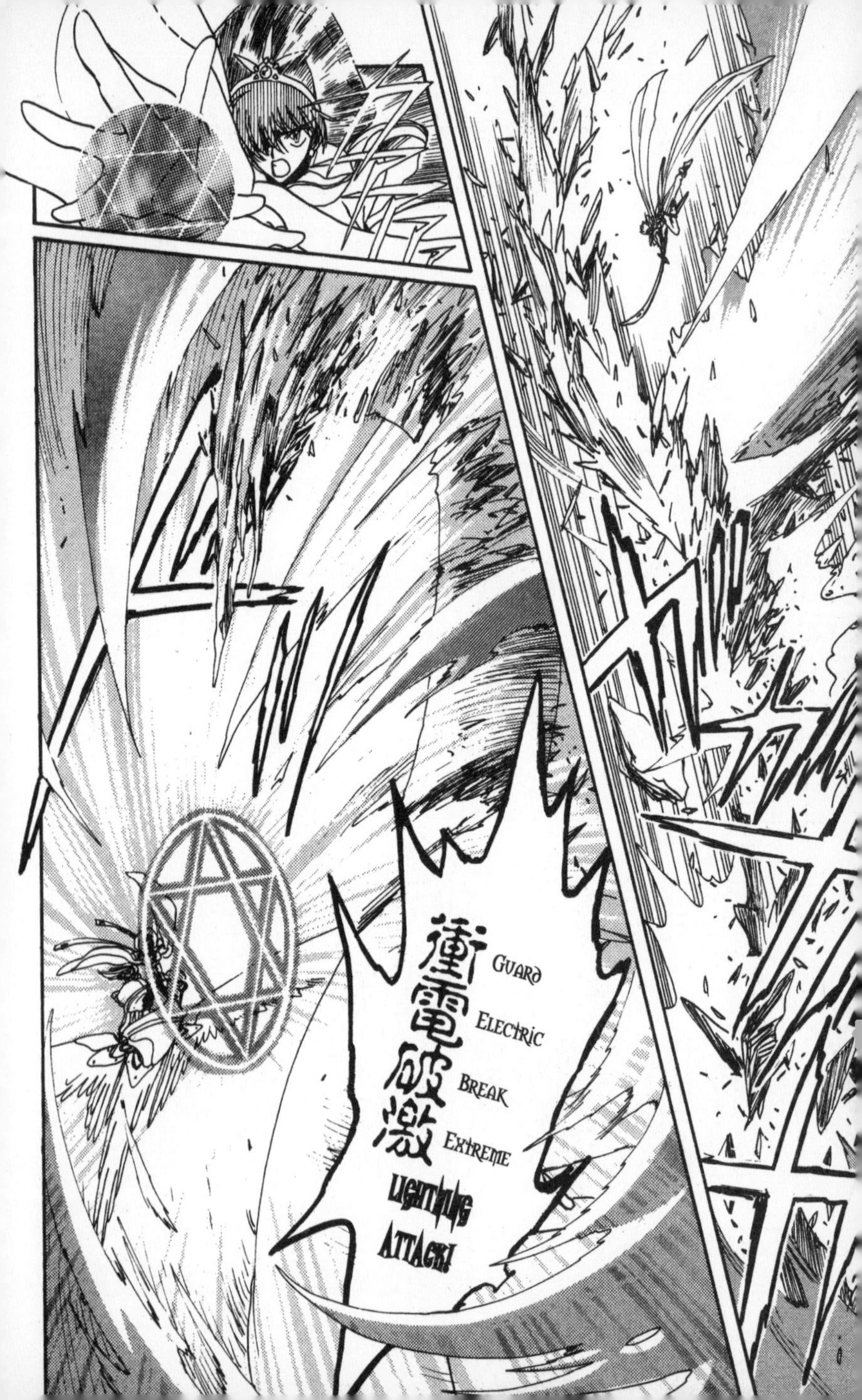
衝雷破激
GUARD
ELECTRIC
BREAK
EXTREME
LIGHTNING ATTACK!

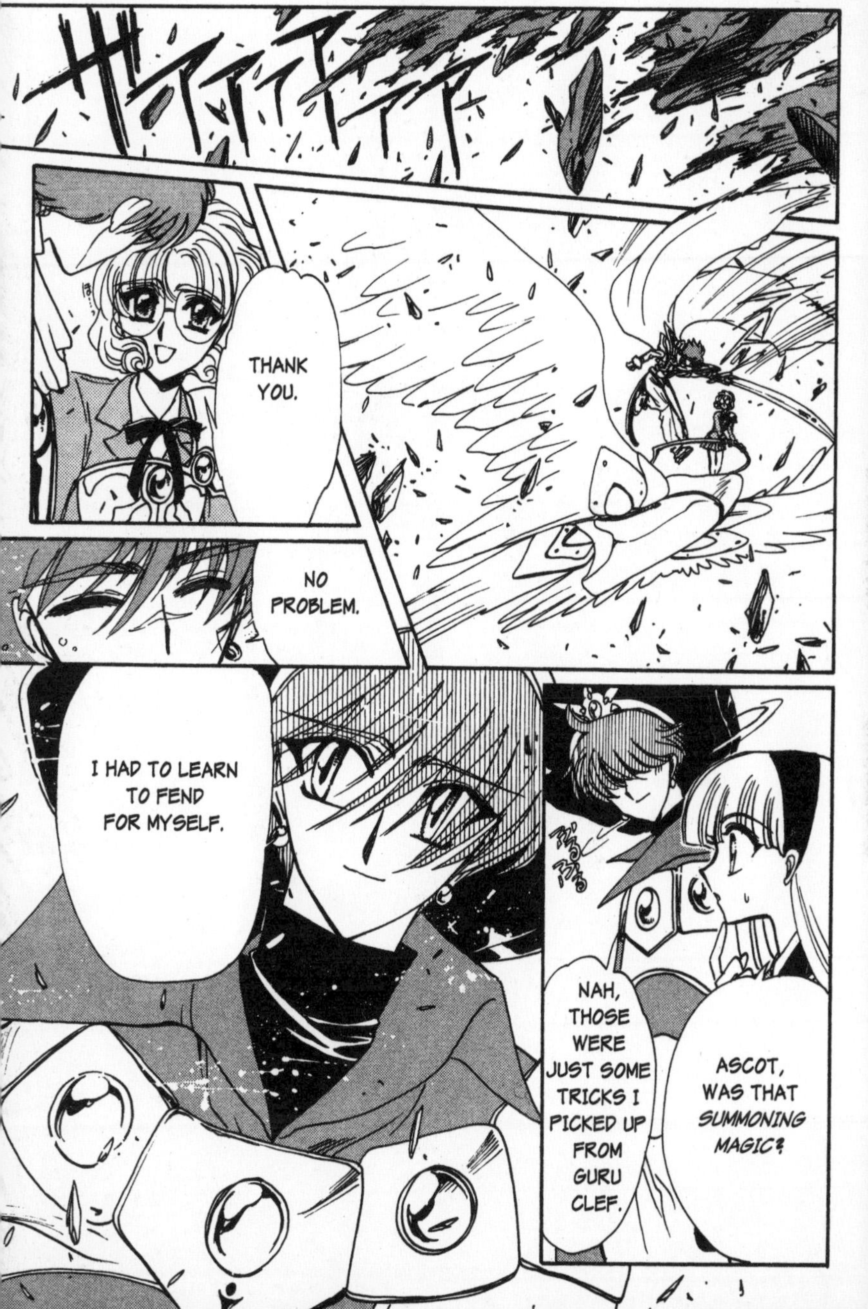
THANK YOU.
NO PROBLEM.
ASCOT, WAS THAT SUMMONING MAGIC?
NAH, THOSE WERE JUST SOME TRICKS I PICKED UP FROM GURU CLEF.
I HAD TO LEARN TO FEND FOR MYSELF.

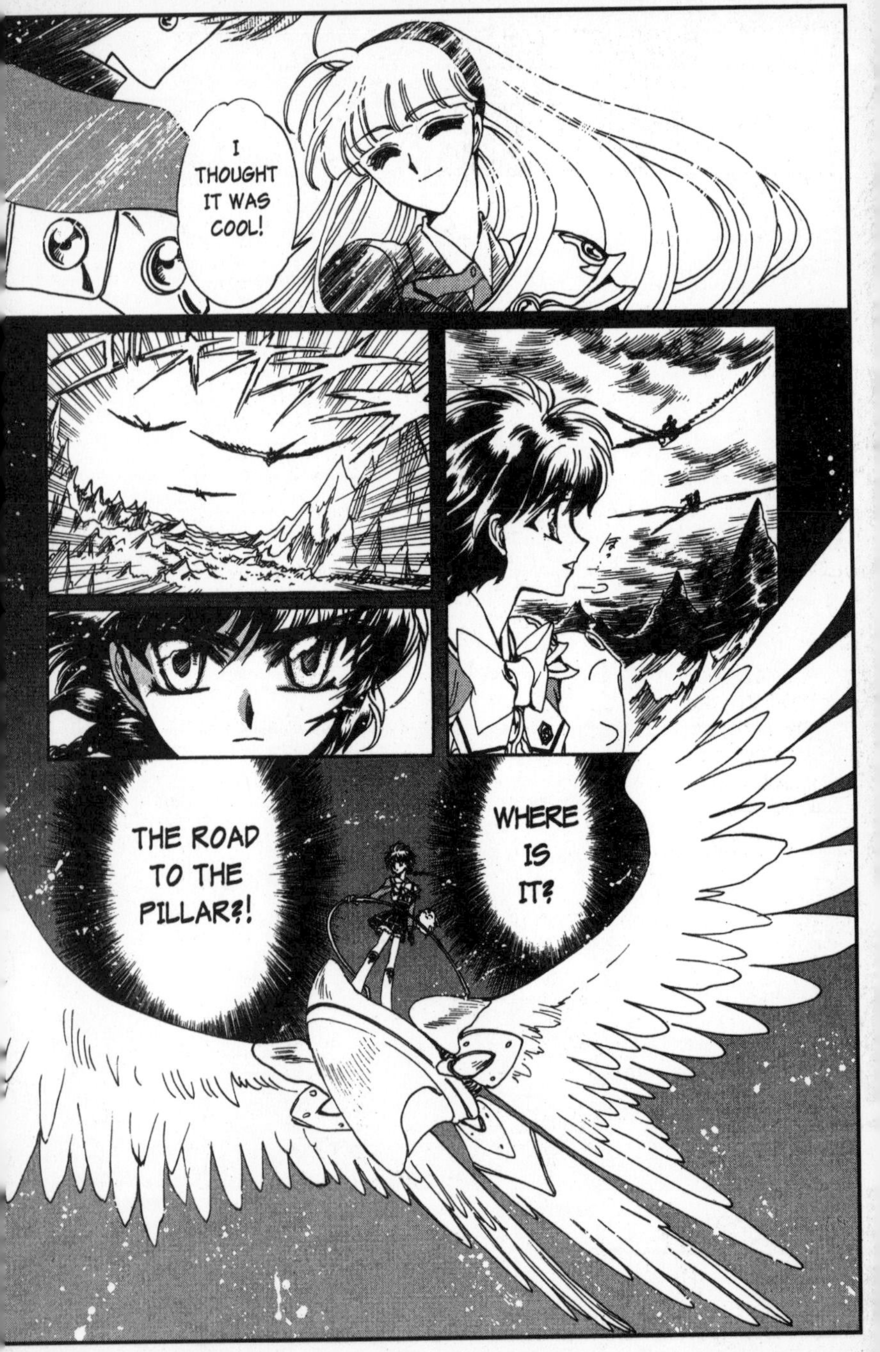
I THOUGHT IT WAS COOL!
WHERE IS IT?
THE ROAD TO THE PILLAR?!

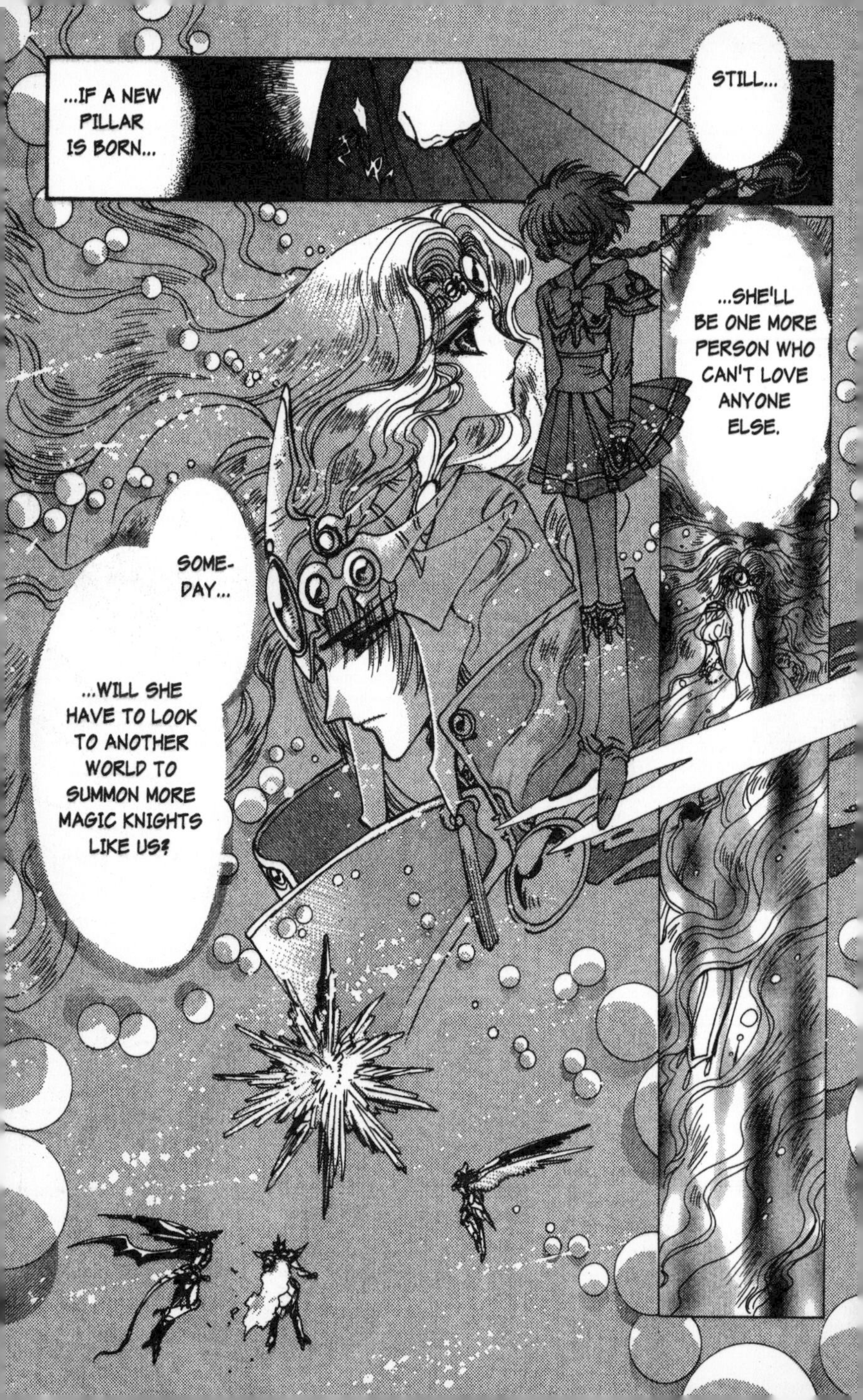
STILL...
...IF A NEW PILLAR IS BORN...
...SHE'LL BE ONE MORE PERSON WHO CAN'T LOVE ANYONE ELSE.
SOME-DAY...
...WILL SHE HAVE TO LOOK TO ANOTHER WORLD TO SUMMON MORE MAGIC KNIGHTS LIKE US?

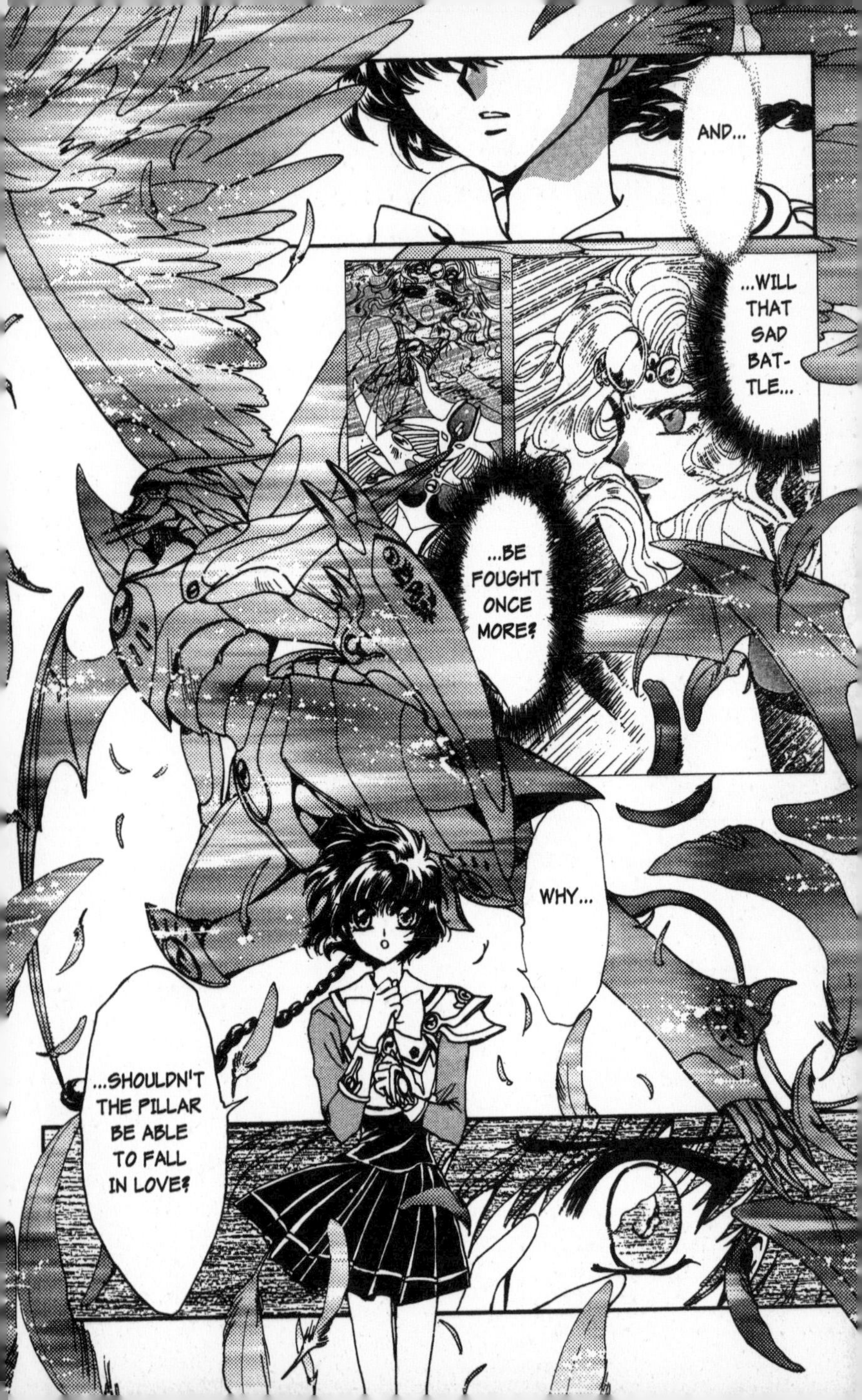
AND...
...WILL THAT SAD BAT-TLE...
...BE FOUGHT ONCE MORE?
WHY...
...SHOULDN'T THE PILLAR BE ABLE TO FALL IN LOVE?

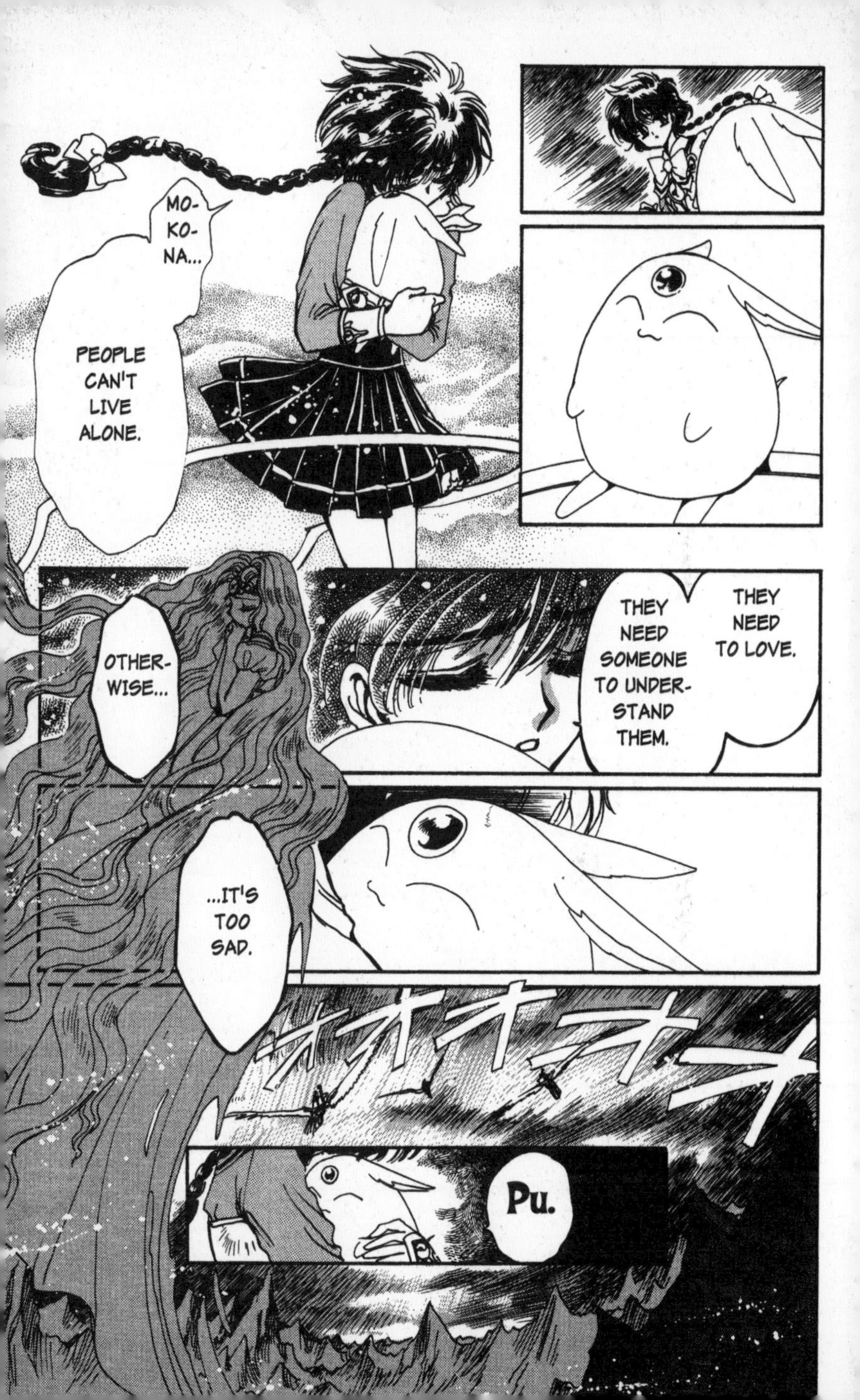
MO-KO-NA...
PEOPLE CAN'T LIVE ALONE.
THEY NEED TO LOVE.
THEY NEED SOMEONE TO UNDER-STAND THEM.
OTHER-WISE...
...IT'S TOO SAD.
Pu.

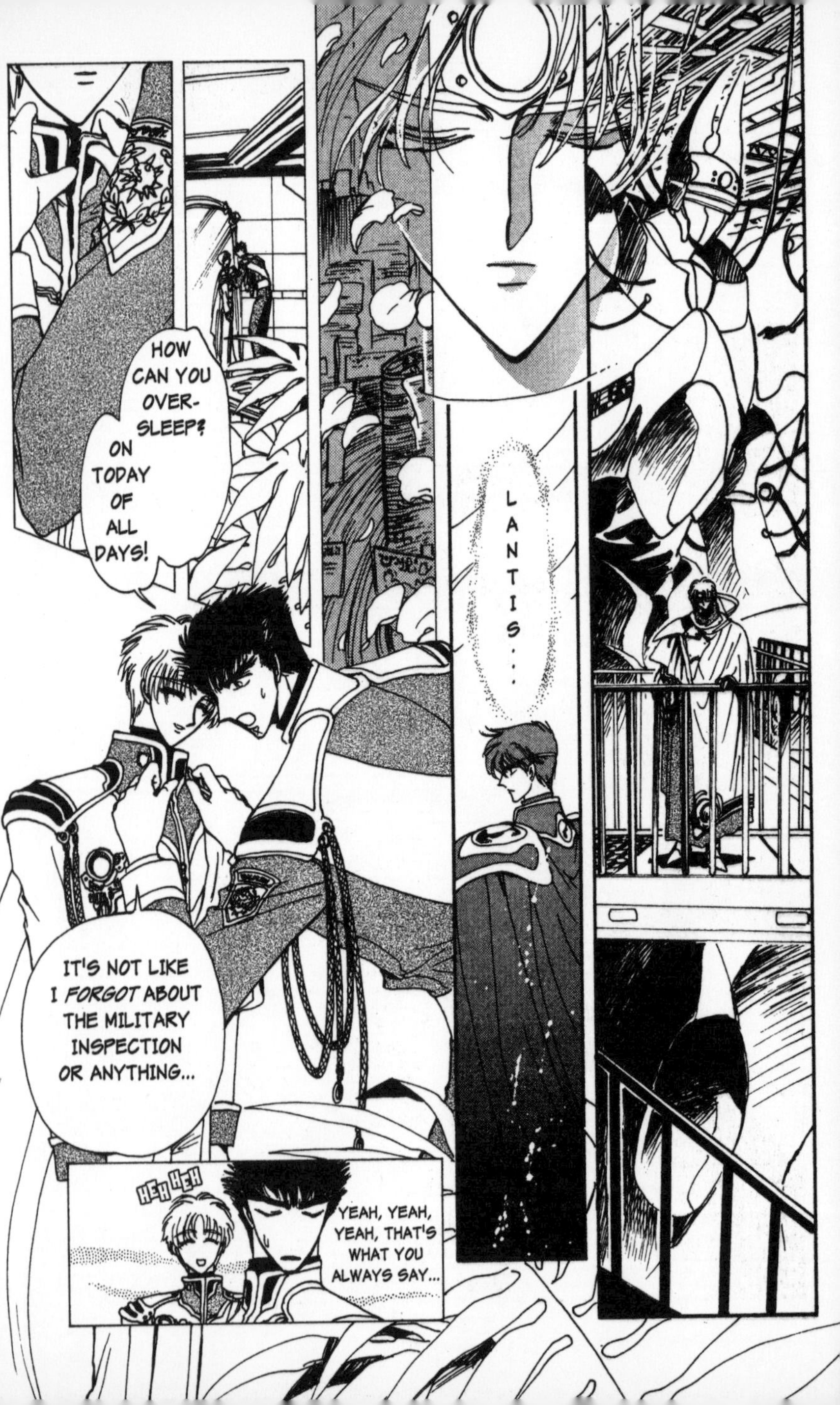
LANTIS...
HOW CAN YOU OVER-SLEEP? ON TODAY OF ALL DAYS!
IT'S NOT LIKE I *FORGOT* ABOUT THE MILITARY INSPECTION OR ANYTHING...
HEH HEH
YEAH, YEAH, YEAH, THAT'S WHAT YOU ALWAYS SAY...

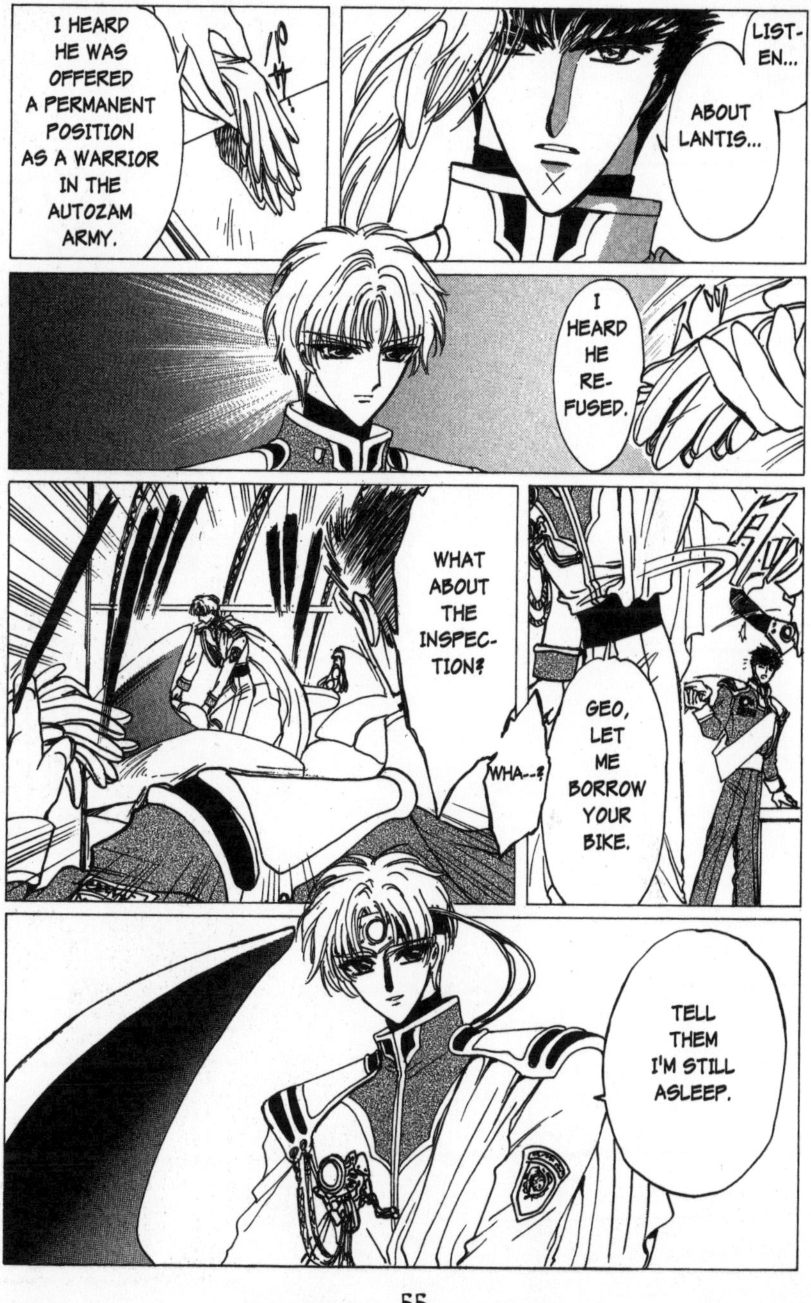
LIST-EN...
ABOUT LANTIS...
I HEARD HE WAS OFFERED A PERMANENT POSITION AS A WARRIOR IN THE AUTOZAM ARMY.
I HEARD HE RE-FUSED.
GEO, LET ME BORROW YOUR BIKE.
WHA--?
WHAT ABOUT THE INSPEC-TION?
TELL THEM I'M STILL ASLEEP.

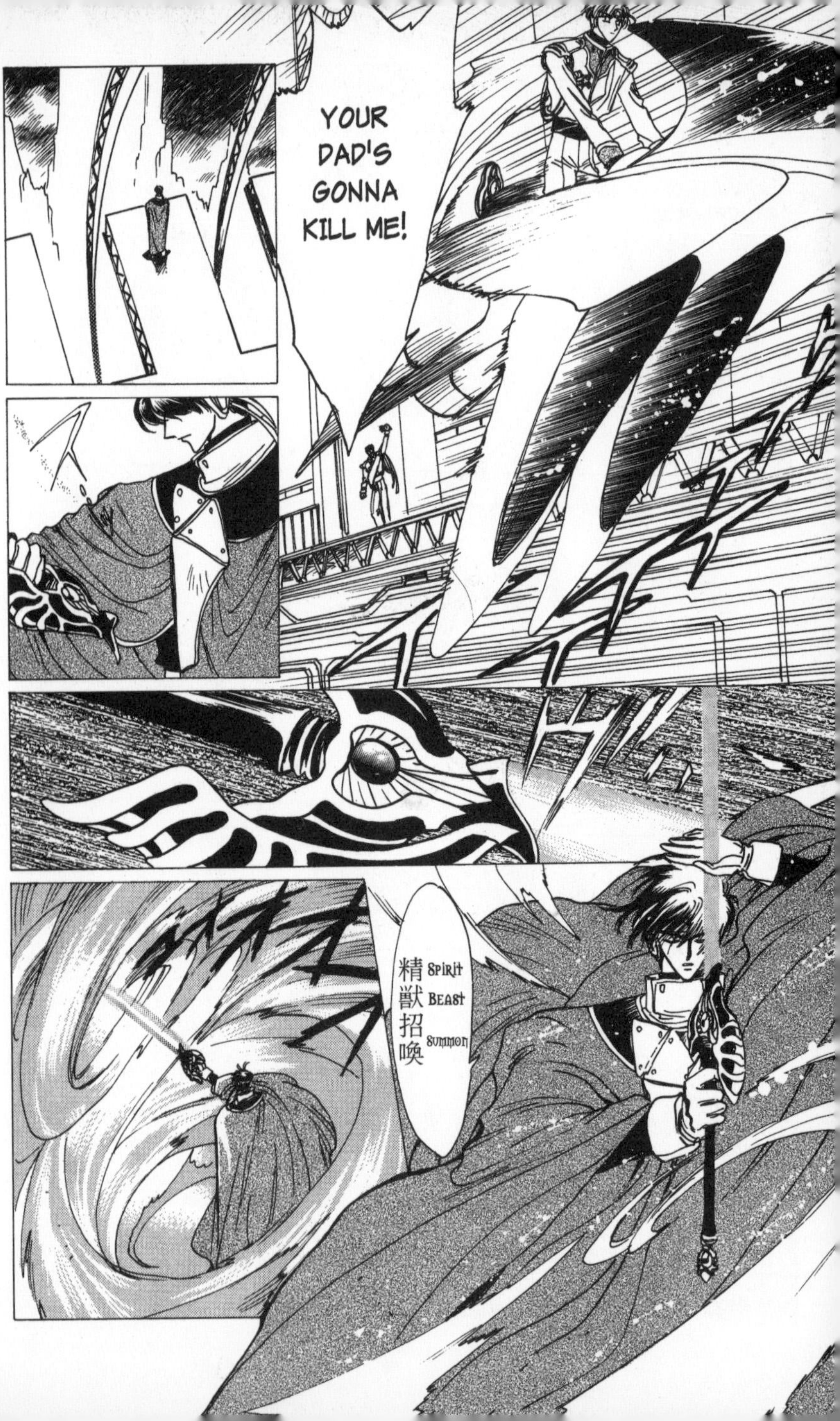
YOUR DAD'S GONNA KILL ME!
精獣招喚 Spirit Beast Summon

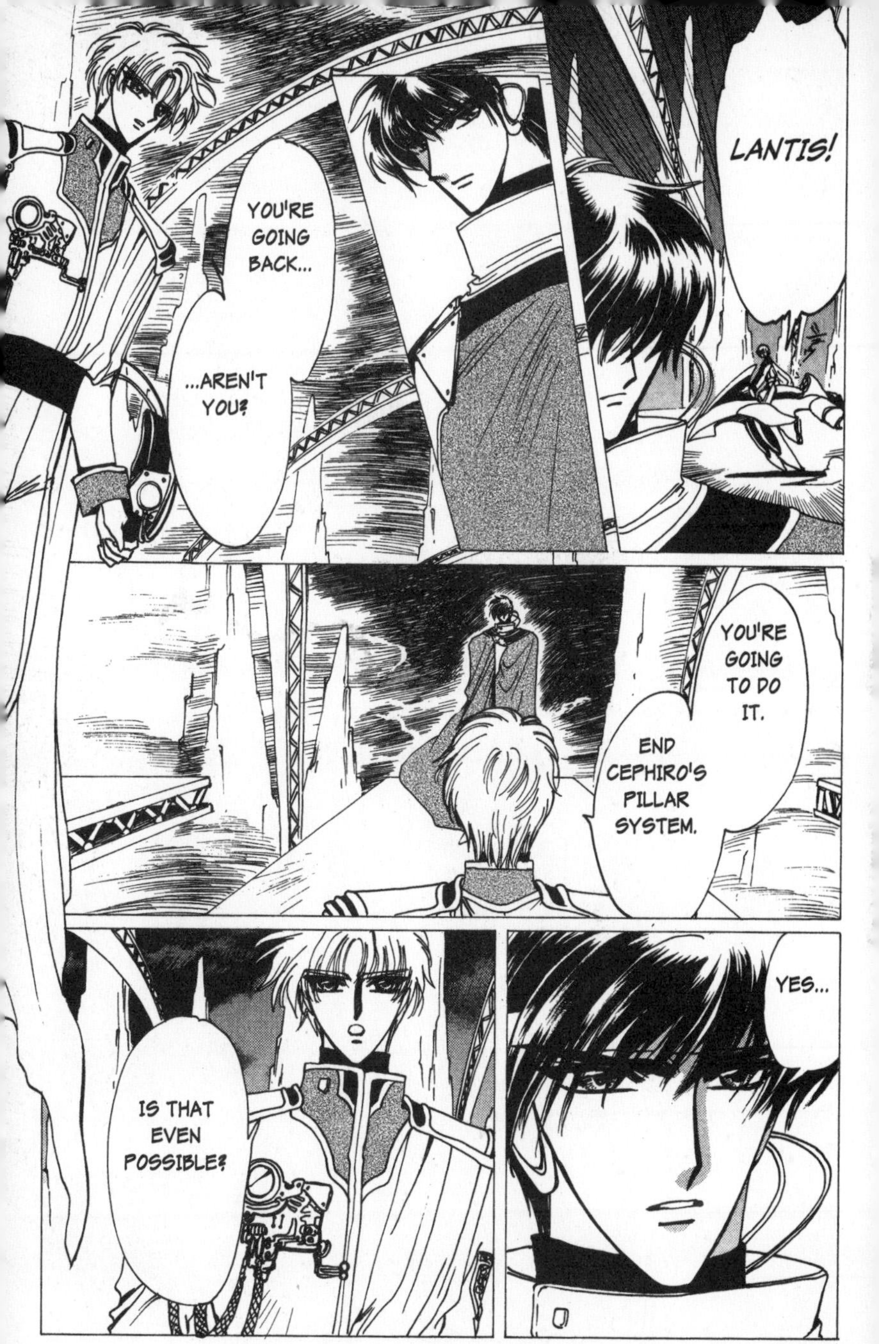
LANTIS!
YOU'RE GOING BACK...
...AREN'T YOU?
YOU'RE GOING TO DO IT.
END CEPHIRO'S PILLAR SYSTEM.
YES...
IS THAT EVEN POSSIBLE?

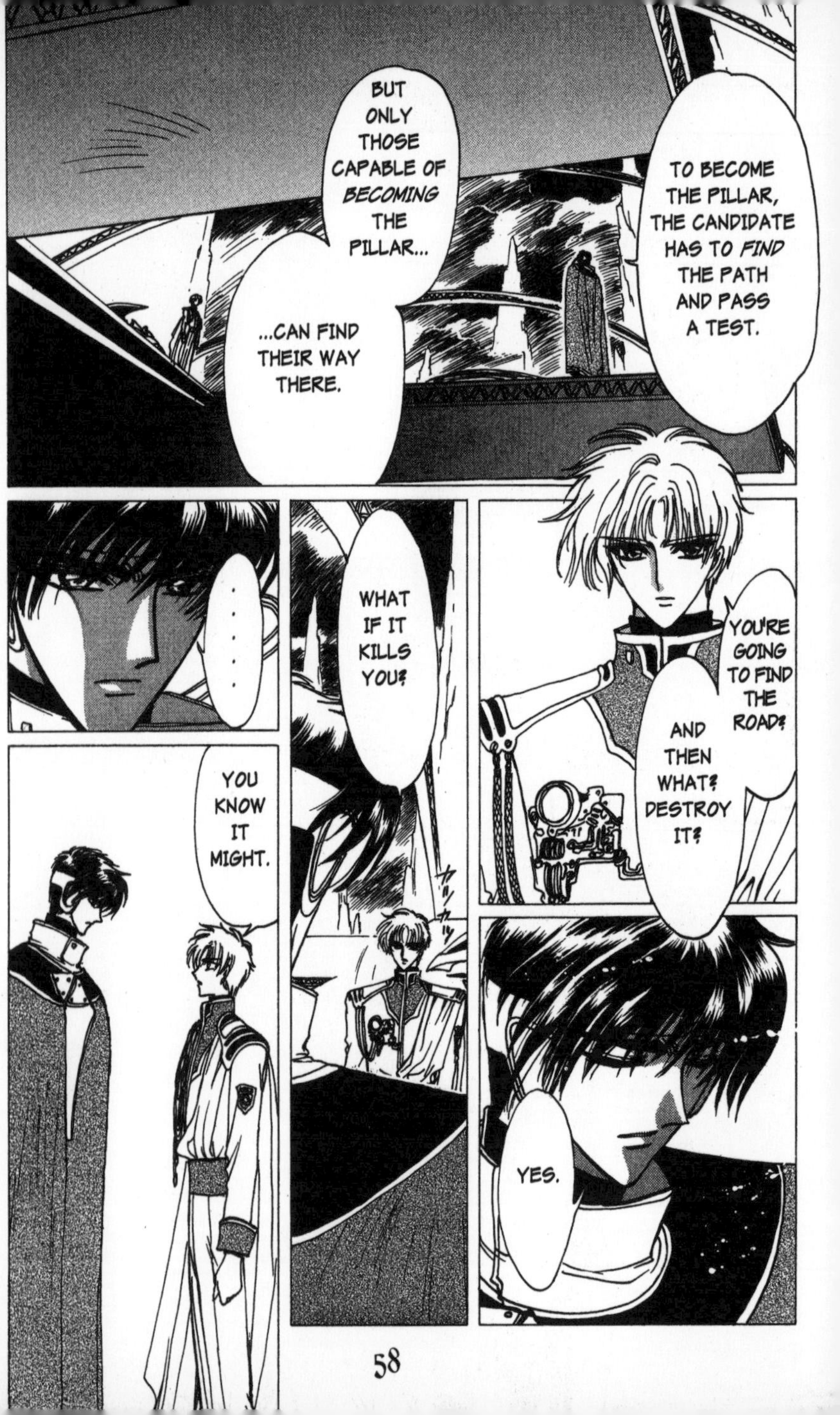
TO BECOME THE PILLAR, THE CANDIDATE HAS TO *FIND* THE PATH AND PASS A TEST.
BUT ONLY THOSE CAPABLE OF *BECOMING* THE PILLAR...
...CAN FIND THEIR WAY THERE.
YOU'RE GOING TO FIND THE ROAD?
AND THEN WHAT? DESTROY IT?
YES.
WHAT IF IT KILLS YOU?
· · · · ·
YOU KNOW IT MIGHT.

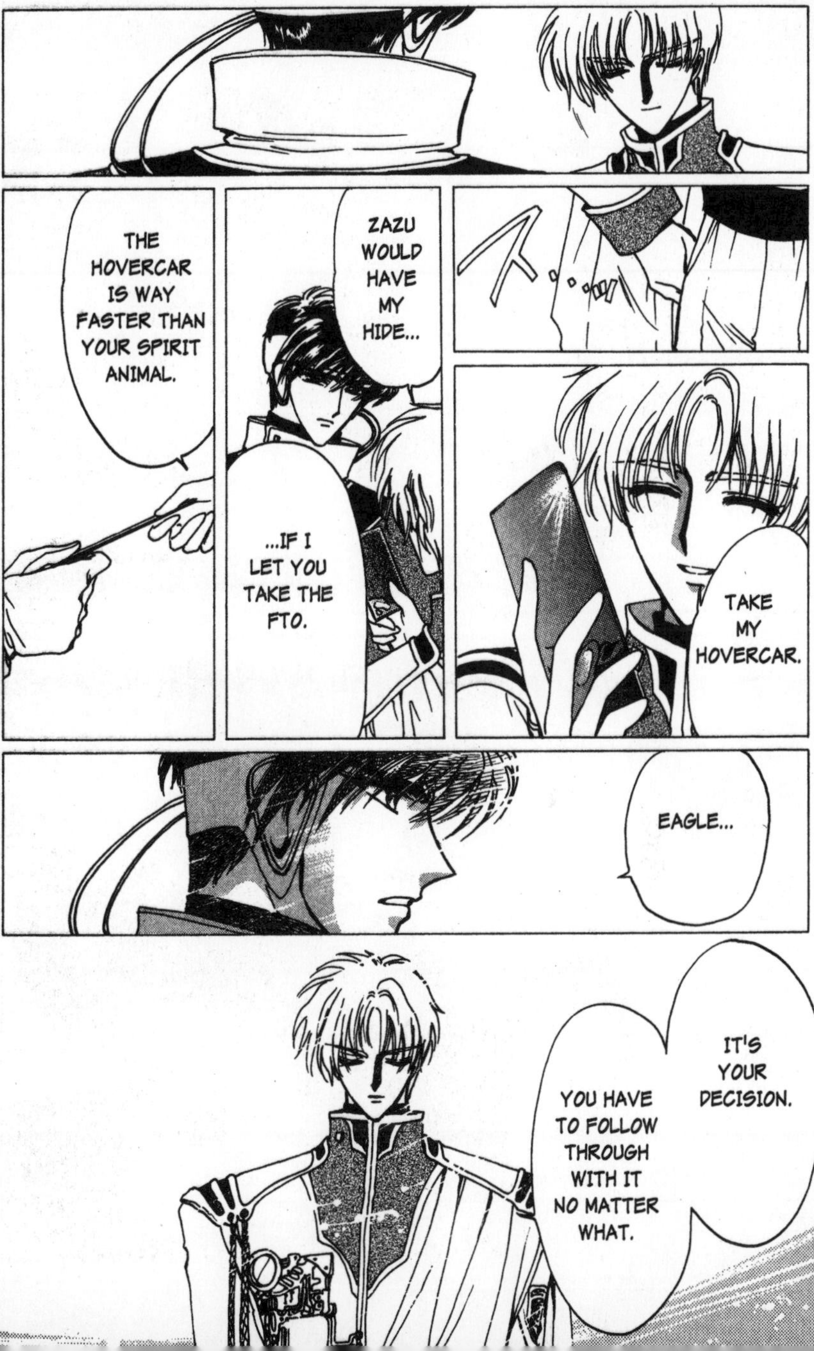
TAKE MY HOVERCAR.
ZAZU WOULD HAVE MY HIDE...
...IF I LET YOU TAKE THE FTO.
THE HOVERCAR IS WAY FASTER THAN YOUR SPIRIT ANIMAL.
EAGLE...
IT'S YOUR DECISION.
YOU HAVE TO FOLLOW THROUGH WITH IT NO MATTER WHAT.

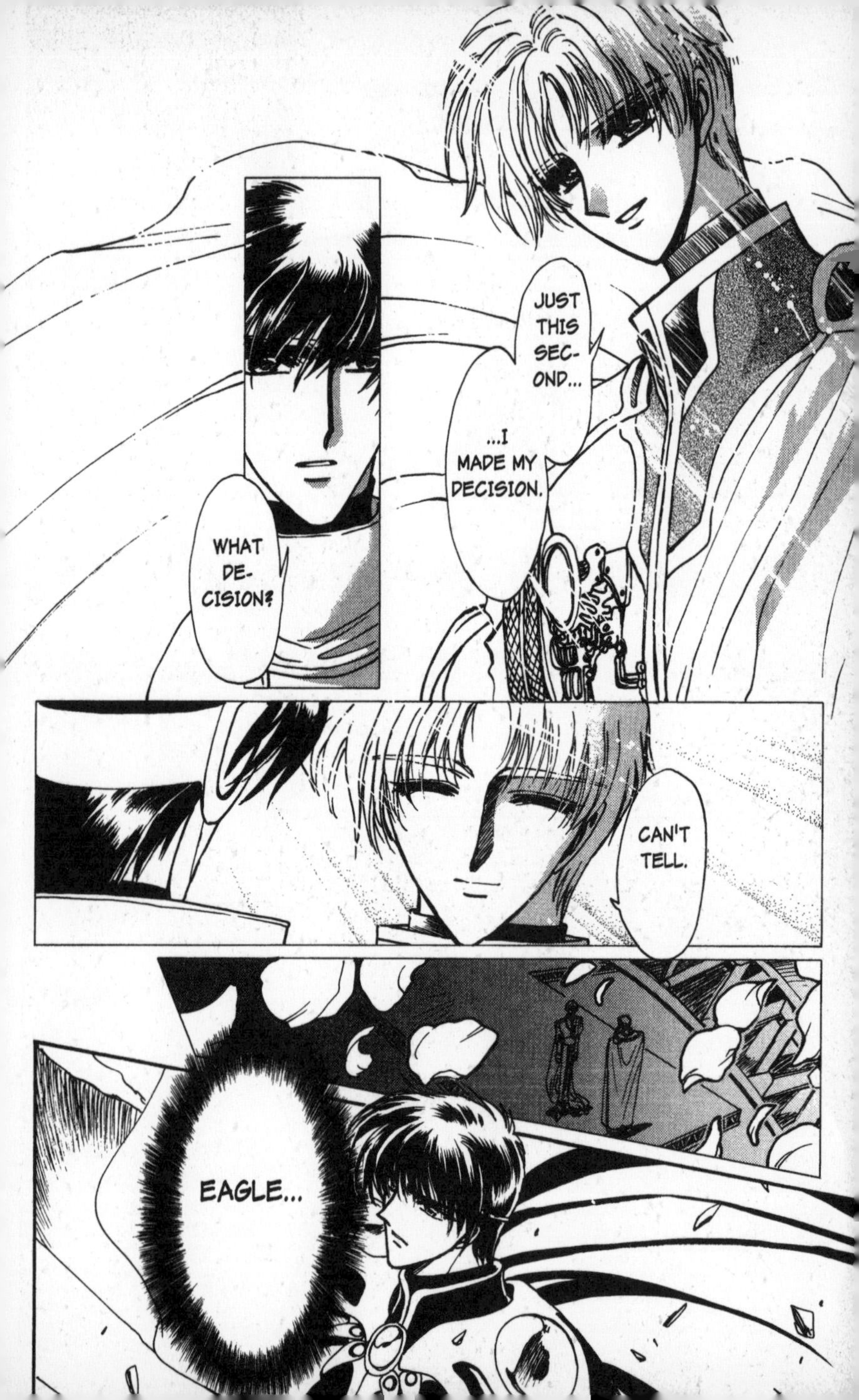
JUST THIS SEC-OND...
...I MADE MY DECISION.
WHAT DE-CISION?
CAN'T TELL.
EAGLE...

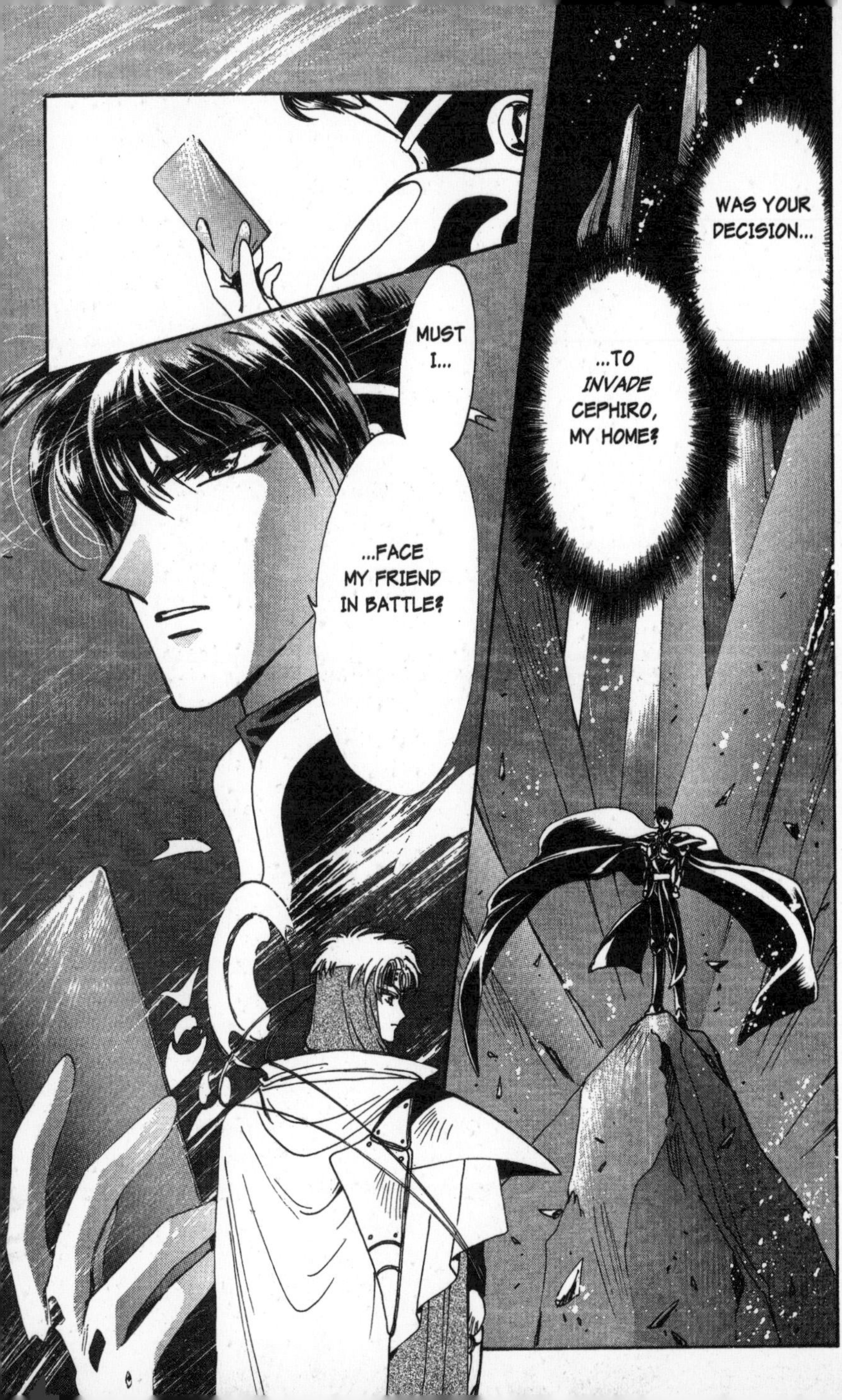
WAS YOUR DECISION...
...TO INVADE CEPHIRO, MY HOME?
MUST I...
...FACE MY FRIEND IN BATTLE?

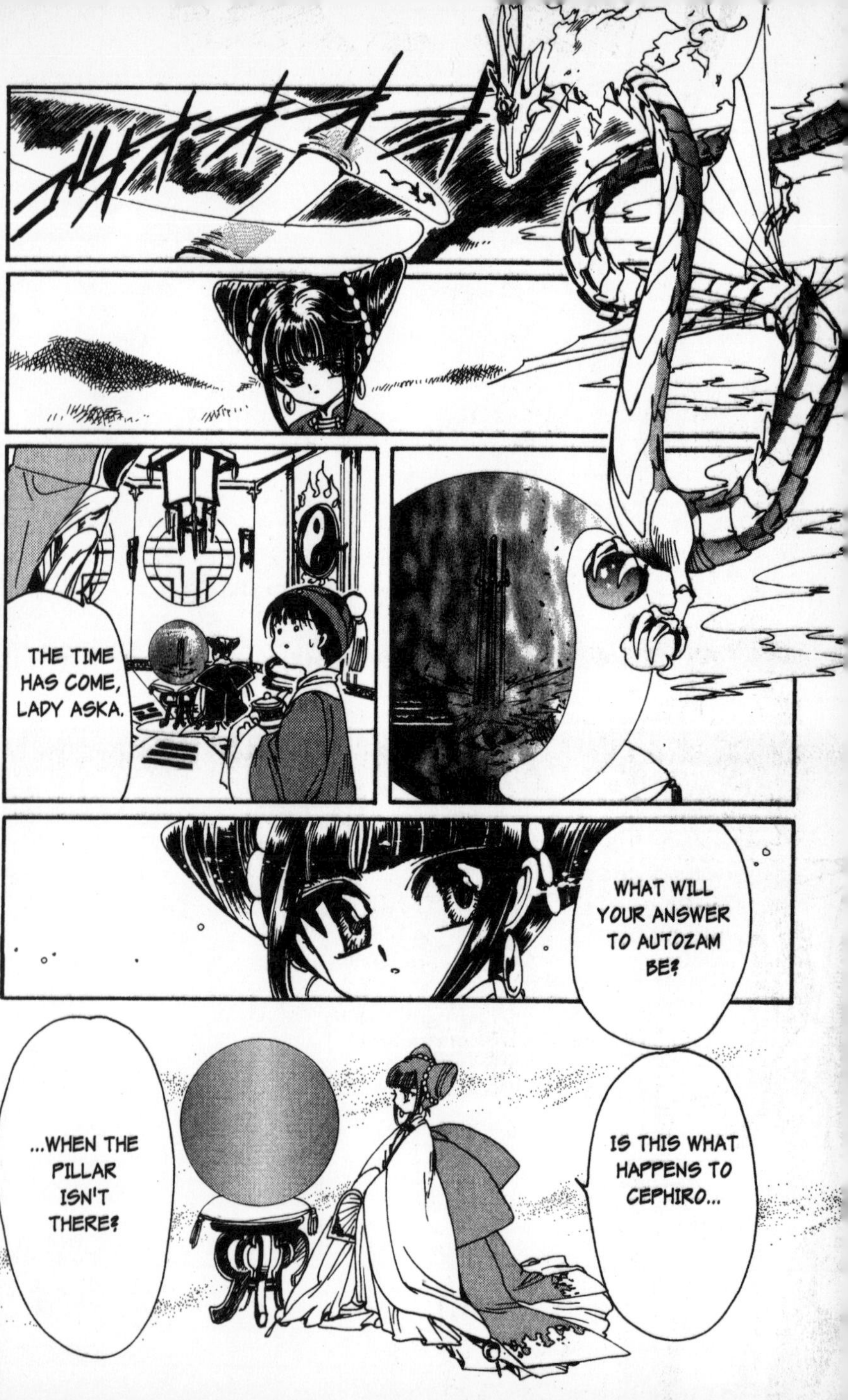
THE TIME HAS COME, LADY ASKA.
WHAT WILL YOUR ANSWER TO AUTOZAM BE?
IS THIS WHAT HAPPENS TO CEPHIRO...
...WHEN THE PILLAR ISN'T THERE?

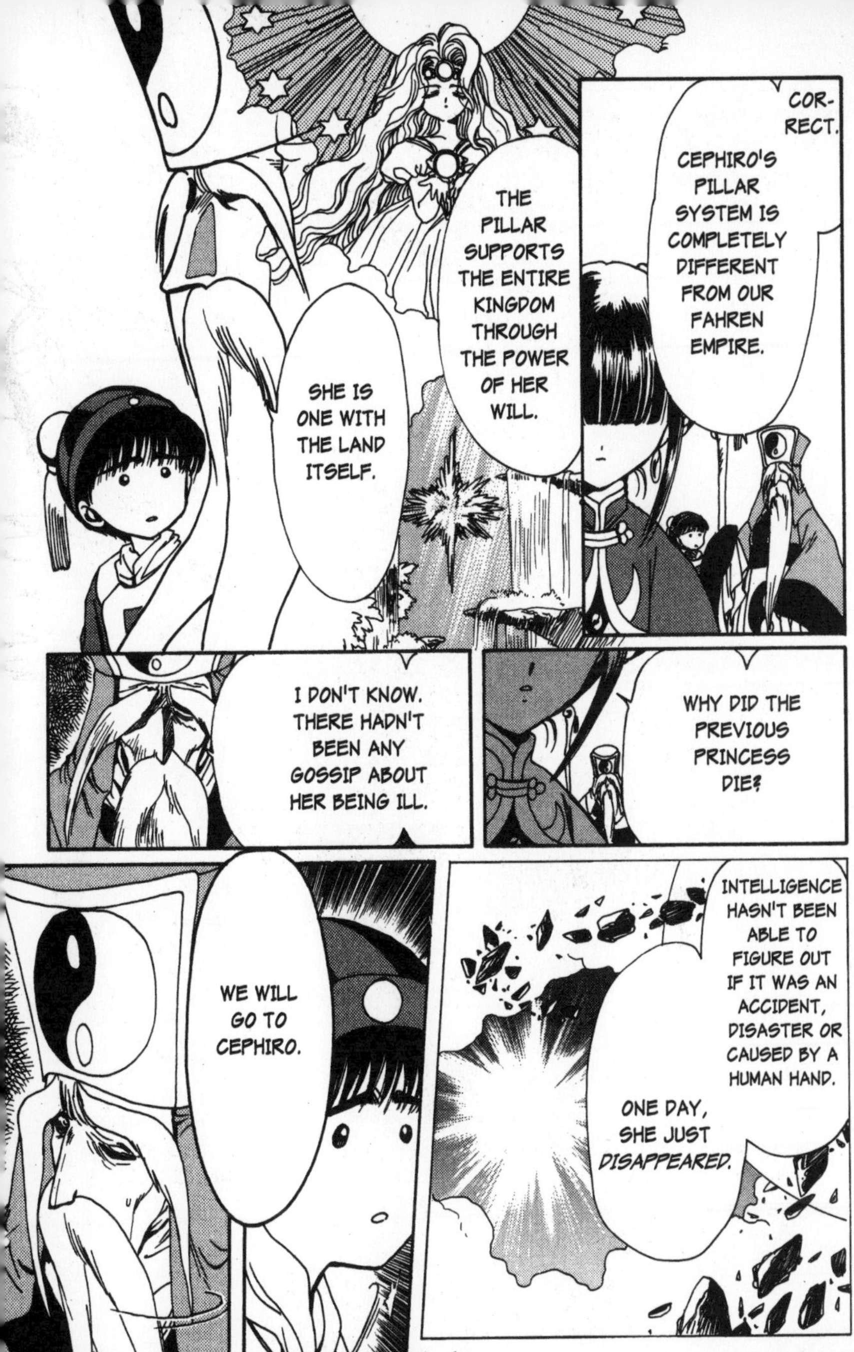
CORRECT.
CEPHIRO'S PILLAR SYSTEM IS COMPLETELY DIFFERENT FROM OUR FAHREN EMPIRE.
THE PILLAR SUPPORTS THE ENTIRE KINGDOM THROUGH THE POWER OF HER WILL.
SHE IS ONE WITH THE LAND ITSELF.
WHY DID THE PREVIOUS PRINCESS DIE?
I DON'T KNOW. THERE HADN'T BEEN ANY GOSSIP ABOUT HER BEING ILL.
INTELLIGENCE HASN'T BEEN ABLE TO FIGURE OUT IF IT WAS AN ACCIDENT, DISASTER OR CAUSED BY A HUMAN HAND.
ONE DAY, SHE JUST *DISAPPEARED.*
WE WILL GO TO CEPHIRO.

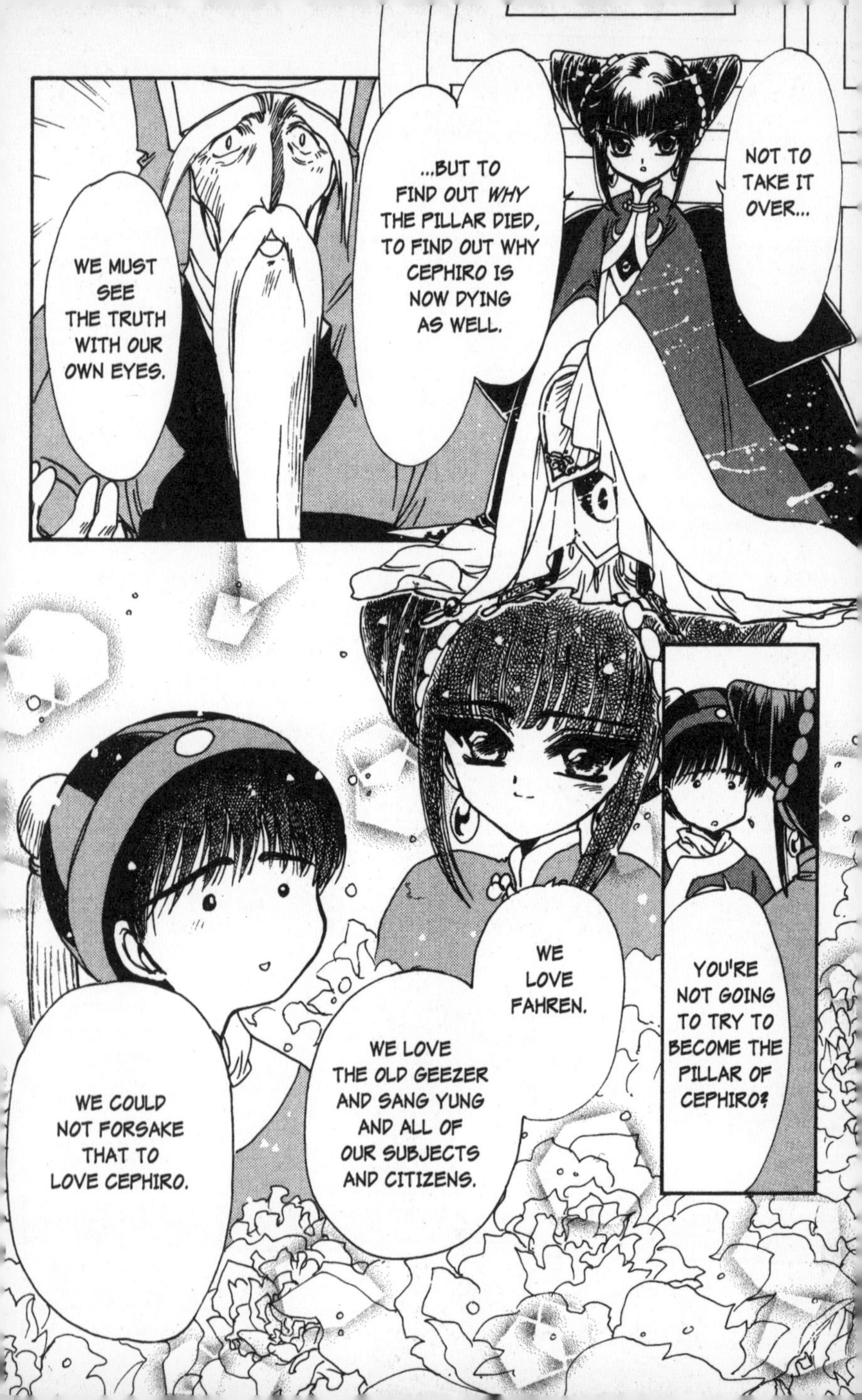
NOT TO TAKE IT OVER...
...BUT TO FIND OUT *WHY* THE PILLAR DIED, TO FIND OUT WHY CEPHIRO IS NOW DYING AS WELL.
WE MUST SEE THE TRUTH WITH OUR OWN EYES.
YOU'RE NOT GOING TO TRY TO BECOME THE PILLAR OF CEPHIRO?
WE LOVE FAHREN.
WE LOVE THE OLD GEEZER AND SANG YUNG AND ALL OF OUR SUBJECTS AND CITIZENS.
WE COULD NOT FORSAKE THAT TO LOVE CEPHIRO.

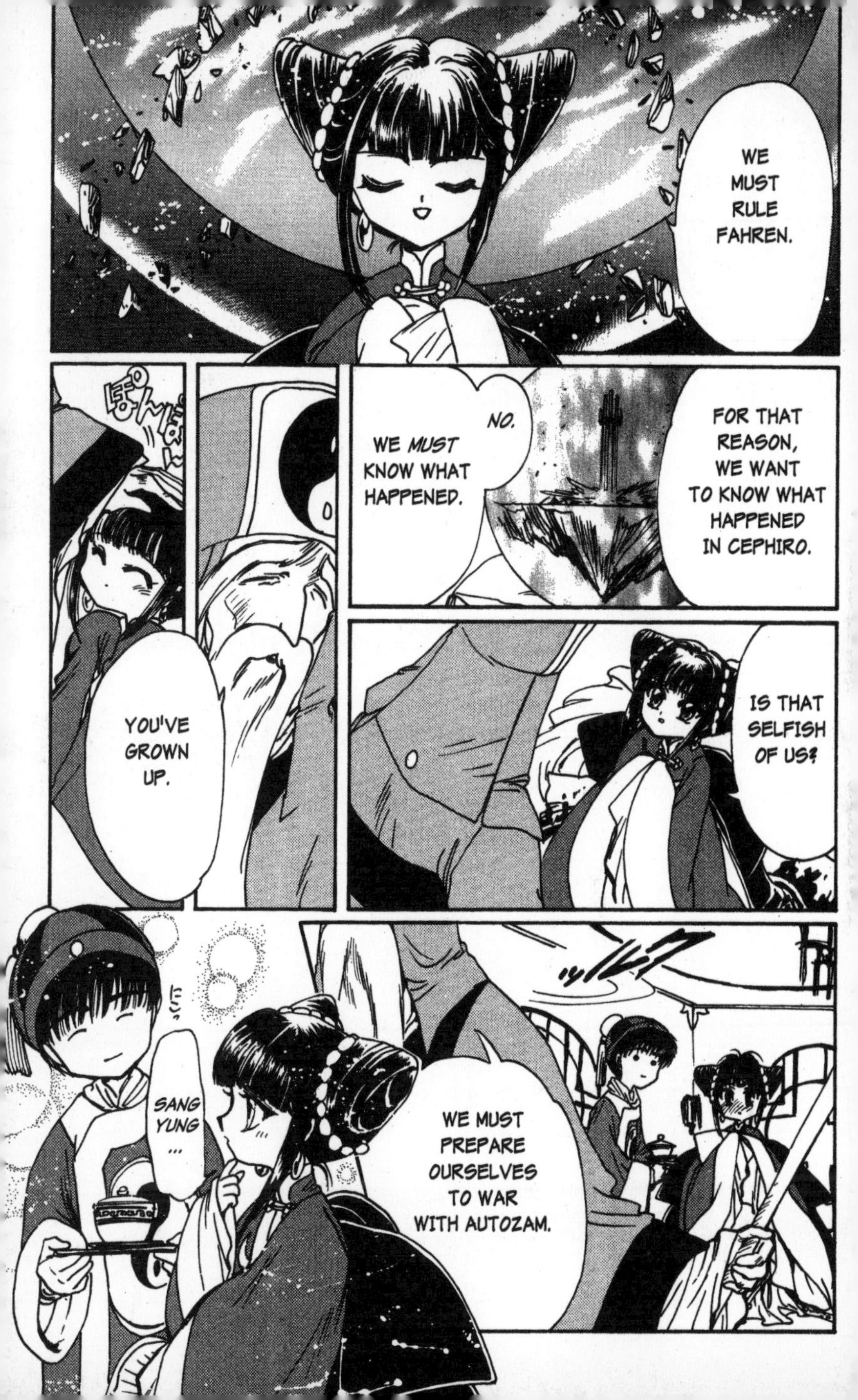
WE MUST RULE FAHREN.
FOR THAT REASON, WE WANT TO KNOW WHAT HAPPENED IN CEPHIRO.
NO.
WE *MUST* KNOW WHAT HAPPENED.
IS THAT SELFISH OF US?
YOU'VE GROWN UP.
WE MUST PREPARE OURSELVES TO WAR WITH AUTOZAM.
SANG YUNG ...

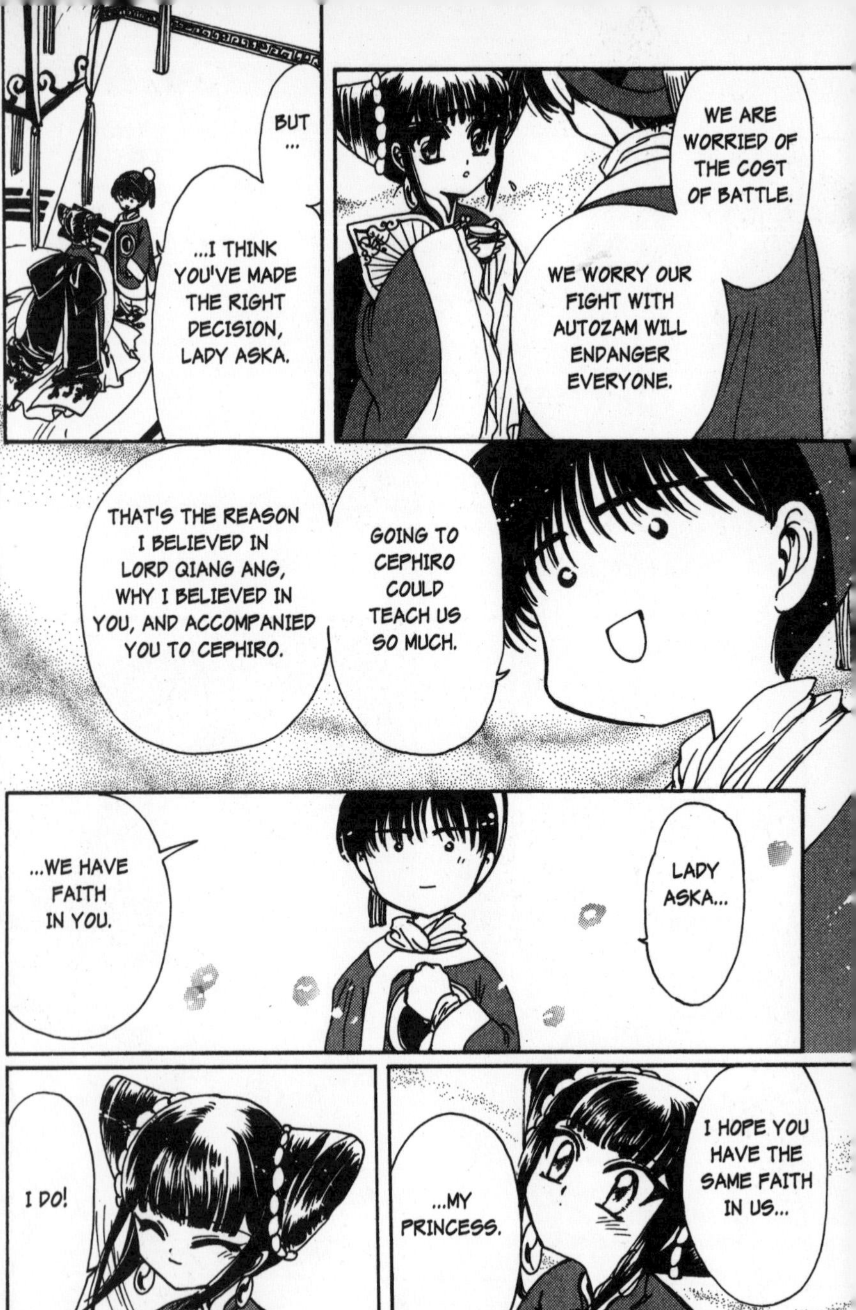
WE ARE WORRIED OF THE COST OF BATTLE.
WE WORRY OUR FIGHT WITH AUTOZAM WILL ENDANGER EVERYONE.
BUT ...
...I THINK YOU'VE MADE THE RIGHT DECISION, LADY ASKA.
GOING TO CEPHIRO COULD TEACH US SO MUCH.
THAT'S THE REASON I BELIEVED IN LORD QIANG ANG, WHY I BELIEVED IN YOU, AND ACCOMPANIED YOU TO CEPHIRO.
LADY ASKA...
...WE HAVE FAITH IN YOU.
I HOPE YOU HAVE THE SAME FAITH IN US...
...MY PRINCESS.
I DO!

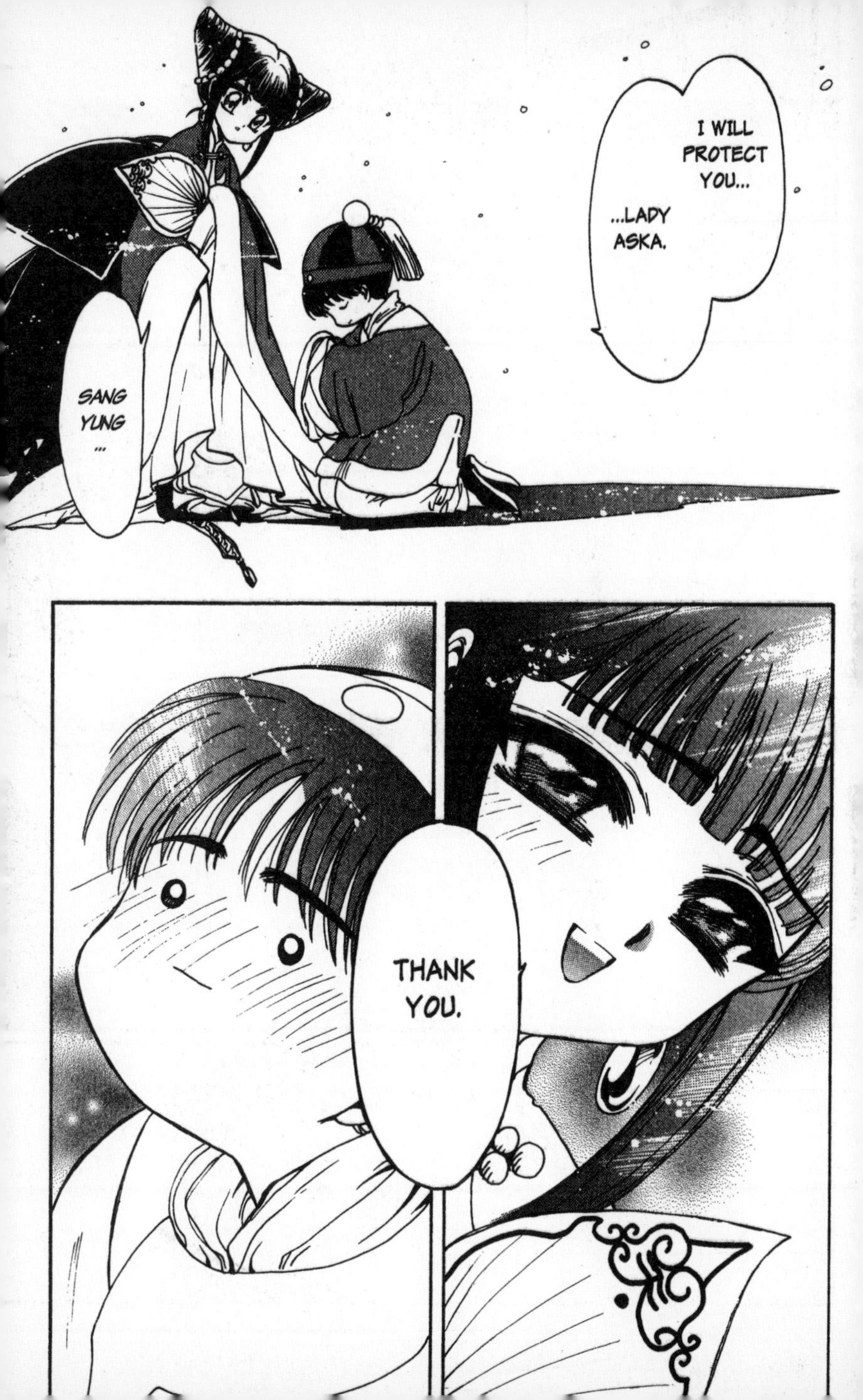
I WILL PROTECT YOU...
...LADY ASKA.
SANG YUNG ...
THANK YOU.

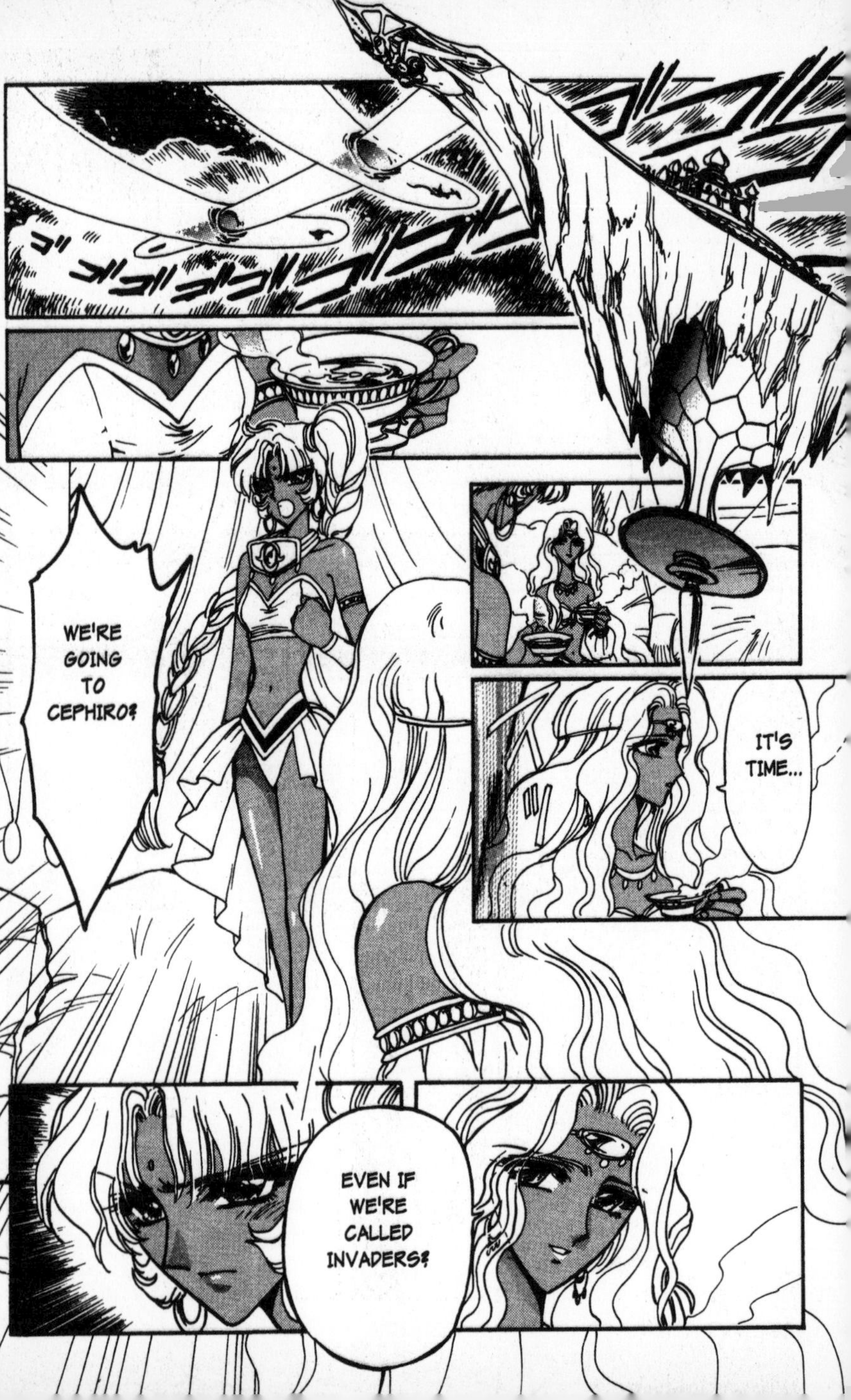
IT'S TIME...
WE'RE GOING TO CEPHIRO?
EVEN IF WE'RE CALLED INVADERS?

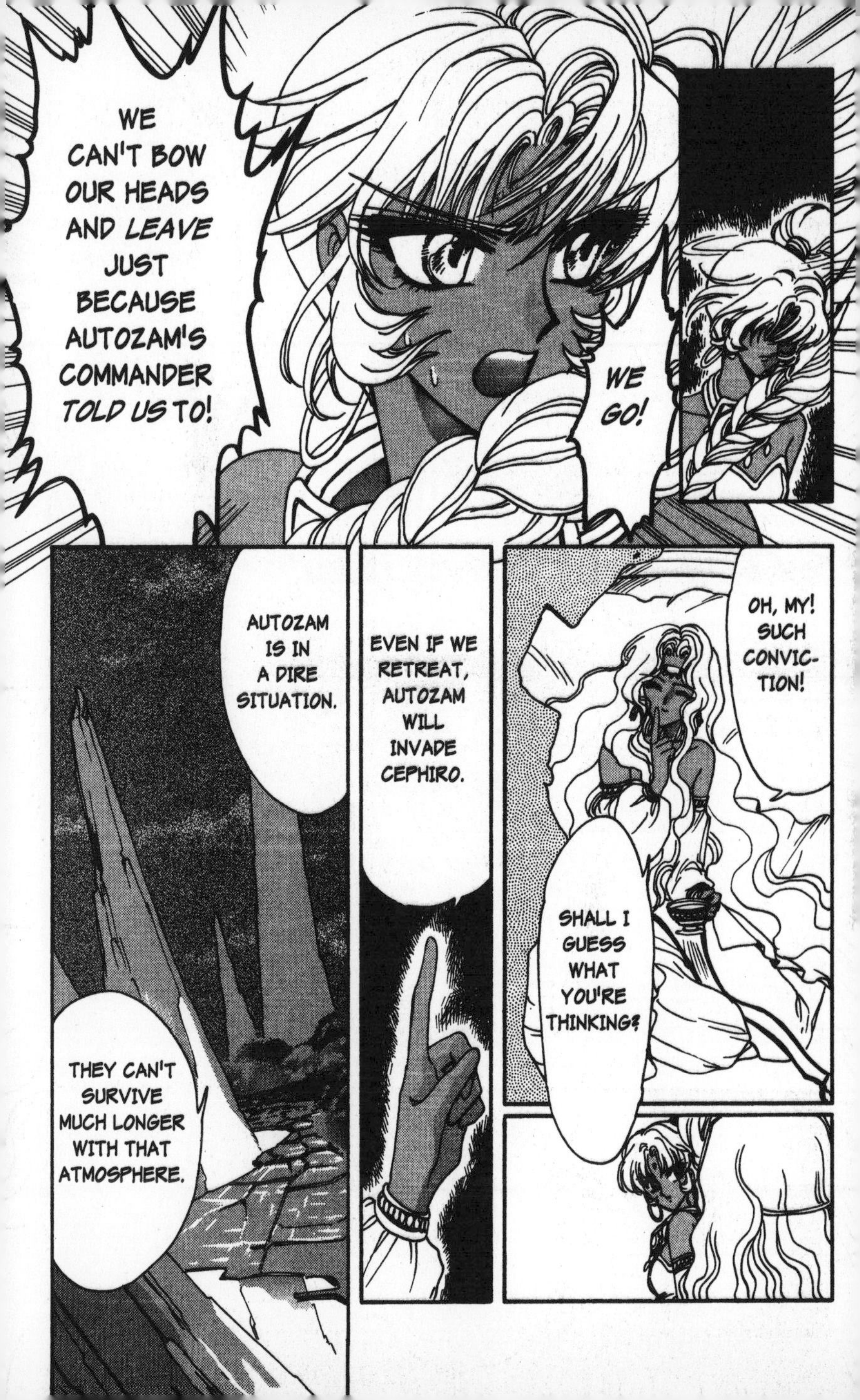
WE CAN'T BOW OUR HEADS AND *LEAVE* JUST BECAUSE AUTOZAM'S COMMANDER *TOLD US* TO!
WE GO!
OH, MY! SUCH CONVIC- TION!
SHALL I GUESS WHAT YOU'RE THINKING?
EVEN IF WE RETREAT, AUTOZAM WILL INVADE CEPHIRO.
AUTOZAM IS IN A DIRE SITUATION.
THEY CAN'T SURVIVE MUCH LONGER WITH THAT ATMOSPHERE.

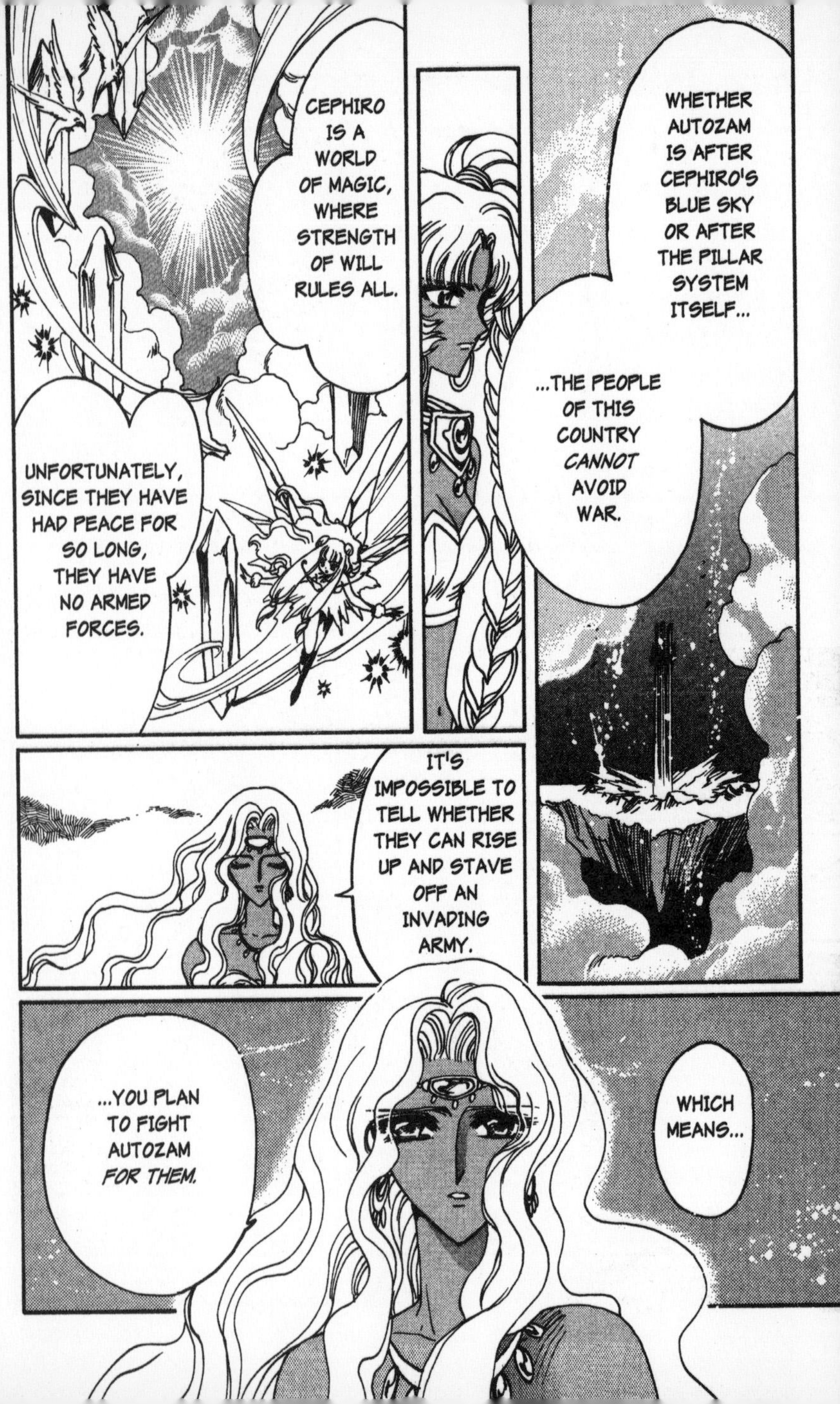
WHETHER AUTOZAM IS AFTER CEPHIRO'S BLUE SKY OR AFTER THE PILLAR SYSTEM ITSELF...
...THE PEOPLE OF THIS COUNTRY *CANNOT* AVOID WAR.
CEPHIRO IS A WORLD OF MAGIC, WHERE STRENGTH OF WILL RULES ALL.
UNFORTUNATELY, SINCE THEY HAVE HAD PEACE FOR SO LONG, THEY HAVE NO ARMED FORCES.
IT'S IMPOSSIBLE TO TELL WHETHER THEY CAN RISE UP AND STAVE OFF AN INVADING ARMY.
WHICH MEANS...
...YOU PLAN TO FIGHT AUTOZAM *FOR THEM.*

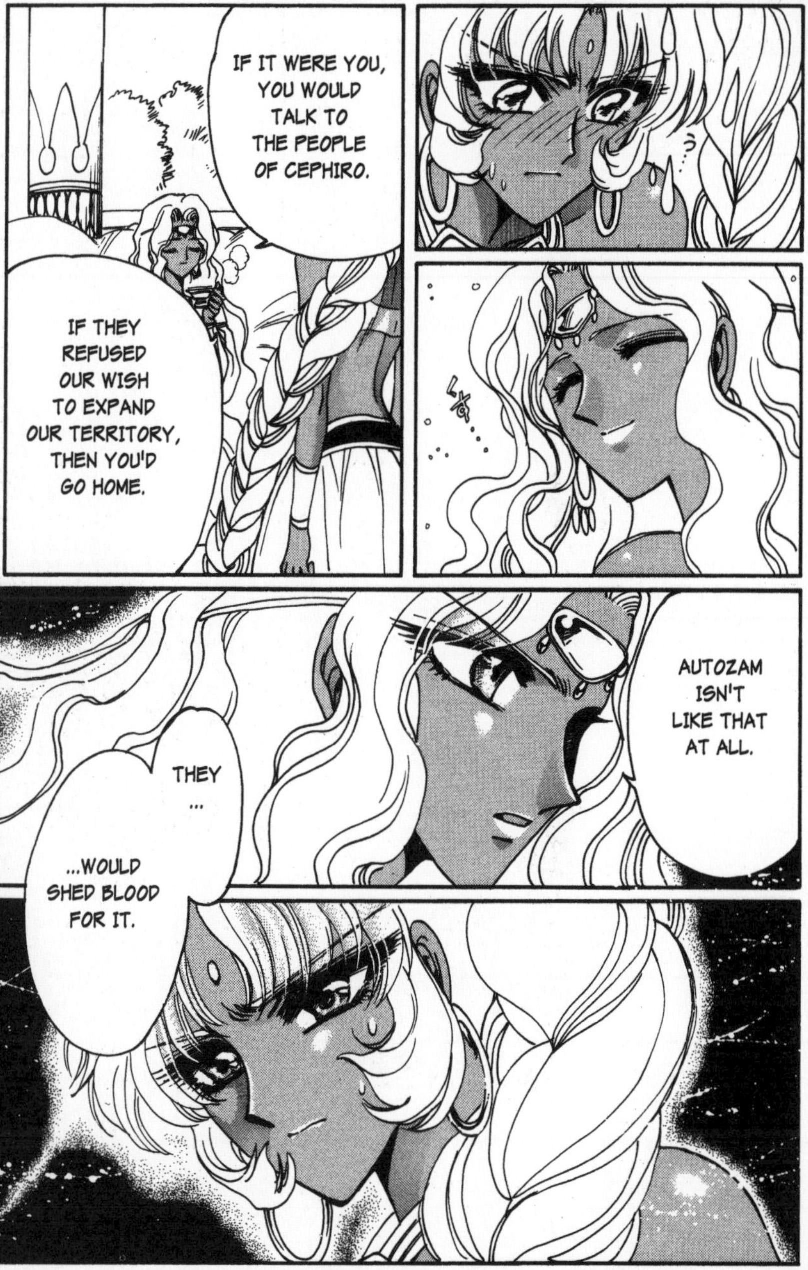
IF IT WERE YOU, YOU WOULD TALK TO THE PEOPLE OF CEPHIRO.
IF THEY REFUSED OUR WISH TO EXPAND OUR TERRITORY, THEN YOU'D GO HOME.
AUTOZAM ISN'T LIKE THAT AT ALL.
THEY ...
...WOULD SHED BLOOD FOR IT.

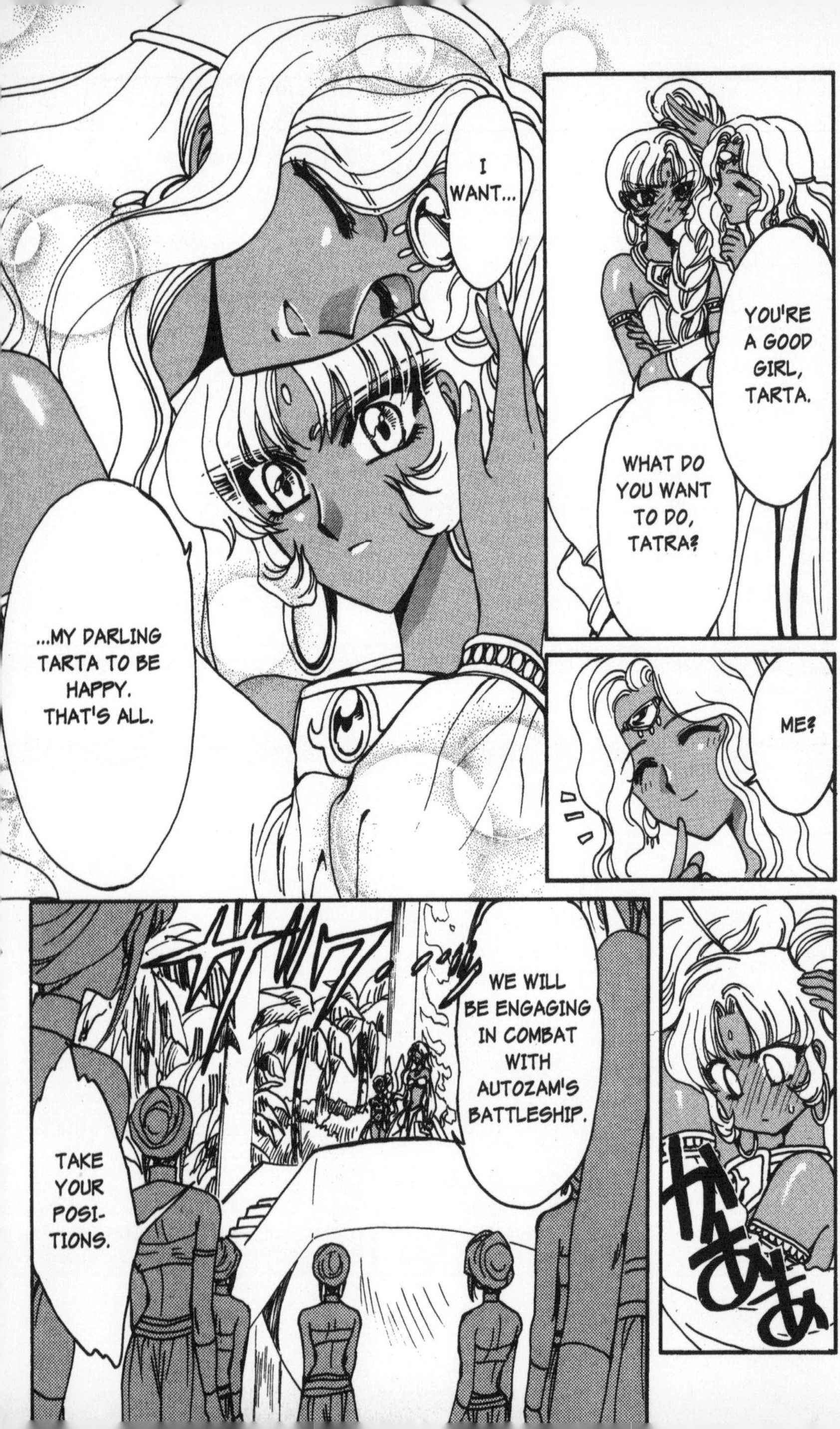
YOU'RE A GOOD GIRL, TARTA.
WHAT DO YOU WANT TO DO, TATRA?
ME?
I WANT...
...MY DARLING TARTA TO BE HAPPY. THAT'S ALL.
WE WILL BE ENGAGING IN COMBAT WITH AUTOZAM'S BATTLESHIP.
TAKE YOUR POSI-TIONS.

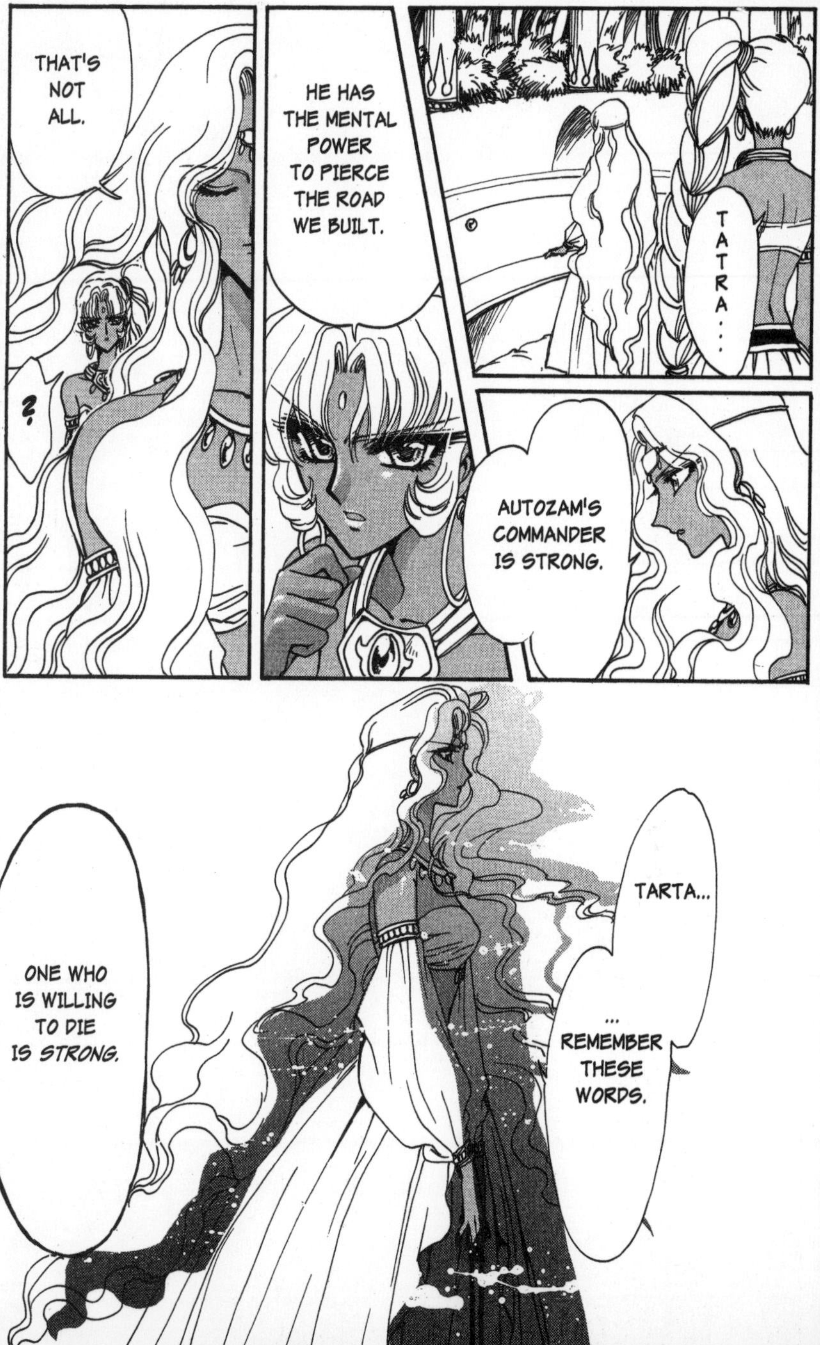
TATRA...
AUTOZAM'S COMMANDER IS STRONG.
HE HAS THE MENTAL POWER TO PIERCE THE ROAD WE BUILT.
THAT'S NOT ALL.
?
TARTA...
...REMEMBER THESE WORDS.
ONE WHO IS WILLING TO DIE IS *STRONG.*

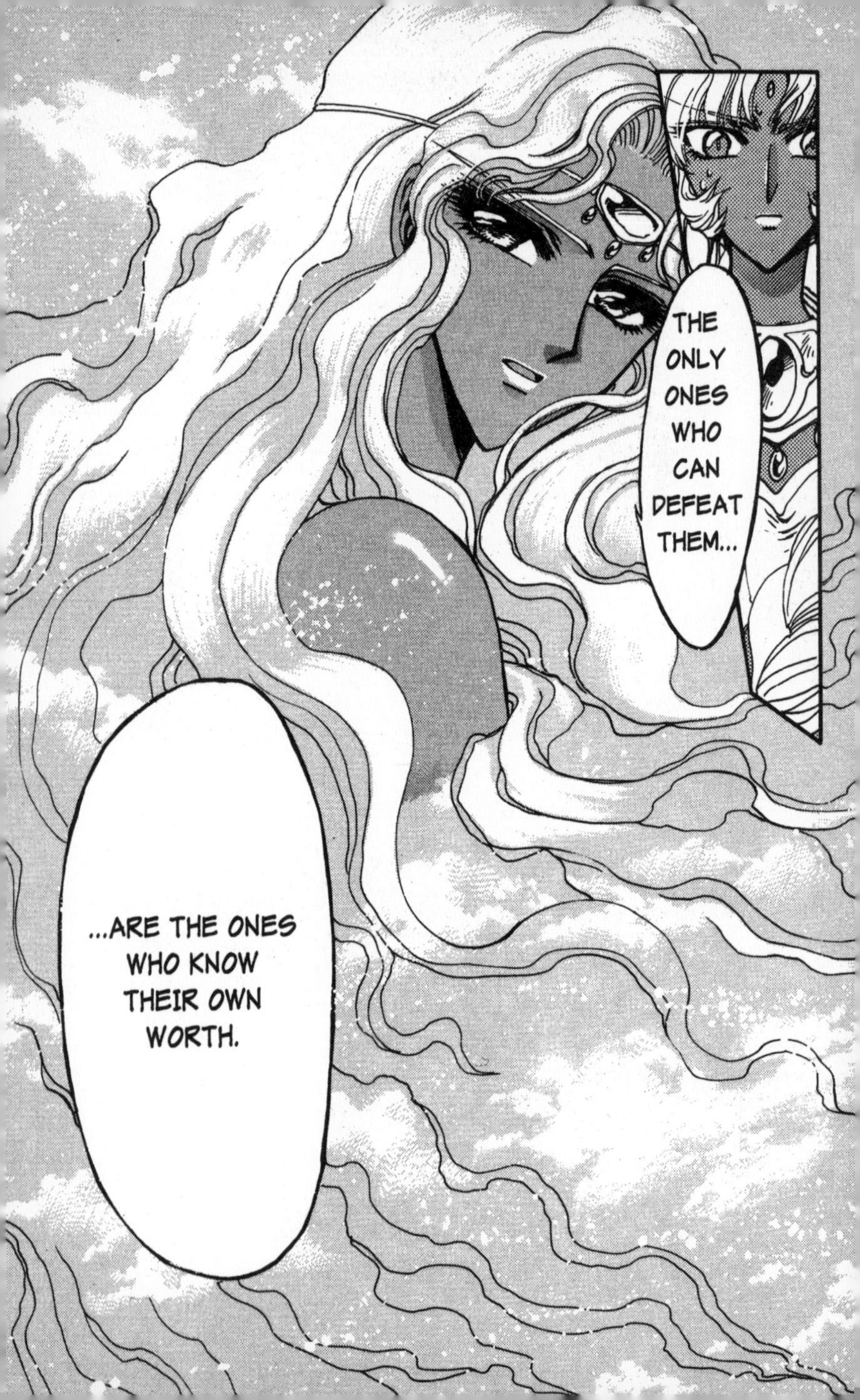
THE ONLY ONES WHO CAN DEFEAT THEM...
...ARE THE ONES WHO KNOW THEIR OWN WORTH.

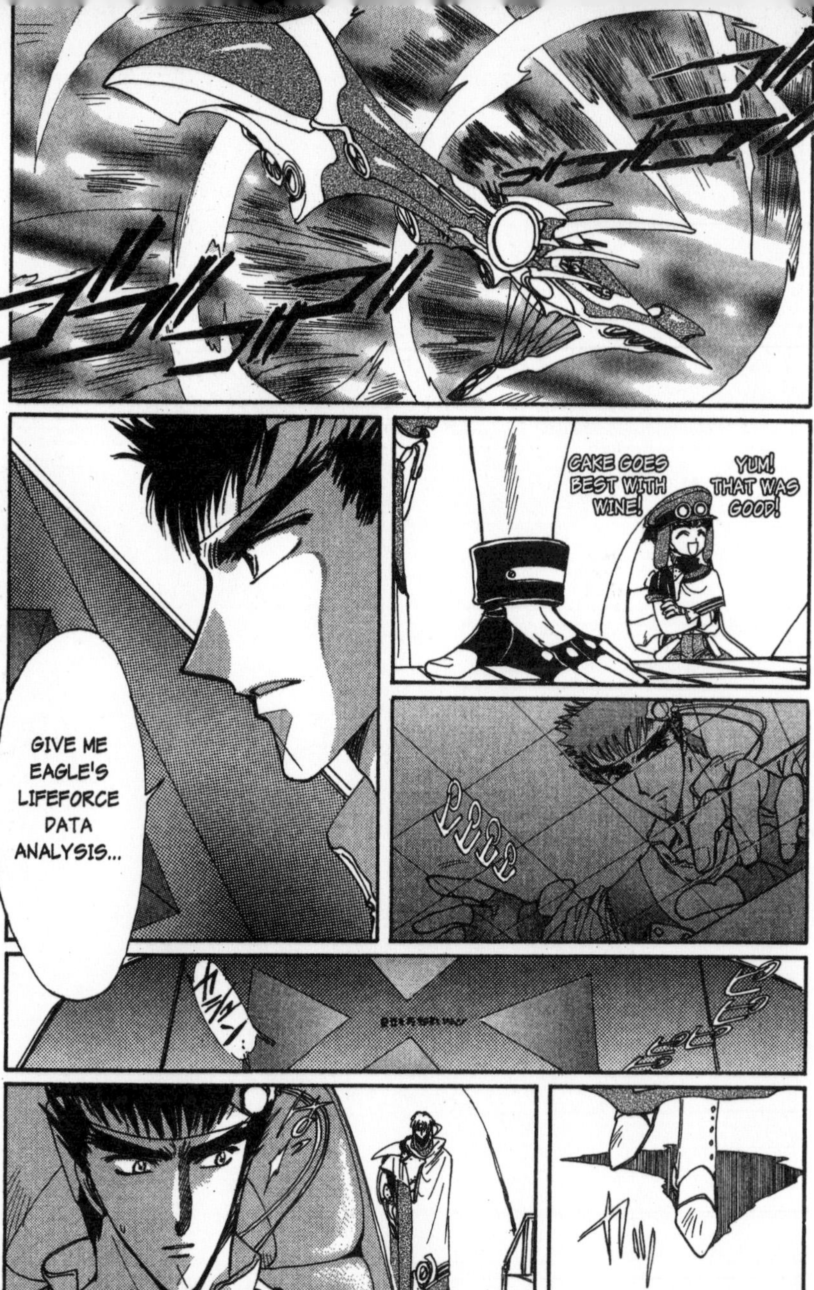
YUM! THAT WAS GOOD!
CAKE GOES BEST WITH WINE!
GIVE ME EAGLE'S LIFEFORCE DATA ANALYSIS...

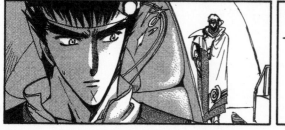

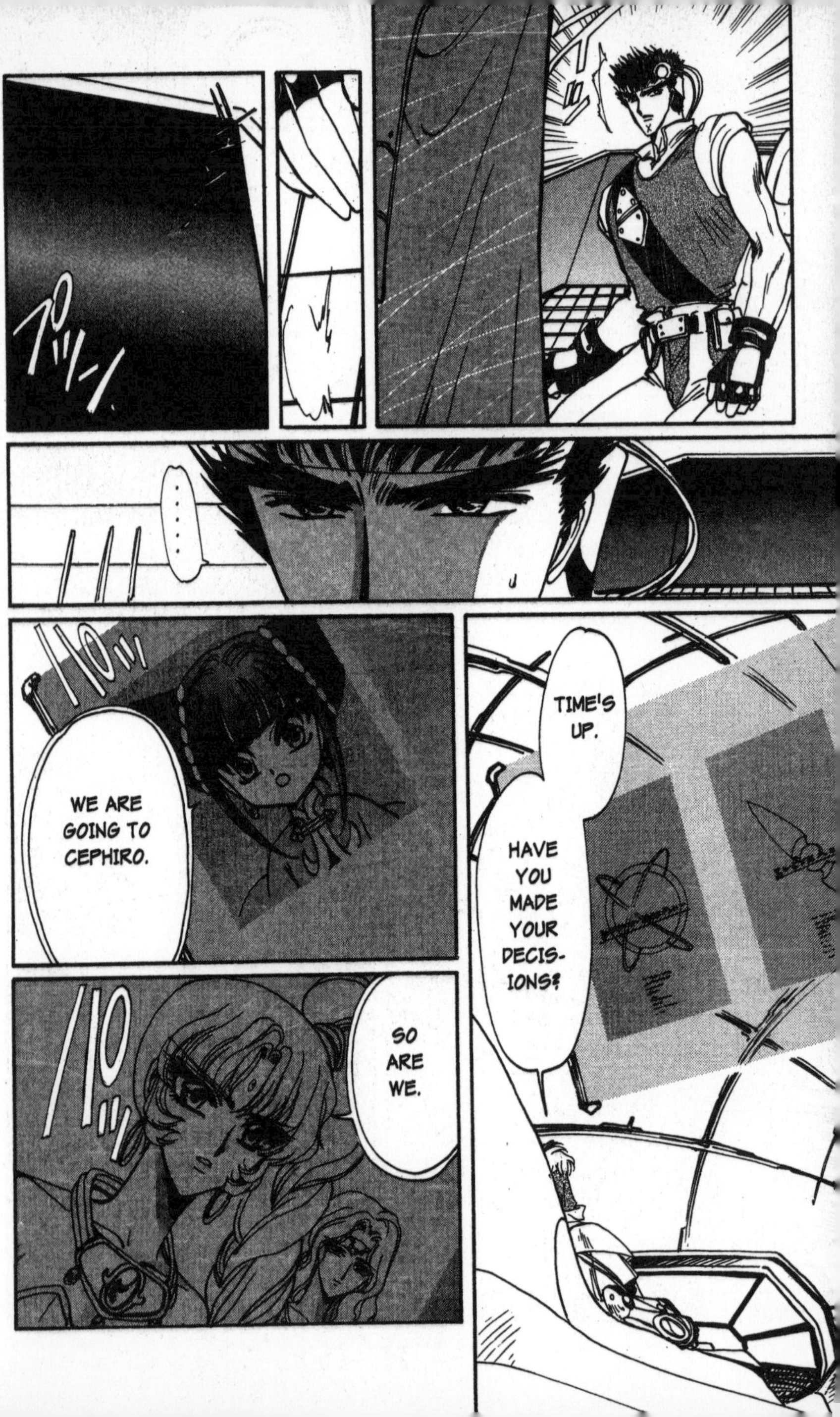
.....
TIME'S UP.
HAVE YOU MADE YOUR DECISIONS?
WE ARE GOING TO CEPHIRO.
SO ARE WE.

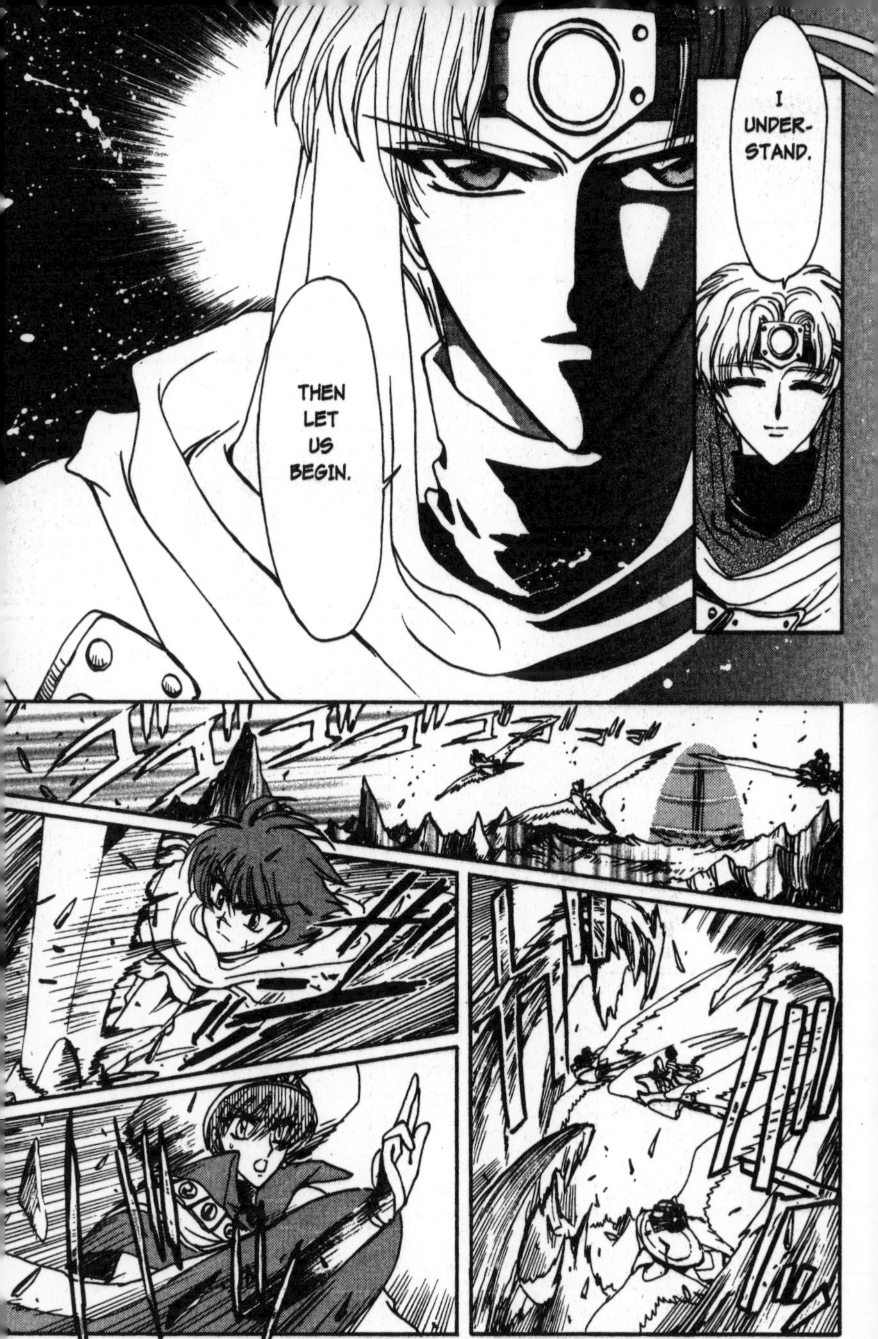
I UNDER-STAND.
THEN LET US BEGIN.

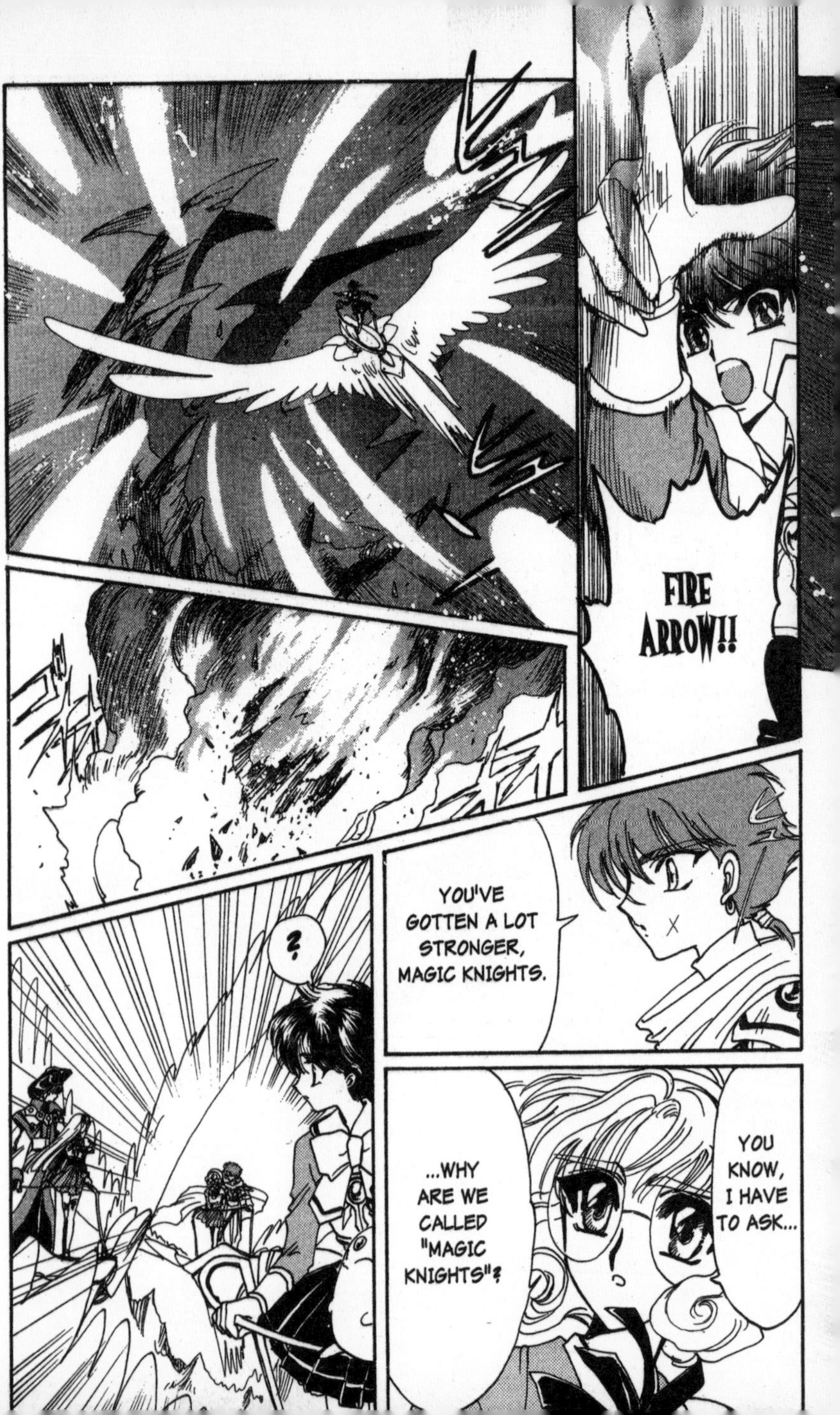
FIRE ARROW!!
YOU'VE GOTTEN A LOT STRONGER, MAGIC KNIGHTS.
?
YOU KNOW, I HAVE TO ASK...
...WHY ARE WE CALLED "MAGIC KNIGHTS"?

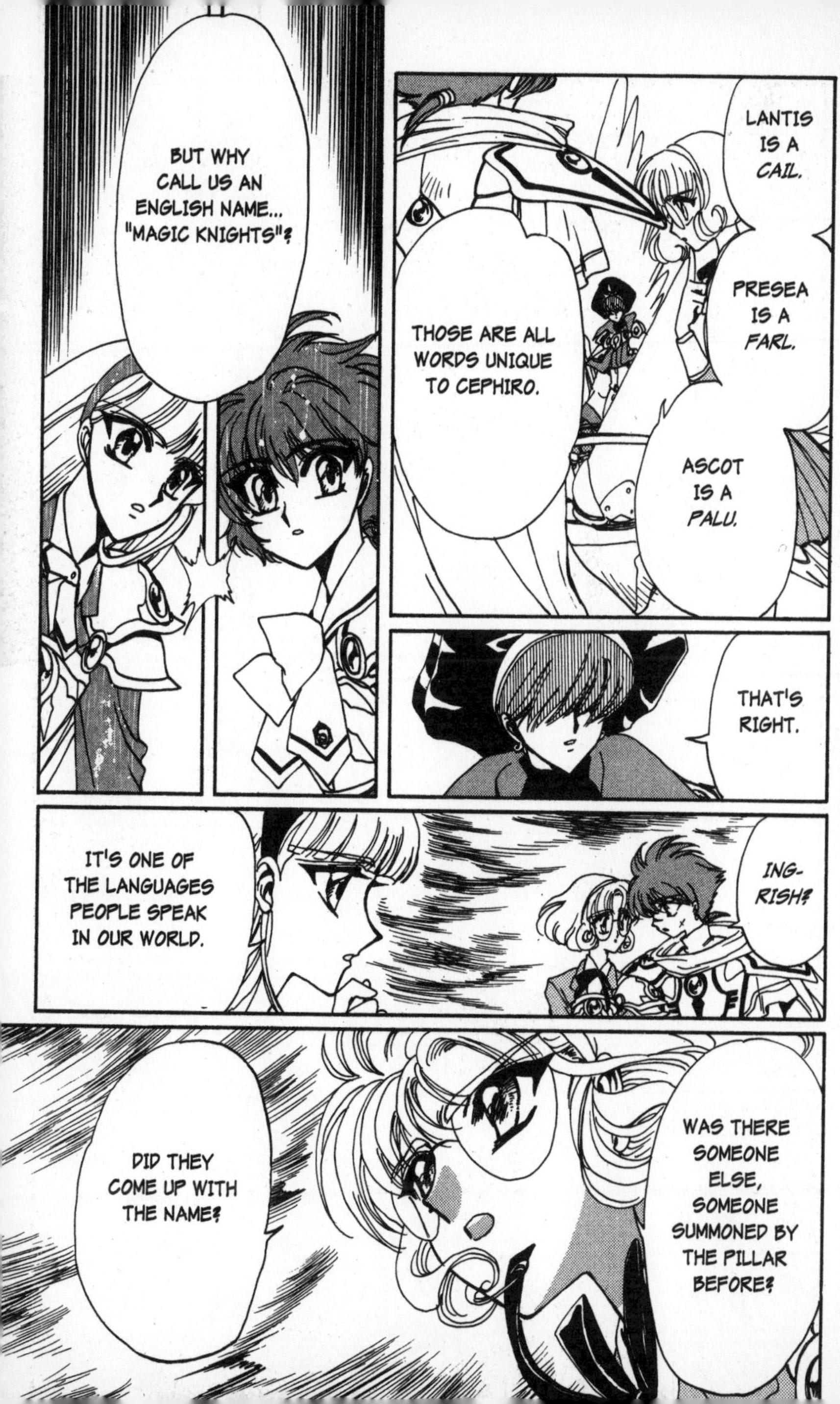

LANTIS IS A *CAIL.*
PRESEA IS A *FARL.*
ASCOT IS A *PALU.*
THOSE ARE ALL WORDS UNIQUE TO CEPHIRO.
THAT'S RIGHT.
BUT WHY CALL US AN ENGLISH NAME... "MAGIC KNIGHTS"?
ING-RISH?
IT'S ONE OF THE LANGUAGES PEOPLE SPEAK IN OUR WORLD.
WAS THERE SOMEONE ELSE, SOMEONE SUMMONED BY THE PILLAR BEFORE?
DID THEY COME UP WITH THE NAME?

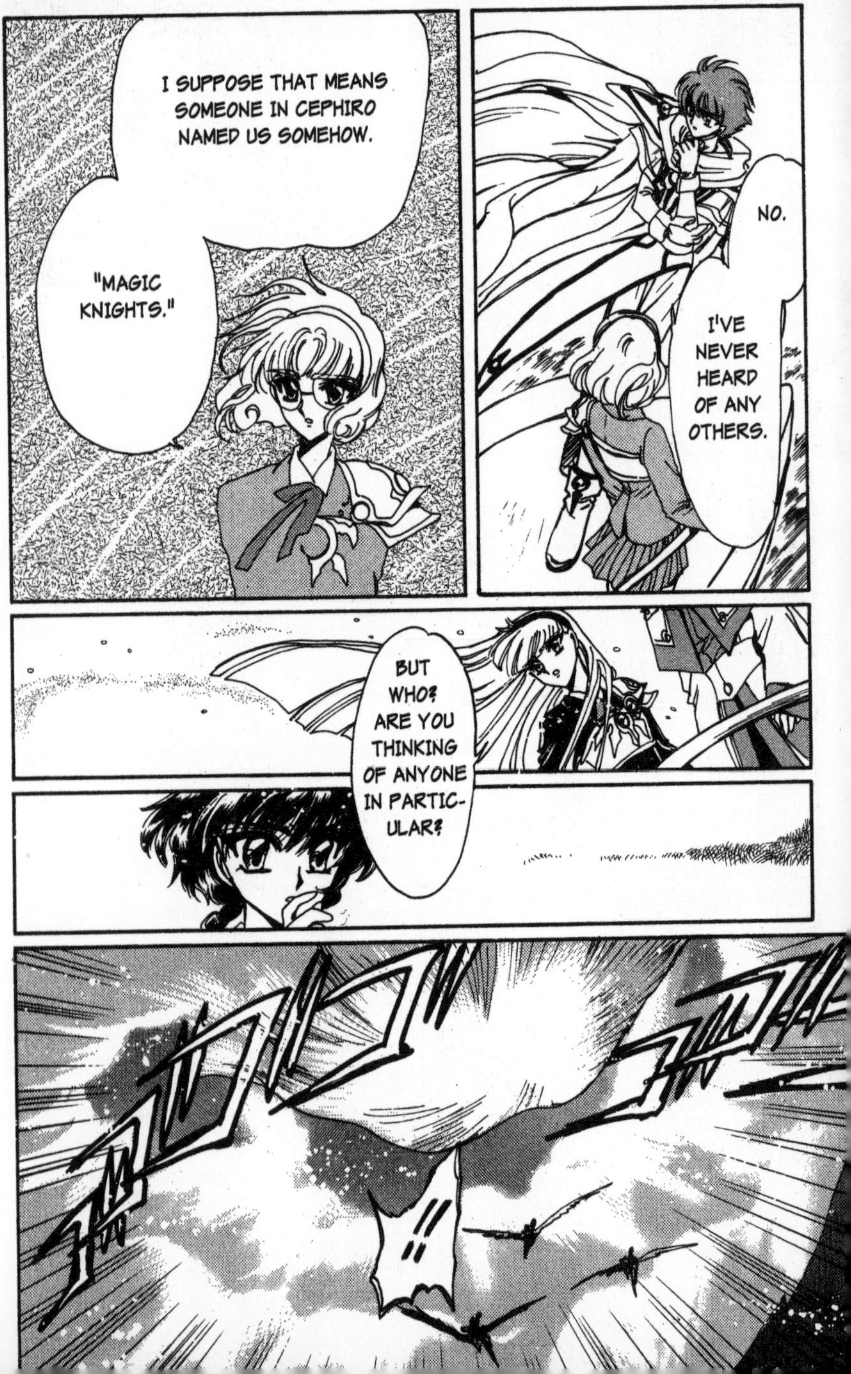
NO.
I'VE NEVER HEARD OF ANY OTHERS.
I SUPPOSE THAT MEANS SOMEONE IN CEPHIRO NAMED US SOMEHOW.
"MAGIC KNIGHTS."
BUT WHO? ARE YOU THINKING OF ANYONE IN PARTIC-ULAR?
!!

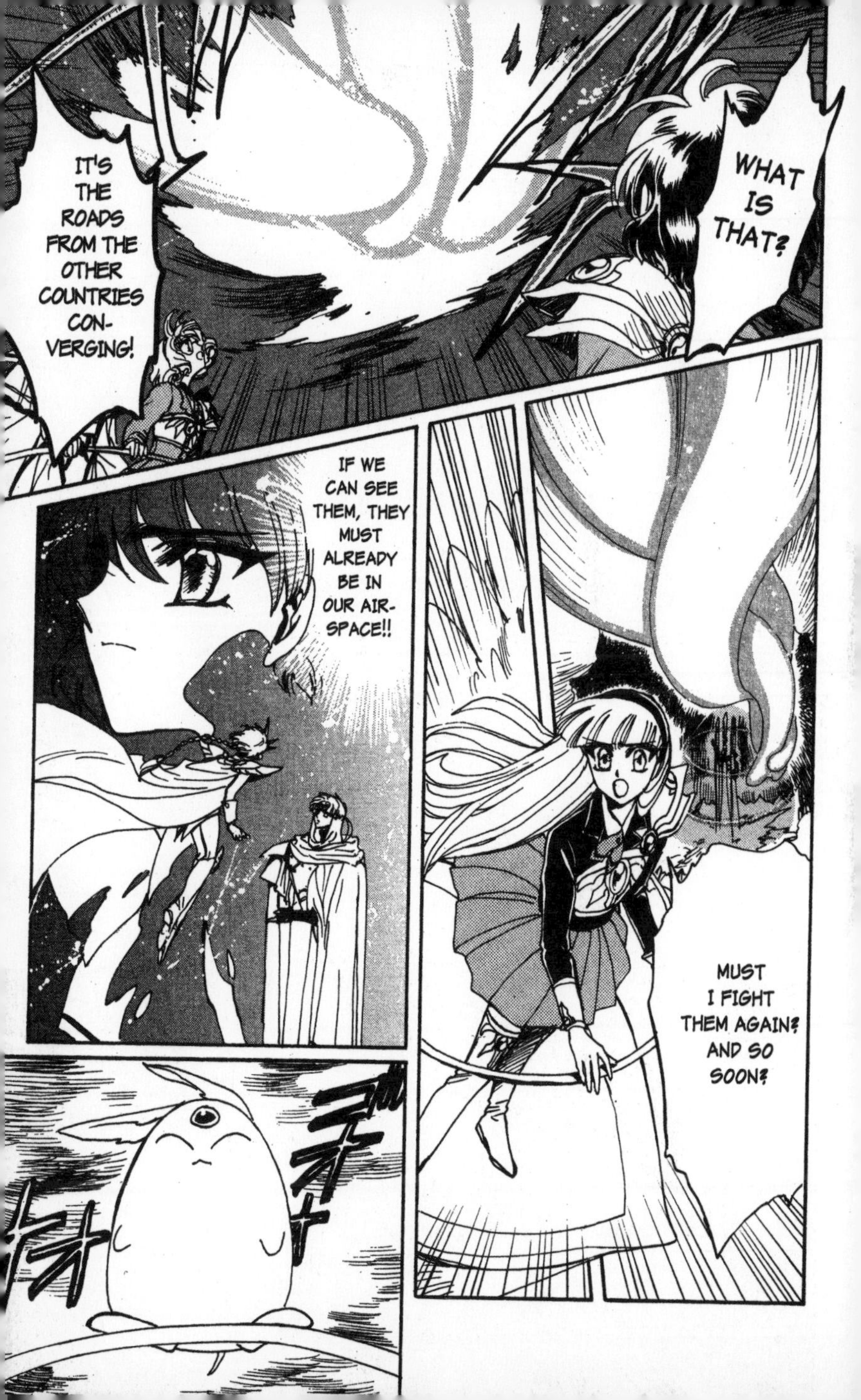
WHAT IS THAT?
IT'S THE ROADS FROM THE OTHER COUNTRIES CON-VERGING!
MUST I FIGHT THEM AGAIN? AND SO SOON?
IF WE CAN SEE THEM, THEY MUST ALREADY BE IN OUR AIR-SPACE!!

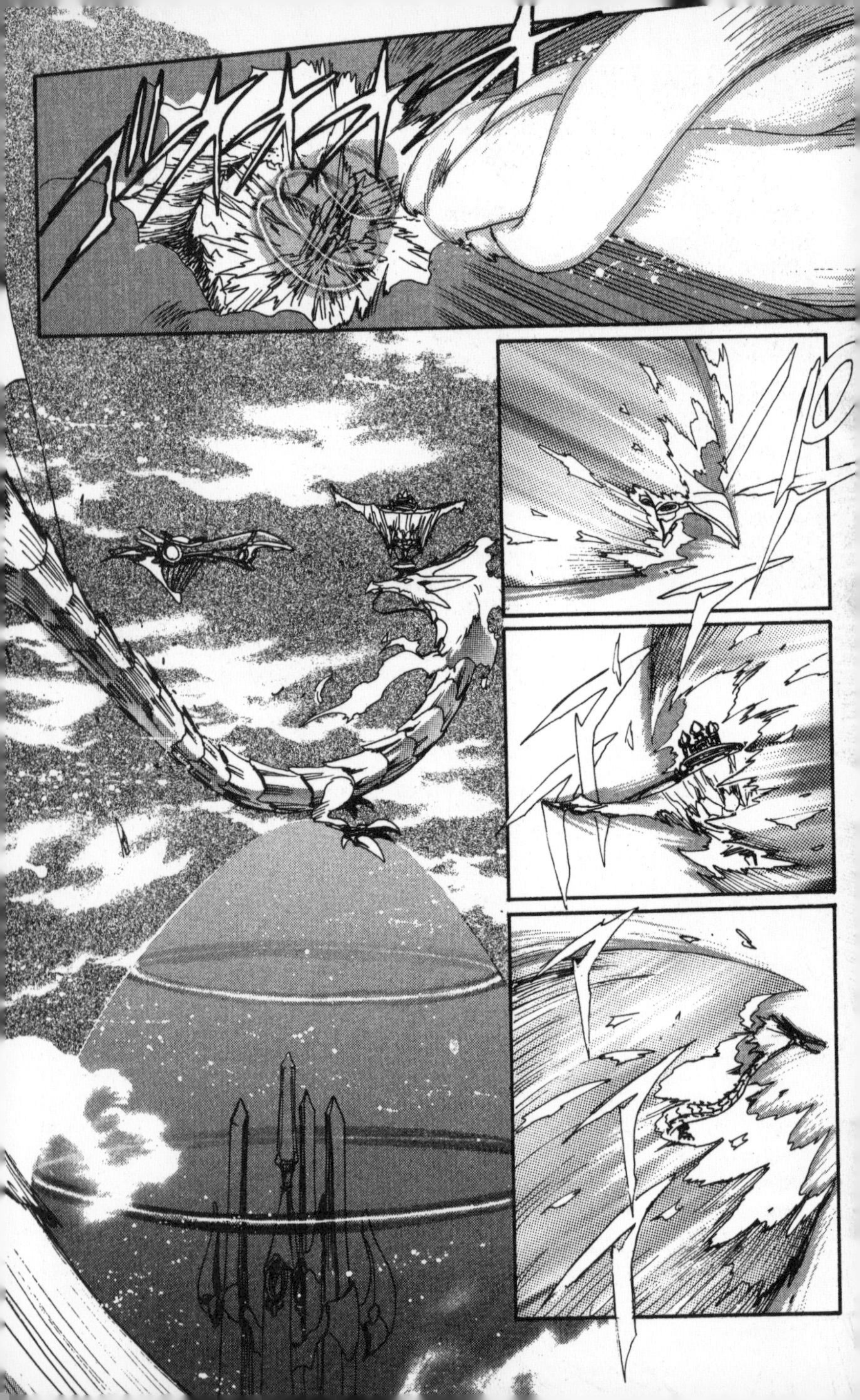

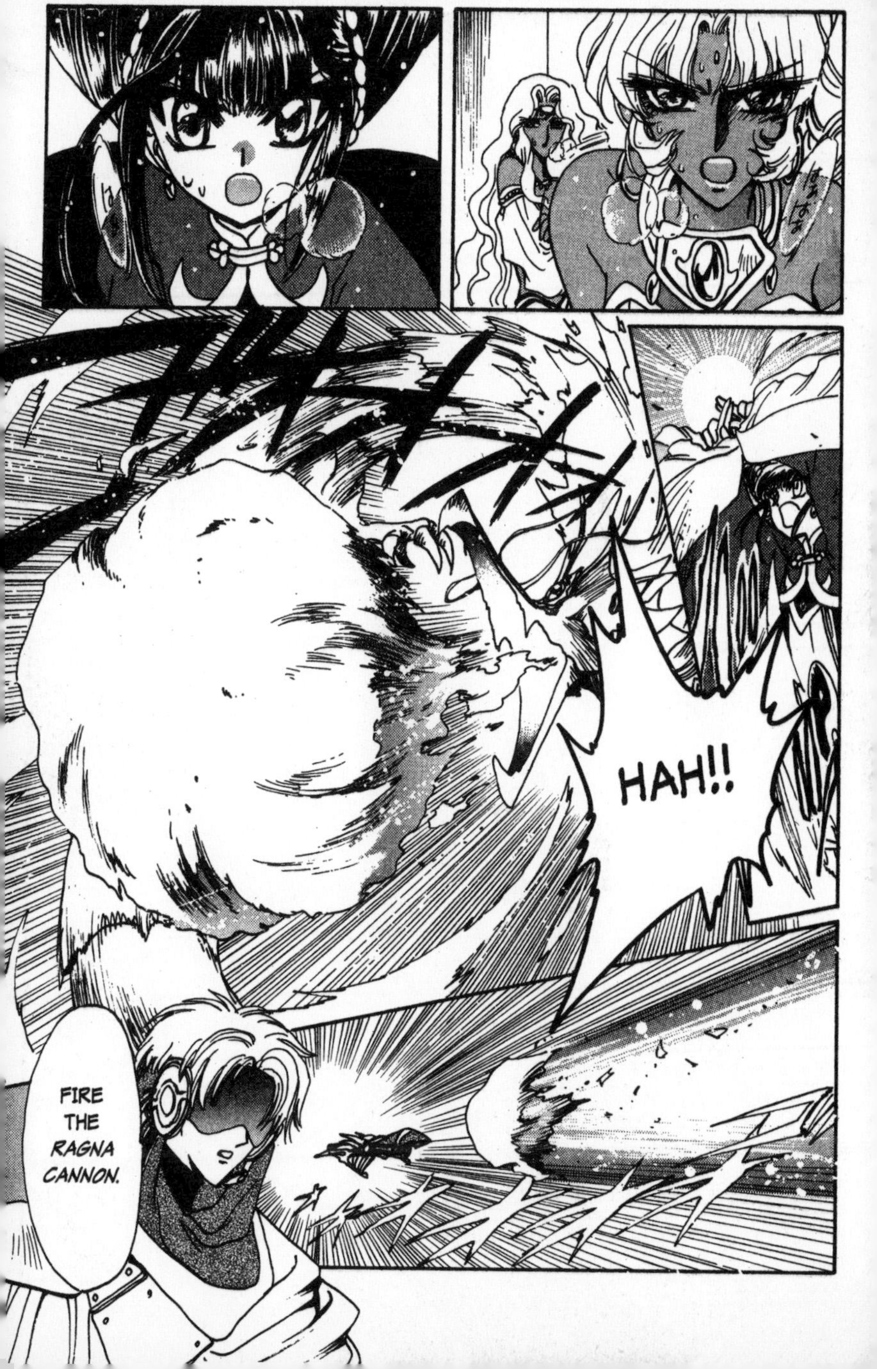
HAH!!
FIRE THE RAGNA CANNON.

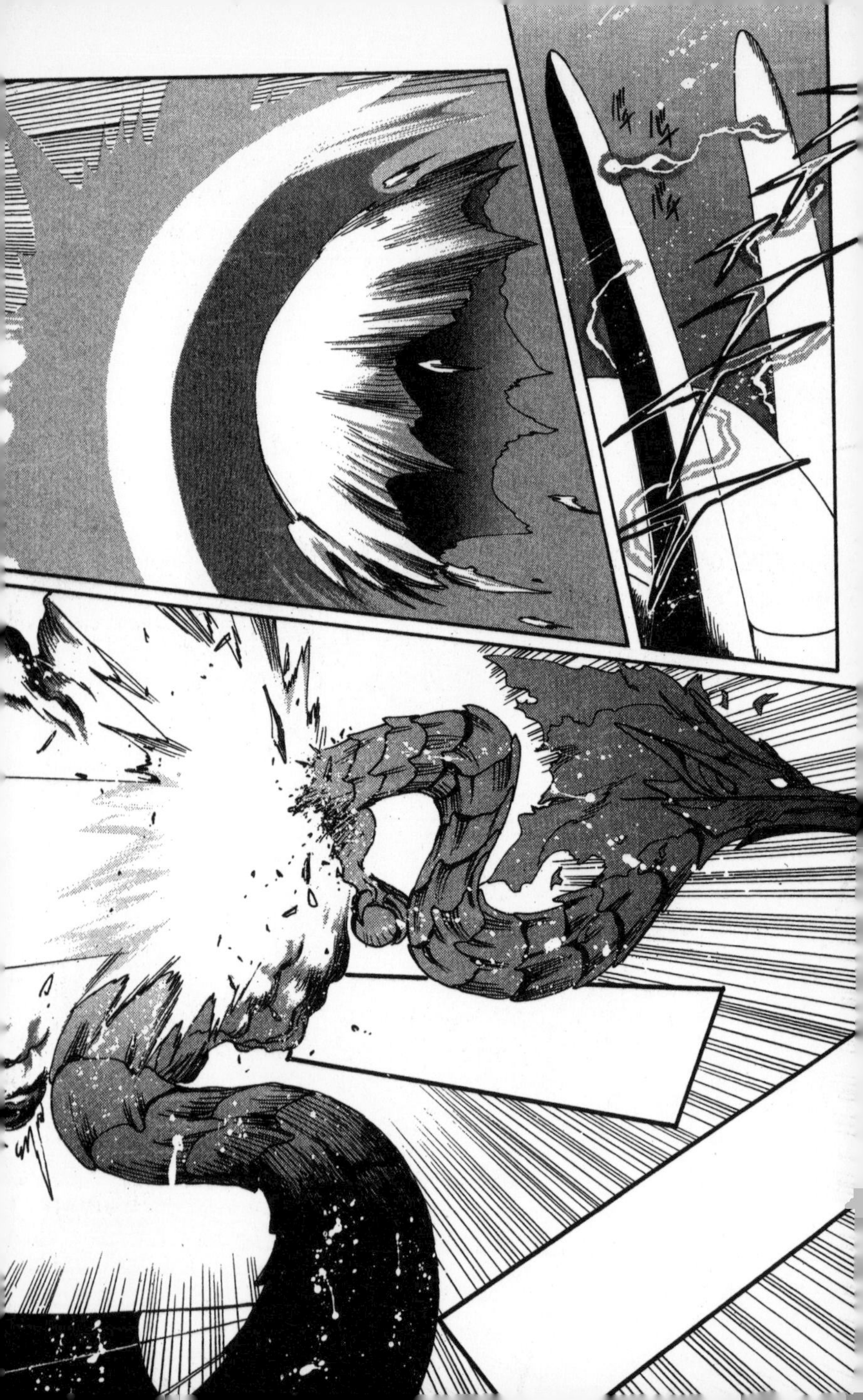
バチ
バチ
バチ

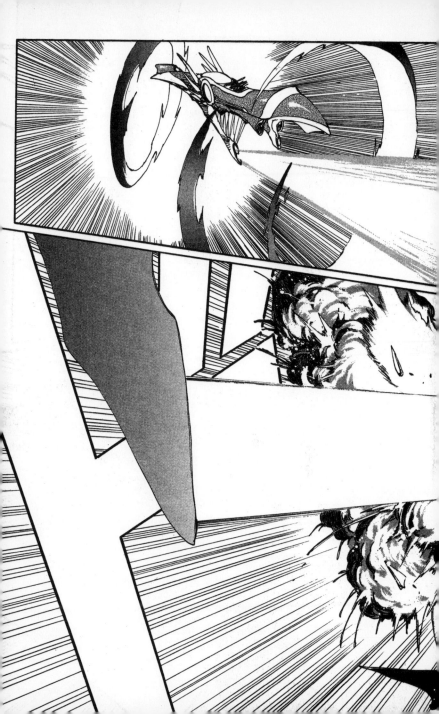

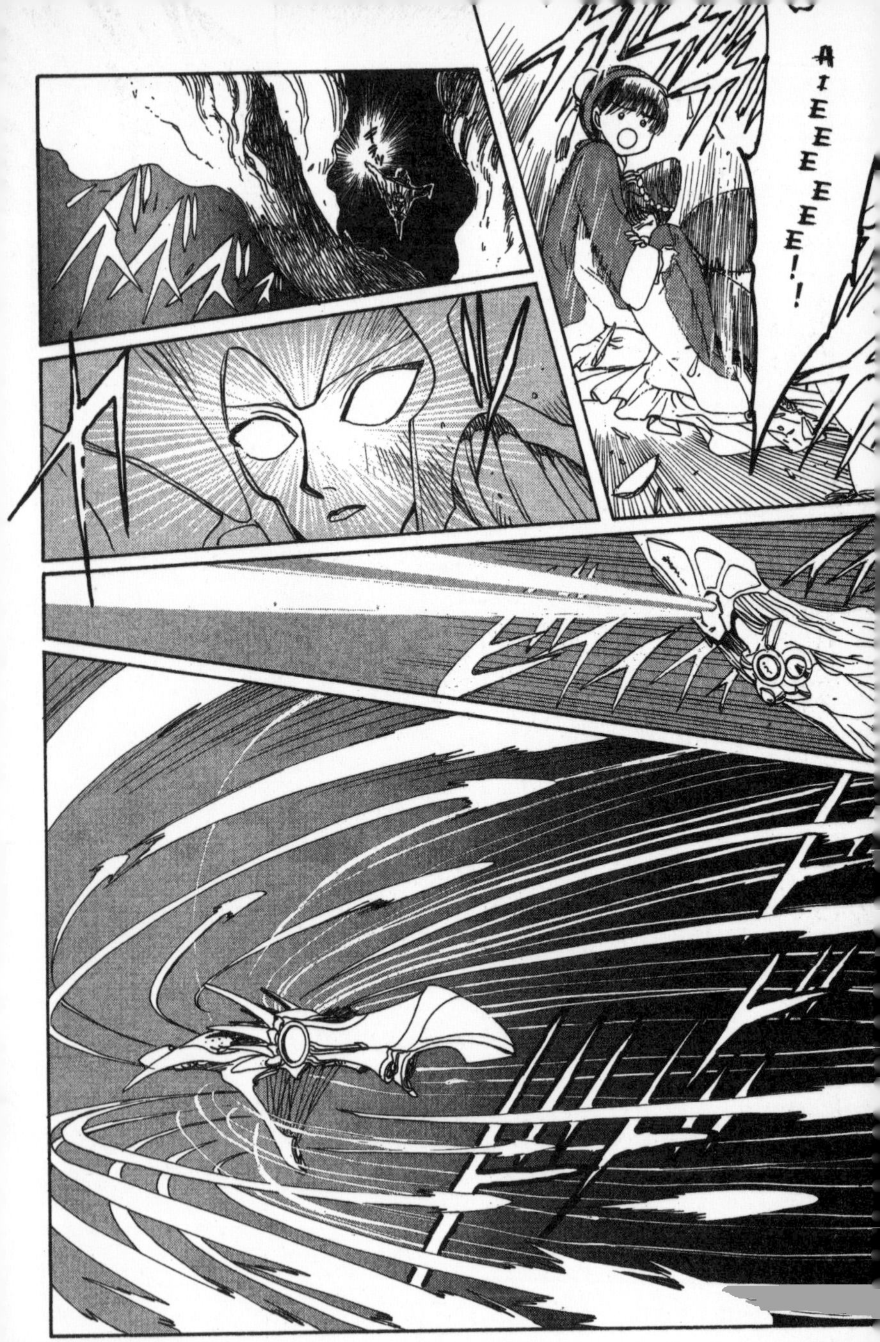
AIEEEEEE!!

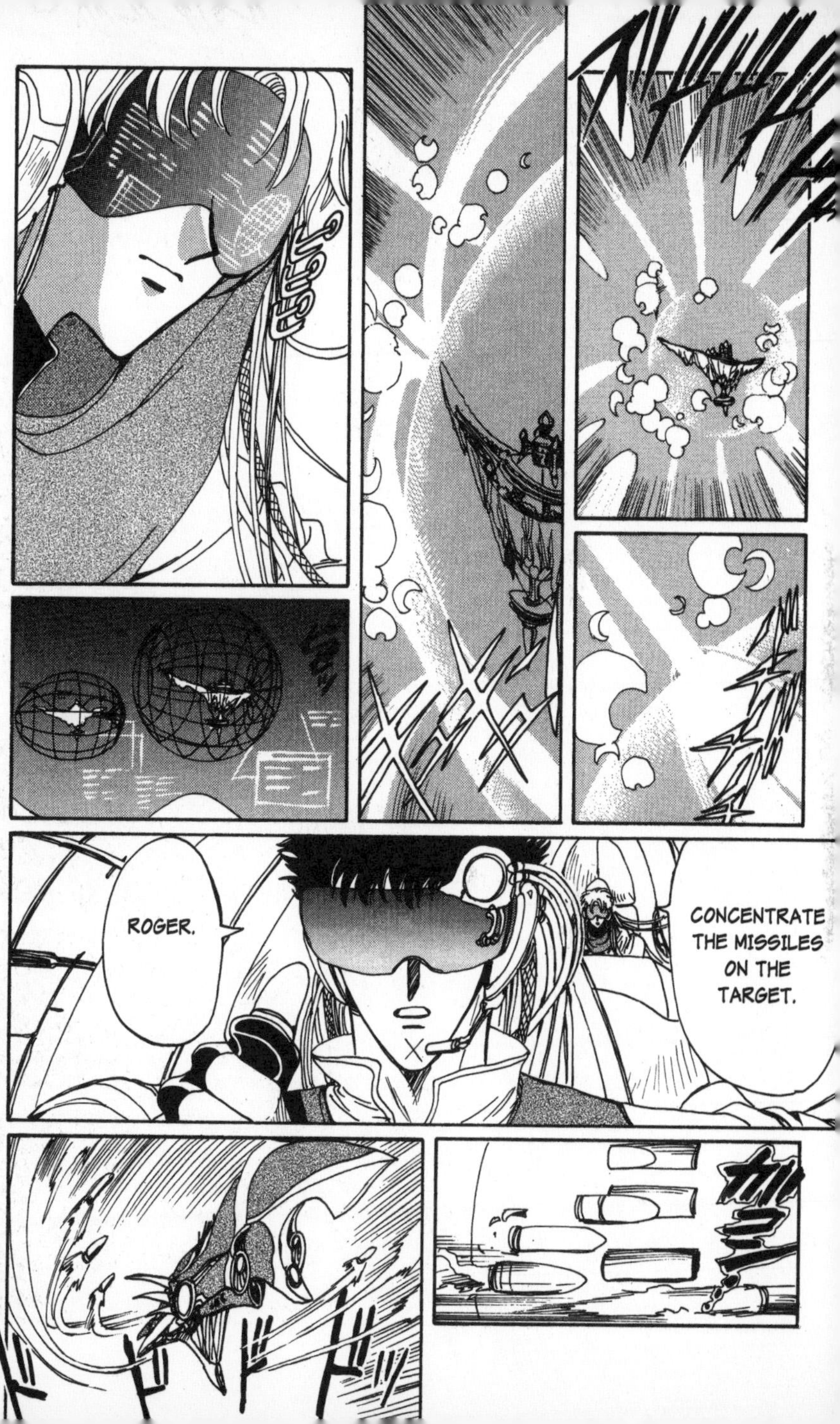
CONCENTRATE THE MISSILES ON THE TARGET.
ROGER.

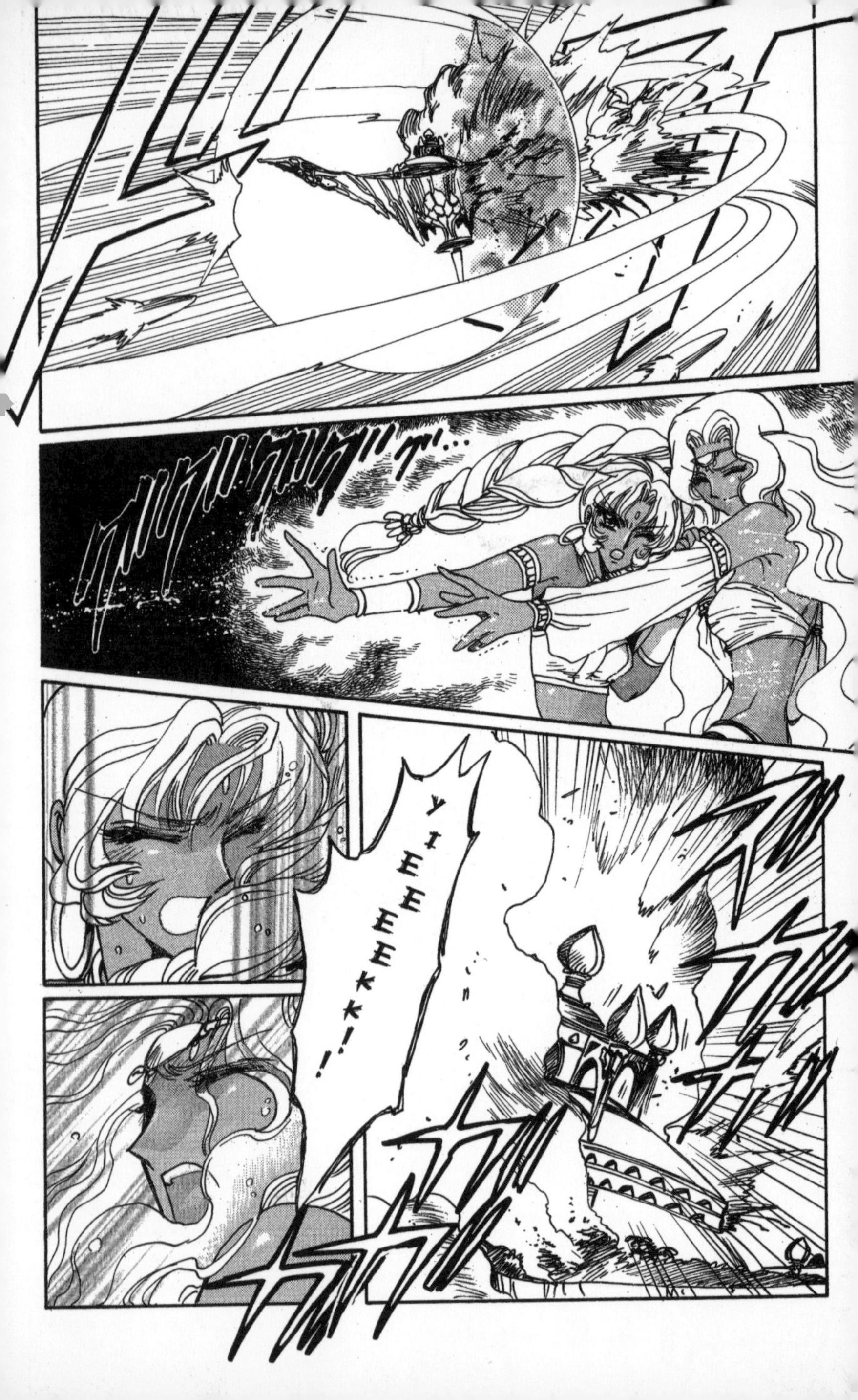
YIEEEEKK!!

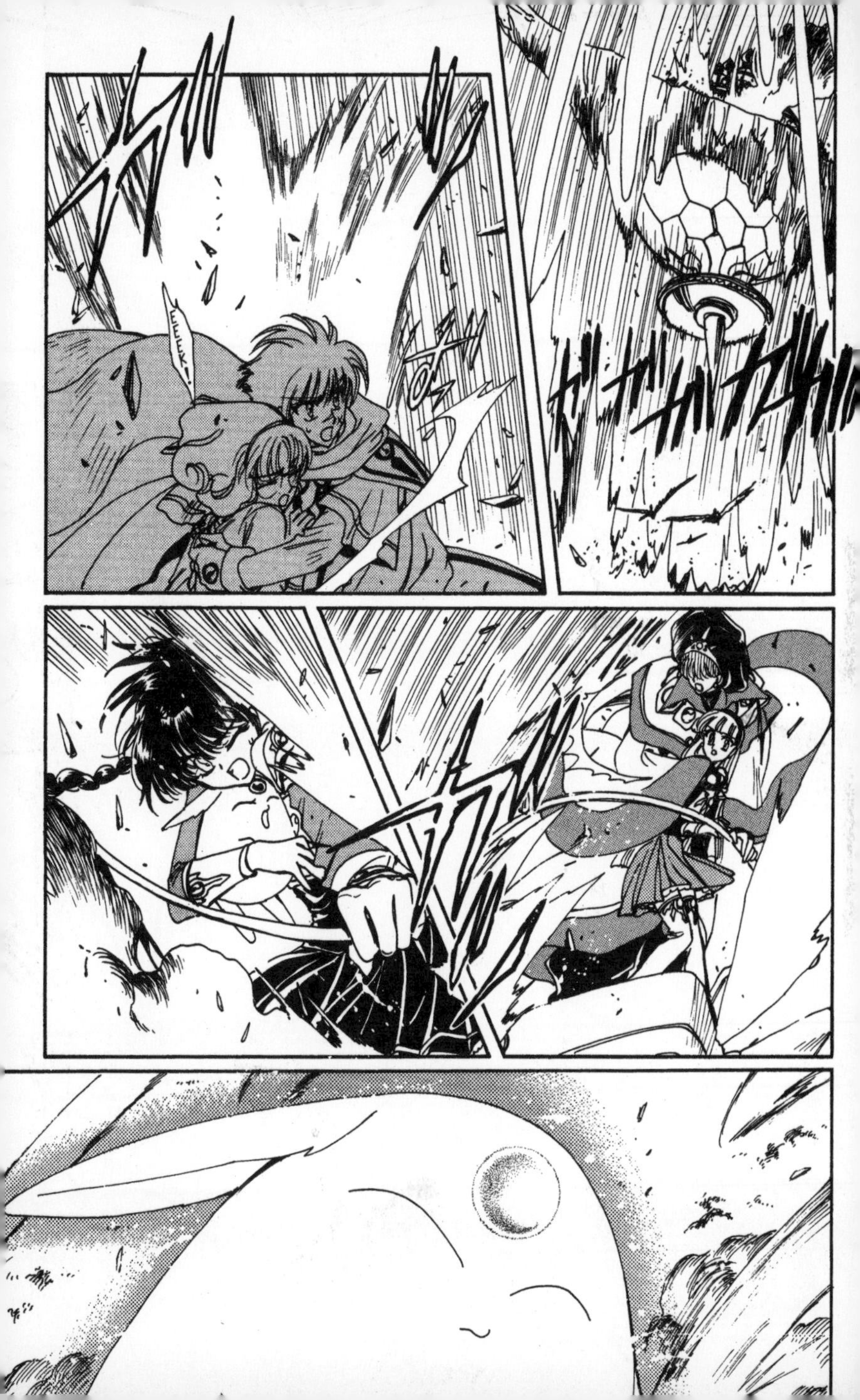
EEEK!

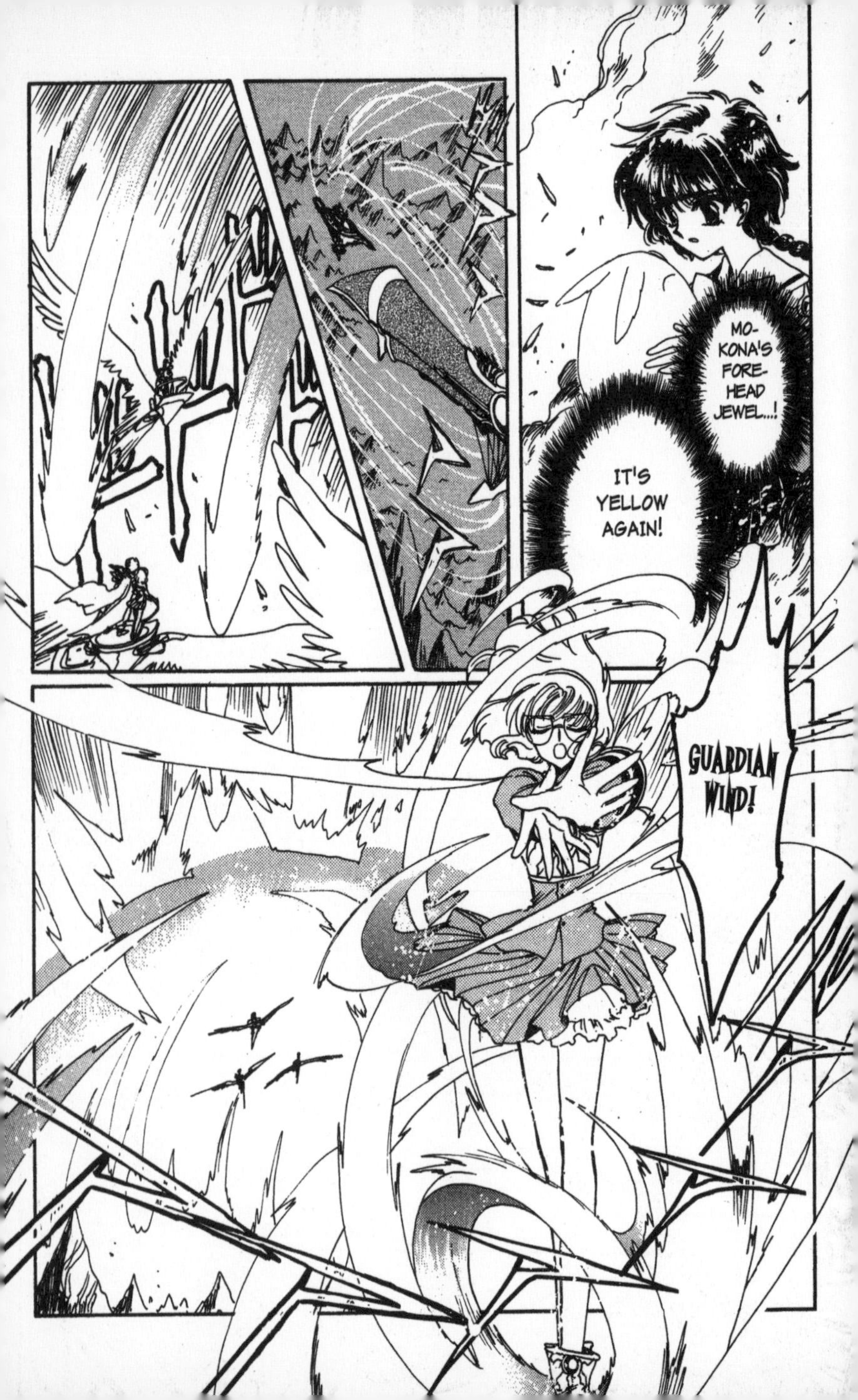
MO-KONA'S FORE-HEAD JEWEL...!
IT'S YELLOW AGAIN!
GUARDIAN WIND!

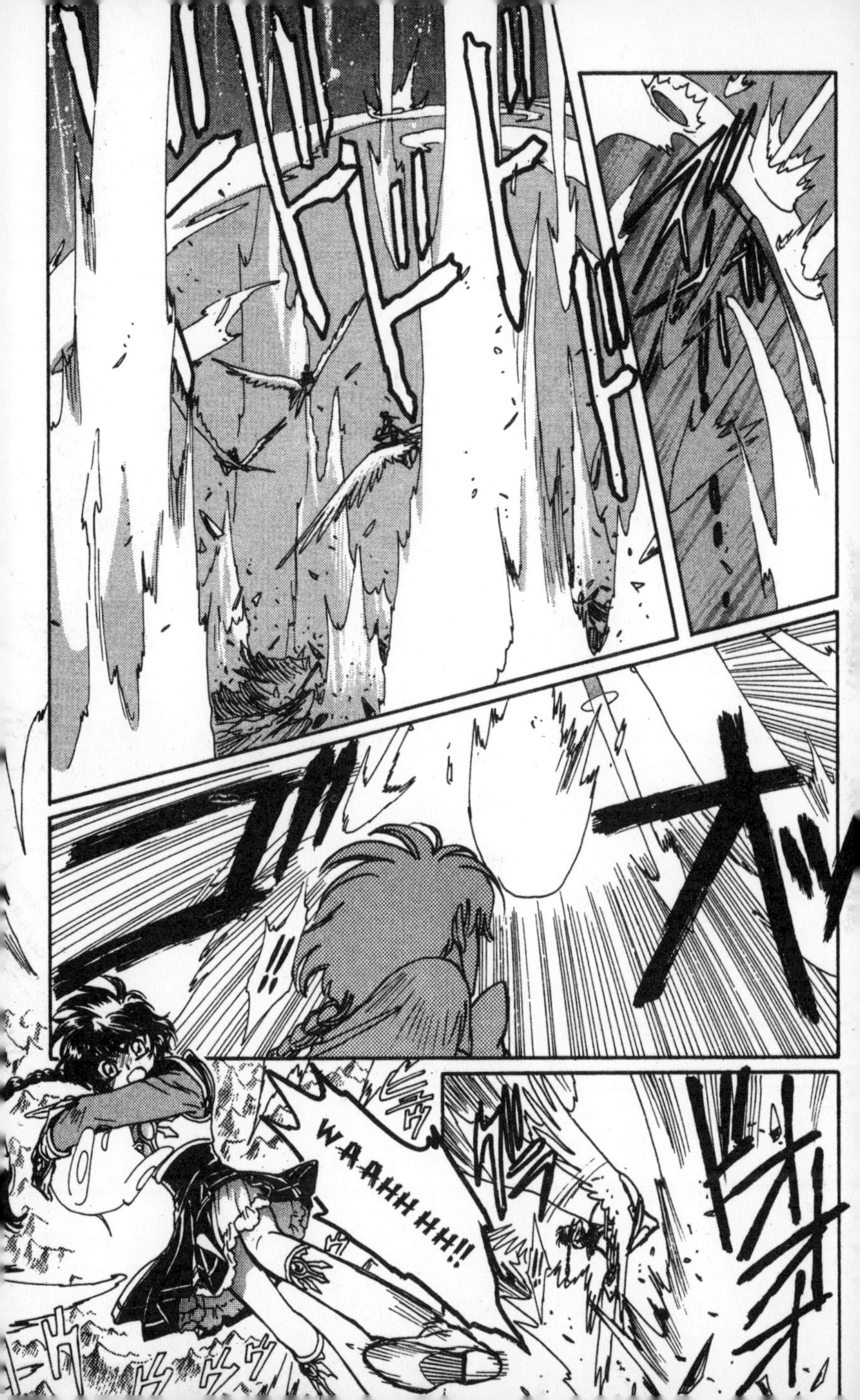
WAAHHHHHH!!

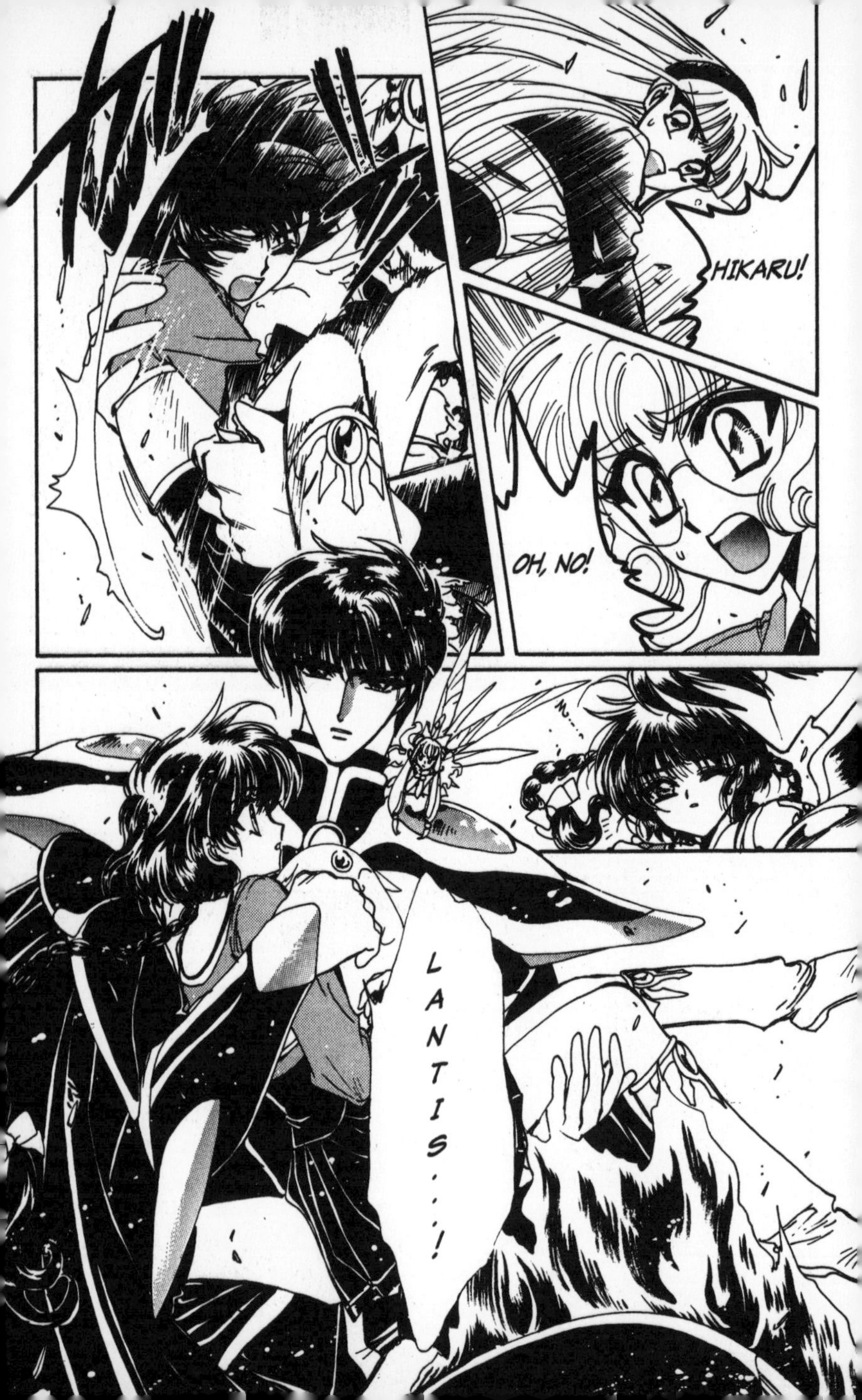
HIKARU!
OH, NO!
M...
LANTIS...!

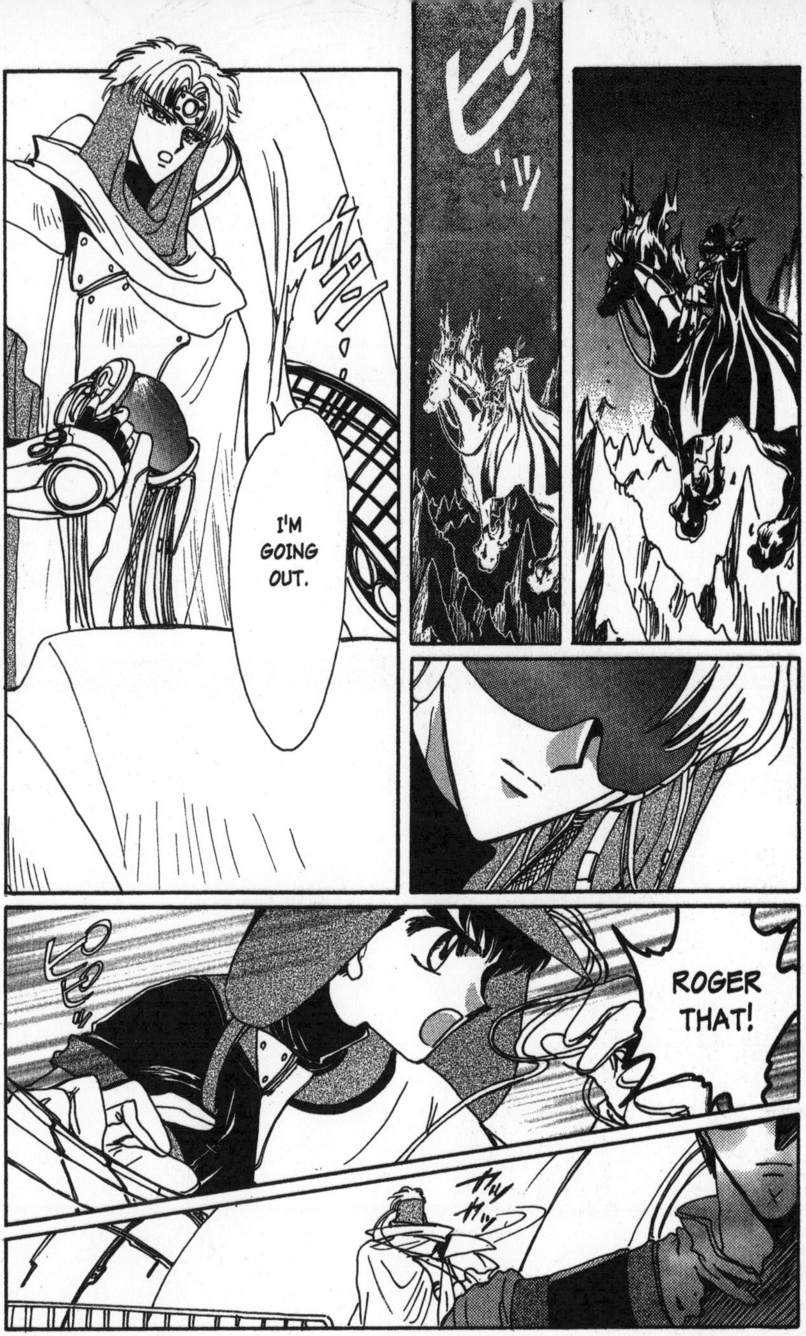
I'M GOING OUT.
ROGER THAT!

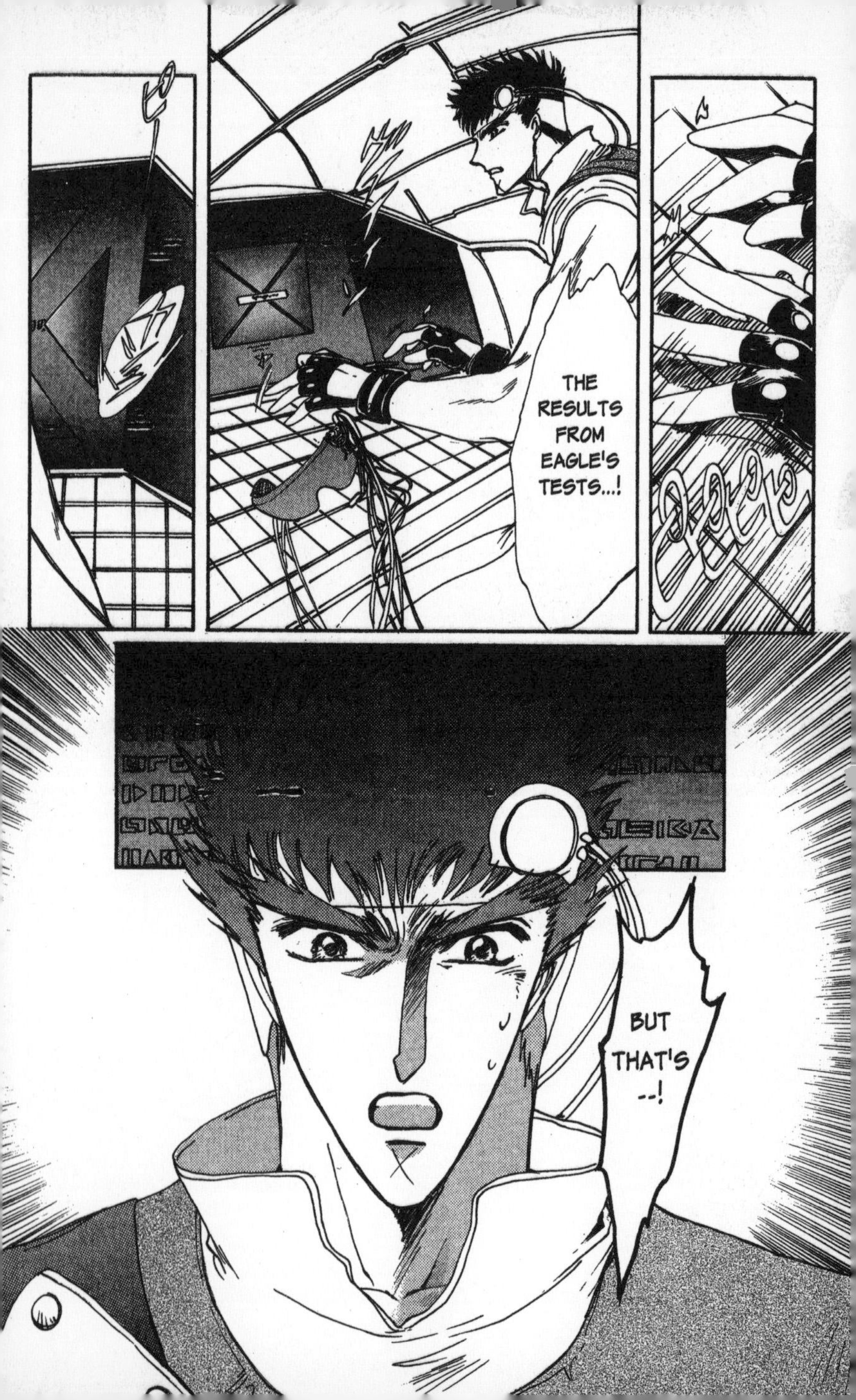
THE RESULTS FROM EAGLE'S TESTS...!
BUT THAT'S --!

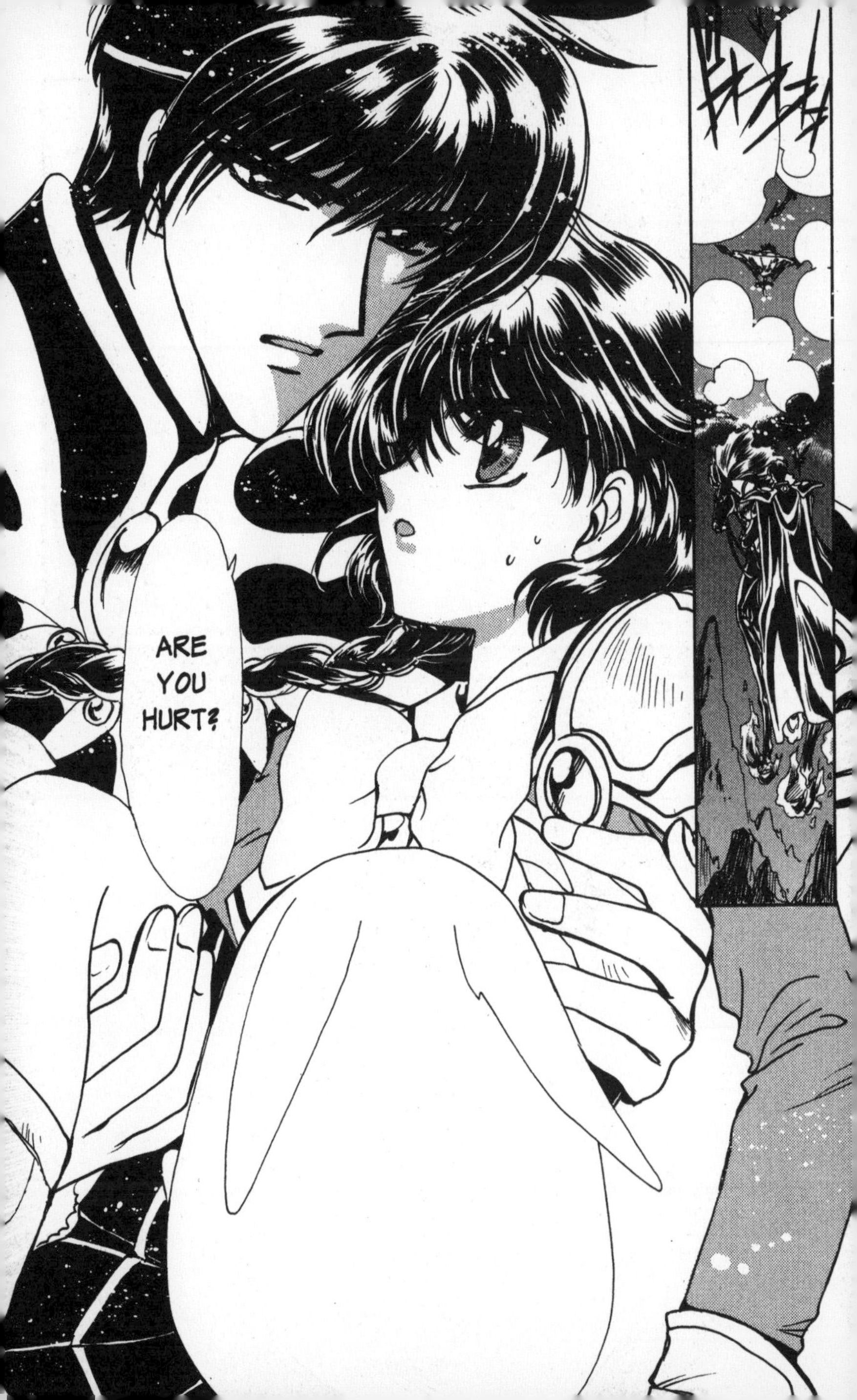
ARE YOU HURT?

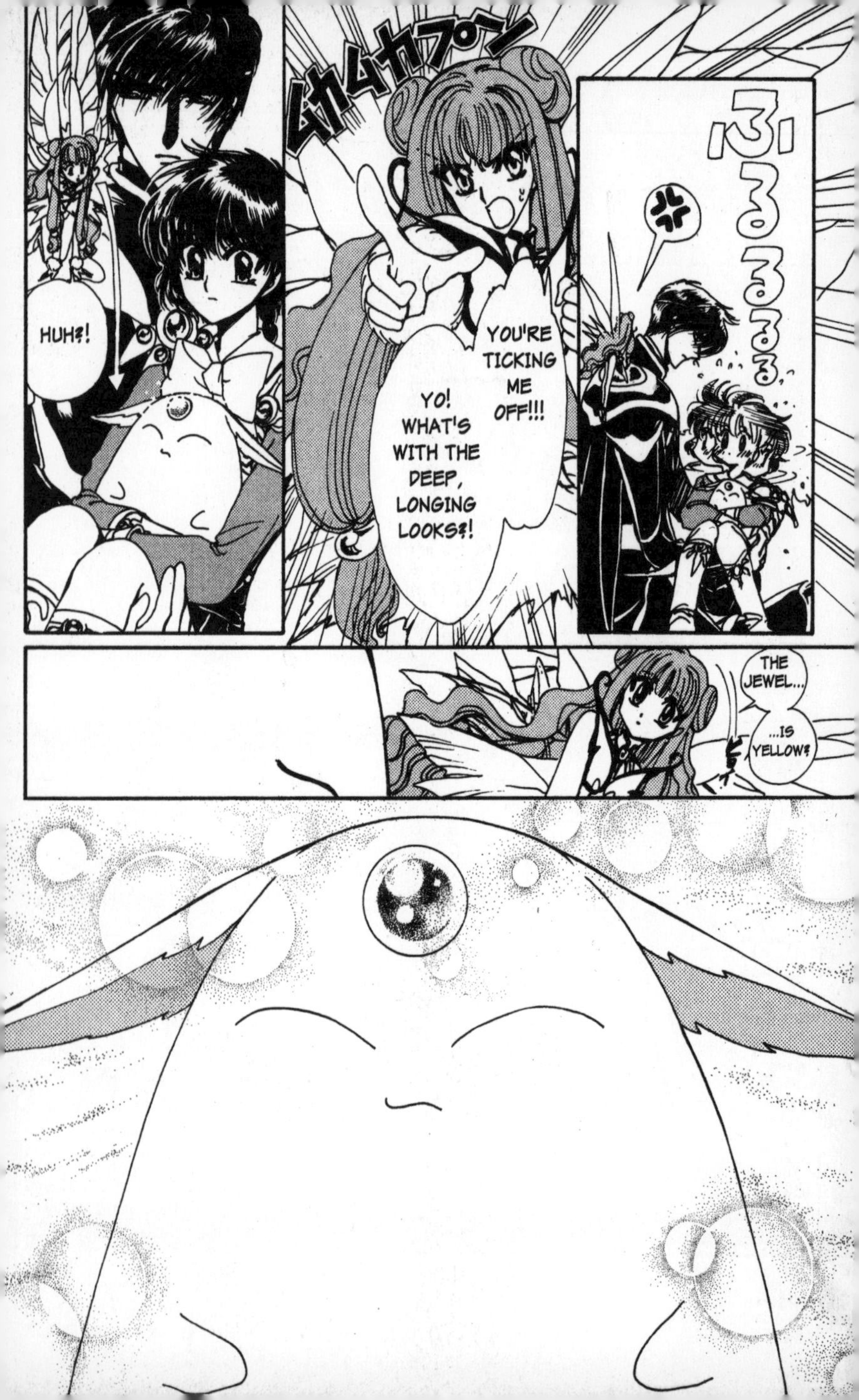
ふるるるる
ムカムカプ〜ン
YOU'RE TICKING ME OFF!!!
YO! WHAT'S WITH THE DEEP, LONGING LOOKS?!
HUH?!
THE JEWEL...
...IS YELLOW?

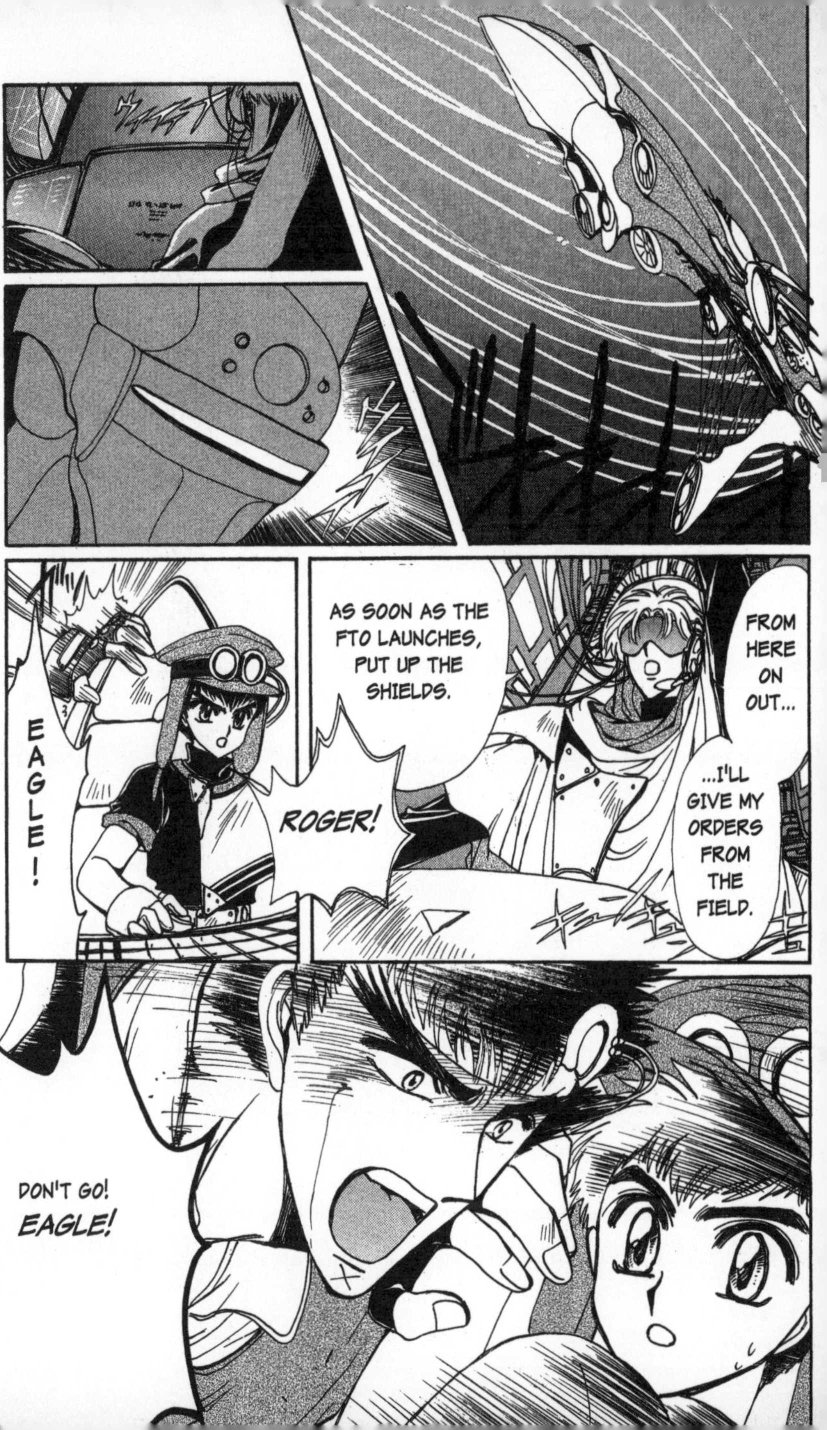
FROM HERE ON OUT...
...I'LL GIVE MY ORDERS FROM THE FIELD.
AS SOON AS THE FTO LAUNCHES, PUT UP THE SHIELDS.
ROGER!
EAGLE!
DON'T GO! EAGLE!

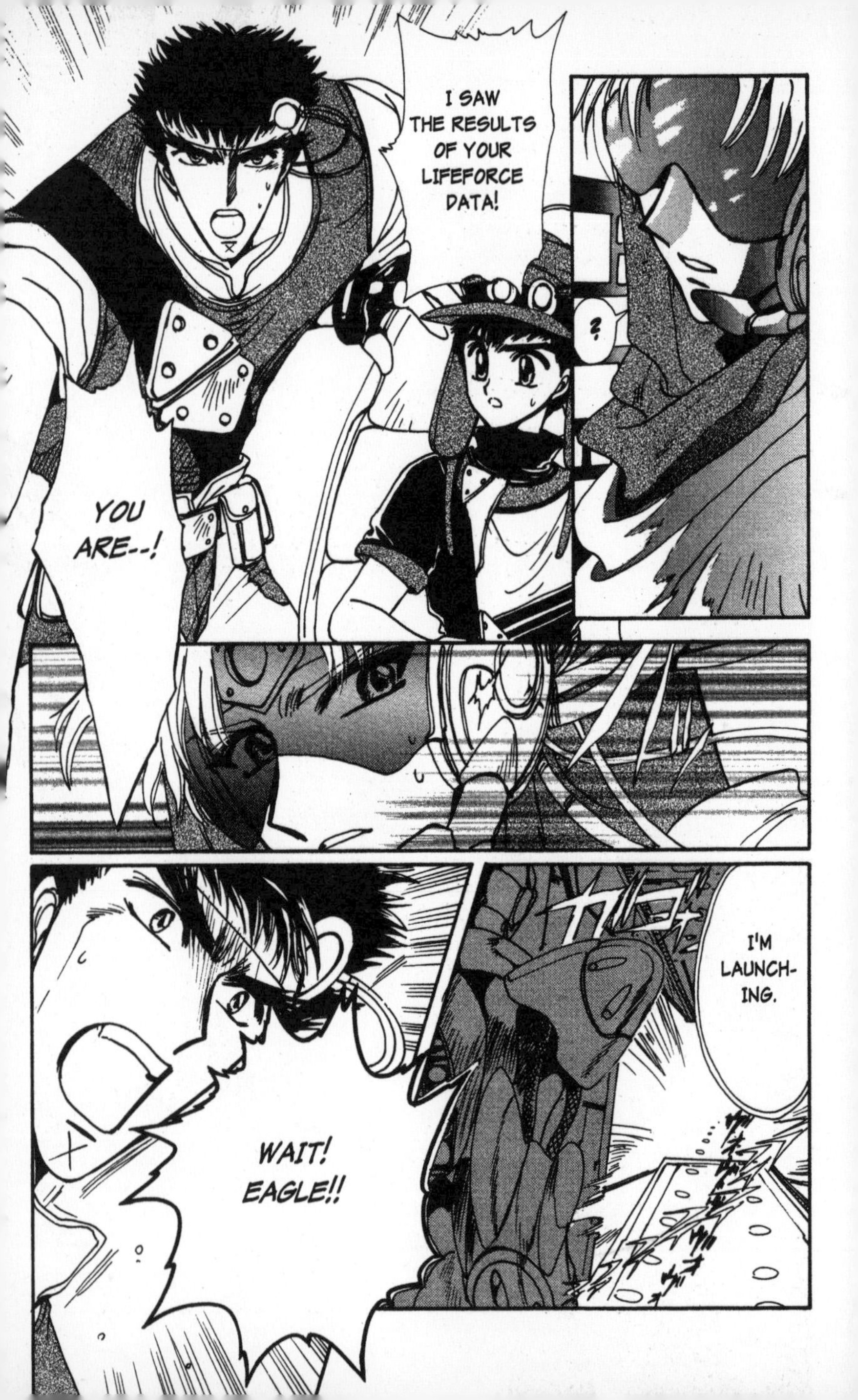
?
I SAW THE RESULTS OF YOUR LIFEFORCE DATA!
YOU ARE--!
I'M LAUNCH-ING.
WAIT! EAGLE!!

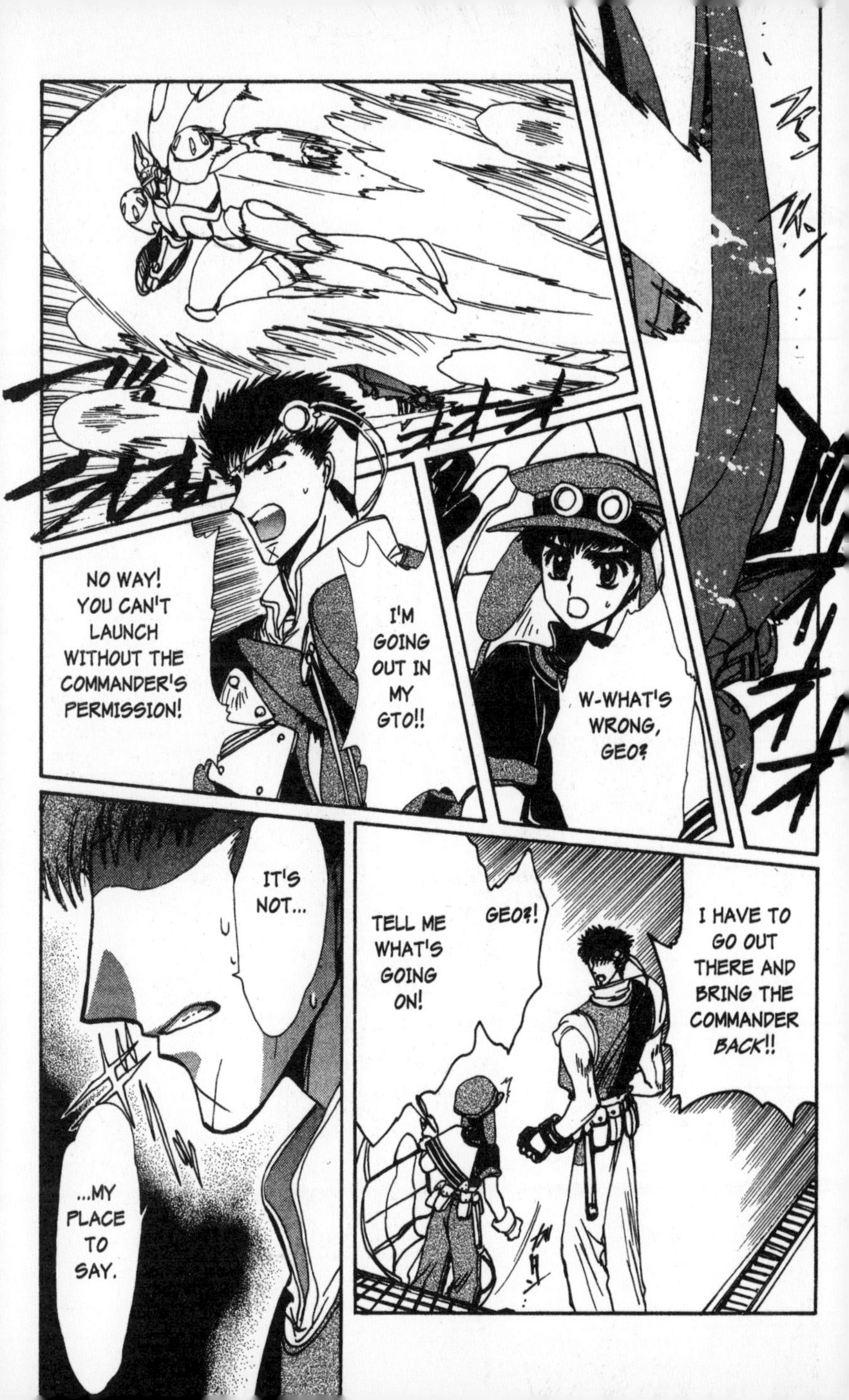
W-WHAT'S WRONG, GEO?
I'M GOING OUT IN MY GTO!!
NO WAY! YOU CAN'T LAUNCH WITHOUT THE COMMANDER'S PERMISSION!
I HAVE TO GO OUT THERE AND BRING THE COMMANDER *BACK*!!
GEO?!
TELL ME WHAT'S GOING ON!
IT'S NOT...
...MY PLACE TO SAY.

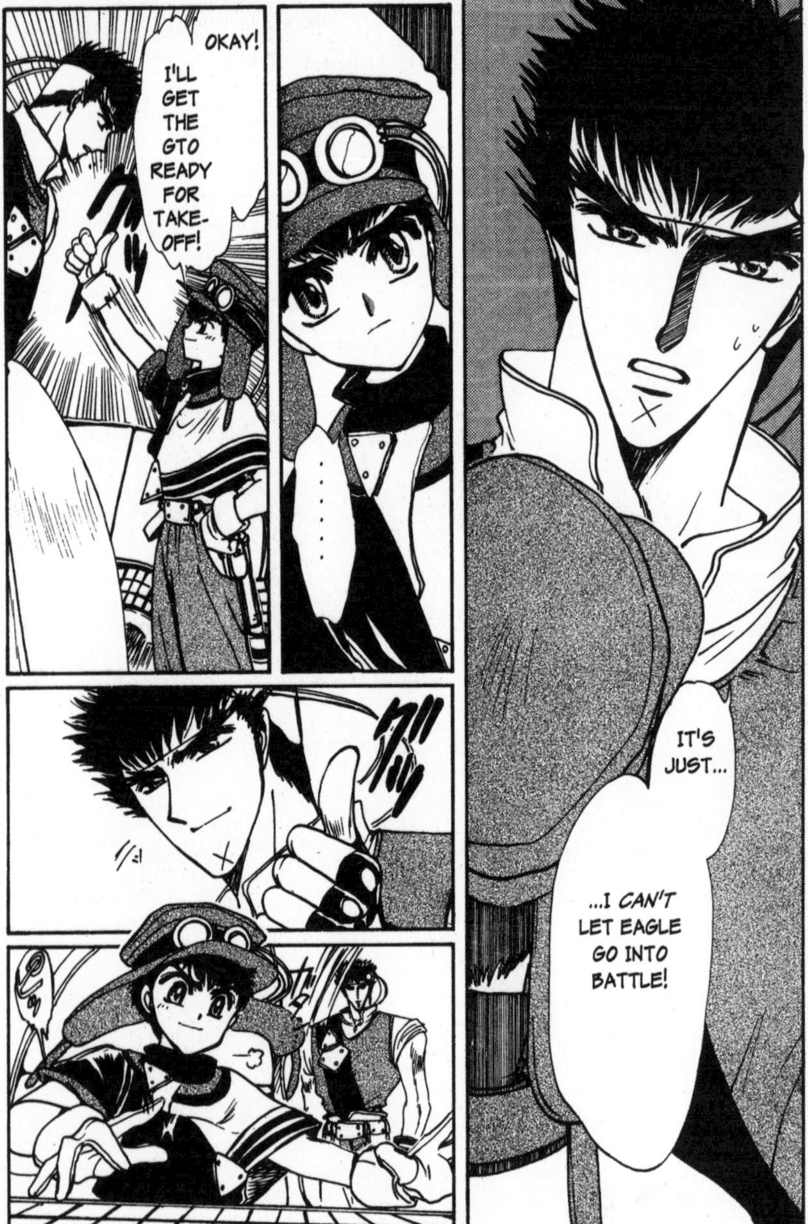
IT'S JUST...
...I CAN'T LET EAGLE GO INTO BATTLE!
OKAY!
I'LL GET THE GTO READY FOR TAKE-OFF!

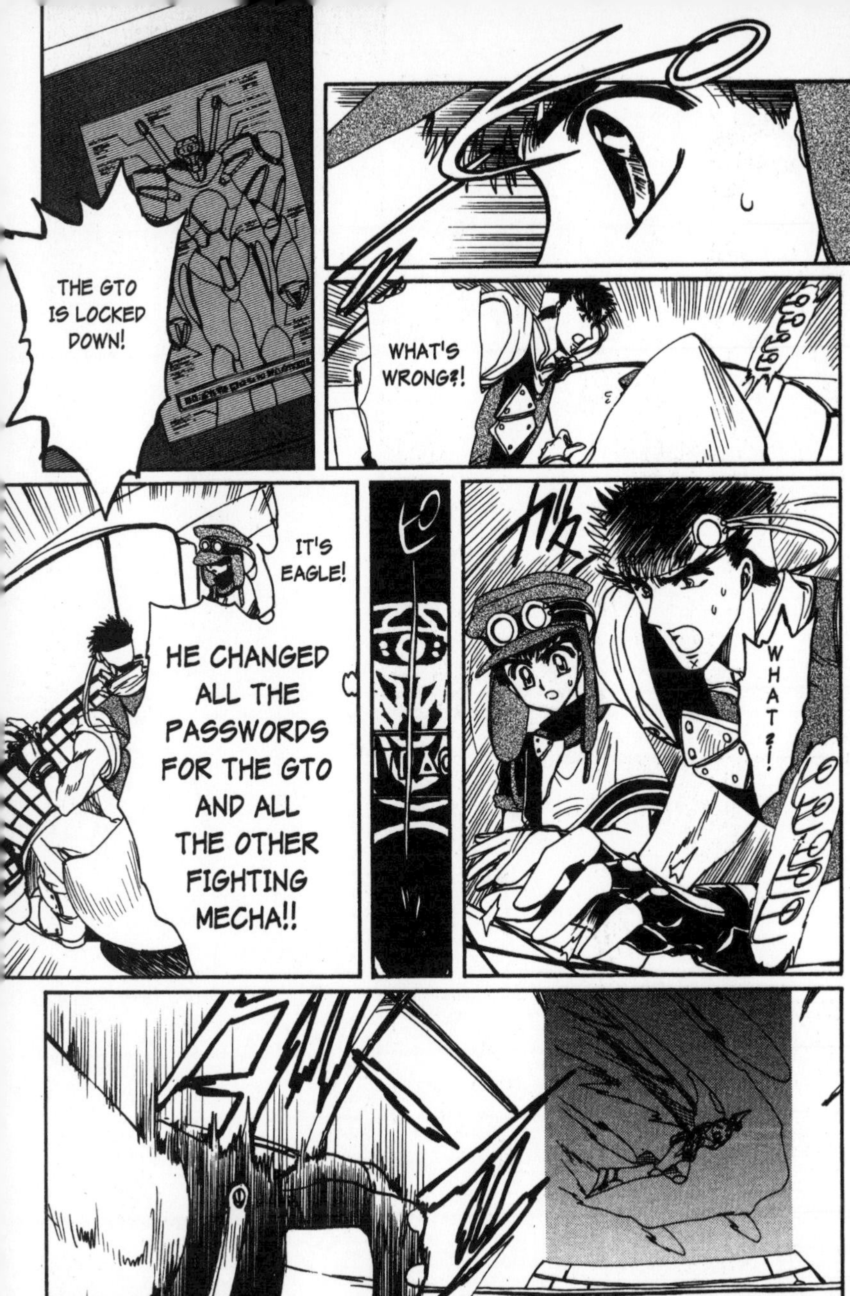
WHAT'S WRONG?!
THE GTO IS LOCKED DOWN!
WHAT?!
IT'S EAGLE!
HE CHANGED ALL THE PASSWORDS FOR THE GTO AND ALL THE OTHER FIGHTING MECHA!!

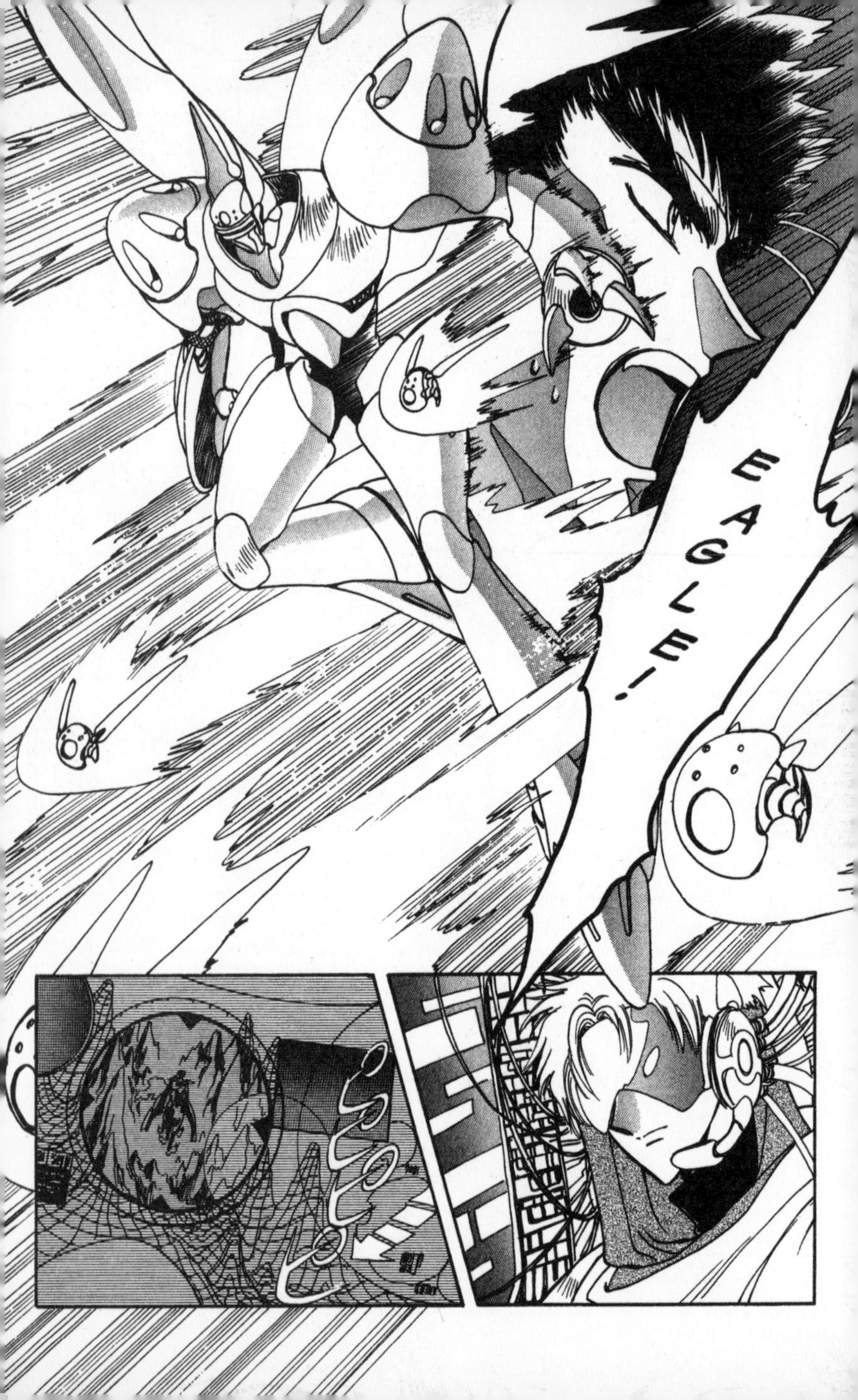
EAGLE!

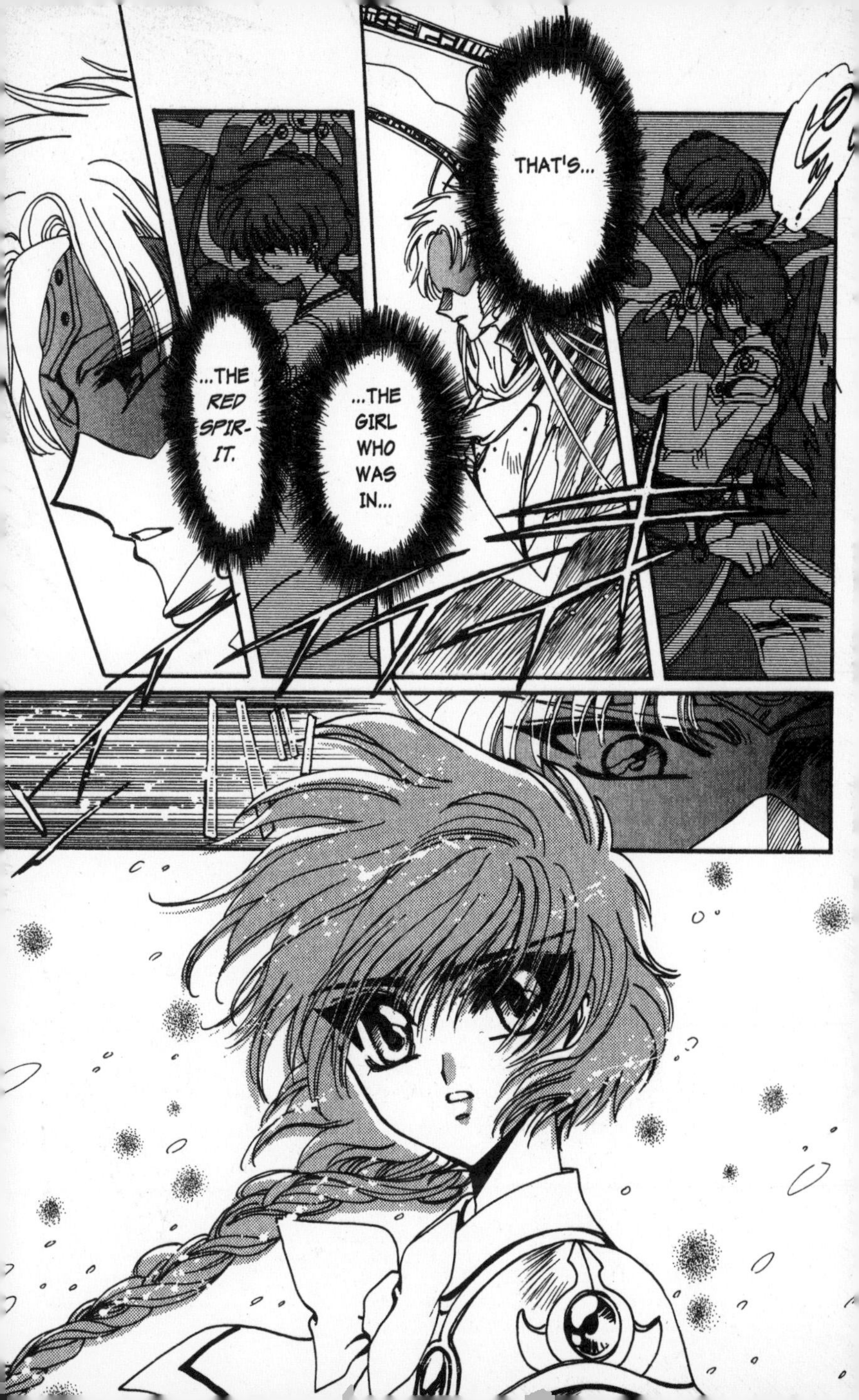
THAT'S...
...THE GIRL WHO WAS IN...
...THE RED SPIR-IT.

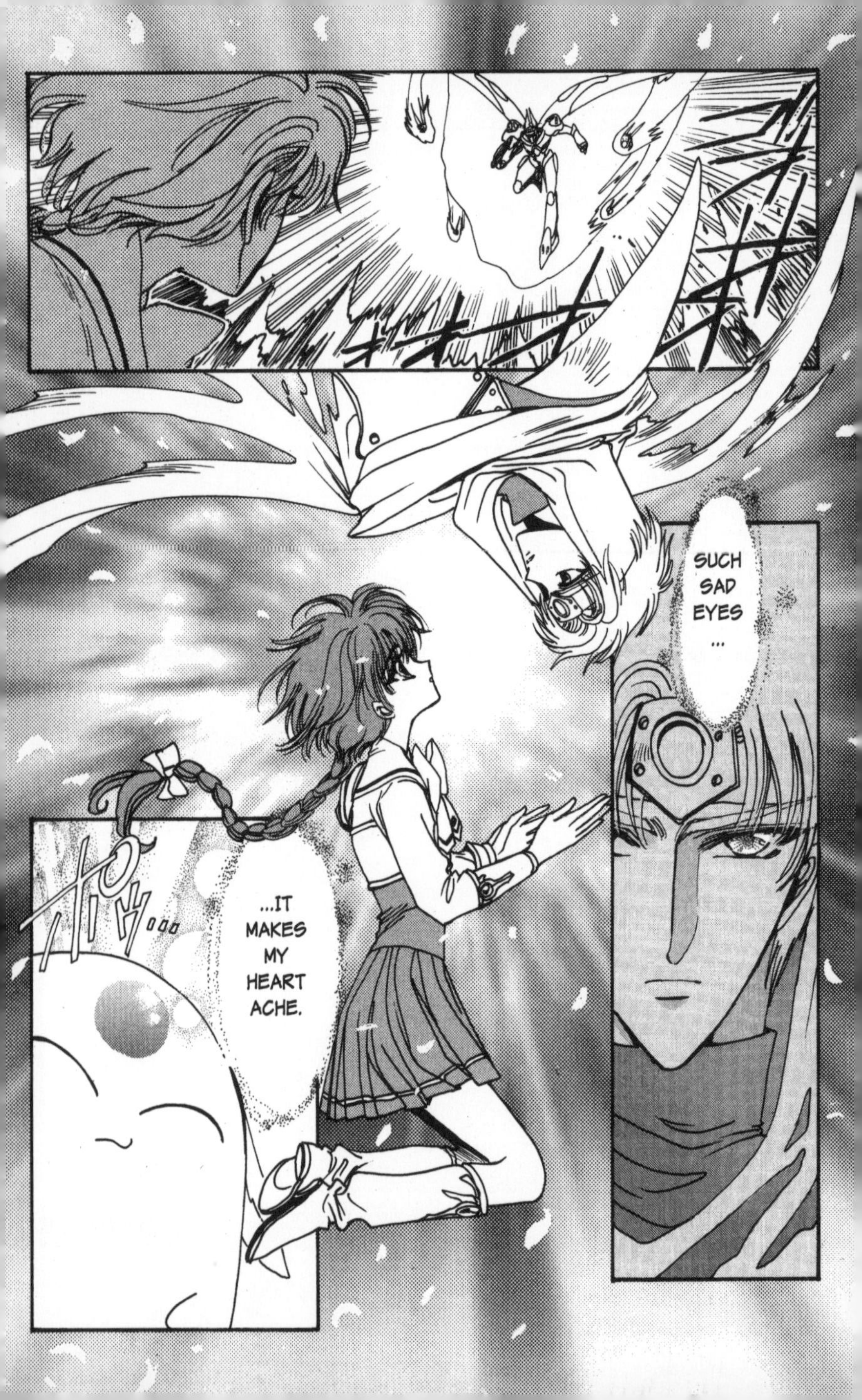
SUCH SAD EYES ...
...IT MAKES MY HEART ACHE.

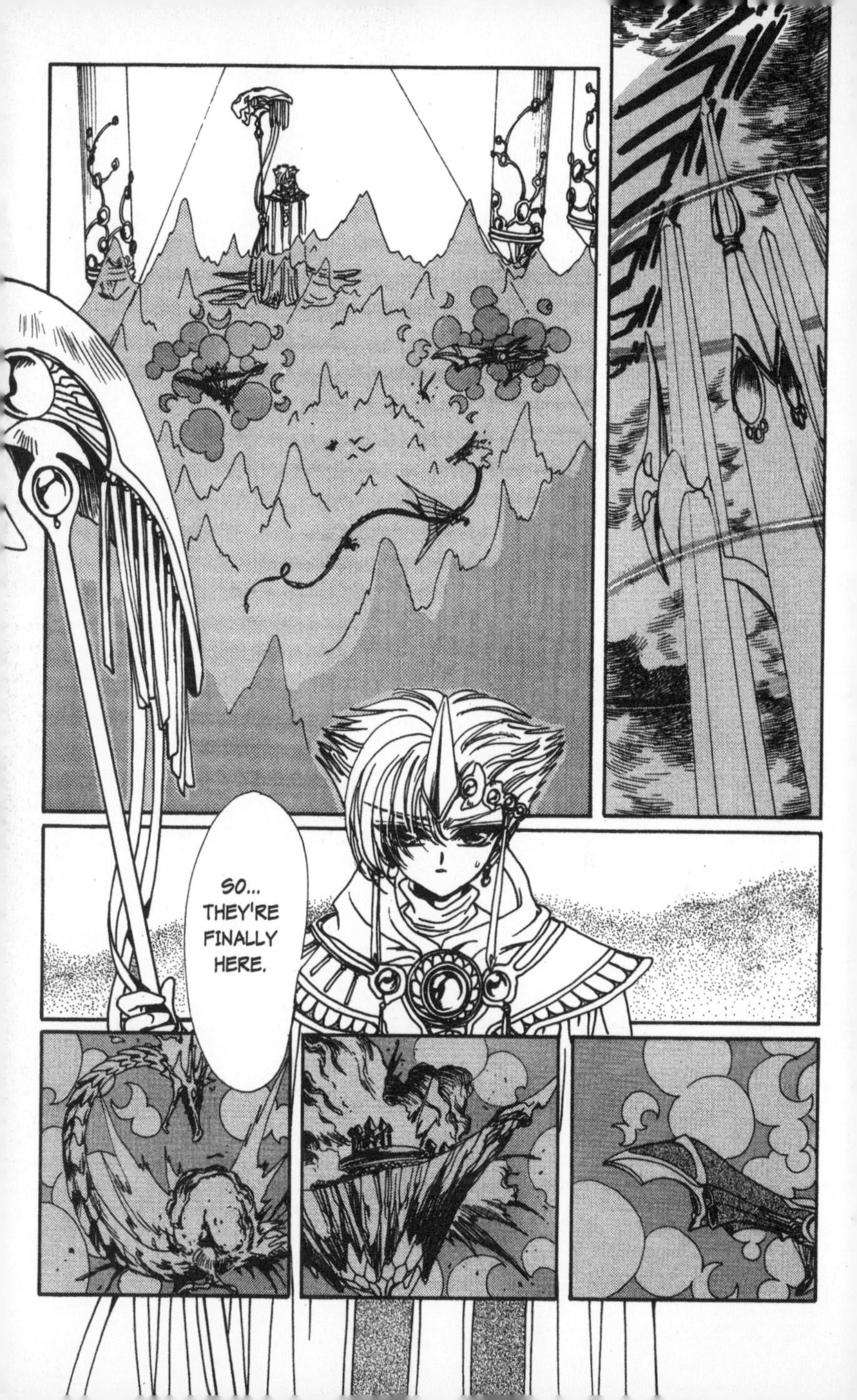
SO... THEY'RE FINALLY HERE.

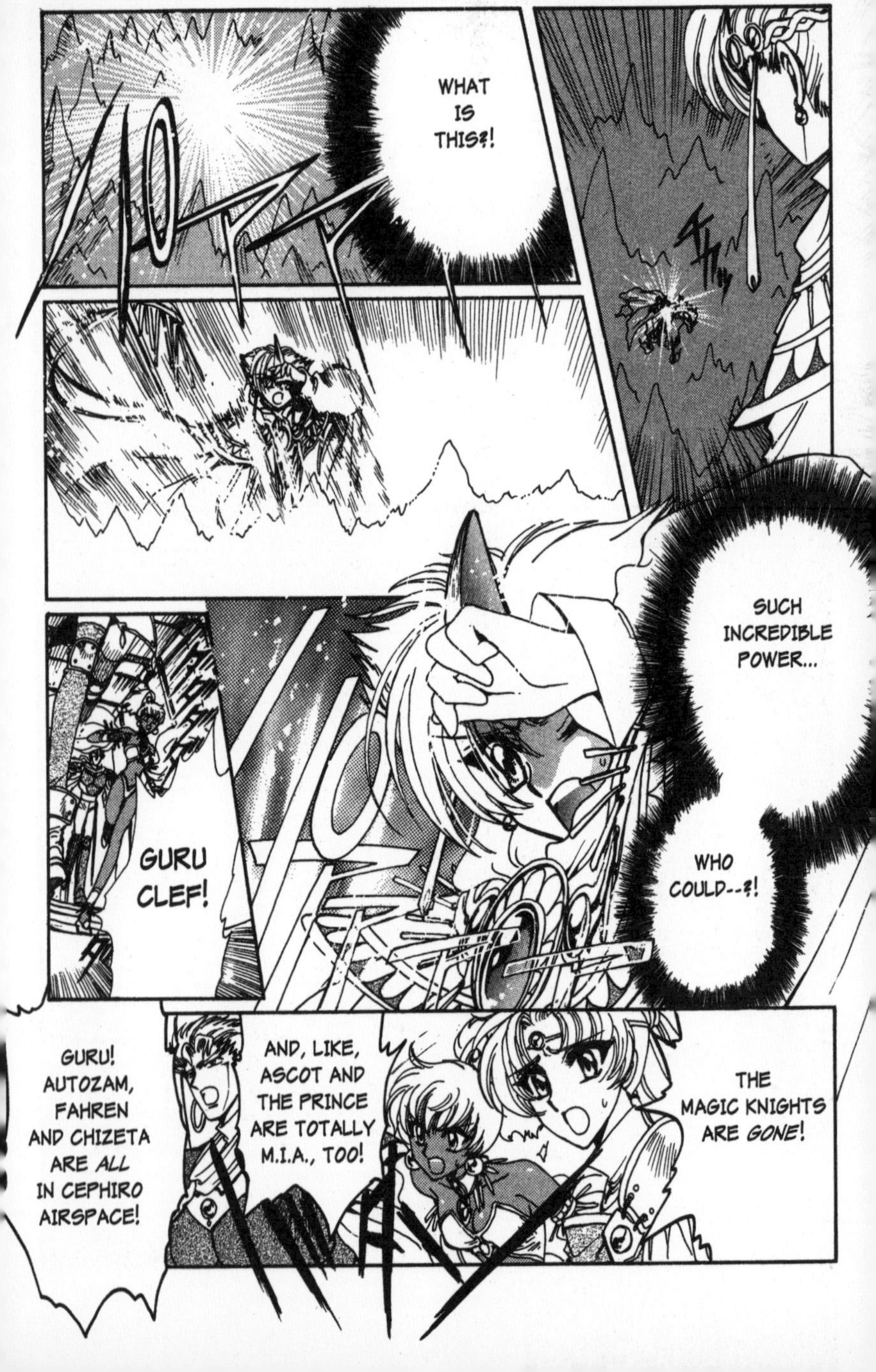
WHAT IS THIS?!
SUCH INCREDIBLE POWER...
WHO COULD--?!
GURU CLEF!
THE MAGIC KNIGHTS ARE *GONE*!
AND, LIKE, ASCOT AND THE PRINCE ARE TOTALLY M.I.A., TOO!
GURU! AUTOZAM, FAHREN AND CHIZETA ARE *ALL* IN CEPHIRO AIRSPACE!

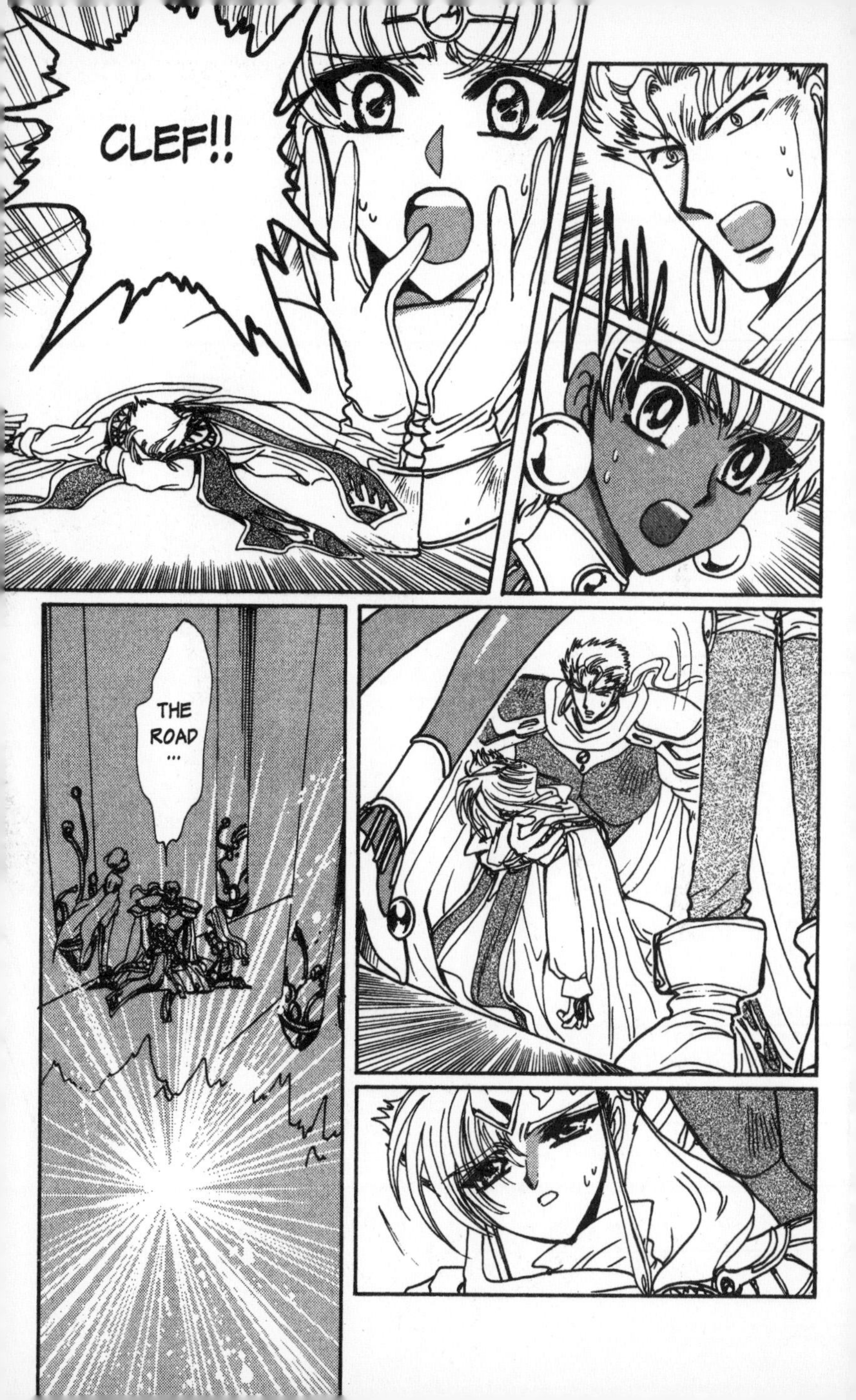
CLEF!!
THE ROAD ...

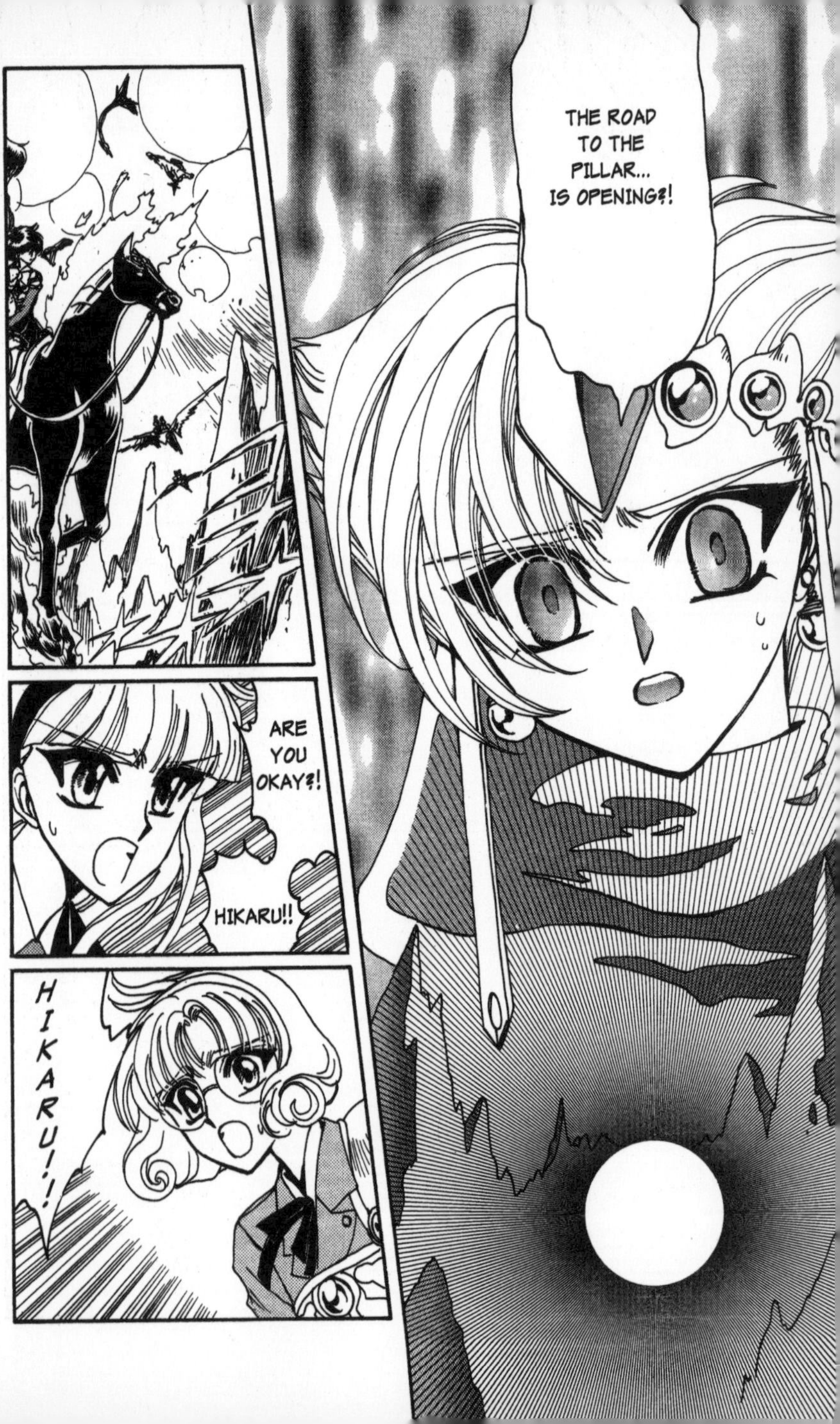
THE ROAD TO THE PILLAR... IS OPENING?!
ARE YOU OKAY?!
HIKARU!!
HIKARU!!!

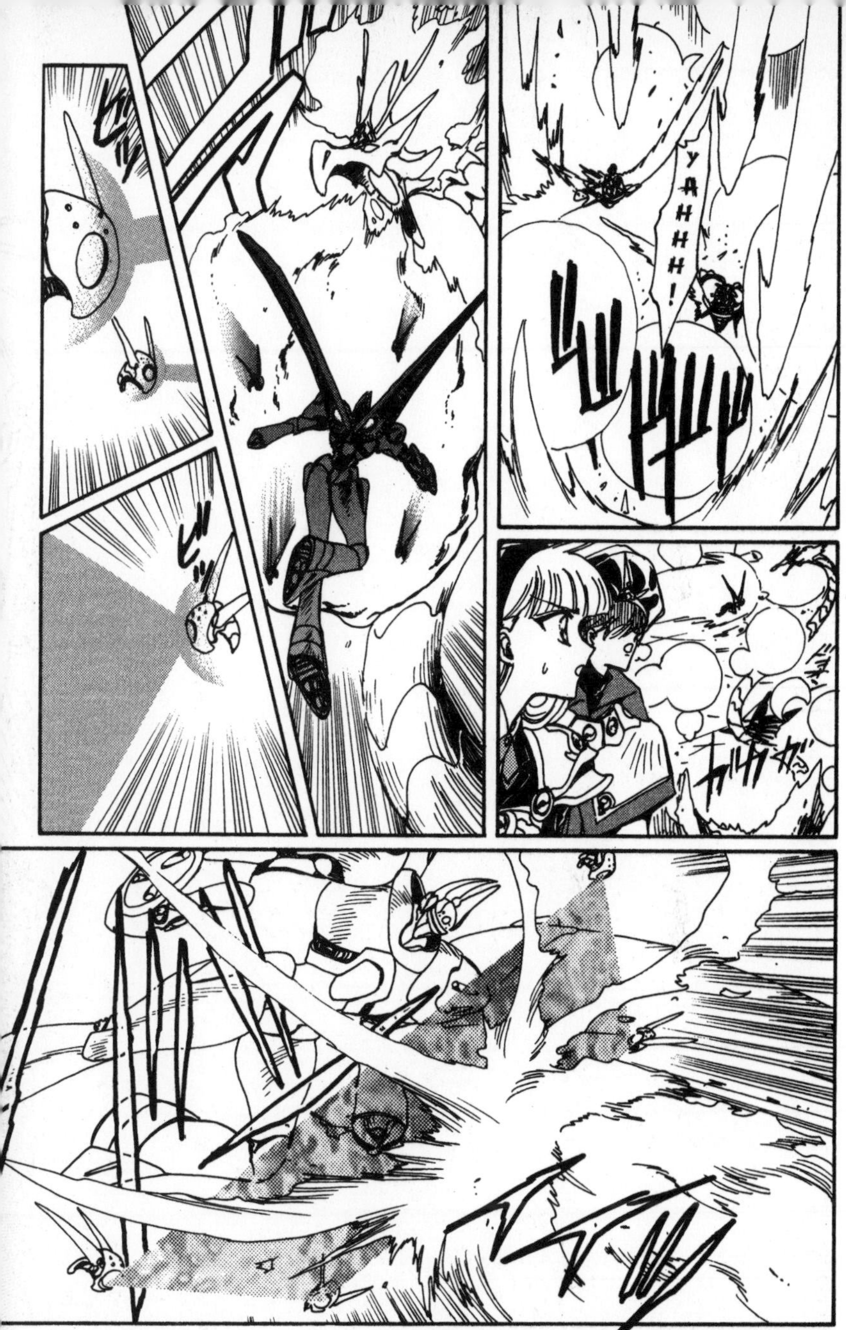
YAHHHH!

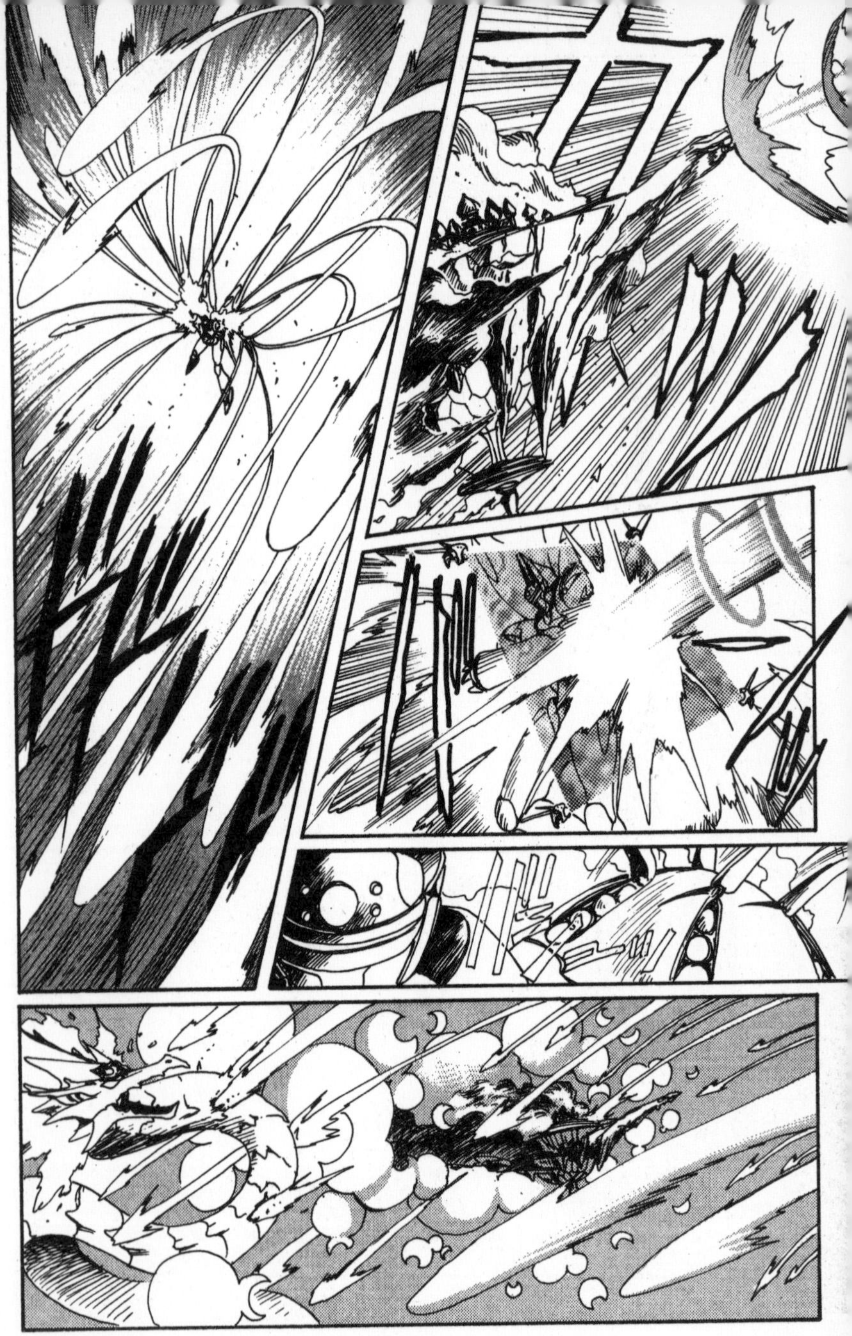

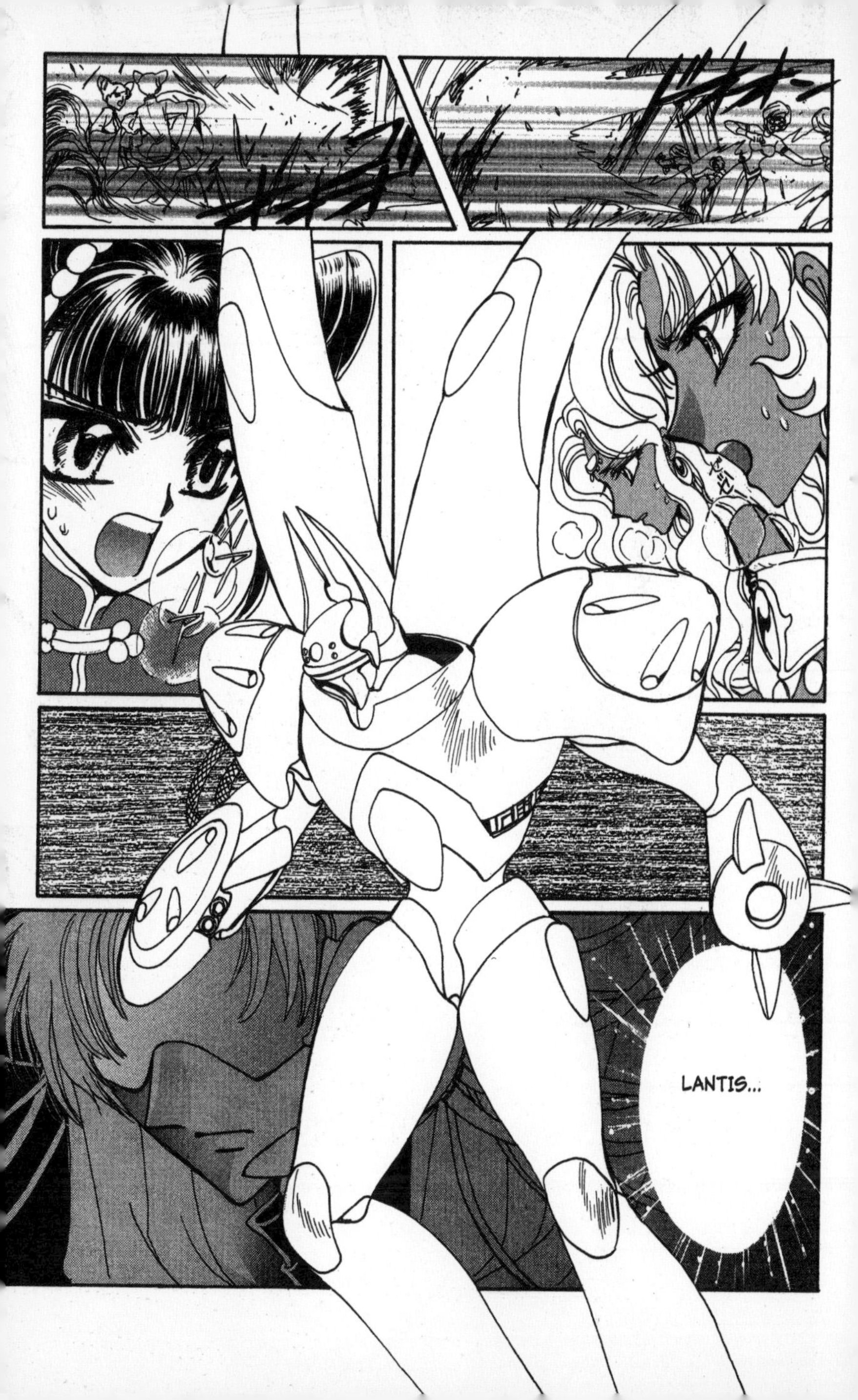
LANTIS...

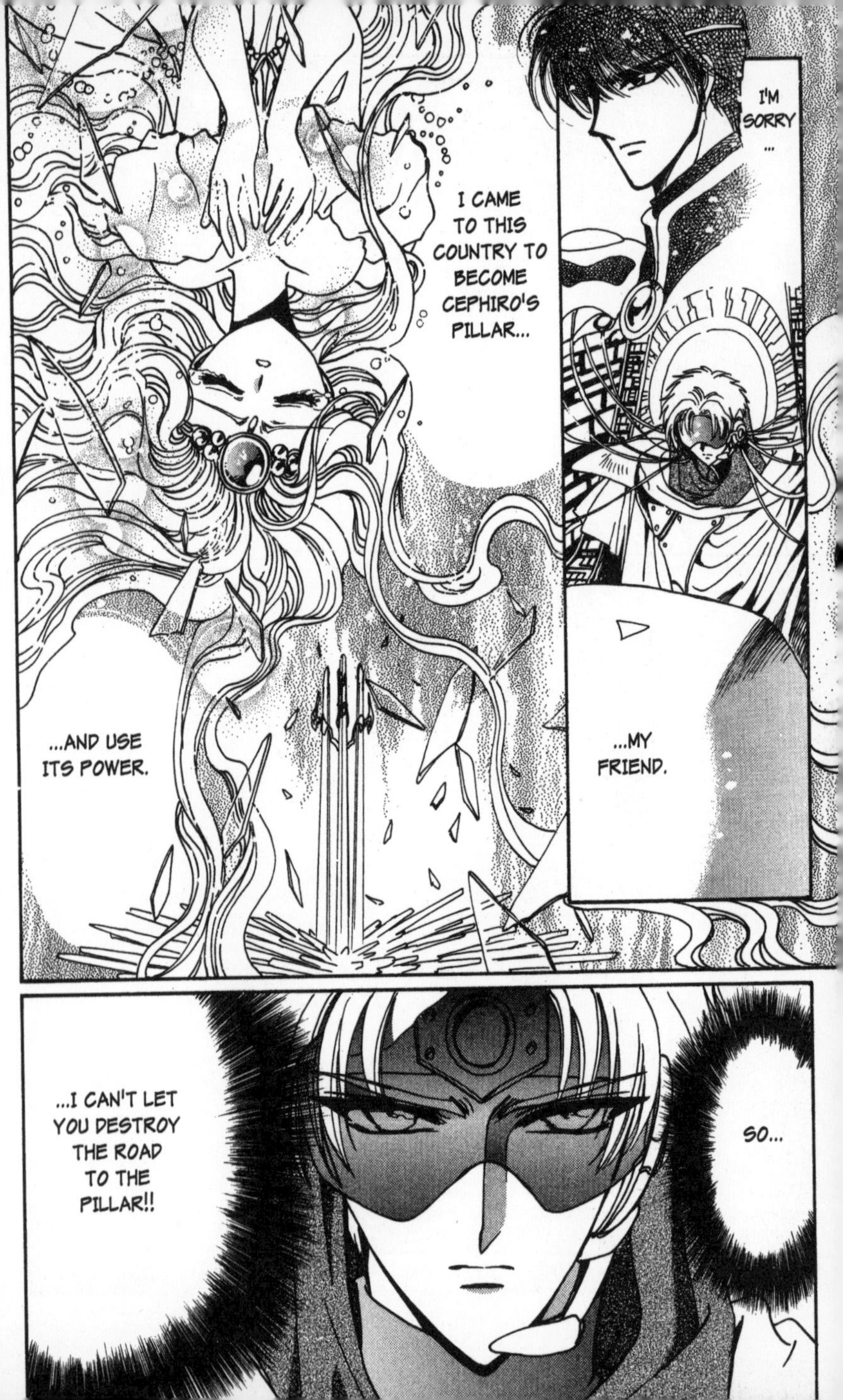
I'M SORRY ...
...MY FRIEND.
I CAME TO THIS COUNTRY TO BECOME CEPHIRO'S PILLAR...
...AND USE ITS POWER.
SO...
...I CAN'T LET YOU DESTROY THE ROAD TO THE PILLAR!!

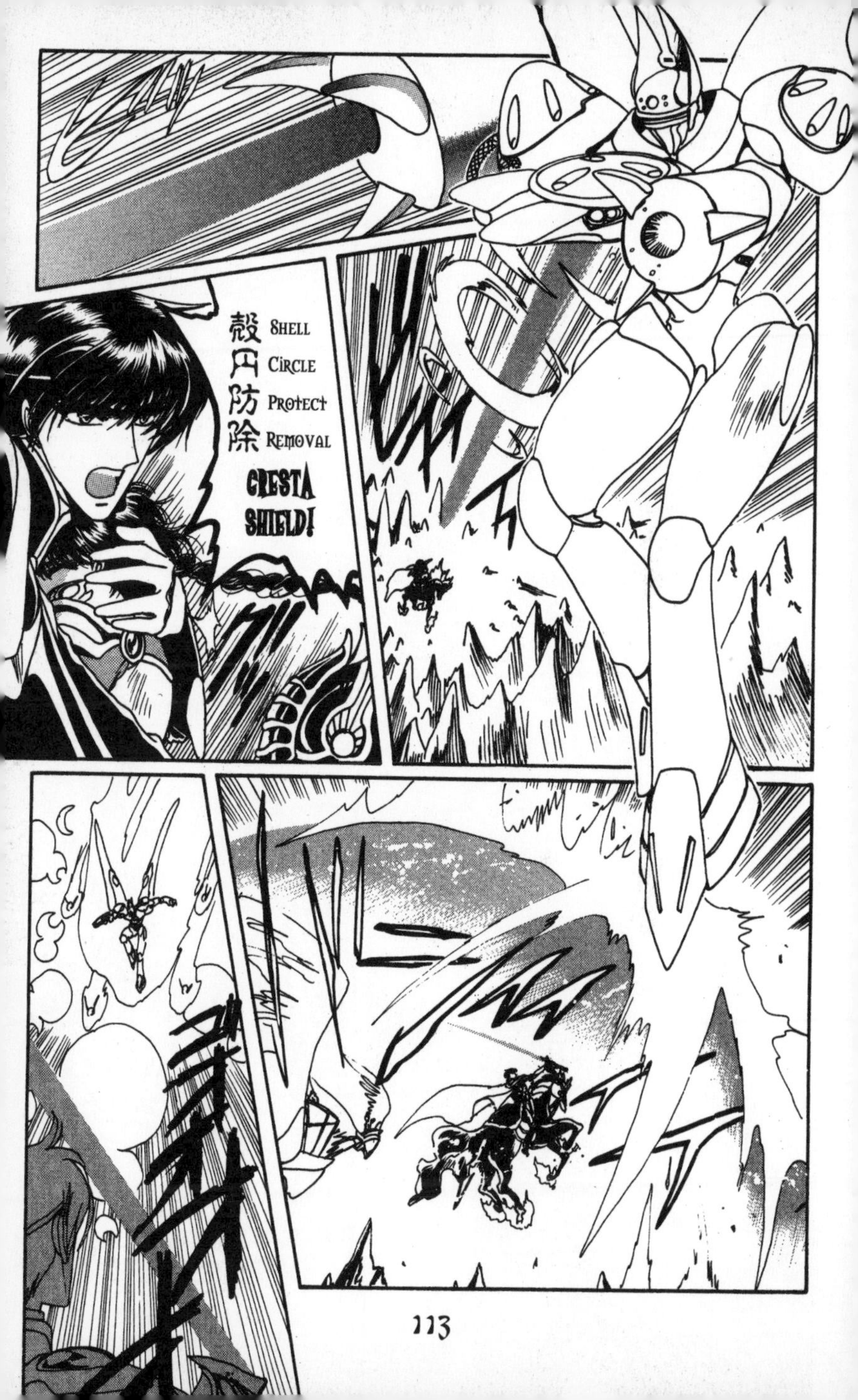
殼 SHELL
円 CIRCLE
防 PROTECT
除 REMOVAL
CRESTA SHIELD!

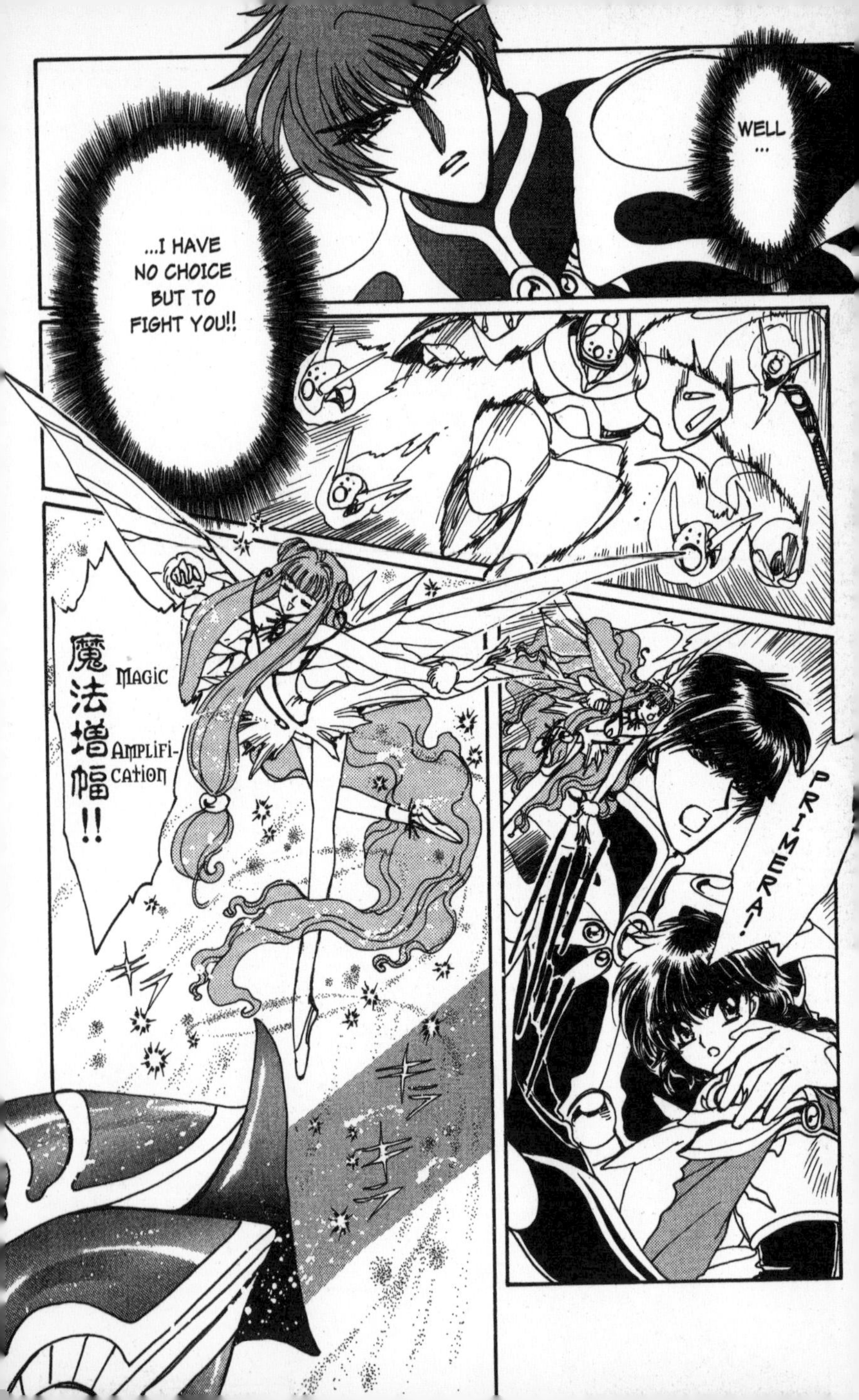
WELL ...
...I HAVE NO CHOICE BUT TO FIGHT YOU!!
PRIMERA!
魔法増幅!!
MAGIC AMPLIFICATION

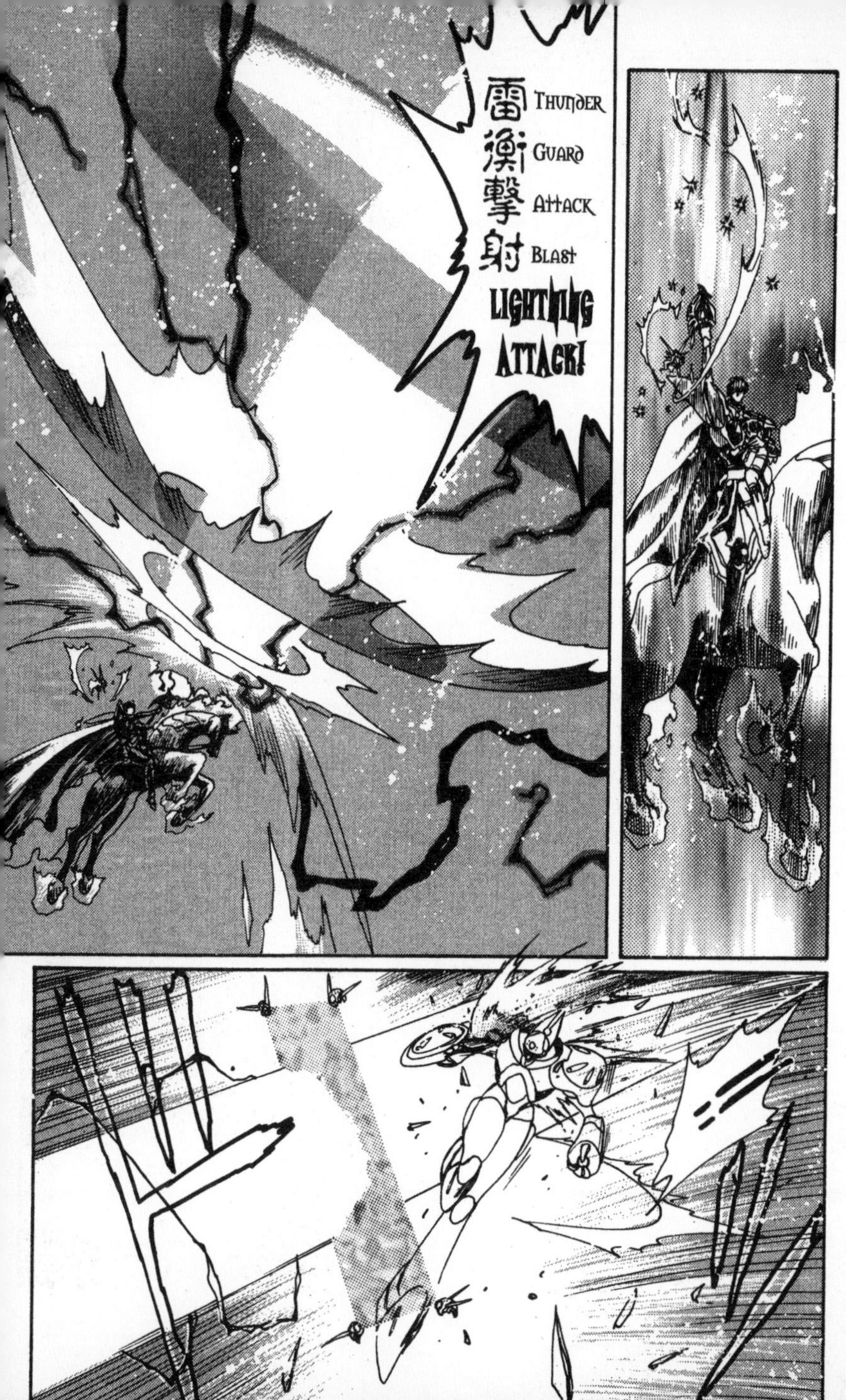
雷衝撃射
Thunder
Guard
Attack
Blast
Lightning
Attack!

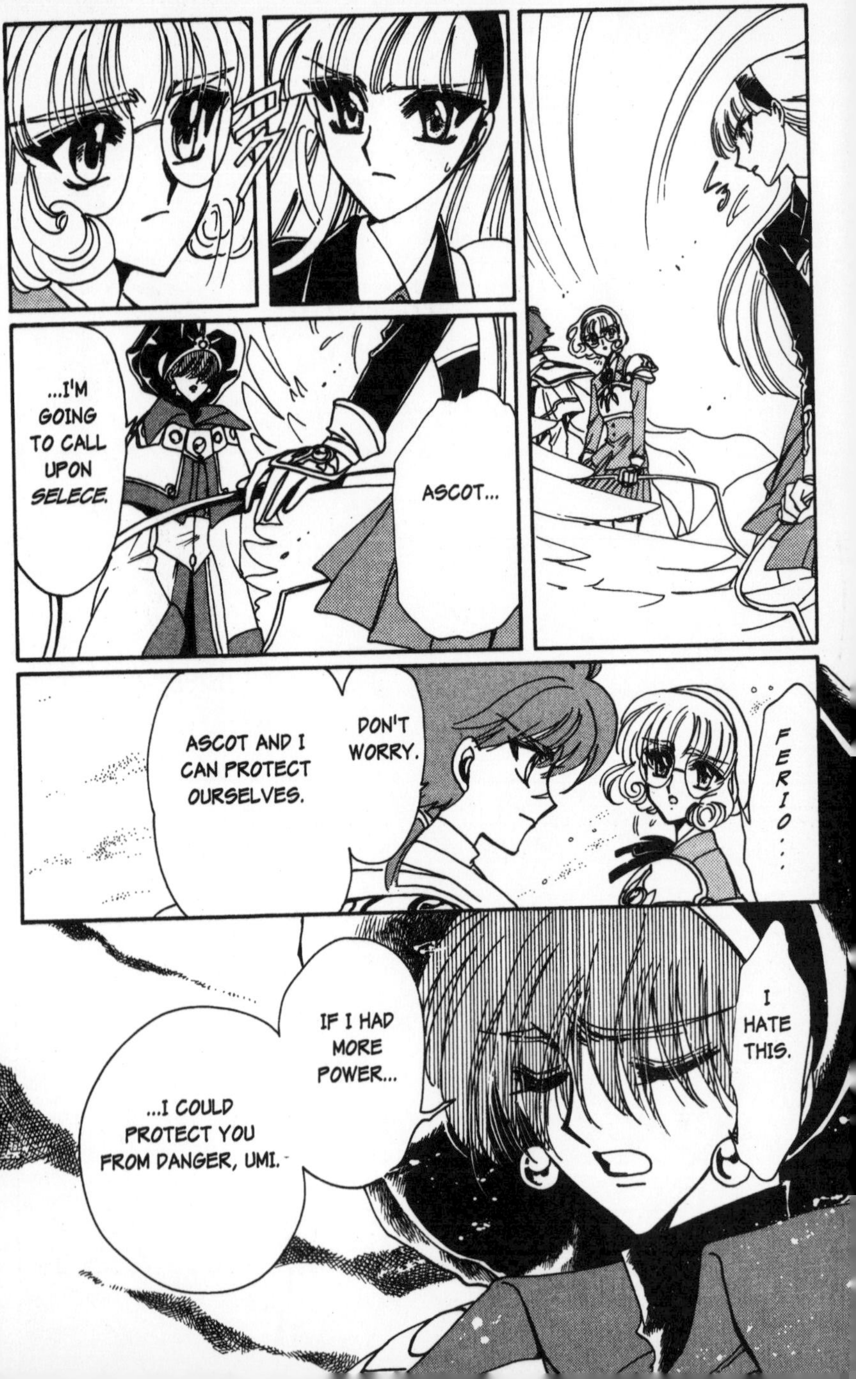
ASCOT...
...I'M GOING TO CALL UPON SELECE.
FERIO...
DON'T WORRY.
ASCOT AND I CAN PROTECT OURSELVES.
I HATE THIS.
IF I HAD MORE POWER...
...I COULD PROTECT YOU FROM DANGER, UMI.

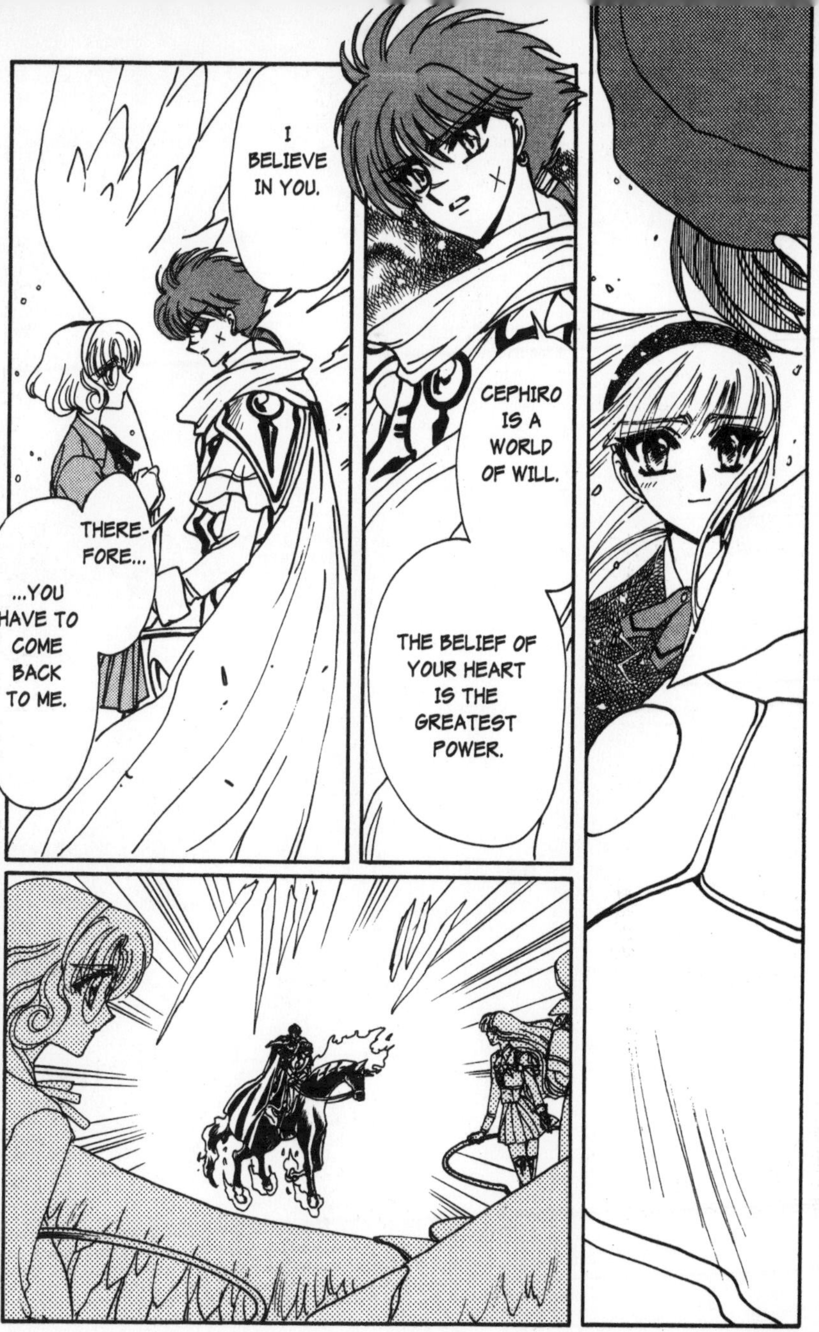
CEPHIRO IS A WORLD OF WILL.
THE BELIEF OF YOUR HEART IS THE GREATEST POWER.
I BELIEVE IN YOU.
THERE-FORE...
...YOU HAVE TO COME BACK TO ME.

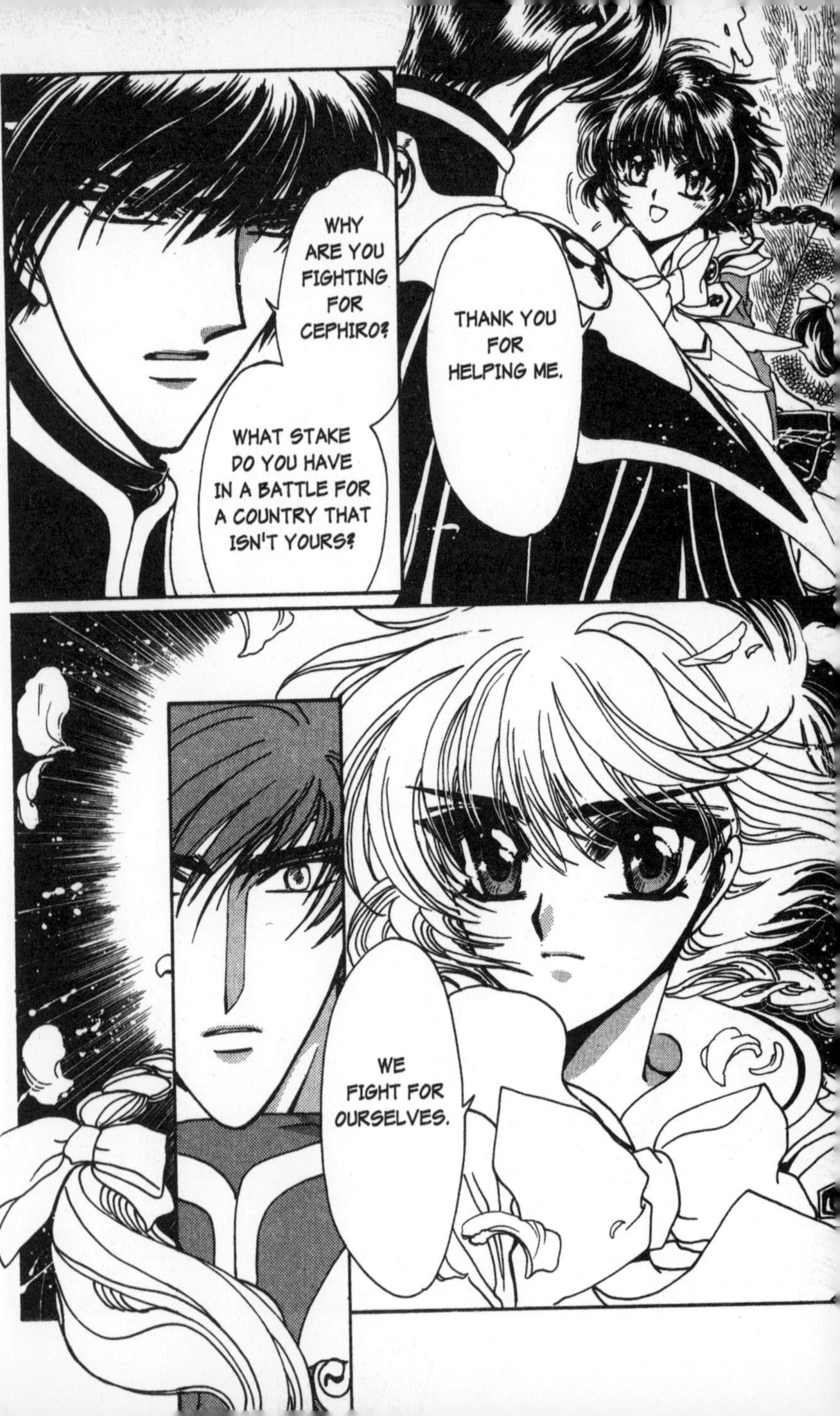
THANK YOU FOR HELPING ME.
WHY ARE YOU FIGHTING FOR CEPHIRO?
WHAT STAKE DO YOU HAVE IN A BATTLE FOR A COUNTRY THAT ISN'T YOURS?
WE FIGHT FOR OURSELVES.

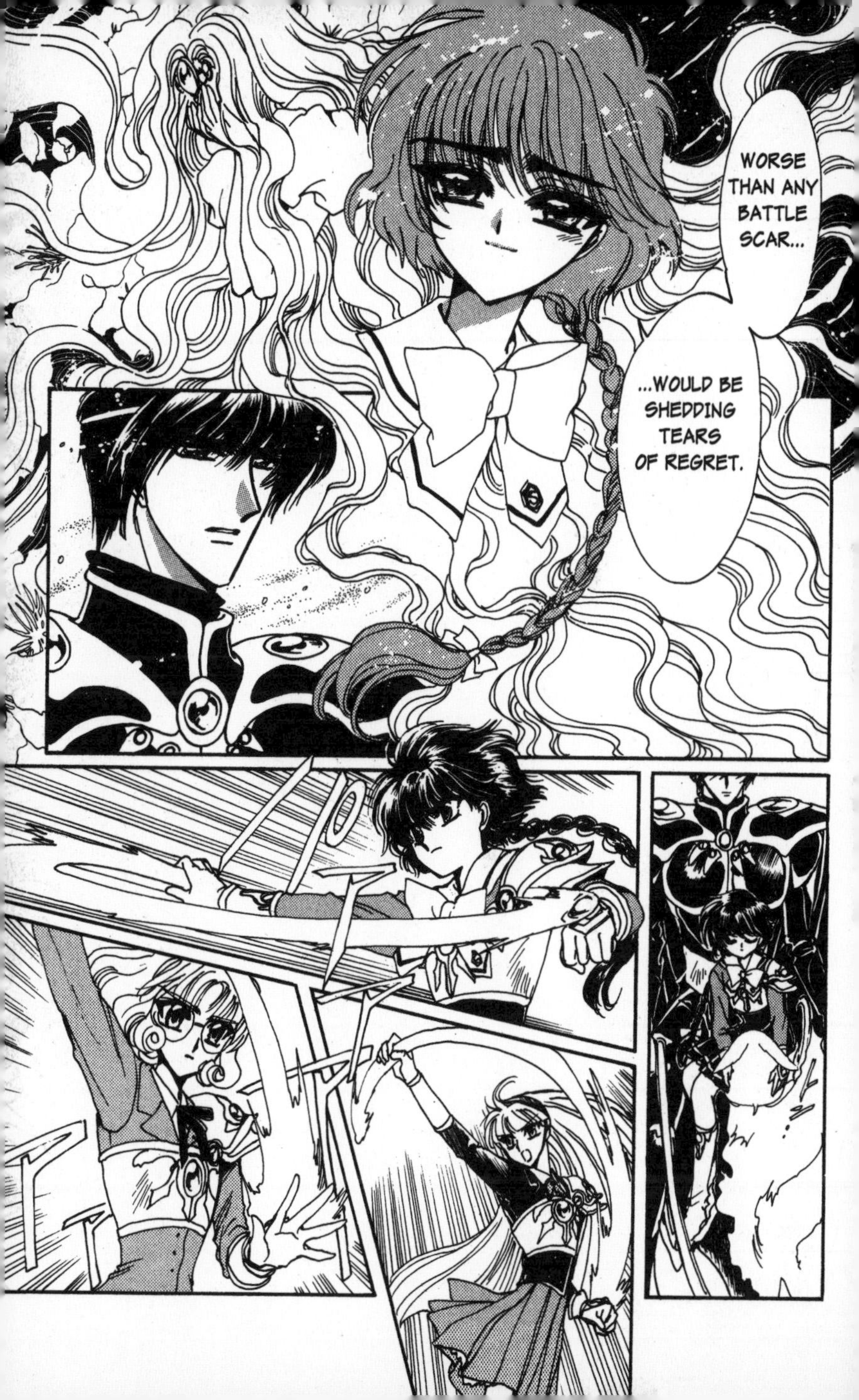
WORSE THAN ANY BATTLE SCAR...
...WOULD BE SHEDDING TEARS OF REGRET.

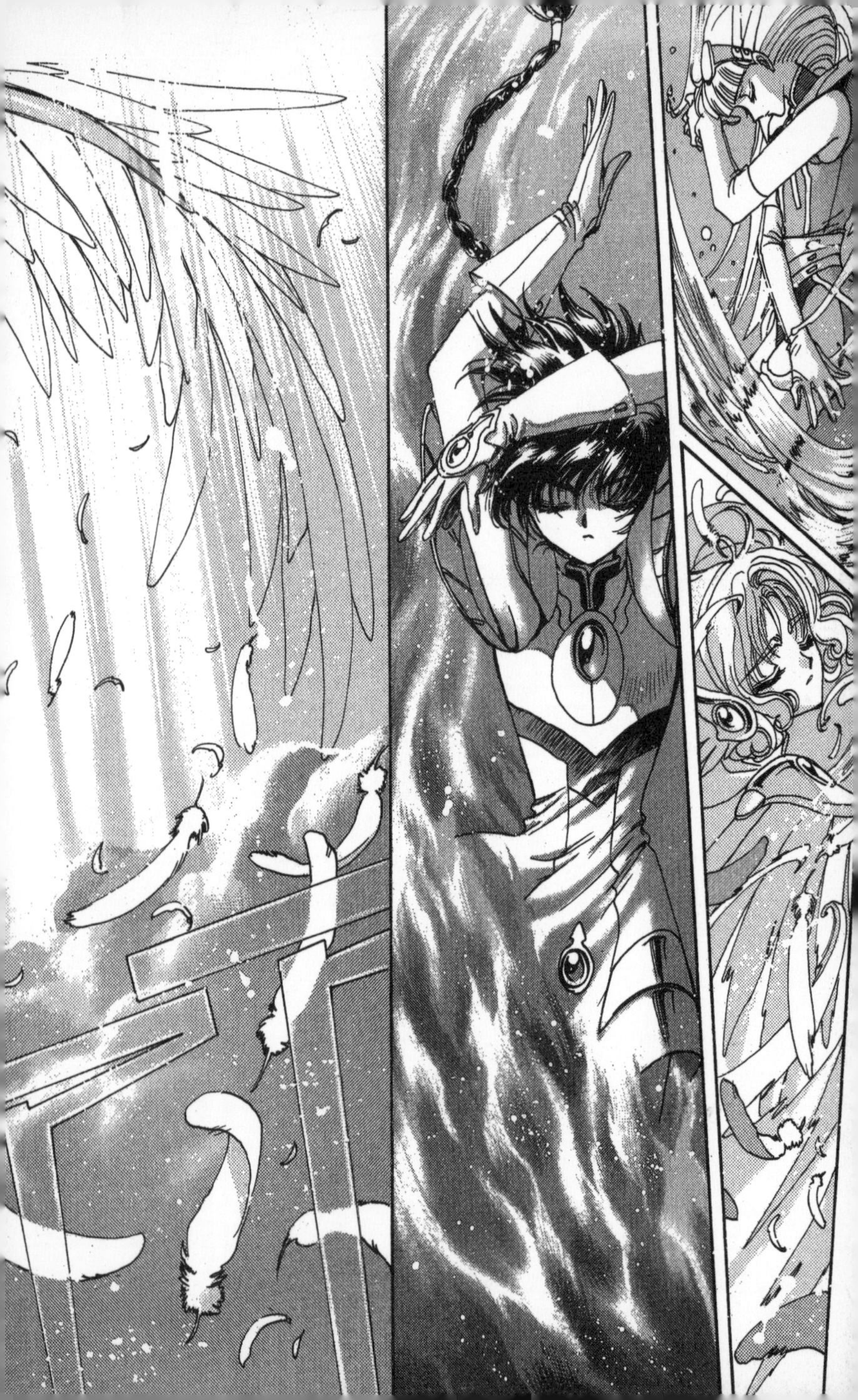

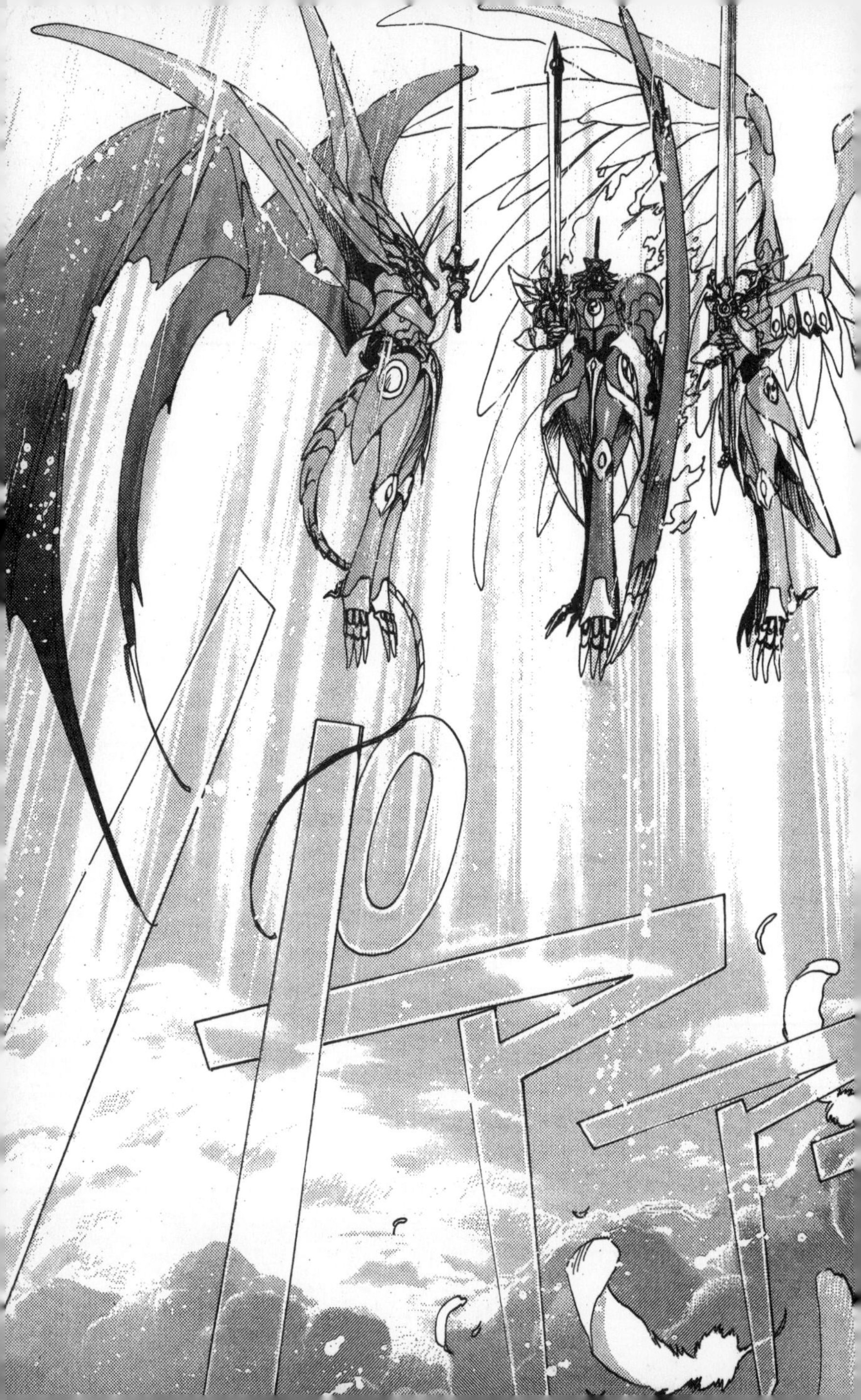

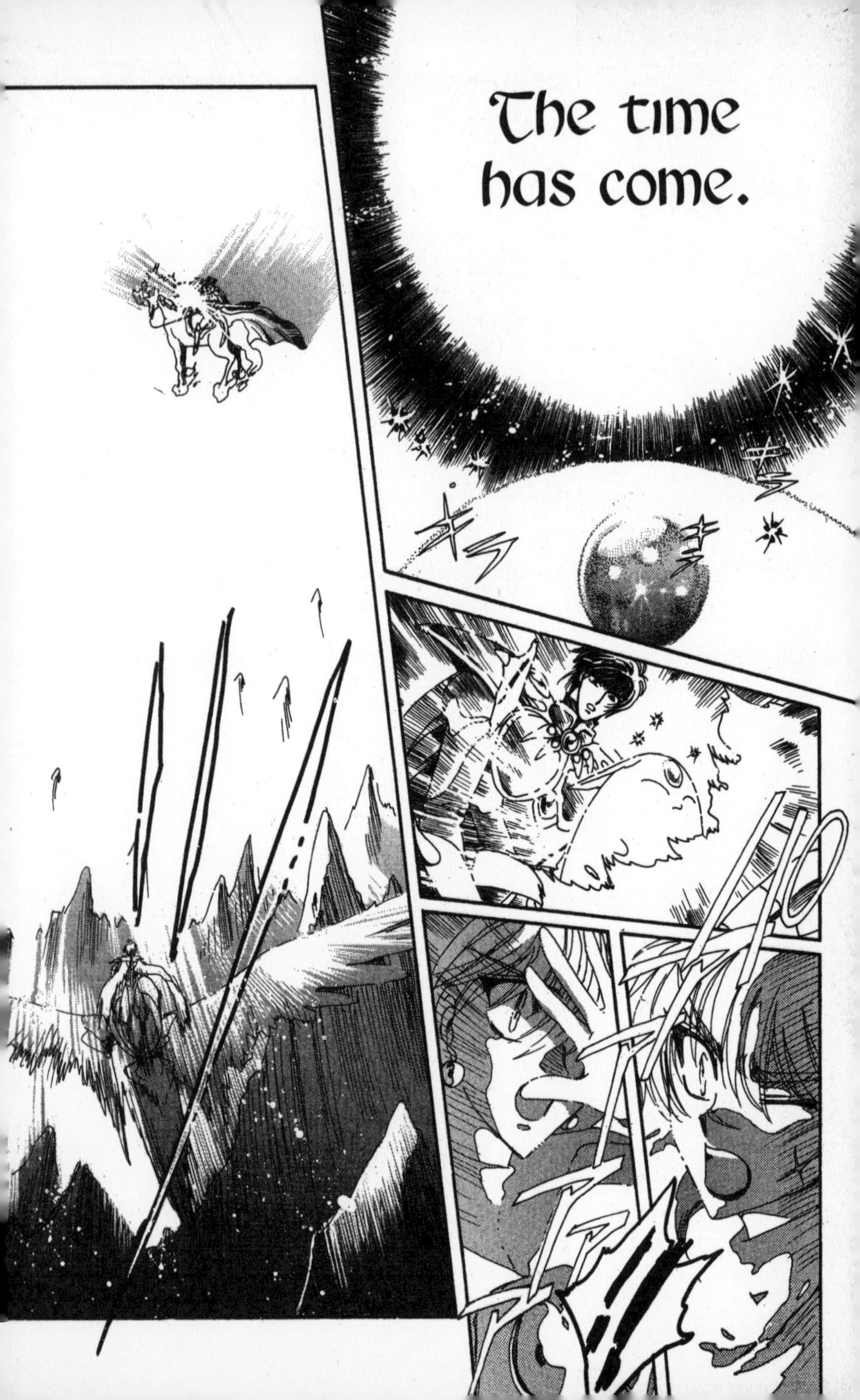
The time has come.

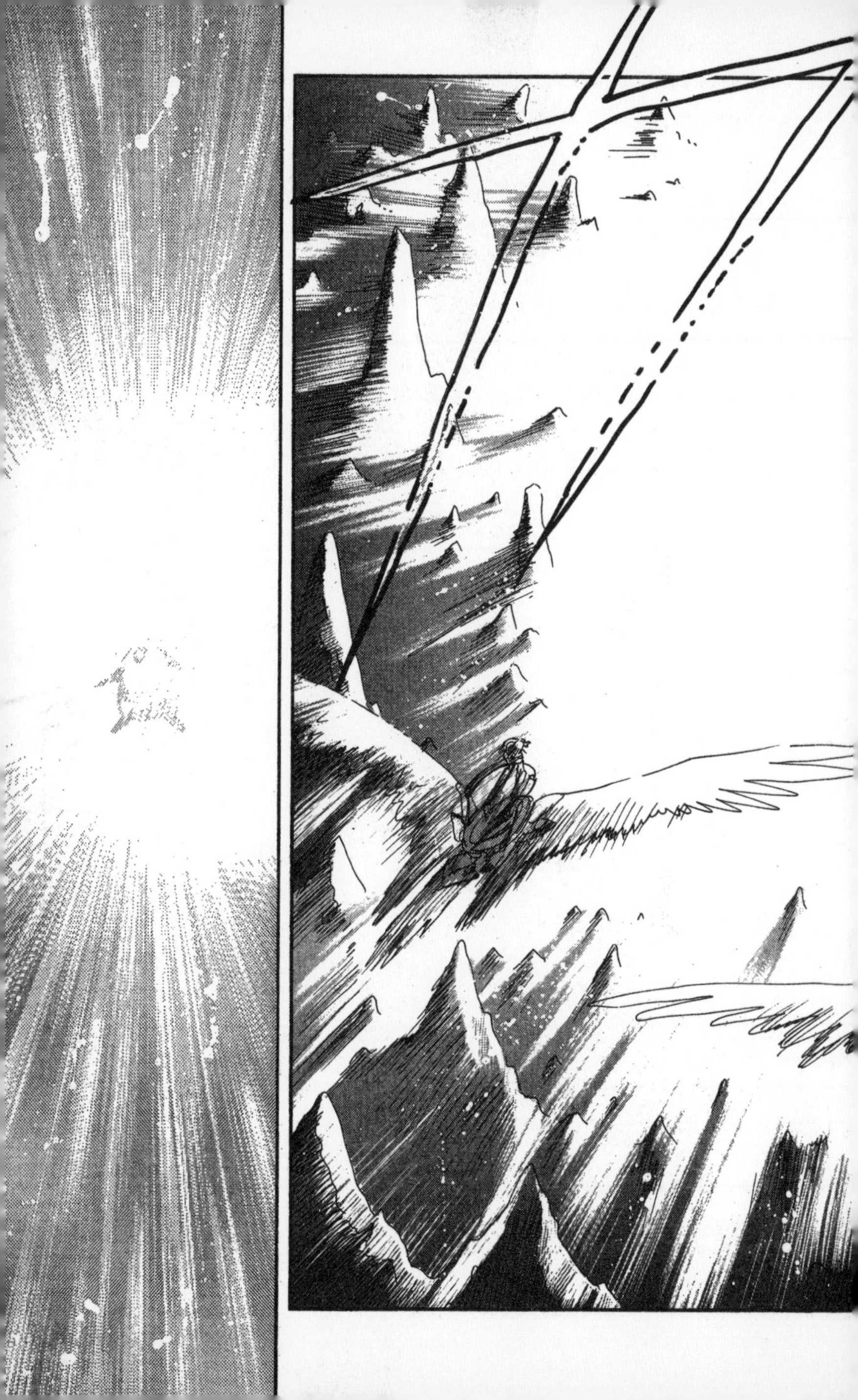

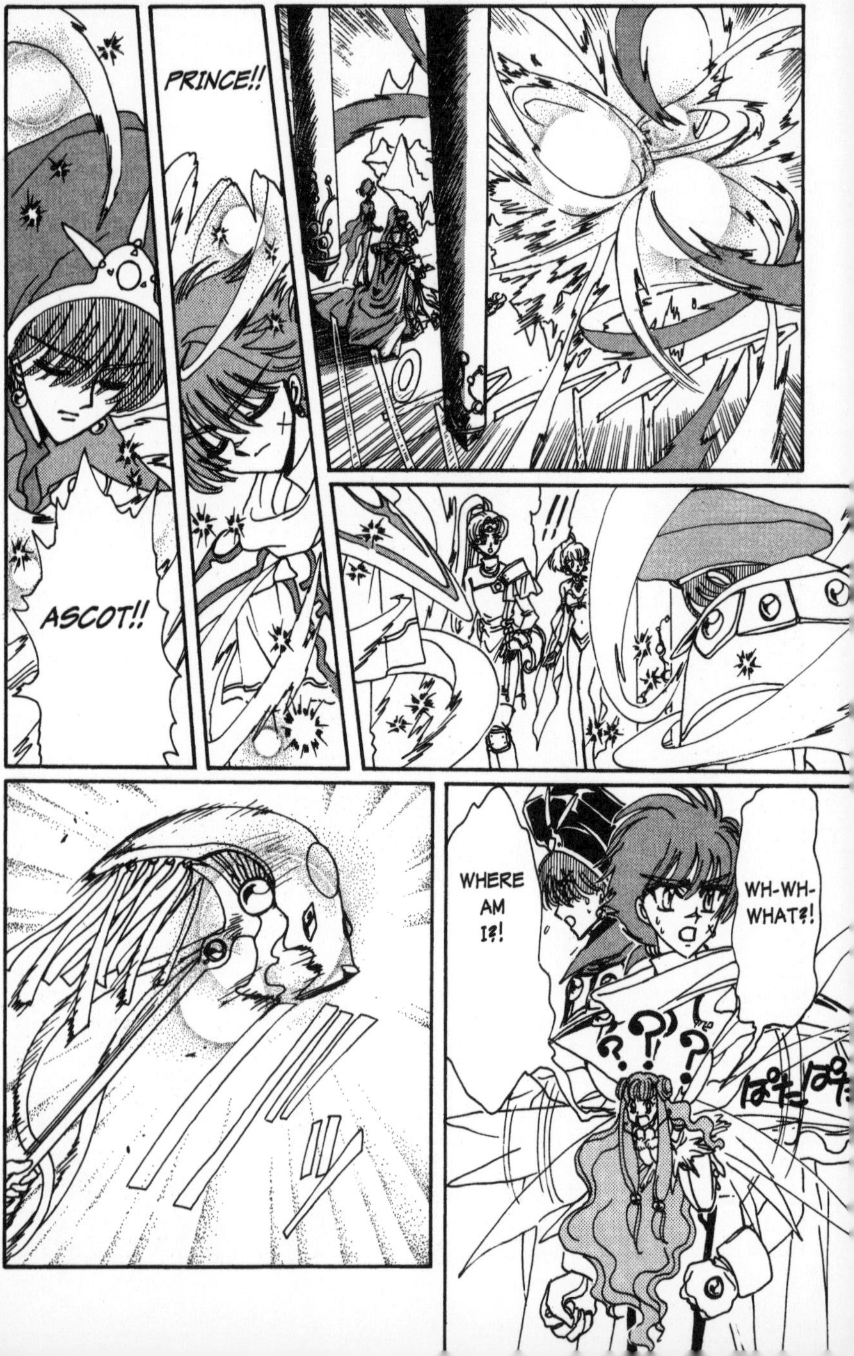
!!
PRINCE!!
ASCOT!!
WH-WH-WHAT?!
WHERE AM I?!
? ?! ?
ぱたぱた

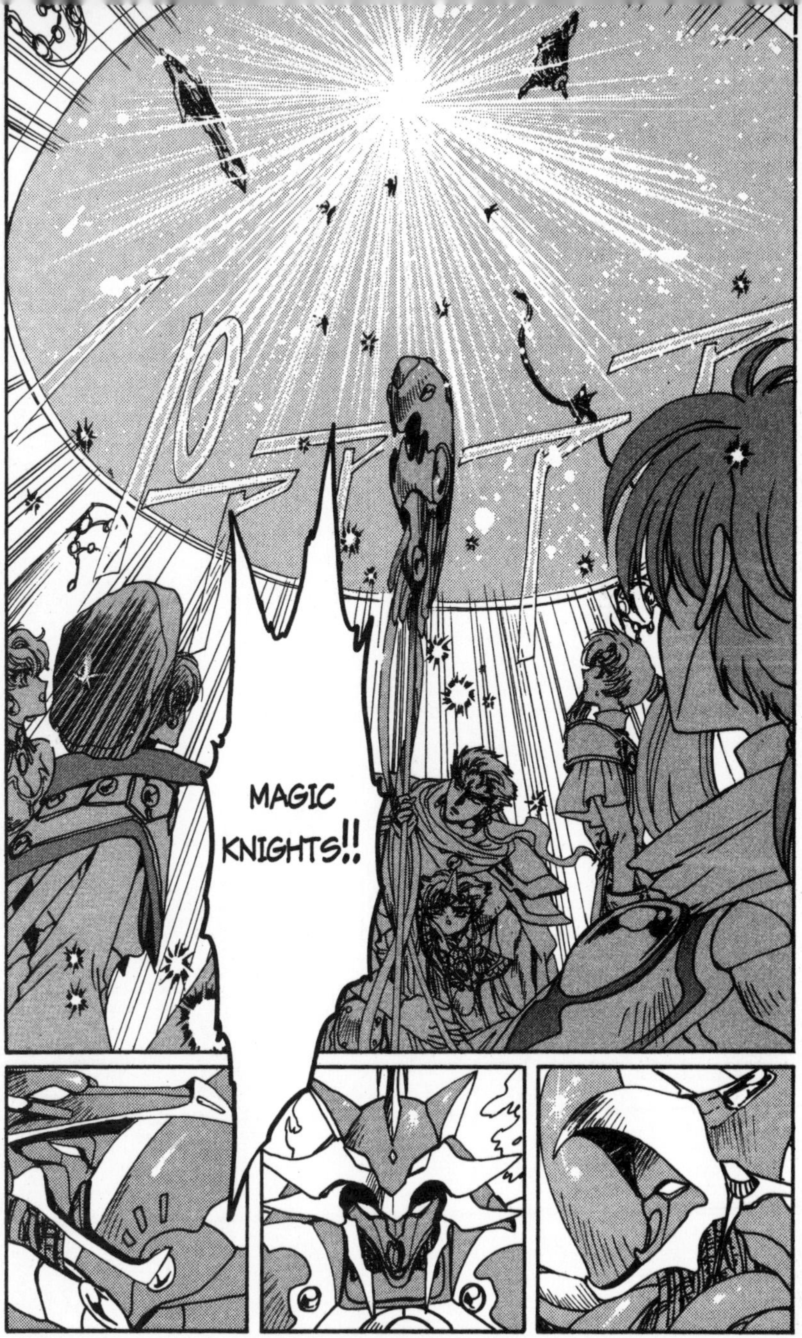
MAGIC KNIGHTS!!

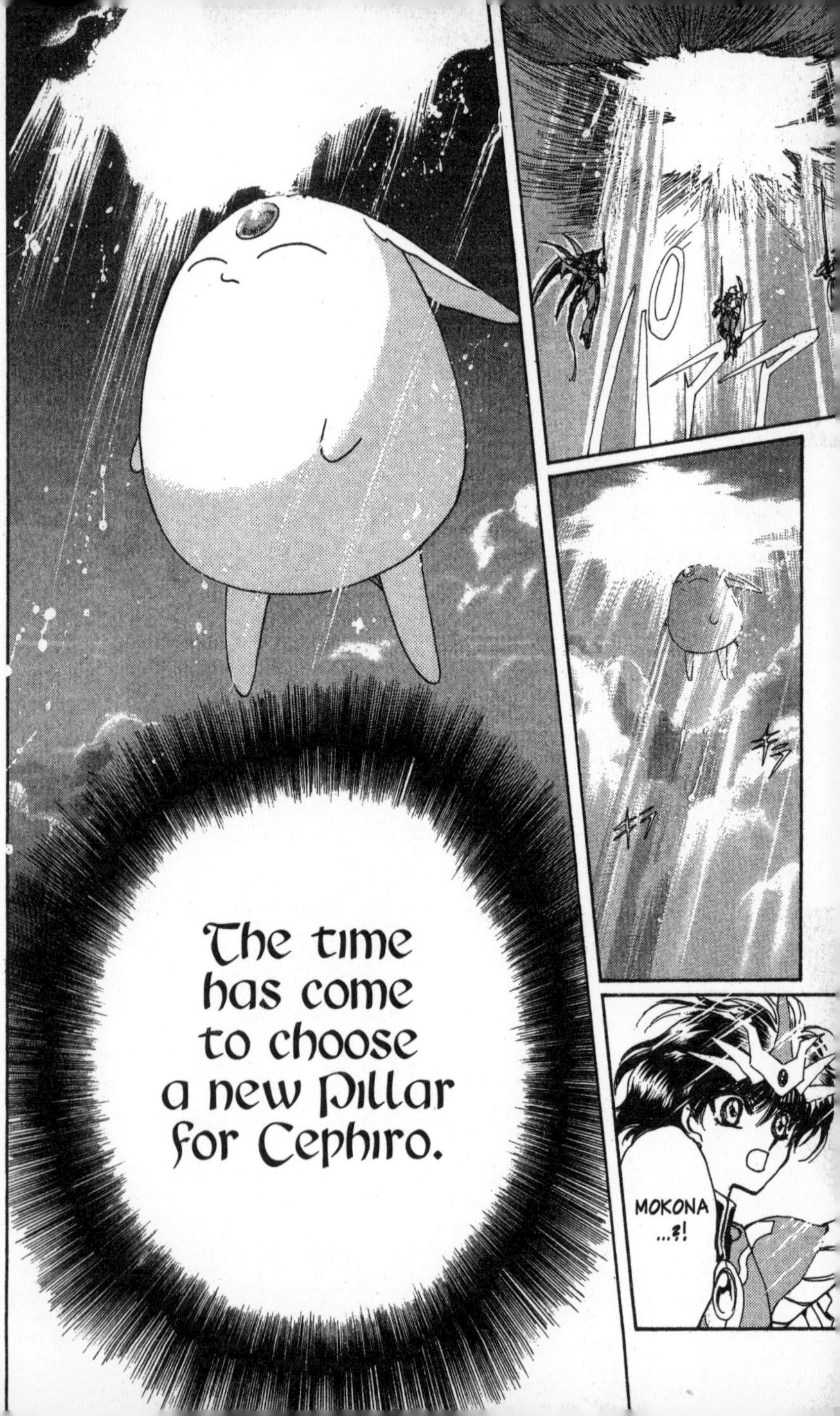
キラ
キラ
MOKONA ...?!
The time has come to choose a new Pillar for Cephiro.

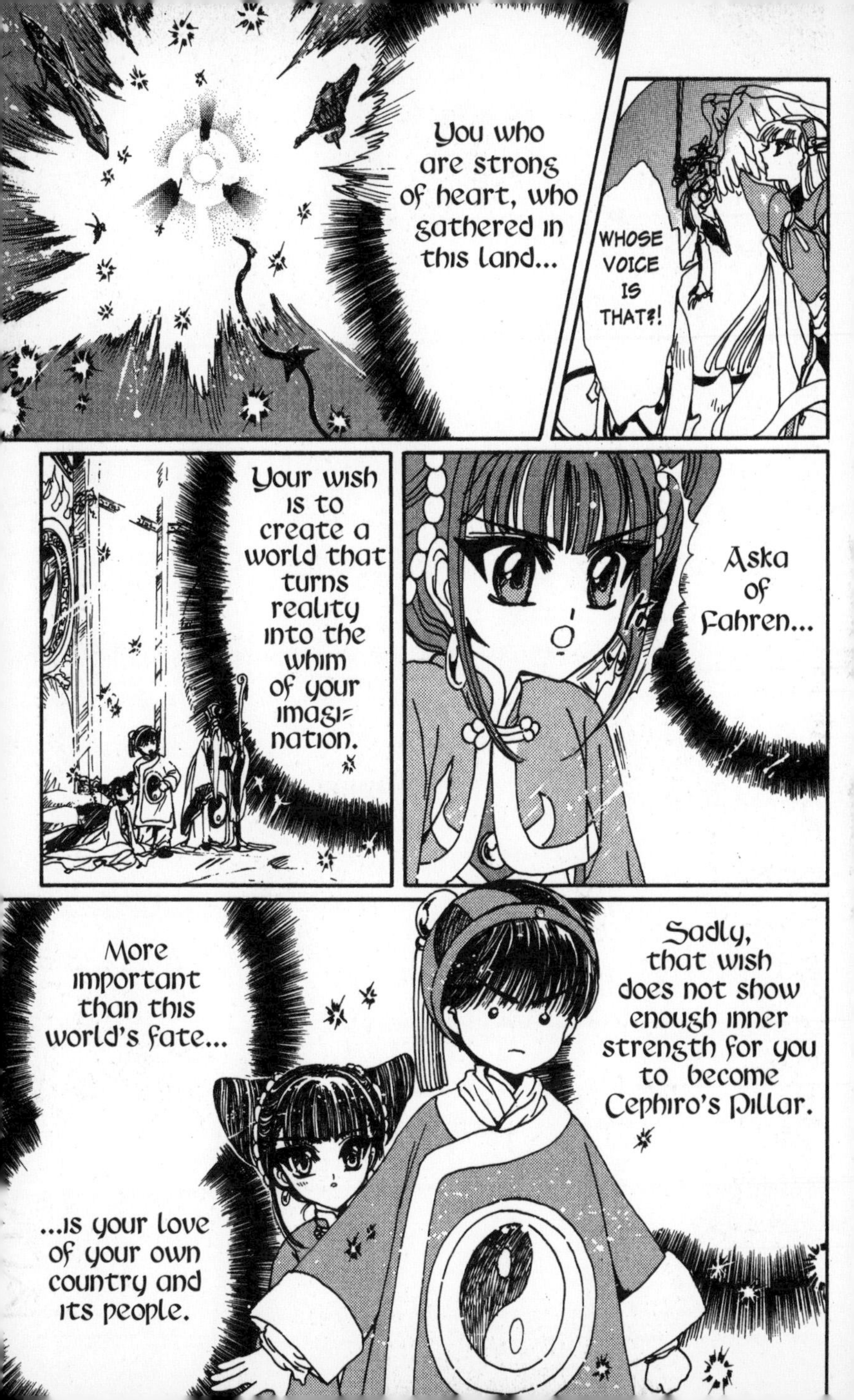
WHOSE VOICE IS THAT?!
You who are strong of heart, who gathered in this land...
Aska of Fahren...
Your wish is to create a world that turns reality into the whim of your imagi-nation.
Sadly, that wish does not show enough inner strength for you to become Cephiro's Pillar.
More important than this world's fate...
...is your love of your own country and its people.

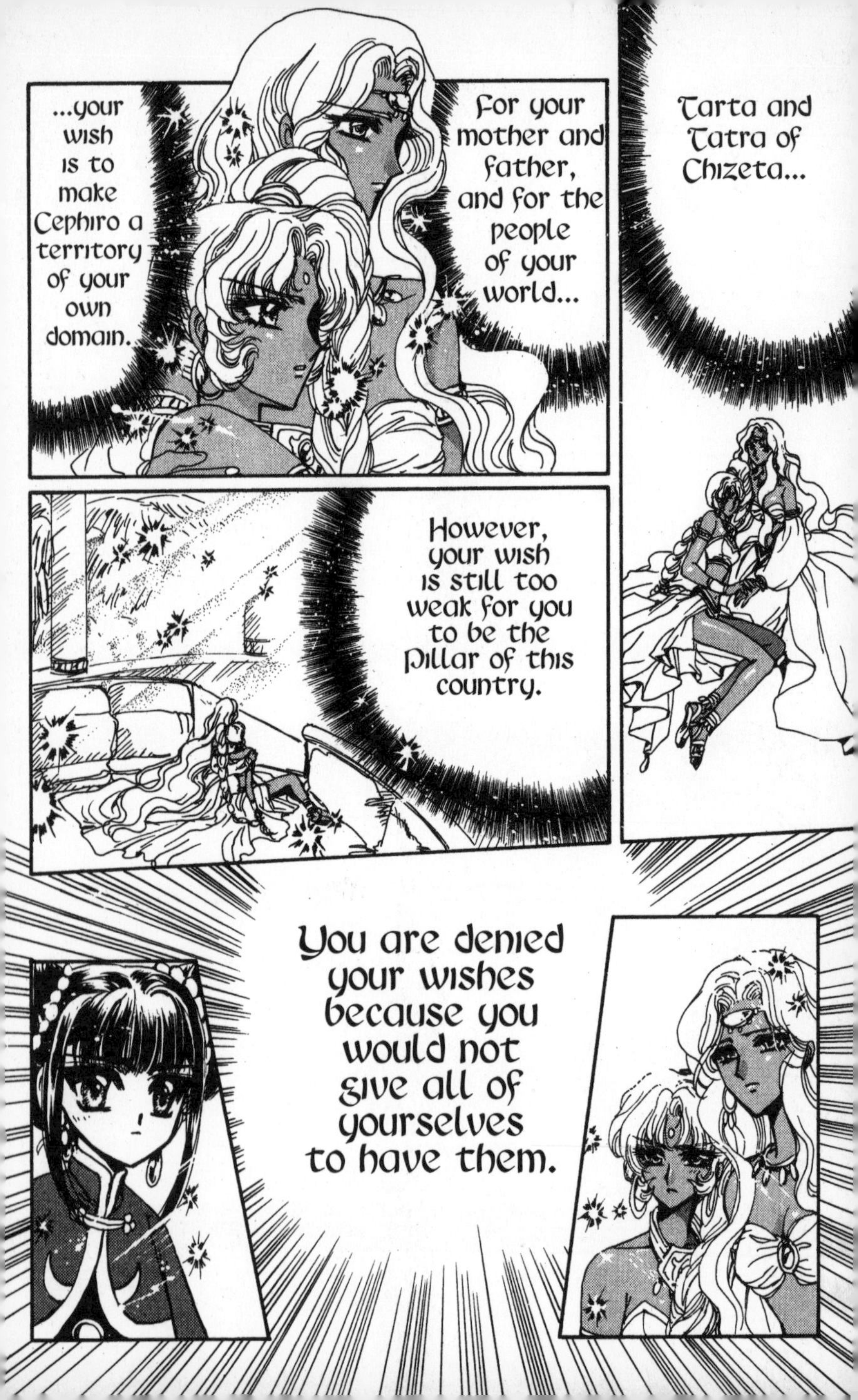
Tarta and Tatra of Chizeta...
For your mother and father, and for the people of your world...
...your wish is to make Cephiro a territory of your own domain.
However, your wish is still too weak for you to be the Pillar of this country.
You are denied your wishes because you would not give all of yourselves to have them.

Lantis
...

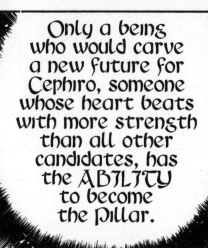

Only a being
who would carve
a new future for
Cephiro, someone
whose heart beats
with more strength
than all other
candidates, has
the ABILITY
to become
the Pillar.

Your
heart is
strong.

129

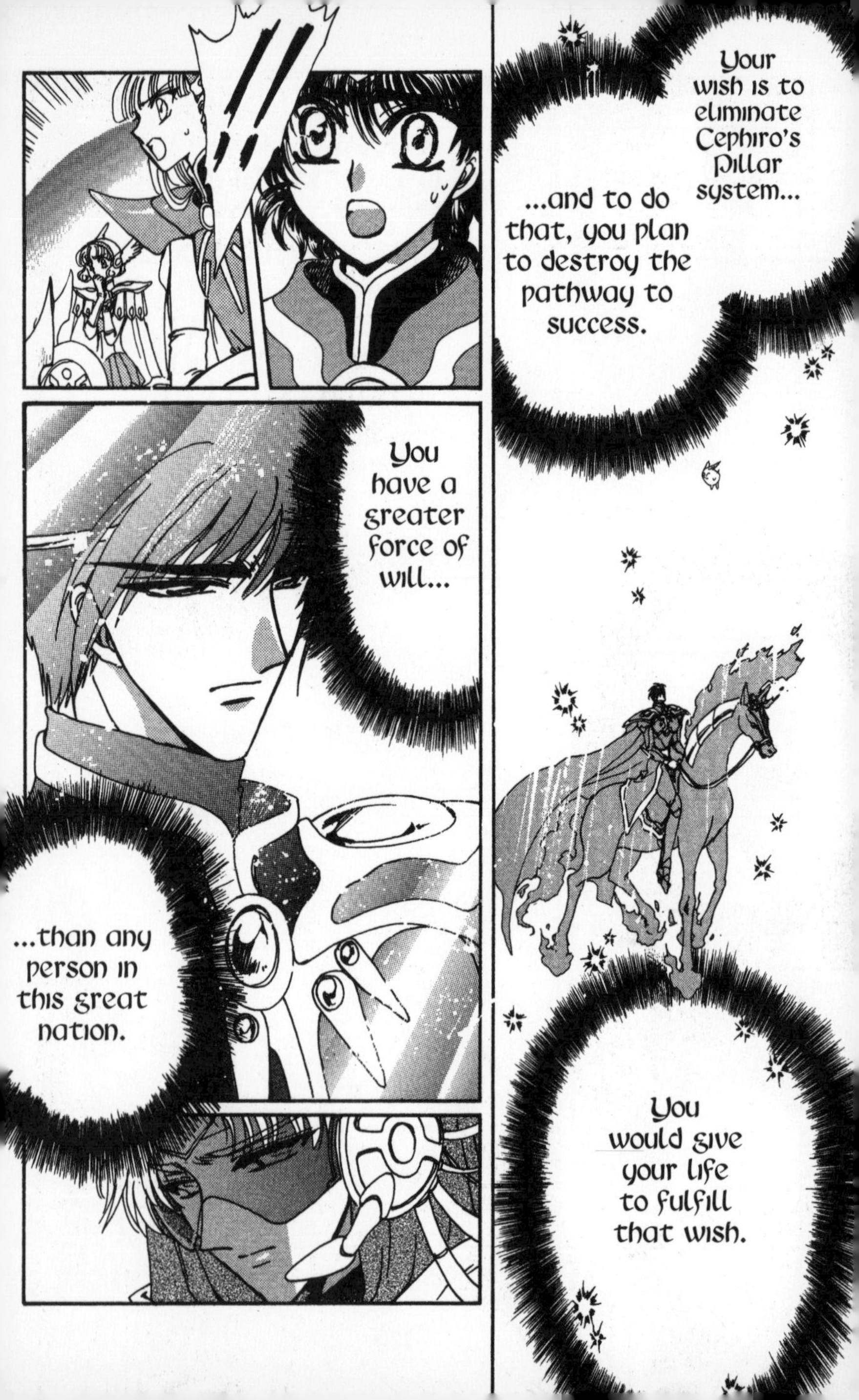
Your wish is to eliminate Cephiro's Pillar system...
...and to do that, you plan to destroy the pathway to success.
You would give your life to fulfill that wish.
You have a greater force of will...
...than any person in this great nation.

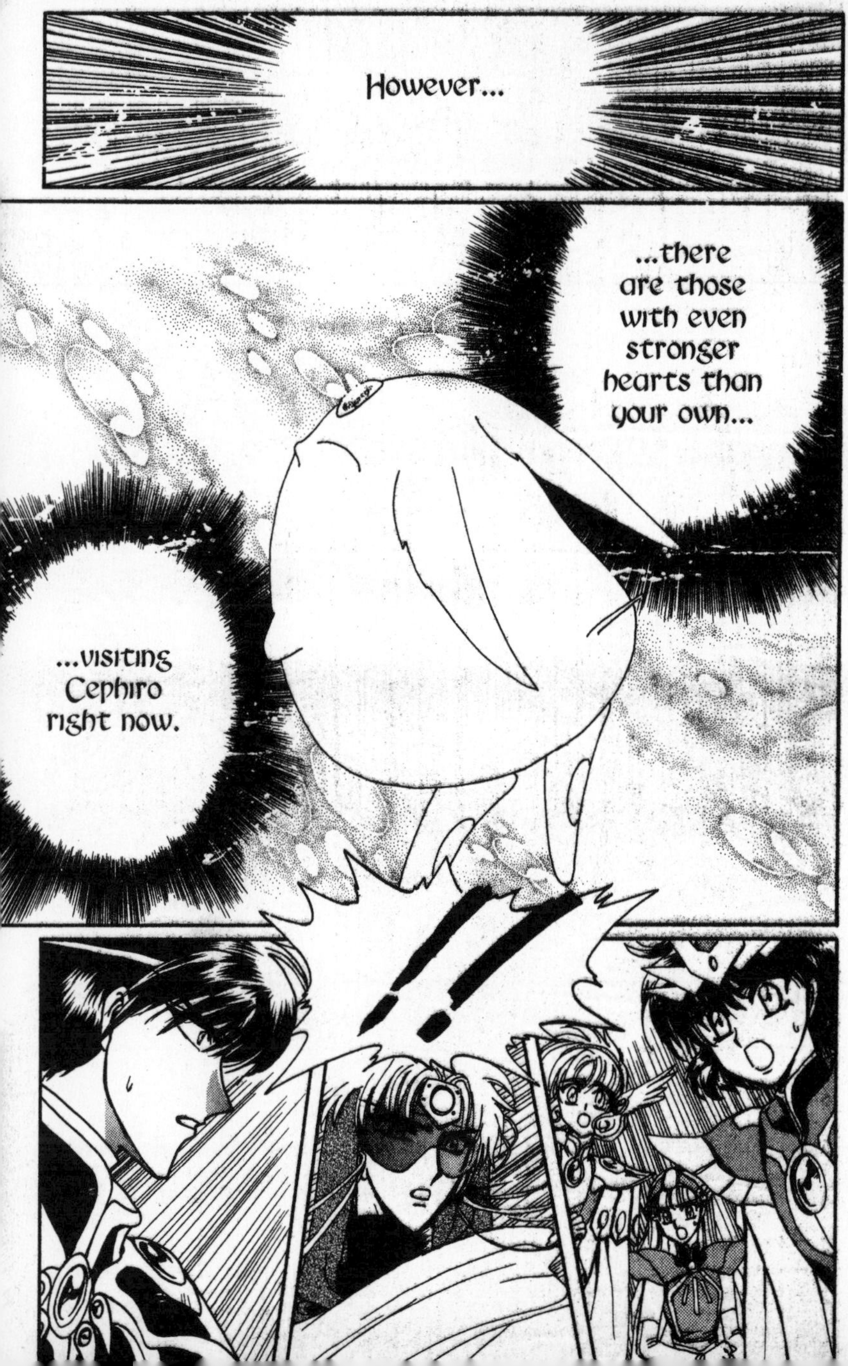
However...
...there are those with even stronger hearts than your own...
...visiting Cephiro right now.
!!

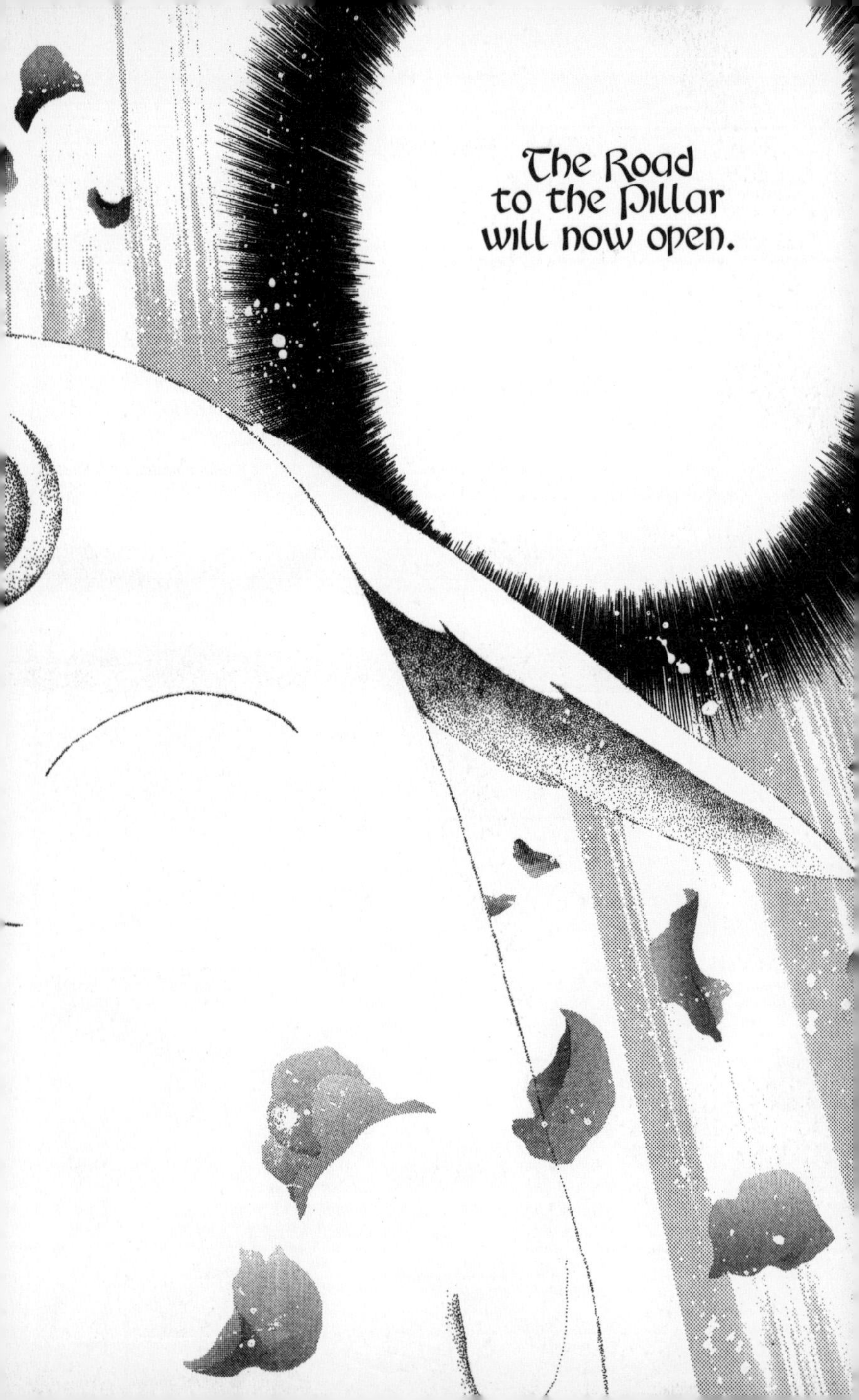
The Road to the Pillar will now open.

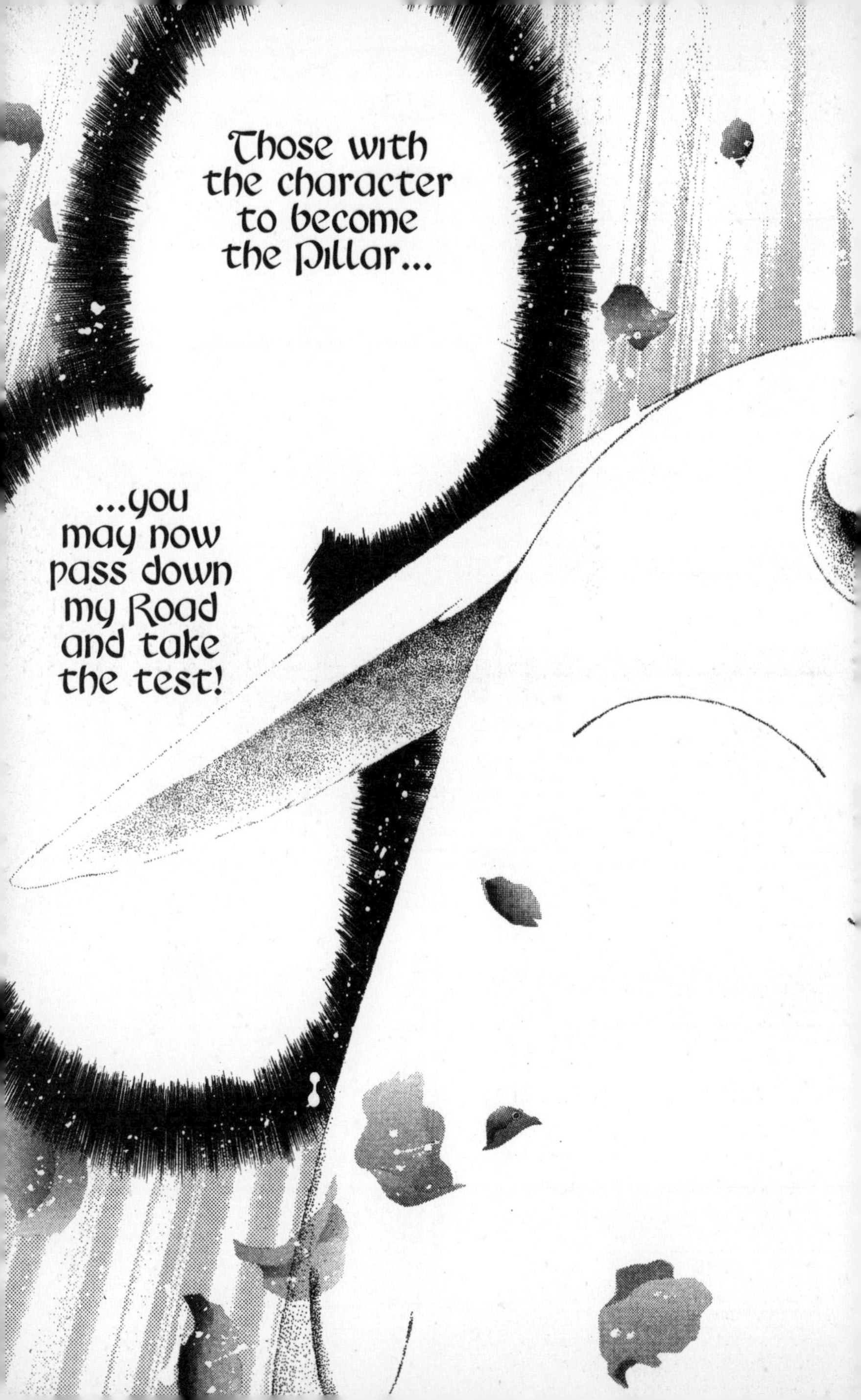
Those with the character to become the Pillar...
...you may now pass down my Road and take the test!

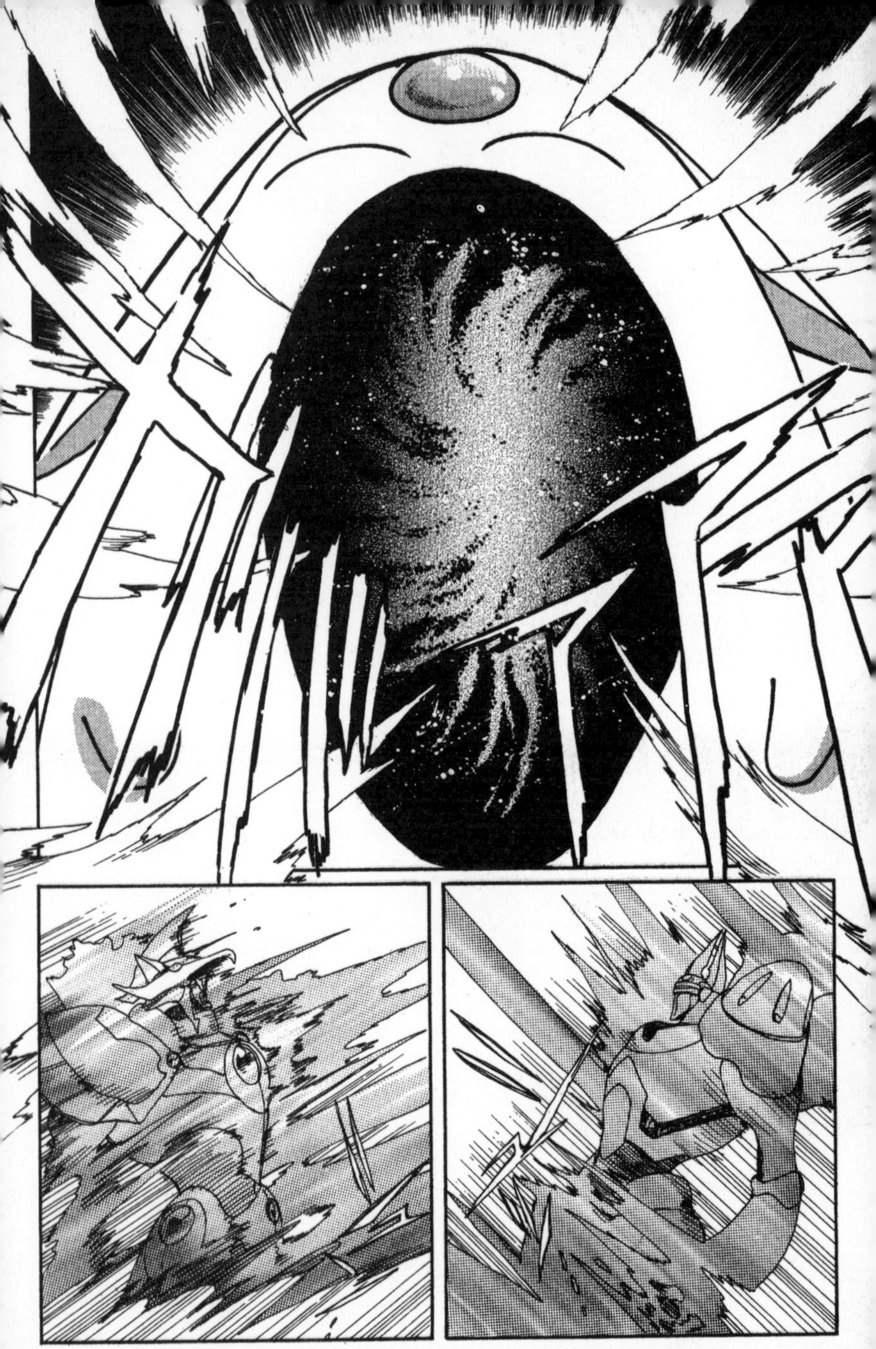

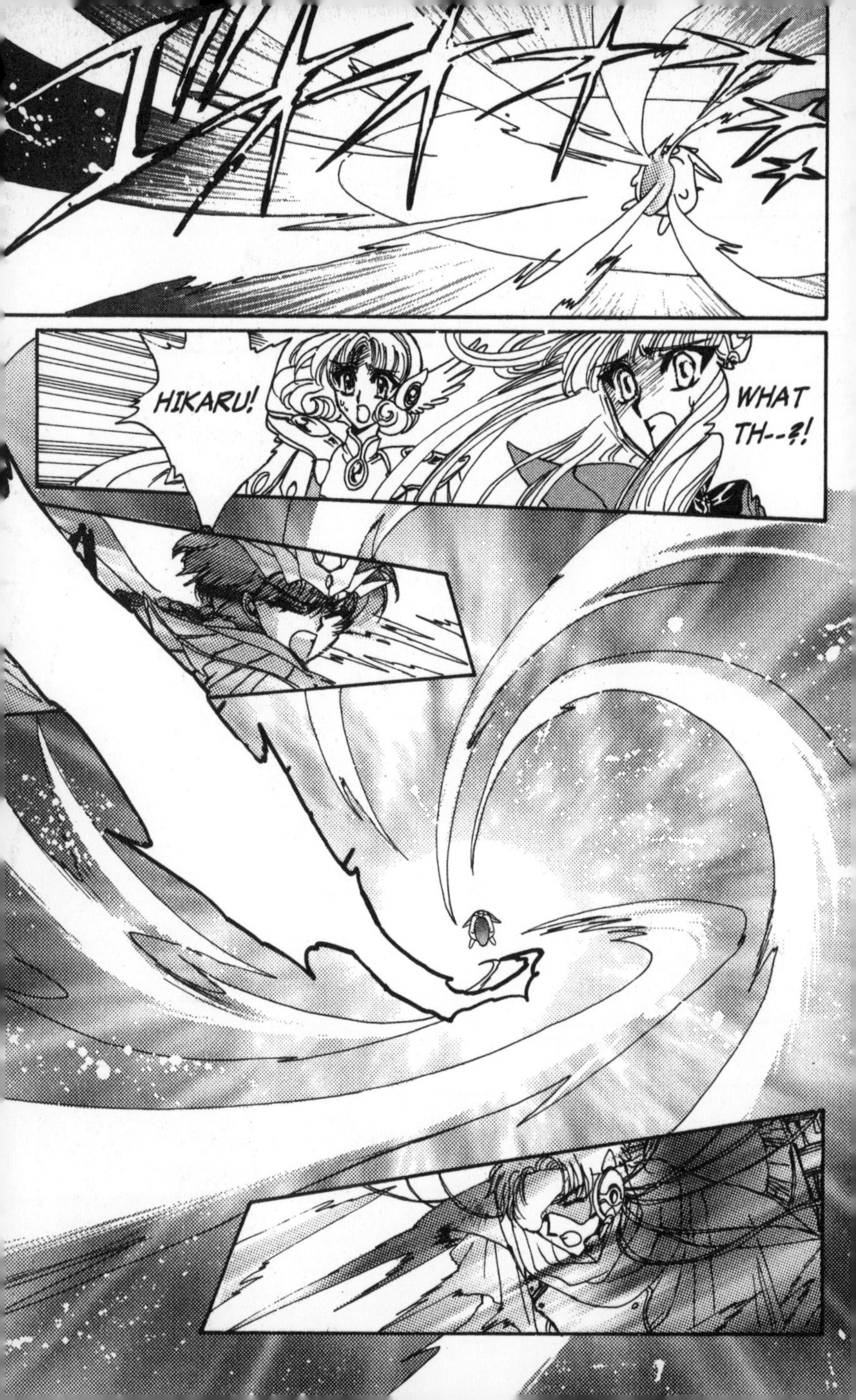
WHAT TH--?!
HIKARU!

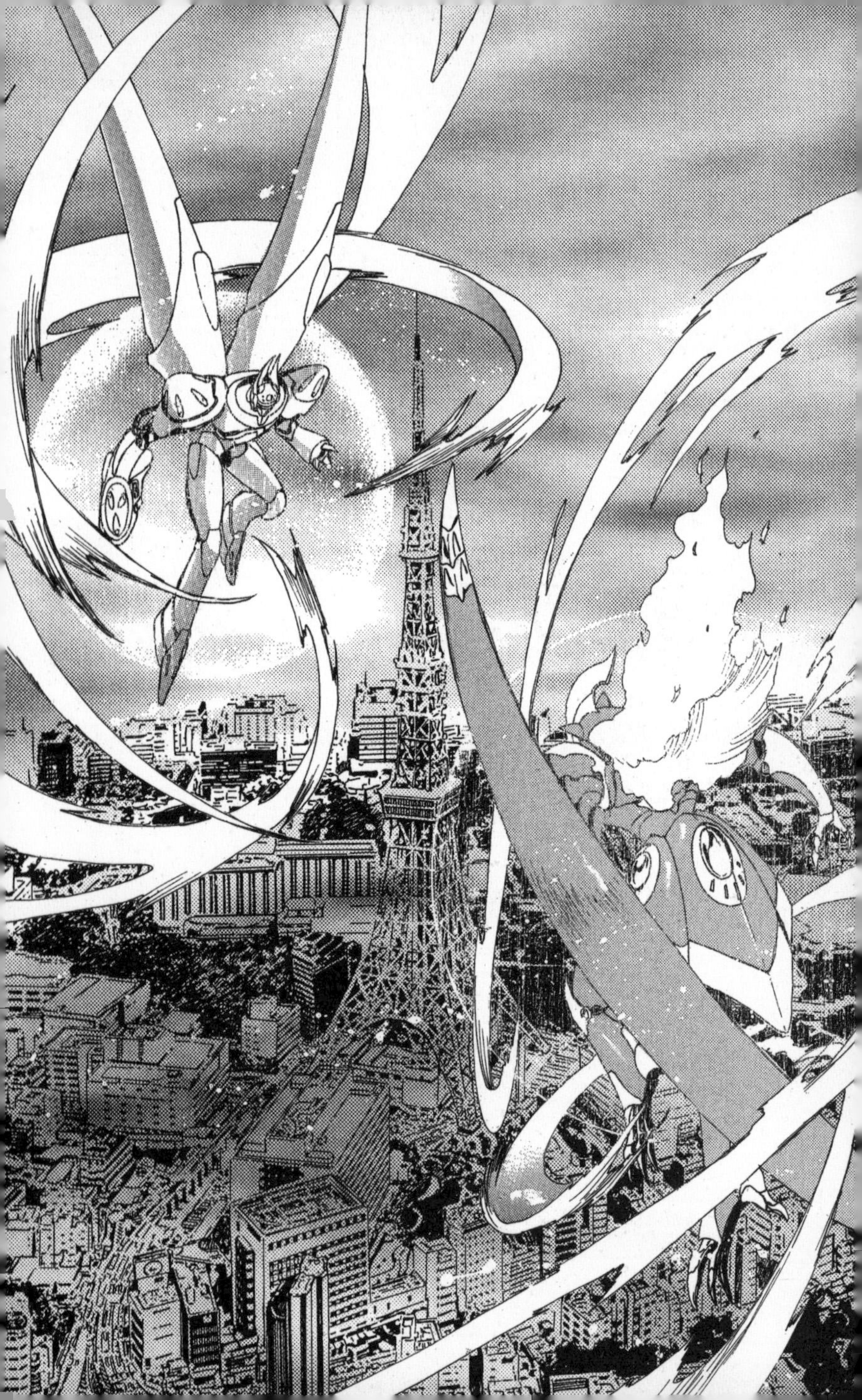

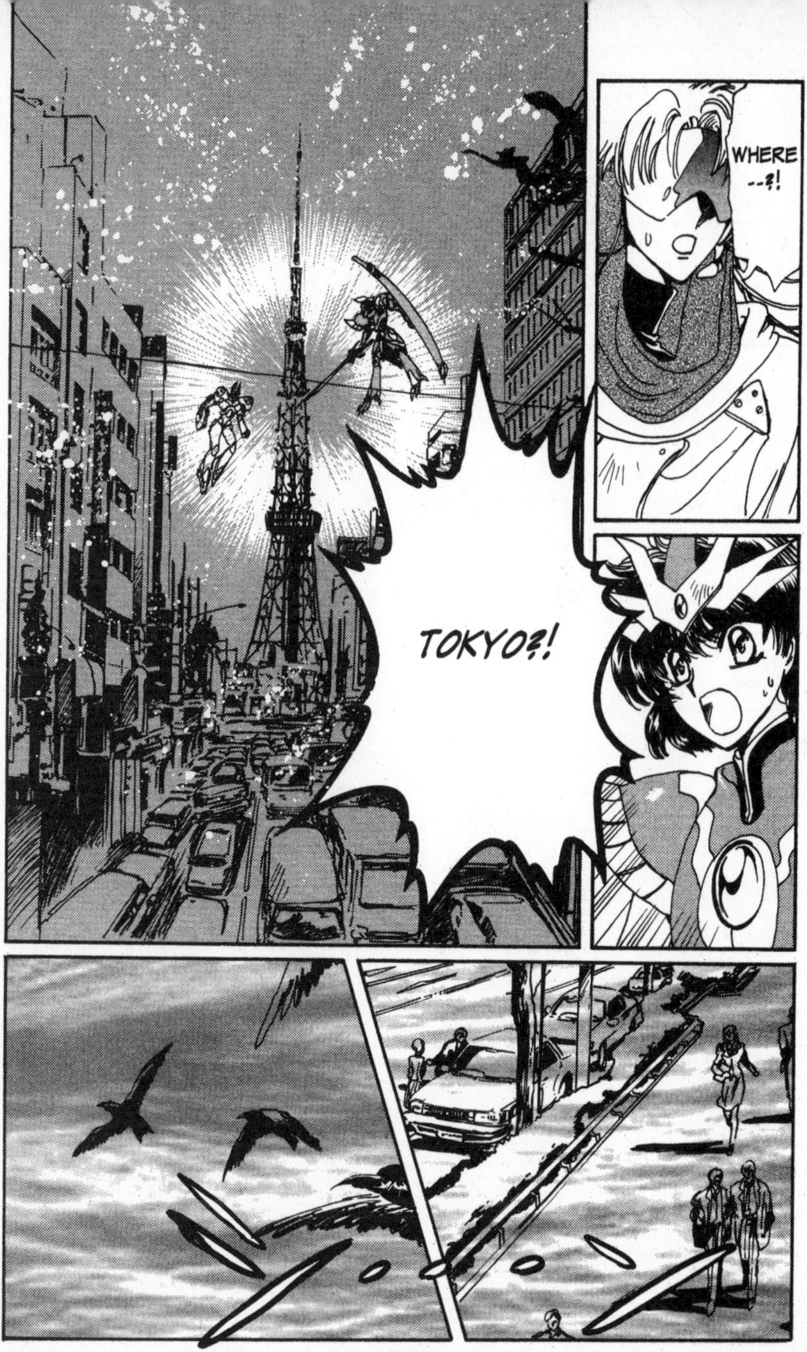
WHERE --?!
TOKYO?!

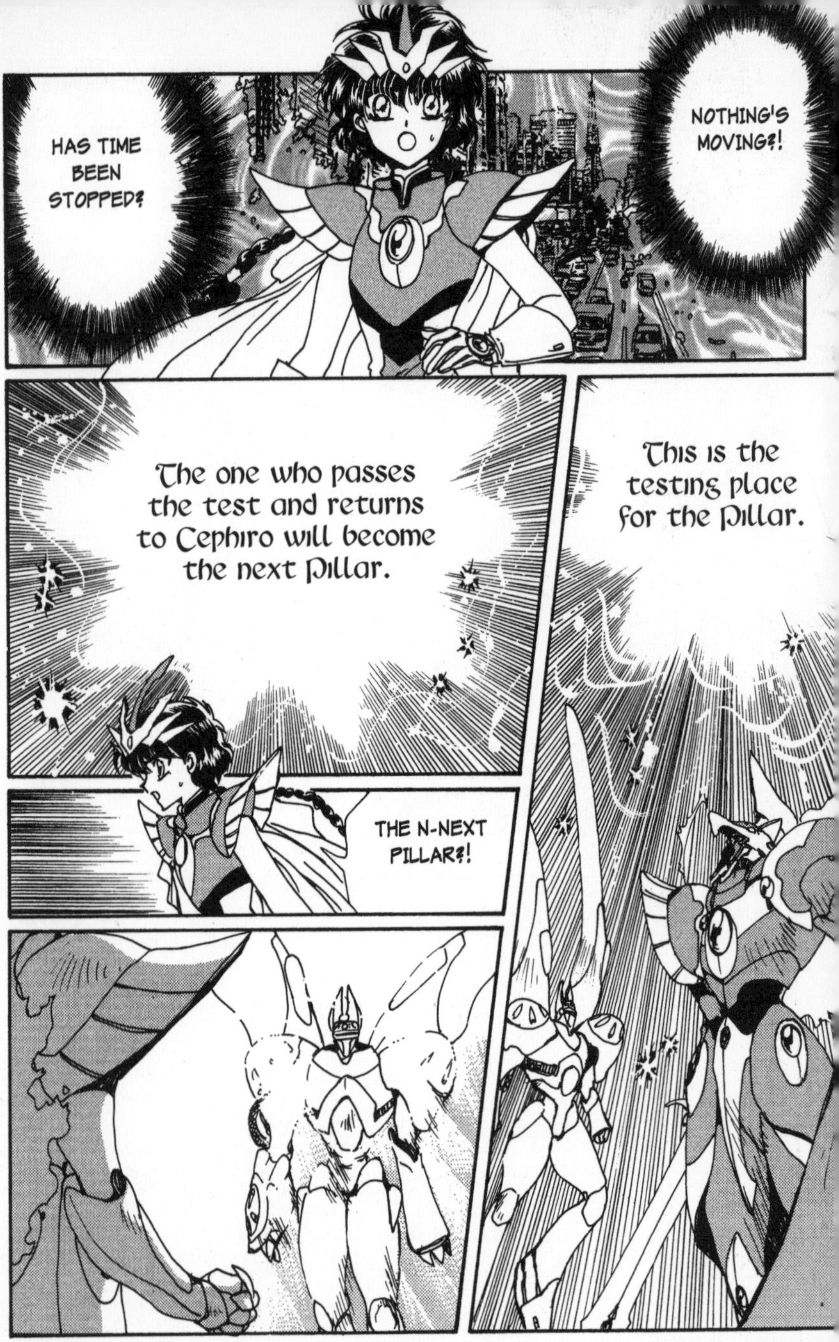
NOTHING'S MOVING?!
HAS TIME BEEN STOPPED?
This is the testing place for the Pillar.
The one who passes the test and returns to Cephiro will become the next Pillar.
THE N-NEXT PILLAR?!

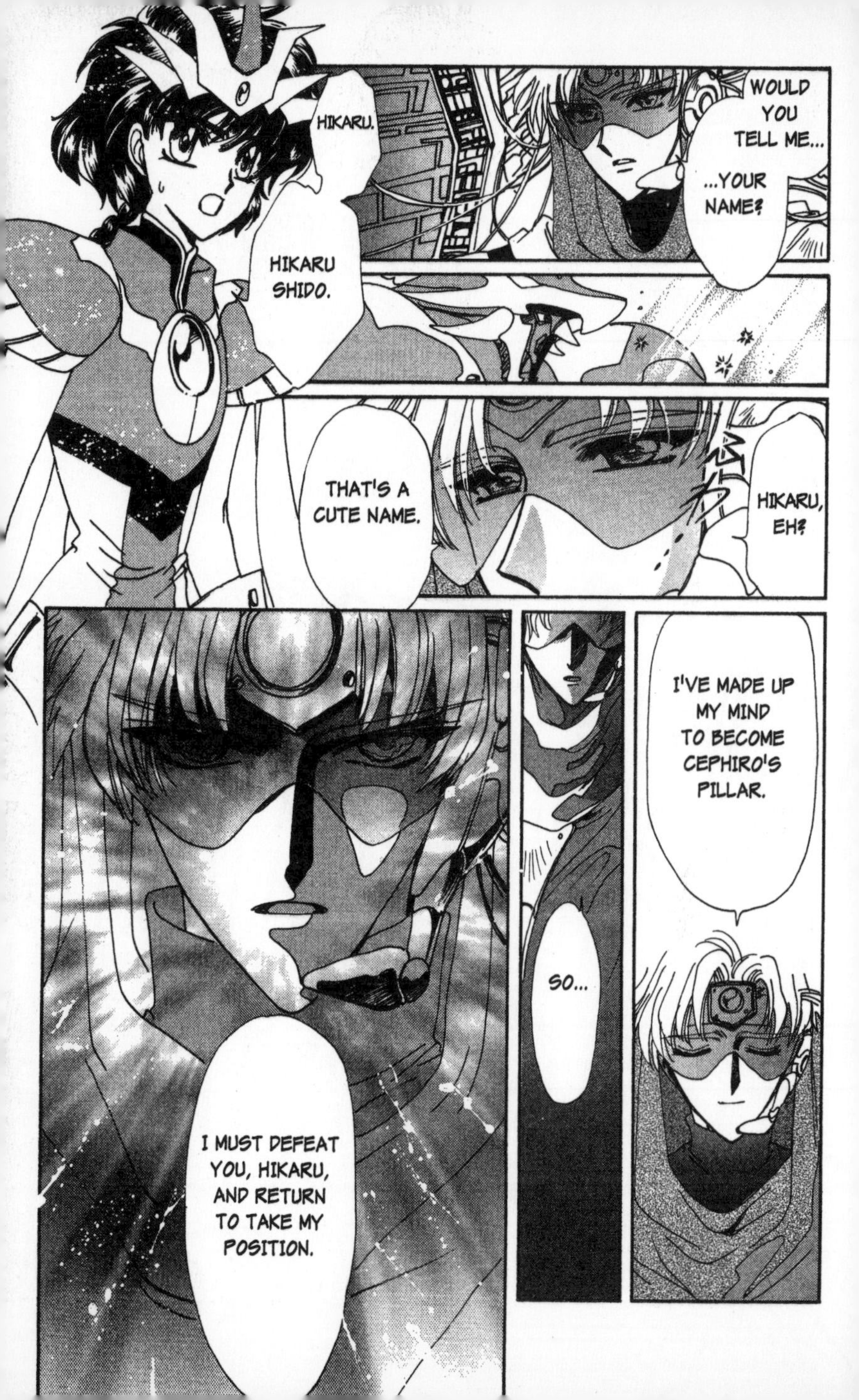
WOULD YOU TELL ME...
...YOUR NAME?
HIKARU.
HIKARU SHIDO.
HIKARU, EH?
THAT'S A CUTE NAME.
I'VE MADE UP MY MIND TO BECOME CEPHIRO'S PILLAR.
SO...
I MUST DEFEAT YOU, HIKARU, AND RETURN TO TAKE MY POSITION.

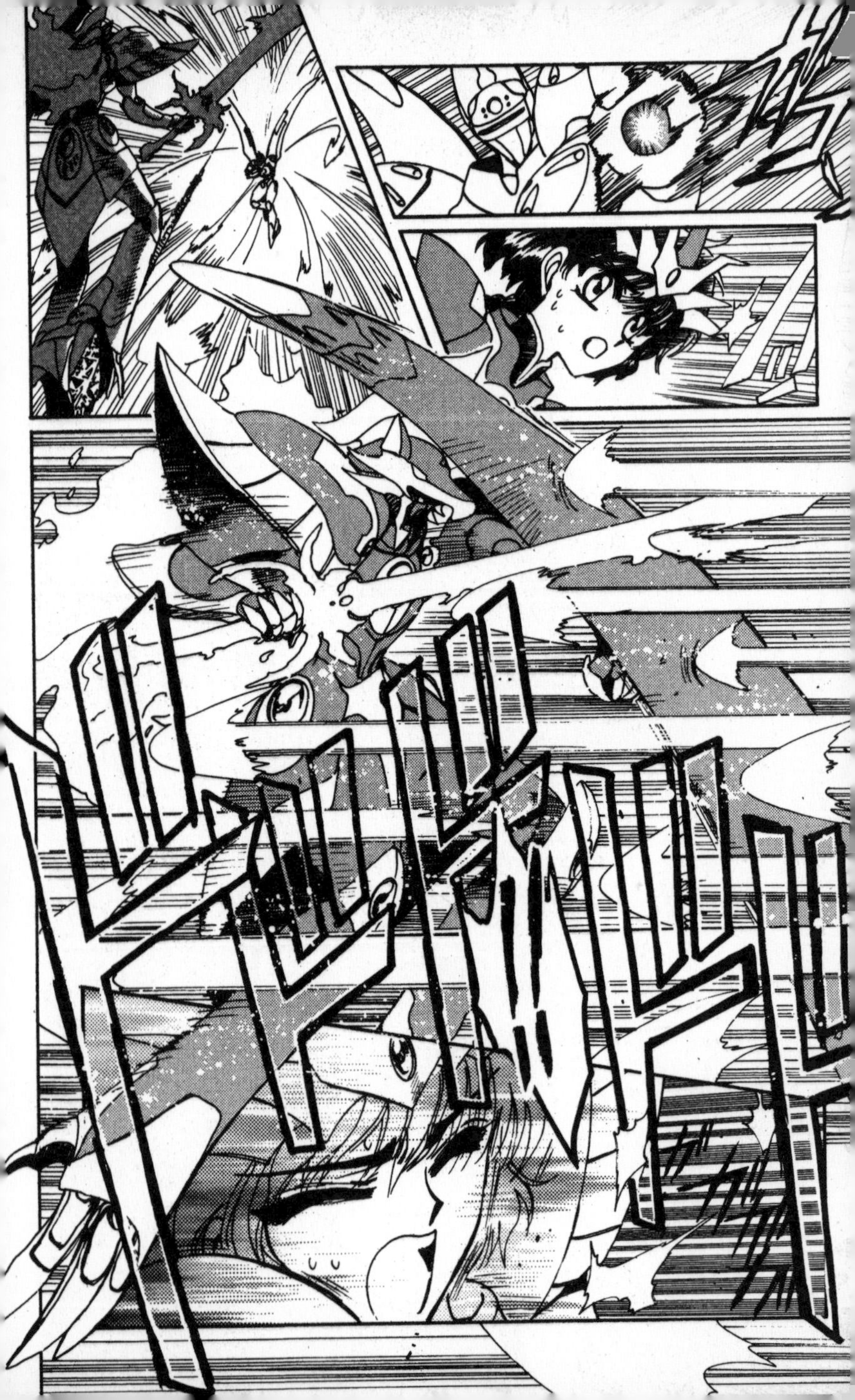

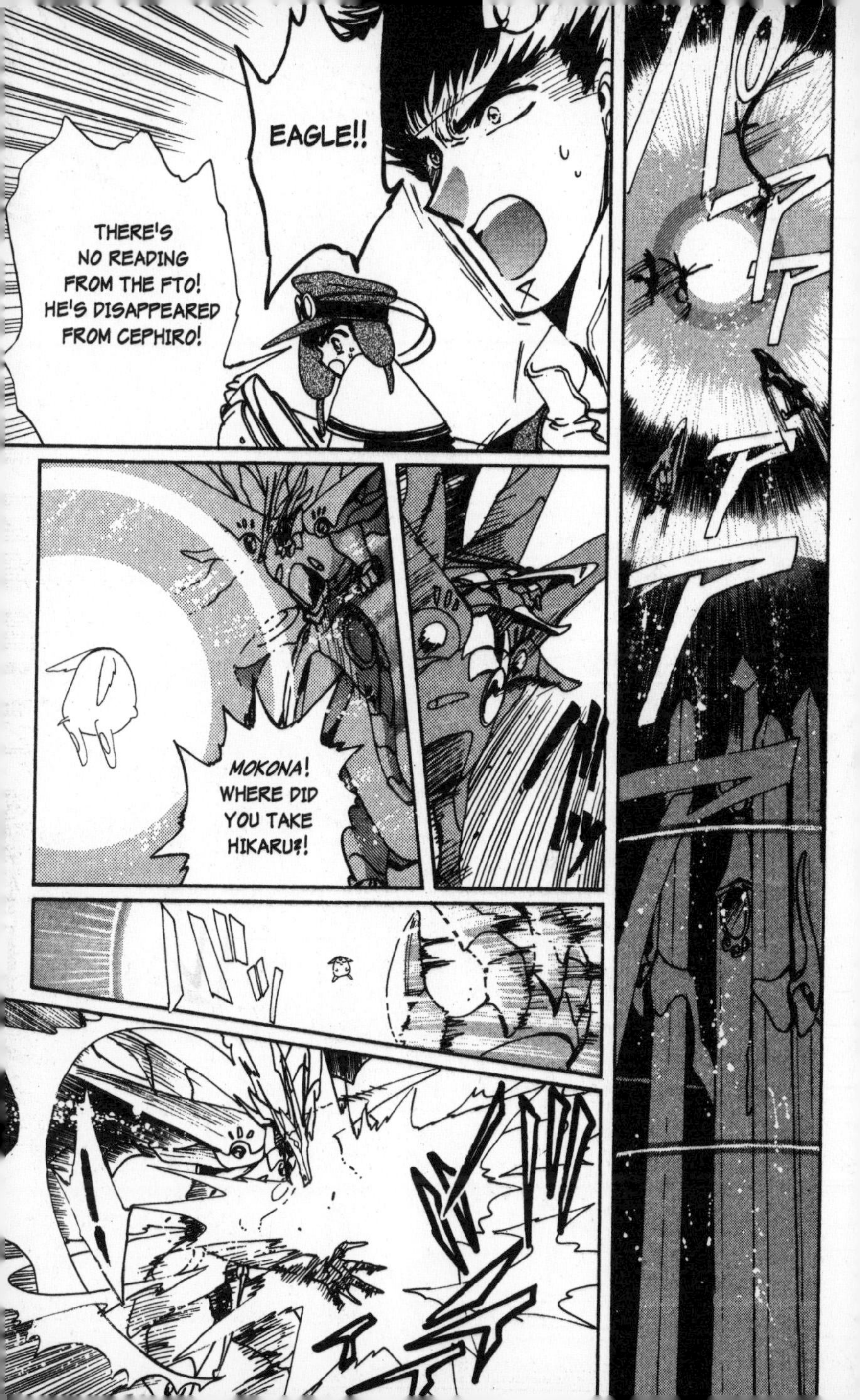
EAGLE!!
THERE'S NO READING FROM THE FTO! HE'S DISAPPEARED FROM CEPHIRO!
MOKONA! WHERE DID YOU TAKE HIKARU?!

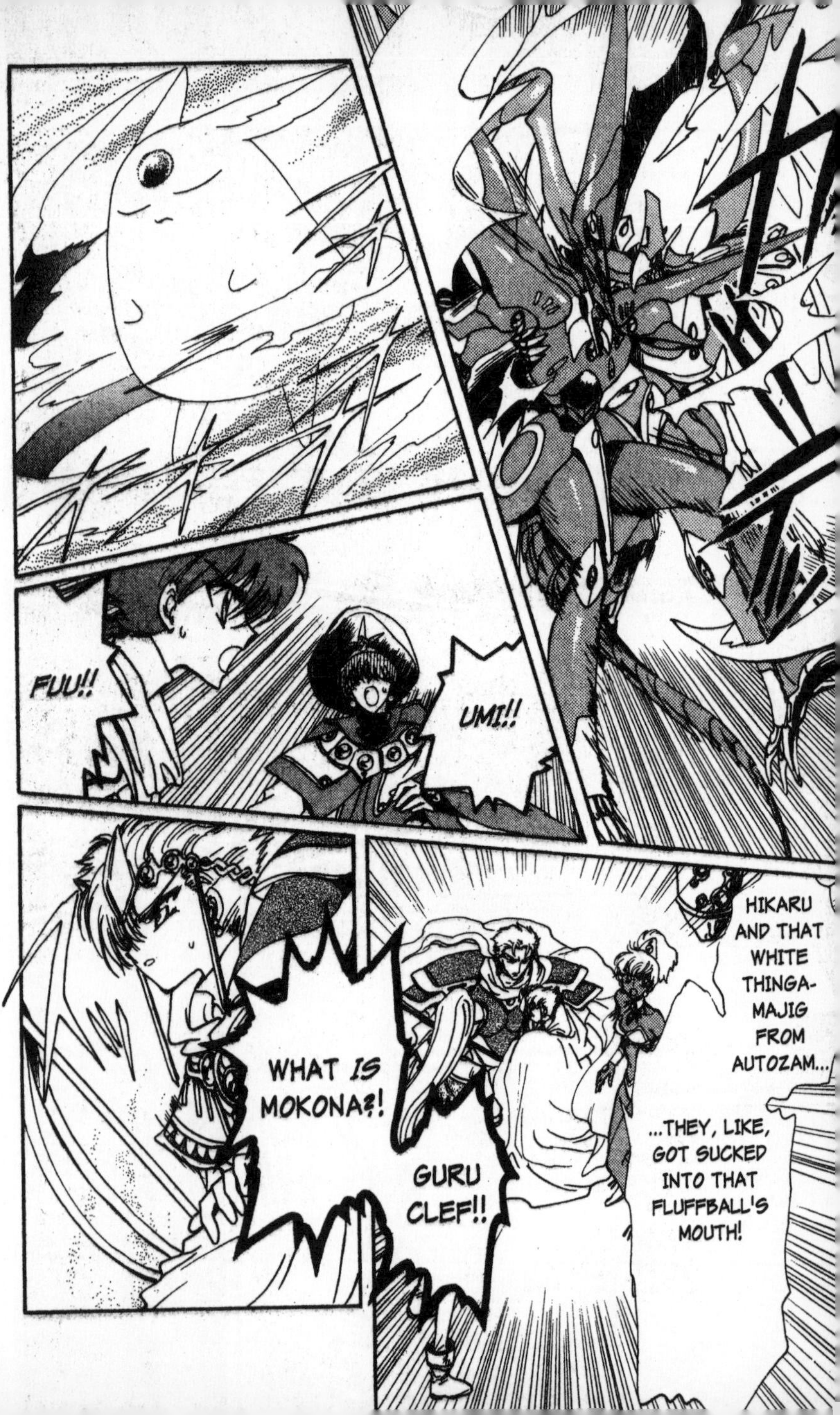
UMI!!
FUU!!
HIKARU AND THAT WHITE THINGA-MAJIG FROM AUTOZAM...
...THEY, LIKE, GOT SUCKED INTO THAT FLUFFBALL'S MOUTH!
GURU CLEF!!
WHAT IS MOKONA?!

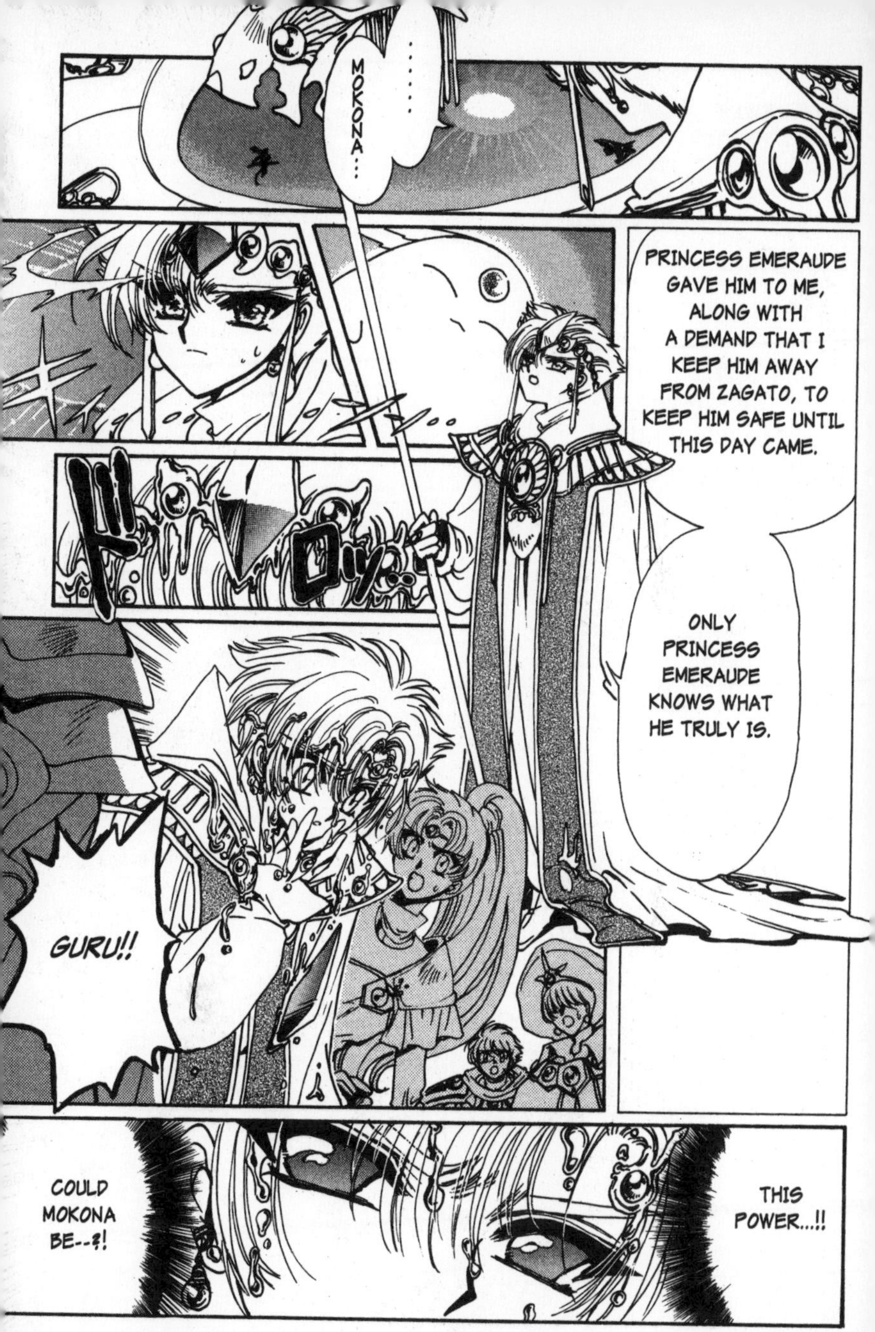

......
MOKONA...
PRINCESS EMERAUDE GAVE HIM TO ME, ALONG WITH A DEMAND THAT I KEEP HIM AWAY FROM ZAGATO, TO KEEP HIM SAFE UNTIL THIS DAY CAME.
ONLY PRINCESS EMERAUDE KNOWS WHAT HE TRULY IS.
ド!!ロッ..
GURU!!
THIS POWER...!!
COULD MOKONA BE--?!

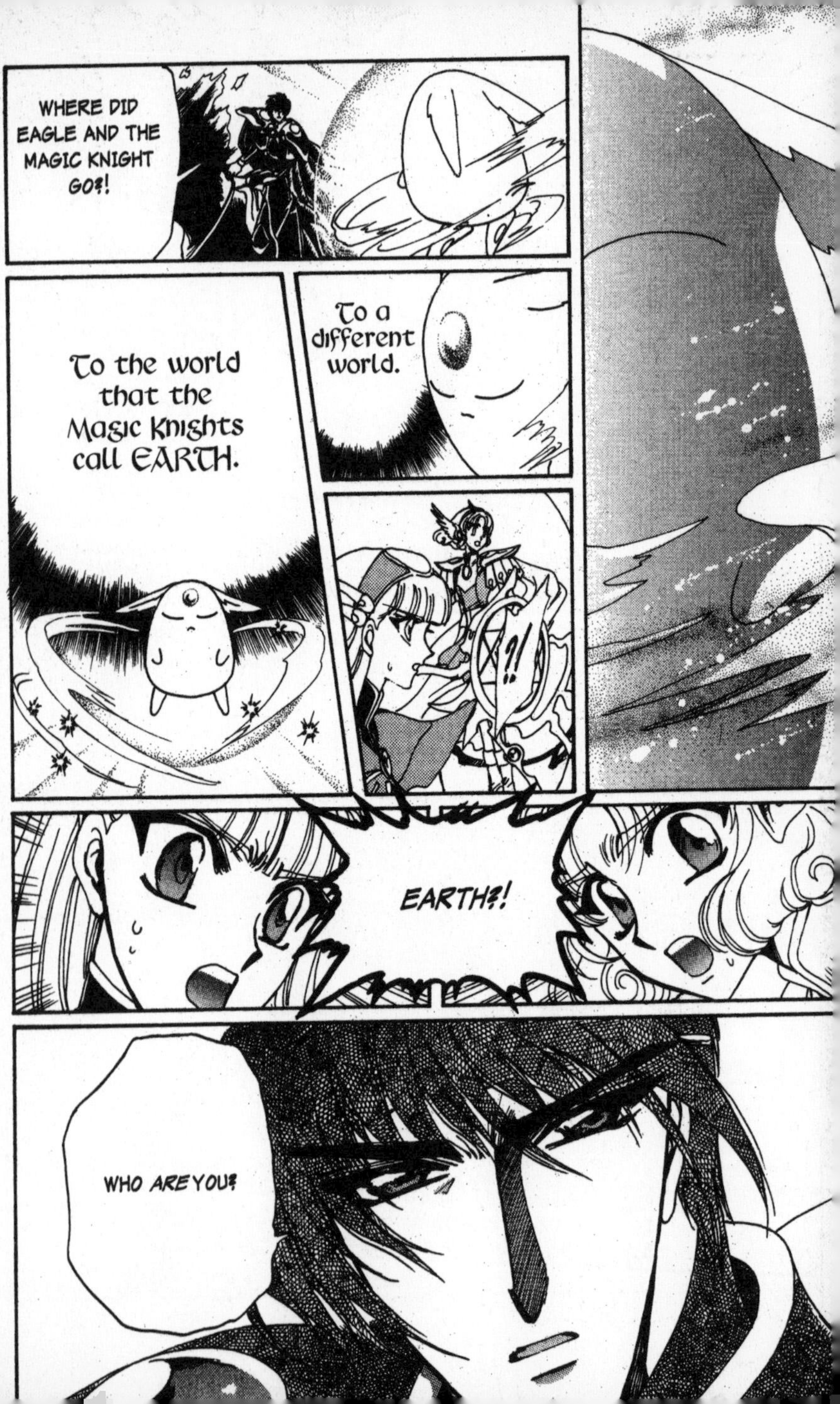
WHERE DID EAGLE AND THE MAGIC KNIGHT GO?!
To a different world.
?!
To the world that the Magic Knights call EARTH.
EARTH?!
WHO ARE YOU?

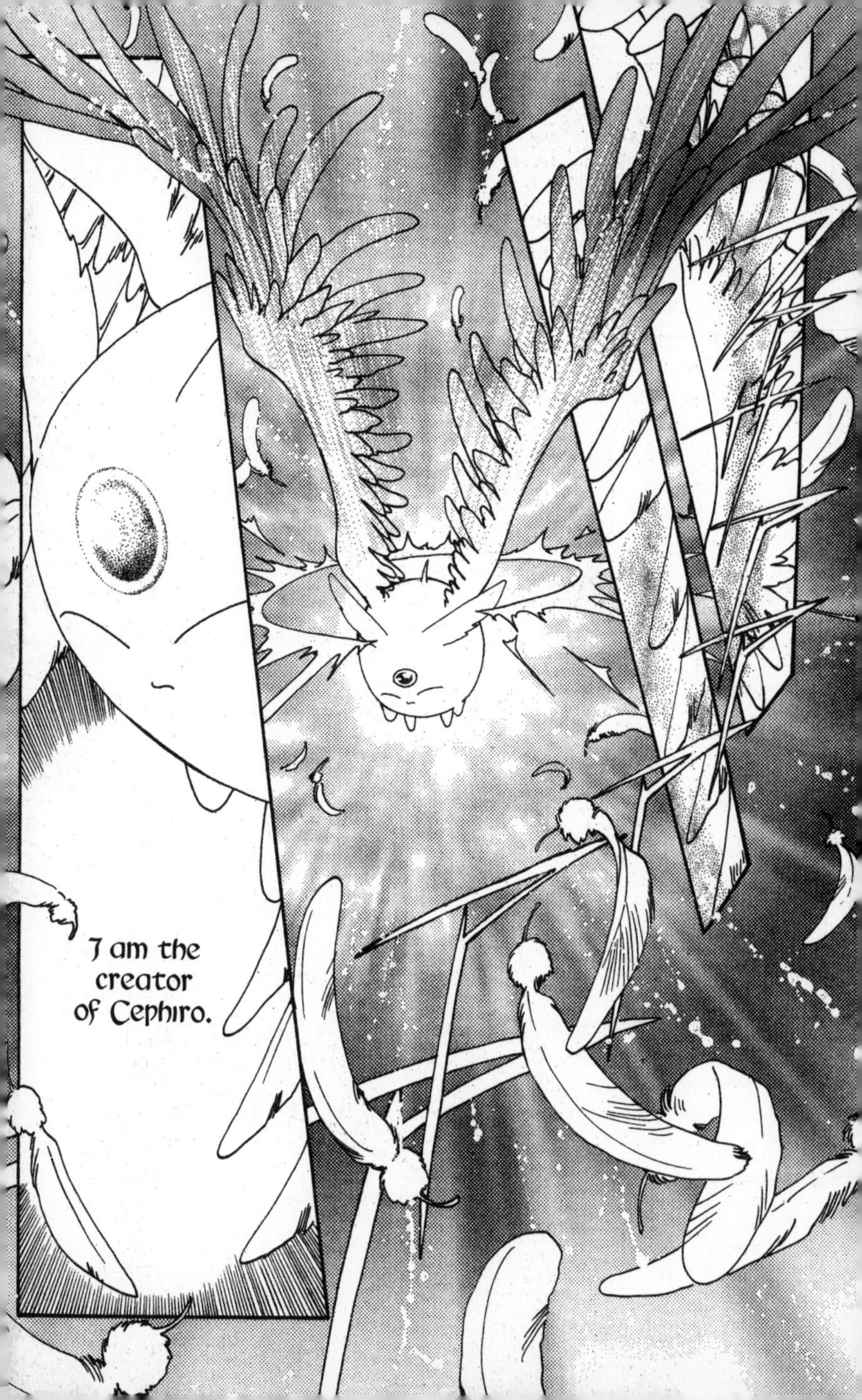
I am the creator of Cephiro.

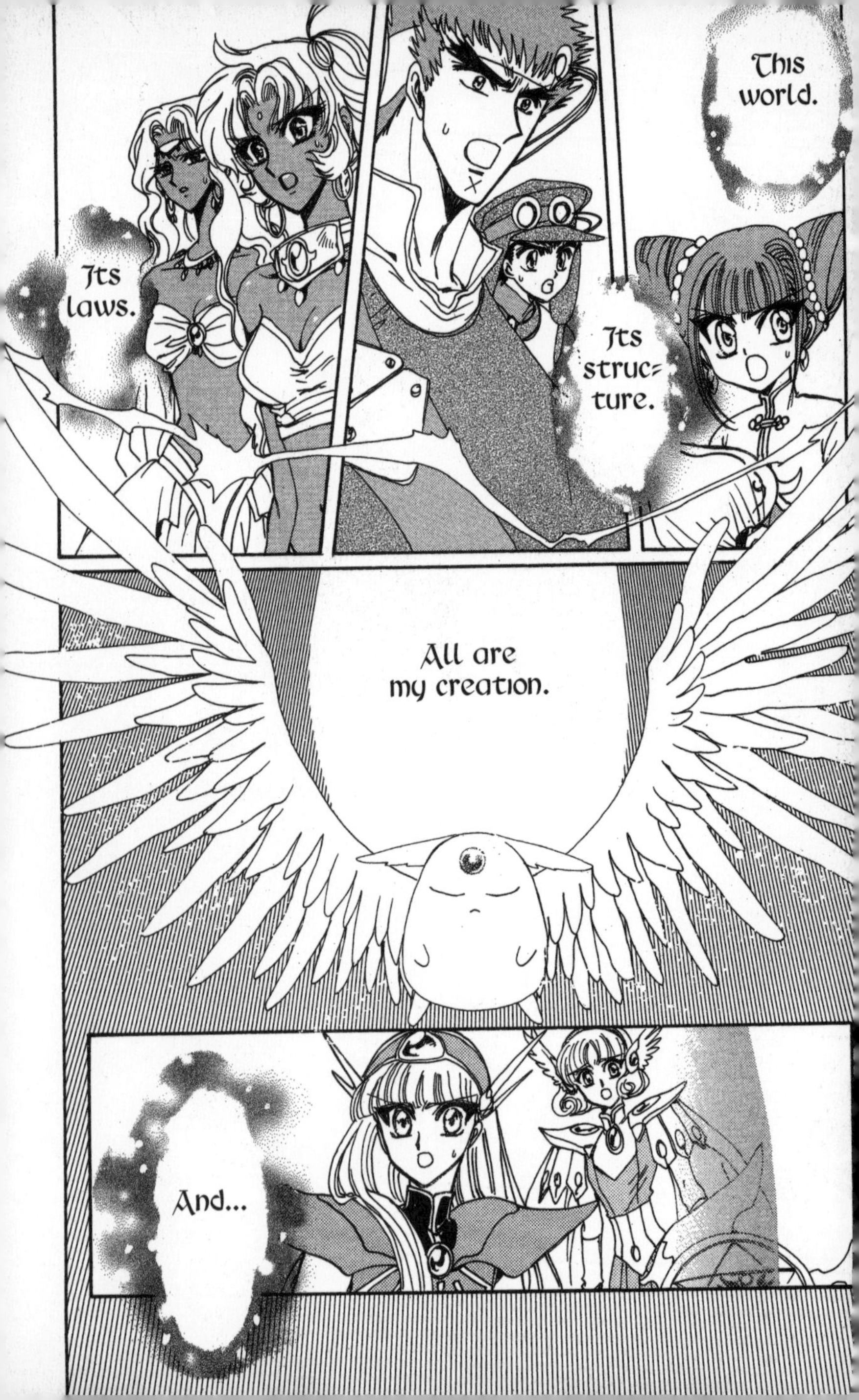
This world.
Its structure.
Its laws.
All are my creation.
And...

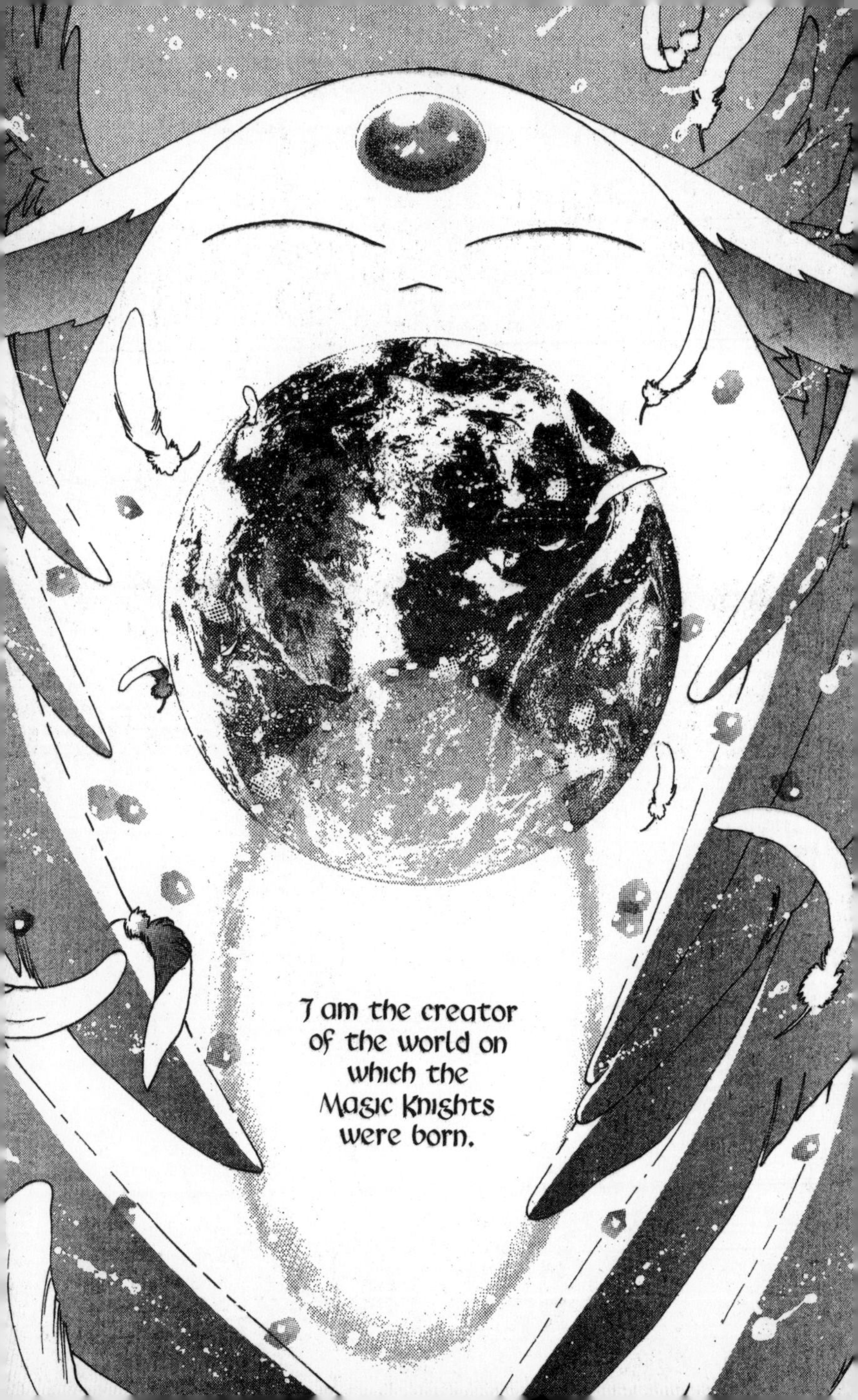
I am the creator of the world on which the Magic Knights were born.

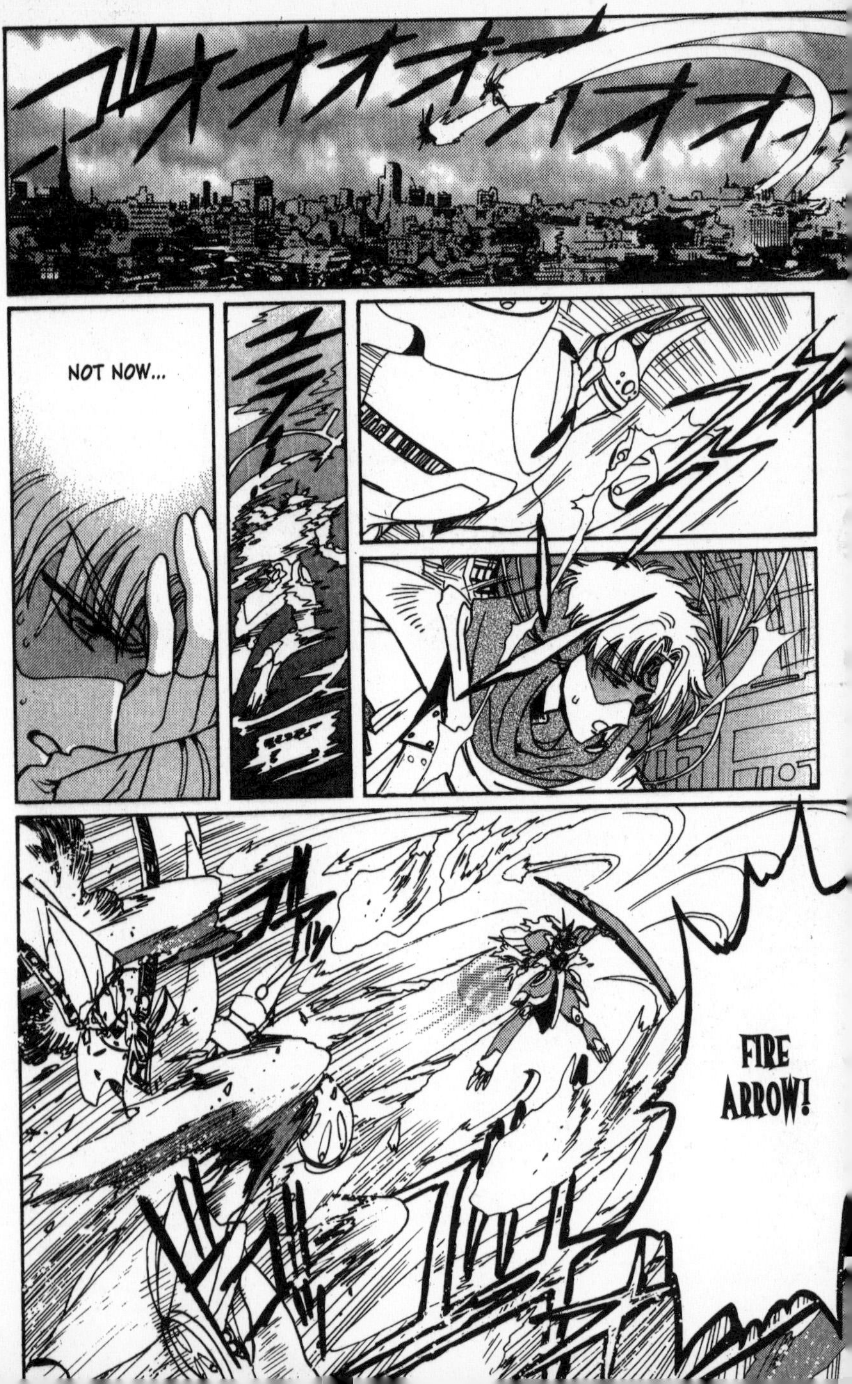
NOT NOW...
FIRE ARROW!

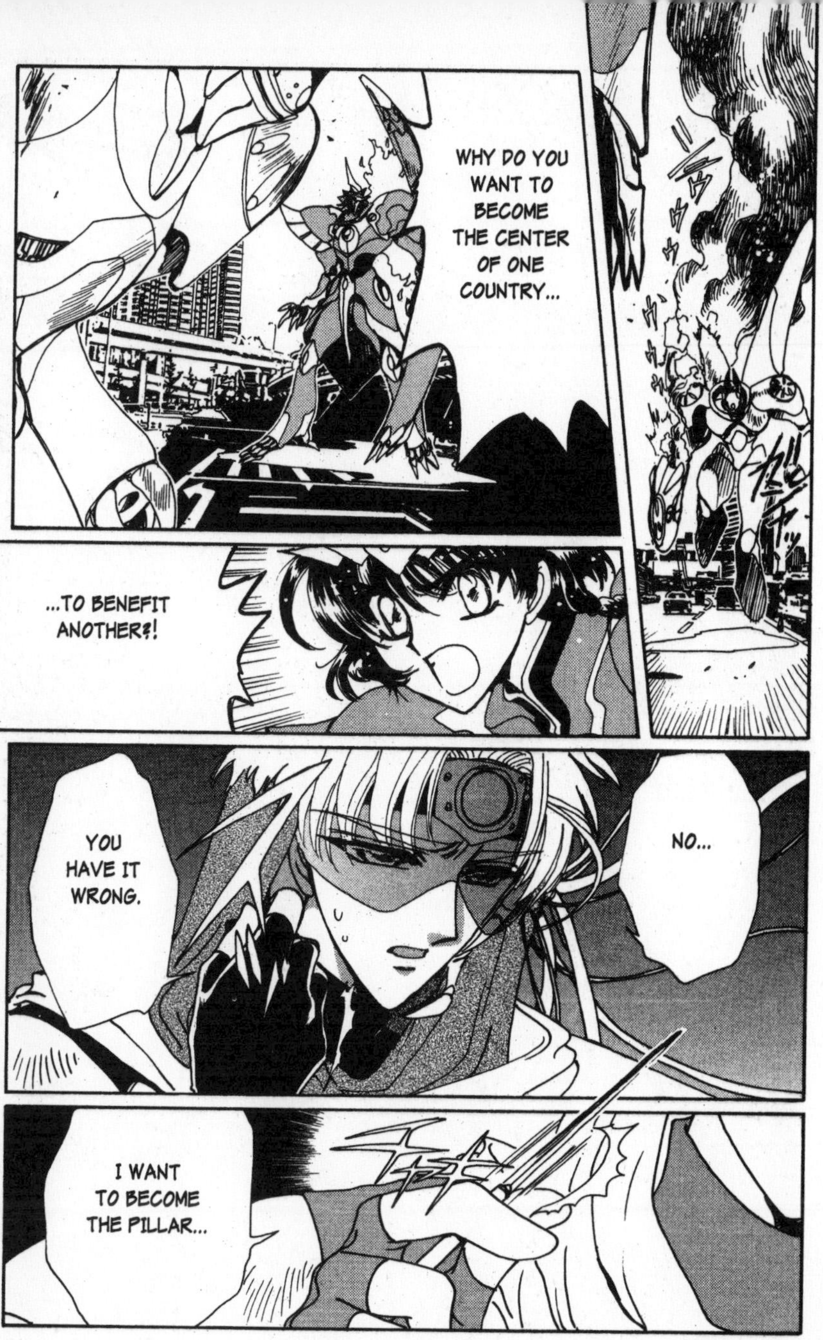
WHY DO YOU WANT TO BECOME THE CENTER OF ONE COUNTRY...
...TO BENEFIT ANOTHER?!
NO...
YOU HAVE IT WRONG.
I WANT TO BECOME THE PILLAR...

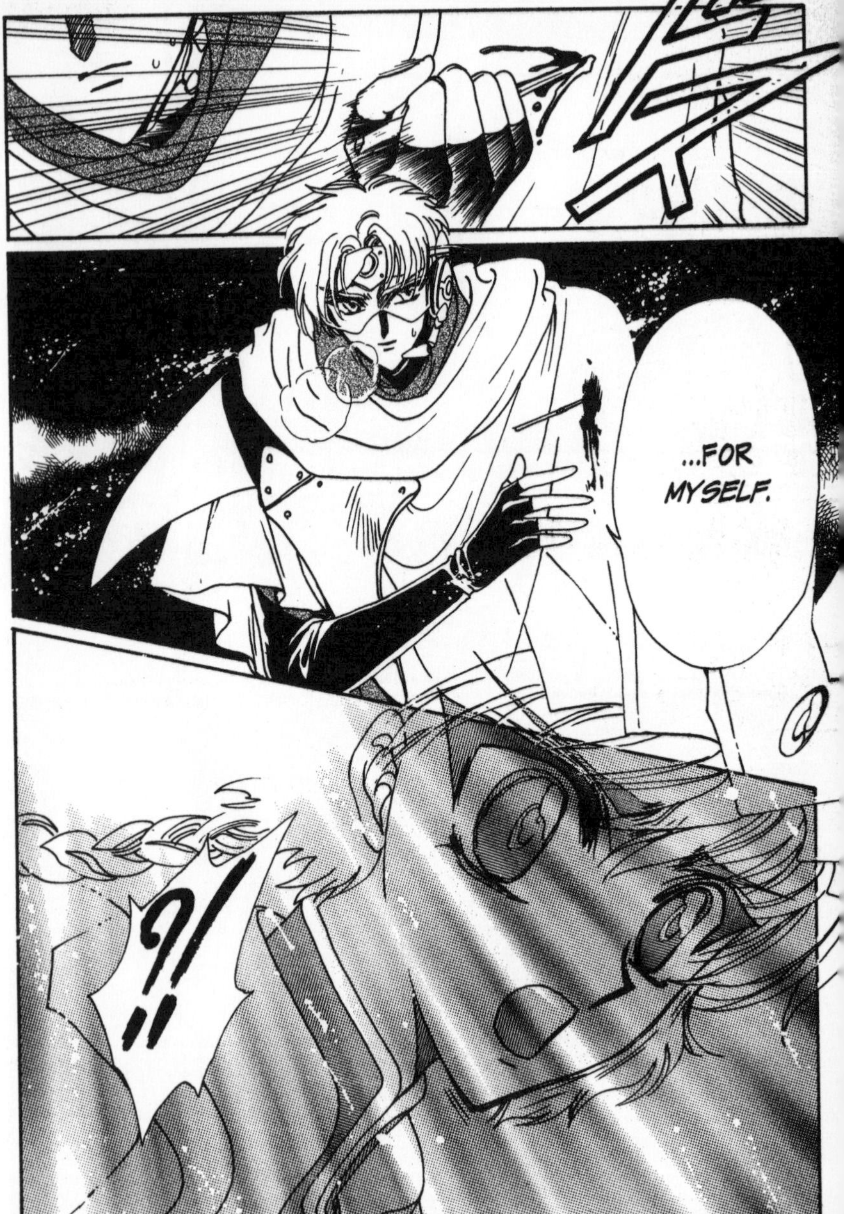
...FOR MYSELF.
?!!

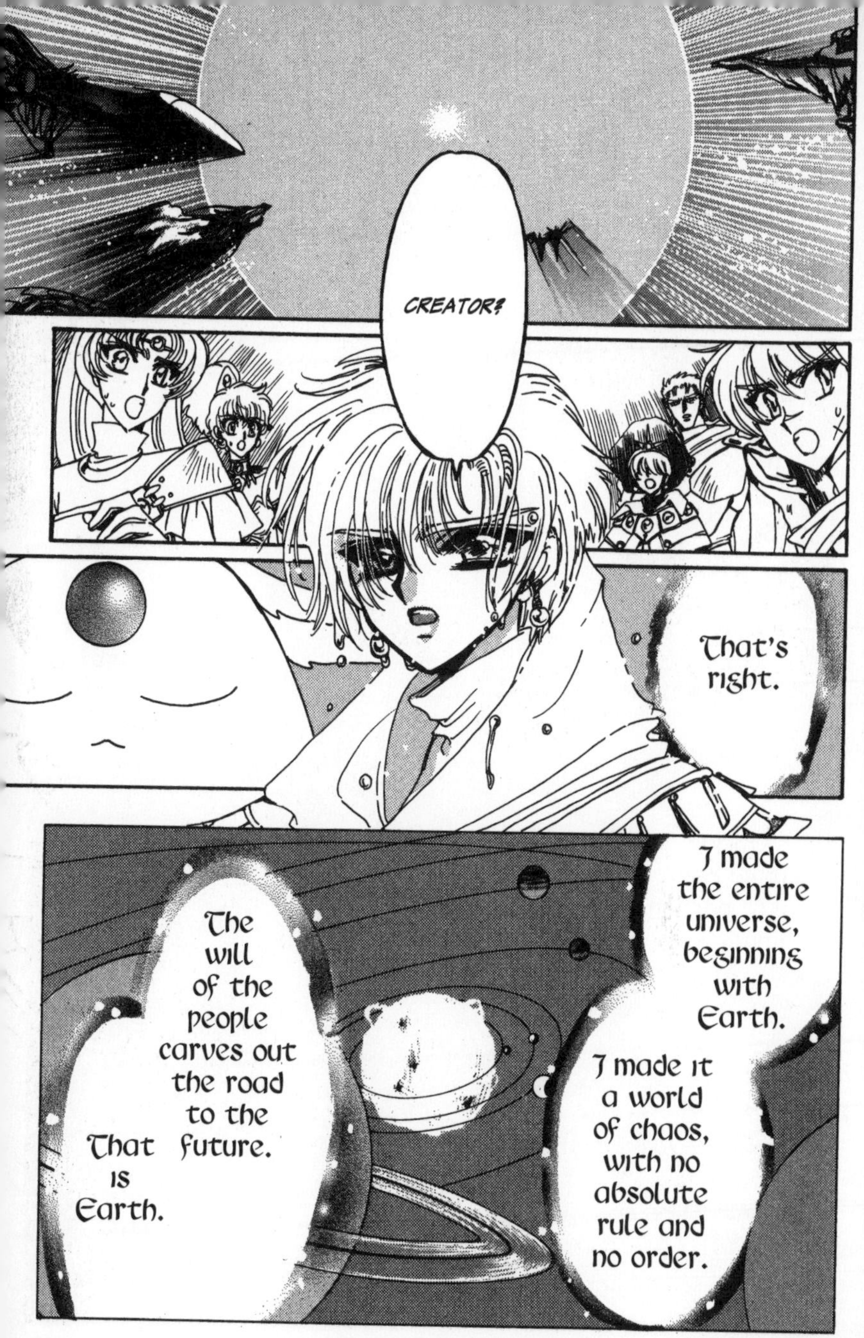
CREATOR?
That's right.
I made the entire universe, beginning with Earth.
I made it a world of chaos, with no absolute rule and no order.
The will of the people carves out the road to the future.
That is Earth.

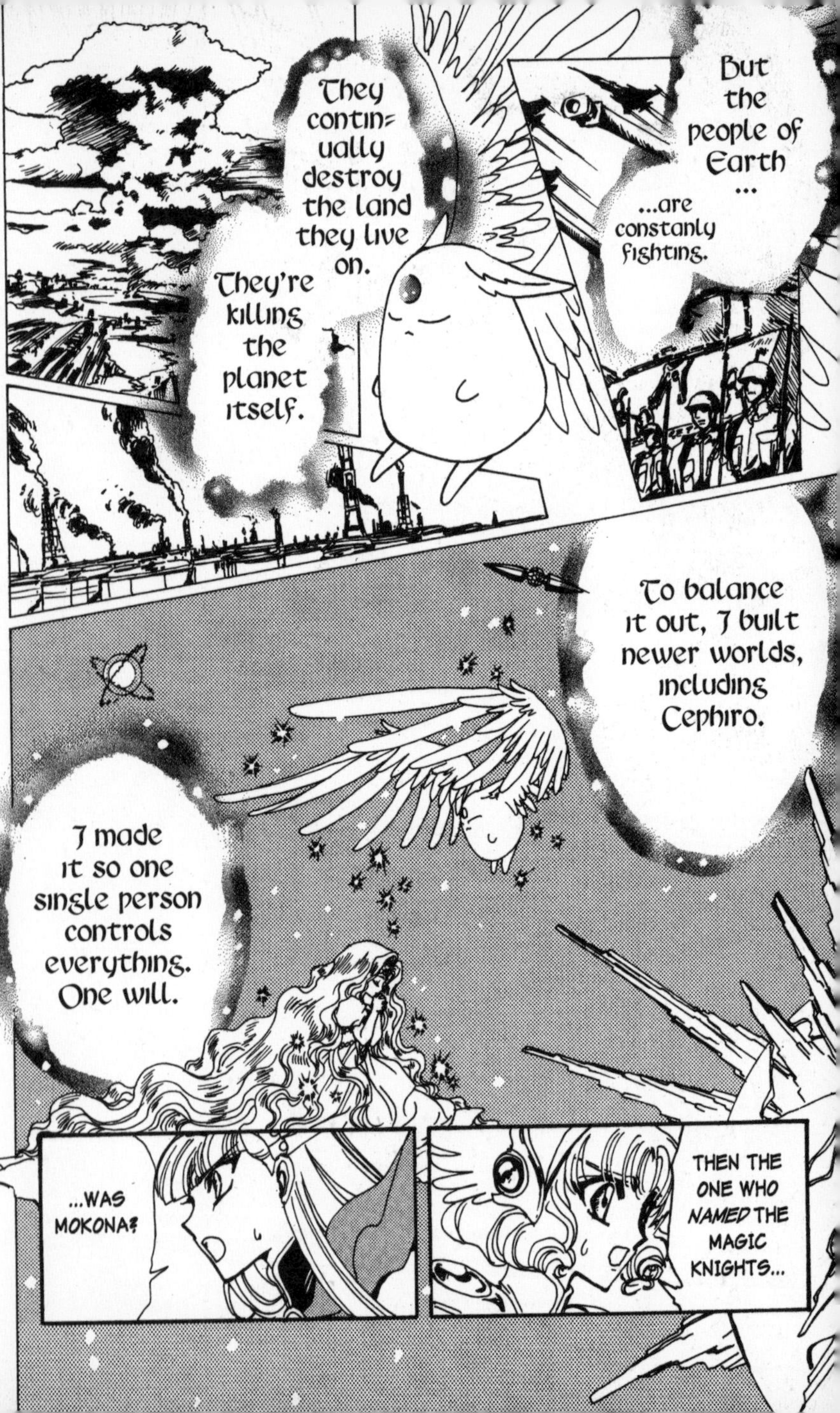
But the people of Earth ...
...are constanly fighting.
They contin-ually destroy the land they live on.
They're killing the planet itself.
To balance it out, I built newer worlds, including Cephiro.
I made it so one single person controls everything. One will.
THEN THE ONE WHO *NAMED* THE MAGIC KNIGHTS...
...WAS MOKONA?

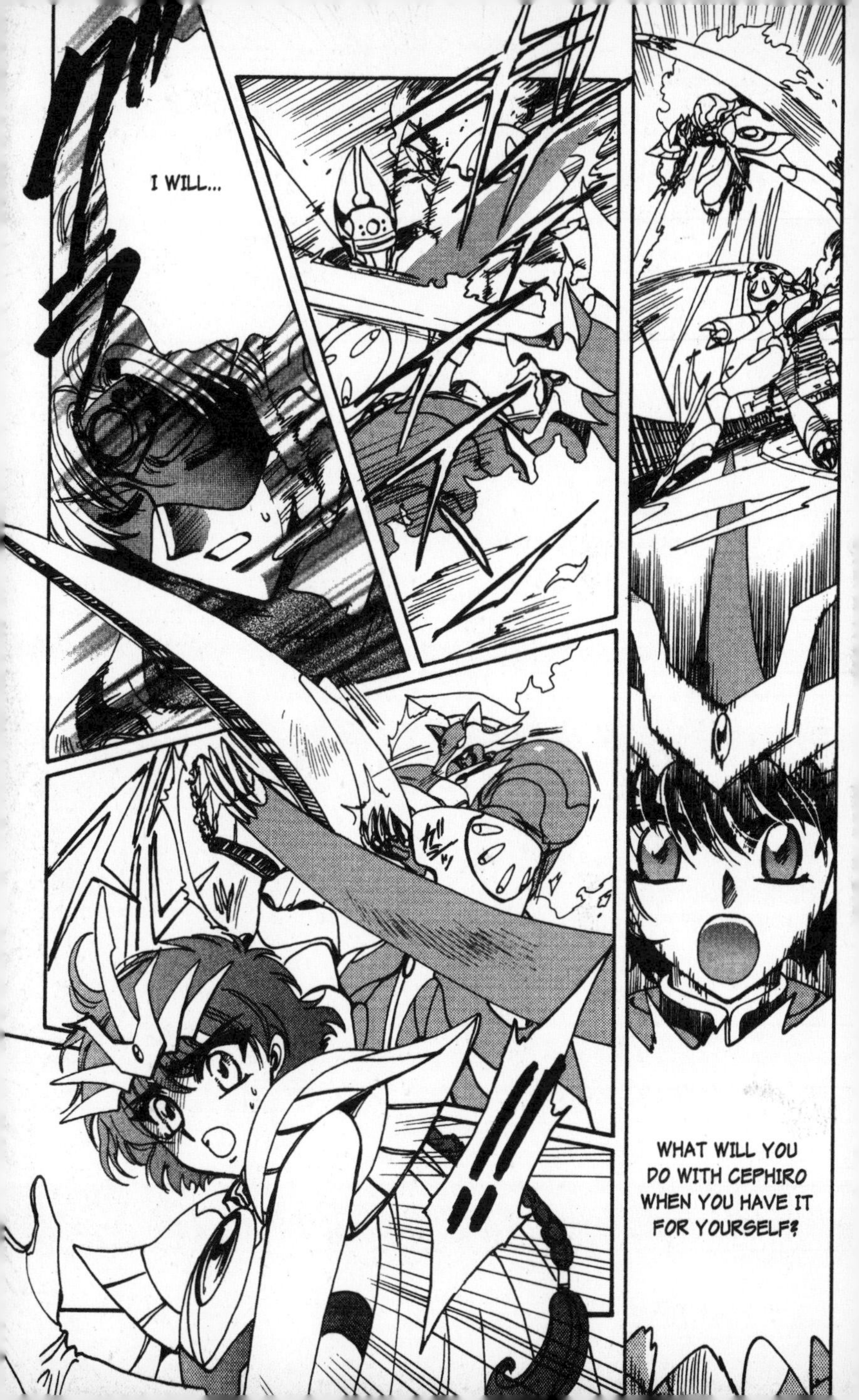
WHAT WILL YOU DO WITH CEPHIRO WHEN YOU HAVE IT FOR YOURSELF?
I WILL...

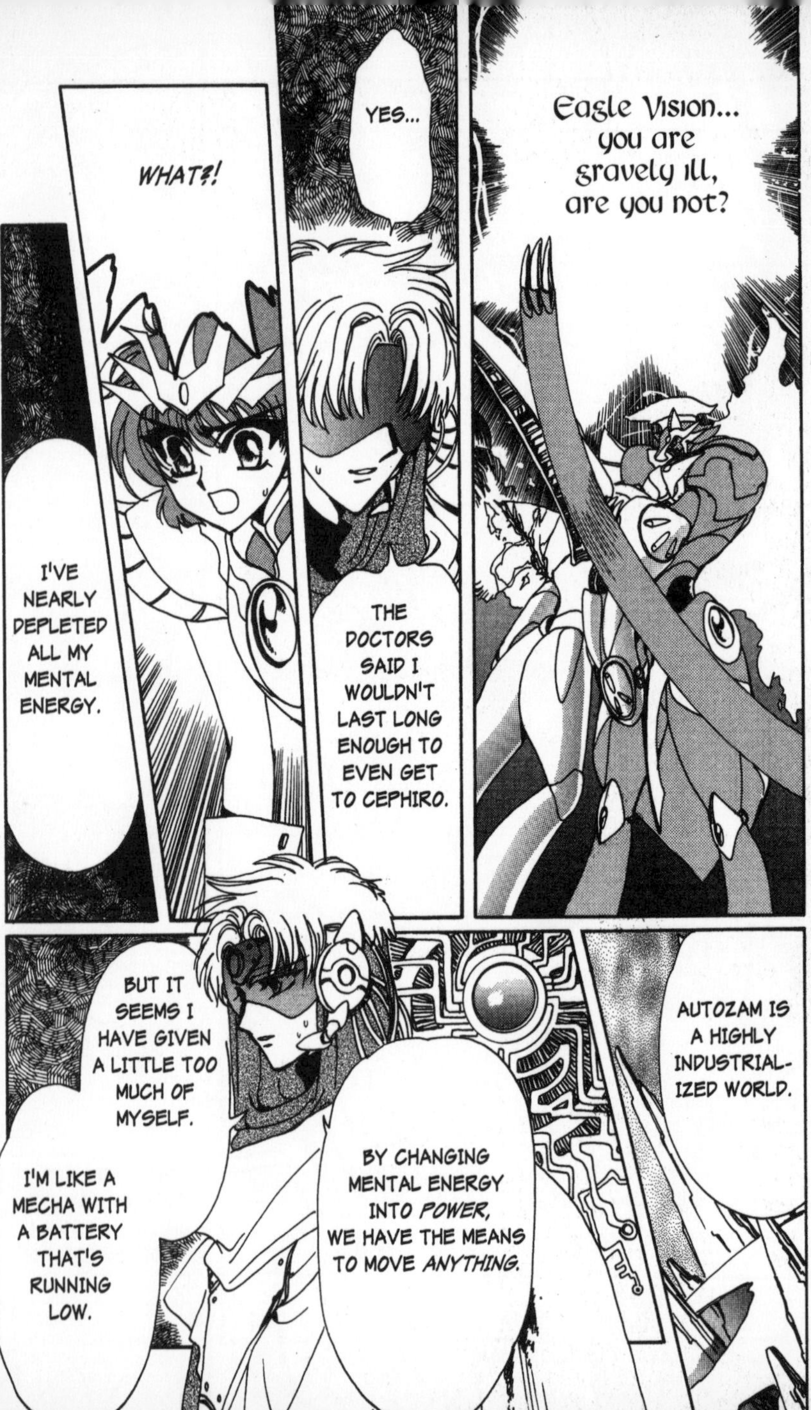
Eagle Vision... you are gravely ill, are you not?
YES...
THE DOCTORS SAID I WOULDN'T LAST LONG ENOUGH TO EVEN GET TO CEPHIRO.
WHAT?!
I'VE NEARLY DEPLETED ALL MY MENTAL ENERGY.
AUTOZAM IS A HIGHLY INDUSTRIAL-IZED WORLD.
BY CHANGING MENTAL ENERGY INTO *POWER*, WE HAVE THE MEANS TO MOVE *ANYTHING*.
BUT IT SEEMS I HAVE GIVEN A LITTLE TOO MUCH OF MYSELF.
I'M LIKE A MECHA WITH A BATTERY THAT'S RUNNING LOW.

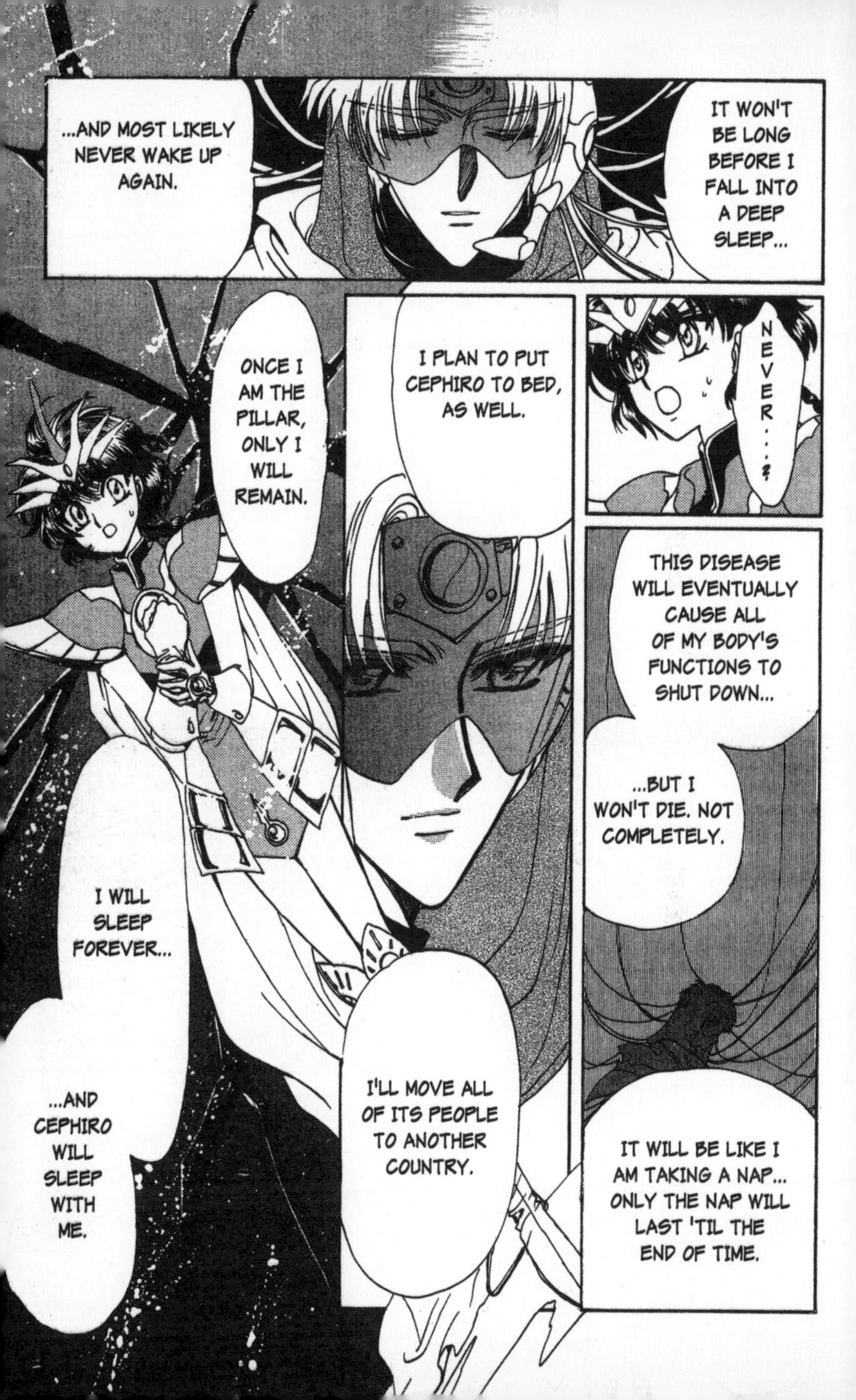
IT WON'T BE LONG BEFORE I FALL INTO A DEEP SLEEP...
...AND MOST LIKELY NEVER WAKE UP AGAIN.
NEVER...?
THIS DISEASE WILL EVENTUALLY CAUSE ALL OF MY BODY'S FUNCTIONS TO SHUT DOWN...
...BUT I WON'T DIE. NOT COMPLETELY.
IT WILL BE LIKE I AM TAKING A NAP... ONLY THE NAP WILL LAST 'TIL THE END OF TIME.
I PLAN TO PUT CEPHIRO TO BED, AS WELL.
I'LL MOVE ALL OF ITS PEOPLE TO ANOTHER COUNTRY.
ONCE I AM THE PILLAR, ONLY I WILL REMAIN.
I WILL SLEEP FOREVER...
...AND CEPHIRO WILL SLEEP WITH ME.

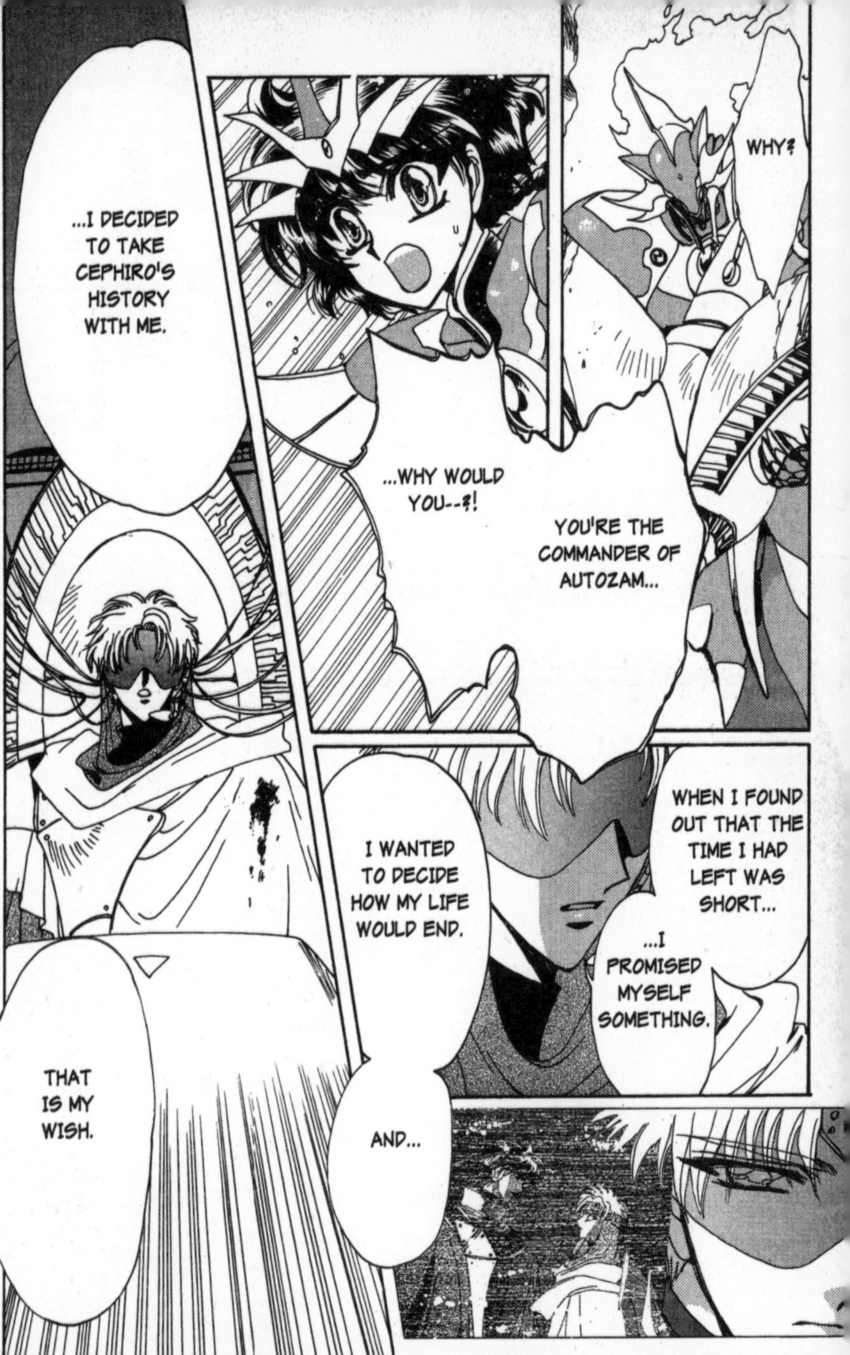
WHY?
YOU'RE THE COMMANDER OF AUTOZAM...
...WHY WOULD YOU--?!
WHEN I FOUND OUT THAT THE TIME I HAD LEFT WAS SHORT...
...I PROMISED MYSELF SOMETHING.
I WANTED TO DECIDE HOW MY LIFE WOULD END.
AND...
...I DECIDED TO TAKE CEPHIRO'S HISTORY WITH ME.
THAT IS MY WISH.

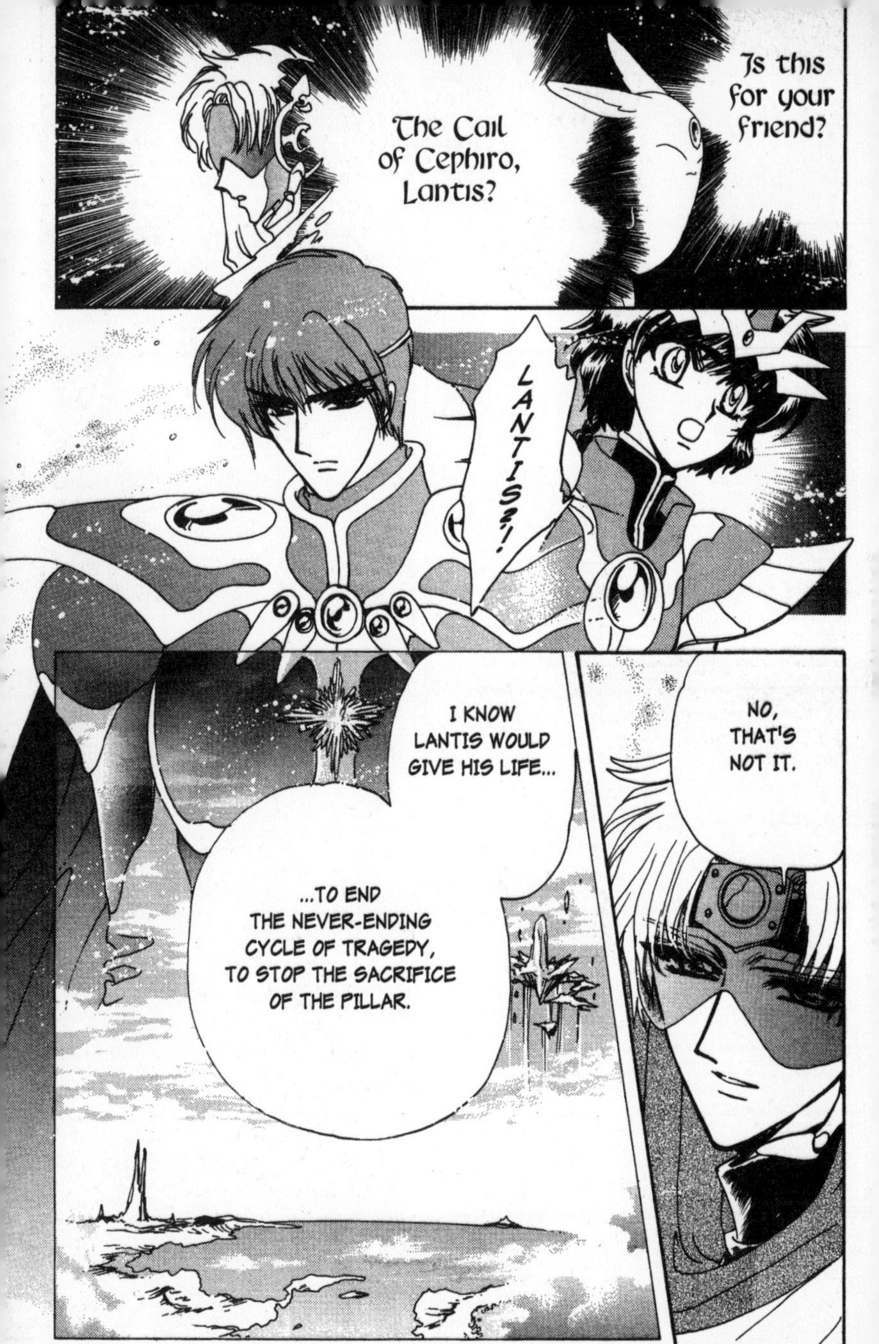
Is this for your friend?
The Cail of Cephiro, Lantis?
LANTIS?!
NO, THAT'S NOT IT.
I KNOW LANTIS WOULD GIVE HIS LIFE...
...TO END THE NEVER-ENDING CYCLE OF TRAGEDY, TO STOP THE SACRIFICE OF THE PILLAR.

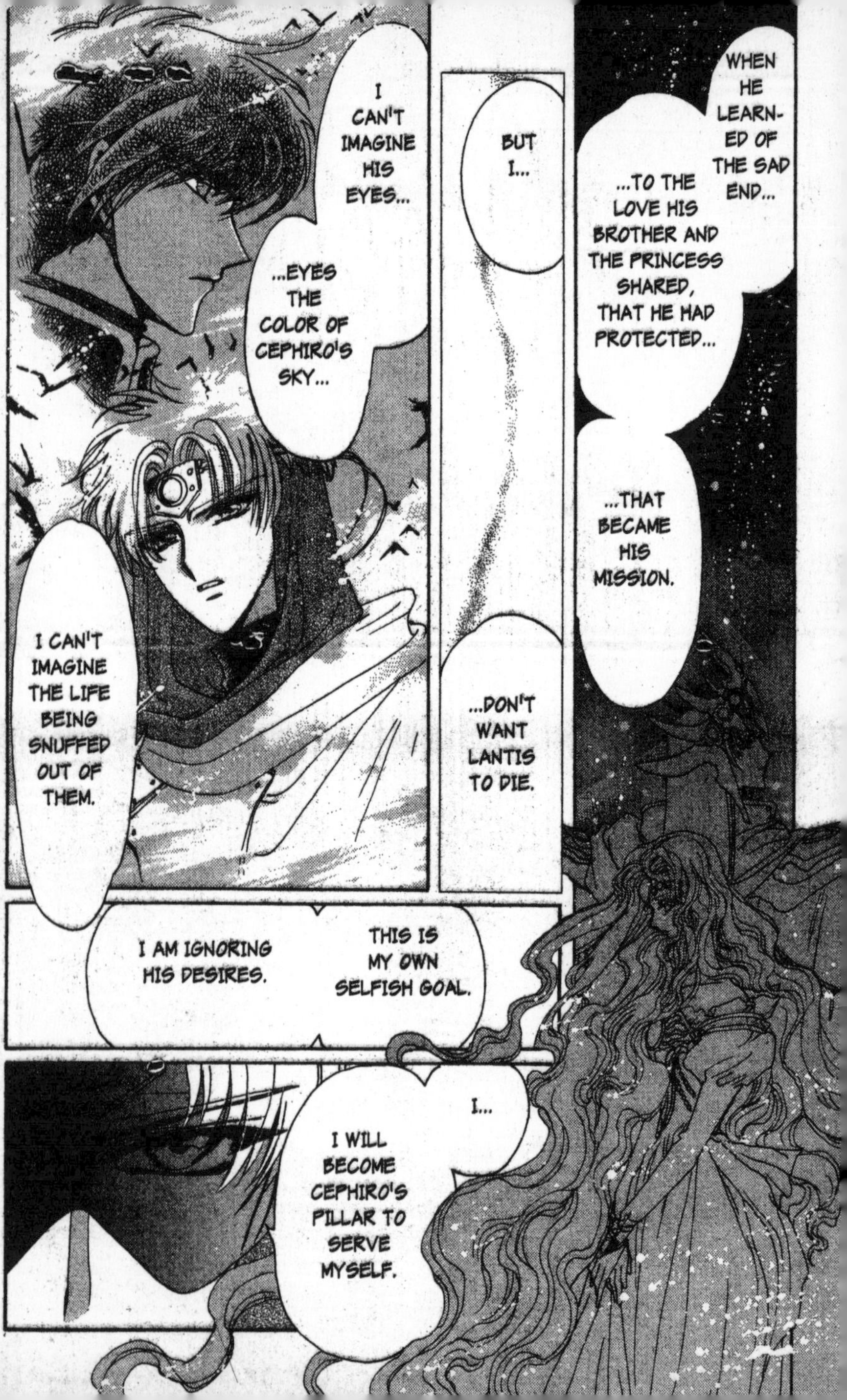
WHEN HE LEARNED OF THE SAD END...
...TO THE LOVE HIS BROTHER AND THE PRINCESS SHARED, THAT HE HAD PROTECTED...
...THAT BECAME HIS MISSION.
BUT I...
...DON'T WANT LANTIS TO DIE.
I CAN'T IMAGINE HIS EYES...
...EYES THE COLOR OF CEPHIRO'S SKY...
I CAN'T IMAGINE THE LIFE BEING SNUFFED OUT OF THEM.
THIS IS MY OWN SELFISH GOAL.
I AM IGNORING HIS DESIRES.
I...
I WILL BECOME CEPHIRO'S PILLAR TO SERVE MYSELF.

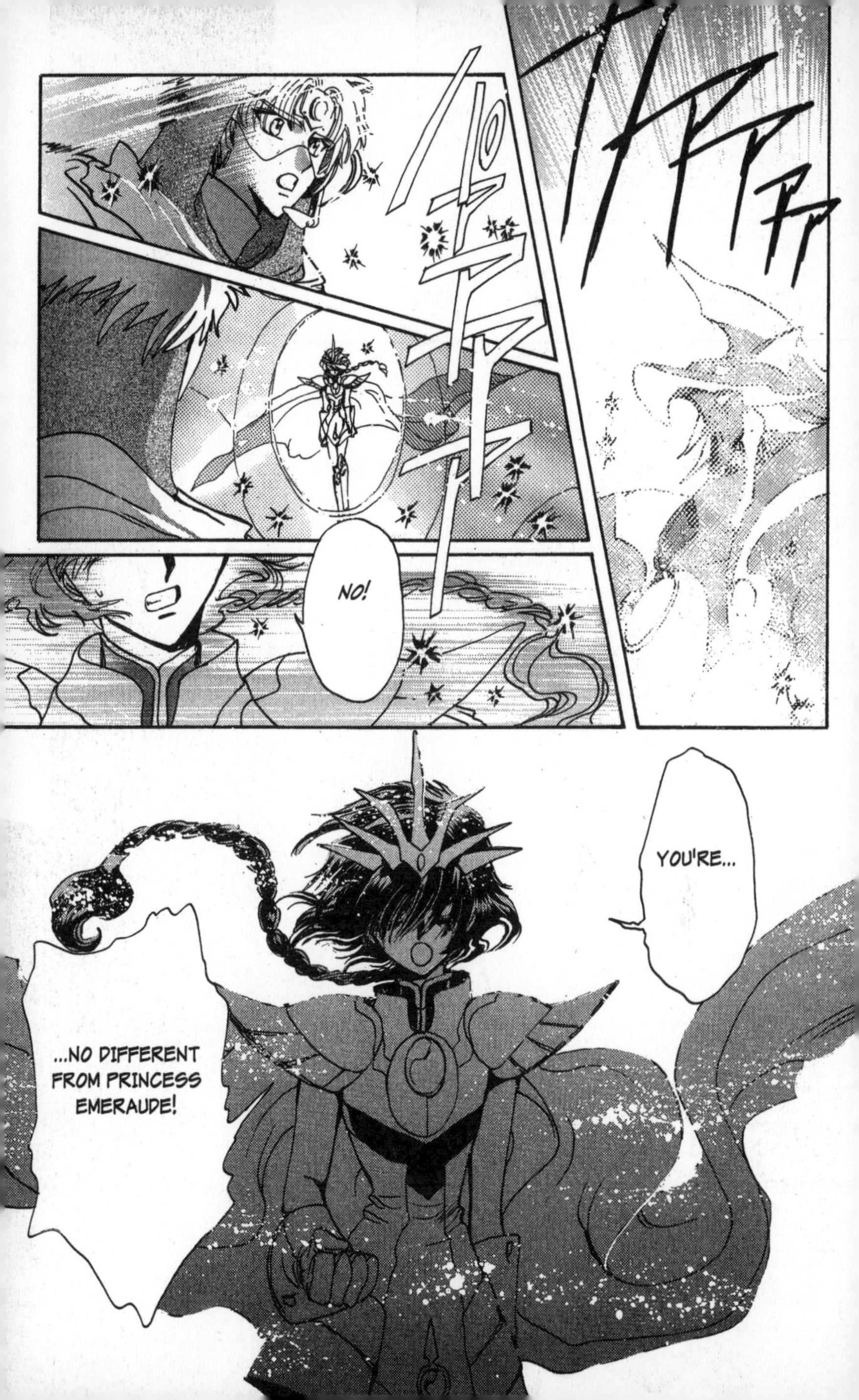
NO!
YOU'RE...
...NO DIFFERENT FROM PRINCESS EMERAUDE!

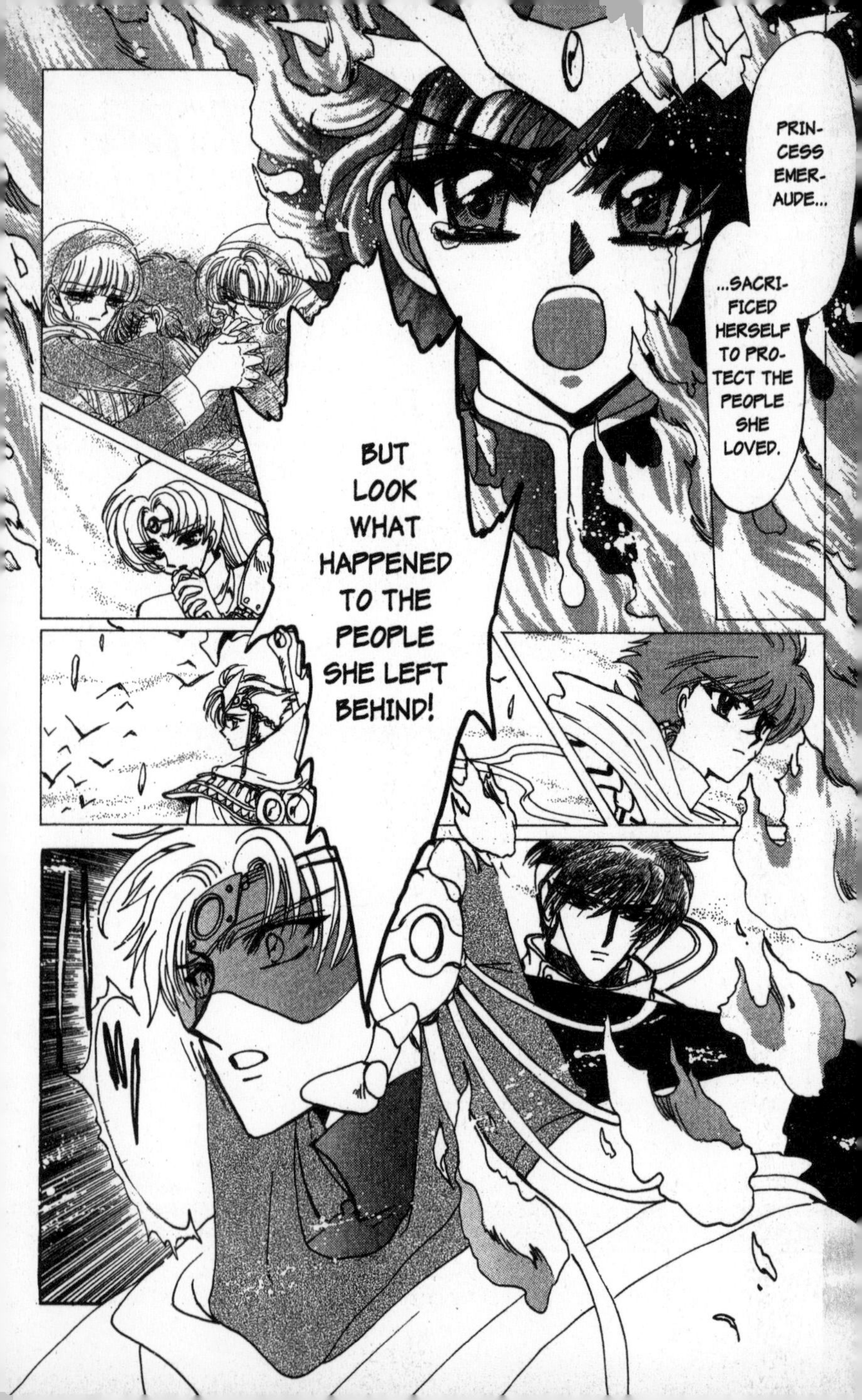
PRIN-CESS EMER-AUDE...
...SACRI-FICED HERSELF TO PRO-TECT THE PEOPLE SHE LOVED.
BUT LOOK WHAT HAPPENED TO THE PEOPLE SHE LEFT BEHIND!

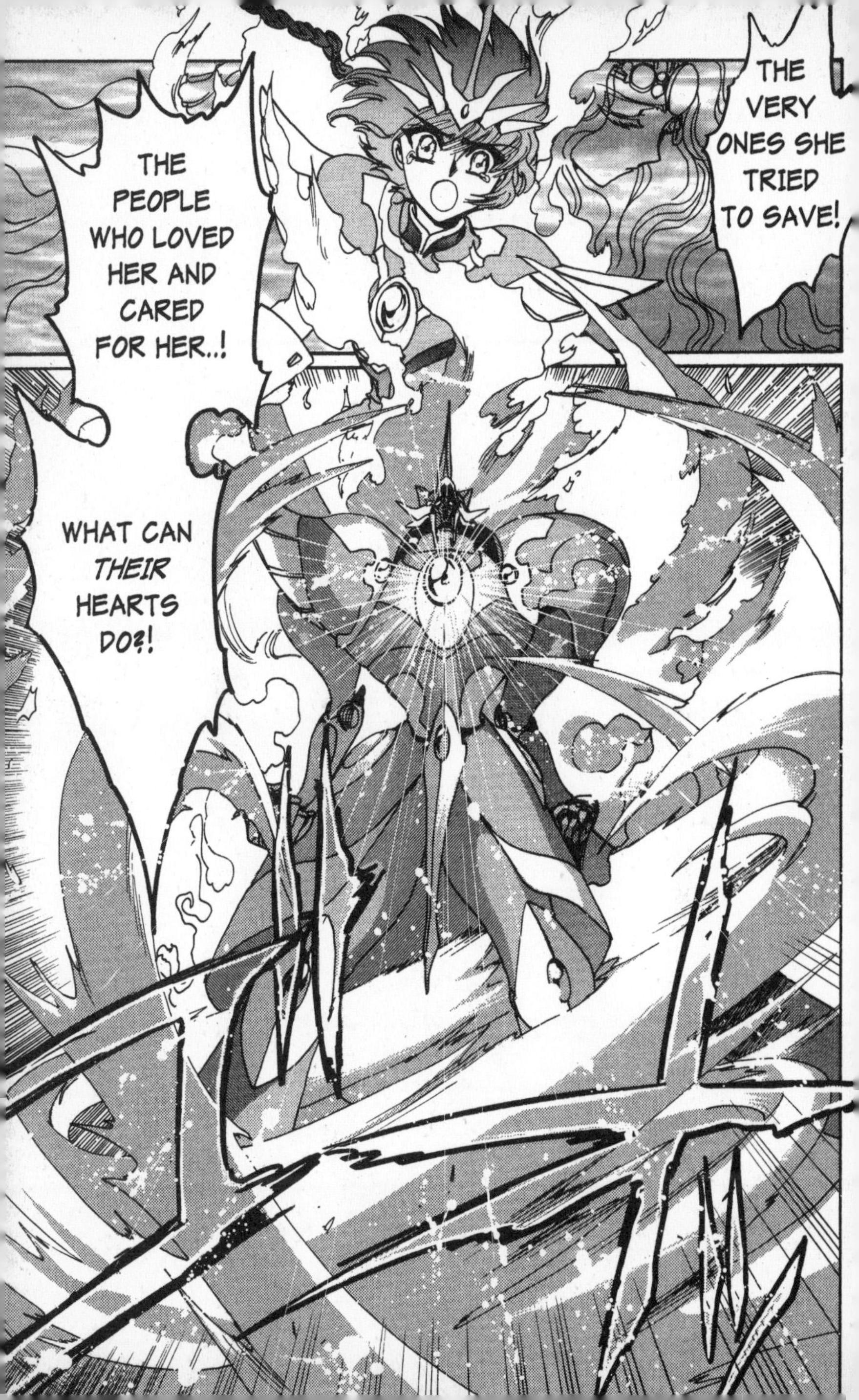
THE VERY ONES SHE TRIED TO SAVE!
THE PEOPLE WHO LOVED HER AND CARED FOR HER..!
WHAT CAN *THEIR* HEARTS DO?!

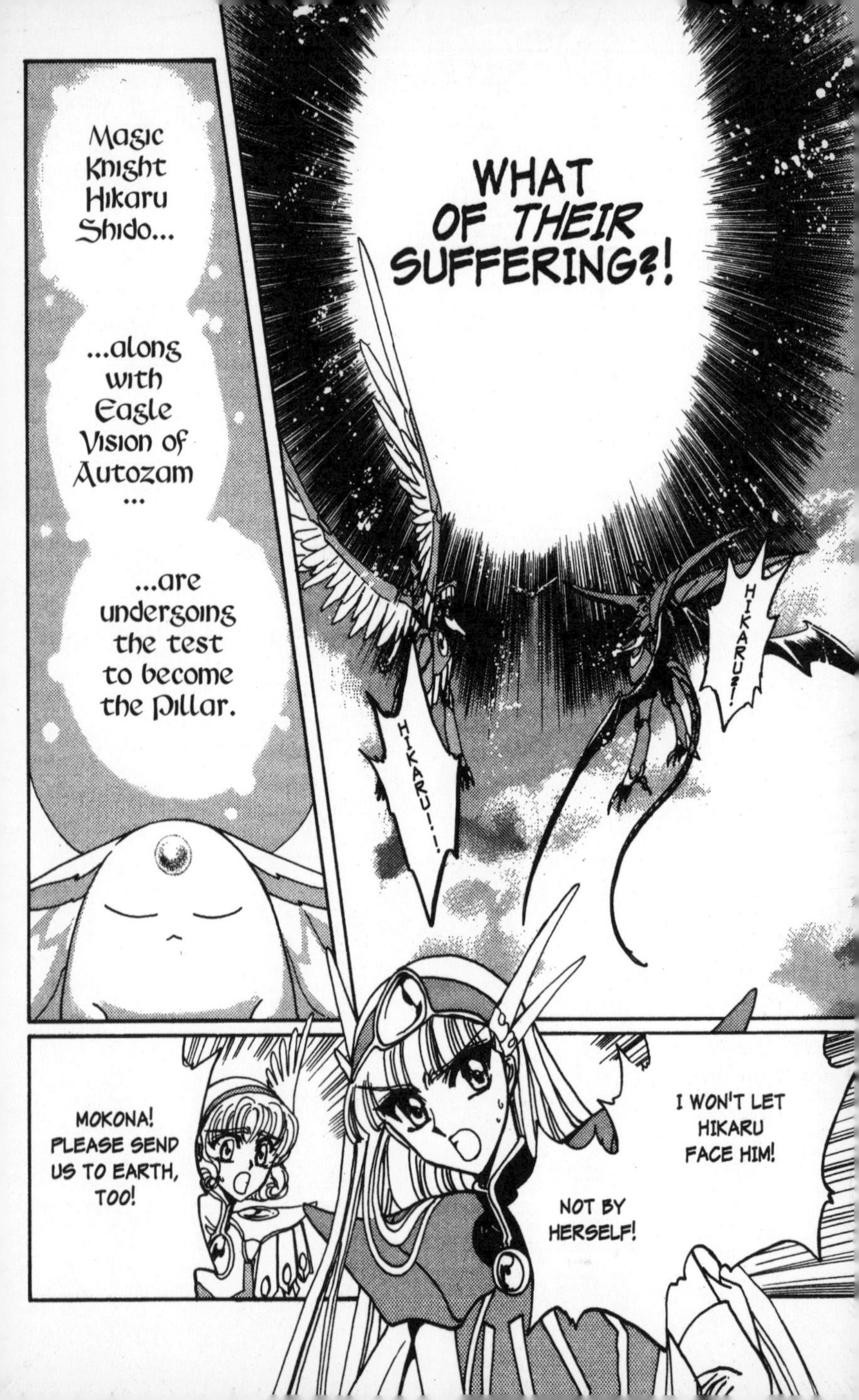
WHAT OF THEIR SUFFERING?!
HIKARU?!
HIKARU!!
Magic Knight Hikaru Shido...
...along with Eagle Vision of Autozam...
...are undergoing the test to become the Pillar.
I WON'T LET HIKARU FACE HIM!
NOT BY HERSELF!
MOKONA! PLEASE SEND US TO EARTH, TOO!

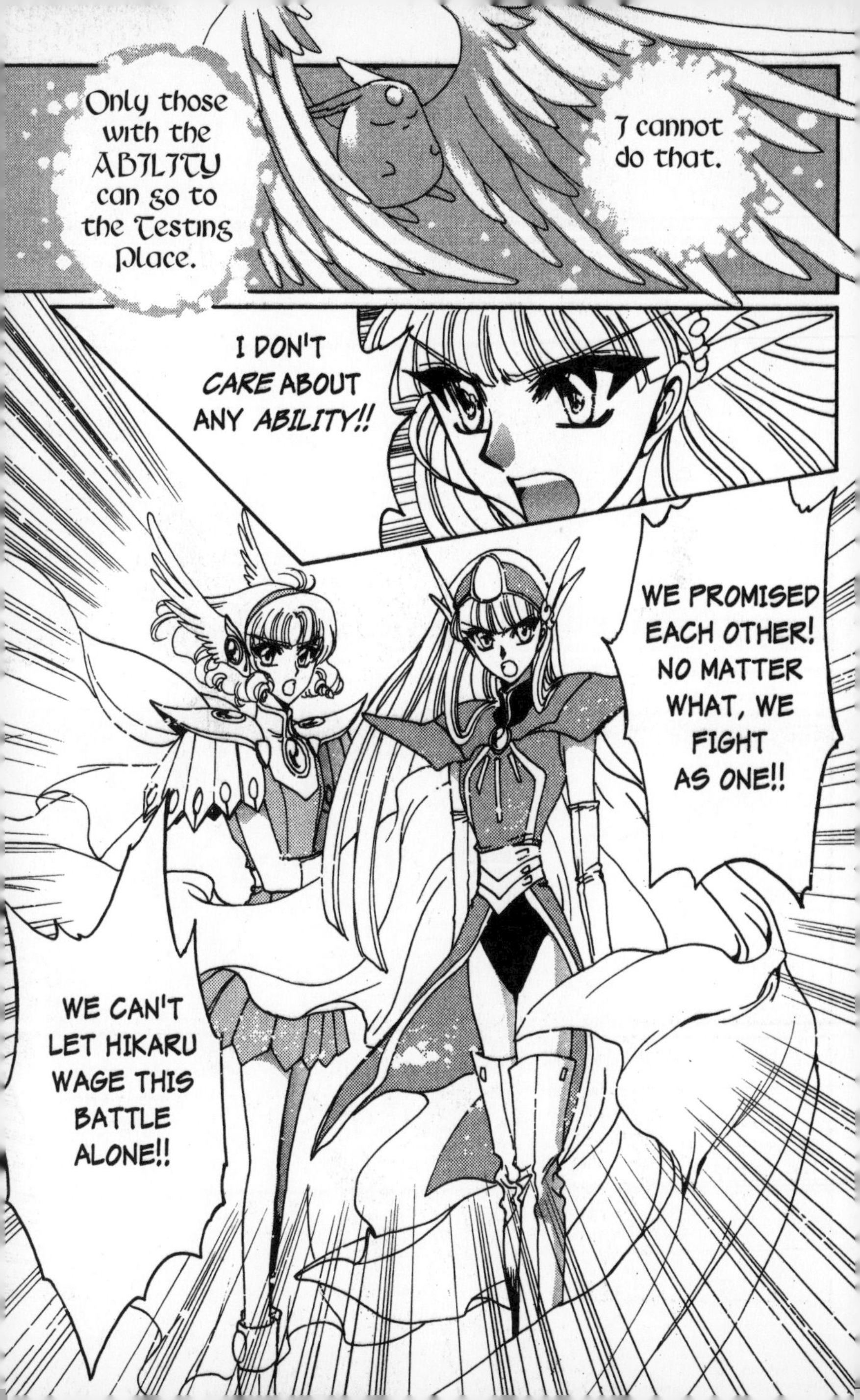
I cannot do that.
Only those with the ABILITY can go to the Testing Place.
I DON'T CARE ABOUT ANY ABILITY!!
WE PROMISED EACH OTHER! NO MATTER WHAT, WE FIGHT AS ONE!!
WE CAN'T LET HIKARU WAGE THIS BATTLE ALONE!!

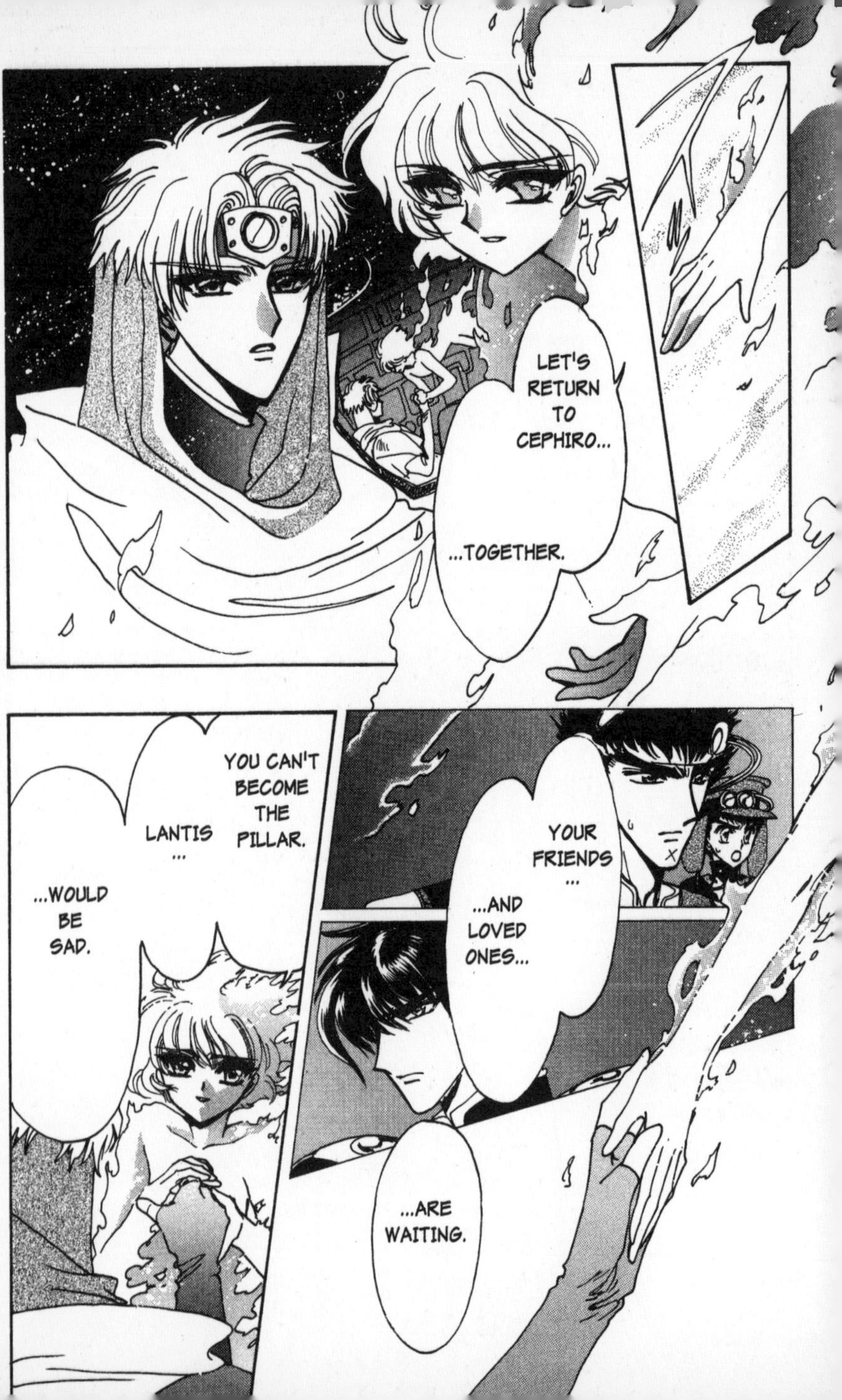
LET'S RETURN TO CEPHIRO...
...TOGETHER.
YOUR FRIENDS...
...AND LOVED ONES...
...ARE WAITING.
YOU CAN'T BECOME THE PILLAR.
LANTIS...
...WOULD BE SAD.

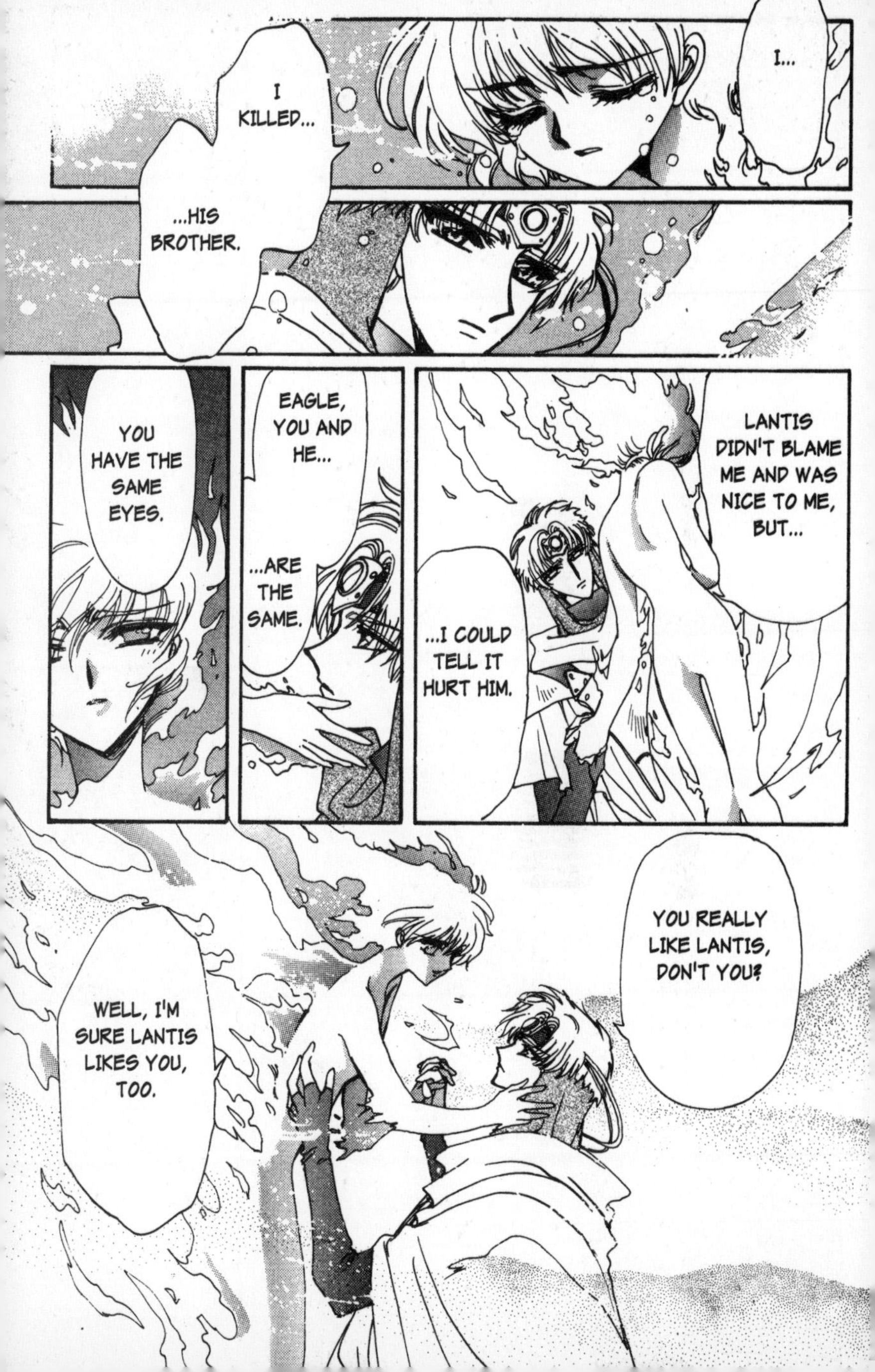
I...
I KILLED...
...HIS BROTHER.
LANTIS DIDN'T BLAME ME AND WAS NICE TO ME, BUT...
...I COULD TELL IT HURT HIM.
EAGLE, YOU AND HE...
...ARE THE SAME.
YOU HAVE THE SAME EYES.
YOU REALLY LIKE LANTIS, DON'T YOU?
WELL, I'M SURE LANTIS LIKES YOU, TOO.

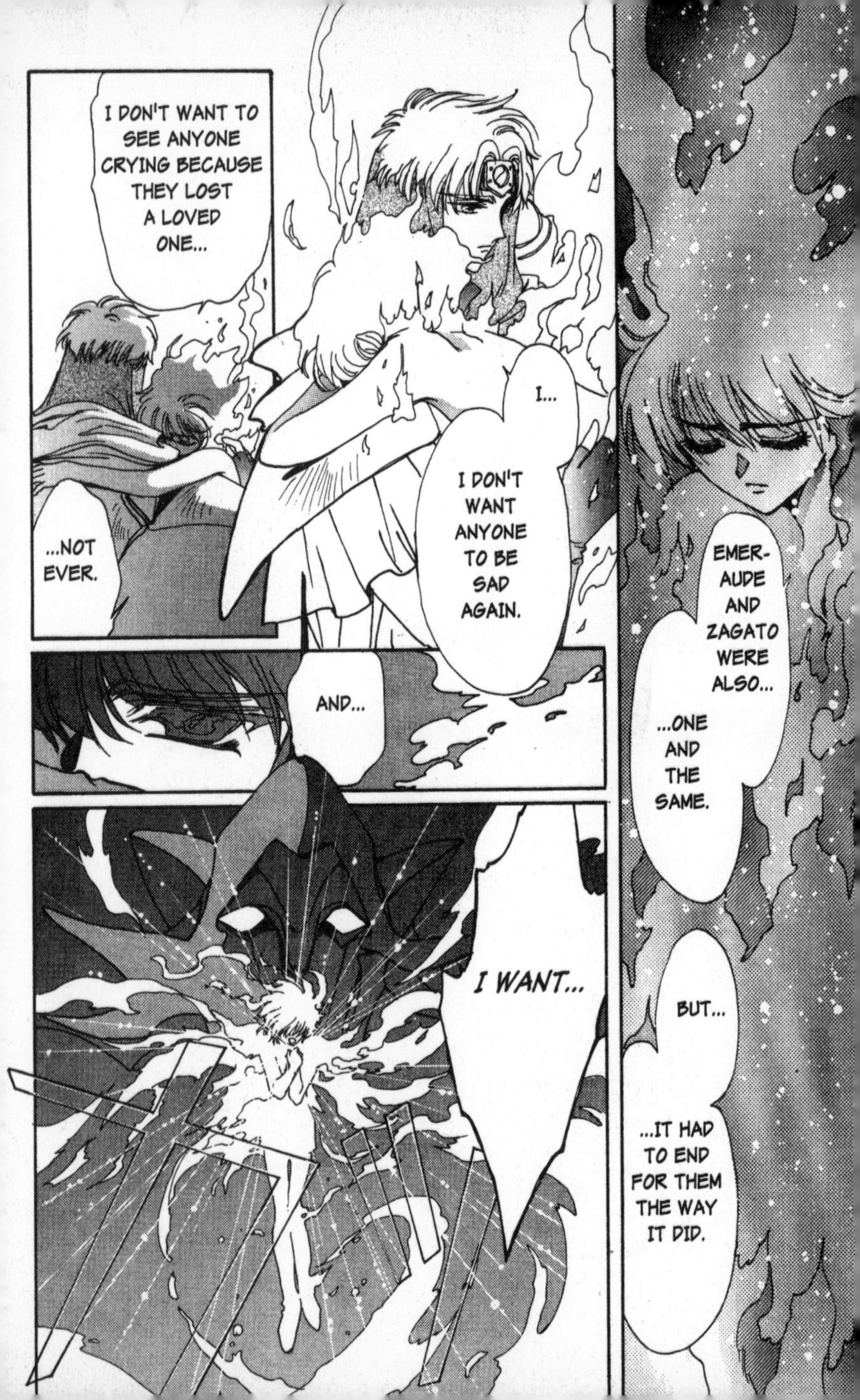
EMER-AUDE AND ZAGATO WERE ALSO...
...ONE AND THE SAME.
BUT...
...IT HAD TO END FOR THEM THE WAY IT DID.
I DON'T WANT TO SEE ANYONE CRYING BECAUSE THEY LOST A LOVED ONE...
...NOT EVER.
I...
I DON'T WANT ANYONE TO BE SAD AGAIN.
AND...
I WANT...

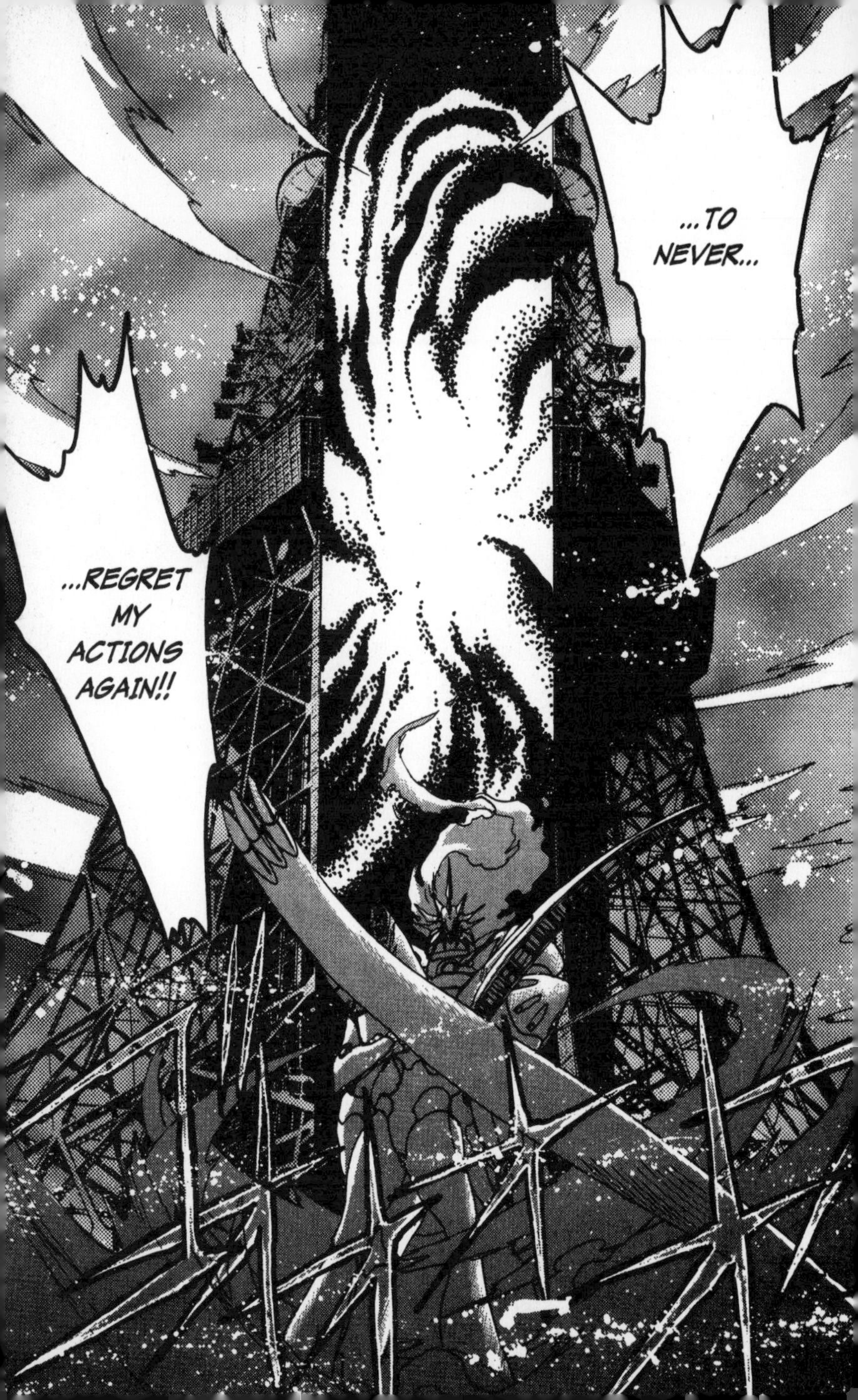
...TO NEVER...
...REGRET MY ACTIONS AGAIN!!

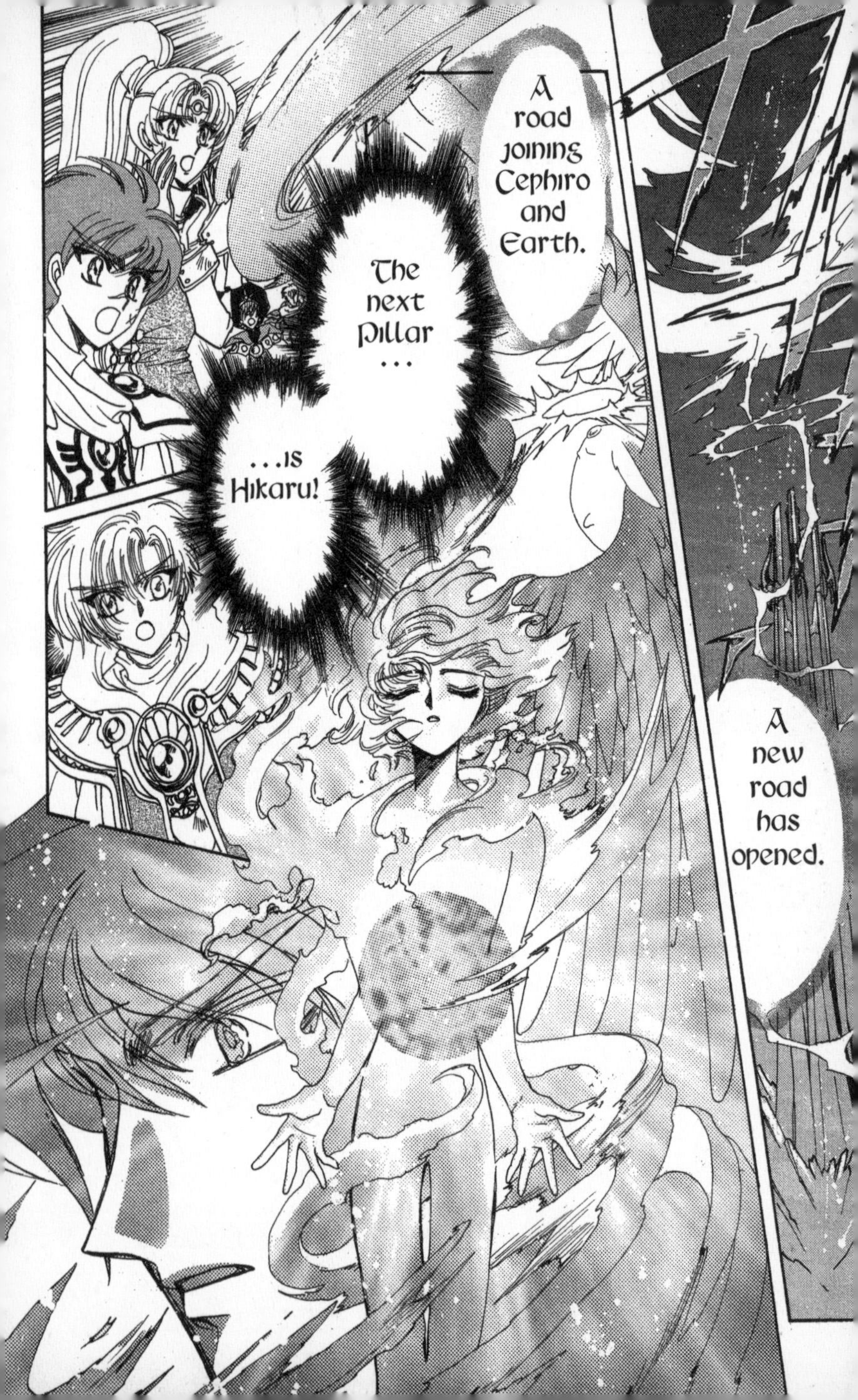
A new road has opened.
A road joining Cephiro and Earth.
The next Pillar...
...is Hikaru!

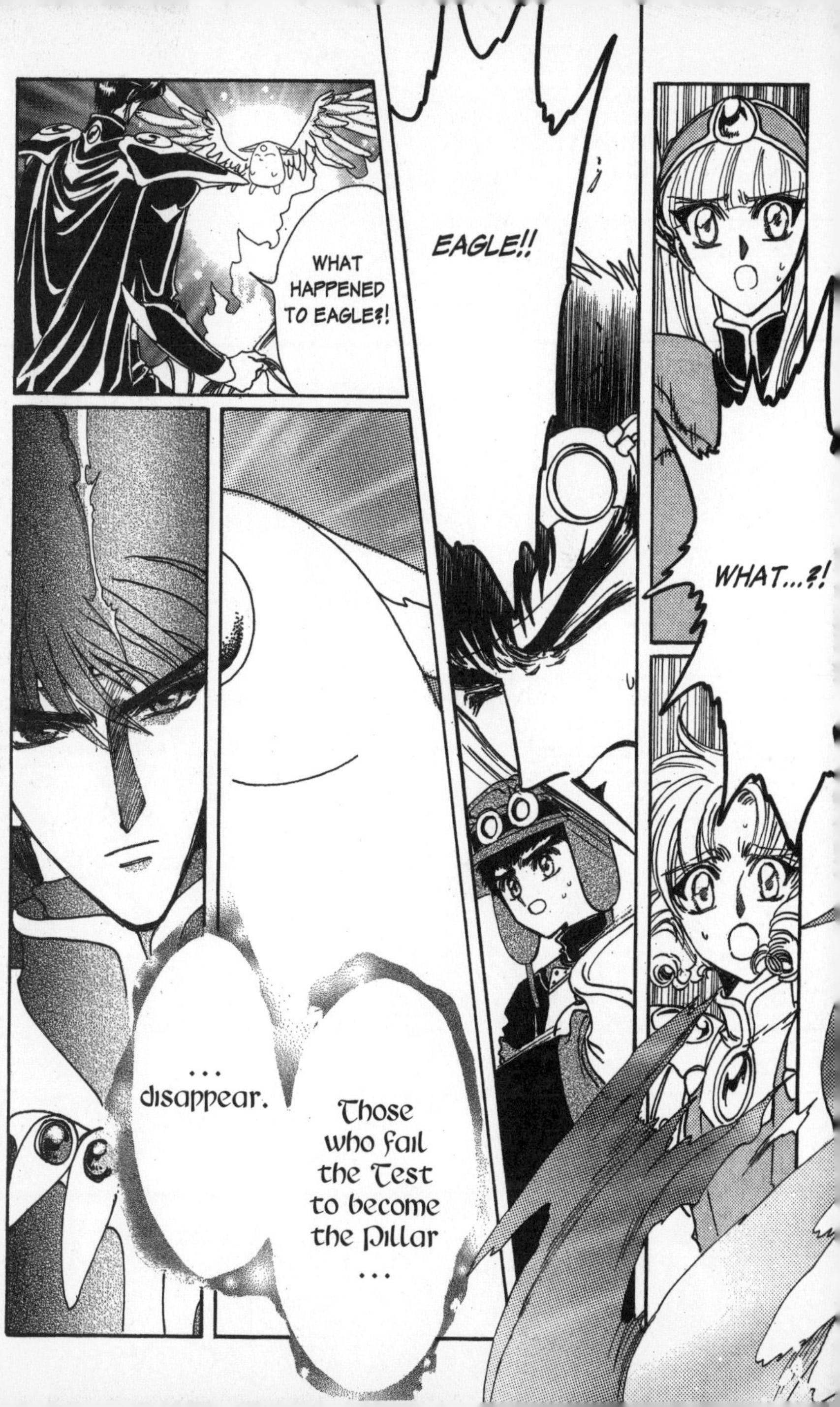
WHAT...?!
EAGLE!!
WHAT HAPPENED TO EAGLE?!
Those who fail the Test to become the Pillar ...
... disappear.

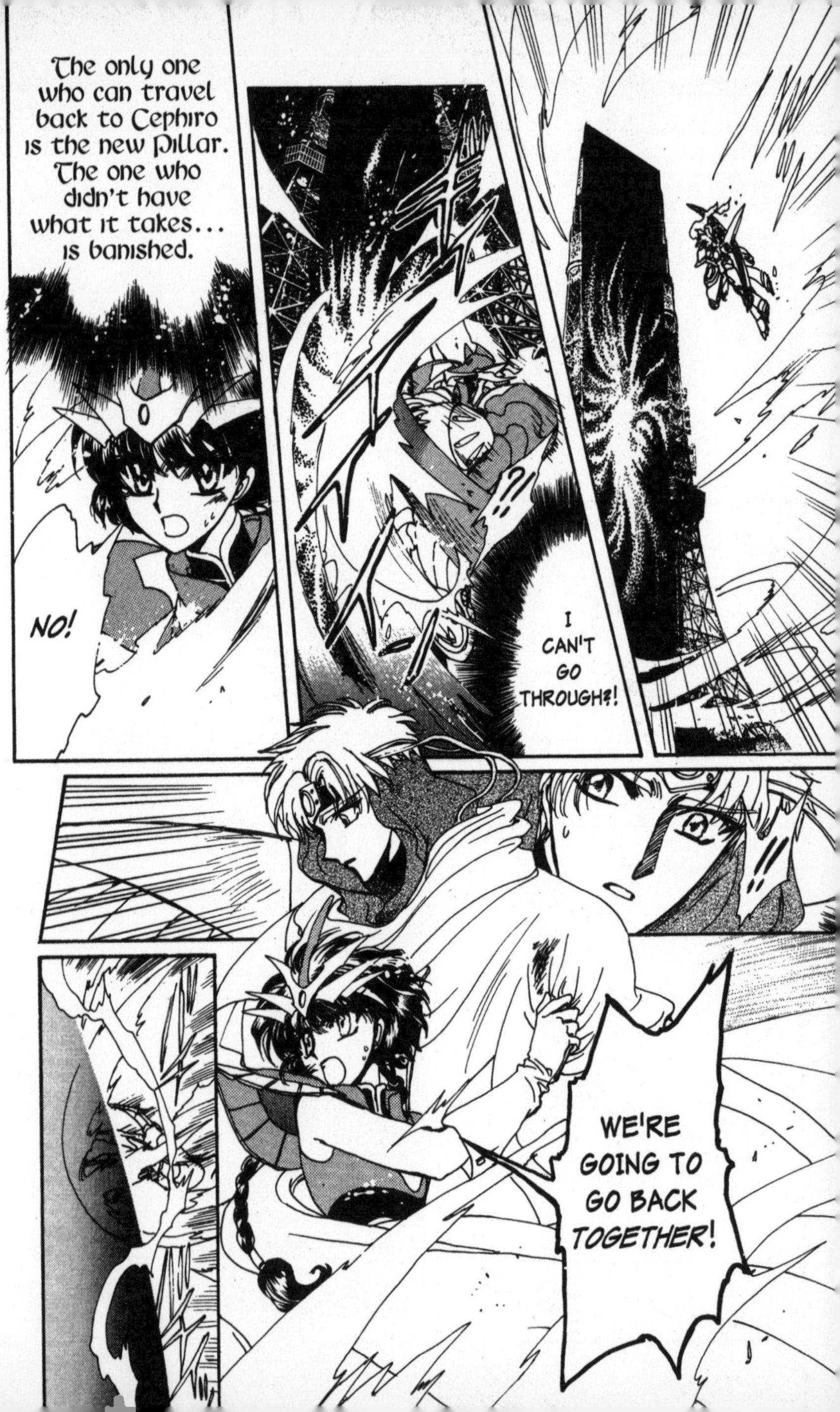
I CAN'T GO THROUGH?!
The only one who can travel back to Cephiro is the new Pillar. The one who didn't have what it takes... is banished.
NO!
WE'RE GOING TO GO BACK TOGETHER!

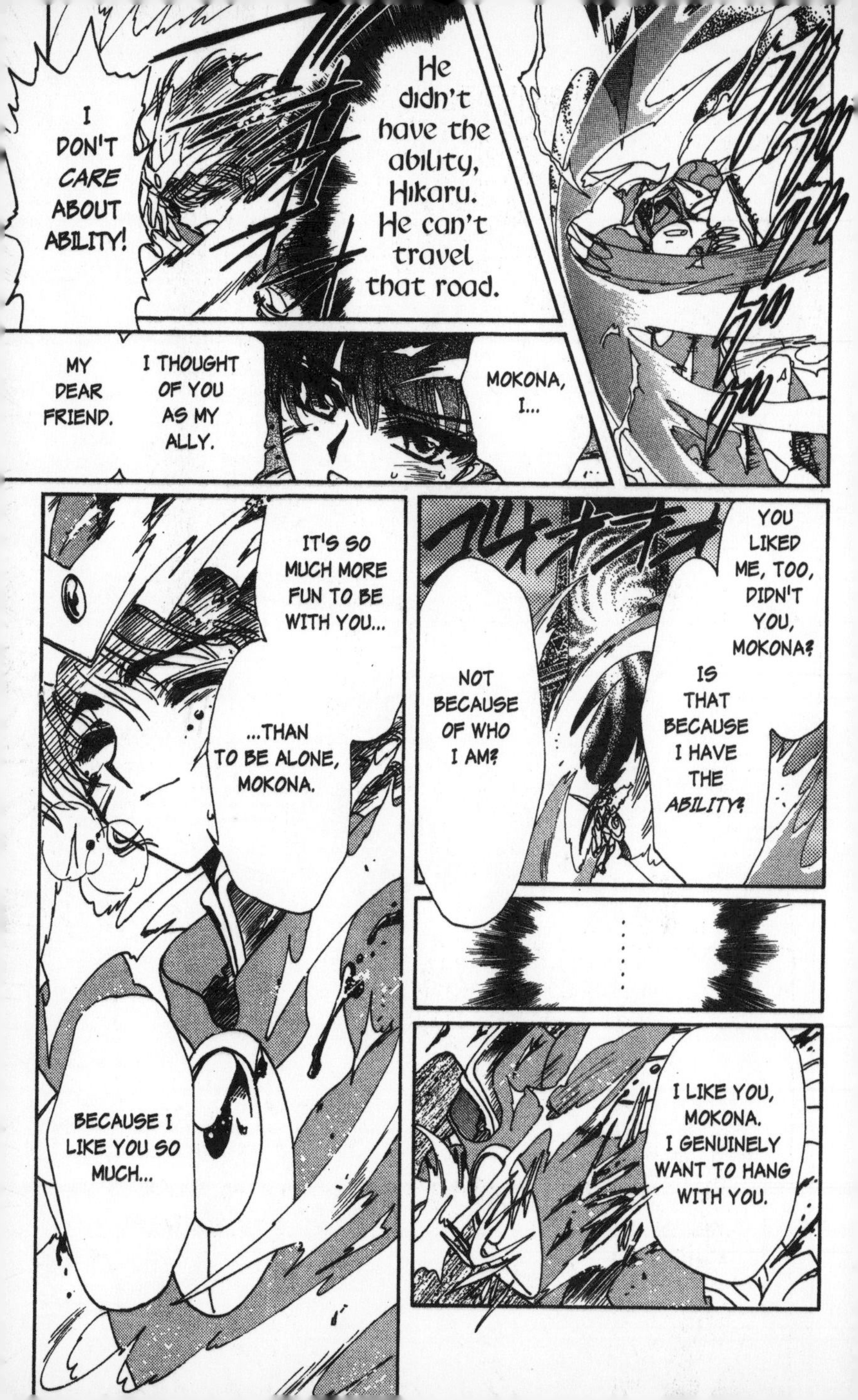
He didn't have the ability, Hikaru. He can't travel that road.
I DON'T CARE ABOUT ABILITY!
MOKONA, I...
I THOUGHT OF YOU AS MY ALLY.
MY DEAR FRIEND.
YOU LIKED ME, TOO, DIDN'T YOU, MOKONA?
IS THAT BECAUSE I HAVE THE ABILITY?
NOT BECAUSE OF WHO I AM?
......
I LIKE YOU, MOKONA. I GENUINELY WANT TO HANG WITH YOU.
IT'S SO MUCH MORE FUN TO BE WITH YOU...
...THAN TO BE ALONE, MOKONA.
BECAUSE I LIKE YOU SO MUCH...

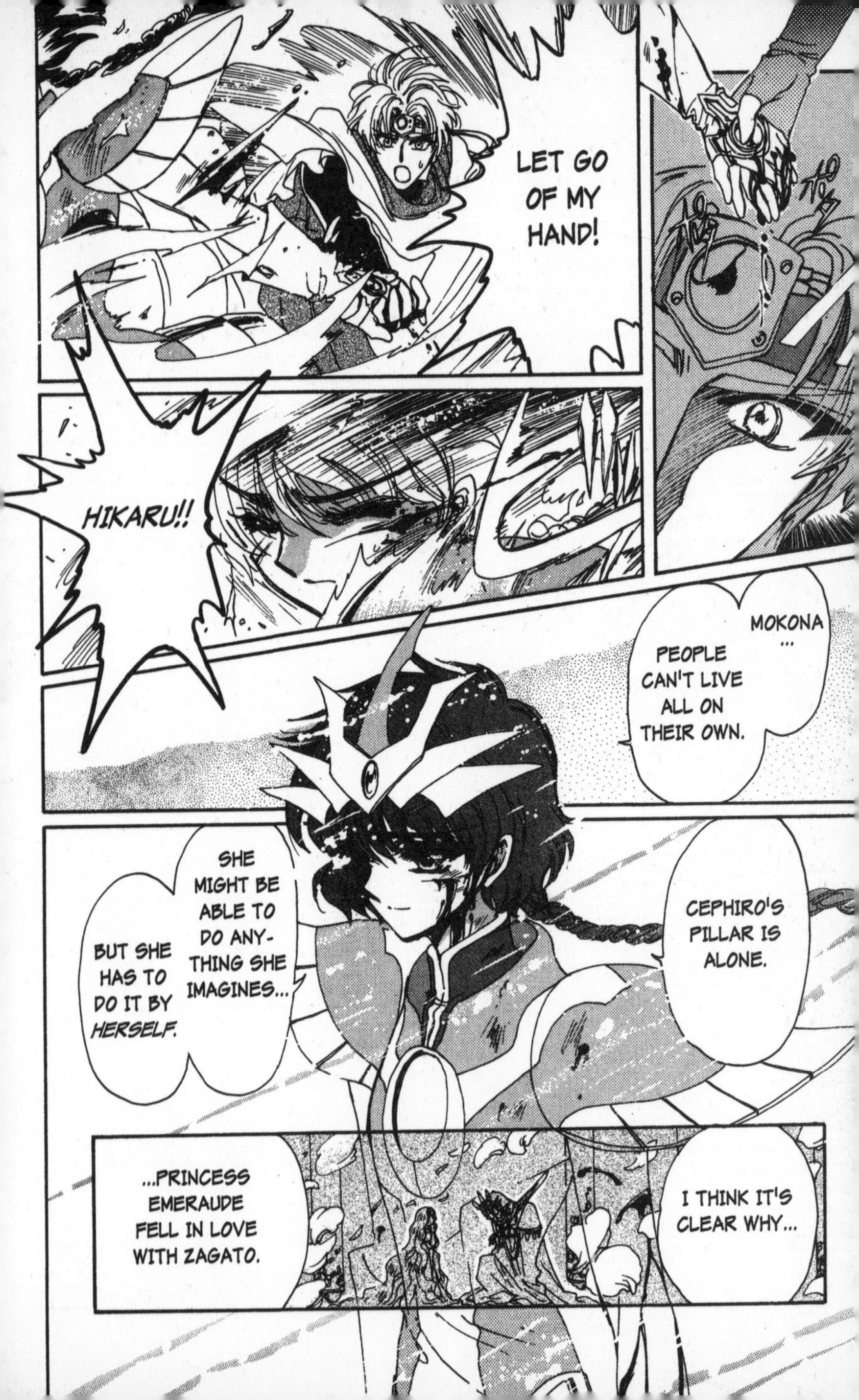
LET GO OF MY HAND!
HIKARU!!
MOKONA...
PEOPLE CAN'T LIVE ALL ON THEIR OWN.
CEPHIRO'S PILLAR IS ALONE.
SHE MIGHT BE ABLE TO DO ANY-THING SHE IMAGINES...
BUT SHE HAS TO DO IT BY *HERSELF*.
I THINK IT'S CLEAR WHY...
...PRINCESS EMERAUDE FELL IN LOVE WITH ZAGATO.

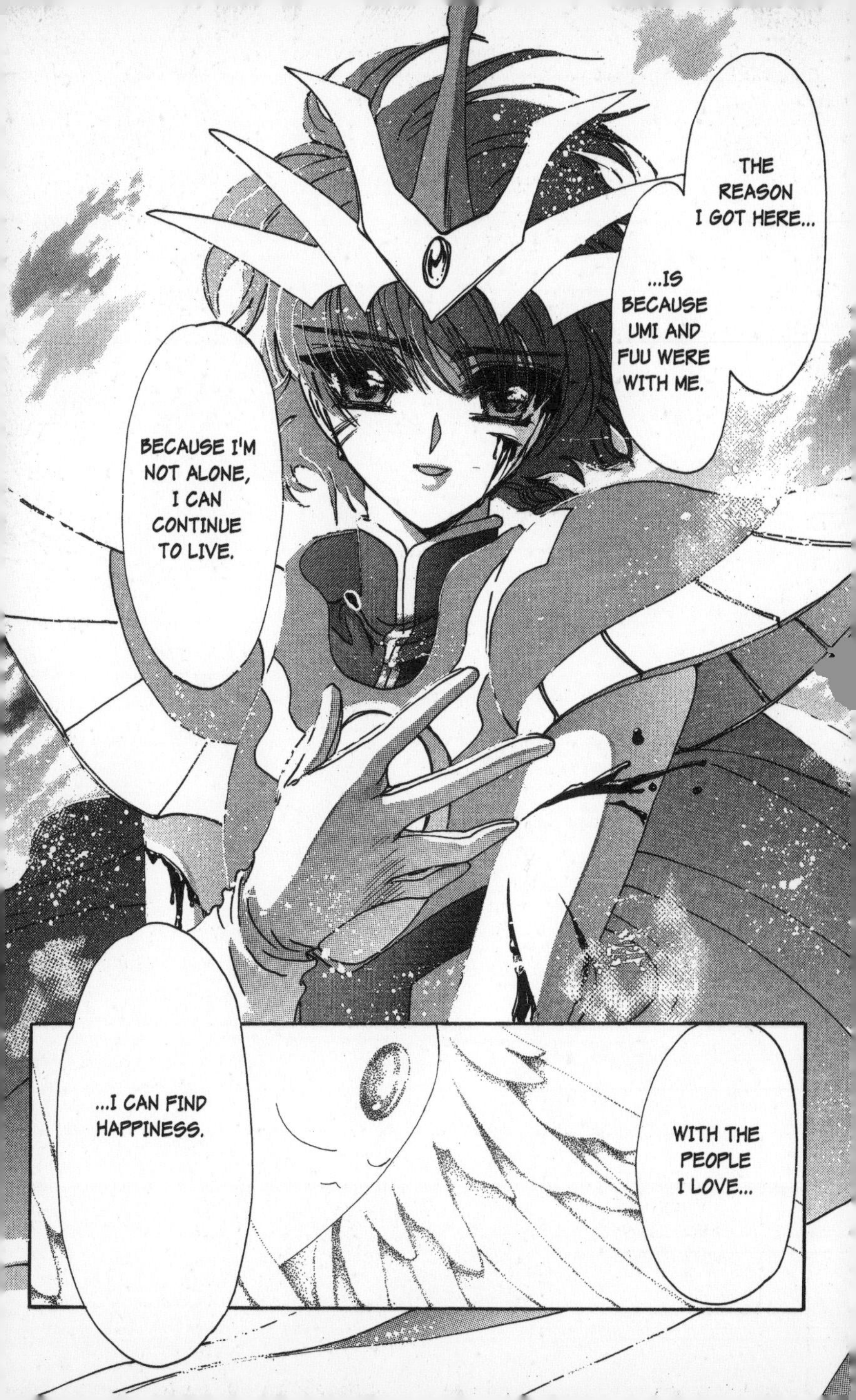
THE REASON I GOT HERE...
...IS BECAUSE UMI AND FUU WERE WITH ME.
BECAUSE I'M NOT ALONE, I CAN CONTINUE TO LIVE.
WITH THE PEOPLE I LOVE...
...I CAN FIND HAPPINESS.

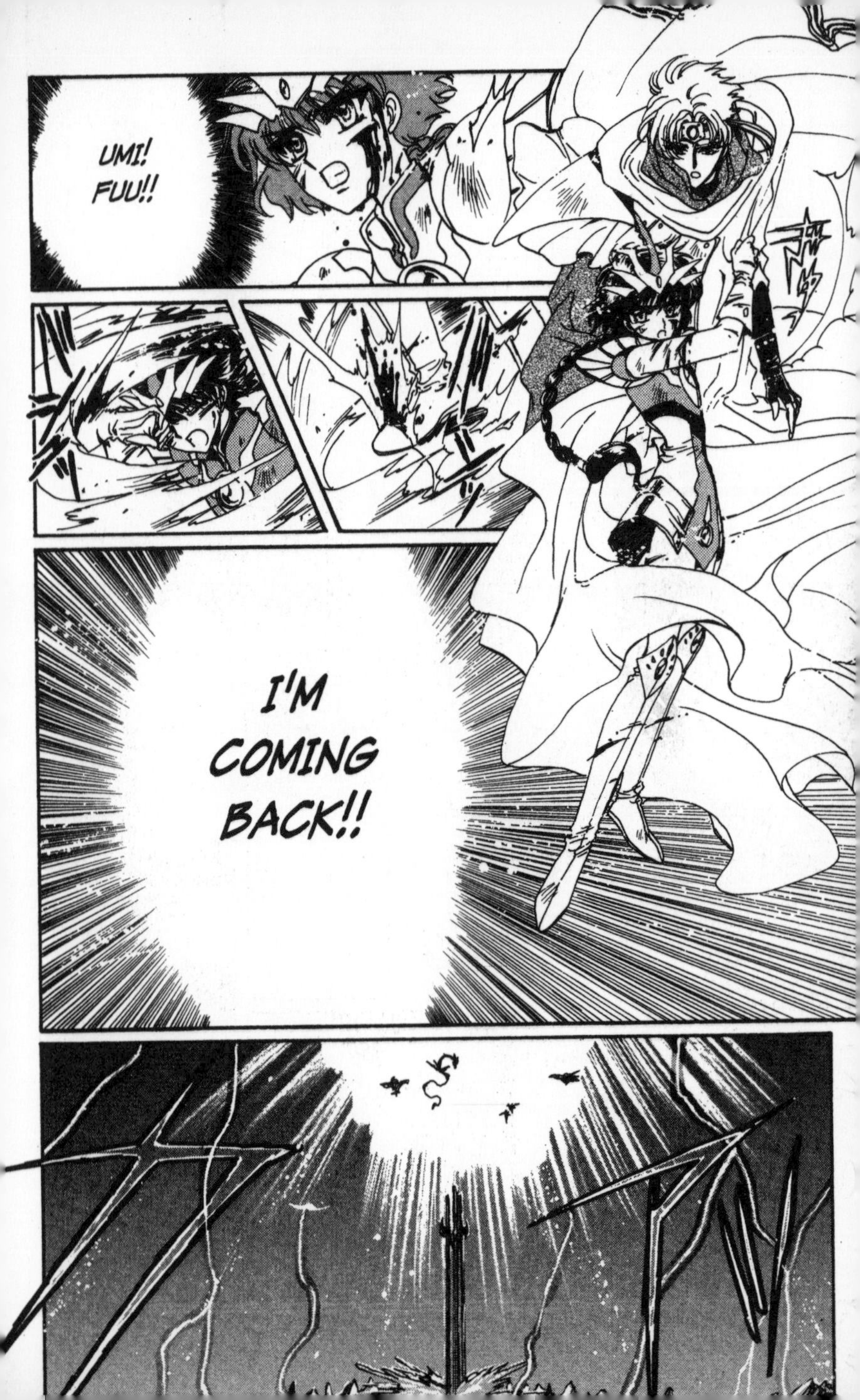
UMI!
FUU!!
I'M
COMING
BACK!!

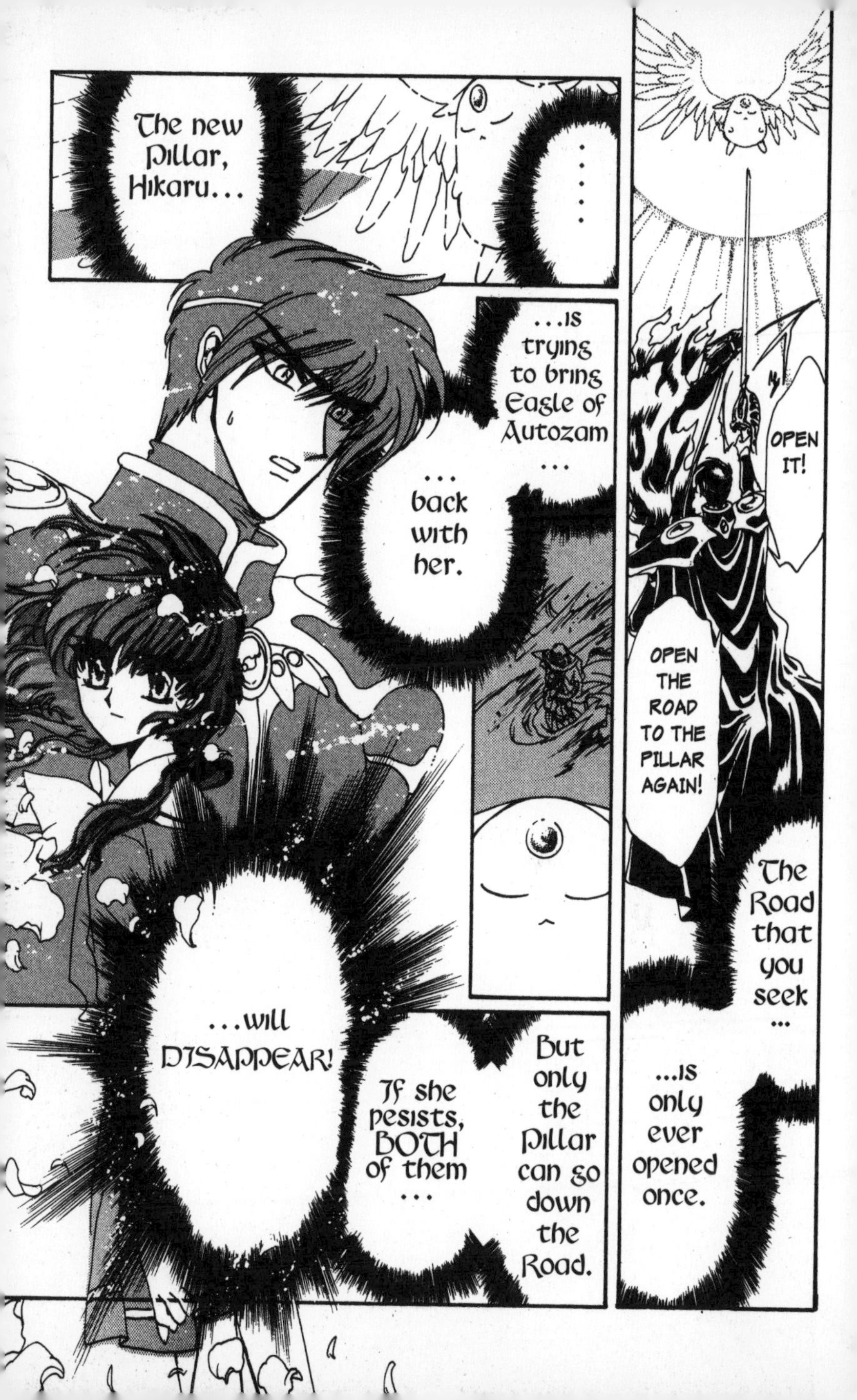

OPEN IT!
OPEN THE ROAD TO THE PILLAR AGAIN!
The Road that you seek ...
...is only ever opened once.
......
The new Pillar, Hikaru...
...is trying to bring Eagle of Autozam ...
... back with her.
But only the Pillar can go down the Road.
If she pesists, BOTH of them ...
...will DISAPPEAR!

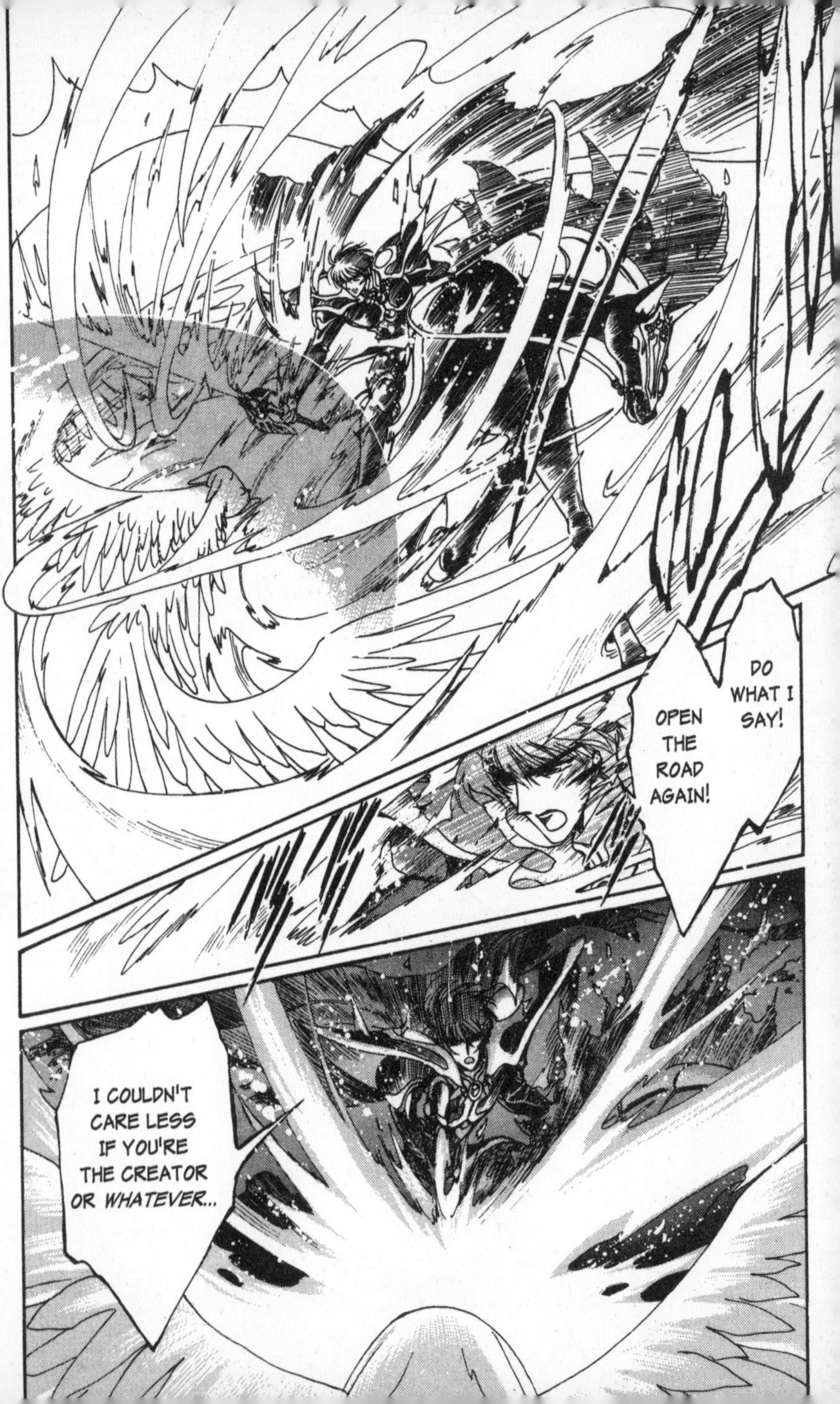
DO WHAT I SAY!
OPEN THE ROAD AGAIN!
I COULDN'T CARE LESS IF YOU'RE THE CREATOR OR *WHATEVER*...

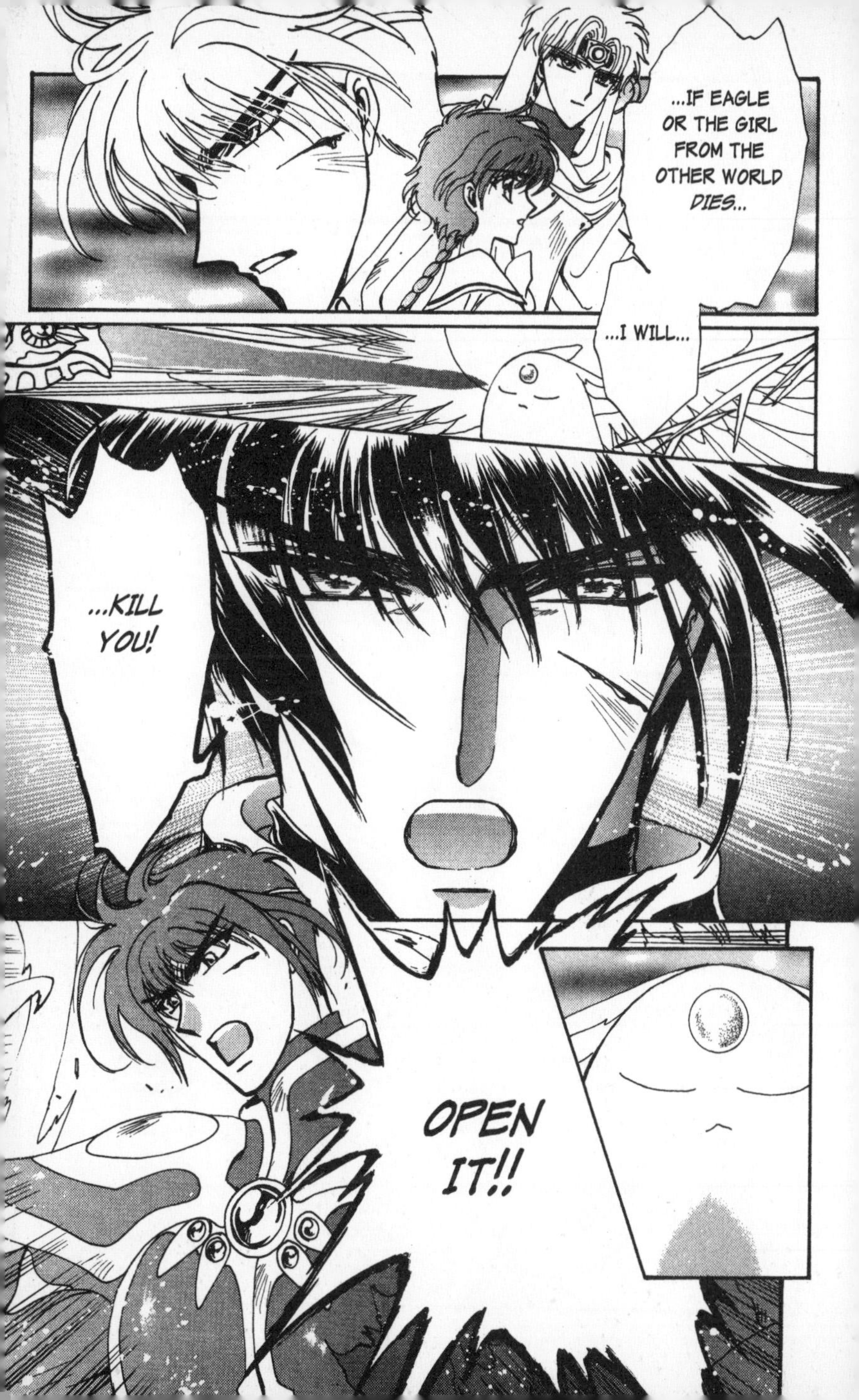
...IF EAGLE OR THE GIRL FROM THE OTHER WORLD DIES...
...I WILL...
...KILL YOU!
OPEN IT!!

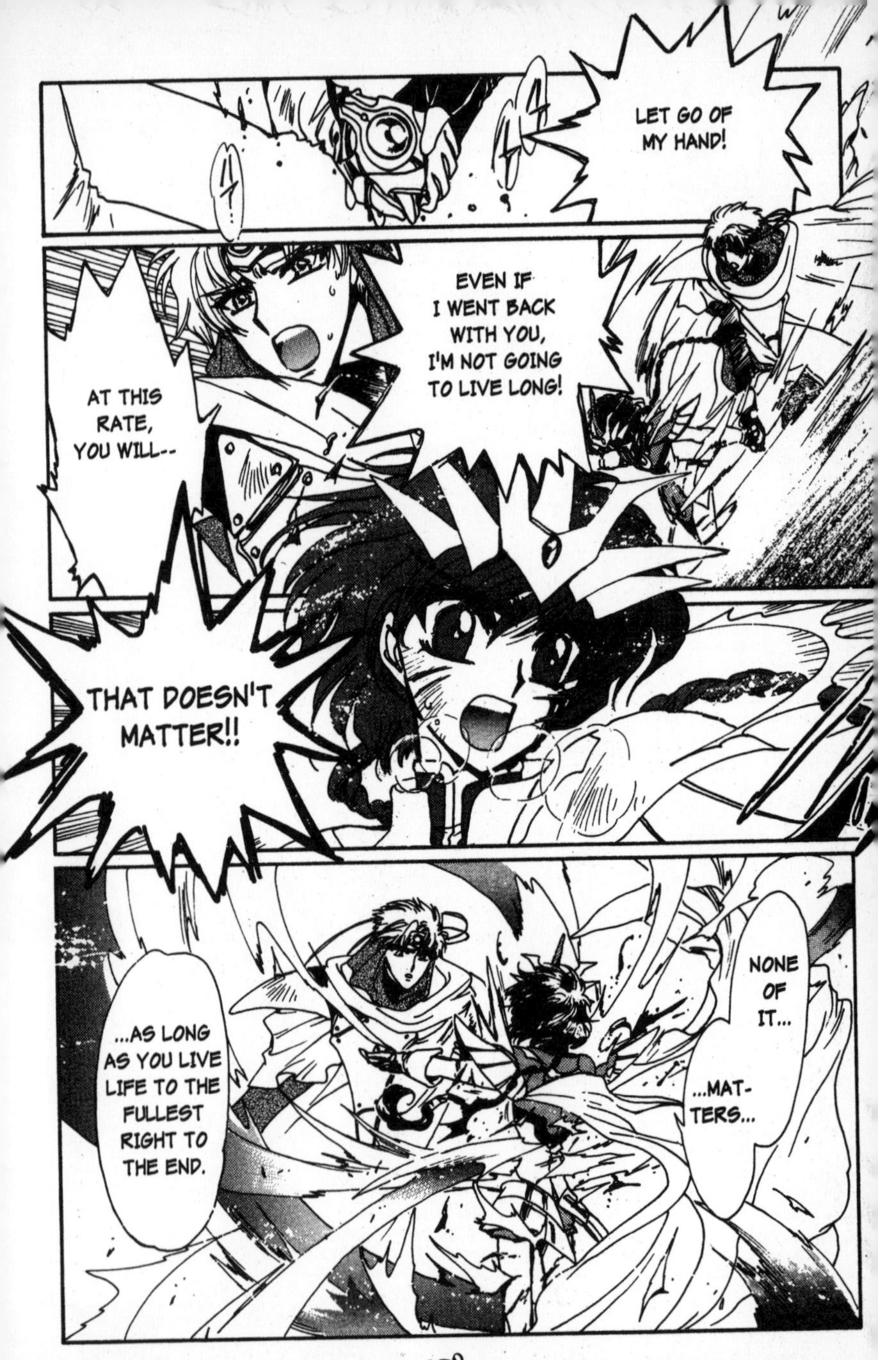
LET GO OF MY HAND!
EVEN IF I WENT BACK WITH YOU, I'M NOT GOING TO LIVE LONG!
AT THIS RATE, YOU WILL--
THAT DOESN'T MATTER!!
NONE OF IT...
...MAT-TERS...
...AS LONG AS YOU LIVE LIFE TO THE FULLEST RIGHT TO THE END.

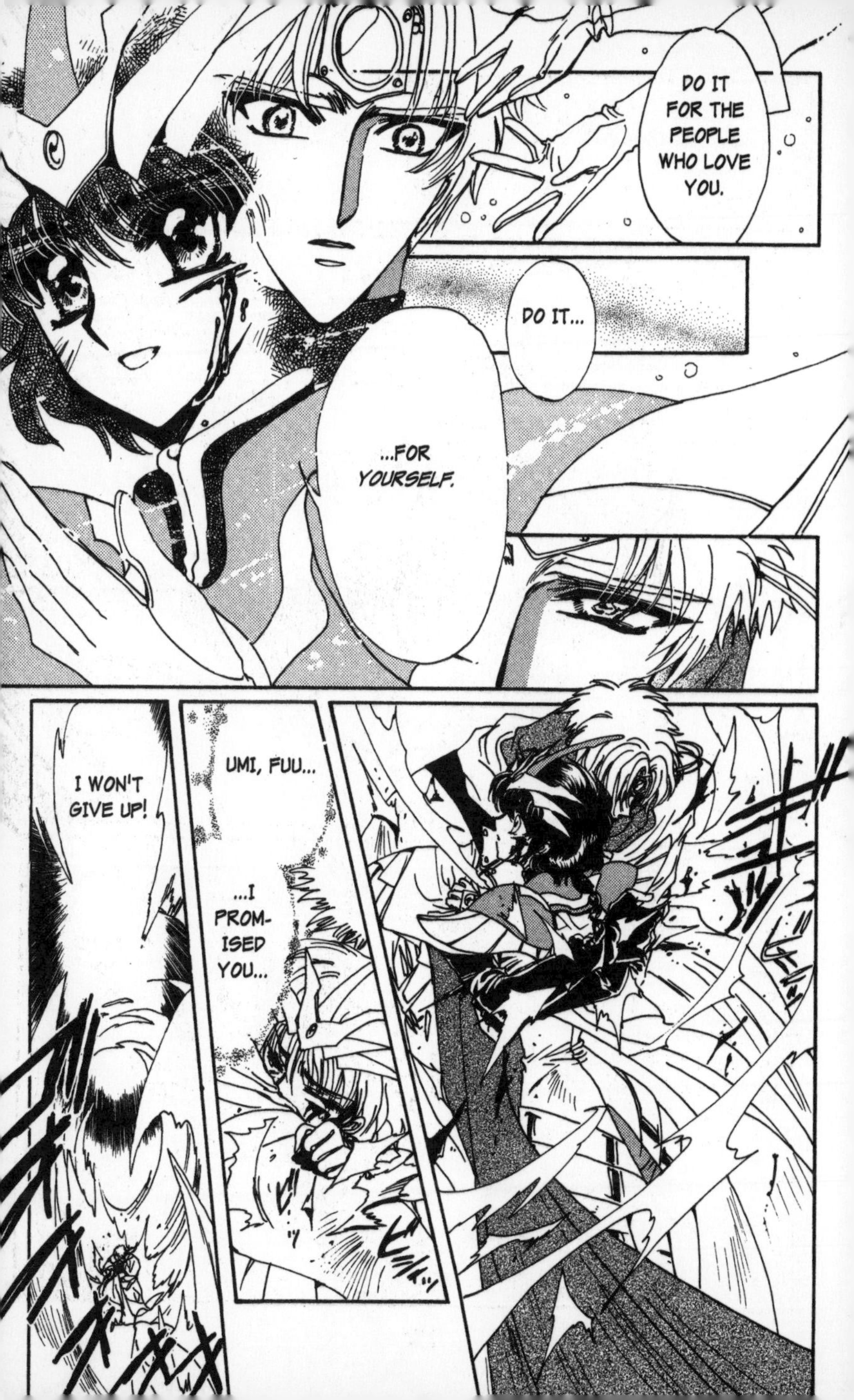
DO IT FOR THE PEOPLE WHO LOVE YOU.
DO IT...
...FOR YOURSELF.
UMI, FUU...
...I PROMISED YOU...
I WON'T GIVE UP!

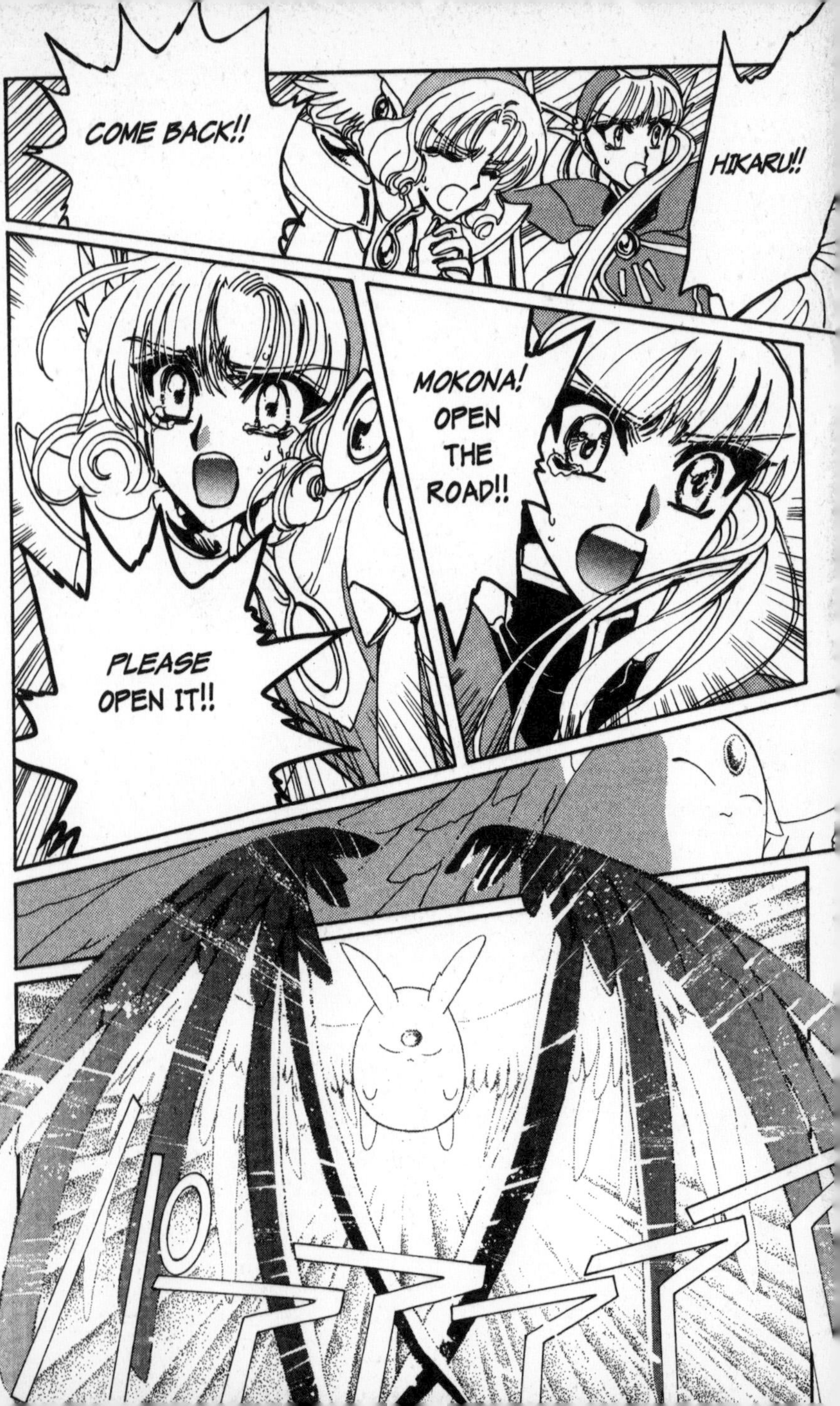
HIKARU!!
COME BACK!!
MOKONA! OPEN THE ROAD!!
PLEASE OPEN IT!!

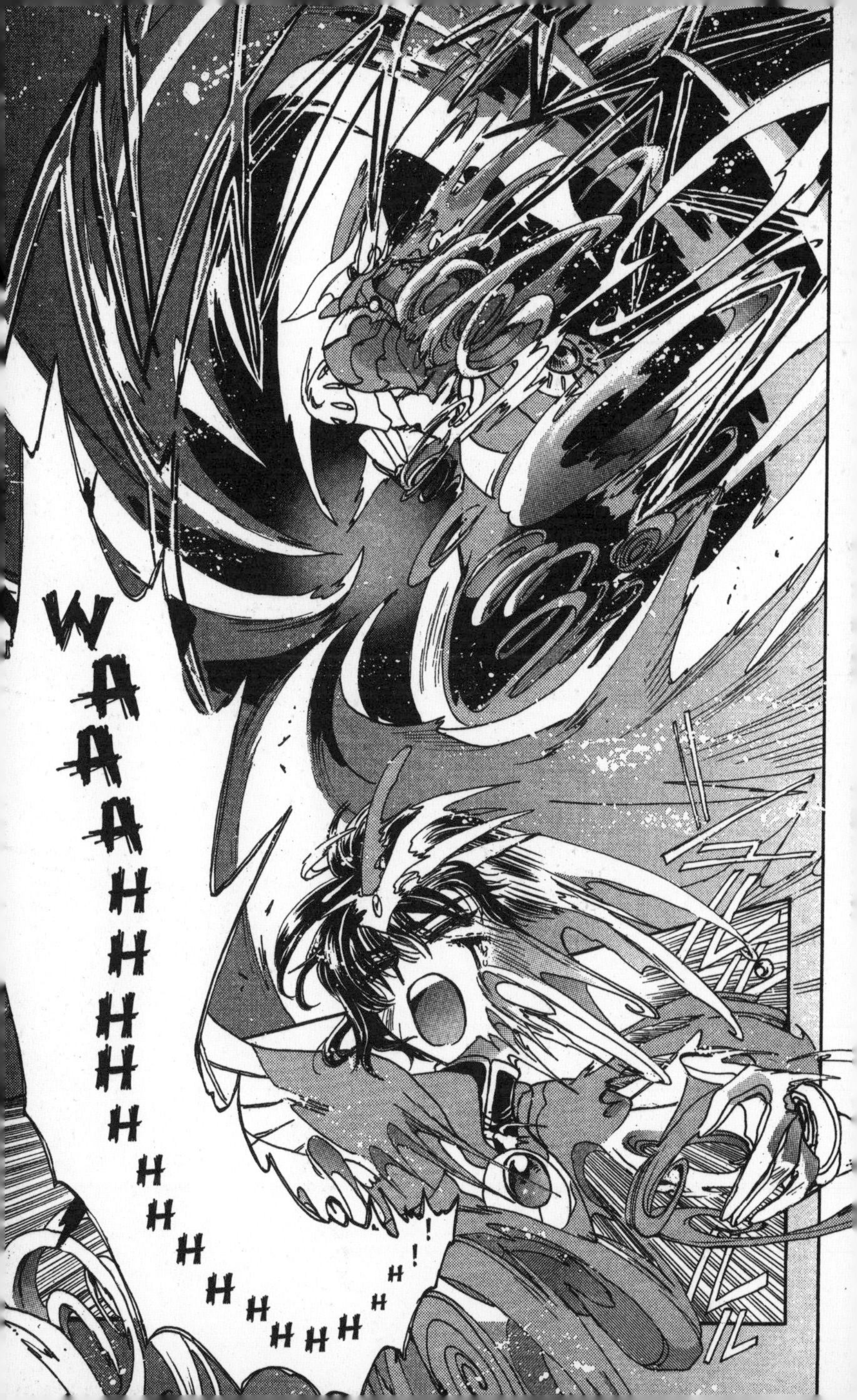
WAAAHHHHHHHHHHHHHHH!!

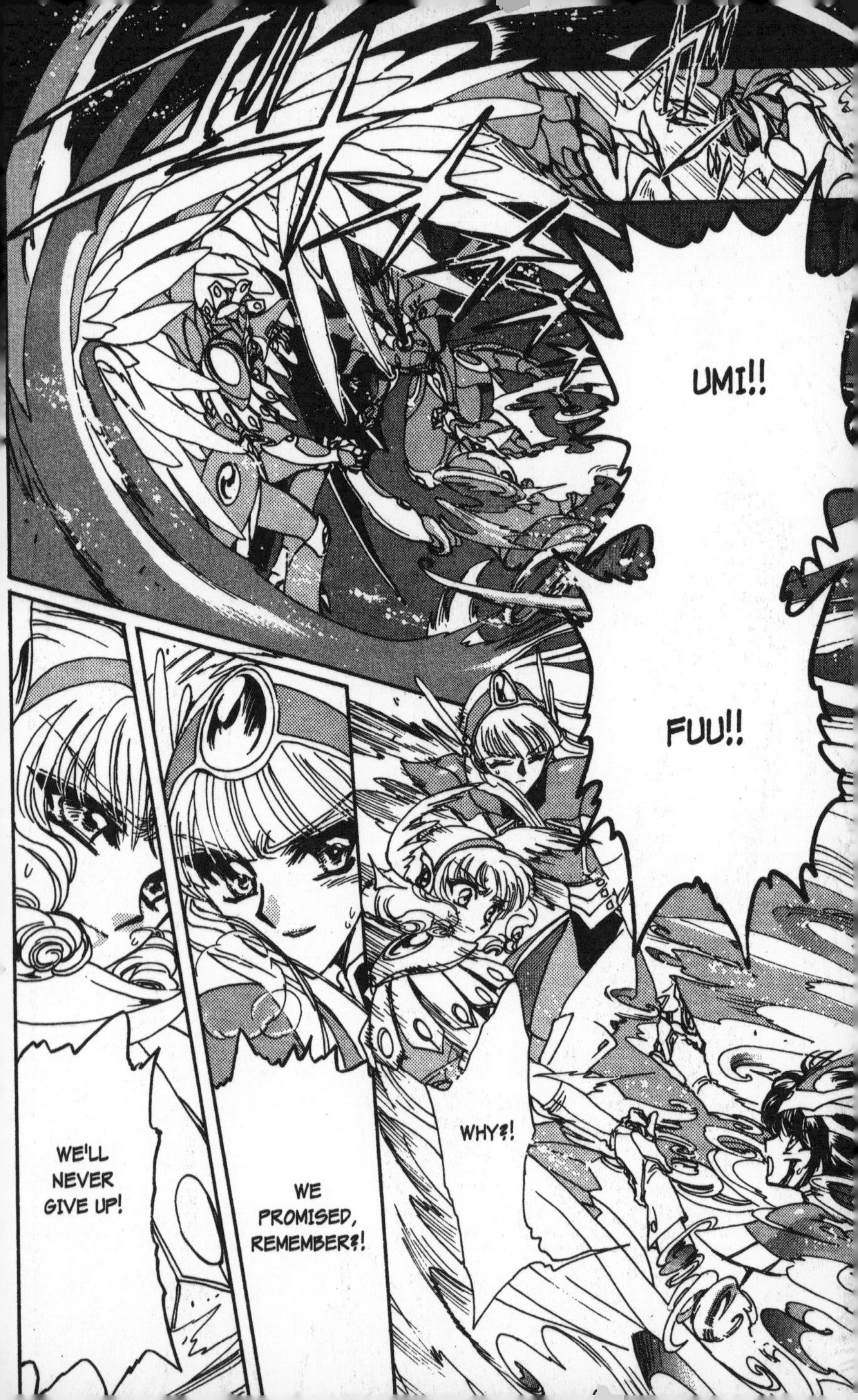
UMI!!
FUU!!
WHY?!
WE PROMISED, REMEMBER?!
WE'LL NEVER GIVE UP!

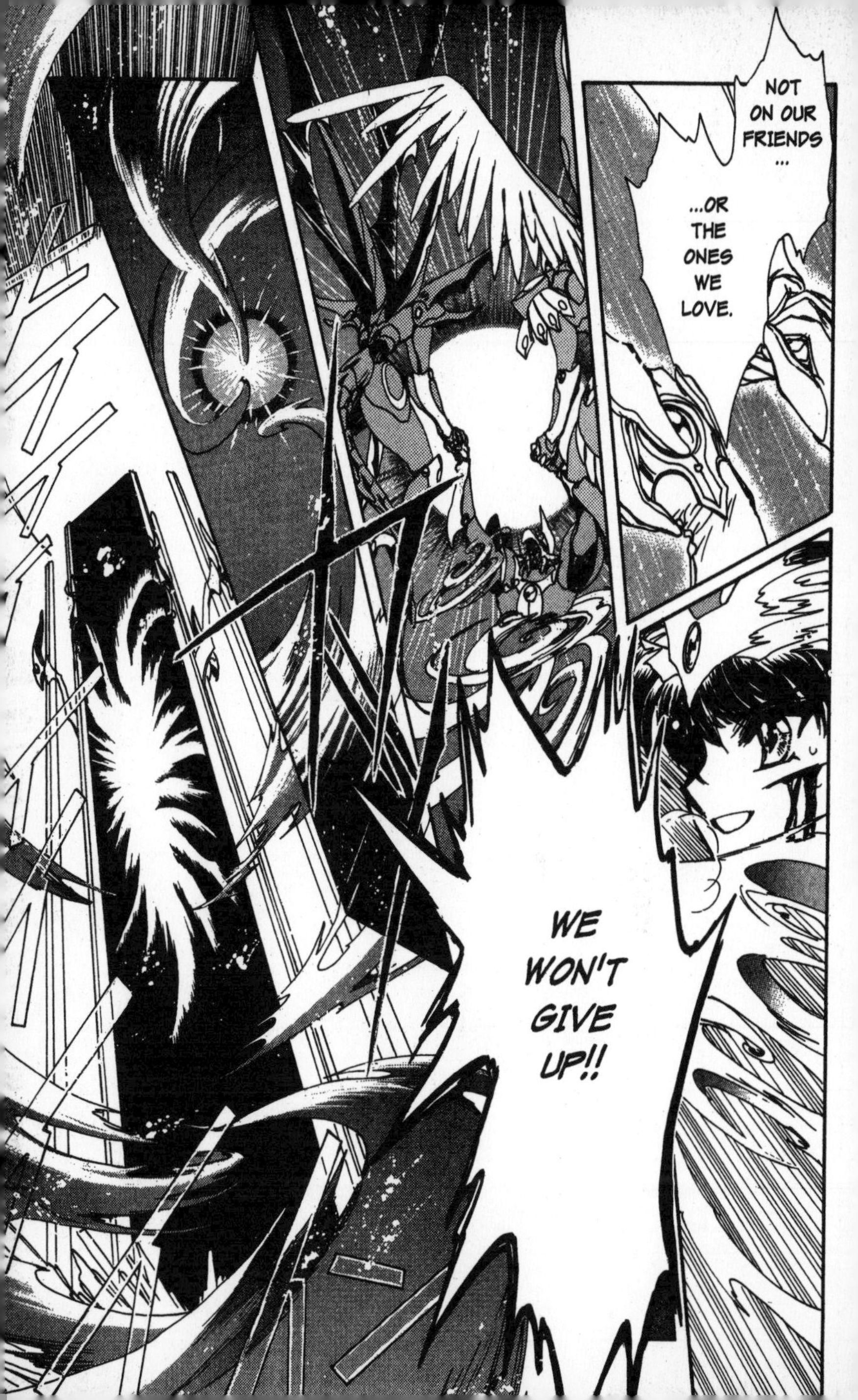
NOT ON OUR FRIENDS ...
...OR THE ONES WE LOVE.
WE WON'T GIVE UP!!

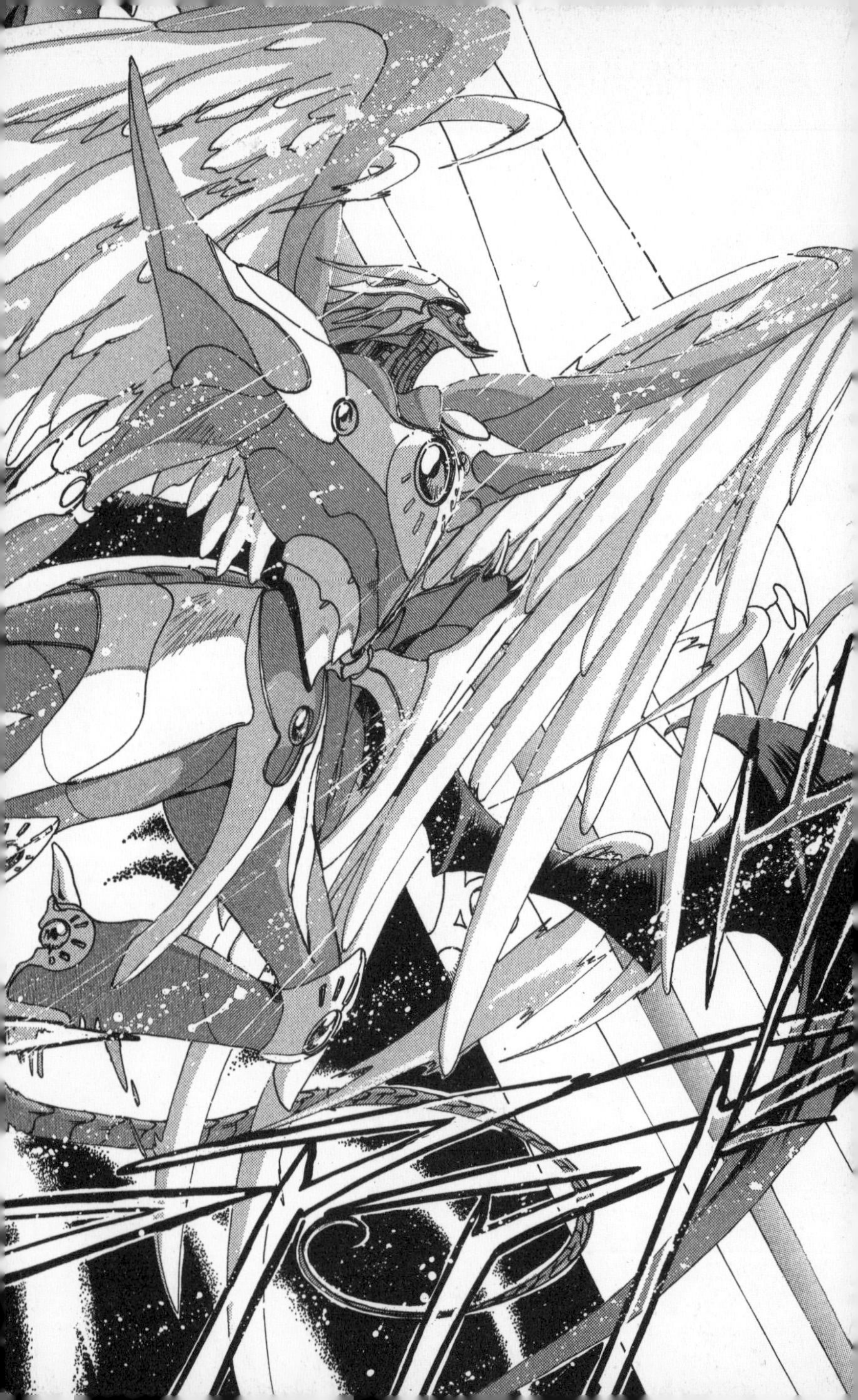

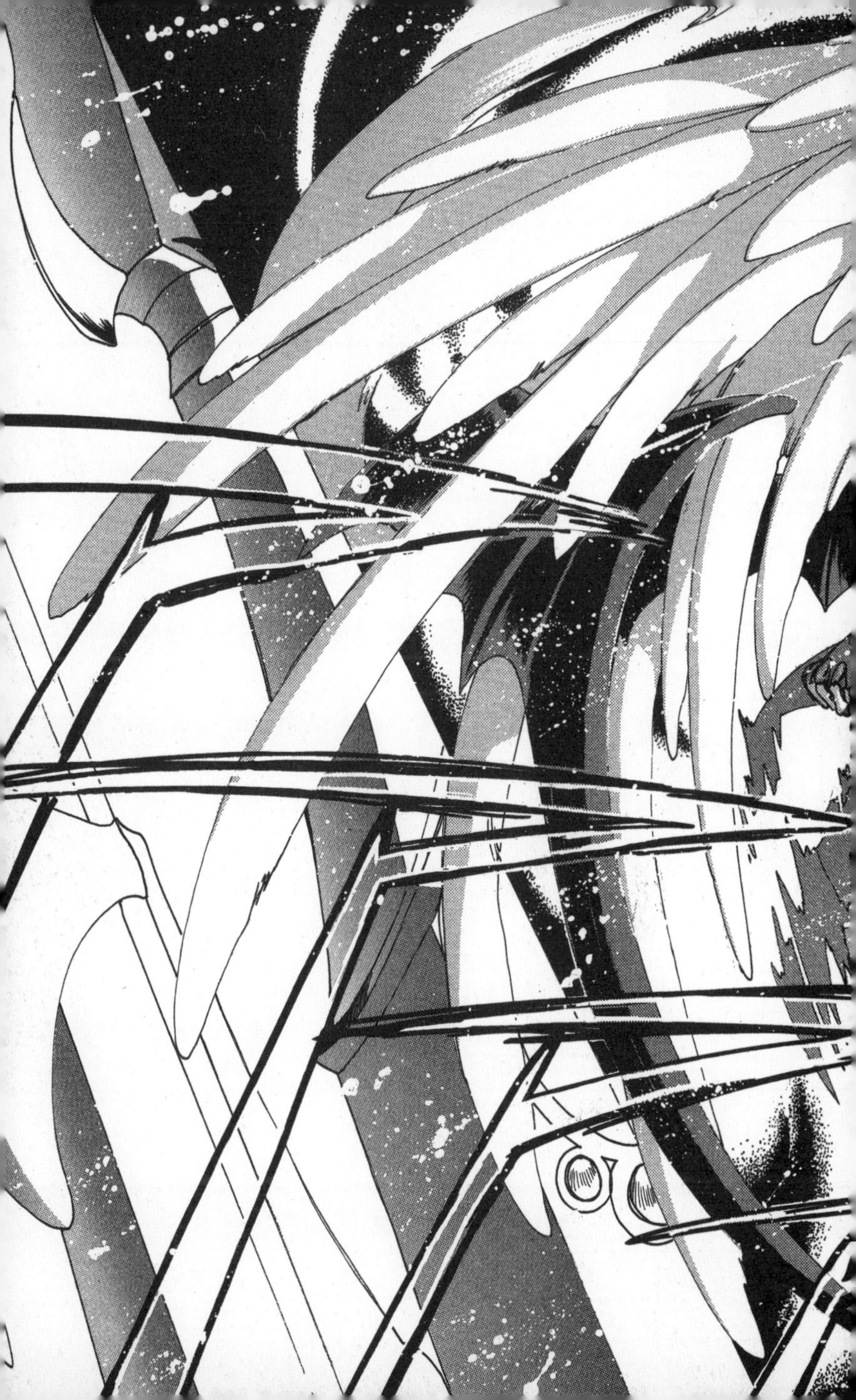

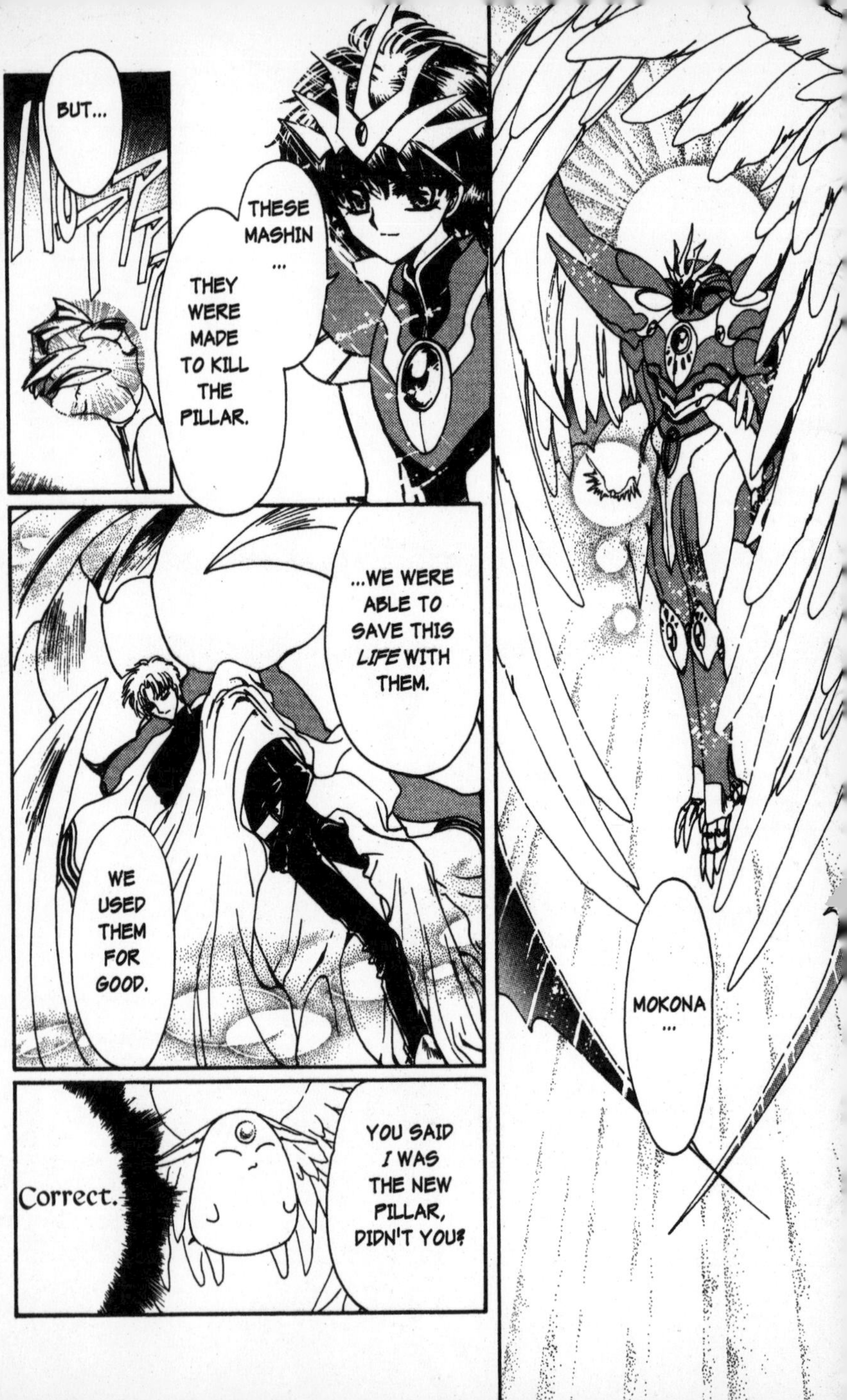
MOKONA ...
THESE MASHIN ...
THEY WERE MADE TO KILL THE PILLAR.
BUT...
...WE WERE ABLE TO SAVE THIS *LIFE* WITH THEM.
WE USED THEM FOR GOOD.
YOU SAID *I* WAS THE NEW PILLAR, DIDN'T YOU?
Correct.

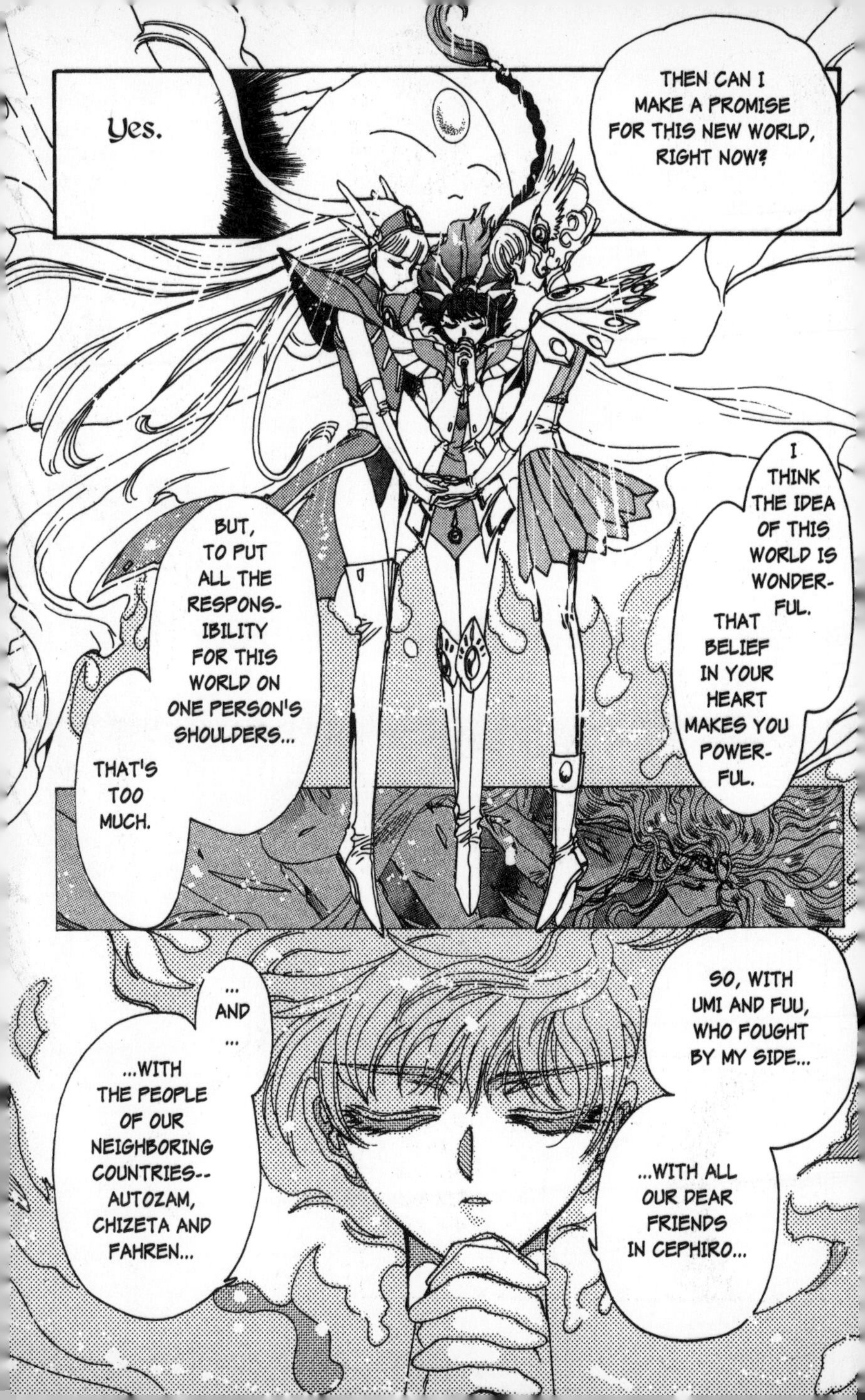
THEN CAN I MAKE A PROMISE FOR THIS NEW WORLD, RIGHT NOW?
Yes.
I THINK THE IDEA OF THIS WORLD IS WONDER-FUL.
THAT BELIEF IN YOUR HEART MAKES YOU POWER-FUL.
BUT, TO PUT ALL THE RESPONS-IBILITY FOR THIS WORLD ON ONE PERSON'S SHOULDERS...
THAT'S TOO MUCH.
SO, WITH UMI AND FUU, WHO FOUGHT BY MY SIDE...
...WITH ALL OUR DEAR FRIENDS IN CEPHIRO...
... AND ...
...WITH THE PEOPLE OF OUR NEIGHBORING COUNTRIES-- AUTOZAM, CHIZETA AND FAHREN...

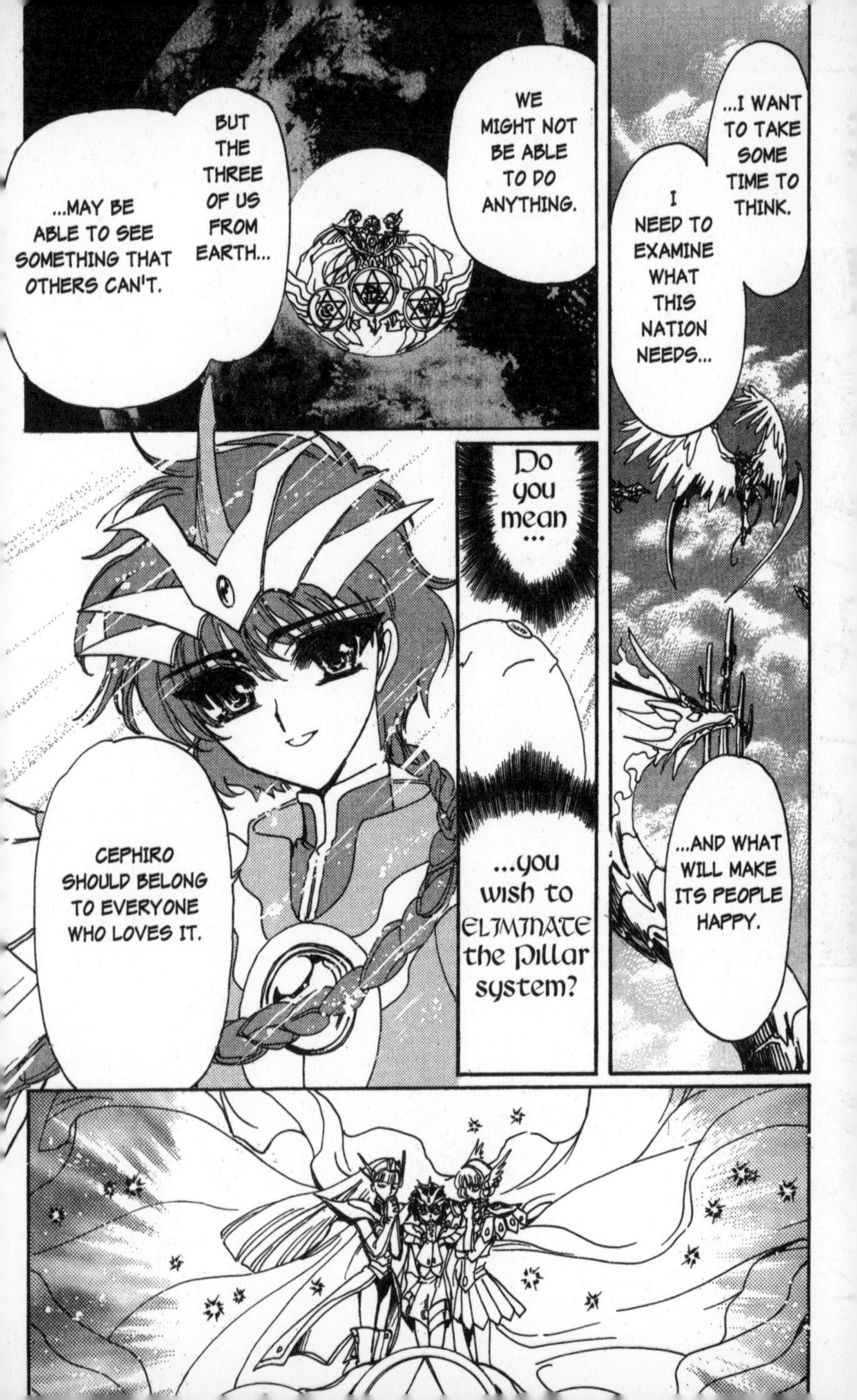
...I WANT TO TAKE SOME TIME TO THINK.
I NEED TO EXAMINE WHAT THIS NATION NEEDS...
...AND WHAT WILL MAKE ITS PEOPLE HAPPY.
WE MIGHT NOT BE ABLE TO DO ANYTHING.
BUT THE THREE OF US FROM EARTH...
...MAY BE ABLE TO SEE SOMETHING THAT OTHERS CAN'T.
Do you mean...
...you wish to ELIMINATE the Pillar system?
CEPHIRO SHOULD BELONG TO EVERYONE WHO LOVES IT.

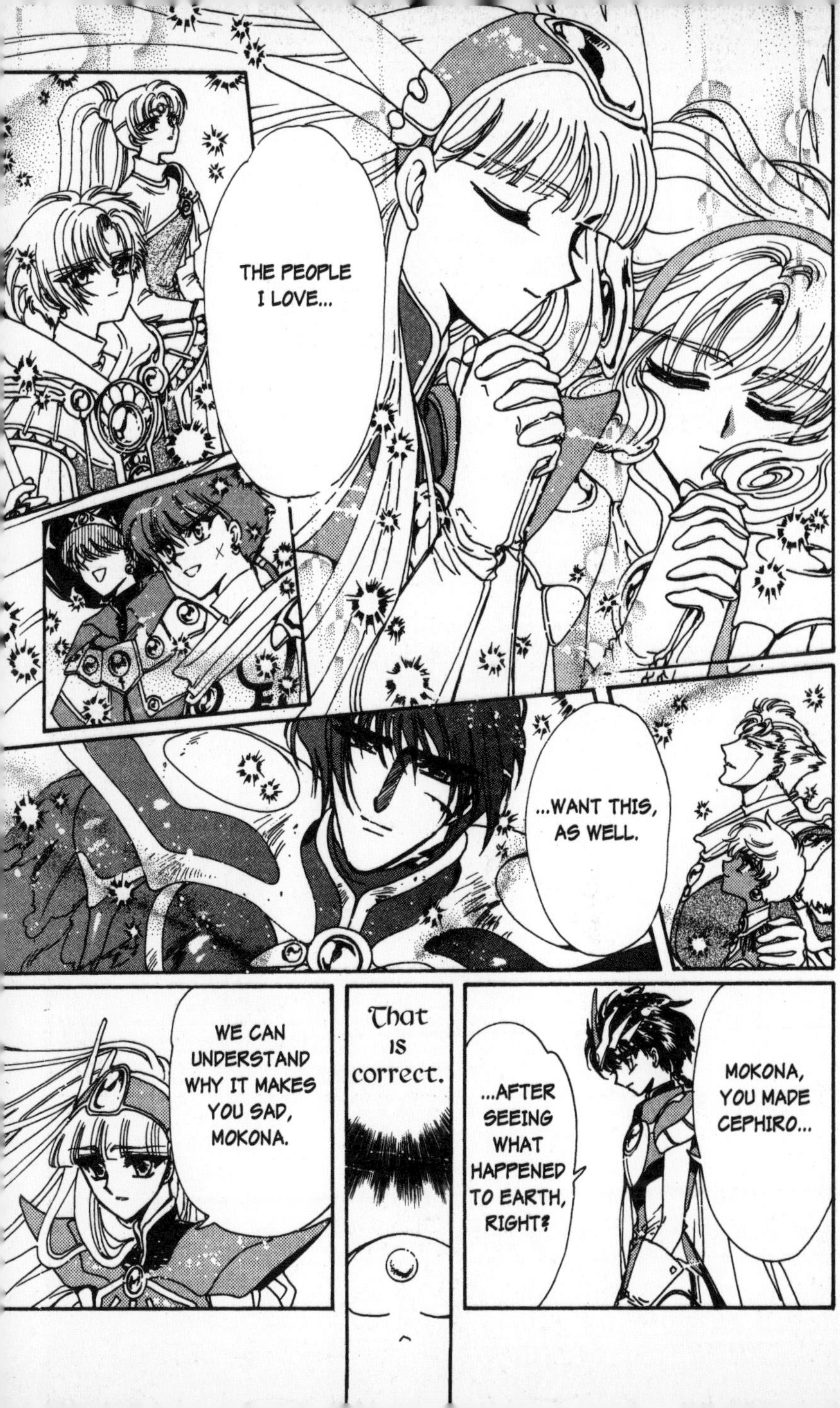
THE PEOPLE I LOVE...
...WANT THIS, AS WELL.
MOKONA, YOU MADE CEPHIRO...
...AFTER SEEING WHAT HAPPENED TO EARTH, RIGHT?
That is correct.
WE CAN UNDERSTAND WHY IT MAKES YOU SAD, MOKONA.

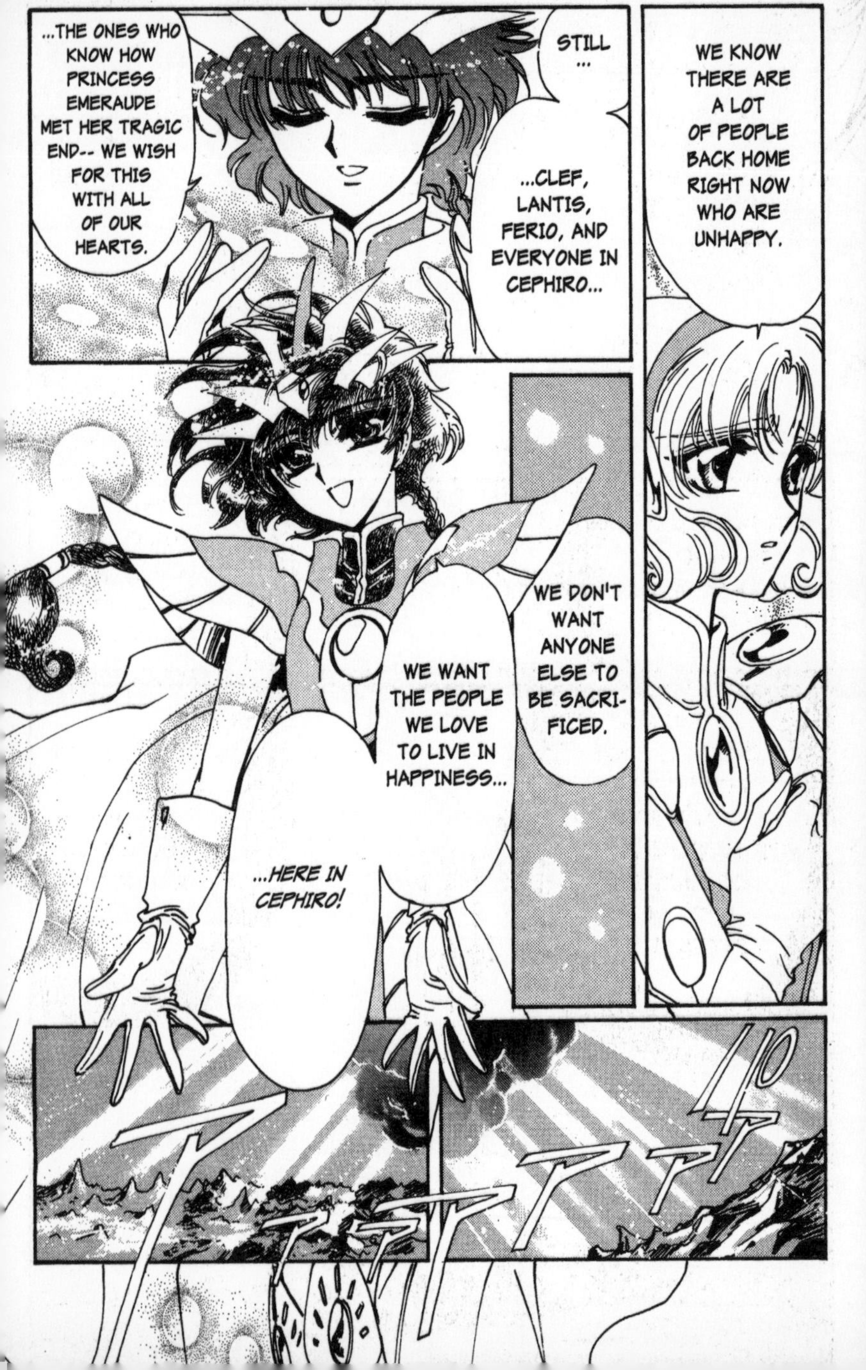
WE KNOW THERE ARE A LOT OF PEOPLE BACK HOME RIGHT NOW WHO ARE UNHAPPY.
STILL ...
...CLEF, LANTIS, FERIO, AND EVERYONE IN CEPHIRO...
...THE ONES WHO KNOW HOW PRINCESS EMERAUDE MET HER TRAGIC END-- WE WISH FOR THIS WITH ALL OF OUR HEARTS.
WE DON'T WANT ANYONE ELSE TO BE SACRI-FICED.
WE WANT THE PEOPLE WE LOVE TO LIVE IN HAPPINESS...
...HERE IN CEPHIRO!

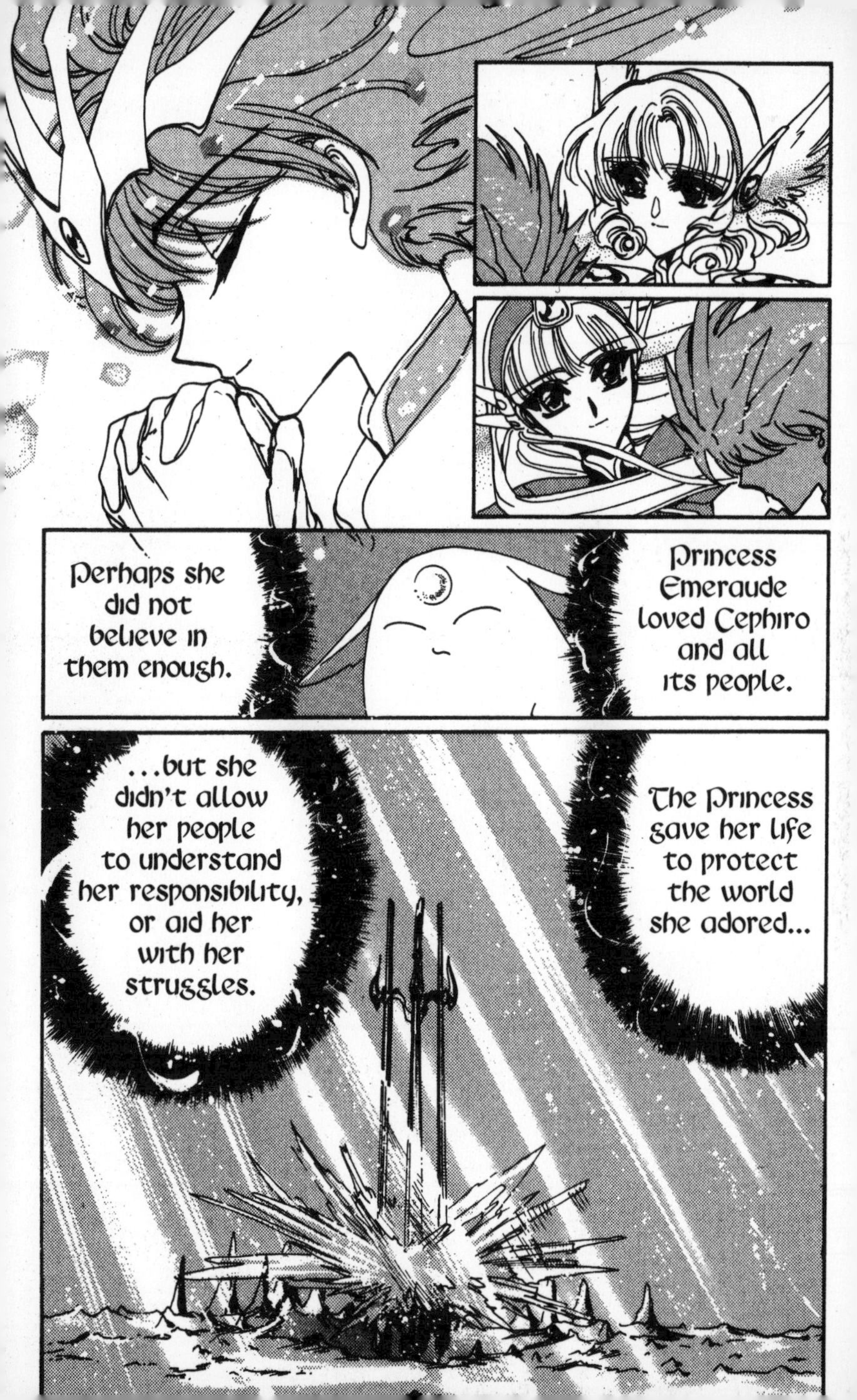
Princess Emeraude loved Cephiro and all its people.
Perhaps she did not believe in them enough.
The Princess gave her life to protect the world she adored...
...but she didn't allow her people to understand her responsibility, or aid her with her struggles.

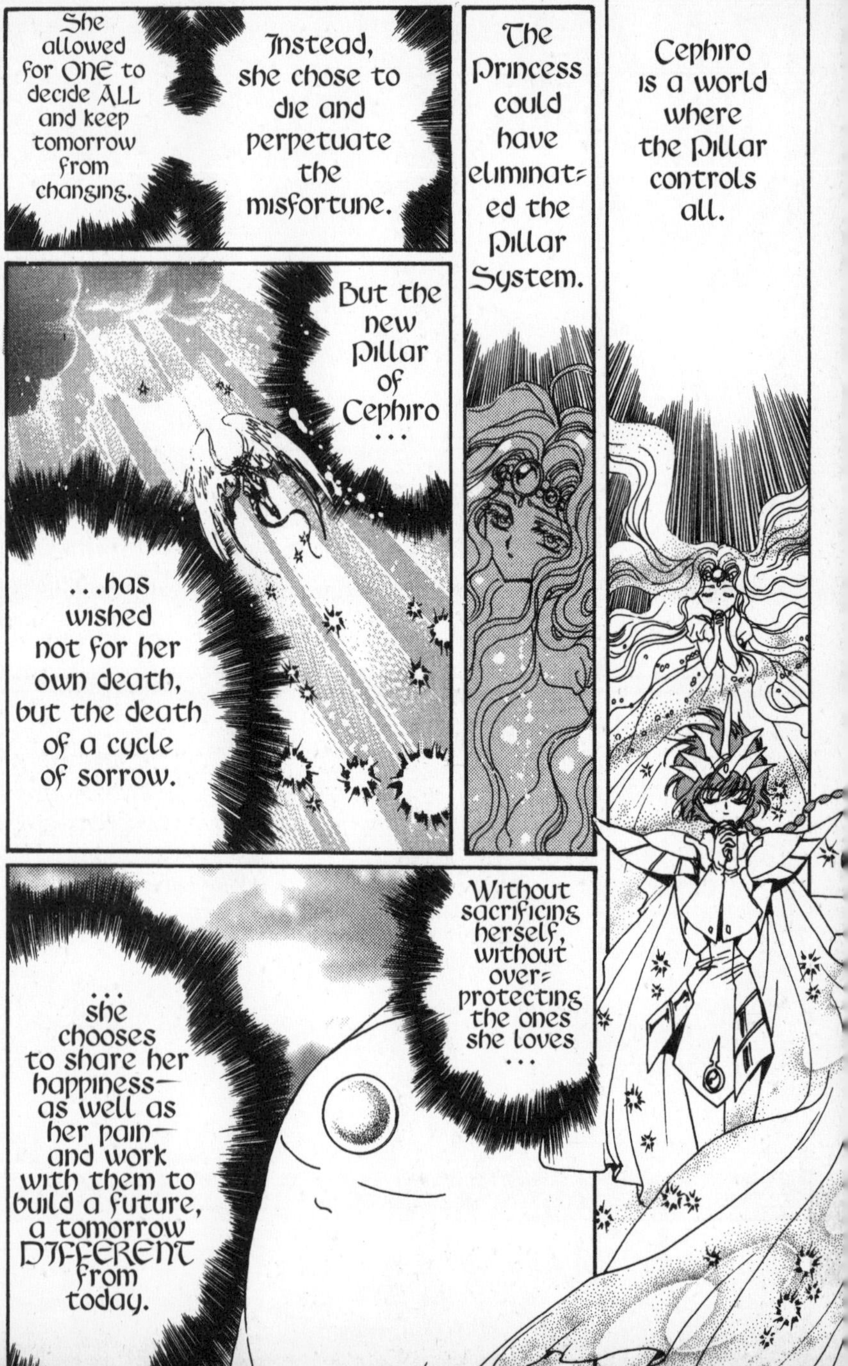

Cephiro is a world where the Pillar controls all.
The Princess could have eliminat-ed the Pillar System.
Instead, she chose to die and perpetuate the misfortune.
She allowed for ONE to decide ALL and keep tomorrow from changing.
But the new Pillar of Cephiro...
...has wished not for her own death, but the death of a cycle of sorrow.
Without sacrificing herself, without over-protecting the ones she loves...
...she chooses to share her happiness—as well as her pain—and work with them to build a future, a tomorrow DIFFERENT from today.

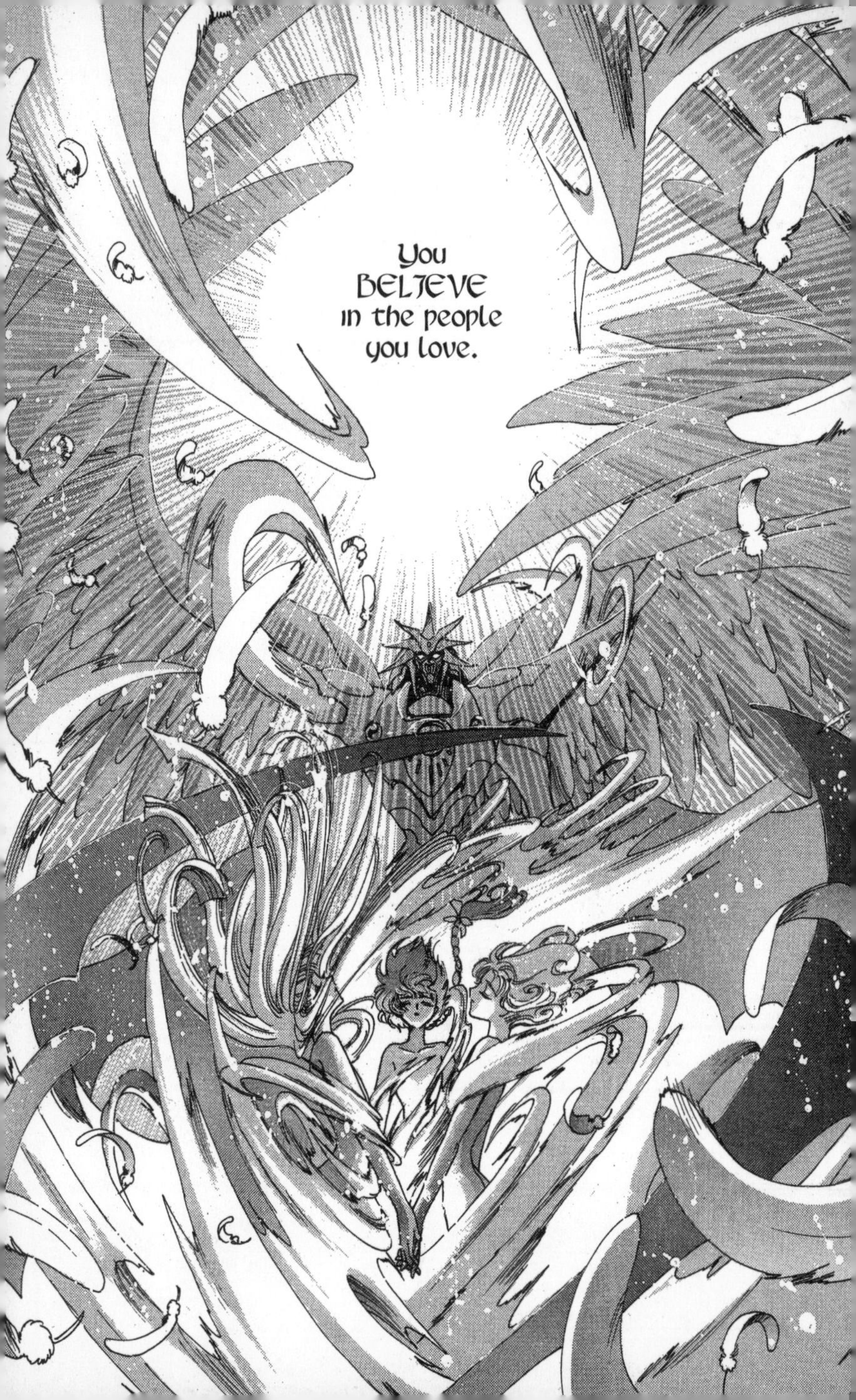
You BELIEVE in the people you love.

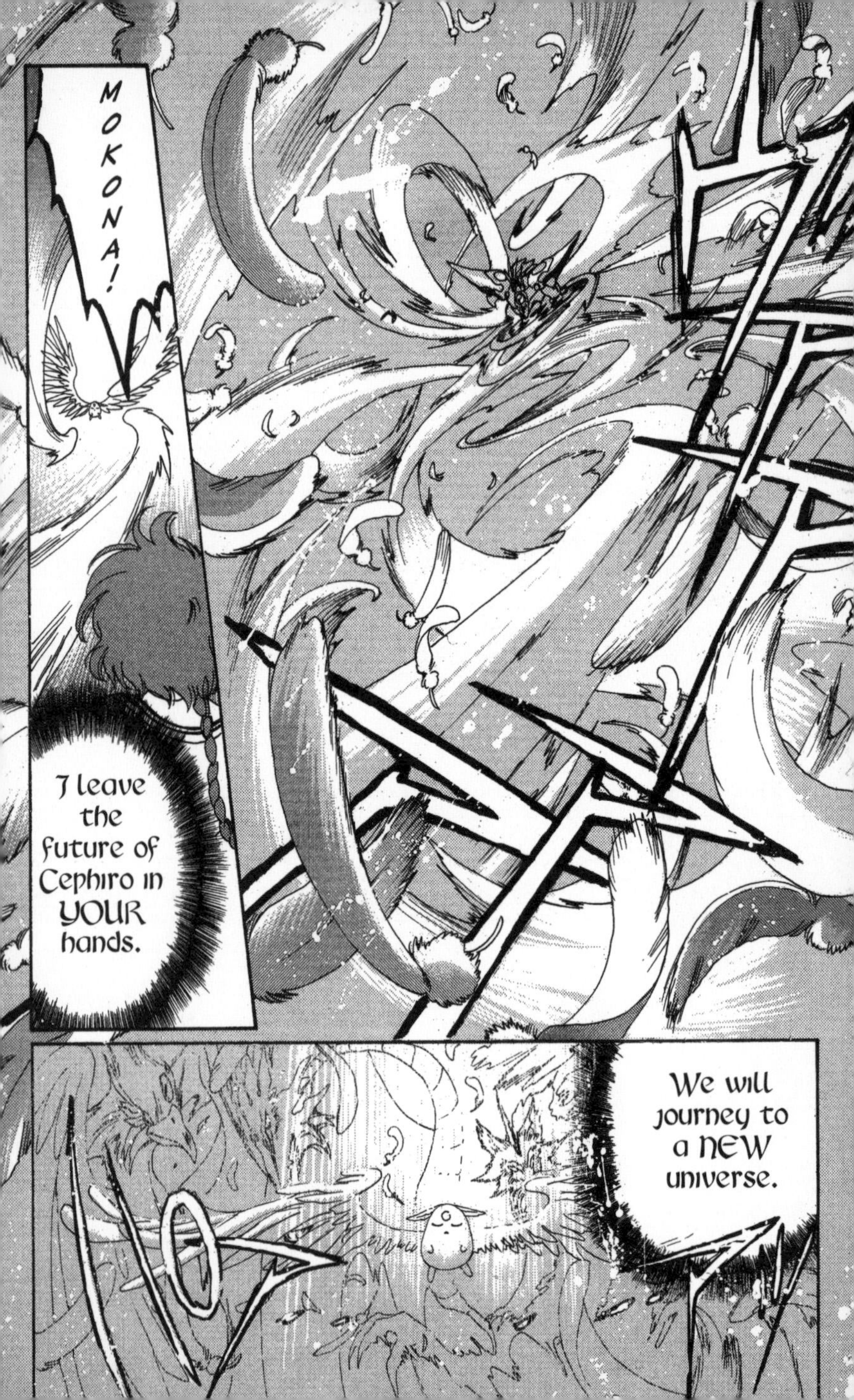
MOKONA!
I leave the future of Cephiro in YOUR hands.
We will journey to a NEW universe.

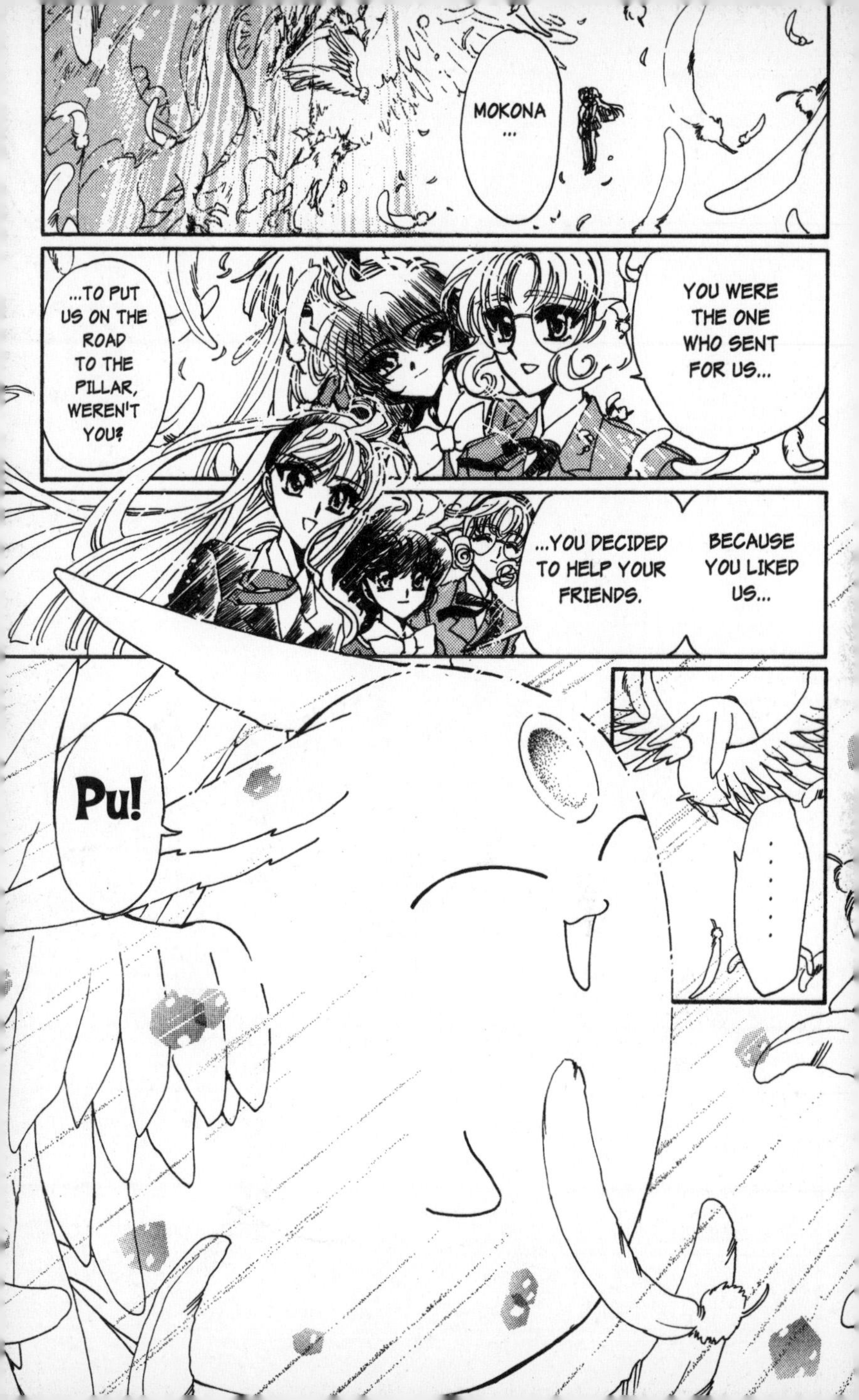
MOKONA ...
YOU WERE THE ONE WHO SENT FOR US...
...TO PUT US ON THE ROAD TO THE PILLAR, WEREN'T YOU?
BECAUSE YOU LIKED US...
...YOU DECIDED TO HELP YOUR FRIENDS.
......
Pu!

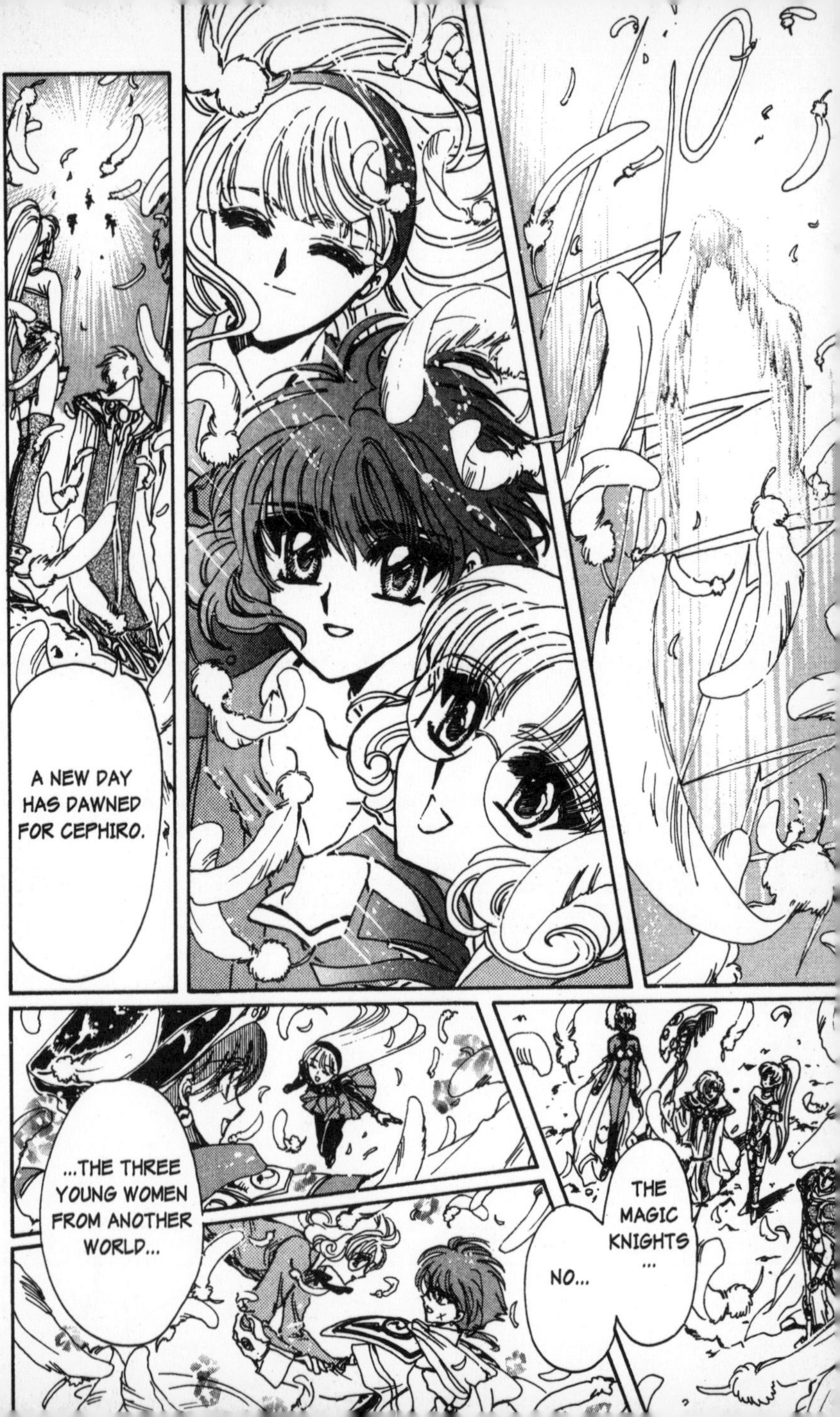
A NEW DAY HAS DAWNED FOR CEPHIRO.
THE MAGIC KNIGHTS ... NO...
...THE THREE YOUNG WOMEN FROM ANOTHER WORLD...

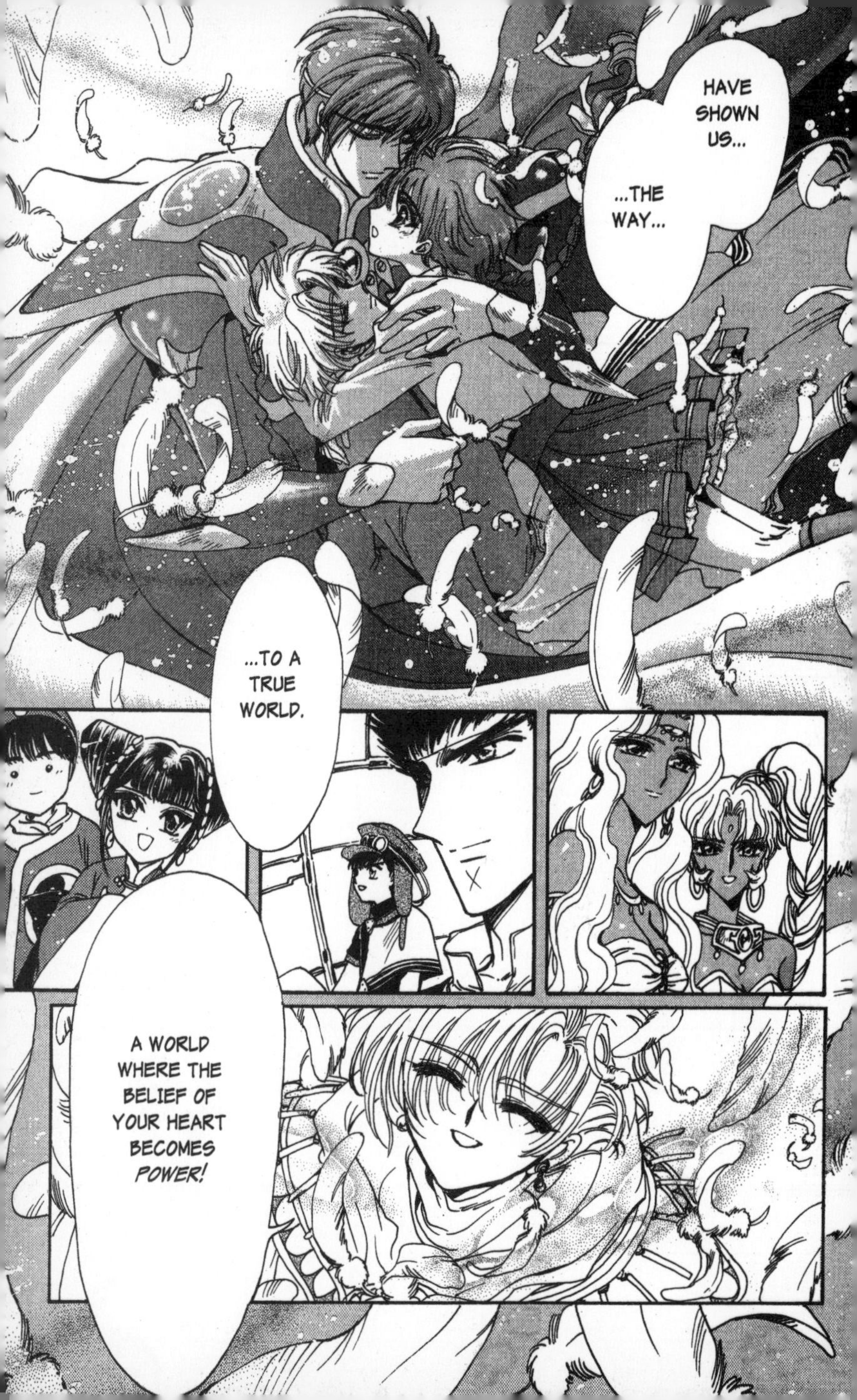
HAVE SHOWN US...
...THE WAY...
...TO A TRUE WORLD.
A WORLD WHERE THE BELIEF OF YOUR HEART BECOMES *POWER!*

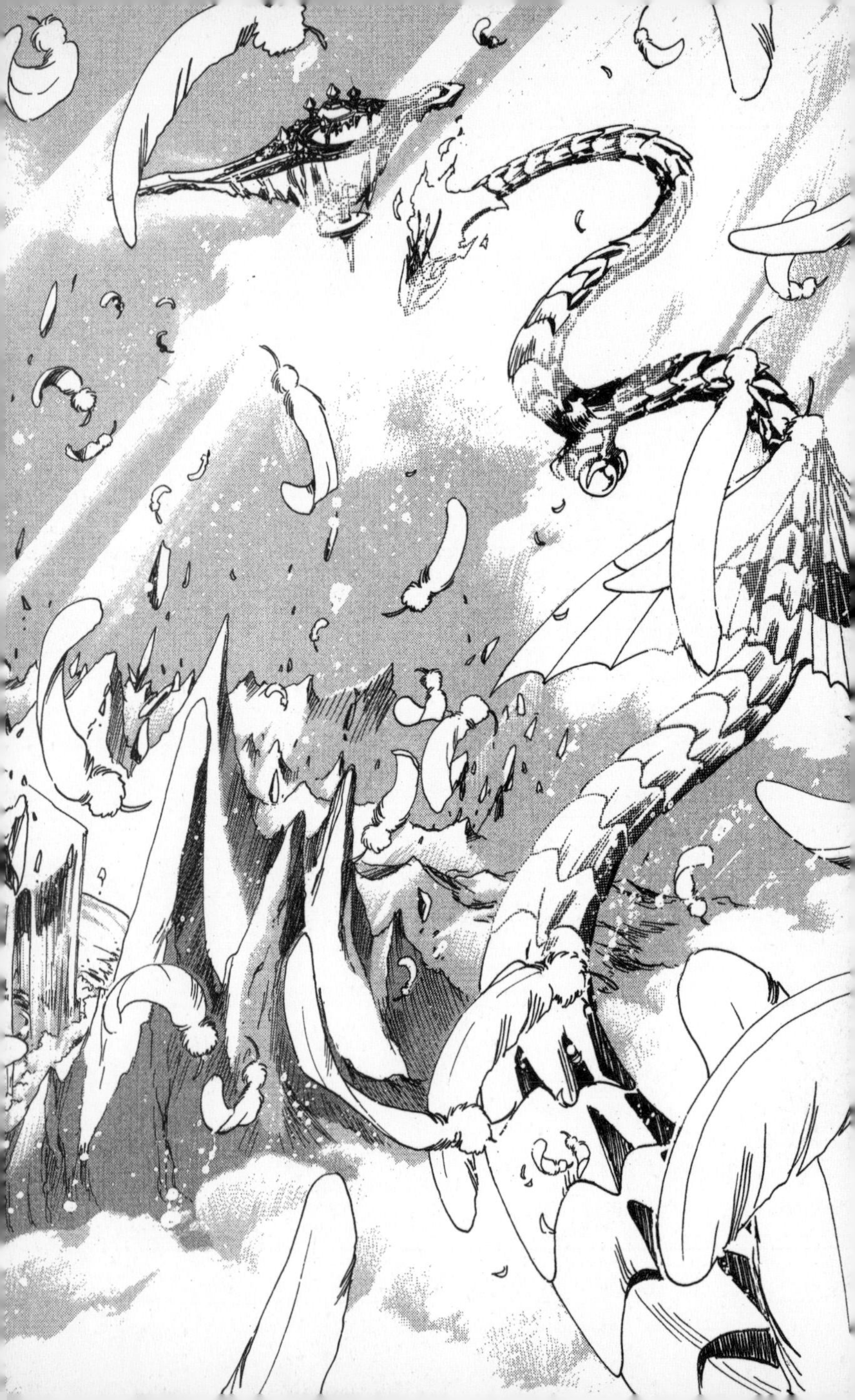

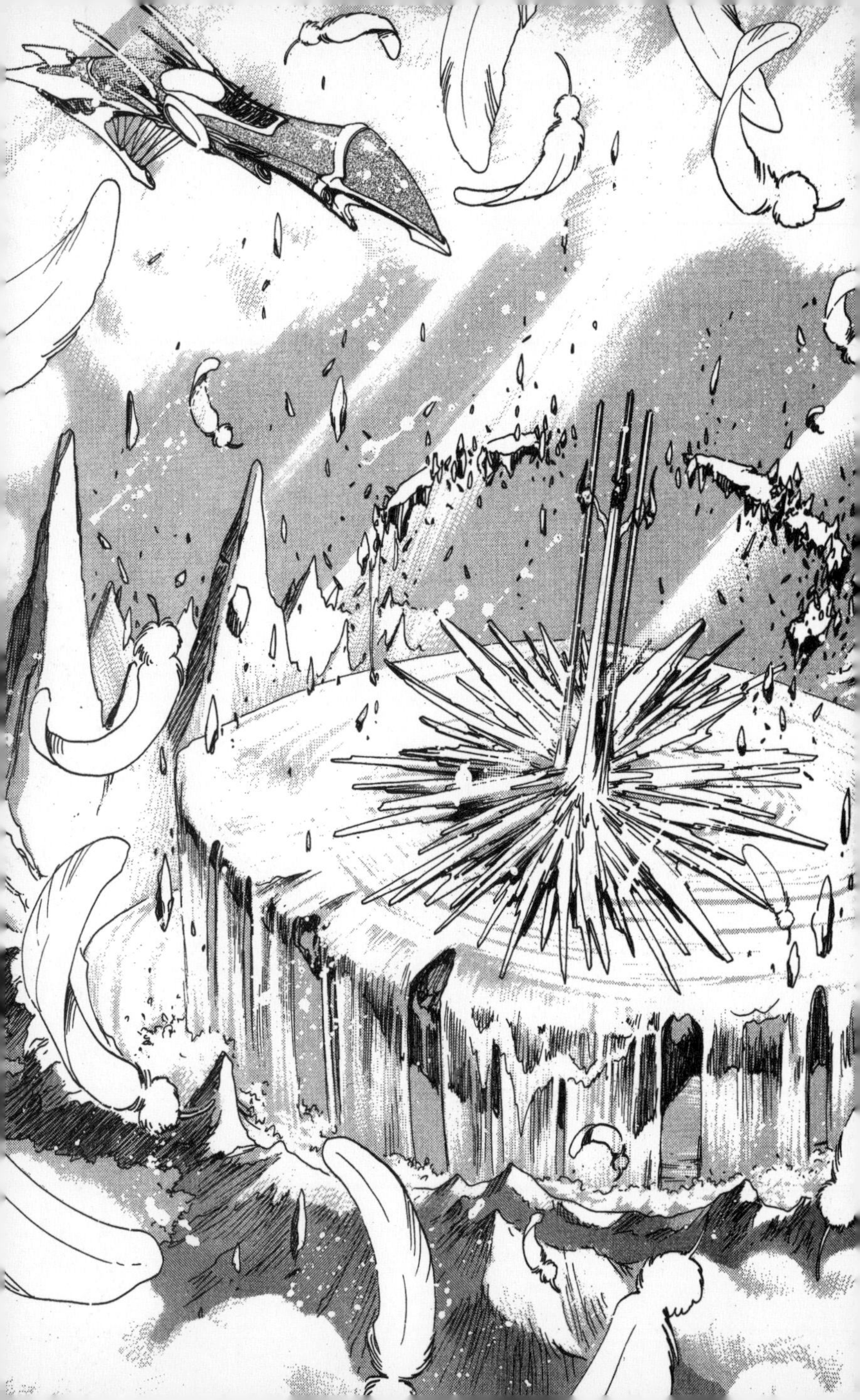

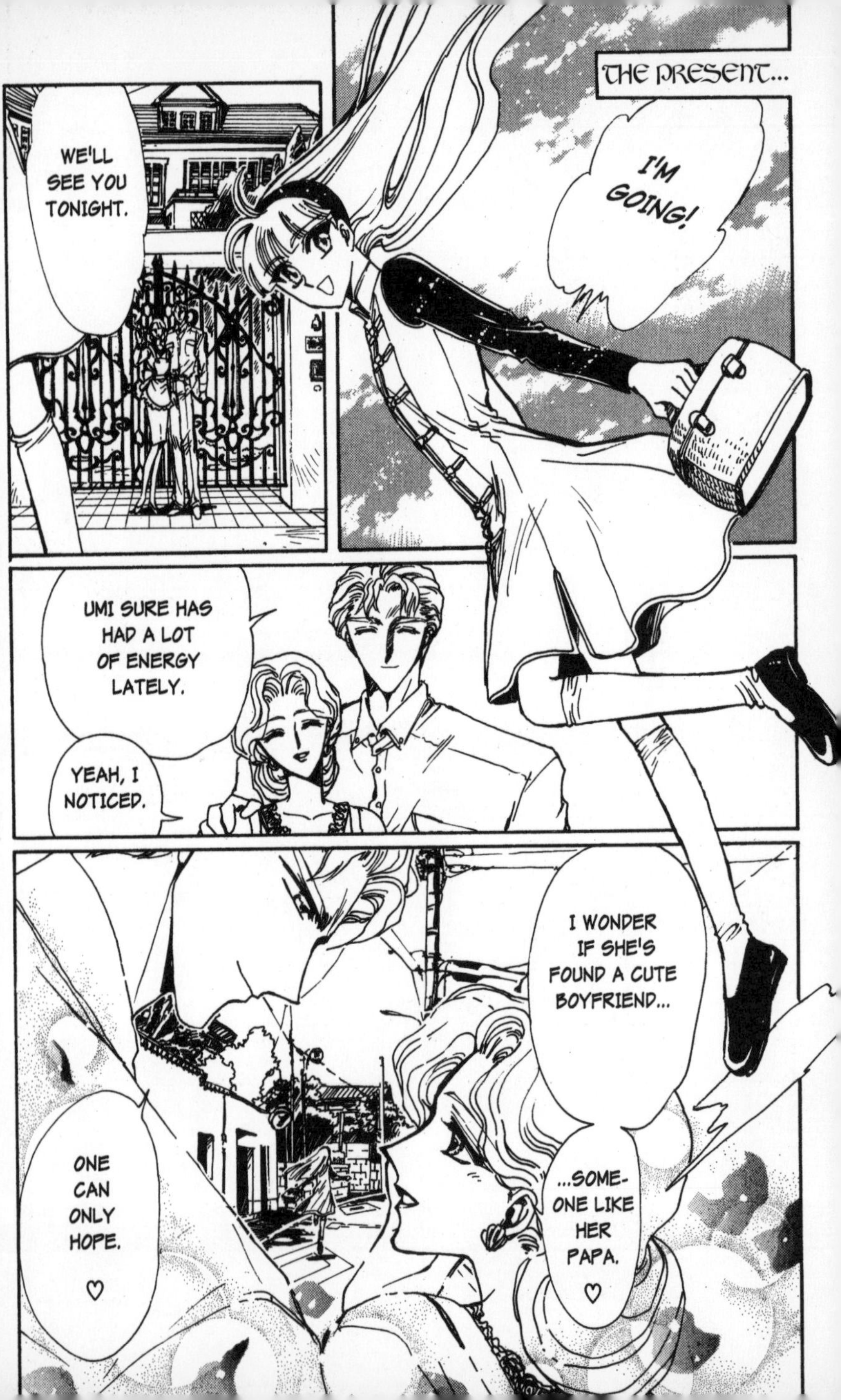
THE PRESENT...
I'M GOING!
WE'LL SEE YOU TONIGHT.
UMI SURE HAS HAD A LOT OF ENERGY LATELY.
YEAH, I NOTICED.
I WONDER IF SHE'S FOUND A CUTE BOYFRIEND...
...SOME-ONE LIKE HER PAPA. ♡
ONE CAN ONLY HOPE. ♡

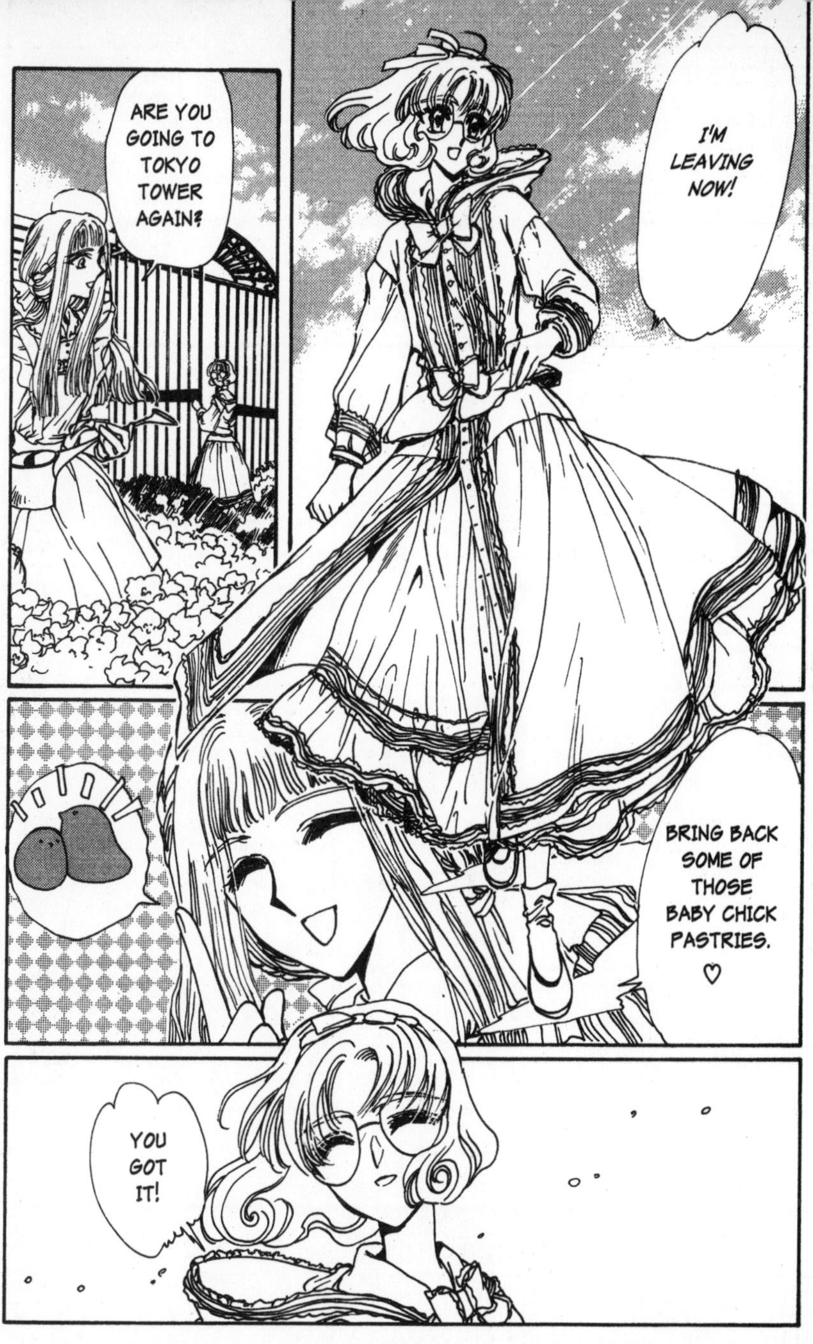
I'M LEAVING NOW!
ARE YOU GOING TO TOKYO TOWER AGAIN?
BRING BACK SOME OF THOSE BABY CHICK PASTRIES. ♡
YOU GOT IT!

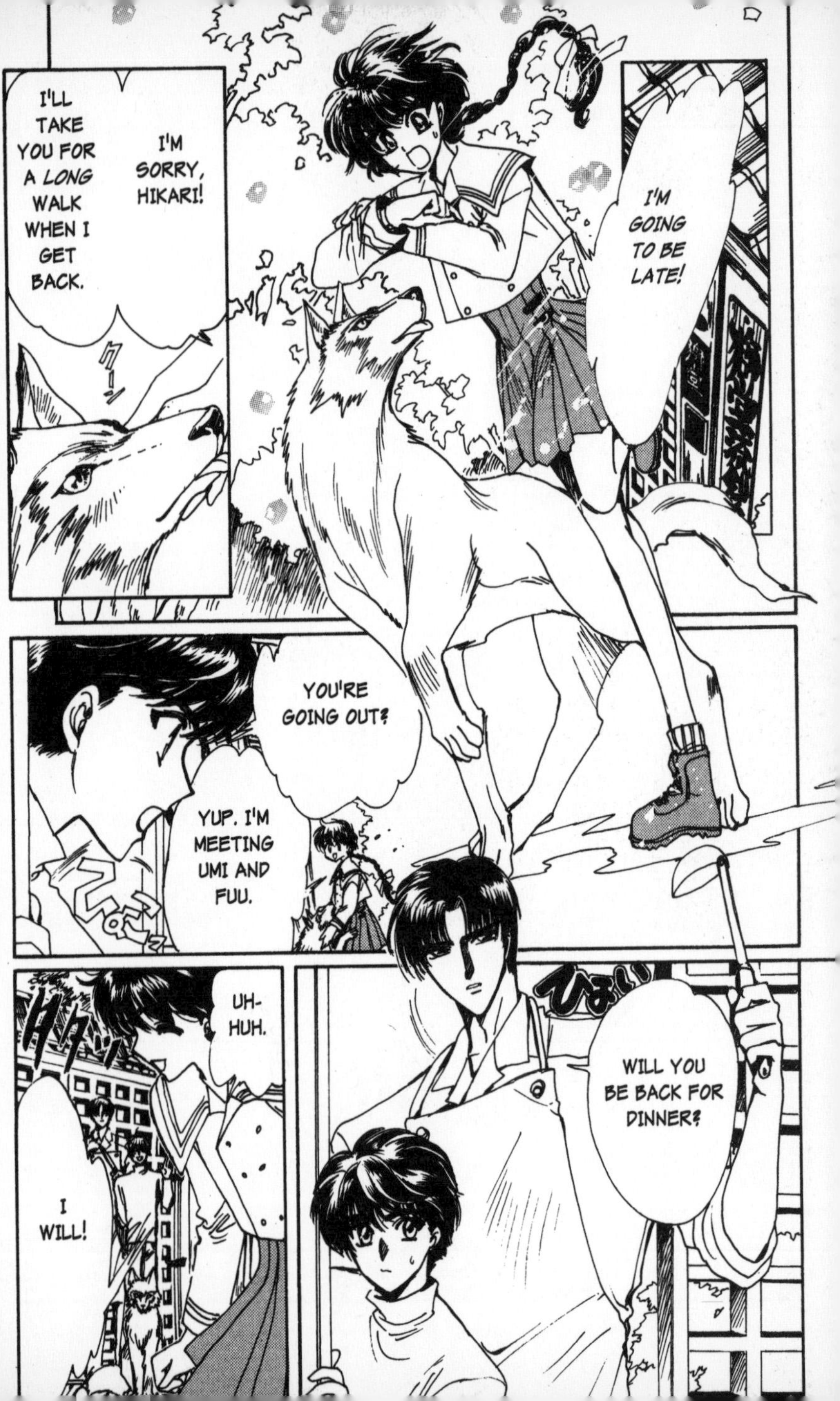
I'M GOING TO BE LATE!
I'M SORRY, HIKARI!
I'LL TAKE YOU FOR A LONG WALK WHEN I GET BACK.
YOU'RE GOING OUT?
YUP. I'M MEETING UMI AND FUU.
WILL YOU BE BACK FOR DINNER?
UH-HUH.
I WILL!

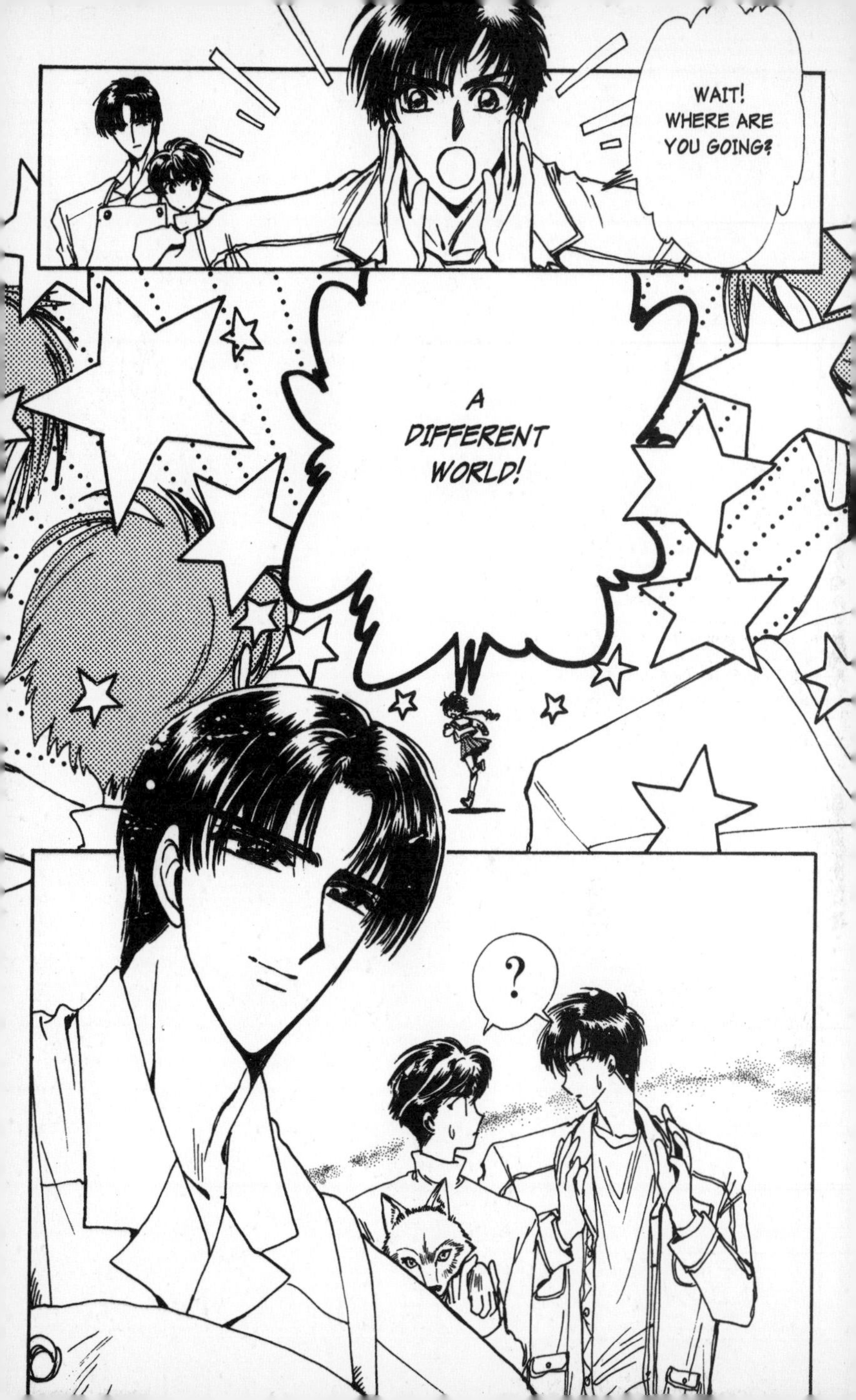
WAIT! WHERE ARE YOU GOING?
A DIFFERENT WORLD!
?

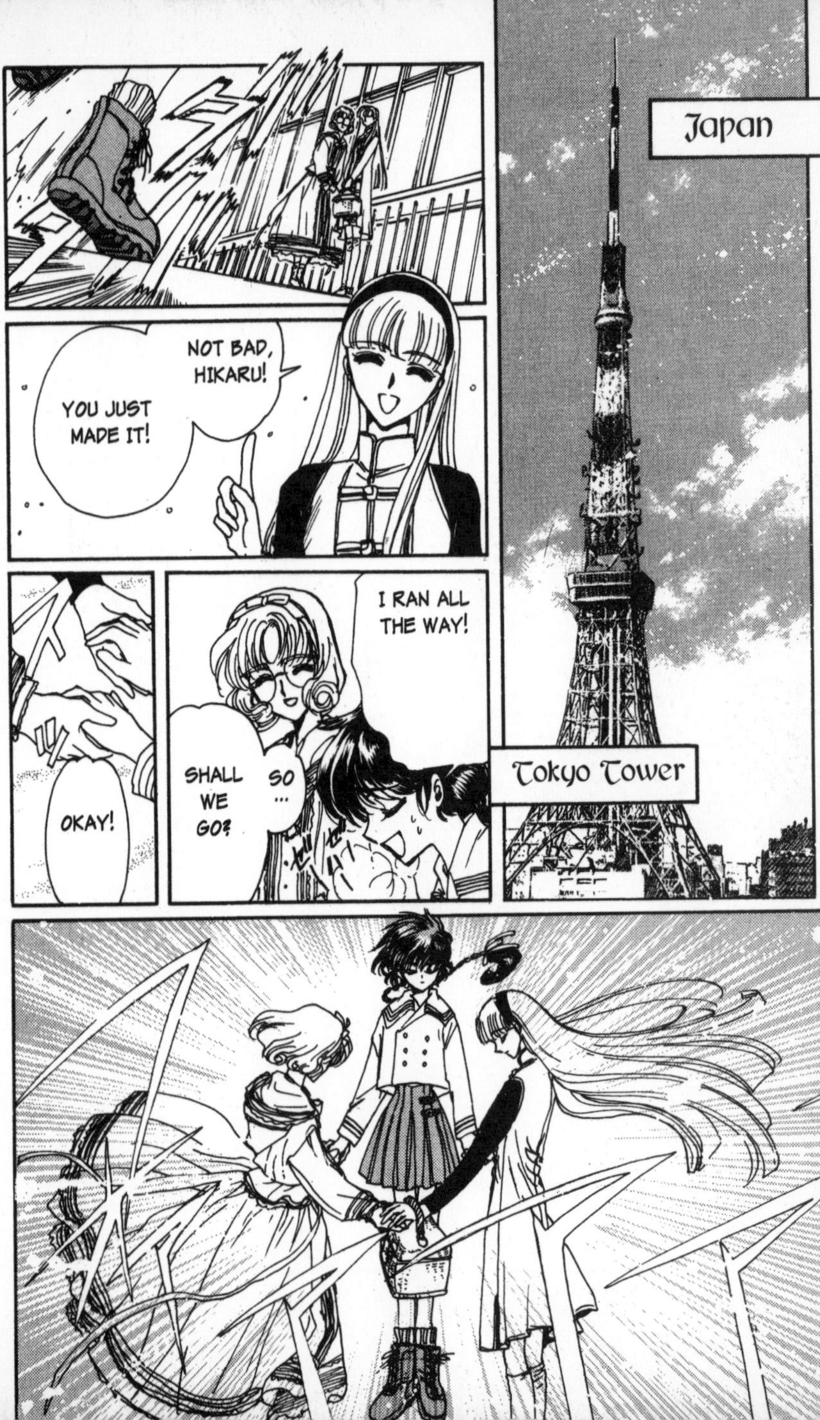
Japan
Tokyo Tower
NOT BAD, HIKARU!
YOU JUST MADE IT!
I RAN ALL THE WAY!
SO ...
SHALL WE GO?
OKAY!

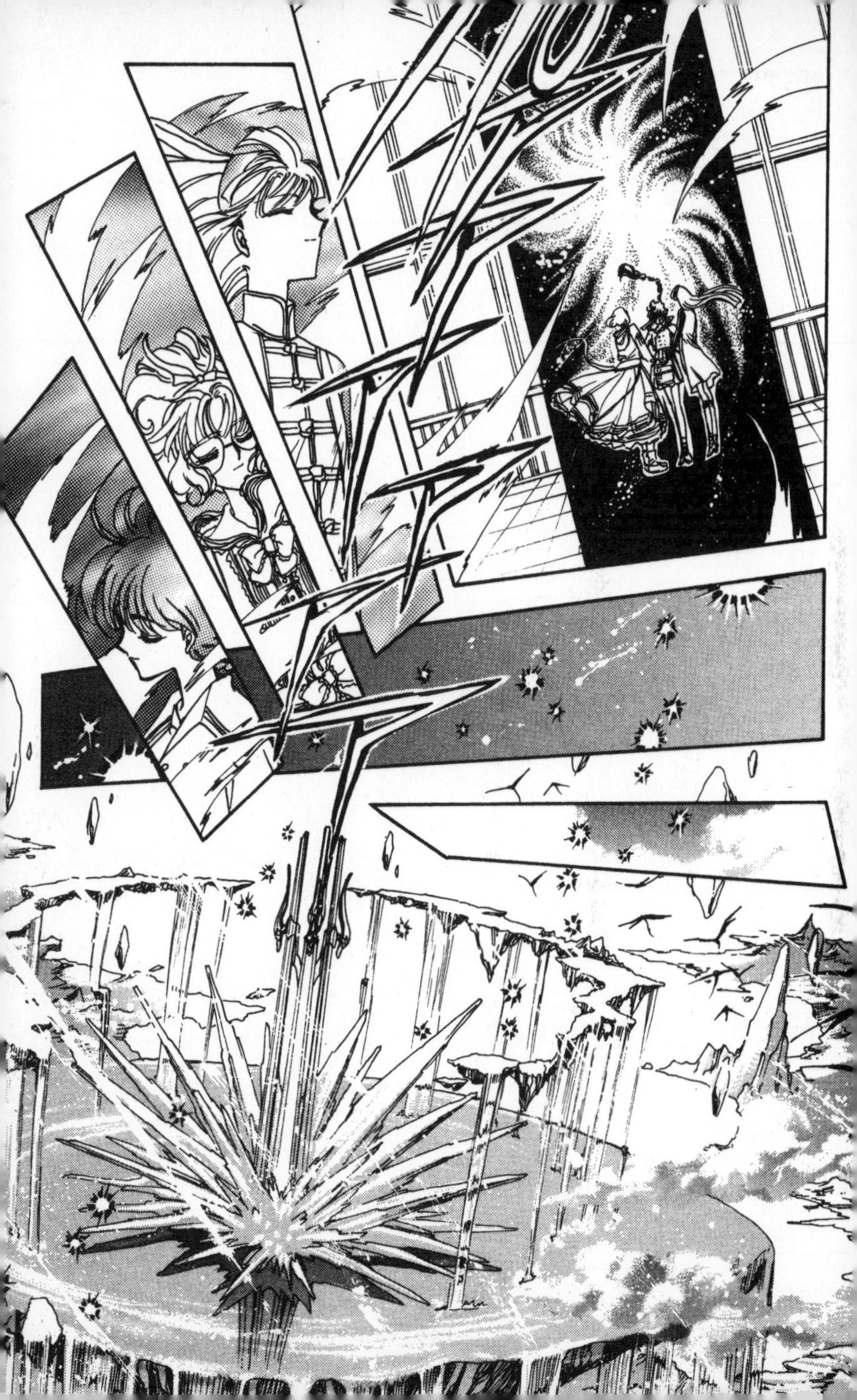

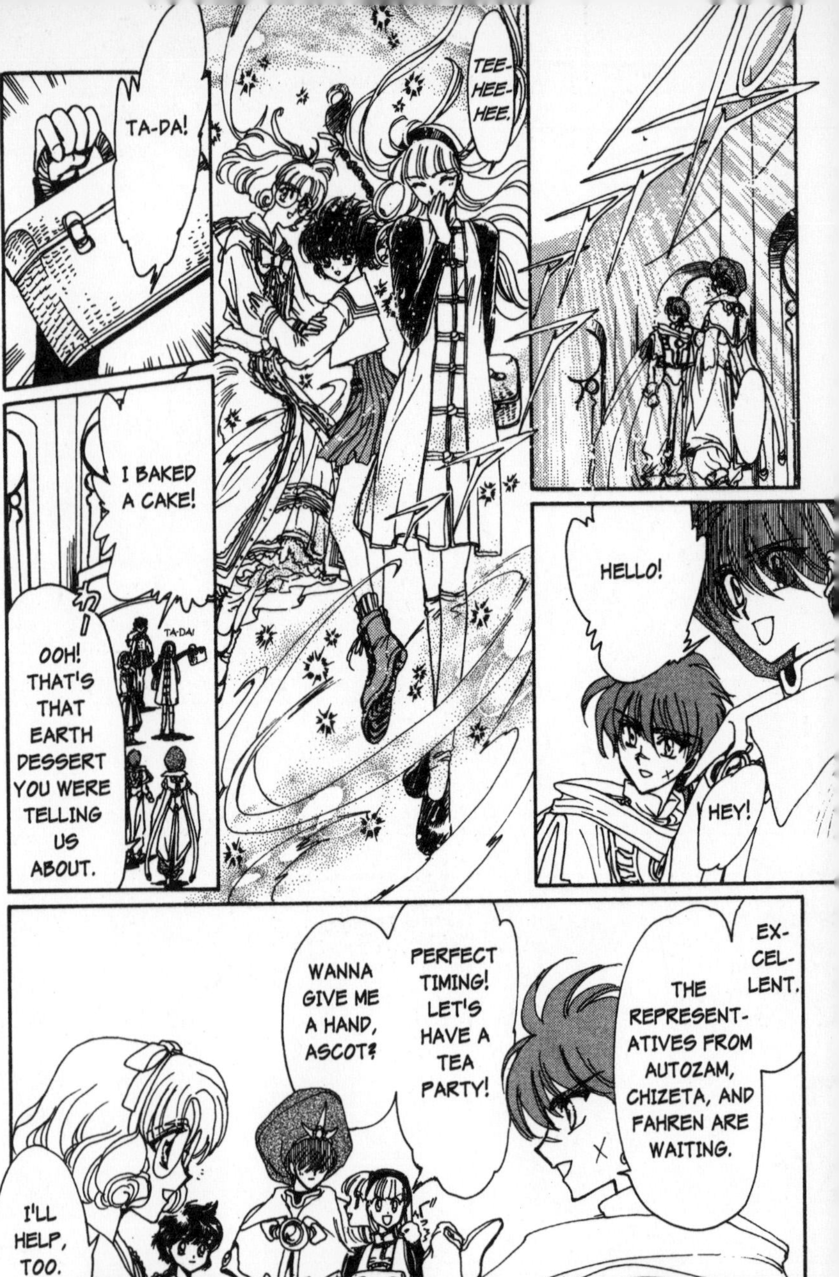
HELLO!
HEY!
TEE-HEE-HEE.
TA-DA!
I BAKED A CAKE!
TA-DA!
OOH! THAT'S THAT EARTH DESSERT YOU WERE TELLING US ABOUT.
EXCELLENT.
THE REPRESENTATIVES FROM AUTOZAM, CHIZETA, AND FAHREN ARE WAITING.
PERFECT TIMING! LET'S HAVE A TEA PARTY!
WANNA GIVE ME A HAND, ASCOT?
I'LL HELP, TOO.

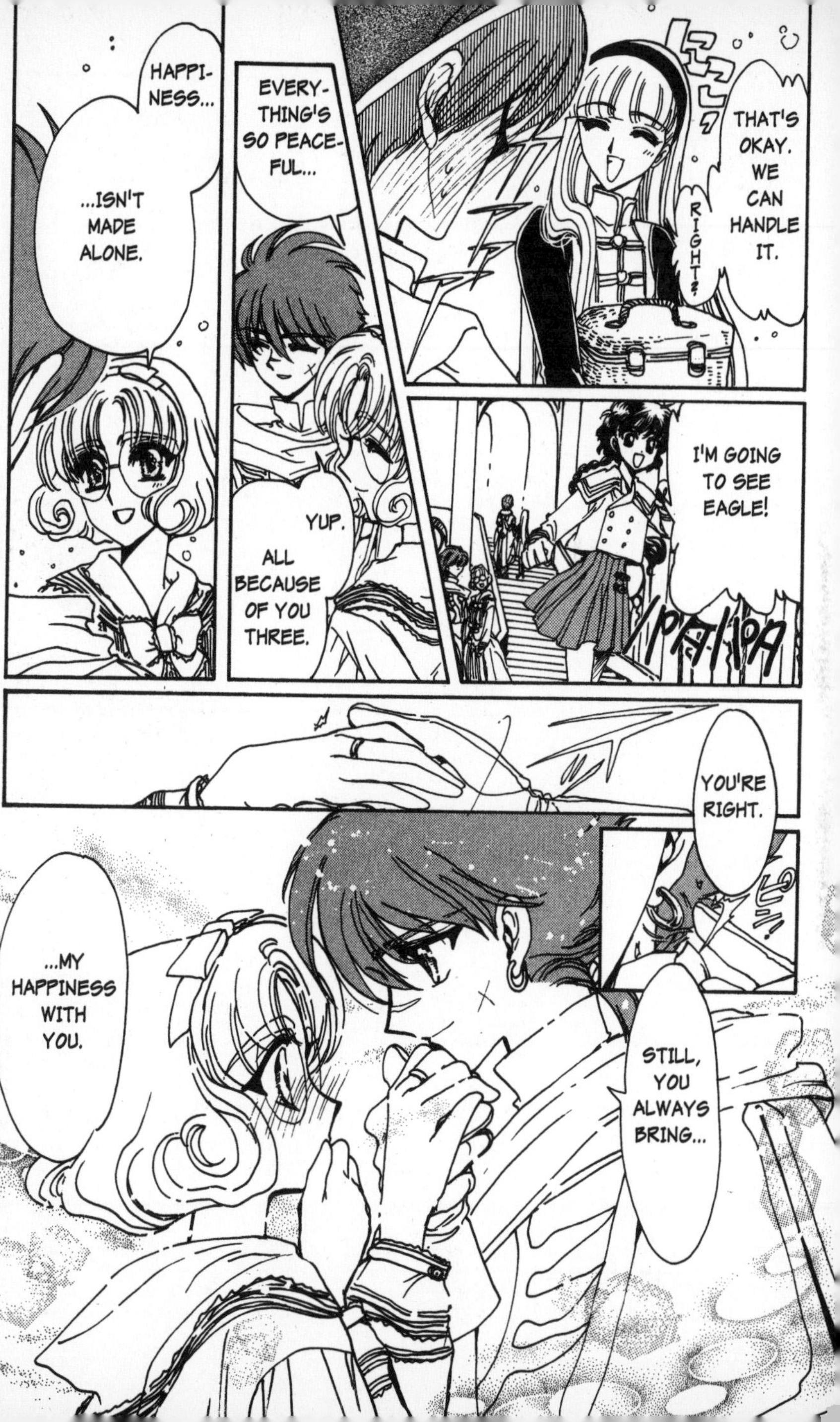
THAT'S OKAY. WE CAN HANDLE IT.
RIGHT?
I'M GOING TO SEE EAGLE!
EVERY-THING'S SO PEACE-FUL...
YUP. ALL BECAUSE OF YOU THREE.
HAPPI-NESS...
...ISN'T MADE ALONE.
YOU'RE RIGHT.
STILL, YOU ALWAYS BRING...
...MY HAPPINESS WITH YOU.

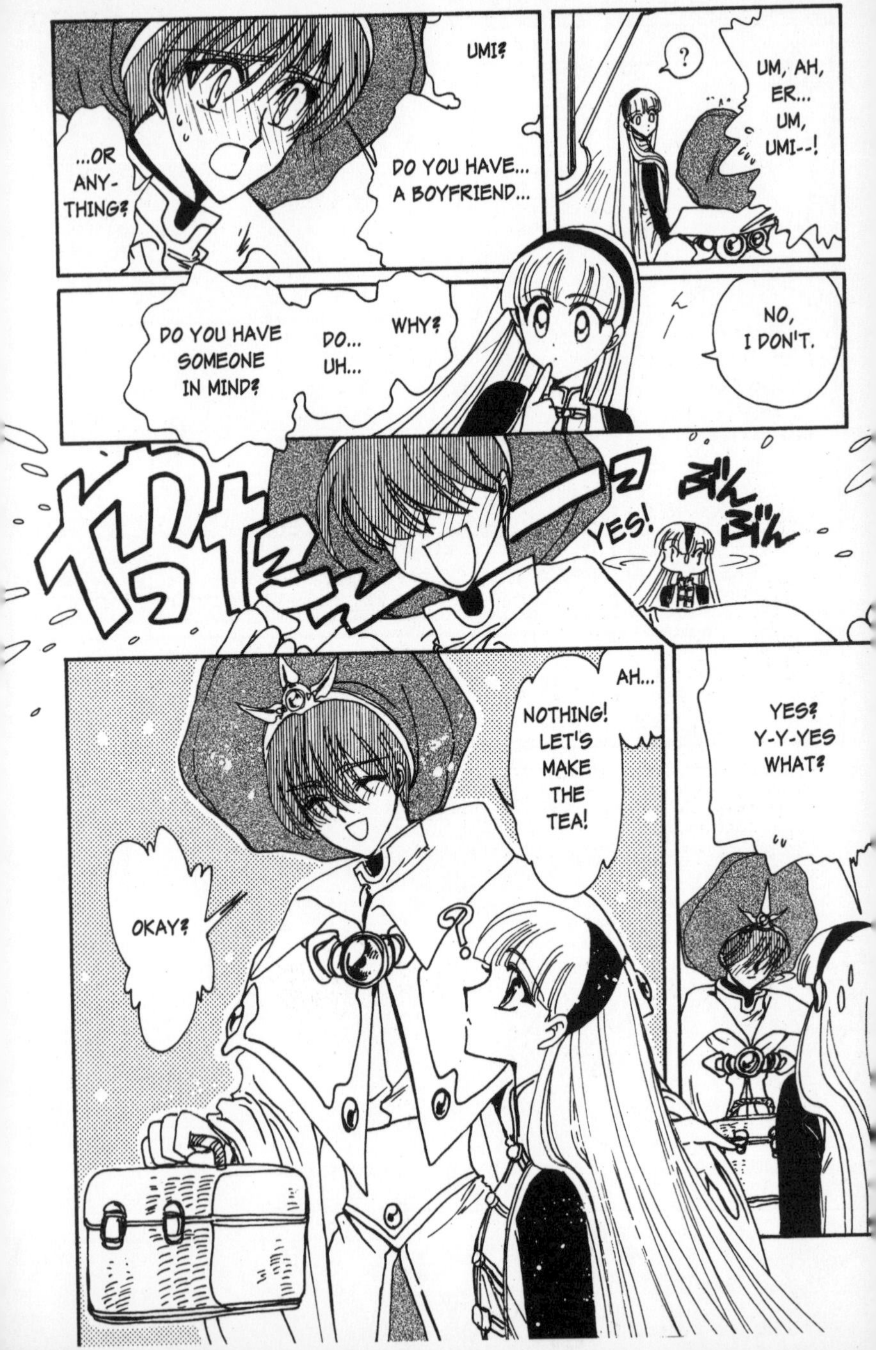
?
UM, AH, ER... UM, UMI--!
UMI?
DO YOU HAVE... A BOYFRIEND...
...OR ANYTHING?
NO, I DON'T.
WHY?
DO... UH...
DO YOU HAVE SOMEONE IN MIND?
ぶんぶん
YES!
やったーっ
YES? Y-Y-YES WHAT?
AH...
NOTHING! LET'S MAKE THE TEA!
OKAY?

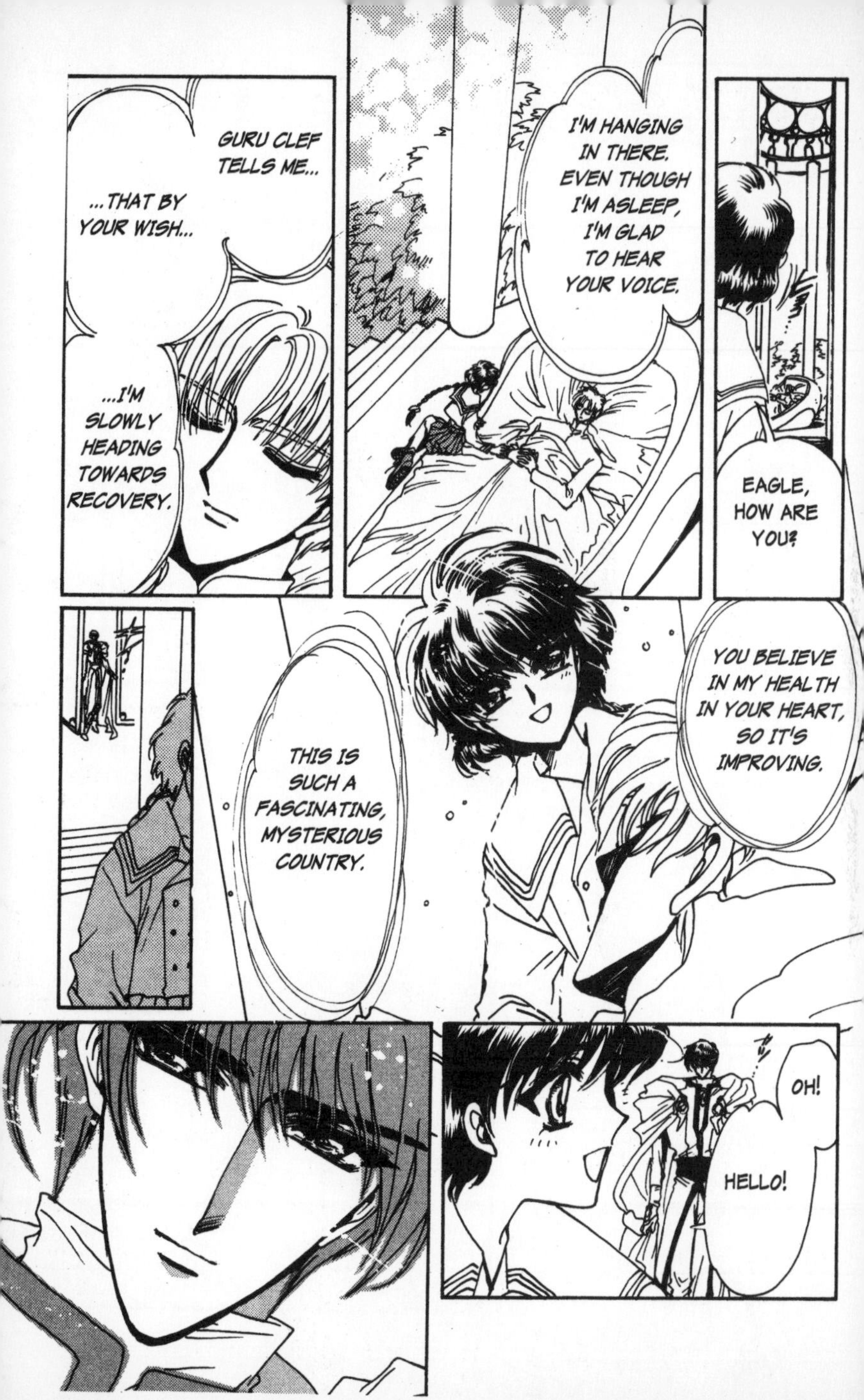
EAGLE, HOW ARE YOU?
I'M HANGING IN THERE. EVEN THOUGH I'M ASLEEP, I'M GLAD TO HEAR YOUR VOICE.
GURU CLEF TELLS ME...
...THAT BY YOUR WISH...
...I'M SLOWLY HEADING TOWARDS RECOVERY.
YOU BELIEVE IN MY HEALTH IN YOUR HEART, SO IT'S IMPROVING.
THIS IS SUCH A FASCINATING, MYSTERIOUS COUNTRY.
OH!
HELLO!

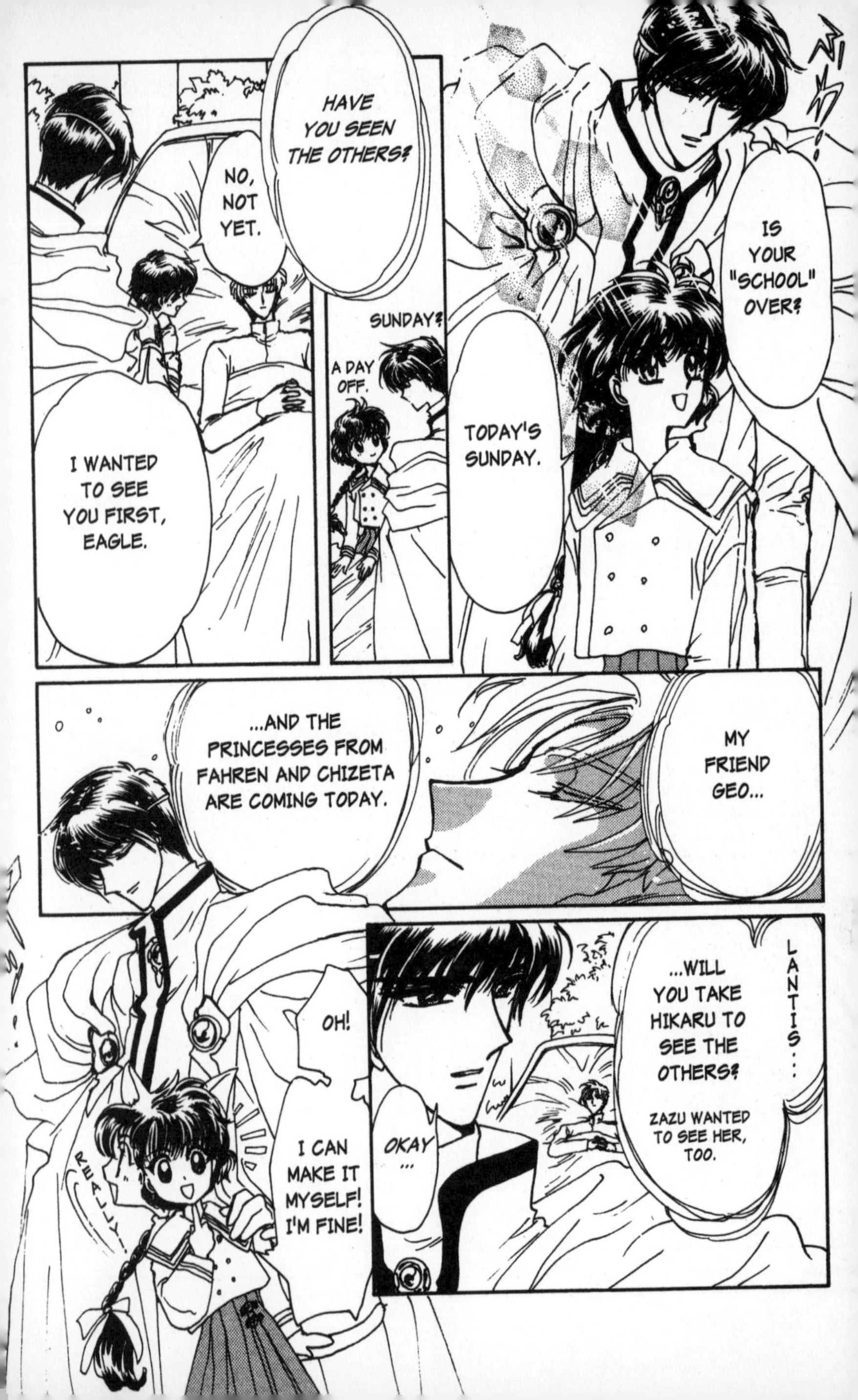
IS YOUR "SCHOOL" OVER?
TODAY'S SUNDAY.
SUNDAY?
A DAY OFF.
HAVE YOU SEEN THE OTHERS?
NO, NOT YET.
I WANTED TO SEE YOU FIRST, EAGLE.
MY FRIEND GEO...
...AND THE PRINCESSES FROM FAHREN AND CHIZETA ARE COMING TODAY.
LANTIS...
...WILL YOU TAKE HIKARU TO SEE THE OTHERS?
ZAZU WANTED TO SEE HER, TOO.
OKAY...
OH!
REALLY
I CAN MAKE IT MYSELF! I'M FINE!

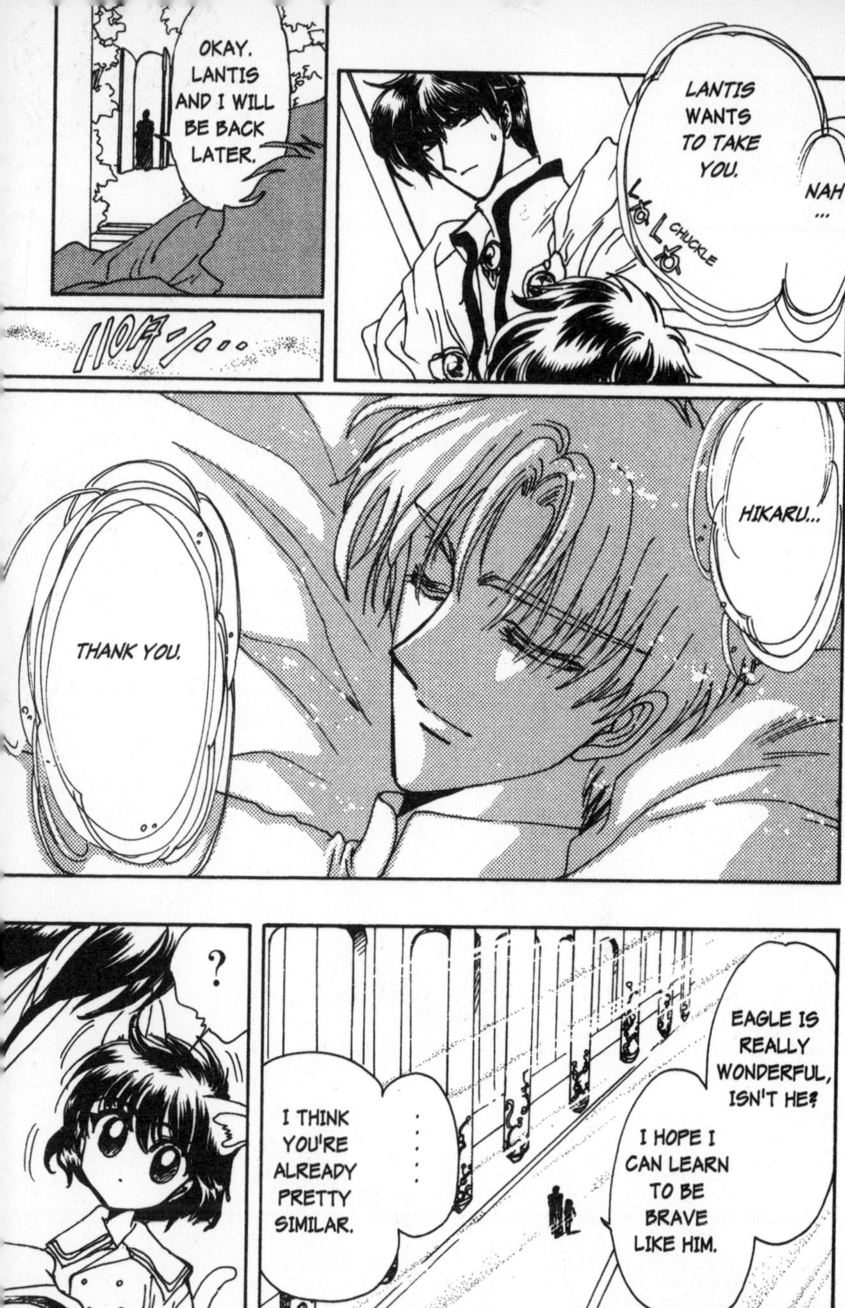
LANTIS WANTS TO TAKE YOU.
NAH ...
CHUCKLE
OKAY. LANTIS AND I WILL BE BACK LATER.
HIKARU...
THANK YOU.
EAGLE IS REALLY WONDERFUL, ISN'T HE?
I HOPE I CAN LEARN TO BE BRAVE LIKE HIM.
......
I THINK YOU'RE ALREADY PRETTY SIMILAR.
?

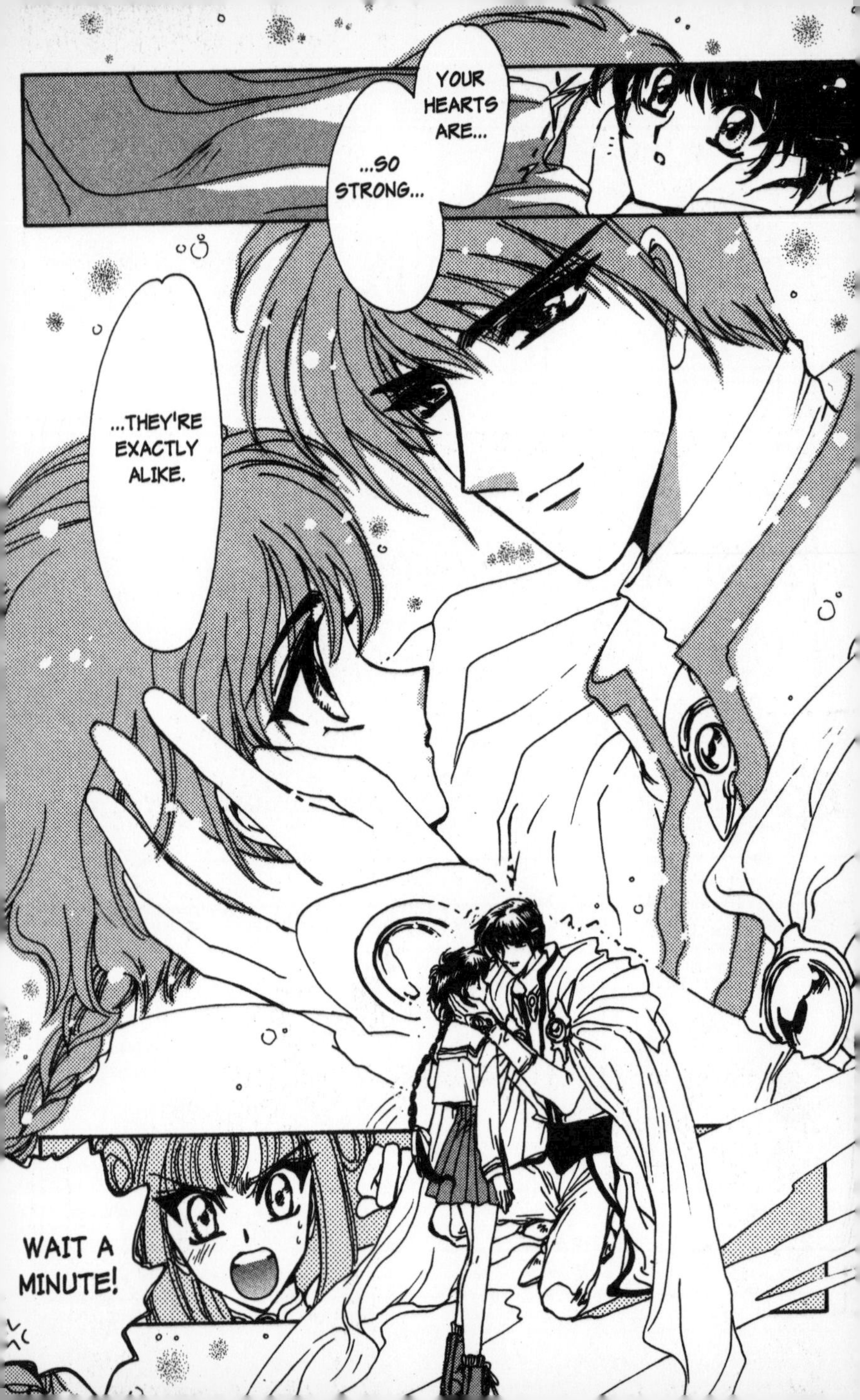
YOUR HEARTS ARE...
...SO STRONG...
...THEY'RE EXACTLY ALIKE.
WAIT A MINUTE!

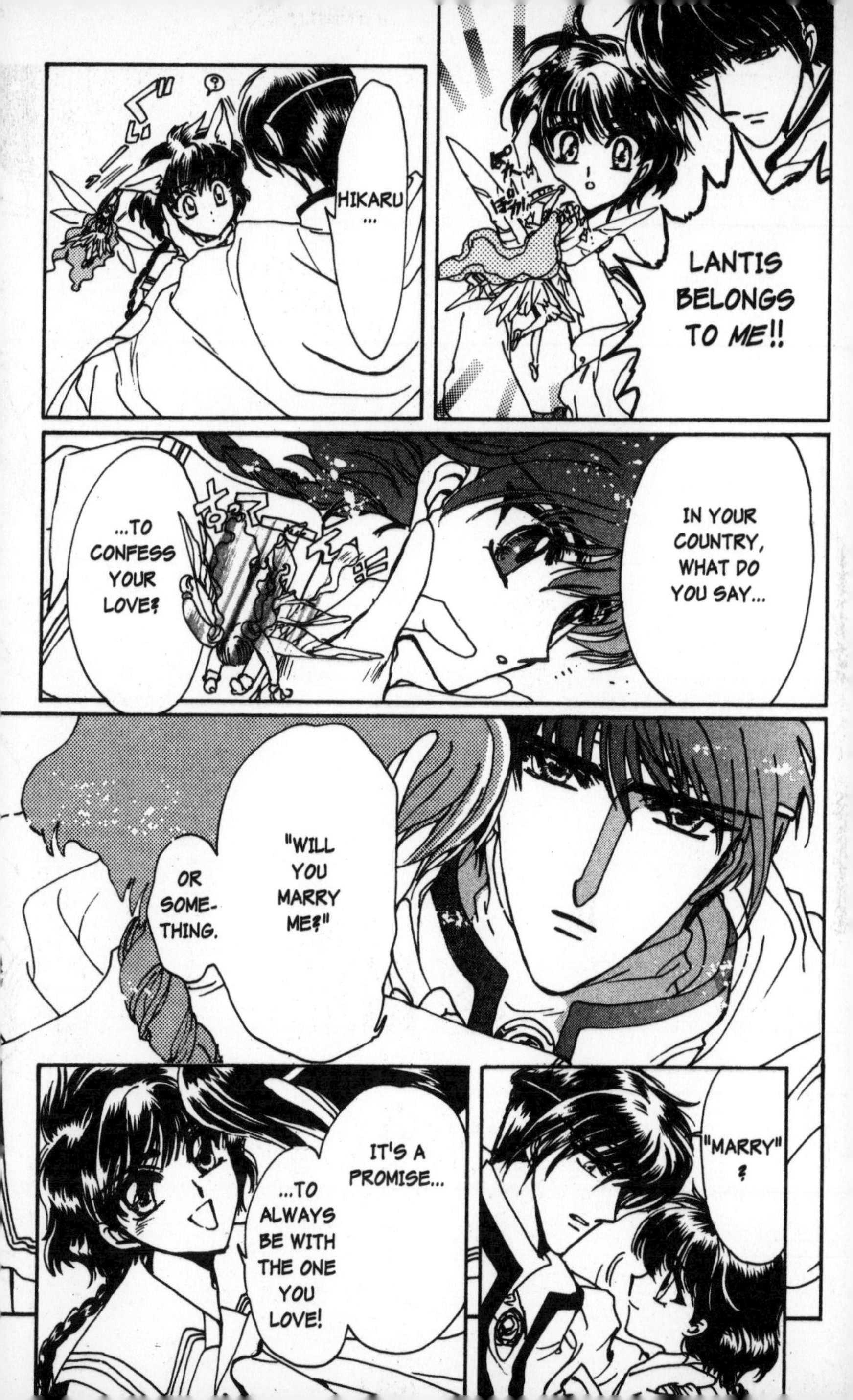
LANTIS BELONGS TO ME!!
HIKARU ...
IN YOUR COUNTRY, WHAT DO YOU SAY...
...TO CONFESS YOUR LOVE?
"WILL YOU MARRY ME?"
OR SOME-THING.
"MARRY"?
IT'S A PROMISE...
...TO ALWAYS BE WITH THE ONE YOU LOVE!

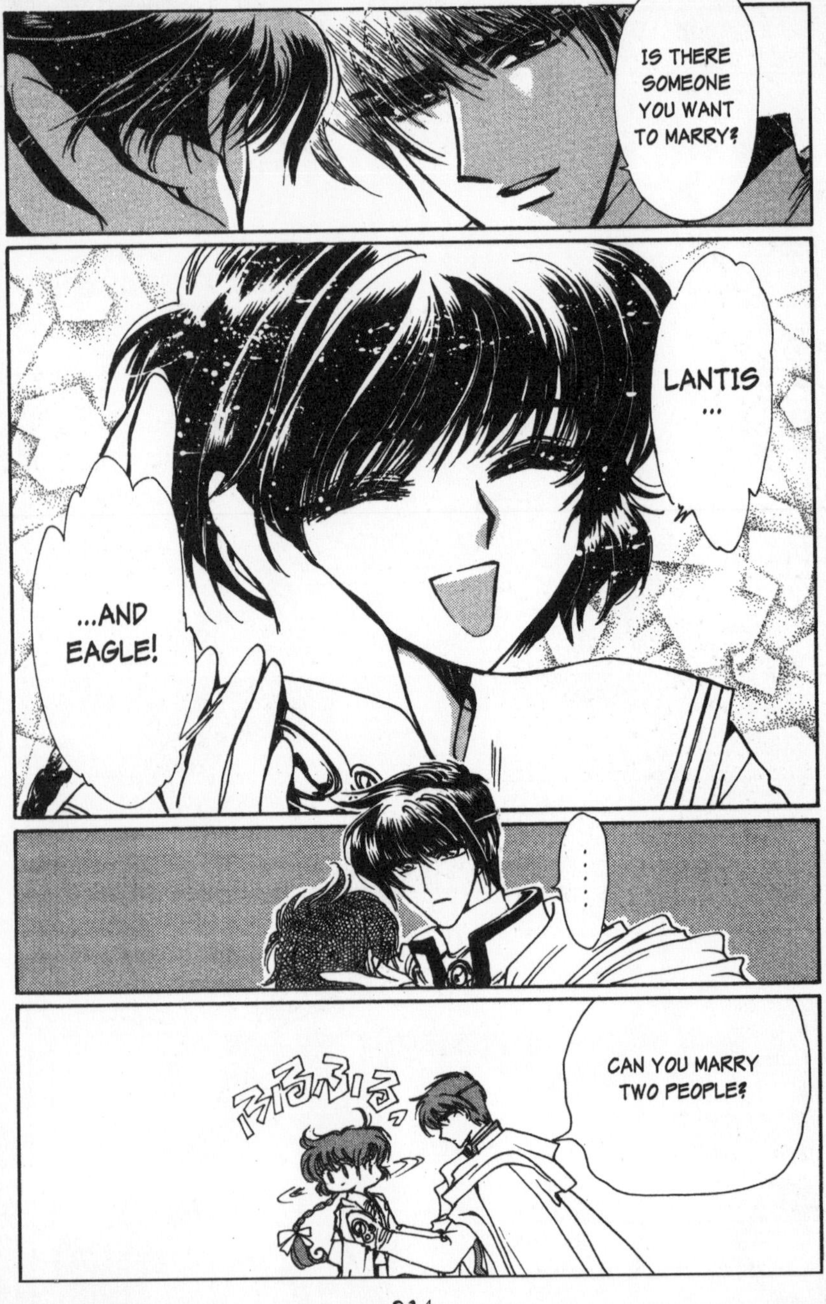
IS THERE SOMEONE YOU WANT TO MARRY?
LANTIS ...
...AND EAGLE!
.....
CAN YOU MARRY TWO PEOPLE?
ふるふる

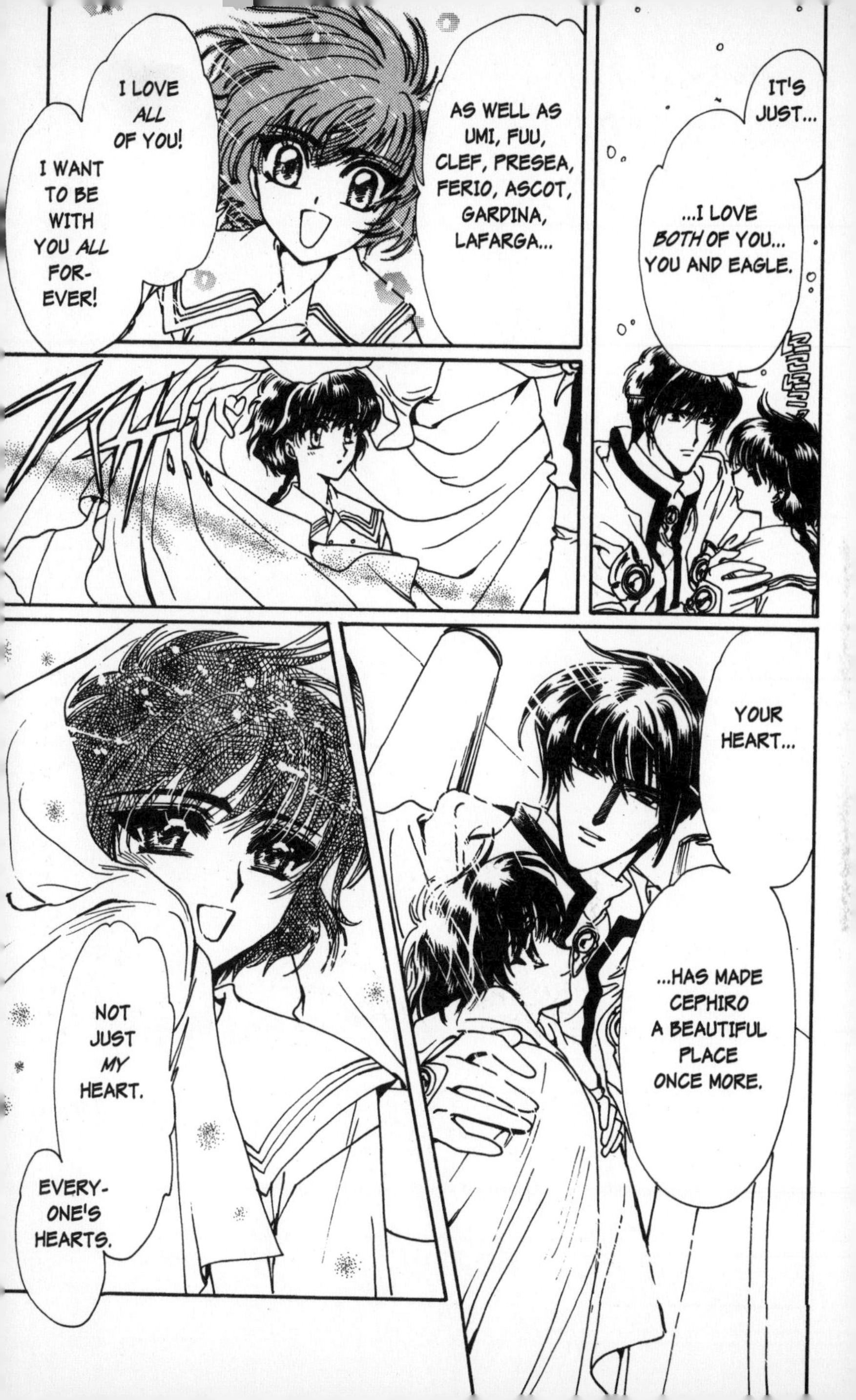
IT'S JUST...
...I LOVE *BOTH* OF YOU... YOU AND EAGLE.
AS WELL AS UMI, FUU, CLEF, PRESEA, FERIO, ASCOT, GARDINA, LAFARGA...
I LOVE *ALL* OF YOU!
I WANT TO BE WITH YOU *ALL* FOR-EVER!
YOUR HEART...
...HAS MADE CEPHIRO A BEAUTIFUL PLACE ONCE MORE.
NOT JUST *MY* HEART.
EVERY-ONE'S HEARTS.

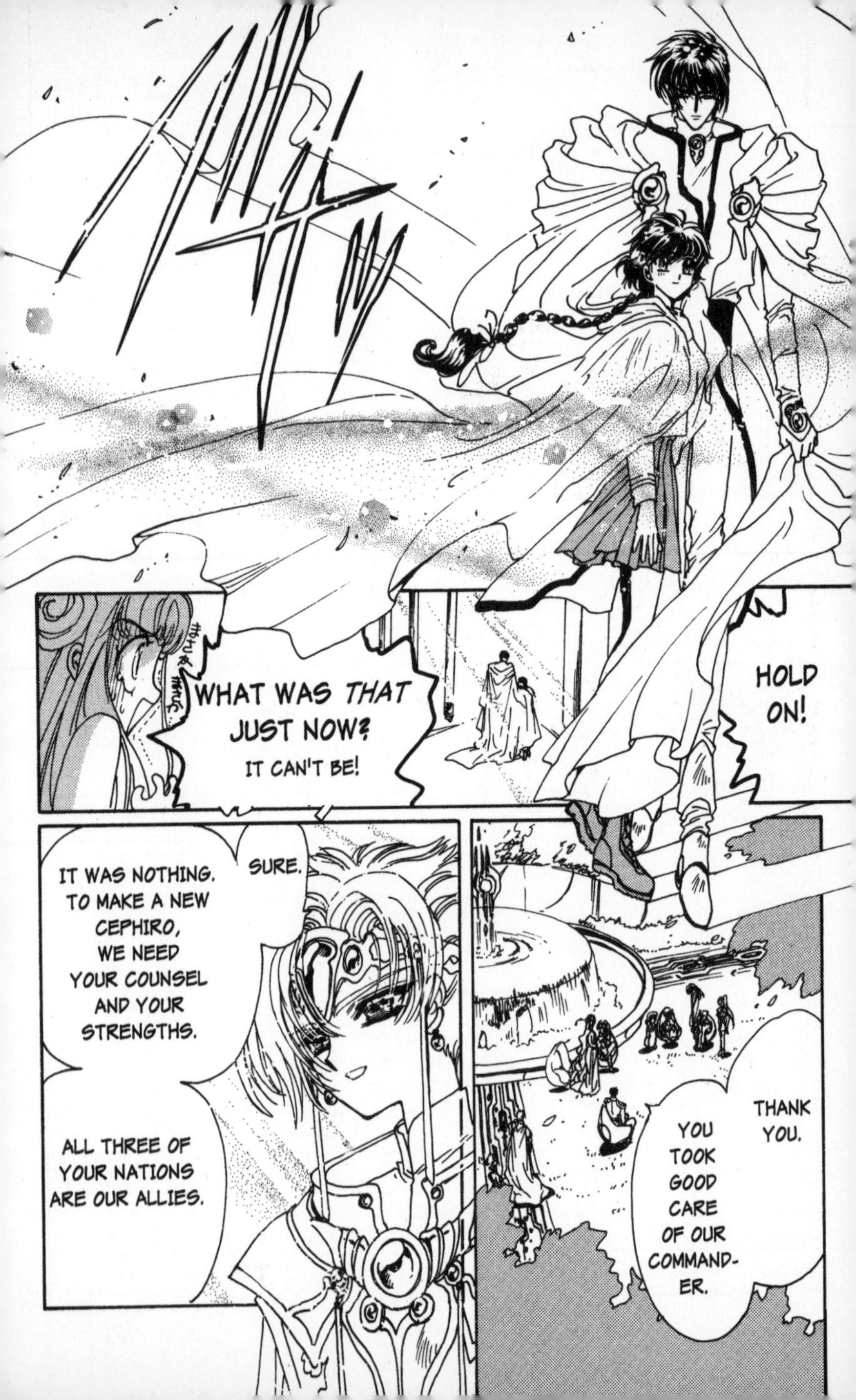
HOLD ON!
WHAT WAS THAT JUST NOW?
IT CAN'T BE!
THANK YOU.
YOU TOOK GOOD CARE OF OUR COMMAND-ER.
SURE.
IT WAS NOTHING. TO MAKE A NEW CEPHIRO, WE NEED YOUR COUNSEL AND YOUR STRENGTHS.
ALL THREE OF YOUR NATIONS ARE OUR ALLIES.

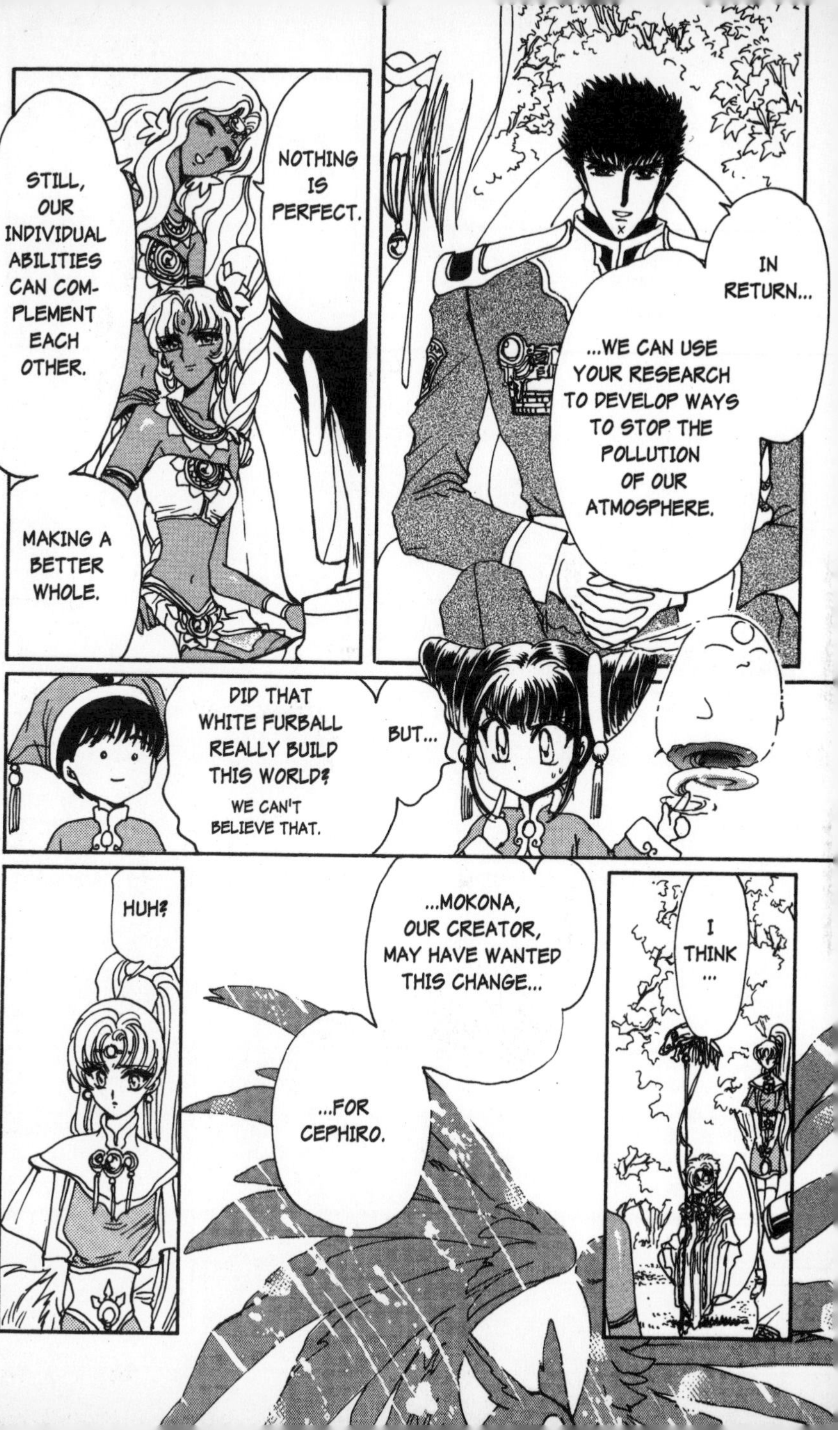
IN RETURN...
...WE CAN USE YOUR RESEARCH TO DEVELOP WAYS TO STOP THE POLLUTION OF OUR ATMOSPHERE.
NOTHING IS PERFECT.
STILL, OUR INDIVIDUAL ABILITIES CAN COM-PLEMENT EACH OTHER.
MAKING A BETTER WHOLE.
BUT...
DID THAT WHITE FURBALL REALLY BUILD THIS WORLD?
WE CAN'T BELIEVE THAT.
I THINK ...
...MOKONA, OUR CREATOR, MAY HAVE WANTED THIS CHANGE...
...FOR CEPHIRO.
HUH?

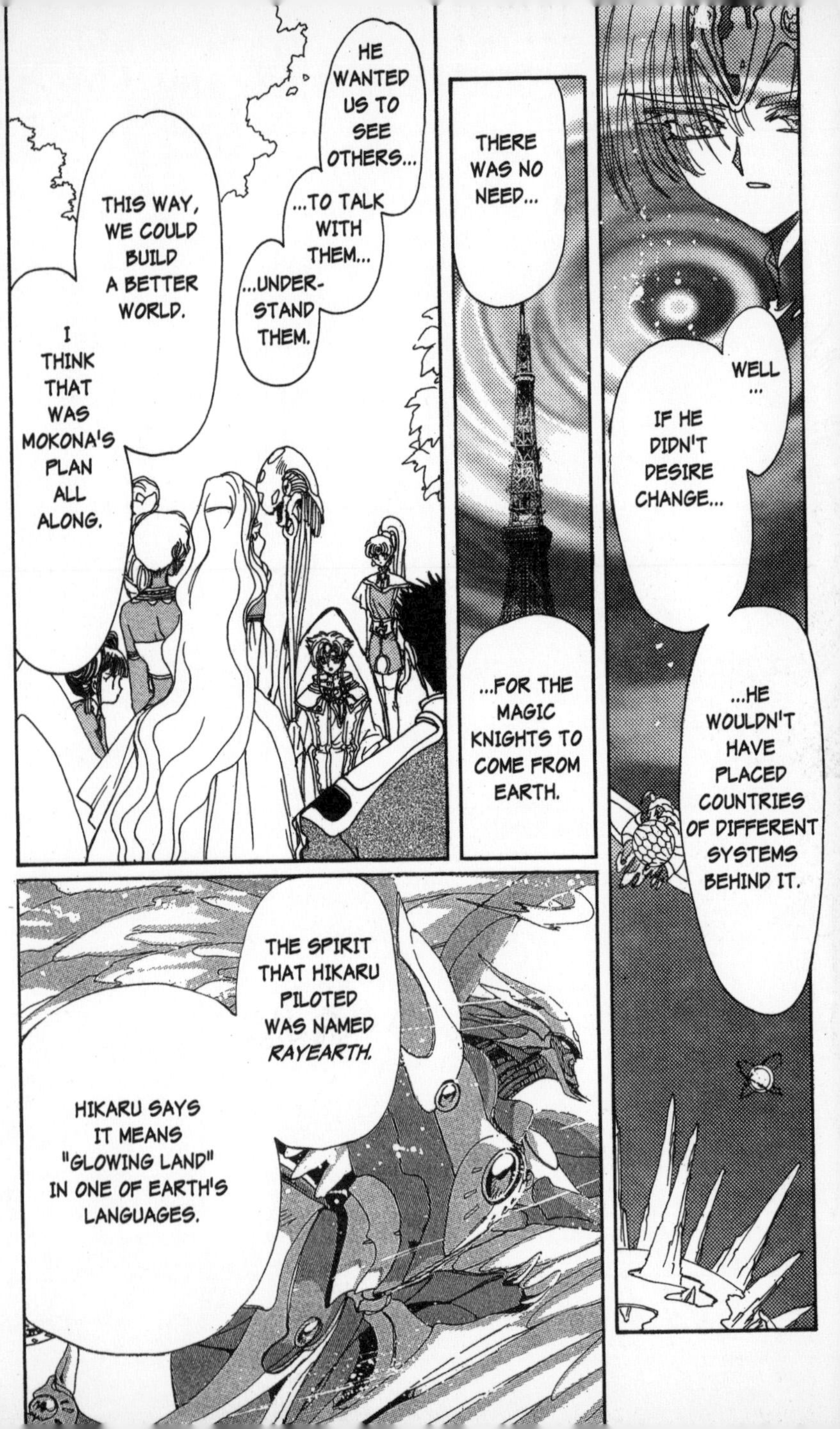
WELL ...
IF HE DIDN'T DESIRE CHANGE...
...HE WOULDN'T HAVE PLACED COUNTRIES OF DIFFERENT SYSTEMS BEHIND IT.
THERE WAS NO NEED...
...FOR THE MAGIC KNIGHTS TO COME FROM EARTH.
HE WANTED US TO SEE OTHERS...
...TO TALK WITH THEM...
...UNDER-STAND THEM.
THIS WAY, WE COULD BUILD A BETTER WORLD.
I THINK THAT WAS MOKONA'S PLAN ALL ALONG.
THE SPIRIT THAT HIKARU PILOTED WAS NAMED *RAYEARTH.*
HIKARU SAYS IT MEANS "GLOWING LAND" IN ONE OF EARTH'S LANGUAGES.

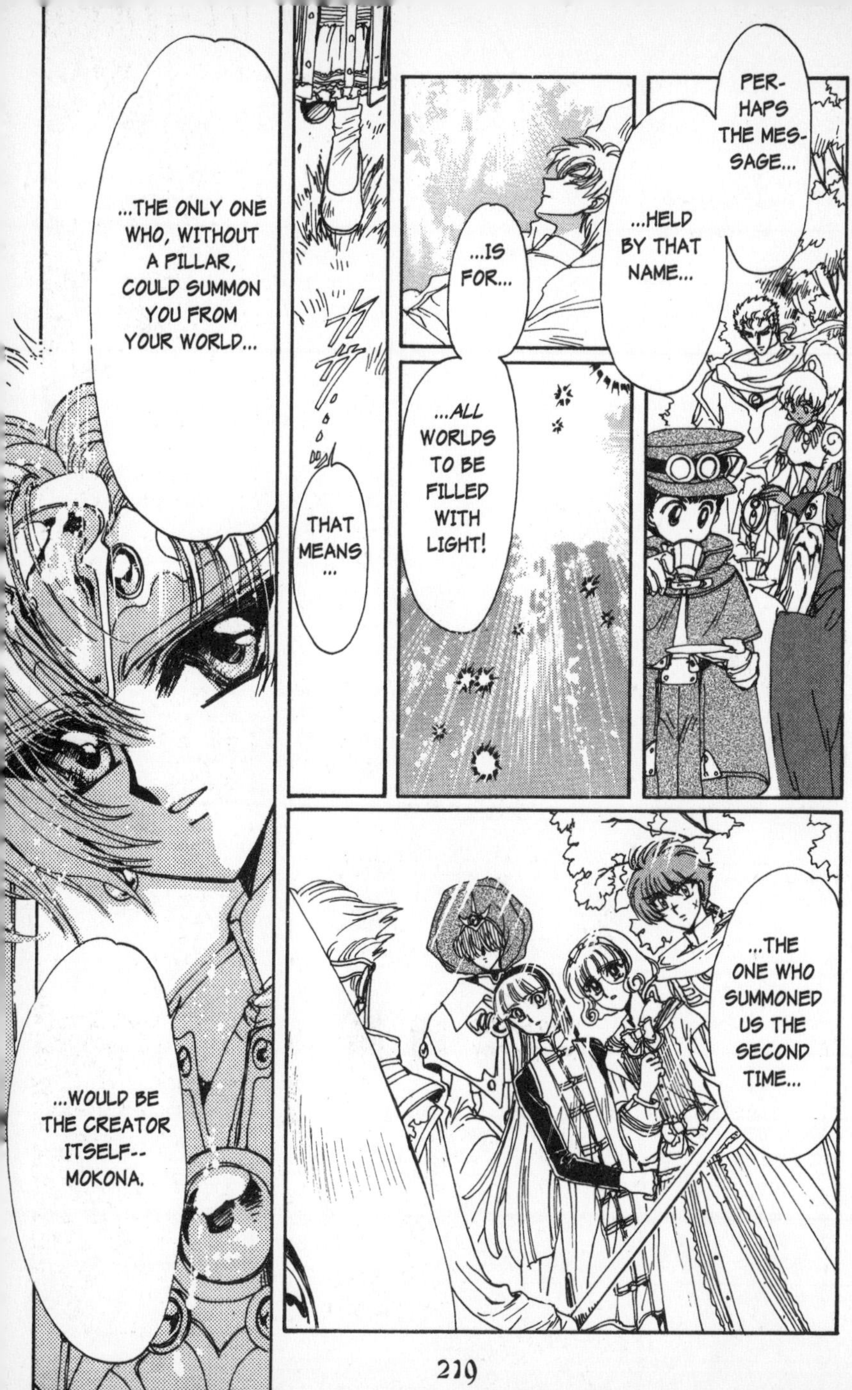
PER-HAPS THE MES-SAGE...
...HELD BY THAT NAME...
...IS FOR...
...ALL WORLDS TO BE FILLED WITH LIGHT!
THAT MEANS ...
...THE ONE WHO SUMMONED US THE SECOND TIME...
...THE ONLY ONE WHO, WITHOUT A PILLAR, COULD SUMMON YOU FROM YOUR WORLD...
...WOULD BE THE CREATOR ITSELF--MOKONA.

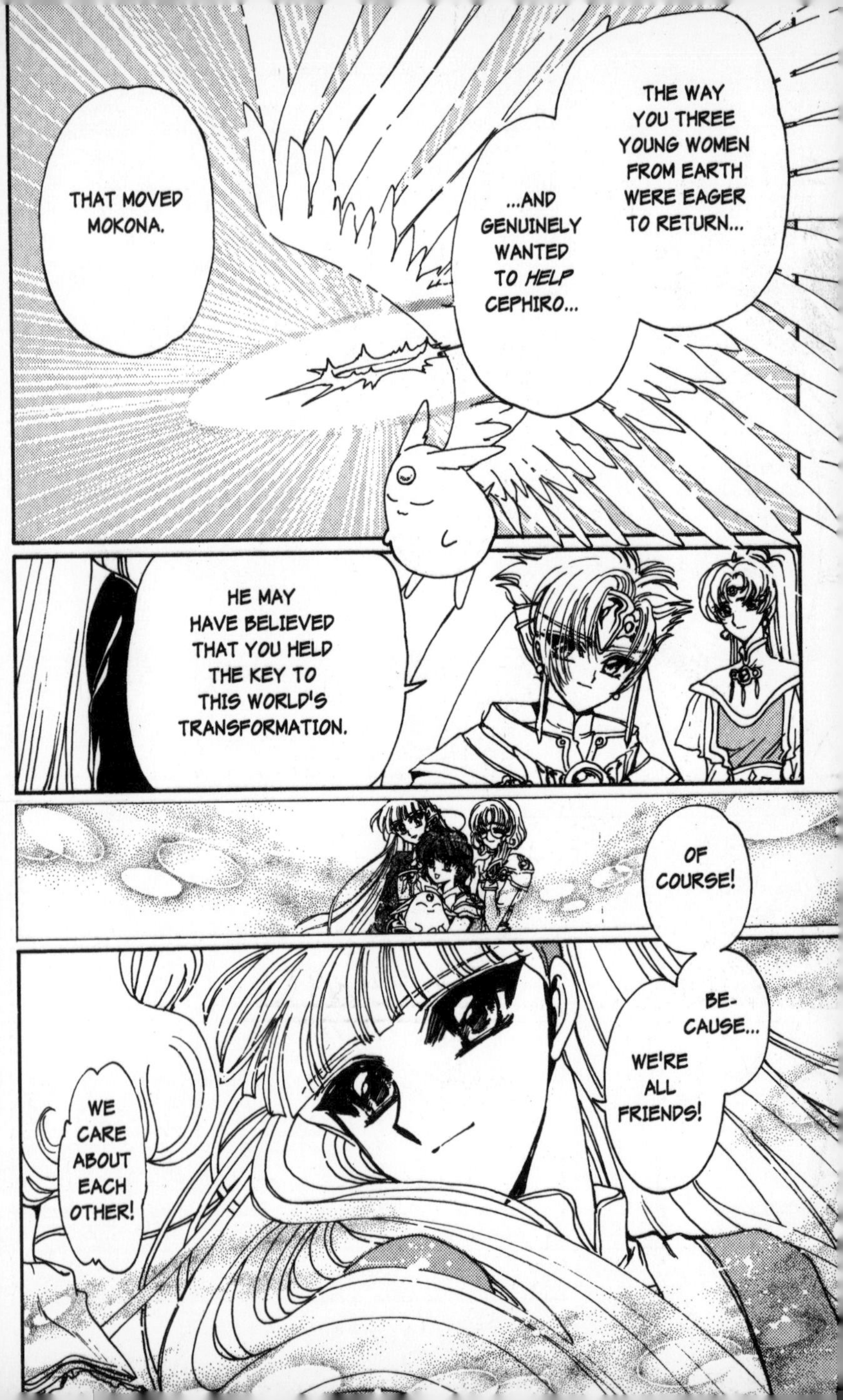
THE WAY YOU THREE YOUNG WOMEN FROM EARTH WERE EAGER TO RETURN...
...AND GENUINELY WANTED TO *HELP* CEPHIRO...
THAT MOVED MOKONA.
HE MAY HAVE BELIEVED THAT YOU HELD THE KEY TO THIS WORLD'S TRANSFORMATION.
OF COURSE!
BE-CAUSE...
WE'RE ALL FRIENDS!
WE CARE ABOUT EACH OTHER!

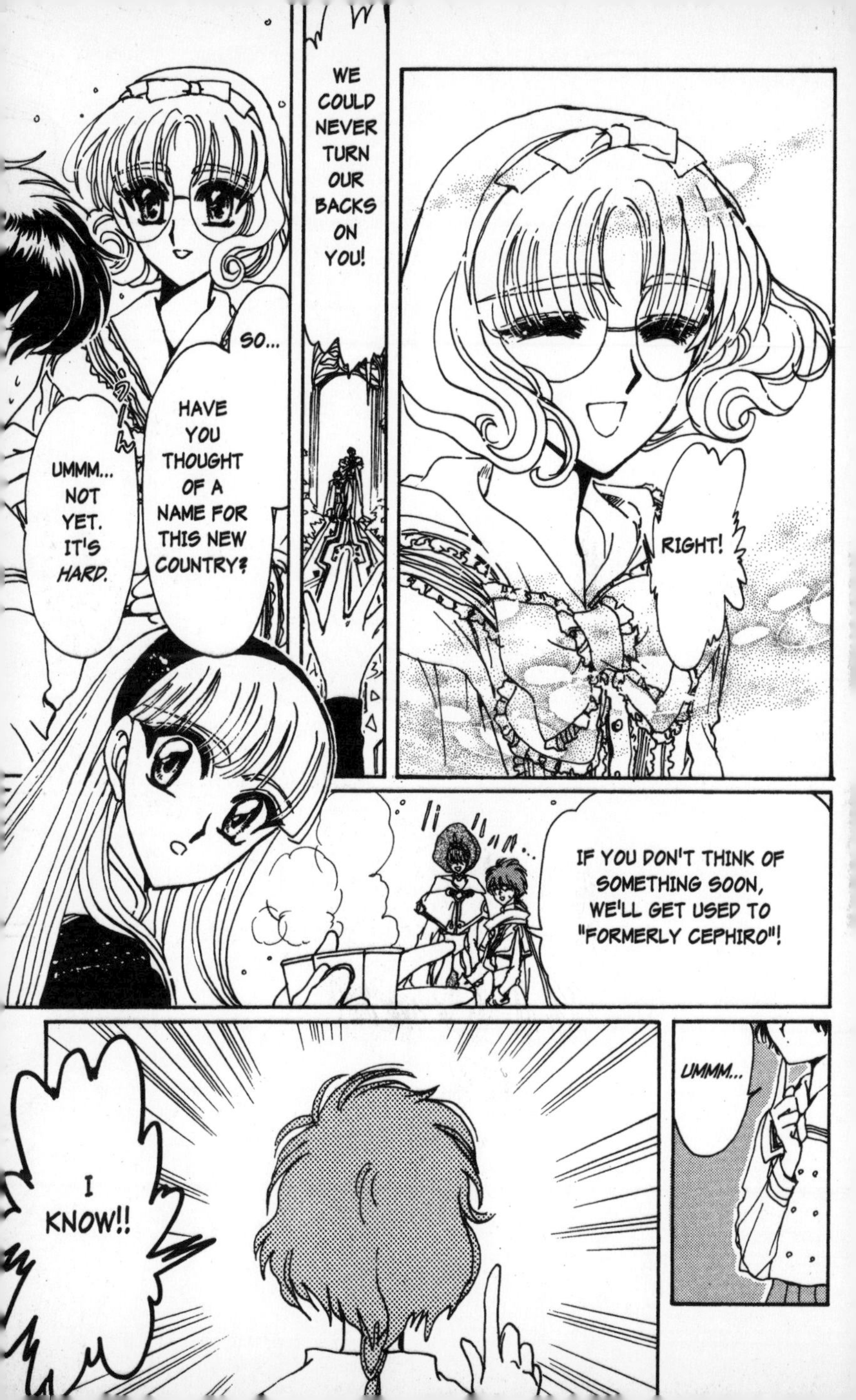
RIGHT!
WE COULD NEVER TURN OUR BACKS ON YOU!
SO...
HAVE YOU THOUGHT OF A NAME FOR THIS NEW COUNTRY?
UMMM... NOT YET. IT'S *HARD.*
IF YOU DON'T THINK OF SOMETHING SOON, WE'LL GET USED TO "FORMERLY CEPHIRO"!
UMMM...
I KNOW!!

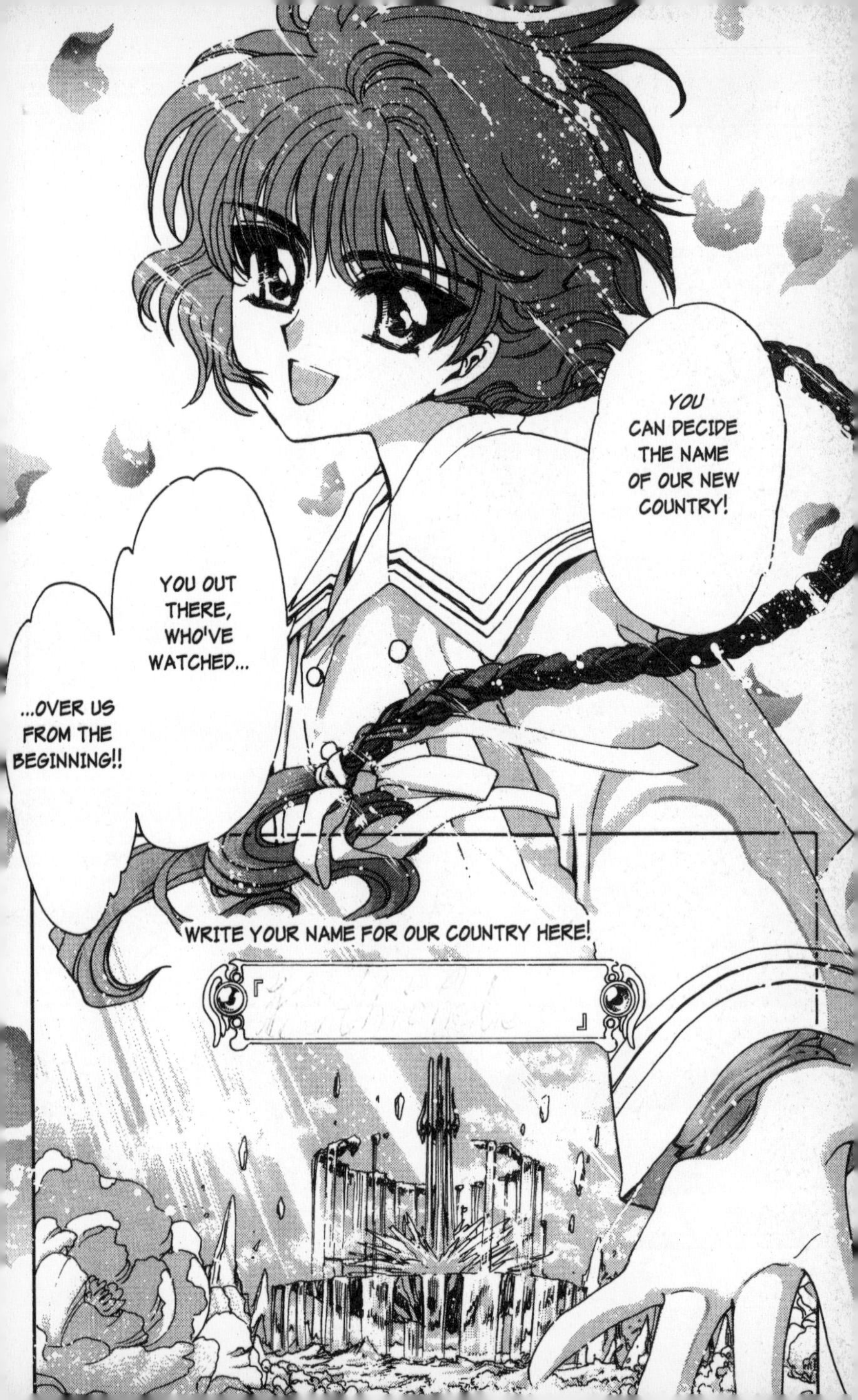
YOU CAN DECIDE THE NAME OF OUR NEW COUNTRY!
YOU OUT THERE, WHO'VE WATCHED...
...OVER US FROM THE BEGINNING!!
WRITE YOUR NAME FOR OUR COUNTRY HERE!

Meet Misaki, the Prodigy.

A lightning-fast fighting doll.
An insane mentor.
A pinky promise to be the best.

ANGELIC LAYER

STOP!

This is the back of the book.
You wouldn't want to spoil a great ending!

This book is printed "manga-style," in the authentic Japanese right-to-left format. Since none of the artwork has been flipped or altered, readers get to experience the story just as the creator intended. You've been asking for it, so TOKYOPOP® delivered: authentic, hot-off-the-press, and far more fun!

DIRECTIONS

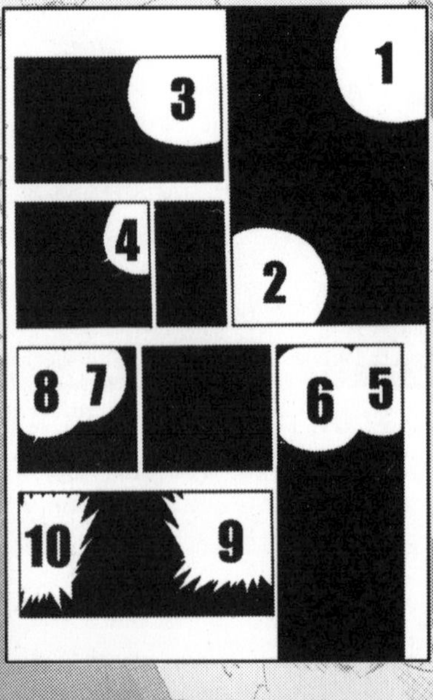

1
2
3
4
5
6
7
8
9
10

If this is your first time reading manga-style, here's a quick guide to help you understand how it works.

It's easy... just start in the top right panel and follow the numbers. Have fun, and look for more 100% authentic manga from TOKYOPOP®!

100% AUTHENTIC MANGA

MAGIC•KNIGHT RAYEARTH II

•CHARACTER COLLECTION•

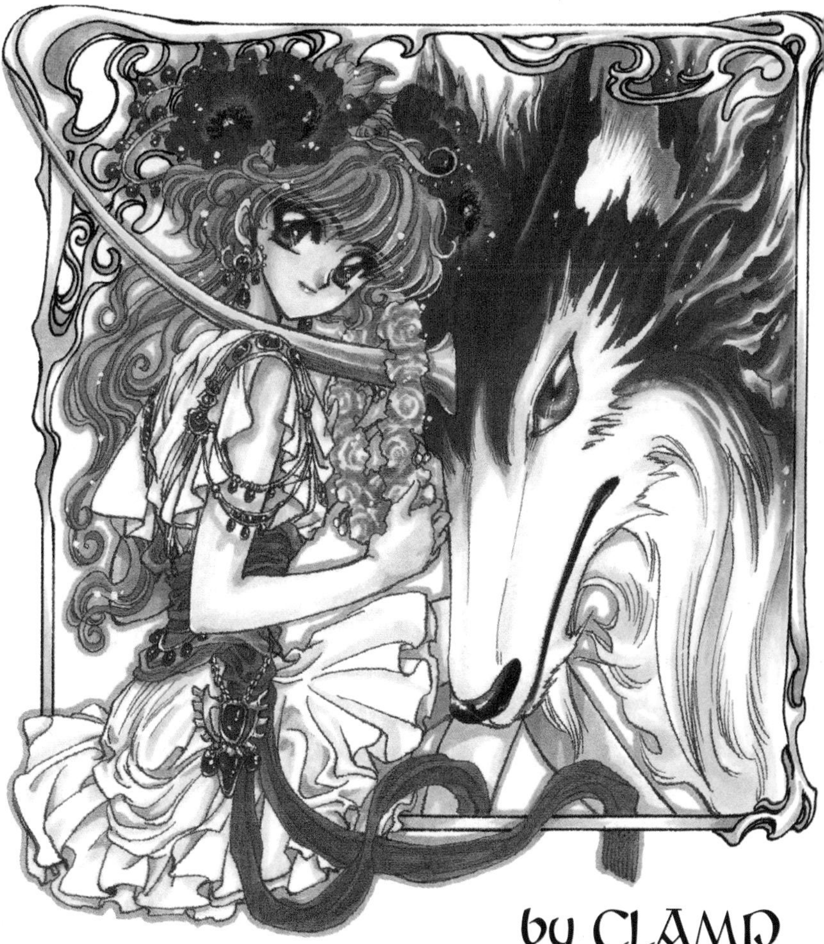

by CLAMP

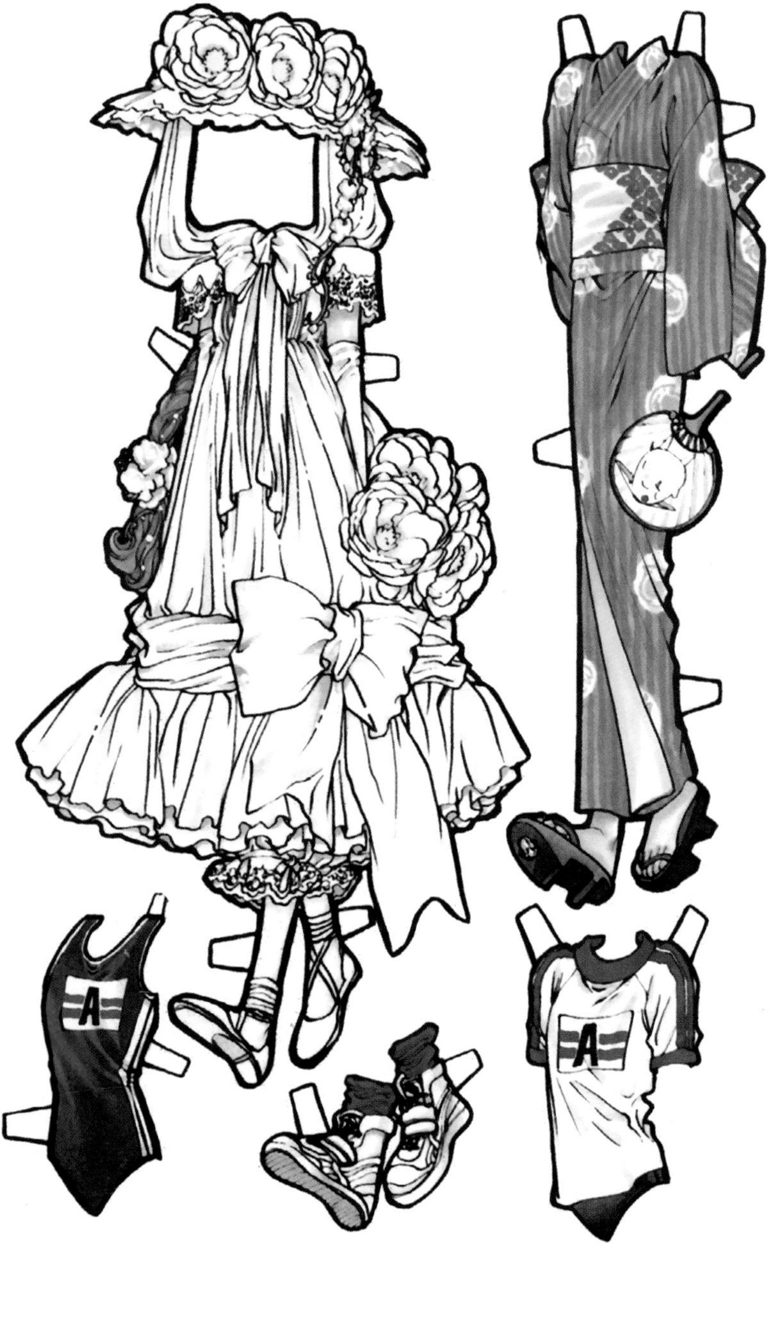
A
A

SHIDOU HIKARU

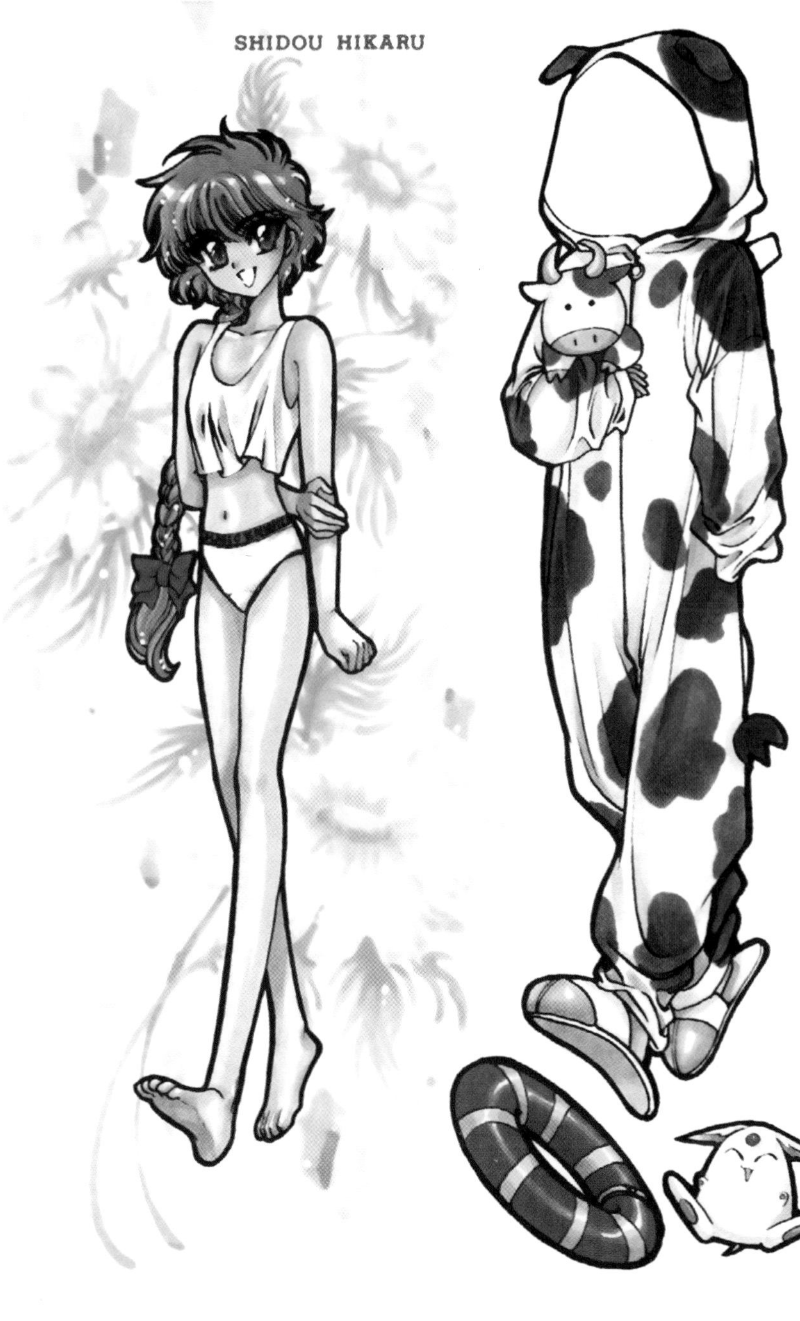

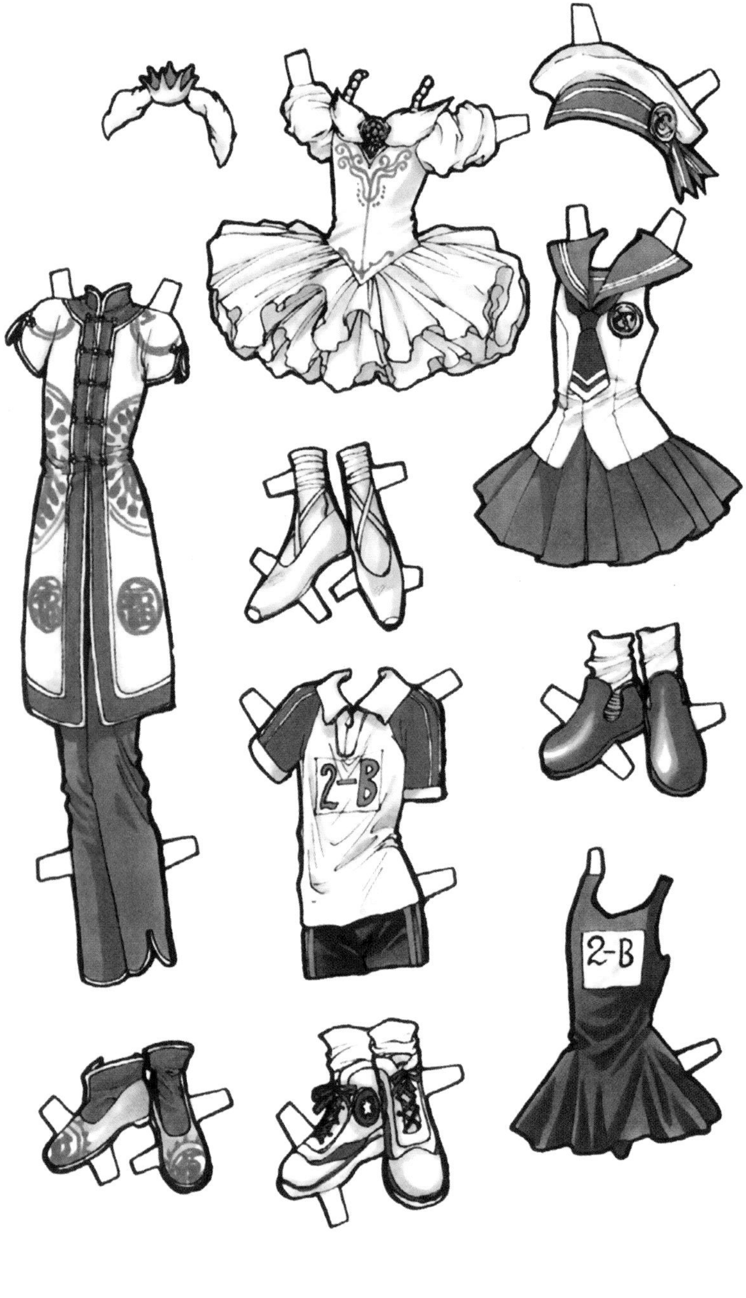
2-B
2-B

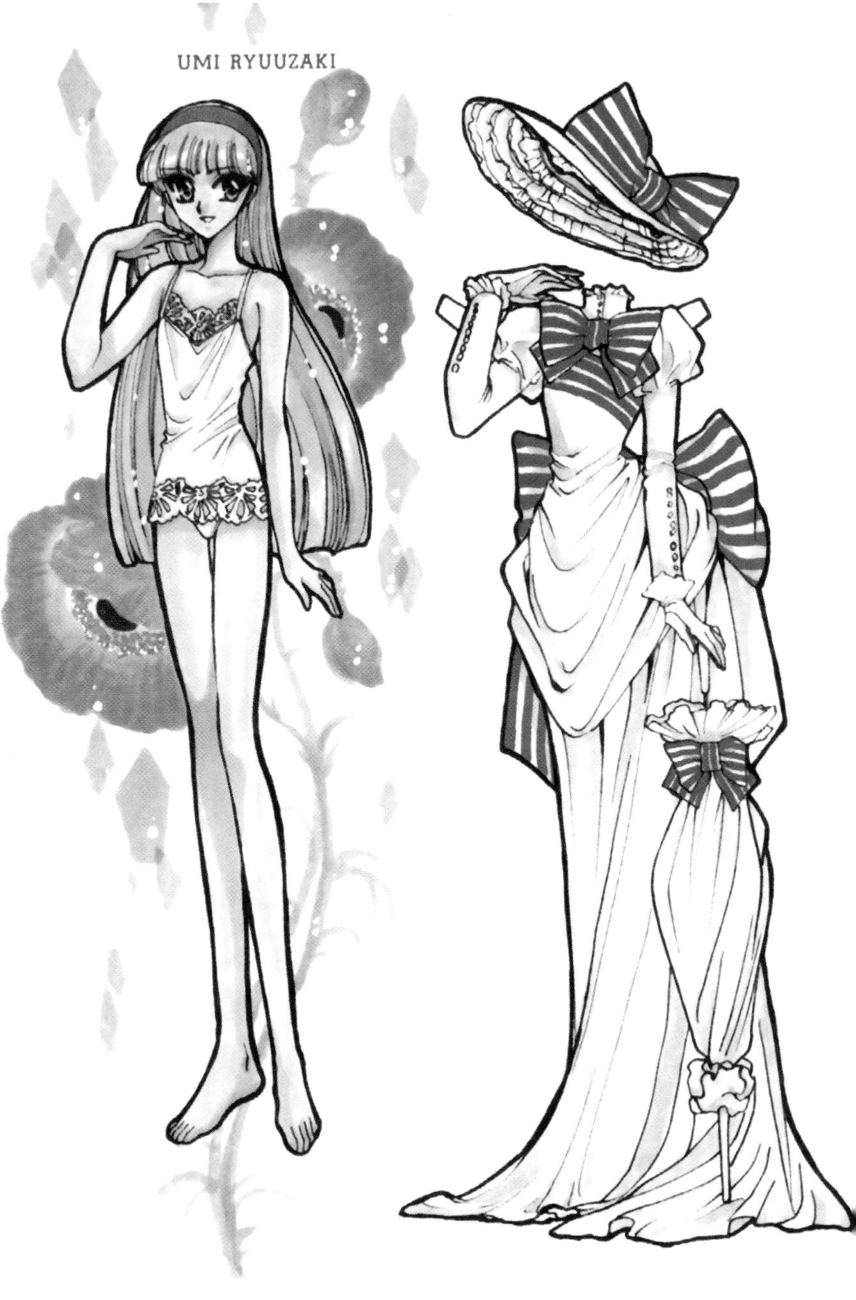
UMI RYUUZAKI

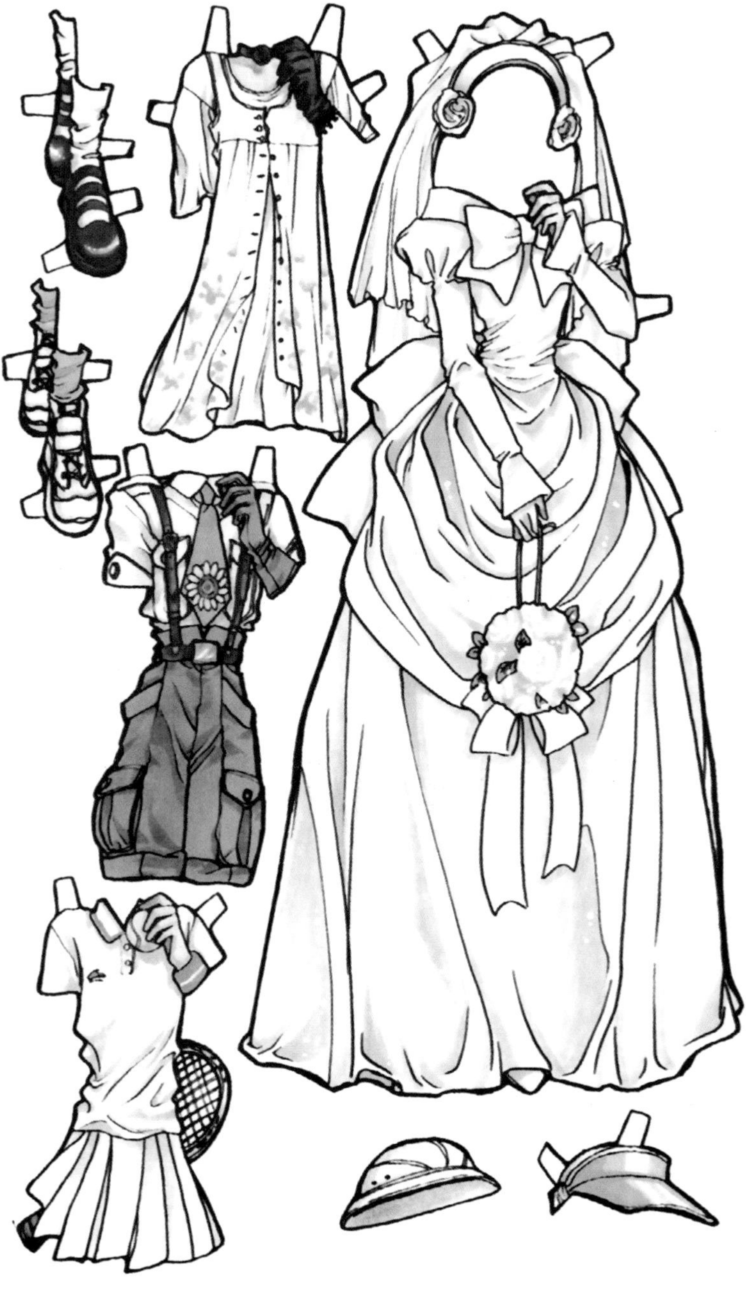

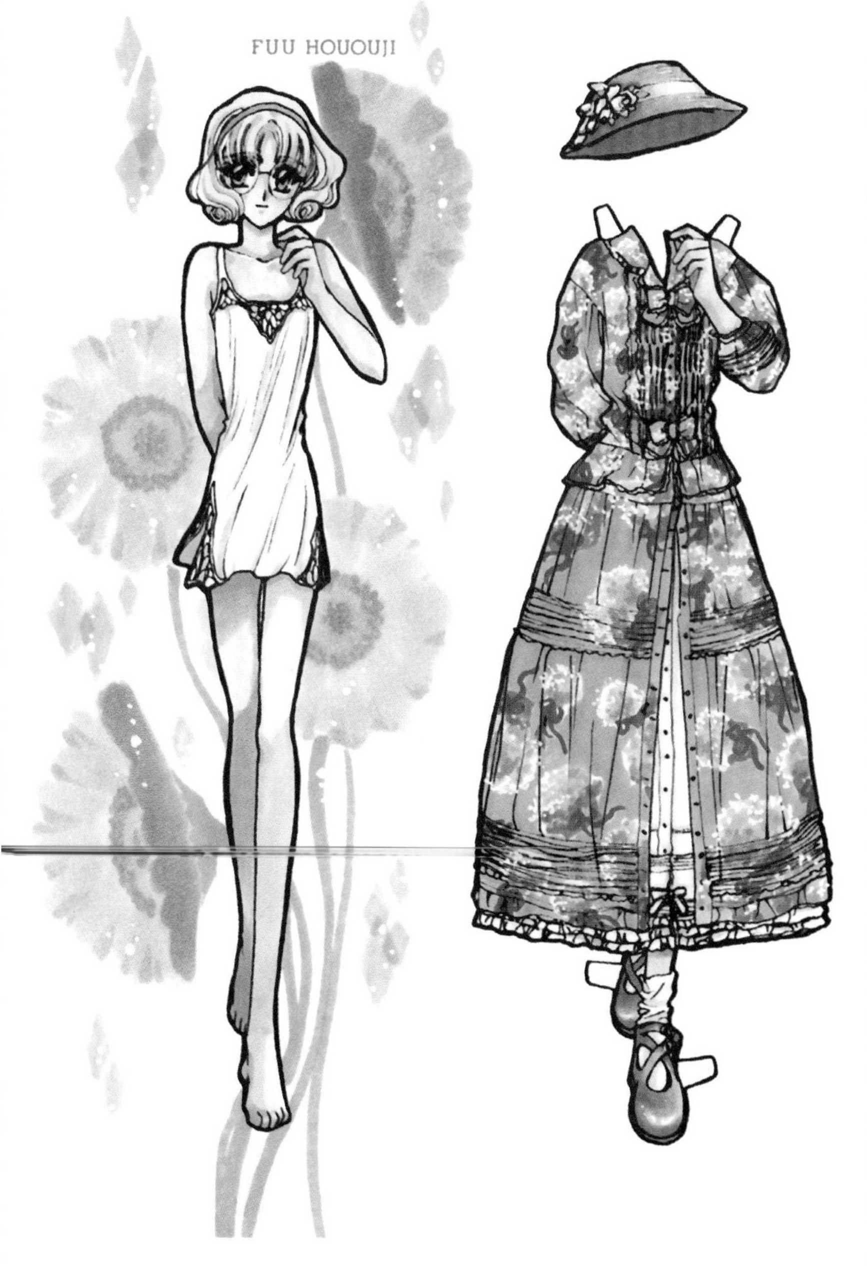
FUU HOUOUJI

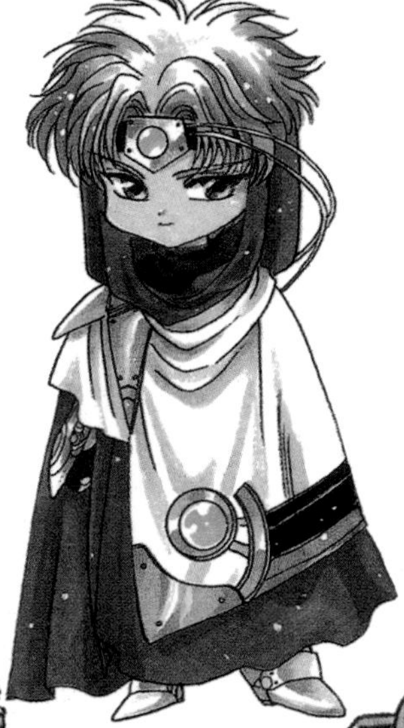

Eagle Vision

Home: Autozam

Favorite Thing: Sweets, Teatime, Naps

Least Favorite Thing: Nothing in particular

The Commander of the NSX, the battleship that leads Autozam's invasion force. He's Autozam's top Mecha pilot, but off the battlefield he's relaxed and always smiling. He loves tea time (especially tea with sweets!) and taking a nice nap afterwards. His increasing sleepiness caused much concern among his friends. Little did they know that he carried with him a terrible secret...

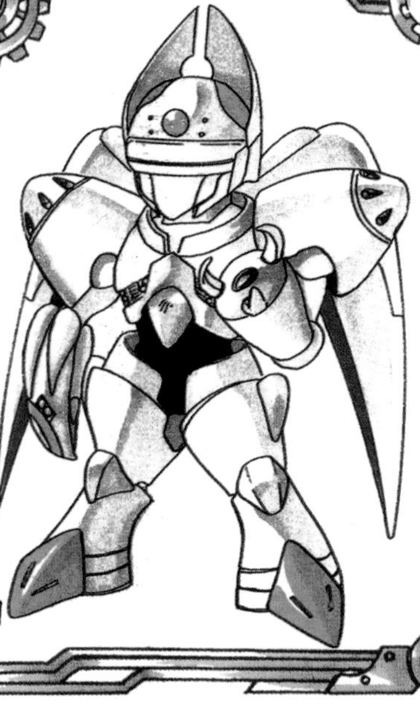

FTO

Home: Autozam

Eagle Vision's custom made Fighter-Mecha. It emphasizes speed and maneuverability over sheer power, but with Eagle at the controls, it's unstoppable. It has a laser sword built into its right hand, and it can also use Vulcan cannons and beam weapons. The usually calm Eagle becomes another person when he gets inside his FTO. Both the FTO and Geo's GTO are custom Mecha, much more powerful than the standard Autozam units.

Lantis (Cail)

Home: Cephiro

Favorite Thing: Naps

Least Favorite Thing: Sweets

    Sol Zagato's younger brother. As Cail, it was Lantis' duty to protect Emeraude, but after seeing the looming tragedy surrounding her and his brother, he left Cephiro to stay in Autozam. He was Guru Clef's most gifted student in the magic arts and is more powerful than even a Dal. His voice is much like his brother's, but their personalities are quite different. A private man, he kept his plans a secret until the very end. He shares a special bond with Eagle Vision of Autozam.

Primera (Pixie)

Home: Cephiro

Favorite Thing: Lantis, Plug and Gear (foods in Cephiro)

Least Favorite Thing: Anyone who stands between her and Lantis

    A Pixie who's stood by Lantis' side ever since he rescued her from a monster in the forest. Her magic is limited to healing and amplification, although she only uses it to help Lantis. Although she realizes that he doesn't reciprocate her feelings, Primera dreams of staying with Lantis forever, and she'll pounce on anyone who stands in the way of that dream.

Tarta

Home: Chizeta
Favorite Thing: Parents, Martial Arts, Tatra

The younger of Chizeta's two princesses, Tarta comes off as stubborn and stern, but she's honest and kind at heart. She is concerned about her country's small size and seeks to annex Cephiro in order to please her parents. Her parents don't mind their nation's size, and would rather their people had peace and happiness. She practices her martial arts daily, and strives to be a better leader, but sadly her older sister always gets the final word.

Tatra

Home: Chizeta
Favorite Thing: Tarta, Tea

The older of Cephiro's two princesses, Tatra comes off as ditzy and overly happy, but she hides a somber, serious side. Her knowledge and combat skills are the greatest in Chizeta. She's fond of having tea at the most inopportune times. Tatra seems to get a kick out of inciting her sister's frustrations.

Geo Metro

Home: Autozam
Favorite Thing: Sweets, Anything tasty, Cooking
Least Favorite Thing: Alcohol

Second in command of the NSX, Geo is an excellent fighter. He's a true friend to Eagle, always watching out for him, especially when Eagle doesn't watch out for himself. He's also friends with Lantis, so Eagle's decision to invade caused Geo great distress. Despite his rougher exterior, he has a sweet tooth and isn't fond of alcohol. He gets along well with the much younger Zazu.

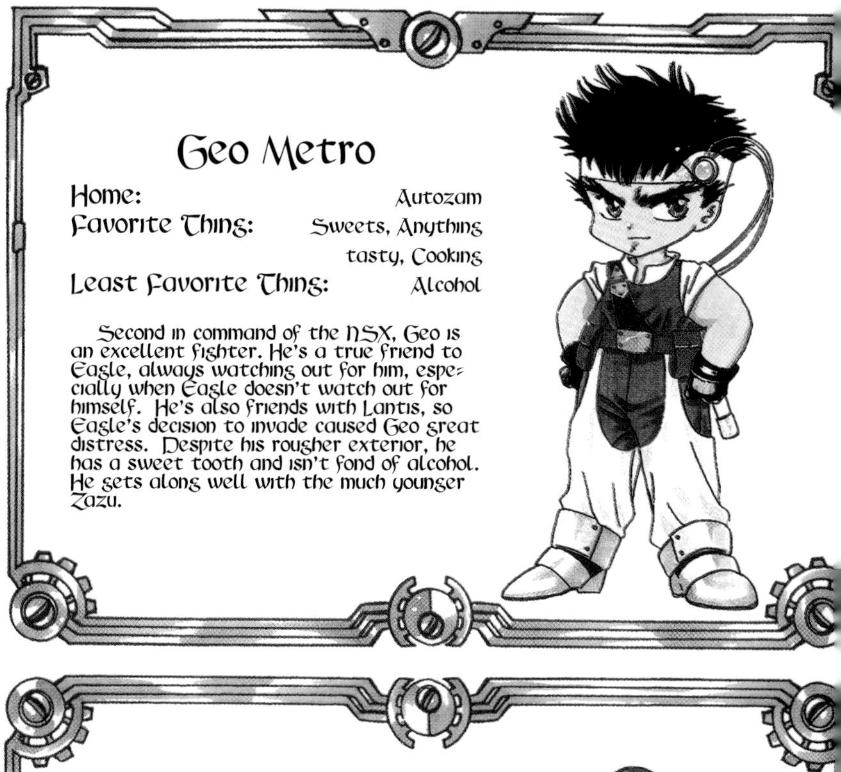

Zazu Torque

Home: Autozam
Favorite Thing: FTO, Alcohol
Least Favorite Thing: People who trash his Mecha

Even though he's the youngest member of the NSX crew, Zazu is the top mechanic. His skills have pulled his crewmates out of numerous jams, as Zazu can fix just about anything. He signed on for this mission so that he could stay close to his favorite Mecha - Geo's FTO. He loves an occasional drink and will take whatever he can get! Ladies, take note! He's currently on the lookout for a girlfriend.

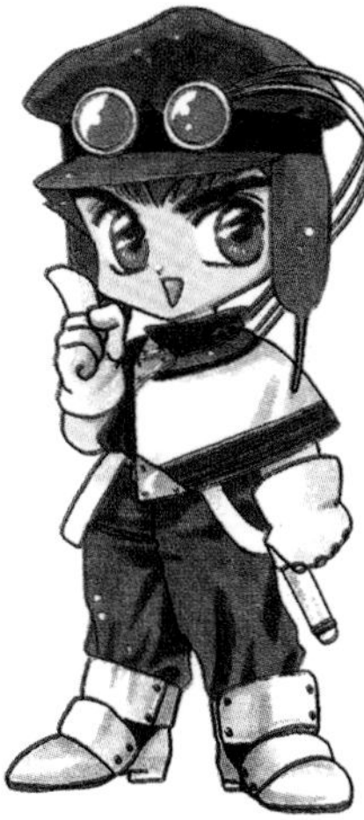

Sang Yung

Home: Fahren
Favorite Thing: Lady Aska, Books

Lady Aska's loyal servant, Sang Yung, grew up by her side. He has a chibi-face, but he's actually very smart and studious. His wish is that when Lady Aska becomes Empress, he can be by her side and provide her with counsel. He can't use the illusionary arts of the royal family, but he's well trained in martial arts and archery. He might be holding a crush for Lady Aska, but due to class differences, he knows nothing could ever come of it.

Qiang Ang

Home: Fahren
Favorite Thing: Apricot Wine,
Massages

The acting regent, he leads the Fahren government until Lady Aska is old enough to take her seat. A relative of the royal family, he has some magical abilities. He sees great potential in Lady Aska, and his unforgiving regimen of study and discipline is his way of showing that he cares. Lady Aska calls him a "preachy old man," but he doesn't mind putting up with her abuse. He hopes that when he's gone, Sang Yung will continue to guide Aska.

Rahkun and Rashid

Home: Chizeta

The guardian Djinns that protect Chizeta's princesses. They have kept Chizeta's royal family safe for generations. Rahkun protects Tarta and Rashid protects Tatra. They may look alike, but their personalities are different. Since they are spirits, they can change shape at will, but they usually maintain the appearance of Djinns.

Lady Aska

Home: Fahren
Favorite Thing: Sweets (especially peach-flavored ones), Mischief, Sang Yung

Still a child, Lady Aska is in training to become Fahren's next Empress. Being the heir to the throne, as well as an orphan, she's grown up spoiled and acts a little selfish, but she has a good heart. Her reasons for coming to Cephiro are purely selfish. She wishes to rule a land where all her dreams come true. Her favorite companion and friend is Sang Yung, the child of her former nanny. She is required to keep her tutor, Qiang Ang, with her at all times, but that doesn't mean she has to listen to him. The illusionary spells she uses were passed down her family line for generations.

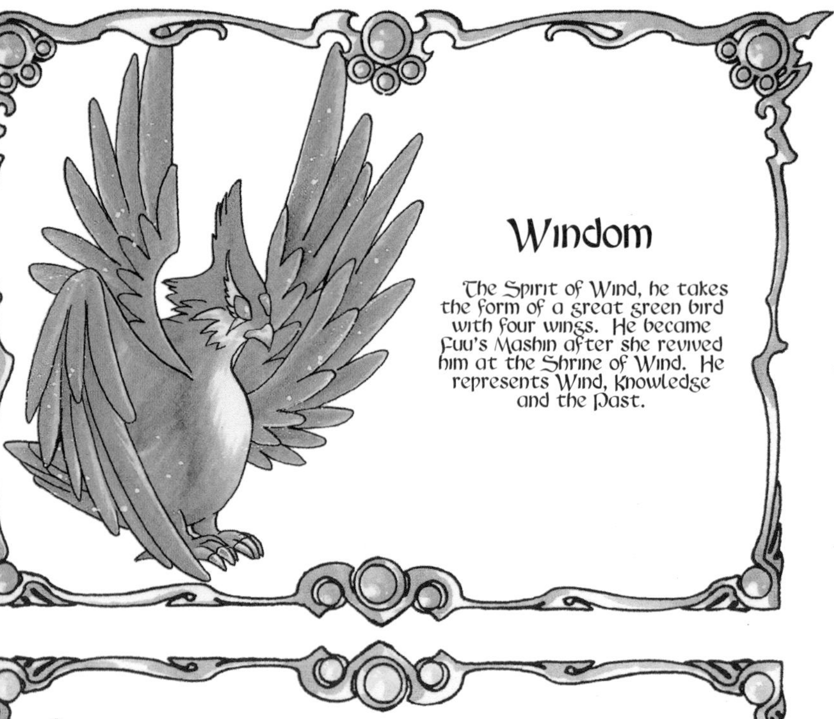

Windom

The Spirit of Wind, he takes the form of a great green bird with four wings. He became Fuu's Mashin after she revived him at the Shrine of Wind. He represents Wind, Knowledge and the Past.

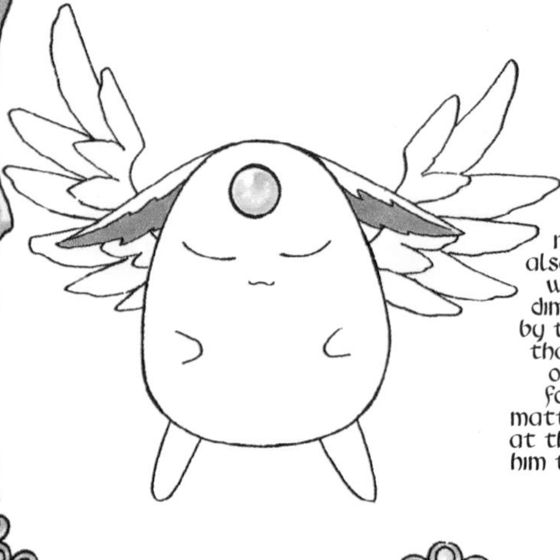

Mokona
(true form)

This Creator made not only Cephiro and its neighboring countries, but also Earth itself. He remained with the Mashin in another dimension until he was needed by the Magic Knights. It is said that his true powers are seen only when the jewel on his forehead glows yellow. No matter how eloquently he speaks at the end, it's still hard to take him too seriously as he still looks like a marshmallow!

Rayearth

The Spirit of Fire, his form is that of a red lion with an ivory horn. Hikaru revived him at the Fire Shrine and he fights with her as her Mashin. As with Mokona, his true form was not revealed until the end of the story. He represents Fire, Passion and the Future.

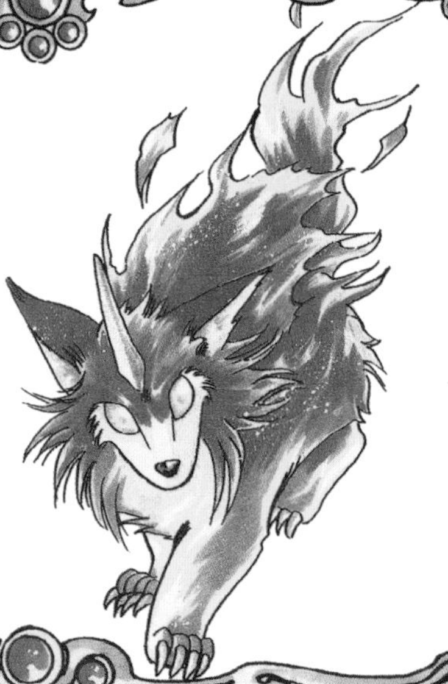

Selece

The Spirit of Water, he's shaped like a blue dragon. Umi revived him at the Shrine of Water, and he's been her Mashin ever since. He represents Water, Kindness and the Present.

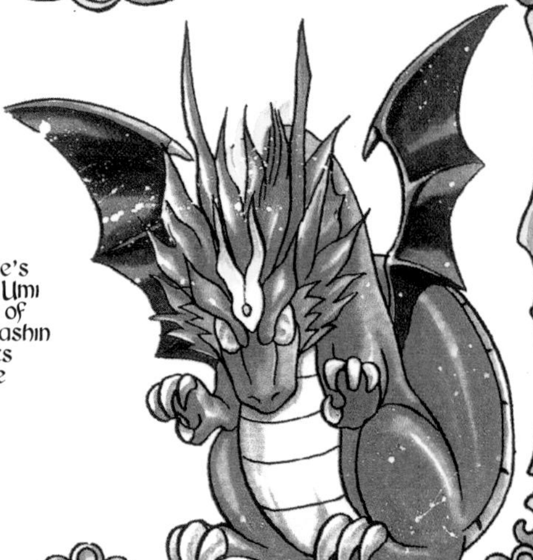

Magic Knight Rayearth II Character Collection ©1995-1996 CLAMP.
First published in Magic Knight Rayearth II vols. 1-3 by Kodansha Ltd., Tokyo.
English publication rights arranged through Kodansha Ltd.

English text © 2003 by Mixx Entertainment, Inc.
TOKYOPOP is a registered trademark of Mixx Entertainment, Inc.

LOS ANGELES * TOKYO